THE HISTORY OF

KEYBOARD MUSIC

TO 1700

Willi Apel

THE HISTORY OF

KEYBOARD MUSIC

TO 1700

translated and revised by

HANS TISCHLER

Indiana University Press

BLOOMINGTON / LONDON

ML
549
.A6413

CONTENTS

PART II. THE SIXTEENTH CENTURY

Contents

Contents

Contents

PREFACE

Soon after the publication of *Geschichte der Orgel- und Klaviermusik bis 1700* in 1967, Mr. Bernard B. Perry, director of the Indiana University Press, expressed his interest in bringing out an English translation, and asked me to do it. Unfortunately at that time I was so strongly committed to other work that I had to decline. The ensuing search for a translator came to a very happy conclusion when my colleague Professor Hans Tischler kindly agreed to undertake this burdensome task.

Professor Tischler has done much more than merely translate the book. He has checked on details, corrected a considerable number of errors, and brought the literature up to date with the aid of information I was able to provide, thus making the present publication a more reliable and accurate book than the original edition. I am profoundly grateful to Professor Tischler for having temporarily forsaken his own research and devoting himself to the task of translating my book with a zeal and unselfish interest which I could not have expected.

Bloomington, Indiana
May 1969

Preface to the First Edition

I CAN TRULY say that this volume, which I am publishing when I am past the age of seventy, has occupied me throughout my life. Even as a student at the University of Berlin I made plans in this direction, for it appeared to me then that Seiffert-Weitzmann's *Geschichte der Klaviermusik* (1899) fell short of the state of research at the time—apart from the fact that it treated only music for stringed keyboard instruments and did not include the organ. In 1884, A. G. Ritter had published a basic work about early organ music, *Zur Geschichte des Orgelspiels*, which, despite its incompleteness, is still not out of date. Another important contribution was A. Pirro's study *L'Art des organistes,* which appeared in 1926 in Lavignac's *Encyclopédie de la musique.* Finally, in 1935 G. Frotscher published his two-volume work, *Geschichte des Orgelspiels und der Orgelkomposition*, which contained many valuable additions, especially to the history of organ playing and organ construction. Yet none of these books (others of less importance I omit here) seemed to fulfil the idea I had conceived: a comprehensive presentation of keyboard music, i.e., music for the organ as well as for the stringed keyboard instruments, up to the time of Johann Sebastian Bach. This is the purpose to which the present volume is dedicated. The limit will be the generation of composers born around 1670, whose work obviously reaches into the early 18th century, but is included in our considerations as long as it does not bear unmistakable signs of a new style, the musical Rococo.

Some readers may find it unsatisfactory that a comprehensive volume on early keyboard music stops just short of Bach's work—that singuar corpus to which everything that precedes seems to point, for which all earlier works seem a mere preparation. The decision not to include Bach was based not only on the limitations of space (one or two chapters would hardly suffice) but also on the realization that his work would put the rest of the book in the wrong light—earlier compositions would not be seen in the full brilliance of their own value but in the lesser light of a preparation or of first steps. It was exactly this that had to be avoided. My task is not only to give a historical overview but to show (and, I hope, to convince the reader) that in the field of keyboard music personalities like Schlick, Cabezón, Byrd, Frescobaldi, and others cannot be passed over as mere precursors of Bach any more than Josquin, Palestrina, Monteverdi, or Schütz can be regarded as such in vocal music. Nevertheless I have tried to point toward Bach on many occasions. These references are assembled in the Index of Names and provide an idea of the many relationships between the keyboard works of Bach and those of his predecessors.

The realization of the task that I set for myself was largely facilitated, indeed rendered possible, by the financial support of the library administration of Indiana University, which put photographs of more than three hundred sources of early keyboard music at my disposal. Most of them were reproduced by the *Deutsches Musikgeschichtliches Archiv Kassel* with such a degree of technical perfection that they are equivalent to the originals. I am very grateful to these two institutions, as well as to the numerous libraries (at Berlin, Munich, Leipzig, Tübingen, Marburg, Vienna, Bologna, Naples, Rome, Paris, Barcelona, Madrid, and elsewhere) that filled my requests for microfilms with an obliging promptness.

Finally I must refer to the valuable help given me by my students, who studied numerous sources and transcribed them into modern notation. If I had had to undertake this work myself, the completion of this volume would have been considerably delayed. To name all of those who helped in this manner would not be meaningful, since their contributions were largely a matter of teamwork. Quite a few, however, were stimulated into undertaking larger tasks that have matured into publications. I herewith express my sincere thanks to all of them for their interest and help.

WILLI APEL

Indiana University, 1966

Translator's Note

Rarely in any discipline does a work appear that is both thorough and wide in scope. Rarely can such a work boast both extensive and intensive coverage, many new ideas, clear and precise presentation, and a scholarly-historical as well as an aesthetic-critical acumen, as this one does. It will probably become a standard reference work for both scholars and musicians and remain so for a long time.

I have endeavored to render it more useful to the reader by 1. structuring its divisions and subdivisions more clearly, 2. standardizing the footnotes so that most scholarly references appear in notes at the end of the text and only a relatively few essential, explanatory remarks appear at the foot of the page (this arrangement has occasioned many small changes in the original text), 3. adding a complete bibliography of all works referred to in the text, 4. completing the Index of Names, and 5. considerably expanding the original *Sachregister* and dividing it into an Index of Works and an Index of Terms. Hundreds of other small changes and additions update and correct the German edition, so that this translation in fact represents a second edition.

HANS TISCHLER

Indiana University
August 1969

THE HISTORY OF

KEYBOARD MUSIC

TO 1700

Explanatory Notes

IN ORDER to reduce the number of musical examples as much as possible, fugue subjects and similar simple melodic items are given in letter notation. The method used to represent the rhythm is illustrated by the following example:

| c | de |f g − a | ge fg -f ec | d/c B | c | =

The abbreviations used to designate the various periodicals and monument editions are given on p.818 (e.g., *MMG* = *Die Musik in Geschichte und Gegenwart*). Works referred to frequently are cited by means of abbreviations that generally consist of the author's name plus a key letter from the title of the work (e.g., Apel N = Apel, W. *Die Notation der Polyphonen Musik, 900 bis 1600*). These abbreviations are given in bold type following the full references in the Selected Bibliography, pp.818–31.

INTRODUCTION

1

General Observations

on Keyboard Instruments

and Keyboard Music

THE WORD *keyboard* in the title of this book is a convenient equivalent for the collective term *clavier*, which is derived from the Latin *clavis* (key), and before 1700 applied to all keyboard instruments. In the 18th century it was extended to the modern pianoforte, which was invented shortly after 1700 but did not come into general use until about 1770, and thus remains outside our considerations. The older meaning still applies in such titles as Bach's *Well-Tempered Clavier* and *Clavierübung*, but in the 19th century, as the harpsichord and clavichord became obsolete, *Klavier* in German came to mean the pianoforte exclusively, and this circumstance accounts for the use of the words "Orgel und Klavier" in the title of the original German edition of this book. The work *keyboard*, similar in meaning to the Spanish *tecla* and the German *Tastatur*, suits our purpose not only because of its brevity but also because it eliminates the need to differentiate between the organ and other keyboard instruments—a decision that is simply not feasible for most types of early keyboard music, such as the canzona, the fantasy, the prelude, and even the ricercar and variation sets (like those by

Sweelinck and Scheidt). We shall therefore use the terms keyboard or clavier throughout, be it for organ, harpsichord, or clavichord.

To be exact, we should add the *organistrum* (hurdy-gurdy, *vielle à roue*), which is documented as early as the 10th century—a violin-like instrument, whose strings were sounded by means of a wheel turned by the left hand, while the right hand operated a keyboard mechanism that shortened the strings. A similar principle was used in Hans Haiden's gamba mechanism (about 1575), which was described by Michael Praetorius in his *De Organographia* (1619) and his *Teatrum instrumentorum* (1620). However, these and similar instruments have had only an ephemeral importance and have not played a recognizable role in the evolution of clavier music.

Common to all clavier instruments is the keyboard, that well-known black-and-white pattern. In an almost symbolic way it characterizes a wide area of music, which in extent and significance takes second place only to the baton, but surpasses the latter both in its more ancient tradition and its greater wealth of forms and styles. It is well worth the effort of pursuing the reasons why the piano and its predecessors hold such a prominent position. Apparently there is nothing more artificial and less artistic in the whole domain of musical instruments than that complicated mechanism of levers, joints, connecting rods, hammers, slides, springs, straps, etc., which constitute a key. A violinist's instrument rests close to his body, his hand holds the bow that makes the strings sound, and in a most literal sense it is his finger-tips' sensitivity that produces the music. With hands and mouth an oboist holds his instrument as though it were a part of himself, his own breath flows through the pipe, and his lips vibrate in closest contact with the reed. Compare him with a pianist or an organist: Both are far removed from the sounding strings or pipes, both are busy depressing lifeless ivories, and both depend on a complicated apparatus, which produces tones as mechanically as the typewriter prints letters and words.

Certainly such an artificial way of making music would never have become so popular if its manifest shortcomings had not been balanced by considerable merits. The most striking is the enormously enlarged array of pitches that are available to the single player: The piano has eighty-eight keys while the violin has four strings; the organ has hundreds and thousands of pipes, the oboe only one. No wonder that the availability of such means has inspired pianists and organists to imitate a whole orchestra or to vie with it. However the extent of tonal possibilities is not the essential reason for the superiority of the keyboard instruments. We recognize this when we compare the piano with the harp, which also has many strings—in some types almost as many as the piano—but has no keyboard. It is therefore not so much the extensive tonal material but the keyboard—more accurately the combination of the two—to which the piano as well as the harpsichord and organ owe their chief advantage. Playing a keyboard instrument is simple and easy; it has what may be called a natural finger technique. Imagine playing a scale or a triad on various instruments, imagine the necessary hand positions and movements of the fingers, and you will recognize the advantages of the keyboard. No other mechanism attains the same degree of correspondence between the motions of the fingers and the pitches produced. Indeed the keyboard represents a nearly perfect reflection of the gamut of tones: the high and low pitch of the tones, the similarity of the octaves, and the distinction between the fundamental diatonic steps and the intervening chromatic ones. Thus it is easy to understand that during the 16th century the keyboard instruments were called *istromenti perfetti* by the Italians.

Let us turn from the claviers to general observations about the music played on them. What interests us here is the justification and meaning of the term "clavier music" as a general designation for music composed for the early keyboard instruments. Obviously the validity of the term rests on two premises: that these instruments had a literature that was common to all of them, and that it can be clearly distinguished from the rest of music literature.

The first point can be proved easily. In early music the organ, harpsichord, and clavichord were not viewed as instruments that required an individual approach or a way of composing that was peculiar to and commensurate with each. Although the instruments are very different in timbre, the manner of playing was so similar that any composition could be presented equally well on any one of them. In the 14th and 15th centuries instruments were never specified, so that we need other clues to determine that we are, in fact, dealing with clavier music. In the 16th century and later, indications such as *Intabulatura d'organo* (Cavazzoni, 1543) or *Balli d'arpichordo* (Facoli, 1588) do appear; elsewhere, however, there are still collective designations such as *pour les orgues espinettes et manicordions* (Attaingnant, 1530), *per ogni sorte di stromenti da tasti* (A. Gabrieli, 1595), *per cimbalo et organo* (Frescobaldi, 1628; Storace, 1664; Strozzi, 1687), or *auff Orgeln und Instrumenten zu gebrauchen* (B. Schmid, 1607). That the designation *fürs Clavier*, which occurs frequently in Germany, is ambiguous, is obvious from Bach's *Clavierübung*.

The second premise is more difficult to establish—the demarcation between clavier music and other fields of music literature, such as purely vocal music, instrumental ensemble music, or music for voices and instruments, which assumes a particularly important place in the 14th century. The essential difference is that clavier music is performed by a single player (rarely two), while in the other instances several performers are always necessary. The difference between solo and ensemble music manifests itself unmistakably in the notation of early music, namely, in the manner in which the various voices of a composition are arranged. Essentially there exist two possibilities, which may be called "single" and "simultaneous placement." In the first, each part is written out by itself in a different place on the same page, on two facing pages (choir-book arrangement), or in different books (part books). In the other, the voices are arranged above each other so that simultaneously sounding tones are placed vertically above or below each other. A modern example of single placement is the four separate parts of a string quartet; examples of simultaneous placement are the orchestral score and the brace used in piano music. If we limit ourselves to the period from 1300 to 1600 (the time during which the problem of demarcation is of real importance), we can formulate the following rule: When a composition is written in single placement, it is ensemble music; if it is notated in simultaneous placement, it is solo music.* In addition to clavier music, solo music comprises lute music, which is easily distinguished because of its peculiar notation (lute tablature). Clavier music is notated either on a two-staff brace with a separate staff for each hand, or in special tablature notations (German and Spanish clavier or organ tablatures).

Around 1575 the score (It. *partitura*) appears, with a separate five-line staff for each of usually four parts. Compared with the notations mentioned above, it is more problematic. The earliest known example is the *Libro di ricercate a quattro voci* (1575) by the Neapolitan Rocco Rodio; the last one is Bach's *Art of Fugue*.[1] In between there exist many other publications or manuscripts for which the question "ensemble or clavier?" can usually be decided without difficulty in favor of the clavier (e.g., Scheidt's *Tabulatura nova*, Coelho's *Flores de musica*, or Frescobaldi's *Fiori musicali*), but not always with assurance. We all know the dispute that arose about the "correct" performance of the *Art of Fugue*. In fact, this question can be much more easily decided in favor of the clavier from internal signs than in the case of several 17th-century Italian publications, such as the posthumous print of Frescobaldi's *Canzoni alla francese* of 1645.

The result—to summarize our discussion—is a well-delineated repertoire of early clavier music. It comprises everything in manuscript or print that is notated on a two-staff brace or in clavier tablature, as well as the majority of polyphonic scores. Pieces that are preserved in single parts do not belong to it.

There have been various attempts to enlarge the field of clavier music in a way that contradicts the above principles, by assigning to the clavier (more spe-

---

* Only very rarely do we find exceptions to this rule. In the Old Hall Ms., the main source of English music of the 15th century, written about 1440, homo-rhythmic ensemble works are notated in simultaneous placement, a practice in which the score notation of the 13th-century conductus apparently lives on. I know of only three instances of solo music in single placement: In Bermudo's *Declaración de instrumentos musicales* (1555), fol.114ff., several pieces are printed in separate parts (choir-book arrangement) with the note "esta musica ser hecha para tañer, y non para cantar" (this music is to be played, not sung); and at the end of Michael Praetorius' *Musae Sioniae* VII (1609) and in his *Hymnodia Sionia* (1611), which are printed in part books, several pieces are presented with the note "pro organicis, sine textu" (for organ, without text). However, he says in a "nota" that an organist who wants to play these pieces must transcribe them "from the notes into tablature." For Bermudo's pieces it is absolutely necessary to make a tablature first; this will be obvious if one tries to play them from the parts of the original print.

cifically to the organ) works notated in single voices. Thus A. Schering maintained in *Die niederländische Orgelmesse der Zeit Josquins* (1912) that many masses of the latter half of the 15th century represent not vocal but organ compositions. We need not enter into a discussion here of the reasoning that led to this theory (which is generally recognized as untenable today). We need only compare one of those pseudo-organ works—perhaps the pieces reproduced in Schering's *Alte Meister der Frühzeit des Orgelspiels* (1913) or Ockeghem's "organ motet" *Ut heremita solus,* printed in his *Geschichte der Musik in Beispielen*—with a genuine organ composition of the period (perhaps a piece from the *Buxheim Organ Book*) to recognize that such a complicated organ style is completely beyond the realm of possibility. Equally wrong are Schering's attempts to assign vocal or vocal-instrumental compositions of the 14th century, such as a Landini ballata, to the organ. Here, too, a comparison with genuine organ music of the time (the *Codex Faenza*) presents clear proof to the contrary, if one is at all necessary.

Another attempt in a similar direction was made by O. Kinkeldey in his important publication *Orgel und Klavier im 16. Jahrhundert* (1910). On the basis of certain observations in Bermudo's *Declaración de instrumentos musicales* (1555), he arrived at the conclusion that a good organist or clavier player was expected to play directly from a choir book.[2] Such a procedure represents at best a singular, virtuoso achievement, certainly not a general practice. Even for the most gifted musician, simultaneously reading four parts written in different places (and without bar lines) and playing them directly on the organ simply transcends the power of the human brain. Even Bermudo admits that this kind of organ playing is extremely difficult and that the most gifted performers can hope to master it only after twenty years of study. We must assume that even life-long studies will only result in a player's retaining a number of works by heart, so that the choir book serves only as an occasional memory aid. Based on Kinkeldey's explanations, J. Wolf goes one step further and counts works by Willaert, Buus, and others, which were published in part books, among the "oldest Italian organ monuments,"[3] although Kinkeldey says that under these circumstances "score playing out of a choir book was impossible" and "the organist had to prepare for himself a score or an organ arrangement."[4] But essentially there is no difference between choir books and part books, for one can arrange the latter on a suitably built music stand just like a choir book.

Whatever one may think of the capabilities and practices of the organists of the period, it certainly does not follow that music played from choir books or part books is organ music. With equal justification one could insist that a string quartet by Mozart is piano music, merely because a pianist succeeded in playing it out of four voice parts—which would, in fact, be much easier than the corresponding performance of modal works of such contrapuntal complexity as a 16th-century ricercar. Neither does the employment or preparation of a score

7

change the situation—after all, there are piano scores of Mozart's string quartets. The earlier counterparts to such piano scores are the innumerable intabulations of motets, madrigals, and chansons, whose peculiarity consists in the many changes made in the vocal patterns, the omission of parts, and the addition of figurations. Thus changed they belong to clavier music as peripheral phenomena, though they unfortunately occupy a far larger part of this field than appears desirable to us today.

2

The Evolution of

Keyboard Instruments

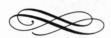

B Y FAR THE OLDEST AND, from the point of view of evolution, the most
interesting keyboard instrument is the organ. It has three fundamental parts: a
number of pipes, each of essentially unalterable pitch, an artificial wind supply,
and a key mechanism that opens and closes the individual pipes to the wind.

According to almost unanimous reports, Ctesibios, a Greek engineer who
lived in Alexandria during the 3rd century B.C., was the inventor of the first organ,
the so-called hydraulis. Pliny the Elder, in his *Natural History* (c.A.D.70), calls it
one of the wonders of the world, along with Archimedes' machines, Chersiphron's
Temple of Diana in Ephesus, the construction of the port of Athens by Philon, and
Deinocrates' plans for the city of Alexandria. A detailed description of the hydraulis is found in Vitruvius' *De Architectura* (c.A.D.14) and in *Pneumatica* by
Heron of Alexandria (2nd century?). We also possess a goodly number of depictions on cameos, mosaics, and coins. Especially important is a small model of
baked clay, which was found in 1885 in the ruins of Carthage. From all this evidence we gain a clear picture of the hydraulis, free from the fantastic and legendary
notions that surrounded the instrument during the Middle Ages, and which even
today are not entirely eliminated. The following is a brief resumé of Heron's
description:[1]

The wind mechanism of the hydraulis has two main parts: an air pump, and
a diving bell submerged in a large container of water (see Fig.1a.). The air pump

Fig.1a.

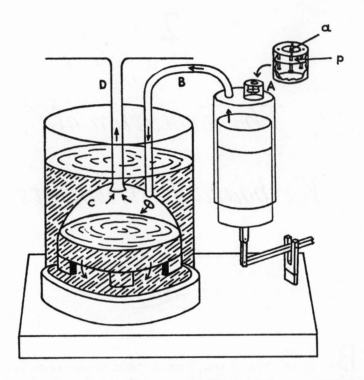

consists of a cylinder in which a piston moves up and down with the aid of a long lever (A is the entry valve, whose opening, a, is closed by a metal plate, the *platysmation*, p, which moves on three or four pins). The air, which is compressed in the cylinder, is conducted through pipe B into the diving bell C (*pnigeus*), which rests on several metal blocks in the water-filled container. From the bell a second pipe, D, leads up to the wind chest and to the pipes. As the pumping continues, the bell fills with air and the displaced water reaches a stationary maximum level. The entire water apparatus thus serves to transform the pulsating air pressure of the pump into an even pressure, which is necessary for the pipes to produce an even sound. The pumper must merely see that air bubbles continue to escape from the bell and appear on the surface of the water.*

Even more interesting than the wind mechanism of the hydraulis is its key mechanism, which Heron describes in great detail (see Fig.1b.). Below each pipe there is a wind-chest with a wooden plate (slider or pallet, S) with a hole in it, which can be moved horizontally. This plate is connected to a lever consisting of two pieces, DC and CBA, which turns around the fixed axis P. When the key is

---

* In the Middle Ages this phenomenon led to the fantastic idea that the hydraulis was activated by boiling water (or even by steam).

Fig.1b.

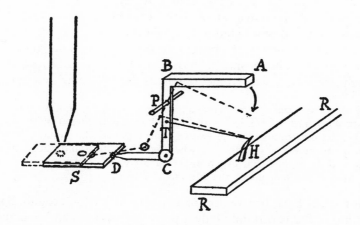

depressed at *A*, the slider moves backward so that the hole lies beneath the pipe's opening and the wind enters the pipe and causes it to emit a sound. In addition, there is a spring mechanism that pulls the slide back into its original position as soon as the finger releases the key. It consists of a lightly curved, elastic piece of horn *H*, whose lower end is fastened to a board *RR*, placed at right angles to the key; the upper end of *H* is connected by a tight thread to point *T* of the lever. When the lever is depressed, the piece of horn is stretched; on being released it pulls the lever back to its original position. Vitruvius reports that in his day the hydraulis had two air pumps, one on the right and one on the left, an improvement that was probably generally accepted rather quickly. All in all the hydraulis represents a solution to the mechanical and aerodynamic problems of the organ that is highly ingenious in its simplicity.

There is a prevailing idea that the sound of the hydraulis was unusually loud and almost terrifying. But this idea, like so many others that arose about the water organ at a later time, is based on a misunderstanding. From the ancient sources one receives a totally different impression. Cicero describes the sound of the hydraulis as a sensation which is as agreeable to the ear as the tastiest fish to the palate; and in Athenaeus' *Deipnosophistae* (c.A.D.220) we read of a hydraulis heard from a neighbor's house, whose sound "was very sweet and gay, so that all of us listened, charmed by its melodies." Similarly the idea that the hydraulis was used chiefly at the circus to accompany the combat of the gladiators is hardly well founded. Essentially we are dealing with a household instrument of agreeable sound, which, on occasion was also built in larger sizes to be used outdoors.

Literary references to the hydraulis are found until the end of the 4th century. In the meantime another type, the pneumatic organ, had been accepted, in which the water mechanism was replaced by bellows. The earliest evidence is generally believed to be an epigram of Julian the Apostate (361–363), in which we hear of a "wind that rises from a cave of ox-skin." But in the *Onomastikon* (c.120B.C.) Pollux speaks of a "Tyrrhenian aulos with metal pipes blown from below: The smaller one is furnished with wind out of bellows, the larger one with the aid of water." The earliest depiction of a pneumatic organ is found on an obelisk erected at Constantinople by Theodosius (d.395). In an *Epistola ad Dardanum* (4th century, wrongly ascribed to St. Jerome) one finds the following description:

> First I want to speak of the organ. . . . One makes a hollow out of two elephant skins, and this is filled [with air] with the aid of fifteen smith's bellows. It emits a strong sound through twelve bronze pipes, like thunder [*tonitrus*], so that it can be heard clearly everywhere within a thousand paces [*per mille passus*] and more, like that organ of the Hebrews which, as is reported, was heard from Jerusalem up to the Mount of Olives.

This is the first time that we hear of an organ with a loud sound. But the comparison with thunder is certainly only a poetic expression, and one must bear in mind that the ears of that period were not used to the sound levels of the modern orchestra or the noise of today's metropolis. Cassiodorus (c.485–580) expresses himself in a similar manner:

> The organ is a kind of tower, built out of a number of pipes which, by means of wind from bellows, give out a very loud sound [*vox copiosissima*]. And in order that the sound may be altered in an appropriate manner, wooden levers are constructed, which are nimbly moved by the fingers of the player, and emit a loud-sounding and very agreeable music [*grandisonam et suavissimam cantilenam*].

Cassiodorus is the last writer of the Mediterranean area who reports about the organ. For the next few centuries only sources from northern France and England are preserved; in these the organ is occasionally mentioned, but without any detailed description. An especially remarkable event in the early history of the organ took place in 757, when the ambassadors of the Byzantine Emperor Constantine V Copronymus presented an organ as a gift to King Pippin. In the year 812 ambassadors of Emperor Michael I Rhangabes brought an organ to the court of Charlemagne at Aachen, obviously to document the superiority of Byzantine culture. Charlemagne gave orders to study the organ secretly and to construct one like it, but this plan did not succeed. Fourteen years later, however, the Venetian priest Georgius built an organ at Aachen for Louis the Pious, and the court poet Ermoldus Nigellus speaks of that event in terms that make it clear that the building of an organ (it almost makes one think of the atom bomb) had become the chief object of the rivalry between the two world powers of that period. "That organ, which France never produced—how proudly the Greeks gloried in that fact—and by which Constantinople thought to surpass Thee, oh Emperor: now it stands at the court of Aachen." Unfortunately we do not know what was so singular and, at that time, so extraordinary about this organ.

From England we have rather early reports of organs of considerable size. Aldhelm (c.640–709) says in his poem "De virginitate" that anyone for whom music for strings and voice is not enough may enjoy "the great organ with a thousand air streams out of wind-filled bellows." Though poetic overstatement may be involved here, the report of the monk Wulstan (d.983) does give us definite facts about the gigantic organ that was erected at Winchester under Bishop Aelfheah (or Elphegus, d.951). It had twenty-six bellows, from which "seventy strong men drive out the wind with all their strength," four hundred pipes, and forty sliders with ten openings each, in front of which "sit two brothers, unified in spirit, each serving his own alphabet." "It sounds so loud that everybody covers his ears with his hands, unable when close by to stand the noise that the various tones give out."

A very important report about organ building from the 10th century is preserved in the so-called Bern treatise, *De fistulis organicis quomodo fiant*. Detailed information about the construction of the bellows, the wind-chest, the pipes, and the playing mechanism is found here. The pipes are said to have different lengths but the same diameter, about the size of a chicken egg. Even as late as the early 15th century, in the famous representation of an organ in Van Eyck's Ghent Altar triptych, one can clearly see that all the pipes have the same width. What is the significance of this principle of construction? In the modern organ, within each rank all the pipes have the same proportion of diameter to length (*Mensur*, mensuration), which causes all of them to have the same quality of sound; e.g., a timbre like a stringed instrument is achieved with narrow pipes, and a flute-like character with wide mensuration. Medieval organs, on the other hand, even those that had several ranks, had only a single register; nevertheless their sound was by no means as uniform as that of a modern *principal*. The uniform diameter of all the pipes caused the mensuration to change gradually from a very narrow one to a very wide one, and the timbre to shift from a string sound in the low register to a flute sound in the high one. If one can compare the modern organ with its many stops to ribbons of different colors, the sound of the Medieval organ is analogous to a single ribbon whose color changes continuously, like the rainbow, from one end to the other.

To pursue the further development of the organ does not serve our present purpose, since it consists more or less of technical improvements of the construction. Only one detail, the playing mechanism, demands our attention, for it is of interest in connection with the early history of organ music to be treated in the next chapter. We have seen that the Greek hydraulis had a keyboard which was similar to that of the modern piano in that the keys were depressed by finger motion and reset in their rest position by a spring mechanism. At a time which we cannot ascertain, perhaps during the 6th or 7th century, this mechanism was supplanted by another, much more unwieldy one. The sliders were no longer moved back and forth by a lever mechanism, but pushed in and pulled out directly

Fig.2 **Fig.3**

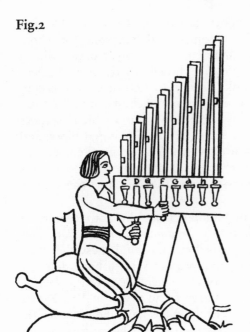

St. Etienne Bible, 11th Cent. (Bibl. Dijon)

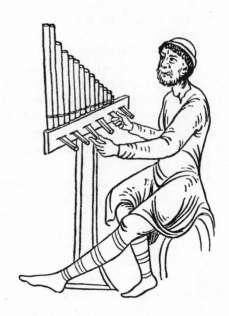

Gräfl. Schönborn'sche Bibl., Pommersfelden,
Cod. 2776, 11th cent.

by hand by means of an elongation of the key. These "tongues" (*linguae*), which protruded from the organ cabinet, are found in all depictions from the 9th, 10th, and 11th centuries. They can be seen in Figs.2 and 3, which also indicate the manner of playing. The introduction of this much more primitive playing apparatus is probably connected with a tendency toward bigger and louder instruments. That the earliest pneumatic organs still had a finger keyboard can be deduced, e.g., from the description by Cassiodorus, given above. But if one looks at the enormous apparatus of bellows for the organ shown in Fig.3, the use of the tongues becomes understandable: The power of the wind pressure made it impossible to use the delicate keyboard of antiquity. Occasionally attempts may have been made to master the great wind pressure of a large church organ by means of a lever mechanism, but it was so unyielding that the keys had to be beaten down with the fist. Admittedly, the only evidence for this technique is a passage in Michael Praetorius' *Syntagma musicum* of 1619, but one need not relegate this report to the realm of fable, despite its late date. However, it is even more inappropriate to represent the "beating by fists" as the normal technique of playing during the Middle Ages, as is frequently done in recent literature. Authentic documentation is available only for the "pulling by hand."

Fig.4

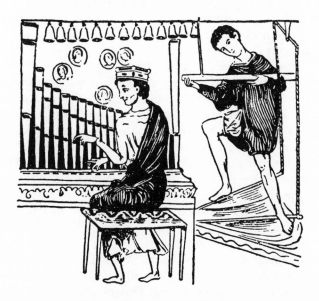

Belvoir Castle *Psalter,* 13th Cent.

It would be interesting to determine when this awkward manner of playing was given up and once more replaced by finger technique. A depiction in the Belvoir Castle *Psalter* (Fig.4) proves that the latter was already known by the 13th century. It shows a light, graceful manner of playing with the fingers of both hands. Evidently this relatively small organ had a key mechanism which was not unlike that of the Greek organ. Indeed, it can be proved that as early as the 10th century the West had detailed knowledge of the hydraulis. The Bern tract, mentioned above, contains a detailed description of the playing mechanism, which is doubtless based on Heron's *Pneumatica*. There are the same elastic pieces of horn (*ex cornu semicirculi*), which are attached to a fixed board (*in quodam ligno ante capsam firmo*), as well as the keys (*lamina*), which are connected to the pieces of horn by means of wire. To be sure, Heron's detailed description of the lever mechanism is missing, but that it was, in fact, included, is clear from the distinction between keys (*lamina*) and sliders (*linguae*), and especially from the mention of *depressa lamina* and *laxa lamina*, i.e., keys in depressed and normal rest positions: "The wire is attached to the piece of horn and the slider in such a way that when the key is depressed, the whole slider is pushed in . . . , whereas at the release of the key it is pulled out." Thus we may infer that we owe a decisive and permanent progress in the construction and playing of the organ—like so many other important results of the Carolingian renaissance—to Greek antiquity.

Let us now briefly assemble the little that is known about the early history of the stringed clavier instruments.

The harpsichord probably derives from the triangular psaltery with the addition of a key apparatus that made the strings sound by means of quills. In a similar manner the clavichord was probably developed from the monochord by increasing the strings (polychord) and adding a keyboard with a tangent mechanism. The earliest evidence of a stringed clavier instrument is found in a letter by King John I of Aragon, written in 1367, in which he commissions his ambassadors to find someone who could play the *exaquir*, an instrument which is described as "semblant d'orguens que sona ab cordes" (similar to the organ but sounded by means of strings). Probably the *exaquir* (*eschaquier, chekker, Schachtbrett*) was a kind of harpsichord. In the *Minneregeln* of Eberhard Cersne (1404) the *Schachtbrett* as well as the *clavicordium* and *clavicymbalum* are mentioned. Both types of instruments probably emerged in the second half of the 14th century.

On the clavichord—as on the monochord—each string was originally used to produce several (two to four) pitches, so that an instrument with twenty-four keys needed only about ten strings. Such an instrument is known as a fretted (*gebundenes*) clavichord, in contrast to an unfretted (*bundfreies*) one, in which each key corresponds to a separate string. The introduction of this improvement is usually ascribed to the Crailsheim organist D. T. Faber (1725).[2] But as early as 1555, Bermudo says in *Declaración de instrumentos musicales* that in his day the clavichord had forty-two strings;[3] and Johann Speth demands in *Ars magna consoni et dissoni* (1693) "that every key (*Clavir*) have its own string and not that perhaps two, three, even four keys touch one."

PART I

CLAVIER MUSIC

BEFORE 1500

3

Antiquity and Early

Middle Ages

IN THE PRECEDING CHAPTER we traced the history of the organ from its beginnings to about the 13th century, a period of about one and one-half millennia. Although many details are unknown and a number of important questions remain unanswered, we are nevertheless able to form an adequate idea of the evolution and changes of the organ in those remote times. As to what music was played on these instruments, however, we are left in total darkness. The earliest extant source of clavier music is from the 14th century; nothing of what was heard on the hydraulis, the early Christian, or the Carolingian organ is known to us. And yet, it is perhaps not impossible to bring a ray of light into this darkness, so that at least some outlines may be recognized. Indeed, it is our knowledge of the mechanics of the various types of organs which, I believe, makes such an attempt possible.

We have seen that the Greek hydraulis, as described by Heron, had a very remarkable mechanism, with keys which could be depressed easily and which returned to their rest position by themselves. Doubtless these instruments were played in a manner very similar to today's organs, or at least to those of the 15th and 16th centuries, mainly with the second, third, and fourth fingers. Indeed in various reports we find explicit references to the ease with which the hydraulis could be played and to the agility of the organist's fingers. Publilius Optatianus Porphyrius (c.325) says in a poem about the hydraulis that "to the smallest movement the agitated keys open themselves," and Claudius Claudianus (c.365–408) praises "the man who with light touch [*levi tactu*] and roving finger [*erranti digito*] brings forth the innumerable tones of the iron field [*segetis aeneae*]" (the pipes of the hydraulis were often compared to the stalks of the wheat field). We have similar evidence relating to the early pneumatic organ. Julian the Apostate in the epigram cited in the Introduction speaks of a "dexterous man who moves the keys with quick fingers [*thoa daktyla*]," and Cassiodorus says that "the wooden levers are dexterously managed by the fingers of the player." From all this we may conclude with certainty that the music that was heard on such organs was just as "light" and "quick" as the movement of the fingers on the keys, probably already quite virtuosic, and certainly quite different in character from what one would conclude from the usual descriptions, according to which the early organs were only able to produce a "thunderous noise."

In fact, without transcending the limits of admissible speculation we may well go a step further and affirm that two-part music was performed on Greek and early Christian organs. Or is it conceivable that for many centuries players sat before a keyboard quite similar to today's without trying to produce tones simultaneously with both hands? It is generally admitted—chiefly on the basis of a passage in Plato's *Laws*—that there existed in ancient Greece a rudimentary kind of polyphony, so-called heterophony. In reality, however, Plato's description indicates not so much heterophony in the modern meaning of the word, as real polyphony, for it speaks of various intervals, pitches, rhythms, and numbers of notes.[1] If it is true, then, that a kind of polyphony, however simple, was already known in Plato's time, we certainly may assume that the hydraulis greatly influenced its further development and gave it new direction.

Whatever picture of the organ music of antiquity and the early Middle Ages one accepts, there is no doubt that a totally different kind of music was heard on the Frankish organs of the 9th and later centuries. One did not play them with the fingers, but the whole hand took hold of the slide protruding from the wind chest. The only kind of music that could be produced was a series of relatively long, sustained, single tones. Indeed, both hands were needed for each change of pitch, one to push back the slider just used, the other to pull out the new one at the same time. The process may be seen in Fig.2, where the melody is changing from *F* to *D* (or vice versa). Note that the pipes are marked incorrectly—the longest should stand on the left side, above the *C*. The organ of that period is thus mainly a monophonic, melodic instrument. The music played on it must have been similar to hymn melodies; it is shown in many pictures accompanying choral hymn singing in combination with other instruments.

A question arises as to the relationship between the organ practice of that period and the early species of polyphonic music called *organum*. More specifically, is the latter derived from the former? Without reservation this question was answered positively by A. Gastoué, who says, "It is impossible not to see that the two parts of the vocal organum are an imitation of the two-part chant executed on the keyboard of the organ, water- or air-driven. . . ."[2] Most scholars, however, say "no," and explain the origin of polyphony in other ways. As far as is known to me, none have used the decisive argument that with the primitive mechanism of the Carolingian organ, the simultaneous sounding of two tones was impossible.

Or was it possible? Could two organists have played simultaneously, each playing his own melody? As improbable as this hypothesis of "four-hand" organ playing seems at first glance, there is conclusive evidence that such a practice did, in fact, exist. In the depiction on the Obelisk of Theodosius there are two men working the bellows, and two players. One of the most famous pictures from the early history of the organ, the hydraulis in the Utrecht *Psalter* (8th century), shows a kind of double organ with two groups of four pipes each, two sets of bellows, each served by two men, and two organists, each of whom seems to spur the pumping assistants to ever greater efforts. Among literary documents, one that is quite explicit is the report of Wulstan about the Winchester organ. Here we read of two brothers, unified in spirit, each serving his own alphabet (i.e., the keys marked with letters; cf.p.13). There can be no doubt that from the 4th to the 10th centuries organs were played by two players. Music thus produced cannot have been radically different from what we know about the earliest polyphony, the organum of the *Musica* and *Scholia enchiriadis* of the 9th century.

The idea that polyphony derived from organ playing is therefore not so absurd; in any case it is more firmly founded than any other theory of its origin. It is even possible that "four-hand" organ playing was of Byzantine origin. It is depicted on the 4th-century Obelisk of Theodosius in Istanbul, and art historians concur that the Utrecht *Psalter*, which dates from the 8th or 9th century, is based on Byzantine archetypes of a much earlier date. In the middle of the 8th century a Byzantine organ, a gift from Emperor Copronymus, came to the court of Pippin, where its arrival was celebrated as an event of uncommon significance (cf.p.12). May we assume that this was a double organ similar to the one in the Utrecht *Psalter*, but perhaps constructed with bellows? Certain sources seem to indicate that organs were known in Gaul as early as the 6th and 7th centuries; if that is so, the great stir produced by the Byzantine organ would be difficult to understand unless it represented a novel type with new sound possibilities. It is probable, therefore, that the organ of 812 was also a double organ, on which two-part music could be played (cf.p.12). The Winchester organ would thus be the counterpart of the Byzantine and Frankish organs of the Carolingian period.

We may therefore imagine that music like that in Fig.5 was heard on organs around the year 800. In moderate tempo fourth followed fourth, fifth followed fifth—a music of dark solemnity and novel, exciting sound, well suited to the

Fig.5

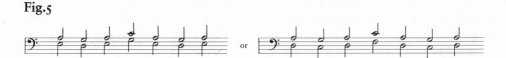

rough voices of the Frankish singers, who surely loved to join in. This initial stage of organ polyphony did not develop further because, after all, the Frankish organ was basically a monophonic instrument, which could only be changed into a polyphonic one by the interesting but rather special use of two players. Depictions from the 10th to the 12th centuries always show only one player, and only the reintroduction of the Greek keyboard made possible the start of an enduring evolution of polyphonic organ music, which we see for the first time in the *Robertsbridge fragment* from the beginning of the 14th century. In the meantime the possible use of the organ was similar to that of the portative at the time of Machaut and Landini; it functioned as a purely melodic instrument in the performance of ensemble music, such as the organa of St. Martial and Notre Dame. It is obvious that the participation of the organ can only be envisioned in connection with the tenors (from the Latin, *tenere*, to hold) with their long, sustained tones; and it is equally obvious that it is exactly these tenors that implied the participation of the organ, nay demanded it—think of the *puncti organici*, pedal points that stretch over whole pages in the three- and four-part organa of Perotin. I deliberately say "participation," for it appears to me that these tenors were primarily meant for singers, if for no other reason than their liturgical, Gregorian derivation. But wherever an organ was at hand, it may well have been used to make the singers' difficult task somewhat easier.

It has been supposed that in the melismatic organa of St. Martial the organ did not play the sustained tones of the tenor, but the very mobile upper part, for this was the *vox organalis*, the "organ part."[3] Here one must first note that the designations *vox principalis* and *vox organalis* were employed only in connection with the note-against-note style of the 9th to the 11th centuries; with the melismatic organum of the 12th century the terms *cantus, discantus,* and later *tenor* (long, sustained notes!) and *duplum* came into use. The question turns on how early a date one assumes for the introduction and general acceptance of the key mechanism, for the upper parts of such organa cannot be executed without it. As we have seen above, it was known shortly before the year 1000, but from pictorial sources of the next centuries we get the impression that (as in the case of Cristofori's pianoforte) it remained a singular attempt for some time.

With the 13th century we again stand on firm ground, thanks to the picture in the *Psalter* of Belvoir (Fig.4). The two-part clausulae of the Perotin period may well have been heard on such organs and may have inspired the composition of original organ music of a similar kind. Admittedly no genuine organ music has reached us from the entire century, but there can be no doubt that a tradition of organ composition and a significant development of two-part organ playing must have evolved some time before the earliest extant monument, the *Robertsbridge fragment*.

4

The Fourteenth Century

The *Robertsbridge Fragment*

U NDER THE NUMBER Add.28550, the British Museum holds a voluminous manuscript with various records referring to the Abbey of Robertsbridge.
Inserted at the end are two sheets of music, which are known as the *Robertsbridge
fragment*. External as well as internal evidence point to the time around 1320.
The content is usually thought of as English, but is probably of French provenance.[1]

The first two pages of the fragment contain one incomplete and two complete compositions. The latter pieces are of considerable length, and by their construction are recognizable as estampies.[2] Originally the estampie was probably a
dance or a dance-song, but the examples in the *Robertsbridge fragment*, like
almost all the others that have reached us (all written for one or two melodic
instruments), represent a later stage of development, in which their dance character is only hinted at. The characteristic form of the estampie, obviously suggested by the sequence, was retained, however; it consists of four, five, or more
sections, called *puncti*, each of which is repeated: AA BB CC . . . . Each *punctus*
has two different endings, *ouvert* and *clos*, which correspond to the modern
prima and *seconda volta*. Usually the two endings of the first *punctus* are used
for all the others, so that the following structure results: A + x A + y ‖ B + x
B + y ‖ C + x C + y ‖ . . . . Sometimes a large part of the preceding material from
the first *punctus* is also taken over into the succeeding ones. This is true of the two
organ estampies that interest us here. They differ, however; in the first estampie
the portion of the *primus punctus* that is taken over into the other *puncti* is always
the same, whereas in the second estampie its length changes.

Estampie no.1 begins with a punctus of 46 measures, the beginning and end
of which are shown in Fig.6. At measure 8 (marked *𝄐*) the original has the legend

Fig.6

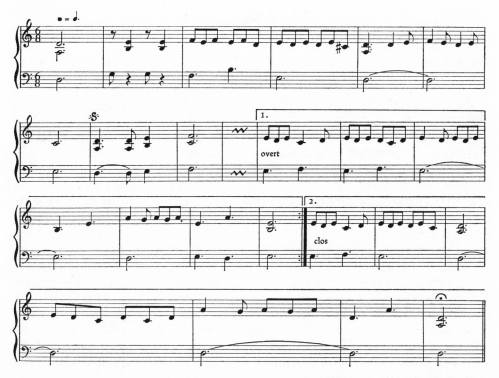

retⁿ (*returnare, retourner*), and each of the three following *puncti* concludes with the same passage (measures 8–9) and the same legend. Obviously this means that also in these *puncti* the notated section is followed by the entire passage beginning at *f*. Since the notated beginnings of the last three *puncti* comprise 16, 20, and 24 measures, respectively, and the continuation taken from the first *punctus* is 38 measures long, the respective lengths are 54, 58, and 62 measures. When the 46 measures of the first *punctus* are added, the total length of the piece is 220 measures, which is then doubled because each *punctus* is repeated. Such a piece is bewildering; it raises questions as to what purpose music of such dimension served and at what occasion it was played.

The second estampie is composed of five *puncti*, but it is only about half as long as the first. The endings taken over from the *primus punctus* are considerably shorter and of varying length. Fig.7 shows the beginning of the *primus punctus*.

This estampie, which carries the legend *Retrove* (Fr. *Retrouvé*) is remarkable, for the two voices move mostly in parallel fifths. In comparison with vocal music of the period, such as the motets of the *Roman de Fauvel* or those by Philippe de Vitry, this style is extremely archaic, but it is known that the organum in paral-

Fig.7

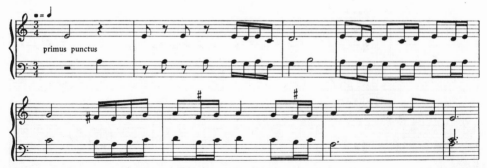

lel fifths continued for a long time as "sunken art music." In the famous bull of 1324 Pope John XXII admitted the organum in parallel fifths as the only polyphonic ornamentation of the service. Note also the hocketing at the start; similar passages are also found in the other *puncti*.

The estampies in the *Robertsbridge fragment* are followed by three works, *Firmissime, Tribum quem,* and *Flos vernalis* (the last incomplete), which are provided with full texts and thus suggest a connection with vocal music. Indeed the first two prove to be organ versions of motets from the beginning of the 14th century, and no doubt the third piece belongs to the same species, although its vocal original is not known. Thus at the very beginning of clavier literature we find the intabulation, which occupies an important place in the sources of the 15th and particularly the 16th centuries—in fact, a numerically much more important place than we would like.

The motets referred to above are *Firmissime—Adesto—Alleluia Benedictus* and *Tribum quem—Quoniam secta—Merito,* both preserved in the musical appendix to the *Roman de Fauvel* (Paris, Bibl. nat. fr. 146), which was completed about 1316.[3] A comparison of the organ versions with their vocal prototypes affords an interesting insight into the practice of arranging in the early 14th century. In *Tribum quem* the organ version is transposed a whole tone up, from *F* to *G.* Another change concerns the number of voices: the motet, following the practice of the period, is in three parts, while the organ version has only two, except for a few places where a three-note chord occurs. But it must be said that the three-part texture of the original is more apparent than real; this motet differs from similar pieces in that it uses rests extensively, so that most of the time only two parts sound simultaneously. Probably it was this peculiarity that influenced the choice of this particular motet; the two-part organ texture, which was normal for this period (and up to the middle of the 15th century) was achieved in *Tribum quem* without difficulty and without essential omissions. In fact, we find that in a few places, where only one voice is heard in the original, the organ arranger has added some freely invented notes to preserve the continuity of the two-part texture from

Fig.8

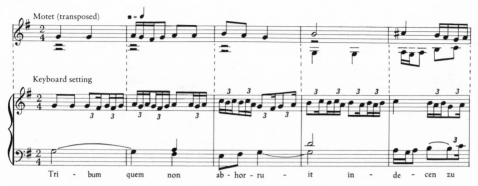

beginning to end. In the first three measures, for example, where the motet starts monophonically, a lower part is added for the left hand, and in measures 8–9 the pause in the triplum is replaced by a freely invented continuation of the upper part.

The decisive element of the clavier arrangement is the addition of ornamental figuration, which is also considered absolutely necessary in all later intabulations. In the present instance it is mainly a revolving triplet figure, shown in Fig.8, which imparts a lively, genuinely clavieristic character to the upper part.

Like *Tribum quem*, the motet *Firmissime* has many rests that frequently reduce the three-part setting to two parts. Nevertheless it contains several passages in which all three voices are active, and these lead to three-part sections in the clavier setting as well. Fig.9 shows two of these. (In the transcription the notes are disposed as in the original: The mensural notation appears in the upper system, the letter notation in the lower one.)

Fig.9

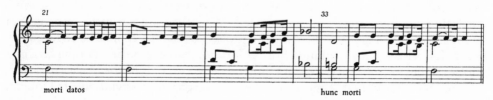

In *Flos vernalis* the movement of the coloratura increases to thirty-second notes (see Fig.10).

The *Codex Faenza*

The next source of clavier music is of Italian provenance. The *Codex Faenza*,[4] discovered—or, more correctly, rediscovered—in 1939, contains a large collection

27

Fig.10

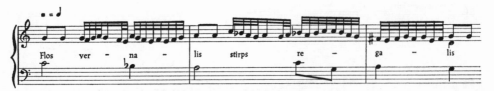

of pieces in a surprisingly modern notation, that is, on two staves with regularly drawn bar lines that mark off groups of breve value. There is no doubt that these pieces represent clavier music, not, as it was first assumed, ensemble music for two melodic instruments. The main reason for this assumption was that the music is in two parts, without the full chords that one expects in keyboard music. But it is precisely this two-part texture, with richly figurated upper part and quietly moving lower part, that points to the organ. It is found not only in the works of the *Robertsbridge fragment* but, even more distinctly, in the German organ settings from the first half of the 15th century.

The *Codex Faenza* contains forty-seven clavier settings, most of which turn out to be intabulations of vocal music: ballades by Machaut (*Hont paour, De tout flors*), madrigals by Jacopo da Bologna (*Soto l'imperio, Non al suo amante, I' mi son un, O ciecho mondo, Aquil' altera*) and Bartolino de Padua (*Qualle legge, La dolce cera, Imperial sedendo*), ballate by Landini (*Che pena questa, Non ara may*) and Antonio Zaccara (*Rosetta che non cangi, Un fior gentil*), etc. In addition we find two groups of Kyrie and Gloria, a single Kyrie, a dance-like piece (*Bel fiore dança*), and some settings that have not been identified.

The intabulations are based on the same principles as those in the *Robertsbridge fragment*, but differ from them in details of style. While some three-part passages occur in the earlier pieces, the two-part texture is now strictly carried through. When the vocal original is in two parts (as in *I' mi son un* or *Imperial sedendo*), the intabulation merely gives the upper part a more florid motion, while the tenor remains practically unchanged. We deliberately use the very general term "more florid motion" because the process of change cannot be reduced to a formula such as "ornamentation" or "coloration," as can be done in the intabulations of the 16th century. Not infrequently the contour of the upper part is so thoroughly altered that it must be called a paraphrase. Particularly striking and interesting is the tendency to "heighten" the melody, to shift it to a higher range and thereby give it greater intensity. Fig.11a. is an example of ornamentation (a portion of the vocalise on "la . . . vidi" from *Non al suo amante*), and b. an example of a heightening paraphrase (the beginning of the *volta* from *I' mi son un*).[5] The tenor, which is left unaltered, is omitted here. (From here on all musical examples in this chapter are reduced 1:4, breve = half note, unless otherwise indicated.) In the second example note that the organ part ascends to *d''* in every

28

Fig.11

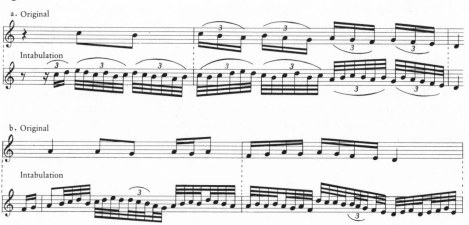

measure, while the vocal original moves between *d'* and *a'*. Such heightening in the paraphrase recalls the boldly ascending figures that Buxtehude and Bach use in their organ chorales. This feature and several other details suggest an inner relationship between the music of the 14th century and that of the late Baroque, a relationship that is also indicated by the fact that Buxtehude's and Bach's organ music have often been called "Gothic."

A number of the vocal originals are in three parts, e.g., the two ballades by Machaut, the ballate by Landini, and Jacopo's *Aquil' altera*. Here the middle part is generally disregarded, except at places where it takes over the melody, i.e., where the upper part descends below the middle part or rests. Otherwise the style is the same: The organ part is often freely formulated and always in a higher range than the vocal original.

In the above examples the figuration consists chiefly of variants of the mordent and the turn, with occasional admixtures of scale fragments. Several times, however, a characteristic formula occurs—a descending appoggiatura of a second followed by a downward skip of a fourth, as in Fig.12 (both passages are from *Imperial sedendo*). This figure is of special interest because it recurs in the German organ settings of the period 1430–1450.

In comparison with the stereotyped intabulations of the 16th century, the methods employed in the *Codex Faenza* are remarkably varied and free. Equally remarkable is the virtuosic finger technique of the right hand. Not until the in-

Fig.12

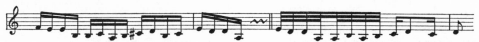

tabulations of the *Buxheim Organ Book*, about one hundred years later, do we again find clavier technique at a similarly high level of development.

In addition to the intabulations, the *Codex Faenza* contains several original keyboard pieces: *Bel fiore dança*, which is best assigned to the clavichord or harpsichord, and some Kyries and Glorias, which are presumably for organ. The dance piece consists of two sections of 20 and 12 measures, respectively. Fig.13 shows the tenor moving in relatively long notes of equal duration (it seems to have a distant, but probably accidental, similarity to the *spagna* tune of the 15th century), while the right hand plays figures of a unified, somewhat monotonous rhythm that underscores the dance character of the piece.

Fig.13

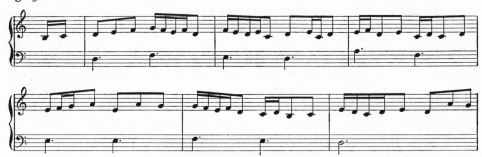

With the Kyries and Glorias the *Codex Faenza* opens the literature of liturgical organ music, which assumes increasing importance during the 15th and 16th centuries. All the Faenza settings are based on the melodies of Mass IV, *Cunctipotens genitor*, which were also frequently employed in later periods. In two instances rudimentary organ Masses are formed by combining a Kyrie with an immediately following Gloria. These two Masses also exhibit the *alternatim* structure obligatory for all later organ Masses, i.e., the alternation of organ movements and Gregorian chant.* Most clearly this structure emerges in the second Kyrie-Gloria (*MD*, XV, pp.85f.). It comprises five movements for the Kyrie and ten for the Gloria, distributed as follows:

Organ	Gregorian Chant
Kyrie: 1. Kyrie I	2. Kyrie II
3. Kyrie III	4. Christe I
5. Christe II	6. Christe III
7. Kyrie IV	8. Kyrie V
9. Kyrie VI	

---

* In the course of this book we will use the terms *alternatim* structure or alternating organ Mass although they may not always reflect the situation correctly. Cf.pp.418–19.

Gloria:

	1. Gloria in excelsis Deo
2. Et in terra . . . voluntatis	3. Laudamus te
4. Benedicimus te	5. Adoramus te
6. Glorificamus te	7. Gratias . . . gloriam tuam
8. Domine Deus, Rex . . . omnipotens	9. Domine Fili . . . Christe
10. Domine Deus, Agnus . . . Patris	11. Qui tollis . . . miserere nobis
12. Qui tollis nostram	13. Qui sedes . . . miserere nobis
14. Quoniam tu solus sanctus	15. Quoniam tu Dominus
16. Tu solus . . . Christus	17. Cum Sancto Spiritu
18. In gloria Dei Patris	
19. Amen	

The alternating distribution in this Gloria is interesting: it is almost exactly the same as that in later Glorias of Italian provenance, but it differs from the German and English Glorias (cf.p.93).

The other "organ Mass" of the *Codex Faenza* (*MD*, XIII, pp.81ff.) has only three movements for the Kyrie: *Kyrie, Christe, Kyrie*. The Gloria shows the same distribution as the one above, but breaks off with the *Qui tollis*. Toward the end of the manuscript there is another single Kyrie movement (*MD*, XV, p.75).[6]

Stylistically all these movements are formulated according to a uniform principle. The Gregorian melody is put into the lower part as a sequence of notes of equal length, each of which fills an entire measure. This kind of presentation assumes a fundamental importance in the subsequent evolution of the organ chorale up to Bach; we shall designate it as *cantus planus*. An upper part fills the time interval between the sustained tones of the *cantus planus* with florid figurations. The brief *Benedicimus te* of the second Mass is an example of this texture (Fig.14).

Fig.14

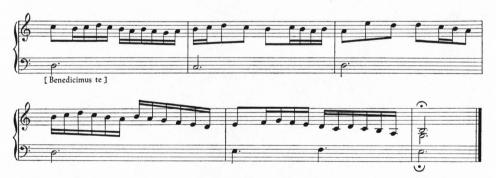

[Benedicimus te]

In the penultimate measure the *cantus planus* is modified by shortening the note values. Nearly every movement of this Mass exhibits such deviations here and there; elsewhere the notes keep their normal distance, but are connected by free insertions (ornamented *cantus planus*), e.g., in the excerpt from Kyrie I in

Fig.15

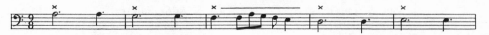

Fig.15. By contrast, the pieces of the first Mass exhibit a strict *cantus-planus* setting, which predominates in later liturgical compositions (e.g., in the organ hymns by Cabezón).

An English *Felix Namque*

From the end of the 14th or beginning of the 15th century we have a recently discovered English organ piece.[7] It is a two-part arrangement of the offertory *Felix namque*, a chant that plays an important role in English organ music of the 16th century. In contrast to the florid figurations of the Italian pieces, the upper part moves mostly in alternate quarter and eighth notes (the time signature is 6/8).

5

The Fifteenth Century

Sources Before 1450

WITH THE BEGINNING of the 15th century the French, Italian, and English traditions of clavier music once again recede for a long time—for over a hundred years. We know that great church organs were built at various places,[1] and some names of organists, like the Florentine Squarcialupi have reached us, but we do not know what music was played on these organs. From the entire 15th century no organ music is extant from France, Italy, or England.

Another area, Germany, emerges at this time. A considerable number of fragments for the period c.1425–1450 have been preserved, as well as Conrad Paumann's *Fundamentum organisandi* (1452) and the *Buxheim Organ Book* (c. 1470), a voluminous collection that may be called the last document of Medieval organ music. A list and a brief description of these sources follow:[2]

C. Vienna, Nationalbibl. Cod. 3617, a motet manuscript of the 13th century. Contains a *Kyrie magnae Deus* for organ as a supplement (fol.10v).
D. Breslau, Staatsbibl. I Qu 438, a cover leaf that comes from Sagan. Contains parts of a Gloria.
E. Breslau, Staatsbibl. I Qu 42, a fragment that comes from the Breslau Dominican monastery. Contains a song arrangement and the beginning of a fundamentum.
F. Munich, Staatsbibl. Cod. lat. 7755, a collective manuscript of medical treatises and an organ tract. Contains a song arrangement at the end.
G. Munich, Staatsbibl. Cod. lat. 5963, a collection of mathematical and astrological tracts. Contains a Magnificat for organ (fol.248).
H. Berlin, Staatsbibl. theol. lat. quart. 290, a collection of sermons (on fol.17 there is an indication of place and date: Wynsem, 1431) with musical entries (on fol.56v–58): *Wol up ghesellen,* Sanctus, Patrem, and two other settings.[3]
I. Breslau, Staatsbibl. I F 687, a fragment that comes from the Breslau

Dominican monastery. Contains *Bonus tenor Leohardi, Tenor bonus III Petri* (or *punctorum?*), a collection of teaching examples, *Der Winter der wyl weychen,* and *Mit ganczem Willen.*

    K. Hamburg, Staatsbibl. N D VI 3225. This manuscript contains alchemistic descriptions and sermons (several of them dated 1457), and two interpolations with organ music, which L. Schrade has designated as Ha and Hb. Ha (fol.1–5) contains teaching examples and two Magnificats (the first being a later entry); Hb (fol.11–15) is inscribed: "Sequitur fundamentum bonum et utile pro cantu chorali valens videlicet octo notarum wolffgangi de nova domo," and contains teaching examples as well as a brief preamble and two arrangements of a song tenor.

    L. Tablature of Adam Ileborgh, 1448 (Philadelphia, Curtis Institute of Music). Contains 5 preambles and 3 arrangements (*mensurae*) of *Frowe al myn hoffen an dyr lyed.*

    M. *Fundamentum organisandi Magistri Conradi Paumanns Ceci de Nürenberga Anno 1452* (formerly Wernigerode Zb 14, now Berlin, Staatsbibl. Ms. mus. 40613). Contains, besides the fundamentum, a Magnificat, an *O clemens,* 12 song settings, and 3 preambles.

    N. Erlangen, Univ.-Bibl. Hs. 554 (now 729?), fourteen pages of a collective volume (fol.127v–133v). Contains a copy of Paumann's *Fundamentum* as well as prelude-like pieces.

    O. *Buxheim Organ Book* (Munich, Staatsbibl. Cim. 352b; *olim* Ms. mus. 3725), a voluminous tome with over 250 pieces of all sorts.

A remarkable fact emerges from this list of sources: At least three different areas of Germany participated in the development of organ music of the 15th century—the South with the organ tract (F), Paumann's *Fundamentum* (M), the Erlangen tablature (N), and the *Buxheim Organ Book* (O); Silesia with the *Sagan fragment* (D) and the fragments of the Breslau Dominican monastery (E, I); and the Northwest with the *Wynsem manuscript* (H)[4] and the tablature of Ileborgh (L), which comes from Stendal. The Hamburg tablature (K), more specifically its second portion, was written by a Wolffgang de Nova Domo and therefore probably comes from a place called Neuhaus, which cannot be identified today.

    We will treat manuscripts C to L, each of which contains only a few pieces, as a unit, and divide the repertoire presented in them into four categories: liturgical compositions, song settings, preludes, and teaching examples. The larger sources M, N, and O deserve separate treatment.

LITURGICAL COMPOSITIONS

The liturgical repertoire of these German sources consists of a Kyrie (in C), a Gloria (in D), three Magnificats (in G and K), and a Sanctus and Credo (in H). Without exception these pieces exhibit the two-part *cantus-planus* setting in the strict form, without the occasional paraphrasing of the *cantus firmus* found in the *Codex Faenza.* The chief difference lies in the formulation of the upper parts, which avoid the fast ornaments and runs of the Italian arrangements and prefer a more expressive, if at times rather awkward, melodic line. In the same way as in the visual arts—compare Italian and German sculpture at the beginning of the 15th century—the contrast between South and North manifests itself here.

The oldest of the extant compositions is probably the Kyrie of the Vienna manuscript (C). It is based on the Kyrie *magnae Deus* (Kyrie V of the present order), whose words are written into the music. The upper part moves in semibreves throughout, the chant tune in notes eight times as long, as shown in Fig.16. The figuration consists of a series of four-note formulae which recur frequently in this or similar forms in German organ music of the 15th century. The "affective" formula at the beginning of measure 3 is particularly interesting. It occurs six times in this piece, always starting on the fifth of the respective tenor note. The cadence formula at the end of the phrase is even more remarkable. It is frequently encountered in the organ music of the period, but cannot be found anywhere else in music literature. Occasionally it occurs in the *Codex Faenza*, although not as an expressive cadence formula but as a fast ornament (cf.Fig.12).

Fig.16

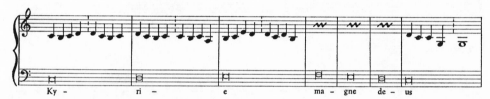

Ky -   ri -   e   ma - gne de - us

The Gloria of the *Sagan fragment* (D) consists of three sections: *Et in terra pax*, *Benedicimus te*, and *Glorificamus te*. It omits the *Gloria in excelsis Deo*, *Laudamus te*, and *Adoramus te*, thereby offering another piece of evidence for the practice of alternation. The chant tune on which this work is based is the Gloria ad lib. I of the Vatican Edition, transposed down a fifth. At the very beginning there is a remarkable change from the skip of a fourth *c–f* (originally *g–c′*) to one of a tritone *c–f♯*, a forceful intensification of expression at the expense of the rules. In the course of the piece the raised fourth is used often, producing a Lydian coloring. Fig.17 gives the beginning of the *Et in terra*. Like almost all organ pieces of the 15th century, it starts with a fast anacrusis. (The symbol x added to notes in this and several other examples indicates that at the particular place the original shows the note form ♪, whose meaning is unclear and variable.) The addition of the upper part is extensively governed by the principle of octave doubling. To connect and bridge the fixed points, figures of a contour similar to those in the *Codex Faenza* are employed, but in a quieter motion, occasionally less smooth, willful, or somewhat awkward. At times peculiarly wooden, repetitive figures occur, as in Fig.18a. and b., from the *Benedicimus te* and *Glorificamus te*, respectively.

Fig.17

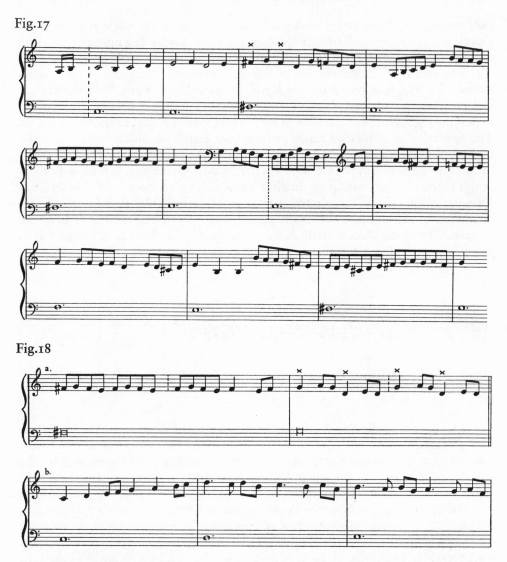

Fig.18

The Berlin manuscript (H) contains a *Summum Sanctus,* which is based on the Sanctus of Mass IV (*Conctipotens genitor*). The first (or third?) *Sanctus,* the *Dominus,* and the *In excelsis* have been composed. The figuration in the upper part is similar to that of the Kyrie discussed above (cf.Fig.16); it does, however, occasionally involve passages that move twice as fast, as shown in Fig.19. The incomplete *Patrem* preserved in the same manuscript shows the same character. In both pieces not only octaves and fifths but occasionally sixths begin to occur as contrapuntal intervals.

36

Fig.19

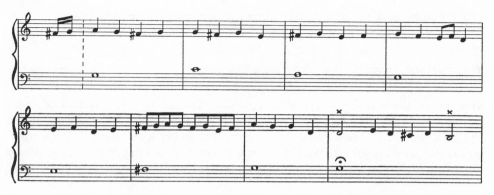

The Munich manuscript (G) contains a brief *Magnificat octavi toni quatuor notarum,* which presents faster motion in both voices: eighth notes in the figuration, half notes in the tenor. In measure 5 we find a full *F*-major triad in the right hand—the first sign of a specifically clavieristic technique (Fig.20).

Fig.20

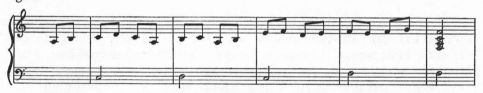

The designation *quatuor notarum* refers to the fact that every measure contains four notes. In several other works, especially in song settings, the meter is indicated by legends like *trium notarum, quatuor notarum, sex notarum,* or *octo notarum.* Their kinship with the *divisio ternaria, quaternaria, senaria,* and *octonaria* of 14th-century Italian music is unmistakable, especially when one contrasts them with the totally different French terminology: perfect and imperfect *tempus* and *prolatio.*

Another (untitled) arrangement of the eighth Magnificat tone is found in the Hamburg manuscript (K) as the last piece of the first musical interpolation.[5] This arrangement also comtains an *F*-major triad, and at the same place as in the Munich Magnificat, but it differs from the latter in that its figuration is more advanced. It is written in 3/4 time and in sixteenth notes (Fig.21).

SONG SETTINGS[6]

We now turn to those pieces whose titles or, when none is given, whose *cantus*

Fig.21

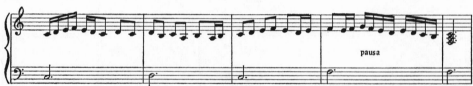

firmi prove them to be arrangements of German songs. The method of composition as well as the stylistic attitude here are basically the same as in the liturgical works. The borrowed tune is entrusted to the lower part, in long, equal notes, one per measure. Above it there is a freely invented upper part in moderate motion, which uses the same formulae as in the liturgical pieces.

Fig.22

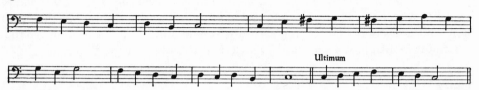

The Breslau fragment (E) contains a setting of a simple melody; its contour as well as its regular structure indicate that it is a popular song (see Fig.22). Each note of the basic melody is sustained for one 6/4 measure, the final note of each phrase for two measures. Fig.23 shows a passage from this setting (measures 9–12), with remarkable affective appoggiaturas followed by broken triads.

Fig.23

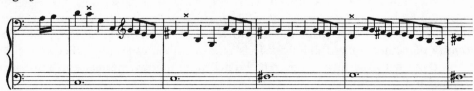

The Munich organ treatise (F) is followed by a piece of some length; the lower part again appears to reveal the regular structure and pronounced C-major tonality of a popular tune. In the arrangement each note occupies a 6/4 measure, and many of the figurations employ the same formulae as the piece from the Breslau fragment. Particularly frequent is a rhythmic group, rather touching in its awkwardness (Fig.24).

The Berlin manuscript (H) contains two song settings: *Wol up ghesellen yst an der tyet quatuor notarum* and *Frysicum* (?), both in 4/4 time (*quatuor*

Fig.24

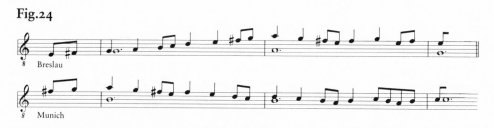

notarum). In the first twelve measures of *Wol up ghesellen* the two-part arrangement is expanded to three parts by using an added line of letter notation. Other
interesting details are that every phrase starts with the two-note upbeat, which is
so characteristic of early organ music; the cadence formula (|*d' c' c' g* | *g*) (cf.
Fig.12) occurs twice; and in the three-voice passage the middle part uses the raised
fourth as a leading tone to the fifth. Fig.25 shows the beginning of the composition.
table appended to his print contains twenty-nine "marques des argreménts," some

Fig.25

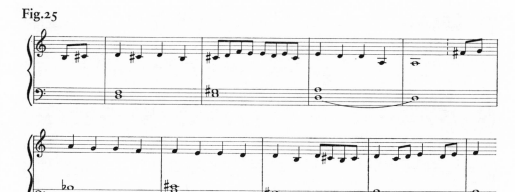

  Two settings of one song are preserved in the Hamburg manuscript (K).[7]
The first one, designated *Tenor bonus duarum mensurarum vz. sub secunda
mensura brevis* (?) *prolationis*, is in 4/4 time, the other is in 3/4.
  The Breslau fragment (I) contains four song settings. The first one, entitled
Bonus tenor Leohardi, is based on a C-major tune of regular structure and impressive contour. It is reproduced in its entirety in Fig.26. The arrangement, for
which the unknown composer chose the swinging motion of 3/4 time, is just as
attractive as the melody. Each note of the basic tune is held for one measure, the
final note of each phrase for two. The C-major tonality of the song is fully
maintained, and reinforced by well-planned cadences in the upper part. The
melodic contour of the upper voice is easily one of the most attractive creations

Fig.26

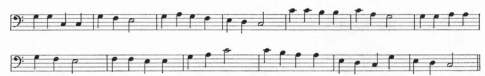

of early organ music. Gently and evenly, inspired by a touching tenderness of expression, it flows on through ever new turns—an impressive musical counterpart of the visual arts of the period. In addition to the two- and three-note anacruses (*a b* | *c'*), (*c' a b* | *c'*), we find for the first time the four-note anacrusis (*c' b a b* | *c'*), which is used almost exclusively by Paumann and in the *Buxheim Organ Book*. Fig. 27 shows the arrangement of the third phrase of this song.

Fig.27

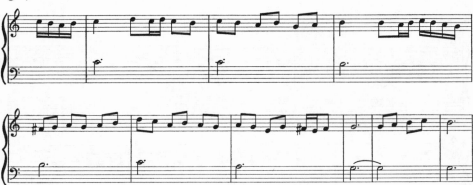

The next piece in this manuscript, *Tenor bonus III [notarum] Petri* (?), has numerous diads in the right hand. It represents an experiment that is not rivaled for a long time. To illustrate the procedure, the final measures are reproduced in Fig.28. The occasional octaves and tenths suggest that the low notes of the upper part were played by the left hand, and that therefore the lower part was probably played on the pedals.

Fig.28

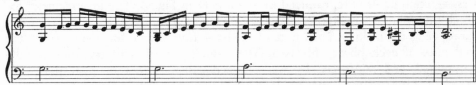

Two song settings conclude the manuscript: *Der Winter der wil weychen* and *Mit ganczem Willen*. They are the first examples of a later practice, that of paraphrasing the basic melody. They are also the first songs that reappear in Paumann's *Fundamentum* and in the *Buxheim Organ Book*. They will be discussed later.

The 1448 tablature of Adam Ileborgh[8] is singular in several ways. In addition to a number of preludes, it contains three arrangements of the song *Frowe al myn hoffen an dyr lyed,* designated as *Mensura trium notarum, Mensura duorum notarum,* and *Mensura sex notarum.* The first setting contains three semibreves per measure (3/4), the second two (2/4), and the third six (6/4). The *Mensura duorum notarum* is in two parts; the others are reinforced by a contratenor, just like the opening measures of *Wol up ghesellen.*

These song settings have an organ style that is clearly different from that of the earlier German sources, particularly because of the very ornamented and occasionally virtuosic treatment of the upper part, which recalls the luxuriant figurations of the Italian organ music found in the *Codex Faenza.* But there is an unmistakable difference between them. In the pieces of the *Codex Faenza* figurations of a unified character follow one another flowingly (cf.Fig.11); but Ileborgh, deliberately or through a lack of ability, changes his design constantly. His inventive faculty exhausts itself at the end of every measure and each measure is filled with new figures. Only in occasional sequential passages do more unified formulations emerge, but neither their elegance nor their expressiveness is impressive.

Fig.29 shows a portion of the first *mensura.* The five-note turn that appears in measure 3 occurs several times in Ileborgh's music; it is also used as an anacrusis to both the first and the third *mensura.*

Fig.29

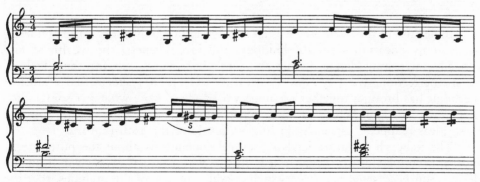

The second *mensura* is less heterogeneous, but very pedantic, because of an excessive use of sequential chains. At two places the sequences employ a peculiar figure that reappears in a similar form in the other two settings (Fig.30). Could

Fig.30

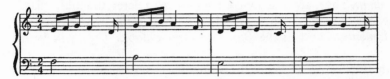

it stem from the influence of 14th-century French syncopation theory? Although the figure corresponds completely to these teachings, they were never applied so awkwardly by the French.

The third *mensura* has even more peculiar formulations or misformulations than the first. It is truly a collection of curiosities, a contrivance in which mechanical labor manifests itself with really touching honesty, as, for example, in Fig.31.

Fig.31

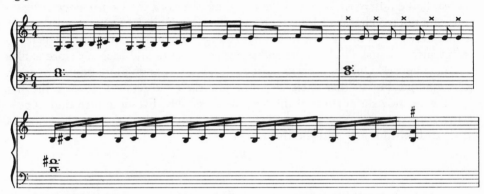

In defense of the composer we can say that although he lacks musical finesse, he certainly does not want for boldness and inventiveness; the wealth of historically interesting details in his *mensurae* fully makes up for their lack of artistic perfection. We may even regard it as a fortunate accident that a musical mechanic has brought together the most varied ideas, from whatever source they may derive, and put before us an extremely instructive museum show. Some of these ideas reappear, especially in English music of the 16th century.

The Ileborgh tablature leads to several conclusions about the purely technical aspects of German organ music in the 15th century. It is clear from the designation *pedale seu manuale,* which is added to one of the preludes, that the lower voice was, or at least could be, played on the pedals. Indeed, from certain considerations (see note 8), one can conclude with certainty that in the three-part pieces both the tenor and the contratenor were heard in the pedals, and that the technique of double pedals, which is usually associated with Tunder and Bach, was in use in Germany as early as the 15th century.

PRELUDES

Earlier writers (cf.Chap.4, note 2) have called some compositions in the *Roberts-bridge fragment* preludes, though without any justification. This type occurs for the first time in the tablature of Adam Ileborgh of 1448, over a hundred years later. Even without the heading: *Incipiunt praeludia diversarum notarum secundum modernum modum subtiliter et diligenter collecta . . . ,* and such titles as *Praeambulum in C* and *Praeambulum bonum,* it would be clear that these are the first essays in a genre that, more so than any other, is the exclusive domain of keyboard music. In Ileborgh's tablature there are no vocal archetypes on which to lean, no borrowed tenors on which to build: The organist creates freely out of his own invention, guided only by the technical capabilities of his instrument. Although one may therefore assume and anticipate a certain freedom of style and an unrestrained flow of ideas in the preludes, it is nevertheless surprising to see how strong these forces are in the first attempts—much stronger, in fact, than in many later works of the same type. One almost has the impression that a long-suppressed aspiration to free oneself from a foreign domination has finally emerged in an elementary manner, and it is perhaps not incorrect to relate the words *"secundum modernum modum"* in the heading to the almost revolutionary style of these preludes. It manifests itself most impressively in the fourth of the five preludes, designated *Praeambulum super d a f et g,** reproduced here in its entirety in Fig.32.

A novel, almost unique, feature in the history of keyboard music is the rhythm of the upper part, which resists all attempts to fit it into a meter or into measures. Completely unrestrained and almost unruly long and short notes form a fantastic soaring line of great tension and expression. A closer look shows, however, that the "unruliness" consists only in a dropping of conventions, not in a lack of intrinsic rules. On the contrary, the rhythmic and melodic movement exhibits a fine sensitivity, an effective construction, a vivacious interplay of external freedom and internal restraint. Note the wide arch of the first section; the low range and quiet motion of the second one, which so effectively prepares the modulation and the ascent of the third; and the long-drawn, calming descent of the last section. All this happens within the simplest harmonic framework, above three tenor notes (*d e d*), which are joined in contrary motion by the reinforcing notes (*a g♯ a*) in the contratenor. It must be assumed that, as in the *mensurae,* the lower parts were executed as double pedals. As elsewhere in Ileborgh, the upper part ends on the third (here, in fact, on the minor third), a practice that was otherwise avoided in final chords until about 1600.

---

* The legend *super d a f et g* seems to point to transposition.

Fig.32

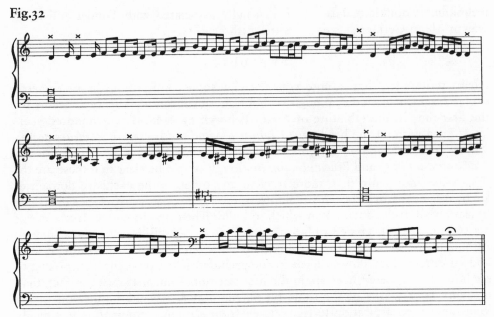

The first prelude of the Ileborgh collection, *Praeambulum in C et potest variari in d f g a* (cf. footnote on p.43), is very similar, but shorter. Except for transposition, the same lower parts are used: (*c d c*) in the tenor and (*g f# g*) in the contratenor. The other three preludes are in two voices and are designated as *manualiter* (one as *pedale seu manuale*). The lower parts consist mostly of descending scales; executing them on the pedals would indeed be rather forced. The second piece, *Praeambulum bonum super C manualiter et variatur ad omnes* (Fig.33) is remarkable, especially for its full final chord.

Fig.33

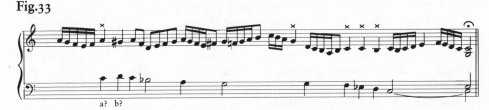

The Hamburg manuscript (K) contains a *Preambulum super g*,[9] in which one can see a first step in the direction of stylistic stabilization of the prelude. It starts with a short series of relatively long notes, of equal duration, and only in the final cadence do free figures similar to those in Ileborgh's preludes appear (Fig.34). Many preludes in the *Buxheim Organ Book* are built on the same principle, except that a free introduction often precedes the "stabilized" section.

Fig.34

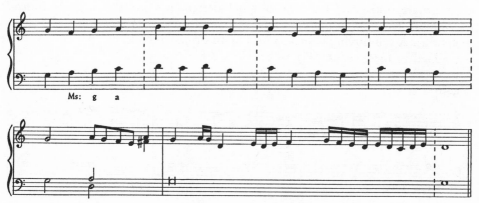

THEORY OF ORGAN COMPOSITION

Several of the sources discussed in this chapter contain explanations, brief examples, or lengthy pieces used to teach organ composition. They give us a fairly clear idea of the technical background of the organ works of the period. Perhaps the oldest document of this type is the recently discovered and published organ tract of the *Munich Codex* (F).[10] It cites a number of four-note formulae, which are differentiated as *ascendentes, descendentes,* or *indifferentes.* The formulae (*c d c d*), (*c d e f*), and (*c b c d*) belong to the first category; (*c b c a*), (*c b a g*), and (*c b b a*) are in the second; and (*c d b c*), (*d c b c*), and (*c d e c*) in the third. By combining two such formulae one arrives at a group of eight notes (semibreves) that coordinates with one tenor note; and care must be taken that the first, fifth, and eighth notes of each group are consonant with the tenor. As an example the author offers an *ascensus,* i.e., a stepwise ascending series of tenor notes, and later also a *descensus,* in which the consonances that have to be watched are indicated by lines. The former is shown in Fig.35. Note that in the

Fig.35

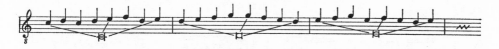

third measure the use of the "indifferent" formula (*f e d e*) leads to an appoggiatura.

Under the title *Incipit fundamentum bonum p[edaliter] in c d a,* the Breslau manuscript (E) contains an *ascensus* and *descensus* that goes from *c* to *b* and uses much freer figures. Even more interesting is a collection of twenty-eight brief teaching examples found in the Breslau fragment (I). They are based on such progressions as *f–g–a* (the original designation for this type is *clausula ascendens*), *f–e–d* (*clausula descendens*), *f–g–f* (*clausula in idem*), and *f–f* (*pausa generalis*). A reinforcing contratenor and an ornamented upper part in 3/4 time are added to these tenors. Fig.36 provides three examples.

Fig.36

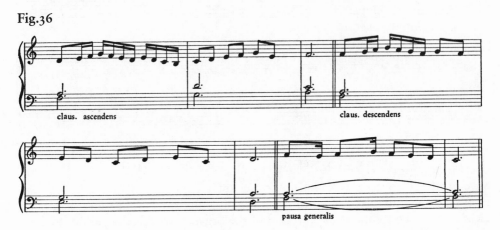

claus. ascendens   claus. descendens

pausa generalis

The Hamburg manuscript (K) begins with an *ascensus* and *descensus* ranging from *c* to *c'*, paired with an ornamented upper part in 3/4 time. This is followed by thirty-two examples with titles such as *Sequitur capitulum de c ut ut* [*c like ut*], *Sequitur capitulum de re ut d* [*re like d*], etc., and finally six *pausae*. In the term *capitulum* one scholar has sought a connection with the liturgy[11] (reading of the *capitulum* from the Scriptures) but in reality it only means "chapter," in the sense of "section." Moreover, these examples obviously do not teach the setting of two voices, but only the figural ornamentation of interval progressions. In Fig.37 the letters do not denote an independent part to which the upper part forms a counterpoint, but merely indicate the interval that is ornamented in the upper part. Thus these pieces are interesting not so much in connection with organ composition as with the later theory of ornamentation in the 16th century.[12]

Fig.37

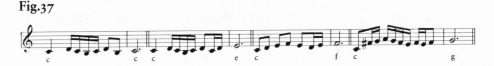

c   c   c   e   c   f   c   g

The second insert of the Hamburg manuscript begins with a *Fundamentum bonum et utile pro cantu chorali valens videlicet octo notarum wolffgangi de nova domo.* This is a practical composition text quite similar in design to that of the well-known *Fundamentum organisandi* by Conrad Paumann. Both present scale-like figures, which, curiously, all start from *B* and generally go up to *b*. In an *ascensus simplex* and *descensus eiusdem* this range is covered stepwise; in the *ascensus* and *descensus in tertias* it is covered in thirds: *B–d, c–e, d–f*, . . . , *g–b* | *b–g, a–f*, etc.; then in fourths; fifths, sixths; and even sevenths, which reduce the series to two skips: *B–a, c–b*. To these didactic tenors the author sets an ornamented upper part, which is in 4/4 time (*octo notarum*), following the older tradition, and seems to be only an awkward attempt. Fig.38 is an example of the *ascensus* and *descensus in quintas*. Note that the first bass note of each measure forms an octave with the counterpoint. This is true of almost all the other teaching pieces.

Fig.38

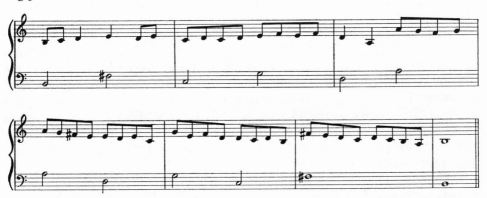

Another *Fundamentum sub secunda mensura minoris prolacionis* follows, in which the same tenor passages are given an ornamented counterpart in 3/4 time. This meter reflects the progressive tendencies that emerge in organ music around 1450—half a century later than in vocal music. Everything in this fundamentum sounds smoother, less uneven than in the first one. The tenor figures no longer start on *B,* but on *c*. The series in fifths may again serve as an example (Fig.39).

Fig.39

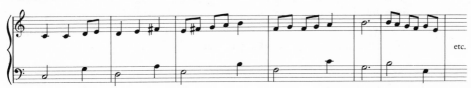

Paumann's *Fundamentum Organisandi*

In Conrad Paumann we meet the first clearly outlined personality in the field of organ music. He was born blind in Nuremberg about 1415, and became the organist at the Sebaldus church there about 1440. In his *Spruchgedichte auf die Stadt Nürnberg* (1447), Hans Rosenplüt praises him as the

> meyster ob allen maystern:
> Solt man durch kunst einen meister kron,
> er trug wol auf von golt ein kron.*

Around 1450 he went to Munich to enter the service of Duke Albrecht III, and later served his successor, Albrecht IV. His fame soon spread into other countries; in 1470 we find him at the courts of Mantua and Ferrara, and in 1471 at Regensburg, where he played the organ for Emperor Frederic III and his retinue. He died in 1473 at Munich, and is honored by a gravestone that can still be seen at the Frauenkirche.

Paumann compiled for his pupils a *Fundamentum organisandi*,[13] dated 1452, in which organ teaching of the 15th century received its classical form. The point of departure is a series of scale-like formulae similar to those of the *Fundamentum Wolffgangi* in the Hamburg manuscript, but they start on *c* and encompass a tenth, up to *e'*. The *ascensus et descensus simplex* is followed by the *ascensus et descensus per tertias, per quartas,* and *per quintas.* Each of these is presented twice (the second *simplex* is erroneously copied after the two *per tertias*). At the end there is also an *ascensus et descensus per sextas,* which consists of only *c–a:a–c.*

Although we cannot be certain about the chronological relationship between Paumann's *Fundamentum* and that of Wolffgang de Nova Domo (whose date is unknown), it is clear that stylistically the former represents a later stage of development. All its pieces are written in *tempus perfectum,* the meter that dominated vocal music almost exclusively since Dunstable and Dufay. Another progressive trait is that the notes of the *cantus firmus,* which in principle are set in the perfect breves of the *cantus planus,* are frequently ornamented or even freely paraphrased. Also, the upper part, which is set to the *cantus firmus,* exhibits more refined features, particularly in rhythmic formulation. In general, when the tenor moves in sustained notes, it is paired with a counterpoint of florid figurations; but when it itself is ornamented, the upper part employs the same note values. Unisons, octaves, fifths, thirds, and sixths are used to connect the two voices. Parallel fifths and octaves are generally avoided, but are still found occasionally. However the dissonant appoggiatura at the beginning of the measure, which gives older organ works the typical expression of Gothic over-

---

* Master above all masters:
  If one crown a master because of his art,
  he would surely wear a crown of gold.

Fig.40

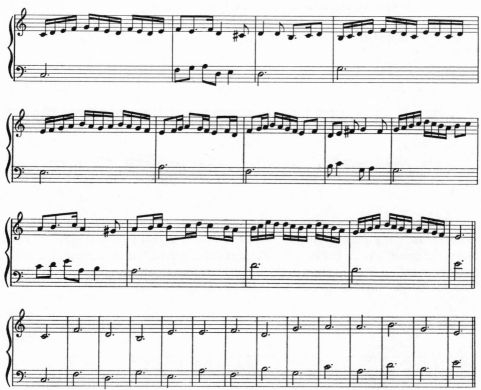

excitement, are almost entirely eliminated. The first *ascensus per quartas* in Fig.40 is a typical example; its skeletal form has been added.

After the *ascensus et descensus* there follows a collection of *pause*, i.e., cadence formulae above sustained or repeated notes, such as occur at the end of a composition or of a section. For each tone of the hexachord three or four examples are given, of which those based on g are cited in Fig.41.

Fig.41

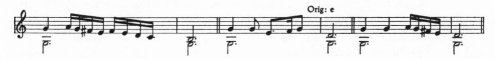

These *pause* are followed by a group of *redeuntes simplices super sex voces*, in which the repeated tones of the *pause* are extended to form pedal points six to twelve measures long. The six examples given present (for those who want to listen!) instructive material on the question of tonality and accidentals in the 15th century. Fig.42 includes several excerpts that show that the remark, "Consistency is not a virtue of the Mediaeval mind" is also valid in this area.

Fig.42

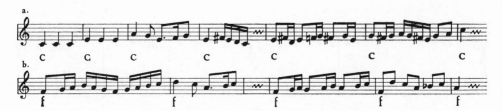

The next section bears the heading *Secuntur redeuntes in idem per duo voces.* Unfortunately it contains only a single example,[14] a real two-part setting above the pedal point on *c*. Because of its particular interest it is reproduced in its entirety in Fig.43 (a few errors in the notation of the rhythm have been corrected). This is the first time that rests are used in the upper part.

Fig.43

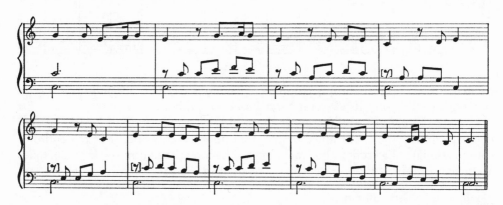

The conclusion consists of a *Fundamentum breve cum ascensu et descensu*, in which brief progressions, such as (*c d c*), (*c e f g*), (*d d e d*), etc., are treated in a fashion similar to that of the above more extended scale-like formulae. This is followed by a more substantial composition without title, which in a way seems to represent the "journeyman's masterpiece," or at least a model for one.[15] At the end of this piece we find the legend, "et sic est finis," which signals the conclusion of the *Fundamentum* proper.

50

In the Wernigerode manuscript a number of compositions are added, most of them probably by Paumann.[16] Among them there are two liturgical settings: *Magnificat* and *O Cle[mens]* (the antepenultimate section of the *Salve regina*); seven arrangements of German songs: *Wach auff mein Hort, Mit ganczem Willen, Des Klaffers Neyden, Ellend du hast, Benedicite Almechtiger Got, Domit ein gut Jare, Mein Hercz in hohen Freuden;* a French song, *En avois;* and an Italian one, *C[on]l[agreme]*. Only one of these pieces, the *Magnificat,* corresponds to the teaching examples of the *Fundamentum:* Its Gregorian tenor is laid out as a *cantus planus* that is occasionally slightly ornamented, and the upper part employs lively motion (sixteenth-note figures in 3/4 time) where the tenor has sustained notes, and moderate motion (quarters and eighths) where the tenor is ornamented.

All the other compositions represent a more advanced stage, mainly in the formulation of the tenor, in which the *cantus planus* is replaced by rhythmically free groupings in alternating half, quarter, and eighth notes. Concomitantly the character of the upper part also changes, as the ornamental formulae are replaced by a quieter, more expressive motion. Thus the complete contrast between the sustained tones of the tenor and the florid movement of the discant vanishes. Both voices join in a sweeping homogeneous duet. The new style may be exemplified by the beginning of *Ellend du hast* (Fig.44).

Fig.44

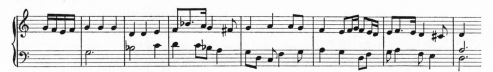

Vocal models for the German song settings that are added to the *Fundamentum* are preserved in the *Lochamer Song Book,* which constitutes the first portion of the Wernigerode manuscript. It offers a welcome opportunity to study the compositional procedures that lead from a vocal setting to an organ piece, in a manner similar to various pieces in the *Robertsbridge fragment* and the *Codex Faenza.* But there is a difference, in that most of the vocal models in the *Lochamer Song Book* are not polyphonic compositions that are intabulated, but monophonic lines (cf. below, pp.53–54) that are presented as *cantus firmi* in the organ arrangements, with an added upper part that may be, and probably is, freely invented.

In two pieces, *Mit ganczem Willen* and *Benedicite,* the organ tenor results from a transformation that may be called an ornamented or paraphrased *cantus planus:* The notes of the song, originally given as semibreves, are expanded to breves or longs, which are then mostly resolved into smaller note values. The same procedure, by the way, was used in the earlier setting of *Mit ganczem Willen* in the Breslau fragment (I). Fig.45 presents the melody of this song from the *Lochamer Song Book* and the tenors of the two organ settings. The general agreement of the two transformations is remarkable: Notes 1–4 appear in lengthened values, the low-lying cadence *d–e–d* (notes 5–7) is paraphrased in a higher range, and the downward skip of a fifth *a–d* (notes 8–10) is ornamented. And the two organ tenors continue to agree in a similar manner. Certain notes of the *cantus firmus* do not enter at their normal places, at the beginning of the assigned measure, but are shifted to the middle or end of the measure (note 6), or at times anticipated (note 5 in the *Fundamentum* setting).

Fig.45

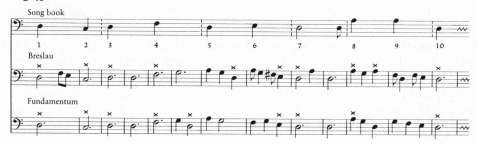

It is interesting that in the 16th and 17th centuries a stricter technique of figuration was taken up, in which the *cantus-firmus* note always appears at the beginning of the measure. In the 15th century a freer procedure was in general use, which was artistically superior, and made it possible for the creative musician to develop a completely original melody from one that was given. Many models for this procedure could be found in the vocal music of Dunstable, Dufay, and other masters.[17]

In *Benedicite Almechtiger Got* a rather strict agreement between the song (which, by the way, appears as early as 1400 in the Mondsee manuscript) and the organ tenor is evidenced: Each note (semibreve) of the song corresponds to a 3/4 measure (breve) in the tenor, which is resolved into ornamental figures.[18] See Fig.46.

Fig.46

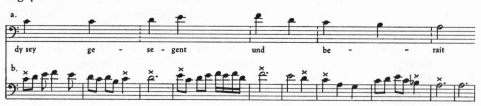

Upper parts, whose general gait has been described and illustrated in Fig.44, are added to these tenors. The difference between the old and the new style becomes particularly clear in a comparison of the two arrangements of *Mit ganczem Willen*. Although they agree very closely in the treatment of the tenors, they differ greatly in their upper parts, as Fig.47 shows (cf.meas.11–13 of Fig.45). A comparison of the two arrangements in their entirety reinforces the impression one receives from the brief excerpt cited here. The formulae and figurations, which often change from measure to measure, are replaced by a quiet, elastic, organically developing melody; the strong contrasts of the earlier lines are mitigated, their angular contours rounded; and the decorative approach is transformed into expression, dry severity into lovely gracefulness. Admittedly *Mit ganczem Willen* represents an artistic high point, which is not quite reached in the other pieces of the *Fundamentum*. Its singular position is confirmed by the fact that it is the only piece in the collection (except for the appendix pieces mentioned in note 16) that has three voices, even if only for the first half. It must be noted that the contratenor follows the tenor note for note and so is not yet a voice with rhythmic independence; and that the tenor and the discant frequently form sixths, which the contratenor completes to full sixth-chords. Here for the first time organ music accepts those harmonious sounds that give the music of Dunstable and Dufay such an unmistakable imprint. Fig.47 shows a brief passage of this kind.

Fig.47

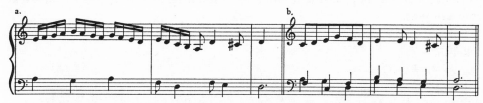

In the remaining German song settings, a comparison with their vocal models produces a substantially different result: Their tenors are taken over, at least in principle, without change; in other words, they are not first expanded to a *cantus planus* and then altered by figurations. True, here and there one finds deviations or ornamental additions, but the basic structure, in particular the number of measures, remains unchanged. The beginning of *Ellend du hast* from the *Lochamer Song Book*, given in Fig.48, will serve as an example; compare it with the beginning of the organ setting in Fig.44.

Whatever the reason for the different treatment—possibly the tunes in the *Lochamer Song Book* are not really "songs" but already ornamented tenors*—

---

* Most of the monophonic songs in the *Lochamer Song Book* are designated as tenors. On p.5, e.g., we read: *Tenor Ellend du hast.*

Fig.48

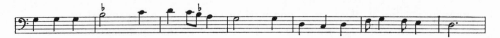

here we are interested solely in the fact that the organ composer took over the tenor part with only insignificant changes, and saw his task exclusively as the addition of the clavieristic upper voice. As examples of this practice we may cite *Des Klaffers Neyden* and *Wach auff mein Hort.* Polyphonic models exist for both organ settings; for the former in the *Lochamer Song Book*,[19] for the latter in the works of Oswald von Wolkenstein.[20] A comparison shows that in both instances the tenor is taken over without substantial changes (the first eight measures of *Wach auff*, it should be noted, are based on a sort of introduction, which is missing in Wolkenstein's song), but the upper parts of the organ settings deviate so strongly from those of the vocal works that they must be looked upon as newly invented.

These two organ works, as well as those based on *Benedicite* and *Mit ganczem Willen,* thus prove to belong to a type that must be called an "arrangement," to differentiate it from a mere transcription or intabulation. But an example of the latter type can also be found in one of the organ pieces added to the *Fundamentum, Domit ein gut Jare,* whose two parts are identical with the discant and tenor of a piece without text in the *Lochamer Song Book,* designated as *Der Sumer.* Fig.49 gives the beginnings of the original setting and of the organ transcription.

Fig.49

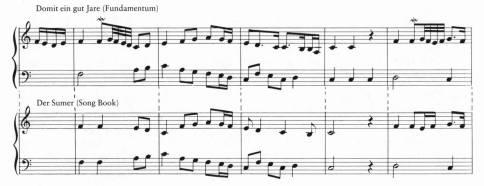

Domit ein gut Jare (Fundamentum)

Der Sumer (Song Book)

We can be brief about the remaining contents of the Wernigerode manuscript. The piece designated as *En avois* (p.70) is a setting of the song (or chanson tenor) *Une fois avant que morir,* which is preserved in the Brussels *Basse-danse*

54

manuscript.[21] The Italian ballata *Con lagreme* by Johannes Ciconia hides under the abbreviation C. l. (p.86).[22] Both melodies also occur in the *Buxheim Organ Book,* the former under the completely distorted designation *Annavasanna.* The song arrangement *Mein Hercz in hohen Freuden ist per me Georg de Putenheim* (cf.p.64) differs from the other settings in its extended use of fast figurations in thirty-second notes, which occur frequently in the *Buxheim Organ Book.* A later supplement (pp.88–92) contains two undesignated pieces—one by Wilhelmus Legrant, the other by Paumgartner—both also preserved in the *Buxheim Organ Book* (nos.113 and 110), and three *praeambula.* The first *praeambulum* consists of three brief sections, each in a different style: three-note chords, continuous motion in sixteenth notes, and dotted rhythms (Fig.50). In contrast to the preludes by Ileborgh, everything follows a regular course, but the result is dry and pedantic. Nevertheless the piece, which is probably by one of Paumann's pupils, is not without a certain interest, since it manifests the principle of contrast with a clarity uncommon for the period.

Fig.50

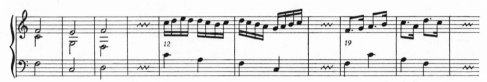

The manuscript in the University Library at Erlangen (N) consists mainly of a copy of Paumann's *Fundamentum.* It differs in some particulars from the one in the *Wernigerode Codex;* e.g., the second *ascensus simplex* appears in its correct place near the beginning of the collection. Several preludes are entered before the *Fundamentum,* but unfortunately in very faulty notation. Nevertheless it is apparent that they belong essentially to the Ileborgh type, in which free improvision is spread over a few sustained notes. But they also involve chordal passages (Fig.51).

Fig.51

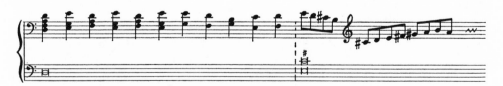

The Buxheim Organ Book

The *Buxheim Organ Book* is one of the most voluminous sources in the field of early clavier music. It was written around 1470, probably in Munich, in the circle of Paumann's disciples. For some time it was held by the Carthusian monastery at Buxheim, and since 1883 it has belonged to the Bavarian State Library in Munich.[23] For a long time only excerpts from this volume were known, but now there exist both a facsimile edition and a complete transcription by B. A. Wallner.[24]

According to the numbering of the new edition, the manuscript contains 256 works,[25] among them about forty liturgical pieces, sixteen preludes, and five collections of teaching examples. The remaining works, as far as can be determined, are arrangements or intabulations of German, French, or Italian songs. All these types are already represented in earlier sources, so that in this respect the *Buxheim Organ Book* does not offer anything new. In the realm of the stylistic evolution, however, some progress is shown, though more in the sense of a termination than of a new beginning. The following observations will serve mainly to clarify this finishing-off process.

The most important advance is the changeover to a full three-part setting. Many pieces still represent the intermediate stage, in which a two-part setting is completed here and there by a third part—usually to a larger extent than was the case earlier—but the majority consist of three complete voices: discant, tenor, and contratenor. The contratenor is not yet a real middle part, but a filler, which moves in approximately the same range as the tenor, so that repeated voice crossings result. Thus keyboard music reaches the stage of technique here that vocal music had long since attained in the secular art song of the 14th and early 15th centuries (Machaut and his successors). Quite frequently the contratenor carries out erratic skips, which only serve to get it to the place where it is needed to fill in the harmony. A particularly crass, but not at all unique, example from the *Magnificat octavi toni* (no.24) is shown in Fig.52.

Fig.52

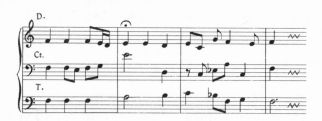

Several pieces have already progressed to four-part texture, e.g., *Jhesu bone* (no.1), which opens the collection, *Creature* (no.111), and in places the *Kyrie de Sancta Maria Virgine* (no.150). However, the tendency is not in the direction of real four-part writing but toward fuller chords with startling voice crossings and dissonances, which make it clear that we are dealing with a pre-mature experiment. Setting organ music on its way to genuine four-part writing was reserved for a later master, Arnolt Schlick.

The *Buxheim* repertoire may be differentiated into three styles: one that follows the *Fundamentum* of 1452, one that is characterized by an increase in figurations, and a third that aims at a simplification dominated by the principle of homophony. The first type appears in three-part settings in which the contratenor already shows a frequent rhythmic independence from the tenor. It is represented by pieces such as *Damadame* (no.3), *Mir ist zerstört* (no.5), *O werder Trost* (no.26), and the untitled composition by Paumgartner (no.110), which is one of the most beautiful works of the time, and which was previously included in the Wernigerode manuscript. *O werder Trost* (Fig.53) has the full charm of a Binchois chanson and is probably French in origin rather than German.*

Fig.53

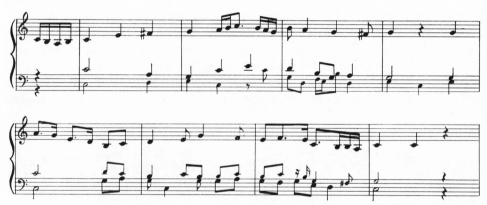

Many of the Buxheim pieces go beyond this style in the direction of increased, indeed profuse, ornamentation, not unlike the style of the *Codex Faenza*. But it cannot be assumed that there is a direct connection with the Italian organ technique of that earlier period. Probably what we have here is the natural end result of a continuous evolution. In three successive generations it leads to ever faster figuration in the upper part—from the quarter notes (semibreves) of the earliest German organ pieces, to the eighth- and sixteenth-note motion in Ileborgh's and Paumann's music, to the thirty-second notes (*fusae*) that give their characteristic imprint to many pieces of the *Buxheim* repertoire. The progress (if one may call it that) becomes particularly clear when one compares two arrangements of the same tune. The beginning of *Ellend du hast* is given in

---

* In this and the following examples from the *Buxheim Organ Book* the contratenor part is printed in small noteheads to differentiate it from the tenor, which is given in the usual size notehead.

Fig.54

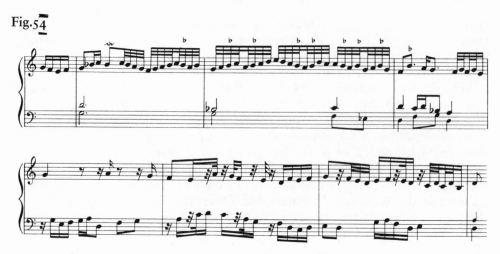

Fig.44 as it appears in the *Fundamentum,* and in Fig.54 according to the *Bux-heim Organ Book* (no.48). The last three measures of Fig.54 exhibit a most curious and artificial technique, as two voices alternate very short notes and rests in the manner of a rapid hocket. Similar breakneck formations are found several times in a *Benedicite* (no.41), which may have been written by the same author (Fig.55). In the last section of the collection, which is written by another

Fig.55

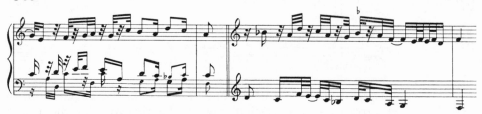

hand, sixty-fourth notes (*semifusae*) appear repeatedly; e.g., several times in the second *Fundamentum* (new ed., vol.III, 333, 336) and in *Selaphasepale* (Dufay's *Se la face ay pale,* no.255), a passage from which is reproduced in Fig.56.

Fig.56

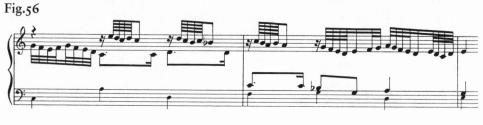

Finally there appear rhythmic forms that stem from the theory of proportions (Fig.57). Interestingly, they reappear in similar fashion a hundred years later in England.

Fig.57

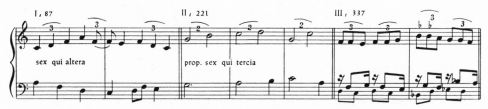

A number of pieces in the *Buxheim Organ Book* are completely dominated by this profuse ornamentation, especially the *Benedicite*, no.41; *Ellend*, no.48; *Collinit*, nos.56 and 57; *Annavasanna*, no.92; *Stublin*, no.136; *Was ich begynne*, no.205; and *Selaphasepale*, no.255. It seems that Paumann himself initiated this development: Pieces like *Jeloymors*, no. 17, and *Con lacrime*, no.38, both designated M.C.C. (*Magister Conradus Caecus*), as well as the *Fundamentum M.C.P.C.*, no.189, clearly belong to this category. It is understandable that such suggestions were eagerly cultivated and pursued by his students to their extremes. The three settings of *Was ich begynne* (nos.205, 207, 208) are especially worth noting. Their designations—*6 sive 12 notarum, Secunda mensura 4^{or} notarum,* and *Tercia mensura 3^{m} notarum*—as well as several details of their style recall Ileborgh's three *mensurae* on *Frowe al myn hoffen*.

Although this may be artistic decadence, the evolution nevertheless represents a remarkable advance in clavieristic technique; in fact it is a masterly achievement comparable to the ones attained about a hundred years earlier in Italy and about a hundred years later in England. At the same time South German keyboard virtuosity of the 15th century excels in that it is not limited to finger dexterity, but also includes pedal technique. The pedal technique of the *Buxheim Organ Book* does not evolve out of the double pedals of Ileborgh's tablature, but out of the state of the art as represented by Ileborgh's *Praeambulum bonum pedale sive manuale,* where the pedals are given the execution of an independent bass part. In that piece (cf.Fig.33) the pedal voice is a simple scale descending in slow motion, but in the *Buxheim Organ Book* the pedals are employed to execute voices that move throughout in quarter, eighth, and at times even in sixteenth notes. Pedal markings in the form of a *p* or *pe* are found particularly in *Salve regina*, no.73; *Kyrie-Gloria de S. Maria*, no.150; *O intemerata virginitas*, no.225; *Leuservituer (Le serviteur)*, no.226; *Bekenne myn klag*, no.227; *Wunschlichen schon*, no.237; and *Ess ist vor als gewesen schercz*, no. 238; as well as in several teaching examples (e.g., new edition, vol.III, p.305).

Fig.58

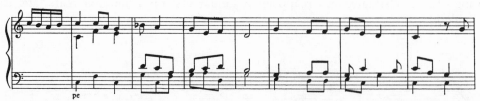

In the last five pieces named the pedals are prescribed for the contratenor, which is notated as usual as the middle part, but clearly has the character of a bass (*contratenor bassus*), since it almost always lies below the tenor, and often exhibits the typical interval skips of a bass voice. Fig.58 shows the beginning of *O intemerata* (bar lines are as given in the original).[26] In the *Kyrie de S. Maria* the pedals again play the lowest part, but here it is not the contratenor, but the tenor that is notated as the lowest part. Curiously, the pedals do not play continuous series of notes, but single notes after the beat, alternating with rests; in this manner their import as the carrier of the *cantus firmus* (from Mass IX) is suitably stressed, as is shown in Fig.59.

Fig.59

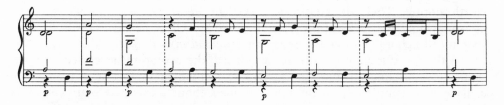

The principle of using the pedals for the lowest part is followed even in compositions where such a part does not exist, i.e., where the tenor and contratenor move in the same range and continually cross, as is the case with most of the *Buxheim* repertoire. The problem is solved by assigning to the pedals notes, measures, or groups of measures taken from one voice or the other, depending on where the lowest notes occur. In the *Salve regina* (no.73), the designation *p* alternates between tenor and contratenor. The two lower parts of the second section, *Ad te clamamus*, are transcribed in Fig.60 (the lines under the parts replace the pedal sign *p* in the original).

Thus the *Buxheim Organ Book* evidences a remarkably high degree of development of both finger technique and pedal playing. Even though only a handful of pieces carry pedal signs, others were probably executed in the same

Fig.60

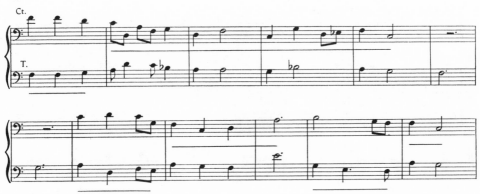

manner. The above analysis shows how this had to be done. It is corroborated by a note at the end of the manuscript:

> *Item nota, quando contratenor altior est tenore, tunc lude tenorem inferius in pedali. Sed quando contratenor ponitur inferius tenore, lude tenorem superius et contratenorem inferius.*
>
> (Note also that when the contratenor lies above the tenor, the tenor must be played below on the pedal. But when the contratenor is set below the tenor, play the tenor above [on the manual] and the contratenor below [on the pedals].[27]

In contrast to the many profusely ornamented pieces in the *Buxheim Organ Book,* there are several compositions in a rather simple style, dominated by harmonic principles, and written mostly in half and quarter notes joined together in homophonic chords. This style is especially evident in several Kyrie settings: the *Kyrie de S. Maria* (no.150, cf.Fig.59), the *Christe* that belongs to it, and the four sections of the *Kyrieleyson de Apostolis* (no.157); it also occurs in a number of preambles (nos.58, 112, 191, 194, 206) and song-like pieces (nos.221, 227, 244). Almost all these pieces are in an even meter; ternary meter (*tempus perfectum*) still dominates in the *Buxheim Organ Book,* though not as exclusively as in the *Fundamentum.* In the vocal music of the 15th century the texture tending toward homophony also appears in connection with the *tempus imperfectum.*

The untitled piece no.253, one of the last entries, proves to be a relatively late composition. It makes extensive use of imitation and it no longer employs the semibreve as the beat unit, but uses the minim instead. Its beginning is given in Fig.61.

Most of the pieces in the *Buxheim* repertoire that have French (or occasionally Italian) titles are probably transcriptions of chansons, i.e., not arrangements but merely intabulations. Several of them can be proved to be such, e.g.:

Fig.61

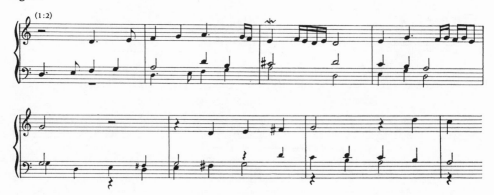

Nos.11, 226: *Leuservituer* = Dufay, *Le serviteur*
No.16, 17, 18, 168, 169, 170, 202: *Jeloemors* = Binchois, *Je loe amours* (cf. J. Marix, *Les Musiciens de la cour de Bourgogne*, 52)
Nos.38, 137, 138, 139: *Con lacrime* = Ciconia, *Con lagreme bagnandome* (cf. Clercx, *Johannes Ciconia*, II, 63)
Nos.39, 104: *O rosa bella* = Dunstable, *O rosa bella*
No.61: *Puisque* = Dunstable, *Puisque m'amour*
Nos.83, 225: *Selaphasepale* = Dufay, *Se la face ay pale*
No.106: *Entrepris* = Bart. Brolo (cf. Ringmann, *Glogauer Liederbuch* I, 80)
No.122: *Sanssoblier* = Joh. Franchois, *Sans oublier* (cf. Ch. van den Borren, *Pièces polyphoniques de provenance liégeoise*, 72)
No.256: *Lesovenir* = Morton, *Le souvenir* (cf. K. Jeppesen, *Der Kopenhagener Chansonnier*, 37)

To give an idea of the technique of coloration of the period, Fig.62 contrasts the beginnings of two *Jeloemors* with the upper part of the original by Binchois.[28] A particularly striking example of the transformation of a simple, singable melody into a clavieristic *perpetuum mobile* is the beginning of Morton's *Le souvenir* (Fig.63); the Chanson was originally written a fifth lower.

The treatment of the lower parts differs considerably from case to case. In *Le souvenir* the original tenor and contratenor are taken over into the organ

Fig.62

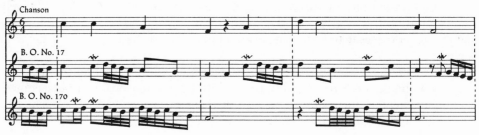

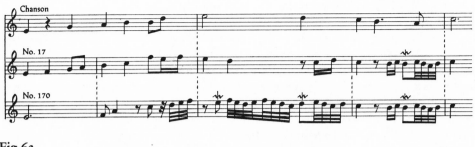

Fig.63

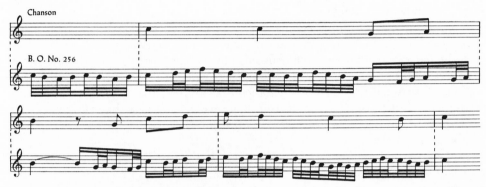

setting almost note for note, while in other arrangements these voices are ornamented or occasionally varied (e.g., in several of the *Jeloemors* pieces), or reduced to a single part by omitting the contratenor (e.g., in *Entrepris*).

As indicated by their titles, most secular pieces in the *Buxheim* collection are derived from German songs. There are about one hundred such compositions, including a number of songs that appear several times, for example, *Der Winter will hin wichen* (nos.32, 33, 34), *Benedicite Almechtiger Got* (nos.41, 68, 69, 70, 224), *Ellend du hast* (nos.48, 49, 50, 94, 95, 96), *Was ich begynne* (nos.97, 98, 205, 207, 208, 209), and others. The question arises whether they are merely intabulations of polyphonic vocal settings or whether there are some genuine organ arrangements, in which only one part, usually the tenor, is taken from the vocal repertoire and used as the basis of a newly created organ setting. This question was already raised in connection with the songs in the *Fundamentum* of 1452, which proved to contain one intabulation (*Domit ein gut Jare*) and several pieces that may be arrangements. The situation in the *Buxheim Organ Book* is probably similar. It contains about fifteen songs (some represented by several works) for which polyphonic vocal models are known, either in the *Lochamer Song Book* or in *Schedel's Song Book*.[29] Nine of them are obviously intabulations, in which all three parts correspond to the respective vocal works (*Mir ist zerstört, Gedenck daran, Seyd ich dich hertzlieb*), or at least in the tenor and discant while the contratenor deviates wholly or in part (*Möcht ich din begern, Ein Froulin, Min trüt Geselle, Der Sumer, Der Winter, Wunschlichen schon*). In five other songs (*Des Klaffers Nyd, Min Hercz in hohen Fröuden, Ellend du hast, Kem mir ein Trost, Ich lass nit ab*) the correspondence is limited to the tenor, which is frequently subjected to certain changes, however. It is possible, therefore, that we are dealing with organ settings based on *cantus firmi;* and that a similar situation obtains in the many cases where only a monophonic model is known to us. The question cannot be decided with certainty, of course, since one can hardly assume that all the vocal settings of the period have been preserved.

Nevertheless we are able to arrive at more positive answers when several organ settings of the same song are preserved, which happens repeatedly in the *Buxheim Organ Book*. In those instances we can investigate whether the discants (and possibly the contratenors, too) are merely ornamental versions of the same melodic line or whether they differ in substance. The former is clearly the case in the three pieces on *Leucht leucht wunniglicher zinnenzin* (nos.27, 28, 29). Despite various deviations, they exhibit melodies that are essentially identical, not only in the tenor but in the discant as well. Here we can assume that all of them are derived from the same two-part vocal model; in other words, we are dealing with intabulations.

A substantially different picture emerges in the five *Benedicite* settings in the *Buxheim Organ Book* (nos.41, 68, 69, 70, 224) and in the piece from the *Fundamentum* discussed above (cf.p.52). All of them are based on the old melody by the Monk of Salzburg, which is the model for all their tenors, each with different figuration. Thus the tenors show quite different melodic contours, but the counterpoints differ so greatly that they cannot be assumed to derive from the same source. The supposition that a different vocal model existed for each of these settings is certainly too forced to be considered seriously. Therefore we may conclude that here most or all of these settings represent genuine organ arrangements.

Min Hercz in hohen Fröuden ist represents a very similar situation. It appears in a vocal version in *Schedel's Song Book* (no.20, fol.26v–28), as well as in three clavier settings: two anonymous ones in the *Buxheim Organ Book* (nos.67, 181) and a third in the *Wernigerode Codex*, which is attributed to Georg de Putenheim. A comparison of the four versions shows that genuine correspondences exist only in the tenors, but that the counterpoints are formulated differently in each setting. Certainly there are occasional similar measures, but such similarities are pure accidents that can hardly be avoided as long as the tenor remains the same. Besides, there are also frequent deviations in the tenors, so that one gains the impression that all four settings derive from a popular song that is not preserved in its original version, that is, if one can speak of an "original" version. Fig.64 shows measures 21–22 of the setting in *Schedel's Song Book* and the corresponding measures in the three clavier versions.

Similar relationships are found in the various settings on *Ellend du hast, Was*

Fig.64

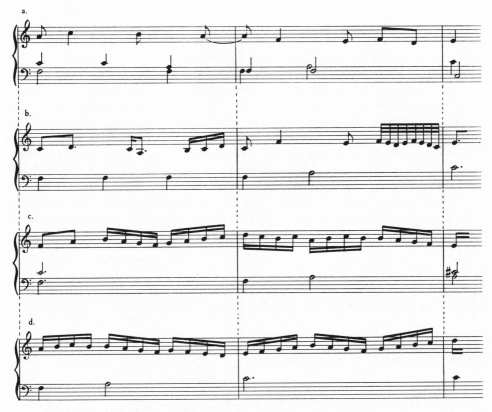

a. Schedel, meas. 20; b. Wernigerode, meas. 20; c. Buxheim, No. 67, meas. 23; d. Buxheim, No. 181, meas. 21.

ich begynne, Vil lieber zit, Crist ist erstanden (or *Cristus surrexit*), and several others. It thus seems that in the repertoire of German songs—in contrast to French pieces—genuine arrangements are relatively frequent.

Several settings in the *Buxheim Organ Book* prove to be arrangements of dance tunes, basse-danse melodies that reach us from three 15th-century sources: the *Libro dell' arte del danzare* by Antonio Cornazano; the sumptuous *Basses-danses manuscript* of the Bibl. royale at Brussels (Ms.9085); and a print by Michel Toulouze, *L'Art et instruction de bien dancer* (Paris, before 1496).[30] Nos. 56–57, entitled *Collinit*, are based on the tenor *Collinetto* (Cornazano); nos.79–82, *Modocomor*, on *La (Ma) doulce amour* (Brussels, no.52; Toulouze, no.18); nos. 135–36, *Stublin*, on *Languir en mille destresses* (Brussels, no.40; Toulouze, no.8), a tune that is found also in the *Lochamer Song Book* with the text *Virginalis flos*

65

vernalis. In all these settings the dance tune is laid out in principle as a *cantus planus*, with one original note per measure, but this note is paraphrased in many measures. A contratenor and a richly ornamented upper part are added.

The history of *Une fois avant* (Brussels, no.24) is not so simple. This basse-danse is related to the tenor of Paumann's *En avois*[31] as well as to the tenors of eight pieces in the *Buxheim Organ Book,* four of which appear under the corrupted designation *Annavasanna* (nos.89–92), and four under the German title *Vil lieber zit* (nos.37, 51, 93, 217). In these pieces the relationship of the tenors to the basse-danse is recognizable in some places, but elsewhere it can only be reconstructed by a forced interpretation. Furthermore the simple correspondence of each basic note to one measure of the tenor, which characterized the above melodies, no longer holds. A more detailed study may perhaps show that the various tenors relate more to each other than to the basse-danse. This would probably mean that they are all based on a variant derived from the basse-danse. Fig.65 gives the beginning of *Une fois* (the original was written in breves and started on *d*), *En avois, Annavasanna* no.89, and *Vil lieber zit* no.37, all transposed to *c.*

Fig.65

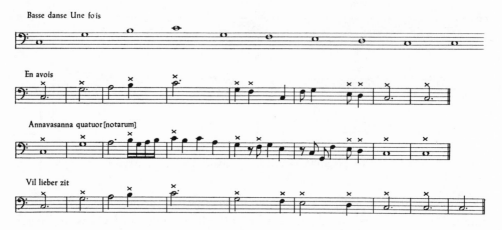

The liturgical organ pieces in the *Buxheim Organ Book* are listed here by types:

1. Ordinary of the Mass: *Kyrie* and *Gloria* (*Et in terra*) *de Sancta Maria Virgine* (nos.150, 151), *Kyrieleyson pascale* (no. 152), *Kyrieleyson angelicum* (nos.153–55), *Sanctus angelicum* (no.156), *Kyrieleyson de Apostolis* (no. 157), *Credo* (*Patrem omnipotentem* no.222), *Kyrieleyson ang[e]licum* (no. 251); *Kyrie* (untitled, no.242).
2. Proper of the Mass: *Gaudeamus* (no.35), *Rorate* (no.36), *Salve sancta parens* (no.149).
3. *Magnificat:* nos.24, 47, 77, 248

4. Antiphons: *Salve regina* (nos.72, 73), *Ave regina* (nos.159, 160, 258), *Sub tuam protectionem* (nos.40, 158), *O florens rosa* (no.2), *Descendi in ortum* (no.161), Salve radix (no.250).
5. Hymns: *Jhesu bone* (no.1), *Maria tu solacium* (no.74), *Virginem mirae pulchritudinis* (no.75), *Veni virgo* (no.76), *Veni creator Spiritus* (no.78), *Pange lingua* (no.163), *Dies est leticiae* (no.167), *O gloriosa domina* (nos.200, 201), *O regina gloriae* (no.211), *O intemerata virginitas* (no.225), *Pulcherrima de virgine* (no.228).

Here, too, the first question is: To what extent are we dealing with transcriptions (which are less interesting) and to what extent with original arrangements of liturgical *cantus firmi*? The three *Ave regina* (which are based on a composition by Walter Frye),[32] the two *Sub tuam protectionem* (intabulations of a Dunstable motet), and *Pange lingua* (which derives from a vocal setting by Touront)[33] are transcriptions. Stylistic features of the settings for the ordinary of the Mass, the Magnificat, and the introits *Gaudeamus* and *Rorate* suggest that they are probably arrangements. For the other pieces the question must be left open.

The pieces for the ordinary of the Mass have been transcribed and analyzed by L. Schrade.[34] Here we must limit ourselves to brief outlines. The *Kyrie* and *Gloria de Sancta Maria* are based on Mass IX; the *Kyrie pascale* on the first part of Mass I; the two *Kyrie angelicum* as well as the untitled piece no.242 on Mass IV; the *Kyrie de Apostolis* on Mass XIV; the *Credo* setting probably on Credo IV; the source of the *Sanctus angelicum* is problematic. The Gregorian melody is always in the tenor, the lowest voice notated (in three-part settings or passages it frequently rises above the contratenor), and mostly without additional figuration. Most Kyrie settings stand out because of their simple, homophonic texture—the *Kyrie de S. Maria Virgine* even more so, because it employs four parts and a peculiar, hocketing pedal line to carry the *cantus firmus* (cf.Fig.59).* The *Gloria* that belongs to it sets the entire text (beginning, as always, with the *Et in terra*), except for the *gratias agimus . . . unigenite Jesu Christe, Domine fili . . . Christe*, and the brief invocation *Jesu Christe* shortly before the end. Such an extended setting of the text is very unusual in organ Masses. It is possible that the three missing passages were omitted in error, and that this is intended to be a setting of the entire Gloria. This would be a unique situation, but it would make more sense than the arbitrary omission of three sections.

The proper of the Mass is represented by three introits: *Gaudeamus* for the feast of St. Thomas, *Rorate* for the fourth Sunday in Advent, and *Salve sancta parens* (set only up to *regem*) for Marian feasts. The chant melodies, as usual, are in the tenor, and are laid out in principle as *cantus plani*, but with many ornamented notes as in the *Benedicite* of Paumann's *Fundamentum*. The essential principle remains the regular distribution: Each measure contains one note of the chant, which may be at the beginning or elsewhere in the measure. Thus a chant

---

* In measures 10–16 the *cantus firmus* is in the contratenor, thereafter apparently back in the pedal part.

Fig.66

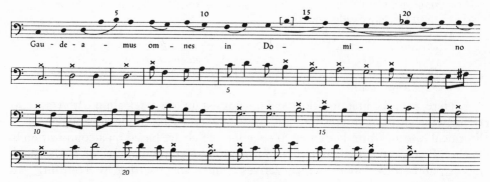

tune of twenty notes always results in an organ tenor of twenty measures, and where occasional deviations are found, one can probably conclude that they are based on variants of the chant tradition. In Fig.66, the beginning of *Gaudeamus*, the two melodies correspond exactly according to the principle: one chant note = one measure. Note 14 is missing from the version in the modern gradual. For notes 11 and 19, which do not appear in the corresponding measures, we have a choice of several explanations: deviating chant tradition, free paraphrase, perhaps even a shift of the note into another voice.

The Magnificats consist (as in Paumann) of the first verse only, except for no.77, in which the third verse, *Quia respexit*, is added. In this latter verse the long text requires that the recitation tone be extended; this is reflected in the organ setting by eleven articulations of the tone *f* (the eighth-mode chant tune is transposed down a fifth). Thus the setting offers a practical application of the *redeuntes* of the *Fundamentum*. Indeed, as Fig.67 shows, the counterpoints are formed exactly according to the model of Paumann's teaching example (cf.Fig.43). The whole passage represents a "pastorale" that is unusually harmonious for that period.

Fig.67

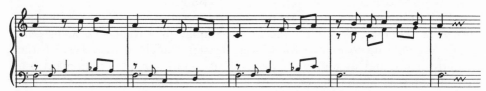

Turning to the Marian antiphons, we shall discuss only the two *Salve regina* (nos.72, 73), since the others (*Ave regina, Sub tuam protectionem*) are intabulations (cf.p.67). Both show the usual alternating structure of organ settings of

68

this famous antiphon: ℣ 1, 3, 5, 7, 9 for the organ, the even-numbered verses *choraliter*. The second arrangement makes special use of the pedals for the lowest part at any given point (cf.p.60). The liturgical melody seems to lie in the tenor, but it is difficult to recognize, even if one looks for some of it in the contratenor or discant. Unlike the introits this work certainly does not employ an ornamented *cantus planus*, but uses a free paraphrase with an irregular distribution of chant notes.

The last third of the *Buxheim Organ Book* is mostly filled with teaching examples, which are divided into five extensive collections:

1. *Incipit Fundamentum M.C.P.C.* (no.189)
2. *Sequitur aliud Fundamentum* (no.190)
3. *Ascensus simplex, etc.* (no.231–34)[35]
4. *Sequitur Fundamentum Magistri Paumann Contrapuncti* (no. 236)
5. *Ascensus simple, etc.* (no.236a)[36]

Altogether these examples occupy about ninety pages of the manuscript. The discussion of this enormous amount of material must be limited to the following brief remarks. There are some *ascensus* and *descensus* and a number of *redeuntes*, but the collections consist chiefly of *clausulae*, i.e., settings based on brief series of notes (for example, *c–g, c′–a, c–f–c, e–e–f–e*, etc.), similar to those in the *Fundamentum breve* of the *Wernigerode Codex* (cf.p.50) and the Breslau fragment (E) (cf.p.45). The third and fifth collections are particularly remarkable because of their full three-part texture, the figuration of the fundamental group by notes, and the rapid motion of the discant. By contrast, the settings of the fourth collection, ascribed to Paumann, stand out for their simple, often purely homophonic texture. Three settings in the first collection, called *Concordantiae M.C.P.C.*, one each on an *ascensus et descensus per tertias, per quartas,* and *per quintas* (new ed., vol.II, p.250), also show a purely homophonic three-part texture. These pieces are probably the most interesting ones in all the *Fundamenta*, for they indicate a turn of

Fig.68

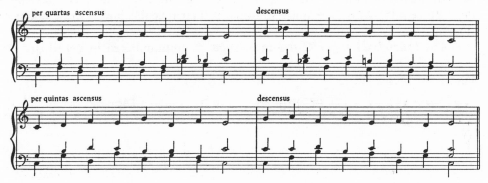

per quartas ascensus   descensus

per quintas ascensus   descensus

events that proves decisive for the future, a change from contrapuntal to chordal thinking, from polyphonic treatment to harmonization. Fig.68 shows the progressions by fourths and fifths. In the two *descensus* the rational principles of harmonic sequence are clearly foreshadowed. Here is another area in which Paumann shows himself as a thinker and teacher seeking new horizons.

The most interesting part of the *Buxheim* repertoire are the preludes. No less than sixteen pieces are designated as *praeambulum*, and possibly one or two other untitled pieces should be counted in this category. Some of the preambles are brief works in chordal texture, e.g., no.58 (Fig.69). Others combine chordal style and passage work (nos.195, 206), as in the prelude in the Wernigerode manuscript (cf.Fig.50). In a number of preludes the rhapsodic style of Ileborgh's preambles returns. The mixture of free improvisational passages, chords, and ornamental runs in these pieces sums up what had developed in the preceding period in both North and South Germany.

Fig.69

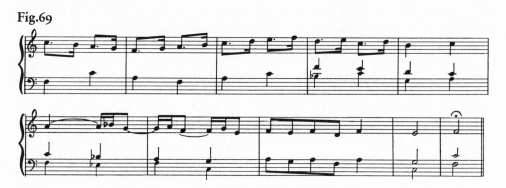

The first prelude of the *Buxheim Organ Book*, *Praeambulum super G* (no.53), is a good example of the combination of Ileborgh's rhapsodic technique and Paumann's chordal texture. The purely monophonic beginning exhibits the very same principle of annunciation (apostrophe) that the North German masters of the 17th century were to employ so often in their toccatas and chorale fantasies (Fig.70).

The *Praembula super C* (no.232), *super D* (unnumbered in vol.III, p.318),

Fig.70

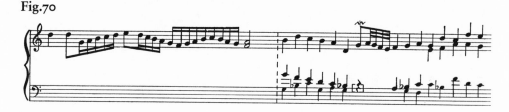

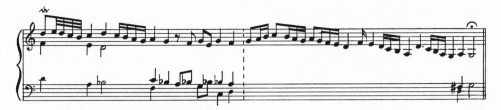

super mi (no.233), *super f* (no.234), and *super f* (no.235), inserted in the third collection of teaching pieces, are patterned like this piece, but more extended. In the
second and the last the concluding passage work is heard above a long-sustained
pedal point of root and fifth. The introductory runs lie in a high register, while the
concluding ones descend steeply, often below the tenor notes. This leads to the
supposition that the upper parts were played mainly on four-foot stops, resulting
in an even brighter sounding beginning.

PART II

THE SIXTEENTH CENTURY

6

General Observations

ONE MAY ATTACH little or much significance to the terms Gothic and Renaissance, and opinions may differ about their applicability and temporal limitation with respect to literature, philosophy, or art, but in the field of keyboard music the time around 1500 clearly represents a boundary between two evolutionary phases for which the designations "Gothic" and "Renaissance" are welltaken. In the course of our study we shall discuss the stylistic differences; right now our aims are not the details but a general view—not the total picture but its size and scope.

Indeed, it is above all a matter of difference in size, like comparing a miniature in a book to a wall painting. The quantity of the source material itself brings about a new situation. In studying the 14th and 15th centuries we had to be satisfied with a few scattered, accidentally preserved, and mostly fragmentary documents. Now a plethora of manuscripts and prints are at our disposal, and only occasionally are they incomplete. Just as important is the spatial broadening of the picture: In the 15th century our knowledge was limited to a single country, but in the 16th century five countries—Germany, Italy, Spain, England, and France (one could also include Switzerland and Poland)—contribute to the development of clavier music. Moreover the veil of anonymity is lifted; instead of the few names that reach us from the early times, we now have a large number of rather well-known personalities. Here and there a differentiation is discernible among the various keyboard instruments, mainly between organ and harpsichord. However it is the creation of new types—toccata, ricercar, canzona, variation, and dance types—that gives Renaissance clavier music a completely new fulness and liveliness.

Agreeable as this extraordinary enlargement of the scope is, it makes the detailed description of the encompassed panorama much more difficult. No matter how one arranges the material—by personalities or types, countries or periods—gaps, overlaps, and interruptions in the continuity will always occur. For the 16th century presentation by types will be the most meaningful and suitable. Its greatest disadvantage is that it destroys the unity of personality by dividing the work of a composer, but the loss is not as great as it would appear to be, for during this period composers usually limited their activity to a few types. (In this respect Cabezón was a remarkable exception.) Moreover, even with all the liberating tendencies of the 16th century, the individuality of the creative musician is not yet as pronounced as in the 17th, where one meets such well-defined personalities as Sweelinck, Frescobaldi, Froberger, and Buxtehude. Nevertheless men like Schlick, Cavazzoni, Cabezón, or Byrd must not become shadowy figures, who try with varying success to influence the inalterable evolution of morphological events. Thus as a necessary corrective of our method of presentation, we first turn to a survey of the most important clavier composers of the 16th century.

Keyboard Composers of the Sixteenth Century

One of the truly great masters in the field of organ music was Arnolt Schlick. He was the author of one of the most important books on organ building, the *Spiegel der Orgelmacher und Organisten* (1511), and of *Tabulaturen etlicher Lobgesang und Lidlein* (1512), in which his works for organ and lute are preserved. His birth is usually put around the year 1460, but it is more likely about 1450, since a letter written by his son in 1511 (printed in the preface of the *Tabulaturen*) refers to him as "an old, wizened man." A recently discovered Trent manuscript[1] contains compositions that he sent to Bishop Clesio along with a long dedication. From the latter we learn that Schlick was still alive at the time of the coronation of Charles V in 1520, that he was in the service of the count palatine of Heidelberg, and had gone blind in his old age. His son mentions that Schlick had played and sung "for many years before emperors and kings, prince-electors, princes, prelates, and also other secular potentates." Ornithoparchus dedicates the Fourth Book of his *Micrologus* (1516) to him, calling him "the most consummate musician and the most eminent organist of the prince-palatine." Nevertheless his son had to exhort him "not to let his life end in silence" before Schlick decided to have a "first sample" of his works appear in print. His compositions are preserved in *Tabulaturen etlicher Lobgesang und Lidlein uff die Orgeln und Lauten* (1512)[2] and in the manuscript Trent, Archivo di Stato, Sez. ted. N. 105.[3]

A somewhat younger contemporary of Schlick's was Paul Hofhaimer, born in 1459 in Radstadt (Province of Salzburg), died in 1537 in Salzburg. About the age of twenty (1480) he was called to service by the Archduke of Tirol and given a life-long appointment as the organist at Innsbruck. After the death of the Archduke in 1490, he was taken over by Emperor Maximilian I (who raised him to nobility in 1515). Later we find Hofhaimer at Torgau, at the court of Frederic the

Wise; at Augsburg in 1509; and at Salzburg after 1519. He not only enjoyed great favor among princes, but also gained the admiration of leading men of his day, such as Konrad Celtes, Paracelsus, Dürer, and Cranach (who painted his portrait), and the reverence of a circle of disciples, whom Othmar Luscinius called *Paulomimi*, i.e., imitators of Paul. His organ playing is praised in several sources, but unfortunately, apart from intabulations of a few songs, only four of his organ pieces are preserved: *Recordare, Salve regina, T'Andernaken,* and a *carmen* (in the tablatures of Kleber, Kotter, and Sicher.)[4]

An outstanding student of Hofhaimer's was Johannes Buchner (Hans von Constanz, 1483–c.1540), born at Ravensburg, and organist at Konstanz (1512) and Überlingen (1526). He wrote (c.1520?) a *Fundamentum, sive ratio vera, quae docet quemvis cantum planum . . . redigere ad iustas diversarum vocum symphonias,* which contains teaching examples and about twenty liturgical organ pieces.[5] A copy, *Abschrift M. Hansen von Constanz* (1551),[6] contains about thirty additional liturgical pieces.[7]

During the same time and in the same area (southwestern Germany and Switzerland) the following men were active: Johannes Kotter (c. 1485–1541), born at Strasbourg, organist at Freiburg (Switzerland) and Bern; Leonhard Kleber (c.1490–1556), born at Göppingen; and Fridolin Sicher (1490–1546), born at Bischofszell, organist at St. Gall. We know them chiefly through their voluminous tablatures—Kotter: Basel, Univ. Bibl. F. IX. 22 and F. IX. 58; Kleber: Berlin, Stb. Ms. mus. Z. 26; Sicher: St. Gall Stiftsbibl. Cod. 530—which contain mostly intabulations of vocal compositions. But Kotter's tablature also includes a number of dances, preludes, and fantasies,[8] Kleber's a series of preludes. Kotter's collection was written about 1513–17, Kleber's 1520–24, and Sicher's 1504–31.[9]

An outstanding English organ master of the same generation was John Redford. Born around 1480, he died in London in 1547, where he had been active as an organist at St. Paul's Cathedral. We have about fifty of his compositions, almost all liturgical organ music. Most of them are preserved in Brit. Mus. Add. 30513, the so-called *Mulliner Book,* and Brit. Mus. Add. 29996.[10]

Marco Antonio Cavazzoni (c.1490–1560) was probably born in Urbino, grew up in Bologna (in his print he calls himself Marco Antonio da Bologna), but was active mostly in Venice. At times he was also in Rome in the service of Pope Leo X (1520–21), and in Padua in the service of Cardinal Bembo (1523), who later befriended him and his son Hieronimo (Girolamo). In 1523 he published a collection of organ compositions under the title *Recerchari Motetti Canzoni Libro primo.* Another ricercar (*Recercada di māca in Bologna*), together with organ works by Jacobo Fogliano (1468–1548), Julio Segni (1498–1561), and others, is included in a manuscript of the Biblioteca Capitolare of Castell' Arquato.[11]

The great Spanish organ master of the 16th century was Antonio de Cabezón (c.1500–66). He went blind as a child. In 1526, after an undetermined length of service under a Bishop of Palencia, he entered the service of Empress Isabella. Immediately after her wedding in the same year to Charles V, she organized a chapel in which Cabezón assumed the position of organist. In 1538 he was appointed in addition to a simliar position with the Emperor, and in the following year the Emperor entrusted him with the musical education of his children, particularly that of the Infante Philipp. When Philipp became Regent of Spain in 1543, he made Cabezón his court organist, whose special duty it was to play a portative for Philipp on his many journeys. It is known that Cabezón visited Italy, Flanders, and Germany in 1548–49, and England in 1554–56. About forty compositions by "Antonio" (doubtless Antonio de Cabezón) are included in the collection of Luis Venegas de Henestrosa's *Libro de cifra nueva para tecla, arpa y vihuela*, printed in 1557; and about one hundred (almost all different from the first collection) in the posthumous publication, *Obras de musica para tecla, arpa y vihuela de Antonio de Cabezón . . .*, brought out by Antonio's son Hernando in 1578.[12]

Thomas Tallis (c.1505–85) was the organist or choirmaster of the Abbey of the Holy Cross at Waltham until 1537. He was then elevated by Henry VIII to membership in the Chapel Royal in London, where, together with his younger colleague William Byrd, he later (about 1574) occupied the position of organist. Most of his organ works—all exclusively liturgical, like Redford's—are contained in the *Mulliner Book*. A few that are preserved in later sources (e.g., in the *Fitzwilliam Virginal Book*) are striking because of their enormous length.[13]

William Blitheman (c.1520–91) was the choirmaster of Christ Church at Oxford in 1564, and was appointed organist of the Chapel Royal in 1585, evidently as Tallis' successor. He was John Bull's teacher. The previous remarks about Tallis' organ works also hold true for Blitheman's.

Contemporary with Blitheman was the very important Italian organ composer Andrea Gabrieli (c.1515–86). He was born in the Canareggio quarter of Venice, entered the chapel choir of San Marco as a singer in 1536, and became the organist at San Geremia in Venice in 1558. Six years later he became the second organist at San Marco, and first organist in 1585, both times succeeding Claudio Merulo, who was much younger. Between 1562 and 1564 he traveled in Bohemia, Austria, and Germany, established contacts with the leading families in Graz, Munich, and Augsburg, and was a member of the court orchestra of Duke Albrecht of Bavaria, which was directed by Lassus. His organ works are preserved mostly in posthumous prints:[14]

> *Intonationi d'organo di Andrea Gabrieli et di Gio. suo nepote* (1593)
> *Ricercari di Andrea Gabrieli . . . Libro secondo* (1595)
> *Il terzo libro de ricercari di Andrea Gabrieli* (1596)
> *Canzoni alla francese . . . Libro quinto* (1605)
> *Canzoni alla francese . . . Libro sesto et ultimo* (1605)

Three organ Masses in manuscript are preserved in the Turin tablatures (Collection Giordano, vol.3).[15]

Hieronimo (Girolamo) Cavazzoni was the son of Marco Antonio Cavazzoni. His organ works reach us in two prints:[16]

> *Intavolatura cioe Recercari Canzoni Himni Magnificati composti per Hieronimo de Marcantonio da Bologna, detto d'Urbino, Libro primo* (1543) *Intabulatura d'organo cioe Misse Himni Magnificati . . . Libro secondo* [undated; the Masses also appeared in a new print, again undated, under the title *Di Hieronimo d'Urbino Il Primo Libro de Intabulatura . . . apresso di Antonio Gardano*]

In the preface to the first print, which is addressed to Cardinal Bembo, the composer speaks of himself as *"anchor quasi fanciullo"* (not much more than a boy), which implies that he must have been born around 1525, about 1520 at the earliest. All we know of his later life is that he served Duke Guglielmo Gonzaga of Mantua as organist of the court church S. Barbara in 1565.[17]

The next Italian organ master is Annibale Padovano, born in Padua in 1527, died in Graz in 1575. At the age of twenty-seven (1552) he had already achieved the position of first organist at San Marco in Venice. In 1566 he gave it up in order to go into the service of Archduke Karl of Austria at Graz. A posthumous print, *Toccate et ricercari d'organo del eccelentissimo Annibal Padoano* (1604), contains Annibale's only known organ works:[18] 3 toccatas and 2 ricercari, as well as 5 toccatas *"d'incerto."*

The chief representative of German clavier music of the second half of the 16th century is Elias Nikolaus Ammerbach. He was born about 1530 in Naumburg, died in 1597 in Leipzig, and is one of the earliest known organists of Leipzig's St. Thomas Church. He published *Orgel oder Instrument Tabulatur*, 1571 (second, partially revised edition, 1583), and *Ein neu künstlich Tabulaturbuch*, 1575. These prints consist of a few dances, about twenty settings of Protestant chorales, and numerous intabulations.

The surpassing importance of Italian organ music becomes clear when one turns to Ammerbach's contemporary, Claudio Merulo (1533–1604), also known as Claudio da Correggio, after his birthplace. At the age of twenty-three (1556) he was the organist of the cathedral at Brescia, but in the following year he was made second organist at San Marco, where Padovano held the position of first organist. When the latter left Venice in 1566, Merulo, barely thirty-three, was advanced to first organist, while the office of second organist was entrusted to the fifty-year-old Andrea Gabrieli. Even this position, the highest that an organist of that period could aim for, did not satisfy Merulo for long. In 1586, after a brief sojourn in Mantua, he went into the service of Duke Ranuccio Farnese of Parma, who raised him to nobility. His organ works are preserved chiefly in the following prints:[19]

> *Ricercari d'intavolatura d'organo, libro primo,* 1567 (1605)[20]
> *Messe d'intavolatura d'organo: libro quarto,* 1568

Canzoni d'intavolatura d'organo: libro primo, 1592; *secondo,* 1606; *terzo,* 1611
[the last two published by his nephew Giacinto]
Toccate d'intavolatura d'organo: libro primo. 1598; *secondo,* 1604

With William Byrd (1543–1623), English clavier music once more steps significantly to the fore, this time in its later development, which is directed chiefly at the harpsichord. Perhaps he was a student of Tallis'; in any case he was in close contact with him (in 1575 they jointly received a monopoly for printing and selling musical publications). In 1562 he became the organist at the cathedral of Lincoln, and in 1572 at the Chapel Royal in London. Although he retained the Catholic faith, he was spared persecution, probably because of the high regard in which he was held. His clavier works are preserved in *My Ladye Nevells Booke, the Fitzwilliam Virginal Book,* the *Parthenia* (printed in 1611), as well as in various virginal books of the early 17th century.[21]

Many other clavier composers were active, e.g., Fatorini, Facoli, Valente, Rodio, Lohet, and Mareschal; but the information we have about their lives is very incomplete. The little we do know about them will be mentioned in connection with their works.

7

Liturgical Organ Music

Liturgical organ music takes first place in the clavier literature of the 16th century. Intabulations of vocal works can compete with it in quantity, but not in historical and artistic significance. Artistically, although liturgical organ music shows more mechanical skill than creative power, it reaches a high level of both technique and intent. Such outstanding organ masters as Schlick, Redford, Cabezón, and Cavazzoni worked exclusively or predominantly in liturgical music and created works of high rank in this field. Its historical significance is revealed by both a comparison with the 15th century and a glance forward, for liturgical organ music, which in the 16th century developed under the auspices of the Roman Catholic Church, became the basis for the brilliant development of the Protestant organ chorale in the Baroque era. Many methods and principles of form evolved, which were used later in the works of Scheidt, Tunder, Buxtehude, and Bach.

Germany

HOFHAIMER

Although Hofhaimer was probably somewhat younger than Schlick, his extant organ pieces doubtless represented an earlier stage of development. In the two liturgical organ works by Hofhaimer that have been preserved, a *Salve regina* and a *Recordare*, the three-part texture, which is quite usual in the *Buxheim Organ Book*, is still fully retained. But an important difference does exist: The voices are clearly separated in register, so that crossings of the two lower parts occur only occasionally. Another difference concerns the treatment of the Gregorian melodies. In the *Buxheim Organ Book* they are used mostly in a greatly changed form, either as extensively ornamented *cantus plani* or freely paraphrased. Hofhaimer sets them mostly as strict *cantus plani*, with long notes of equal duration, sub-divided only here and there. Thus he reverts—consciously or unconsciously—to an older technique, which had been used in the *Codex Faenza* and in the early German sources, and which also predominates in the later evolution of liturgical organ music.

The *Salve regina* consists, as usual, of five organ movements alternating with four sections performed *choraliter*.* In each organ movement the chant tune is presented as a *cantus planus* (occasionally ornamented) as follows:

Salve regina: c.f. in the middle part in 𝅝
Ad te clamamus: c.f. in the upper part in   𝅗𝅥
Eya ergo: c.f. in the middle part in   𝅗𝅥
O clemens: c.f. in the middle part in   𝅗𝅥
O dulcis: c.f. in the upper part in   𝅗𝅥 𝅘𝅥

The lowest part is always a freely invented bass, which quite frequently shows the typical progressions by fourths and fifths that make a freer development of harmony possible. In general, however, it still preserves enough independence and melodic life to save it from becoming a mere support part. In some movements that offer the *cantus firmus* in the middle voice, the bass tends to follow the florid upper voice in parallel tenths. Fig.71, from the first movement of the *Salve regina*, is an example.**

Fig.71

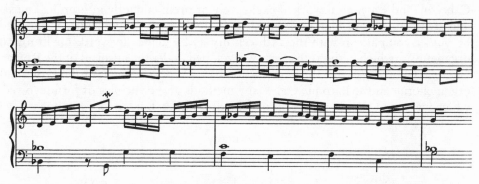

It is certainly no accident that the first movement employs notes of double value and that it is therefore about twice as long as the other movements. Planning is particularly evident in the treatment of the *cantus firmus* of the last movement, *O dulcis Maria*. Not only does it lie in the upper part, which in itself signifies

---

* The *Nobis post hoc* inserted by Kotter does not belong to it; it is not compatible with the complete design or the style.

** If not otherwise noted, all musical examples in Part II: The Sixteenth Century are reduced by 1:2 (semibreve = half note).

an important step toward the Lutheran "discant chorale," but it also has a livelier, more song-like rhythm, | ♩ ♩ |, is slightly varied on occasion (unless, as is always possible, a variant of the Gregorian melody is involved), and even ornamented here and there. Fig.72 shows the process of transformation in three phases: a. the Gregorian tune, b. its new rhythmic formulation, and c. its final form. Thus there is a planned progress in the five movements of Hofhaimer's *Salve regina* from the oldest type of *cantus-firmus* treatment to more modern methods.

Fig.72

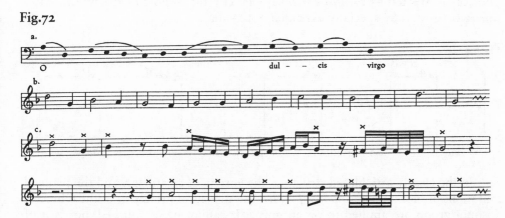

Further progress is found in his *Recordare*, which must be considered as a later work.[1] It is based on the offertory *Recordare virgo mater*[2] and the following prosa (tropus) *Ab hac familia*, which forms the *secunda pars* of the composition. The *Recordare* begins with an extended section in the style of the *Ad te clamamus* (see above), i.e., with the melody in the upper part in half notes. The same technique is employed for the end (*indignationem tuam*). In between there are two short sections in which the chant tune appears in notes of half the length, at first in the upper part of a duo of tenor and bass, then as the lowest part of a three-voice setting. Thus considerable variety emerges within the narrow limits of the *cantus-planus* technique. The scheme is presented graphically in Fig.73.

While the possibilities of the *cantus-planus* technique are exploited to its very limits in the *Recordare* (the presentation in quarter notes should probably

Fig.73

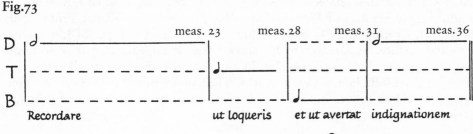

be regarded in this light), the attached *Ab hac familia* employs a method that is both new and extremely important for the future—the imitative treatment of the *cantus firmus*. The plan is again shown graphically; see Fig. 74. The Gregorian tune is divided into five phrases. The first is performed twice in succession, first in the tenor, then, lightly ornamented, in the discant; the second phrase appears in two strettos, of the fifth above and the octave below; the third phrase enters first in half notes in the discant, then in diminution in the tenor; and the last two phrases are treated as a *cantus planus*, whereby the import of the words *Virgo Maria* is stressed by specially extended note values.

Fig.74

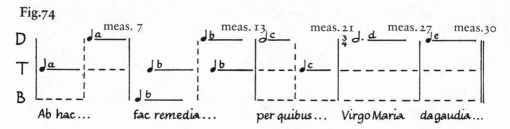

In the clearly articulated structure, the variety of treatment, and the planned imitations of Hofhaimer's *Ab hac familia,* the structural principles of the Obrecht-Josquin group are applied to organ music. It cannot be established, nor is it of particular importance, that it occurs here for the first time. What is essential is that around 1500 liturgical organ music became enriched through another technique, the imitative treatment of a *cantus firmus* divided into subsections, a technique that was to assume the greatest importance in its future evolution, and especially in the Protestant organ chorale.

In many ways the style and expression of Hofhaimer's organ works still appear to be related to the Gothic past, particularly in the filigree-like tracing of the voices, whose course is still quite dominated by the idea of a self-sufficient figuration without a definite goal. Totally different principles of formulation are encountered in the works of Arnolt Schlick.

SCHLICK

Schlick's *Tabulaturen etlicher Lobgesang* of 1512 contains a *Salve regina* of five sections; organ settings of *Pete quid vis, Hoe losteleck, Benedictus, Primi Toni, Maria zart, Christe,* and *Da pacem* (three); as well as a number of lute pieces. From the preface, his answer to his son's letter, it appears that they were all composed around 1511 for this print. In any case, they are stylistically more developed than Hofhaimer's organ works. Hofhaimer never goes beyond three parts, but Schlick proves himself a master of four-part setting and of a highly developed technique of imitation.

He places the *Salve regina* at the beginning of his collection (an introductory poem ends with "Zum ersten facht mein Salve an"). The design is as follows:

Salve regina:	4-part, *c.f.* in the tenor in ♩. (♩ ♩)
Ad te clamamus:	4 part, *c.f.* in the bass in ♩
Eya ergo:	3-part, *c.f.* in the discant in ♩
*O pia:**	4-part, *c.f.* in the alto in 𝅝. (♩ ♩ ♩)
O dulcis:	3-part, *c.f.* in the bass in ♩

The *O pia* seems to be most archaic. With its long, sustained notes, breves in *tempus perfectum,* its low register, and its many voice crossings (the alto, which carries the *cantus firmus,* lies below the tenor most of the time), it reminds us of Ockeghem. In this movement, moreover, initiation is only suggested, whereas it plays a rather important role in the other four movements. In *Ad te Clamamus* and *Eya ergo* it is employed for the beginning of the *cantus firmus,* as Fig.75 shows (figuration is indicated by a line). In the second example the procedure assumes the character of mature fore-imitation, which plays such an important role in the subsequent development of the organ chorale. In addition, all five movements include more or less extended imitations that are not related to the *cantus firmus* but employ motifs that emerge in the counterpoints. Schlick's technique here is almost equal to that of vocal music of his day, particularly as represented by Obrecht.

Fig.75

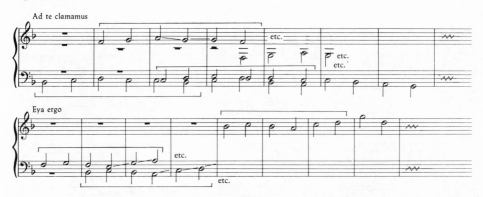

Indeed, some features seem to anticipate a much later stage of evolution. If one looks at the example in Fig.76 without prejudice, Sweelinck's methods of creating complementary motifs will probably come to mind, rather than the imitation methods of the early Netherlanders: Brief snatches of imitation like those from the *O dulcis Maria,* in Fig.77, are more in step with his time. The beginning

---

* *O pia* replaces the *O clemens* used by Hofhaimer; both sections have the same melody.

Fig.76

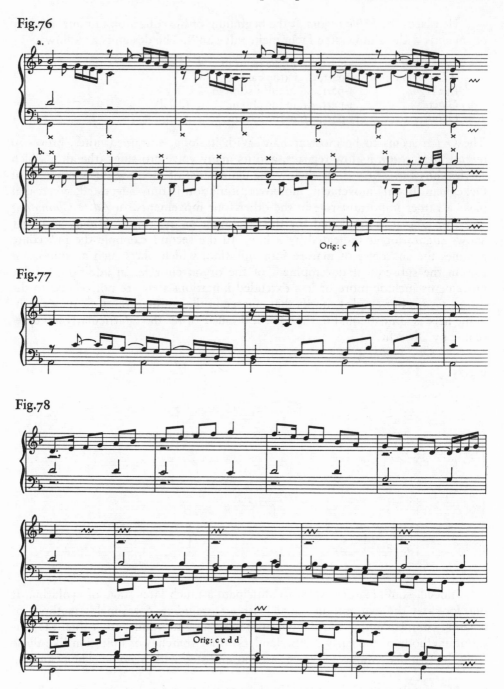

Orig: c ↑

Fig.77

Fig.78

Orig: c c d d

86

of the *Salve regina,* shown in Fig.78, is most unusual and impressive in this respect. One counterpoint after another enters at long intervals with an extended ascending and descending scale. Although this musical idea was doubtless inspired by Obrecht, such convincing élan is not to be found in his works.

This first show of confidence in the strength of the scale is something new in the development of organ music. The scale appears here not as the structural *cantus firmus* (as in Paumann), not as an ornamental filler (as in the *Codex Faenza*), but as meaningful, weighty substance. What this step means emerges most clearly if we compare Schlick's *Salve regina* with Hofhaimer's setting. Above the same tenor Hofhaimer has written a finely chiseled but purely decorative upper part that turns rather aimlessly around its own axis, whereas Schlick's *Salve* is one of the truly great masterpieces of organ art, perhaps the first one to deserve to be so ranked. It still breathes the strict spirit of the Middle Ages, which brought forth so many wonderful works, but new forces are already at work that lend this composition a novel fulness of expression and sound.

Among the other liturgical pieces in Schlick's *Tabulaturen,* the three settings of *Da pacem* are close in style to the *Salve regina.* They are based on an antiphon[3] which is performed throughout as a strict, totally unornamented *cantus planus* in half notes. In the first setting it becomes the top part of three; in the other two it is the tenor and bass, respectively, in four-part settings. The three pieces together may well be called the earliest example of chorale variations, about one hundred years before those of Sweelinck, who in fact treated the same theme in four variations. To the *cantus planus* Schlick adds two or three counterpoints, which move up and down in beautifully curved lines. The passage from the second piece, shown in Fig.79, may be especially noted; for in it appears the "fremd und süss lautende Konkordanz" (strange and sweet-sounding consonance) that Schlick mentions in his *Spiegel der Orgelmacher,* and for whose sake he prefers to have the circle of fifths of his system of tuning (a meantone temperament using natural thirds and small fifths) conclude on *A flat* rather than on *G sharp.* Naturally, in this system the *A flat*-major triad sounds quite different from the *C-* or *G*-major triads—"strange and sweet-sounding."

Fig.79

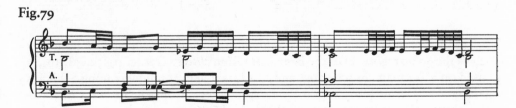

Schlick gives the name *Primi toni* to a piece that has not yet been identified. It presents three voices of a rather similar character. The middle one may be an ornamented *cantus planus*, but attempts to unravel the basic tune do not lead to a satisfactory result. There is hardly a trace of imitation. Imitation affects two other compositions all the more, a *Christe* and a *Benedictus*, both in three parts. The *Christe* begins with an extended duet by the upper parts, after which the bass enters, as shown in Fig.80. The basic motif is a five-tone scale fragment, which is spun out with rhythmic variations in a manner reminiscent of Obrecht. The same motif is also found in the upper parts in variously ornamented forms, e.g., at the very beginning of the discant. One is almost moved to call the piece a contrapuntal fantasy on the theme *A B C D E*.

Fig.80

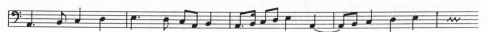

The imitative motif plays an even greater role in the *Benedictus*, especially when we remove the coloraturas and reduce the setting to its simple, basic form. That such a basic form is its model is shown by the fact that the middle section, apart from the figuration of the upper part, proves to be a strict canon of fourteen measures (meas.22–36). Fig.81 shows the beginning of this passage, omitting the coloraturas of the discant. In the other sections of the work imitation is also very important, e.g., right at the start, where the three voices enter one after the other with the same idea, in a truly fugal manner. For this reason G. Frotscher called the *Benedictus* an organ ricercar; but in all probability it is not an original organ composition but a transcription of a Mass movement, probably by Obrecht or Isaac. The same is true for the *Christe*.

Fig.81

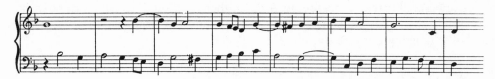

The *Maria zart* from Schlick's *Tabulaturen* deserves a place of honor as much as the *Salve regina*. Like the *Benedicite Almechtiger Got* (cf.pp.52, 58, 59), it is based on a German church song, and this fact makes it unique among Schlick's organ works. The melody, which is also preserved in one of Schlick's lute settings,[4] shows the characteristics of the later Lutheran chorale: short phrases, mostly of four main beats, separated by rests, constituting a simple, folk-like tune. It is a new type of religious music, which does not express the sublime idea of the liturgy but the pious spirit of the people—a music that did not grow in the mystic darkness of the altar but in the sunlight of the church square. The fitting place for such a tune is the upper part, and it is there that Schlick puts it in his arrangement for organ (though in the lute setting it serves as the tenor). Easily heard, it sings out there not as a strict *cantus planus* but in its natural flow—measured but not stiff and gracefully decorated here and there. Two finely drawn lower parts, which often ascend and descend along the scale, join in to create a three-part texture of a most delicate expression and exquisite beauty. The melody is divided into thirteen brief sections separated by rests.[5] Almost every phrase is treated imitatively, frequently in the form of a free canon. The procedure is so remarkable that it is worthy of a special presentation (Fig.82), but it will be necessary to reduce the expressive lines to mere skeletal sketches.

Fig.82

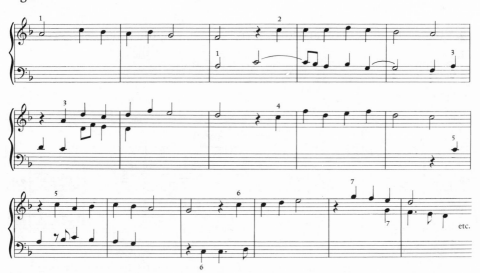

A recently discovered Trent manuscript[6] reveals two aspects of Schlick: As a teacher of counterpoint he wrote eight settings of the sequence verse *Gaude Dei genitrix* and a bicinium on the antiphon *Ascendo ad Patrem meum*,[7] and as an organ virtuoso he produced a ten-part organ setting of the same antiphon. Schlick says in the preface that the arrangements of *Gaude Dei genitrix* are "etwas news vor ungehortz . . . keins dem andern gleich, sundern yedes mal ander Contrapunct" (something new and never heard before . . . none similar to another, but each time another counterpoint), also that he "uff yede Compositz eigen Regel gefunden und gemacht, die so gewiss sein, leichtlich allen chorgesang uff die art zu setzen"

(found and made a separate rule for each setting, which are so clear that it will be easy to set all chants in the same manner). Indeed, these settings can be called a new *Fundamentum organisandi*, a practical guide to the treatment of any chant on the organ. In each arrangement Schlick demonstrates another type of treatment; all of them, however, are based on the principle of reinforcing the sound of a two-part setting—a *cantus-planus* chorale with a moderately florid counterpoint—with parallel thirds, fourths, or sixths. The following outline illustrates the various methods:

c.f.		counterpoint
I.	simple	with tenths
II.	with lower fourths	with tenths
III.	with sixths	with thirds
IV.	with thirds and lower fourths	with tenths
V.	with lower thirds	with lower thirds
VII.	with thirds	simple
VII.	with lower tenths	simple
VIII.	with lower thirds and lower sixths	with thirds

Fig.83 reproduces the beginnings of several of the settings.

Fig.83

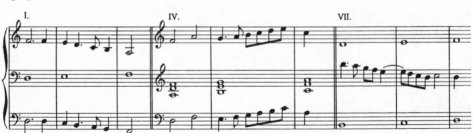

Schlick uses the antiphon *Ascendo ad Patrem meum* to demonstrate two types of treatment that are as contrasting as can be imagined—one for two voices and one for ten. Both represent novelties in organ music, the first because it dispenses with all figuration and has a simplicity that evidently derives from vocal models (duo sections in Masses), and the second because of its incredible fulness of sound and massiveness. We need not discuss the bicinium here, since we shall come across similar settings later, particularly in Cabezón's music. The other piece, however, is not only a novelty but also a unicum in organ literature: a ten-voiced setting with four parts for the pedals—an almost unbelievable feat of virtuosity, in which Schlick suitably glories: "Unnd zu dem hab ich uff den chorgesang Ascendo ad Patrem zu wegen brocht zehen stim; die man in Organis spiln mag, vir stim in dem pedal und sechs in dem manual, als ich sehen und hören lassenn kann."

(And I have succeeded in setting the chant *Ascendo ad Patrem* for ten voices, which one may play on the organ, four parts on the pedals and six on the manual, as I can illustrate for the eyes and ears of an audience). Not every modern organist would be able to perform this feat, even if he wore special shoes, as Schlick must have, to enable him to depress two keys at the interval of a third with either foot. Aside from the aspect of virtuosity, the work is also highly impressive musically, a masterpiece of both contrapuntal and harmonic arrangement. In the aural impression the chordal element obviously predominates, but the harmonies do not follow each other merely for the sake of their own sound, but as the logical and necessary results of melodic progressions. The beginning shown in Fig.84 gives some impression of the power of the work, though not of the full brilliance it acquires with the use of reedy mixtures.

Fig.84

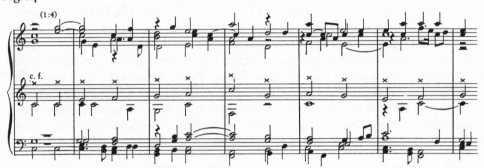

Such sounds provide a completely new, unsuspected insight into the organ art of Arnolt Schlick. He emerges even more clearly as one of the greatest masters who have left their imprint on the history of organ music. The serious dignity of the *Salve regina*, the loveliness of the *Maria zart*, and the massiveness of the *Ascendo ad Patrem* proclaim a creativity that is inferior to Frescobaldi or Bach in quantity only.

BUCHNER AND HIS CONTEMPORARIES

Hans Buchner is the most outstanding of Hofhaimer's students. His *Fundamentum* (cf.p.77), which reaches us in three copies, is an important document of organ music. It methodically teaches the contrapuntal treatment of a *cantus firmus*, and a good number of liturgical organ pieces are added to it to demonstrate the practical applications of the theory. The *Fundamentum* has three sections: the *ars ludendi* (fingering, keyboard, scale, note values, explication of the tablature), the *ars transferendi* (transcriptions of vocal works), and the *fundamentum* proper, which is designated as "brevis certissimaque ratio quemvis cantum planum redigendi in iustas duarum, trium pluriumque vocum symphonias" (brief and sure guide for treating any *cantus firmus* in a correct setting of two, three, or more voices). This composition text is illustrated by a number of *tabulae*, in which scales, intervals, and sustained notes (*redeuntes*) are arranged in various settings —somewhat as in Paumann's *Fundamentum*, but much more systematically. Of course it is conceived from the point of view of a later style, that of a three-part texture of imitative counterpoint, to which a special *tabula fugandi artem complectens* is devoted.

The instructional portion is followed by a collection of fifty liturgical compositions in which the theory is applied. It includes 10 introits, a gradual, 2 responsories, 4 sequences, 9 hymns, a Magnificat, 5 Kyries, 4 Glorias, 5 Sanctuses, and 5 Agnuses, but no Credos.[8] In at least one instance a Kyrie, Gloria, Sanctus, and Agnus, all consecutive (Päsler, nos.7–10), are connected and designated as "penthecostales" to form a complete organ Mass.

Almost everywhere the *alternatim* practice is recognizable. In the responsory *Judaea et Hierusalem* the response is set for the organ; the verse *Constante estote* is not set and was thus performed as a chant; the partial repetition of the response, *Cras egrediemini* (called *Repetitio*), is again left to the organ, to be followed by the Gregorian *Gloria Patri* and the repetition of the organ setting for *Cras egrediemini*. In the sequences only the odd-numbered lines are set for organ, without regard to whether it is a sequence of the older type, starting with a single verse, or one of the more recent variety, in which all sections have double versicles. Compare the following two designs (organ settings are given in capitals):

Congaudent angelorum	*Natus ante secula*
1. CONGAUDENT	1a. NATUS ANTE
2a. quae sine	1b. per quem fit
2b. FILIUM QUI	2a. PER QUEM DIES
3a. nam ipsa	2b. quem angeli
3b. IN TERRIS	etc.
etc.	

The movements of the Mass ordinary are treated in similar fashion. Thus the Kyrie regularly contains two *Kyries*, one *Christe*, and two more *Kyries*, which produce the following order:

KYRIE Kyrie KYRIE Christe CHRISTE Christe KYRIE Kyrie KYRIE

For the Sanctus four movements are provided, thus:

SANCTUS, Sanctus, SANCTUS DOMINUS DEUS SABAOTH.
Pleni sunt caeli et terra gloria tua. HOSANNA IN EXCELSIS.
Benedictus qui venit in nomine Domini. HOSANNA IN EXCELSIS.

The Agnus consists mostly of two organ settings, for the first and for the third invocations.

The table below compares Buchner's disposition of the Gloria with several other Glorias. The one in the *Buxheim Organ Book* (cf.p.67), is omitted because of its completely deviating structure.[9]

Comparative Treatment of the Gloria
(O = organ movement)

	F	B	R	A	CA	C	M
1. Gloria in excelsis Deo							
2. Et in terra . . .	O	O	O	O	O	O	O
3. Laudamus te							
4. Benedicimus te	O			O	O	O	O
5. Adoramus te							
6. Glorificamus te	O			O	O	O	O
7. Gratias agimus . . .			O				
8. Domine Deus rex . . .	O	O		O	O	O	O
9. Domine Fili . . .			O				
10. Domine Deus agnus . . .	O	O		O	O	O	O
11. Qui tollis . . . nobis			O				
12. Qui tollis . . . nostram	O			O	O	O	O
13. Qui sedes . . . nobis		O	O				
14. Quoniam tu solus . . .	O			O	O	O	O
15. Tu solus Dominus		O					
16. Tu solus Altissimus . . .	O			O	O	O	O
17. Cum Sancto Spiritu		O	O				
18. In gloria Dei Patris	O	O	O	O			
19. Amen	O		O		O	O	O

F = Faenza (cf.p.31); B = Buchner; R = Philip ap Rhys (cf.pp.154–55); A = Attaingnant (cf.p.106); CA = Castell' Arquato (cf.p.112); C = Cavazzoni (cf.p.116); M = Merulo (cf.p.122).

As in vocal settings, the intonation is performed in chant, so that the organ enters with ℣ 2, in contrast to the Kyrie, Sanctus, and Agnus, in which the organ starts out with the first verse. In the remainder of the Gloria the organ is generally heard in the even-numbered verses, most consistently in the Italian settings. Almost the same disposition, deviating only at the end, is followed by the two Glorias in the Attaingnant print. The design of the Gloria by the Englishman Philip ap Rhys is entirely different: The four short invocations (℣ 3–6) are given to the choir as a unit, after which the organ is regularly employed for the odd-numbered verses (omitting ℣ 15). Buchner's settings are striking in that he omits not only the four invocations but also the following long ℣ 7, and later he changes from setting the even-numbered verses (8, 10) to working out the odd-numbered ones (13, 15, 17).

Let us now turn from the liturgical consideration of Buchner's organ settings to their musical features. Often the movements are designated as *m* (*manualiter*) or *p* (*pedaliter*). Many of them carry legends indicating how the basic chant tune has been treated. Designations such as *choralis in discantu* or *in basso* point out the traditional procedure that assigns the *cantus firmus* to a single voice. In a good number of pieces, however, we find such legends as "fugat in quarta," "fugat in tenore cum discantu in octava," "in unisono utriusque tenoris," "in discantu alto tenoris et basso," "in ombnibus vocibus," "in commutatione vocum," "in tenore et aliarum vocum permutatione," etc.—all signifying that the chant is heard in several parts.

Essentially this is done in two ways, either by "permutation," in which a fragment of the tune appears first in one voice, then in another; or by "fuguing," i.e., in the manner of a stretto. Fig.85 shows one example of each method in simplified notation: a. *Kyrie. Choralis in tenoris et aliarum vocum permutatione* (Päsler, p.132); b. *Sanctus. Choralis in basso cum fuga octavae* (Päsler, p.115). Buchner's indications, however, are not always trustworthy; a Sanctus[10] is designated *fugat in basso et discantu*, but it actually presents a *permutatio per omnes voces,* since the motif (|*c c A* | *B♭ B♭A G* | *F*) (beginning of Sanctus XVII?) is heard four times, once each in the bass, discant, tenor, and alto.

Fig.85

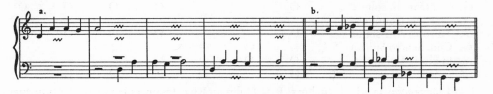

In several instances the imitation becomes a strict canon, as in *Infunde unctionem tuam* (Päsler, p.157). In two verses of the *Magnificat*[11] the same melody is treated first as a canon at the fifth (*Choral in discanto et alto fugat in quinto*), and then as a canon at the fourth (*Choral in discanto et alto fugat in quarto*). How this interesting problem is resolved is shown in Fig.86. The canon at the fourth reminds us of the "egg of Columbus"; incidentally, it is used in the very same form about one hundred years later by Ulrich Steigleder in one of his *Variations on Vatter unser* (cf.p.405).

Fig.86

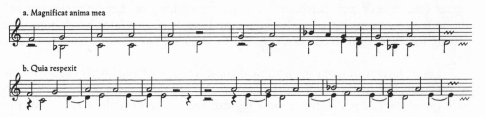

a. Magnificat anima mea

b. Quia respexit

Buchner's general musical style seems to point to the fact that he was more interested in teaching than in art. Certainly these two goals are not so disparate that they cannot be combined, but to do so demands a skill and an intellectual superiority that Buchner did not possess. One cannot deny that his pieces have a dignified seriousness, a posture suitable to their liturgical purpose, but their pedagogical aim is all too clear, especially in the shorter movements, the Kyries, the Agnuses, the many sections of the sequences, etc. Moreover, the too frequent use of stereotyped ornaments is disturbing, particularly his use of the turn, which appears at every possible occasion. Here we see the beginning of that ill-famed technique of "coloration," which affected a wide range of clavier music throughout the 16th century. To be sure, Buchner still applies this method in a relatively moderate manner. The decisive point, however, is not so much the extent but the manner of its use, which more and more takes on the character of a system. Some pieces of the *Buxheim Organ Book* are much more ornamented than any composition of the 16th century, but their figurations still possess an attractive vitality, freedom, fantasy, and even capriciousness. In the works of Schlick and Hofhaimer figuration is ennobled and becomes beautiful decoration, which enlivens the music. With Buchner, and even more so with many of the later musicians, it freezes into a mechanical routine, a predetermined recipe, which is applied according to a rule. As an example Fig.87 reproduces the section *Per quem dies: Choral in discanto* from the sequence *Natus ante secula* (from the Zurich manuscript).

Fig.87

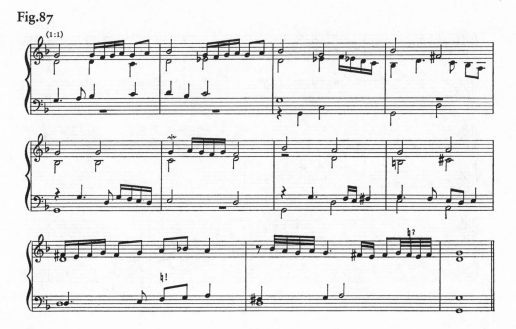

Four-part texture is almost as frequent as three-part. Occasionally Buchner even writes pieces for five and six voices, but they are so shot through with rests that they actually constitute four-part writing. Some are really written for five parts, e.g., the Gloria Patri of the introit *Resurrexi* (in the Zurich manuscript), but, then, the polyphonic texture is replaced by a purely chordal one with an ornamented upper voice.

Three compositions by Buchner that are on a higher artistic level than the works in the *Fundamentum* are preserved in Kleber's and Sicher's tablatures: *Recordare, Maria zart,* and *Sancta Maria.*[12] The *Recordare* is very similar in style and structure to the arrangement by Hofhaimer discussed above and is also its equal artistically. It is probably an early work in which Buchner consciously followed his teacher's composition. His liking for the turn is already apparent here: The discant of Hofhaimer's setting contains seventeen turns, while Buchner's has more than twice as many.

While Buchner's *Recordare* points to Hofhaimer, the model for his *Maria zart* was certainly Schlick's setting of the same church song. Like Schlick, Buchner treats the various phrases of the melody imitatively, but goes far beyond his model by employing a four-part texture and systematically exploring the possibilities of canonic imitation. The very first line of the melody enters in a stretto of two voices; the second line is used twice as a counterpoint to the first one; various ideas enter in diminution and fugato before they are heard in the

Fig.88

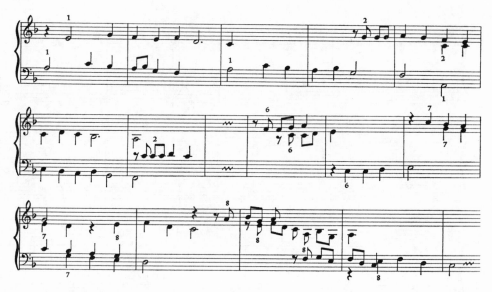

main voice, which appears to be the bass; etc. Kleber calls the work a *fuga optima*, and it certainly deserves this title. It is probably the earliest known example of a fully developed chorale motet, the type in which Bach, too, created his greatest chorale settings, e.g., *Wenn wir in höchsten Nöthen seyn*, which he dictated to his faithful friend Altnikol shortly before his death. It is unfortunate that Buchner's *Maria zart*, a fairly long composition, is not available in a modern print. To give an idea of the structural relationships several passages are reproduced in Fig.88 in outline (i.e., without the connecting figurations). Compare this design with that of Schlick's arrangement (Fig.82).

Buchner's *Sancta Maria*, like *Maria zart*, is motet-like, but more concisely formulated. The imitative treatment of each line takes on more of the character of a fore-imitation with a concluding statement in the bass. Occasionally Buchner involves the principle of diminution, e.g., in the passage in Fig.89. At first we hear the motif of the first double versicle (1 = 2), then that of lines 3–6 is added above it, and this is followed by another contrapuntal combination of the two motifs. The passage cited is the second setting of line 3.

Fig.89

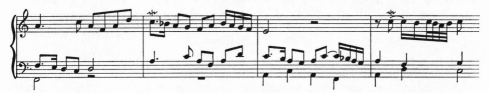

The tablatures of Kleber, Kotter, and Sicher contain a few additional liturgical movements, including a *Resonet in laudibus* by Bernhard von Salem, a *Pleni sunt* by Konrad Brumann, and a *Sancta Maria* by Leonhard Kleber.[13] Structurally as well as stylistically they are very close to Hofhaimer's works, and therefore add nothing new to our picture of German organ music at the start of the 16th century. An exception is an anonymous *In dulci iubilo* from Sicher's tablature, which differs from the rest in its brevity and simplicity. It does not contain a single ornament. Even more unusual is the melody, which probably originated in the 14th century; with its folk-like key of *F* major and gently moving 6/8 time, a new type, the Christmas cradle song, *pastorale*, or *siciliano*, is realized for the first time. But the most astonishing feature is the treatment of the tune as an accompanied two-part canon, which is very similar to what Bach did two hundred years later. Fig.90 shows the beginning and end of this particularly charming composition.

A tablature in the Breslau Library from the middle of the 16th century was described by F. Dietrich in 1932,[14] but has been missing since World War II.

Fig.90

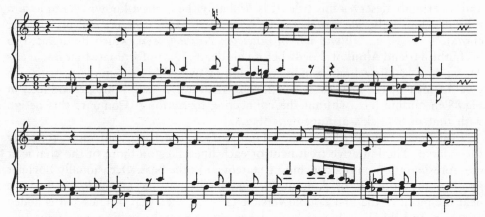

According to Dietrich's account it contained Magnificats, numerous settings of psalm tones, a *Te Deum,* and a German chorale *Wir gläuben all an einen Gott.* Stylistically the pieces seem to follow Buchner's *Fundamentum.* According to Dietrich[15] they are all the work of one composer and were all written down shortly after 1565.

THE PROTESTANT ORGAN CHORALE

In the Breslau tablature there is only one example of the German Protestant organ chorale, but in slightly later sources it assumes a considerably greater role. The first of these sources is the *Orgel oder Instrument Tabulatur* by Elias Nikolaus Ammerbach, which was published in two somewhat different editions (1571 and 1583).[16] Together the two prints contain about twenty different settings of Lutheran chorale tunes, mostly songs of praise and thanks from the early period of the Lutheran tune repertoire, of which only a few survived into the 17th century. *Gelobet seist du Jesu Christ* (1583, no.10) is the only one that also appears frequently in the organ literature of the 17th century.

Ammerbach arranges these melodies in concise four-part settings, which one may call homophonic with polyphonic features—the same method used later in the one hundred chorales in Samuel Scheidt's *Görlitz Tablature* of 1650 and in the chorales that conclude Bach's cantatas. Such arrangements are often called vocal, and indeed they are in Bach's case; however, there is no doubt that Ammerbach and Scheidt wrote their settings for the organ or a household clavier instrument. Occasionally the pieces in Ammerbach's tablature still follow the earlier practice and put the chorale melody in the tenor (e.g., in 1571, no.1: *Wo Gott der Herr nicht bei uns hält*), in the alto (1571, no.2: *Herr Gott nu sey gepreyset*), or in the bass (1583, no.6: *Herr Gott nu sey gepreiset, Idem et ultimum in Bassu*)—but it usually lies in the upper part.

In his article "Ammerbach" in *MGG*, W. Ehmann writes: "The Leipzig municipal documents give a vivid picture of how he experienced much tribulation and sorrow in these thirty-five years during which he held his office because he was such a thoughtless genius. . . ." His organ chorales also show traits that one may call the results of thoughtless genius: Archaic turns and breaches of the rules are ubiquitous, but there are also audacities that anticipate a later evolution of musical style, particularly in the treatment of dissonances. Of course one has to take into account the possibility of occasional printer's errors, but enough remains that can be explained only as the expression of an original, personal style, interesting for its individuality. As examples Fig.91 presents the beginning of a setting of *Herr Gott nu sey gepreiset* (1583, no.3) and two passages from other chorales. Note the simultaneous sounding of *F* and *F sharp* (the *punto intenso contra remisso* of Correa de Arauxo) in b. (1571, no.8) and the highly "modern" and correctly resolved supertonic six-five chord in c. (1571, no.3).

Fig.91

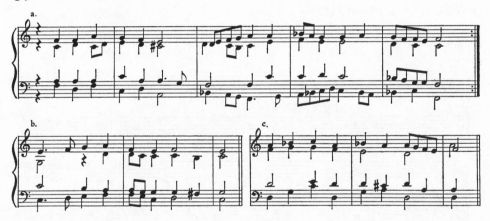

The tablatures that follow Ammerbach's—those by Bernhard Schmid the Elder (1577), Jacob Paix (1583), and Christoph Löffelholtz (1585), and the manuscript Berlin, Stb. 40115 (1593)[17]—together contain about fifteen chorale settings, all probably intabulations of vocal pieces. Orlando di Lasso and Stephan Zirler are named as the authors of several of them; others are evidently harmonizations of an ornamented melody (a style known as cantional style).

Augustus Nörmiger's *Tabulaturbuch auff dem Instrumente* of 1598 is another important source for the early history of the German organ chorale. The manuscript opens with a collection of seventy-seven chorales, "So des Jahres über in der Christlichen Kirchen und sonsten zu gebrauchen verordnet" (as they are ordered to be used throughout the year in Christian churches and elsewhere), as we read on the title page. This is the earliest complete cycle and in the usual order: Advent, Christmas, Passiontide, Easter, Ascension, Whitsuntide, Trinity, and finally, catechism and psalm songs. For the first time in clavier literature we find a large number of those chorales that were repeatedly set during the 17th and 18th centuries: *Nun komm der Heiden Heiland, Vom Himmel hoch da komm ich her, Christ lag in Todesbanden, Vater unser im Himmelreich, Ein feste Burg, Aus tiefer Not,* and many more. Nörmiger employs a method of arrangement similar to Ammerbach's, but with a more correct texture and with hardly any breaches of the then valid rules of counterpoint and harmony.

Finally there are four chorale settings by Simon Lohet. Born about 1550 in Liége, he lived in Stuttgart from 1571 until his death in 1611 (and there he taught Adam Steigleder). His chorale settings, preserved in Johann Woltz's *Nova musices organicae tabulatura* (1617), are: *Nun welche hie ihr Hoffnung gar* (Psalm cxxv), *De tout mon coeur* (Ps.ix), *Erbarm dich mein o Herre Gott* (Ps.li), and *Media vita*.[18] These are the beginnings of a more artistic treatment of the chorale, for the first line is set in imitative style. The opening section of *Nun welche hie* is given in Fig.92.

Fig.92

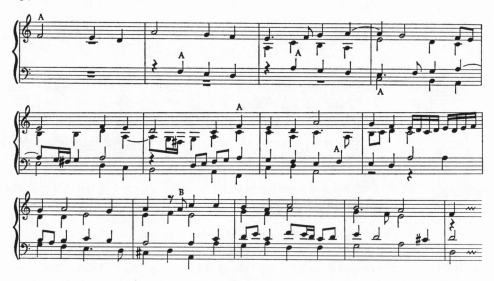

Poland

A very extensive repertoire of liturgical organ music is preserved in several Polish tablatures of the 16th century. The most important of these sources is a collection of over five hundred pages assembled during the years 1537–48 by Johannes of Lublin, a canon of the Krasnik monastery.[19] It starts with an extended treatise, which is arranged somewhat like Buchner's *Fundamentum*, but surpasses it in detailed discussion and number of teaching examples—*ascensus, descensus, clausulae, conclusiones, concordanciae,* etc. This is followed by an unordered collection of about 250 compositions: liturgical organ pieces, preludes, dances, intabulations of motets and vocal works with German, French, Italian, and Polish titles, as well as some untitled and unidentifiable works. The pieces are mostly anonymous, but occasionally names are given: Phynk (Finck), Stolczer, N. C. (Nicolaus Cracoviensis?), and others.

The liturgical repertoire of this manuscript is as follows:

Mass proper: 13 introits, 7 sequences, 2 hymns
Mass ordinary: 3 complete Masses, 9 Kyries, 1 Gloria, 2 Credos, 2 Sanctuses
Offices: 5 hymns, 2 antiphons, psalm tones singly and in groups

The introits include *Ressurrexi* (N. C., with Gloria Patri), *Cibavit eos* (N. C. 1540, with verse), *Benedicta sit Sancta Trinitas* (N. C., with Gloria Patri), *Puer natus est nobis,* and *Spiritus Domini.* Of the sequences, *Lauda Sion* (12 verses) and *Congaudent angelorum* (5 verses) are worth mentioning. The hymns of the Mass are *Tantum ergo* (from *Pange lingua*) and *Crux fidelis.*

Two of the three Masses (*Officium de Dominica* and *Officium solemne*) include the Credo; one (*Officium per Octavas*) does not. The Kyries, both those included in the Masses and the separate ones, consist mostly of four movements: *Kyrie, Kyrie tertium, Christe,* and *Kyrie ultimum.* The Gloria usually consists of three movements: *Et in terra, Domine Deus Agnus, Qui sedes* or *Qui tollis;* while the Credo has two: *Patrem* and *Qui propter;* the Sanctus three: *Sanctus, Sanctus III, Osanna;* and the Agnus one: *Agnus Dei.*

Among the pieces for the Daily Offices the following may be singled out: *Salve regina* (N. C.), *Regina coeli, De profundis, Exempla octo tonorum* (1542), *Toni valentes ad cantum,* and *Toni transpositi, Primus . . . Septimus* (1543).

Let us now look at the musical treatment of the Gregorian tunes. In the introits it is difficult to determine the method in detail because the chants often deviate strongly from those printed in the modern (i.e., mediaeval) Graduale, particularly in their concluding sections. The basic principle consists in assigning the melody, section by section to various voices, in other words, to treat it as a migrant *cantus firmus.* Two examples will illustrate this procedure:

Fol.84v: *Introitus de Corpore Cristi (Cibavit eos)*

Cibavit . . . frumenti:	fore-imitation, then *c.f.* in bass
alleluia:	*c.f.* in tenor
et de petra, melle:	beginning of *c.f.* in discant, then in bass
saturavit eos:	*c.f.* in discant
alleluia (different):	*c.f.* probably in tenor

Fol.80: *Officium de Nativitate Cristi* (*Puer natus*)

Puer . . . nobis:	beginning of *c.f.* in alto, tenor, discant, then the whole *c.f.* in bass
et filius . . . nobis:	beginning of *cf.* in discant, then in bass
cuius imperium:	*c.f.* in tenor
super humerum etc.:	unclear, but *c.f.* surely in various voices.

In principle, the chant, wherever it appears, is treated as a *cantus planus* in semibreves (half notes), but quite often connecting and decorating tones are added. The first *alleluia* of *Cibavit eos,* e.g., whose chant tune is ([c f] f e d d e d d), appears as in Fig.93.

Fig.93

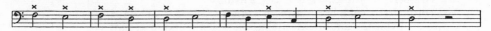

The sequences consist of a considerable number of short versets, most of which start with a fore-imitation and then present the whole segment in one part. Nevertheless there are also examples of the migrant *cantus firmus* or of imitative treatment of each phrase, so that one may perhaps speak of a motet-like setting of the entire verse.

Several of the pieces for the Mass ordinary are based on melodies whose identification is difficult. For example, in the *Officium per Octavas* (fol.21v) the Kyrie and Gloria use the well-known melodies of Mass IV. The Sanctus and Agnus, however, are based on almost identical tunes (*c' ac' gaff* . . .), but neither is found in any of the generally accessible sources; in both movements it appears as *cantus planus* in breves.[20]

One of the settings for the Daily Offices is the *De profundis super discantum* (fol.206v). The upper part of this arrangement is identical, note for note and rest for rest (i.e., in line arrangement), with the Protestant chorale *Aus tiefer Not schrei ich zu dir,* whose text is a paraphrase of Psalm cxxx, *De profundis clamavi ad te.* Both the German paraphrase and the melody connected with it are found in Walther's *Gesangbüchlein* of 1524, and were surely known in Catholic Poland before 1548 This composition is of such extraordinary interest that it is reproduced in its entirety in Fig.94.

Fig.94

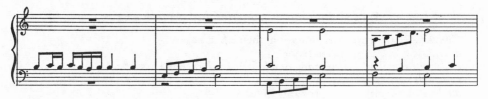

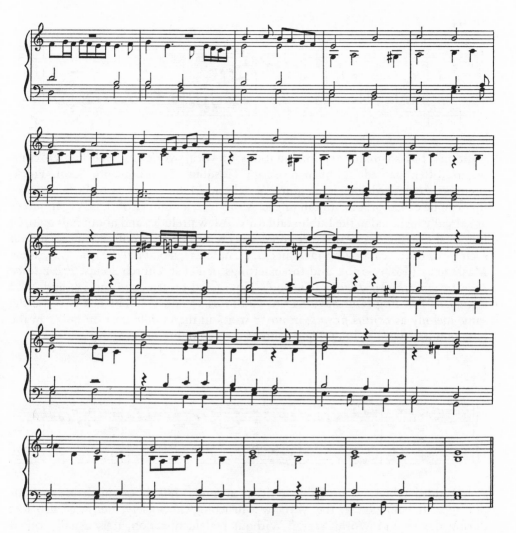

Finally a few remarks about the psalm tones. The *Exempla octo tonorum* (fol.191v) are brief settings in which only the endings of the recitation formulae are considered. The *Toni valentes ad cantum* (fol.195v) are arrangements of the first four psalm tones. The seven *Toni transpositi* (fol.229v) in which the tones appear transposed down a fourth are the most richly executed of all. The beginning of the *sextus tonus* is a good example (Fig.95).

A second Polish source reaches us in a tablature dated 1548, which originally belonged to the Cracow Order of the Holy Ghost. Later it passed into private Polish hands, and was lost during the Second World War, but fortunately a photographic copy has been preserved.[21] It contains one hundred and one com-

Fig.95

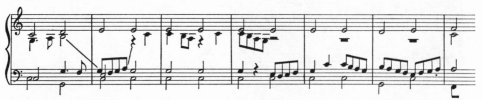

positions, but so many are intabulations of vocal works by well-known composers, often named in the manuscript (Josquin, Tromboncino, Senfl, Finck,
Breitengasser, Verdelot, Jannequin, Gombert, Mahu), that very little remains
that can be called original organ music. Moreover, a number of these organ pieces
are already included in the Lublin tablature. A few preludes and about half a dozen
liturgical organ works can be counted as new additions, among them a *Tantum
ergo* (no.4 of the catalog by Jachimecki, cf. note 21), a *Salve regina* (no.32), a few
Mass items (nos.95–100), and three settings of Polish church songs: *Przez thwe
szwyete zmarthwywsthanye* (Through Thy sacred resurrection; no.11) and *Nasz
Zbawiciel Pan Bog* (Our Savior Lord God; nos.17 and 31). The last two use the
same melody as *cantus firmus;* in no.17 it lies in the middle part, in no.31 in the
bass in notes twice as long. Fig.96 shows the beginning of no.17.

Fig.96

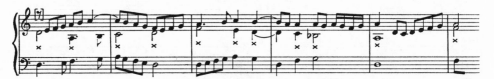

A third tablature, probably written around 1580, is of much greater importance. It belonged to the Warsaw Musicological Society, but was also lost
during the Second World War.[22] Without real justification, it is usually called
Tablature of Martin Leopolita. For many years this manuscript was known only
by way of a very inadequate dissertation, which does not even contain a table
of contents.[23] A short time ago, however, G. Golos treated it in two articles, on
which the following explanations are based.[24]

The manuscript consisted of ninety-eight folios containing seventy-five compositions, all of them liturgical music. Formerly these pieces were generally
thought to be transcriptions of vocal music, but the alternating plan of the
Kyries, sequences, Marian antiphons, Magnificats, etc., as well as the occasional
use of added voices and other clavieristic features prove that most of them are
genuine organ music. Only a few pieces are marked by initials, which are inter-

preted to mean Christoph Clabon, Martin Leopolita, Martin Wartecki, and possibly Jakob Sowa.

The manuscript consists of 47 introits, 8 sequences, 12 pieces for the Mass ordinary (of which four, nos.16–19, form a *Missa solenne*), and 8 Magnificats. The participation of the organ in the introits and sequences is even more prominent than in the Lublin tablature. Many compositions show the technique, so favored during the 16th century, of fore-imitation followed by the complete presentation of the *cantus firmus* in one of the parts. The style is generally that of Netherlandish counterpoint, but occasionally one finds passages that herald the approaching 17th century. Quasi-polychoral formations appear, e.g., which perhaps derive from Venetian models, such as the excerpt from the Magnificat in Fig.97.

Fig.97

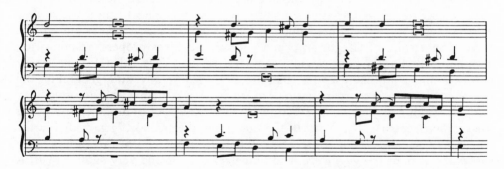

France

The earliest known sources of liturgical organ music in France—unfortunately also the only ones from the 16th century—are two prints by Attaingnant from 1530 (early 1531 according to the modern calendar): *Tabulature pour le jeu d'Orgues Espinetes et Manicordions sur le plain chant de Cunctipotens et Kyrie fons . . .* and *Magnificat sur les huit tons avec Te deum laudamus et deux Preludes, le tout mys en la tabulature des Orgues Espinettes et Manicordions. . . .*[25] The reference to spinets and "manicordions" (probably clavichords) shows that the pieces were used not only in church but also for private edification.

The first print contains two organ Masses, *Cunctipotens* and *Kyrie fons.* These two Masses and Buchner's approximately contemporary composition (cf.p.93) are the first known examples of the complete organ Mass, comprising all five (or at least four) movements of the ordinary. The type of Mass composition that prevailed almost exclusively in the vocal literature of the 15th and early 16th century—one in which all the movements are related by the use of the same *cantus firmus* (*Alma redemptoris mater, L'homme armé,* etc.)—is completely unknown in organ music. The organ Masses all belong to the so-called *missa choralis* type, in which the various movements—Kyrie, Gloria, etc.—are based on Gregorian Kyrie, Gloria, etc., melodies, i.e., the whole Mass is based on one of the various cycles of the Mass ordinary. Of course these cycles were organized relatively recently; the earliest ones originated in the 13th century, but the majority of those in use today were put together as late as the 19th century by Dom Pothier and Dom Mocquereau. The oldest cycle, and the only one that has been preserved without change, is the *Missa Cunctipotens genitor,* the Mass IV of the modern collection. None of the others were established or unified by the 16th century.

This situation is clearly reflected in the organ Masses of the Attaingnant print. The *Missa Cunctipotens* is based throughout on the melodies of Mass IV. The *Missa Kyrie fons,* despite its title, uses only the Kyrie of today's Mass II; for the Credo it uses the melody of Credo I and for the remaining movements the melodies of Mass IV. Not only was the order of the melodies in the Mass ordinary subject to strong variations, but so were the melodies themselves, as they were sung in the 16th century, much more so than the pieces that belong to the original repertoire of Gregorian chant, such as the Mass propers, responsories, antiphons, etc. For the purposes of a comparative analysis it is therefore necessary to draw on chant manuscripts that are both temporally and geographically close in origin to the organ settings to be investigated; but this is often very difficult. Take, for example, the section *Domine Deus Rex* from the Gloria of the *Missa Cunctipotens:* The Vatican Graduale has the melody (g ge fg e) for the words *Rex caelestis,* while a French Graduale from the end of the 14th century shows the variant (g f gagf e ef). The latter version, or one very similar to it, is employed in both organ Masses.[26]

All the Mass movements are composed according to the *alternatim* principle. The disposition of the Gloria has already been given in a table (see p.93). For the Agnus we find two movements, as in Buchner's work; for the Sanctus, however, there are three: *Sanctus, Sanctus,* and *Benedictus,* which leads to a different division of roles. The Kyrie of the *Missa Kyrie fons* has the usual five movements, which produce the *alternatim* order (O = organ, C = chant): O C O | C O C | O C O. The *Missa Cunctipotens,* however, has six movements; two Kyries, two Christes, and two Kyries. It is not impossible that two different compositions for the Christe are presented to provide a choice; but it is more probable that another disposition is intended, in which each of the three main sections is presented in the same order, thus: O C O | O C O | O C O.[27]

In the *Missa Kyrie fons,* we see the Credo in complete form for the first time. The sections are *Patrem, visibilium, Et ex Patre, Et incarnatus est, Et homo, Et exspecto,* and *Amen.* Using the modern division of the text into nineteen sections (indicated in the *Liber Usualis* by double bars), we find that the following passages are entrusted to the organ: 2 beginning, 2 end, 4, 8 beginning, 8 end, 17, and 19—a very arbitrary disposition, to be sure. The participation of the organ in the Credo of Italian masses (Cavazzoni, cf.pp.116–17; A. Gabrieli, Merulo) is much more regular.

The second Attaingnant print contains a *Te Deum* of fifteen short segments, and a number of Magnificat settings (as well as two preludes, cf.p.217). Scattered organ pieces for the Magnificat occur in the early Munich fragment (G) (cf.p.37), in the *Buxheim Organ Book*, and in Buchner's music. With Attaingnant, however, they assume a systematic treatment for the first time, for they are set to each of the eight tones to which the text is sung (according to the mode of the preceding and concluding antiphon), and entitled *Magnificat primi toni, secundi toni,* etc. The Magnificat consists of ten verses (twelve with the Gloria Patri), so that five or six organ movements are needed for an *alternatim* performance. But since all the verses are sung to the same melody, the organ settings may be repeated, and fewer of them are needed. In the Attaingnant collection each *tonus* is represented by two verses, except the *quartus tonus,* which has five, and the *octavus tonus,* which has four.

The principal difference between French and German organ music of this period is the importance of four-part writing. It is well-developed in Schlick's works around 1510, and is treated as routine by Buchner around 1520, but here it plays a very subordinate role. In the first print, which contains the two Masses, it does not appear at all, and in the second it appears only in the *Te Deum*.[28] Although in this respect French organ music lags considerably behind the German, it is more progressive in the frequent application of added voices. In the organ Masses we repeatedly find a three-note chord at the end of a two-part movement, or a four-note chord concluding a three-part setting. The movements of the Magnificat show even more changes in the number of parts and insertions of full chords. Fig.98 shows such a passage from the *Magnificat quarti toni,* which is conceived in three voices.*

To be sure, many settings in Paumann's *Fundamentum* and in the *Buxheim Organ Book* make use of free voices, adding a third voice here and there to a two-part setting. But there it is done to achieve a denser polyphony, while in Attaingnant's collection the purpose of the full chords is to reinforce the sound. This genuinely clavieristic use of free voices is found for the first time in Marco Antonio Cavazzoni's *Recerchari Motetti Canzoni* of 1523. In the French as well as in the Italian print the music is notated on two staves. In Germany the so-called German organ tablature, essentially a score notation, was retained throughout the 16th century. It is obvious that the former method favors free voices, just as the latter renders their use more difficult, if not impossible. At the beginning of the 17th century this contrast between "Germanic" and "Latin" organ music (and notation) still persists, as between Scheidt and Frescobaldi.[29]

---

* The note values in the musical examples taken from Attaingnant are not reduced.

Fig.98

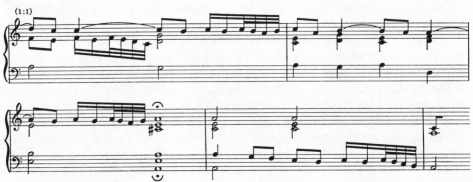

French and German organ music at the beginning of the 16th century also differ in the use of imitation. When we consider that around 1520 Buchner treats the technique of imitation systematically in his *Fundamentum* and also employs it frequently in his compositions, it is surprising to see how rarely and in some ways how imperfectly it is employed in the Attaingnant collections. Not even one piece approaches pervading imitations. The one that comes closest to this style is the *secundus versus* of the *Magnificat octavi toni,* but it is transcribed from a vocal setting by Richafort (cf. note 28). Otherwise imitation is limited to three or four pieces, which start with a brief imitation. The most highly developed example is probably the beginning of the *Benedictus* from the *Missa Cunctipotens,* shown in Fig.99.

Fig.99

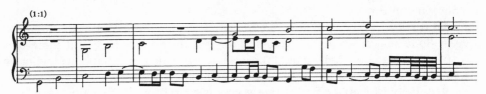

The prevailing method of composition consists in creating counterpoints in regularly flowing scale figures above a *cantus planus.* Fig.100 shows a typical example, the beginning of the *Gloria* from the *Missa Kyrie fons.* This style is rarely found in German organ music of the 16th century, i.e., occasionally in some preludes; however it has a very important role in Italy. There are other features in the French music: held chords, homophonic progressions, sequences, etc., which often succeed each other rather abruptly, giving an impression of lack

Fig.100

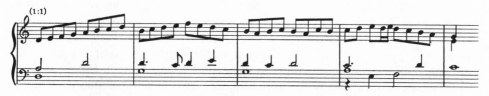

of unity and planning. Moreover, there are many errors in the counterpoint, some of which may be due to carelessness in printing. All in all the pieces are obviously mediocre products.

Italy

MARCO ANTONIO CAVAZZONI AND HIS CONTEMPORARIES

The development of liturgical organ music, indeed of clavier music as a whole, is far more significant in Italy than in France. Important Italian organ music emerges as early as the end of the 14th century, in the *Codex Faenza*. In view of its early prominence it is particularly regrettable that from the next hundred years we know the names of but a few organists (among them Antonio Squarcialupi, who died in 1475) and some reports about organ construction. It is only in 1517 that the veil begins to lift, thanks to a collection of *Frottole intabulate da sonare organi, libro primo*, published by the Roman printer Andrea Antico.[30] As the title indicates, it contains only intabulations of frottole, and is thus of little interest for the history of keyboard music.

The next source, the *Recerchari Motetti Canzoni* by Marco Antonio da Bologna (Marco Antonio Cavazzoni), 1523, is one of the most significant and interesting documents of organ music from the early 16th century.[31] Its contents are as follows:

1. Recercare primo
2. Salve Virgo
3. Recercare secondo
4. O Stella maris
5. Perdone Moi sie folie
6. Madame vous aves mon cuor
7. Plus ne regres
8. Lautre yor per un matin

The titles of nos.2 and 4 obviously point to a relationship to liturgical music. What this relationship may be, however, remains uncertain. In the title of the print these pieces are called *motetti;* they may thus be intabulations of vocal motets. But the term *motetti* may have only the general meaning of church music (in contrast to the secular *canzoni*); if so, it is quite possible that they are not transcriptions of polyphonic vocal works but arrangements of liturgical melodies, most probably hymns. Even so, the problem of identification remains. There are a number of hymns that start with the words *Salve Virgo* or *O stella maris*, but differ from each other further on in the text.[32] Which of these is intended is rather difficult to determine, since quite often the same hymn text is sung to different melodies and different texts are set to the same melody.

The musical style of the two *motetti* is almost as problematic as their liturgical background. They represent an exception to the organ music of the time, and are hardly comparable to anything else. Several details are taken from the motet style of the period, especially the imitative duos that bear the stamp of Josquin; these occur in both pieces, as well as repeatedly in organ pieces by Buchner. Unlike the Buchner pieces, the *motetti* do not carry the motet style through systematically, but mix it with purely clavieristic style elements similar to those in the Attaingnant prints. Imitation is also used, again not systematically, but in a highly original manner, in suggestions and free variants that resist a real analysis. This is by no means meant to imply a negative judgment. On the contrary, the mixture of styles and the freedom of treatment give the two works a particular charm and raise them far above the average.

Fig.101

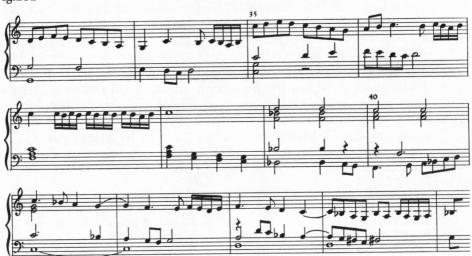

Their structure can be described only approximately. In the *Salve Virgo* we can discern perhaps three main sections: a beginning, which is dominated by the ascending motif (*f g a b♭*); a shorter middle section (meas.31–40) in a free, non-imitative style; and an extended conclusion (33 measures), in which a descending scale motive (*c' b♭ a g f e f*) occurs repeatedly with a quasi-thematic importance. Fig.101 shows the end of the middle section and the beginning of the third one. Note the free entry of a new voice in a higher register in measure 35, and the "imitation" of an idea in the same part in which it has just been heard in measure 43. The piece begins with a duet of ten measures, which is then repeated Josquin-fashion an octave lower; another imitative duo (of two plus two measures) occurs in the third section (meas.50–53). These are just about the only passages in the entire piece that are built "according to the rules."

The *O stella maris* causes even greater difficulties for an analytic-synthetic approach. The impressive starting motif (| *c c* | *e f♯* | *g* |) never returns. It is followed by a duet of ten measures, which is heard again in abbreviated form an octave lower. Further along in the piece several passages are repeated: measures 55–56 = 62–63 (in the same register), 71–73 = 75–77 (an octave lower), 82–83 = 85–86 (a fourth higher). Toward the end there is a section in triple meter; the beginning of it is reproduced in Fig.102.

Fig.102

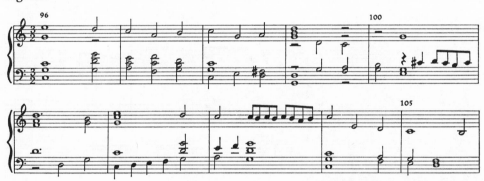

This is the first appearance of parallel 1–5–8 chords in the accompaniment. Objectionable as they may have been to theorists, they play an important and quite justified role, especially in Italy. The passage quoted in Fig.102 is followed by a literal repetition of measures 96–103, and then by a few measures in duple meter, which give a dignified, festive conclusion to the whole composition. In its details as well as in its entirety this work is most interesting and impressive.

Each of the two *motetti* is preceded by a *recercar*, which doubtless represents a kind of prelude. This is indicated not only by the order but also by the identity of tonality: *F* major in the first pair and *G* major in the second. It is therefore tempting to try to prove the existence of motivic relationships as well, but the search leads to no tangible results.[33] We shall return later to the *recercari*, which are artistically superior, and to the *canzoni*.

In the 1940s several manuscripts were discovered at the main church of Castell' Arquato (not far from Piacenza). They contain valuable material for the history of Italian clavier music from about 1530 to 1550.[34] The liturgical repertoire is represented in them by a *Missa in Solemnitatibus Beatae Mariae*, a *Messa de la Dominica*, a *Messa dell' apostoli*, two single Credos, as well as settings of *O gloriosa Domina, Assumpta est Maria*, etc.

The organ Masses, as is always the case in the 15th and 16th centuries, are arranged for alternation. The Marian Mass is a setting of the Kyrie and Gloria of Mass IX of the *Graduale*. The Kyrie consists of four movements (*Kyrie primus, Christe, Kyrie, Kyrie ultimus*), the first of which was surely repeated as *Kyrie tertius*. The Gloria has eleven movements, and concludes with the troping pieces *Mariam sanctificans, Mariam gubernans*, and *Mariam coronans Jesu Christe*. The music is basically formulated as a three-part *cantus-planus* setting with the melody mostly in semibreves (in the first and second *Kyrie* it is in breves) in the middle voice (in the first *Kyrie* it is in the bass). But toward the end of each movement the setting broadens into four parts or into a fuller chordal texture. Fig.103 shows the beginning and end of the *Kyrie ultimus*.

Fig.103

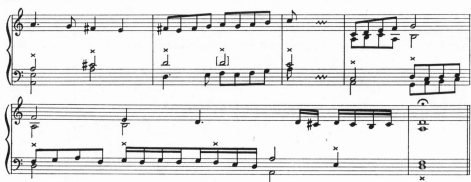

The name of the author, Jaches, appears at the end of the *Kirie ultimus*[35] in the *Messa de la Dominica*, and he is probably the author of the entire Mass. Jeppesen conjectures that he is the organist Jacques Brumel, who was active at the court of Ferrara from 1533 to 1564. The tendency to add free chordal reinforcements, observed in the Marian Mass, is even stronger in this Mass. Its versets —five for the Kyrie, nine for the Gloria, two for the Sanctus, and one for the Agnus —are basically cast in a four-part setting. But it is very often interspersed with full chords of five, six, or even seven notes, and may also be reduced abruptly to three voices for a measure or two. What a difference between this treatment of the organ and the strict counterpoint of the German school of Schlick and Buchner! One of the most peculiar products of this style, which is so strongly dominated by the effect of the sound, is the passage in Fig.104 (the beginning of the *Domine Deus Rex*), in which a chord is treated like a kind of pedal point. Similar passages

Fig.104

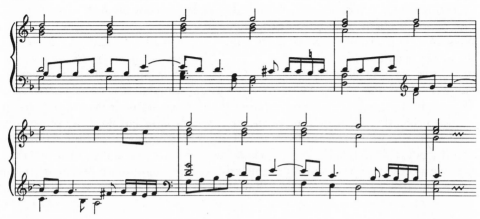

may also be found in the first ricercar of Marco Antonio Cavazzoni (cf.Fig.159).

How much the technique is dominated by the idea of organ sound is also shown by the free, even careless, treatment of the rules of counterpoint, e.g., the frequent use of parallel octaves and fifths. Josquin does not entirely avoid parallel fifths (it is to him rather than to somebody like Palestrina that we must look for a comparison), but in the organ works of the period they occur much more frequently and with more emphasis. Not infrequently they also occur in the form of parallel triads, as in Fig.105 (from the *Gloria*). To maintain that these and similar events (e.g., sharp dissonances like B♭ against B) prove "lack of knowledge" or "poor mastery of the craft" will probably not occur seriously to anybody today. They are as justified in the clavier style of the period as the "strict style" in Palestrina's vocal music is.

Fig.105

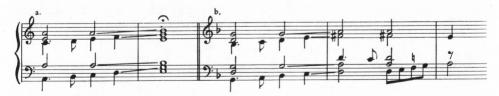

The treatment of the *cantus firmus* in this Mass by Jacques Brumel is of special interest. For the Kyrie and Gloria the melodies of today's Mass XI are used, for the Sanctus and Agnus those of Mass XVII. These melodies do not appear as continuous parts within a contrapuntal setting—the extensive use of free voices alone makes this impossible—but appear as needed, at times in the

113

upper part, or in one of the middle voices, if one may speak of voices here at all. Sometimes the liturgical melody is actually divided into single notes, one of which may sound in the highest part, the next one in a middle voice, and another at the bottom of a chord. Nevertheless the *cantus-planus* idea is strictly carried out insofar as each note of the chant corresponds to one full measure of the arrangement (two semibreves in the original). Occasionally it looks as though a measure contains two notes of the chant, or none at all, but this is probably a result of variants in the Gregorian tradition rather than of deviations from a clearly recognizable principle. The beginning of the *Et in terra pax* in Fig.106 is an illustration of this treatment. The various notes of the chant change position within the chords, but always extend over a whole measure.* In the eighth measure there are two notes (8 and 9) of today's melody, but we may safely assume that this composition is based on a version that lacks note 8, an assumption that is con-

Fig.106

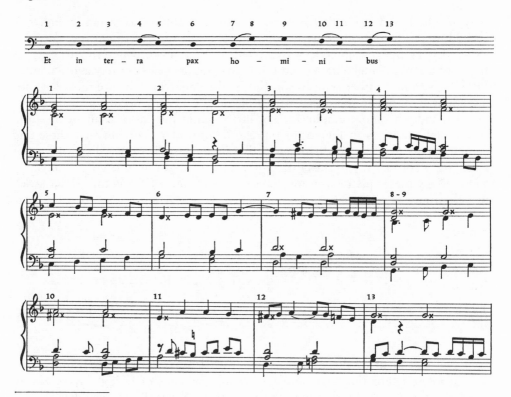

---

* In each measure the note is articulated twice, as often happens in the organ music of the period; cf., e.g., Schlick's *Salve regina*.

firmed by the corresponding section from the *Messa Domenichal* by Andrea Gabrieli.

The two single Credos from Castell' Arquato—one written at the end of the *Messa de la Dominica*, the other in a separate fascicle (not listed by Jeppesen)—represent methods of composition that belong to a later stage of Italian organ music. The first one makes extensive use of short imitations, and thus proves to be a later addition to Jacques Brumel's Mass, in which imitation hardly ever appears. Whether it is based, as Jeppesen thinks,[36] on the so-called *Credo Dominicalis* (Credo I) is questionable, since this melody is only recognizable in the first section, the *Patrem*, if at all. The situation in the second *Credo* is much clearer. It is based on Credo IV (known in the 16th century as *Credo cardinalis*), and the melody is treated in a very simple manner in most movements—as a harmonized discant. This piece certainly belongs to the latter half of the 16th century (the handwriting is doubtless of a later date than that of the other liturgical pieces, the ricercars, and the dances), but even for that period a chorale harmonization is unusual and therefore remarkable. Fig. 107 shows the beginning of the *Genitum non factum*.

Fig.107

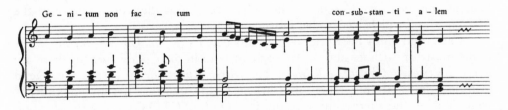

GIROLAMO CAVAZZONI

By far the most significant liturgical organ music in 16th-century Italy is that of Girolamo Cavazzoni. It appeared in two prints, the first of which is dated 1543,[37] and comprises the following:

Libro primo

4 hymns: *Christe redemptor omnium, Ad cenam agni providi, Lucis creator optime, Ave maris stella*
2 Magnificats: *primi toni* and *octavi toni*
(At the beginning of *libro primo* there are, in addition, 4 ricercars and 2 canzonas.)

Libro secondo

3 Masses: *Missa Apostolorum, Missa Dominicalis, Missa de Beata Virgine*
8 hymns: *Veni creator Spiritus, Pange lingua gloriosi, Exsultet coelum laudibus,*

Iste confessor, Jesu nostra redemptio, Jesu corona virginum, Deus tuorum militum, Hostis Herodis impie
2 Magnificats: *quarti toni* and *sexti toni*

Here, for the first time in Italy, is a rather extensive and varied repertoire of liturgical organ music.

The Magnificats all consist of five movements: *Magnificat, Quia respexit, Deposuit, Suscepit,* and *Gloria Patri* (i.e., ℣ 1, 3, 7, 9, 11), omitting ℣ 5, *Et misericordia.* Probably one of the other verses was used for this one since all the verses are based on the same melody, the repeated Magnificat tone. This practice already appeared in the Attaingnant prints, in which the majority of the Magnificats consisted of only two organ settings.

The *Missa Apostolorum* is based on the chants of Mass IV (*Cunctipotens genitor*), completed by the Credo IV, which Cavazzoni calls *Credo cardinalis.* The *Missa Dominicalis* is based on Mass XI (*Orbis factor*), but with the Agnus of Mass XII, and completed by the Credo I, which is called *Credo dominicalis.* The *Missa de Beata Virgine*, which has no settings for the Credo, employs the chants of the Marian Mass IX (*Cum iubilo*), and the Gloria is expanded by the well-known Marian trope *Spiritus et alme.* All the Masses have the same structure, with three versets for the Kyrie, nine each for the Gloria and Credo, two for the Sanctus, and one for the Agnus. The only exception is the troped Gloria of the Marian Mass, which has twelve movements.*

Cavazzoni limits his Kyrie to three movements (*Kyrie, Christe, Kyrie*), while in the music of Buchner and of Attaingnant (and in the *Codex Faenza*) there are five (2 *Kyries*, 1 *Christe*, 2 *Kyries*). The *Missa Apostolorum* carries the legend "Chirie primus. Iterum repetitur—Christe—Chirie quartus. Iterum repetitur,"[38] which implies the alternating structure O C O | C O C | O C O. The prescription *Iterum repetitur* is made possible here by the fact that this Kyrie is of the type a a a | b b b | c c c'. The chant melody of the Kyrie of the *Missa Dominicalis* has the form a a a | b b b | a a c. Here the legend reads, "Chirie primus. Iterum repetitur—Christe—Chirie," and the second *Chirie* represents the *Chirie ultimus,* since it is based on melody c. The alternating structure is probably the same as above, except that the *Chirie primus* is to be repeated for both the third and the seventh invocation. On the other hand, the Kyrie of the *Missa de beata Virgine* has the form a b a | c d c | e f e', so that, according to the same scheme, sections a, d, and e would be played by the organ. Actually the *Chirie primus* is composed to melody a, the *Christe* to melody c, and the second *Chirie* to melody f. Thus the result for the total performance is the irregular order O C O | O C O | C O C.

The structure of the Gloria has been given earlier, in a table that compares those by Buchner, Attaingnant, and others (cf.p.93). The Credos have organ

---

* The movements are the same as in the Marian Mass from Castell' Arquato with an added setting for the *Amen.*

settings for the following sections of the modern text disposition: 2, 4, 6, 9, 11, 13, 15, 17, 19. In contrast to the Credo of the Attaingnant print (cf.p.106), the organ playing is distributed equally over the whole, according to a well thought-out plan. The change from even- to odd-numbered sections (from ℣ 6 to ℣ 9) can probably be explained by the fact that in the 16th century sections 7 and 8 (*Qui propter nos* and *Et incarnatus est*) formed a single section. According to this assumption the organ movements of Cavazzoni's Credos would comprise all even-numbered verses, exactly as in his Glorias. The Credo of the Mass from Castell' Arquato shows the same disposition, except that the last three movements are missing, probably because the manuscript is incomplete.

For the Agnuses Cavazzoni provides only a single organ section, which was probably used for the first and the third Agnus, since all three Agnus melodies belong to the type a b a. The intended arrangement of the Sanctuses is more problematic. In each of the three Masses the Sanctus consists of a *Sanctus primus* and *Sanctus secundus*. The former obviously belongs to the first *Sanctus;* the only clue to the position of the other, however, is offered by the thematic substance of the organ setting. In the *Missa Dominicalis* it points to the section *Pleni sunt* (Sanctus XI), and in the *Missa Apostolorum* to the *Pleni sunt* (Sanctus IV) or to the various other sections that share the same melody (*g b c' d' c' b . . .*): the second *Sanctus,* the *in excelsis*, *Benedictus*, and the concluding *in excelsis*. In the *Missa de Beata Virgine* (based on Sanctus IX) the *Sanctus secundus* is based on the same idea (*g e c d c*) as the *Sanctus primus*; but since this motif occurs only at the beginning of the chant tune, it suggests no logical place for the second setting. Is it to be assumed that it may replace the first one, if one so chooses? In any case, in the Sanctus of Cavazzoni's Masses no clear disposition for the participation of the organ is recognizable. It first becomes clear in the Masses of Andrea Gabrieli and Merulo, where the two settings always belong to the first and third *Sanctus*.

Several of the hymns appear in the modern *Antiphonal* with changed texts. They are listed with these designations in Benvenuti's new edition as follows:

Ad cenam agni providi	as *Ad regias agni dapes*
Christe redemptor omnium	as *Jesu redemptor omnium*
Exsultet coelum laudibus	as *Exsultet orbis gaudiis*
Hostis Herodis impie	as *Crudelis Herodes, Deum*

The melodies employed by Cavazzoni are correctly listed by Benvenuti, except for *Iste confessor,* which is based on the melody on page [49] (not [51]) of the *Antiphonal,* and for *Ad cenam,* which is in the sixth mode and based on a tune no longer in use.[39]

Knowledge of the relations between organ composition and chant tune, which were discussed in great detail in the preceding pages, is always of importance, but it is particularly valuable in studying Cavazzoni, who opened very novel avenues to the field of organ music—avenues that can be recognized only

Fig.108

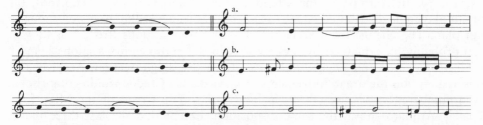

a. *Missa Apostolorum:* Glorificamus; b. *Missa Dominicalis:* Et ascendit; c. *Missa de Beata Virgine:* Kyrie II.

by comparing his compositions with the chants on which they are based. First one notes the freedom with which he treats the traditional chants of the Roman Catholic Church. For him the Gregorian chant no longer represents a sanctified tradition, but material that he uses as a point of departure—material that he can dispose of as a sovereign artist. It is difficult to escape a comparison with Michelangelo, in whose canvasses we recognize a very similar attitude vis-à-vis the subjects from the histories of the Saints. Cavazzoni's liturgical organ works are not so much arrangements as bold and independent paraphrases on the various chants of the Mass and the Offices. Occasionally the musical substance of his compositions deviates so strongly from the melodies on which they are based that only a general similarity of line can be recognized. Of course variants in the tradition of the Gregorian chant also play a role, but the decisive element is the free will of the composer. Schlick, Buchner, Attaingnant, Redford, Cabezón, and others generally preserve the Gregorian melody faithfully and at most decorate it or expand it occasionally with figures, but Cavazzoni often uses it as material for new and individually conceived motifs, omitting or adding notes, changing the intervals, and assigning an important role to a free rhythmic formulation. Fig.108 presents a few of the many examples of this process of transformation. The *Magnificat primi toni* provides further very instructive illustrations, for a different initial motif is derived from the Gregorian intonation formula for each verse (Fig.109).

Cavazzoni also takes new directions in structure. The traditional *cantus-*

Fig.109

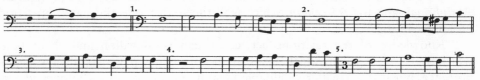

planus method is rather unimportant in his music, and hardly ever occurs in its strict form, but where it is employed it is almost always anticipated by an introduction in imitative style. This presentation of the chant is most apparent in the hymns. In four of them (*Christe redemptor, Lucis creator, Exsultet coelum,* and *Jesu corona*) the chant lies in the bass, in two (*Deus tuorum* and *Hostis Herodis*) in the upper part, and in one (*Jesu nostra*) in the tenor, always in semibreves. In *Ad cenam* the hymn enters after an extended fore-imitation with the first line in semibreves in the bass. Then the whole tune is heard in the soprano in alternating semibreves and minims (half and quarter notes in the reduced transcription) in the triple meter that is often looked upon as the authentic rhythm of the Ambrosian hymn. It is interesting that in the original this triple meter is notated in a quadruple measure (Fig.110).* *Veni creator* may also be included in the category of the *cantus-planus* setting with fore-imitation, except that the tune, which is heard in the upper part, is enlivened by figurations at several places.

Fig.110

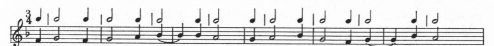

The three remaining hymn settings differ from those just discussed in that they are divided into several sections, each treating the chant in a particular way. Thus in the *Ave maris stella* the first line of the tune is set in fugal style, the second is paraphrased in the soprano after a brief fore-imitation, the third is presented as a *cantus planus* in the bass, and the fourth is similarly presented in the soprano. *Iste confessor* and *Pange lingua* consist of several sections in fugal style and may thus be classified as chorale motets. In *Iste confessor* the beginning of the first verse (*gag e f g g*)[40] is imitative throughout, whereas its continuation (*a f a c' ba g*) is heard slightly decorated in the upper part. The other three lines are handled similarly, but the passage *meruit beatas* is strangely omitted. Cavazzoni's arrangement of the Corpus Christi hymn *Pange lingua* is particularly intense. Everything is worked out with superior mastery and grand eloquence: At the beginning the intonation of *Pange lingua* is fashioned in a nearly spoken rhythm and presented four times in an ever higher register; the theme of the section *fructus ventris generosi* is heard seven times in close strettos; and the final section, shown in

---

* Cf. the transcription by Schering (see note 39). As strange as this notation may appear today, it is completely sensible within the framework of the notational system of the period—in fact it is necessary to indicate the correct tempo relationship between the quadruple and triple meter sections, that is, the equivalence of the beat ($\quarternote = \quarternote$), not of the measure ($\quarternote = \dottedhalfnote$), which would produce a triplet rhythm ($2\quarternote = 3\quarternote$).

Fig.111

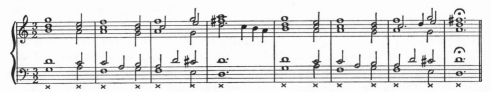

Fig.111, with its broad triplet rhythm, full chords, and reaffirming repetition, gives the work a triumphant conclusion.

In Cavazzoni's Masses we find essentially the same methods of composition as in the hymns; the difference is, of course, that in the Masses we are not dealing with twelve extended pieces but with over seventy short ones, each comprising about eight to twenty measures. The briefest among them consist of single points of imitation, which derive from the often freely transformed head motif of the Gregorian tune. In other instances this tune is treated as a *cantus planus* with fore-imitation. Often the chant melody is divided into two subsections, which are treated separately, e.g., each in its own point of imitation, or the first as a fugato and the second as a *cantus planus*. Sometimes the entire chant melody is used, sometimes motifs are extracted from it, and occasionally one finds ideas, insertions, or concluding passages that have no recognizable connection with the chant. Freedom of formulation and an independence of the creative artist emerge everywhere; in the organ music of the 16th century these are completely new and unique phenomena.

In each Magnificat, the Gregorian chant tune is presented in five settings, or variations. There is a plethora of forms here, a wealth of ideas to which general explanations or rubrics cannot do justice. The prevailing method is to divide the Magnificat tone into its two natural phrases (A = intonation and tenor; B = tenor and termination), and to treat each as a separate fugato. We intentionally say "fugato," for the imitation is frequently not limited to a single point of imitation but is extensively developed, so that we can indeed speak of short fugues. This term applies especially to the second sections, in which the idea being developed usually appears in a well-articulated rhythm and in repeated strettos. For example, in the *Magnificat octavi toni* two themes are extracted from the Gregorian *tonus* and appear with slight changes in all five verses, strangley transposed from G to F (Fig.112). The quieter theme A is developed in a single point of imitation and thus appears only three or four times in each verse, while B is heard ten times in the first verse, eleven times in the second, etc., mostly in two strettos separated by a brief episode. In this manner every verse reflects the same idea: the intensification of musical events.

Of course the general style of Cavazzoni's liturgical pieces is based on the contrapuntal-imitative vocal style of the period, but his work stands out for its

Fig.112

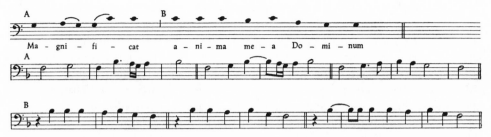

flowing lines and clear polyphonic web, which excels the work of many a famous vocal composer (e.g., Willaert). The frequent admixture of free voices and toccata-like elements proves that his is not merely an imitation of motet style.

ANDREA GABRIELI AND MERULO

The organ works of Andrea Gabrieli that reach us in prints contain no contributions to liturgical music, unless one counts his *Intonazioni* as preludes meant for church use. Nevertheless it had to be assumed that he was active in this field, and, indeed, in the 1960s three organ Masses by him were discovered in one of the Turin tablatures (vol.3 of the Giordano collection): a *Messa Domenichal,* a *Messa della Beata Vergine,* and a *Messa Apostolorum.* Like Cavazzoni's Masses, these works are based on Mass XI (with Credo I), Mass IX (without a Credo), and Mass IV (omitting the Agnus and using a Credo melody that is no longer found in the modern *Gradual*), respectively. For the Kyrie Gabrieli composed four movements for each of the first two Masses (*Kyrie, Christe, Kyrie, Kyrie*), and three for the last one. A comparison with the chant tunes produces the usual structure for the *Kyrie Domenichal:* O C O | C O C | O C O, and the deviating order O C O | O C O | O C O for the *Kyrie della Beata Vergine;* for the *Kyrie Apostolorum* either formula is possible. The remaining Mass sections follow the same order as Cavazzoni's.

Gabrieli generally treats the chant in a manner similar to Girolamo Cavazzoni's, but his somewhat more conservative approach is shown by the fact that several times he employs the strict *cantus-planus* arrangement, which does not occur in Cavazzoni's Mass settings. In the *Messa Domenichal,* e.g., five sections belong to this type: *Kyrie I, Et in terra, Benedicimus, Glorificamus,* and *Sanctus I. Kyrie II* and *Et exspecto* start with fore-imitations followed by a rhythmically free and partially ornamented presentation of the entire chant melody. The remaining movements consist mostly of two or three points of imitation based on sections of the chant melody. A similar situation obtains in the other two Masses.

Gabrieli's frequent use of the toccata style is notable. For the *Messa*

Domenichal he writes an introductory movement, which is formulated exactly like his *intonazioni*. Other examples are found in the *Amen* of the Gloria and at the end of this Mass, as well as in the *Et in terra* and *In gloria* of the Marian Mass and in the two *Amen* settings of the *Messa Apostolorum*. Also in the fugal movements Gabrieli often inserts fast passage work and stereotyped ornaments, which do not enhance them. The frequent use of a stumbling figure that serves to "decorate" the progression of an ascending third is particularly disturbing; this figure also plays a disagreeable role in the Masses of Merulo and the ricercars of Annibale Padovano. A passage from the *Domine Deus Rex Caelestis* of the Marian Mass will serve as an illustration (Fig.113). It is certainly no sin against the spirit if we eliminate or soften such flaws. Special features worth mentioning are the Josquin-like imitative duo that starts the *Et unam Sanctam* of the Sunday Mass and the especially long chant tones, each sustained for three full measures, in the *Quoniam* of the Marian Mass.

Fig.113

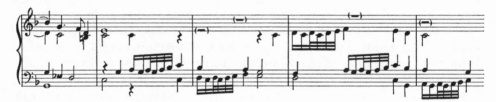

In 1568 Claudio Merulo published a print, *Messe d'intavolatura d'organo*,[41] which again consists of the three usual Masses—a *Missae [sic] Apostolorum*, a *Missae in Dominicis diebus*, and a *Missae virginis Marie*. Separately there are also three Credos—*in Dominicis diebus, Angelorum*, and *Cardinalium*. Like Cavazzoni's and Gabrieli's Masses, Merulo's are based on Masses IV, XI, and IX, and the Credos are based on Credo I, III, and IV of the modern *Gradual*. For each Kyrie Merulo writes five movements (*Kyrie, Kyrie, Christe, Kyrie, Kyrie*). In the Marian Mass, in contrast to Cavazzoni (cf.p.116), Merulo uses sections a, d, and e of the Kyrie (a b a | c d c | e f e'), so that the normal alternating structure results. The Gloria is disposed like Cavazzoni's; the one in the Marian Mass is again expanded by the trope *Spiritus et alme*. For the Sanctus Merulo writes two settings, based on the first and third invocations—and so does Gabrieli—whereas the position of Cavazzoni's second setting is not fixed.

In his treatment of the chant melodies, Merulo often writes the initial imitation in the form of an inversion fugue, i.e., using the inverted subject, as in the *Kyrie II* and *Sanctus II* of the Sunday Mass, in the *Sanctus II* of the *Missa virginis*, and in the *Et exspecto* of the *Credo Cardinalium*. The following are several other movements that have some special features:

1. *Missa Apostolorum, Kyrie III:* The movement starts with the *cantus planus* on "Kyrie" in the soprano, and after a free interlude, closes with a fugal section on "eleyson."

2. *Missa Dominicalis, Agnus:* After an eight-measure point of imitation the tune of "Agnus . . . tollis" appears in the bass and "peccata . . . nobis" in the soprano.

3. *Missa virginis Marie, Et in terra:* A fugal section on the head motif (g a e f g) is continued in free counterpoint; then the entire melody is heard in the soprano.

4. *Missa virginis Marie, Qui sedes:* After a brief point of imitation we hear "Qui . . . dexteram" in the bass, then "miserere nobis" three times in the soprano.

5. *Missa virginis Marie, Agnus:* For the fore-imitation the inversion of the head motif is used; then "Agnus . . . tollis" follows in the soprano (meas.12). The semibreves are syncopated, always entering on the second and fourth beats of the measure. The concluding section (meas.19–31) bears no recognizable relationship to the end of the Gregorian melody, but the inverted motif of the beginning appears twice.

6. *Credo Dominicalis, Crucifixus:* The movement starts with a fugal section on an apparently freely invented theme; then we hear "Crucifixus . . . nobis" in the tenor and "sub Pontio . . . sepultus est" in the soprano, both in a rhythmically free formulation.

7. *Credo Dominicalis, Et ascendit:* The entire movement consists of a fugue on a canzona-like theme, which shows no recognizable relationship to the chant.

8. *Credo Dominicalis, Amen:* The Georgian tune (a g f g a g f e d) (omitting the Phrygian cadence on e) appears five times in the soprano; a free postlude follows.

Fig.114

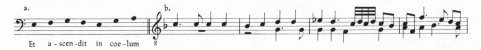

No. 7 is most peculiar, Merulo does not treat the chant tune a., but a freely invented theme b., as shown in Fig.114. The treatment of the *Amen* (no.8) recalls the *soprano ostinato* of the English school (cf.pp.145f.), but here the repetition of the theme obviously has liturgical significance, as it has in the Amen fugues of Bach and Handel (the threefold *Miserere* in no.4 doubtless has the meaning of a repeated entreaty for pity). On the whole, the *Credo Dominicalis* has a freer formulation than the other works. The *cantus planus* in more or less regular note values (semibreves) is replaced in almost all the movements by a rhythmically free presentation of the chant (cf.no.6 above); portions of the chant are not always recognizable, or are interrupted or replaced by extended free interludes, as in the *Genitum non factum*.

Merulo's organ Masses are highly artistic creations, in which contrapuntal technique frequently serves expressive melodic lines and individual harmonic

Fig.115

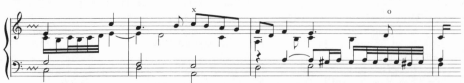

events. Fig.115, an excerpt from the *Domine Deus Agnus Dei* of the *Missa Dominicalis*, shows some of the characteristics of his style in the dissonant line of the alto in one measure (x) and the intimation of a dominant seventh chord in the next one (o). A particularly effective vehicle of expression that Merulo employs a number of times is the 6–5 appoggiatura, as shown in Fig.116 (from the *Qui tollis* of the *Missa Dominicalis*).

Fig.116

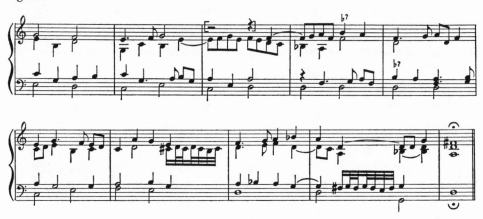

With these figures the solemn realm of sound of the Italian high Renaissance acquires an increase in emotion that suggests the first breath of the spirit of the Baroque. Merulo's organ Masses are among the most beautiful and valuable contributions to the liturgical organ music of the 16th century. It is most unfortunate that they are not generally accessible in a new edition, nor even represented in collections of old organ music. A collection of fifty-six *Versetti di Ms. Claudio,* probably for the Magnificat (cf.Chap.6, note 20), are also awaiting publication.

As a sort of footnote it should be mentioned that Girolamo Diruta (1557–1612) sets twenty-one hymns and the eight tones of the Magnificat for organ in the *Seconda Parte* of his *Transilvano* (1609). The latter are also given in various transpositions, e.g., *un tuono più alto (basso), alla terza più alto (bassa),* etc. All of these are brief settings, meant primarily as didactic material, and must be judged as such.

At the beginning of the last quarter of the 16th century, Naples, representing a new locale and a new approach, joins the northern Italian cities of Bologna and Venice in the evolution of liturgical organ music. In Naples there was an active group of clavier composers, who occupied an interesting historical position; on the one hand they received stimuli from Spain (Cabezón), and on the other they developed several traits that characterize the forms and style of Frescobaldi.[42]

The earliest representatives of the Neapolitan school are Antonio Valente and Rocco Rodio. Valente was the organist of the Neapolitan church of Sant' Angelo à Nido. He was probably born around 1520 and died around 1600. In early childhood he went blind, as we learn from the accolade added to his first print: "Cieco dà i'soi teneri anni della puetrita." In 1576 he published an *Intavolatura de cimbalo*,[43] containing a fantasy, 6 ricercars, a *Salve regina*, intabulations, and dances; and in 1580 a collection of *Versi spirituali*. Of Rodio nothing certain is known. He was born in Bari, probably between 1530 and 1540, and died in Naples between 1615 and 1626. In 1575, a year before Valente's first book, he published a *Libro primo di ricercate a quattro voci con alcune fantasie sopra varii canti fermi*, the earliest source of keyboard music notated in score (cf.p.6). It contains 5 ricercars, and 4 "fantasies on a cantus firmus": on *La mi re fa mi re, Iste confessor, Ave maris stella,* and *Salve regina*.[44] The first *cantus firmus* is none other than the *spagna*, the famous basse-danse melody of the 15th century, which was still used by Zacconi as late as 1622 as a *cantus firmus* for contrapuntal exercises.[45] The other *cantus firmi* are liturgical melodies. Like the *spagna*, they are presented as strict *cantus plani* in breves. Against the sustained *cantus-planus* tones three counterpoints play lively motifs, clavier figures, and sixteenth-note passages in skillful imitation and charming alternation. Fig.117 shows the beginning of the fantasy on *Salve regina*.

A striking alternation between diatonic steps in one voice and their chromatically altered forms in another occurs frequently. Even though in some

Fig.117

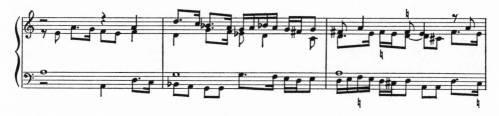

125

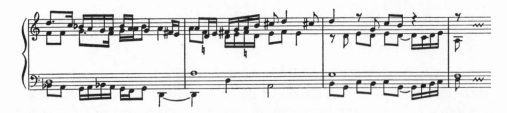

passages the extent to which accidentals remain valid is uncertain, there can be no doubt that Rodio intentionally employs a characteristic harmonic vocabulary, a vocabulary that will be repeatedly used in early Baroque music. Interestingly, Rodio's fantasies (as well as his ricercars) contain passages that can barely be executed on the organ, even if we assume that the *cantus planus* is played on the pedals. Fig.118 shows two such passages: a. from *Ave maris stella;* b. from *Iste confessor.* Since in Rodio's print the music is not notated in a keyboard brace but in score, at first glance one might assume that it is to be performed by four melody instruments. But on what instrument could one play the extended *cantus-planus* part, which runs on without a rest, if not on the organ? After all, compositions of this type become meaningful only when the ear can grasp the contrast between the sustained tones and the living lines of the counterpoints. Perhaps the situation can be explained by the fact that in southern Italy organs had narrower keys, on which tenths—which almost always present difficulties—could be executed without too much discomfort.[46]

Fig.118

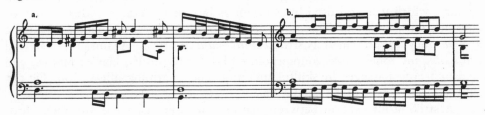

Antonio Valente's *Intavolatura de cimbalo* appeared one year after Rocco Rodio's print, also in Naples. Only one piece in it interests us, a *Salve regina*. It is strange that it appears in a collection that, according to its title and contents, was meant for the harpsichord. As in Rodio's music, the Marian antiphon is presented as a strict *cantus planus* in breves with three lively counterpoints. But since Valente writes his compositions in a kind of fingering notation for each hand, the individual notes of the antiphon do not always appear as sustained notes, but are frequently reiterated by the other hand. Valente's *Salve regina,*

like most of the other pieces in his print, is quite mediocre. Fig.119 shows its beginning and measures 21–22, which illustrate more clearly the individuality of his clavier style.

Fig.119

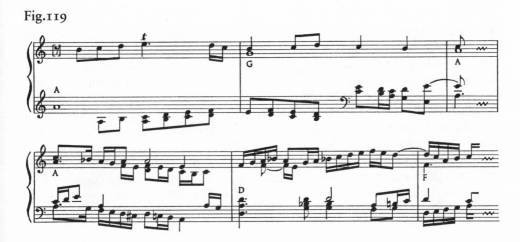

Valente's second publication, the *Versi spirituali* of 1580,[47] is far more important, historically as well as artistically. It is a collection of 43 short organ pieces, "sopra tutte le note," for the use at "Messe Vespere, et altri Officii Divini," as the title says. It consists of six versets each for the tones *ut, re, mi, fa, sol, la,* and *fa di be fa be mi,* i.e., according to modern usage, C major, D minor, E minor, F major, G major, A minor, and B-*flat* major. At the end a single *Verso sopra il b molle di E,* i.e., in E-*flat* major, is added. As is to be expected, the pieces are still somewhat modal; nevertheless for the first time there is a new idea of tonality, for which the term "key" is far more apt than "church mode." The decisive factor is that Valente drops the differentiation between authentic and plagal church modes, which is, in fact, an artificially retained fiction in the field of polyphonic music, except for polyphonic arrangements of the eight psalm or Magnificat tones, as in Cabezón's *Salmodia.* The *Versi* of Valente do not belong to this type because they are also meant for the Mass, where the presentation of psalms is out of the question.

Indeed one can see immediately that these versets have no relationship whatever to the recitation formulae of the psalms or the Magnificat, but that they are freely composed. Each is a brief setting of about ten to twenty measures, starting with a point of imitation and then continuing mostly in free polyphony. In the sixth verse of each mode two voices are treated in strict canon, while the other two join in with free imitations. Frequently the compositions begin with a two-part passage, comprising a subject and a countersubject, which is then repeated in the other voices. Some of the themes have a lively, canzona-like character, e.g., *Verso V sopra il Re;* on the other hand, *Verso V sopra il Mi* is written in the style of Gabrieli's *Intonazioni.* Fig.120 shows the beginning of the particularly lively *Verso IV sopra il Re.*

The versets of Valente have a remarkable historical importance; for the first time liturgical organ music is freed from its close ties with the chant. One or two freely composed pieces are already found in Merulo's organ Masses, but they are isolated and somewhat experimental, whereas Valente provides freely invented music, which occasionally sounds quite secular, for the entire liturgy, the Mass as well as the Daily Offices. He served as the organist of Sant' Angelo à Nido from 1565 to 1580. One wonders what the clerics and the congregation must have thought at the Sunday Mass when the organ rang out, during the solemn *Kyrie Orbis factor,* with the lively fugue whose beginning is reproduced in Fig.120. Let us hope that they understood the musical value of these pieces well enough to overcome their ecclesiastic doubts. Most of the pieces keep well within the limits appropriate for the service and would still serve today as its dignified ornament.

Fig.120

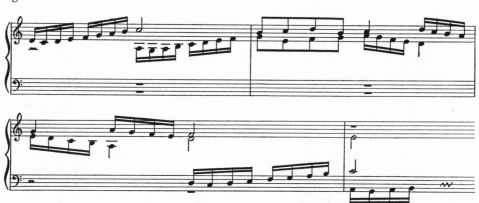

In 1598 an anonymous collection of versets appeared at Venice under the title *Intavolatura d'organo facilissima.*[48] It contains two pieces for each of the eight church modes in the form of brief and simple fugatos. The first of each pair is apparently based on a freely invented idea, while the second is occasionally based on the *initium* of the corresponding Magnificat tone. The *Primo del terzo tono,* e.g., begins with the motif (| *c'* — *c' c'* | *a c' b* — |), and the *Secondo* with (| *g* — *a c'* | — *b a* — |). On the title page we read that the versets may serve to "risponder à Messe, à Salmi, ed à tutto quello che è necessario al Choro," in other words, just like the versets of Valente.

128

Spain

CABEZÓN

Spanish liturgical organ music is represented principally by a ·single master, Antonio de Cabezón (cf.p.77). His liturgical compositions, as contained in his *Obras* (1578) and in small part in Venegas' *Libro de cifra nueva* (1557), consist of 32 hymns (among them 14 settings of *Ave maris stella* and 8 of *Pange lingua*), a *Salve regina*, 9 Kyries, and 3 collections of versets for psalms and Magnificats. The preponderance of organ pieces for the Daily Offices probably reflects a Spanish tradition; Spain, more than other countries, resisted the invasion of the organ into the Mass.

The individuality of Cabezón's liturgical organ music emerges when compared to Girolamo Cavazzoni's extensive works. We are struck by Cabezón's conservatism, which is partly explained by the fact that Spanish music in general was more hesitant in matters of "progress" than Italian music, and partly by the fact that Cabezón is closer to Marco Antonio's generation than to that of Girolamo. The decisive element, however, was probably the dramatic contrast between their personalities and life histories. The differences become almost tangible in our imagination: here the vicacious Italian, a child of fortune, perhaps a child prodigy, to whom it was given to create lasting masterpieces and present them to the world in prints while still a youth; there the serious, meditative Spaniard, who lost his sight in early childhood and had to toil hard to make his way to the height of excellence. Nothing was further from his mind than the craving for freedom, the "natural genius," which is so clearly recognizable in Cavazzoni. His creativity found its realization within the framework of the rule, in the fulfillment of tradition.

With few exceptions his many hymns are based on the strict *cantus-planus* style. Indeed, no organ master crystallized this style so purely, filled it so perfectly with content, as Cabezón. The writing without *tempus,* i.e., in a series of semibreves, which Cavazzoni uses exclusively, is found in only a few instances in Cabezón's music. Cabezón frequently employs the *tempus perfectum,* in which three semibreves form a *brevis-perfecta* unit. Since he always divides his music into semibreve measures, one must combine three such measures into a larger unit. Where the *tempus imperfectum* appears, the larger unit contains two measures. The following is a survey of the meters employed in Cabezón's *cantus-planus* hymns and those set in other styles (P = Pedrell H; A = Anglés M):

1. *c.pl.* in 𝄵·: *Christe redemptor* (P III, 58)
2. *c.pl.* in 𝄵∘: 8 *Pange lingua* (P III, 17 = A 115; P III, 19; P III, 60; P III, 62; A 1; A 111; A 113; A 117); 2 *Te lucis* (P III, 10; A 140); *Sacris solemniis* (A 156)
3. *c.pl.* in 𝄵: 8 *Ave maris stella* (P III, 4; P III, 5; P III, 7; P III, 8; P VII, 27; A 122; A 123; A 130); *Quem terra pontus* (A 149)

4. *c.pl.* in ⊙: 4 *Ave maris stella* (P III, 48; P III, 48; P III, 49; A 121); *Beata viscera* (P VII, 31)
5. Motets: 2 *Ave maris stella* (P III, 50 = A 127; A 125); *Veni creator* (P III, 52); *Christe redemptor* (P III, 54); *Ut queant laxis* (P III, 56)
6. Chordal setting: *O lux beata Trinitas* (A 134)

By far the most numerous are Cabezón's settings of *Pange lingua* and *Ave maris stella,* the former melody always presented in alternating breves and semibreves, the latter in equal note values, either in breves or semibreves. An interesting exception is the fourth *Ave* of group 4. above; it consists of three sections (differentiated in Anglés M as *1ª*, *2ª*, and *3ª diferencia*), each of which presents the tune once. It is heard in the first section in whole notes, in the second in halves, and in the third in quarters. It is almost like coming upon a last remnant of the isorhythmic motet of Dunstable or Dufay.

Cabezón's hymns, like all his other works, are written in a strict contrapuntal texture of two, three, or four parts.* Free voices, which play such an important role in Attaingnant and the two Cavazzonis, do not appear in his music; in fact they cannot be symbolized in Spanish organ tablature. Cabezón's melodies, except for those used for *Ave maris stella* and *Veni creator*, are not the ones in use today. The melody of *Pange lingua,* which probably goes back to Mozarabic times, is the one that is traditional in Spain, and is always used in the arrangements by other Spanish organ masters.[49] The liturgical melodies are always used in their pure forms, without any additional notes or figurative or ornamental expansions, though they had been in normal use in organ music as far back as Paumann. A strictness in the musico-religious position is expressed, which once again strikes a contrast to the willfulness with which Cavazzoni bends the chant tunes to his use.

Cabezón connects the strictly stated chant tunes with counterpoints whose intrinsic spirit and expressiveness proclaim the hand of a great master. His compositions attest most impressively to the artistic validity of the *cantus-planus* style, that style which palpably and convincingly realizes the medieval principle of *coincidentia oppositorum,* the unification of opposites.

Among the two-part settings, the *Te lucis* (P III, 10) stands out; it is given in its entirety in Fig.121. What an admirably rich life unfolds from such a simple frame! What a free yet intrinsically orderly interplay—slower and faster groups of tones, ascending and descending motion, scales and skips, continuous passages and incisive pauses! Some details in the contours of the lines and in the combined sound of the voices recall the late Gothic style and its special idiosyncrasies, but it is through them that the music acquires that austere expression by which it differs from other works of the period. To be sure, one needs only add a few additional accidentals, such as a *b flat* in the eighth and tenth measures, to

---

* Five or six voices appear only in a number of intabulations.

Fig.121

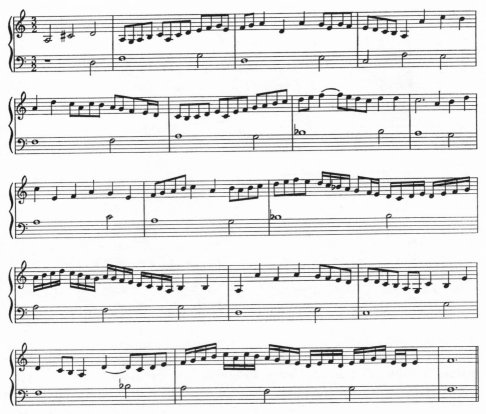

soften this austerity, which is obviously considered a fault by most modern observers.

The three- and four-part hymns also exhibit conservative traits, especially in their harmonic approach. There is an almost complete absence of cadences and functional-harmonic progressions. This is all the more surprising since in the great majority of hymns the chant tune lies in the tenor, or occasionally in the alto or discant, so that there is always a lower part that could have been formulated as the bass of something approaching a functional-harmonic setting. It is clear from a comparison with other compositions of the period that this was not Cabezón's intention. Fig.122 shows the ending of *Ave maris stella* as arranged by Cavazzoni and by Cabezón (P III, 48). In both works the chant lies in the top part of a four-voice setting (a very rare arrangement for Cavazzoni), but the harmonic interpretation is completely different. Cavazzoni derives from the chant tones a functional chord progression, whose cadential effect is fully assured by the subdominant, which enters at exactly the "correct" place, and by

Fig.122

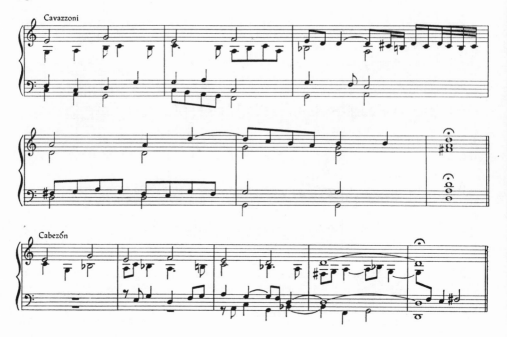

a leading tone (*c sharp*), which is not present in the chant—an effect that he then appropriately underscores in the last two, triumphant measures. Cabezón's setting, on the other hand, shows an ambivalent harmonization such as one might find in Ockeghem's music. Nothing is further from his mind than an emphatic final gesture that points heavenward: He lets the sounds die away gradually in the dark depths.

An ornamented counterpoint prevails in the two-part hymns, but quieter counterparts, which approach the imitative vocal style, are associated with the *cantus planus* in the three-part and particularly the four-part arrangements. The four *Ave maris stella* from the *Obras* (P III, 48ff.) are especially beautiful examples of this kind. They present the chant in the tenor, discant, alto, and bass, respectively, while the counterpoints are frequently derived from imitative motifs. The second of these pieces begins with a fore-imitation, and so does the two-part *Te lucis* (shown in Fig.121) in a rudimentary fashion. But while Cavazzoni starts every *cantus-planus* setting with a fore-imitation, Cabezón does so only rarely, in the two instances just mentioned and in two *Pange lingua* (P III, 62; A 117) and a *Te lucis* (A 140).

Finally let us turn to the hymns, in which the chant is treated as in a chorale motet. In an *Ave maris stella* from the Venegas print (A 125) the imitative treatment of the melody is only partially carried through, chiefly in the second line of the chant ("Dei mater": *d' g a c' b♭ a g*), which enters as a counterpoint near the end of the first line (meas.40–49); then, after a seemingly free interlude, it appears in the tenor (meas. 68–80); and finally in semibreves and lightly ornamented in the discant (meas.81–89). The other lines of the tune appear as a *cantus planus* in the tenor, the first one with an extended fore-imitation.

The chorale motet type appears especially pure in three pieces that follow each other in the *Obras,* obviously grouped together intentionally by Cabezón (or his son?): *Veni creator, Christe redemptor,* and *Ut queant laxis* (P III, 52ff.). Each composition consists of four or five sections in which the phrases of the chant are successively treated in imitation, mostly with the imitation itself based on the head motif of the phrase, whereupon the entire phrase is heard in the discant. In these settings Cabezón occasionally transforms the chant freely, a procedure that he never permits himself to use in *cantus-planus* settings. Thus in *Veni creator* the last three notes of the first line (*c' d' c'*) are expanded from three to six measures (meas.21–26) through a free paraphrase. In *Christe redemptor* the melody of the hymn (which can be deduced from the *cantus-planus* setting in P III, 58) is divided into five sections, each of which is treated separately, the last one with remarkable fulness: the final phrase (*a g f d f g a g f g*) is heard seven times (meas.59ff.), three of them in the discant.

Common to all three chorale motets is a very quiet motion, in minims almost throughout (half notes in Pedrell H), as is usual in the vocal music of the period. But this is no reason to believe that they are transcriptions. If they were, they would certainly include lively coloraturas. Although these compositions represent a later type of chant treatment than the *cantus-planus* settings and may possibly belong to Cabezón's later works, they nevertheless exhibit some traits that sound rather archaic for the 16th century and give the pieces a characteristic quality of austerity. The beginning of *Ut queant laxis* given in Fig.123 is an ex-

Fig.123

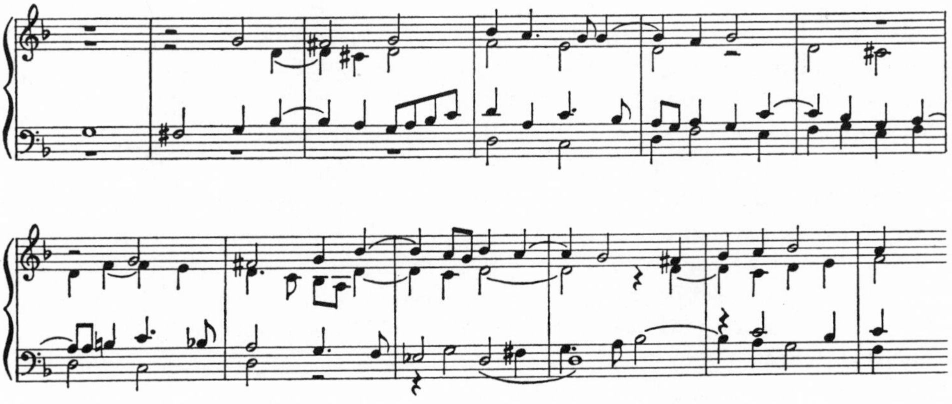

ample. The chord (*a c♯ f♯*) in measure 3 is particularly interesting: a dominant harmony with two leading tones, which recalls Machaut, and which is found at times as late as the 17th century.

The Mass is represented in Cabezón's music by nine Kyries. One (P III, 12) is in three parts and consists of three movements; the other eight form a group (P IV, 26–45), all of them in four parts and consisting of four versets. The three-part Kyrie is called *Kyrie de Nuestra Señora,* and the first of the four-part Kyries is called *Tema Rex virginum,* but the others carry very unusual headings for Kyries: *de primer, segundo, . . . , septimo tono* (the *quinto tono* has been placed at the end, undoubtedly by accident). In four Kyries the basic chant tune is easily recognized: *Nuestra Señora* and *Rex virginum* both use the well-known Kyrie IV (*Cunctipotens genitor*), *primer tono* uses the Kyrie ad lib. II of the modern *Gradual,* and *segundo tono* the ad lib. III. In the *quinto tono* the first two movements derive from the first phrase of the modern Kyrie ad lib. IV, but in the two remaining sections no relationship to the chant melody can be discovered. For the other Kyries no Gregorian models can be proved with certainty.[50]

The three-part *Kyrie de Nuestra Señora* originally carries the designations *K[yrie]*, *Segundo Kyrie,* and *Terzer Kyrie,* but in reality consists of Kyrie, Christe, and Kyrie (K Ch K). The four movements of the remaining Kyries are untitled, but, as can be easily established, follow the order K K Ch K. No reason can be found for representing the first Kyrie by two settings and the second by only one. There can be no doubt that both Kyries were performed according to the alternating plan, O C O, the first one with two different settings for the organ, the second with a repeated setting. It can easily be established that the Christe was also performed in the order O C O. The chant tunes of the *Kryie de primer* and *de segundo tono* (ad lib. II and ad lib. III) have the outlines a b a | c d c | e f e, in other words, have different melodies for the middle invocations. In both cases Cabezón's Christe setting is based on the first phrase, c, and not on the middle one, d. The result, therefore, is the form O C O | O C O | O C O, and one is probably justified in assuming that this formulation is also valid for the other Kyries.

The musical style of the *Kyrie de Nuestra Señora* is singular not only because of its three-part setting but also because all three movements are written in *cantus-planus* style, with breves in the tenor throughout. The other eight Kyries are written in motet style, except for the second versets, which are all built on a *cantus planus* in semibreves. The strict plan that these pieces follow has a surprising aspect: The *cantus-planus* technique, which represents an older tradition, a greater simplicity, and an easier intelligibility than the motet style, is employed for the second Kyrie, not for the first. A further sign of planned procedure is seen in the *Kyrie de primer, . . . , septimo tono,* for toward the end the last movements all switch to a section in triple meter, which is always followed by a few concluding measures in which the weightier and more dignified duple meter has the last word; only the *tercer tono* contains no such section.

Finally there are Cabezón's compositions for the psalms and the Magnificat. For the psalmody he wrote two collections of *versillos* (versets), a *Salmodia para principiantes* (P III, 21ff.), and one that is called *Fabordon y glosas del primer, segundo, . . . tono* (P III, 32ff.).[51] Except for a few anonymous *fabordones* in Venegas's *Libro de cifra nueva*, Cabezón's pieces are the earliest documentation of the use of the organ in conjunction with the psalmody of the Offices, in particular during Vespers. In the 16th century *fabordon* (in Italian *falso bordone*) meant a texture that may be regarded, and at the time was regarded, as a later development of the *fauxbourdon* of Dufay and Binchois. It meant the four-part harmonization of a melody, especially of the psalmodic recitation formulae. Such simple harmonizations (*fabordon llano*) were also written with fast figurations in one voice or another and called *fabordon glosado* (glossed). Cabezón's collection, the *Fabordon y glosas*, comprises four versets for each psalm tone. The versets are listed in the table of contents as *llano, glosado con el tiple* (glossed in the discant), *glosado con el contrabaxo* (ornamented in the bass), and *glosado con las vozes de en medio* (ornamented in the alto and tenor, either alternately or also simultaneously). Fig.124 shows the first and last versets of the *primer tono*. The Gregorian tune lies in the discant, but as is always the case with psalm versets, the intonation (*f g a*) is not included in the composition, since it was sung by the choir.

Fig.124

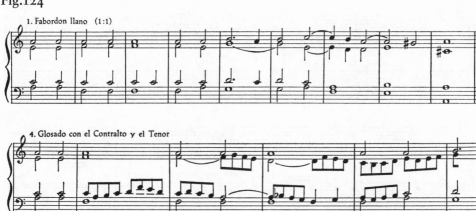

The versets of the *Salmodia para principiantes* are very different. They are written in *cantus-planus* style throughout, with the psalm tone occurring consecutively in the discant, alto, tenor, and bass in the four versets that belong to each *tono*. Even though they are brief and are written "for beginners" (this designation was perhaps inserted by the editor or the publisher), the versets of the *Salmodia* are among the most significant creations of the Spanish organ master.

135

The counterpoints added to the *cantus planus* are always treated in imitation (this is only rarely so in Cabezón's *cantus-planus* hymns, for example). Corresponding to the bipartite psalmodic formula there are two separate points of imitation, based on different subjects. The articulation and expressive power of these subjects is as admirable as the skillful treatment within their small framework. Among the many jewels, the third and fourth versets of the *sexto tono*, given in Fig.125, are of particular brilliance. Here and there in Cabezón's music there are some curious passages that at first appear to be mistakes in dictation or printing, e.g., the chromatic variants in the first motif of the third setting, or the Lydian cadence in the final measure of the fourth one. But on a closer inspection they prove to be sensible and correct according to a higher wisdom.

In his Magnificats Cavazzoni writes five organ versets for each of the four

Fig.125

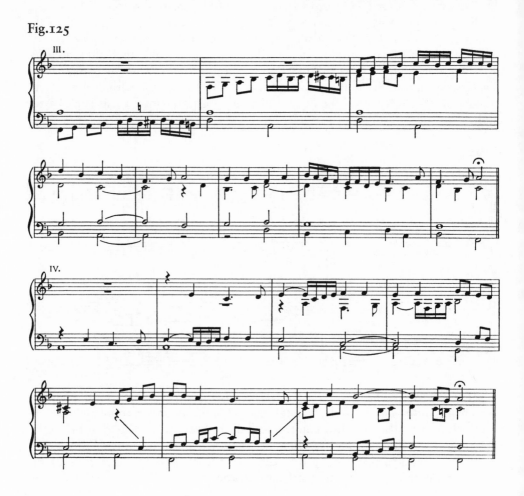

tones he sets, i.e., one less than would be needed for the twelve verses of text. But Cabezón, in his *Salmodia para el Magnificat* (P IV, 1ff.), provides not only the full number of six versets, but in most cases seven (for tones 1, 4, 6, 7, and 8). Perhaps the seventh section served as a free organ postlude, or one of the long verses (℣ 3?) was divided at the time, so that the total number of lines increased to thirteen.* Several details of the arrangement are not clear, e.g., the treatment of the intonation. In the Magnificat—in contrast to the psalms—each verse begins with the intonation. In many of Cabezón's versets the intonation is included in the composition, but not in all. In the *primer tono*, e.g., it is recognizable only in the second, third, and fifth versets, in the *quinto tono* in all but the third. From these two examples it is apparent that no regular approach can be observed. Also in other respects the chant model in this collection is treated with a liberty that is surprising in Cabezón. Not only are the liturgical recitation formulae often freely changed or expanded (exactly as in Cavazzoni), but also in quite a few instances the versets show no discernible relationship to them (e.g., versets IV and VII of the *primer tono*).

The great majority of the Magnificat versets are arranged in motet style, rather similar to Cavazzoni's, but mostly shorter. There is an occasional glossed fabordon setting (e.g., *segundo tono* no.V) and one group of four *cantus-planus* settings in the same order as in the *Salmodia para principiantes* (*tercer tono* nos.III–VI). In several groups the final verset is written in triple meter. Perhaps the collection does not achieve an artistic level quite as high as that of the other *Salmodia,* but it, too, contains many beautiful and skillful works. One illustration is the concise third verset of the *cuarto tono* (Fig.126). Note the ambivalent

Fig.126

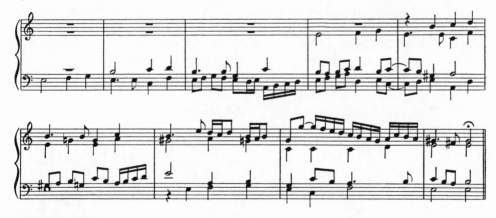

---

* Another possibility is that the Magnificat versets were also intended for the canticle *Benedictus* (*Ant. Rom.* p.10), which is sung to the same melody, but has fourteen verses (cf. *Liber Usualis,* p.402).

cross relations between g♯ and g′ in the sixth measure and the augmented fifth (c′–g♯′) in the last measure. The latter occurs so often in Cabezón's music that Pedrell calls it, with justification, *"caractéristique et vraiment personnel au style de Cabezón."*[52]

BERMUDO, PALERO, AND OTHERS

Compared with the comprehensive and magnificent works of Cabezón, all other liturgical organ music created in Spain pales, but it cannot be disregarded. His contemporary, Juan Bermudo (about 1510 to 1565?), wrote an important theoretical book, *Declaración de instrumentos musicales* (1555),[53] to which he added several organ pieces, responding "to requests by friends, particularly several from the New World."[54] They consist of five hymn settings: *Ave maris stella, Conditor alme siderum, Vexilla regis prodeunt, Veni creator Spiritus,* and *Pange lingua;* and four free compositions (tientos). All these pieces are printed in single voices in choir-book format, but Bermudo explicitly states that "esta musica ser hecha para tañer, y no para cantar" (this music is made to be played and not to be sung).[55]

The hymns are short four-part pieces (*Vexilla regis* is in five parts), which begin with a fore-imitation of three or four measures and then present the liturgical melody continuously in the upper part: in semibreves (*Ave maris stella* and *Vexilla regis*), in alternating breves and semibreves (*Conditor alme* and *Pange lingua*),* or in a freer rhythm (*Veni creator*). The contrapuntal setting is remarkable for its extension into the low register: In each piece the bass reaches D or C several times, producing a characteristic full and dark sound. Bermudo's style also includes several oddities that may be held to reflect a lack of skill or, with equal justification, an ingenious peculiarity (almost as in Berlioz). For one who has not completely subscribed to the idea of the superiority of "strict counterpoint" the latter interpretation is certainly preferable. The empty sounds, the chords without thirds or fifths, are especially striking, and have a distinctive, austere beauty. As an example, see the passage from *Conditor alme* in Fig.127 (meas.7ff).

Fig.127

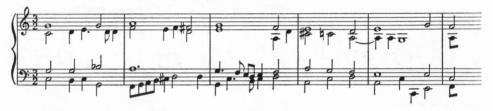

---

* *Pange lingua* is given in semibreves and minims, but with the augmenting effect of the *prolatio perfecta.*

In his *Libro de cifra nueva*, Venegas de Henestrosa preserves two organ hymns by Palero, who is identified in Pedrell A (p.IV) as Francisco Fernandez Palero, the organist of the court chapel at Granada in 1568. The three-part *Ave maris stella* (Pedrell A, no.87) puts the chant tune in the bass and the various lines of the chant are separated by extended rests and introduced by fore-imitations. In the four-part *Veni redemptor quaesumus* (no.91), on the other hand, the melody is treated in the usual manner, as a continuous *cantus planus* (in the alto).

A *Sacris solemniis, Joseph vir* by Morales (no.92) is the only known organ piece by that great master of Spanish vocal music. The melody on which it is based is the same that Cabezón used in his *Sacris solemniis* (no.110). In Morales's work it appears in alternating breves and semibreves in the top part of a quietly animated setting of beautiful sound, whose beginning is shown in Fig.128. The fact that the full text is added to this composition suggests that it is probably a vocal work.

Fig.128

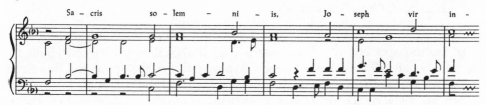

This is certainly true of *Salmo II, Qui habitat* and *Salmo III, Cum invocarem* (nos.94, 95), two pieces by Luys Alberto, one of the many Spanish composers about whom nothing else is known. They present the full text below the music (xc, 10 and iv, 9, respectively), are in five parts (which occurs nowhere else in Venegas), and show no connection whatever with a psalm tone. Thus they obviously represent transcriptions of psalm motets. In the table of contents these two pieces are combined with several others to form a group called *Completas de Quaresma* (Compline of Lent).

The last contribution to the liturgical organ music of Spain in the 16th century is an *Ave maris stella* by Hernando de Cabezón, which he included in his edition of his father's *Obras*.[56] It is a three-part *cantus-planus* setting, very similar to those by Antonio and entirely equal to them artistically. The two counterpoints are often related to one another through imitation, particularly in the passage in Fig.129. Why didn't Hernando write more pieces like *Ave maris stella*, or if he did, why didn't he include them in his edition? Was it because he felt that he could only imitate his father's work but not add anything new to it? He did not lack talent or taste, for his intabulations are decidedly above the average of his time. We shall return to them in a later chapter (cf.p.290).

Fig.129

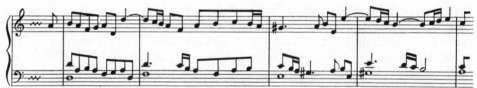

England

A very voluminous repertoire of liturgical organ music, until now only partially studied, is found in a number of English manuscripts from the period about 1530 to 1560; they are listed below in an approximate chronological order:

1. London, Brit. Mus. Roy. App. 56
2. London, Brit. Mus. Add. 15233
3. London, Brit. Mus. Add. 29996
4. Oxford, Christ Church College Ms. 371
5. London, Brit. Mus. Add. 30513 (Mulliner Book)[57]

The manuscripts consist almost entirely of liturgical organ pieces, about two hundred in all. Most numerous are the hymns and then the antiphons, those compositions that are meant for the Daily Offices (probably first of all for Vespers). There are a few pieces for the Mass, particularly offertories, among them the frequently composed *Felix namque* for Marian feasts. A Mass ordinary by Philip ap Rhys and a Mass proper (for Easter Sunday) by Thomas Preston are unique works. The systematic treatment of psalm and Magnificat tones, especially as found in Spain, is completely absent.

Many of the pieces are anonymous, but for a good number the authors' names are given: Alwood, Master Avere (Avery Burton?), Blitheman, Carleton, Coxsun, Farrant, Kryton, Parsons, Phelyppe Apprys (Philip ap Rhys), Preston, Redford, Shelbye, Shepherd, Tallis, Taverner, Thorne, and others. Most of these composers are represented by only two or three pieces and nothing is known about their lives. But for four of them, John Redford, Thomas Preston, Thomas Tallis, and William Blitheman, a large number of works have been preserved and many more biographical details are known. Redford, Tallis, and Blitheman were included in our survey of 16th-century organ masters (cf.pp.77, 78). In recent years some information about Preston's life has come to light. He was probably born around 1500, was the organist at Magdalen College in Oxford in 1543 and the organist at St. George's chapel, the Chapel Royal, in Windsor from 1558 to 1563, and probably died in 1563 or 1564.[58] Thus chronologically he probably belongs between Redford (d.1547) on the one hand, and Tallis (d.1585) and Blitheman (d.1591) on the other.

We have many more works by the earliest of these organ composers, Red-ford, than by any of his successors; over forty can be assigned to him with cer-tainty.[59] Whatever the reason—greater productivity, higher esteem on the part of his contemporaries, or fewer sources lost—we are fortunate that such an exten-sive collection of this outstanding early master has been preserved. It therefore will not only be the point of departure for our observations on the organ music of the Tudor period, but also its very center.

REDFORD

Four offertories (*Iustus ut palma, Precatus est Moyses, Tui sunt celi,* and *Felix namque*), 11 antiphons (3 *Glorificamus,* 3 *Lucem tuam,* and 5 *Miserere*), 25 hymns (among them *A solis ortus cardine, Christe qui lux, Eterne rerum conditor, Iste confessor, Iam lucis orto sydere, Veni redemptor*), 2 *Te Deum,* and an *Agnus* are definitely identified as Redford's. Pfatteicher R contains about twenty more pieces, some of which are so close to the style of these works that they can be accepted as Redford's compositions.[60]

It is best to consider Redford's works as a whole, from the two points of view that correspond to his creative processes as a composer: first the treatment of the liturgical melodies, and then the addition of the counterpoints. This discussion will be limited to those works that are definitely known to be Redford's.

In the treatment of the liturgical melodies Redford's position is midway be-tween Cabezón and Girolamo Cavazzoni. His methods are much freer than Cabezón's, but he does not go so far as to use the chant merely as a point of de-parture, as Cavazzoni often does. The strict *cantus planus,* which plays such a big role in Cabezón's settings, is found in only six pieces: three of the short *Miserere* (Pfatteicher, R, p.22, nos.a[=b], c, and d[=e]), *Eterne rerum, O lux,* and *Agnus* (pp.41, 50, 86). In other pieces the chant is occasionally ornamented, e.g., in *Glorificamus,* the three *Lucem tuam,* and *Ad cenam* (pp.17, 18, 19, 20, 27). Fig.130 shows a passage from the third *Lucem tuam* together with its Gregorian model.[61] In this piece fifteen of the sixty-six notes of the chant tune are para-phrased by additional notes or figures, but in the embroidered passages the chant notes also occur in their regular distribution, each occupying the time of a semi-breve (a half note in Fig.130). This principle has appeared several times before: in the *Benedicite* in Paumann's *Fundamentum* (cf.p.52), in the introit *Gaudeamus*

Fig.130

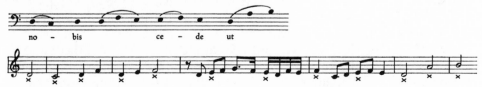

in the *Buxheim Organ Book* (cf.p.67), and in the *Et in terra* from Jacques Brumel's Mass (cf.p.113). In Redford's music it also plays a basic role.[62]

In a number of compositions Redford goes one step further and embroiders the entire chant melody. Complete paraphrasing occurs above all in the three great offertories, which open the new edition, and also in *A solis ortus, Angulare fundamentum, Christe qui lux* (pp.26, 28, 33 bottom[63]), and several other arrangements. Here, too, the paraphrase is based on a regular distribution of the chant notes. Deviations occur here and there, but in most instances they must be considered the result of a divergent chant tradition.

A very peculiar method of transforming Gregorian chants, one apparently employed only in England, is known as *faburden*. According to the usual explanation it consists in the frequent replacement of the chant notes by the third above.[64] More correctly put, they are replaced by the sixth below, which can then be shifted up an octave. That the real meaning of *faburden* is the substitution of the sixth is confirmed by the etymological relationship to *fauxbourdon*, in which the *cantus firmus* is accompanied by a tenor consisting mostly of sixths below the melody. The substitution of the sixth is clearly operating in the single piece by Redford that bears the designation *faburden*, the organ hymn *O lux on the faburden* (Pfatteicher R, p.50). Fig.131 shows part of the chant melody of *O lux beata Trinitas* and the part derived from it, which is the bass of the composition. The hymn has the form a a b a; Fig.131 shows the first and third sections.

Fig.131

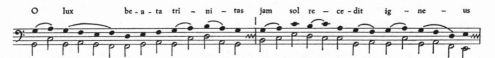

This is not a simple transposition of the whole melody down a sixth. Here and there a chant note is shifted to the octave below—particularly at the beginning and end—exactly as is done in the *fauxbourdon*. Thus the derived melody does not move in the same way as the original one, but differs from it in the frequent occurrence of skips: a fourth instead of a second, a third instead of a unison, a fifth instead of a third. This is probably the reason for the use of faburden. It enabled the composer to insert some larger intervals and thus create a bass part that is more appropriate for a polyphonic setting than one that proceeds mostly in seconds. The faburden is therefore rarely used in the upper part,[65] but mostly in the bass or tenor where larger intervals and changes in the original melody are particularly likely to please.

In addition to this hymn, Redford's works include a series of other faburden pieces that are not designated as such: *Iste confessor*, two *Salvator*, *Te lucis*, *Verbum supernum*, ℣ 2, and the two *Te Deum* (Pfatteicher R, pp.45 top, 56, 57,

Fig.132

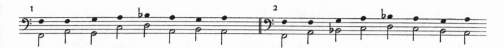

58, 63, 75, 80), and various pieces that are not completely authenticated, e.g., *Eterne rerum*, ℣ 1–2 (pp.39f.). These works afford a more accurate insight into Redford's handling and modifications of the faburden technique. The pure faburden, with lower sixths and octaves, is found again in *Verbum supernum*, ℣ 2, and *Eterne rerum*, ℣ 1–2. The two verses of the latter show how two different faburden parts may be derived from the same tune (Fig.132). In other instances the faburden part is shifted up an octave, so that a sixth lower becomes a third higher, and an octave lower becomes a unison. This procedure occurs in a number of anonymous organ hymns found in Brit. Mus. Add. 29996 (fol.158–178v) with the following legend: "All these are uppon the faburden of these playne songs."[66] We have a single example of this kind by Redford, *Iste confessor* (Pfatteicher R, p.45;[67] Fig.133). Again, we can see how the faburden, which serves as the *bassus* of a two-part setting, differs from the chant tune mainly in the size of its intervals. Near the end two chant notes are surprisingly replaced by their fifths—a procedure that can in no way be derived from the principles of faburden (or *fauxbourdon*).

Fig.133

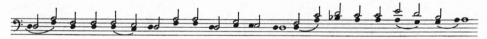

Another modification of the faburden, almost as striking, consists of substituting the lower third rather than sixth for the chant, not just for an occasional note, but throughout. This method seems to have been the one preferred by Redford. He uses it in the two *Salvator*, *Te lucis*, ℣ 1–2, and in many sections of the two *Te Deum* (Pfatteicher R, pp.56, 57, 58, 75, 80), where it is indeed often difficult to establish the chant version. In almost all these pieces the lower third is replaced here and there by the lower fifth (just as in *Iste confessor* the upper third is replaced by the upper fifth). The beginning of the first *Salvator*, given in Fig. 134, is an example of this practice.

These examples show to what degree the original melodies can be dis-

Fig.134

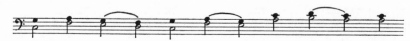

guised by the faburden methods of the English school. In some instances the derived melody is even further changed by figurations and inserted notes. But despite all the liberties of alteration the idea of the Gregorian melody is retained throughout its full length. The complete freedom of handling the chant found in Cavazzoni's works is as far from Redford's style as the strict adherence characteristic of Cabezón's music.

Let us now turn to the second consideration, that of the counterpoints that are added to the *cantus firmus* and the resulting polyphonic texture. In contrast to the Continental practice of the period, four-part writing is the exception in Redford's settings. The only four-voiced pieces are a *Glorificamus*, two *Lucem tuam*, and ℣ 2 of a *Salvator* (Pfatteicher R, pp.17, 19, 20, 56). About twenty settings are in two parts, the rest in three. The strong preference for a limited number of voices shown by Redford, and by early English clavier music in general, is most surprising since by the end of the fifteenth century English composers were already writing vocal works for six, eight, and nine voices.[68]

Even a superficial examination of Redford's organ works reveals several different types of composition, some of which are in strong contrast with each other. Compare, e.g., the stiff, mechanical figurations of one of the *Miserere*[69] (Pfatteicher R, p.23, middle) with the highly subtle texture of the *Salvator with a meane* (p.57).[70] Between these extremes we find several other more or less clearly differentiated types. They can be categorized according to a principle that is not limited to Redford—in fact, it may be used as a guide to the entire evolution of *cantus-firmus* settings from Leonin to Bach—but which proves particularly useful in his case. It is a classification based on the degree of the melodic relationship between the *cantus firmus* and the counterpoints according to a scale that goes from total independence to complete fusion.

At the beginning of this scale there are pieces like the above *Miserere*, in which a strict *cantus planus* in half notes is linked with a completely contrasting counterpoint in continuous eighth-note motion. The *Agnus* (Pfatteicher R, p.86), Redford's only composition for the Mass ordinary[71] is quite similar. In the three-part settings of this type Redford adds a rhythmically similar voice to the *cantus-planus* part, as in the first *Miserere* (p.22, top), or to the counterpoint, as in *O lux on the faburden* (p.50), part of which is given in Fig.135. There are only a few examples of this stiff, mechanical type in Redford's works; from the aesthetic-

Fig.135

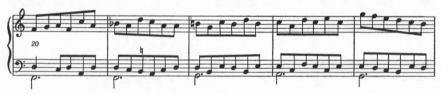

artistic point of view this is not regrettable. But strangely enough it was increasingly cultivated and developed by his younger contemporaries and successors, who used very similar formulae, marked by skips and angular contours.

Another procedure is that of contradictory rhythms, which were introduced in a modest way by Redford, but later on were used a great deal and driven to extremes. In one of the many *Miserere* (Pfatteicher R, p.22, bottom) the three voices move from beginning to end in the following rhythms: upper part | ♩♪♩♪ |, middle part (*cantus firmus*) | ♩ ♩ ♩ |, and lower part | ♪ ♩ ♪ ♩ |.

A third type is represented by pieces in which the counterpoints are still independent of the *cantus firmus* (mostly ornamented *cantus plani*), but are related to one another by means of identical motifs. A lovely example is the *Glorificamus* (p.17), which starts with four entrances of a distinct motif (Fig.136). This motif then recurs here and there in the course of the composition (occasionally slightly altered), almost acquiring the character of an ostinato.

Fig.136

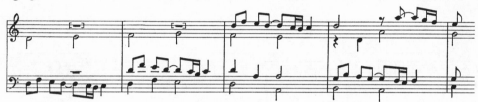

This type, which we may designate as *soprano ostinato*, emerges even more clearly in a section of the first *Te Deum* (p.78, meas.282–295; probably on the word *dignare*). The top part consists entirely of repetitions of a rhythmically incisive dance-like motif (Fig.137). Another example of this technique, which is

Fig.137

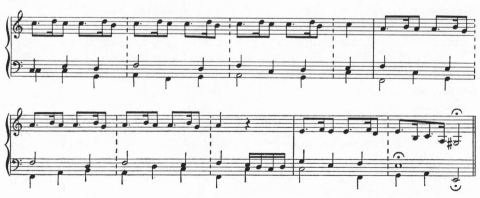

Fig.138

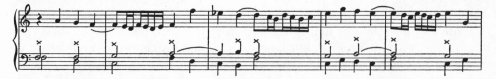

characteristic of Redford, is an *Eterne rerum conditor* (p.41, bottom). The top part again consists of repetitions of one motif, which is transposed to various levels in order to agree with the notes of the *cantus firmus*.* An excerpt is given in Fig.138. Several other pieces represent the ostinato type, but they differ in that the dominating motif appears in all the parts, including the *cantus firmus*. A fine example of this type of writing is the *Eterne rex* (p.42), a section of which is shown in Fig.139. Note that the ostinato motifs used in *Glorificamus, Eterne rerum,* and *Eterne rex* (Figs.136, 138, 139) are related. In an *Iam lucis* (Pfatteicher R, p.48) the same idea reappears in a somewhat expanded form.

Fig.139

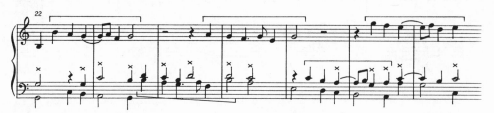

When the ostinato motif also appears in the *cantus firmus,* as it does in the *Eterne rex* and *Iam lucis,* we are well on the way to an ever greater assimilation and fusion of the voices. There may be several intermediate stages, but for our purposes it will suffice to characterize the final one, which is represented most impressively by the four three-part offertories: *Iustus ut palma, Precatus est Moyses, Tui sunt celi,* and *Felix namque* (pp.3, 6, 12, 72=73).** All these are compositions of considerable length, and we must keep in mind that the choral intonations of the Gregorian melody are not included in these settings, which usually begin the soloistic continuation at the words *ut palma Moyses, celi,* and *namque,* respectively.

---

* Cf. the discussion of *discantus ostinato* in Pfatteicher, p.40. Such ostinati are probably found for the first time in Ockeghem (e.g., *Missa De plus en plus, Gloria,* meas.104ff.), later in Obrecht and Isaac. In general, several stylistic details of old English organ music can be traced to the early Netherlanders.

** The setting of offertories, and especially of the *Felix namque,* is one of the many features that differentiate the liturgical organ music in England from that on the Continent. It will be recalled that a *Felix namque* is preserved from as early as about 1400 (cf.p.32).

As mentioned earlier, the chant melodies in these offertories are subjected to very free paraphrasing, which leads to a complete reformulation. It is important and essential that the formulae used for the paraphrasing affect the counterpoints as well, in other words, that the *cantus-firmus* ornamentation and the counterpoints are closely related. Particularly impressive examples of this technique are found in *Iustus ut palma,* from which a typical passage is given in Fig.140. The very high range of the upper part is also of interest. Even though the g''' reached here represents an extreme case, there are quite a few passages in Redford's music in which the upper part moves into the three-line octave. Other English composers also employed this peculiar way of writing.

Fig.140

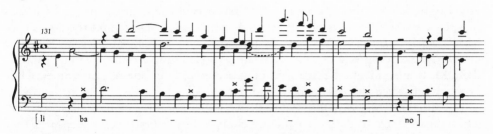

[li - ba - - - - - - - - no]

In many of his compositions Redford shows himself as a great master of the organ. The basic approach in his music is still wholly medieval: He aims at transparency, not fullness; at linear tracing, not chordal sound; at melodic intensity, not the sustaining power of harmony. In pursuing these aims he sometimes does without additional decoration entirely, using no enlivening figures and ornamentation. A piece like *Veni redemptor* (Pfatteicher R, p.61), in its ascetic simplicity and austere introspectiveness, is one of the most stirring creations in organ music. The contrast between masterpieces such as this and some of Redford's other (mostly brief) pieces, with their dry, pedantic, and downright unmusical figurations, is so striking that the latter almost appear spurious. But the same dualism occurs in the music of almost all the English organ masters, from Redford to Tomkins.

PRESTON AND HIS CONTEMPORARIES

Thomas Preston is the most important of Redford's successors. His organ works—chiefly a number of offertories and a Mass proper for Easter Sunday—are all found in the manuscript Brit. Mus. Add. 29996, which also includes many works by Redford and pieces by Robert Coxsun, John Thorne, Richard Wynslate, and others. Another manuscript, Brit. Mus. Roy. App. 56, contains a number of anonymous liturgical organ works that probably belong to a somewhat earlier time; we shall therefore discuss them first.[72]

The manuscript starts with a *Felix namque*, which consists of three sections (A, B, C). A and B are in three parts and C in four;[73] A contains the chant melody from "namque" to "Maria" (the chorally sung incipit "Felix" is, as usual, omitted from the composition), B goes from "et omni" to "sol," and C from "iustitiae" to "noster." The chant lies in the upper part throughout as a *cantus planus*, but it is given a different rhythm in each of the three sections. In A each note is represented by a breve followed by a minim, which makes a total of five minims and results in a time signature of 5/4 in the transcription; in B each note is treated as a semibreve plus a minim, and thus fills a 3/4 measure; finally, in C it is presented as a simple minim, and the series of these minims may be transcribed in 3/4 time just as well as in 4/4. Thus we have a construction with two diminutions of the basic values which recalls the isorhythmic motets of Dunstable and Dufay. There are also models for the 5/4 plan of the first section in the music of the 15th century, e.g., in the *Qui tollis* of Obrecht's *Missa Je ne demande* and the *Sanctus* of Isaac's *Missa paschalis*;[74] we may assume that one or both of these works were known to the composer of this *Felix namque*. There is a difference however: In these Mass movements the five-beat plan occurs only in one or two voices, while in the organ piece it governs the entire setting.

Against the *cantus planus* we hear two lower parts (three in the last section), whose character and design frequently change. In the first twelve measures they

Fig.141

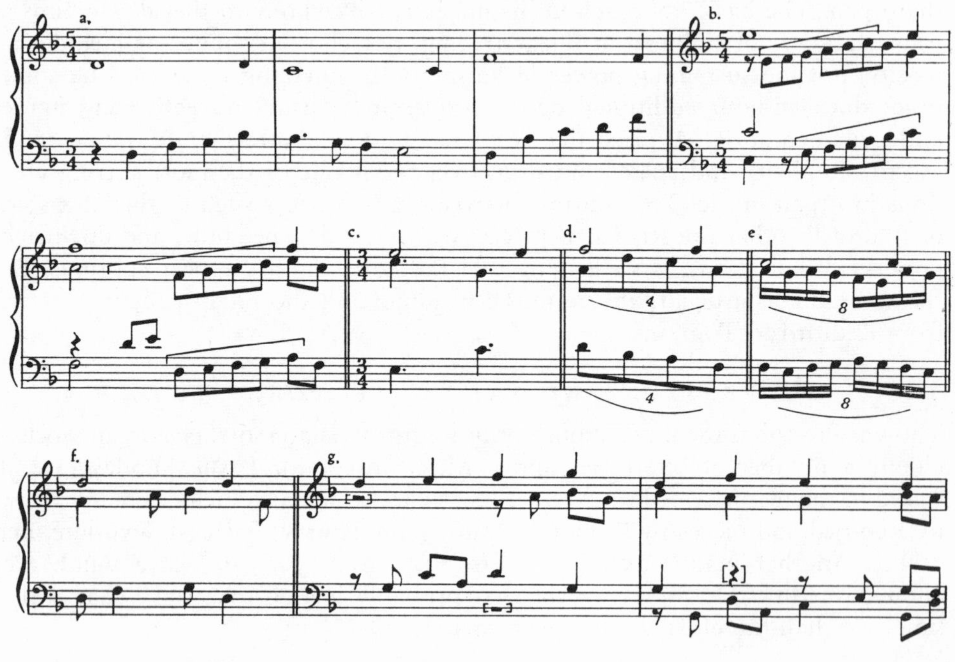

develop imitatively from a pithy quarter-note motif (Fig.141a.). In measure 20 they involve a figure of a special kind that reappears in English clavier music of the 16th century in hundreds of repetitions and variants—in parallel thirds (tenths) or in sixths with a quasi-imitative entry (Fig.141b.). Section B unfolds in normal 3/4 time, but now various rhythmic complications enter in the lower parts: groups of two, four, and eight notes against the three beats of the *cantus planus* (Fig. 141c.–e.); this subsection is followed by an extended passage in which each voice consistently develops another rhythm (Fig.141f.), very similar to one of Redford's *Misereres* (cf.p.145). In the brief concluding section C, the *cantus planus* and the counterpoints combine to form a unified, "normal," four-part texture, which does not occur too often in English organ music (Fig.141g.).

A second *Felix namque* in Brit. Mus. Roy. App. 56 is notated in only two parts, but at the end the melody of the offertory is added in Gregorian notation with the legend, "play the playne songe in lonke." In reality the melody must not be added as a series of longae, but as one of perfect breves. Fig.142 shows a passage from the middle and one from the end of this piece. In both of them, and in other passages, the top part crosses below the *cantus planus*. Was it played on a second manual, or on the pedals, or sung by a choir?

Fig.142

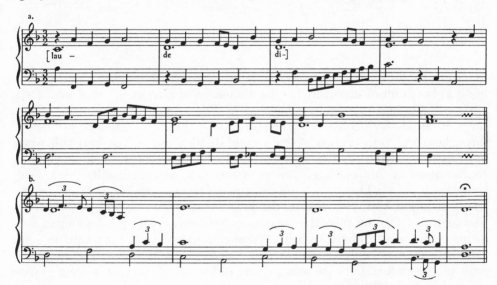

The second *Felix namque* is much more unified than the first, and artistically superior to it. It is a very long composition—140 measures—but from beginning to end the two counterpoints flow in organic lines, supporting and connecting the sustained notes of the chant with ever new turns. However, as in so much of English organ music, there are many rough, awkward details; in the music of the 16th century they affect us like foreign bodies, hostile to the senses, like obstinate carry-overs of medieval asceticism. Compare, e.g., this *Felix namque* (to say nothing of the first one!) with Schlick's *Salve regina*, which is based on the same structural principles!

A *Beata viscera* in the same manuscript has the Gregorian melody[75] in the discant as a *cantus planus* in breves. The two counterpoints add quiet imitative duets at the beginning and end, and in the middle there is a section of figurations in parallel thirds and tenths.

Of the remaining liturgical pieces in the collection only one deserves special mention, a *Kyrie-Christe*, mainly because in England—in contrast to the Continent—compositions for the Mass ordinary are very rare. But its style is also unusual; one part with long, sustained *cantus-firmus* notes, plus a richly ornamented upper voice—a manner of writing that one occasionally finds in Ockeghem's music. Compare, e.g., the excerpt given in Fig.143 with the *Agnus Dei III* from Ockeghem's *Missa L'homme armé*.

Fig.143

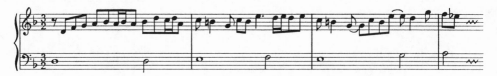

Let us return to the first *Felix namque* from Brit. Mus. Roy. App. 56, and use it as the point of departure for the discussion of a series of other works that are spiritually and technically related to it. This composition, with its strange turns, is not at all singular, but represents a type that was cultivated in England throughout the 16th century. Even around 1650 Thomas Tomkins still wrote in this style, which at its very first appearance sounds almost archaic. It may be characterized as follows: To a *cantus planus* two, or occasionally three, lively counterpoints are added, which are constructed from a number of varied figures. The figures are best described as the product of geometric and arithmetic invention rather than of musical imagination—geometry seemingly determines their melodic contours, arithmetic their rhythmic relationships. This results in some extremely curious compositions—dry and pedantic, and without sensuous appeal—that seem foreign to the music of the 16th century. Yet just because of their strangeness they offer some interesting aspects.

Almost all English keyboard composers employed this style of writing, which we may call "design style." It is used in many liturgical works written for the organ, such as a number of offertories, particularly the frequently composed *Felix namque* (Preston, Farrant, Tallis), as well as in *Exsultabunt sancti* (Thorne of

York), *Diffusa esta gratia* (Preston), *Veritas mea* (Coxsun), and others. Blitheman was one of the first to transfer this style to the antiphon *Gloria tibi trinitas*, which became the mainstay of English instrumental music under the name *In nomine*.[76] Hymns, too, were composed in this manner, e.g., *Christe redemptor* (Blitheman, Bull) and *Christe qui lux* (Heath). The *cantus firmus* usually lies in the upper or the middle part, less often in the bass.

Some of the diverse figures that appear in the counterpoints result from rhythmic considerations. They mostly aim at producing a conflict between the two moving parts or between the moving parts and the *cantus planus* of the chant tune. Three types may be differentiated, depending on the cause of the conflict: a. proportional contrasts in note values—three notes against two, four against three, or nine against eight; b. different rhythmic groupings, such as ♩♪ against ♪♩, or ♫♩ against ♩♫ (polyrhythm); or c. different divisions of the measure, e.g., 3/8 against 4/8 (polymeter). The examples in Fig.144 may be added to those from the first anonymous *Felix namque* given in Fig.141, especially c.–f.

Fig.144

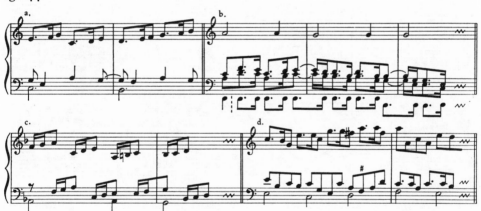

a. Preston, *Felix namque* (Stevens A, p.8); b. Preston, *Diffusa est* (Brit. Mus. Add. 29996, fol.49); c. Farrant, *Felix namque* (Stevens M, p.16); d. Heath, *Christe qui lux* (Stevens M, p.78).

There are other rhythmic oddities that are of even greater interest because they introduce the virtuoso style of the virginalists. This style, which is so decisive in the evolution of clavier technique, did not emerge from the secular music of the Elizabethan era, but arose much earlier, from the liturgical organ pieces of the early Tudor period. In Redford's music we find several features that point in this direction, and there are clearer indications among his successors—Preston, Blitheman, Tallis, and their contemporaries. Many of the well-known keyboard figures characteristic of the virginalists already appear in the liturgical organ pieces written about 1530 to 1560. In Preston's *Diffusa est*, e.g., both ornamented counterpoints must be played by the left hand in diads from beginning to end. It is a long work, more than 160 measures, a veritable "etude for the left hand," which may offer even the modern pianist some stimuli for improving his technique. The same melody is used by Blitheman in the second half of his *Gloria tibi trinitas* II (Stevens M, p.68), where the left hand is given some rather fast passages in sixths. Fig. 145 shows several typically clavieristic figures that reappear in similar fashion in later English keyboard music.

Fig.145

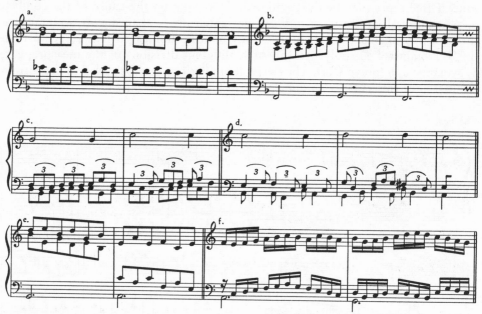

a. *Beata viscera* (Brit. Mus. Roy. App. 56); b. Wynslate, *Lucem tuam* (Brit. Mus. Add. 29996, fol.19v); c., d. Preston, *Diffusa est;* e., f. Preston, *Felix namque* (Stevens A, pp.8, 9).

Let us now describe briefly the individual works of the early English masters. Preston's output by its very extent takes first place. It comprises 12 offertories—8 on *Felix namque,* and settings of *Diffusa est, Confessio, Reges Tharsis,* and *Benedictus* (*sit Deus pater*),[77] an arrangement of the antiphon *Beatus Laurentius,* and a Mass proper for Easter Sunday.[78] The strange contrast that pervades Redford's works—pieces with stiff, mechanical figurations side by side with those in which genuinely contrapuntal voices combine in a unified whole—also marks Preston's output. Two of his offertories, *Diffusa est* and the *Felix namque* published in Stevens A (p.6), are typical products of the design style. The remaining offertories, however, are completely different; they are similar in style to Redford's and at least equal to them artistically. Free of all figuration, they are dedicated throughout to strict counterpoint, to inner life rather than external motion. All seven *Felix namque* that belong to this type are in four parts. The first four are built on a *cantus planus* in breves, which lies in the discant, bass, alto, and tenor, respectively. No.7 puts the Gregorian melody in the alto in semibreves with occasional light ornamentation. In contrast to these arrangements, the *Felix namque* nos.5 and 6 do not offer a recognizable *cantus firmus*, which is probably an indication that they are transcriptions of motets. *Reges Tharsis* is in three parts with the freely paraphrased chant tune in the bass; *Benedictus* has four voices and a *cantus planus* in breves in the discant; and *Confessio* is in four parts with a *cantus planus* in semibreves in the alto.

The main differences between Preston's offertories and Redford's are the former's preference for four-part writing and the treatment of the Gregorian melodies as strict *cantus plani*. The music also has a greater sonority and fulness of sound, not only because Preston writes more parts but also because he avoids placing the upper part too high above the others—indeed this is hardly possible in a four-part setting. Nevertheless the archaic, modal character of the harmony remains the same. It is almost unbelievable that half a century after Josquin a composer could combine four voices to produce such antiquated sounds. But how beautiful these sounds are in their serious dignity, their awe-inspiring strictness!

On the other hand, the influence of the Netherlandish style is evidenced by the rather frequent employment of imitation between counterpoints. In Redford's music imitation usually involves complementary motives, but Preston uses it in the sense of *ars fugandi*, in other words, as an imitative chain or stretto, the usual technique of the motet style during the period. There are also passages in which the imitation stretches over several measures and acquires the character of a canon. In measures 6–13 of the offertory *Benedictus*, e.g., the alto and the bass constitute a strict canon at the interval of a half note.

Fig.146 shows the beginning and a later passage from the *Felix namque* no.4 (Brit. Mus. Add. 29996, fol.57). The chant melody (starting with *namque*) is heard as a *cantus planus* in the tenor, transposed up a fourth. A consistent key signature of *B flat* and *E flat* ensures the strictly model character of each part and of the whole work. Note the descending scale passages, which often give the impression of a quasi-ostinato; they occur in similar fashion in many other English organ compositions. A four-part work quite similar to this *Felix namque* is Preston's

Fig.146

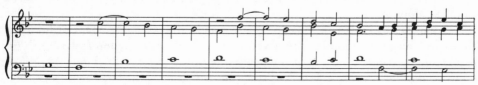

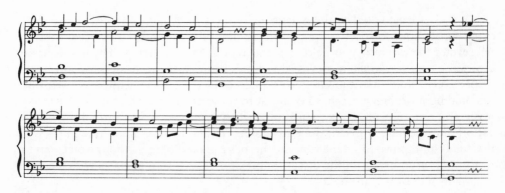

setting of the antiphon *Beatus Laurentius*. The *cantus firmus* lies in the upper part, presented mostly as a *cantus planus*, but here and there it is paraphrased simply.

Finally, Preston left a unique composition, a Mass proper for Easter Sunday (Brit. Mus. Add. 29996, fol.62vff.),[79] which is curious for several reasons. It consists of the following pieces:

Resurrexi—Tu cognovisti—Resurrexi:	introit and verse
Hec dies—Confitemini:	gradual and verse
Alleluia—Versus I (Pascha nostrum)—	
Versus II (Epulemur):	alleluia and two verses
Fulgens, versus I–XIII:	sequence

The offertory and the communion are omitted; possibly some folios of the manuscript are lost. But even the preserved portions make up an extensive work, which is the only known instance of a comprehensive Mass proper for organ. It is a curious conglomeration of styles, and contains the most varied treatment of chant tunes. The first of the three pieces of the introit is written in two parts, with many syncopations and oddities, and without a recognizable *cantus firmus* (possibly it should be added in *cantus-planus* fashion as in the *Felix namque* mentioned on p.149). The introit verse is in three parts and in a normal contropuntal setting, with the lightly paraphrased *cantus planus* in the tenor. The third section is in the same style but has four voices. *Confitemini* is one of the most abstruse examples of the design style, with proportional counter-rhythms 2:3, 4:3, and 8:3. Its lower part is the Gregorian melody; however, it does not move in the usual long note values (breves or semibreves), but mostly in quarter notes (minims). Fig.147 shows a passage near the end. Finally, the various sections of the *Fulgens praeclara*[80] come close to being a catalog of the pedantic design style in all its diverse manifestations.

A parallel to Preston's Mass proper exists in the complete Mass ordinary by Philip ap Rhys, which is also preserved in Brit. Mus. Add. 29996 (fol.28v).[81] The author's name, which is given at the beginning of the work as Phelyppe Apprys off Saynt Poulles [St. Paul's] in London, suggests a Welsh origin. The organ Mass con-

Fig.147

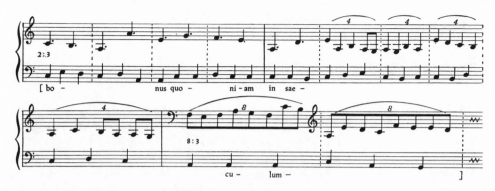

[bo -   nus quo -   ni - am   in   sae -

cu -   lum —   ]

sists of: [*Kyrie*] *Deus creator omnium, Gloria, Credo in unum Deum* (the music for which is not entered), *Offertorium in die Sanctae Trinitatis, Sanctus,* and *Agnus Dei.* It thus constitutes a complete ordinary with an inserted offertory. Each portion of the ordinary contains several sections, which alternate with portions performed *choraliter.* The structure of the *Gloria* is given in the table on p.93. The musical formulation is much more homogeneous than Preston's Mass proper. Apart from the offertory, the Mass consists of sixteen movements, which are about six to ten measures long in the *Kyrie* and *Gloria,* and somewhat longer in the *Sanctus* and *Agnus.* Some are in two parts, others in three; some are contrapuntal, others given to figuration; some have the *cantus firmus* in the top part, others in the bass or the middle part. Perhaps the most unusual is the last movement of the *Kyrie,* in which the Gregorian tune (from Kyrie XIV) appears in the discant in an uninterrupted series of quarter notes (minims), supported by two low-lying voices that progress in the same note values. The result is a strictly homophonic setting, rather a rarity in English organ music. Brit. Mus. Add. 29996 also contains a *Miserere* and a *Felix namque* by Philip ap Rhys (fol.6v and 41).

The same manuscript includes two compositions by Robert Coxsun, a *Veritas mea* and a *Letamini in Domino,* both offertories. Here again the Janus face of English organ music emerges. *Veritas mea* has only two ornamental voices, to which the chant melody in the form of a *cantus planus* must probably be added—as in the second *Felix namque* of Brit. Mus. Roy. App. 56 (cf.p.149)—but this problem has not been solved. In any event, the two notated parts are one of the most fantastic products of the design style. Fig.148 gives some impression of the character of this piece. The sixteenth-note passage in the last measure of the excerpt is derived from a motif that is employed in the same manner in the next five measures, always in a syncopated rhythm that contrasts with that of the lower voice. The *Letamini in Domino,*[82] however, is completely different. In its free paraphrase of the chant melody (as usual, the initial *Laetamini* is not included in the composition), in the very high register of the upper part, and in the occa-

Fig.148

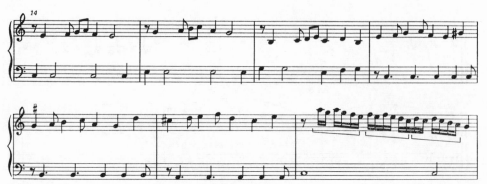

sional points of imitation, it comes close to Redford's *Iustus ut palma*, but it has an even more ascetic sound. Brit. Mus. Add. 29996 also contains two *Misereres* by Kyrton, a *Miserere* by E. Strowger, a *Te Deum* by Avere (Avery Burton?), a *Lucem tuam* by Wynslate (cf.Fig.145b.), and an *Exsultabunt sancti* by Thorne of York.[83]

The manuscript also contains a collection of anonymous settings "upon the faburden" (see above, p.143). It is a cycle of twenty organ hymns, each of which is represented by three, four, or five verses—a total of seventy-one pieces. The hymns follow the order of the liturgical calendar: first three for Advent, then four for Christmas, etc., until the third Sunday of Lent. This is by far the largest collection of music in the faburden technique (see the discussion on pp.142ff. in connection with the works of John Redford). Most of the pieces employ the upper third in transforming the original melodies, a few the lower sixth or lower third. Occasionally the faburden does not appear in the bass but in the part next to the lowest, as, e.g., in the last verse of *Veni redemptor gentium* (Stevens A, p.21[84]). The first verse of every hymn is in two parts, the second usually in three, the third in three or four, and others that may follow again in three. The first verses mostly begin in syncopated counterpoint, but soon lapse into fast runs; the final verses are written mostly in a mechanical design style with contrasting rhythms, e.g., twelve notes (eighths) in the upper part, three (halves) in the middle part, and two (dotted halves) in the lowest. As a rule the verses in between show a polyphonic technique, with occasional imitations or with an ostinato in the top part. In four hymns (*Salvator mundi*, *Christe redemptor*, *A solis ortus*, and *Bina celestis II*) the second verses are written as two-part canons above the faburden voice, while in the corresponding verse of *Hostis Herodis II* the faburden part itself is presented as a canon in the two lower voices.

TALLIS, BLITHEMAN, AND THEIR CONTEMPORARIES; BYRD

The previous observations concerned the earlier phase of England's liturgical music, from about 1520 to about 1550. The chief source for the later phase is the

Mulliner Book,[85] which for the first time preserves works by Tallis and Blitheman, the most significant English organ masters active in the second half of the 16th century. Both are represented by several pieces in later sources also, e.g., in the *Fitzwilliam Virginal Book*. Other composers active at the time were Richard Alwood, Nicholas Carleton, Richard (John?) Farrant, and William Shelbye, each of whom is known for a few organ works. The liturgical organ repertoire of the period consists predominantly of hymns and antiphons, among which the Trinity antiphon *Gloria tibi trinitas* occupies a special place. Of the numerous offertories of the earlier period only the *Felix namque* persists, and there is a single *Te deum* by Blitheman.

Among Thomas Tallis' works we find several settings of hymns and antiphons that represent a new type of English organ music. The most important features of this type are the four-part texture, the treatment of the Gregorian melody as a lightly paraphrased *cantus planus* in semibreves, and the utilization of a motif in all voices. There are 8 compositions of this kind by Tallis: 2 *Veni redemptor*, 2 *Ecce tempus*, an *Ex more docti mistico*, and 3 arrangements of the antiphon *Clarifica me*.[86] The four-part texture and motivic unification of this type approaches the normal style of the 16th century, but some oddities still cling to these compositions, rendering them different from the Continental four-part writing of the period. Tallis' music is no less archaic-modal than Thomas Preston's offertories; indeed it goes one step further, for the modal harmonies are pervaded by bold dissonances, which reinforce the austerity of the sound. Most often they derive from, and are justified by, the consistent reuse of the basic motif. Fig.149 shows several pertinent passages from *Ex more docti*.

Outside England formulations of this kind are found only in Spain, in Cabezón. There is a clear relationship between the keyboard music of the two coun-

Fig.149

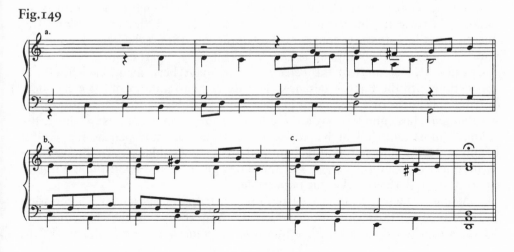

tries.[87] The final measure in Fig.149c. shows a frequent device in English music, which provides further evidence of this relationship. The minor seventh is used as the turning point of a scale passage, creating a cross-relation with the major seventh, which is used as the leading tone. This is sometimes called the "English Seventh." The cross-relation here is rather mild because of the relatively large time interval between the two tones, but it asserts itself far more sharply in other places, at times even in simultaneous dissonance, as in Fig.150. These passages, as well as the one shown in Fig.149b., are early examples of what Correa de Arauxo calls *punto intenso contra remisso* (cf.pp.528, 533).

Fig.150

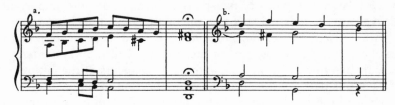

a. Stevens M. No. 99, meas.18; b. No. 101, meas. 8.

The full four-part sound, the motivic unification of the texture, the modal coloring of the harmony, the bold but always logical treatment of dissonance—all of these contribute to making Thomas Tallis' hymns and antiphons, despite their brevity (twenty to twenty-five measures), some of the most impressive products of 16th-century English organ writing.

His two-part arrangements of antiphons, one on *Natus est nobis*, the other on *Gloria tibi trinitas* (Stevens T, pp.40, 32), are completely different. The former is an insignificant little work with running passages in the left hand, but it is interesting because the liturgical melody is cast in the 6/8 "lullaby rhythm" frequently used in Christmas songs. In the *Gloria tibi trinitas* the very freely paraphrased melody of the antiphon is handled as a free two-part canon.

Tallis' two settings of the *Felix namque*[88] have been mentioned briefly in connection with the English design style. I do not hesitate to call them the most horrible specimens of a genre that is always quite problematic. It is almost unbelievable that these monster works—the first is more than 200 measures long, the second almost 270—full of banalities, come from the same pen as the skillful hymns and antiphons so full of real musical life. One would prefer to forgive them as products of youthful excess, but the dates given in the *Fitzwilliam Virginal Book*, 1562 and 1564, make this impossible.

As unsatisfactory as they are from the artistic point of view, it is interesting to trace them to their Gregorian models. Both are based on the chant melody, which is transposed up a fourth in the *Felix namque I*, and up a fifth in *II*.[89] In both settings the initium *Felix* is included in the composition, in *I* as a *cantus-planus* setting of eight measures, in *II* as a fore-imitation of fourteen measures derived from the ornamented head motif (*d f g f d*). In *I* the introductory *cantus-planus* setting is followed by a fore-imitation on the head motif of *namque* (*d c f*); measure 16 starts the main portion, in which the chant appears as a *cantus planus* in the top part, beginning with *namque* (similarly in *II*, where it is heard in the middle part).[90] Curiously, in both cases the offertory melody occupies only about three-quarters of the composition—measures 16–145 in *I*, and measures 15–178 in *II*. Another melody of about forty notes is employed for the final section; the beginning of this melody is shown in Fig.151 at the original pitch. Possibly it represents the verse *Beata et venerabilis*, which followed the offertory in an earlier era.[91]

Fig.151

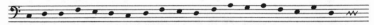

Tallis' two *Felix namque* enlarged the repertoire of English figuration formulae by a number of figures based on arpeggios, figures that anticipate forms that play an important role in later clavier literature. They are found particularly in *I*, from which Fig.152 quotes a few examples. The first example shows that Tallis occasionally presents the notes of the chant tune in the form of full chords, something that none of his predecessors had attempted. The second illustrates the juxtaposition of related triads (here *E flat* major and *C* minor), so frequent in English chord arpeggiations, and a genuine Alberti bass almost two hundred years before Alberti. As for the third passage, is it not reminiscent of Chopin?

The *Felix namque II* shows Italian influence in various details. It is most apparent in the coda (meas.26off.), which is written in exactly the same style as the intonations or toccatas of Andrea Gabrieli. Italian influence also informs the

Fig.152

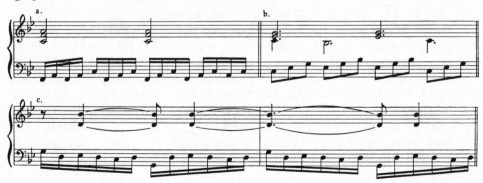

introduction, where the first five notes of the offertory melody are reconstituted as a regular ricercar theme, which is presented in a regular point of imitation.[92] The Italian character continues even further in the main section of the work until measure 40, where typically English figuration motifs enter to give the piece a completely new character. The Gregorian melody is treated as a *cantus planus* in breves (more accurately in pairs of semibreves) as in the *Felix namque I*, but here and there free paraphrases take the place of sustained notes. Fig.153 shows three such paraphrasing measures (meas.78–80). The *cantus-firmus* notes are (*a g b g*), the beginning of the melody for (*di*) *gnissima* (the second note is modified here by a sharp).

Fig.153

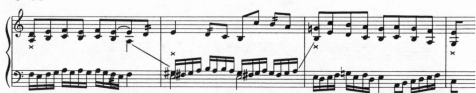

In general Blitheman's organ works are similar to Tallis', but they maintain a more even artistic level. He does not quite reach the high point that the hymns and antiphons of his compatriot do, but he avoids the excesses indulged in by Tallis in the two *Felix namque*. Blitheman's chief contribution to the organ hymn are four settings of *Eterne rerum conditor* (Stevens M, nos.49–52). They seem to form a liturgical unit, since they represent the even-numbered verses of this hymn in nine stanzas. While Tallis follows a unified style in his hymns, Blitheman writes in a different manner in each of the four settings. In the first one the strongly paraphrased *cantus firmus* lies in the lower part and combines with an upper part of similar character to produce a duet of remarkable unity and impressive vitality. The second setting has three parts, with an occasionally ornamented *cantus planus* in the lowest voice and a rising scale motif (| — *fg abb c'* |) connecting the two upper parts. The third verse, in four parts and with a somewhat ornamented *cantus planus* in the tenor, is designated as *melos suave;* indeed it distinguishes itself from its neighbors by its song-like discant, which one could almost take for a Lutheran chorale.[93] There is a sharp dissonance *c♯'–c''* (*punto intenso contra remisso*) in measure 15, and a dominant seventh chord in the concluding IV V I cadence. In the last stanza Blitheman writes the same way as Preston in *Diffusa est:* The right hand plays a strict *cantus planus* in semibreves (half notes in the transcription) while the left hand plays diads throughout. But here these parts are not exercises for the intellect or the fingers but form a lively background from which the hymn melody stands out in relief. Fig.154 shows the beginning of this setting.

Fig.154

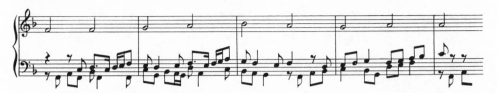

An arrangement of the hymn *Christe qui lux* (Stevens M, no.22) is formulated in three parts on a freely paraphrased *cantus firmus* in the middle part. With its sharp dissonances, sudden changes from a minor to a major third, and *Mixolydian* cadences (a minor dominant before a major tonic chord), this composition is one of the most typical, and at the same time most beautiful, examples of the English style.

Blitheman's *A excellent meane* (Stevens M, no.32), an extended composition, is really a Felix namque.* In contrast to Tallis' *Felix namque*, this one is written in a very quiet, almost homophonic texture, with three parts that move almost exclusively in quarter notes. The chant melody lies in the bass, lightly ornamented, and completely regular in the disposition of two notes of the chant in each measure.

In his *Te Deum* (Stevens M, no.77), Blitheman closely follows earlier compositions of the song of praise in the overall design (alternate verses for chant and for organ) as well as in style. Like the two *Te Deum* by Redford and the one in Brit. Mus. Add. 29996 by Master Avere, the organ verses are set for either two or three parts, some with ostinato motifs, others with stereotyped figures. All of them are written in the faburden method, which appears here for the last time. This is doubtless an early work of the master. To illustrate the faburden method once more, Fig.155 coordinates the four different transformations of the beginning of *Tu ad liberandum* (all transposed to the original pitch notation).

Finally, Blitheman wrote six settings of the *Gloria tibi trinitas* (Stevens M, nos.91–96). This melody, under the title *In nomine,* had a very wide diffusion in England, especially in the field of instrumental ensemble music.[94] The first five settings are very similar to each other. They are in three parts; use the antiphon melody as a *cantus planus* in half notes; add decorative voices; and divide into two or more sections, which are contrasted by changes in the figuration. The last one, however, has four parts; it paraphrases the chant, which lies in the bass, by inserting quarter and eighth notes, and creates counterpoints in the three upper parts that exhibit the idea of unity and relationship with the *cantus firmus*, instead of change and contrast. It is obviously on a different artistic level; in every respect it approaches Tallis' hymns and antiphons.

---

* It was reprinted in Hawkins' *History of Music* (1776), Appendix to vol.V, no.9.

Fig.155

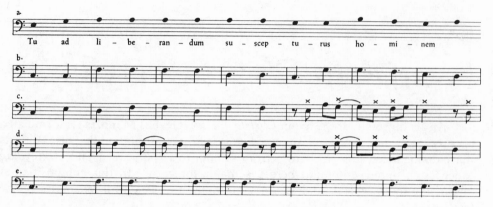

a. Chant (deviates toward the end from the version in the modern Antiphonale Romanum, p.67*);
b. Redford I; c. Redford II; d. Master Avere (Burton?); e. Blitheman.

Richard Alwood, probably a contemporary of Tallis and Blitheman, also wrote a piece entitled *In nomine* (Stevens M, no.23), but it shows no recognizable relation to the general type. It is most interestingly constructed around the motif (*f g a bb a*), which recurs seven times, always in the soprano and always in half notes, but each time it is altered, as the various notes are variously extended by repetitions or interrupted by rests. By combining the repeated notes into single notes, we obtain the formulation of the upper part shown in Fig.156. This method

Fig.156

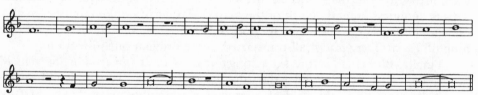

of deriving a whole voice from a five-note idea recalls the manner in which Obrecht, in his Masses *Si dedero* and *Je ne demande*, derives a whole tenor part from a brief motif, which he repeats in various mensurations. Alwood does not adhere strictly to the mensurations, but presents the motif in free rhythmic transformations not unlike those found in some of Frescobaldi's ricercars and capriccios. The manuscript Brit. Mus. Add. 30485 preserves two more *In nomine* by Alwood (fols.48v and 55v), in which the melody of the *Gloria tibi trinitas* is arranged in a simple-four part setting.

Among Alwood's other works are two settings of the Easter hymn *Claro paschali gaudio*, which again demonstrate the dualistic character of England's liturgical organ music. One (Stevens M, no.21) is a somewhat pedantic *cantus-planus* setting, which shows features of the English design style toward the end; the other (no.18) is a homogeneous work, dominated by a descending scale motif, which takes a rightful place next to the most beautiful pieces by Redford and Tallis.

Liturgical pieces by several other organists are included in the *Mulliner Book:* Nicholas Carleton's *Gloria tibi trinitas* and an untitled piece, which for reasons unknown is called *Audi benigne conditor* in the new edition (Stevens M, nos.3 and 4); a *Felix namque* by Farrant (cf.Fig.144c.); a *Christe qui lux* by Heath (cf.Fig.144d.); a *Felix namque* and a *Miserere* by Shelbye (Stevens M, nos.34 and 41); an *In nomine* (no.45, which was surely an ensemble piece originally, and a *Benedicamus Domino* (no.84), which just as clearly originates from vocal music, both by (Robert?) Johnson; and a *Quia fecit* by Shepherd (no.24), which is taken from a six-part Magnificat.[95]

William Byrd's liturgical organ music is insignificant compared to his output in the field of secular clavier music, both in quantity and in artistic and historical stature. He almost always follows in the footsteps of the older tradition of Tallis and Blitheman. Surprisingly, that impressive type of liturgical organ music, which is most beautifully represented by Tallis' short hymn and antiphon settings, never appears in Byrd's works. The extended *cantus-planus* arrangement with ornamented counterpoints prevails almost exclusively.

Byrd's extant opus in the field of liturgical organ music consists of two compositions on the hymn *Veni creator Spiritus* (Tuttle B, pp.8 and 10; the first carries the legend "Upon a plainesong," the second has no title), a *Gloria tibi trinitas* (Tuttle B, p. 6), and three pieces entitled *Miserere* (Tuttle B, p.12, and FW, II, pp.230 and 232). In the first *Veni* the melody lies in the upper part as a strict *cantus planus* in semibreves; the left hand adds running passages in the first section, and diads in triplets in the second. Evidently a piece like Blitheman's *Gloria tibi trinitas* (Stevens M, no.92) served as a model. Fig.157 shows two very similar passages from these two pieces (a. Blitheman; b. Byrd).

Fig.157

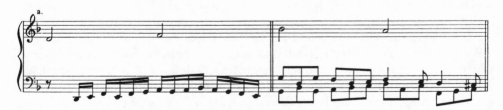

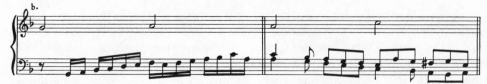

Of the three pieces that are called *Miserere* only one (Tuttle B, p.12) is based on the frequently set antiphon *Miserere mihi;* the other two use an entirely different melody, which is identical with *Gloria tibi trinitas* at the beginning but later deviates rather strongly from it. In the last of these settings (*FW*, II, p.232), the *cantus planus* can easily be established with the aid of the other setting (*FW*, II, p.230). It is occasionally paraphrased in the same way as Tallis does in the second *Felix namque* (compare Figs.153 and 158).

Fig.158

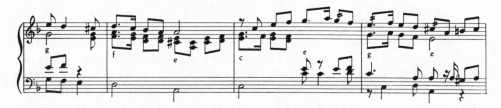

The *Two pts. Gloria tibi trinitas* is based on a very free paraphrase of the Gregorian melody. However the regular distribution of the chant notes is observed throughout. (The arrangement begins with *tibi;* the first three notes are set as breves, the remaining ones as semibreves.) The addition of the discant creates a setting noteworthy for its concatenation of heterogeneous elements. A very attractive beginning is imitatively developed; a passage in the most perverse design style follows; and finally there are a few concluding measures of grace and loveliness such as could come only from Byrd.

Two pieces by Byrd based on the hexachord are, as far as we know, the earliest organ settings on this subject, one that was later treated very often. In the first *Ut re mi fa sol la* (Tuttle B, p.86) the ascending and descending hexachord is played five times as a high-lying top part by a second player ("The playnesong briefes [breves] to be played by a second person," says a legend at the end), while the first player executes a rich and varied "accompaniment." In the second piece (*FW*, I, p.395 = Andrews N, p.68) the subject is presented in semibreves and subtly woven into the contrapuntal texture. Occasionally it is transposed from G to C, D, A, F, and B♭. Finally there also exists an *Ut mi re* (*FW*, I, p.401), a very interesting contrapuntal study on the subject (*c e d f e g f a*), i.e., on the *ascensus per tertias* of Paumann's *Fundamentum*.

8

Imitative Forms

ONE OF THE MOST significant characteristics of the musical evolution
of the 15th century was the gradually spreading use of imitation, especially in
the works of Arnold de Lantins, Busnois, Obrecht, Isaac, and finally, Josquin. In
the 16th century this more or less sporadically applied method became fundamental. The so-called pervading-imitation technique was elevated to a general
principle of composition, mainly by Nicolas Gombert (c.1490–c.1560). It proved
particularly fruitful for the motet (and is sometimes called the motet style) because it made possible a close connection between text and music. The connection
did not aim at an interpretation of the text, as in the madrigal, but, in keeping
with the more transcendental-abstract character of the motet, at a purely formal
coordination. The text is divided into brief segments of about three or four words,
and for each of these a musical motif is invented and presented consecutively by
the various voices. The result is a brief point of imitation, and the motet in
essence consists of a chain of such points of imitation, usually with dovetailed
endings and beginnings.

As early as the end of the 15th century the imitative technique was transferred to instrumental music. In particular Obrecht (c.1450–1505) and Isaac
(c.1450–1517) wrote a number of pieces for instrumental ensembles (three or
four viols, recorders, etc.) that could be called instrumental motets or chansons.
At the start of the 16th century the evolution of similar compositions for keyboard
instruments began. They appeared under the names *ricercar, canzona, fantasia,*
and *tiento.*

One of the most widely discussed problems in the field of early keyboard
music is the specific and meaningful distinctions among these types, particularly
between the ricercar and the fantasia. Seiffert G (p.32) quotes the explanations

given by Michael Praetorius in his *Syntagma musicum* (vol.III, 1619, p.21). He concludes (but not with complete justification) that Praetorius saw the chief difference between them as the number of thematic ideas employed, that the fantasia used several ideas and the ricercar only one. Seiffert declares that this definition is erroneous and asserts that, on the contrary, the fantasia was monothematic and the ricercar polythematic. It was soon established that neither Praetorius' nor Seiffert's explanation could be maintained, and the fatalistic view was adopted that the two designations were equivalent. G. Frotscher expressed it especially plainly: "Fantasia and ricercar canot be differentiated either at the time of their birth or in their later evolution, not even if we assume a confusion of the terms."[1] So categorical a pronouncement falls wide of its mark. It would be better to say that the two titles are occasionally used as equivalents, particularly in music for the lute and instrumental ensembles, but that in general they represent two completely different phenomena. In clavier music especially there can be no thought of equivalence, as will be shown in the following discussion.

The Ricercar

The term ricercar, derived from the Italian *cercare* (search), was used in the 16th and 17th centuries as a designation for various species of composition that, at first glance, have nothing in common with each other. Thus a lute ricercar from about 1510 is completely different from an organ ricercar by Andrea Gabrieli from the middle or the second half of the 16th century or the two-part ricercars found in a number of prints from about 1580 to 1650. Nevertheless all these types represent various manifestations of a common principle, which may be best described by the concept of "examination" or "study," corresponding to the literal meaning of the word ricercar.

Such a study can be directed at various goals. It may be anticipatory, in the sense of a technical and, at the same time, spiritual preparation for the playing of an instrument. This seems to have been the original meaning of the ricercar. The lute ricercars in the prints of Petrucci (1509/10), as well as the earliest organ ricercars, by Marco Antonio Cavazzoni (1523), are more or less improvisational preparations or introductions. Other ricercars resemble instructional studies, like the later etude, but are not directed so exclusively to the purely virtuosic element. The ricercars (*recercada*) for viola da gamba in Ganassi's *Regola Rubertina* (1542) and Diego Ortiz's *Tratado de glosas* (1553), as well as the many vocal ricercars (mostly textless duets), such as the *Ricercari a due voci* by Francesco Guami (1588), and a number of similar publications in the 17th century belong to this type.[2] The main type, however, is the imitative ricercar, which is a study of imitative counterpoint. Some of the later lute ricercars approach this type, e.g., those by Francesco Canova da Milano (1536, 1547) and others, though they are mostly called fantasies (e.g., those by Valentin Bakfark and Simon Gintzler). This type is more pronounced in the ensemble ricercars for three or four instruments (viols, recorders, etc.) or singers, such as the *Fantasie Recercari Contrapunti a tre voci di M. Adriano et de altri Autori appropriati per cantare et sonare d'ogni sorte di stromento* (1551)[3] and similar collections from the mid-16th century.

The base of the imitative ricercar, however, is organ music. The organ ricercars of Girolamo Cavazzoni (1543) started an evolution, which was nourished by ever new ideas, and continued far into the 17th century. After two centuries it found its peak in Bach's *Musical Offering*. An incipient stage of this evolution is represented by Marco Antonio Cavazzoni's ricercars, a few by Jacobo Fogliano, Jacques Brumel, and Julio Segni, and some that are anonymous. We shall consider these very peculiar works first.

MARCO ANTONIO CAVAZZONI AND HIS CONTEMPORARIES

Marco Antonio's *Recerchari Motetti Canzoni* contains two ricercars at the beginning of the collection in the order: *Recercare primo—Salve virgo—Recercare secondo—O stella maris*, so that each ricercar is followed by a "motet" (cf.p.109). This order is certainly not accidental, but indicates that the ricercar still possesses its original character, that of a kind of introduction to the following organ motet. In fact, the ricercars are in the same key as the motets that belong to them: The first pair is in F major, the second in G major.

Both ricercars are of considerable length: The first comprises 126 measures (of a breve each), the second 149. For this period the only piece that is comparable in length is Buchner's *Maria zart* with its 105 *tempora*. One must admire how well this large musical space is filled with a living, always changing, but coherent content. Full chords, ascending and descending scales, motivic continuations, and suggestions of imitation pass in free sequence, and forcefully hold the listener's attention. Bold dissonances recall the organ music of the Gothic era, while the spirit of the Renaissance reveals itself in the many cadences using the dominant with an ornamental turn on the leading tone. The most heterogeneous elements are handled with great freedom, liberties only a master of the art can take without suffering poor results.

The genuine clavieristic texture of free voices, which appears for the first time in Marco Antonio's music, is handled in an even bolder manner than in Attaingnant's. The most varied textures, from full chords of six or seven notes to purely two-part settings, follow each other freely. This style of writing presupposes a totally different type of organ from that for which the strictly polyphonic music of Arnolt Schlick was written. In comparison with the "Gothic" organ of the North, with its many individual registers, its two manuals, and its pedals, the Italian Renaissance organ is of striking simplicity, for it is limited almost exclusively to the open diapason rank and a single manual. Jeppesen has made a detailed and interesting presentation in which he concludes that "the art of the Italian organist consisted in creating a spirited variety within the rather narrow limits of possible sounds, and giving, through gradations of light, life and soft contours to this almost too brilliant clarity."[4] Indeed, typically Italian pieces, such as Marco Antonio's ricercars, Merulo's toccatas, and the imitative ricercars of Girolamo Cavazzoni and Andrea Gabrieli, can only be shown off to advantage on such an organ.

For that time the range of these ricercars is unusually wide. It extends over four octaves, from F to *f'''*, and is exploited several times for special sound effects: Both hands may play on the upper half of the keyboard (as in *Recercare I*, meas. 114–18), or the right hand may play in the highest range while the left is in the lowest (*Recercare I*, meas.35; *Recercare II*, meas.118). In the 16th century other dispositions of this kind are found only in the early English repertoire, especially in Redford's music.

Although Marco Antonio's ricercars do not belong to the imitative type, this does not mean that they contain no imitations.[5] For example, in measure 25 of *Recercare I* we hear a motif (*a* | *b a* — *g* | *f*), which is answered a fourth higher in measure 27, and serves complete points of imitation in measures 62–75, 83–90, and 112–18. In measures 57–60 a brief motif (*a g f e d*) is treated to a regular stretto, which is resumed in measure 109–11 and 122–24. *Recercare II* is based on an idea (*a* | *b a* — *g* | *f e d* — |), which is an extended variant of the main motif of *Recercare I*. At first it appears alone (meas.40, 42, 55, abbreviated in 51, and in the lower part in 61 and 65), then in immediate repetition (meas.82–87), in stretto (meas.110–16 and 132–36), and alone again in the highest octave of the keyboard as a final confirmation (meas.142–44). But this accounts for only the completely obvious manifestations of the subject. In other places it is adumbrated more or less clearly in rhythmic variants, possibly already in measures 6–8 (in the shorter form of the first ricercar), and indubitably in measures 12–13 (in diminution; with free imitation by the lower part?). Also, what we have called the first single entry of the subject (meas.40) may on closer observation—or further hearing—reveal itself to be the start of a rather extended imitational section, in the course of which the subject appears in various guises, and which concludes with the exact repetition of the model in measures 55–57. In these ricercars the idea of imitation is thus not aimed at exact repetitions in a four-part texture, but at improvisatory allusions within a free-voiced organ setting.

Both ricercars include many interesting and original stylistic details, two of which are illustrated in Fig.159. At the beginning of the first ricercar, just as in the *Domine* of Brumel's *Messa de la Dominica* from Castell' Arquato (cf.Fig.104), a right-hand chord is treated as a pedal point; and in a passage from the second one, "peculiar, 'romantic'-sounding sixth chords," as Jeppesen[6] puts it, bring about a stirring climax.

More light is shed on the early history of the organ ricercar by material in the manuscripts of Castell' Arquato, to which we also owe the earliest Italian

Fig.159

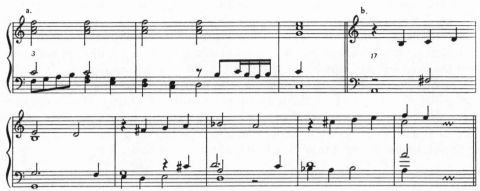

organ Mass (cf.p.111). There is another ricercar by Marco Antonio, four by
Jacobo Fogliano (1468–1548; organist at Modena), two by "Jaches" (most probably Jacques Brumel, who was the organist at Ferrara from 1533 to 1564), one by
Julio da Modena (i.e., Julio Segni, 1498–1561, pupil of Fogliano and second
organist at San Marco in 1530), and two anonymous ones.[7] Marco Antonio's
ricercar (*recercada*) is somewhat similar to the two preserved in print. But
toccata-like elements, held chords, and connecting scale passages are stressed
even more, and there is practically no suggestion of imitation. This ricercar would
seem to represent a still earlier stage of development, closer to the lute ricercar,
than the two long ones, in which counterpoint, thematic invention, and imitation
play a significant role. Fig.160 shows the very impressive beginning of this piece
(cf. Benvenuti M, p.70; Jeppesen O[2], II, p.67).

The four ricercars by Jacobo Fogliano (Benvenuti M, pp.59ff.) are similar

Fig.160

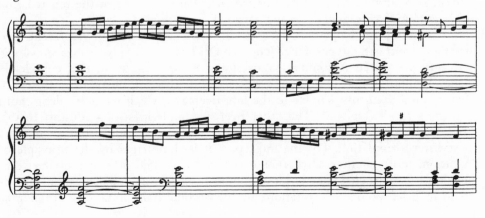

in length to Marco Antonio's manuscript ricercar (about 40–60 measures), but they are contrapuntal-imitative studies, which either omit the toccata-like element entirely (nos.1, 2, and 3) or employ it only toward the end as an improvisatory cadence (no.4). This character is most evident in the second ricercar, which does not start with a full chord, but with an imitative stretto on a subject of impressive contours, based on skips of fourths (Fig.161). It is abandoned soon (in meas.4) in favor of a new subject, which, like many in Fogliano's music, has a truly song-like, or more exactly, chanson- or canzona-like character. Fogliano's ricercars also have other features that recall the canzona, such as a cantabile melody (no.2, meas.17ff.), homophonic declamation with repeated tones (no.2, meas.14 and 36), or literal repetition of a passage (no.1, meas.21–28; no.3, meas.21–28; 29–34).

Fig.161

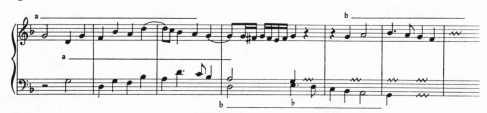

Julio Segni's ricercar has the subtitle "musica ficta per la via di G sol re ut," a legend that most probably refers to the frequent flatting of the sixth degree (*E flat*). "It is a big, magnificent piece, constructed mainly with a view toward creating full chordal effects, with only suggestions of imitations or none at all, and with some, though moderate, use of passage work."[8] The first of the two anonymous ricercars (*recerchade*) (Benvenuti M, p.78) starts with a rather free introductory portion, and continues with two quite complete points of imitation (meas.18–21 and 25–31), the first of which is based on one of the repercussion subjects found so frequently in the canzona.

According to Jeppesen,[9] Jacques Brumel's two ricercars represent two strikingly contrasting types. One (Jeppesen O[2]; II, p.71) is only 31 measures long, and close to Marco Antonio's manuscript ricercar in style. It, too, completely eschews imitation and unfolds in a free series of chordal, melodic, and pseudo-contrapuntal segments, similar to the lute ricercars, which its ambivalent chord sequences recall (Fig.162). The other ricercar stands in strong contrast to this brief study, first of all in length—it comprises 130 measures—but even more in stylistic formulation. For the most part it is dominated by the principle of imitation, more so than any other organ ricercar. The first half of the composition is constructed exactly like a motet: Six or seven subjects enter one another in brief points of imitation. In the second half imitations are not as

Fig.162

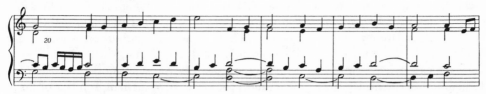

recognizable; nevertheless the texture remains wholly contrapuntal and eschews not only chords and scale passages but also the cadence trills so indispensable in the organ music of that period. Though one may feel that this tendency toward strict counterpoint is desirable in principle, the result is nevertheless unsatisfactory. The subjects have too little character, and the texture is too uniform to fill such a large time span with meaningful content.

Let us sum up briefly our observations on the early organ ricercar from about 1510 to 1540. Although the extant compositions represent only a small portion of the original repertoire, they furnish an outline of a stylistic evolution that moves from the completely free "technical study" almost to the contrapuntal "imitational study." We may put Marco Antonio's ricercar from Castell' Arquato and the shorter ricercar by Jacques Brumel from the same source at the beginning of this evolution. Both may be regarded as organistic counterparts to the lute ricercars of 1510. The next stage, and incidentally the artistic climax of this early evolution, is represented by the two printed ricercars by Marco Antonio, which differ from those just mentioned in length, but even more importantly in their admixture of imitative features. Another step is reached in the four pieces by Fogliano, which are almost entirely beholden to the contrapuntal-imitative technique, but in some details show the influence of the chanson. At the end of this evolution we find the longer ricercar by Brumel, in which the motet style of the period is transferred to the organ. It may be regarded as the immediate forerunner of Girolamo Cavazzoni's ricercars of 1543, with which the long development of the imitative ricercar begins.

For a long time it had been assumed that the imitative ricercar derived from the motet. Riemann, e.g., speaks of a "direct imitation of the motet,"[10] and Frotscher says: "The motet form becomes and remains the ideal and the model for the composition of ricercars"; indeed he explains even the "developments and changes . . . mainly by the variety of the motet models."[11] However, the early history of the organ ricercar (only recently more accurately mapped) shows that its roots are quite different. Even if we speak only of the imitative ricercar, views like those quoted cannot be maintained. One of the few ricercars that may be called a replica of a motet is the longer ricercar by Jacques Brumel. Possibly others of this type existed, but in the works of Girolamo Cavazzoni and of his successors, principles of form emerge that definitely differ from those obtaining in the motet. Furthermore, it must not be forgotten that fully pervading imitations were introduced in the motet by Gombert around 1540, which is about the same time as this principle succeeded in the ricercar. The truth is that about the same time both the motet and the ricercar achieved new formulations, which were based on the same idea, but which led to very different results.

We can briefly formulate the difference as follows: The motet consists of a large number of short points of imitation, the ricercar of a small number of large imitative sections. In the motet a musical idea normally enters four or five times and then immediately gives way to a new idea, which is treated in similar fashion. In the ricercar the fast-passing motif gives way to a real subject, which is presented extensively in a long section with numerous imitations. The fundamental difference may be seen from the fact that the monothematic ricercar is found as early as Andrea Gabrieli's music, while a monothematic motet is an obvious absurdity. It is easy to see that the different, even contrary, handling of the same compositional principle springs from the difference in the problem or the goal. In the motet, imitation is very closely related to the text and functions only as a means to an end, to coordinate the music with the text in a logical manner. In the ricercar such a relationship does not exist. Imitation is employed for its own sake, as a purely musical device. It inspires the composer to new solutions, indeed to intentional complications such as augmentation, diminution, inversion, and polythematic texture—things that would be completely out of place in the motet. Thus the ricercar emerges as a thoroughly independent and autonomous type, with only a point of departure in common with the motet.

GIROLAMO CAVAZZONI AND BUUS

Girolamo Cavazzoni's four works of 1543, with which the history of the imitative ricercar starts, exhibit the characteristics of this species.[12] They are rather long compositions, each comprising about one hundred measures and consistsing essentially of a series of imitative sections. In relation to their length, the number of sections—or, to put it differently, subjects—is rather small: The first ricercar is constructed from four subjects, the second from nine, and the third and fourth from seven or perhaps eight. A pervading-imitation motet of the same length would surely need about twenty subjects or motifs. The peculiarity of the ricercar asserts itself in the fulness with which many of the subjects are presented. Sections with eight or nine subject entries appear several times, and sometimes the number of imitations reaches seventeen and nineteen. The joy of thematic exploration, which is so characteristic of the imitative ricercar, announces itself here. The chordal element, which plays such an important role in the earliest ricercars, is totally excluded, but not the toccata-like passage work. Each of the first three ricercars by Girolamo contains a passage with ascending and descending scales, which, however, are not supported by chords (as they usually are in toccatas), but by contrapuntal voices. The basic construction of Cavazzoni's four ricercars may be read from the following schematic presentation:

No.1: A || B || C || D — || E — $\wedge\!\wedge$ —
(upper: 16, 41, 56, 60, 67 76, 82, 87–95; lower: 5, 17, 5, 4, 4)

No.2: A || B(s) || C || D || E(s) || F(s) || G $\wedge\!\wedge$ || H(s) || I(s)
(upper: 17, 19, 31, 40, 46, 53 62, 68, 90–99; lower: 7, 7, 6, 3, 4, 9, 8, 13, 7)

No.3: A || B(s) || C(s) || $\wedge\!\wedge$ || D || E || F || G || H || I
(upper: 14, 20, 38, 46, 73, 80, 88, 96, 103–114; lower: 5, 4, 19, 12, 5, 3, 6, 4, 3)

No.4: A || B(s) — || C || D(s) || E, E' || F(s)
(upper: 14, 23, 29, 37, 54, 84–101; lower: 5, 9, 6, 6, 9 8, 9)

A, B, etc., indicate the various subjects, — contrapuntal sections without subject, $\wedge\!\wedge$ sections with passage work. The upper series of numbers indicates measure numbers, the lower one the number of imitations in the thematic sections. Subjects that are treated mostly in stretto, are symbolized by (s).

Fig.163

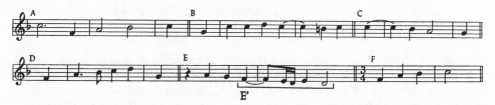

Obviously such schematic presentations give only a general contour of a work, and do not do justice to Cavazzoni's ricercars, which are distinguished from later ones by a greater freedom and elasticity of treatment. The fourth ricercar is particularly interesting and impressive. Its subjects are given in Fig.163. In their individuality, and even more in their succession, we recognize artistic purpose and great musical sensitiveness: for example, in the contrast between the sustained character of the first subject and the lively rhythm of the second; or in the change from descending to ascending motion that pairs the third subject with the fourth, and the last two with each other. Subjects A, D, and F are related by the use of the same melodic segment (*f a b♭ c′*). Is this planned or accidental? It is certainly not planned in the sense of conscious transformation, as it occurs in Frescobaldi's variation ricercars and canzonas, but it is probably not sheer accident either—not an accident we can disregard, but rather the result of an immanent inclination toward form, which imbues the work with a feeling of unity.

The fifth idea is the subject of an unusually extended imitative section. At the start the full subject (E) is heard only once, and then is immediately shortened to become a motif (E'), which occurs in repeated strettos, all pushed together into the space of six measures, as though by an outside force. This is followed by a chordal transition of a few measures, in which the musical events quiet down. They soon lead to the reentry of the complete subject, which is now presented fully in several imitations. The proudly ascending motion and triple meter of the sixth subject (F) are in strong contrast to the falling lines of the preceding section, in which (F) is clearly anticipated (meas.74: *d f g a*). At the very end (F) is heard once more, triumphantly broadened, and supported by full chords.

Another detail worth noting is that the first subject of ricercar no.1 appears at the end of the section in augmented note values, as shown in Fig.164. This is probably the earliest example in the evolution of the organ ricercar of the use of augmentation. It is exploited consciously as an important structural principle in Andrea Gabrieli's works, but appears only as a spontaneous inspiration in Cavazzoni's. Despite their dependence on the imitative technique, Cavazzoni's ricercars generally preserve the character of freedom and freshness. It is exactly this trait that gives them their chairm and artistic value.

Fig.164

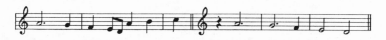

In the 1540s and 50s several collections of ricercars appeared in the form of part books; *Musica nova accomodata per cantar et sonar sopra organi et altri strumenti*, 1540, with works by Julio Segni, Willaert, and others (cf. note 8); *Recercari da cantare et sonare d'organo et altri stromenti*, 1547 and 1549, by Jacques Buus; *Fantesie et recerchari da cantare et sonare per ogni instrumento*, 1549, by Giuliano Tiburtino; *Fantasie recercari contrapunti per cantare e suonare d'ogni sorte di stromenti*, 1551, by Willaert and others; and *Il primo libro de ricercari*, 1556, by Annibale Padovano. The works in these collections have often been included in the evolution of the organ ricercar, but this procedure is not justified. Publications in the form of part books belong to the field of ensemble music, not that of organ or other keyboard music. Moreover it is clear from the original titles that these ricercars were primarily meant as vocal music (*da cantare*), in which each part was presented by a singer as a pure vocalise—a practice that would surely be worth reviving and imitating.[13] Obviously they could be executed just as well on any *stromenti*, i.e., on melody instruments such as viols, recorders, or zinks. They belong to the organ in the same sense and in the same measure that any music created in the 16th century—motets, chansons, or madrigals—can be rewritten in score, provided with the required ornaments, and played on a keyboard instrument.

It is a different case when such a transcription was made by the composer himself, just as original transcriptions by Bach, Mozart, or Brahms belong to a category other than those made by Messrs. X or Y. The only known example of an original transcription is a ricercar from the 1549 part-book print by Buus (*libro secondo*), which reappears as an organ composition in a publication of the same year, *Intabolatura d'organo di recercari* (in clavier score, as the title indicates). Comprising more than 270 measures, it is probably the longest ricercar ever written. O. Kinkeldey has reprinted the organ transcription together with the first 38 measures of the part-book print.[14] We will forego the analysis of this piece, since its chief interest lies in the fact that it demonstrates the intabulation procedure, which is mainly a matter of adding coloraturas and abandoning the consistent differentiation of the voices. Fig.165 reproduces measures 20–22 of both versions. Note how the *d* in the alto in the third measure is dropped in favor of an ornament in the tenor.

Fig.165

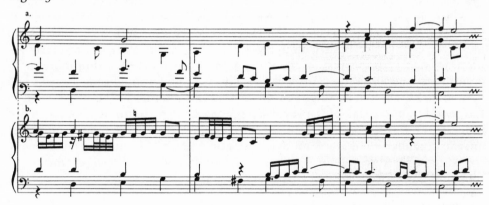

Buus's *Intabolatura* contains three more ricercars; the next one, with 227 measures, approaches the length of the first piece, but the other two keep within more modest limits, about 160 measures each. It has often been maintained that these pieces are also transcriptions from the part-book prints, but this is not the case.[15] We must assume that they are genuine organ ricercars, although they are probably based on a version that presented the four-part texture more clearly than the organ composition does. Like all early ricercars, those by Buus are notated in keyboard score, in which more attention is given to the distribution of the material between the left and right hands, while the definition of the contrapuntal voice leading is neglected. Buus goes even further in this direction than Girolamo Cavazzoni. Four-part passages alternate abruptly with phrases in three or two parts; notes from the same voice are given to either hand as needed; and rests are inserted very sparingly. Often they do not serve to indicate the entry or drop-

Fig.166

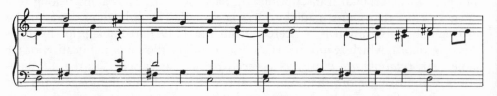

ping out of a part as much as to induce the player to lift a finger, as in measures 47–50 from the *Recercar secondo*, shown in Fig.166.

Despite some arbitrariness in details, the free notation corresponds well to the musical substance, which is formulated freely, with elan, and with great variety. In the preface to his edition of ricercars nos.3 and 4, M. S. Kastner stresses that Buus is unjustly known as a dry and pedantic contrapuntist—a reputation that derives chiefly from the 1547 part-book print of ricercar no.4, published by Wasielewski[16] and by Riemann.[17] It is, indeed, a monstrous work of 223 measures, in which a single subject appears over one hundred times. The other ricercars of the two part-book prints avoid this excessive monotony, and each treats several ideas. Nevertheless sections with thirty, forty, or even fifty entries of a subject are no rarity either. In this respect the three organ ricercars keep within more moderate limits, and also offer some welcome changes in occasional cadence trills and figurations. Occasionally there are things that are unusual in the organ style of the period (not to speak of the vocal style), e.g., the deft stretto of a concise motif in measures 92–98 from the *Recercar secondo*, given in Fig.167, which produces an effect similar to that of motivic work in the 17th century. The thematic structure of the three organ ricercars may be outlined as follows (cf. the corresponding table for Cavazzoni's ricercars, p.173):

Fig.167

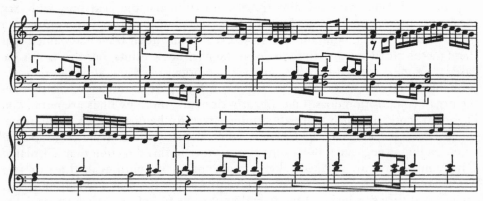

No.2: A $\overset{50}{-}$ || $\overset{58}{B}$ || $\overset{73}{C}$ || $\overset{91}{D(s)}$ $\overset{99}{-}$ || $\overset{106}{E(s)}$ $\overset{124}{-}$ || $\overset{133\ 149}{F}$ $-$ || $\overset{164\ 173}{G}$ $-$ || $\overset{184\ 200-227}{H}$ $-$

$\quad\quad\ \underset{11}{}\quad\ \underset{2}{}\quad\ \underset{9}{}\quad\ \underset{8}{}\quad\quad\ \underset{10}{}\quad\quad\ \underset{7}{}\quad\ \underset{5}{}\quad\ \underset{6}{}$

No.3: A || $\overset{88}{B}$ || $\overset{123-158}{C}$

$\quad\quad\ \underset{38}{}\quad\ \underset{10}{}\quad\ \underset{11}{}$

No.4: A || $\overset{40}{B}$ || $\overset{53}{C}$ || $\overset{62\ 86}{D}$ $-$ || $\overset{93}{E}$ || $\overset{116-165}{F}$

$\quad\quad\ \underset{11}{}\quad\ \underset{3}{}\quad\ \underset{4}{}\quad\ \underset{9}{}\quad\quad\ \underset{8}{}\quad\ \underset{18}{}$

Ricercars nos.2 and 4 have about the same number of subjects as Cavazzoni's, but since they are much longer, this amounts to a tendency to limit the number of subjects. This tendency is quite unmistakable in the *Recercar terzo*, which has only three subjects, and devotes more than half the composition to the first one. In the *Recercar secondo* considerable space is given to free counterpoint. Buus does not use toccata-like passage work, at least not at cadence points as Cavazzoni does. In the free and elastic use of his subjects, Buus goes even beyond Cavazzoni. It is often uncertain in which measure or in which voice a suggestion of a subject or a free formulation is intended. Thus it must be understood that the numbers given in the schematic outlines are intended to indicate only an approximate picture of the frequency of the various subjects. There are, moreover, a number of sections that are not based on genuine subjects but on brief motifs, such as ascending or descending scale fragments or other characteristic progressions, which repeatedly emerge in the texture. Section H of the *Recercar secondo* is based on the motif ($|-g\ a\ b\ |\ c'-b\ |$), which appears in many rhythmic variants; and a similar motif ($|-d\ f\ g\ |\ f$) dominates section B of the *Recercar terzo*. In the final section (C) of this ricercar, the motif $a\ b\flat\ a$ (or $d\ e\flat\ d$) in various note values is heard again and again; it is also heard with the first note repeated, e.g., as ($|\ a-a\ a\ |\ b\flat-a-\ |$); and shortly before the end Buus uses this pattern in greatly lengthened note values in the bass. Similarly, the motif of section B appears twice in augmentation, first in the bass and then in the soprano (cf. Kastner's new ed., p.6, lines 3 and 4).

Buus almost always puts his subjects in the highest or lowest part, not in a middle voice where they would not be heard as easily. Whether this is a virtue or a fault, it certainly proves that in composing his organ ricercars Buus did not proceed as a learned contrapuntist, but as a practical musician.

ANDREA GABRIELI

Andrea Gabrieli's ricercars are preserved in two posthumous publications, 1595 and 1596. Although Andrea was about fifteen years older than Girolamo Cavazzoni, his ricercars represent a later stage of development. They were probably written about 1560, for Andrea Gabrieli seems to have become active as a composer only in his later years.[18] The relationship of the two Italian masters may have been similar to that between the slow-maturing Haydn and the precocious Mozart.

Gabrieli's *Libro secondo* (1595) contains 11 of his ricercars (and 2 by his nephew Giovanni), his *Libro terzo* (1596) offers 6 more, all identified by key designations (*primo tono, secondo tono,* etc.). There are 4 more pieces in the *Libro quinto* of 1605, all called *ricercari ariosi,* and 3 that are derived from chansons (*Ricercar sopra Martin menoit,* etc.); these pieces are discussed later (cf.p.199) in connection with the canzona. No other composer was so intensely occupied with this species, and none contributed so decisively to its evolution as this Venetian master. In his hands the ricercar acquired the character, which it preserved during its later development, that of a strict contrapuntal setting entirely dominated by imitation, making conscious and systematic use of the devices of "higher counterpoint." The ricercar thus became a display piece for musical learnedness, and was still used in this manner by Bach.

Gabrieli's ricercars, like all his works for organ, are printed as an *intabulatura,* i.e., on two staves, like those by Cavazzoni and Buus. Nevertheless their contrapuntal character as four-part settings is carried through much more strictly than in Buus's music. Genuine free voices rarely occur, unless we count the absence of rests where a part pauses for some time. The chief collection in the *Libro secondo* (designated as II in the following discussion) is ordered according to the twelve Church modes, but the *primo tono* is represented twice and the pieces in *ottavo* and *decimo tono* are added by Giovanni to complete the cycle. The *Libro terzo* (which we shall call III) contains one ricercar each in *primo* and *secondo tono* and two each in *quinto* and *nono.*[19]

One indication that Gabrieli's ricercars represent a later stage of evolution than Cavazzoni's and Buus's is that the tendency toward limiting the number of subjects goes one step further, arriving, in some instances, at a monothematic composition. Of the seventeen ricercars in II and III, only one (II, 5), which has five subjects, is comparable to Cavazzoni's in this respect. Five of Gabrieli's ricercars use only three subjects each, six are based on two, and the remaining five are constructed from single subjects.

Another sign of a later date is the extended use of coloratura-like ornaments in sixteenth and thirty-second notes (*fusae* and *semifusae* in the original). In Cavazzoni and Buus such quick figures occur only as cadenza-like passages at the ends of sections and as transitions between them; Gabrieli employs them every-

Fig.168

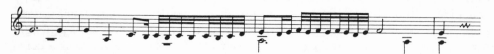

where, often as an integral part of a subject, e.g., in ricercar III, 6 (Fig.168). Although this kind of embroidery is typical of 16th-century practice, it is not an artistic gain, particularly when it occupies so much space in such a serious and, in a way, abstract species as the ricercar. Many products of the visual arts of the late 16th century suffer from a similar excess of ornaments and flourishes. We may be justified in omitting many of the ornaments or at least simplifying them for modern performances of Gabrieli's ricercars.

Gabrieli's most important contribution to the evolution of the ricercar is that he turned it into the medium of the learned style, the "higher counterpoint." In almost all of his ricercars he applies at least one of the artifices that have always been considered evidence of contrapuntal mastery: inversion, invertible counterpoint, stretto, augmentation and diminution, or the combination of several subjects. With this step the ricercar moved even farther from the motet and became more a form of its own. The idea of a "monothematic motet" is absurd, and so is a motet in which a subject is sung in quadrupled note values.

An artifice that is not so well known but which nevertheless played an important role in the history of the ricercar is the double subject.[20] The complete subject, A (the first subject is almost always the one involved), consists of two portions, A_1 and A_2, in which A_2 is the counterpoint to the second entrance of A_1. This method can be represented by the schematic formula $\frac{A_1\ A_2}{A_1}$. A_2 is not an indifferent counterpoint, but has thematic significance. Later on the two portions of the subject sometimes reappear in their original combination (as, e.g., in double fugues by Handel), are treated individually, or are sometimes recombined in a different way, as in the example in Fig.169. In this excerpt from ricercar II, 4 the ornaments, which were written out in the original, are indicated by "t".

Fig.169

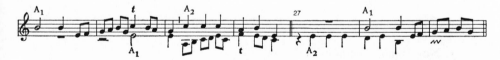

The following table, in which the seventeen ricercars of II and III are schematically presented, is similar to the table of Cavazzoni's ricercars above, but without the lower series of numbers that indicated the number of imitations (cf. p.173). The symbols A^2, A^3, A^4 indicate augmentation by doubling, tripling, and quadrupling the note values; $A_{1,2}$ a double subject; A/B the contrapuntal combination of two subjects; A^i the inversion of a subject; and A(i) the subject in both its normal and its inverted form. The figures after the title, such as (1, 3), refer to volume and page in Pidoux G.

Libro secundo (II)

1. Primo tono (1, 3)   A $\parallel$ A^4 ; A^2 $\parallel$ A^3
   (with markers: 49 over A^4; 98–128 over A^3)

2. Primo tono alla quarta alta (1, 8)   A $\parallel$ A^4/A $\parallel$ A^2/A
   (35 over A^4/A; 78–114 over A^2/A)

3. Secondo tono alla quarta (1, 12)   A $\parallel$ A^4/A
   (47–99 over A^4/A)

4. Terzo tono (2, 26)   A$_{1,2}$ $\parallel$ B $\parallel$ B/C
   (32 over B; 45–65 over B/C)

5. Quarto tono (2, 29)   A $\parallel$ B(e) $\parallel$ C(e) $\parallel$ D(e) $\parallel$ E(s)
   (34 over B(e); 67 over C(e); 76 over D(e); 97–128 over E(s))

6. Quinto tono (1, 16)   A$_{1,2}$(i) $\parallel$ B/A$_1$ $\parallel$ C(s) $\parallel$ A$_1$^{1}
   (58 over B/A$_1$; 71 over C(s); 76–82 over A$_1$^{1})

7. Sesto tono (1, 20)   A $\parallel$ A/B $\parallel$ C
   (23 over A/B; 50–100 over C)

8. Settimo tono (1, 24)   A$_{1,2}$ $\parallel$ B(s) $\parallel$ C(s)
   (25 over B(s); 41–65 over C(s))

9. (10.) Nono tono (1, 28)   A $\parallel$ B $\parallel$ A(i)
   (42 over B; 51–112 over A(i))

10. (12.) Undecimo tono (1, 33)   A$_{1,2}$
    (1–49 over A$_{1,2}$)

11. (13.) Duodecimo tono (1, 36)   A$_{1,2}$ $\parallel$ B(i); A$_1$, A$_2$
    (54–88 over B(i))

Libro terzo (III)

1. Primo tono (2, 3)   A
   (1–47 over A)

2. Secondo tono (2, 6)   A$_{1,2}$ $\parallel$ B(s)
   (26–58 over B(s))

3. Quinto tono (2, 10)   A $\parallel$ B
   (39–98 over B)

4. Quinto tono (2, 14)   A $\parallel$ B
   (21–48 over B)

5. Nono tono alla quarta alta (2, 16)   A $\parallel$ A/B
   (20–64 over A/B)

6. Nono tono (2, 19)   A $\parallel$ B $\parallel$ C(s)
   (26 over B; 65–118 over C(s))

Among the monothematic ricercars III, 1 is outstanding for its simplicity. It is limited to the presentation of one, very long subject, which appears fourteen times in 47 measures, mostly in stretto. Exactly because of this feature it seems to be the most progressive work of all; it may almost be called a fugue. The beginning is shown in Fig.170. In II, 10 we see the seeds of the double fugue of Bach or Handel. But the two portions of the double subject are exploited separately more than was usual later on. (In the 18th century subjects of this kind, consisting of

Fig.170

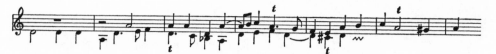

an antecedent and a consequent phrase, were called *andamento*.) The remaining monothematic ricercars (II, 1; II, 2; II, 3) are divided into sections devoted to different contrapuntal approaches, a method that probably represents the chief difference between the older imitative types and the genuine fugue. The structure is based on the principle of augmentation, as the composer repeatedly seizes the opportunity to employ the original subject as a counterpoint against its own augmentation, similar to what Bach did in his *Art of Fugue;* see, e.g. meas.35–41 of II, 2 (Fig.171).

Fig.171

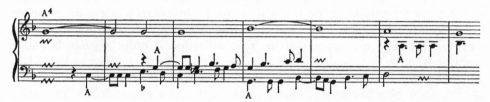

Among the ricercars with two subjects, three (III, 2; III, 3; III, 4) have the simple structure A B; in other words, they consist of two monothematic ricercars without a break. In the first two pieces the two sections are connected by introducing the second subject as the counterpoint of the last presentation of the first one. In another bi-thematic ricercar, III, 5, this contrapuntal combination continues throughout the second section; and in II, 9 a third section develops the first subject in inversion. The contrapuntal artifices applied in Ricercar II, 11 (no. 13 in the original count, which includes the two ricercars by Giovanni Gabrieli) are particularly interesting. In the first section the two portions of a double subject (Fig.172a.) are combined in various ways. At one point the second portion appears in inversion (Fig.172b.). The second section introduces a new subject and its inversion (Fig.172c.); the new subject is also combined with both portions of the original (double) subject (Fig.172d.).

The ricercars with more than two subjects do not add anything new to this picture, except for II, 6, whose wealth of contrapuntal artifices makes it the equal of II, 11. In the first section a double subject is answered by its own inversion, and thus becomes the earliest example of a so-called inversion fugue. Again the two portions of the subject are largely developed independently. Thus in measure 7 A_2, rather than $A_1 + A_2$, enters in the third voice. In measure 71 A_1 appears in

Fig.172

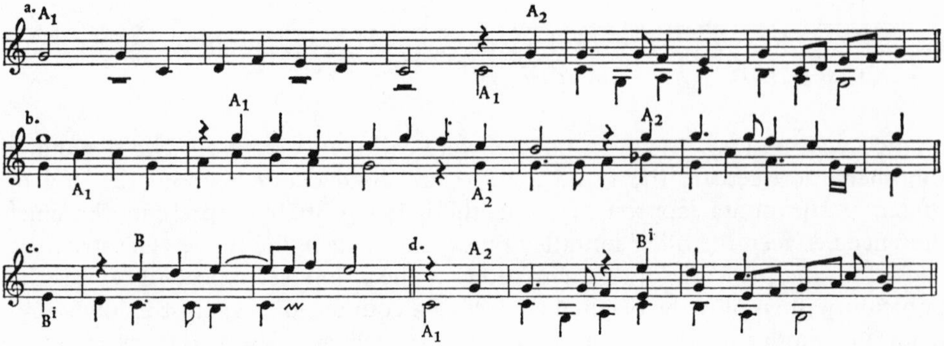

the bass in halved note values, the only known example of diminution in Gabrieli's ricercars.

The table on p.180 shows that the ricercars of the *Libro terzo* are contrapuntally simpler than those in the *Libro secondo*. Is this mere accident or are there two different phases of development in Gabrieli's style? If so, which is the earlier one? The thematic elaboration of the first collection is more mature, but it is doubtful whether this is the decisive factor. At all events, a ricercar like III, 1 anticipates the simple fugue, while the ricercars of the *Libro secondo* are the starting point of a historical evolution that comes to a climax in Bach's *Art of Fugue*.

PADAVANÒ, BERTOLDO, AND MERULO

Annibale Padovano's ricercars published in 1556 (cf.Chap.6, note 18) belong to the field of ensemble music and are related to the organ, if at all, with the same reservations as the ricercars of Willaert, Tiburtino, and others. However, two genuine organ ricercars by Annibale are preserved in a print that appeared in 1604—almost thirty years after his death—under the title *Toccate et ricercari d'organo del eccelentissimo Annibal Padoano*.[21] Their thematic structures may be presented as follows:

No.1: A $\overset{13}{\|}$ A/B $\overset{47}{\|}$ B $\overset{58}{\|}$ C $\overset{77-108}{\|}$ D(s)   No.2: A $\overset{40}{\|}$ B $\overset{58}{\|}$ B/C $\overset{80-101}{\|}$ C

Padovano evidently develops one of Gabrieli's ideas; he provides continuity among the various sections by introducing a new subject as a counterpoint to the preceding one, and then treating it independently. In the first ricercar this method is applied to subject B, in the second to subject C. In its own way each composition tries to enlarge the traditional limits of the tonal resources of the 16th century. In the first ricercar it is done by using an unusual key, *D* major; in the second, by using a first subject that consists of the intervals of a seventh chord; a third subject in lively motion points ahead to the style of the Baroque era. Fig.173 shows the three subjects of the second ricercar. The progressive character of these details justifies the assumption that Padovano wrote these ricercars shortly before his death, around 1570. Also progressive, but not in a good sense, is the frequent employment of the figure that appears at the end of Fig.173 and serves to "ornament" an ascending third. It is particularly disturbing when it occurs three times in rapid succession, as in measure 25 of the second ricercar.

Fig.173

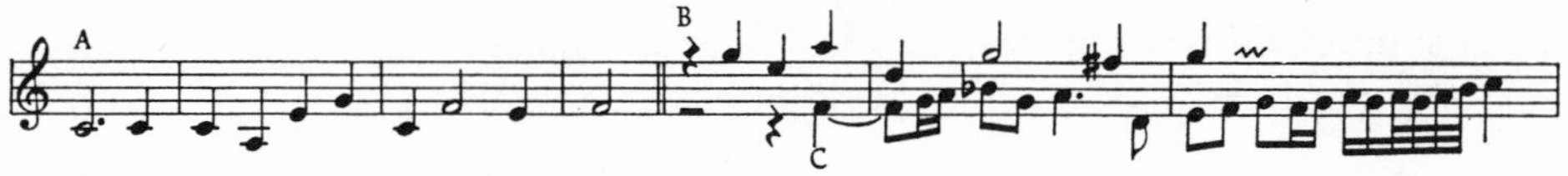

Three ricercars are contained in the posthumous print *Tocate ricercari et canzoni francese intavolate per sonar d'organo* (1591) by the organist of the Padua cathedral, Sperindio Bertoldo (c.1530–70). The first, *del sesto tuono*, has as its subject (| c' — a d' | c' f' — e' | f'), which is only very lightly developed. Bach used exactly the same subject as the basis of his great organ fugue in *E flat* major. The other two ricercars, *del primo* and *del terzo tuono*, are shortened and some-what ornamented intabulations of two ensemble ricercars (nos.IV and I) from Annibale Padovano's *Ricercari* of 1556 (cf.Chap.6, note 18).[22]

Claudio Merulo (1533–1604) left four prints containing ricercars, but only one is important to us, the *Ricercari d'intabolatura d'organo, libro primo*, published in 1567 (reprinted in 1605). The other three are *Ricercari da cantare a 4 voci* (1574, 1607, 1608), published in part books, in other words, ensemble music for four singers. The first collection contains eight ricercars averaging one hundred measures in length. They are entered in the order of the eight church modes (*primo, secondo . . . tuono*), but with the fifth and sixth modes replaced by the eleventh and twelfth, which merely underscores the fact that Lydian had in effect become Ionian (major).[23] Five ricercars (in modes I, II, IV, XI, and XII) are transposed down a fifth; one (in mode VIII) is transposed twice, i.e., from G to *F*.

Two of Merulo's ricercars (in modes I and VII) approach the ricercar type of Girolamo Cavazzoni, for they use a relatively large number of subjects—seven or eight. The others mostly employ three or four subjects. The monothematic ricercar, which plays such an important role in Andrea Gabrieli's works, is not represented at all. Ricercar II comes closest; it is based almost entirely on one idea (A) and its inversion (A¹), though beginning in measure 40 a second subject (B) is added, first as a counterpoint to A¹, then independently. Toward the end of

Fig.174

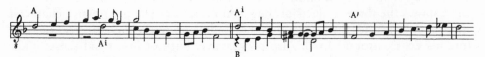

the ricercar (meas.8off.) the main idea and its inversion appear in modified forms (cf.A′ in Fig.174).

Except for this "inversion fugue," Merulo's ricercars contain none of the artifices of the higher counterpoint, which Andrea Gabrieli had introduced. Even such a simple and obvious device as the double subject is used only once, in the first section of ricercar VII, whose beginning is given in Fig.175.

Fig.175

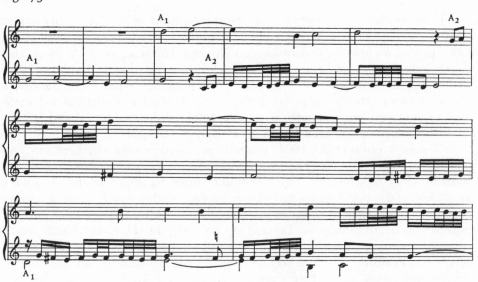

Merulo's contrapuntal style suffers from a lack of sharp rhythmic contour and individuality. The voices move in quarter notes almost throughout, and one has to look far and wide for a passage in which a voice stands out from its surroundings, e.g., by dint of a pithy motion in eighth notes. The example in Fig.175 seems to contradict this statement, but in reality the rhythmic liveliness is limited to stereotyped ornaments. There are frequent and unpleasant appearances of the figure already noted in connection with Gabrieli and Annibale Padovano. Only in his canzonas and toccatas did Merulo develop a technique of ornamentation that is individual and artistically significant.

Twelve ricercars in *primo* to *duodecimo tuono* are printed by Diruta in the *Seconda Parte del Transilvano* (1609, 1622): two by Luzzaschi (1545–1607, Ferrara), four by Gabriele Fatorini (born c.1575, organist at Faenza), two by Adriano Banchieri (1567–1634), and four by Diruta himself.[24] The fact that they all have the same length, 24 breve measures, indicates that these ricercars are not genuine compositions but rather illustrative examples written on commission. The two pieces contributed by Luzzaschi, are probably the most remarkable. The first, a *Ricercare del primo tono*, is based on the subject (| $d - a -$ | $a - d' -$ |); the second, *del secundo tono*, is based on its inversion: (| $d' - a -$ | $a - d -$ |). The print also contains a more extended ricercar by Diruta, of which he says: "qual feci nel principio de' miei studii con le fughe riverse" (I made this at the beginning of my studies of inversion fugues). He inserts this inversion fugue in order to illustrate how one makes an *intavolatura* on two staves from an open score.

I have been unable to obtain a copy of a print by Ottavio Bariola, *Ricercate per sonar d'organo,* published in Milan in 1585. Frotscher, who evidently consulted one, describes Bariola as an "emulator of Merulo, who transforms the mobility and technical complexity of his model into superficial effects."[25] These ricercars are probably preserved in the Turin tablature, Giordano collection 8, together with hitherto unknown ricercars by Biancardi and Francesco Porta.[26]

RODIO AND VALENTE

The Neapolitans Rocco Rodio and Antonio Valente were discussed in connection with liturgical organ music. Rodio's *Libro primo di ricercate* of 1575 contains five ricercars.[27] The thematic structure of the first four may be presented as follows:

No.1: A || B(s) || C(s) || Coda
No.2: || A², A♭, A♯, A⁴
No.3: A, A² || B(s) || C || D, D♯
No.4: A/B || C(s), A, B || A³, A'

In the first ricercar the second idea (d | g -f e a | -g fe $d -$ |) is treated strikingly in strettos of varied interval and range. The four-measure coda is a brilliant little virtuoso piece, in which a rapid figure is presented with surprising finger acrobatics. Fig.176 shows the next to the last measure.[28] Such things are

Fig.176

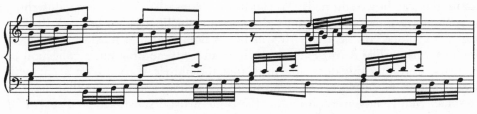

completely outside the stylistic limits of the ricercar, but are the first signs of the virtuosic early Baroque.

The second ricercar has only one subject, which is presented quite ingeniously in various rhythmic shapes.

The fourth ricercar begins with a section in which two subjects are used; right in the first exposition A is answered by B. This very unusual method is also found in a ricercar by Antegnati (no.2; cf.p.412). As Kastner notes,[29] Rodio's ricercar is also quite progressive in its harmony and modulation. The passage given in Fig.177 is remarkable for its use of a *D sharp* and for a voice leading that contradicts all the rules of Palestrina counterpoint. Passages like it announce the advent of the *seconda prattica*.

Fig.177

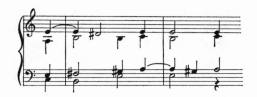

The fifth of Rodio's ricercars represents the high point of his work in this field. It was not included in the above table because its essential features cannot be presented in a schematic outline. As in the second ricercar, only one subject is presented in various rhythmic shapes, which cannot be defined by such categories as augmentation or diminution. Rodio rather aims at subjecting the five notes of the main idea—recognizable as the well-known *Lascia fare mi (la sol fa re mi)*— to the most fanciful rhythmic formulations. This ricercar takes a well-deserved place between two famous compositions on the same subject: Josquin's *Missa La sol fa re mi* and Frescobaldi's *Capriccio sopra Lascia fare mi*.

In the preface to his publication of Rodio's works, M. S. Kastner quotes a passage from F. Abbiati's *Storia della musica* (1943), in which Rodio is called an "arido contrappuntista e spirito conservatore." Kastner disagrees with this characterization and says that, on the contrary, Rodio's ricercars prove him to be a "contrappuntista alacre, artista abilissimo dotato d'immaginazione."[30] We do not need to say how right he is: To call Rodio "conservatore" is certainly wrong. In general we must guard against the common inclination to criticize the old ricercars as "dry" or "learned." It was not so long ago that musicians spoke in similar terms of *The Art of Fugue,* which is, after all, nothing but a collection of ricercars. Certainly this does not mean that the old ricercars are on a par with Bach's unique masterpiece, and some are really so long and uniform that they are tiresome. Many, however, thrive on the same artistic substance as *The Art of*

Fugue, and anyone who reveres this work as one of the greatest musical creations will probably find quite a few of the old ricercars worth his attention. Rocco Rodio's fifth ricercar is one.

The *Intavolatura de cimbalo* by the blind Neapolitan, Antonio Valente, appeared one year after the publication of Rodio's print. Its six ricercars are noteworthy primarily because of the variety of their formulation. The first one, *Recercata del primo tono a cinque con la quinta parte in canone al unisono del tenore,* starts as usual with imitative entries of the five voices, the third and fourth of which continue throughout the 100 measures of the composition as a canon at the distance of four measures. The subject enters only three more times, twice in the bass and once in the soprano (meas.26, 34, and 42). Thus the idea of the ricercar has been radically altered.

The same method is applied to the fourth ricercar, *Recercata del sesto tono a quattro voce con lo basso in canone a l'ottava del contralto,* but the subject is more consistently developed, within the canon as well as in the other two parts. The fifth, *Recercata del septimo tono,* has a very different structure. It is a brief, unusually lively piece, which is based on two interesting subjects, shown in Fig.178a. and b.

Fig.178

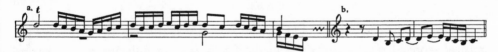

In the other three ricercars (no.2, *primo tono;* no.3, *terzo tono;* and no.6, *ottavo tono*) the contrapuntal-imitative element plays only a secondary role. The subjects serve mostly as points of departure for choral and running passages in the toccata style. The *Recercata del primo tono* starts with a section of about twenty measures in the usual imitative style, but the texture never achieves a genuine four-part aspect, and the vagueness of the voice leading is more akin to a lute texture than to the clavier. The subject (| *d –d ef ge* | *f*) is then heard three times in doubled note values and finally five times in quadrupled note values. But it does not contribute to a contrapuntal texture; it is always the lower or upper voice of chordal settings ornamented by passage work. *Recercata del terzo tono* is more in keeping with the idea of a contrapuntal texture (mostly of two or three parts), but it is completely overrun with stereotyped passages and trills. And Valente is one of the first to use the letter *t* to symbolize ornaments like trills or mordents that are not written out. *Recercata del ottavo tono* begins with an eight-measure section of imitations, followed by two sections in toccata style, the last one in 6/4 time with chordal pulses in a dance-like rhythm of alternating half and quarter notes (meas.31–45).

The Tiento

In Spain the tiento corresponds to the Italian ricercar. Even its name has a similar meaning: *Tentar* literally means "to touch" and has therefore often been equated with *toccare*. In a more general sense, however, it means "to touch intellectually," i.e., "examine" or "scrutinize," the same as the Italian *ricercare*. The musical practice also shows considerable correspondence. The earliest tientos, those in Luis Milan's *El Maestro* (1536), are "studies" in lute playing, very similar to the lute ricercars in the Petrucci prints. When transferred to the organ, the tiento acquired the character of a study in contrapuntal-imitative texture, as was the case with the ricercar.

The earliest source for the organ tiento is the *Libro de cifra nueva* by Venegas de Henestrosa (1557). This collection contains 28 tientos: 4 anonymous, 2 each by de Soto and Vila, 3 each by Julius de Modena (Segno) and Palero, and 14 by Antonio de Cabezón.[31] In addition 12 tientos by Cabezón are preserved in his *Obras de musica* (1578), and about 30 more are extant in a manuscript of the University Library at Coimbra (Ms.242; c.1580), half of which seem to be the work of the Portuguese composer Antonio Carreira, while the rest are mostly anonymous.

CABEZÓN

The largest collection of tientos by one composer is the one by Cabezón. The musical score of the 14 contained in the *Libro de cifra* indicates a very unified character. Except for no.51 they are all written in long note values—semibreves, minims, and semiminims (half, quarter, and eighth notes in our transcription) and show a very quiet motion, such as predominated in the vocal music of the early 16th century. Quick ornaments or toccata-like passages, like those that appear in Marco Antonio's works, are completely absent. In most of these tientos Cabezón uses three or four subjects, the first of which is the most characteristic one, the one most articulately developed. The others are often taken from the common stock of motet motifs (Gombert); in some instances they are only briefly touched on, in others they are presented in numerous strettos. Non-imitative sections are frequently inserted. Possibly this indicates a connection with the early, non-imitative ricercar type, which is still recognizable in Italy in the works of Girolamo Cavazzoni, but disappears completely in Andrea Gabrieli's. In the tiento the free-contrapuntal texture continued in use throughout the 16th century and occupied an even greater role in the 17th. Almost all of Cabezón's tientos contain a number of rather long sections that must be called non-imitative. They do not exclude the possibility of occasional use of imitation, but it is done only by way of suggestion, as motifs enter and disappear, change or yield to others, and lead to new developments and events. It is because of this totally free treatment of

Fig.179

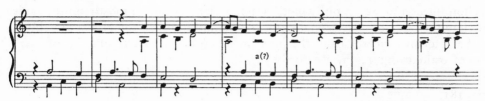

the contrapuntal-imitative texture that these sections are among the most interesting creations of the 16th century in this field.

The artifices of imitative counterpoint are limited—as in the ricercars of Girolamo Cavazzoni—to the stretto, which is used especially with subjects of a more conventional type. In a few tientos a subject occasionally occurs in inversion, e.g., in no.16, measures 21ff., and in no.26, measures 21ff. Only very rarely does Cabezón involve the augmentation of a subject, as in no.32, measure 7. Being exceptions, such singular instances only confirm the fact that the various artifices of strict counterpoint, which play so important a role in the Italian ricercar of Andrea Gabrieli and his successors, are basically alien to the Spanish tiento, not only to Cabezón's but also to those of the later organists of the Spanish peninsula.

On the other hand, we find certain techniques that never entered into the strictly systematic construction of the Italian ricercar. One of these is the use of extended duet sections, such as the ones in no.31, measures 82–94, and no.51, measures 74–83 and 88–96, and the development of imitations into a kind of ostinato. In no.26, measures 45ff., a two-part combination is heard four times in a row, alternating between the two lower and the two upper parts, in a Josquin-like manner (Fig.179). The ostinato character is even clearer in the concluding section of tiento no.36, where a motif of remarkable contour (*d | a c′ a d | a*), is heard four times in a row in the bass (meas.125–39). The most remarkable tiento in this respect (and others) is no.44, which Anglés justifiably calls "una de las piezas más inspiradas."[32] It is 182 semibreve measures in length and has at least ten subjects, surpassing all the others in both respects. In measures 61–69 a brief phrase is repeated four times almost without change, while the upper part consists of a single pitch sounded four times, like a bell tone (cf.Fig.180)—reminiscent of Busnois' famous motet *Anthoni usque limina*. Immediately thereafter a subject

Fig.180

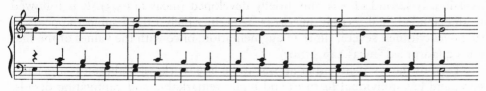

(e″ | c″ d″ e″ a′ |) is heard five times in a row in the soprano. In the extended final section (meas.136–82), a pithy motif appears eighteen times, mostly on the same pitch in the bass, but occasionally transposed and in other voices. Fig.181 shows a characteristic excerpt from the bass (meas.149ff.), which recalls the frequent use of ostinato figures by Redford.

Fig. 181

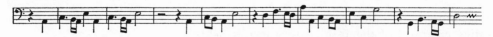

The twelve tientos preserved in the *Obras de musica* form a compact group (fols.50–68v).[33] The six odd-numbered pieces in particular harbor many novelties. They make extended use of small note values, i.e., *fusae* and occasionally *semi-fusae* (sixteenth and thirty-second notes in our transcription), while the even-numbered ones show the quiet motion that prevails almost exclusively in the *Libro de cifra*. The six livelier tientos surely belong to Cabezón's later works, between 1557 (the date of the publication of the *Libro de cifra nueva*) and 1566 (the year of his death). The other six were probably composed earlier, and Hernando was surely aware of this fact when he consistently placed an earlier work after one from his father's last period.

The older tientos (or, in any case, those written in an earlier style) do not add any new features to the picture sketched above. Two of them are based on borrowed subjects: *Tiento sobre Qui la dira* (Pedrell H; IV, 55) on a chanson by Crecquillon, and *Tiento sobre Cum Sancto Spiritu* (VII, 9) on the corresponding section from Josquin's *Missa de Beata Virgine*. It is very interesting to compare the latter with its model. Cabezón treats only two brief motifs of the Mass movement imitatively; he does this at the beginning, and then abandons imitation completely in the rest of the tiento. Instead he adds new counterpoints to extended quotations from Josquin's music, e.g., to the entire soprano melody for the *Amen*.

The *Tiento de tercer tono* (IV, 59) unmistakably shows the influence of the Gabrieli type of ricercar. From beginning to end it is worked strictly imitatively, lacking entirely the free-contrapuntal sections that are so characteristic of Cabezón's other tientos in the earlier style. It starts with a long imitative section of 113 measures that systematically employs the techniques of the double subject and inversion. A second idea is only briefly developed (meas.113–43). It is followed by an extended final section (meas.143–262), in which a third subject appears at least twenty times, several times in augmentation, once with the values of the first notes quadrupled (meas.229, tenor).

Each of the six tientos that appear to be late works of Cabezón is a masterpiece, and has individual features and many remarkable and captivating details.

The use of smaller note values marks them externally as a group, and they also have a common tendency toward longer and more characteristic subjects. Fig.182 shows the most remarkable ones, among them some whose chromatic steps transcend the usual limitations of the 16th century and point to the Baroque era. (The number of the tientos is indicated by I, II, etc., the subjects by A, B, etc.) Many features in these tientos suggest and anticipate the Baroque, but they often occur side by side with formulae that recall the style of the late Gothic era. We have the impression that two very different, yet somehow related, periods—both with an inclination toward tension, intensity, and pathos—join hands, while the tendencies toward evenness, clarity, and balance, usually regarded as the essential achievements of the Renaissance, are disregarded.

Fig.182

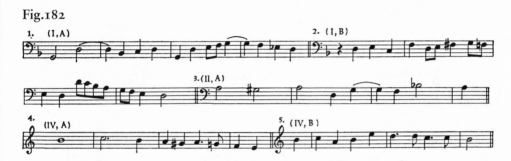

The first tiento (Pedrell H; IV, 46) is based on two long subjects (cf.Fig.182, 1. and 2.), the second of which is introduced (Pedrell, H; p.47, meas.7 from the end) as a counterpoint to the first, but thereafter appears independently. Despite their length and individuality, both A and B are presented in strettos; B is even treated in a triple stretto (p.48, meas.8). Fast notes appear only once (near the beginning of p.47), as a purely figural counterpoint to A. Although such decorative counterpoints are common in Cabezón's hymns, they are a real novelty in the tiento. The last presentation of subject B (p.48, line 4) is combined with a counterpoint in triplet rhythm, which takes the form shown in Fig.183 near the end of this passage. After this forceful action the concluding coda, with its soothing, descending lines, has the effect of a propitiatory gesture.

Fig.183

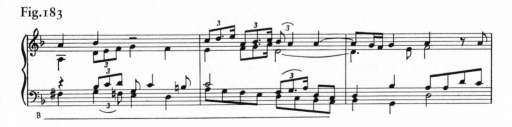

The second of the later tientos will be described at the end of our discussion. The third one (Pedrell H; IV, 57) consists of three thematic sections and a coda. Subject A appears regularly on the tonic or dominant, a procedure that is rarely found in the 16th century. Most of the time B and C are treated in the same way, and are also presented in strettos. Once again the coda has a calming effect after the preceding dangers, but it, too, contains a moment of excitement as the B-minor sixth chord enters as a leading-tone harmony before the C-minor triad (meas.86).

The first and third tientos look like first essays in a new style, but in the fourth one, *Tiento del cuarto tono* (Pedrell H; IV, 63), the style is fully developed and mature. The work is based on four subjects (the first two are shown in Fig.182, 4. and 5.), all of which are presented in strettos, the first one even at its first appearance. As unusual as such a treatment is at the beginning of a tiento, this Josquin-like opening is one of Cabezón's most beautiful innspirations. The other strettos of subject A all differ in their time and pitch intervals. The last presentation of the subject is in the bass, and is combined with the highly expressive lines of a running counterpoint in the two upper parts (Fig.184). With its dotted rhythm the second subject (cf.Fig.182,5.) deviates conspicuously from the usual practice of the 16th century. The third thematic section is in triple meter for contrast.

Fig.184

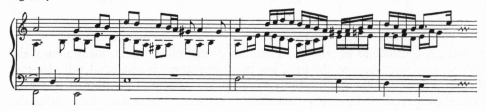

The coda of the next tiento of this group (Pedrell H; IV, 69) is in the style of a *fabordon glosado* (cf.p.135). The use of a complementary figure in measures 110ff. is definitely a Baroque trait.

The *Tiento del sexto tono con primera y segunda parte* (Pedrell H; VII, 2) outstrips all the others in length, with 259 semibreve measures: 177 in the first section and 82 in the second. Five subjects are developed in the first section, and almost every imitative passage is followed by a lengthy postlude in free counterpoint. The last subject is not presented in a point of imitation but in a sixfold sequence with a stretto between tenor and bass (p.5, meas.9 from the end). Finally, at the end of the *primera parte* there is a remarkable extended pedal point on F. The second section starts with two or three motif-like subjects in triple meter, then moves to a subject in duple meter, which is presented in numerous strettos, and concludes with a strangely ununified coda, in which rhythmically intricate sixteenth-note passages suddenly appear and disappear. Although this work contains some interesting details, it is not completely satisfactory.[34]

The *Tiento del primer tono,* the second in the group of the later tientos (Pedrell H; IV, 51), has been saved for last because in every respect it represents the climax of Cabezón's works. It is based on three subjects, the first of which has a bold contour (cf.Fig.182, 3.). In the course of its presentation the upper parts offer figurations of a very individual character and an almost forced, heightened expressivity (meas.29ff.). Even more striking is the insertion of a section in which the sustained starting notes of the subject are transformed into an extremely lively motif through diminution by eight. This motif is then employed in several strettos and as a figural counterpoint to the original form of the subject. Such a procedure is not employed again until fifty years later, by Sweelinck. In similar manner the second subject is transformed into a lively motif, whose dotted

Fig.185

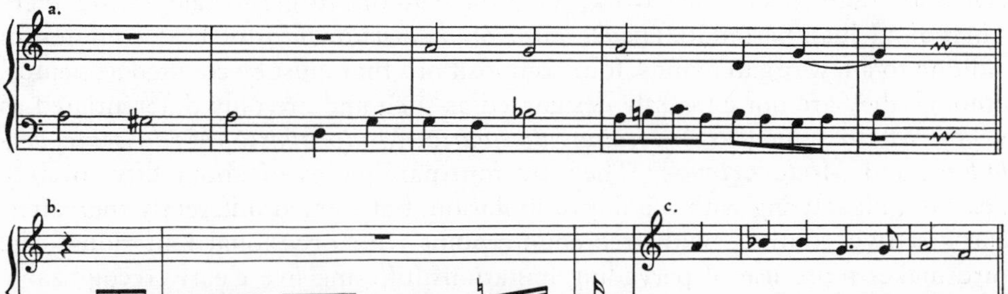

a. beginning, subject A; b. subject A in diminution; c. subject B; d. subject B altered; e. final chorale.

rhythms are a complete novelty in the music of the period. A third idea, presented first in strettos, then with a figural counterpoint, and finally in a free conclusion, is even more astonishing and surprising than what precedes: We suddenly hear, in full chords of the right hand above a variegated running bass in the left, a veritable Lutheran chorale, whose beginning recalls *Vom Himmel hoch da komm ich her*. We shall not try to explain this "heavenly" apparition. Let us take it as the happy inspiration of a musical genius with visionary power, who anticipates the period of Buxtehude and Bach. Fig.185 may illustrate more clearly the masterful work of Cabezón's old age, which we have just tried to describe. Deeper study will uncover many other things to admire in it, e.g., the inner logic in the changing figurations of the "basso continuo," above which the final chorale is heard.

BERMUDO, VILA, DE SOTO, PALERO, AND CARREIRA

Other musicians besides Cabezón were active in the field of the tiento, but we have only fragments of their work. As in the field of liturgical organ music, there is first of all Juan Bermudo. His *Declaración de instrumentos* of 1555 contains, in addition to a few organ hymns, four compositions that must be counted as tientos, although they are not expressly designated as such and are only differentiated as to key: *Modo primero con resabios de quarto, Modo quarto, Modo sexto verdadero,* and *Modo octavo*.[35] They are four-part pieces of about fifty to sixty measures, all starting with a point of imitation, but treated differently thereafter. The first two continue with free counterpoint with occasional imitations. The third makes more use of pervading imitations, offering five clearly recognizable subjects, one of which is even presented in inversion. The last one employs a mixture of free counterpoint and points of imitation. The textural peculiarities observed in Bermudo's organ hymns (cf.p.138) are found here again, even more pronounced. The range of the keyboard is fully exploited, from C up to a″. Despite this large range, everything can be played by the two hands. The left hand frequently involves tenths, but they were easy to reach in the short octave in use during the period (Bermudo described it in detail). In these pieces, too, various oddities occur; to use Pirro's phrase: "on remarquera, comment certaines pauvretés d'écriture y sont rachetées en général par l'empleur et parfois par l'heureuse étrangeté de l'harmonie" (one will note how certain faults of writing are generally ransomed here by the fulness and sometimes by the strangeness of the harmony).[36] Very frequent use is made of the genuine Lydian cadence, with leading tones to both the fifth and octave, which sounds like an archaism from the 14th century. It is found in all the tientos, mostly transposed and leading to the triads of G or D, as in Machaut. Fig.186 shows a few instances.

The *Libro de cifra nueva* by Venegas de Henestrosa, which was published two years after Bermudo's *Declaración* (1557), contains a special collection of

Fig.186

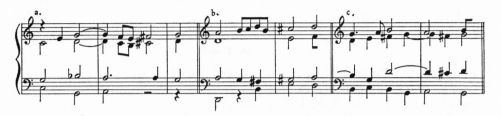

a. *Modo quarto* (meas.34ff.); b. *Modo primero* (meas.42f.); c. *Modo octavo* (meas.13f.).

Tientos de Antonio y de otros tañedoros, comprising nos.34–55 (no.48 is a *Verso de Morales glosado de Palero*). Among the tientos of the "otros tañedoros" there are two by Pedro Alberto Vila (1517–83), organist at Barcelona.[37] They differ from similar works by Cabezón in that they exhibit a more definitely Renaissance-like counterpoint and greater euphony. Vila also published a *Libro de tientos* of his own, which is unfortunately lost. There was a copy in the library of King John IV of Portugal, which was destroyed by the earthquake of 1755.[38]

Francisco de Soto, who served together with Cabezón at the imperial court at Madrid, is also represented among the "otros tañedoros." His two tientos (nos.49 and 50)[39] are imitative only at the start, and otherwise more homophonic, with song-like passages. In general they have a lyrical, graceful character, which clearly contrasts with Cabezón's tientos.

Venegas preserves 14 works by Francisco Fernandez Palero, who is better known than Vila or de Soto. Unfortunately they prove to be rather disappointing; most of them are ornamented intabulations of vocal works, such as the two *Kyries* from Josquin's *Missa de Beata Virgine* (nos.100, 101), motets by Jaquet, Verdelot, and Mouton (nos.114–16), and Spanish romances (nos.104, 105). The original works consist of 2 organ hymns (cf.p.139) and 3 tientos (nos.53–55), which conclude the group "de Antonio y de otros tañedoros." The organ hymns were at least cleanly worked out, but the tientos bear such an obvious stamp of mediocrity, even amateurish uncouthness, that one must wonder why Venegas included them in his collection.

Portuguese organ music appears for the first time in the second half of the 16th century. A number of tientos by Antonio Carreira (c.1525–c.1590) are preserved in Ms. mus. no. 242 of the University Library of Coimbra.[40] In several instances the ascriptions are ambiguous, for the composer is sometimes designated only as *Ca,* which may also apply to Cabezón and in one instance definitely does. The three works published by Kastner are based on one subject each, and they differ from Cabezón's tientos in the lack of non-imitative sections. In this respect they approach the stricter character of the Italian ricercar. These and other stylistic characteristics may decide whether the ambiguously designated tientos belong to Carreira or to Cabezón.

Canzona and Fugue

The earlier assumption that the ricercar developed from vocal music is, as we have seen, hardly valid. This is not the case with the second most important type of imitative clavier music of the 16th century, the *canzona* or, as it is often called, *canzona francese*. Even the name indicates a connection with the French chanson, that combination of light poetry and graceful music that enjoyed unparalleled favor for over one hundred years. Instrumental music could not fail to adopt this species, even though one of the chief attractions of the original, the charming and frequently rather suggestive text, was lost. The earliest examples of this kind are by Jacob Obrecht. Several of his instrumental pieces carry the designation *carmen,* evidently the humanistic translation of *chanson.*

Under this title the first chansons appear in keyboard music—by Paul Hofhaimer and his successors, the "Paulomimes." A *Carmen magistri Pauli* (Moser H, p.110) is a three-part piece of sixteen measures, which falls into four sections, each of which opens with a brief point of imitation on a different motif. In the first motif, with its reiterated notes, the relationship with the chanson is especially plain, as Fig.187 shows (the ornamental notes are given in small notes).

Fig.187

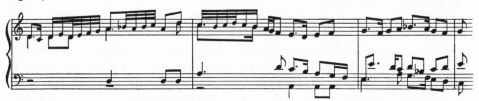

A *Carmen in sol* by Johannes Kotter (Merian T, p.66) is very similar but somewhat more imitative. It, too, begins with a repercussive subject, this time combined with a downward skip of a fifth ($|\ d' - d'\ d'\ |\ g\ ...$). In both cases, as well as in several others, it is difficult to decide whether the pieces are original keyboard compositions in the chanson style or merely intabulations of vocal works. In the first decades of the 16th century the French chanson was certainly transferred to the clavier in Germany, but this episode was brief. Apparently the light, and sometimes even frivolous, character of the French form did not suit the German organists for long.

In Italy it was different. The process apparently started there a little later, but was then developed more consistently, so that the Italian *canzona d'organo* became one of the most important types of keyboard music, one that Bach still knew and cultivated.

MARCO ANTONIO CAVAZZONI AND GIROLAMO CAVAZZONI

The documented history of the organ canzona begins with the print of Marco Antonio da Bologna of 1523. It contains four pieces that bear French designations—*Perdone* (for *Pardonnez*) *moi sie folie, Madame vous aves mon cuor, Plus ne regres,* and *L'autre yor per un matin*—which clearly represent the *Canzoni* included in the title of the print. It is obvious that they are imitations of vocal chansons of the Josquin period, but unfortunately none of the models for the four pieces have been located. Thus it cannot be decided whether Marco Antonio's canzonas are merely ornamented transcriptions or relatively free settings of ideas from chansons. Each canzona has one of the repetitive forms typical of the vocal chanson:

$$\text{I: } \overset{20\ 62}{A\ B\ A} \qquad \text{II: } \overset{22\ 54\ 75}{A\ B\ A}\ \text{Coda} \qquad \text{III: } \overset{23\ 45}{A\ A\ B} \qquad \text{IV: } \overset{19\ 35\ 81}{A\ A\ B\ A}$$

Marco Antonio's canzonas are similar in style to his ricercars, but they lack the latter's grandeur and freedom. Josquin's duo-imitations and the immediate repetition of a duo passage in the higher or lower octave appear repeatedly.

The second stage in the evolution of the Italian organ canzona is represented by Girolamo Cavazzoni, whose role here is very similar to the one he played in the history of the ricercar. He gave the type those features that remained standard for its entire subsequent development: lively movement throughout, four-part texture in an imitative setting, brief and precise subjects presented mostly in strettos, a starting subject that almost always has threefold tone repetition, and frequently the repetition of sections.

His *Intavolatura . . . libro primo* (1543) contains two canzonas: *sopra Il e bel e bon,* based on Passereau's chanson *Il est bel et bon,* and *sopra Falte dargent,* based on Josquin's *Faulte d'argent.*[41] These are definitely not mere intabulations of vocal music; instead Cavazzoni employs the motifs of these chansons to create a new contrapuntal-imitative texture, and treats the subjects in separate imitative sections, as in his ricercars. For example, he extracts two ideas from the beginning of Josquin's *bassus,* each of which is imitated four times, the first subject in measures 1–8, the second in measures 9–17. Fig.188 illustrates this procedure (the original distribution of the notes for the right and left hands is retained). These two imitative sections are followed by a third, which employs the chanson's motif for the words "se je le dis" (| /*d e f♯* | *g*), and by two more based on subjects that do not occur in Josquin's work (| /*d d c♯* | *d b♭ a* — | and | *a -a b♭ g* | *a*). Despite this very different treatment, the A B A form of the chanson is retained. The A contains the first four subjects, and B the fifth. In the canzona *Il e bel e bon,* Passereau's chanson is similarly transformed into a new work.

Fig.188

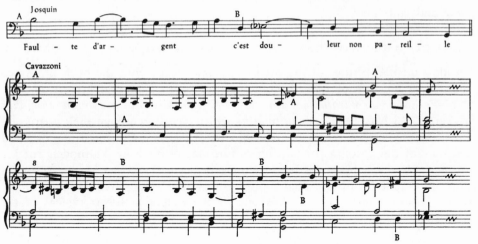

ANDREA GABRIELI, BERTOLDO, AND MERULO

Two of Andrea Gabrieli's posthumous publications are devoted to keyboard canzonas: *Canzoni alla francese per sonar sopra istromenti da tasti, Libro V* and *VI*, both of 1605. They contain pieces with titles such as *Suzanne un jour d'Orlando, Martin menoit di Janequin, Un gai berger di Crequillon,* and *Orsus au coup di Crequillon,* as well as some without indication of authorship, such as *Petit Jacquet, Le bergier,* and *Con lei foss'io.*[42] Several of these canzonas carry the legend "Tabulata di Andrea Gabrieli," and indeed, all those that can be compared with their vocal models prove to be mere intabulations, differing from the originals only in the addition of ornaments. In this matter Andrea goes far beyond what the German colorists dared to do. A particularly crass instance is the *Canzon francese detta Or sus di Jacob* (obviously a wrong attribution, since this is another setting of Crecquillon's *Orsus au coup*), in which the predominantly homophonic model is ornamented from beginning to end with *semifusae* (sixteenth notes; cf. Pidoux G, V, p.23). Thus most of Gabrieli's canzonas belong to the same category as the many hundreds of intabulations that take up so much boring space in 16th-century sources.

But Gabrieli also wrote a few pieces that follow the canzonas of Girolamo Cavazzoni, in which a chanson is not intabulated but freely paraphrased—one could also say parodied. To distinguish them from the intabulated *canzoni,* Gabrieli calls them *ricercari,* but they are a part of the history of the canzona rather than of the ricercar. *Libro V* contains three such "ricercars," on *Martin menoit* (Janequin), *Orsus au coup* (Crecquillon), and *Pour ung plaisir* (Crecquillon); and *Libro VI* includes a fourth, on the madrigal *Con lei foss'io* (Ponte).

Each immediately follows a corresponding "canzona," which offers all the material needed for a comparison, except for *Orsus,* where no recognizable relationship exists between canzona and ricercar. In the chanson or madrigal the motifs follow one another without break. As in Cavazzoni's canzonas, the transformation consists in treating the motifs individually with varying amounts of imitation. For example, measures 12–14 from *Martin menoit* (reproduced in Fig.189 without Gabrieli's ornaments) engender a paraphrase of twice that length in the ricercar (meas.20–27). When the model itself is imitative, Andrea shows how the motif may be imitated in other ways; compare, e.g., measures 20–23 of the canzona with measures 37–43 of the ricercar. The treatment of the madrigal *Con lei foss'io* is especially ingenious; here a purely homophonic vocal piece of forty measures is turned into a strictly contrapuntal paraphrase almost three times as long, with twelve subjects, each in four or more points of imitation. *Martin menoit* uses the same number of motifs, while the other two make do with five or six. The differences between Andrea's chanson-ricercars and his genuine ricercars lie in the large number of subjects, the motet-like technique of pervading imitations without using the artifices of the higher counterpoint, the canzona-like character of many of the subjects, and the confirming repetition of the concluding section (in *Martin menoit* and *Pour ung plaisir*) or the beginning (in *Orsus au coup*).

Fig.189

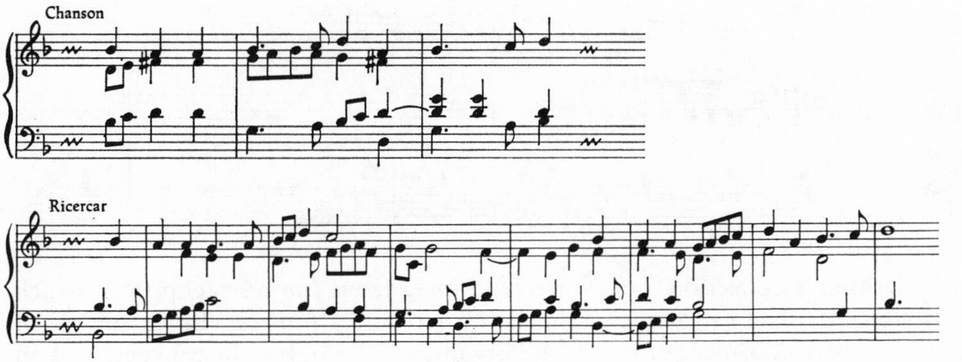

Four compositions entitled *Ricercar arioso,* which are preserved in *Libro V,* are closely related to these canzonas. The appellation evidently indicates a relationship to secular music, which possibly consists in taking subjects from French chansons or Italian canzonets. Indeed, they are far more lively than those on which the ricercars proper are based. In three of these pieces, the repetitions of entire sections are written out, as is usual in the secular vocal repertoire of the 16th century: A A B C C (no.1), A B B (no.3), and A A B C C C (no.4), and in each

Fig.190

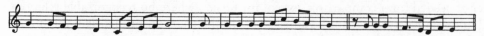

case the final repetition is followed by a coda (*ripresa*) of four measures. In the remaining piece (no.2) the first section (meas.1–12) returns at the end in an ornamented variant. The subjects of the fourth *ricercar arioso*, shown in Fig.190, may give an idea of the general character of these pieces, which are among the most attractive creations in the keyboard repertoire of the 16th century.

In 1591 Giacomo Vincenti of Venice published the *Canzoni francese intavolate per sonar d'organo* by Sperindio Bertoldo (c. 1530–1570), who had been active as the cathedral organist at Padua. This print contained ornamented intabulations of *Un gai berger, Hor vien za vien, Petite fleur,* and *Frais e gagliard.* How conventional the treatment of such intabulations was is shown by Fig.191, in which the beginnings of Andrea Gabrieli's and Bertoldo's settings of *Un gai berger* are reproduced (cf. the new edition mentioned in note 21).

Fig.191

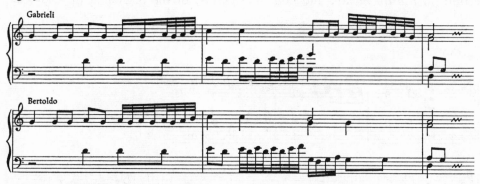

Bertoldo's collection *Tocate ricercari et canzoni francese* (cf.p.183), which was also published in 1591, contains another *canzone francese.* In his volume of canzonas Bertoldo mentions only the organ as the required instrument, and so does Merulo, but Gabrieli speaks of *istromenti da tasti.* One need not take such references too literally, but there is no doubt that the organ was used for secular music much more than one would think today.

Merulo left three books of *Canzoni d'intavolatura d'organo,* published in 1592, 1606, and 1611, the last two of which were brought out posthumously by his nephew Giacinto Merulo. Altogether they contain 23 canzonas. Only five refer to French chansons: *Petit Jacquet* (I, no.9; by Courtois?), *Petite Camusette* (II, no.1; Willaert?), and the three five-part canzonas that constitute the *Terzo*

Libro: Languissans di Crequillon, Content di Crequillon, and *Suzanne un giour di Orlando Lasso.* All the others carry Italian designations, such as were used around 1550 for galliards (cf.p.238): *La Leonora, La Rosa,* and *La Gratiosa,* and also strange names like *La Bovia* ("bove" = ox), *La Zambeccara* ("zambecco" = wild goat), and *La Albergata* ("albergo" = lodging). No models have been found for any of these canzonas; indeed it is very improbable that pieces with such titles are derived from vocal compositions. Manifestly they are intabulations of instrumental ensemble canzonas (*canzone da sonar*), a type that first appears in Florentio Maschera's *Libro primo de canzoni* of 1584, with very similar designations: *La Capriola, La Duranda, La Rosa,* etc. In the third part of his *Nova Musices Organicae Tabulatura,* 1617, Johann Woltz transcribed into tablature a number of such "beautiful, lovely, selected fugues and concerts or, as the Italians commonly call them, *canzoni alla francese.*" He included ten by Merulo, among them *La Leonora, La Gratiosa,* and *La Zambeccara.* Four canzonas from the 1592 print appear as unornamented ensemble pieces in the *Canzoni per sonare* of 1608 published by Raverii. Thus there is no doubt that Merulo's organ canzonas are merely transcriptions, some from French chansons, but most of them from his own ensemble canzonas.

Everything else that was created at the time in the field of the canzona belongs to the category of the intabulated chanson (e.g., *Sortemeplus de Filippo de Monte* in Valente's *Intavolatura de cimbalo* of 1576), or to the intabulated ensemble canzona (e.g., the *Canzoni de sonare a quattro voci* by Florentio Maschera, 1584, and the *Capricci overo canzoni a quattro* by Ottavio Bariola, 1594.[43] To sum up, then, the 16th century had no independent organ canzona, which might be placed on the same level as the organ ricercar. Girolamo Cavazzoni achieved a significant step in the direction of an independent evolution when he created the paraphrasing canzona, in which the motifs or subjects of a chanson were treated in a new manner. He was followed by Andrea Gabrieli with his ricercars on *Martin menoit,* etc., and perhaps with his *ricercari ariosi.* Otherwise, Gabrieli, Merulo, and their contemporaries limited themselves to ornamented transcriptions of chansons or of ensemble canzonas.

PELLEGRINI

It is only shortly before 1600 that the organ canzona becomes an independent type with an individual and original character. It emerges in the *Canzoni de intavolatura d'organo fatte alla francese,* published in 1599 by Vincenzo Pellegrini (c. 1560?–1631?, active first in Pesaro and later in Milan). This print contains 13 canzonas (*La Berenice, La Gentile,* etc.),[44] which manifest a very important and basic principle of the further evolution, that of contrast. They consist of a number of sections, which differ not only in subject matter but also in texture, rhythm, and tempo. *La Capricciosa,* e.g., consists of three rather long sections (of about

36, 26, and 22 semibreves), the first of which is written in a lively imitative style, the second one homophonically and in triple meter, and the third more chordally and employing a rapid figure. At the same time the first two sections are connected through the use of the same musical idea, an arrangement that suggests the principle of the variation canzona, which plays so decisive a role in Frescobaldi. Fig. 192 shows the beginnings of the three sections.

Fig.192

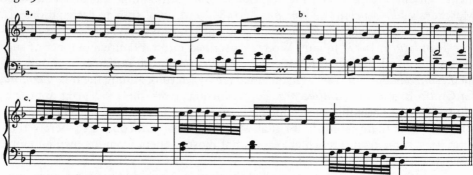

The credit for having introduced this type of canzona, which became standard for the entire further evolution of the species, does not go to Vincenzo Pellegrini, but to a greater master, Andrea Gabrieli. The earliest posthumous publication of Gabrieli's works, a part-book print that appeared three years after his death, *Madrigali et ricercari di Andrea Gabrieli a quattro voci* (Gardano, 1589), contains seven ensemble ricercars.[45] The last one, *duodecimo tono*, exhibits all the typical characteristics of the contrast canzona. This composition is historically very significant and at the same time musically very attractive. That Gabrieli called it a ricercar, not a canzona (if the designation is authentic), may perhaps be explained by the fact that for him the term canzona was still inseparably connected with the idea of the intabulated chanson—so much so that he designated even paraphrases of chansons as ricercars. As far as we know Pellegrini was the first to transfer this original type to the organ and give it the name of canzona, which remained connected with it.

THE DEVELOPMENT IN GERMANY

In Germany the canzona had a very different development. It first received a new name, then a new content. The new name is *fuga*, an expression that had existed for a long time, but with an entirely different meaning—as the designation of a canon. As early as 1420 Oswald von Wolkenstein (1377–1445) used the word in this sense, and Glarean still called a mensuration canon by Josquin a *fuga trium* *temporum.* It first appears with a new meaning in Kleber, who calls Buchner's freely imitative paraphrase of *Maria Zart* a *fuga optima.** Bernhard Schmid the Younger then identifies *fuga* with canzona. His *Tabulatur-Buch* of 1607 contains a group of pieces inscribed: "Fugues (or as the Italians call it) *Canzoni alla Francese.*" Ensemble canzonas by Brignoli, Gabrieli, Malvezzi, Maschera, and other Italians are intabulated and designated as *Fuga prima, Fuga secunda*, etc.[46]

The term *fuga* appears in Woltz's tablature of 1617 with the meaning changed again—and this is the decisive step. Twenty compositions by Simon Lohet are described by the legend "Fugas sequentes a Clarissimo Viro, Aulae Wirtembergicae quondam Organoedo celeberrimo, Domino Simone Lohet . . . olim communicatas . . . huic apponere placuit . . ." (It is a pleasure to append hereto the following fugues, communicated some time ago by the famous Mr. Simon Lohet, once the very celebrated court organist at Württemberg).[47] The novelty of these works lies above all in their brevity. At a time when ricercars and canzonas often ran to more than one hundred measures, it is not only a difference of degree but also one of concept when a composer limits himself to about twenty-five measures and realizes this concept in twenty different compositions. Eight of the pieces employ only one subject, and they come much closer to the later idea of the fugue than one would think possible one hundred and fifty years before Bach. Despite the new name and the new content, the connection with the canzona is still recognizable, particularly in the frequent use of subjects with initial tone repetitions. The subjects of *fugae* 1, 5, 8, and 10 are shown in Fig.193.

Fig.193

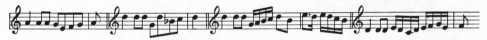

All eight monothematic fugues, nos.4, 6, 9, 11, 12, 14, 17, and 19, are based on ricercar-like subjects, and no.17 is a regular inversion fugue. Eight others, nos.1, 2, 3, 7, 13, 15, 18, and 20, consist of two sections, the first one imitative with a canzona subject, the second one either imitative with a subject in stretto or more freely formulated with complementary motifs and clavieristic figures. Nos.8, 10, and 16 consist of three sections: one with a canzona subject, one with strettos, and one with clavieristic figures. No.5 also consists of three sections, all of them imitative. The twenty fugues are arranged by keys: Nos.1 and 2 end on *D*, nos.3–9 on *G*, nos.10–13 on *C*, nos.14–16 on *F*, and nos.17–20 on *E*. Whether this order originates with Lohet or with Woltz we do not know.

Several of the monothematic, ricercar-like fugues are available in new edi-

---

* Cf.p.97. The term *fuga* probably does not refer to the piece as a whole but to the various imitative, often canonic beginnings of the lines, and we should probably read *fugae optimae.*

Fig.194

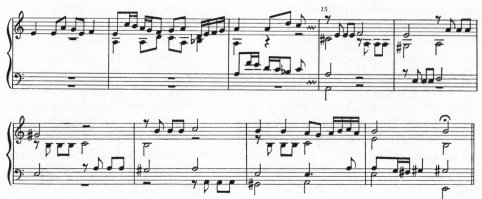

tions (cf. note 47). In the others the clavieristic formulation of the final sections is particularly worthy of note, e.g., in the *Fuga vigesima* (no.20), whose beginning and end are reproduced in Fig.194.

After the twenty fugues, Woltz adds another piece by Lohet, which he calls *Canzona*,[48] but which is really a very brief monothematic fugue with inversion of the subject. Like the preceding *fugae*, it is in the key of E.

Three "fugues" preserved in the Ms. F. IX. 49 of the University Library at Basel are by Samuel Mareschal (born at Tournai in 1554, active in Basel, where he died in 1640). Two are formulated exactly like Lohet's; the third is somewhat longer and concludes with a kind of free postlude.[49]

The Fantasy

A number of 16th-century keyboard pieces bear the designation *fantasy*. Various scholars have tried to explain this term by relating it to the ricercar, some emphasizing their differences, others their similarities (cf.p.165). We can come close to the meaning only by interpreting the term in a literal sense, the same procedure that served to clarify the term ricercar. While the ricercar always relates to "examination" or "study," the fantasy is just what its name implies—a free or freer handling of musical invention or inspiration. This definition is as true of the fantasies from the 16th century as it is of Bach's *Chromatic Fantasy*, Mozart's *D minor Fantasy*, Beethoven's *Sonata quasi una fantasia*, or Liszt's *Don Juan Fantasie*. It does not preclude the possibility of a fantasy's occasionally assuming more definite contours, as in those by various 17th-century composers: Sweelinck, Frescobaldi, Froberger, etc. But even in these instances the term by no means indicates a unified type; instead, each of these masters creates a type of his own, quite different from those of the others.

Of course the "free" invention that represents the characteristic feature of the fantasy is free only within the framework of conventions in force at the time, in other words, in relation to the more firmly structured forms and types of the period. From them the fantasy takes over the elements and principles of style, but treats or combines them in ways that differ somewhat from the rules in current use. Since imitation is of basic importance in the music of the 16th century, it is understandable that most fantasies of the period show some influence of the imitative style, although this is not always the case.

GERMANY, ITALY, SPAIN, AND FRANCE

In lute music the term fantasy was employed rather frequently in the 16th century, mostly for quasi-polyphonic and quasi-imitative pieces, for which the designation ricercar did not seem proper. It appears only sporadically in keyboard music of the period, for the first time in connection with clavier compositions in the tablatures of Kotter and Kleber (around 1520). A *Fantasia in ut* by Kotter[50] unmistakably represents a type whose real development began one hundred years later and reached its glorious climax another hundred years thereafter—the prelude and fugue. The piece starts with nine measures of three-part, lightly ornamented chords. This prelude is followed by a section of twenty-five measures, in which a single, chanson-like subject is treated imitatively, and which can definitely be called a fugue. Fig.195 shows the prelude and the fugue subjects in simplified form, with the figurations omitted.

Fig.195

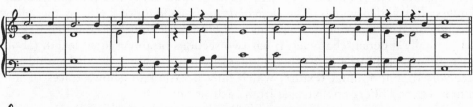

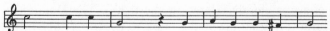

Two more fantasies are found in Kleber's tablature.[51] The *Fantasy in Fa* (fol. 56) begins with a twelve-measure prelude of three-part chords enlivened by scale passages, followed by a longer section (52 measures) in imitative style, and then a brief postlude in which the right hand executes a long run (ascending from *f* to *f″*, then falling back to *c′*) above a pedal point on *F* and *c* in the left hand. In the imitative section various chanson-like subjects are presented and treated in Josquin fashion, in duo-imitation or pairwise imitation.* Thus this fantasy may be characterized as a kind of clavier canzona with prelude and postlude. The *Fantasy in Re* (fol.119v) consists of a single section in three-part counterpoint with occasional suggested imitations, but more frequently with sequential treatment. The style recalls the ensemble pieces of Obrecht and Isaac.

To sum up, we may be justified in saying that these three early fantasies deviate from the norms of the time and therefore deserve the designation *fantasy*, indeed require it.

Organ fantasies of an entirely different kind are found in Italian sources, all from the second half of the 16th century. The best known is Andrea Gabrieli's often cited *Fantasia allegra* from the *Terzo libro de recercari* (1596).[52] Essentially this piece represents a ricercar with two subjects, but it differs from the usual type in its looser construction, the lively, canzona-like character of the subjects, and in the fact that the second subject often appears in figural variants, mostly in stretto with the unornamented form, as in Fig.196.

Fig.196

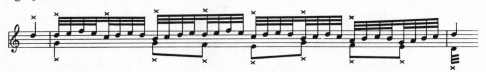

The four fantasies of 1575 by the Neapolitan Rocco Rodio are again completely different. They are settings of pre-existing melodies—of three hymns and the *Spagna*. Even within the narrowest limits of space and time, the notion of the fantasy thus varied widely. The *Intavolatura de cimbalo* of 1576, by the fellow Neapolitan Antonio Valente, contains a *Fantasia del primo tono*, which has another totally different character. It has two sections of about equal length (about 45 measures each), the first of which is written in toccata style, the second in a free-voiced contrapuntal texture, which only occasionally shows traces of imitation. Fig.197 offers one passage from each section.

In Spain the organ fantasy is closely related to the tiento. The Dominican monk Tomás de Sancta Maria (d.1570?) devoted a book to it, *Arte de tañer fantasia* (1565). It teaches meter, keyboard, fingering, ornaments, counterpoint, cadences, etc., in detail, so that the reader can learn to improvise a fantasy. The explanations and some of the appended examples show that improvisation kept strictly to the style of imitative counterpoint, excluding all elements of freer treatment, like that found in the "preludes" of the fantasies by Kotter, Kleber, and

---

* We distinguish between duo-imitation: b—a— and pairwise imitation: a—a—.

Fig.197

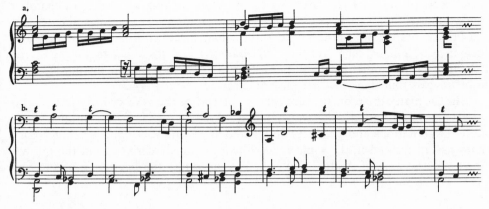

Valente. The pieces used to illustrate the numerous explanations are proper classroom examples without marked individuality.[53]

In France the hundred years between Attaingnant (1529) and Titelouze
(1623) yield only a single piece that is expressly for clavier, a *Fantasie sus orgue
ou espinette* by the chanson composer Guillaume Costeley (c.1531–1606).[54] It
is a rather pleasant piece, which uses a variety of approaches, and may be regarded
as a precursor of the English fantasies. Fig.198 gives the beginning (the manuscript's most obvious errors, mostly wrong clefs, have been corrected).

Claude le Jeune (c.1530–1600), a contemporary of Costeley, left three fantasies in his posthumous *Second livre des meslanges* (1612). Two are in four parts
and one is in five (a paraphrase of Josquin's motet *Benedicta es caelorum regina*),
but they unmistakably bear the marks of ensemble music.[55] The same is true of

Fig.198

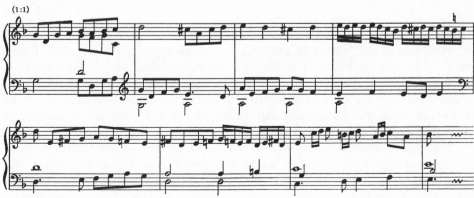

the 42 *Fantaisies à III, IV, V, et VI parties* by Eustache du Caurroy (1549–1609), which were printed one year after his death.[56] They belong to the field of chamber music, indeed they "seem to us to be the contrapuntal heritage of a classicist of the French period of counterpoint, rather than pieces meant for practical performance."[57] Finally there are the *Vingt-quatre Fantasies à quatre parties* by the Belgian Charles Guillet (d.1654), published in 1610. A glance at the modern edition[58] reveals that they, too, are ensemble music.

In Germany the fantasy reappears at the end of the 16th century in a manuscript preserved at Gdansk (Danzig; State Archive Vv 123). It contains some motet intabulations and 17 pieces designated as *Phantasia primi . . . octavi toni*.[59] They are all written in the same style, which obviously derives from the intonations and toccatas of Andrea Gabrieli. Fig.199 offers the beginning of the first piece, *Phantasia primi toni*.

Fig.199

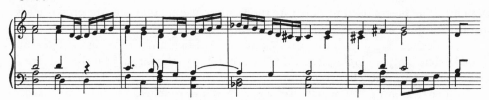

The tablature of Jacob Paix, *Ein Schön, Nutz und Gebreuchlich Orgel Tabulaturbuch* (1583), contains two very different fantasies, a *Phantasia primi toni* and a *Phantasia septimi toni*, which would be called polythematic ricercars today. There are occasional two-part episodes, to which Ritter probably gives too much importance when he sees in them "an essential step toward the later fugue."[60] Frotscher thinks that Paix "took [these pieces] from an Italian source,"[61] an assumption that is quite plausible.

ENGLAND

The evolution of the fantasy in England was much more interesting and significant than on the continent. The reason is probably that the stricter imitative-contrapuntal forms, the ricercar and canzona, did not flourish in England, where the principle of imitation was accepted late and hesitatingly. The fantasy, or, as the English said, the fancy, was cultivated all the more—so much so that it emerged there as a rather clearly defined type.

The earliest known example, a *Fansye* by Newman[62] in the *Mulliner Book*, is a brief three-part composition similar to Kleber's *Fantasy in Re*, which still stands outside the real development of the English fantasy and certainly shows no recognizable relation to the later type. A *Fantasy* by Thomas Tallis[63] represents a singular case, but a very remarkable one because of its closeness to the imitative style. It is 37 measures long, and successively presents nine or ten thematic ideas in imitation. The first subject is treated in a complete four-part point of imitation; the others are more cursorily presented in an uninterrupted three-part setting, which increases in liveliness. It concludes with a few free measures in which the right hand plays parallel sixths. If one insists on relating the fantasy to the ricercar, this is the most appropriate example to use. What ricercars with a like number of subjects (e.g., Girolamo Cavazzoni's) would present more thoroughly and at much greater length is suggested in this fantasy in a free and easy manner within a relatively small framework.

The singular fantasies by Newman and Tallis are followed at the end of the 16th century by an extensive output, which leads to the crystallization of the type. Its chief characteristic consists in a concatenation of sections in various styles, from the contrapuntal to the dance-like. This type first appears in the works of the great master of English clavier music, William Byrd, and then in Giles Farnaby, Peter Philips, John Mundy, Benjamin Cosyn, John Bull, Orlando Gibbons, and others. In England the fantasy had acquired such importance and such a clear contour by the end of the 16th century, that Byrd's pupil Thomas Morley (1557–1603) called it the main type of instrumental music. In his *Plaine and Easie Introduction to Practicall Musicke* of 1597 he described it as follows:[64]

> The most principal and chiefest kind of music which is made without a ditty is the fantasy, that is, when a musician taketh a point at his pleasure and wresteth and turneth it as he list, making either much or little of it as shall seem best in his own conceit. In this may more art be shown than in any other music, because the composer is tied to nothing but that he may add, diminish, and alter at his pleasure. And this kind will bear any allowances whatsoever tolerable in other music, except changing the air [mode] and leaving the key, which in fantasy may never be suffered. Other things you may use at your pleasure, as bindings with discords, quick motions, slow motions, proportions, and what you list. Likewise this kind of music is with them who practise instruments of parts [ensemble] in greatest use, but for voices it is but seldom used.

This is indeed a very apt explanation of the English fantasy. The word "point" does not necessarily mean that the composition is based on a single idea. On the contrary, multiplicity of subjects or ideas is as characteristic and necessary as variety and freedom in their treatment. How these principles of formulation were translated into actuality can be seen and heard in William Byrd's six fantasies. A description of the process or its result is much more difficult, because the ideas are frequently "wrested and turned" in a manner for which no adequate terminology exists. In the final analysis we can only refer the reader to the music itself—a recommendation that is all the more justified, since these works are among the most ingenious and captivating creations in the field of keyboard music. Nevertheless we shall attempt to characterize briefly the contents of two of these fantasies to give the player a "guide through the work." In the following analysis the first number refers to the section; the number in parentheses indicates the length of the section in semibreves (whole notes in the new edition); indications such as 6/1 refer to the length of a phrase (= six whole measures):

> I. *FW*, I, pp.37ff.: 1 (30), ricercar; 2 (12), 6/1—phrase with echo repetition; 3 (21), imitation of a lively subject with strettos; 4 (16), 4/1—phrase heard four times; 5 (6), 3/1—phrase with duo-imitations à la Josquin; 6 (12), 2/1—phrase heard six times; 7 (10), march-like, with figurations; 8 (34), corranto with increasing motion; 9 (4), cadence figuration.
>
> II. *FW*, II, pp.406ff.: 1 (57), ricercar (twelve imitations numbered in the original); 2 (71), ricercar, somewhat freer; 3 (27), imitative, with a lively subject; 4 (22), freely imitative play with motifs; 5 (24), similar, with a scale motif; 6 (11), song-like, with figurations; 7 (15), motif play with a dance-like accompaniment; 8 (43), corranto with increasing motion and two echo repetitions; 9 (12), chords with figurations.
>
> The fantasies in *FW*, I, p. 406 (= Andrews N, p.204) and Andrews N, p.237 are of similar structure.

Common to these fantasies—and to most others written in England—is a beginning in imitative counterpoint and an ending with ornamented chords. In between there is much variety in free alternation: canzona, toccata, song, dance, march, and other forms served as inspirations. Frequently there are sections in which a phrase of two to four measures is repeated several times, but always with some changes that lend charm and interest to the repetition. Everywhere Byrd proves himself a master of invention, an original musician of the highest rank. The two corrantos (I, 8 and II, 8 above) are especially attractive, and their increasing liveliness recalls Hugh Aston's *Hornepype* (cf.pp.249ff.).

Another fantasy by Byrd (Tuttle B, p.92) deviates from the general type in that it omits the freely formulated sections entirely and limits itself to the imitative treatment of nine or ten subjects or motifs. It is written in a strict three-part polyphony throughout, and approaches the English ensemble fantasies of the period so strikingly that it may be regarded as a clavier transcription of a fantasy for three instruments.

The last of Byrd's fantasies appears in *FW*, I, p.188. It is an unmistakable keyboard fantasy, which deserves a special place because of its length and wealth of original ideas. It consists of four separate sections and an introduction, a *Praeludium to ye Fancie* (entered elsewhere in the manuscript; *FW*, I, p.394), which is a brief, but particularly impressive, prologue to the four scenes of dramatic and aural play. The first two sections captivate us with their inexhaustible supply of contrapuntal and figural formulations; then we are removed to a totally new province, something like an idyllic-pastoral landscape. Above a harmonic bass that alternates gently between the tonic and dominant we hear an entrancing web of small melodic figures and echo fragments in 6/4 time, which we could imagine being intoned by recorders. Gradually the exchanges become livelier, are smoothed out into eighth-note figurations, and are followed by triplet figures in 9/4, first in halting rhythms, then (in section 4) in quarters, and finally in eighth notes, until the increasing motion flows into a broadly conceived and richly ornamented plagal cadence. The piece recalls Aston's *Hornepype* even more than the corranto sections of the first two fantasies.

A few of the most remarkable tableaux may be singled out from the fulness of this fantasy: two two-part canons in the first section, both of which are repeated an octave lower; a high-spirited clavier figure (Fig.200a.) and a passage with a 6/8 figure above chords in 4/4 (b.) in the second section; echo effects (c.) that anticipate Sweelinck in the third; and a passage with boldly syncopated chords (d.) in the fourth section. Byrd changes key several times in this work; according to Morley, this is something that "in fantasy may never be suffered." The prelude and the first section are in *A* minor; the second section starts in *F* and ends in *C;* the third begins in *C*, modulates to *A*, and concludes in *C* again, but shortly before the end (at the meter change to 9/4) a very bold and unexpected turn occurs: a progression from the dominant of *A* minor (with *G♯*) to a triad on *F* with a *B♭* appoggiatura; the fourth section starts in *C* and proceeds to a broadly expanded plagal cadence in *A* major. Thus the tonal-harmonic element lends further color to the amply designed canvas.[65]

Fig.200

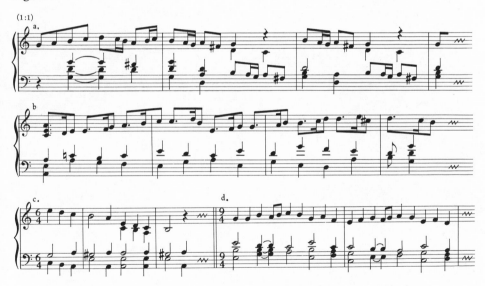

Byrd laid the foundation of the fantasy, and most of the later virginalists, especially Farnaby, Bull, and Gibbons, contributed to its growth, but none surpassed the old master. The evolution occurred for the most part in the early 17th century, and will be considered later, in connection with these composers' other works.

In conjunction with the English fantasies two specifically English types of keyboard music may be mentioned—the point and the voluntary. "Point" means a point of imitation, and serves as the title of very short pieces, eight to twelve measures long, in which a thematic idea is imitatively presented. Six such miniature fugal settings are found in the *Mulliner Book*, four anonymous ones and one each by Shepherd and Tallis. The name "voluntary"—something like "As you like it"—may refer either to the freedom and ease of formulation or to an *ad-libitum* use in the religious service.[66] The earliest known examples, one each by Alwood and Farrant, are found in the *Mulliner Book*. The former is 34 measures long, and treats two or three ideas in a freely imitative style; the latter is a miniature of 7 measures, which might better be called a point. *Ladye Nevells Booke* preserves three voluntaries by Byrd,[67] one of which is comparable to Alwood's in both style and length. Another one, entitled *A Lesson of Voluntary*, is a keyboard transcription of an extended fantasy for five string instruments. The third begins with a brief prelude, then proceeds to a freely imitative treatment of various subjects, and concludes with a postlude with lively figurations.[68]

9

Free Forms

IN CHAP.5 we discussed the evolution of the prelude in the 15th century. If we compare the beginning and end of this evolution, that is, a preamble by Ileborgh with one from the *Buxheim Organ Book* we will see that during the twenty-five years between them the original scope was enlarged but not essentially changed or abandoned. Only in the 16th century did the prelude acquire new characteristics—traits that can be described as Renaissance-like, since they tend toward clarifying the idea, solidifying the structure, and regularizing the technique. Where to draw the line between the later Middle Ages and the Renaissance—whether around 1500 with Josquin, around 1450 with Ockeghem, or even earlier with Dufay—is a much-debated question (cf.p.75). In the special field of keyboard music the time around 1500 proves to be an important and essential line of demarcation. In the history of the prelude the line is particularly clear.

The Prelude in Germany, France, and Poland

Two German manuscripts, the tablatures of Kleber and of Kotter, open the 16th-century literature of the prelude. The former contains 14 *praeambula*, and 2 postludes, designated as *finale;* the latter preserves 7 preludes, some with humanistically learned titles, such as *Prooemium* or *Anabole* (Greek for "beginning").

The preludes of the Kleber collection still show a connection with the earlier prelude in that many of them contain monophonic passages, mostly at the beginning or end. Such passages played an important role in the preludes of the 15th century, but here they manifest another character, for the free, rhapsodic lines are replaced by a more ordered motion in regular note values that consciously uses the scale as the structural basis. Fig.201 reproduces the *Preambulum in sol*

Fig.201

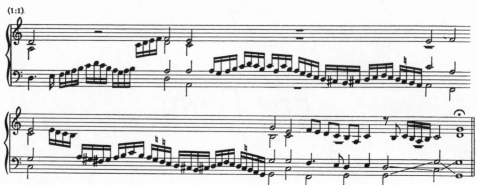

(fol.65v), signed V. S., which employs such figures at various places to extend certain chords, and assigns some of the fast passage work to the left hand. It anticipates the characteristic elements of the Italian intonations and toccatas in a remarkable fashion.

Other preludes of Kleber's collection consists exclusively of four-part chords that follow each other in a firm rhythmic framework and exhibit a secure feeling for purposeful progression, i.e., for functional harmony. A piece like the *Preambulum in re* (fol.4v), shown in Fig. 202 breathes self-confidence, boldness, and pride, in a genuine Renaissance spirit.

Fig.202

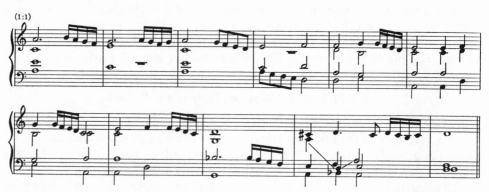

The highest artistic achievement among Kleber's preludes is probably the *Finale in re seu preambalon*,[1] toward the end of the tablature (fol.162v). With its 33 measures it is the longest of the preludes. It divides into three sections, separated by fermatas: a four-part beginning and ending, plus a shorter two-part

214

passage in the middle. If the first and last sections are played on the full organ, and the middle one is played on solo stops, as was certainly the practice of the time, there emerges an organ piece of impressive strength, even by today's standards. This is one of the earliest pieces to demand a change of registration in its structure, even though it was not yet prescribed.

The preludes included in the other tablature are all signed by Kotter, and are presumed to have been composed by the collector of the manuscript.[2] Here the toccata-like passage work disappears entirely. Like the *Preambulum in re* mentioned above, an *Anabole in fa* is purely chordal. It contains two sections each ten measures long; the first consists of chords in whole notes, the second of chords that move twice as fast. The same elements are found in the *Preludium in la*, but in a greatly expanded framework (sixty-six measures). It divides into four sections: a. chords in whole notes, first without, then with connecting ornaments (meas.7ff.); b. chords in half notes above a steadily moving bass line; c. the same with ornamental turns in the upper part; and d. the same without any figurations. Fig.203 shows the beginnings of these sections. It must be admitted that the attempt to give form to this extended piece through structure and alternation has gotten bogged down in technical externalities.

Fig.203

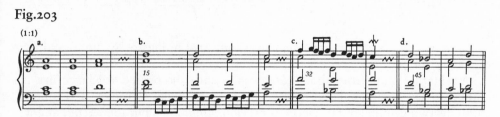

In the remaining preludes Kotter tries to adapt the vocal style of his time to the organ. His chordal preludes are in four parts, but three-part settings prevail in the polyphonic ones. Occasionally one finds suggestions of imitation, and some passages of echo-like duo-imitations in the Josquin manner. Adapted to the organ, they can be made particularly effective with changes in manuals and registration. However, the meaning and purpose of the prelude is no longer maintained. These pieces can hardly be distinguished from what Kotter calls elsewhere *fantasia, harmonia,* or *carmen*.

A *Preambulum in re* from the same period, and probably from the same locale, is preserved in a Trent organ tablature.[3] Toward the end it contains two arresting groups of measures, in which full chords move in a syncopated rhythm, as follows: | ♩ ♩ | ♩ ♩ ♩ |. It would be completely wrong, however, to assume that in an early 16th-century prelude the effect of real syncopation was intended, as it is in modern dance music. In truth, such groups, which occur repeatedly later on, mean that two 4/4 measures are regrouped into one 2/4 and two 3/4 measures

Fig.204

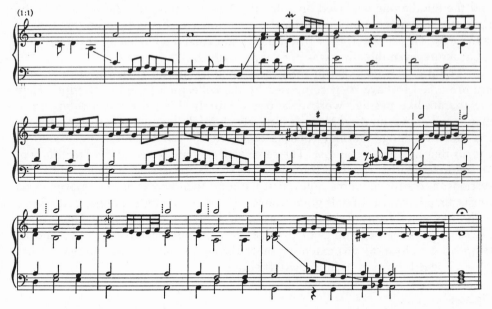

$(4 + 4 = 2 + 3 + 3)$. This arrangement is indicated in Fig.204 by notes and bar lines above the staff.[4]

A tablature book from about 1550 was recently discovered at Klagenfurt. In addition to several intabulated motets (by Josquin, Senfl, Verdelot, and others) it contains two genuine organ pieces, a *Praeambulum 6 vocum Lud. Senfl*, and an anonymous *Exercitatio bona*.[5] It comes as a pleasant surprise that Senfl (c.1486–c.1543), the great German master of motet and song, also wrote for the organ. Indeed, the prelude is a creation of high rank, equal to his vocal works. The piece is rather long (74 breve measures), and is clearly intended for four-part playing

Fig.205

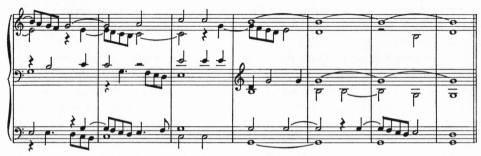

on the manual and two-part execution on the pedals; it thus furnishes additional documentation for the highly developed pedal technique already evidenced in the works of Ileborgh and Schlick. It was probably written for a special festive occasion, which demanded music full of magnificence and dignity. The conclusion (in Fig.205) has an unusual harmonization: The penultimate chord of the subdominant (*C* major) is replaced by the mediant (*E* minor).

The *Exercitatio bona* from the same manuscript is not, as one might think, a kind of finger exercise, but a long piece of 125 breve measures, in four parts. It should probably be called a prelude, but may also be considered a primitive ricercar. It includes numerous suggestions of conventional imitations and is distantly reminiscent of Marco Antonio Cavazzoni's ricercars.

A manuscript of the Fürstlich Thurn- und Taxis'sche Hofbibliothek at Regensburg (FK 21) also contains a number of short *preambula*,[6] which were probably written in the second half of the 16th century.

The prelude was also cultivated in France. Unfortunately only three examples are extant, two in Attaingnant's print *Magnificat sur les huit tons avec Tedeum et deux préludes* of 1530, and another in his *Treize Motets et un prélude* of 1531. The last one is a brief piece, which lacks the characteristic traits of the German preludes; if it were not expressly called a *prélude*, one would take it for a verset from Attaingnant's organ Masses. The two preludes from the *Magnificat* print exhibit the same, rather dry style of figurations, but they are much longer. The first one runs to 45 measures, and the second, *Prélude sur chacun ton*, with its 85 measures, is one of the longest preludes preserved from this period. Its content, however, is much too scanty to satisfy this grand scale. Except for a few full chords at the start, it exhibits a two- or three-part texture filled mostly with formalistic and amateurish figures, with so many sequences that it gets tiresome.

The evolution represented by Kotter's and Kleber's preludes was continued in Poland, where organ music was cultivated intensively under the influence of German organists. The tablature of Johannes of Lublin from about 1540 contains a very voluminous repertoire of pieces used during the service. The preludes interspersed in the tablature and presumably played during the Mass, the Vespers, or on similar occasions probably belong to this repertoire. The Lublin tablature contains 21 preludes,[7] the Holy Ghost tablature 3 more (cf.p.103). Their style is close to Kleber's. In both Polish tablatures the basic setting is a four-part chordal texture, enlivened or loosened up in a quasi-polyphonic manner by occasional figures or ornaments in one voice or another. The number of voices is frequently increased to five, particularly in the first few measures, and at times there are even six-part chords. The pedals were no doubt used in such instances, and in various places they are expressly prescribed. Each prelude begins with a full, festive chordal section, without the introductory passages frequently found in the *Buxheim Organ Book* and in Kleber's tablature. But the final chord is very often extended and stressed by toccata-like runs, as, e.g., in the *Preambulum*

Fig.206

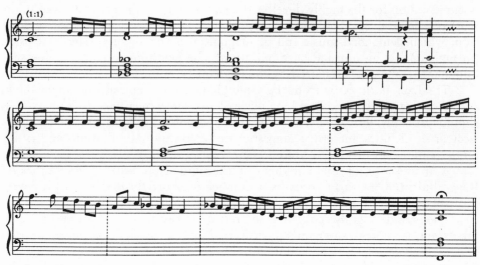

super FF (Lublin, fol.98v; new ed., p.7), whose beginning and end are reproduced in Fig.206.

Most of the Polish preludes are substantially longer than Kleber's, but do not go beyond what seems appropriate. In about twenty to thirty measures there unfolds a mixture of festive chords, enlivening polyphonization, and concluding passages of improvisation that does full justice to the demands of a liturgical prelude. With these pieces the first chapter in the history of the prelude reaches a dignified conclusion; it lasted exactly one hundred years, from Ileborgh (1448) to the Holy Ghost tablature (1548).

The Italian Intonations

The second chapter was written in Italy, under the title of *Intonazione*, by Andrea and Giovanni Gabrieli. In 1593 the *Intonationi d'organo di Andrea Gabrieli, et di Giovanni suo nepote* appeared, containing 8 intonations by the older organ master and 11 by the younger. Unfortunately the late date of the publication (for Andrea it is obviously posthumous) gives no clue to the time of origin of this type. But that date can be deduced from other evidence: Both collections are ordered according to the church modes (*Intonazione del primo tono*, etc.), but Andrea's takes into account only the traditional eight modes. It may therefore be assumed that it was conceived before the twelve-mode system of Glareanus (*Dodecachordon*, 1547) was printed or generally known, probably between 1550 and 1560.

Andrea Gabrieli's eight intonations present a remarkably unified type. Within a frame of twelve to sixteen measures we hear a series of sustained chords; in the first two or three measures they are presented as pure block chords, but thereafter they are connected by continuous chains of fast passages played by either the right or the left hand, while the other hand plays three-part chords. The *Preambulum in sol* in Kleber's tablature (cf.Fig.201) remarkably anticipates the basic elements of the Italian intonations, but this should not be taken as suggesting an evolutionary relationship. Now the same elements are related in a different way. In the earlier pieces passage work provided interludes for the purpose of expansion, but here it takes on the character of a continuous connection and enchainment, like a garland suspended between the columns of the chords. Listening to this music evokes a festive mood, as this comparison suggests. Like the polychoral motets of the Venetian school, these preludes reflect the aura of magnificence of the city and period in which they were written. Fig.207 gives the *Intonazione del secondo tono*.

Such lively and often individually conceived lines should not be referred to

Fig.207

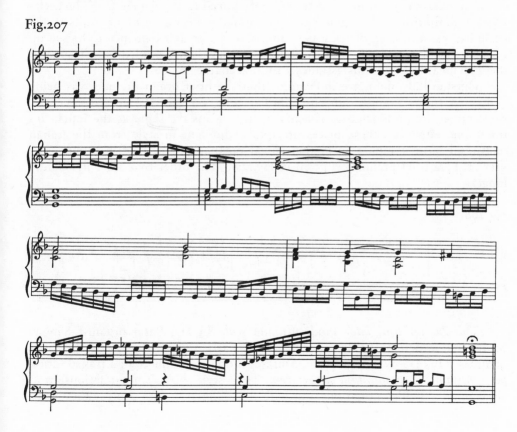

as "passages" or "runs," but there do not seem to be any less pejorative or colorless designations available. In any event, such figures should not be equated with virtuosity and finger agility, as has been often done. Tension is sustained by expressive lines that follow the unwritten laws of musical gravity and elasticity. A characteristic figure will occasionally recur in adjacent measures and thereby acquire the force of a motif, as, e.g., in the *quarto tono*, measures 9–11, or in the *settimo tono*, measures 8–9 and 14–15. Artistically these figures are on a much higher level than the purely ornamental passage work that permeates the innumerable intabulations of motets and chansons, particularly in Gabrieli's own *canzoni alla francese*.

Giovanni Gabrieli added eleven intonations of his own to those of his uncle. As would be expected from one born in 1557, he takes cognizance of the completed system of Glareanus, but the third and fourth mode have a common intonation *del terzo e quarto tono*.[8] Each intonation is, moreover, transposed either a fourth up or down or a fifth up or down. They are shorter than Andrea's pieces, mostly about five to eight measures in length. Perhaps Giovanni, whose other works are certainly not inclined to be brief, bowed to the demands of the ecclesiastical authorities, who again and again found it necessary to set limits to the organists' expansive tendencies. Giovanni shows a greater tendency to loosen up his chords polyphonically and to limit his passage work, which is restricted to the final measures and thus assumes a routine character.

Outside Italy there are indications that the brief organ prelude was being cultivated. In the Spanish *Libro de cifra nueva* by Venegas de Henestrosa (1557), three pieces are designated as *entrada*, which means the same as the Italian *intonazione*. However, these pieces are totally different in style from the Italian ones, and most comparable in their fugal manner to the English points. The first of these brief preludes is given in Fig.208.[9] The other two are only slightly longer.

Fig.208

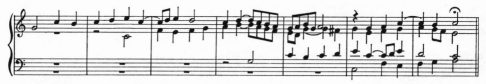

The *Zwölff toni oder modi utraque scala* by the Basel organist Samuel Mareschal, which probably come from the early 17th century, are also brief preludes.[10] Like Giovanni Gabrieli, Mareschal offers each piece in a transposition *per quartam* or *per quintam superiorem*. Their style shows some relationship to Giovanni Gabrieli's intonations, but with this difference: The contrapuntally en-

Fig.209

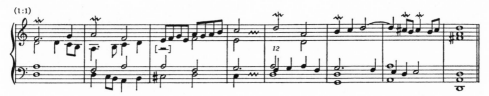

livened chords are used throughout the piece and there is no concluding passage work. Fig.209 shows the beginning and end of the *primi toni: Dorius*.

The English Prelude

The evolution of the 16th-century prelude found its conclusion in England. Two preludes by Byrd (*FW*, I, p.83; Tuttle B, p.127) indicate the direction in which this evolution moved: toward greater vivacity, playfulness, and—unfortunately—shallowness. The first piece shows a slight similarity to the intonations of Andrea Gabrieli, but the expressive figurations are replaced by trills and scales. The second has only outward vivacity but no inner liveliness. The brief prelude that opens the collection of the *Parthenia* is on a higher level.

The *Fitzwilliam Virginal Book* includes seven preludes by John Bull, which move still further in the same direction, for they involve fireworks of real bravura: broken octaves in the left hand (*FW*, II, p.259), arpeggios (*FW*, II, p.22), rapid tone repetitions (*FW*, I, p.418), and virtuosic scales through more than three octaves (*FW*, II, p.274). The prelude *FW*, II, p.23, is interesting for a different reason: It leans heavily on the style of the Italian intonations, but differs from them in a remarkably forward-looking use of harmony. Despite the designation *Dor.* (Dorian), it is written in a pure *F* major, which is firmly established at the start by a clear I IV V I progression. Fig.210 shows this beginning, but the sequentially repeated runs are only suggested.

As much as this technique may have been admired by Bull's contemporaries, the modern listener can hardly help smiling. When one hears what was revolutionary in 1600, modern in 1800, and antiquated today, one is moved to murmur:

Fig.210

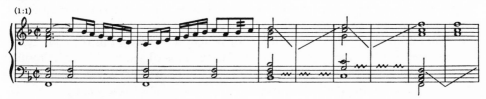

"Sic transit gloria mundi." Several preludes from other sources, which are published in the complete edition of Bull's keyboard works,[11] are of similar character. There are also a number of anonymous preludes in the *Fitzwilliam Virginal Book*, but they do not add any new features.

The Toccata from Andrea Gabrieli to Merulo

We now turn to the second main type of free organ music of the 16th century, the toccata. Like the canzona, it may have originated in a different field, perhaps in music for festive functions with trumpets and timpani, only to be adapted later to the organ.[12] As far as we know, this adaption was done by Andrea Gabrieli, whose *Intonationi d'organo* of 1593 also contains four toccatas.[13] As in the case of his intonations, we lack a definite indication of their date of composition, since the collection was published seven years after his death. The same is true of Annibale Padovano, who died in 1575, and whose toccatas and ricercars appear in a print of 1604. In this situation Padovano could well be regarded as the "inventor" of the toccata, but inner criteria speak in favor of Gabrieli's claim.

Two of Andrea's four toccatas—a *Toccata del primo tono* and one *del ottavo tono*[14]—give themselves away as the earliest examples of their species because of their simple construction. Both begin with two or three measures of quiet chordal polyphony, followed by chords connected by passage work. They are thus quite similar to the intonations, but longer, the first comprising 18 measures, the second 45. The essential difference is that the figurations of the toccatas lack the forceful expression, the liveliness, and the variety that informs the intonations. The profusion of mechanical scale runs in very fast motion (*semifusae*) is particularly disturbing. In the intonations they appear here and there among figures of other types; in the toccatas this relationship is reversed, especially in the *Toccata del ottavo tono*, which moves almost exclusively in rapidly ascending and descending scales for forty measures. Here the inner weakness of the "free" keyboard style becomes manifest. A style whose roots originate not in composition, but in improvisation, satisfies only within a small framework. Thus a new element had to be incorporated into the toccata to enable it to outgrow the miniature form of the intonation.

Andrea Gabrieli recognized this need and started on the road that was to prove the most fruitful in the future, though it was not the only one. He connected the style of free improvisation with the one that contrasted most with it, the strictly polyphonic style of the ricercar. His toccatas *del sexto tono* and *del nono tono* both adopt this principle of construction. A section in ricercar style is inserted between the opening and concluding sections of passage work. Although the free sections in these toccatas are monotonous in themselves, they achieve greater meaning and significance as parts of the whole. In one of these toccatas the three sections are 26, 27, and 14 measures long, respectively, in the other 41,

19, and 14 measures. Measures 14–15 from *Toccata del nono tono* are given in Fig.211. Note the use of the minor seventh as the turning point in a scale figure, in close proximity to the major seventh representing the leading tone. This particularly expressive cross-relation is frequently found in English vocal and organ music of the 16th century (cf.p.158). In Italian music its occurrence is much rarer.

Fig.211

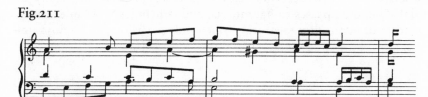

Annibale Padovano left three toccatas in the posthumous print *Toccate et ricercari d'organo* of 1604.[15] The second and third (*sesto, ottavo tono*) exhibit the three-section form within a total length of about 50 measures. The first one (*primo tono*) is by far the longest and lacks the concluding section of passage work. An introduction of 45 measures is followed by a ricercar of 80 measures, in which two subjects are treated successively with great detail. It constitutes a kind of prelude and fugue. The introductory portion shows a tendency to distribute the passages and chords systematically between the two hands. In Gabrieli's pieces the passages change from one hand to the other quite often, without apparent planning, and frequently a chord is sounded by one hand and taken over by the other. In Padovano's toccatas, however, the alternation produces four sections of almost equal length, each set off by a definite cadence. Throughout the entire toccata section letters are given below the staff to indicate a pedal part with long, sustained tones. This is the first unmistakable documentation of the use of pedals in Italy, while in Germany it is established as early as about 1450. Fig.212 shows the beginning of the *Toccata del primo tono*.

Fig.212

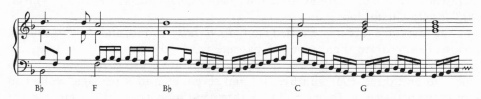

Padovano's print of 1604 also contains five toccatas *d'incerto autore*, which may have been written at the same time as the three by Padovano, i.e., in the 1560s. Nos.6, 7, 8, and 10 of the collection[16] consist of passage work throughout, like the two early toccatas by Andrea Gabrieli, while no.9 exhibits a more developed structure. In no.6 the figurations repeatedly assume the character of motifs or subjects. In no.10 the figuration is assigned exclusively to the right hand in the first half, and to the left hand in the second half; in two places these passages descend to contra *F*, a fact that probably necessitates a revision of prevailing ideas about the range of the organs of the period. Fig.213 shows one of these passages. Toccata no.9 starts with a brief section of eleven measures in a polyphonically enlivened chordal style, then passes to figurations, and concludes with an extended polyphonic section of about fifty measures, which only occasionally employs imitation of a brief motif (/ *a a f* | *g − a*).

Fig.213

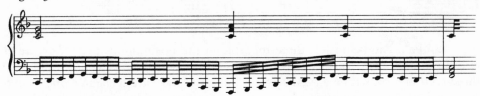

In 1591 there appeared a posthumous print by the Paduan cathedral organist, Sperindio Bertoldo, which contains two toccatas: *Tocate ricercari et canzoni francese* (cf.p.183). They differ from the Venetian toccatas not only in length—the first one is only about forty measures, the second about thirty—but also in their general abandonment of the passage work so characteristic of the latter. Apart from a number of written-out cadential trills, *Tocata prima* is written in a chordal-contrapuntal style throughout, with a brief middle section hinting at imitations. *Tocata seconda* includes a few measures of running scale passages, which, however, are overshadowed by the many written-out trills.

The picture of the early Italian toccata is completed by Girolamo Diruta in the first part of his *Il Transilvano* (1593, 1597, 1612, 1625). Thirteen toccatas are inserted in this important theoretical work: 4 by Diruta (nos.1, 2, 3, and 13), 2 by Andrea Gabrieli (nos.5 and 12), and one each by Merulo, Giovanni Gabrieli, Luzzascho Luzzaschi, Antonio Romanini, Paolo Quagliati, Vincenzo Bell'Haver, and Gioseffo Guami (nos.4 and 6–11).[17]

The first three toccatas, entitled *di grado, di salto buono,* and *di salto cattivo,* serve to demonstrate three types of passage work: the purely scalar type, the "good skip," and the "bad skip." The good skips are those that occur between notes two and three, four and five, six and seven, etc., of a passage, while bad skips occur between notes one and two, three and four, five and six, etc. Fig.214 shows a characteristic passage from each of the two "skip toccatas." The differentiation of these three types of progressions is not without interest. The figurations of the Italian intonations and toccatas to a large degree combine passages of these kinds, but without singling out any one of them. As a matter of fact, Diruta does

Fig.214

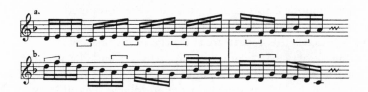

not take cognizance of arpeggios, which combine *salti buoni* and *salti cattivi*. This is all the more striking, as he employs a rather extensive section with arpeggios in his *Toccata del XI. e XII. tuono* (no.13). Thus in Diruta's systematic presentation a category is missing, the one Frescobaldi called *"non uscir di grado"* (nonstop skipping), one that he surely understood as something much more ingenious than mere chordal figures.

One of Andrea Gabrieli's two toccatas in *Il Transilvano* (*decimo tuono;* no. 12) is limited entirely to chords and figurations, while the other contains a ricercar section in the middle. The toccata by Bell'Haver (organist at St. Mark's, died 1587) is also in three sections, with a weak middle portion in routinely ornamented pseudo-polyphony. The toccatas by Luzzaschi (1545–1607, Ferrara), Romanini (organist under Prince Sigismund Báthory of Hungary), Quagliati (Roman organist, died 1628), and Gioseffo Guami (organist at Munich, Venice, and Lucca, c. 1540–1611) are all without subdivisions. The most interesting and certainly the most progressive is Quagliati's piece, which contains occasional formulae reminiscent of English music, like those in Fig.215. Such figures would be mild and usual in virginal music, but they are a novelty in Italy.

The 16th-century toccata reaches its climax in the works of Claudio Merulo, who devoted the greater part of his output to this species. In 1598 he published a collection *Toccate d'intavolatura d'organo, libro primo*, with 9 toccatas in the

Fig.215

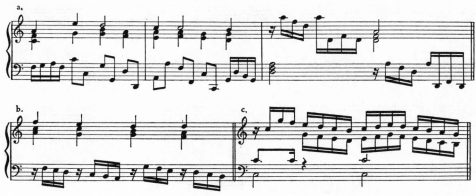

first to fourth modes, and in 1604 a *libro secondo* of the same title with 10 pieces in the fifth to tenth modes. Several more toccatas are contained in the Turin manuscripts (collection Giordano, vol.2) and elsewhere.[18]

First let us discuss this repertoire from the point of view of formal structure. Several toccatas (Libera M, I, nos.1, 4, 6; II, no.3; and the majority in III) are entirely in toccata style; but most (I, nos. 2, 3, 5, 7, 8, 9; II, nos. 4, 5, 6, 8, 9; III, no.1) have a section in ricercar style near the middle, and exhibit the contrast type that is so important for the later development of the toccata, and that is found in some toccatas by Andrea Gabrieli and Annibale Padovano. In several toccatas of *Libro secondo*, Merulo takes another step in this direction by interrupting the play of free improvisation with two fugal sections. This five-part formulation can be seen in II, nos. 1, 2, 7, and 10. It prevailed in the later evolution of the toccata, especially in Germany. Froberger, Buxtehude, and Bach employed it repeatedly.

No less significant are Merulo's innovations in style—the musical content with which he informs the structure. The free sections are derived principally from the same elements as Gabrieli's, i.e., from chords and passage work; however, they are no longer contrasted as separate elements but woven into a unified texture. Only a few of the manuscript toccatas (III, 2, 4, 6) still exhibit the older style of sustained chords with ascending and descending figurations moving above or below them. In the others the long, sustained block chords are replaced by a contrapuntal texture in which now this voice, now that one progresses, leading to a continuously changing harmonic background in which the figurations play an integral role. The figurations are no longer limited to scalar formulae, but appear in changing, often quite expressive, lines in various degrees of rapidity and differentiated rhythms: eighths, sixteenths, thirty-second notes, occasionally even dotted and syncopated. Fig.216 presents a section from II, no.4.

Fig.216

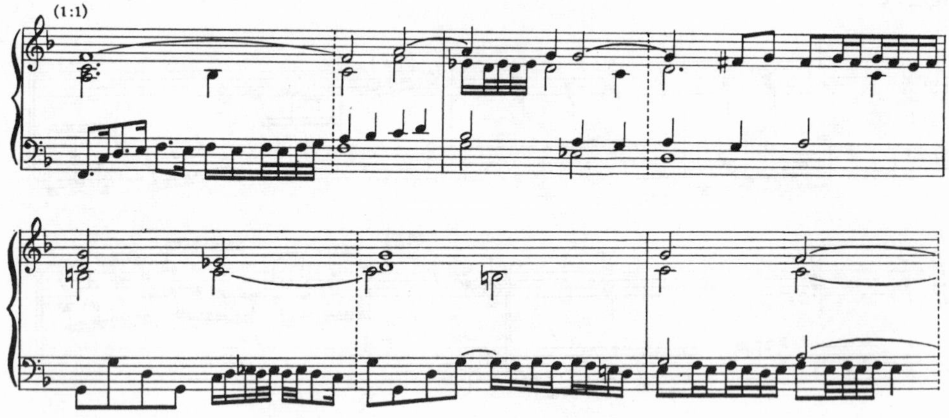

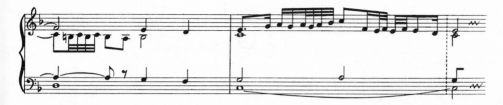

Some of the fugal sections are very short, particularly in nos.3, 5, and 8 of *Libro primo*, but more often they are quite extensive. They are frequently based on two or more subjects, as in I, nos.2 and 7, and II, nos.4, 8, and 9. With few exceptions the subjects do not exhibit the sustained character of ricercar subjects, but move mostly in quarter and eighth notes. In some toccatas, especially in the *Libro secondo*, the ricercar is not separated from the preceding free section by a clear cadence, but enters gradually, so that a continuous transition is created from one section to another. Compare, e.g., II, no.5, measure 24, and especially II, no.9, measures 21ff., where a subject is announced twice in half notes before it enters in measure 26 in shorter note values as the subject of the ricercar.

The manuscript toccatas of vol.III do not represent a unified style. There are works in the earliest toccata style, like no.6, as well as others with remarkably progressive features, particularly no.8, which includes a lengthy passage with complementary motifs in the style of Sweelinck. In toccata no.9 the free postlude is limited to the figurative ornamentation of the penultimate chord and is therefore structurally insignificant: Once again, as in one of Padovano's toccatas, the form that plays such an important role in the clavier music of the subsequent period, the prelude and fugue, emerges by chance. Merulo's authorship of nos.6, 8, and 9 is not absolutely certain, since these compositions are not signed, and his name appears only in the table of contents (*tavola*), which was apparently added in the 19th century. No.7 is identical with the one that Diruta printed in *Il Transilvano*.

10

Dance Music

IN COMPARISON WITH THE PRECEDING CENTURY, keyboard music of
the 16th century represents a basic change, and in no other field is this change as
striking as in dance music. As though touched by a liberating magic wand, a
marvelous richness suddenly unfolds, and a steady stream of varied and colorful
new phenomena appear.

At first the basse-danse is still cultivated, but it soon sinks into oblivion and
is replaced by new dances in the prevailing fashion. The most important are the
pavane and the galliard, which appear around 1510, followed by the passamezzo
and the saltarello about 1520. In addition there are the branle and the tourdion,
the hornpipe and the dompe, the piva and the calata, the hoftanz and the zeuner-
tanz, and, toward the end of the century, the first examples of those dances that
were to play important roles later on: the allemande, the courante, and the gigue.

Sixteenth-century dance music reaches us largely in lute books. Some prints,
such as Francesco Bendusi's *Opera nova de balli* (1553) and Claude Gervaise's
Livre de danceries (1547, 1550, 1557), preserve dances for instrumental ensembles. A third group of sources contain clavier dances.

The Kotter and Kleber Tablatures

The earliest sources of keyboard dance music are the manuscripts of Kotter and
of Kleber, in which the following dances are found:

1. *Spanieler,* by Kotter (Merian T, p.44)
2. *Spaniol Kochersperg* (Merian T, p.46)
3. *Spanyöler Tancz* and *Hopper Dancz,* by Weck (Merian T, p.48)
4. *Spaniol,* by H. von Constantz (Merian T, p.50)

228

5. *La Spania in re* (Kleber, fol.29v)
6. *La Spania in re*, by H. B. (Kleber, fol.60v)
7. *Tancz der Schwarcz Knab* and *Hopp Tancz*, by Weck (Merian T, p.52)
8. *Dantz moss Benczenauher*, by H. v. Constantz (Merian T, p.54)
9. *Ein ander Dancz* and *Hopper Dencz*, by Weck (Merian T, p.56)

Nos.1–6 have similar titles, and in fact belong together. They are all based on the same melody, *Il re di Spagna* (The King of Spain), which is one of the many basse-danse tunes in the 15th-century dance books.[1] There these tunes are notated as monophonic pieces in long notes of equal value (mostly breves), not as dance tunes in the real sense, but like the tenors that underly the *cantus-planus* settings of Schlick and Cabezón. They were probably played on a trumpet or a trombone, while shawm players executed livelier counterpoints that provided the melody and rhythm of the dance. Probably these melodies were improvised like the 17th-century *divisions upon a ground* or like modern jazz. Among Kotter's keyboard dances there is one that illustrates this procedure in a very interesting way.

Fig.217

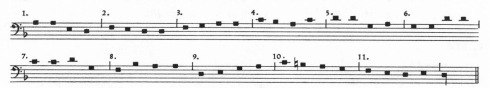

Fig.217 shows the tenor that was known as *Il re di Spagna*, or simply as *Spagna* (the dividing lines and numbers have been added). From Cornazano's treatise we know that a tenor that was notated in this fashion could be used for four metrically different dances: the *saltarello*, the *quaternaria*, the *cacciata* (or *piva*), and the *bassa danza*. The saltarello had three beats for each note of the tenor ("tre botte per nota"), the quaternaria four, the piva four, but at a faster tempo, and the bassa danza six. The saltarello was also called *alta danza* or simply *alta*, a designation that may be preferable for the 15th-century type to avoid confusion with the 16th-century saltarello. The difference between bassa danza and *alta* (the two other variants do not interest us here) can be demonstrated by the way they use the spagna tune (Fig.218).

In the Kotter and Kleber tablatures, nos.1–6 prove to be arrangements of the *spagna* tune in the meter of the alta danza throughout, not in the meter of the bassa danza. The bassa-danza scheme leads to extremely slow changes of har-

Fig.218

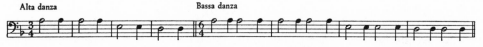

Alta danza   Bassa danza

mony; this fact probably explains why the alta meter, with progressions that move twice as fast, was more favored by the composers of the 16th century.[2]

An interesting historical evolution can be seen in the different treatment of the counterpoints that were added to the *cantus firmus* in these six examples. A transition from a purely functional dance to a stylized type of purely musical significance takes place. At the beginning we have the *Spaniol Kochersperg* (no.2), which has such archaic features that it has been called "musically unintelligible."[3] Indeed its setting is very peculiar; elements of the ancient organum in parallel fifths seem to combine with the fauxbourdon of the Dufay period. It is written in three voices, the lowest of which carries the spagna tune while the other two essentially parallel it in fifths and octaves; the result is a 1–5–8 organum setting. This texture is enlivened by the use of passing tones and ornamental turns, which appear almost identically in the two upper voices, and thus form parallel fourths. An excerpt is given in Fig.219; the piece is quite attractive, despite its primitive quality. This method represents more of an improvisation practice than a genuine method of composition, a kind of recipe, according to which one could create music above a basse-danse tenor. The method is essentially the one that Simon Tunstede describes around 1350 as *discantus supra librum*.

Fig.219

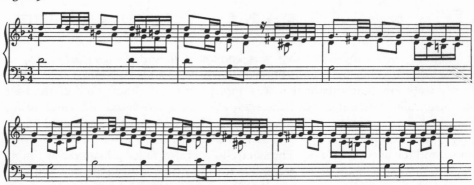

The character of the *Spania in re* from Kleber's tablature (no.5 above) is completely different. The texture is again three-voiced, but the *cantus firmus* lies in the middle part, supported by a harmonically oriented bass and overlaid with a richly ornamented upper part, which employs mostly scale-like figures. This texture is similar to the one found in the clavier music of the *Buxheim Organ Book*. The beginning is given in Fig.220.

Two other dances, the *Spanieler* by Kotter and the *Spaniol* by H. von Constantz (nos.1 and 4), seem to be close to Hofhaimer's organ technique. H. von Constantz is probably Hans Buchner, who, like Kotter, was one of Hofhaimer's students. Again the *cantus firmus* lies in the middle voice, but the bass is not just

Fig.220

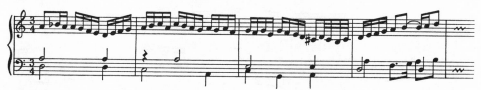

a filler part. Its line is as lively as the discant's; in fact it often parallels it in tenths. The similarity to Hofhaimer's *Salve regina* (cf.p.82), even the identity of technique, is obvious. The beginning of Kotter's *Spanieler* is shown in Fig.221.

Fig.221

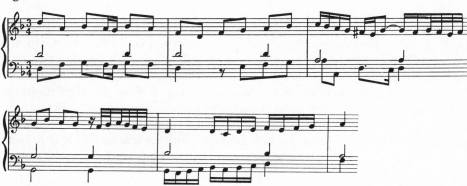

The other *Spania in re* (no.6) is signed H. B. (Hans Buchner) and dated 1520. It presents the spagna tune in alternating breves and semibreves, which become alternating whole and half notes in 3/2 time when the usual reduction is applied. This fact is somewhat obscured because the *cantus firmus* is rather richly ornamented and the composition starts with two introductory groups, each a semibreve in value, that have the character of a fore-imitation and stand outside the metric scheme. The *cantus firmus* again lies in the middle voice, and is joined by two additional parts, which are also full of rich, freely changing figurations. In comparison with the pieces discussed so far, this one shows much greater artistry and command of compositional technique—so much so that it almost becomes "too much of a muchness." In any event, such a work is a far cry from a functional dance, and is definitely art for art's sake. Fig.222 shows the beginning (the letters indicate the structural notes of the spagna tune).

The *Spanyöler Tancz* by Hans Weck (no.3) differs from all the other spagna settings in that it presents the melody in the top voice rather than in a lower part. Its relationship to the other spagna settings is thus analogous to that of Schlick's *Maria zart* to his *Salve regina*. In its field Weck's dance represents as high a level

Fig.222

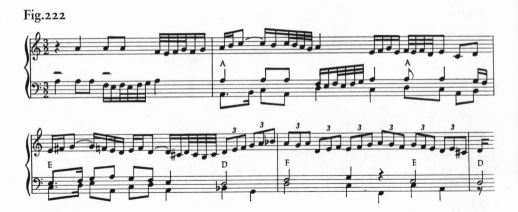

of artistic formulation as Schlick's work does in liturgical organ music. The *cantus firmus* is no longer ornamented in a stereotyped manner, but transformed in an ingenious way into a new melody with individuality and a life of its own. The voices are increased from three to four, and the lower parts assume a new character, that of a purely harmonic foundation that stresses the rhythm. In this explicit contrast of flowing melody and rhythmically punctuated harmony, we find for the first time a dance type that remained standard throughout the subsequent evolution of dances in the 16th century. With its unmistakable expression of self-assurance and vitality, it stands squarely on Renaissance ground. Fig.223

Fig.223

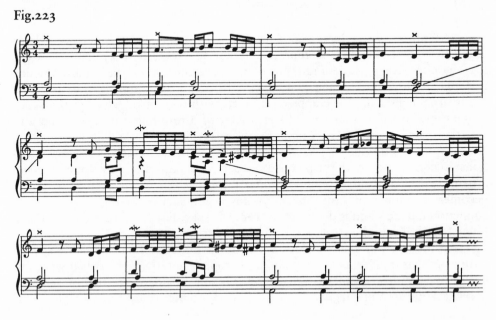

shows the beginning, with the structural notes of the spagna tune marked "x."[4]

The *Spanyöler* is followed by a *Hopper Dancz* in triple meter at twice the speed. This is the first appearance of a dance and an after-dance. The latter obviously belongs to the species of the piva, in which, according to Cornazano's description, each note of the basic tune is represented by four fast beats (of unequal duration). In this instance, as well as in the pivas preserved in Petrucci's fourth lute book of 1510, an alternating rhythm of quarter and eighth notes is employed. Fig.224 shows the beginning of the *Hopper Dancz* (the letters below the staff indicate the bass notes), together with a tentative reconstruction of the underlying melody (notes 1–8 correspond to the excerpt).

Fig.224

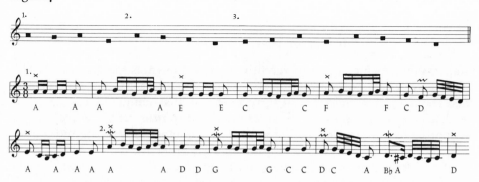

In addition to the spagna settings, Kotter's tablature contains three dances of the same general type, but based on other tunes. Weck's *Tancz der Schwarcz Knab* (no.7) uses the *Schwarzknab* melody, which is also used in many German lute dances, often entitled "hoftanz."[5] Weck puts it, lightly ornamented, in the tenor of a three-part setting, whose character is the same as the spagna settings of Kotter and Buchner (nos.1 and 4). The melody of the *Dantz moss* (dance measure) *Benczenauher* by H. v. Constantz (no.8) is the *Bentzenauer,* which is also known from lute settings.[6] The present piece is notated in 2/4 time, but must be read in 3/4 time. Here again the basic tune lies in the tenor of a three-part setting, with a lower part that is more of a support bass. Weck's piece, simply called *Ein ander Dancz* (no.9), seems to be based on the tune given in Fig.225; the tune is found in the second highest of four voices, and becomes harder to recognize toward the end.

Fig.225

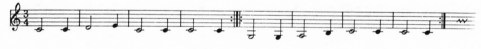

As in his *Spanyöler Tancz,* Weck also adds hopper dances to the *Schwarcz Knab* and the *Ander Dancz,* and each of these represents another type of after-dance. The one following the *Spanyöler* is based on a different tune, and is completely independent of the main dance. In the *Schwarcz Knab,* the main dance and and the after-dance are based on the same *cantus firmus,* curiously have the same rhythm, but add different counterpoints. In the *Ander Dancz* both dances are derived from the same material, but the time changes from 3/4 to 3/8.

To summarize briefly—all the dances from the Kotter and Kleber tablatures belong to a single species, which may be called *cantus-firmus* dances, or perhaps tenor dances, even though the basic tune does not always lie in the tenor. They derive from the basse-danse practice of the 15th century, but none are genuine basse-danses. Six of these dances employ the spagna tune in the metric scheme of the alta, and one of the after-dances follows the rhythm of the piva.

Italian Keyboard Dances to 1550

An Italian source, which has only recently become known, is the manuscript Ms. it. Cl. IV, No. 1227 (collocazione 11699) of the Biblioteca Marciana in Venice, written about 1520, a collection of forty brief and unassuming dances, concluding with a *Veni creator spiritus* and an *Et exsultavit spiritus meus.*[7] While it dates from approximately the same period as the German tablatures, it does not represent an end, but rather a new start in the field of keyboard dance. The titles of most of the dances point to popular songs, e.g., *La bella franceschina, Tuó la straza furfante,* or *Vegnando da Bologna,* but the manuscript also includes *Padoana im piva* (no.1), *Pavana in passo e mezo* and *Saltarello de la pavana* (nos. 4–5), *Passo e mezzo* (no.22), and *Saltarel del roy* (no.28)—the earliest instances of the new dance types of the 16th century.

Some of the dance songs are written in 4/4 (originally as four minims in ₵), even though their musical rhythm is doubtless ternary (6/4 or 3/2). This practice is also found in many later pieces, e.g., Frescobaldi's *Romanesca* (cf.Chap.16, note 45). As an illustration see the beginning of *Le roto el caro,* in Fig.226. It is probably best to consider such dances as galliards.

A dance entitled *La cara cossa,* shown in Fig.227, represents an early form

Fig.226

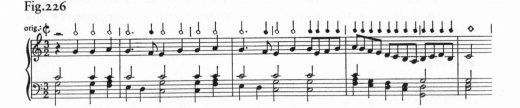

of the folia, which reappears around 1550 in various Spanish sources: in the lute
books of Valderrábano (1547) and Pisador (1552), in the *Tratado de glosas* by
Diego Ortiz (1553),[8] and in Venegas de Henestrosa's *Libro de cifra nueva* (1557).[9]
In contrast to the later folia, all these pieces begin with the dominant, not the tonic.

Fig.227

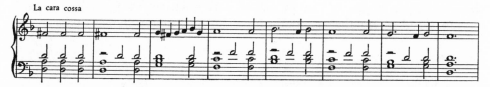

La cara cossa

Besides such dance songs, the manuscript contains some dances designated
as to type. The *Passo e mezzo* (no.22) represents the earliest known instance of
the *passamezzo antico*, which plays a very important part in the evolution of
dance music. Passamezzos are not freely invented dances, but in a sense are
variations on one of two bass themes (the *antico* and the *moderno* or *novo*), which
acts as a framework. The notes of the theme—the pillars of the framework—are
placed two full measures apart. Fig.228 shows the *Passo e mezzo* from the Venetian
manuscript and the theme.

Fig.228

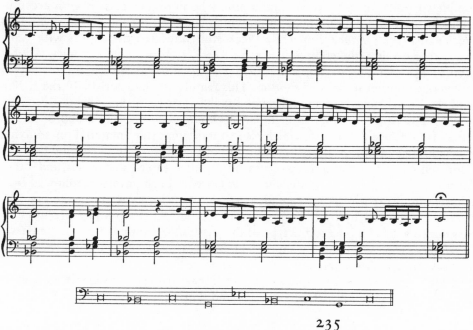

235

All passamezzos anticos are based on the same scheme, and—like the spagnas
—form a family that is held together by the same melodic idea. It is strange that
this theme appears as a bass tune that lacks even the rudiments of melodic form.
Indeed, it is hard to imagine that such a thing could have been invented at a time
when the "fundamental" import of the bass had not yet been discovered. This
bass is surely something secondary, and the real seed of the passamezzo antico
will have to be sought in a simple melodic formula. Such a formula is given in
Fig.229, together with the bass, in the usual key of G minor. In many passamezzos

Fig.229

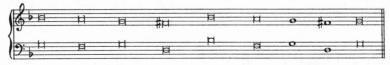

this discant tune does not emerge as clearly as the bass and the resulting harmonic
progression, but this is not really surprising, for in variations the bass of a theme
is generally a more stable element than the melody. Of course, there are instances
in which the melody is clearly preserved, e.g., in one of Attaingnant's galliards
(cf.Fig.236).

The Venetian dance collection represents a turning point, not only with
respect to types but also in the field of style. The contrapuntal, linear texture,
which still dominated the *cantus-firmus* dances of the early German tablatures, is
completely gone. In its place we find a purely homophonic texture with accentu-
ating chords and a figural upper voice, which was seen for the first time in Hans
Weck's *Spanyöler Tancz*. But while Weck still connected the chords with "correct" voice leading, the composer here proceeds with far fewer scruples. Almost
every dance contains passages in which two or more triads (1–3–5 or 1–5–8)
follow one another in parallel motion. This feature is characteristic of the Italian
(and the French) clavier dance throughout the 16th century.

A somewhat later source of Italian keyboard dances is the group of manuscripts from Castell' Arquato, which also contain important material for studying
the evolutions of liturgical organ music and of the ricercar. In one of the fascicles
(Jeppesen's no.1) we find 14 pavanes, in another (no.2) 2 pavanes and other
dances, and in a third (no.3) a *Pavana a la batiglia*. Each pavane is followed by a
saltarello and usually by an extended *represa* or *coda* as well; in one case the
pavane is followed by both a ripresa and a coda. All the pavanes are in effect
passamezzos, 8 belonging to the type of the passamezzo antico and 9 to the passamezzo moderno. As frequently happens in dance music, a newly introduced dance,
the passamezzo, uses an already established name before it appears under its own
title. Here the passamezzo antico appears in two forms that deviate somewhat
from the usual one: (B♭[forG] F G D . . .) and (G F G D G [for B♭] . . .).[10]

In each passamezzo (pavane) the basic scheme is presented twice. This is the first step in the direction of the passamezzo variations (cf.pp.270ff.). The saltarellos that follow are similarly constructed. The rather extended ripresas usually repeat a formula of two notes (dominant–tonic) ten or twelve times, or even more often. Fig.230 illustrates the structure with the bass scheme of a passamezzo moderno (no.2 of fascicle 1) (the small notes indicate the basic rhythm of the left hand).

Fig.230

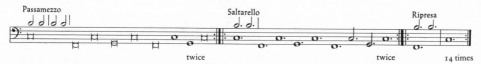

The dances from Castell' Arquato are very simple in style and retain the character of functional dance music. In many of them the left hand plays recurring 1–5–8 chords, while the right hand executes simple figurations. The beginning of the pavane outlined schematically in Fig.230 is a good example (Fig.231).

Fig.231

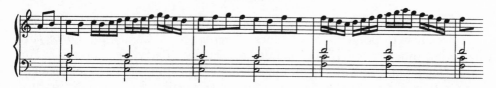

Fascicle 2 contains about a dozen dances with titles such as *La Delfina, Il Cremonense,* and *Zorzo.* Most of them are in 3/4 time and thus seem to be saltarellos or galliards. Two of the dances in duple meter, *Il Bersonello* and *Ciel Turchin,* consist of three-measure phrases, like the branles in the Attaingnant print.

The early history of Italian keyboard dances reaches the end of a first phase with a collection printed in 1551: *Intabolatura nova di varie sorte de balli da sonare Arpichordi, Clavicembali, Spinette e Manachordi raccolti da diversi eccelentissimi Autori, Libro primo* (Gardano, Venice),[11] in which the final transition from the pavane to the passamezzo is made. Only one of the twenty-five dances is still called a pavane, *Fusi Pavana piana* (but the dance entitled *Le forze d'Hercole* probably belongs to the same category). By contrast, the after-dance in triple meter is still predominantly the galliard, and the only example of a saltarello, *Saltarello del Re,* can barely be distinguished from a galliard.

The collection begins with three dances called *Pass'e mezo nuovo,* which are subsequently contrasted by a group of three *Pass'e mezo antico* (nos.14–16). In comparison with the earlier passamezzos, the dance rhythm is more stressed (by repeated chords), and the phrase endings are emphasized by a stereotyped broken-chord formula, as illustrated in Fig.232. In the second example a tendency emerges that is important for the subsequent evolution. The harmonic framework is enlivened not only by figuration but also by rhythmically staggered chords.

Fig.232

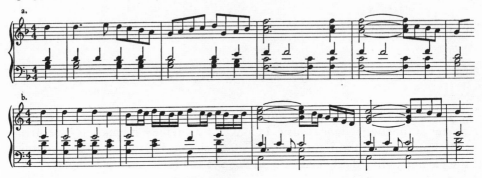

a. Pass'e mezo antico (No. 14); b. Pass'e mezo nuovo (No. 3).

The great majority of the dances are galliards, all with individual titles. Several titles seem to point to vocal tunes (*L'herba fresca Gagliarda, Tu te parti Gagliarda*), others possibly to localities or persons (*Lodesane Gagliarda, Fornesina Gagliarda*). This usage continued for a long time in Italy, particularly in connection with the livelier dances in triple meter (galliard, saltarello, corranto). Later it was transferred to other lively types, especially to the canzona. As in the Venetian manuscript, these galliards are mostly notated in 4/4 time, although their rhythm is definitely ternary. Hemiola figures, which are also found in the galliards of the Attaingnant print (cf.Fig.238), appear repeatedly. Figure 233 shows the beginning of the *Mezza notte Gagliarda* (the original measure units are indicated by small bars above the staff).

The structure of the passamezzos is, of course, given by the basic scheme. The *Fusi Pavana piana* has the form AA′ BB′ (with varied repetitions), in which A comprises four measures and B seven. The galliards, with few exceptions, have

Fig.233

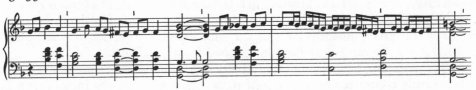

the form AA BB (each letter standing for four 6/4 measures) or aa bb cc (each letter indicating two measures). The *Saltarello del Re* has the form aa bb CC.

Attaingnant's Dance Collection

There is a single, but rather significant, source for the evolution of keyboard dances in France, a print brought out by the Parisian publisher Attaingnant, probably in 1530: *Quatorze Gaillardes neuf Pavennes sept Branles et deux Basses Dances le tout reduict de musique en la tabulature du jeu d'Orgues Espinettes Manicordions et telz semblables instruments musicaulx.*[12] The legend "reduict de musique en la tabulature" should probably be interpreted to mean that the dances were orginally written for an instrumental ensemble and were then transcribed into clavier tablature (a brace of two staves of five lines each) and ornamented with the usual figurations. It is noteworthy that for the execution "jeu d'orgues" is mentioned first; it is surely not the church organ that is intended, but the small house organ (such as the so-called bible regal), which was then in wide use. The number of dances given in the title is not quite correct: In reality there are fifteen galliards and eight pavanes.

There are only two examples that are designated as basse-danses (nos.7 and 8), and, in fact, they do not belong to the species, but merely bear its name. The essential feature of the basse-danse, the *cantus firmus,* has completely disappeared. Both pieces are song-like, and consist of three brief sections. One is in 4/4 time, the other in 3/4. Structurally and stylistically they should be counted as branles or as a pavane and a branle. This is another example of the use of an earlier name for a new dance. (cf.p.236).

The branle existed in a large number of subspecies, which probably differed mainly in the dancers' movements. Musically only two types can be distinguished: the *branle commun* (or *simple*) in 4/4 time (e.g., no.4) and the *branle gay* in 3/4 or 6/4 time (e.g., no.5). Most branles comprise two sections, each of which is usually repeated. Interestingly, most of these sections are of irregular length. In four branles (nos.4, 5, 12, and 14) each section consists of six measures, or, more accurately, of a three-measure phrase that is repeated with a different ending. Fig.234 shows the first section of branle no.12 (all musical examples from Attaingnant are given without reduction in note values). Only one branle is built "regularly," no.16, which contains four sections of four measures each.

Fig.234

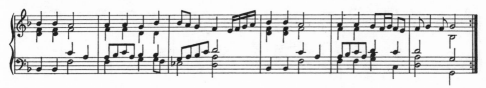

Like the branle, the pavane and the galliard exhibit distinctive features, but in contrast to it, these two types evolved further. The pavanes are all in duple meter (4/4), the galliards in triple (3/4 or 6/4).[13] Some show a two-part structure ‖ : A : ‖ : B : ‖, but most of them are tri-partite, A B A or A B C, usually with each section repeated, although sometimes the repetition is not indicated, possibly erroneously. The A B C form is the one that later became standard, particularly in the English pavanes and galliards. It is especially clear in pavanes nos.1 and 27 and galliards nos.1a and 28. In three instances a pavane combines with the succeeding galliard in a variation pair, in which the second dance represents a tripla variant of the duple-meter main dance (nos.1–1a, 11–11a, and 21–21a). In the first and third pairs each 4/4 measure (semibreve) of the first dance becomes a 3/4 measure (dotted minim) in the second one, but in the second pair it is expanded to two such measures. Fig.235 shows the beginnings of the first and second pairs (giving only the upper parts).

Fig.235

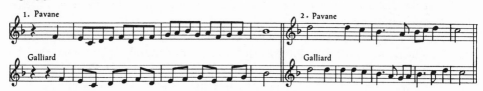

Some pavanes and galliards of the Attaingnant print really represent a later type of dance—the passamezzo antico and moderno. The antico structure (cf.Fig. 229) is very clear in galliard no.6, where not only the bass scheme but also the associated melody can be recognized (Fig.236).[14] As in the passamezzos from Castell' Arquato, a variant of the usual bass line is employed—the one with the tonic (instead of the mediant) as fifth note (cf.p.236). This galliard consists of

Fig.236

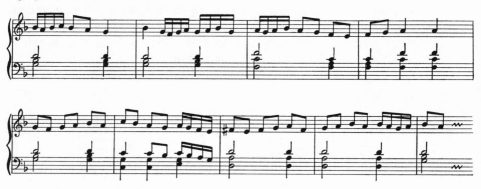

three variations on the double theme, with a repeated *ripresa* based on the formula | c | d | g | g | inserted between the second and third variations. The original intent of the ripresa is clear here—to confirm by repetition the closing formula of the main idea. The passamezzo moderno first appears in this collection—in the third of the pavane-galliard pairs (nos.21–21a)—but in a form that deviates somewhat from the one generally used thereafter. Fig.237 puts the two forms side by side.

Fig.237

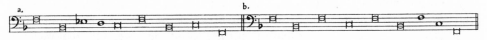

Just as the branle (or the pavane) is offered under the name of the basse-danse, the passamezzo appears under that of the pavane. The memory of this substitution lived on in the designations *pavane passemaize* and *passamezzo pavane* for the passamezzo antico, and *quadren paven* for the passamezzo moderno.[15]

In style the French dances are similar to the Italian ones from the Venice and Castell' Arquato manuscripts. The contrapuntal texture is predominantly replaced by homophony, in which parallel motion of fifths and octaves is not at all rare. However, the left hand is not given block chords exclusively, as in the Italian dances, but is also entrusted with filling passage work or contrapuntal fragments, as, e.g., in galliard no.25 shown in Fig.238. This passage also offers an early example of a hemiola rhythm, i.e., of the change from 6/4 to 3/2 time, which is characteristic of the courantes of the 17th century.

Fig.238

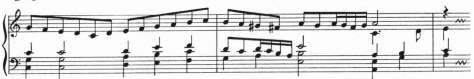

The Dances in the Lublin Tablature

The tablature of the Polish canon Johannes of Lublin contains thirty-six dances, written about 1537 to 1547,[16] about the same time as the galliards, pavanes, and other dances collected by Attaingnant. The titles reveal a varied repertoire, international in character, with dances assembled from many countries. Names like *Conradus* (nos.1 and 25), *Ferdinandi* (no.2), and *Paur Thancz* (no.27) point to Germany; *Italica* (nos.18, 32, and 36) to Italy; *Poznanie* (nos.8, 9, 23, and 24) to Poland; *Hayduczky* (no.31) to Hungary; and *Hispaniarum* (no.35) to Spain.

241

Several dances bear the general designation *chorea;* others remain untitled. Almost all pieces consist of a main dance in 4/4 time and an after-dance in 3/4 that uses the same melody. Space permits only a few remarks about the individual dances and their tunes. The *Czayner Thancz* (no.29) is essentially identical with the *Zeuner Tanz* in Neusidler's lute book of 1540. Dances nos. 6 and 26 start with exactly the same four-measure phrase as Josquin's frottola *In te Domine speravi,* $(\mid a - a - \mid bb - a\,g\,f \mid e\,f - e \mid f - f - \mid).$[17]

Four dances of the Lublin tablature, *Chorea super duos saltus, Alia super duos saltus, Alia Poznanie,* and *Ad novem saltus* (nos.15, 21, 24, and 30), have a very unusual rhythm. In contrast to the other dances they consist mainly or entirely of three-measure rather than four-measure phrases, each of the form $\mid \downarrow \downarrow \mid \downarrow \downarrow \downarrow \mid \circ \mid$, i.e., with syncopation in the second measure. The real meaning of this figure, however, is not one of syncopation but of measures of different length: $\mid \downarrow \mid \downarrow \downarrow \mid \downarrow \downarrow \mid \circ \mid$. Fig.239 shows the beginning of the *Chorea super duos saltus,* with the original disposition of the measures indicated above the staff. This is the same peculiar rhythm that was found in an early 16th-century prelude (cf.Fig.204).

Fig.239

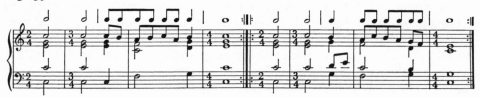

Dances nos.5, 13, and 14 are early examples of the passamezzo antico. No.14, *Jescze Marczynye* ("Once more, Martin"), is of special interest, for in it the basic chord structure is filled out with motifs, not with figurations, as shown in Fig.240.

Fig.240

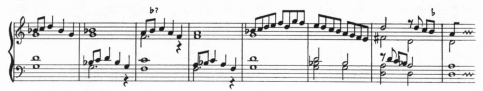

The Dance Collections by Facoli and Radino

Two later sources of Italian keyboard dances are prints by Marco Facoli of Venice and Gio. Maria Radino of Padua. *Il secondo libro d'intavolatura di balli* by Facoli (1588)[18] contains a *Pass'e mezo moderno in sei modi* and *Saltarello del pass'e mezo ditto in quattro modi,* 4 *Padoane,* 12 pieces designated *Aria,* 2 *Napolitane,* and 2 *Tedesche.* The *Passamezzo and Saltarello* is a variation set (cf. p.274). The paduanas are a well-defined type, quite different from the pavane, which is occasionally called a paduana. They are all in 6/4 time (originally six minims) and are formulated in eight clearly articulated four-measure phrases, four of which are varied repetitions of the other four. The first two paduanas, *Marucina* and *La Chiareta,* have the scheme | A A' | B B' | C C' | D D' |; the third, *La Finetta,* treats the last two phrases as a unit: | A A' | B B' | C D C' D' |; while the fourth, *La Marchetta,* does so in the first two phrases: | A B A' B' | C C' | D D' |. The fourth one is even followed by a lively figural variation of the entire piece: *Alio modo.*

The stylistic details of these dances are interesting. The left hand is limited to sharp rhythmic chords, which completely disregard, even scorn, the prohibition against fifths—a prohibition that, in fact, has no justification at all in music so strongly rooted in percussive rhythm. In every cadence measure (meas.4, 8, etc.) there is a stereotyped, interestingly notated broken-chord figure (see Fig.241). The upper part has a strikingly winged line, which anticipates or echoes the dance movements in quite a pictorial way, often by placing fast figures on the last of three beats. An ascending slide[19] is frequently employed. Fig.241 shows the beginning (A A') of the second paduana.

Facoli's twelve arias are among the earliest examples of this type and are therefore important for the pre-history of the genuine aria of the 17th century.

Fig.241

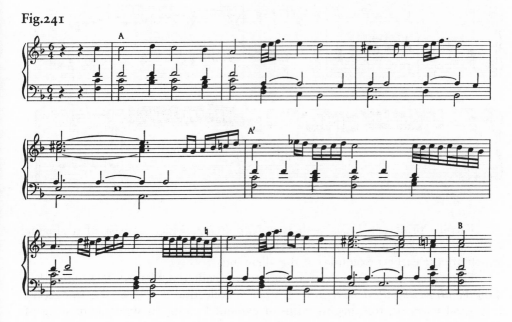

They are called *Aeri* in the title, confirming the hypothesis, first put forth by P. Nettl,[20] about the etymology of the term (from *aere* = air, wind). Most of Facoli's arias have titles such as *Aria della Signora Cinthia* (*Lucilla*, etc.); but there are also two *Arie della Comedia* and an *Aria da cantar Terza Rima*, in which the later meaning of aria, as a model usable for various texts of the same verse form, clearly emerges.

Facoli's arias are all in 6/4 time (originally six minims in ₵ 3, exactly like the paduanas), and are all twelve measures long. In several of them the last four measures are inscribed *Le Riprese*. They are obviously clavier accompaniments to dance songs: The various stanzas of the song were sung to the first eight measures, and a ritornello was danced between the stanzas. The contrast between song and dance often receives palpable expression in the music, as, e.g., in *Aria della Signora Michiela* (Fig.242).

Fig.242

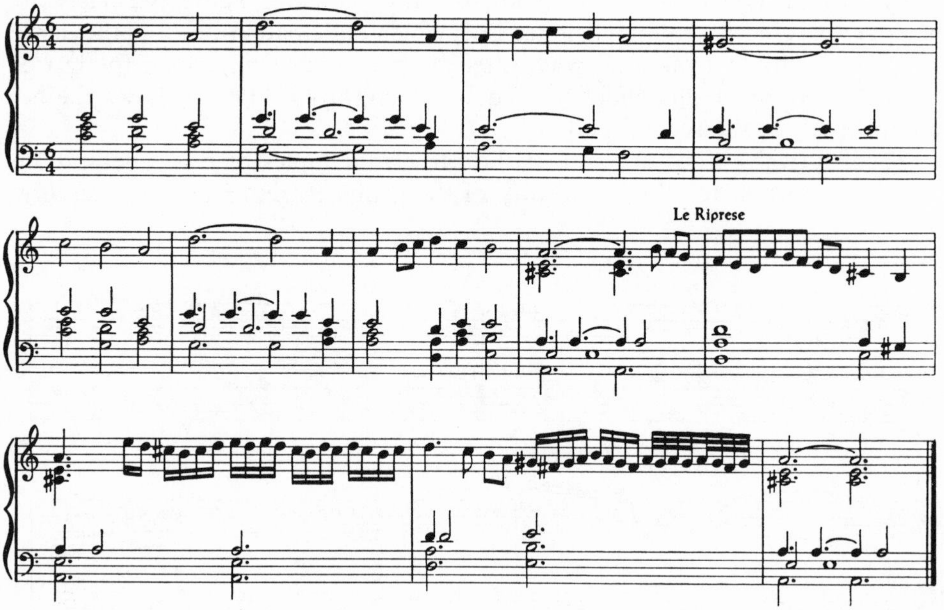

Facoli's print concludes with two *Napolitane,* which consist of a singing part with text and a rudimentary keyboard accompaniment, and two *Tedesche,* which are the earliest examples of the allemande.

Four years later Gio. Maria Radino of Padua published *Il primo libro d'intavolatura di balli d'arpicordo* (1592),[21] a collection that is similar to Facoli's in several ways. It, too, begins with an extended variation work, consisting of a *Pass'e mezo* and *Gagliarda*, each with six variations (cf.p.274). It is followed by two paduanas and four galliards. The two paduanas, like those by Facoli, are in 6/4 time, but they are somewhat differently formed. They have four eight-measure phrases, the second of which is a varied repetition of the first: A A′ B C. Each paduana is followed by a variation of the entire piece, called *Seconda parte.* The galliards also are in 6/4, but differ from the paduanas in form. The first three have the characteristic structure of the galliard, which consists of three sections, each of which is repeated in varied form: | A A′ | B B′ | C C′ |. In the fourth galliard the form is reduced to A A′ B B′. Usually each section comprises four measures, but in three instances there are sections of different length: In no.1 section A contains three measures and B two, and in no.2 section B has five measures. Similar irregularities also occur in the galliards (and the pavanes) of the virginalists.

In general Radino's dances are quite similar to Facoli's. The ascending slide recurs in his music, although in the slower rhythm of two sixteenth notes and an eighth. Facoli follows an earlier custom of giving the left hand only chords to play, while Radino occasionally entrusts it with figurations and motivic figures. In Radino's galliards not only does the rhythm change from 6/4 to 3/2 time but also from 3/4 to 6/8, a change that leads to interesting rhythmic passages. A particularly striking one is shown in Fig.243; it is taken from the *Gagliarda seconda* (beginning of section B).

Fig.243

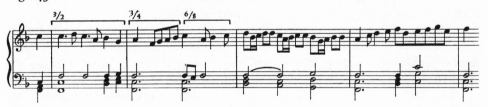

In conclusion let us mention two more sources—manuscripts probably written around 1570: Florence, Bibl. naz., Magliabechiana XIX, 115 and 138. The first contains twenty-three pieces, among them *La Monaca, La Spagnoletta, Corrente, Aria di Santino da Parma, Terza rima,* and songs such as *Era di maggio* or *Dalle porte d'Oriente.* The second includes a *Gagliarda di S.* (probably Santino) *da Parma, Ruggiero, Spagnoletta,* and *La Monaca,* as well as a number of clavier settings with full texts written below, e.g., *Lungo età verde riva* and *Dhe se ti mova un cor,* which are probably the earliest songs with keyboard accompaniment. About one hundred years later Storace employed the spagnoletta from this manuscript, with the key changed from *G* major to *A* minor, for a number of variations.

German Sources of the Late 16th Century

Keyboard dances are found in a number of German prints and manuscripts from the last three decades of the 16th century:[22]

1. Elias Nikolaus Ammerbach, *Orgel oder Instrument Tabulatur* (1571, 1583)
2. Bernhard Schmid (the Elder), *Zwey Bücher einer neuen kunstlichen Tabulatur auff Orgel und Instrument* (1577)
3. Jacob Paix, *Ein schön, nutz und gebreuchlich Orgel Tabulaturbuch* (1583)
4. Christoph Löffelholtz, Manuscript Tablature, 1585 (Berlin, Staatsbibl. mus. ms. 40034)
5. Anonymous Tablature, 1593 (Berlin, Staatsbibl. mus. ms. 40115)
6. Augustus Nörmiger, Manuscript Tablature, 1598 (Berlin, Staatsbibl. mus. ms. 40089 [not 40098])
7. Bernhard Schmid (the Younger), Tabulaturbuch ... (1607)

Following A. Ritter, music historians call the authors of these books (especially of the prints) colorists[23] because they busied themselves with the transcription of motets and other vocal works, "all ornamented (*coloriert*) with great diligence," as Paix says. This pejorative designation is somewhat unjust, for coloration was practiced everywhere throughout the 16th century. Moreover, Ritter took no notice of the fact that in addition to the mechanically ornamented vocal works of Arcadelt, Crecquillon, and Lassus, the colorists' books contain a great number of very valuable, independent pieces—the dances—which make these tablatures significant. They give us a lively and complete picture of German dance music toward the end of the 16th century. The books contain the international Italian dances, a great many German dances of various kinds, and dances from other countries, such as Prussia, Poland, and Hungary.

The Italian dance types include the passamezzo in several stages of evolution: antico, moderno, and freely composed. In the first category there are 5 pieces by Ammerbach (1583 edition, nos.97, 98, 105, 106, 107; no.97 is erroneously entitled *Passamezzo nova;* 3 dances by Schmid the Elder (MeT,* pp.92f., nos.29, 30, 33), 2 by Paix, MeT, p.125, nos.53, 54), one by Löffelholtz (*Passa mezo Venetiano;* MeT, p. 167, no.1), and 2 in the anonymous tablature (MeT, p.200, nos.25–26). In all of them the standard bass and the basic melody of the passamezzo antico can be recognized easily. The passamezzo moderno is represented by 3 Ammerbach pieces (nos.93, 94, 95, which are erroneously called *Passamezo antico*); a *Passamezo comun* by Schmid the Elder (MeT, p.92, no.31); a *Passemezo* in the anonymous tablature (MeT, p.214); and 2 *Passo è mezo italiano* by Schmid the Younger (MeT, p.263, nos.77, 78). The freely composed passamezzos are the *Engelische Passamezo* by Ammerbach (no.101), the *Passomezo ungaro* by Schmid the Elder (MeT, p.93, no.32; complete in H. Halbig, *Klaviertänze des 16. Jahrhunderts,* p.12); and the *Pass'è mezzo novo, Pass'è mezzo La Parenzina,* and *Un altro Pass'è mezzo novo* by Paix (MeT, pp.126f., nos.55, 56, 57).

---

* Abbreviation for Merian T.

In most instances the passamezzo is followed by a saltarello, which is usually derived from it by a transformation into triple meter—a tripla or proportz. Occasionally a ripresa is added to the passamezzo or the saltarello, e.g., Ammerbach's *Alia Passamezo—La Reprisa—Saltarello vel tripla proportio* (nos.98–100). Paix's *Pass'è mezzo antico* (complete in MeT, pp.135ff.) is an extended composition, consisting of passamezzo, ripresa, saltarello, and ripresa, each section having several *modi*, i.e., variations. The two *Passo è mezo italiano* by Schmid the Younger (the second is complete in MeT, p.264) are also extended variation sets. We shall return to them in the chapter on variations. Finally there are also twelve galliards by Schmid the Younger.

Most of the pieces preserved in the German tablatures are not the Italian dance types, but indigenous social music from the end of the 16th century, which has much more variety and individuality than the Italian repertoire. The German tablatures consist primarily of dance songs like *Die Megdlein sind von Flandern, Es het ein Baur sein Freylein verlohren,* or *Wir trinken alle gehren,* but they also contain processions, mask dances, German and Polish dances, and other numbers. Nörmiger's collection, which was made "upon serene demand" of Duke Friedrich Wilhelm of Saxony for "Miss Sophia, Duchess of Saxony," especially abounds in variety and color. It contains first "D. Martini Lutheri deutzsche Geistliche Lieder auff die fürnemsten Feste"—seventy-seven chorales in simple keyboard settings—which constitute an important source for the history of the Protestant chorale (cf.p.99). They are followed by "schöne weltliche Lieder," such as *Ach höchster Schatz auf dieser Erdt* and *Ach Elselein du holder Bule mein,* and by nearly one hundred dances—intradas, paduanas, passamezzos, galliards. A variety of other pieces give a very vivid picture of the ceremonial and social life at the Saxon court toward the end of the 16th century—*Churf. Sachs. Witwen Erster Mummerey Tanntz* and *Frewlein Sophien Erster Mummerey Tanntz, Fürstliche Aufführunge zum Tantz* and *Fürstliche Abfürunge vom Tantz, Der Heyligenn drey Könige Auftzugkh* and *Der Mohren Auftzugkh, Mattasin oder Toden Tantz,* and *Der Schefer Tantz.* These pieces are brief, with very individual and charming melodies, which are particularly agreeable because the usual ornaments are omitted. There are some picturesque figures, such as the "fearful" rhythms of the *Mattasin oder Toden Tantz,* or the "swaying" motion of the *Kerabe* (refrain) that concludes *Der Schefer Tantz* (Fig.244).

Fig.244

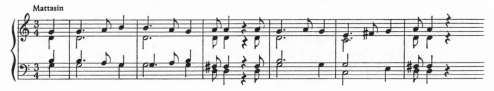

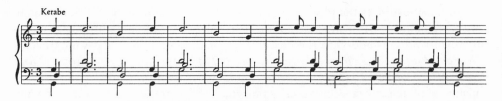

The intradas are not really dance music, but are closely related to it. As the name indicates, they accompany festive entrances of groups or individuals, and were probably used mostly as introductions to dancing. The anonymous tablature of 1593 includes six intradas (MeT, pp.210–14), and Nörmiger's contains ten (of which four are published in MeT, pp.239f.). Nörmiger's *Fürstliche Aufführunge zum Tantz* (MeT, p.240) also belongs here. The intradas are not a standardized type. Some are in duple meter, others in triple, and some alternate between the two. Interesting irregularities in rhythm and phrasing indicate that the intradas were not really danced, but rather interpreted by individual pantomime. The remarkable individuality of the intradas in Nörmiger's collection is exemplified by *Ein ander Intrada* (MeT, p.240), reproduced in Fig.245. Note the dissonance F♯–F in the fifth measure, which confirms the legitimacy of such occurrences (cf.Fig.91b.). Successive 1–5–8 chords occur in the accompaniment, but the voice crossings avoid parallel fifths and octaves.

Fig.245

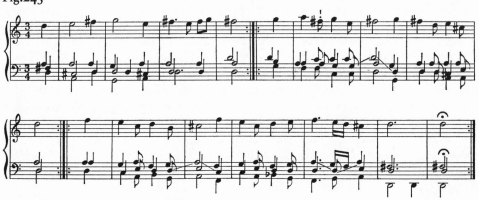

English Keyboard Dances Before Byrd

The picture of Renaissance dance music that emerges in Germany, France, Poland, and Italy is significantly enlarged and completed in England. Dance music received its rounding-off and achieved its highest fulfillment in the island kingdom, which is so often decried as unmusical. The development moved along conventional roads in Italy and France, and led to an attractive, though rather modest achievement of its own in Germany, but in England it rose to truly artistic heights with such masters as William Byrd, John Bull, and Orlando Gibbons.

The beginning as well as the end-result of English dance music are extremely interesting. Unfortunately there are very few early remains. The only source earlier than 1550 is the manuscript Roy. App. 58 of the British Museum, written about 1530; it is, however, a very important one for the history of dance music, since all the clavier pieces contained in it are dances: *A Hornepype* by Hugh Aston, *My Lady Careys Dompe, The Short Measure off My Lady Wynkfylds Rounde, The Emperors Pavyn, A Galyarde, The Kyngs Pavyn, The Crocke, The Kyngs Maske (Marke?)*, and *A Galyard*.[24]

Hugh Aston's *Hornepype* is doubtless one of the most remarkable works of all keyboard literature.[25] First of all its length is surprising: no fewer than 118 measures in 6/4 time. But surprise yields to admiration when one discovers how alive the content is in this extended span—a content that not only aims at changing figures but also at intensification of the material. The total construction discloses a feeling for dynamic development, which has no equal in the music of the 16th and 17th centuries. The piece divides into a number of sections that produce a continuous increase in tempo and intensity. It begins with eleven measures that have the character of an introducton. This section is dominated by a swaying, idyllic motif (cf.Fig.246a.). The dance proper follows: first in a sort of *allegro moderato,* with rhythms that are clearly marked, but sound intentionally reticent

Fig.246

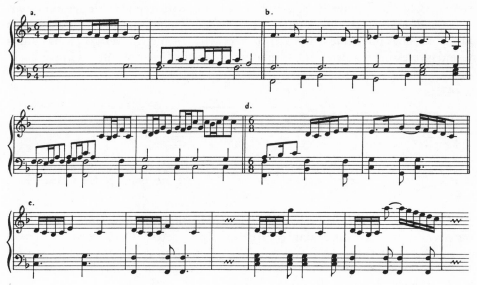

(b.); then in faster motion, *allegro*, presenting motifs in which one can almost recognize the dancer's gestures (c.). The main portion of the piece is an extended *presto* section in which veritable fireworks of constantly changing, captivating ideas are unleashed (d.). In one especially arresting passage the same motif is heard eleven times, with consistent widening of the interval skip from a third to a thirteenth (e.). This colorful variety continues with undiminished, and even increasing, liveliness, until the last eight measures, when the motion slows up, as though in a state of exhaustion, which one is surely justified in expressing by a gradual *ritardando*.

The astonishing wealth of melody and dynamics contrasts with the extremely simple harmonic construction—the continuous alternation of tonic and dominant. Expressed in terms of 16th-century composition technique, it is an alternation of F and G, each sounding for a whole measure, most often in the highest part of the accompaniment. Thus the entire hornpipe is based on a two-note ostinato; it is the earliest example of the *ground*, which plays an important role in English keyboard music. A particularly fine touch occurs in the eleven-measure introductory section, where the ostinato appears in reverse order, *G–F,* in a kind of upbeat form, before it assumes its normal shape at the start of the dance proper. In this way, introduction and dance relate to one another like question and answer, like attempt and realization.

The next piece in the manuscript, *My Lady Careys Dompe*,[26] is also a ground with continuous alternation of tonic and dominant. In contrast to the *Hornepype*, where the ostinato is completely covered by the other parts, its ostinato stands out clearly and furnishes the dance rhythm, as shown in Fig.247a. Above this bass the right hand plays a melody that unfolds with remarkable freedom and liveliness, despite all the accommodation to the harmonic scheme. Although this dance piece does not achieve the artistic excellence of the *Hornepype*, it has many fine and interesting features. The beginning of the upper part is offered in Fig.247b.

Fig.247

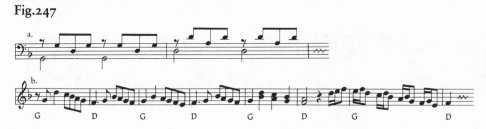

The dompe is followed by *The Short Measure off My Lady Wynkfylds Rounde*, an attractive little dance piece in triple meter, which consists of two musical phrases in the order A A B B A A B B. Both phrases are of irregular length: A has nine measures and B ten. Decorative turns, as shown in Fig.248, give the melody a characteristic and charming shape.

Fig.248

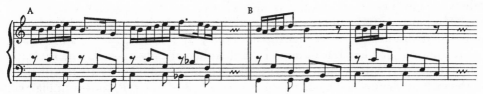

The remaining dances in the manuscript Roy. App. 58 are pavanes and galliards. They are the first English examples of these two types, which were to play an important role in the development of English dance music. As keyboard literature these pieces are of little interest, since they are probably all transcriptions of ensemble dances.[27] Their strict three-part texture, which frequently includes "unplayable" intervals—tenths and twelfths—in the left hand, differs decidedly from the genuine clavier style of the *Hornepype*, *Dompe*, and *Rounde*.

The earliest known example of an English pavane for clavier, a *Pavyon* by Master Newman, is contained in the *Mulliner Book*, written about 1560.[28] It consists of four repeated sections of six, seven, six, and six measures, respectively. Apart from a few full chords at beginning and end, it is written in four parts and exhibits a contrapuntal mastery that is unusual in dance music of the period. The last two sections, particularly, remind one of the masterful polyphonic-motivic style of William Byrd. In tonal technique Newman's pavane is remarkable, first because it is in C minor, a key that is hardly ever found in the 16th century and was only rarely employed even in the late 17th century. Even more unusual is the conclusion of the piece, where an augmented sixth chord A♭–C–F♯ appears.[29] The turning figures are particularly beautiful and impressive. They are used motivically in the last section, with the highest note often representing an expressive appoggiatura. There is a suggestion of that gentle melancholy that to a large degree characterized the mood of Elizabethan England and that found its most touching expression in one of Orlando Gibbons' pavanes. The last section of Master Newman's pavane is given in Fig.249.

The next stage of English dance music is represented by a manuscript written about 1570. It is the possession of Trinity College in Dublin, and has been published under the title of *The Dublin Virginal Book*.[30] It contains 30 unnamed

Fig.249

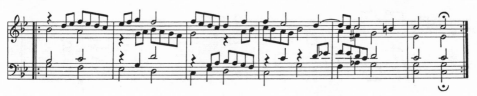

pieces, some of which prove to be variations on the passamezzo antico, while others are pavanes, galliards, allemandes (almans), branles, and dance songs.

The pavanes and galliards already exhibit characteristics of their later evolution. There are five pavane-galliard pairs (nos.3–4, 5–6, 7–8, 21–22, and 26–27), related not only by key but in most instances thematically as well. The thematic relations are particularly clear in the first three pairs, although they are less obvious in the melody than in the bass, as, e.g., in section B of nos.5–6, shown in Fig.250.

Fig.250

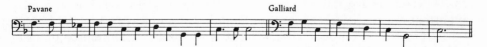

Galliard no.22 and pavane no.26 consist of four sections, like Master Newman's pavane; the others show the three-section form, which occurs occasionally in Attaingnant's print and which is almost exclusively employed later. Usually each section is repeated, either exactly or with an ornamented variant of one measure or another, most often in the final measures. Only once, in section B of pavane no.26, is the repetition varied throughout. The sections are usually four measures long, occasionally eight. An interesting exception is pavane no.5, with three sections of five, four, and six measures, respectively.

The texture of these dances is free-voiced contrapuntal, with the material distributed equally between the two hands in strong contrast to the Italian texture found in the *Intabolatura di balli* of 1551 and in the dances of Facoli and Radino. Occasionally there are suggestions of imitative and motivic techniques, e.g., in pavane no.3, which is ascribed to a Master Taylor. Its first section is given in Fig.251. As in Master Newman's pavane, there is a tendency toward artistic formulation, which later leads to the complete stylization of the dance in the works of the virginalists. The artistic highpoint of the collection is pavane no.21. The grand approach and impressive lines, especially in the first and last sections, make one suspect that it is a youthful work by Byrd.

Most, if not all, of the other dances in the *Dublin Virginal Book* are simple arrangements of popular tunes, and are often quite charming. Several of them, e.g., the branle *Hoboken* (no.12) or the alman *Prince* (no.15), are found in other

Fig.251

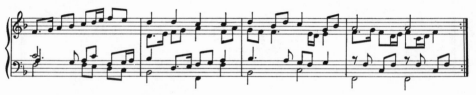

sources as ensemble or lute dances and can thus be identified.[31] In style, and probably in their social or cultural function as well, they belong to the same type as the German dances from the end of the century, most of which are also based on popular tunes. The last piece in the collection (no.30) is quite different; its style and form mark it as a paduana. It consists of two sections of four and six measures, respectively, both repeated in lightly varied form, followed by a variation of the entire piece and a ritornello (meas.41), in which a two-measure ground (dominant and tonic in alternation) is varied eight times.[32]

Byrd's Pavanes and Galliards

The period of Queen Elizabeth I witnessed the artistic climax of 16th-century dance music. Until then it was cultivated by more or less skilled musicians and dance teachers; now it bloomed as a mature and highly stylized art in the hands of a series of outstanding masters, especially William Byrd, John Bull, and Orlando Gibbons, the "three famous masters" (as they are called on the title page of the *Parthenia*), who represent with almost mathematical exactness three generations of English music (their birth dates are, respectively, 1543, 1562, and 1583). This astonishing development was certainly favored, if not made possible, by the fact that it was confined to a narrow field. It was limited to the two dance types that were already preferred in the earliest English sources of the century—the pavane and the galliard. The virginal books include other dances: allemandes, courantes, and gigues, but historically, as well as stylistically and artistically, they represent the beginning rather than the final stage of an evolution.

Byrd's dance compositions occupy first place chronologically as well as quantitatively. They include 21 pavane-galliard pairs, 5 single pavanes, and 7 single galliards, as well as the *Passamezzo Pavana* (FW, I, p.203) and the *Quadran Paven* (FW, II, p.103), which are variations on the passamezzo antico and moderno (cf.p.271), and the pavane-galliard pairs *Delight* and *Lachrymae* (FW, II, pp.436 and 42), which are arrangements of lute works by Johnson and by Dowland. It is not easy to treat this extensive repertoire and give an adequate impression of it. Let us begin with the structural factors.*

Almost all the pavanes and galliards show the three-section form that had already become the norm in the *Dublin Virginal Book*. A novel feature is that each section is repeated in varied form, as in the paduanas and galliards of Facoli and Radino. The basic structure is thus A A' B B' C C'. Occasionally the varied repetitions are omitted throughout (e.g., in the pavane FW, II, p.394, and in the galliard FW, II, p. 258), or in the last section (in the pavane FW, II, p.226, and in the *Pypers Gagliarde*, TB, p.80). In two galliards (FW, II, p.202; AN, p.99) the two

---

* The new editions of Byrd's works (cf.p.80) are abbreviated in the next two sections as follows: FW = *Fitzwilliam Virginal Book*; AN = H. Andrews, *My Lady Nevell's Book*; P = *Parthenia*; TB = S. Tuttle, *William Byrd*.

halves of the last section are varied separately, in the form C_1 C_1' C_2 C_2'. Significant deviations are found in only two instances: in the well-known pavane and galliard *The Earle of Salisbury* (P, p.12), in which both dances consist of only two sections each, without varied repetitions, and in *Galliards Gygge* (AN, p.54), which shows the completely different form, A B C B, with varied repetition of each section, followed by a variation of the entire piece. Even the title indicates a mixed type, similar to the *Passamezzo Pavana*.

The sections, as expected, are generally of regular proportions, but there are some instances of irregular length, and they are interesting from the historical point of view. In 16th-century dances, bar lines in both the sources and the new editions frequently result in groups of different numbers of beats, and cannot be used for counting measures. Instead it is preferable to define the length of the sections by the number of semibreves in each (whole notes in the new editions), and use a formula like 8.8.8, which means that each section of a pavane or galliard consists of eight semibreves (in the galliard, of course, they are always dotted). The varied repetitions are disregarded in these formulae, since they are of the same length as the corresponding main sections.

Fundamentally Byrd constructs his pavanes and galliards in very simple and regular proportions. The former have sections of sixteen semibreves, except for four pieces (FW, II, pp.200 and 398; AN, p.96; and TB, p. 55), whose sections all comprise eight semibreves; and the latter always have sections of eight dotted semibreves. Twelve pavane-galliard pairs have the form 16.16.16–8.8.8, and three have the form 8.8.8–8.8.8 (four, if we count the two-section *The Earle of Salisbury*, 8.8–8.8). Only in the following five pavane-galliard pairs does Byrd deviate from this normal form, which corresponds to the nature of the dance:

1. TB, p.60: 8.8.12–8.8.8
2. TB, p.40: 12.12.12–8.8.12
3. FW, II, p.226: 16.16.24–8.8.8
4. TB, p.55: 8.8.8–5.4.6
5. TB, p. 98: 16.16.16–4.7.7.4

In the first three of these pairs the deviation consists only in the enlargement of regular phrases by half their length, a procedure that is hardly irregular, but that represents a digression from the norm for Byrd. Only two of his dances, the galliards of the last two pairs, are really irregular. Almost all the dances with abnormal structure occur in TB, whose contents derive from later sources. May we conclude that they belong to a later period of the master's activity? This supposition becomes more probable when one considers the pavanes and galliards of Morley or John Bull, in which irregular structures are the norm. On the other hand, Master Newman's earlier pavane also consists of sections of irregular length, 12.14.12.12.

Another important element that is closely related to structure is the tonal formulation. No form offers more interesting insights into the tonal and modulatory practices of the late 16th century than the English pavanes and galliards. Their three-part structure suggested a differentiation of the sections based not only on musical content but also on key changes. Byrd and his successors were fully conscious of the significance of the problem, and found a large variety of solutions for it, even to the extent of using many a modulation within a section in order that the section might begin and end in different keys. In key changes an important and impressive role is played not only by the dominant and sub-dominant but also by keys a second and a third apart. Beautiful effects, similar to unexpected lighting, are created when an E♭ major chord follows a section that closes in G major (AN, p.105), or when a cadence in E major is followed by a beginning in F major (TB, p.42). The *Eighte Pavian* (AN, p.121) is especially rich in interesting color contrasts and modulations. Its first section moves from E via C to A. Thus there are two key changes at the distance of a third between sections, and another between the end of section 3 and its repetition, and one at the interval of a minor second that results from the repetition of the second section, which moves from F to E.

In almost all instances the key and modulation schemes of the galliards differ somewhat from those of the corresponding pavanes. The pavane-galliard FW, II, p.384 (= AN, p.90) may serve as an illustration; the course of harmonies may be shown as follows (the lower-case letter symbolizes a minor key):

Pavane	Galliard
$a - A \parallel F - E \parallel A - A$	$A - C \parallel F - A \parallel D - A$

This difference alone indicates that the galliards are not derived from the pavanes, and this suspicion is confirmed by the melodic-thematic content of the dances. Except for a common basic key, the members of a pair are completely independent. There are occasional similarities in the melodic lines of the first few measures—one of the most obvious occurs in the *Sixte Pavana* and *Galliarde* of *My Ladye Nevells Booke* (AN, p.110)—but after the opening measures the two dances are totally different, and the similarity of the beginnings may just be accidental. A single exception that confirms the norm shows how Byrd proceeded when he derived a galliard from a pavane: In the *Paven-Galiard* from Add. 30485 (TB, p.55; cf. the list on p.253) the fact that both dances have exactly the same strikingly simple tonal scheme ($C\ C \mid C\ G \mid C\ C$) immediately suggests a relationship, which is fully confirmed by the thematic content. The melody of the galliard is derived from that of the pavane, but the transformation is much more complex and far more interesting than in the usual after-dance. The simple change from duple meter to triple, which is common in a proportz, seems to have been consciously avoided by Byrd. After the regularly built pavane (8.8.8), he places a galliard of totally irregular structure (5.4.6). The basic melodic forms of the three sections of the pavane and the galliard have been placed next to each other in Fig.252 in order to show how Byrd constructed them from the same thematic material. (In the following figures the note values have been reduced 1:2, so that each semibreve of the original corresponds to a half note.)

Fig.252

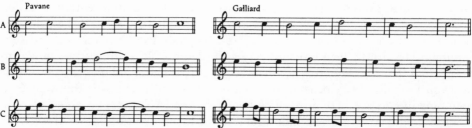

These explanations will suffice to characterize the structural bases of Byrd's pavanes and galliards, but the manner in which this framework was filled with content can only be described generally and to a limited degree. Like Beethoven's *Sonatas,* these dances are not so much representatives of a unified type as individual works of varied character. Far removed from any routine, like the one that predominates in the Italian dances, Byrd formulates his pavanes and galliards in ever new and original ways. Never does he lack for a clever idea or a new turn, and in only one respect does he observe convention—in the final measures, which almost always exhibit the same, rather pedantic broken-chord figure, shown in Fig.253. It is quite admissible, even desirable, to omit this disturbing feature at a performance.*

Fig.253

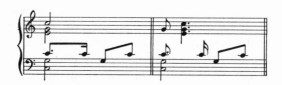

Despite all their individual differences the pavanes and galliards naturally share certain basic stylistic principles. Their individuality is pointed up by a comparison with the dance pieces of Facoli and Radino, the time of whose composition coincides approximately with Byrd's main creative period.[33] A glance at any pavane by Byrd and the examples from the Italian prints (cf.Figs.241–43) will show the great differences in the textures. The Italians were generally satisfied with a purely homophonic setting, in which the right hand is given the melody

---

* This also applies in part to the rapid runs and trills that sometimes occur without preparation before the final chord, e.g., in the *Pavana Ph. Tr.* (*FW,* I, p.367). In the varied sections, which are ornamented throughout, they are obviously quite germane.

and the left hand has block chords to bring out the rhythm. Byrd is one of the greatest masters of vocal polyphony, and his polyphonic workmanship also provides the pervasive lifeblood of his clavier dances, skillfully adapted to the possibilities of the instrument and the player. Imitative passages are frequently woven into the texture with admirable adroitness, as, e.g., in the first section of the *Pavana Ph. Tr.* (Philipp Tregian; *FW*, I, p.367), whose beginning is shown in Fig.254.

Fig.254

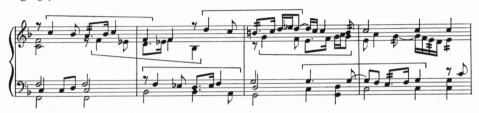

Even more frequent and more typical is the employment of brief, affective motifs, which pervade the musical substance and lead to an extraordinary density and fullness of the musical events. One of the most beautiful examples is the *Firste Pavian* of *My Ladye Nevells Booke* (AN, p.77), designated as "the first that ever hee made" in the *Fitzwilliam Book* (*FW*, II, p.204). Is it an accident that it is in C minor, the same key as Master Newman's *Pavyon?* In any event, there is an unmistakable relationship between the two in technique and in feeling, but the later master brings to fulfillment what the earlier one only promises. As in Newman's pavane, the beginning of Byrd's is simply formulated, but in the second and third sections motivic work engenders an extraordinary intensity of propulsion and expression. A few measures from the third section are given in Fig.255. Note the unexpected and, therefore, all the more impressive change to major toward the end. Many other examples of this kind can be cited, e.g., the *Pavane Bray* (*FW*, I, p. 361), the pavane *FW*, II, p.226 (which is the only one of these pieces to omit the conventional runs and broken-chord figure at the end), and the pavanes *FW*, II, pp.200 and 389; AN, pp.102 and 110, and TB, p.118.

Fig.255

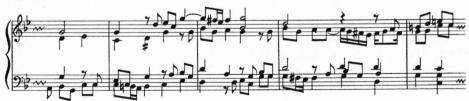

In these pieces we frequently find melodic turns that intensify the expression, particularly the sixth as an unprepared appoggiatura to the fifth, and the minor seventh in a bold cross-relation with the leading tone. Fig.256 gives a number of such passages.

Fig.256

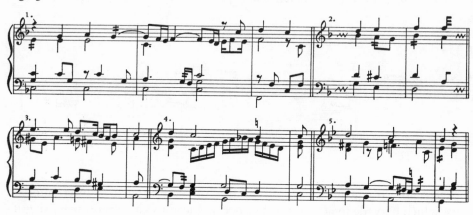

In addition to these "elaborated" and intense pavanes there are others that are simpler, and whose charm lies in their relaxed mood, gentle expression, and natural grace. The pavane-galliard pairs TB, pp.40, 55, 60, and 70, are but a few of the most obvious examples of this type. The culmination of this species is probably the pavane-galliard *The Earle of Salisbury,* which received the well-deserved honor of being included in the *Parthenia.* Since none of these pieces is preserved in the earlier collections of *My Ladye Nevells Booke* and the *Fitzwilliam Book,* can we assume that this simplified, melody-oriented style represents a later stage of Byrd's work?

The single pavanes and galliards do not add any new features to the picture. In the pavane *FW,* II, p.427 (= AN, p.117), designated "Canon. Two parts in one," each section is a canon of the two upper parts above a freely added substructure. The imitation is always at the lower fifth and at the distance of two semibreves. This combination of two such incongruous elements as canon and dance is probably the earliest and, at the same time, one of the most beautiful examples of this species, to which Haydn, Mozart, and Schubert later contributed their canonic minuets, scherzos, and trios. The *Galiardo Mrs. Marye Brownlo,* contained in the *Parthenia,* is a very lively and brilliant piece that is a kind of counterpoint to the canonic pavane. Here Byrd proves that he is a master not only of strict counterpoint but also of virtuosic keyboard style. Playful figures of changing form and original character enliven the main sections as well as the varied repetitions, which in other works are frequently constructed with the aid of conventional passage work. We have to admit that the numerous ornaments, indicated by oblique bars or double bars, are entirely appropriate and even necessary here, whereas in the dances written in polyphonic style they are disturbing.

Allemande, Courante, and Gigue

Byrd is important to the history of keyboard dance not only because he carried the traditional pavane and galliard to the peak of their artistic perfection but also because he was one of the first to show an interest in the new dance types, the allemande and the courante, which were to play a dominant role later on. Around 1550 the allemande occurs in various dance collections of English, French, and Dutch provenance, intended for instrumental ensembles or for the lute.[34] As a clavier dance it is first found in the tablature book of B. Schmid the Elder (1557), which contains an *Alemando novelle* (Merian T, p.111). It is a typical example of what was originally a very simple and somewhat heavy-footed dance; Thomas Morley in his *Plaine and Easie Introduction to Practicall Musicke* refers to it as "fitly representing the nature of the people whose name it carrieth."[35] Fig.257 reproduces the beginning of this piece.

Fig.257

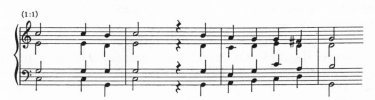

Under the name of alman or almayne, the allemande became the most popular dance of fashion in the England of the late 16th and the early 17th centuries. The *Fitzwilliam Virginal Book* includes 23 almans: 5 by Byrd, 3 by Johnson, one each by G. Farnaby, Hooper, Marchant, Morley, Peerson, and Tisdall, and the rest anonymous. Many more are found in the virginal books of Will Forster, Benjamin Cosyn, and others. The usual allemande consists of two sections of four or eight measures, but there are a number of examples written in three sections like the pavane. In one such alman, by Byrd (*FW*, II, p.182), as in most of the others, each section is repeated in varied form. In his *Monsieurs Alman* the allemande proper is followed by four variations (one in *FW*, I, p.234, the others separately in *FW*, I, p.238, and AN, p.221).

Stylistically Byrd's allemandes are far above the level of functional music, but far below the degree of artistic formulation and technique that characterize his

pavanes. This judgment is not a negative one, but merely an affirmation of the
fact that around 1600 the pavane has reached the end of its evolution while the
allemande is only at its beginning. Many years later, with Chambonnières and
d'Anglebert, the allemande reaches a stage of high stylization, and then, once
again, it is the more recent dances—the minuets, gavottes, and bourrées, like the
allemandes of Byrd and his contemporaries—that charm the listener with the
natural simplicity of their melodies and rhythms. A most attractive piece of this
type is an anonymous *Alman* (*FW*, II, p.266), whose first section is shown in
Fig.258.

Fig.258

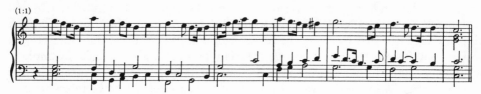

The allemande also acquires a companion, the courante of the Italian variety,
called *corrento,* which differs from the French *courante* even as late as Bach.
Except for a *Corante du Roy* by Schmid the Elder (Merian T, p.112) which cannot
be distinguished from a saltarello, the courante appears first in the English sources.
And it often appears there with the dotted rhythms and peculiar "running" figure
that later characterize Frescobaldi's correntes. A *Coranto* by Byrd (*FW*, II, p.359)
shows both features (Fig.259). One anonymous coranto (*FW*, II, p.308) shows a
singular rhythmic treatment: It starts in 6/2 time and ends, one might say, twice
as fast, in 6/4 time.

Fig.259

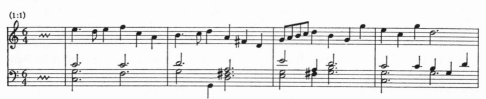

The gigue, too, begins to occur, though to a limited extent and not too
clearly formulated. Two pieces in the *Fitzwilliam Virginal Book* that are designated *Gigge,* one by Giles Farnaby (*FW*, II, p.46), the other by his son Richard
(*FW*, II, p.162), have nothing to do with the dance type of the gigue, but belong
to the repertoire of English comedians' songs, known as jig. One by Byrd (*FW*,
II, p.237) and two by Bull (*FW*, II, pp.257, 258) are, by contrast, dances in 6/4

time. In the last one the melodic line is full of the skips that are characteristic of the 17th-century gigue, especially near the end, which is shown in Fig.260.

Fig.260

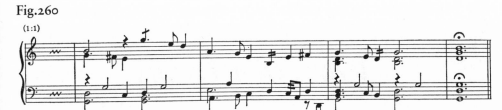

There is also a Dutch source, the clavier book of Susanne van Soldt (Brit. Mus. Add. 29485), written in 1599 for the twelve-year-old daughter of a well-to-do merchant who had moved from Antwerp to London around 1576.[36] The manuscript contains 23 pieces, among them pavanes, galliards, allemandes, and a number of tunes from the Dutch psalter (*sallem*) in simple harmonizations. *De quadre pavanne* and *De quadre galliard* (nos.22–23) are arrangements of the passamezzo moderno, and the melody of *Allmande de La nonette* was used for the chorale *Von Gott will ich nicht lassen* in Germany and for the noël *Une vierge pucelle* in France.

11

Variation Forms

Less is known about the origins and early evolution of the variation form than about any other form of keyboard music, or of music in general. When it first emerges in Spain around 1530, it has already reached a stage of incipient perfection and maturity that presupposes a previous development of some duration. How that development proceeded is unknown.

Our first task is to distinguish between *variation form* and *variation technique*. The latter is a very old element of musical evolution, which, in European music, plays an important role as far back as the Gregorian chant. It emerges clearly in the ornamented intabulations of the 15th and 16th centuries, which are nothing more than varied treatments of vocal works. A rondeau from the late 14th century, *Di molen van pariis,* which is preserved in a basic version and in three different ornamented ones, has been regarded as the earliest example of the variation form.[1] But this opinion can only be accepted with reservations. Admittedly we have several differing versions of the same composition, but, mostly because of the great length of the rondeau, it is rather doubtful whether they form an entity—which is one of the most essential features of the variation form. The same reservation applies to similar examples from the 15th century, e.g., the three arrangements of *Frowe al myn hoffen* in the tablature of Adam Ileborgh (1448), and the various intabulations of *Annavasanna* in the *Buxheim Organ Book.*

Even if these pieces are considered part of the early history of the variation form, there still remains a large gap in technique and methods between them and the Spanish variation sets of the 16th century. They all employ only a single type of variation, the coloration of the upper part with more or less rich figures, which is a far cry from the diverse and refined methods found in the Spanish *diferencias,* e.g., those by the lutenist Narvaez (1538) or those in the *Libro de cifra nueva* by Venegas de Henestrosa (1557).

The Spanish Diferencias

The diferencias are the starting-point as well as the center of our observations, for several themes appear among them that were repeatedly chosen by the Spanish lute and clavier masters: *Las vacas, Conde claros,* and a pavane tune in which the 17th-century *folia* is anticipated.

Las vacas, or *O guardame las vacas* (Oh, let us put the cows to pasture), or *Romanesca O guardame las vacas* is a popular Spanish tune, similar to the soprano formula of the passamezzo antico, but it usually lies a third higher, as shown in Fig. 261 (cf.p.236, Fig.229). The corresponding bass notes, and therefore the harmonies as well, are identical, except that in the romanesca (as we shall call this two-part tune henceforth) the bass does not start with the tonic (*D*) but with the mediant (*F*). They differ also in rhythm: The passamezzo uses duple meter, the romanesca triple. Again the question arises of where the thematic essence is to be found—in the melody or in the bass? In the passamezzo this question was answered in favor of the melody, and the same decision may be made here, with even more assurance. The name itself, *Guardame las vacas,* unequivocally indicates a song-like item. This conclusion is further borne out by the fact that the theme is occasionally called *Seculorum del primer tono,* obviously referring to the (*a g f e d*) line of the melody, which is identical with the chief termination, i.e., the *Seculorum, Amen,* of the first psalm tone.[2]

Fig.261

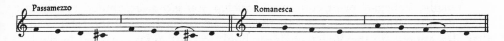

Some of the simplest examples of variation technique are to be found in the anonymous *Cinco diferencias sobre Las vacas* (Anglés M, p.186) in Venegas' *Libro de cifra nueva*. The theme is set in pure homophony and furnished with figurations—ascending and descending scale passages that pervade the harmonic texture like diagonal threads. Despite the simplicity of the principle, the five variations possess remarkable individuality and expressive power. The third variation is given in Fig.262.

The *Cinco diferencias sobre Conde claros* in the same work (Anglés M, p.185) represents a type that may be called *continuous variations.* This type uses a brief theme, two to four measures in length, and the variations follow one another without breaks. It includes the English grounds and the passacaglias and chaconnes of the 17th century. The continuity is especially pronounced in the many

Fig.262

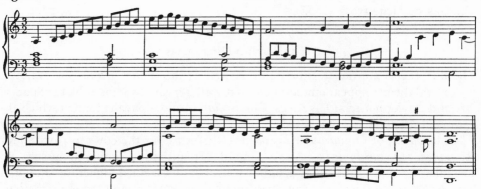

instances where the theme and each of its variations close on the dominant, as in *Conde claros,* or on the subdominant. The theme and the first variation of *Conde claros* are given in Fig.263.

Fig.263

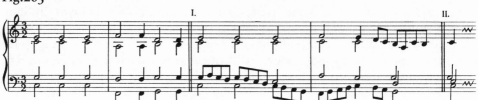

Finally, Venegas' print contains a *Pavana con glosa,* attributed to Antonio (de Cabezón) (Anglés M, p.191). Its theme is an earlier form of the folia, a form that also appears in the Venetian dance book (c.1520) (cf.p.234) and in the lute books of Valderrábano (1547) and Pisador (1552).[3]

Cabezón's *Obras de musica* contains a number of very outstanding variation works, listed here with their original titles. The number of variations is given because Pedrell's new edition contains some insufficient or misleading statements.

1. *Diferencias sobre las Vacas* (Pedrell H, VII, p.70) 3 var.
2. *Pavana italiana* (VII, p.73) 6
3. *Diferencias sobre la Gallarda milanese* (VIII, p.1) 2
4. *Diferencias sobre el canto del Caballero* (VIII, p.3) 5
5. *Diferencias sobre la Pavana italiana* (VIII, p.6) 5
6. *Diferencias sobre el canto de La Dama le demanda* (VIII, p.10) 6
7. *Diferencias sobre el villancico De quién teme enojo Isabel* (VIII, p.13) 7
8. *Diferencias sobre las Vacas* (VIII, p.20) 6
9. *Otras diferencias de Vacas* (VIII, p.25) 4

Fig.264

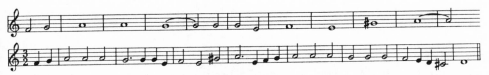

Cabezón's variation works have two basic characteristics: The theme in its simple form is taken for granted, and the composition starts with the first variation (the numbers above take account of this situation); and the variations are always connected by transitions, which sometimes make it difficult to determine the structure. The difficulty is further increased by the fact that dividing the theme —more accurately, the first variation (and with it, the following ones)—into measures is sometimes a puzzle. The bar lines in the original do not correspond to the measures of the modern system but, in keeping with the custom of the period, they correspond to the beat unit, the semibreve. As in Cabezón's hymns (cf.p.129), two or three original "measures" must then be combined and the note values halved, in order to produce measures that are comprehensible to modern readers and players. In nos.2, 5, 6, and 7 of the above list two original measures must be combined (*tempus imperfectum*), and in nos.8 and 9 three form a unit (*tempus perfectum*). In nos.1 the meter is veiled by the lack of bar lines in the first variation. Fig.264 gives the beginning of the melody in the original notation, and a reconstruction that results unequivocally from the succeeding variations. The melody of the *Canto del caballero* (no.4) is the most difficult, but also the most interesting in this respect. Basically it is cast in duple meter, but it contains two symmetrically placed passages in irregular meter, as shown in Fig.265. This is one more instance of the division of two 4/4 measures according to the equation $4 + 4 = 3 + 3 + 2$.[4]

Fig.265

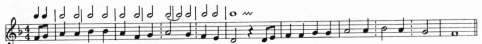

Nos.1, 8, and 9 have the same theme, *Las vacas,* or the romanesca. *Pavana italiana* (no.5) and *La dama le demanda* (no.6) are also based on identical themes. The first half of each of them coincides with a piece that Thoinot Arbeau cites as

Fig.266

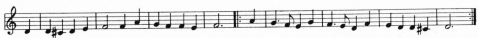

Fig.267

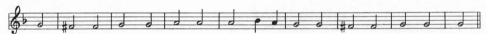

a model of the pavane in his *Orchésographie* (1588). The melody used by Cabezón is given in Fig.266. No.2 is also called *Pavana italiana,* but its theme differs from that of no.5; it appears again in John Bull's *Spanish Paven* and in Sweelinck's *Pavana Hispanica.* Its basic form is shown in Fig.267. We can skip the *Gallarda milanese* (no.3), for the theme can be recognized easily enough from the original. On the other hand, understanding the basic form of the melody of the villancico *De quién teme enojo Isabel* ("About Whom Does Isabel Grieve?") is particularly important because it is greatly altered in the variations. The song is a lovely popular tune of eight measures, with an added ripresa that repeats the last two measures. In Fig.268 the measures are numbered for later reference.

Fig.268

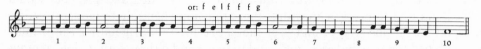

Let us now turn from the themes to the variations themselves and the means that Cabezón uses to give a theme a new shape. Variation always implies the cooperation of two contrasting principles: preservation and renewal. In some way the substance of the theme must be preserved even though something new must be added. Thus every variation must be discussed from two different but equally important points of view: the degree of the retention of thematic elements and the changes resulting from variation. In the themes of the variation works of the 16th and 17th centuries, one can distinguish three elements that may remain fixed in various degrees: structure, harmony, and melody. The structural features of a theme, which express themselves in length and phrasing, are the most stable element. Similarly the sequence of harmonies is usually unalterable, but occasionally one harmony or another may be replaced by a related one. But with respect to the melody there are four possibilities: The melody may be taken over into the variation without extensive changes and in the same function, i.e., as the top part; it may be put into another voice, again without substantial changes; it may remain in the upper part, but in an ornamented form; or it may be replaced by a new melody. These four methods are of basic importance in variation technique, at least from Cabezón to Sweelinck and Scheidt. Unfortunately, here, as elsewhere in the area of variations, there is no established terminology. In the following discussion these methods are therefore simply designated by letters as follows:

A. Melody of the theme in the top part of the variation
B: Melody of the theme in a lower part of the variation
C. Ornamented melody of the theme in the top part of the variation
D. Melody of the theme not recognizable in the variation

Attempts to classify artistic efforts always contain imperfections, and it will certainly not be possible to assign every variation clearly to one of these categories. A variation may begin in one of these styles and continue in another, in which case a designation such as A–D may be used; and occasionally it will be impossible to make a definite decision between types C and D. Nevertheless this sytem is useful in studying variation technique in the 16th and 17th centuries because it reflects rather accurately the methods consciously employed by the composers of the period. In variations of types B, C, and D the treatment of the melody always differs in some way from its appearance in the theme. This difference provides a primary variation element, to which others may be added. In variations of type A the theme is preserved in all its characteristic features, and the variation technique consists mostly in the figuration or some other new treatment of the lower parts.

On the whole, the variation works of Cabezón remain structurally constant, as is the rule with almost all variations, at least up to Mozart. Occasionally one finds deviations from this rule, but in most instances they seem to be printers' errors. For example, in the third variation of no.2 above (*Pavana italiana*) one of the three measures (Pedrell H, VII, p.74, second brace, meas.103) is superfluous, and two measures are missing at the end of the fifth variation. Only in the variations on the *Isabel* theme (no.7) is the principle of retaining the structure consciously relinquished, as will be shown below.

The harmonic plan of the theme also remains basically the same in all the variations. There are occasional insignificant deviations, mostly substitutions of a mediantal harmony; e.g., in the last variation of no.9 the note E in measure 6 of the romanesca theme is harmonized not by three C-major triads, but by two C-major triads and one A-minor triad.

In Cabezón's treatment of the melody, all four types are represented, and they are usually easy to recognize. The following are schematic outlines of three of the works:

var.	I	II	III	IV	V	VI
No.2:	C	C	A	C(?)	D–A	C–D
No.5:	C	C	A	B	B	
No.9:	A	B	B–D	D		

In other words, in no.5, e.g., the melody of the *Pavana italiana* appears ornamented in the upper part in the first two variations, then unchanged in the upper part of the third, and in a lower part in the last two variations (both times in the tenor). The fifth variation in no.2 begins with a freely invented upper part, which leads back into the melody of the theme toward the end; and the last variation starts with an ornamental figuration of the theme and ends with freely invented figurations.

In Cabezón's variation works type A occurs twelve times, B ten times, C six times, D eight times, and another six variations are of a mixed type. The number of variations with a freely invented melody (D) is relatively high. In general it is the early variations in a set that preserve the melody as well as the structure and harmony of the theme. One of the many signs of Cabezón's creative power is that he often prefers to free himself from melodic ties. He knows how to formulate his new lines with a great variety of lively figures. Similar melodies, sometimes even more expressive, grace the top part of those variations in which the theme lies in a lower part (B). One of the many beautiful examples of this type is the fourth variation on the *Caballero* theme (no.4), shown in Fig.269. Intrinsic life and intensity inform these figures. The great art of Ockeghem seems to be revived in the spirit of the Renaissance!

Fig.269

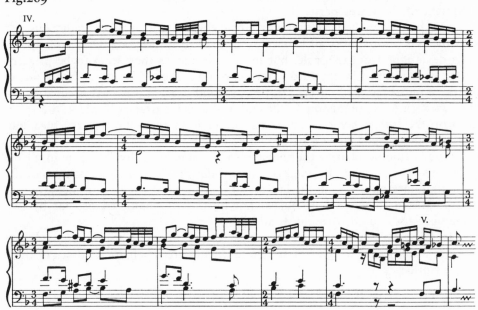

Cabezón's variations on the *Isabel* theme (no.7) deserve special attention, for they treat the structural plan very freely. In the second variation (no.1 of the new ed.), *A*, the first note of measure 6 (cf.Fig.268), is tripled in value, as shown in Fig.270. This expansion is not a mistake in printing since the corresponding note in measure 8 is treated in the same manner. The purpose of the expansion is to make possible the echo-like repetition of the figural ornament—a very charm-

Fig.270

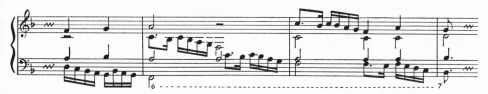

ing effect. All the remaining variations present the theme in doubled note values, so that each measure of the theme corresponds to two measures in the variation. More extensions occur toward the ends of variations II, III, and IV: Measure 9 of the theme is represented by four and one-half measures in variation II (actually nine measures in the original; new ed., p.15, meas.18–26); measure 8 by four measures in variation III (eight measures in the original; new ed., p.16, meas.16–23), and five in variation IV (ten measures in the original; new ed., p.17, meas. 21–30). The *Isabel* variations are an intellectualized work, not easily accessible, which renounces one of the chief attractions of the variation form, the audible relationship to the theme. In its stead it offers a more sublime charm by making demands on the understanding of the listener.

The *Otras diferencias de Vacas* (no.9) presents a totally different picture. The structural and harmonic elements are simple and clear, and the melody is always audible, as is usually the case in Cabezón's variation works. The special import of the *Otras diferencias* lies in their novel stylistic features, which were to have a significant effect on subsequent developments. In general Cabezón's variations preserve the individuality of each voice; in this respect he is still wholly beholden to the Ockeghem tradition. But in the *Otras diferencias* two voices are repeatedly related through imitative stretto, and much use is made of brief motifs heard in immediate succession in various voices. Fig.271 shows one of these passages (the end of the first variation). The beginnings of this technique of complementary motifs was seen in Schlick's music (cf.p.85). Cabezón employs it almost as systematically and with almost as much consciousness of its importance as Sweelinck and Scheidt did later on. No less significant, aesthetically and historically, is the use of a very vivid, almost wanton, clavieristic figure in the

Fig.271

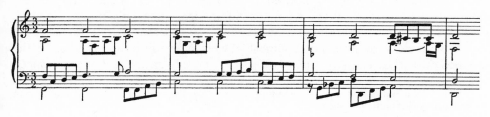

concluding measures of the work. The passage is so fascinating that it is reproduced completely in Fig.272. Such things are not expected from so serious and
strict a master. This work is surely a late one; along with several of the tientos, it
heralds the advent of the Baroque era.

Fig.272

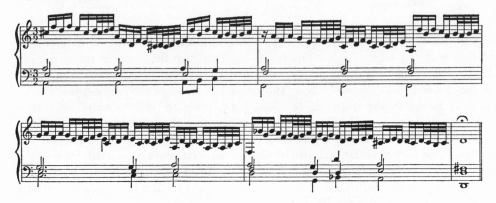

The Passamezzo Variations

About 1570, shortly after Cabezón's death, the variation form emerges in three
other countries: Germany, Italy, and England. The German sources of the 16th
century contain only two variation works: a passamezzo by Schmid the Elder
(1577) and a passamezzo by Paix (1583.)* The contribution of Italy is more extensive: one passamezzo each by Andrea Gabrieli, Facoli (1588), and Radino
(1592), and 6 variation works on various themes by Valente (1576). At the top—
in quantity as well as quality—are the variations of the English virginalists. Two
variation sets on the passamezzo theme in the *Dublin Virginal Book* of about
1570 are probably the earliest examples. They are followed by the voluminous
and significant output of William Byrd; and by the variations of John Bull, Giles
Farnaby, Orlando Gibbons, and others, which take us into the third decade of
the 17th century.

The passamezzo theme, which is common to all three countries, demands a
particular variation technique. The passamezzo antico, even when it appears
without additional variations, is itself a variation of a basic theme (cf.pp.235f.).
Although the theme is derived from a melodic idea, often only its bass is used,
which establishes the harmonic scheme. This scheme always retains the same
length, with the structural notes almost always succeeding one another at the
distance of a long, i.e., two breve measures (two 4/4 measures in our reduced

---

* This discussion will cover only genuine variation works, and not the many dances with
varied repetition of individual sections.

transcription). It is understandable that it was an attractive task for the musicians of the period to fill these expanded intervals with lively, varied, and always new content. The schematic character of the theme requires individual formulation not only of the top part but also of the bass line because only the first note of every other measure is fixed. This is the difference between the variation technique of the passamezzo and of other variations, for in most of the others the melody or the bass of the theme is retained, often both.

There are about twenty variation works based on the passamezzo antico and twenty based on the passamezzo moderno, its variant in major. Usually the passamezzo is followed by an after-dance—a galliard or saltarello—which is also presented in several variations. The following table shows the chief stages of an evolution that can be traced through more than one hundred years (P = passamezzo, G = galliard, S = Saltarello; the numbers indicate the number of variations):

Passamezzo antico

A. Gabrieli	*Terzo libro*, 1593 (Pidoux G, vol.I)	P:5
Valente	*Intavolatura de cimbalo*, 1576	P:6
anonymous	*Dublin Virginal Book* (Ward D, p.1)	P:4–G:4
	(Ward D, p11)	P:10
Schmid the Elder	*Zwey Bücher . . . Tabulatur*, 1577	P:4–S:3
Paix	*Orgel Tabulaturbuch*, 1583 (Merian T, p.135)	P:5–S:4
Byrd	Passamezzo Pavana (*FW*, I, p.203)	P:6–G:8
Philips	Passamezzo Pavana (*FW*, I, p.299)	P:7–G:8
Picchi	*Balli d'arpicordo*, 1620 (Chilesotti P, p.9)	P:6–S:2
Scheidt	*Tabulatura nova*, 1624 (*DdT* I, p.40)	P:12
Storace	*Selva di varie compositioni*, 1664	a. 8 var.
	(cf.p.681)	b. 8 var.

Passamezzo moderno

Facoli	*Intavolatura di balli*, 1588 (new ed., Apel, *CEKM* no. 2, p.1)	P:6–S:4
Radino	*Intavolatura di balli*, 1592 (new ed., Harding, p.31)	P:6–G:6
Schmid the Younger	*Tabulaturbuch*, 1607 (in F)	P:6–S:4
	(in C; Merian T, p.264)	P:6–S:5
Byrd	Quadran Paven (*FW*, II, p.103)	P:4–G:6
Bull	Quadran Pavan (*FW*, I, p.99)	P:4
	(*FW*, I, p.107)	P:4–G:6
Sweelinck	Passamezzo (Seiffert S, p.243)	P:6
Storace	*Selva di varie compositioni*, 1664	8 var.
	(cf.p.681)	

In several of these works the basic structures indicated above are expanded by ripresas, which are added at various places. Twelve variations of a ripresa conclude the saltarello by Schmid the Elder, e.g., and Paix ends his passamezzo

Fig.273

Continued on
opposite page

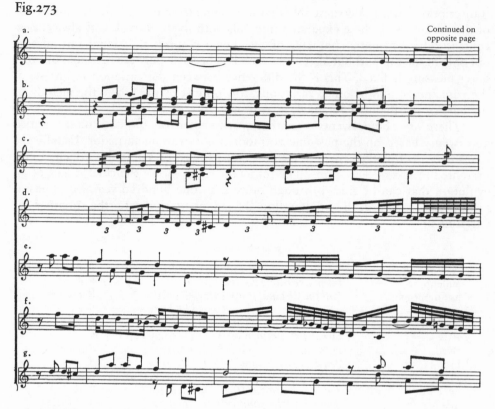

a., b. Gabrieli, var. I and V; c., d. Byrd, var. II and IV; e., f. Picchi, var. III and VI; g. Scheidt, var. V.

with four variations of a ripresa and his saltarello with two variations of another ripresa. The order differs in Facoli, where each variation (*parte*) of the main dance consists of passamezzo plus ripresa (i.e., $P_1R_1P_2R_2P_3R_3$ etc.), while in the saltarello the ripresa is placed at the end. The approach of Byrd and of Bull in their *Quadran Pavans* is to follow every two variations of the passamezzo and the galliard with two variations of the ripresa: $P_1P_2R_1R_2P_3P_4R_3R_4$. In contrast to the passamezzo (and its after-dance), whose bass and harmonic scheme are completely unalterable, the ripresa appears in several forms, though all of them start with the dominant. Schmid the Elder writes it in two double measures, harmonized | V | I IV |, Paix in four, harmonized | V | I | IV V | I |. After the main section Facoli adds a *prima* and a *seconda ripresa,* which are as long as the main section; the sequence of harmonies is about as follows: | V | V | I V | I || V | V | IV V | I |. The English Quadran pavans also have double ripresas equaling the passamezzo in length. In the original they are not differentiated as such, but are numbered consecutively with the variations of the main melody, so that they appear as vari-

Fig.273 (cont.)

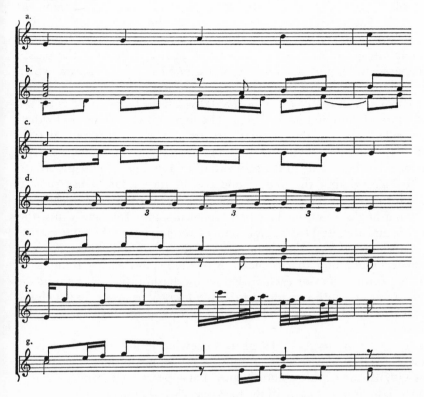

ations III, IV, VII, and VIII of the work. Their harmonic scheme is not clear; in Bull's quadran pavans the following scheme seems to be used: | V | V II | V II | V || IV | V | I V | I | (the II represents a second dominant).

In the works listed in the above table there are 110 variations on the passa-mezzo antico and its after-dances and 81 on the passamezzo moderno. This voluminous repertoire can be used for a comparative study. Fig.273 demonstrates the diverse phenomena that can occur within the same framework. It shows the first three measures of the passamezzo antico as arranged in several particularly interesting or characteristic variations. Only the top parts are given, and to make the comparison easier the key of D is used for all the examples (some of the variation works are in G, C, or A) and the note values have been reduced equally (semibreve=half note).

Fig.273 gives but a minute segment of the whole field of passamezzo varia-tions. The simplest and most primitive are the variations by Valente and the sec-ond set from the *Dublin Virginal Book.*[5] They differ from the other works in that each note of the theme is set as a breve instead of a long, so that the span to be filled is reduced to half the usual size. The filling out is accomplished with corresponding simplicity; only the top part changes while the chordal accompaniment remains unaltered. The other passamezzo of the Dublin manuscript shows a somewhat more advanced style in the usual framework of longs. In its harmonic scheme the tonic always appears as a major triad, probably because the passamezzo is transposed to C, and would have necessitated C-minor chords, which the composer apparently did not dare use.

With the *Pass'e mezzo antico in cinque modi* by Andrea Gabrieli we enter the level of artistic formulation and intrinsic life. The first two variations (individual variations are called *parte* in the original) are treated in a contrapuntal style similar to that of his ricercars, while the third and fourth lean on the toccata style of his intonazioni. The beginning of the fifth variation uses a motif in triple stretto (second half of Fig.273), but the middle and end of the variation use runs in toccata style. This is one of the earliest instances of a change in style, technique, and motif within a single variation. This practice occurs quite frequently in variation works before and after 1600—similar instances, though not of the same clarity, are found in Cabezón's works. This is just one of the many differences between early variation technique and that of Bach, Mozart, Beethoven, or Brahms, in which the unified formulation of each variation is a basic principle. One of the few exceptions is the sixteenth variation of the *Goldberg Variations,* in which the first half is conceived as the introduction and the second as the fugal section of a French overture.

The *Pass'e mezzo moderno* by Facoli is somewhat monotonous because it strongly stresses a dance-like scheme: Almost every other measure becomes a cadence point with the same broken-chord figure that appears often in his paduanas (cf.p.243, Fig.241). In the *terza parte* of the passamezzo and in the fourth variation of the saltarello a group of eighth notes (of the form −g ef | g) appear several times in various voices like a complementary motif. This use of a brief, characteristic motif as the chief melodic element of an entire variation becomes very important later in the evolution.

Radino's variations are on a much higher level. Their vivid, varied formulation anticipates several things that are expressed with greater power and genius in Giovanni Picchi's masterpiece. Some of Radino's variations (var. III and IV of the passamezzo and var. IV and V of the galliard) may be called toccata-like, and belong to the same type as some by Gabrieli. The passage work, however, does not consist of scale runs only, but occasionally involves broken chords and other characteristic figures as well. The remaining variations are mostly of the motivic type, which takes clearer shape here than in Facoli's work. Fig.274 gives a number of motifs used by Radino, and the beginning of the *seconda parte,* in which motif 1. plays a leading role (in its second half motif 1a. appears, which is more striking).

Fig.274

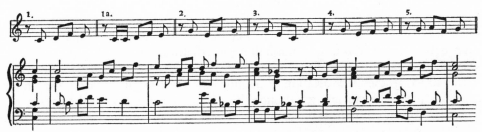

The culmination of the Italian passamezzo variations is the *Pass'e mezo antico* by the Venetian Giovanni Picchi.[6] From start to finish it is filled with exciting, fresh ideas. Picchi creates an intoxicating fullness and magnificence of sound on the harpsichord. His is a virtuoso piece in the best sense of the word. One of the many fascinating details is a written-out trill on *d*, which does not start with *e* as the upper auxiliary but with *e* flat. It is employed as an ornament to the D-minor triads that conclude the *prima, quarta,* and *quinta parte.*

The German passamezzo variations are inferior to the Italian ones. While one does not expect as much from Bernhard Schmid the Elder as from Andrea Gabrieli, it is nevertheless surprising to see how he stays completely within a purely technical compass. On the occasions when he tries to transcend the limits of the most elementary variation techniques—runs above chords—he invents figures of a touching naiveté, like the passage at the start of the third variation given in Fig.275. Paix makes a serious attempt to replace runs and block chords with real four-part writing, but the intent is more praiseworthy than the result.

Fig.275

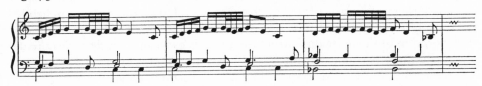

The two passamezzi by Schmid the Younger are more interesting. He is obviously influenced by Italy, and in fact, he goes beyond the usual limits of influence, for in his passamezzo in C he includes almost literally three variations from Radino's passamezzo (var. I, V, and VI). Such borrowing was permissible during this period and even later on; moreover, the title *Passo è mezo italiano* sufficed for the necessary amenities. His unpublished passamezzo in F is also called *italiano* and probably contains borrowed material, too.

In his passamezzo Sweelinck frequently employs a certain figure that is repeated in every measure of a variation. This technique of the "figure" variation stands out particularly in the last variation.

Scheidt's *Tabulatura nova* contains a varied passamezzo (antico), whose structure deviates from the usual one. The first structural note is expanded from four to five measures (four and one-half measures in var. I). The principle of figure variation is applied more clearly than in Sweelinck, especially in variations III, VIII, and IX. In the fifth variation he employs the same motif as Picchi does in his third one (cf. Fig. 273e. and g.), though the similarity exists only at the beginning. The fiery, restless Italian soon moves to other, increasingly accelerating figures, while the serious, methodical German consistently retains the motif throughout and changes to another only in the last quarter of the variation.

It goes without saying that the English filled the wide frame of the passamezzo with all the effervescent wealth of their highly developed art of the variation. The individuality and forcefulness of the clavieristic figures Byrd employs in some of his variations on the passamezzo antico surpass anything that was invented in this field. The playful, dance-like triplet figures that he uses in the fourth variation have a special charm. A sample is given in Figure 273d. Under the title *The Passinge Measures* this work appears in *My Ladye Nevells Booke;* it was thus composed before 1591.

The *Passamezzo Pavana* by Peter Philips—composed in 1592, according to a notation in the *Fitzwilliam Virginal Book*—is closer to the virtuosic type. Variations III and IV of the passamezzo have fast runs in thirds and sixths for the right hand, and variation V of the passamezzo and variation VI of the galliard have "break-neck" passages for the left hand. The last variation of the passamezzo is arranged in three different episodes, almost like a little ballet scene.

In the quadran pavans (passamezzo moderno) by Byrd and by Bull the basic structure is expanded to twice its length by the insertion of long ripresas. Here one really needs "the wrong end of the binoculars" to compress the large dimensions and clarify them at least for the eye; to what degree they can be comprehended by the ear is another question. In accordance with the major mood of the theme the elaboration of the individual structural notes is even more lively and more detailed than in the passamezzo antico, and one's attention is even further diverted from the form and directed toward the figures. A comparison of these quadran pavanes with a passamezzo of the *Intabulatura di balli* of 1551 shows the extent of the change that has taken place in the course of half a century: A living organism has been turned into an abstract scheme that must now be filled with significant content and new life in a totally new manner.

Valente's Variation Works

In addition to the passamezzo (cf.p.273), Antonio Valente's *Intavolatura de cimbalo* of 1576, preserves five other variation sets: *Zefiro* (12 *mutanze*), *Lo ballo dell'intorcia* (7), *Tenore grande alla Napolitana* (6), *Romanesca* (5), and a *Gagliarda napolitana con molte mutanze*.[7] It is the only source in the continental repertoire that contains variations on other themes. The romanesca theme is the same one Cabezón used, but it is expanded from eight to ten measures by a two-measure ripresa of the type | IV V | I |. The *Zefiro* is a variant of the romanesca, related to it in the same way as the passamezzo moderno is related to the antico. In other words, the romanesca is the passamezzo-antico theme in 3/2 (both in minor), and the zefiro is the passamezzo-moderno theme in 3/2 (both in major). Closely related to both is the *Tenore grande*, another eight-measure theme in 3/2, but with a slightly different bass: | B♭ | B♭ | e♭ — f | B♭ || B♭ | f | g c d | G |. *Lo ballo dell'intorica* (is the name derived from *torcere*, to turn, or from *torcia*, the torch?) has the same harmonic scheme as the passamezzo antico, but its tempo is four times as fast, as each harmony or bass note occupies a 2/4 measure (a semibreve in the original).

The *Gagliarda napolitana* belongs to another type of dance music. It is based on an ostinato subject of two measures, which is varied 39 times. The subject, which emerges more clearly in later variations than at the beginning, shows a similarity to the Spanish *Conde claro*s (cf. Fig.263) that is surely not accidental, especially in the continuous change between 3/2 and 6/4 time. Fig.276 gives the first and seventh *mutanze*. Note the parallel triads in the first measure, which also occur often in the Neapolitan villanella of the period.

Fig.276

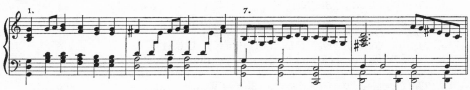

The level of Valente's variation technique is very primitive, that of the figure variation, in which a figural ornament, adapted to the individual harmonic situation, recurs in each measure. This technique repeatedly appears in the later evolution of the variation form (even Reger used it in his *Telemann Variations*). To illustrate it Fig.277 gives the opening measures of the *Ballo dell'intorcia* and of some of its variations.

Fig.277

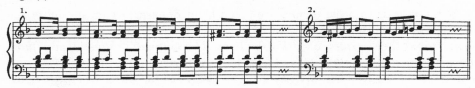

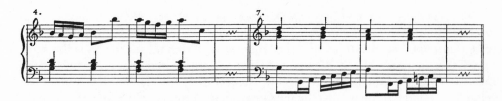

Byrd's Variation Works

Around the time that Valente was contributing his rather poor addition to the evolution of the variation form in Naples, one of the greatest masters in the field, William Byrd, was active in the North. A high art miraculously flowered in his hands, for we cannot find any preparation or antecedents for it. Even Cabezón's output of variations, as important as it is, offers no explanation for all the novel features in Byrd's variations. The only explanation is that a great master transformed the tradition from the depths of his own creative power, and created such a new life for it that the historical context is without significance and only the creative process is essential. There are many such examples—didn't the same phenomenon occur two hundred years earlier with another Englishman, Dunstable?

Byrd's works in this field fall into two main categories: variations on songlike themes and grounds (cf.pp.285ff.). The following pieces belong to the first category. The first seven are contained in *My Ladye Nevells Booke* (*Nev*), and were therefore written before 1591.

1. *The Woods so wilde* (*Nev*, p.144 = *FW*, I, p.263), dated 1590   14 var.
2. *The Maydens Song* (*Nev*, p.149 = *FW*, II, p.67)   8
3. *Walsingham* (*Nev*, p.173 = *FW*, I, p.267)   22
4. *All in a Garden green* (*Nev*, p.181 = *FW*, I, p.411)   6
5. *Lord Willobies welcome home* (*Nev*, p.186) = *Rowland* (*FW*, II, p.190)   3
6. *The Carman's Whistle* (*Nev*, p.189 = *FW*, I, p.214)   9
7. *Sellengers Round* (*Nev*, p.211 = *FW*, I, p.248)   9
8. *Jhon come kisse me now* (*FW*, I, p.47)   16
9. *Fortune* (*FW*, I, p.254)   4
10. *O Mistrys myne* (*FW*, I, p.258)   6
11. *Callino Casturame* (*FW*, II, p.186)   6
12. *Gipseis Round* (*FW*, II, 292)   7
13. (untitled) (Tuttle B, p.104)   10
14. *Goe from my Window* (Tuttle B, p.113)   7
15. *Bonny sweet Robin* (Tuttle B, p.139)   4

Without exception the themes are taken from English folk music—more accurately, from English popular music. Many of the texts and a few of the tunes are known from other sources, e.g., *Walsingham*, *The Carman's Whistle*, and *Jhon come kisse me now*.[8] *Callino Casturame* is a Bowdlerization of the Irish *Cailinog a stuir me* ("Young Maiden, My Love"). The history of the theme of *Fortune* (no.

9) is most interesting. It derives from the tenor of the chanson *Fortuna desperata* by Busnois, which starts with (| $f - f\,g$ | $a\,g$ | f).[9] Both Obrecht and Josquin used it as the *cantus firmus* of a Mass, and Ludwig Senfl used it in a piece in which the melody is combined with *voces musicales*, i.e., with fragments of the hexachord scale, in the manner of a quodlibet.[10] In England it occurs in minor with the text *Fortune my foe*, beginning (| $g - g\,a$ | $b\flat\,a$ | g |), and continuing in an altered form with a popular flavor. It was used in this form as the theme for variations not only by Byrd but also by Sweelinck (with the German text *Von der Fortuna werd ich getrieben*) and by Scheidt.

No country in Europe can boast of such an old tradition of beautiful folk tunes as England. During the 16th century a treasure trove of tunes arose, full of graceful charm and gentlemanly elegance—genuine children of the Renaissance spirit. Byrd seems to have been the first to recognize the musical significance of this treasure, for a good number of these song or dance tunes appear first or exclusively in his variation works. Even in the choice of his themes Byrd emerges as an innovator in the field, for he is always intent on preserving and stressing their character. And so the expression of gentle gaiety, and occasionally of gentle melancholy, which pervades these English folk tunes, carries over into the variation works and lends them a new color. The variations on *Walsingham* or *The Woods so wilde* contrast with Cabezón's *Isabel* variations in the same way as Mozart's variations on *Unser dummer Pöbel meint* contrast with Bach's *Canonische Veränderungen über Vom Himmel hoch*.

Only four themes—*Lord Willobie*, *Jhon*, *Fortune*, and *Goe* (nos.5, 8, 9, and 14)—are in duple meter; all the others use 3/2 or 6/4 time and thus have a somewhat more dance-like character. This is particularly true of *Sellengers Round* and *Gipseis Round* (nos.7 and 12), as their titles indicate. The former was included by Augustus Nörmiger in his dance collection of 1598 under the legend *Ihr Für(stlicher) G(naden) Vierder Mummerey Tantz* (Merian T, p.236). Some melodies exhibit unusual and charming turns of harmony, which then recur in the variation set, e.g., *Walsingham*, in which an unexpected change from minor to major occurs in the penultimate measure, or *The Woods so wilde*, which executes a graceful shift with an ascent from F to G at the end.

To analyze Byrd's treatment of these themes in his variations, let us apply the same categories—A, B, C, and D (cf. p.267)—as we used in the discussion of Cabezón's variations. In toto Byrd wrote about 130 variations; about 50 have the melody of the theme in the top voice (A), 25 in the alto, tenor or bass (B), ten in the top part, but in an ornamented form (C), and 15 do not use it (D). The remaining variations are mixed types, in which the melody is heard in the top part as originally presented in the first half, and in an ornamented form in the second half (A–C). In variations of type B Byrd most frequently presents the melody in the alto; he does so particularly in final variations—in those of nos.2, 3, 4, 6, 7, and 8 in the above list.

The four basic types occur in Byrd's variations with about the same relative frequency as in Cabezón's. Byrd, too, definitely prefers a "polyphonic" treatment of the theme, as represented by type B, to the figural treatment of type C. Freely invented melodies (D) occur chiefly in *The Woods so wilde* and in the variations on an unnamed theme (no.13). The retention of the bass, an approach that continuously gains in importance in the subsequent evolution, is more frequent in Byrd's variations than in Cabezón's. This principle does not yet play an important role in Cabezón's music, though there are individual instances (especially in *La Dama le demanda*). In Byrd those variations in which the bass of the theme is retained are still definitely in the minority,* but in some of his sets there is a tendency to treat the bass as a thematic element, especially in *The Woods so wilde*, *Callino Casturame*, and the untitled variations. A fixed bass occurs in all four types of variations, most often in type D, where it replaces the fixed melody.

The following schematic presentation of four of Byrd's variation works gives the basic type of each variation. The variations with a fixed or approximately fixed bass are marked with an asterisk:

> *The Woods so wilde* (no.1)
> A A B* D* D* B* A D* D D* D* D–B* B A
> *All in a Garden green* (no.4)   A A–C* A–C A–C D–C* B*
> *Callino Casturame* (no.11)   A A* C* A C* D–A*
> *Goe from my Window* (no.14)   A A A A B A–C B

In *The Woods so wilde* the number of variations with a new melody is striking. Most of them take over the bass of the theme (D*), but variation IX is independent of the theme in this respect as well; its relationship to the theme is limited to the harmonic and structural elements. The figural approach (C) is not represented in this set. In three variations the melody is shifted to a lower part (B), twice while retaining the bass of the theme (B*). In *All in a Garden green* the second half of the theme is frequently ornamented. In *Callino Casturame* the theme is retained in a simple or ornamented form almost throughout, and so is the bass; this treatment approaches the standard type of later variation works. In *Goe from my Window* the melody is also retained throughout, but without figurations, while the bass is formulated in a new way each time. In two variations the melody appears in the tenor.

The study of thematic retention, as interesting and important as it is, is only an introduction or preparation for the discussion of the principles of variation. Through it we can evaluate the creative contribution of the composer, recognize the characteristics of his style, and indicate his part in the evolution of the form. But there is an intrinsic difficulty in describing these factors satisfactorily; and the more they are marked by the power of creative imagination, as is true of Byrd to a very high degree, the more difficult it becomes. Therefore the following

---

* Disregarding the grounds of course (cf.pp.283ff.).

attempt at presentation must be regarded as only a guide to his works and an invitation to the reader to study them.

In general the strict four-part (occasionally three- or two-part) manner of writing, which is always the basis of Cabezón's variations, hardly ever occurs in Byrd's music. His style, to a large extent, still shows the influence of polyphony, but it is not worked out strictly; rather it serves as a starting point for creating life, variety, and color within an essentially clavieristic texture. Liveliness of expression, variety of technique, and a worldly spirit are the outstanding qualities of his art of variation, in complete contrast to the strict seriousness, inner discipline, and depth of Cabezón's variations. In technique as well as in spirit Byrd is the founder of an art that finds its meaning and fulfillment in light-hearted playfulness and gay entertainment—he is a genuine ancestor of Mozart and Schubert.

From an analysis of the technique of this great body of material—the aesthetic and moral attitude is implicit—we may extract certain basic methods that represent guiding principles of formulation. The first is the art of figuration, which also plays an important role in Cabezón's variations. But even in this special area certain distinctions emerge. The figuration of the entire theme, so ingeniously applied by Cabezón, is rather rare in Byrd, who mostly applies a playful ornamentation of individual notes, measures, or sections, such as the first or second half of a variation; for example, in variations VII and XII of *Walsingham* or in variations II and VI of *The Carman's Whistle*. It is fully developed in only three or four variations—most beautifully in variation III of *Fortune*, but less successfully in variation III of the unnamed variations (no.13). Byrd uses free figurations much more frequently as a contrast to or as a background for the theme, in the upper part, in the bass, or distributed among several parts. In variation VI of *The Woods so wilde*, e.g., the theme is heard in the alto with an ornamented upper part above it; and in variation VII the melody is in the soprano with a figural bass beneath it. In variation IV of *The Maydens Song* the figuration is distributed in a charming alternation among the lower voices, and occasionally affects the notes of the theme, which is carried by the soprano. The figurations most often employ scale fragments, occasionally interspersed with jagged lines or broken triads. The latter are very typical of English keyboard music. They are present in the liturgical organ works of the earlier English generations (e.g., in Tallis' *Felix namque*, cf.p.159, Fig.152), but were increasingly cultivated by the virginalists. In some variations Byrd uses figurations in diads, mostly for the left hand (e.g., in var. XIV of *Walsingham*, var. VI of *Sellengers Round*, and var. VIII of *Jhon come kisse me now*)—figures such as are already found in Thomas Preston's music (cf.p.152, Fig.145). The basic features of Byrd's figural technique were developed long before him; what distinguishes him from his predecessors is the unforced and graceful application of this technique.

Byrd's second most important type is the motivic variation. He employs it so

Fig.278

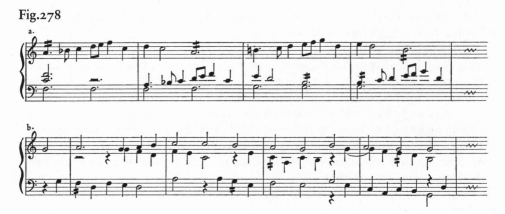

a. *The Woods so wilde*, var. V; b. *The Maydens Song*, var. III.

extensively and in so many varied and ingenious manifestations, that he may be called the founder of this technique. Motivic variation is used with particular frequency in *The Woods so wilde* (var. IV, V, VIII, IX, XI), *The Maydens Song* (var. II, III, VII, VIII), *Walsingham* (var. II, III, IV, VI, X, XI, XVIII, XXI), and *Jhon come kisse me now* (var. III, IV, XI, XV). There are two kinds of motivic variation, as illustrated by the examples in Fig. 278. In a. the motif is presented in two voices in regular alternation, while in b. the motif is used in an imitative interplay of all the voices with irregular entries that often cross the bar line. It is useful to distinguish the two methods as "complementary motifs" and "imitative motifs." Both methods play an important role in variation technique, indeed in all keyboard music, of the early 17th century.

The motif is sometimes derived from the melody of the theme. In the two examples in Fig.279 the motif is formed by diminution of the beginning of the

Fig.279

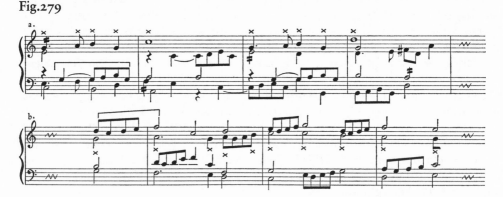

a. *Jhon come kisse me now*, var. XV; b. *The Maydens Song*, var. VIII.

melody (shown by "x"). Similarly, in variations III, IV, VI, and VII of *Walsingham*, Byrd very ingeniously uses the ascending third (*b♭ c′ d′*), with which the tune starts, as the starting-point for an imitative motivic texture.

A third variation type is characterized by a texture of full harmonies pervaded with polyphonic elements. Byrd uses it discriminatingly for several final variations (in *The Woods so wilde, All in a Garden green, The Carman's Whistle,* and *O Mistrys myne*) and occasionally elsewhere (e.g., var. XX of *Walsingham* and var. VII of *Sellengers Round*).

Byrd does not limit himself to a single type of treatment within each variation, but frequently changes the style or the motifs. Indications of this idea are found in Cabezón, and a fully developed example occurs in the final variation of Andrea Gabrieli's passamezzo (cf.p.274), where the change from a motivic to a toccata-like style is probably dictated by structural reasons—in order to achieve a brilliant conclusion. Only in Byrd does the changing variation—as we may designate it—appear as an established and frequently employed technique. It occurs in *Walsingham* (var. XV, change of motif), *Jhon come kisse me now* (var. IX, change of figuration), and *Goe from my Window* (var. IV, change from complementary motivic technique to figurations in the left hand). A particularly colorful interplay of changing ideas marks the variations on *Fortune* and on *O Mistrys myne*. Both are based on relatively long themes, in which some phrases are repeated, and thus offer opportunities for variations within a variation, opportunities that Byrd did not miss.

The overall structure of some of the variation sets shows a rather unified character, e.g., *The Carman's Whistle, Sellengers Round,* and *Callino Casturame*. The gentle pastoral character of the theme carries over to the whole work, and it becomes somewhat dull. The meaning of the variation form lies in change, and one need only look at *The Woods so wilde, Walsingham,* or *Jhon come kisse me now* to see how fully Byrd understood this meaning and gave it expression. Nevertheless he, like many after him, sees to it that justice is done to the principle of order. Thus he often makes the first three or four variations of a set very simple and similar, using them as a quiet introduction and preparation to the color play of the succeeding ones; or he formulates the last variation as a confirming, crowning conclusion in a full, chordal texture, and lets the melody ring out clearly one last time. The ordering principle of the variation pair, which still plays an important role in Mozart, Beethoven, and Brahms, is probably employed for the first time by Byrd, e.g., in *The Woods so wilde* (var. VI–VII) and in *Walsingham* (var. VIII–IX and XVI–XVII).

Grounds

An important separate category of English variations is that of the grounds. They are based on a bass figure that is repeated many times without interruption, and are thus essentially *basso-ostinato* works. In principle there is no relationship, or only a very loose one, between ground and variation form. This becomes clear in the earliest examples of grounds—a number of 13th-century motets whose tenors are constructed from several repetitions of a brief formula, such as ($\|$: f — $e\,g$: $\|$) in *Amor potest conqueri*, or ($\|$: a | c' — $b\flat$ | $ag\,a\,f$ | a : $\|$) in *Or ne sui*.[11] What differentiates such ostinato compositions from genuine variations is the treatment of the upper parts. They are only contrapuntally related to the tenor, and pay no heed to the harmonic-structural element (to do so at that early time would have been an anachronism). The same treatment reappears in ostinato motets of the 15th century, in which the repeated formula is transposed to various scale degrees, e.g., Busnois' *In hydraulis*.[12]

The earliest English grounds of the 16th century belong to the same type. Aston's *Hornepype* and *My Lady Careys Dompe* (cf.pp.249f.) are each based on an ostinato of two notes, a formula that is interpreted harmonically to a degree— as an alternation of tonic and dominant—but is too short to be treated structurally in a variation set. On the contrary, the upper parts move in freely flowing lines that consciously avoid cadential breaks. *Uppon la mi re*[13] (Brit. Mus. add. 29996) is based on the ostinato motif (*a e d*) played in half notes (originally semibreves) and repeated 53 times without a break. Above this bass lies a middle part that is constructed in the very same manner, for the same motif is transposed up a fifth and shifted by a quarter note, so that the two voices form a kind of canon. The top part is faster moving, and its free lines and constantly changing figures are reminiscent of the *Hornepype*, but it is much more independent of the substructure. It divides into periods of varied length, which never lean on the regular construction of the lower parts, but often cross them at the most unexpected places. The upper part is often constructed from repeated sequence-like formulae, a quarter note in length, in contrast to the fundamental motif, which is six quarter notes long. Fig.280 shows a formula in dotted rhythm in a syncopated position, shifted by an eighth note from the basic rhythm. The harmonic implications of the ostinato motif—I V IV in modern terms—are expressed in the top part only occasionally and, it would seem, unintentionally. The top part moves mostly in the highest register, often three octaves above the bass note, thereby creating another contrast to the substructure—one of pitch. All these incongruent elements produce one of the strangest compositions in keyboard literature—a work whose intractability irritates as much as it fascinates. Fig.280 shows the beginning and two later passages.

In the latter part of the 16th century the character of the ground changes. The rudimentary and "open-ended" oscillating motifs are replaced by formulae of greater length, which usually close on the tonic and thus constitute complete units. Moreover, the upper parts give up their independence and begin to follow the harmonic and structural outlines of the ostinato bass, interpreting it in a continuous chain of variations on the ostinato theme. The primary difference

Fig.280

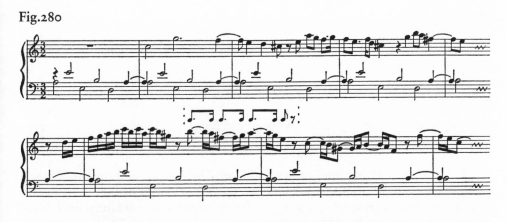

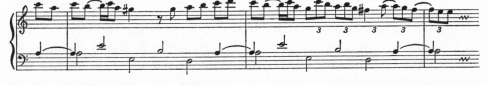

between ostinato variations and song variations is that new melodies appear throughout the former—of necessity, since the theme does not possess a melody as such. As a rule the ostinato theme is a short phrase of four measures, with no breaks between the repetitions, but there are also grounds with themes twelve to thirty-two measures long.

Even as Byrd was a master of song variations, he was also first—chronologically, quantitatively, and artistically—in the composition of the later grounds. The following list of his grounds is arranged like that of his song variations, giving the length of the theme as well as the number of variations:

1. *My Lady Nevells Grownde* (Nev, p.1)	32 meas.	6 var.
2. *The Huntes upp* (Nev, p.58, FW, I, p.218) =		
Pescodd Time (FW, II, p.430)	16	11
3. *The Second Grownde* (Nev, p.163)	12	16
4. *Hughe Ashtons Grownde* (Nev, p.194) =		
Tregians Ground (FW, I, p.226)	16	12
5. *Malt's come down* (FW, II, p.166)	8	9
6. *The Bells* (FW, I, p.274)	1	140
7. *A Ground of Mr. Birds* (Tuttle B, p.13)	4	37
8. *A Grounde* (Tuttle B, p.22)	4	20
9. *A Ground* (Tuttle B, p.26)	4	23
10. *A Hornepipe* (Tuttle B, p.31)	4	50

All the grounds are in 3/4 time (originally 3/2). The same is true of the ostinato variations of the 17th century: the passacaglias and the chaconnes. Fig. 281 shows the themes of nos.5 to 10.

Fig.281

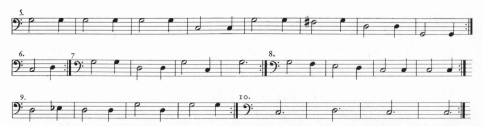

The Bells (no.6) occupies a special place. The brevity and open-endedness of the theme indicate that this famous composition belongs to the early type of ground, in which the upper parts move freely above the oscillating bass. Byrd finds new ways to interpret the basic motif in one hundred and forty repetitions. The motion constantly increases and the bell sound grows fuller and more swirling. This work is impressive proof of his great artistry.

Grounds nos.1 to 4 are contained in *My Ladye Nevells Booke* and therefore must have been written before 1591. The length of their themes is unusual. Possibly they derive from song-like melodies, of which Byrd has retained only the bass. In that case they would be in the same class as the many variation sets on the passamezzo, in which only the bass of the original melody is retained. This assumption is most likely true for *The Huntes upp* or *Pescodd Time,* no.2, whose title seems to point to a popular tune,[14] and *Malt's come down* no.5, may also belong to the group of grounds whose themes are derived from songs. The song variations *The Carman's Whistle,* on the other hand, are designated as *Ground* in Forster's Virginal Book, although the bass is different in each variation.

Nos.7 to 10 are grounds that are ostinato variations in the proper sense. They are based on four-measure themes that close on the tonic and usually appear in the bass of each variation. But Byrd does not limit himself strictly to this regular treatment; in the course of a composition he moves to freer methods. He surrounds the ostinato idea with figurations, puts it into an upper part, or omits it entirely so that only the harmonic frame informs the variation.

The *Hornepipe* (no.10) is remarkable. Its fifty variations are divided into three sections, each based on a different theme. Variations I–XXIX employ the theme that appears in the first four measures of Fig.281, with the first note (c) occasionally replaced by the lower dominant (G). Beginning with variation XXX the meter changes from triple to duple with triplets. For variations XXX–XXXVI the first ostinato theme is replaced by the formula ($\|$: $c - | f g | c - | f g$: $\|$), which is reversed to read ($\|$: $f g | c - | f g | c -$: $\|$) for variation XXXVII to the end. Fig.282 shows the transition from the first to the second section.

Variation pairs appear repeatedly in Byrd's grounds, i.e., two successive variations connected through the use of the same or a similar motif, which often

Fig.282

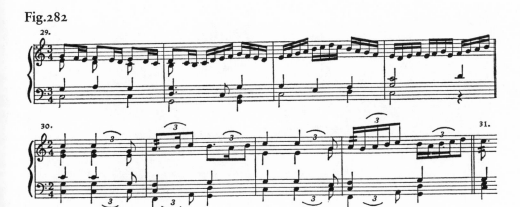

appears first in the right hand and then in the left. Particularly clear instances occur in the following grounds:

No.7: var. V–VI, XIII–XIV, XV–XVI, XXXVI–XXXVII
No.8: var. XII–XIII
No.9: var. IV–V, VI–VII, VIII–IX, XIII–XIV
No.10: var. XIII–XIV, XV–XVI, XVII–XVIII, XIX–XX

This method plays an important role in the chaconnes and passacaglias of the 17th century; therefore it is of special interest to find that Byrd anticipates it in his grounds. Another of his fine touches is the introduction of the characteristic motif of a variation in the last measure of the preceding one in order to establish a fluid connection and an inner relationship, e.g., between variations V and VI of *A Ground,* no.9 (Fig.283).

Fig.283

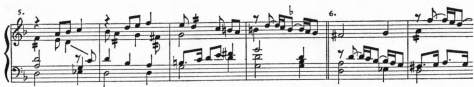

12

Intabulations

THE CLAVIER MUSIC of the 16th century includes innumerable intabulations, which occupy a much larger space than they deserve relative to their historical and artistic significance. A fraction of their number suffice to indicate how a technically satisfactory keyboard texture is created from a vocal model—how the four or more voices of a motet, chanson, or madrigal are distributed or occasionally omitted and stereotyped figurations added whenever opportune. Examples of this practice are found in the very earliest manuscript of clavier music, the *Robertsbridge fragment* from the beginning of the 14th century, and many more occur in the Faenza codex and the *Buxheim Organ Book*. In the 16th century they are absolutely without number—a sign of the increasing importance of the keyboard instruments and the growth of a class of music lovers for whom the intabulations of a Josquin motet or a Lassus chanson possessed the same value as four-hand arrangements of Classical symphonies had for the amateurs of a later epoch. This phenomenon is of particular interest to students of the sociology of music.

The contents of many manuscripts and prints of the 16th century consist exclusively or predominantly of keyboard intabulations of vocal compositions. The following is a list of such sources, but it does not claim to be complete:

1. *Frottole intabulate da sonare organi*, 1517, by Andrea Antico (containing works by Bartolomeo Tromboncino, Marco Cara, and others). Partial new ed. in Jeppesen O.
2. Kotter's tablature (chiefly Isaac and Hofaimer). Cf. Merian T, pp.37ff.
3. Kleber's tablature (Josquin, Isaac, Brumel, Senfl, etc.).
4. Sicher's tablature (Obrecht, Josquin, Isaac, Senfl, etc.). Cf. W. R. Nef, *Der St. Galler Organist Fridolin Sicher und seine Orgeltabulatur* (1938).

5. *Dixneuf chansons (Vingt et cinq chansons, Vingt et six chansons) musi-cales reduicts en la tabulature des Orgues Espinettes Manicordions* . . . , 1530, by Attaingnant (chiefly Claudin de Sermisy). New ed. in A. Seay, *Pierre Attaingnant: Transcriptions of Chansons for Keyboard* (1961).

6. *Treze Motetz musicaulx avec ung Prelude le tout reduict* . . . , 1531, by Attaingnant (Obrecht, Brumel, Févin, etc.). New ed. in Y. Rokseth, *Treize Motets et un Prélude* (1930). Cf.p.217.

7. Munich, Staatsbibl. Mus. ms. 2987 (Sandrin, Jannequin, Gombert, etc.). New ed. by J. Bonfils in *Le Pupitre*, book 5 (1968); cf. W. Apel, "Du nouveau sur la musique française pour orgue au XVIᵉ siècle," *La Revue musicale*, XVIII (1937) pp.96ff.

8. Cracow tablature from the Order of the Holy Ghost, 1548. Cf.p.103.

9. E. N. Ammerbach, *Ein neu kunstlich Tabulaturbuch, darin sehr gute Motetten . . . auff die Orgel und Instrument abgesetzt* . . . , 1575 (Lassus, Clemens, Scandellus, etc.).

10. B. Schmid the Elder, *Zwey Bücher einer neuen kunstlichen Tabulatur auff Orgel und Instrument* . . . , 1577 (mostly Lassus, but also Clemens, Arcadelt, Crecquillon, Cipriano de Rore, etc.), Cf. Merian T, pp.79ff.

11. *Musica di diversi autori* . . . , 1577, by Gardano (Jannequin, Crecquillon, Clemens, Lassus, etc.).

12. Jacob Paix, *Ein schön, nutz und gebreuchlich Orgel Tabulaturbuch*, 1593 (Lassus, Palestrina, Philippe de Monte, Striggio, Cipriano de Rore, Crecquillon, Jannequin, etc.). Cf. Merian T, pp.114ff.

13. Sperindio Bertoldo, *Tocate ricercari et canzoni francese intavolate per sonar d'organo*, 1591. Cf.pp.183,200.

14. Andrea Gabrieli, *Canzoni alla francese* . . . *Libro V, VI*, 1605. Cf.pp.198ff.

15. Claudio Merulo, *Canzoni d'intavolatura d'organo*, 1592, 1606, 1611. Cf.p.200.

16. Manuscript tablature of Johannes Fischer of Mohrungen, *Künstlich Tabulaturbuch darinnen sehr gutte Motetten von den vornehmsten Componisten . . . abgesetzt . . . Liber secundus*, 1595 (Thorn church archive, Arch. woj. w Torunin Rps. XIV 13 a, contains about 150 intabulations).

For a more detailed study of the technique of intabulation the new editions of nos.1, 5, 6, and 7 are particularly valuable, for the vocal models are reproduced alongside the intabulations. Individual examples of this kind may be found in many other publications, e.g., in Kinkeldey O, p.264, where Lassus' *Susanne un jour* is printed together with its intabulations by Andrea Gabrieli and Ammerbach.

In almost all these sources the intabulations are treated routinely, especially with respect to the added figurations. Around 1570 there are indications of a change in approach, changes in two directions, in fact—toward abandoning added figurations completely, on the one hand, and toward creating them in an original fashion, on the other. The former was probably first tried by Ammerbach, whose *Orgel oder Instrument Tabulatur* of 1571 contains a voluminous collection under the heading "Folgen die gekolerierten Stücklein." He omits the collection from the second edition of 1583, but several of the "gekolerierten" pieces reappear in it in a very simple garb, e.g., *Gott ist mein Liecht* (1571, no.1 = 1583, no.34) and

Petercken sprack (1571, no.4 = 1583, no.36). The other tendency emerges in Cabezón's *Obras de musica,* not so much in his "composiziones glosadas," which more or less keep within the limits of the usual,[1] but in those that are glossed by Hernando: *Ye pres en grey* (Pedrell H, vol.VII, p.11; probably Crecquillon's *Je Prends en gré*), *Dulce memoriae* (ibid., p.17; Pierre Sandrin's *Doulce memoire*), *Susana un jur* (ibid., p.33; Lassus' *Suzanne un jour*), and *Pis ne me pulvenir* (ibid., p.42 ; Crecquillon's *Pis ne me peut venir*).[2] Hernando deals so freely with his vocal models that these pieces can hardly be called intabulations. A good example is *Dulce memoriae,* which follows Sandrin's chanson rather closely at the start, but reinterprets or paraphrases the model very freely toward the end, as complementary figures, very individual, abstruse rhythms, and other free and original ideas emerge. Fig.284 shows a passage shortly before the end, together with the corresponding passage of the chanson. Note that the second measure of the original is reduced to half a measure in the arrangement. Similar instances are repeatedly found in Hernando's settings.

Fig.284

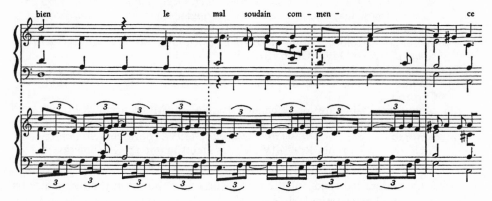

PART III

THE FIRST HALF OF

THE SEVENTEENTH

CENTURY

In the entire history of keyboard music no century presents so many important and interesting personalities as the seventeenth—Sweelinck, Bull, Gibbons, Frescobaldi, Titelouze, Scheidt, Froberger, Chambonnières, Tunder, Weckmann, Poglietti, Muffat, Buxtehude, Pasquini, D'Anglebert, Cabanilles, Pachelbel, Alessandro Scarlatti, Kuhnau, Böhm, Fischer—and many composers who are not as well known but who are equally interesting. With such an array of personalities, a different arrangement of the material is necesary. The creative individuals, not the musical forms, are our chief interest and must furnish the basis for discussion.

The great growth of keyboard literature at the turn of the 16th century is followed by a much greater one as we enter the 17th. To preserve some degree of historical order, the material has been divided into two sections, corresponding approximately to what has been called the early and the middle Baroque. The former comprises mainly the first half of the 17th century, the latter the second half; the former, the works of the masters who were born about 1560 to 1610, the latter, the works of their successors up to the generation born around 1670.

13

England

ABOUT THE YEAR 1611 a beautifully engraved print appeared in London. It was entitled *Parthenia or the Maydenhead of the first musicke that ever was printed for the Virginalls. Composed by three famous Masters: William Byrd, Dr. John Bull and Orlando Gibbons.* These three masters were selected from the many virginalists as particularly famous and significant—a judgment that is still correct today. They represent three successive generations, for Byrd was born in 1543, Bull in 1562, and Gibbons in 1583—almost exactly one hundred years before Bach. Byrd is the only known representative of the first generation, but Bull and Gibbons are surrounded by a good number of virginalists, among them Thomas Morley (1557–1603), John Mundy, (c.1560–1630), Peter Philips (1560–1628), Giles Farnaby (c.1565–c.1640), and Thomas Tomkins (1571–1656). An art that is amazing in its richness, brilliance, liveliness, and variety flowered in the hands of these masters—and died after forty years as suddenly as it had sprung up. By a strange coincidence almost all its contributors died around the same time, in the 1620s. Byrd died at eighty, only shortly before Gibbons, at forty-two. Only Tomkins survived the catastrophe and continued the tradition, by then old-fashioned, into the second half of the century.

Morley and Mundy

The great works of William Byrd, especially in the dance, the variation, and the fantasy, constitute a brilliant conclusion for the keyboard music of the 16th century. His pupil Thomas Morley (1557–1603) was the publisher of many madrigal prints and the author of the famous treatise *Plaine and Easie Introduction to Practicall Musicke* (1597). His keyboard works include 3 pavane-galliard pairs, 1 or 2 variation works, and 5 single pieces: a galliard, a passamezzo antico, a passamezzo moderno, an allemande, and a fantasy.[1]

Morley's pavane-galliards must be discussed in connection with Byrd's. In most instances Byrd's fall into three sections of regular length, and only once is the galliard thematically derived from the pavane. Morley's also have three sections, but they tend toward irregular structures throughout, as the following table shows (as in the survey of Byrd's pieces, the varied repetitions of each section are not considered):[2]

    1. (Dart, nos.1–2): 20.16.20–14.13.11
    2. (Dart, nos. 5–6): 16.20.16–13.8.14
    3. (Dart, nos. 8–9): 15.16.16–8.8.9

The pavane and galliard in no.3 are thematically completely independent, but the legend "The Galiard to the Pavane before" confirms the fact that they belong together. In no.2 the thematic relationship is limited to the first two measures of the first section. By contrast, the first and second sections of the galliard melody of no.1 are derived from the pavane, but the third section is unrelated. As in Byrd's *Paven-Galiard* pair (cf.pp.255f.), the transformation is rather complex—and therefore interesting. On the whole the note values are retained (in the proportion 1:1) and only the bar lines are moved to enclose three rather than two half notes. This is a very unusual procedure, as the strong beats of the measure are shifted. A few measures, however, are transformed according to the proportz principle, in which the measures are preserved intact, but the note values are changed. Fig.285, which shows the first half of the first section of each dance (in a somewhat simplified from), illustrates the transformation.*

Fig.285

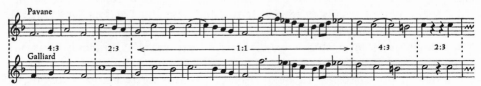

According to English custom the two passamezzos (Dart, nos.3 and 4) are designated as *Quadro Pavan* and *Passymeasures Pavan*. In every respect they conform to the general picture sketched earlier (cf.pp.270ff.). The *Quadro Pavan* is formulated $P_1P_2R_1R_2P_3P_4R_3R_4$ (R = ripresa), exactly as in Byrd and Bull. Several sections clearly show the influence of the Italian toccata style.

Morley's *Fantasia* (Dart, no.12; *FW*, II, p.57) begins with a long section whose style is reminiscent of the intabulated canzonas of the Italians (A. Gabrieli,

---

    * From here on all musical examples are given without reduction of note values, unless otherwise indicated.

Merulo), and closes with a shorter one (Dart, meas.45; FW, II, p.61, meas.13) that proves to be a simple air in three phrases, each of which is heard twice with different ornamental figurations. Inserted between them is a brief, playful middle section (Dart, meas.40; FW, II, p.61, meas.4) in which an augmented sixth chord Bb–$g\sharp$–d' occurs near the beginning.[3]

Nancy (Dart, no.11; FW, I, 57) is a variation work. The charming, folk-like theme of three sections is followed by two variations, within which each section is repeated in varied form. Unfortunately the variation technique is limited almost entirely to runs and trills.

The eight variations on *Go from my Window* (Dart, no.13; FW, I, p.42) are far superior, but they are also preserved as a work by John Mundy (FW, I, p.153). In his few extant compositions Mundy (or Munday, c.1560–1630) proves to be a musician of ideas and originality—one can hardly say this about Morley—so that this attribution seems better founded. Furthermore, the very interesting final variation is omitted in the Morley version. The feature that raises this work above others of the period—even above Byrd's variations on the same theme—is the free treatment of the melodic element, i.e., the replacement of the song by other melodies. In itself this is nothing new, for there are instances of this technique in Cabezón's and Byrd's music (symbolized by letter D). The novelty in Mundy's variations lies more in the approach than in the use. After the folk-like, serene air of the theme (= var.I, Fig.286a.), variation II (Fig.286b.) enters with a dreamy, gently descending scale idea. One is reminded of the beginning of the *Diabelli Variations*, except that Mundy ties the knot with a delicate hand while Beethoven severs it with a sword. Variations III and IV are just as individualistic, and in variation IV the *A*-major chord that concludes the second of the four phrases is extended by an insert of two measures. The conventional approach of the next three variations (var.V–VII) contrasts effectively with what preceded as well as with the final variation, which is once more highly individual in formulation. It

Fig.286

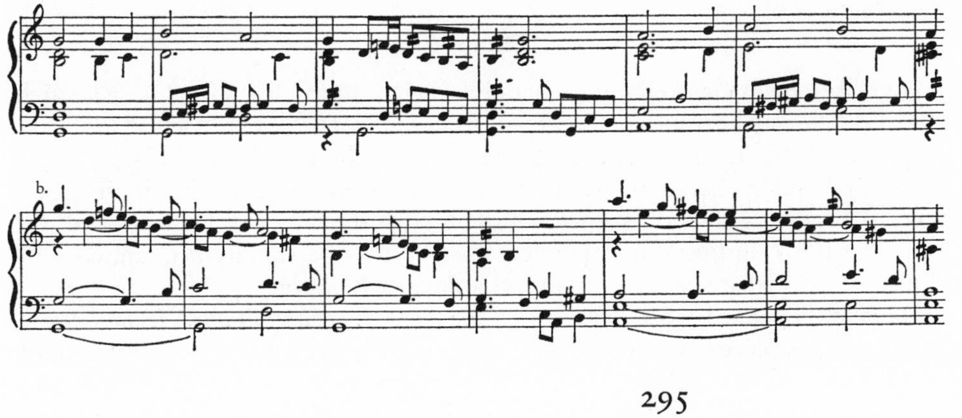

also exhibits a remarkable shift in form, as the first phrase is reduced from four to three measures, the second is expanded from four to five measures, as shown in Fig.287, and the last phrase is expanded to six measures. Thus Mundy's *Go from my Window* proves to be a variation work in which the structural as well as the melodic component of the theme is treated with unusual freedom.

Fig.287

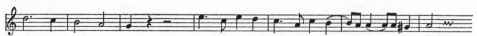

Mundy wrote two lesser pieces—*Robin* (FW, I, p.66), a song with two figural variations; and *Munday's Joy* (FW, II, p.449), a kind of galliard in two sections with repetitions—as well as two fantasies. The fantasies are entered in the *Fitzwilliam Virginal Book* as the second and third works, immediately after John Bull's famous *Walsingham* variations. The first one (FW, I, p.19) consists of some six rather brief sections, the first of which is based on a theme that is unusually lively for the period (Fig.288). This section is followed by various short ideas, a section with figures in sixteenth and thirty-second notes, and a very attractive, longer concluding section in a dance-like 9/8 meter. All in all, it is a work that is worthy of being ranked with Byrd's fantasies. The other fantasy is the well-known piece of program music in which Mundy describes a storm with "Faire Wether," "Lightning," "Thunder," and "A cleare Day." To the modern listener, who is acquainted with Beethoven's *Pastoral Symphony,* it seems rather naive, but some details are quite remarkable, e.g., the several sudden transitions from good weather to lightning.

Fig.288

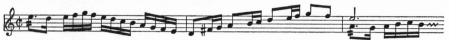

Philips

Recent research has clarified several details of Peter Philips' life (cf. J. Steele's article in *MGG*). He was born in 1560 or 1561 and died in 1628 at Brussels. More than half his life, from 1582 to his death, was spent on the Continent, in Italy, Spain, France, and finally Belgium, where he was active as the organist of the court chapel at Brussels. Thus he was one of the first to transmit the English art of the virginal to the Continent. It is possible that he was personally acquainted with Sweelinck, who wrote two variations on a *Pavana Philippi.*

Philips' keyboard works are found chiefly in the *Fitzwilliam Virginal Book,* where 19 of his pieces are entered as a continuous group (nos.70–88), many with dates, ranging from 1580 to 1605. Nine of these pieces are intabulations of chansons or madrigals, and the remaining ones may be reduced to 7: *Pavana-Galiarda Pagget* (nos.74–75), *Passamezzo Pavana-Galiarda* (nos.76–77), *Pavana-Galiarda Dolorosa* (nos.80–81), *Pavana* (no.85), *Galliardo* (no.87), and two *Fantasias* (nos. 84, 88). In other manuscripts there are 2 more fantasies, 4 galliards, an allemande, and several intabulations.

The single pavane (*FW*, I, p.343) is dated 1580 and inscribed "The first one Philips made." It consists of three irregular sections (13.11.15), each of which is repeated in varied form as is usual; but in the third section the song-like melody in the upper part is surprisingly replaced by a *cantus planus* in whole notes. The same procedure is found in a pavane by Morley (*FW*, II, p.209).

The *Passamezzo Pavana-Galiarda* (*FW*, I, p.299), dated 1592, is a passamezzo antico, comprising seven variations of the main dance, eight variations of the galliard, and a repeated ripresa called *Saltarella*. Several variations are quite original: In the last one of the pavane several structural harmonies are laid out in reiterated block chords *alla battaglia* (Fig.289a.), and Variation VII of the galliard has syncopated sixth chords (Fig.289b.), but their continued reiteration does become tiresome.

Fig.289

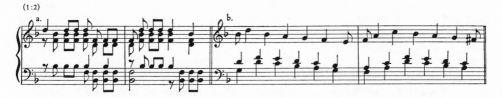

Philips' *Pavana-Galiarda Pagget* (*FW*, I, p.291)[4] has the outline 16.16.32–8.8.16, but the real proportions are not as simple and regular as these figures would indicate. The melodies of sections A and B of the pavane are composed of phrases of nine and seven measures. The C section evolves from a descending-scale motif, which keeps appearing in new shapes. There is a remarkable structural relationship between the melodies of the pavane and those of the galliard. Since the latter are exactly half as long as the former, one might suppose that they are derived by proportional transformation, i.e., that two 4/4 measures are compressed into one 3/2 measure. Philips does derive the galliard from the pavane, but in a far more complex, even devious, manner, as is illustrated by Fig.290, which shows the melodies of the corresponding sections A and *A* in simplified form.)* The final sections, C and *C*, are related like A and *A*, but B and *B* have

---

* In what follows A, B, C symbolize the melodies of the pavane; *A, B, C,* those of the galliard, and A', *A'*, etc., the varied repetitions.

Fig.290

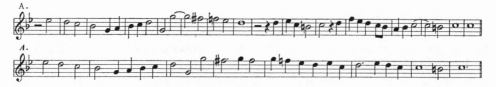

completely different melodies; and while B is irregularly phrased 9 + 7, B has two regular phrases 4 + 4. Nevertheless they are related through their basses; the bass of *B* is largely, but not completely, transformed from that of B in the proportion 4:3, as shown in Fig.291. The varied repetitions of the sections are dominated by agreeable and varied figurations. In A' there is a measure of thirds for the right hand, one of the earliest signs of the re-emerging virtuosic style developed by Farnaby and Bull.

Fig.291

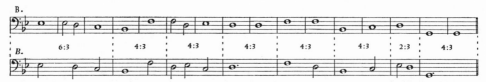

The *Pavana-Galiarda Dolorosa* (FW, I, p.321) is dated 1593. All its details are so similar to the work just discussed that it must be considered the work of Peter Philips, although its melody may well be by Francis Tregian.[5] Except for the somewhat routine figurations in sections B' and C', this piece is one of the most important and thoughtful creations of the period. It starts in a low-lying C major, which produces just as touching a mood of lament as a tragic minor could. The second section is particularly beautiful; a "wailing" motif of great forcefulness is heard in it repeatedly (Fig.292). In section C an uninterrupted melody

Fig.292

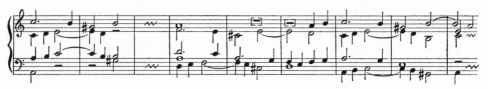

298

Fig.293

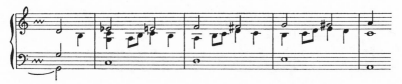

spans 32 measures. An ascending chromatic line, shown in Fig.293, appears four times—probably the earliest instances of its kind in clavier music. The galliard uses essentially the same ideas in a somewhat compressed form, but without the fast figurations in the varied repetitions.[6]

Philips' four fantasies represent quite different types and prove once again the changeableness of the concept. One is a youthful work, dated 1582 (*FW*, I, p.352); it is obviously the earliest reflection of his Italian sojourn (he was accepted into the English College at Rome in October 1582). It may be characterized as a kind of ricercar, with its contrapuntal texture hidden beneath toccata-like elements, full chords, and figurations. Toward the end (top of p.355) a second idea appears several times (| *c — c c* | *d — e —* | *f — d —* | *c —* |), followed by a seemingly free conclusion in toccata style. It is certainly no accident that this piece is in *F* major, a key that was as usual in Italian keyboard music as it was unusual in England. A *Fantasie de Petro Philippi*, preserved in Ms. 888 of the University Library at Liége, is a toccata of the Italian type, but here and there it includes Sweelinck-like keyboard figures.[7] Another fantasy from the same source is an intabulation of Striggio's madrigal *Chi fara fede*.[8]

The fantasy in *FW*, I, p.335, is most interesting. It proves to be a long monothematic ricercar, whose subject (| *g — g g* | *a –g ef g* |) is taken from a fantasy by Byrd (*FW*, II, p.406). The 39 entrances of the subject are numbered in the original. The work falls into four clear divisions: 1. subject in original note values (nos.1–18); 2. subject in diminution and stretto (nos. 19–27 ; the stretto to no.19 is unnumbered); 3. subject in augmentation (nos.28–31); 4. subject in original note values (no.32), in diminution and stretto (nos.33–34; the strettos are unnumbered), in diminution with a melismatic counterpoint (nos.35–37 and 39), and in diminution with note values quartered (no.38). This composition is unmistakably close to the fantasies of Philips' contemporary, Sweelinck. Which one gave, and which received?

Four more pieces by Philips are preserved in Oxford, Christ Church Ms. 1113 (formerly 1175): an *Almande, Deggio dunque* in three sections, *Le Rosignol*, and a *Benedicam Dominum*. The last three are probably intabulations of vocal works, but the *Almande* is a genuine keyboard work, which shows this dance well on its way to becoming a stylized work of art. It comprises two ten-measure sections,

Fig.294

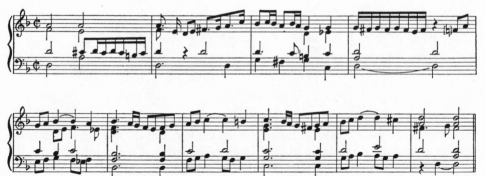

each repeated in varied form, followed by another variation of the entire piece, *altro modo*. The first section is given in Fig. 294.

Farnaby

Except for the "three famous Masters," no virginal composer has such an extensive output as Giles Farnaby. Little is known of his life, however. He was born around 1565 in Truto and died in 1640 in London. In the Foreword to his print *Canzonets to foure voices* (1598) he calls himself, with a touching modesty, "a sely [silly] sparrow who presumeth to chirpe in presence of the melodious Nightingale." Proof that his contemporaries enjoyed his "chirping" is borne out by the great number of his pieces that were preserved. The *Fitzwilliam Virginal Book* contains 52 of his compositions, including 14 variation works, 8 fantasies, 7 pavanes, and 2 galliards. He was also known in Germany, for his *Kempes Moris* (i.e., moresca of the famous clown Kempe) is preserved in Lynar A 1.

It seems only proper to compare Farnaby's variations with Byrd's. While Byrd (the "melodious Nightingale?") prefers extended lyrical melodies of a song-like character, Farnaby tends to use short, piquant tunes, probably taken from English folk dances. *Kempes Moris, Muscadin, Put up thy Dagger Jemy, Quodlings Delight, Rosasolis, Up Tails All,* and *Wooddy-Cock* are gay dance tunes. Even the titles of the third and sixth pieces convey their saucy character. The "sely sparrow" comes to the fore in melodies like the one in Fig.295. More

Fig.295

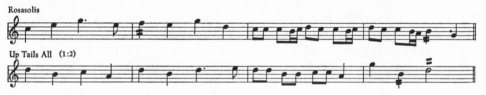

song-like themes are *Bony sweet Robin* (the only theme common to Farnaby and Byrd), *Daphne, Loth to depart, Pawles Wharf, Spagnioletta, Tell mee Daphne,* and *Why aske you.*

Up Tails All, with 19 variations, and *Rosasolis*, with 12, lead the others in length. In *Kempes Moris, Muscadin, Pawles Wharf,* and *Spagnioletta* Farnaby limits himself to two presentations of the theme with varied repetition of the sections, i.e., A A′ B B′ + variation. *Daphne* is a kind of galliard in three sections, treated as follows: A A′ B C B′ C′ + variation.

The main difference between Farnaby's variation technique and Byrd's is the almost total absence of contrapuntal-motivic settings, which Byrd mastered so admirably. Farnaby's strength lies in figuration, in the invention of new figures, which often have a virtuosic character. His music (and that of his contemporary Bull) contains the first examples in virginal music of passages with skips of octaves or tenths, rapid arpeggios and broken octaves, tone repetitions, rapid simultaneous runs in both hands, trills in thirds in one hand, even hand-crossings (cf. *FW*, II, p.80, 5th–6th brace), and similar bravura tricks. Fig.296 includes several such artifices. Such virtuosic figures were employed extensively as early as the mid-16th century in liturgical organ music, especially in Tallis' *Felix namque*, dated 1562. It is strange that Byrd, who was Tallis' friend and possibly his student, kept away from them completely. Farnaby, Bull, and their contemporaries took them up again and made them an integral component of virginal style.

Fig.296

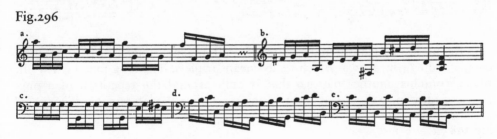

a. *FW*, II, p.73, 6th brace; b. *FW*, II, p.464, 6th brace; c. *FW*, I, p.201, 3rd brace; d. *FW*, II, p.464, 5th brace; e. *FW*, II, p.142, 5th brace.

Farnaby's eight fantasies, like Byrd's, consist of several sections of very varied formulation.[9] But their contents are more amusing than significant. They do not lack charming details, but neither do they lack banalities; above all, Farnaby does not possess the power to carry through and to unify, which is so important, especially in such a loose structure as a fantasy. Both his virtues and his shortcomings reveal themselves in the fantasy *FW*, II, p.82. The first section, in which a very graceful subject and a related motif are presented in a new light, again and again, is one of the most beautiful creations of the literature of the period. The next passage (p.83, 4th brace, meas.4) is equally outstanding; as often occurs in

Byrd's works, too, a single measure is repeated several times, each time ingeniously altered. A second main section starts with a charming dance song in 9/4 time, but soon goes astray in empty passage work and sheer tinkling. It finally arrives at a toccata ending that has no relation to what precedes it, and thus a promising beginning ends in disappointment and defeat.

Farnaby's most unified and on the whole successful fantasy is probably *FW* No.208 (II, p.270). Two or three organically connected episodes can be distinguished. The last section (p.272, 2nd brace, meas.1) is particularly charming. A short scale motif (*d'–c' b ag*) recurs fourteen times in consecutive measures: It starts on *d* four times, then six times on *a*, and four more times on *d*, each time passing from one octave to another. It is an ingenious handling of a trivial technique. A characteristic of Farnaby's keyboard style is the repeated occurrence of skips in the left hand from the middle to the lowest register of the keyboard. A unique, strikingly bold modulation, shown in Fig.297, enharmonically equates *e♭* and *d♯* and *b♭* and *a♯* (p.270, 5th brace).

Fig.297

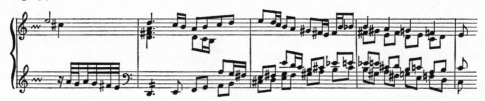

An interesting feature in the fantasy *FW*, II, p.489, is the frequent alternation of 4/4 and 6/4 measures, which really means triplets. The long fantasy, *FW*, II, p.323, contains another passage that is built around the repetition of a one-measure idea (p.328), but at most it amuses rather than fascinates (Fig.298).[10]

Fig.298

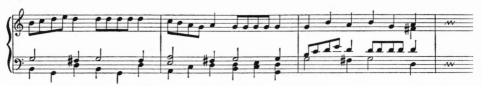

Farnaby was clearly a master of the miniature, and proves it in a number of brief pieces—in a sense the first "bagatelles" in the history of music. Some of them have romantic-sounding titles, e.g., *Farnabye's Conceit* or *Toye* (FW, II, pp.424, 421), little jokes of twelve and thirty-two measures, respectively; or *Giles Farnaby's Dreame, His Rest, His Humour* (FW, II, pp.26off.), a cycle of three pieces consisting of a tuneful pavane, a charming galliard, and a merry humoresque. In the last section Farnaby inserts, as a successful joke, the pedantic *ut re mi fa sol la*—it reminds one of the "Grossvatertanz" from Schumann's *Carnaval*. Four pieces are entitled *Maske* (FW, II, pp.264, 265, 273, 350), and apparently represent music to accompany masques—scenic performances that enjoyed extraordinary favor under Elizabeth's successor, James I (1603–25). The first one is particularly charming; it consists of a chain of six short, song-like sections that probably served to accompany a ballet or a pantomimic presentation.

The shortest of Farnaby's miniatures is the eight-measure *For two Virginals* (FW, I, p.202), a piece for two harpsichords or for one double virginal with two keyboards. The first player presents the melody, which is an early form of the famous bergamasca, in a simple, homophonic setting, and the second plays the same setting with dextrously inserted figurations and arpeggios. This piece and a *Canción Belle sans paire a doce para dos instrumentos*, which is found in Venegas' *Libro de cifra nueva* (Anglés M, p.158), are the only known examples of clavier music for two instruments before Pasquini and Couperin. There are four English pieces for two players at one instrument: one for three hands, *Ut re my fa sol la* by Byrd (Tuttle B, p.86), a very long piece by Bull with the possibly satiric title *A Battle and no Battle* (Mus. Brit. vol.XIX, No.108), a *Verse for two to play on one Virginal or Organ* by Carlton, and *A Fancy for two to play* by Tomkins.[11]

Bull

There is a contrast in personality and way of life between the withdrawn Farnaby and his famous contemporary, John Bull (1562–1628). Bull was educated by William Blitheman. At the early age of twenty (1582) he became the organist at the Hereford Cathedral, and in 1585 he entered the Chapel Royal, where he had been a choir boy. He is perhaps the first composer to follow an academic career: He graduated as Bachelor of Music from Oxford University in 1586, received the Doctor of Music from Cambridge University in 1592, and was called to the newly founded Gresham College in London in 1596 as Professor of Music. In 1601 he traveled through France, Germany, and the Netherlands, celebrated everywhere as a great virtuoso. For reasons that are not clear (religious persecution? political enmity? moral offense?) he left England in 1613 and went to Belgium, where he was active as the organist at the Antwerp cathedral from 1617 until his death.

We know about 140 clavier works by Bull. They are preserved in a large number of manuscripts, the most important sources being the *Fitzwilliam Virginal Book*, Paris Conservatory Rés. 1185 (formerly 18548), Brit. Mus. Add. 23623, and Vienna Nationalbibl. Ms.17771,[12] and six pieces appeared in *Parthenia*. Earlier attempts at a catalog and a new edition[13] of his works have been outdated by a complete edition in two volumes by *Musica Britannica* (vols.XIV and XIX:

John Bull, Keyboard Music I and II), referred to in the following discussion as *BK*.[14] It contains a total of 143 compositions, among them 15 fantasies, 30 settings of liturgical subjects, 12 preludes, 15 variation works, 12 pavane-galliard pairs, 3 pavanes, 12 galliards, 3 settings of the passamezzo moderno (quadran pavane and galliard; passamezzos 2–3 appear as a single work in *FW*), 3 compositions on the hexachord, 5 arrangements of Dutch folk tunes, 9 corantos, 8 almans, and various smaller pieces (*Toy, Welsh Dance, My Self, My Grief,* etc.).

Current opinion tends to regard Bull as just a clavier virtuoso, as the Franz Liszt of the 16th–17th century. But such a judgment does neither him nor Liszt any justice. It would be even more incorrect to imagine him as the well-nourished, red-cheeked "John Bull" of newspaper cartoons, a picture evoked not only by his name but also by a very frequently cited work, the somewhat brutal *King's Hunt.* An Oxford portrait of him at the age of twenty-six gives a very different impression; it shows a man of delicate and noble features, with the expression of spiritual melancholy that marks many faces of the period. In his work he proves to be a very versatile and complex musician, whose art cannot be expressed in a simple formula. Many of his pieces are virtuosic and brilliant, some trivial, others learned and pedantic; some bear witness to his contrapuntal mastery, his depth of feeling, and his religious devotion. Three periods can be distinguished in his output: an early one, during which he writes organ works in the cerebral "design" style of the Tudor period; a middle period, during which he turns to the virginal; and a late one, in which he returns to the organ, but as a changed, matured master.

Among the early works there is a series of pieces in which a liturgical melody is laid out as a *cantus planus,* i.e., as an uninterrupted row of equally long notes (breves, semibreves, or dotted semibreves). Two counterpoints with lively figurations of essentially the same type are usually added—just as in the offertories by Preston, Farrant, Tallis, and other Tudor composers. As in these earlier compositions, the chant merely serves as a scaffolding for a series of unconnected passages of pedantic formulae or for clavieristic acrobatics, which often assume etude-like characteristics. However, the ornamental formulae are generally somewhat more modern than those in the earlier pieces, and some of them are not uninteresting, particularly a few that consist of brief complementary motifs, e.g., in *Christe redemptor omnium* (*BK*, I, p.103; *FW*, II, p.64), measures 36–37, given in Fig.299.

Fig.299

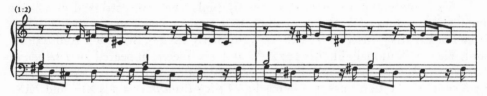

Another example of this style is a *Veni redemptor gentium* (BK, I, p.124; FW, I, p.138).

In a *Miserere* (BK, I, p.105; FW, II, p.442) and a *Salvator mundi* (BK, I, p.111; FW, I, p.163) the chant tunes are set three times consecutively, like chorale variations. Here the heterogeneous figurations, often changing unexpectedly, are replaced by passage work of a more unified character, which has an even more tiring effect. All through the first section of the *Miserere* the whole notes of the *cantus planus* in the top part are accompanied by a counterpoint in quarter notes in the middle voice and one in eighth notes in the lowest voice. This changes to eighth and sixteenth notes in the second section. In the third section the *cantus planus* is shifted to the middle part and the upper and lower voices take over the sixteenth- and eighth-note figurations, respectively. How monotonous this can become is illustrated in Fig.300 by an excerpt from the last section (meas.70ff.):

Fig.300

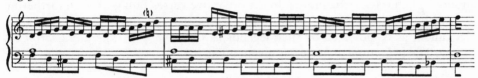

There are twelve *In nomines* by Bull (BK, I, nos.20–31), some of which are called *Gloria tibi Trinitas* in the sources. Most of them show the same approach as the other liturgical compositions, but there is one that occupies a special place not only in Bull's output but in the total repertoire of early organ music as well. Technically as well as historically the work that is often called the "great *In nomine*" (BK, I, p.86; FW, II, p.34) belongs to the design style, but here it is developed into something new and more meaningful. Even the layout is unusual: Each note of the *cantus firmus* is presented as the value of semibreve + semibreve + minim + semiminim, i.e., 4 + 4 + 2 + 1 = 11 semiminims, eleven quarter notes in modern terms, forming two measures of 4/4 and one of 3/4.* Thus the entire composition consists of a regular succession of irregular blocks, and this peculiar scheme helps to raise this work above others of its type. In the final section each building block is dotted and thereby expanded by one half, so that each chant note comprises two measures of 6/4 and one of 9/8. At first this gigantic structure may look discouraging, but on closer examination it proves to be a very successful work. Despite all the variety of ideas, the details produce a unified total impression of magnificence and grandeur. An important contributory feature is the fact that, in contrast to the usual practice, the *cantus planus* is given to the bass. The three

---

* A section of the anonymous *Felix namque* from Roy. App. 56, is similarly based on a series of 5/4 measures (cf.p.148).

contrapuntal upper parts maintain a dense polyphonic imitative texture of great vitality for long stretches. The several figural passages do not disturb the overall style but constitute a meaningful contrast. All in all this *In nomine* is more than an early piece; it is an early masterpiece.

All the compositions discussed so far belong to the *cantus-planus* type, but in a number of pieces the liturgical melodies are treated in other ways. They probably belong to John Bull's late period (after 1613), for all of them are contained in the Antwerp and Vienna manuscripts, both written on the Continent (cf.note 12). First there is a very terse and simple *Te lucis ante terminum,* in which the melody of this compline hymn is heard in the top voice and is harmonized in the four-part style of a simple hymn setting. Bull omits all figuration, all virtuosic brilliance, and chooses a style that was usual at the time for the Protestant chorale.

A *Telluris ingens conditor* in seven verses shows the transformation of the clavier virtuoso into the serious contrapuntalist. In the first two verses the *cantus firmus* is accompanied by three counterpoints that are closely united through imitations of characteristic motifs. In the other five verses Bull goes even further in the direction of strict counterpoint, and presents two of the counterpoints as a strict canon, as is indicated by such legends as *Canon a 4 in superdiatessaron* or *2 in una.* The beginning of verse 4 is given in Fig.301.

Fig.301

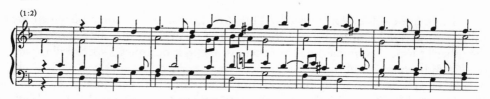

Bull's *Salve regina* consists of the usual five verses, which probably correspond to the five odd-numbered verses of the Marian antiphon—"probably," because the melodies are not easily recognized in the organ settings. Apparently they are very free paraphrases, starting with an imitative presentation of the head motif but continuing independently of the chant; their texture is very interesting and combines contrapuntal, motivic, and figural elements. In verse 4 the brief melody of the *O clemens* occurs three times in a row in the discant, first with one counterpoint, then with two. This work, also, gives the impression of mature mastery.

The three works on the hexachord (*Ut re mi fa sol la*) may also be counted as liturgical pieces. They provide the clearest examples of the early, middle, and late periods of Bull's creativity. In the earliest setting (*BK,* I, p.56; *FW,* II, p.283), the ascending and descending hexachord is heard 23 times (always on g) as a *cantus planus* in the soprano, supported first by one part, then two, and finally by three. The lower voices employ the stereotyped figures of the English design style, and

Fig.302

(1:2)

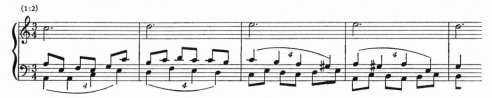

the left hand is repeatedly assigned extended passages in thirds and sixths and in very complicated rhythms. Fig.302 shows an example of the latter (meas. 142–46).

The "chromatic" *Ut re mi fa sol la (BK*, I, p.53; *FW*, I, p.183)[15] is much more mature and interesting. In one of his settings on the hexachord, Byrd had transposed the subject to various pitches; now Bull exploits this possibility to a surprising and singular extent for the time—he transposes the hexachord to each of the twelve steps of the chromatic scale. In doing so he uses a very remarkable scheme, which in a sense anticipates the principle of the whole-tone scale by about three hundred years: The hexachord first appears on the six steps of the whole-tone scale ascending from G *(G, A, B, Db, Eb, F)*, then on those ascending from Ab *(Ab, Bb, C, D, E, F♯)*, and finally five times on G, as a kind of well-deserved rest after the hazardous journey through uncharted areas. Indeed, this enterprise must have appeared really foolhardy and nearly impossible to the contemporary observer and listener, and even today one cannot deny one's admiration for the boldness of the concept. Each presentation of the hexachord comprises thirteen semibreves, twelve for the ascent and descent and one for the transition to the next hexachord, so that this work, like the great *In nomine,* is built of a regular series of irregular blocks (five measures in 2/2 time and one in 3/2 in the modern reduction). The two works are similar in style and probably close to one another in time, for both seem to have been written during the last years of Bull's stay in England, around 1610.

Since in the course of the work each chromatic tone also appears in its enharmonic equivalent (*c♯* and *db, d♯* and *eb*, etc.), the question arises of how this could be realized on the keyboard instruments of the period. Several authors have answered to the effect that "obviously a kind of 'equal temperament' was already in use."[16] It is much more likely, however, that Bull intended this piece for an *arcicembalo* or *arciorgano,* which had separate keys—and of course separate strings or pipes—for *c♯* and *db, d♯* and *eb*, etc. Niccolo Vincentino demanded these very complex instruments as early as 1555 and 1561, respectively, and at the beginning of the 17th century several instruments with more than twelve keys per octave were built and used. The *Universal-Clavicymbel* built by Charles Luython (1557/8–1620) was praised by Praetorius in his *Syntagma musicum* of 1619 as "*instrumentum perfectum si non perfectissimum.*"[17]

The hexachord theme appears throughout in the various voices of a contrapuntal four-part setting, which is free of all figurations. Fig.303 shows a passage —the transition from the third presentation of the hexachord idea on B to the fourth one on Db—in which the enharmonic equivalents occur particularly close to one another.

Fig.303

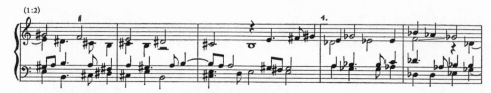

The third composition on the hexachord (*BK*, I, p.65) does not appear in the *Fitzwilliam Virginal Book,* but in the Antwerp manuscript, which was written shortly after Bull's death. There it is called *Fantasia sopra ut re mi fa sol la,* and indeed the subject is no longer used as a *cantus planus,* but is woven freely into a dense, purely contrapuntal texture, nearly always in a different rhythm and often only suggested by an ascending or descending line. There is no doubt that this work presupposes an acquaintance with the Italian clavier literature, and Frescobaldi's *Fantasie* of 1608 are likely direct models.

Most of the fifteen fantasies, which open the complete edition (*BK*, I, nos. 1–15; no.16 is clearly a prelude), consist of several sections of varying content, like Byrd's fantasies. No.10, the only one contained in the *Fitzwilliam Virginal Book,* is most interesting. Its first section is a long duet, whose voices are extensively related through the imitation of various subjects or motifs. It is followed by another two-part section in which the lower voice consists of twelve repetitions of an ostinato of a peculiar, rotating design, shown in Fig.304. The piece concludes with a coda in a full, clavieristic setting pervaded by a scale motif.

Fig.304

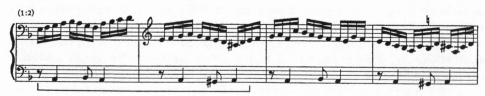

Bull's preludes were discussed earlier (cf.p.221). Only the specifically "virginalistic" works remain: the variations on secular themes, the pavanes and galliards, and the many smaller pieces.

Among the variation sets the one on *Walsingham* (BK, II, p.46; FW, I, p.1) is by far the most notable. During Bull's lifetime it was obviously already very famous, for it was entered as the first composition in the *Fitzwilliam Virginal Book*. In thirty variations Bull offers a survey of the many details of virginalistic technique, the like of which is not found in any other work of the period. Van den Borren describes this work in very enthusiastic terms,[18] but I cannot quite agree with his judgment. One look at Byrd's variations on the same theme will reveal how far Bull's composition lags behind that of the older master in artistic quality. To begin with, the fact that the theme always appears in the top part—mostly in a very simple form, though sometimes garbed in brilliant if rather hollow passage work—shows a certain "superficiality" that marks the whole work; and the lower parts of the variations are mostly given to mere finger acrobatics—but even today they are astonishing. Fig.305 gives the beginning of variation XXVIII, which must be played with crossed hands.

Fig.305

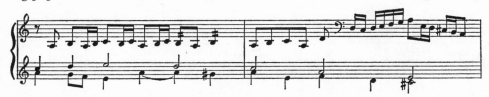

Whatever one may think about Bull's *Walsingham* variations, one cannot deny that they represent a feat of brilliant virtuosity. The other variation sets, e.g., those on the *Spanish Paven* (BK, II, p.31; FW, II, p.131), *Revenant* (BK, II, p.94), *Les Buffons* (BK, II, p.97), *Go from my Window* (BK, II, p.137), and *The New Bergomask* (BK, II, p.140) lack even that spark. The most attractive seems to be the first set of variations on *Why ask you* (BK, II, p.1) and perhaps one or two variations from the two other cycles on the same theme (BK, II, pp.3, 4). All these variation works were probably written before *Walsingham*, which certainly represents a high point in Bull's virginalistic, virtuosic output, and which was probably composed in the first decade of the 17th century, before he left England. Bull also wrote four grounds (BK, II, nos.75, 102a, 102b, 108); the second and third, particularly, are of a disarming triviality.

Bull's pavanes and galliards are the artistic culmination of his entire keyboard opus. In these compositions the wealth of his personality, the versatility of his feelings, and the greatness of his musical genius find their clearest expression. It is no accident that some of these pieces carry designations such as *Fantastic Paven, Melancholy Paven, Trumpet Paven,* and *Pavana Sinfoniae.* Whether they originated with Bull or with others, they show that people recognized definite meanings in these pieces, which can be recognized here and there even today. The second

Fig.306

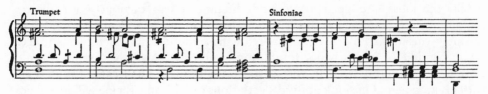

section (B) of *Trumpet Paven* may well have sounded like a trumpet call to the listener of the period, and in the second section of the *Pavana Sinfoniae* there is a passage that brings to mind a concertante ensemble work of the time (Fig.306).[19] Of course the *Fantastic Paven* and the *Melancholy Paven* are both in minor, but the melancholy expression of the latter is more obvious than the mysterious mood of the former.

Fig.307

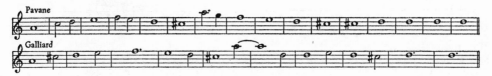

Several of Bull's pavanes and galliards are interesting because of their structural proportions. The pavane-galliard *Lord Lumley* (*BK*, II, p.181; *FW*, I, pp.149 and 54) has the form 11.11.8–8.8.10, and the D-minor pavane (*BK*, II, p.8; *FW*, II, p.121) the form 16.8.16–10.6.10. One galliard (*BK*, II, p.27; *FW*, II, p.251) has the particularly irregular form 8.9.14. Like Morley and Philips, Bull has several pavane-galliards in which the melody of the galliard is derived from the pavane in a free transformation of the rhythm. A fine example is offered by the first section of the D-minor pavane-galliard, which is reproduced in simplified form in Fig.307. In the *Fantastic Paven* (*BK*, II, p.60; *FW*, I, p.124) the first section of the galliard is also related to that of the pavane in a very free, interesting relationship, as seen in Fig.308.

Fig.308

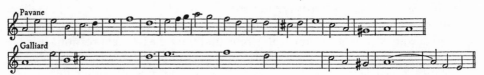

Many of Bull's short pieces are as charming as Farnaby's. In some of his *Almans* the allemande loses its "German heaviness," which Morley ascribes to it in his *Introduction to Practicall Musicke*, and assumes an expression of playful grace, as, e.g., in the *Duke of Brunswick's Alman*. For the Duchess of Brunswick he writes a playful bagatelle—*Duchess of Brunswick's Toy*—in a similar mood, and the *Irish Toy* is no less charming. Finally Bull, like Farnaby, writes several self-portraits: *My Self, My Grief, My Choice*, and *Bull's Good Night. My Grief* (in FW, II, p.258, this little piece appears under the meaningless title *A Gigge*), in which he expresses his sorrow, is particularly pretty. Instead of a dark minor, he uses a gay G major with a lively rhythm and skips for an amusing game of self-ridicule. Perhaps the two measures with cross-rhythms of two notes against three suggest what he, with typical English understatement, keeps to himself.

John Bull's stay in the Netherlands inspired his arrangements of several Dutch folk tunes, *Den lustelijcken Meij, Een Kindeken is ons geboren*, and *Laet ons met herten reijne* (BK, I, nos.52–56), which he treats in simple contrapuntal settings with ornamented repetitions or variations. The last of these pieces is the most beautiful; it opens with a prelude, in which the beginning of the song inspired Bull to write one of his most beautiful and purest settings. Fig. 309 gives the beginnings of the prelude and the song arrangement.

Fig.309

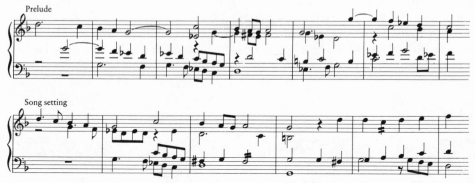

Cosyn, Carleton, Tisdall, and Others

Benjamin Cosyn (c.1570 to after 1644) is known chiefly for *Cosyn's Virginal Book* (Brit. Mus. Roy. 23.L.4), a voluminous collection containing a number of his own compositions as well as pieces by Bull and Gibbons. Several more of his pieces are found in a manuscript of the Paris Conservatory (Rés. 1185) and in one at Oxford Christ Church College (Ms. 1113). His is a rather extensive output—2 preludes, 3 pavane-galliards, 10 galliards, 11 variation sets, 8 fantasies, and other

Fig.310

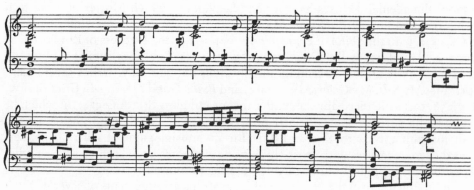

pieces. Only a few have been published, some incompletely, and justifiably; mostly they continue with variations that are nothing but very banal figurations whose value is out of proportion to the space they would occupy.[20] Cosyn also uses a plethora of English ornament symbols, the single and double oblique bar, and even inserts them in Bull's and Gibbons' pieces much more frequently than they appear in other manuscripts. The beginning of a pavane (Cosyn Ms., p.15) in Fig.310 is an illustration. It is certainly not inspired music, and Cosyn's other compositions do not exceed the level of harmless mediocrity either; indeed they often fall below it, if one considers the often silly variation technique. In one of his variation sets, *A Ground* with eight variations, formulae like those shown in Fig.311 are pursued for eight or sixteen measures of the thirty-two measure theme (Cosyn Ms., pp.19ff.

Fig.311

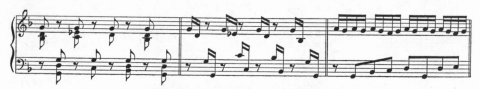

The superficial virtuosity of the pieces in Cosyn's own manuscript is in striking contrast to the eight compositions preserved in the Oxford manuscript.[21] These pieces have no titles and only a monogram, B. C., at the end, which, however, can only mean Benjamin Cosyn. They are written in a free-voiced, contrapuntal, freely imitative texture, mostly employing several subjects or motifs. They are best classified as fantasies or voluntaries. Some details bring Redford to mind, e.g., the beginning of no.70 (p.156) of the collection, reproduced in Fig.312.

Fig.312

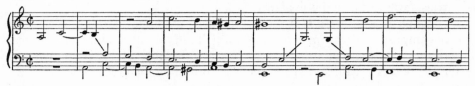

Nicholas Carleton (or Carlton; c.1570–1630, younger of course than the Nicholas Carleton in the *Mulliner Book*) is known by a small number of pieces from Brit. Mus. Add. 29996, but some are of special interest.[22] A prelude compares favorably with other English preludes of the period because of its pure polyphony, free of all virtuosic additions; it is also unusual because of its very low range, from A_1 to d'. Fig.313 shows the end of this attractive piece of twenty-four measures, with its serious, dignified expression.

Fig.313

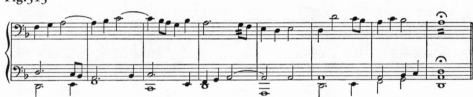

A *Verse of four Parts* is a longer piece in four-part polyphony, in which such distant keys as *F♯* major and *B♭* minor are touched on, and *Upon the Sharpe* moves entirely within the sharp keys (with *d♯, a♯, e♯*, and *b♯*). The *Verse for two to play on one Virginal or Organ*, one of the earliest four-hand pieces (cf.p.303 and note 11) is an *In nomine*, in which the Gregorian melody (*Gloria tibi Trinitas*) is heard in the second highest voice of a four- to five-part setting as a *cantus planus* with occasional paraphrases. Fig.314 shows a passage from this interesting work.

Fig.314

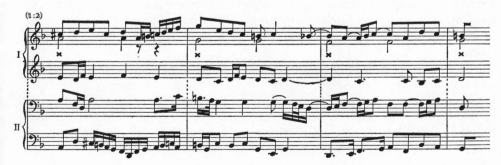

As in his other compositions, Carleton relies completely on the carrying power and intrinsic value of a vital polyphony.

William Tisdall (born c.1570) seems to have favored secular music. We have 7 dance compositions by him: 3 pavanes, a galliard, an allemande, and 2 jigs.[23] The pavanes and the galliard definitely rank with those of better known and greater composers. Again and again one is surprised by the great variety and the beauty, color, and flavor of the English pavane, even in the hands of lesser masters. Tisdall's *Pavana Chromatica* (*Mrs. Katherin Tregians Paven; FW*, II, p.278) consists of three sections of 13, 12, and 15 measures, respectively, that move from *B* major to *E* major, from *G* major to *G* major, and from *E* minor back to *B* major. Although it is free of genuine chromaticism, it nevertheless offers a number of notably bold turns, such as those shown in Fig.315. The gaiety and vivacity of the third section of the galliard (*FW*, II, p.486) are reminiscent of Farnaby.

Fig.315

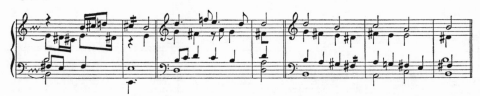

Thomas Weelkes (d.1623), one of the most important English madrigalists, was also active as an organist (in Winchester and Chichester). Unfortunately only 4 clavier compositions of his are preserved; 2 voluntaries, a pavane, and a galliard.[24] All of them are written in a pure, mostly four-part setting, totally free of figurations and other virtuosic elements, except for a number of written-out trills in the varied sections of the galliard. Although they are not particularly original, these pieces take a worthy place within the great tradition of Elizabethan keyboard music.

Several pieces by John Lugge (c.1587?–c.1647; organist at Exeter Cathedral from 1602 to 1645), are available in modern prints.[25] His three voluntaries are written for the double organ, i.e., an organ with two manuals, which gradually came into general use in England after 1600. With their successive changes of subjects or motifs these voluntaries correspond to the English fantasy in form and style.

A number of other composers appear in the various manuscripts of the 17th century, each represented by a few pieces: Edmund Hooper (c.1553–1621), Ferdinand Richardson (c.1558–1618), Martin Peerson (c.1571–1650), Thomas Holmes (d.1638), Robert Johnson (c.1583–1633), John Amner (d.1641), Marchant, Kinlough, Bickrell, Afonso (Ferrabosco), James Harden, and others.

Tomkins

Thomas Tomkins was the organist at Worcester Cathedral from about 1596 to 1646, received a Bachelor of Music degree from Oxford in 1607, and was made the organist of the Chapel Royal at London in 1621. He is perhaps the most peculiar personality among the virginalists. If ever the word "anachronistic" is justified it applies to him and his work. He was born in 1572, outlived all his contemporaries, even younger men such as Gibbons, for he died in 1656. Although he was a pupil of Byrd's, as late as the mid-17th century he wrote pieces in a style reminiscent of Blitheman and Tallis and even earlier English organ masters. One is reminded of the composers of the *Old Hall Manuscript*—Cooke, Damett, Pycard, Sturgeon—who two hundred years before Tomkins retained a long-antiquated tradition with similar tenacity.

A complete edition[26] allows a detailed study of this eccentric late-comer. It comprises 73 compositions, among them 2 (3?) preludes, 18 liturgical organ pieces, 7 *Ut re mi fa sol la*, 12 free contrapuntal works (fancies, voluntaries, verses), 2 grounds, 20 pavanes and galliards, 5 variation sets, and some single pieces. The most important source for Tomkins' works is an autograph at the Paris Conservatory (Rés. 1122) that Tomkins evidently wrote near the end of his life; he first entered pieces by Byrd and by Bull, and then about 50 compositions of his own. Thirty bear dates from the last decade of his life (September 1646–September 1654), and it is generally assumed that they refer to the time of composition. Tomkins would therefore have written these works between the ages of 74 and 82.[27] The 20 undated pieces were probably also written after 1630, for the handwriting is obviously that of an old man. Another Tomkins autograph, the portion of Brit. Mus. Add. 29996 written by him,[28] exhibits much firmer characters. This manuscript must certainly be twenty to thirty years older, and furnishes an approximate time for the pieces contained in it (new ed., nos.27, 32, 40, and 57[29]). Another five pieces (nos.39, 56, 58 62, 65) are included in the *Fitzwilliam Virginal Book*, and can therefore be dated earlier than 1619. Thus it is with some assurance that we can speak of a group of about 10 early pieces and one of at least 30 later ones among Tomkins' keyboard works.

In the *Fitzwilliam Virginal Book* Tomkins is represented, first of all, by an A-minor pavane (new ed., no.36; *FW*, II, p.51), an expressive and expansive composition (of the form 16.20.26). Like so many pavanes and galliards of the period, it unfortunately suffers from the abrupt contrast between the very sustained character of the main sections and the cheap virtuosic effects of the varied repetitions. The third section employs the descending chromatic fourth throughout with striking effect, as shown in Fig.316. Interestingly, this pavane won the distinction of being rearranged by Tomkins' older contemporary Peter Philips. It is found in the Düben Tablature (fol.8v) under the title *Pavana Anglica Thomas Tomkins Collerirt di Pietro Philippi.*

Fig.316

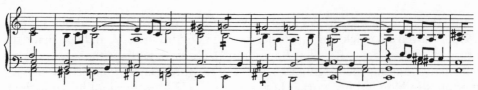

In *Barafostus' Dream* (new ed., no.62; *FW*, II, p.94) Tomkins treats a popular, song-like theme in eight variations, all of type A (melody retained in the upper part). A good many figurations à la Bull or Farnaby are involved, as well as exceedingly big skips in the left hand, both illustrated by Fig.317. In the second half of the concluding variation there are some peculiar rhythmic figures, which are interpreted as quadruplets in 3/4 time in the new edition. Various devices in the three remaining pieces in the *FW* also remind one of Bull: the parallel thirds in the left hand in the *Grounde* (new ed., no.39; *FW*, II, p.87), the arpeggiations in the *Hunting Galliard* (new ed., no.58; *FW*, II, p.100), and the octave skips in *Worster Braules* (new ed., no.65; *FW*, II, p.269).

Fig.317

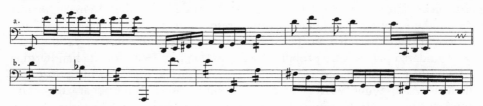

The pieces preserved in Brit. Mus. Add. 29996, include a four-hand *Fancy for two to play* (new ed., no.32). The manuscript carries the legend "Another of the like Tho. Thomkins," a note that obviously refers to Carleton's *Verse*, which is also for four hands and which Tomkins had entered in his collection shortly before (fol.197–200). Even today Tomkins' *Fancy* can claim a place of honor in four-hand literature. The style tends more toward a homophonic-harmonic setting than Carleton's piece. Several passages with polychoral echo effects, like the one given in Fig.318, are especially attractive.

The *Ground* from the same autograph is a kind of companion piece to the one preserved in the *Fitzwilliam Virginal Book* (cf. new ed., nos.39 and 40).[30] Both are based on subjects of four 3/4 measures in the rhythm | ♩ ♩ | —an ostinato of the same type that Byrd used repeatedly. In addition, both start in the very same manner—with a single-voiced announcement and a two-part stretto of the subject, which are given in Fig.319. In the first ground (from *FW*) this is followed by more than forty variations, most of which have the ostinato in the top part rather than

Fig.318

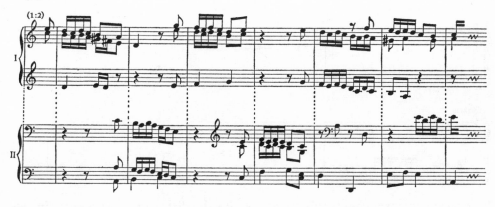

Fig.319

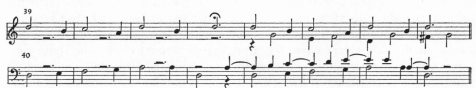

in the bass, and add passage work of the usual type. Thus the natural function of the ground is altered in a way that is interesting as a curiosity but a mistake artistically, for the exposure and audible reiteration of the rather insignificant formula soon becomes tiresome and unbearable. In the second ground, which runs to only twenty-four variations, this fault is largely avoided, but a comparison with any ground by Byrd shows the difference between a great master and a diligent pupil.

Tomkins' works discussed so far were certainly written before 1620. They are not outstanding, but they are appropriate contributions to the musical repertoire of the period. This is not true of the works in the Paris manuscript, which were written between 1646 and 1654, when the great tradition of English clavier music was long a thing of the past. To preserve or revitalize this tradition or an even earlier stage of the evolution seems to have been Tomkins' goal in his last years.

More than half of these late works are liturgical organ pieces on themes already employed by Redford, Blitheman, and Tallis as bases of their organ compositions: *Miserere, In nomine (Gloria tibi)*, and *Clarifica me*. It is not so much the retention of the old themes—the *In nomine*, e.g., was cultivated in instrumental ensemble music by 17th-century English composers as late as Purcell—but the treatment that reminds one of the Tudor design style, that strange, abstract, dry, and pedantic way of writing, in which a sustained *cantus-planus* part is combined with two figural counterpoints consisting of a succession without plan of the most

Fig.320

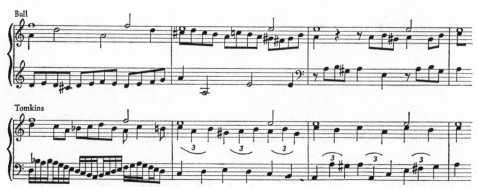

heterogeneous formulae. If this style was already alien and anachronistic in the 16th century, how strange it must have appeared around 1650! To be sure, Tomkins' figures and motifs are somewhat more progressive than Preston's, Farrant's, or Tallis', but the principle remains the same. The treatment of harmony is also the same or similar, and everywhere there are archaic modal turns, like those that result when a composition is dominated by linear voice leading. Bull had initiated greater unity and continuity of figuration as well as greater harmonic clarity in his three-part *In nomine* (FW, I, p.135)—not to speak of his great *In nomine* in A minor (cf.p.305). Compared with these pieces, which were probably written about 1610, Tomkins' *In nomines* sound as though they were written twenty years earlier rather than thirty to forty years later. Fig.320 gives three corresponding measures (notes 32–34 of the Gregorian melody), as set by Bull and by Tomkins (new ed., no.10) (for easier comparison the passage from Bull's work is transposed up a fifth).

The situation becomes even more curious when one realizes that around 1620, during his main period of creativity, Tomkins wrote three-part *In nomines* for ensemble that exhibit a very continuous and unified style, such as one would expect in English instrumental music of the time.[31] Perhaps Tomkins' strange anachronistic return to a much earlier style can be explained by the fact that he became the owner of the manuscript Brit. Mus. Add. 29996, and added much of his own music to it. The very oldest portions of the manuscript bear many of his notes, and testify to his careful study of the works of his musical ancestors. On fol.65 he says of the alleluia for the Easter Mass by Preston, "a good sharpe verse," and of the anonymous Easter hymns on fol.159–178 "good," "very good," and "a good old indeed very good." The many bar lines on these folios, often crooked or broken, are in his hand, and show how attentively he studied every piece.[32] Consequently this century-old organ music may have appeared like a revelation to this old man, who had become a stranger to his own time, like a spring of youth from which he could draw new inspiration for his own composition.

318

Tomkins adopted this archaic style in all his *In nomines* (eight, among them two variants) as well as in several *Misereres* (new ed., nos.13, 16, and 17). An exceedingly curious piece that falls in this category is the *Offertory* (new ed. no.21) contained in the Oxford manuscript and dated 1637. More than 400 measures (semibreves) in length, it is surely one of the longest pieces ever written for the clavier. From beginning to end it is based exclusively on a single theme of seven notes (*a c′ b c′ d′ b a*); this subject is treated imitatively in an introductory portion (new ed. meas.1–15) and then as an ostinato in various voices no fewer than 57 times without interruption: the first 39 times in semibreves (to meas.216), then 16 times in minims (to meas.280), and finally twice more in semibreves (to meas.292; meas.293ff. are a coda). Since the two or three other parts with which the ostinato is combined have to deal with such an enormous length, they exhibit a great variety of formulae, nearly everything that English organ and virginal music produced throughout its evolution.

Not all of Tomkins' later works are of this kind. Among the liturgical pieces there are some that are briefer and more unified, e.g., the *Clarifica me* and two *Misereres* (new ed., nos.4, 19, and 20). These works are undated, however, and may possibly belong to a slightly earlier period. One of his freely imitative works, a *Fancy*, dated 1648 (new ed., no.25), treats three subjects in lively rhythm with great dexterity and fine taste (Fig.321).

Fig.321

(1:2)

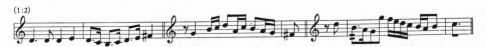

Tomkins' late pavanes and galliards (new ed., nos.41ff.) bring a great English tradition to a worthy end. To be sure, they lack the inner verve, the expressive power, and the melodic richness of the pavanes by Byrd, Bull, or Gibbons, and many a detail sounds labored, as, e.g., the sequences in the *Galliard Earl of Strafford* (no.42), the galliard no.46, and the pavane no.52. The tendency toward irregular phrasing seems to be pushed almost too far, but it does lend some charm and individuality, and prevents these pieces from descending to the level of everyday dance music. Pavane no.47 consists of three sections (8.8½.7½), with the first section phrased 3+3+2. The first section of pavane no.52 begins with four phrases in sequence, each of three beats (minims, or half notes), giving the impression of a galliard. Although Tomkins' late pavanes and galliards offer these interesting details, in artistic value they lag behind two earlier works that are closely related in style: the pavane in the *Fitzwilliam Virginal Book* (new ed., no.56), and the *Pavan Lord Canterbury* in Brit. Mus. Add. 29996 (no.57).[33]

Gibbons

Orlando Gibbons (1583–1625) is the last of the "three famous Masters" whose works were included in the *Parthenia*. Born in Oxford, he became a singer in the choir of King's College at Cambridge in 1596 and an organist in the Chapel Royal at London in 1605. Like John Bull, he also earned academic degrees and honors: in 1606 the Bachelor of Music at Cambridge, in 1607 a Master of Arts at Oxford, and in 1622 a Doctor of Music h.c. from Oxford. He died at Canterbury, where he had gone for the reception of King Charles I and his French wife, Henrietta Maria.

Gibbons' keyboard compositions were published in the 1920s,[34] but a better edition is now available which is the basis of the following observations.[35] It contains 45 pieces, among them 4 preludes, 10 fantasies, 4 pavanes, 7 galliards, 5 variation sets, and several allemandes, courantes, and masks. A first appendix contains 5 doubtful compositions, a second one the beginnings of 9 pieces that are considered spurious.[36]

The first two preludes consist exclusively of fast passage work (no.1 is called *A Running Fantasia* in the manuscript) blended, with a fine understanding for climax and contrast, with harmonies that are remarkably modern for the period. The second prelude was incorporated into the *Parthenia* as its conclusion. The other two preludes are brief pieces, whose simple contrapuntal yet chordal setting is more meaningful to us today than the passage work of the first two.

Two of the fantasies should perhaps be classed as voluntaries because of their brevity.[37] Most of the others divide into several more or less clearly recognizable sections, and they differ from Byrd's fantasies in that they are marked by unity rather than by change and contrast. The multiplicity and variety of ideas, so characteristic of Byrd and even of Farnaby, are completely lacking, and so are the dance-like, song-like, playful, and virtuosic features. Enthusiastic effu·siveness gives way to a moderate approach and a refinement in taste. In their way Gibbons' fantasies are no less significant and no less fascinating than Byrd's. One of Gibbons' most admirable talents is his mastery of the art of the "unending melody," the capability to carry on and develop a musical idea again and again, beyond its "natural" conclusion. It is an art that only a few of the best composers really mastered. No less remarkable is Gibbons' way of leading the musical material in almost every fantasy to a climax shortly before the end by setting his lines into a slow but decisive ascending motion, mostly in sequential phrases. He is perhaps the first to understand the intrinsic dynamics of a musical idea. In the field of keyboard music he certainly had no predecessor in this respect, and, for a long time, no successor. A section of no.11 (Glyn IV, no.6) serves as an illustration (Fig.322).

Several fantasies limit themselves to three voices, yet do not in the least lack fulness of sound or richness of events. Sectional articulation is particularly clear in

Fig.322

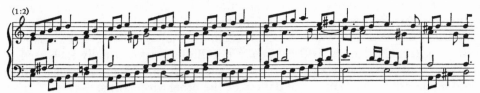

fantasy no.10 (Glyn IV, no.9), the only one that contains a section of passage work. The others continue in a more or less unified contrapuntal texture, within which various subjects or motifs occur more or less clearly. Great maturity, even cleverness of contrapuntal technique is shown in Gibbons' way of working his ideas into the lattice of voices, letting some of them unobtrusively take an effect within it rather than presenting them clearly, as is usual in an imitative texture. The *Fantasia for Double Organ* (no.7; Glyn V, no.19) is especially noteworthy in this respect. An extended composition whose pervasive three-part polyphony eschews all genuine thematic material, it is nevertheless finely molded from start to finish. The four-part fantasy no.12 (Glyn V, no.16) is the direct opposite of this work, for it consists of six thematically differentiated but organically connected sections. It is written in Gibbons' favorite key, A minor, and is one of his most beautiful creations; it was incorporated in the *Parthenia* (as *Fantazia in foure parts*) with good reason. The excerpt in Fig.323 is one of the most impressive examples of the dynamics of musical intensity.

Fig.323

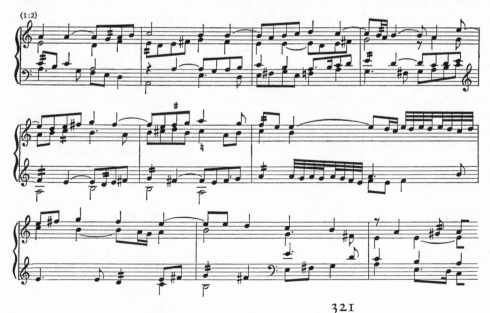

All of Gibbons' pavanes and galliards have come down as single pieces. Even the *Pavane Lord Salisbury* and the *Galliarde Lord Salisbury* (nos.18 and 19) do not form a pair, or at least do not exhibit any thematic relationship. Except for the *Galliarde Lady Hatton,* which has two sections, they consist of three sections, mostly of irregular length, as they often are in Bull's works. Usually each section is followed by a figural repetition with passage work that generally keeps within more moderate limits than in the dances of the other virginalists.

In his pavanes and galliards, even more than in his fantasies, Gibbons proves to be the great master of melodic continuity. From the first to the last measure, each section describes a single curve, equally impressive in its length, its sustaining power, and its buoyant tension. The D-minor pavane (no.15; Glyn III, p.8), is especially admirable in this respect. It is the only pavane with regular sections, sixteen measures in length. But these sections are quite different from the usual examples of four-beat regularity, whose banal schematicism is the exact opposite of sustaining power and buoyancy. The *Pavane Lord Salisbury* is outstanding among all the masterpieces Gibbons created in this field. It is a work of extraordinary spirituality and depth of expression. Clearly and forcefully Gibbons shows himself to be a late master, whose artistic personality holds an even greater fascination when one senses in his work the approaching end of a great epoch. This work represents the culmination of an evolution that perhaps began with Byrd's pavane dedicated to the same noble house and in the same key of A minor —an evolution comparable to the one that leads from a Mozart Adagio to the finale of Beethoven's op.111. Gibbons wrote this pavane—as well as the equally important *Fantazia in foure parts*—at a rather early age. Both are found in the *Parthenia,* which probably appeared in 1611, when Gibbons was about twenty-nine. This pavane and the variations on *The Woods so wilde* are Gibbons' only compositions in the *Fitzwilliam Virginal Book.*

Gibbons' variation works are less important than his fantasies, pavanes, and galliards.[38] In *The Queene's Command* and *Whoop, do me no harm* he does not reach beyond insignificant ripples of figurations. The variations entitled *Ground* (no.26; Glyn II, p.7) are interesting because of the subject on which they are based, which is essentially identical with the passamezzo antico. Fig.324, which shows the beginning of the first variation, will clarify this relationship, and it really makes no difference whether one seeks or finds the traditional subject in the

Fig.324

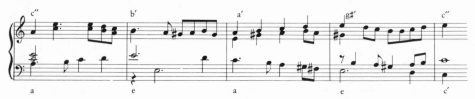

melody (*c′ b a g♯*), in the bass (*a e a e*), or in both at the same time. Gibbons treats the theme in seven variations, whose contrapuntal-motivic style is obviously inspired by Byrd. The upper parts are different in each variation, as one would expect in a ground, but the bass is also extensively altered. Only the harmonic framework is retained as an unchanging and essential element.

In striking contrast to the uniformly contrapuntal *Ground*, the nine variations on *The Woods so wilde* are beholden throughout to figuration technique, which does not lack a certain elegance, but is essentially empty. A comparison with Byrd's variations on the same theme suggests itself. Gibbons uses the following variations types in his set: A B* A A D* A D* B D. The analogous schematic presentation for Byrd's set is given on p.280.

Fig.325

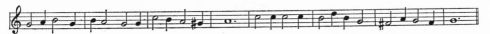

The fourteen variations on *The Hunt's up* (*Peascod Time*) also suggest a comparison with Byrd's variations on the same theme. Byrd's work resembles a ground, but Gibbons' definitely does not. This confirms our earlier suspicion that *Peascod Time* is not really a ground but a popular tune, which is easily recognized in variations III (Fig.325), XI and XIII. *Peascod Time* is probably Gibbons' most important variation work. A number of variations are filled with flowing figurations—especially the middle group, VIII–X—and others are captivating in their ingenious contrapuntal-motivic texture. Variation VI, given in Fig.326, develops an especially interesting motif with great dexterity.

Fig.326

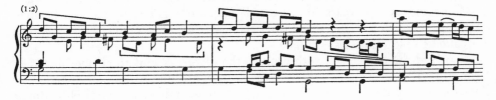

14

The Netherlands

THE NETHERLANDS (present-day Holland and Belgium) played such a leading role in the development of vocal music in the 15th and 16th centuries, that it is strange that they contributed almost nothing to the evolution of keyboard music of the same period or—to put it more circumspectly—there are practically no signs of such activity in the extant manuscripts. The great masters of the 15th century—Ockeghem, Obrecht, Isaac—would not be expected to compose for the organ, for they still held to the medieval attitude that the rank of the *organista* was far below that of the *musicus*. But even in the 16th century the Netherlanders —contemporaries of Schlick, Redford, Cavazzoni, Cabezón, and Gabrieli—do not seem to have very much interest in organ music. In any event, we know only six organ pieces by Dutch composers that were written earlier than 1550: the organ Mass and the two ricercars from Castell' Arquato ascribed to Jacques Brumel, (cf.pp.112–15, 170–71) and the three ricercars from Jacques Buus' *Intabolatura d'organo* of 1549 (cf.pp.175–77.).

Toward the end of the 16th century the picture begins to change. Between 1548 and 1570 seven musicians who were to contribute to the development of clavier music were born in the Netherlands: Giovanni di Macque (c.1548), Simon Lohet (c.1550), Samuel Mareschal (1554), Charles Luython (1556), Pieter Cornet (c.1560), Jan Pieterszon Sweelinck (1562), and Henderick Speuy (c.1570). The four oldest followed the Dutch tradition of seeking employment outside their country: Macque in Naples, Lohet in Stuttgart, Mareschal in Basle, and Luython in Vienna and Prague. Their works are discussed in connection with the music-historical evolution of the countries in which they worked. The other three were active as organists in their homeland—Cornet, the Belgian, in Brussels and the two

Dutchmen, Sweelinck in Amsterdam and Speuy in Dordrecht. They are the only representatives of a genuine Netherlandish keyboard music. The main difference between it and the keyboard music of other countries is its close relationship with English virginal music.

Sweelinck

Jan Pieterszon Sweelinck (1562–1621) was the son of Pieter Sweelinck, who was the organist at the Oude Kerk (Old Church) at Amsterdam until his death in 1573. In 1580 (or earlier) Jan succeeded his father in this office and held it until his own death. Early biographies follow a statement by Mattheson and report that Sweelinck lived in Italy from 1578 to 1580 and studied with Zarlino, but today this account is generally considered unfounded.

Sweelinck's keyboard works are preserved in many manuscripts, which have gradually become known. In 1884 when Ritter wrote his book *Zur Geschichte des Orgelspiels,* he knew of perhaps a dozen pieces. Ten years later Seiffert opened his complete edition of Sweelinck with an entire volume of *Werken voor Orgel of Clavier,* containing 36 pieces. In the 1930s new sources (chiefly the Lynar tablatures) became available to him, so that he was able to publish a second edition with 69 compositions in 1943. Another 5 pieces were found in the Turin tablatures and were printed in a *Supplement* (1958) edited by A. Annegarn. The last two publications are the basis for the following observations.[1]

Seiffert divided the material he knew in three categories:

Works for organ or harpsichord: 13 fantasies (nos.1–13), 6 echo fantasies (nos.14–19), and 13 toccatas (nos.20–32);
Works for organ: 1 prelude (no.33) and 24 chorale settings (nos.34–57);
Works for harpsichord (mostly variations): 7 secular songs (nos.58–64) and 5 dance tunes (nos.65–69).

Seventeen of these pieces (nos.7, 11, 13, 19, 34, 36, 39, 40, 42, 43, 44, 47, 49, 50, 55, 57, 61) are anonymous and were incorporated in the edition because they were similar in style to, or were in immediate propinquity with, authentic works in the sources. This procedure seems to be more justified in the fantasies than in the chorale settings, for Sweelinck's German pupils wrote very similar chorales. Annegarn's *Supplement* contains two "ricercars," which are similar to Sweelinck's toccatas, and three fantasies.

FANTASIES

Some of Sweelinck's fantasies may be early works, for they are very dependent on the English techniques and only suggest the structural principles characteristic of

325

Sweelinck's mature compositions. The pieces concerned are nos.9 (7),* 11, 12,[2] and 13 (8). They may be called ostinato fantasies, since all of them treat their subjects not so much imitatively as in ostinato reiteration. In the following schematic outlines the first column indicates the section of the fantasy in Roman numerals and its starting measures in parentheses in Arabic numerals; the second column indicates the number of voices and the voices in which the subject is heard; and the third column gives the number of subject entrances (S = subject)·

No.12. Subject: | c | g | f | e |

I	2 highest	18 S on c
II (77)	3 highest	11 S on c
ending (120)	3 all	S in diminution

No.13. Subject: same as in no.12

I	3 all	26 S on c
II (119)	2 highest	3 S on c
ending (134)	3 all	Identical with no.12

No.9. Subject: | d' | — c' | b — a g | f♯ g | e f♯ | g |

I	2 lowest	3 S on g, 3 S on c, 3 S on d
II (57)	2 highest	3 S on g, 2 S on c, 3 S on d
III (107)	3 middle	3 S on g, 3 S on c, 3 S on d
interlude (161)	3	
IV (170)	4 all	½ of S imitative

No.11. Bipartite subject: | a | e' | c' c♯' | d' f' | e' || e' | d' c' | a c' | b | a | ; the two halves of S are designated as T and U below.

I	2 highest	4 S on a, a, e, d; 2 U on c, a
II (49)	2 lowest	3 S on a, e, d; 3 U on g, c, a
III (90)	3 middle	2 S on a, d; 3 U on g, c, a
IV (119)	3 all	½ of T and ½ of U partly imitative, partly in highest voice
V (164)	4 all	T imitative
VI (194)	4 all	U (expanded by one measure) imitative
VII (211)	4 all	¼ of T and ¼ of U imitative, S once at the end

No.12 has a four-measure subject of very primitive design, which is repeated twenty-nine times in the top part without change (thirty times if we count an introductory anticipation in the lower part). To bring this stiff material to life, Sweelinck employs decorative counterpoints, first in one, then in two voices. The

---

* The numbers in parentheses refer to Seiffert's first edition, Sweelinck, Gesammelte Werke, vol.1.

Fig.327

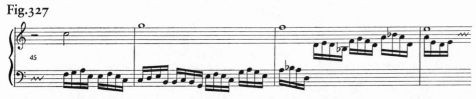

figurations do not lack variety in motion or formulation, but even a greater master than Sweelinck could not have filled such a huge "empty space" with musical life. Obviously this is an early student work, in which he tried to learn the idiom of the English design style. A piece like Blitheman's *Christe redemptor* (*Mulliner Book*, no.108) or John Bull's *Ut re mi fa sol la* (*FW*, II, p.281) may have served as a model, particularly the latter, for its upper part, too, is formed out of numerous reiterations of a basic formula. Sweelinck, however, makes more use than the English of formulae that ornament a skip, as in the passage shown in Fig.327. The most remarkable part of this fantasy is the ending, given in Fig.328, in which the subject is transformed by diminutions to one eighth of the note values, and even to one sixteenth.

Fig.328

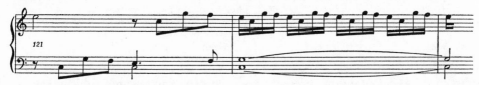

No.13 is a second arrangement of the same subject. It makes much more moderate use of figurations and the regular subject appears in every voice. In nos.9 and 11 the subject is transposed, and in no.11 it is also treated imitatively. In general, proceeding according to a plan is very characteristic of Sweelinck, and each section is reserved for a different treatment of the subject.

Let us now turn form the ostinato fantasies to the others (nos.1–8 and 10). Their subjects are not treated in consecutive repetitions but in imitation. Once again there is a definite plan as the extended compositions are divided into three main sections. In the first section the subject is employed in its original form, in the second usually in augmentation, and in the third in diminution. Sometimes the augmentation, and more often the diminution by two (S^2, $S^{\frac{1}{2}}$) is followed by a transformation in which the note values are quadrupled (or quartered). Several fantasies have additional concluding sections, in which the diminution is canceled. The following table shows the outlines of these fantasies and indicates the starting measures of the various sections:

No.	A		B		C	Ending
	S	S^2	S^4	$S^{\frac12}$	$S^{\frac14}$	
1 (1)		104	—	149	184	
2 (2)		123	168	242	276	$S^{\frac12}$ (290), S (300)
3 (3)		84	164	182	208	S (219)*
4		—	—	103	—	S^2 (118)
5 (4)		159	—	235	251	$S^{\frac12}$ (260), S (289)
6 (5)		—	—	137	183	$S^{\frac14}$ (213)
7		68	—	136	147	
8 (6)		131	—	203	—	S (256)
10		108	130	196	256	S (264)

The sections shown in the table are usually quite long. They fall into sub-sections that are differentiated in various ways, mostly by the use of new counter-subjects or countermotifs, and occasionally by figural counterpoints, strettos, or variants of the subject. To convey some idea of this "filigree work" we shall analyze two fantasies in detail, although even the most detailed analysis cannot present all the features but can only act as a map. Countersubjects are symbolized by A, B, etc., shorter countermotifs by lower-case letters. The subsections are numbered in Arabic numerals, and the numbers of the starting measures are in parentheses.

No.1. Subject: | a | a a | g♯ g | f♯ f | e |

1	2 (56)	3 (70)	4 (94)	5 (104)	6 (119)	7 (126)	8 (140)
S+A	S stretto	S+B	C	S^2+C	S^2+D	S^2+E	S^2+fig.

9 (149)	10 (161)	11 (171)	12 (184)
$S^{\frac12}$+fig., 2-voiced	$S^{\frac12}$+fig., 3-voiced	$S^{\frac12}$ stretto	$S^{\frac12}$

Subsections 5–8 contain one presentation each of the augmented subject, each in another of the four voices and with different counterpoints. The countersubject of section 5 is introduced in section 4 in the form of a fully developed fore-imitation.

No. 10. Subject: | e' | b d' | a f' | e' |

1	2 (22)	3 (52)	4 (74)	5 (89)	6 (108)
S+A	S stretto	S+b	S var.	S var.+C	S^2+D

7 (132)	8 (144)	9 (159)	10 (181)	11 (196)	12 (206)
S^4+fig.	S^4+e	S^4+f	S^4+g	$S^{\frac12}$+h	$S^{\frac12}$+fig.

13 (214)	14 (220)	15 (237)	16 (256)	17 (264)	18 (280)
$S^{\frac12}$+fig.	$S^{\frac12}$ var.	$S^{\frac12}$ var.	$S^{\frac12}$	S+I	coda

In the only surviving source, Padua, Univ. Libr. Ms.1982, this fantasy is called a ricercar. It is one of Sweelinck's longest compositions, and also one of his most important. The unusually individual subject includes two fourths and a sixth, and is not only transformed by augmentation and diminution but is also varied and

---

* This fantasy, which is based on a bipartite subject, is the only one in which Sweelinck makes consistent use of inversion. S^4 is replaced by S^3.

Fig.329

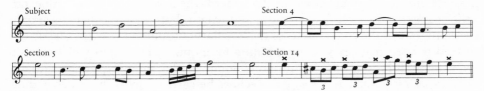

ornamented, as shown in Fig.329. The long section C, in which the subject is treated in diminution (subsections 11–16), is very interesting and full of different ideas. The approach changes every few measures, especially in subsection 15. Fig.330 singles out two echo passages, one at the beginning of subsection 15, the other at the end of subsection 16.

Fig.330

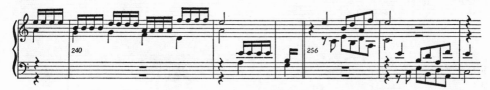

In addition to the ostinato fantasies and the fantasies based on imitation, there is a third type, the echo fantasy, the "Fantasia auf die Manier von ein Echo," as it is occasionally called in the sources. Here, too, Sweelinck proceeds according to a plan of three sections, which may be approximated as fugue—echo—toccata. The echo is found in music as early as the 14th century. The caccia *Tosto che l'alba* by Gherardello da Firenze includes a particularly nice example; in the ritornello a fanfare-like signal reverberates in canonic imitation. The duo imitation, so frequently used by Josquin, comes very close to the echo effect, and Lassus' *Libro de villanelle* of 1581 contains an ingeniously humorous echo piece, *O la, o che bon eccho.* But Sweelinck was probably the first to use the organ for echo effects.[3] It was his nature to give this idea profound thought, particularly in fantasy no.15 (10). Except for a fugal introduction of 13 measures, this composition of 96 measures consists exclusively of echoing repetitions. The briefest echo section is the one in no.18 (13), which comprises only 19 measures. In the other fantasies it usually runs to about 50 measures. The echoes mostly use short, characteristic motifs, one or one-half measures in length. Only in no.15 (10) are the phrases longer, up to 6 measures. As expected, the repetitions are sounded on the same pitch (or an octave lower), but in some exceptional cases they are transposed sequence-like, by an interval of a second (e.g., in no.14, meas.113–16).

Although Sweelinck often goes overboard on this technique, at least for today's taste, one must nevertheless admire the dexterity with which he avoids the danger of unbearable monotony. In this regard it is important not only that the motifs change in their outline, rhythm, and length, but also that their harmonic basis is still free of the conventions of the late Baroque and of the early Classic era that tend toward regularity. Only within a harmonic technique in which chords have varying durations and can progress dominantally, modally, or sequentially can an experiment such as Sweelinck's echoes be carried out without descending to triviality and banality. The colorful invention of motifs and harmonies is beautifully illustrated in fantasy no.17 (12), from which Fig.331 is taken.

Fig.331

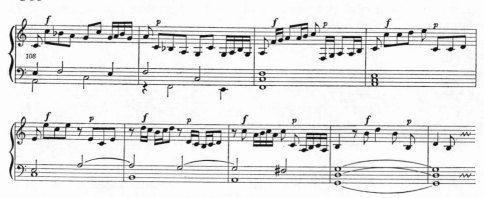

What is the historical significance of Sweelinck's fantasies? What place do they occupy in the evolution of keyboard music, especially of the imitative forms? The ostinato fantasies are probably early works, in which the Dutch master, with the methodical perseverance that characterizes all his work, incorporates the musical language of the virginalists into his technique. In these early works he already stresses the monothematic principle, which he continues to employ in a much more significant way in his major works, the imitative fantasies. Doubtless Sweelinck was the first to regard thematically unified formulation not as one possibility among others but as a high-ranking artistic principle. Of course, in his fantasies the realization of the monothematic idea is quite different from that of a fugue—on the level of planning rather than of formulation. The multiplicity of sections and counter-subjects, the variety of means, and even the great length of his pieces show that Sweelinck's aim was not to create a unified form but a comprehensible framework. Occasionally writers have seen in Sweelinck's fantasies an important and decisive link in the evolution from the (polythematic) ricercar to the fugue, but in reality any monothematic *fuga* by Lohet or Mareschal is closer to the end-product of this evolution than Sweelinck's fantasies are.

TOCCATAS

In his thirteen toccatas Sweelinck follows the Italian tradition of Andrea Gabrieli and Merulo. Except for chordal introductions, nine of them (nos.24 [18], 25 [19], 26, 27–31 [20–24], and 32) consist exclusively of figurations of partly Italian and partly English types. The other four (nos.20–23 [14–17]) include, in addition, imitative sections or sections with complementary motifs. The form of no.20 (14) is the most complete: introduction (meas.1–13)—complementary motifs (meas.14–24)—figurations (meas.25–40)—imitations (meas.41–66)—figurations (meas.67–99).

The imitative sections are not ricercar-like as in Merulo, but use canzona subjects in multiple strettos. Hints of complementary motifs can be found one hundred years earlier in the organ works of Arnolt Schlick (cf.p.85), and in the second half of the 16th century their use becomes somewhat more freqeunt, mostly in variations by Cabezón, Facoli, Radino, Byrd, and others. But Sweelinck is generally considered the first to employ this artifice to a greater extent and with full consciousness of its importance. How much such a thing was "in the air," can be gathered from the fact that around the same time it was used in an equally systematic manner by two Neapolitans, Mayone and Trabaci. In the sections of figurations, the Venetian toccata style, with its sustained chords and ornamental passages, emerges most clearly in no.20 (14), while the English figuration style, with its various formulae—angular motifs, arpeggios, etc.—appears particularly in nos.21 (15) and 31 (24).

The introductory sections with their solemn chord chains, which are often combined with a suggestion of imitation or a quiet melodic line, are particularly impressive. Here Sweelinck has reproduced most beautifully the magnificence of Venetian organ music, perhaps even excelled it. The introduction to no.23, e.g., is based on the same idea as that of Merulo's *Toccata ottava, quarto tono* of 1598, but, as Fig.332 shows, it exhibits a more modern harmonization, clearer articula-

Fig.332

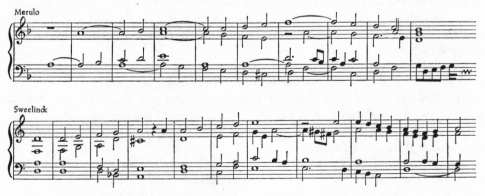

tion, and more consistent development. The introductions of toccatas nos.21 and 22, both in a serious but not at all gloomy A minor, are also very beautiful. In the former, Sweelinck enlivens the basic chordal texture with a quiet motif that returns in every measure, but always in an altered aspect; in the latter he employs a canon between tenor and bass. The introduction of no.30 is based on a five-measure phrase, which appears three times on different pitches.

Two pieces in Annegarn's *Supplement* are called ricercars in the original manuscript (Turin tablature), but are obviously toccatas. The second one (no.5) begins with a series of full chords that are almost too pompous. In two passages (middle of meas.24 and meas.36) the chords are arranged in 3/2 (rather than 2/2) measures, a feature that occurs in several other works (e.g., in the echo fantasy no.16, meas.77ff.).

ORGAN CHORALES

Seiffert's first edition of Sweelinck's organ works contained only two liturgical works: a *Da pacem,* an antiphon of the Roman antiphonal; and *Psalm cxl.* Both are related to the religious conditions prevailing in Holland in Sweelinck's time, for in the 1580s the formerly Catholic country began to turn to Calvinism, which permitted the singing of psalms as the only musical ornament of the services. The recent discovery of additional sources has increased the Sweelinck repertoire by a number of arrangements of Lutheran chorales, which are related to the German Protestant rite. Considering how hostile Calvinism and Lutheranism were to each other during the period, this phenomenon is very surprising. How did Sweelinck get to know these tunes, and why did he set them? The answer to the first question is simple: through his German pupils. The second question is more difficult to answer. For Lutheran chorales to be heard in Calvinist services is certainly impossible. It is more likely that they may have been played as edifying music at the daily organ concerts, which were among the obligations imposed on Sweelinck by the council of the city of Amsterdam, and which were not subject to the supervision of the church authorities. Or perhaps he did not compose the chorales for any definite use, but only because the beautiful melodies pleased and inspired him.

In his expanded second edition Seiffert also included a number of chorale settings that are anonymous in the sources. They are similar to the authenticated works, but hardly more so than those in the same sources that are ascribed to some of Sweelinck's students. We shall limit ourselves to the authenticated works, which are numerous enough and contain everything that is characteristic of Sweelinck's style and treatment.[4]

All these works are chorale variations, i.e., compositions in which the ecclesiastic melody is arranged several times in different ways. In itself this is nothing new; it was done in the Magnificats with their five or six versets or, to cite an example that is closer to the genuine variation technique, in Cabezón's *fabordon* and *glosa* pieces for psalmody. In these instances, however, the individual sections do not form a continuous organ piece, since they were performed in alternation with Gregorian chant. The same practice must be assumed for Blitheman's four arrangements of the *Eterne rerum conditor* (cf.p.160). Schlick's three settings of *Da pacem* (cf.p.87) may more justifiably be called a variation set, for here —in an antiphon—a non-musical reason for the repeated arrangement does not exist. In any case there is no doubt that Sweelinck composes in a genuine variation form; in fact, he frequently connects one variation with the next one by a transition, exactly as Cabezón does in his variations on secular songs. Thus Sweelinck may be regarded as the creator of the chorale variation, which plays an important role in the subsequent evolution of the organ chorale, culminating in Bach's chorale partitas.

From the Gregorian repertoire Sweelinck takes two melodies, the old compline hymn *Christe qui lux es et dies* (no.37) and the antiphon *Da pacem* (no.38).[5] *Puer nobis nascitur* (no.53) is a popular Christmas song, probably of the 16th century. For *Psalms cxvi* and *cxl* (nos.51, 52) Sweelinck uses the tunes of the *Geneva Psalter* by Marot and Beza (1562). The remaining themes are Lutheran chorales (nos. 35, 41, 45, 46, 48, 53, 54, 56; the omitted numbers are not authenticated).

Most of these compositions consist of four variations, some of only three, and one (*Erbarm dich mein*, no.41) of six. A number of variations carry designations (not necessarily originating with Sweelinck) that refer to the texture and the treatment of the chorale, e.g.:

Ich ruf zu dir (no.46)	*Vater unser im Himmelreich* (no.54)
1. *Bicinium, coral in cantu*	1. *a 4 voc.*
2. *a 3 voc., coral in basso*	2. *a 4 voc., coral in cantu*
3. *a 3 voc., coral in tenore*	3. *a 4 voc., coral in cantu colloratus*
4. *a 4 voc., coral in cantu*	4. *a 4 voc., coral in basso colloratus*

These designations represent all the methods Sweelinck employs. Of the 49 variations 11 are for two voices, 22 for three, and 16 for four; the chorale is heard 30 times in the soprano, once in the alto, 10 times in the tenor, and 8 times in the bass; 7 variations have a *cantus colloratus*, i.e., a soprano that is ornamented throughout (in a few others it is partially ornamented), and one has a *bassus colloratus*. It is striking that Sweelinck limits himself to the most elementary treatment. Nowhere is the chorale distributed by lines among several voices; nowhere is it treated imitatively like a chorale motet. Even fore-imitation, which had been widely accepted in the 16th century, is only occasionally found, e.g., in variations III and V of *Erbarm dich mein* (no.41) and in variation IV of *Ich ruf zu dir* (no.46).

In the bicinia the sustained tones of the chorale tune are combined with lively counterpoints whose variety of rather pedantic figures and formulae exhibits an unmistakable kinship with the English design style. Sometimes Sweelinck arrives at such tasteless passages as the ones given in Fig.333. In several bicinia the chorale is ornamented here and there, so that the stark contrast between the two parts is softened. Variation II of no.35 is the most successful bicinium, the only one in which the antithesis becomes a synthesis.

Fig.333

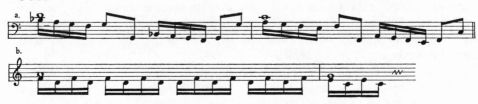

a. *Ich ruf zu dir* (No.46), var. I; b. *Psalm* cxl (No.52), var. II.

Sweelinck employs three-part texture most often. Among these pieces, too, there are some in a dry figural style (e.g., no.37, var.III; no.52, var.III and V), but others are written in a smoother manner. Variation II of *Nun freut euch* (no.48) deserves to be singled out, because every one of its lines starts with a fore-imitation, and sometimes the beginnings of the lines are presented in diminished note values and used as contrapuntal motifs. Of all of Sweelinck's chorale variations this one comes closest to the chorale motet, especially in the section reproduced in Fig.334.

Fig.334

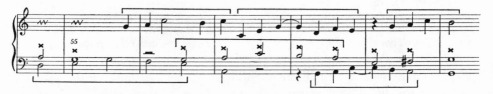

Only in the four-part chorale settings did Sweelinck find the medium in which he could disclose his real powers and prove his mastery. The English design style still affects some of these variations, e.g., variations II and IV of *Herzlich lieb* (no.45) and variations III and IV of *Psalm cxvi* (no.51); but it is certainly no accident that all these variations include passages of various lengths in three parts. In the other four-part variations we find figurations, but figurations of a different kind—free of mechanical dross and transmuted into pure playfulness. A beautiful example is variation III, *Coral in cantu colloratus*, of *Vater unser* (no.54). The noblest of all of Sweelinck's chorale variations is probably variation III of *Erbarm*

dich mein (no.41); the chorale melody in the tenor and the three simple counter-points, which are only occasionally enlivened by figuration, are embedded in the severe harmonies of the Phrygian mode.

In the chorale variations—as in the fantasies—Sweelinck proves to be a master of the miniature, not of the large form. In almost all these works one finds variations of impressive workmanship and great artistic significance side by side with purely mechanical products, which have only historical interest. Only a few can be called successful masterpieces; perhaps the four variations on *Allein Gott in der Höh* (no.35) come closest to it.[6] Omitting the less significant variations will certainly not harm the performance.

VARIATIONS ON SECULAR THEMES

We know seven variation works on secular songs by Sweelinck: *Est-ce Mars, Ich fuhr mich über Rheine, Mein junges Leben hat ein End, More palatino, Soll es sein, Unter der Linden grüne,* and *Von der Fortuna werd ich getrieben. More pala-tino* is anonymous, but there is good reason to count it among Sweelinck's compositions.

The song themes are all bipartite tunes, with both sections repeated (a a' b b'). The individual sections are often irregularly formed (i.e., not in four-measure phrases)—a wholly desirable deviation from the norm. Omitting the repetitions, these themes have the following forms: 4 + 5, 7 + 7, 4 + 6, 4 + 8, 6 + 6, 8 + 10, and 4 + 8, respectively.

Sweelinck's variation techniques are almost entirely limited to categories A (appearance of the unaltered melody of the theme in the top part) and C (the ornamented melody in the top part).[7] Only three variations, variation VII of *Est-ce Mars* and variations V and VIII of *Soll es sein,* belong to type B (melody in a lower part), while type D (freely invented melody) does not occur at all. Considering how frequently types B and D occur in the works of Cabezón and Byrd, Sweelinck's turning toward the simpler, in a sense, more "natural" methods that subsequently dominate the field is a conspicuous change. Sweelinck very clearly formulates the principle of the changing variation, which plays an important role in Byrd. He almost always treats each section of the theme differently, e.g., a and b present the theme simply and a' and b' add figurations; more often the change occurs in the lower parts as each section employs new motifs or figures; but even within the same section the formulation often changes, sometimes from measure to measure. Thus there emerges a variation type of great variety and vivacity, which is probably Sweelinck's most significant contribution to the evolution of variation technique.

The changing variation is treated most beautifully in the variations on *Mein junges Leben hat ein End.* Sigtenhorst Meyer[8] notes that only six of the twenty measures of the theme are really different and claims that this sameness causes a certain monotony that can be corrected somewhat by a lively tempo and a variety of touches. He is certainly right with respect to the theme, but it is just this dry material that kindles Sweelinck's inventiveness and produces veritable fireworks of color, the very opposite of monotony. The ideal instrument for this enchanting work, one of the most outstanding creations in the field of variations, is the Baroque organ.

Fig.335

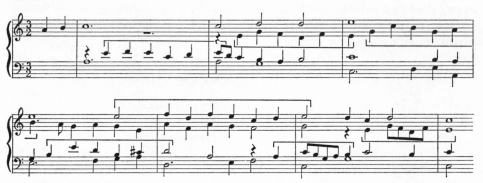

The variations on *Ich fuhr mich über Rheine* is a serious, inward-looking work. The first two variations are especially beautiful; they are written in a motivic-contrapuntal style of greatest maturity and perfection. Fig.335 shows the beginning of variation II.

Fig.336

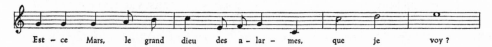

Est – ce Mars, le grand dieu des a – lar – mes, que je voy?

In a sense *Est-ce Mars* stands midway between these two works—serene and gay, mischievous and bold—reflecting the character of the melody as well as of the text, in which the grim god of war is vanquished by Amor.[9] The first phrase, which is repeated, is given in Fig.336. The next two measures exhibit a variative treatment that is interesting for several reasons. Some of the transformations (each variation contains two) are given in Fig.337. The skip of a fifth in the melody is treated in stretto at the lower octave in a., in stretto at the lower fifth in b., and in quadruple stretto in c. In d. the skip is surrounded by a kind of bell figure, which in itself is rather unimportant, but in this work and at this place it sounds just right. In each of these six transformations, moreover, the progression | e'' | a' | is harmonized differently.[10] Here Sweelinck gives us a particularly impressive sample of the harmonic language of the period. Chord substitutions were possible

Fig.337

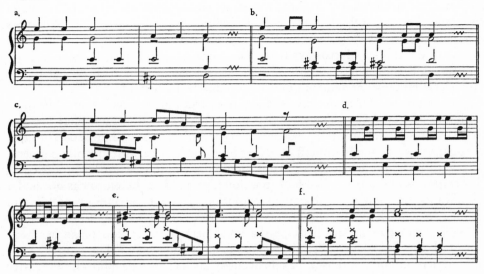

a. var. I; b. var. I; c. var. II; d. var. V; e. var. VII; f. var. VII.

to a much greater extent in Sweelinck's time than in the functionally oriented harmony of the late Baroque.

Several of Sweelinck's compositions throw some light on his relation to the music of other countries. The *Fortuna* theme (no.64) was also used by Byrd. The *Paduana Lachrymae* (no.66) is an arrangement of Dowland's famous *Flow my tears;* it is similar to arrangements by Byrd, Morley, and Farnaby, but more restrained in the use of superficial figurations.[11] *Pavana Philippi* (no.69) is a new arrangement of a pavane by Peter Philips, who lived the greater part of his life in the Netherlands. Philips' composition is dated 1580 and was therefore written during his English period, but it appears in *FW*, I, p.343, in what may be called a purified shape, freed from the "clinkers" of free voices and figurations in the English style. The *Passamezzo* (no.67) is one of the many variation sets on the Italian passamezzo moderno (cf.p.271); Seiffert's remark[12] that "a melodic concordance has hitherto not been found" shows that in 1942 the true nature of the passamezzo was not yet generally known. The *Pavana Hispanica* (no.68) is based on a theme found in Cabezón under the title *Pavana Italiana* (cf.p.266); the variations are partly by Sweelinck and partly by Samuel Scheidt, and may be taken as a joint work with more justification than the series of variations on *Allein Gott in der Höh* (no.35; cf. note 6 above).

Sweelinck's organ music has at times been judged rather negatively by scholars whose competence in these matters cannot be gainsayed. Ritter, e.g., says

337

that Sweelinck "does not always like depth, on the contrary stays too close to the surface."[13] Van den Borren characterizes his works in terms such as "enlevé la spontanéité et la sensibilité," "l'ennui et lassitude," "ton doctoral," or "modèles académiques," and calls Sweelinck "un génie hautain et professoral."[14] With regard to the toccatas Pirro says that Sweelinck "ne prend que les procédées des maîtres qu'il suit, leur inspiration lui reste étrangère," and with regard to the fantasies, that they "ne satisfont que les curieux de mathématiques."[15]

It cannot be denied that there is a core of truth in such assertions, but these criticisms are too severe. There are dry, pedantic compositions, but there are also those that testify not only to an extraordinary technical mastery but also to original thought and vital imagination. It does Sweelinck no service, as frequently happens, to regard his approach to form as his chief contribution. What he produced in this respect is but a product of logic and intelligence, and therefore has not had a significant effect on the subsequent evolution. His artistic importance lies in details, in what happens within this framework. His works—at least the most valuable among them—are perhaps the most perfect realization of an aesthetic approach that might be called "the enjoyment of pure play." The word "pure" applies here in both its senses: "exclusiveness" as well as "cleanliness," the latter having always been regarded as a characteristic of the Dutch people. Everything follows well-ordered pathways; as in a walk through a well-cultivated garden, the eye is continually directed to a new flower, a new color. Everything unfolds in a game that is equally gay and serious, totally unhampered by emotion, sometimes too correct, but mostly stimulating and captivating—music for entertainment in the best sense of the word.

Speuy and Cornet

Only recently has a small but not uninteresting counterpart to Sweelinck's work become generally known: the psalm settings of Henderick Speuy, printed in 1610 under the title *De Psalmen Davids gestelt op het Tabulature van het Orghel en de Clavecymmel.*[16] Speuy was born at Den Briel near Rotterdam (around 1575, according to Noske, but an earlier date, roughly contemporary with Sweelinck, appears possible), became the organist at Dordrecht in 1595, and died there in 1625. His print consists of twenty-four arrangements of Calvinist psalm tunes, all set according to the same scheme: as bicinia with an ornamented counterpoint. In three pieces (nos.2, 13, 19) the *cantus firmus* is in the superius, in four (nos.14, 18, 20, 24) in the bass, and in the remaining settings each line is in a different part. The style is quite similar to Sweelinck's bicinia (e.g., no.38, var.I, or no.52, var.II), but Speuy avoids the pedantic formulations that occasionally creep into Sweelinck's music. In contrast to Speuy's many settings with a migrating *cantus firmus* there are none in Sweelinck's works, except in no.55, *Wie nach einer Wasserquelle.*

338

This piece, however, is spurious, and is actually a work by Speuy (no.11: *Als een Hardt ghejaeght*).

While Speuy's compositions are closely related to Sweelinck's, the output of a contemporary Belgian master, Pieter Cornet, is quite different. All that is known about him (from a letter by his widow) is that he was the organist of the court chapel at Brussels for thirty-three years, and that he was still alive in September 1625. It is therefore assumed that he was active as the organist from 1593 to 1626 and that his dates are c.1560–1626. The chief source for his works is the manuscript collection Berlin Staatsbibl. 40316 (formerly Mus. Ms. 191). It contains nine compositions by Cornet, some with such legends as "mandatomi alli 3. Septembre 1625," from which one can conclude that the scribe was an Italian pupil of Cornet's. Most of these pieces have been published in Guilmant A, vol. X; several were published earlier by Ritter. Two other pieces in the manuscript Lynar A 1 have remained unknown or at least neglected until now. The following is a list of Cornet's known works, as they appear in the complete edition by W. Apel:[17]

1. *Fantasia del primo tono* (Berlin, fol.20; Guilmant A, X, p.183)
2. *Fantasia del 2. tuono* (Berlin, fol.22; Guilmant A, X, p.202)
3. *Fantasia 3. toni* (Berlin, fol.17v; Guilmant A, X, p.192)
4. *Fantasia del 5. tuono . . . sopra ut re mi fa sol la* (Berlin, fol.16v; Guilmant A, X, p.211)
5. *Fantasia 8. toni . . . mandatomi alli 3. Septembre 1625* (Berlin, fol.65; Guilmant A, p.215; Ritter B, p.60)
6. *Fantasia* (Lynar A 1, p.313)
7. *Toccada del 3. tono* (Berlin, fol. 25; Guilmant A, X, p.219)
8. *Salve (regina)* (Berlin fol.28; Guilmant A, X, p.223; partly in Ritter B, p.63)
9. *Tantum ergo* (Lynar A 1, p.310)
10. *Courante . . . mandatomi da luy di 6 Novembre 1624* (Berlin, fol.63; beginning in Guilmant A, X, p. 231)
11. *Corranta* (Berlin, fol.64v)

The five fantasies in the Berlin manuscript represent a novel type, in which the structural approach of the Italian ricercar is combined with the style elements of English virginal music. Except for no.5, which comprises only 86 measures, they are all rather lengthy compositions. This is particularly true of no.4, for which 102 measures are written out and a legend reads "mancano doi terze parte" (two-thirds are missing). Nos.4 and 5 are each based on a double subject, symbolized here as A–B, while the others have four to six subjects. The following analysis illustrates the thematic-structural outlines:

No.1: A, $A^{\frac{1}{2}}$ || B, A (55) || C, C^4 (98) || C/D (134) || $A^{\frac{1}{2}}$, B, C, D (188–243)

2: A–B, A^2, $B^{\frac{1}{2}}$ || C (90) || D (133) || E (158–245)

3: A–B, $A^{\frac{1}{2}}$, $A^{\frac{1}{2}}$, $B^{\frac{1}{2}}$, B^2 || C (75) || D, E (104) || F, F^2 (178–254)

4: A–B (A is the ascending hexachord, B the descending one)

5: A–B

Fantasy no.6 differs from the others in both its brevity and its content. It is not a ricercar but a canzona with a toccata ending, and shows Cornet's dependence on the Italian tradition. Was this tradition transmitted to him through that unknown pupil to whom he gave his pieces to be copied?

The thematic elaboration shows several interesting details. At the beginning of no.4 the ascending and descending hexachord is used as a double subject, with the descending form serving as a counterpoint to the ascending one (cf.Fig.338a.). It is characteristic of Cornet that he uses this first combination only once, in the exposition, but combines the two shapes in various other contrapuntal ways later on (Fig.338b., c., d.). In general he avoids getting tied to a particular configuration and would rather invent new rhythmic formulations. The slow ascent in d., e.g., is followed by a descent at four times the speed, in a very nice, quick change from dignity to gaiety. The same change is even clearer in another passage (meas.47–56), where six tones ascend thoughtfully in whole notes, only to trip down again in a dotted rhythm. Because of the vivid and always variegated presentation of the subject, Cornet's hexachord fantasy is a cut above most other works of this type, including those by Byrd, Bull, or Sweelinck. How unfortunate that this particular composition is incomplete!

Fig.338

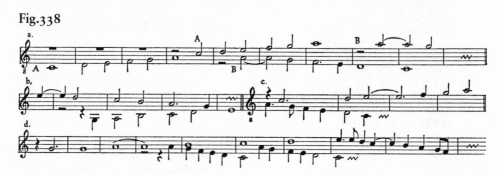

a. meas.1; b. meas.18; c.meas.28; d. meas.81.

In the other fantasies, too, many details show a tendency to avoid a schematic treatment of the subject matter. The augmentation of the subjects is not realized by an exact doubling of the note values, but is done mostly in an irregular manner, doubling one note, tripling another, or leaving one unchanged. The transformation of the subject in fantasy no.2 is shown in Fig.339. Moreover, aug-

Fig.339

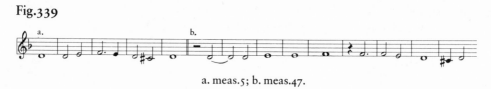

a. meas.5; b. meas.47.

mentation and diminution are not—as in Sweelinck's works—applied systematically, but only here and there where it seems appropriate.

Cornet's fantasies derive their character from the thematic treatment as well as from the figurations. Figurations occur in combination with the subjects or in interludes of various lengths. They lend these works a certain vitality and lightness, in direct contrast to the dignity of the Italian ricercars, and place them close to the English fantasies. Of all the virginalists Peter Philips is probably the intermediary, since he lived in Belgium from 1590 until his death, and was probably the court organist at Brussels and Cornet's official colleague[18] from 1611 on. Indeed the works of the two masters are quite similar overall and in several details.

The English influence on Cornet is most evident in his use of the ornamentation symbol of two oblique bars. This sign occurs particularly often in fantasy no.5, and applies to both long and short notes, exactly as in the works of the virginalists. In addition Cornet's fantasies contain various figures, such as the ones shown in Fig.340, which at the time occur nowhere else but in English keyboard music. However, the extreme virtuosic figures, such as those used by Bull and Farnaby—wide skips, thirds and sixths in the left hand, broken octaves—are not found in Cornet's music.

Fig.340

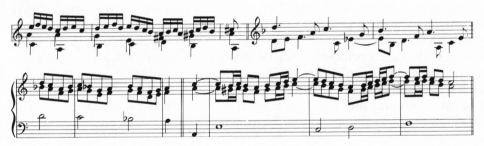

Cornet avoids schematic and formulistic approaches in his figurations, just as he does in the elaboration of his themes. He is always able to say something new, so that despite their great length the fantasies never become tiresome. They also possess a certain "depth of feeling" or "warmth of expression." Such a combination of intelligence, imagination, and expressiveness cannot but result in works of high artistic rank. This synthesis is achieved most perfectly in the *Fantasia del primo tono* (no.1), a work that belongs to the truly great creations in the field of early clavier music.

Cornet's remaining compositions do not in any way rank below the fantasies. The toccata proceeds without fugal sections in figurations whose colorful changes are only rarely halted by sequential repetitions, which do not occur elsewhere in Cornet's music. A lengthy passage (meas.48–54) is obviously intended as an echo effect; this is another singular example in Cornet's music of a popular technique. Van den Borren maintains quite correctly that this piece shows "qualités de solidité, de vigueur, d'élégance et de fougue" that are found in only a few contemporary works.[19] The harmonic treatment of this toccata is also interesting. Van den Borren points to the "marche extrêmement favorable" of the bass in a long two-part passage (meas.55ff.). Perhaps even more noteworthy is the functional harmony of measures 66–69, given in Fig.341.

Fig.341

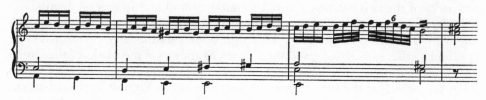

Cornet's *Salve regina* consists of five sections: *Salve, Ad te clamamus, Eia ergo, O clemens,* and *Pro fine.* The first three are worked out as chorale fugues on the initial motifs of the corresponding lines, and here, as in the fantasies, thematic elaboration and figurations combine in a very successful manner. In the *O clemens* the Gregorian melody is presented as a *cantus planus,* first in the soprano, then once more in the tenor. In the final section, called *Pro fine,* the *Salve* melody is combined with its inversion in a setting into which figural elements are again woven, and which is as ingenious as it is impressive. Cornet's *Salve regina* is doubtless one of the most significant creations in the field of liturgical organ music. The dark warmth of expression increases here to religious fervor, to a mystical ecstasy that says in music what cannot otherwise be said. There are passages in it that anticipate the Elevation toccatas in Frescobaldi's *Fiori musicali,* e.g., measures 19–25, from the first section, given in Fig.342. The striking conclusions of the *Ad te clamamus* and the *Pro fine* are both formed with the intensifying augmented fourth of the Lydian mode (*a g♯ a* above *D*). The same formula is employed by Cornet at the end of fantasies nos.2, 5, and 6 (cf. also no.3, meas.19–20).

A lovely counterpart to the *Salve* is the *Tantum ergo* from the Lynar manuscript, an arrangement of the verse *Tantum ergo Sacramentum* from the Corpus-

Fig.342

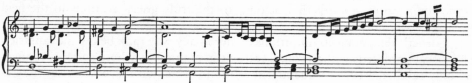

Christi hymn *Pange lingua gloriosi corporis*. Here, too, there is an admirable mixture of tradition and freedom, of sustained chords and fast, winged passages, of contrapuntal texture and motivic interplay, of modern and archaic harmony. The piece also includes several passages that are incorrect according to the rules, but only a Beckmesser would criticize them. Fig.343 gives several passages from it.

Fig.343

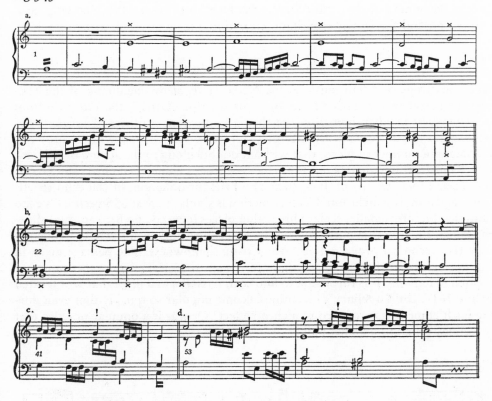

The two courantes are modeled on the English corrantos. Each consists of two sections with varied repetition: A A′ B B′, but the first courante is followed by three variations of the entire piece.

Cornet was a very important artist, but unfortunately far too little of his output has been preserved. Did he receive the recognition due him during his lifetime? Or was he overshadowed by his contemporary, Sweelinck, whose fame attracted so many pupils, who copied his works and preserved them for later generations? There is no doubt that Sweelinck has a much more important role in the evolution of music, but the decision is not so simple when the artistic value of their works is compared. Not many of Sweelinck's works can rival Cornet's best compositions, such as his *Fantasia del primo tono* or his *Salve regina*. Nor can one agree with Seiffert's judgment that "Italian form and English treatment contrast abruptly in Cornet's music" while "Sweelinck led them to a harmonic, mutual interpenetration, and after their fusion transformed them into a new artistic unity."[20] Indeed, one may claim just the opposite with greater justification. In any case, Cornet and Sweelinck must be regarded as masters of equal stature, who together give us a well-rounded picture of keyboard music in the Netherlands at the end of the 16th and the beginning of the 17th century: the Flemish Catholic, full-blooded, dark, and warm; and the Dutch Protestant, clear-thinking, controlled, and cool.

The *Liber Cruciferorum*

Our knowledge of organ music in the Netherlands at the beginning of the 17th century is somewhat rounded out by a manuscript of 1617, the *Liber Fratrum Cruciferorum Leodiensium* (Book of the Cross-Bearing Brothers of Liége).[21] Besides works by Andrea Gabrieli, Merulo, Philips, Sweelinck, and William Brown,[22] it contains a number of pieces that without doubt belong to the sphere of Belgian-Dutch music, although only one bears the composer's name—*Echo* by Frater Gerardus Scronx (new ed., p.79). It consists of a brief introduction, fifteen echo repetitions, and a short conclusion. Its construction is similar to that of Sweelinck's echo fantasies, but on a smaller scale. Three other pieces (new ed., pp.81, 140, 142) show the same structure. Compared to Sweelinck's echo technique, the echoes frequently represent technical progress but more artistic shallowness. The passage given in Fig.344 occurs in the second of these pieces (in the original the repetitions are written in red ink). It is surprising to find such passages in a piece that was written before 1617. Did Sweelinck's invention become popular so quickly that even during his lifetime it was reduced to a cheap effect? Or was it a popular practice that Sweelinck raised to a higher plane?

Fig.344

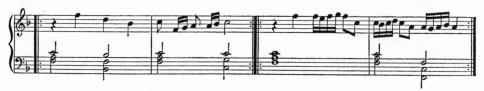

Several of the pieces that are called *Echo* have no echo repetitions at all. The term is obviously meant in the sense of change of registration, as in the *Echo pour trompette* (new ed., p.66), in which various bass passages, designated by long slurs, are to be played on a trumpet stop. In fact, this is one of the earliest organ pieces with definite registration. More remarkable proof of advanced technique is offered by an untitled piece (new ed., p.73), in which the right hand plays partly above and partly below the left hand, as shown in Fig.345. It seems obvious that a solo stop must be used for the right-hand manual, which is heard alternately at the top and in the bass. The harmony in the passage shown is also interesting: Both cadences seem to belong to the second half of the 18th century rather than to the beginning of the 17th.

Fig.345

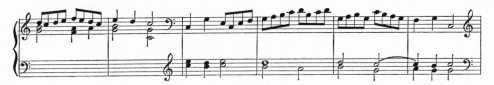

15

Germany

Germany plays only a modest role in the evolution of keyboard
music in the 16th century, but it rises to a leading position after 1600. In no other
country were there so many important masters or so many cities in which music
for organ, harpsichord, and clavichord was cultivated and advanced. Ritter recognized the fact that one cannot follow a single line of evolution in the German clavier
music of the 17th century—a thing that is quite possible in England or France—but
that it divides into three clearly differentiated areas of musical (and general) culture: South Germany, Central Germany, and North Germany. We will follow Ritter's basic plan, but deviate somewhat from his map (as well as from Frotscher's),
for it is not the geographic frontiers but the musico-cultural factors that determine
the areas. We shall therefore include Nuremberg and its masters in Central instead
of South Germany, since Pachelbel's voluminous output of Lutheran chorales, for
example, obviously does not belong to the Catholic South but to the Protestant
Center. Similarly, Samuel Scheidt, from Halle, does not belong to the Central area,
where both Ritter and Frotscher put him, but to North Germany.

A. NORTH GERMANY

As early as the 15th century the cultivation of organ composition is documented in
North Germany by the tablature of Adam Ileborgh, written in 1448 at Stendal, and
by the somewhat older Wynsem fragment. From the next one hundred and fifty
years nothing reaches us from this area, but around 1600 a development begins
that with surprising rapidity leads North German organ music to an eminent position within the entire field of organ music in the 17th century.

The Celle Tablature: Johann Stephan

The earliest extant document of this development is probably a manuscript that Ritter described in his basic study *Zur Geschichte des Orgelspiels* under the title "Das cellische Tabulaturbuch v. J. 1601."[1] It originally contained about 75 chorale settings, 60 of which are preserved completely. The collection begins with a *Kyrie dominicale* in 6 short sections, which is followed by 6 different settings of *Allein Gott in der Höh sei Ehr*, 3 on *Ach Gott vom Himmel sieh darein*, 2 on *Dies sind die heilgen zehn Gebot*, 3 on *Allein zu dir, Herr Jesu Christ*, 4 on *Ich ruf zu dir, Herr Jesu Christ*, 5 on *Vater unser im Himmelreich*, and others. All the pieces are anonymous except for the following (the numbers refer to the new edition cited in note 1):

> No. 7: *Allein Gott in der Höh sei Ehre* . . . Am 7. Juli Ao. 1601 in Zell: Ab O. D. comp. (Ritter B, no.72)
> No. 10: *Ach Gott vom Himmel sieh darein* . . . Johan. Stepha. Or[ganist] in Lüneburg (beginning in Ritter B, no.73)
> No. 13: *Allein zu dir Herr Jesu Christ*. O. D.
> No. 14: *Allein zu dir Herr Jesu Christ* . . . O. D. comp.
> No. 49: *Jesus Christus unser Heiland*. Johannis Stephani Org. in Lü[neburg]
> No. 56: *Wir glauben alle an einen Gott*. O. D. composuit

The Johann Stephan named in nos.10 and 49 is "surely that Lüneburg organist Johann Stephan [Steffens, born at Itzehoe and died in 1616] who was one of the 54 examiners of the Organum Gruningense in 1596."[2] The initials O. D. are interpreted in marginal notes (probably in M. Seiffert's hand) as O. Dithmers, and by L. Schierning as Organist Dedekind[3]—for what reasons and with what justification I do not know. The date of 1601 given in no. 7 furnishes a very welcome indication of the time the manuscript was written and of the compositions contained in it, which was evidently shortly before 1600.

A few chorale settings in the Celle tablature are similar to those of Ammerbach and Nörmiger, for they are brief and limit themselves to an ornamented harmonization of the melody. There are others, however, that take a more pretentious approach and are much longer—compositions that suggest much that was developed and employed by the 17th-century masters. The second setting of *Ach Gott vom Himmel* (no.9), e.g., is a fully developed five-part chorale motet, in which each of the five lines of the chorale is treated fugally. Fig.346 shows the treatment

Fig.346

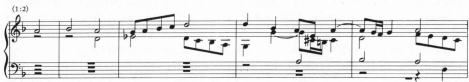

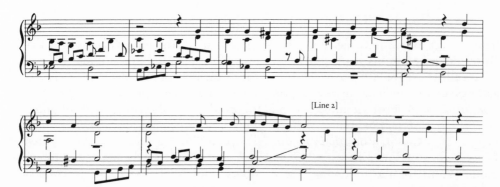

of the first line. The final chords are expanded by means of a figure that has the character of a significant gesture, as frequently occurs in the organ chorales of Scheidemann, Tunder, or Buxtehude (Fig.347).

Fig.347

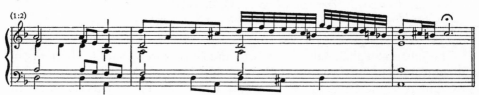

The chorale settings that are signed O. D. (nos.7, 13, 14, and 56) are also motet-like and very long (especially no.14); one of them (no.56) has five voices. With its dark sound and strict approach, *Allein Gott in der Höh* (no.7), reproduced by Ritter, is a lovely example of this unknown composer's mastery of the early North German organ chorale.

Craftsmanship of an even higher order is shown in the two compositions by the Lüneburg organist Johann Stephan, nos.10 and 49. Both works are in five parts and of large dimensions, the former comprising 160 semibreve measures,[4] the latter 120. Both unmistakably suggest the treatment that became characteristic of the chorale fantasy—free use of the most varied means, such as ornamentation, fragmentation, and echo effects. They clearly show a turning away from a vocally oriented manner of writing to a new, definitely instrumental style, with faster motion and brief motifs. Fig.348 presents two passages from Stephan's *Jesus Christus unser Heiland* (no.49). Stephan is a significant predecessor of the later North German masters: Michael and Jacob Praetorius, Scheidemann, and Tunder.

Another work by this composer, a *Fantasia Johan Stephani Orga: Lüneburg*, is found in the Mus. ms. 1581 of the Munich Library (fol.38v). It treats a single subject (*e' | e' e' | f' e' | d' c' | b | a*) in three imitative sections, first in its original

Fig.348

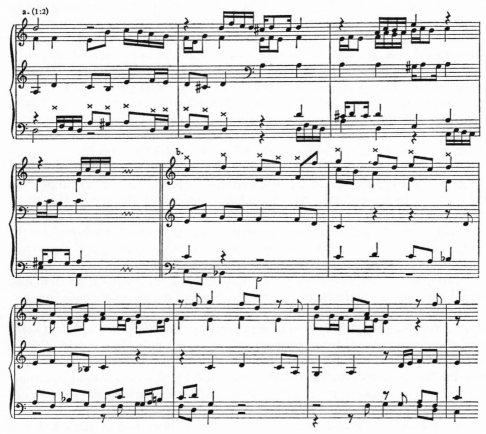

note values, then in diminution, and finally in augmentation. In the concluding section it also occurs several times in still another shape, beginning with note values reduced to one-half, and continuing at one-fourth the original note values. This composition was surely influenced by Sweelinck's fantasies. A *Veni redemptor gentium* in the Calvör Library Ms. Ze 1 has not been available to me.

Hieronymus Praetorius

The most important center of North German organ music at the beginning of the 17th century was Hamburg. During the 16th century Jacob Praetorius the Elder (died 1582?) was active there as an organist at the Jacobskirche. He was followed by his son Hieronymus (1560–1629), and finally by Hieronymus' son Jacob the Younger. Hieronymus' motets, Magnificats, and Masses reveal him to be an important representative of the German-Venetian school.[5] As an organ composer he is known only by a complete cycle of Magnificat settings preserved in an organ tablature of 1611, which belongs to the cathedral chapter at Visby (Sweden). According to the original title this manuscript was written by Berendt Petri at Jacob Praetorius' home in Hamburg. Later it came into the possession of the Visby cathedral organist Johan Bahr, who inserted several leaves containing his own compositions.[6] Petri was obviously a student of the younger Jacob Praetorius, and he incorporated two of Jacob's pieces, a *Magnificat Germanicae* and a *Grates nunc omnes*, in his collection. The remaining works in the original manuscript— 19 Latin hymns, 9 Kyries, an organ Mass without Credo, and 5 sequences—are all anonymous, but some may be the work of Petri or Jacob Praetorius.

Hieronymus Praetorius' Magnificat cycle[7] consists basically of three settings for each of the eight tones. In the first setting the chorale tune always appears in the tenor, in the second in the discant, and in the third in the bass, e.g.: *Magnificat primi toni im Tenore; 2. Versus im Discanto; 3. Versus im Basso.* For the third, fourth, and eighth tones there are four settings. In the *Magnificat septimi toni* the three normal settings are followed by 4. *Versus sopra 2 Clavier,* and then, curiously, by two settings of *Ach Gott vom Himmel sieh darein.*

Five-part texture generally prevails, though here and there it is reduced to four parts by rests or the omission of a voice. Although all the pieces are based on melodies with about the same number of notes, their length differs considerably, from about 40 to 140 measures. With only one exception, an *Alio modo Fuga des Quarti toni,* the chorale tune is heard throughout in the part given in the title—discant, tenor, or bass—and handled like 16th-century *cantus-planus* settings, but Praetorius does not tie himself to a particular note value. He also occasionally interrupts the sequence of sustained tones with figural paraphrases. Such details show an unmistakable tendency toward greater freedom, and this tendency is openly avowed by the free sections in each piece that expand the chorale-based setting. A free interlude is always inserted between the first and the second half of the *tonus,* and in most pieces there are other additions at the beginning, the end, or elsewhere. In this manner Hieronymus Praetorius succeeds in constructing organ compositions of more than a hundred measures from chorale tunes of little more than a dozen notes, and thereby sets the stage for the still longer chorale settings of the later North German masters. A schematic presentation of two of his Magnificat settings follows (I and II signify the first and second halves of the *tonus;* the Arabic numbers indicate the measures):

Magnificat III. toni 2. Versus sopra 2 Clavier (melody in the discant)

1	II	21	33	
fore-imitation	I	free interlude	fugato on a derived subject ‖	

44		50	62		77–85
fore-imitation		II	fugato on a derived motif	II	

Magnificat III. toni 3. Versus im Basso

I		10	27		38	
fore-imitation	I		free interlude		fugato on the intonation ‖	

52–104
free fantasy on II

In the interludes and postludes Praetorius sometimes uses a method that was also used in Johann Stephan's chorale settings, and which plays an essential role in the chorale fantasies of later North German masters. The chorale tune is divided into fragments from which pithy imitation motifs or clavieristic figures are derived. Thus from the termination of the third Magnificat tone (*c′ c′ c′ c′ a c′ b a*), the motif (| / *c′ c′ c′* | *a* |) is formed; Fig.349 illustrates the manner in which it is employed (meas.83–89).

Fig.349

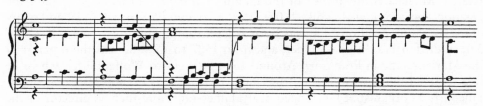

The Magnificat cycle of Hieronymus Praetorius represents an anacrusis to the organ music of North Germany, and announces the magnificence and greatness of this art in a very significant way. Indeed, one cannot imagine a more beautiful or more impressive preface to this century-long musical evolution than the solemn sounds of the first Magnificat (Fig.350).

Fig.350

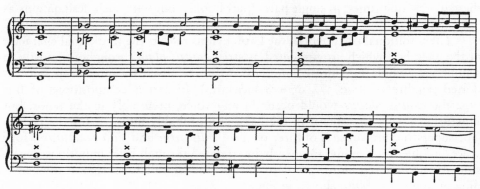

351

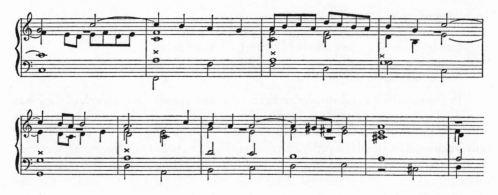

Michael Praetorius

Michael Praetorius is much better known than Hieronymus, to whom he is not related. Michael is the author of the famous *Syntagma musicum* (1615–20), the gigantic *Musae Sioniae* (9 vols., 1605–11), the *Hymnodia Sionia* (1611), and many other vocal compositions. He was born at Creuzburg, Thuringia, in 1571 (1572/3?), studied at Frankfurt on Oder, and from 1587 to 1590 he was the organist at the Marienkirche in Frankfurt. Around 1594 he went to Wolfenbüttel, where he later entered the service of the Brunswick court, first as organist (serving simultaneously as organist at Gröningen near Halberstadt) and then as director of the orchestra (in 1604). After the duke's death in 1613 he went to Dresden. Between 1616 and 1619 he lived at various places as a musical adviser, and finally returned to Wolfenbüttel, where he died in 1621.

We know 10 organ works by Michael Praetorius, 4 on German chorales (*Ein feste Burg, Christ unser Herr zum Jordan kam, Wir glauben all an einen Gott*, and *Nun lob mein Seel*) and 6 on Latin hymns (*Alvus tumescit, A solis ortus, Summo parenti, Vita sanctorum, O lux beata Trinitas*, and *Te mane laudum carmine*). The chorale settings are added to the *Musae Sioniae*, vol. VII (1607), and the hymns to the *Hymnodia Sionia* (1611). Like the vocal compositions in these collections, these works are printed in single parts (part books), but with such designations as "Pro Organico."[8]

The traditional treatment of the Latin hymns reflects the traditional character of the melodies, which are presented as strict *cantus plani* throughout, mostly in semibreves (whole measures), but once in breves (two measures) and once in dotted semibreves (two 3/4 or 6/8 measures). In earlier compositions of this type the *cantus planus* would occur in any voice, preferably in the tenor, but Praetorius always presents it in the bass, and probably meant it for the pedals. The superstructure consists of three or (in *A solis ortus* and *Vita sanctorum*) four voices in quiet polyphony, frequently interrelated through brief imitations. Occasionally the imitated motifs are derived from the chorale tune, e.g., at the beginning of *Summo parenti*, shown in Fig. 351.

Fig.351

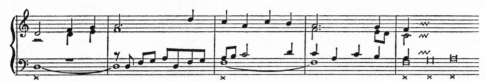

In several hymns, especially in *Summo parenti* and *Vita sanctorum*, the upper parts assume Baroque-like touches toward the end: passage work, clavieristic figures, and complementary motifs. In *O lux beata Trinitas* the chorale tune is laid out in dotted notes, obviously to symbolize the Trinity. The superstructure consists of a longer section in 3/4 time and a shorter one in 6/8, the former in quietly flowing motion, the latter like a pastorale (Fig.352).

Fig.352

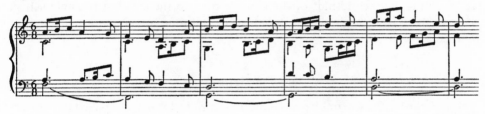

Michael Praetorius' organ hymns are works of restrained expression and serious beauty. The listener is captivated by masterful fashioning of the contrapuntal texture and the well-chosen harmonies, with regular, archaic modal progressions resulting from the *cantus planus* carried by the bass.

The four compositions on Lutheran songs are completely different. Praetorius writes two variations on the chorale *Nun lob mein Seel den Herrn*, both of which carry the lovely melody in alternating half and quarter notes (3/4 time) in the top voice. The three lower parts offer lively figurations, which often invade the chorale tune. Praetorius, the German master, creates a much fuller life for the Lutheran tunes than Sweelinck, the Dutchman, does in similar works. Praetorius writes from the heart; he repeats the last line of the chorale, "those that suffer in thy realm" twice in the first variation and eleven consecutive times in the second one, each time in a different manner. With similar feeling, an unknown master of the 9th or 10th century ended the offertory *Vir erat* with seven repetitions of Job's yearning call *ut videat bona*.[9]

In the other compositions on Lutheran melodies, *Ein feste Burg, Christ unser Herr*, and *Wir glauben all*, Praetorius creates a new type of chorale arrangement, the grand chorale motet. In their lengths, 257, 411, and 310 measures, respectively, and contents these works go far beyond the usual scope. The form of the chorale motet was not unknown during the 16th century; works such as Buchner's *Fuga optima* on *Maria zart*, Cavazzoni's *Pange lingua*, or Cabezón's *Christe redemptor* exhibit it clearly. But all these pieces are of modest length, and treat the individual hymn lines about as fully as in a vocal motet. In Praetorius' compositions the size expands so much and there are so many kinds of treatment that a new type emerges, fittingly called the grand chorale motet.[10] In *Christ unser Herr*, e.g., the last line alone occupies more than a hundred measures, and it employs simple imitations as well as augmentation and diminution by two and by four. The imitative methods of the 16th century combine with the figurations, clavieristic figures, and motifs of the Baroque to form powerful, monumental works. There is hardly another master capable of filling such gigantic spaces with vital, always significant content. In one instance Praetorius himself gave up in the face of the immensity of his enterprise. In the setting of *Wir glauben all*, the presentation of the first five lines takes 265 measures. Similar treatment of the remaining six lines would have resulted in a piece of more than 500 measures. Praetorius therefore decided to limit the second half of the chorale tune to the smallest possible space, and presented it in a simple harmonization without any imitation or figural ornaments.

Jacob Praetorius

Jacob Praetorius, the son of Hieronymus, was born in 1586. He traveled to Amsterdam around 1600, where he studied under Sweelinck, and in 1603, at the age of 17, he became an organist at St. Peter's at Hamburg, a position he retained until his death in 1651. Unlike the other two Praetoriuses, he is known chiefly as an organ composer, although by only a small number of works: a *Magnificat Germanicae* and a *Grates nunc omnes* (a Christmas sequence) from the Petri tablature, and 3 organ chorales and 3 preambles from the Lynar and Lüneburg tablatures.[11]

The two settings on Latin chant tunes are early works, written before 1611 (the date of the Petri tablature). They are traditional pieces, of modest length and simple workmanship, that curiously omit all the stylistic features one would expect from a Sweelinck pupil. The chant melodies are treated partly in brief imitations and partly as *cantus plani*.

One of the German organ chorales, *Christum wir sollen loben schon*, shows similar features. The lines of the melody are heard as a *cantus planus* in the bass, a treatment that is unusual for Lutheran chorales. The first three lines are introduced by fore-imitations, as the whole notes of the *cantus planus* are reduced to half notes in the first line and to quarter and eighth notes in the second, while remaining unchanged in the third line—again a most unusual procedure. The counterpoints are figural and motivic, but much more restrained than Sweelinck's. In *Herr Gott dich loben wir* the six lines of the German *Te Deum* are treated in short sections of impressive simplicity. The composition is dated 1636.

354

A striking contrast to these pieces is provided by the arrangement of *Durch Adams Fall ist ganz verderbt*. Unfortunately it is preserved incompletely (in Lynar B 5, with the legend: *a 5. Echo. auff 3 Clavier*), but the fragment is long enough to recognize the plan of a grand chorale motet. The 133 measures that treat the first two lines and the repetition of this A section and 5 additional measures of the beginning of the B section of this barform are extant. The whole composition may have run to about 300 measures. The format of this remarkable work is the same as that of the chorale motets of Michael Praetorius. But stylistically it goes considerably beyond them in the direction of the chorale fantasy, in which the North German penchant for bold overstatement, fantastic formulation, rhapsody, and improvisation expresses itself most clearly. This magnificent work by Jacob Praetorius is full of lively figurations, daring exploding passages, fragmentation of thematic material, bravura effects, innumerable echoes, abrupt contrasts, and similar artifices of great variety. Fig.353 shows one of the most remarkable passages (the purely harmonic lower parts are omitted or only suggested). In a. there are two especially interesting presentations of the first line of the chorale (| / *e'* | *e' e'* | *d' e'* | *c' b* | *a* |). Both start with fragments of the tune, followed by the entire line, which is expanded by a boldly ascending figure in the second presentation. Each fragment is repeated by an echo. Note the 3 + 2 + 3 rhythm at the beginning of the example.[12] Fig.353 b. and c. show some of the most striking bravura effects from this chorale fantasy. In measures 116–25, the motif (*a b c'*) (derived from *a c'* at the beginning of the second chorale line) rises through two full octaves with the aid of a sequence in thirds.

Fig.353

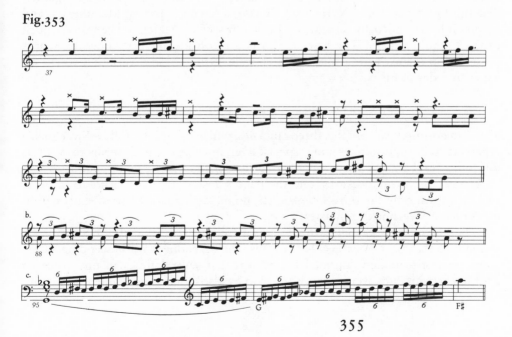

The three *Praeambula* by Jacob Praetorius are the beginning of an evolution that leads to the prelude and fugue of Bach's time. To be sure, this combination is found sporadically as early as the beginning of the 16th century,[13] but it took another hundred years for its aesthetic value to be fully appreciated. Praetorius' *Praeambula* consist of a chordal prelude of eight to sixteen measures and an extended fugal section, about five times as long, on one subject. Their historic significance emerges when they are compared with other works of the period, e.g., with the two preludes by David Abel (d.1639) preserved in Lynar B 3. Both are purely chordal settings in the suspension style of the Italian *durezze e ligature;* the second one (*pedaliter*) is indeed a very beautiful and expressive example of this species.[14]

Samuel Scheidt

With Samuel Scheidt (1587–1654), northeastern Germany also enters Sweelinck's sphere of influence. Except for three student years at Amsterdam (about 1605–1608), Scheidt apparently lived all his life at Halle. Fortunate circumstances enabled him to publish his organ works in two prints and thus pass them on to his heirs in a much more complete condition than other Sweelinck students were able to do. His *Tabulatura nova* came out in 1624 and his *Tabulatur-Buch hundert geistlicher Lieder und Psalmen* in 1650.

The *Tabulatura nova*[15] consists of three volumes. The first two contain an unordered series of fantasies, fugues, echoes, settings of Latin hymns and German chorales, song variations, dances, and a collection of canons—26 works altogether. The third part contains a Kyrie (and Gloria), a Credo, a psalm, Magnificats, and hymns fully intended for use in the Lutheran service, which still retained much of the Catholic liturgy. The first two parts are considerably expanded by works preserved in manuscript: 3 toccatas, 4 chorale settings, and 6 variation works on songs and dance tunes.[16]

FANTASIES, FUGUES, AND TOCCATAS

The *Tabulatura nova* contains three fantasies, which essentially follow Sweelinck's type, but go beyond it in certain respects. Even in length Scheidt seems to want to outdo his teacher. The *Fantasia super Io son ferito lasso* (I, no.2) comprises 330 measures (165 breve measures) and the *Fantasia super Ut re mi fa sol la* (I, no.4) 383 measures; only the third *Fantasia* (II, no.6), with 214 measures, stays within the limits of Sweelinck's fantasies.

The *Fantasia super Ut re mi fa sol la* follows the principle of Sweelinck's ostinato fantasies. The subject—as always, the ascending and descending hexachord—is not genuinely imitated but is repeated several times in one voice or another. Scheidt, however, expands the plan by also employing augmentations and diminutions of the subject in the structural scheme. The following is a schematic analysis, similar to those given earlier for Sweelinck's ostinato fantasies:

Section and Measure	Number of Voices	Voice with Subject	Presentations of the Subject
I	2	top	4 S in ○ on C; 4 S in ♩ on C
II (78)	3	top	4 S in ○ on C; 4 S in ♩ on G
III (154)	3	middle	4 S in ○ on C; 4 S in ♩ on G
IV (230)	4	bass	2 S in ○ on C; 2 S in ○ on g; 1 S in ◻ on C; 1 S in ♩ on C; 1 S in ♩ on G
V (316–83)	4	all	

The subject appears 31 times in large note values, filling 315 measures. Like Sweelinck, Scheidt tries to fill this framework with musical life by adding first one, then two, and finally three counterpoints—an attempt that was even less successful than his teacher's. The many sequences ascend and descend the notes of the hexachord with such pedantic orderliness that the shape of an entire sequence can be indicated by the first note, as in Fig.354.

Fig.354

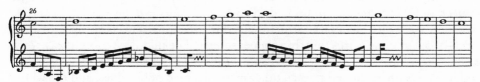

The *Fantasia II,* no.6, is in three parts throughout. It divides into about nine sections, in which the subject is presented partly in imitation and partly in successive repetitions. The final section, in which the subject is fragmented into motifs, is the most interesting.

The *Fantasia super Io son ferito lasso* reflects the imitative fantasies of Sweelinck, but it is not monothematic. It is constructed as a *Fuga quadruplici,* and treats four subjects on an equal basis. The first one, (| e | e e | d c | f | e |), is taken from Palestrina's madrigal named in the title; the second one may be interpreted as its cancrizans form (| / e | f c | d e | A |); the third is the frequently used chromatic tetrachord (| / a | g♯ g | f♯ f | e |); and the fourth is its inversion (| / e | f f♯ | g g♯ | a |). The simultaneous employment of four subjects suggests an Italian influence, such as the *Fantasie a quattro soggetti* in Frescobaldi's first printed publication (1608). Except for this, Scheidt's fantasy definitely follows Sweelinck's lead, in its overall structure of three sections (original note values, augmentation, diminution) and in many details of style. The subjects are mostly presented in contrapuntal combination and imitation, but in the middle section they are added to each other to form a total subject of twenty-five whole notes, which appears once in each voice. In the third section the subjects are reduced in various degrees and occasionally altered in rhythm. Toward the end they are all contrapuntally combined, as shown in Fig.355, in a passage called *Concursus et coagmentatio omnium quatuor fugarum*. In this fantasy Scheidt proves himself a great master of the contrapuntal-imitative technique. Omitting all figurations, he presents the subjects in an abundance of captivating combinations. However, the middle section is somewhat too long.

Fig.355

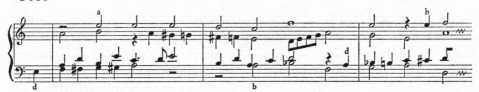

The second part of the *Tabulatura nova* contains two pieces entitled *Fuga*, which are written exactly like Sweelinck's fantasies, for they focus on a single subject. In *Fuga contraria* (II, no.1) the subject (| g | bb c' | d' bb | eb' | d' |) and its inversion are treated in a large structure of three sections. This is really a gigantic form—194 breve measures (nearly 400 measures!). The middle section (meas.56ff.) is constructed like the middle of the *Fantasia super Io son ferito lasso:* The subject and its inversion are added to each other in quadrupled note values, and the whole group of 28 measures is presented once in each part. Scheidt works hard to create variety in the counterpoints, but he frequently relies on sequences again, which no longer possess the sustaining power that they may have had in his time. The third section (meas.114ff.; cf. Seiffert's new ed., p.92, brace 1, meas.5) starts with echoes on the reduced subject and its inversion; it is followed by a passage of strettos in triple meter; a passage with ornamented countersubject, which is inverted simultaneously with the subject; a fourth passage in which the greatly reduced subject is changed into a clavieristic motif; and finally one in which both the subject and its inversion are reduced to quarter notes, sequentially repeated, and combined with figurations in sixteenth notes. In the penultimate subsection (meas.157–73), with the aid of the clavieristic motif, Scheidt forms a phrase of five breve measures, which he repeats literally on three different pitches: G, F, and D. This literal repetition of a long phrase is characteristic of Scheidt's methodical manner of writing. In the entire German organ repertoire there is scarcely a similar instance, but it is interesting to note that the same technique plays an important role in Spanish organ music around 1650 (cf.pp.519, and 547).

The other *Fuga* (II, no.3) shows the same large form in three sections. We must be charitable about a page-long section in which a dotted rhythm is hounded to death. But there are also many interesting details in this piece, particularly in connection with the motivic fragmentation of the subject.

Between the two *Fugae* Scheidt placed two echo compositions (II, no.2), in which he imitates Sweelinck's style with about the same success as the apprentice has with the sorcerer's exorcism.

The three manuscript toccatas (suppl. nos.1–3) start, as usual, with chords and then continue with figurations. Their content is not too remarkable, but their conciseness does recommend them. At the end of the third toccata, shown in Fig.356, the purely chordal outline of the figurations foreshadows tendencies that play an important but often artistically objectionable role later in the century.

Fig.356

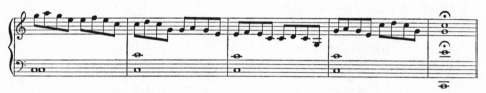

At the end of part I of the *Tabulatura nova* there is a group of twelve canons, most of which can be disregarded since they are only of theoretical or didactic interest. But some of them (nos.4, 8, 9, 11, and 12) represent a type that also plays a role in musical practice. A melody, usually a *cantio sacra,* as Scheidt calls it, is set as a *cantus planus,* and two faster-moving counterpoints that form a canon are added. Fig.357 presents the beginning of Scheidt's canon no.9 on the *Magnificat VIII. toni.* The importance of this type is that with sufficient contrapuntal skill canons can be added to any melody. Since Zarlino devoted a detailed description to such canons in Book III of his *Istitutioni harmoniche* (1558),[17] let us call them Zarlino canons.

Fig.357

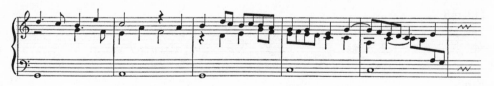

CHORALE SETTINGS

The chorale settings occupy the largest space by far in Scheidt's organ works. They comprise 11 compositions on Protestant chorales,[18] 7 on Latin hymns, one on a psalm (*In te Domine speravi*), 9 Magnificats, a Kyrie (with Gloria), and a Credo. Twenty-five of these works are chorale variations: all the Protestant chorales, except for *Fantasia super Ich ruf zu dir* (I, no.13) and *Allein Gott in der Höh* (suppl., no.5); all the hymns; and all the Magnificats. The number of variations (called *versus* in the original) varies between two and twelve, and the total is more than 150. In this enormous repertoire of chorale variations a number of types can be more or less clearly identified. The following table indicates the frequency of their occurrence in the Protestant chorales (C), the Latin hymns (H), and the Magnificats (M):

		C	H	M	Examples*
2-part	1. figural counterpoint	5	1	2	I–5, VII; III–3, III
	2. imitative	1	3	1	III–9, III; III–13, II
	3. *contrapuncto duplici*	3	1	1	I–3, IV; III–5, III
	4. *complexus mutui*	1	–	–	II–5, III
3-part	5. figural counterpoint	18	6	5	I–1, III; II–7, VI
	6. simple counterpoint	1	2	–	I–12, II; III–16, V
	7. canonic counterpoint	–	–	2	III–4, Vb; III–9, Vb
	8. *choralis coloratus*	2	–	–	I–3, VIII; II–4, II
4-part:	9. *c. f. in cantu*	14	6	8	I–1, I; II–7, I
	10. *c. f. in alto*	1	5	4	II–7, V; III–4, III
	11. *c. f. in tenore*	2	5	5	I–3, II; II–7, IV
	12. *c. f. in basso*	–	2	5	III–3, V; III–11, V
	13. *c. f. in 2 parts*	3	2	5	II–5, V; II–7, IX
	14. canonic counterpoint	–	2	1	III–13, VII; III–16, VII
	15. *choralis coloratus*	6	–	–	I–3, IX; II–9, VII
	16. motet-like texture	1	6	9	III–11, I; III–18, I
	17. chordal setting	–	–	9	III–4, VI; III–7, VI

The two-part texture (bicinium) occurs most often in the form in which Sweelinck employed it, that is, with lively and varied figurations contrasting with the sustained tones of the *cantus firmus* (type 1). A new form (type 2) is the imitative bicinium, in which fragmentation, as well as imitation, plays an important role. The *cantus firmus* is divided into motifs, which are heard in both voices in imitation, often in sequential repetitions also. Fig.358 gives the beginning of III–18, II (*Jesus Christus unser Heiland*). Note that such imitative bicinia occur only in part

Fig.358

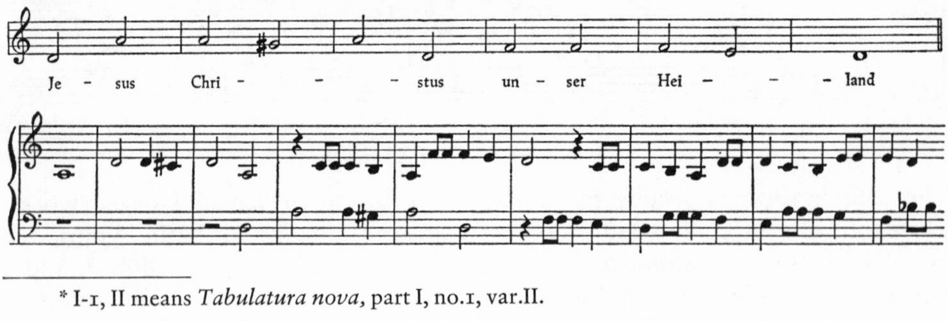

Je - sus Chri - - - stus un - ser Hei - - - land

---

* I–1, II means *Tabulatura nova*, part I, no.1, var.II.

Fig.359

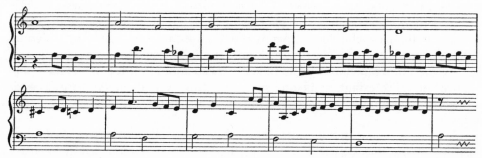

III of the *Tabulatura nova* (in III–14, III; III–16, II; and III–18, II, in addition to the examples given above).

A number of Scheidt's chorale variations are called *Bicinium contrapuncto duplici* (type 3). Each line is combined with a figural counterpoint, and this combination is then repeated in inverted counterpoint at the twelfth (in II–7, VII, at the octave), e.g., in I–3, IV (*Vater unser im Himmelreich*, Fig.359). Although this method smacks somewhat of learnedness, the new illumination that each line of the melody receives in this way is not without artistic effect.

The *Bicinium complexus mutui*, variation III of *Christ lag in Todesbanden*, is a unique piece. Even its length of 167 measures surpasses the usual limits (the other variations of this set run from 50 to 80 measures). "*Complexus mutui*" (mutual envelopment) probably refers to the fact that each line of the chorale is presented twice in succession, first in the upper part, then in the lower one. In addition, each line is introduced by an extended fore-imitation in the style of the imitative bicinia.

Among the three-part variations we may differentiate those with figural counterpoints (type 5) from those with quietly proceeding counterpoints (type 6), although the line between them cannot be rigorously drawn. The former type is found particularly often in the variation sets on Protestant chorales. Fig.360 gives two excerpts from the third line of *O lux beata* (III–16, V and VI) that show the difference. The two Zarlino canons and the examples with ornamented *cantus firmus* (types 7 and 8) will be discussed below, in connection with the corresponding four-part examples.

Fig.360

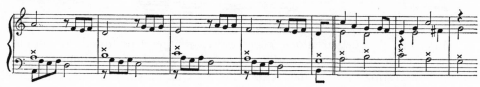

361

Four-part writing is by far the most frequent.[19] The *cantus firmus* may be given to a particular voice—soprano (type 9), alto (10), tenor (11), or bass (12). Type 9 predominates in the arrangements of Protestant chorales, while the other types occur almost exclusively in hymns and Magnificats. Here is another example of the tendency to treat the melodies of the Catholic liturgy as mystic symbols and those of the Lutheran church as audible expressions of faith. It is understandable that Scheidt, a Protestant, had better success in presenting the latter. Settings such as the first variation on *Vater unser* are among the most beautiful creations of the period.

Several four-part settings present the individual lines of the chorale successively in two voices (type 13). This method is expressly indicated in *Versus 4* of the *Magnificat VIII. toni* (III–9, IV), which carries the legend *Choralis in alto et tenore.* The other instances of this technique are inscribed only as *Choralis in basso,* but should really be entitled *Choralis in tenore et basso.* The following pieces in part III share this method: 5, V; 8, V; 9, Va; 10, V (all settings of the fifth verse of the Magnificat); 14, V; and 18, VI.[20]

Scheidt uses a canon between two counterpoints (types 7 and 14) in five variations, all in part III, with designations such as *Canon in subdiapason post minimam.* In all of them the *cantus firmus* is entrusted to the bass. Two of these variations (4, Vb; 9, Vb) are pure Zarlino canons in three parts; in the others (9, Vc; 13, VII; 16, VII) a free fourth part is added.

The method of ornamenting the *cantus firmus,* already employed by Sweelinck (cf.p.333; e.g., var. VI of *Erbarm dich mein*), is used by Scheidt exclusively in arrangements of Protestant chorales (types 8, 15). The ornamented melody is either in the discant (*cantu colorato:* I–3, VIII; I–3, IX; I–5, XII; II–4, II) or in the bass (*basso colorato:* II–9, VII; II–9, VIII). *Versus 2* of *Herzlich lieb* (II–4, II), which is inscribed *coloratus per omnes voces* is a special case; the figuration migrates from section to section from the *cantus firmus* to the counterpoints. The ornamental figures are diverse and changing, but always purely geometric and decorative. There is no trace of an attempt to make them expressive or intensive, as Jacob Praetorius occasionally did. In the last verse of *Vater unser* (I–3, IX) Scheidt uses the *imitatio violistica,* illustrated in Fig.361, for the formulation of the third line.[21]

Fig.361

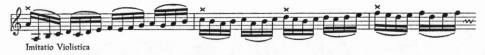

Imitatio Violistica

Motet-like chorale variations (type 16) are another type found only in part III, where they occur in every variation set and always as the first setting. They are the most interesting and significant of Scheidt's chorale variations. Each line is treated imitatively, mostly with extensive application of thematic fragmentation, the importance of which was mentioned in connection with the imitative bicinia (type 2). Usually Scheidt starts with an imitation based on the first line, followed by a fragmented treatment of this line, and concludes with a confirming statement in simple harmonization. The remaining lines are treated in the same manner, but without the opening imitation. The first variation on *Christe qui lux es et dies* (III–13, I; the four lines of the hymn are designated as A, B, C, and D) will illustrate the procedure:

A. meas. 1–11: 5 imitations; 11–14: 4 strettos in diminution; 14–17: imitative-sequential treatment of the last three notes of A (*bb a g*); 17–21: A in the soprano
B. meas. 20–23: strettos in diminution; 23–30: imitative and echo-like treatment of two fragments (the concluding statement is omitted)
C. meas. 31–33: imitative and echo-like treatment of two fragments; 34–37: C twice in the soprano
D. meas. 38–49: fragment (first half of the melody) in many strettos plus two whole measures in four-fold sequence; 50: D in diminution; 51–53: D in the tenor

Section C is reproduced in Fig.362. The corresponding settings for the Magnificats are shorter, since the melody consists of only two lines. The chorale motet on *Jesus Christus unser Heiland* (III–18, I), the only Protestant chorale that starts with such a setting, is especially impressive.

Fig.362

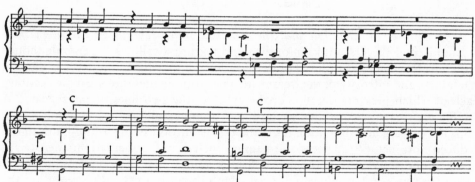

The last category is the presentation of the *cantus firmus* in a simple chordal setting (type 17). Scheidt uses this method exclusively in Magnificats, each of which opens with a motet-like setting and concludes with a chordal one.[22]

Let us now turn to the chorale settings that are not composed in the form of variation sets. Part III of the *Tabulatura nova* contains a Kyrie (and Gloria) and a Credo (nos.1 and 17). The Kyrie consists of three and the Gloria of nine brief sections, which alternate in the traditional manner with sections that are sung. The melody on which the Kyrie settings are based has not been determined. The melody of Mass XII in the modern repertoire is used for the Gloria. The *Credo*, however, is not based on a Gregorian tune but on the melody of the Lutheran translation *Wir glauben all an einen Gott;* thus it is not composed of several sections but is a continuous setting of the entire chorale.

The *Toccata super In te Domine speravi* (II–12) is a very curious piece. According to the title it is a setting of *Psalm xxx* (or *lxx*), which was taken into the Lutheran chorale repertoire as *In dich hab ich gehoffet, Herr.* But the music shows no relationship to a psalm tone or to the chorale melody. Instead Scheidt employs a subject, either traditional or of his own invention, which he also used in one of his canons (no.10) (| *g a* | *b c′* | *d′ e′* | *d′ g* |).[23] In the *Toccata* it appears in various shapes: inversion, diminution by four and eight, fragmentation, indeed even in cancrizans (cf.Fig.363). The work concludes with a long section with various dry figural passages, which do justify the title "toccata," but are even less satisfactory than what precedes. All in all, this is one of Scheidt's least successful works.

Fig.363

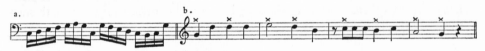

a. Diminution by eight; b. Cancrizans.

In contrast to this *Toccata,* the *Fantasia super Ich ruf zu dir* (I–13) is a masterpiece of the first rank. In outline and texture it follows the chorale motets with which Scheidt opens his chorale variations in part III, but it exceeds them in the fulness and intensity of the treatment. The work divides into six main sections, each of which presents one line of the chorale (the two lines of the repeated A section are treated as one line) according to a unified plan, which is admirable in both its devising and execution. First the line is introduced by a fore-imitation in reduced note values (quarters), sometimes including fragmentation; then it appears in one voice after another in full note values, first with one counterpoint, then with two counterpoints, and finally with three; in the final presentation the chorale line sounds in the soprano above a simple harmonization, giving a very impressive summation and culmination of what preceded. The excerpts from the second section ("den rechten Glauben") shown in Fig.364, provide some of the details of this scheme. In a^1. the last three notes of the chorale line become the object of a sequence, which rises like an intensely repeated supplication to *c″*, where a more echo-like treatment of the initial motif (the first four notes) of the line takes over. Among the most impressive details in this fantasy is the extended

Fig.364

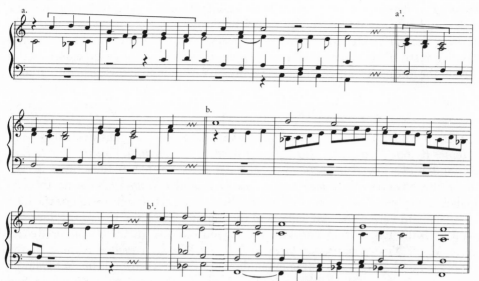

presentation—perhaps it would be better to call it development—of the line "Dir zu leben," from whose simple melody (*f e d c*) Scheidt forms a triple imitation, which then recurs five times in a rising sequence, shown in Fig.365. What is it here that gives the trivial and often pedantic technique of the sequence the effect of a revelation?

Fig.365

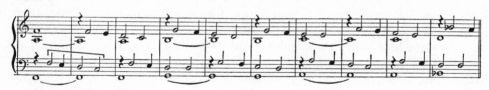

The setting of *Allein Gott in der Höh* (suppl. no.5) represents a briefer but no less beautiful realization of the same plan. The harmonized summation at the end of each line emerges even more clearly, especially since the fugal treatment of each line is cast in duple meter and the final presentation is in triple meter.

The contents of Scheidt's second publication, the *Tabulatur-Buch hundert geistlicher Lieder und Psalmen* of 1650, are exclusively chorale settings. This work is usually called the *Görlitz Tablature*,[24] after the place where it was printed. It contains one hundred chorales in predominantly chordal four-part settings, with some polyphonic enlivening of the lower parts. Perhaps these simple settings were meant primarily as organ accompaniments for the singing by the congregation.

But they could also be used for domestic edification: Part of the title reads "mit der Christlichen Kirchen und Gemeine auff der Orgel desgleichen auch zu Hause zu spielen und zu singen. . . ." In any case Scheidt has created a collection that is as valid for the early Baroque as Bach's chorales are for the late Baroque. In fact, Scheidt's restrained, one might say objective, presentations may be closer to the spirit of the Lutheran church than Bach's affective, sometimes too learned creations.

VARIATIONS ON SECULAR THEMES

Scheidt's *Tabulatura nova* contains seven variation sets on songs or dances: *Ach du feiner Reiter, Also geht's also steht's, Est-ce Mars, Fortuna, Passamezzo, Soll es sein,* and *Wehe Windgen wehe.* Several more are extant in manuscripts: *Bergamasca,* three *Galliardas, Niederländisches Lied,* and *Paduana hispanica,* the last one being partly by Sweelinck. In some of these sets the first expression of the idea of "theme and variations" appears, and the numbering of the variations does not begin with the first setting but with the second one—as in *Ach du feiner Reiter, Est-ce Mars, Niederländisches Lied,* and *Wehe Windgen wehe.* In most of the others the numbering starts at the beginning, but the first setting is made so simple that it may well be called "theme." Only *Fortuna, Paduana hispanica,* and *Soll es sein* still start in the older manner, with the first variation.

The theme of the *Passamezzo* set is based on the passamezzo antico (cf.p.235). Four themes, those of *Est-ce Mars, Fortuna, Paduana hispanica,* and *Soll es sein,* were also arranged by Sweelinck. The *Bergamesca* theme appears earlier in Farnaby's *For Two Virginals;* Scheidt uses only the first half of the melody. The theme of the second *Galliarda* (suppl.p.35) proves to be a proportz of the entire bergamasca tune. The first galliard (suppl.p.31) carries the legend *Galliarda Dulenti Varirt Sam. Sch.* in the original manuscript, meaning that its theme comes from John Dowland, the famous English lutenist.

On the whole Scheidt's technique and methods of variation are similar to Sweelinck's. Types A and C (cf.p.267) predominate, but type B is somewhat more frequent, for it is represented by variations IV and VI of *Also geht's,* variation IX of *Est-ce Mars,* variation VII of *Soll es sein,* and variations IV, V, VI, and IX of *Wehe Windgen.* In all of them the melody is heard in either the tenor or the bass, as is frequently the case in variations of the 16th century. Type D, which does not occur in Sweelinck's works, reappears, mostly in the passamezzo variations, which traditionally belong to this type; but we find it elsewhere, too, e.g., in variations II, III, and V of the third *Galliarda* (suppl.p.37).

More significant differences between the two masters emerge in their approach to variation. The changing variation, which Sweelinck treats with so much favor and mastery, is only rarely found in Scheidt. He tends more toward a unified presentation, which comes dangerously close to pedantry at times, especially in the monotonous repetition of one and the same formula in the passamezzo variations.

The bicinium, which Sweelinck employs only rarely in his secular variations, is found in almost every one of Scheidt's variation sets, several times in some. A number of these bicinia are very attractive, e.g., variation IV of *Wehe Windgen,* while others are rather dry, e.g., variation X of the same set or variation VI of *Soll es sein.* Two variations are entitled *Bicinium duplici contrapuncto* and use the invertible counterpoint at the twelfth. In the *Variatio triplici contrapuncto* of *Est-ce Mars* (var.IV), this method is applied within a three-part texture. In the *Bicinium imitatione Tremula Organi duobus digitis in una tantum clave manu tum dextra tum sinistra* of *Ach du feiner Reiter* (var. V) Scheidt elaborately parades finger changes on the same key in both hands.

Very few of Scheidt's variation sets are convincing in their totality. None reaches the artistic excellence of Sweelinck's *Mein junges Leben hat ein End* or *Ich fuhr mich über Rheine.* The variations on *Wehe Windgen wehe* are the most successful. Even their theme stands out among the others because of its simple, sincere melody and its irregular construction (6+4 measures), and because the sectional repetitions, which are always dangerous in variation sets, are omitted. Scheidt presents the tune in various ways, always being careful to introduce agreeable change without involving pedantries or exaggerations. Furthermore, the transitions with which he connects the individual variations are very lovely and convincing. As he often does in his variation sets, he writes the final variation in triple meter, but without following a schematic transformation according to the proportz idea; instead he presents a quasi-free fantasy on the motifs of the tune, which he expands from ten to twenty-one measures—one of the most remarkable examples of that rare type, in which the structure of the theme is altered. A brief coda in duple meter, in which Scheidt dextrously inserts his favored *imitatio violistica,* concludes the work.

To characterize Scheidt's total output for the keyboard it is necessary to compare him with his teacher. All in all his work equals Sweelinck's. He did not add anything essentially new to the evolution of keyboard music, but as a faithful disciple he preserved the heritage of his teacher and transplanted it to Germany. The two masters share an uneven quality—mediocre works side by side with the sublime, ephemeral techniques next to lasting masterpieces. What differentiates them can be seen by holding their portraits side by side: The Dutch face expresses cultivation, elegance, good breeding, and candor; the German is honest, plain, serious, and reserved. The former is at his best in the clever display of fantasies and secular variations, the latter in the meaningful polyphony of his chorale motets. The former erects a lasting monument for himself with his variations on *Mein junges Leben hat ein End*, the latter with his composition on *Ich ruf zu dir, Herr Jesu Christ.*

Scheidt's position and importance in the evolution of German keyboard music, it seems to me, has not always been judged correctly. We know that he had a number of students, but none of them played any role in the field of organ music. There is no trace of an immediate influence of his *Tabulatura nova* on other composers. The development that led from Sweelinck to Bach did not proceed via out-of-the-way Halle, but via Hamburg and Lübeck—not via Scheidt, but via Jacob Praetorius and Heinrich Scheidemann, the teachers of Weckmann and Reincken.

Scheidemann

Heinrich Scheidemann was born about 1596, the son of the Hamburg organist Hans Scheidemann. From 1611 to 1614 he studied with Sweelinck, and in 1625 he became his father's successor as organist at the church of St. Catherine at Hamburg, a position he retained until his death in 1663. Mattheson contrasts Scheidemann's personality with that of his friend Jacob Praetorius.[25] "Praetorius always showed himself as very grave and somewhat peculiar," whereas Scheidemann "was friendlier and more affable, and approached everyone freely and gaily." Weckmann studied under both and thus had an opportunity "to moderate the Praetorian seriousness with Scheidemann's gentleness." Scheidemann's playing was "nimble with the hand, merry and full of humor," whereas "Schultzen's [Praetorius'] things were more difficult to play and demanded more work."

Until recently about 50 keyboard works by Scheidemann were known, chiefly from the Lüneburg tablatures, which now replace the Lynar tablatures as the main source of North German organ music. This repertoire has been considerably enlarged by the discovery of two manuscripts in the Calvör Library at Clausthal-Zellerfeld (Ze 1 and 2), which contain 28 works by Scheidemann, mostly chorale settings that were hitherto unknown, and by another four organ chorales found in the Pelpin tablatures. A study by W. Breig, *Die Orgelwerke von Heinrich Scheidemann* (1967), pp.107ff., presents an index of 56 authentic organ works, 18 that are preserved anonymously but probably genuine, and 12 of doubtful authenticity: 14 preludes, 2 toccatas, 7 pieces in imitative polyphony, 51 organ chorales, and 12 intabulations.[26] In addition to these 86 compositions we also have about 20 dance pieces.

Most of Scheidemann's preludes are brief pieces of chordal texture, into which occasional motivic repetitions, echo effects, suggested imitations, or toccata endings are woven. Two of them (Seiffert O, nos.9, 10) consist of an introduction, a fugal setting, and a postlude, and one (no.11) has the form of a prelude and fugue, which also appears in Jacob Praetorius (cf.p.356). Especially noteworthy are two passages given in Fig.366: the final figuration of the *Praeambulum* no.8, dated 1637, and the transition from the fugal middle section to the postlude in no.10—the former because such formulae recur again and again later on in the literature, the latter because of the inserted rest, which tangibly indicates a change in registration to full organ. In no.11 the prelude is followed by a long fugue, in which two countersubjects are added to the subject. The second countersubject is

Fig.366

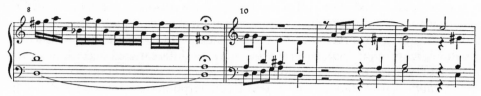

the descending chromatic tetrachord, which was frequently employed in this manner. (It would be interesting to list all the subjects with which it was contrapuntally combined from Scheidt to Bach.) The Lüneburg tablature KN 207, book
15, from which Seiffert published eleven preludes by Scheidemann, contains two
more, both simple preludes in the same style as Seiffert's no.3.

In the Lüneburg tablature KN 208[1] there is a toccata by Scheidemann[27] that
follows Sweelinck's toccatas rather closely. Imitative sections are omitted; instead
echo effects are introduced at various places. The figurations are more modern
than Sweelinck's, especially at the end, where they become an extended arpeggiation. This toccata also occurs in the Lynar tablatures (book B 6), but in a much
longer, highly virtuosic arrangement.[28] Except for occasional variants and a small
expansion after measure 5, the first 30 measures of the two versions are identical.
At measure 31, however, a completely new composition starts. Only here and
there does it suggest the other, mostly in the concluding measures. What is the
relationship of the two versions? If I understand M. Reimann correctly, she is
inclined to the supposition that the Lynar version represents the orginal, and the
Lüneburg version is an abbreviated parody probably by an unknown arranger.[29]
I think it very possible and even probable that both versions originated with
Scheidemann, one from an early creative period, the other from a later one, perhaps around 1650. A comparison of the two versions is a veritable classroom example of the change from the formal early Baroque to the fantastic middle Baroque.
There is also a *Tokkate H.S.M.* (the usual monogram for Scheidemann), which is
preserved in the manuscript Uppsala, Univ. Libr. Ihre 284.[30]

Four of Scheidemann's compositions belong to the field of imitative polyphony. A *Fuga* (Seiffert O, no.12) is a real, terse fugue with a brief, sequential interlude (meas.18–20). A second *Fuga* (no.15) gives the impression of a somewhat
formless youthful production, which may be beholden to an Italian ricercar. The
Canzone (no.13) is dated 1657 and thus probably belongs to Scheidemann's later
works. Indeed it is a variation canzona in three sections, which presupposes an
acquaintance with Frescobaldi's organ canzonas. A *Fantasia* (no.14) belongs to
the same type and probably to the same period; its subject is treated in five sections, alternating duple and triple meter.

Let us discuss the chorale settings that are authenticated first (Breig's index
nos.1–29). The Zellerfeld discoveries prove that chorale variations still dominate

369

the field, as they did in the works of Sweelinck and Scheidt. The Magnificat settings always consist of several verses for liturgical reasons (Scheidemann always composes four). There are fifteen other variation sets—seven with two verses or variations, five with three, and three with four. As in Sweelinck's and Scheidt's variations (cf.pp.333, 360), several types may be differentiated according to the number of voices, the presentation of the melody (*cantus planus*, ornamented *cantus planus*, or imitative), and type of counterpoints. In contrast to Scheidt, Scheidemann's chorale variations are clearly influenced by Sweelinck. Indeed, several pieces in the Fock edition also appear in Seiffert's Sweelinck edition (Fock, nos.4, 6, 12, 27 = Seiffert, nos.40, 42, 44, 50). Nevertheless there are also important differences, e.g., the great preponderance of four-part texture, which is used in 23 variations, while nine variations have three voices and four have two (this count does not include the unpublished Magnificat settings).

The bicinia (Fock, pp.14, 32, 43, 117) are always formulated like Sweelinck's, i.e., as *cantus-planus* settings with a very ornamented counterpoint, rather like Scheidt's, which employ imitation and invertible counterpoint. But Scheidemann's counterpoints are generally simpler and more unified than Sweelinck's. Almost all of Scheidemann's three-part pieces are *cantus-planus* settings, too. The two ornamented counterpoints are presented in parallel runs or in contrasting or complementary phrases (e.g., Fock, pp.8, 33, 36, 44). The most noteworthy four-part verses are those in which the chorale tune is basically laid out as a *cantus planus*, occasionally lightly ornamented, or rather paraphrased, thereby becoming much more expressive. *A solis ortus*, var.II, and *Kyrie summum, Christus* are two examples of this method, one that Buxtehude later led to a high point of dramatic affect. In settings with an ornamented melody Scheidemann also arrives at formulations that open a new field of expression, e.g., in *Erbarm dich mein*, var.II, and in *Mensch willst du*, var.III. The latter work, consisting of four verses, concludes with a cadenza, which includes quintuplets and, in the final measure, an abruptly rising gesture of great colorfulness. Fig.367 shows the last four measures; the sustained chords are indicated by letters. From the variations on *Vater unser* I, Fig.368 gives a passage from verse II (Fock, p.116; Gerdes C, p.209), which is typical of Scheidemann in its combination of formality and impressive gesture. It is on the boundary between early and middle Baroque. In Dietrich G (p.55, etc.) formulae like the ascending one at the end of this example are called "apostrophes." Such apostrophes at the beginning of a phrase occur somewhat later (cf.p.377), but they occur occasionally in Scheidemann's works (cf. Fock, p.57, meas.38).

Fig.367

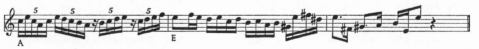

Fig.368

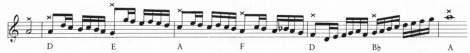

D   E   A   F   D   B♭   A

The second verse of *Lobet den Herren* is especially interesting. Here the chorale tune is not only richly ornamented but also occasionally divided into fragments, which are repeated in the manner of an echo. For example, the line "Sein Lob ist schön," which begins in measure 55, is introduced by a long echo passage, starting in measure 44,[31] in which the initial notes of the line, *d″–b′*, are variously suggested, as shown in Fig.369 (R = Rückpositiv; O = Organ). This setting—like Johann Stephan's *Jesus Christus unser Heiland* and Jacob Praetorius' *Durch Adams Fall*—foreshadows the chorale fantasy. It is represented by at least three other extended chorale arrangements that are not parts of variation sets: *In dich hab ich gehoffet* I, *Jesus Christus unser Heiland,* and *Vater unser* II.

Fig.369

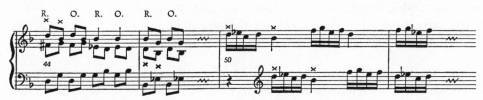

R.   O.   R.   O.   R.   O.

Two of the four organ chorales in the Pelplin tablatures, *Gott der Vater* and *Jesus Christus unser Heiland,* are short pieces, with the melody as a *cantus planus* in the bass. The others, *Ein feste Burg* and *Allein zu dir,* are fantasies.[32] *Ein feste Burg* also appears in Lüneburg KN 208[1] as an anonymous composition. The Lüneburg version is in three parts, however, without pedals, while the Pelplin version is in four parts with pedals. But the difference is not just in the number of voices. The former is an ornamented discant chorale of 48 measures,[33] while the latter is a chorale fantasy of no less than 267 measures, in which the melody is treated twice. The relationship of the two versions is similar to the one discussed above between the shorter and longer versions of the toccata. Measures 1–9 are essentially identical; Lüneburg, measures 38–42 ("Auf Erd ist nicht seins gleichen") occur in Pelplin as measures 250–54, i.e., at the end of the second setting (followed by a concluding coda). Although it is quite possible that both versions of the toccata are by Scheidemann, I believe that the original version of the chorale is the one in the Pelplin tablatures, and that the Lüneburg version is an abbreviation and patchwork arranged for use in a small town. One confirmation of this assumption is the abrupt transition from *A* major to *C* major in Lüneburg, measures 37–38.[34]

Dance music also plays a role in Scheidemann's output, as may be expected of a composer who "approached everyone freely and gaily," according to Mattheson. A galliard (in Uppsala Ms.408, fol.3v) follows the English models and consists of three sections, each of which is repeated, and a *Variatio* of the whole piece. An *Englische Mascarada oder Jüden-Tantz* (handwritten in the Copenhagen copy of G. Voigtländer's Odes, 1642[35]) is a song with a variation. A *Ballett* (in the *Klavierboek Anna Maria van Eijl*[36]) is an agreeable little dance of English flavor, in fact, it is written with English ornamentation symbols. An allemande, 2 courantes, and a *Mascharata* are preserved in the Lüneburg tablature KN 146 (nos.194–97), and there are 15 dances in the recently discovered *Celle Klavierbuch* of 1662, cf.p.384).

Abel, Siefert, P. Hasse the Elder, Düben, Schildt, and Others

There were a number of North Germans, contemporary with Jacob Praetorius, Scheidt, and Scheidemann, who are known by only a few keyboard works: David Abel (Äbel? Ebel?, died 1639), organist at Wismar in 1617 and from 1619 on at Rostock; Paul Siefert (1586–1666) at Warsaw and Gdansk (Danzig); Peter Hasse the Elder (c.1585–1640) at Lübeck; Andreas Düben (c.1590–1662) at Stockholm; Melchior Schildt (c.1592–1667) at Hannover; and Gottfried Scheidt (1593–1661) at Altenburg. Except for Abel and Hasse, they are all known to have been students of Sweelinck's. Their works are preserved mostly in the Lynar tabulatures B 1 and B 3.

We know two short preludes by Abel (cf.p.356), and we may probably attribute to him a *Praeludium ex clave G Ab Org.*[37] and a *Currant Ab., Anno 1626* from the Copenhagen Ms.376.

The Uppsala Ms.408 preserves a *Paduana a Paul Sibern* (Siefert), which is modeled after the English pavanes—in three sections of irregular length (14.16.17), each with a lightly ornamented repetition—and is similar to them in content and feeling. The end of the last section is shown in Fig.370. In Lynar B 1 there is a

Fig.370

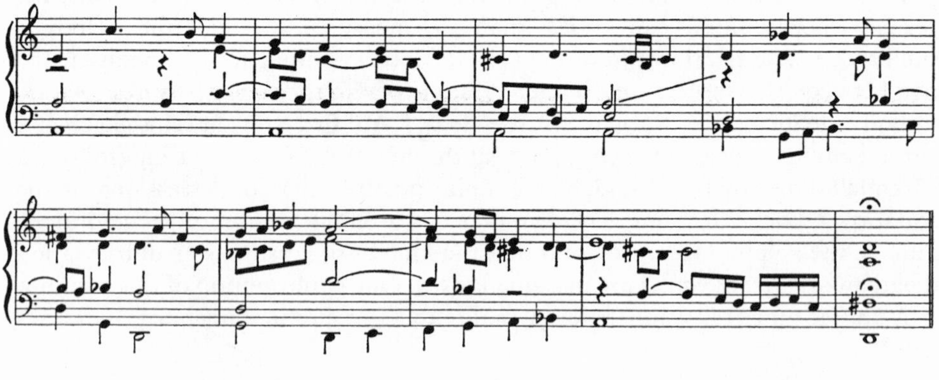

Puer natus in Bethlehem a Paulus Sivert,[38] consisting of a set of eight variations written in a much simpler and more unassuming manner than one would expect from a Sweelinck pupil. Finally, twelve anonymous fantasies in Ms.II.2.51 of the Leipzig Stadtbibliothek have been attributed to Siefert, because the first of them reappears as *Fantasia a 3 Paul Sivert* in Ms.XIV.714 of the Vienna Monastery of the Brothers Minor.[39] These pieces do not have much more in common with Sweelinck's fantasies than the name. The first one develops an eight-measure theme over 105 measures, then develops its diminution in a second section. Three other fantasies are monothematic (nos.5, 6, and 9), but unrelated to the large three-section form that is characteristic of Sweelinck. The remaining fantasies all treat three subjects in brief sections, often as inversion fugues, and may be modeled on Italian ricercars. All twelve have a three-part texture and a manner of writing that does not go beyond dry formulae and unimaginative repetitions. Siefert's memory is certainly not honored by ascribing these pieces to him, especially on the basis of a manuscript that is rather unreliable in indicating composers.[40]

Peter Hasse, the father of Nicolaus and grandfather of Peter Hasse the Younger, contributed two settings signed "P. Hassen" to the collection of organ chorales on *Allein Gott in der Höh sei Ehr* in the Ms. Lynar B 1 (cf.Chap.14, note 6), and a *Praeambulum pedaliter P. H.* (in Lynar B 3[41]). All three pieces are written in simple settings and in good taste. The prelude consists of a dignified solemn opening in a lovely harmonization, a fugal middle section on a descending subject, and a concluding section that is enlivened by motif work and ends with a confirming restatement of the subject.

Andreas Düben was the ancestor of a family that dominated the musical life of Sweden for more than a century. The widespread custom adopted in North German collections of indicating composers by their initials is particularly disturbing in studying Düben. The following is a list of the organ works attributed to him in recent literature, with their original inscriptions:[42]

1. *Allein Gott in der Höh;* var. V: *A. Düben;* var. VI; *A. D.; var.* VII: *M. Düben* (Lynar B 1)
2. *Wo Gott der Herr, Andrae Düben* (Lynar B 1)
3. *Erstanden ist der heilige Geist,* M. D. (Lynar B 1)
4. *Praeludium ex E vel A, A. D. O.* (Lynar B 3)
5. *Praeambulum pedaliter,* M. D. O. (Lynar B 3)
6. *Praeludium,* M. D. O. (Lynar B 3)

A. D. and *A. D. O.* are no doubt abbreviations for "Andreas Düben" and "Andreas Düben Organista." In *M. D.* the first letter may well mean "Magister," but it might conceivably stand for another given name, such as that of an otherwise unknown brother of Andreas. It is not my wish to inject a new assumption here, but only to throw some light on this matter.

Düben's variations on *Allein Gott in der Höh* are all in three parts. The second one (var.VI of the collection), in which each line of the chorale starts with an impressive fore-imitation, is especially beautiful. *Erstanden ist der heilige Geist* consists of a harmonization of the entire chorale and three variations; the first one, "Auff 2 Clavir," is especially remarkable. It is a simple chorale motet, in which the opening line is treated imitatively; the other three lines are played twice each, first in the soprano, then in the bass—an arrangement that Scheidemann used also. *Wo Gott der Herr,* on the other hand, is a grand chorale motet, comparable to those by Michael Praetorius or to the chorale fantasy on *Durch Adams Fall* by Jacob Praetorius. Note the original indications of registration: *forte* and *pian* at an echo passage (Fig.371a.) and *Rück Postiff* and *RP manu* at two ornamented presentations of the fourth line of the chorale, the first one in the soprano, the second in the bass (Fig.371b.) The manner in which Düben ornaments this chorale and accompanies it with chordal interjections recurs in later works of this species.[43]

Fig.371

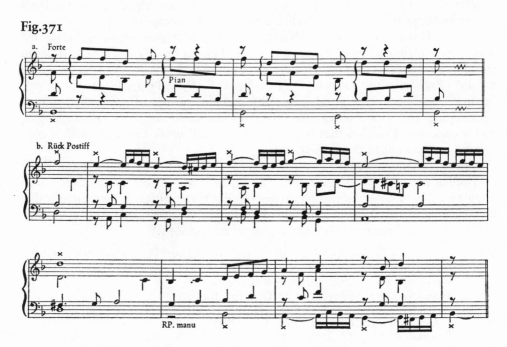

Düben's three preludes are quiet, solemn introductions to a liturgical service quite similar in style to those by Abel, i.e., with many *durezze e ligature* and without fugal sections. The first prelude (no.4 in the above list) carries the designation "ex E vel A" but is in *A* minor throughout. The third one (no.6), however, is entirely in *E* minor, the "mystic" key that Frescobaldi uses in his *Toccate per l'elevazione.* The end of this (until now unpublished) piece is given in Fig.372.

Fig.372

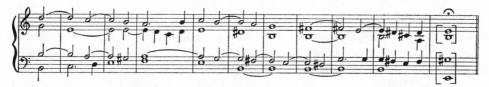

The manuscript Lüneburg KN 207 (book 15) preserves two unimportant preludes by Melchior Schildt, and KN 209 contains an arrangement of *Allein Gott in der Höh,* which fits well into the collection in the Lynar tablature.[44] The five variations on *Herr Christ der einig Gottes Sohn,* with their extensive use of figuration, copy Sweelinck's chorale variations more closely than do the works of any other German Sweelinck student, with the possible exception of Scheidt. This is even truer of Schildt's *Herzlich lieb hab ich dich,* in which the chorale tune is presented in the early-Baroque manner of a *cantus coloratus* e.g., at the beginning of the second line, as shown in Fig.373. But more modern ideas also occur, which reappear in later organ music, e.g., the passage in the same line shown in Fig.374 (R = Rückpositiv; O = Organ). The piece concludes with a lengthy coda (meas. 67–83), in which a very remarkable figure is heard in the passage work—a chromatic scale in sixteenth notes descending through one and one-half octaves— probably a unicum in the keyboard literature of the 17th century. The Zellerfeld Ms. Ze 2 contains an extended *Magnificat I modi* by Schildt, which has not been available to me.

Fig.373

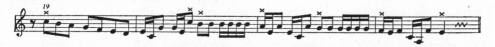

Two contributions, signed G. S., in the collection of variations on *Allein Gott in der Höh* in the Lynar tablature B 1 are generally, and certainly with justification, attributed to Samuel Scheidt's younger brother Gottfried. The first variation (no. 12) is a simply ornamented bicinium, the second (no.13) a tricinium of similar character.

Fig.374

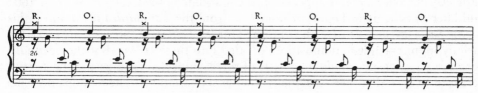

375

A more interesting piece is an arrangement by W. Karges, inscribed *Allein Gott a 3 vocum Choral in Bass*,[45] which is found in the same manuscript as a kind of appendix to the main collection. Most of the lines are heard in one of the upper parts before they are presented in the pedals, so that a very attractive interplay of changing colors results. (This W. Karges is definitely not the Wilhelm Karges who lived from 1613 to 1699, and was active at the court of Brandenburg.)

Johann Decker (1598–1668), D. Meyer, Marcus Olter, and Anton Neunhaber are each known by only one composition.[46]

Delphin Strunck

Delphin Strunck, born in 1601, probably the son of the organist Joachim Strunck, was active in Wolfenbüttel, Celle, and Brunswick, where he died in 1694. The manuscript Lüneburg KN 209 preserves his *Toccata ad manuale duplex, Magnificat noni toni: Meine Seele erhebet den Herrn, Ich hab mein Sach Gott heimgestellt auff 2 Clavier*, and three intabulations of motets—*Surrexit pastor bonus Orl. di Lasso, Tibi laus tibi gloria auff 2 Clavier*, and *Verbum caro factum est*. The Walther manuscript, Berlin Staatsbibl. 22541, contains his *Lass mich dein sein und bleiben*.[47]

The toccata is an enormous work—more than 310 measures. Except for two brief imitative sections it is filled at first with figurations, later on with echo effects on two manuals, and toward the end with figurations on "Rug.Pos." and "Org." plus "Pedel" (which seems to be needed throughout). In the early-Baroque manner, the figurations are very rigid and expressionless, but not necessarily pedantic or schematic. Within this formal framework Strunck invents many interesting and novel figures, some of which are shown in Fig.375 (R = Rückpositiv; O = Organ). Each figure is retained for a section of varying length and adapted to the sustained harmonies on which the whole piece is based. This method is very similar to that in the obras and tientos of contemporary Spaniards, such as Bruna and Jimenez, a similarity that (as elsewhere) certainly does not indicate a dependence or influence, but is rather explained as the "spirit of the period."

Strunck's *Magnificat* has the designation "noni toni." It uses the *tonus peregrinus*, which deviates from the other eight in the employment of two different recitation tones, *a* in the first half and *g* in the second. The resulting melody is (*a c′ a a a a a b♭ a g f ‖ a c′ g g g d f e d*). Curiously it is this melody that was generally employed (even by Bach) for the German translation of the Magnificat, *Meine Seele erhebet den Herrn*. It appears for the first time in the Celle tablature of 1601 and later in Scheidt's *Magnificat noni toni* from the *Tabulatura nova* and in his *Meine Seele erhebet den Herrn* from the *Görlitz Tablature*. Strunck arranges the melody in an extended composition, divided into three *versus*. But the *Secundus versus auf 2 clavier manualiter* consists of three connected settings and the *Tertius versus* of two, so that there is actually a set of six variations. The first one presents

376

Fig.375

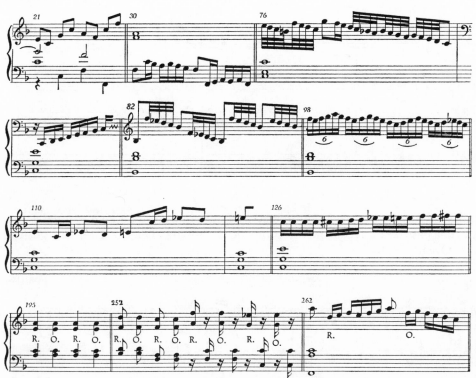

the melody as a *cantus planus* in whole notes, the first half in the discant, then the
whole melody as the tenor part in the pedals, combined with various quietly moving motifs in the other voices. Johann Gottfried Walther incorporated this variation as an independent composition in one of his collections (Ms. Berlin Staatsbibl.
22541).[48] The second variation is similar, but it presents the entire melody in the
discant. In the next three variations Strunck uses a more characteristic approach,
that of lively figuration. In the third variation most of the melody notes are embroidered with sixteenth-note and, occasionally, thirty-second-note passages; the
first note, *a*, e.g., appears as part of a quickly ascending scale figure—one of the
earliest examples of the "apostrophe" (cf.p.370), which plays an important role
in the subsequent evolution of North German organ music. Fig.376 shows the
beginning of this variation (it starts with the final measure of the preceding one).
The last variation shows the characteristic features of the chorale fantasy. The first
melody line is presented in eight measures, followed by a development of twenty
measures, which is filled with fragments that are repeated on various degrees of
the scale, each time followed by an echo. The treatment of the second line is freer

Fig.376

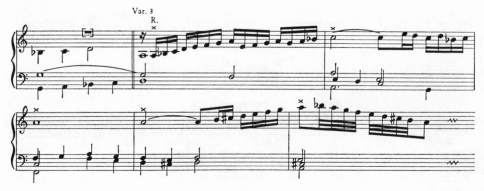

and the notes are no longer considered as a unit, but inspire a high-spirited game, e.g., in a passage derived from the *initium a–c'*, shown in Fig.377 (R = Rückpositiv; O = Organ).

Fig.377

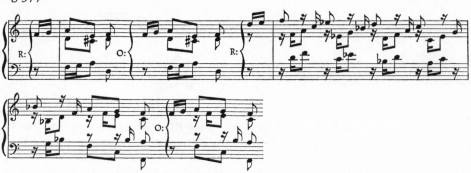

Strunck's setting of *Ich hab mein Sach Gott heimgestellt* consists of four variations, which are similar to those on the Magnificat. The final variation is again an extended fantasy, but less successful than the one in the *Magnificat*.

Strunck's treatment of *Lass mich dein sein und bleiben* is very different. This work is contained in a much later source, the Berlin Walther manuscript. With their expansiveness and formalistic show of technique, the *Magnificat, Meine Seele,* and *Ich hab mein Sach Gott* fit into the picture of North German organ music of the first half of the 17th century. *Lass mich dein sein und bleiben*, on the other hand, is a simple, lyrical, expressive chorale prelude, doubtless belonging to a later period, and representing a work of Delphin Strunck's old age. Or is Walther's ascription erroneous? Perhaps this piece, too, is only the beginning of a

378

longer composition that consists of several variations, and Walther took it out of its context. The melody is the same as Hassler's song *Mein Gmüt ist mir verwirret*, which was also used for the texts *Herzlich tut mich verlangen, Ach Herr mich armen Sünder*, and *O Haupt voll Blut und Wunden*.[49]

Morhardt, Bahr, Kniller, and Woltmann

Nine organ chorales in the manuscript Lüneburg KN 209 are signed P. M. or P. M. H. and are justifiably attributed to Peter Morhardt (Mohrhardt), who was an organist of the Michaeliskirche at Lüneburg from 1662 until his death in 1685. He shows a definite preference for a number of chorales that were hardly used by other composers, e.g., *Alle Welt was lebet und webet, Wacht auf ihr Christen alle, Was fürchst du Feind Herodes (Crudelis Herodes)*, and *Kyrie fons bonitatis*. He also set *Allein zu dir, Aus tiefer Not* (with the tune in the major mode (| *c′* | *b c′* | *d′ d′* | *c′ d′* | *e′* |)), *Gelobet seist du* (dated 1663), *Herr Gott dich loben wir* (*Te Deum*), and *Meine Seel erhebet den Herrn* (Magnificat).[50]

Fig.378

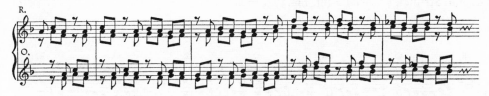

The genuine chorale variation is no longer represented. Several settings, e.g., *Alle Welt* and *Meine Seel*, treat the chorale twice, first in the usual manner with the melody in one or several voices and figurations or chords in the other parts, and then in the form of an extended fantasy with frequently repeated fragments and echoes. In *Meine Seel erhebet den Herrn*, the *Primus versus* comprises only nine measures, while the *Secundus* has more than eighty. Fig.378 shows a passage from the *Secundus versus* in which the first line of the tune (*a c′ a a a bb a g f*) is transformed into an enchanting sound effect. Further on in the piece there are sound effects such as the one shown in Fig.379. Unfortunately Morhardt does not know how to stay within reasonable limits, but fills page upon page with figurations that repeatedly follow the same recipe. In the settings that treat the tune only once,

Fig.379

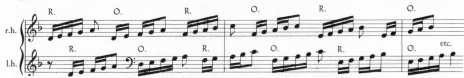

he applies various playful sound effects, mostly at the end of the figural or imitative presentation of a line.

Johan Bahr composed in the same style as Delphin Strunck and Morhardt. Bahr was the organist at St. Mary's at Visby from 1633 to 1670, and later the owner of the Petri tablature.[51] He entered four of his own works in this tablature, two for organ: a *Magnificat octavi toni in Basso* and an *O lux beata Trinitas* (dated 1655), and two vocal works with instrumental accompaniment.

The *Magnificat* consists of three verses; it offers nothing of particular interest, except perhaps the end of the third verse, where the *terminatio* of the eighth tone (*c′ c′ b c′ a g*) appears five times in succession as a transposing basso ostinato and the first two notes are replaced by *c′ g c g c′*. His *O lux beata* is, however, a noteworthy early example of the extended chorale fantasy replete with echoes and echo-like sound effects. The imitative presentation of the first line (*a gfgf d f f ga a g*) with an ornamented upper part is followed by a section in which this line is heard as a *cantus planus* in the pedals while the hands play figurations that alternate between Rückpositiv and Oberwerk (Fig.380; R = Rückpositiv; O = Organ). There is also a long passage with echo repetitions of individual chords, as in Delphin Strunck's *Toccata* (cf. Fig.375, meas.195).

Fig.380

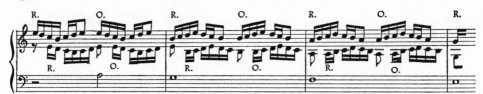

Two other organists are known by only one composition each (preserved in Lüneburg KN 209): A. (Anton?) Kniller (who must not be mistaken for the much later Andreas Kneller) and M. Woltmann. Woltmann's *Von Gott will ich nicht lassen* is a very insignificant, dry, pedantic piece. The first half is given over to innumerable, partly transposed repetitions of the first two lines of the chorale. The remaining lines are presented in echo chords. Kniller's *Herr Gott dich loben wir* (*Te Deum*) consists of four brief sections: *Praeambulum, Herr Gott dich loben wir, Du König der Ehren Jesus Christ*, and *Täglich Herr Gott*. It, too, is not much more than the modest work of a pupil, but the prelude, at least, is of some interest as an early example of the abrupt gestures that play a large role in Buxtehude's music. Fig.381 shows the beginning of this eight-measure piece.

The Anonymous Repertoire

The manuscript collections in which the works of Sweelinck, Praetorius, Scheidemann, Strunck, and Morhardt are preserved also contain many anonymous pieces.

Naturally they are of less interest than the works of composers who are named, but they must not be entirely neglected, particularly when they add something to the total picture. There are also some manuscripts whose contents are all anonymous.

Fig.381

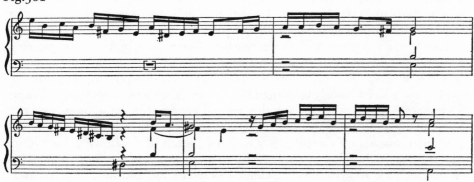

In addition to works by Hieronymus and Jacob Praetorius, and appendices by Johan Bahr, the Petri tablature of 1611 contains 19 Latin hymns, 8 Kyries (all consisting of *Kirie—Alio modo—Christe—Kirie ultimum*), 5 sequences with three to six verses, and a complete organ Mass (without Credo), which is certainly one of the last examples of this species in Germany. These pieces show solid workmanship without originality, and may possibly have been written by Petri.

A completely different world opens up in the manuscript Helmstadt 1055 of the Wolfenbüttel library. It contains only anonymous pieces: 4 preludes (one by Bull = *FW*, II, 274), 18 German chorales (some with *Alio modo*), and 20 dances. All the pieces are simply treated, carry extensive indications of ornaments and fingerings (at the beginning of the manuscript there are also some finger exercises), and were manifestly meant for use at the harpsichord or clavichord in the home. Among the dances there are a *Bergamasca, Sösskenn Tanz, Deutsche Fackell Tanz, Variegrad Tanz*, courantes, balletts, and an *Alman* (English for allemande). Fig.382 reproduces the *Variegrad Tanz*.

Fig.382

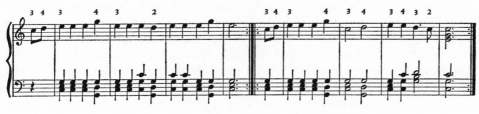

Copenhagen, Royal Library, Ms. 376 contains song and dance settings (cf. p.505) and several pieces for organ: 2 preludes, 2 brief intonations, 5 simple chorale settings (*Vom Himmel hoch, In dulci iubilo*, etc.), and 4 very similarly treated settings of psalm songs: *Der 3. Psalmen, Wie viel sindt* (with the additional remark "angefangen 1639 3. Januar"); *Der 5. Psalmen, O Herr Dein Ohren zu mir; Der 103. Psalmen, Nu preiss mein Seel*; and *Der 91. Psalmen, Wer in des Allerhöchsten Hut*. The tunes are taken from the Geneva Psalter. These pieces are noteworthy, for psalms rarely occur in German organ music.[52]

The Lynar manuscripts[53] are extensive. There are about eighty pieces in collection A 1; for most of them the authors are indicated or easily established from other sources. The most interesting anonymous composition is a suite inscribed at the end, obviously later than the rest, consisting of allemande, courante, and sarabande (cf.p.555). A 2 contains several anonymous intonations and canzonas that suggest an Italian origin (they are inscribed directly after T. Merula's *Capriccio cromatico*). Tablatures B 1 to B 10 contain the following anonymous works: 14 organ chorales (excluding the variations on *Allein Gott in der Höh*, some of which are anonymous), 7 psalms, 19 preludes, 5 fantasies, 2 fugues, and 2 ricercars.[54] One very unusual prelude from B 9 is written in five-part chords throughout, and clearly demands the pedals for the bass; its beginning is given in Fig.383. Four psalm settings in Lynar B 7 treat the tunes from the Geneva Psalter in short variation sets, like Protestant chorales, e.g., *Ps. 5, 2 Vari. in Basso, 3. V. im Tenor*. The manuscript B 11 (also designated as C 1) contains the melodies to all 150 psalms in the simplest of harmonizations, probably transcribed from vocal settings in "hymn" style.

Fig.383

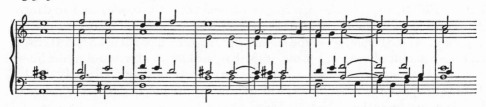

The famous Lüneburg tablatures, which have been known for a long time, contain works by Scheidemann, Jacob Praetorius, Schildt, Weckmann, Tunder, and others, as well as much anonymous material, which was probably written during the period 1630–60.[55] A substantial part of this material is now available in two new editions[56] that contain all the preludes, fugues, canzonas, and toccatas from these manuscripts that Seiffert did not publish. These prints contain many good works, but nothing unusual. A number of preludes in KN 207 (Shannon, nos.17–20) combine extreme brevity—each piece is about ten measures long—

with a surprising vivacity of content. They are surely the work of one composer. It would be nice to know who he was.[57] The prelude in "C b-moll" exhibits such a "modern" C minor that one can transcribe it with the key signature used today (Fig.384).

Fig.384

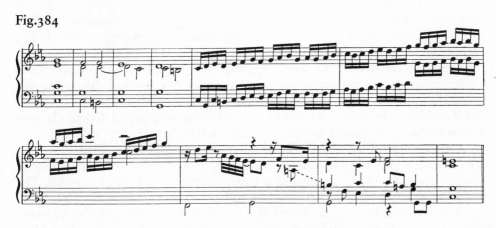

Among the hitherto unpublished works of the Lüneburg tablatures, the anonymous chorale settings, which are especially frequent in KN 208[2] and KN 209, are probably the most noteworthy.[58] Analyzing them in more detail and finding possible ascriptions to well-known masters would be an important and satisfying task. The valuable material still left to be discovered is exemplified by the beginning of a *Herr Jesu Christ du höchstes Gut* (KN 209, no.28) reproduced in Fig.385.

Fig.385

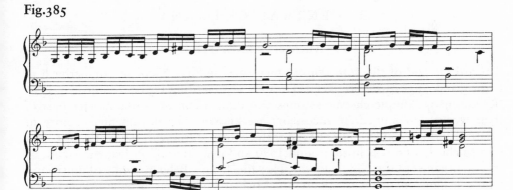

Lüneburg KN 146, written by Joachim Drallius in 1650, is a collection of 240 pieces—simple chorale settings, songs, some preludes, and many dances, especially courantes. Some of the titles are *Türkische Intrada* (no.21), *Juden Tantz* (no.

63), and *Barro Frostart Treme* (no.231), i.e., *Barafostus' Dreame* from the *Fitzwilliam Virginal Book* (no.18). KN 148 is a smaller collection of a similar nature, which was written in 1655–59 by Franciscus Witzendorff of Lüneburg. It contains the same *Türkische Intrada* (no.85), a *Ros Ballet* ("Horse Ballet," no.65), and a group of sixteen *Auftzug* (no.66), the first of which is called *Auftzug der Behren Tantz* ("Bear Dance"). Several pieces from KN 149 are of special interest: *Praelude di C. S.* (cf. note 57, above), several *Taniec* (nos.18, 25, 34) (probably Polish dances), and two *Trezza* (nos.10, 35).

A recently discovered "Celler Klavierbuch von 1662"[59] contains a repertoire of anonymous dances and songs similar to those in KN 146 and 148; 15 dances by Scheidemann; 11 "Tantz und Nach Tantz" and 2 song variation sets by Wolfgang Wessnitzer (1629–97), a Schiedemann student; and, most importantly, two hitherto unknown variation works by Sweelinck (cf.Chap.14, note 1).

A manuscript of the Leipzig Stadtbibliothek (Ms. II, 6. 16), which may have been assembled around 1650 or somewhat later, may be called the *Clavierbuch of Elisabeth Angelina Eygers* because of a poem that appears at the beginning. The manuscript starts with a collection of free pieces in the order of keys (D, G, A, etc.), in which each key is represented by a group such as: *Principal, Fuga, Perambulum, Fuga, Subvenia, Principal.* This is followed by a collection of spiritual songs, e.g., *Lytgen (Liedchen) Dulce coelum dulce nomen*, some with an additional "Phargazion" (variation). This collection, obviously made by a good, diligent, middle-class girl, is without any artistic or music-historical significance, but it has a certain cultural-historical value as a document of the provincial dilettante musician. The chorales and even the preludes and fugues exhibit unmistakable signs of Baroque family songs.

B. CENTRAL GERMANY

Michael and Klemm

Toward the end of the 16th century men such as Elias Nicolaus Ammerbach at Leipzig and Augustus Nörmiger at Dresden were writing keyboard music in Central Germany. Simple chorale settings and dances constitute the greater part of their works. No immediate successors are known. The documented history of Central German clavier music of the 17th century starts with the works of Christian Michael, who was born around 1590 and died in 1637 in Leipzig, where he was an organist of the Nikolaikirche. He came from a Belgian family of musicians, whose original name was apparently Michel. His father, Rogier Michel, was Heinrich Schütz's predecessor at the Dresden court chapel and the teacher of Johann Herman Schein.

Christian Michael's keyboard works are preserved in a beautifully engraved tablature print, which appeared posthumously in 1645: *Tabulatura darinnen etzliche Praeludia, Toccaten und Curanten uff das Clavir Instrument gesetzt.* It contains 18 preludes—9 each in three and four parts, 6 toccatas, and 10 courantes.[60] As in other works of that time, such as Steigleder's ricercars of 1624, a modern consciousness of tonality is indicated by the fact that the pieces are no longer designated by church modes but by keys, e.g., *Praeludium à 3 D* or *Toccata à 4 E.*

The preludes are brief pieces of about ten to twenty measures, most of them set imitatively and employing one or two well-conceived subjects, so that they may well be called fughettas. Several show the mixture of homophonic and contrapuntal elements that is typical of the prelude. A few are somewhat dry and pedantic, but many others are successful and impressive examples of a miniature art that is characteristic of, and acted as a standard for, the later evolution of Central German clavier music.

Fig.386

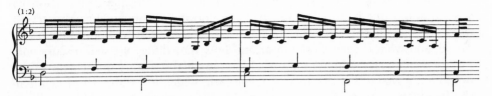

The toccatas, of course, show the Italian influence, but tend to be briefer and more moderate than their models. Occasional imitative sections are based on canzona-like motifs. In the toccata-like passages Venetian scale figures predominate, but arpeggios occur occasionally, e.g., in the passage from the *Toccata à 3 F* given in Fig.386. Its harmonic and melodic features also sound remarkably modern. Christian Michael is also familiar with the *durezze* toccata of the Frescobaldi type, and he expects his audience to know it. In his foreword he says: "I do not doubt that the manner of foreign intervals and durezze . . . is widely known, so that I do not have to make excuses for it in my little work." How well he has studied his model is shown by Fig.387, the end of the *Toccata à 4 A durez.*

Fig.387

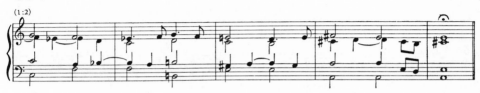

Ten courantes "à 3" (the last one is actually in two parts) conclude the collection, and prove that this dance, which was in such wide favor at the beginning of the 17th century, was also known in Saxony. Michael's courantes are simple pieces, set with dexterity. They often employ a head motif, e.g., (a | a e ag | f [or g] | f# d g | a), which then recurs in other voices.

A contemporary of Christian Michael's, Johann Klemm (or Klemme), was born about 1593 at Öderan (near Zwickau) and died after 1651, probably at Dresden, where he had served as court organist since 1625. He was also active as a publisher, and brought out Schütz's *Symphoniarum sacrarum secunda pars* (1647) and *Geistliche Chormusik* (1648), among others. In 1631 he published *Partitura seu tabulatura italica exhibens triginta sex fugas, 2, 3, 4 vocibus*, a collection of thirty-six fugues ordered according to church modes, twelve each in two, three, and four voices. Each composition is based on one subject—occasionally a double subject—which is developed in a clean contrapuntal style without subsections. These pieces come quite close to what was later called a fugue.

The real significance of this collection lies in its usefulness in studying the early evolution of this species, which received its final Baroque formulation by J. S. Bach about one hundred years later. The print presents extensive materials that permit one to see what the first and last stages of this evolution have in common, and what is even more important, how they differ. We will discuss only one of the many features that might be cited, the tonal structure of the exposition. How close are we here to the answer at the fifth, which is a standard principle in Bach? In Klemm's pieces the older principle of imitation at the fourth predominates. The subject is repeated on the fifth step in the expositions of only five fugues: in the two-part fugues nos.1, 5, and 10; the three-part fugue no.15; and the four-part fugue no.36. But neither the three-part nor the four-part work shows the alternation of tonic and dominant, I V I V, which is typical of the classical fugue. No.15 has the scheme I V V, and no.36 uses I V I I. The three-part fugues mostly have the tonal sequence I IV I, but sometimes I I IV (no.16), I IV IV (no.19), or I I I (no.24). The four-part fugues have schemes such as I IV IV I (nos.25, 26), I IV IV IV (no.28), and I IV I I (no.32). Seven of the four-part fugues are based on double subjects (nos.27, 29, 30, 31, 33, 34, 35), and the expositions are devised so that one of the voices (usually the third one) enters with the second part of the subject. The beginning of fugue no.29, reproduced in Fig.388, is an example of this unusual procedure.

Fig.388

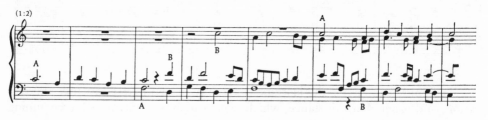

Kindermann and Schedlich

The southern-most musical center of the Central German Protestant area in the 17th century was Nuremberg. Johann Erasmus Kindermann lived there from his birth in 1616 to his death in 1655. Active as the second organist at the Frauen-kirche from 1636 to 1640, and then as an organist at St. Egidien, he published many vocal and instrumental works (*Deliciae studiosorum*) as well as a collection of organ pieces, the *Harmonia organica* of 1645. In addition, a number of dances are preserved in manuscript.[61]

The *Harmonia organica* begins with a group of fourteen short *Praeambula*. The first six cover all the church modes, since each of them serves both the authentic and the plagal mode, e.g., no.1: *1. et 2. toni*, no.2: *3. et 4. toni*, etc. The next six preludes repeat this series in the transposition down a fifth, i.e., with the *finales* G, A, B♭, c, d, and f. Finally there are two additional preludes in the transposition to the second above, one from C major (*11. et 12. toni*) to D major, and one from G major (*7. et 8. toni*) to A major. Unlike Christian Michael, Kindermann still holds on to the Church modes, but at least he drops the differentiation between authentic and plagal modes, which had become pure fiction as early as the 16th century.

The preambles comprise about fifteen to twenty measures each. They are simple and unassuming, and are attractive for this very reason. Even today they are quite usable as brief preludes to a liturgical action. The element of imitation, which plays quite an important role in Michael's preludes, is completely absent from Kindermann's. Each prelude starts, as becomes such a piece, with a full entrance of all voices and then unfolds in a contrapuntal texture with chordal and decorative inserts. Fig.389 shows the beginning of the *Praeambulum 5. et 6. toni* (no.3), in which the Lydian *b* is retained almost everywhere, at first as the augmented fourth above *F* and later as the leading tone to *C*, thereby conforming to modal concepts in appearance, at least.

Fig.389

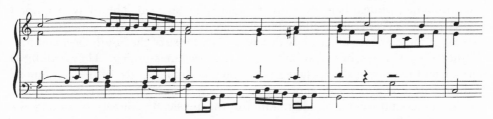

The fourteen preludes are followed by a number of pieces that are called *Fuga*. Some of them—like those by Klemm—are genuine fugues, limited to the terse presentation of an individually conceived subject (nos.18, 19, and 20). Others are based on chorales, and mostly employ the first two lines. In no.25 (*Was mein*

Gott will), e.g., line 2 appears as the answer to line 1, while in no.24 (*Herr Jesu Christ*) line 2 is used for interludes (in meas.25–28 and 34–36). No.21 is an early example of the simple chorale fugue, which limits itself to the first line—a formulation as characteristic of the Central German tradition as the large chorale motet and chorale fantasy are of the North German. In a *Drifache Fuge* (no.16) the first lines of three chorales—*Christ lag in Todesbanden, Christus der uns selig macht,* and *Da Jesu an dem Creuze stundt*—are combined in a simple, stirring setting. Fig.390 shows a passage in which the three tunes occur in close succession.

Fig.390

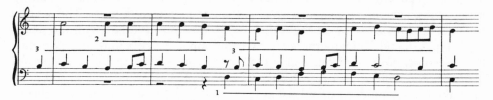

Kindermann's *Harmonia organica* concludes with a *Magnificat octavi toni I.–VI. versus.* The first verse begins with a full-sounding prelude of fourteen measures, followed by an imitative treatment of the two halves of the eighth Magnificat tone. Verse 2 has the "Choral im Discant"; verse 5 is in the bass. The remaining three sections are worked out freely, verse 3 as a fugue, verse 4 as an echo (one of the most charming examples of this type), and verse 6 as a full-sounding postlude.

A manuscript of the Berlin Staatsbibliothek (Mus. ms. 40147), which is now lost, contained 30 dances signed J. E. K. They have been attributed, probably correctly, to Johannes Erasmus Kindermann, and have been incorporated in the new edition. As far as can be established, the dances are individually designated as courante, ballett, etc., but in part occur in tonally unified groups that may be regarded as suites. Two suites (nos.III and IV of the *DTB* volume) consist of allemande, courante, and sarabande; two others (nos.II and VII) of ballett, courante, and sarabande; while others are more irregularly constituted. They may be modest counterparts to Froberger's suites, which were written about the same time. The content of these dances is certainly different from those of the South German master, not only shorter but also simpler and more unassuming. They exhibit a normal, so to speak healthy, clavier technique, without a trace of the cunning or of the intellectual and aural refinement of Froberger's music. Froberger writes for an elite of connoisseurs, Kindermann for the musically interested among the burgher class. But he does so with charm and taste.

David Schedlich (1607–87) was also active in Nuremberg. Born nine years before Kindermann, he outlived him by more than thirty years. He was an organist at various Nuremberg churches, but no organ compositions of his are preserved. A manuscript of the Vienna Nationalbibliothek (Cod. 18491), known as the

Clavierbuch of Regina Clara im Hoff, and dated 1629, contains a *Couranta Da. Sch.*, an *Aufttzug D. S.*, and a *Ballet a David Schedlich*, attractive little pieces similar to Kindermann's dances,[62] plus several anonymous dances. Three additional pieces signed D. S. were a part of the lost Berlin manuscript mentioned above, and are lost together with it.

C. SOUTH GERMANY

The term South Germany usually covers the large area north of and within the northern Alps: Switzerland, southern Germany, and Austria. This area was the scene of an important evolution in organ music in the period 1450–1520. It produced Paumann and the *Buxheim Organ Book* in Munich, Schlick in Heidelberg, Hofhaimer in Augsburg and Salzburg, Kleber in Göppingen, and Buchner and Kotter in Switzlerland. Then the line breaks, and reemerges only toward the end of the century. As in the central German area, it is Belgian musicians who appear first: Samuel Mareschal in Basle, Simon Lohet in Stuttgart, and Charles Luython in Vienna and Prague. Lohet's and Mareschal's works (cf.pp.203f., 220) still belong to the 16th-century tradition, but Luython's music definitely points toward the future.

Luython and Adam Steigleder

Charles Luython, born in Antwerp about 1557/58, was a choir boy in Vienna from 1566 to 1571, became chamber musician to Emperor Maximilian II in 1576, and in 1582 became court organist to Emperor Rudolf II in Prague, where he died in 1620. Luython published printed books of madrigals (1582), motets (1603), lamentations (1604), and Masses (1609). His preserved organ works include three fantasies, a ricercar, and a canzona in Codex XIV.714 (formerly Mus. ms. 8) at the Vienna monastery of the Brothers Minor, a *Fuga suavissima* in Woltz's *Nova Tabulatura* of 1617, and two ricercars in Berlin Staatsbibl. Ms. 40316.[63] In his *Syntagma musicum* II (1619), Praetorius describes an arcicembalo with special keys for sharps and flats that belonged to Luython.

The pieces from the Vienna codex (new ed. nos. 1–5) offer nothing remarkable. They are brief works, in which two or three subjects are treated imitatively in succession in a quiet Italianate counterpoint, without figurations. Parts of nos.1 and 4 are in five voices.

The other three compositions belong to another type because of their considerable length—233, 272, and 218 whole-note measures, respectively—and because they are much livelier. Diminution of the subjects by two and four, augmentation of the main theme, countermotifs, and moderate figurations fill the expansive framework with a rich, varied content. A schematic presentation follows (short motifs appear in lower-case letters):

389

No. 6: *Fuga suavissima* A/B || A‡, A‡, A || C || D/e, e‡, D‡
  ⁸⁶ above, ¹⁰⁶ ^{152–233}

No. 7: Ricercar   A/B || C, B, A || B‡, C‡, A‡ || B, A^2
  ⁸⁴ ¹⁰³ ^{245–272}

No. 8: Ricercar   A || A‡, A || A‡ || free, b || A, A‡, A^{1‡}, c || A^2
  ⁶⁴ ⁹¹ ¹⁰⁸ ¹²⁷ ^{173–218}

No. 8 is based on one subject, the ascending chromatic tetrachord, which is also used in inversion; the other two pieces are polythematic. The name *Fuga suavissima* for no.6 is not at all unjustified. This composition is full of variety and good sound effects, although the third section (subject C) is a bit too long. Passages like the one in Fig.391, which have successive modulations to the upper fifth, while still partly beholden to the modal concept, are the first forays into a hitherto uncharted territory.

Fig.391

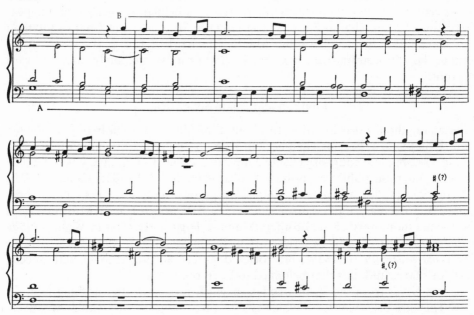

Around the same time Adam Steigleder (1561–1633), a student of Lohet's, was active in southwest Germany, as the organist at Ulm. Unfortunately we know only two pieces by him. One is a *Passa è mezo* recently discovered in Munich Staatsbibl. Mus. ms. 4480.[64] It is a passamezzo antico with two variations, followed by a third one in the form of a *Galliarda*. The other piece is a *Toccata primi toni*, which Woltz incorporated in his tablature.[65] The toccata starts with an imitation of an impressive subject, possibly taken from the hymn *Veni redemptor gentium*

(| / d | a b♭ | a g | − f | e |). This is followed by a toccata-like section in modal harmonies and expressive eighth-note lines that conclude the composition in the same serious manner as it began. The end of this work is given in Fig.392. A third work, a *Fuga colorata*, which Woltz ascribes to Adam Steigleder, reappears in the Turin tablature Foà 3 as a canzona by Giovanni Gabrieli. Judging by the style, Gabrieli may be the author (cf.p.410).

Fig.392

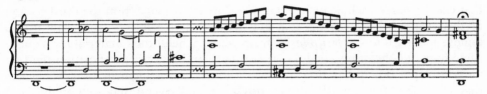

Hassler

Hans Leo Hassler, the son of the organist Isaac Hassler, was born in Nuremberg in 1564. He was one of the first Germans to go to Venice, where he studied with Andrea Gabrieli in 1584. On his return to Germany in 1585 he became an organist for the Fugger family at Augsburg. In 1601 he went to Nuremberg, in 1604 to Ulm, and in 1608 to Dresden, where he died in 1612, after a lengthy illness. Together with his brothers, Kaspar and Jacob, he was much involved in monetary affairs on behalf of the Fuggers and Emperor Rudolf II. In addition to his work as a composer, he was interested in the construction of mechanical musical instruments.

For a long time Hassler has been known chiefly as a composer of vocal music —madrigals, German songs, motets, Masses, and psalms—and in comparison his organ compositions seemed to play only a modest role. A collection of 16 organ pieces published in *DTB*[66] was all that was known until the recent discovery of numerous organ works in the Turin tablatures. At present we know more than 110 keyboard works by Hassler, among them 24 ricercars, 29 canzonas, 12 fugues, 16 toccatas, 7 introits, 14 Magnificats, an organ Mass, 5 intradas, and various other pieces. This list does not include the German chorales published by Woltz in his *Nova . . . tabulatura* of 1617, all of which are probably intabulations of vocal settings. These works, in the German-Venetian style, are just as impressive as Hassler's vocal compositions. The discussion that follows is based first of all on the published works, and some of the unpublished compositions are adduced to complete the picture.

Most of Hassler's ricercars are very long—some are more than 150 double measures—and treat several subjects in several sections. Three of them are outlined schematically here:

No. 2: A || B/C || A, B, C || (3)* D || toccata ending

No. 5: A || A/B || C || C♯ || D

No. 6: A || B || C

Despite their great length, these works are lively and captivating. The subjects are much more individual and vivacious than the usual ricercar themes and these qualities inform the entire work. The main subject of no.2 has an energetic curve that encompasses a whole octave. Fig.393 shows a passage from the third section of this ricercar. For ricercar no.8 Hassler uses two subjects from Palestrina's famous madrigal *Io son ferito lasso,* from which Scheidt took material for a quadruple fugue (*Tabulature nova* no. 2; cf.p.357). In Hassler's composition the two ideas also appear in diminution and in various degrees of augmentation. The pieces that are called "fuga" or "fantasia" (nos.9, 10, and several that are unpublished) are, at least in part, extended ricercars that were copied under different titles.

Fig.393

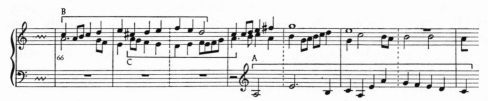

The two canzonas printed in *DTB* (pp.94ff.) do not give a reliable idea of Hassler's output in this field, since in their only source, Padua Univ. Libr. 1982, they are attributed to Christian Erbach.[67] On the other hand, the canzona that appears in the appendix (p.155) is ascribed to Hassler in both the Padua manuscript and the Turin tablatures (Foà 3, fol.33v). It consists of two sections (the first one repeated), each with its own subject. A few subjects from the unpublished canzonas are given in Fig.394. They show Hassler's inclination to energetic lines, which often span an octave, like the subject from ricercar no.2 given in Fig.393.

Fig.394

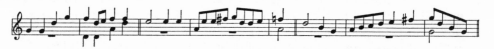

Hassler's toccatas usually begin with a few measures of sustained chords, a solemn opening that is missing in the toccata included in *DTB* (no.16, p.119). Fig.

---

*The fourth section of no.2 is in triple meter

Fig.395

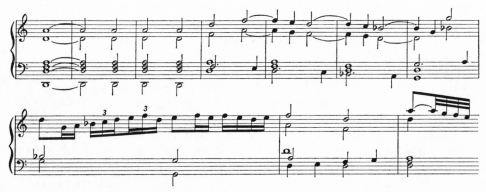

395 gives a typical example, the beginning of the *Toccata del primo tono* in the Padua manuscript. This is followed by a long section in the toccata style of Andrea Gabrieli, a fugue, and a toccata-like postlude. The introits are very similar in form, at times even longer. There are three very beautiful examples in *DTB* (nos.13–15). The chordal passage on p.109, brace 3, is obviously inspired by the double-choir technique of the Venetian style. In both the toccatas and the introits the fugal middle sections are not usually built around sustained ricercar subjects, but use lively themes in quarter and eighth notes.

Hassler's liturgical compositions have remained almost unknown. An organ Mass preserved in the Turin tablatures (Giordano 5, fol.114ff.) includes settings for the Kyrie, Gloria, Sanctus, and Agnus, plus a *Vers Ach Gott vom Himmel sieh darein* inserted after *Cum Sancto Spiritu*. In Giordano 3 and 5 and in Munich, Bayer. Staatsbibl. Ms. 1581, 14 Magnificats by Hassler are preserved, each consisting of six verses. Several intradas (in Foà 7) and a *Sonata, prima parte* (Foà 8) are probably instrumental ensemble works.*

Erbach

Christian Erbach was born in 1573, probably at Algesheim near Mainz, where his family can be traced back to 1543. Around 1596 he became the organist for Count Max Fugger at Augsburg, where he stayed for the rest of his life. In 1602 he was named the organist at St. Moritz at Augsburg as well as the city organist, a position that had been vacated by Hassler's departure. From 1625 until his death in 1635 he officiated as an organist at the Augsburg cathedral. He was also active as a teacher and was widely recognized.

In addition to many vocal compositions, which were printed between 1596 and 1630, Erbach wrote organ works that are preserved in manuscript. About 20

---

* Two organ pieces by Hassler's brother Jacob (1569–1622) are published in *DTB* IV. 2.

compositions are available in new editions, mostly in *DTB*.[68] As in Hassler's case, the new editions represent only a fraction of Erbach's preserved works. Recent research has uncovered more than 150 organ compositions, an output even larger than Hassler's. It consists of 35 ricercars, 10 fugues, 38 canzonas, 43 toccatas, 11 introits, 9 Magnificats, 5 Kyries, and several other liturgical pieces.[69]

The ricercars vary considerably in length—from 45 whole-note measures to more than 400 (e.g., no.2 in *DTB*). Most of them are based on two subjects, but several are monothematic, and there are some that treat three or four subjects. All the ricercars tend to have a unified form, i.e., without the subdivision into sections with different subjects or different treatment that is characteristic of Andrea Gabrieli and his immediate successors. When several subjects are used, all of them normally enter at the beginning—often in the form of a double theme—and in the course of the piece they combine in various ways, as, e.g., in ricercar no.1 in *DTB*. Erbach employs the artifices of inversion, augmentation, and diminution in only two or three ricercars, which differ greatly from the majority. He usually concludes the compositions with a few measures in toccata style.

Fig.396

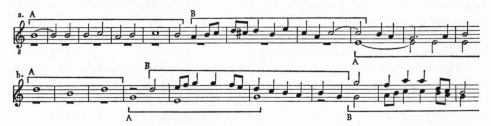

a. Berlin Staatsbibl. Ms. 40316 (formerly no.191), fol.47v; b. Autograph (cf. note 69), fol.18v.

In the ricercars with two subjects Erbach strives to invent contrasting themes; he associates a quiet main idea with a livelier, more playful second subject. In most cases the two subjects enter as the first and second halves of a double theme, as in the two examples given in Fig.396. The total impression is actually determined not so much by the sustained main subject as by the vivacious second one, so that Erbach's ricercars are often playful and gay, rather like canzonas. A good example is the *Ricercar del primo tono* of the autograph. A subject that is itself interesting and individual is joined by a motif that sounds like a teasing bird call (Fig.397). The subject of *Ricercar del nono tono* in the Turin tablature Giordano

Fig.397

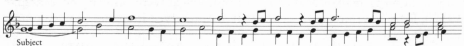

Subject

394

Fig.398

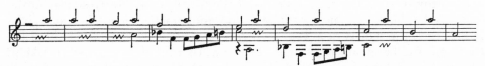

6, fol.123v., shown in Fig.398, has a bold, instrumental character. Its ever-widening skips sound like a premonition of a famous Bach theme; indeed it even surpasses the latter in "weight." A brief, lively motif is inserted here and there in the skips—almost like adding a dwarf to a giant. The treatment is as unusual as the subject. Contrary to his usual manner, Erbach divides this ricercar into two sections. The second one starts with an interesting stretto, followed by four presentations of the subject in augmentation, which seems to double its weightiness. At the end the note values are cut in eight, and the diminution transforms the subject into a clavieristic figure. This ricercar is reminiscent of several of Sweelinck's fantasies. Fig.399 shows the stretto and the diminution.

Fig.399

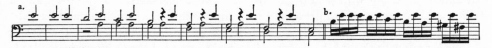

Some of the compositions called *Fuga* resemble the ricercar, while others, because of their brevity and the conciseness of their subjects, approach the genuine fugue.

Several of Erbach's genuine canzonas (some are named canzona incorrectly, e.g., the ricercar in *DTB*, p.5, which is entitled *Canzon cromattica* in the Berlin manuscript) are similar to the ensemble canzonas of the period. The Turin tablatures, particularly, contain several pieces that may be classified with some assurance as ensemble canzonas to which toccata-like figurations were added to adapt them for the keyboard.

Erbach's toccatas generally follow the Venetian tradition. Some of them are written in toccata style throughout, like the older models; others include a fugal middle section, e.g., the one printed in *DTB* (p.46). The material of the toccata-like sections mainly consists of the usual scale passages and trills, above or below sustained chords. Occasionally one finds more modern devices—complementary

Fig.400

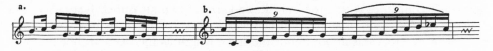

a. Padua, Univ. Bibl. 1982, fol.89; b. Berlin, Staatsbibl. Ms. 40316, fol.54v.

395

figures, dotted rhythms, or continuous arpeggios. Fig.400 shows two particularly noteworthy figures. The fugal sections of the toccatas are mostly similar to the ricercars, but here, too, one occasionally finds more modern ideas. The one given in Fig.401 is the subject of a *Toccata octavi toni*, which is preserved in both the Padua and the Turin tablatures (it is the same work from which Fig.400a. is taken). This toccata and some of the twelve toccatas in the Turin tablatures Giordano 1, 2, and 5 are probably later, more mature works.

Fig.401

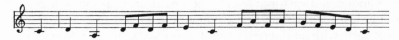

The pieces called *Introit*, two of which are reproduced in *DTB*, are related to the toccatas. They consist of a toccata-like prelude and a shorter, imitative *Versus*. Were they intended to be liturgical, to be played as introductions to the Mass, instead of introits with verse?

Erbach's ricercars, canzonas, and toccatas appear in various manuscripts, but almost all of his liturgical organ works—Magnificats, Kyries, a Gloria, and a *Jesu nostra redemptio*—are preserved in a single source, Munich Staatsbibl. Ms. 1581. The Magnificats generally consist of six verses (one has seven), the Kyries of four (one has five), and the Gloria of seven. Some of this repertoire is available in *DTB*, pp. 49ff., though it is arbitrarily selected and in no particular order.

From these remarks it should be apparent that the compositions printed in *DTB* do not convey an accurate idea of Erbach's works for the organ. We shall have to wait for the complete edition (cf. note 69) to get a true and more vivid picture.

Von der Hofen and Holtzner

Carl (Carolus) von der Hofen was another Belgian organist who was active in South Germany. He is said to have been born around 1589, possibly the son of the Antwerp lutenist and composer Joachim van der Hove (born c. 1570). He was a court organist at Salzburg and still occupied this office in 1647. The manuscript Munich Staatsbibl. Mus. Ms. 1581 preserves the following works by Von der Hofen: a ricercar (no.54), two toccatas (nos.55 and 57), and possibly another ricercar (no.56), which is placed between the toccatas.

The first ricercar is a monothematic piece of about forty measures, in which a quite forward-looking subject is presented within a strikingly archaic, modal texture. It concludes with a toccata-like cadenza of two measures. Just before the cadenza the copyist apparently omitted several measures of the manuscript by mistake. The two toccatas are of about the same length as the ricercar, but toccata-like throughout, without imitation or sectional subdivisions. E. Valentin says that both toccatas "seem to be incomplete and only sketches of expositions";[70] this assertion is erroneous, and is probably caused by the author's unfamiliarity with the usual practice in German tablatures of the 17th century of continuing each brace across both pages of the open volume. Both toccatas are essentially complete, but include occasional obvious errors; in the second toccata however, as in the ricercar, it seems that measures are omitted at two places. It is regrettable that these pieces have been handed down in such a poor fashion, for they are valuable and interesting works. As in the ricercar, modern and archaic features are combined in the toccatas, and this ambivalence creates a peculiar tension, a certain depth and warmth of expression, that is reminiscent of another Belgian master, Pieter Cornet. Fig.402 shows the beginning of the *Toccata primi toni.*

Fig.402

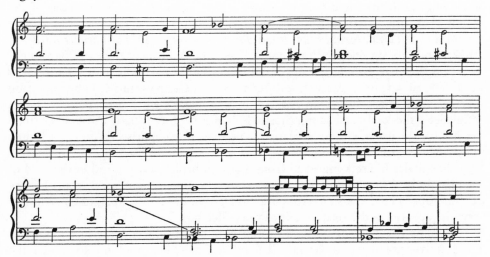

The same manuscript also contains a *Toccata primi toni C. V.* (no.141). L. Schrade interprets the initials to mean Carl Vanderhofen.[71] The attribution is not impossible, but this toccata is much more conventional in its harmony and figuration than nos.55 and 57. It closely follows the style of the Italian intonations and toccatas, as found, e.g., in Andrea Gabrieli's music. Four more ricercars, signed C. V. D. H. (obviously Carl von der Hofen), have been discovered in the Turin tablature Giordano 8.[72]

All that is known about Anton Holtzner is that he was active in Munich and that he died in 1635. The same Munich Mus. Ms. 1581 preserves three of his canzonas, which can be included in keyboard literature only with reservations, for several details indicate that they represent instrumental ensemble music. The one printed in Ritter B, p.112, is a rather long variation canzona, in which the last appearance of the subject exhibits the typical "violistic" manner. This canzona is also preserved in Berlin Staatsbibl. Ms.40615, along with two shorter canzonas. One is a variation canzona in three sections; the other shows neither thematic development nor subdivisions.

Johann Ulrich Steigleder

Hassler and Erbach are still at the transition between the periods, but Ulrich Steigleder is the first South German organ master of the Baroque, comparable to his contemporaries in the North, Scheidt and Scheidemann. He was born in 1593 at Hall in Swabia, the son of Adam Steigleder. In 1613 he became the organist of the Stephanskirche in Lindau, but left in 1617 to assume the position of organist at the abbey in Stuttgart. From 1627 on he served as an organist at the court of Württemberg in the same city. He died in 1635 at an early age, a victim of the plague. His organ works are preserved in two prints, a *Ricercar Tabulatura* (1624) and a *Tabulaturbuch darinnen das Vatter unser 40 mal variiert wird . . .* (1627). Both are significant monuments of the organ music of the early Baroque.[73]

The *Ricercar Tabulatura* appeared in the same year as Scheidt's *Tabulatura nova*. The two prints represent new departures in German music. Letter notation is replaced by musical notes in both of them; Scheidt's work uses the open score, Steigleder's the keyboard score. Steigleder's print, moreover, is the first German example of the use of engraved plates; to be sure, in comparison with early Italian plates (Merulo or Frescobaldi prints) they are very clumsy. According to the title page, Steigleder himself engraved them. He also broke new ground in the field of tonality by replacing the modal designations (*primi, secundi, . . . , toni*) by key designations. The first six ricercars are "in D, in E, in F, in G, in A, in C," and this series is repeated in the second half of the collection.

Perhaps the most remarkable thing about this collection is its attempt to avoid conventional methods and all fixed schemes, i.e., not only to render the various pieces in a new manner but also to make them individually different. This tendency is suggested by the fact that only the first four ricercars are written in the traditional four-part texture, the rest are in three parts. The individual compositions have very different lengths: Nos.1, 2, 3, and 11 are each about 230 measures long, while the others vary from 70 to 160 measures. Nor does Steigleder follow a pattern in the number of subjects he uses; five ricercars (nos.2, 6, 7, 9, and 10) are strictly monothematic, four (nos.1, 3, 4, and 11) are built on double themes, and in the remaining three (nos.5, 8, and 12) additional subjects are introduced in the course of the piece. The novelty and individuality of the subjects is even more noteworthy. Hardly anything from the period can be compared with ideas such as those in Fig.403.

The decisive element, however, is the originality of the methods, the variety of means employed in these compositions. No ricercar is like another; none can be

Fig.403

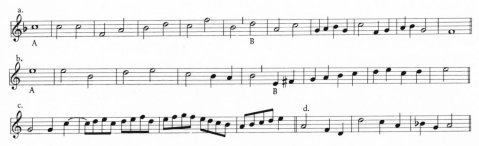

a. Ricercar no. 3; b. Ricercar no. 11; c. Ricercar no. 6; d. Ricercar no. 7

traced to a model. Even when the composer manifestly leans on other masters—especially on Sweelinck—he creates something new and completely personal.

The settings of ricercars nos.6 and 10, both in three parts and monothematic, are particularly simple. Their novelty consists first of all in the use of much livelier subjects than is usual in the ricercar of that period—quarter notes in no.10 and mostly eighth notes in no.6 (cf.Fig.403). Even more important is the systematic articulation in a number of expositions of the subject (A) separated by extended interludes (I):

$$
\begin{array}{cccccccccc}
 & 33 & 54 & 73 & 82 & 90 & 96 & 110 & 129\text{--}44 & \\
\text{No. 6:} & \text{A} & \text{I} & \text{A} & \text{I} & \text{A} & \text{I} & \text{A} & \text{I} & \text{A}
\end{array}
$$

$$
\begin{array}{ccccccc}
 & 10 & 22 & 31 & 44 & 56 & 68\text{--}101 \\
\text{No. 10:} & \text{A} & \text{I} & \text{A} & \text{I} & \text{A} & \text{I} & \text{A}
\end{array}
$$

Fig.404

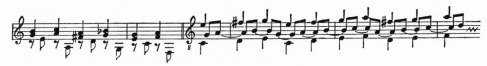

The interludes are mostly constructed with the aid of sequences, and employ either complementary motives or clavieristic figures often featuring notes that regularly fall after the beat. Fig.404 shows two examples, the first from no.6, the second from no.10. Occasionally an interlude is formulated imitatively using a secondary idea, e.g., the fourth one in no.6, which is based on a subject that is as simple as it is original—a scale ascending through an octave in quarter notes: $(c \mid d \, e \, f \, g \mid a \, b \, c)$. The simple and clear structure of these two ricercars represents a novelty in the evolution of the imitative types. In contrast to other structural innovations—e.g., the principles of Sweelinck's fantasies—this one proved to be of permanent significance.

Fig.405

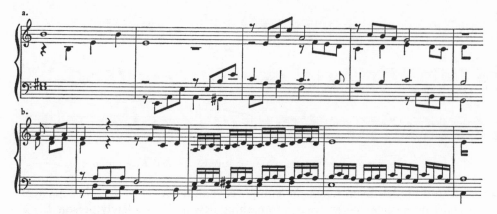

In the other monothematic ricercars Steigleder uses the subject in diminution and augmentation:

$$
\begin{array}{lllll}
 & & 87 & 186 & 202\text{--}51 \\
\text{No. 2:} & \text{A} & \text{I} & \text{A}^{\frac{1}{2}} & \text{A}^2
\end{array}
$$

$$
\begin{array}{llllll}
 & & 38 & 47 & 62 & 88 & 106\text{--}13 \\
\text{No. 7:} & \text{A} & \text{I} & \text{A} & \text{I} & \text{A} & \text{A}^{\frac{1}{2}}
\end{array}
$$

$$
\begin{array}{lllll}
 & & 45 & 64 & & 75 & 88\text{--}99 \\
\text{No. 9:} & \text{A} & \text{A}^{\frac{1}{2}} & \text{A in 3/2} & \text{A}^{\frac{1}{2}} & \text{A}^{\frac{1}{3}}
\end{array}
$$

The enormously long interlude of ricercar no.2 consists of a large number of lively motifs, which follow one another in brief points of imitation, sequential repetition, and other, constantly changing, captivating configurations, far from any schematic or pedantic approach. The two passages given in Fig.405 provide an idea of how everything sparkles with life and spirit. The material of the second interlude of ricercar no.7 is largely derived from the triad motif with which the subject begins (cf.Fig.403). Steigleder starts with a figure that is as simple as it is unheard-of at the time—a stroke of genius worthy of Beethoven (Fig.406). In ricercar no.9 a simple subject (*c'* | *b* | *c'* | *a* | *bb* | *c'* | *f*) is presented, in the manner of Sweelinck, in various degrees of diminution; by the end whole notes have been reduced to eighths.

Fig.406

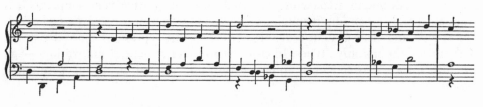

Two of the three ricercars with several subjects are rather simply constructed:

No. 8: $\overset{67}{A} \quad \overset{75}{A} \quad \overset{95-112}{B} \quad A$ No. 12: $\overset{22}{A} \quad \overset{38}{B} \quad \overset{54-72}{I} \quad A$

As in the other ricercars discussed so far, a relatively quiet motion prevails, mostly in quarter and eighth notes. The other ricercars are largely given to vivacious clavieristic figurations, as in Sweelinck's fantasies, and make much use of diminution and augmentation of the subjects. Here, too, Steigleder proves his originality, his abundance of ideas, and his endeavor to avoid pedantic and schematic formulae. One of the most remarkable passages, in the interlude of ricercar no.1, is reproduced in Fig.407. But not everything reaches the same high level of artistic inspiration. Toward the end of ricercar no.11 the figurations that Steigleder places against the sustained notes in the left hand—the second half of the subject (cf.Fig. 403) is presented here in quadrupled note values—are just as monotonous and dry as those that appear in John Bull's or in Sweelinck's early fantasies.

Fig.407

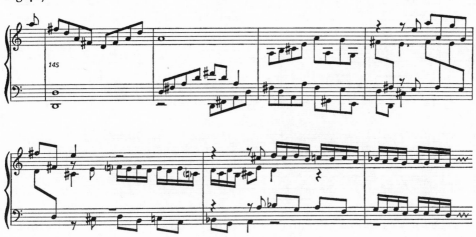

Perhaps the most original and curious of the ricercars is no.3. It starts with an unusually long double subject (cf.Fig.403), which is extensively developed in the first and last sections, each about eighty measures long, where the two portions of the subject appear together and separately in augmentation and diminution. Between these two sections there is an equally long interlude, dominated by the cuckoo's call. In contrast to Frescobaldi, who introduces the bird call here and there in his *Capriccio sopra il Cucu*, Steigleder repeats it without letup (as the bird so often does) about 120 times. One would think that this is too much of a good thing, but by using small variants of the motif—transposition, shift from upbeat rhythm to stressed position—and by adding a great variety of counterpoints,

Steigleder succeeds in avoiding the impression of hypertrophy. One passage is given in Fig.408.

The title of Steigleder's second print informs us that "the *Vater unser* is varied forty times." Naturally such a large number of chorale variations does not represent a unified composition in the same sense as a group of six or eight variations on a chorale or song theme. Steigleder rather presents a collection from which the organist may choose what he wishes: a short piece or a long one, easy or difficult, in one style or another. Each setting carries an explanatory legend, e.g., *Coral im Bass, 3 vocum; Coral im Discant mit einem collerierten Bass, 3 vocum; Coral im Discant colleriert; Fugen Manier;* etc. The collection begins with a *Fantasia* and ends with a *Toccata*.

Fig.408

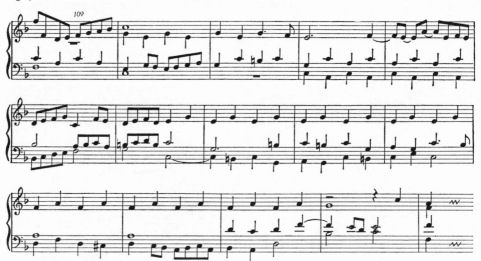

The forty variations fall into the following groups, according to the treatment of the chorale:

1. Chorale as *cantus planus* in the discant:
   11 pieces (nos. 4, 7, 9, 16, 17, 18, 23, 30, 32, 37, 39)
2. Chorale as *cantus planus* in the tenor:
   7 pieces (nos. 5, 11, 15, 20, 25, 26, 27)
3. Chorale as *cantus planus* in the bass:
   7 pieces (nos. 6, 8, 14, 19, 31, 33, 36)
4. Ornamented chorale:
   4 pieces (nos. 10, 28, 34, 38)
5. Chorale in two voices:
   5 pieces (nos. 12, 13, 24, 29, 35)
6. Chorale motets and fantasies:
   6 pieces (nos. 1, 2, 3, 21, 22, 40).

Three settings (nos.12, 13, 22) are bicinia, 19 are written in three parts, and 18 in four.

The predominant treatment is that of the *cantus planus*. The chorale is heard most often as a chain of half notes, but it is written in whole notes seven times, and once (no.39) in triple meter with alternating wholes and halves. In several of these pieces Steigleder indicates the possibility of stressing the chorale with the help of an instrument or a singer. Thus we read in no.4, the first *cantus-planus* setting: "A boy may sing the text to this part or a fiddle or another discant instrument may play along." Similarly in no.5, the addition of a tenor or a tenor instrument is recommended, and in no.6 a bass or a bassoon is suggested. In no.7 a note reads: "Since it has happened several times in this book that we found it suitable to sing the chorale or add a musical instrument to it, everybody will . . . know how to follow this advice and do so without further notice."

The difference between the various *cantus-planus* settings lies in the counterpoints. Steigleder always invents new possibilities, which can only be indicated here. Decorative counterpoints of a unified character are found in nos.25 (sixteenth-note runs), 26 (thirty-second-note trills in the bass), 27 (thirty-second-note trills in the soprano), and 9 "mit einem collerierten Bass" (arpeggios occasionally injected in the eighth-note progression). In no.16 the chorale is heard in the discant against two rapidly moving lower parts that employ parallel sixths or tenths, a hocket-like manner, interchange of motifs, and tone repetitions. Fig.409 shows three measures from this variation, which is possibly influenced by the English virginal style. In striking contrast to this variation, which sounds archaic, the pervasive use of a single motif in no.17 (Fig.410) seems to foreshadow Bach's *Little Organ Book*.

The pieces with ornamental counterpoints are mostly in three parts. In the four-part settings the counterpoints added to the *cantus planus* assume more of the

Fig.409

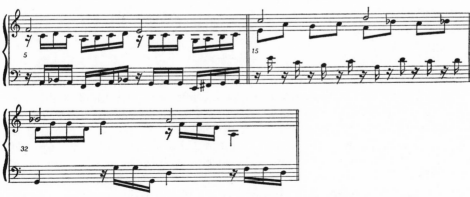

Fig.410

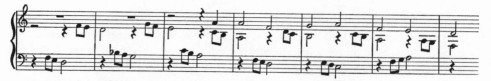

character of a polyphonic texture, e.g., in nos.4, 5, and 6, or in no.37, where the counterpoints are chromatic throughout. Fore-imitations are found in nos.18, 23, and 31. No.15 is especially artful: Three counterpoints are added to the whole-note *cantus planus* in the tenor, and these counterpoints are for the most part derived from diminutions of the lines of the chorale by four and eight. These chorale motifs often enter earlier than the line from which they are derived. Line 3, e.g., is combined with a counterpoint developed from line 4, and line 4 with motifs derived from lines 5 and 6, etc. Fig.411 shows the chorale lines 4 and 5 (the *cantus planus* lines are denoted by Roman numerals, the derived motives by Arabic numerals).

Fig.411

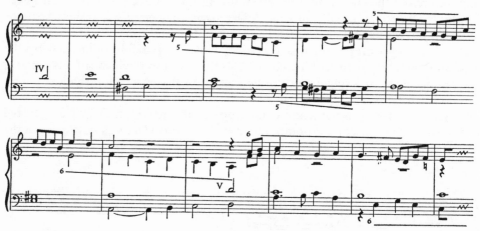

The variations of the fourth group need no further explanation. In the fifth group the chorale appears in two voices, and a different approach is used in each piece. No.13 is a *bicinium contrapuncto duplici* of the same type as in Scheidt's *Tabulatura nova*. In no.35 the chorale is divided between two voices so that the first half of each line is heard in the discant and the second half in the tenor. In three variations Steigleder sets himself the special problem of treating the chorale canonically. In no.12 he solves it by occasionally admitting rhythmic variants. In no.29, on the other hand, each chorale line is set as a strict canon of bass and

Fig.412

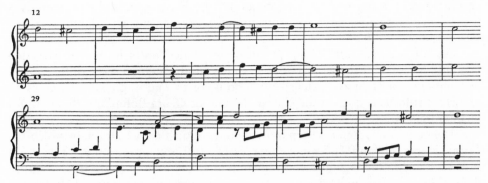

discant within a three part texture, in which the middle part is constructed as a kind of free ostinato. Fig.412 shows the third chorale line as set in each of the two canons. Alongside these two masterpieces of canonic art, the third canon, no.24, "Coral in zwo Stimmen zumal," is important only as a successful idea. It is interesting mainly because it is found one hundred years earlier in Buchner's works. Compare Fig.413 with Fig.86b. The Lydian cadence with two leading tones, which results from the strict application of the canon at the fourth, is one of the last examples of a formula that goes back to the 14th century.

Fig.413

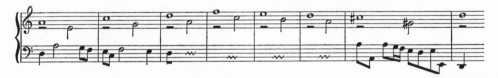

The last group, chorale motets and fantasies, comprises only a few pieces, but they are significant. Three among them outclass all the others even in their length: the introductory *Fantasia* (263 measures), no.22, just about the middle of the collection (129 measures), and the concluding *Toccata* (136 measures). The *Fantasia oder Fugen Manier* belongs to the same type as Scheidt's *Fantasia super Ich ruf zu dir Herr Jesu Christ*—the grand chorale motet. In Steigleder's setting each chorale line is heard about twelve times, usually first in diminution, then in normal note values as a sequence of half notes. The diminutions consist not so much of quarter notes as of irregular mixtures of quarters and halves, and thus appear in many rhythmic variants in which the natural accents of the melody are often neglected. This gives the composition a somewhat dry, learned character; moreover, it is much too long for its content. Perhaps Steigleder was conscious of this, for he followed this extended treatment with a similar but much shorter one (no.2) "for those whom long fugues do not serve well," and another (no.3)with the legend "brief and easy like the preceding one." Both are successful representatives of the type, captivating in their contrapuntal workmanship and dignified in expression and sentiment.

One of the most interesting pieces of the collection is no.22, an extended bicinium. Its contents make it a chorale fantasy (in the modern sense of the word). Each chorale line is quoted extensively in both voices, and fragmentation plays an important role, as it does in the chorale bicinia of Georg Böhm and the youthful Bach (cf.pp.633f.).

The fantasy character is even more definite in the final variation, in which the chorale is treated "auff Toccata Manier." In fact, this composition is a toccata in three sections; in the second section the individual chorale lines are treated imitatively, though occasionally brief toccata-like passages (t) are inserted between the individual lines:

$$\begin{array}{c}
\quad\quad 44 \quad 57 \quad 64 \quad 73 \quad 78 \quad 94 \quad 99 \quad 107 \quad\quad 113\text{--}36 \\
\text{T} \parallel \text{I} \quad \text{t} \quad 2 \quad 3 \quad 4 \quad 5 \quad \text{t} \quad 6 \parallel \text{T}
\end{array}$$

In the imitative sections the chorale lines often appear in irregular and arbitrary rhythmic variants, a procedure that is more appropriate in the "free atmosphere" of this composition than in the introductory *Fantasia*. Particularly interesting is the transformation of line 5 into motivic figures (shown in Fig.414), which continue into the toccata section that follows. The many novel and bold figures that appear in the toccata sections are most remarkable. In a surprising way, around 1625 a South German master is anticipating many features that characterize the North German toccata of the second half of the 17th century. Thus in both his ricercars and his chorale settings Johann Ulrich Steigleder proves to be one of the most gifted and most original organ masters of his period.

Fig.414

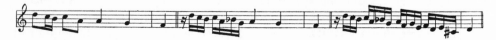

The first sixteen leaves of a manuscript collection in the British Museum (Add.34898) contain a number of anonymous liturgical organ pieces (hymns, Kyries, etc.) written in German organ tablature. Merely on the basis of conjecture F. Hirtler calls these works "newly discovered organ pieces by J. U. Steigleder."[74] The same manuscript includes seven ricercars (fol.23v–31), of which nos.1, 3, and 5 bear the signature Johann Benn. According to recent research, he was born about 1590, worked as the organist at the convent of St. Leodegar at Lucerne from 1638 to 1655, and died around 1660.[75] The first two ricercars are for four voices, the last for three. They do not offer much of special interest. The beginning of the first one is given in Fig.415. It is clearly a double subject, whose second portion is separated from the first by a rest, and is employed independently further on in the composition. With the aid of an additional countersubject (| − a b | c′ b a g | f |), a kind of triple fugue is created.

Fig.415

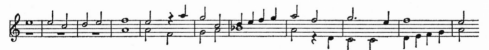

16

Italy

A. FIRST GENERATION, NORTH ITALY

Giovanni Gabrieli

Tʜᴇ ᴛʀᴀᴅɪᴛɪᴏɴ of North Italian organ music, founded by the two Cavazzonis and further developed by Andrea Gabrieli, Padovano, Merulo, and others, was brought to its conclusion by Giovanni Gabrieli. A nephew of Andrea Gabrieli's, he was born in Venice in 1555 (1557?), served from about 1575 to 1579 under Lassus at the Munich court chapel, and became second organist at St. Mark's in 1584 and first organist in 1586, both times as his uncle's successor. He died in Venice in 1612 (1613?). His compositions for the organ seem to have been written in the latter part of his life; in any event they reach us in prints dated 1593 to 1608 or in posthumous manuscripts.

Until about 1930 only a few organ pieces by this famous master of vocal and instrumental ensemble music were known, chiefly those contained in Italian prints of the 1590s: 11 intonations from the *Intonazioni d'organo di Andrea Gabrieli, et di Giovanni suo nepote* (1593), 2 ricercars from the *Ricercari di Andrea Gabrieli* (1595), and a toccata from Diruta's *Il Transilvano* I (1593). In addition there was a canzona in Winterfeld's *Johannes Gabrieli und sein Zeitalter*, vol.III, p.65 (1841), and a ricercar in Ritter B (no.8), both of which were taken from the manuscript Berlin Staatsbibl. 40316. In 1931 this repertoire was enlarged by five compositions, which G. Tagliapietra found in a manuscript of the Vereeniging voor Nederlandse Muziekgeschiedenis and printed in Tagliapietra A, II (nos.20–24). In a publication by G. S. Bedbrook, *Giovanni Gabrieli: Werke für Tasteninstrumente* (1957) two pieces from Munich Staatsbibl. Mus. ms. 1581 were added to the list of works (pp.17, 29).[1] About the same time a two-volume edition by S. Dalla

Libera, *G. Gabrieli: Composizioni per organo* (1956/57), appeared. The first volume disregards the Munich manuscript, but adds four canzonas from a print by Raverii, *Canzoni per sonare* ... (1608); the second presents 23 new pieces, all of which are taken from the Turin tablatures. (In the following observations citations not otherwise identified refer to this edition.) These various publications result in a total of 50 keyboard works by Giovanni Gabrieli.

However, this total—or at least the total of authenticated works—must be reduced somewhat. The four canzonas from the Raverii print (I, nos.6–9) must be eliminated because both the source and the style prove them to be ensemble compositions.[2] The five pieces published by Tagliapietra from the "Dutch" manuscript and accepted by both Bedbrook and Dalla Libera are more problematic. This manuscript (compare the facsimiles inserted in Tagliapietra A, I) is a 19th-century copy of pieces from one of the Lübbenau organ tablatures (Lynar A, 1, pp.42–55). But in that source (as well as in the copy) only the first of the five pieces, the *Fantasia quarti toni* (I, no.13; Tagliapietra A, II, no.20) is attributed to Giovanni Gabrieli, while the next four (I, nos.11, 12, 14, 15; Tagliapietra A, II, nos.21–24) are anonymous. We shall return to the question of whether the style of these works fits into Gabrieli's organ opus.

Giovanni Gabrieli's intonations were discussed in connection with those by Andrea (cf.p.220). In discussing the ricercars, let us start with two that are definitely authentic, those that Giovanni included in his own edition of the *Ricercari di Andrea Gabrieli, Libro secondo* (1595). The *Ricercar dell' ottavo tono* (I, no.3) begins with an exposition of two subjects (they could also be regarded as a double theme), which are joined by a third one in measure 23. As in Andrea Gabrieli's works, the three subjects occur in various combinations, and in other respects as well this ricercar follows tradition closely. There may be a somewhat greater freedom in handling tonal relationships, which shows itself in the occasional shifting of the subjects from the field of *G* to that of *A,* which almost gives the impression of a modulation (cf.meas.59–75).

The second ricercar, *Ricercar del 10⁰ tono* (I, no.4), is quite different. Riemann published it in his *Musikgeschichte in Beispielen* (no.52), and pointed to its progressive character when he called it "the oldest real fugue with divertissements." Indeed it discloses a consistent alternation between expositions of the subject and

Fig.416

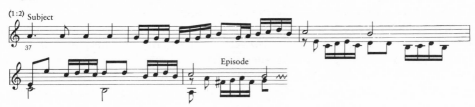

interludes derived from a lively clavieristic figure (Fig.416). The very same structure, only within a smaller framework, is found in the piece that Winterfeld published under the title canzona (I, no.5). Its overall style is also very similar. Fig.417 shows the subject and the motif that is used for the episodes. The ricercar published by Ritter (I, no.10) also receives its characteristic shape from the repeated appearance of a clavieristic figure that is almost identical with the episode motif of the second ricercar above (I, no.4); but here it has added thematic significance, since it is introduced at the beginning as a counterpoint to the main subject. Thus these three works represent a novel type, in which Giovanni Gabrieli attempts to mollify the seriousness of the ricercar by introducing playful—even humorous— elements.

Fig.417

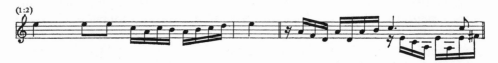

In the Turin tablature Giordano 6 six ricercars and two *Fugas* (II, nos.1–8) appear successively, but only the first piece, a rather short, monothematic ricercar, carries the designation Gio: Gabrieli. It exhibits the quiet movement of the older style, free from all playful elements. The second ricercar is identical with the Winterfeld piece (I, no.5), but omits seven measures (23–29). The last piece of this group recurs in Lynar A 2 with the legend *Ricercar 9. toni Johan Gabriel.*[3] It too, is monothematic, but it is based on a lively canzona subject. Whether this ascription is authentic and whether it permits any conclusion about the authenticity of the intervening pieces (II, 3–7), must remain an open question.

The Turin tablature Foà 3 contains five canzonas attributed to Giovanni Gabrieli[4] (II, nos.9–13). Probably all of them are genuine even though the first one appears in Woltz's *Tabulatura* of 1617 as *Fuga colorata Adami Steiglederi* and the last two are ascribed to Erbach in other manuscripts.[5] Pirro says that the first canzona, the "fuga colorata," is "fort curieuse par sa diversité."[6] This gay and charming piece is best described as a contrast canzona. It consists of about six brief sections, in which imitations, complementary motifs, echo passages, chords, and toccata-like figures alternate. The second canzona is particularly interesting. It consists of nine short sections, alternating between duple and triple meter, and all the duple-meter sections are identical, so that a rondo form A B A C A D A E A results. The triple-meter sections are also very similar to one another, but different enough to give the whole piece the needed variety. A similar variety is given to the transitions from these sections, which open all the ritornellos (A). Several stylistic details are just as remarkable as the form of the piece, especially the polychoral effects in the ritornello. Fig.418 shows a few passages from this very attractive

Fig.418

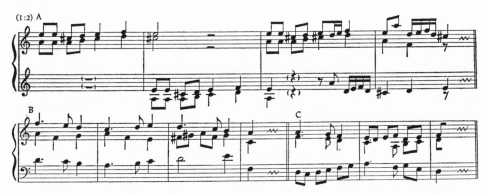

composition; but, like so many canzonas of the Turin tablatures, it may be an intabulation of an ensemble piece.

The Turin tablature Giordano 2 contains ten toccatas (II, nos.14–23) all of which are probably by Giovanni Gabrieli, although only the first two are expressly ascribed to him. They are short pieces, about as long as Andrea's intonations and in Andrea's style, that is, without imitative sections, although such sections are found in some of Andrea's toccatas. The same is true of the *Toccata del 2° tono,* which Diruta preserves in *Il Transilvano* I (I, no.2).

Let us now return to the five pieces from Lynar A 1, which were incorporated by Tagliapietra, Bedbrook, and Dalla Libera in their editions. The first piece, *Fantasia del quarto tono* (I, no.13), is the only one that carries Gabrieli's name. It is really a brief monothematic ricercar in the old style with a toccata ending, very similar to the first ricercar in the Turin collection (II, no.1). The first of the un-signed pieces, a *Toccata* (I, no.12), unlike all the authenticated toccatas by Giovanni Gabrieli, contains a middle section in imitative texture. The presence of this section is certainly not conclusive proof that this work is not his, but it does not support his authorship either. The *Ricercar del 7° e 8° tono* (I, no.11) presents such a dry, pedantic clavieristic figure and at times such a clumsy technique that one can only hope that it can be eliminated from the master's output. The *Fuga del 9° tono* (I, no.15) is similar to the ricercar published by Ritter (I, no.10); in both a lively, playful counterpoint is added to the main subject at the very be-ginning, and further along in the piece the subject and the counterpoint alternate. As early as 1934, in my review of *Tagliapietra A,*[7] I said that the *Fantasia del 6° tono* (I, no.14) "raises doubts regarding its authorship, because it contains numer-ous melismas and echo effects peculiar to the Sweelinck style. If one wants to insist on Gabrieli as its author, this would mean that this style, which is based on a free use of organ registers, originated in Italy. At this time this seems rather im-probable." M. Reimann, in her review of the Bedbrook edition,[8] expressed a similar opinion when she called the "echo octave transpositions at the start, the scale sequences at the end, and the development of the clavieristic figure in the middle . . . typically North German." The Fantasia is certainly not by Gabrieli. Thus the doubts about the unsigned pieces, which were accepted along with his organ works by Tagliapietra, Bedbrook, and Dalla Libera, are reinforced. It would certainly be unwise to base any important conclusions on them, such as those concerning the role the great Venetian master played in the evolution of organ music. It is, after all, modest and, in comparison with what he created in other fields, somewhat disappointing.

Antegnati and Cavaccio

Costanzo Antegnati (1549–1624) was the organist at the cathedral of Brescia, and famous as an organ builder and as the author of *L'Arte organica* (1608), one of the most important treatises for the history of organ building and the art of registration. A collection of twelve ricercars, *primo* to *duodecimo tono*,[9] is added to it, under the title *L'Antegnata, Intavolatura de ricercari d'organo*. Three are polythematic: Nos.1 and 4 have the form A ‖ B, while no.2 may be schematically outlined as A/B ‖ C/d/e (the lower-case letters symbolize shorter secondary subjects of motivic character). The other nine are monothematic, but the subject is often varied, either by rhythmic transformation, or by melodic changes, such as partial inversion or partial transposition. Ricercar no.5 is especially rich in variants; Fig.419 shows the reformations of the subject. At the end Antegnati arrives at a formulation that is completely different from the subject of the beginning, but which results from progressive changes.

Fig.419

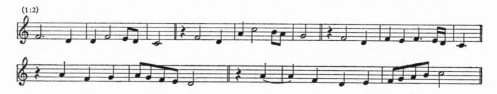

In many other details Antegnati's ricercars also show a tendency toward a freer treatment, which is unusual for the period, especially for a man who was born in the middle of the 16th century. The normal motion of the voice texture is frequently increased by quick figures; elsewhere it reaches the firmness of homophonic progressions. Here and there Antegnati injects parallel sixth chords into the free contrapuntal texture, and he does not eschew parallel fifths or triads either. Several ricercars conclude with rather extended sections in toccata style. Occasionally Antegnati finds ways and means of creating effects of tension and intensification. In ricercar no.12, e.g., the presentation of the subject (including its inversion and diminution) is followed by a second section with toccata-like runs, at the end of which the subject is introduced once more in block chords, like a fanfare. The treatment of the second section of no.1 is equally interesting and unusual. The subject (| / *a f b♭* | *a*) is worked out not so much imitatively as in the form of an insistent ostinato. Fig.420 shows the final measures of this work.

Fig.420

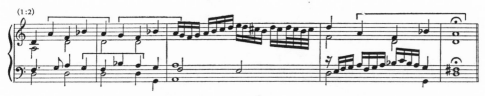

A contemporary of Antegnati's was Giovanni Cavaccio (c.1556–1626). He was born in Bergamo, and became the music director of the local cathedral in 1581 and of Santa Maria Maggiore in 1604. Just before his death a collection including 4 toccatas, 8 ricercars (4 each in three and four parts), and 20 canzonas appeared under the title *Sudori musicali* (1626).[10] The *Toccate* have nothing in common with the musical type of the same name, but are composed in a purely contrapuntal manner without any figuration. Why Cavaccio, who surely knew the toccatas of Andrea Gabrieli or Merulo, used this title in such a misleading way is inexplicable. The first and third toccatas are peculiar in that, in addition to a number of imitatively treated ideas, they have a kind of main theme in long note values, which recurs like an ostinato. In the first toccata (*d g f g c d*) is heard three times in the bass, with each tone extending over two breve values (*longa imperfecta*). In the third one (*d' c' b♭ g a*) is heard once each in the alto, soprano, tenor, and bass, with each tone occupying three breve values (*longa perfecta*). The latter subject is the well-known *Lascia fare mi* (*la sol fa re me*), and it is possible that the former has a special meaning, too. In the second toccata there is also a "main theme" (*a d b♭ a c' f g a d* in breves) but it appears only once, in the bass. The fourth toccata, however, exploits homophonic sounds, and suggests imitation only here and there. Its beginning is shown in Fig.421. All things considered, Cavaccio's

Fig.421

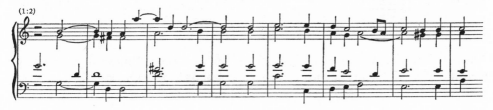

toccatas resemble what Giovanni Macque, and later Frescobaldi, called "capriccios."

Some of Cavaccio's ricercars are polythematic, and some employ only one subject to which countersubjects are sometimes added. In the *Ricercar quarto à 3* the entire bass is written as an ostinato that repeats the formula (e | g a | e g | f e |) in semibreves eleven times, alternating between the original pitches and a transposition a fifth higher. Among the four-part ricercars nos.1 and 3 have unusual subjects, which are given in Fig.422.

Fig.422

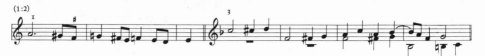

From the words "Quali canzon francese altre volte stampate di nuovo escono in luce" on the title page we learn that the canzonas are taken from an earlier publication, perhaps the part-book print *Musica di Giovanni Cavaccio,* which appeared in 1597. They definitely give the impression of ensemble music, particularly the last one, which is written for eight voices.

Cavaccio's toccatas and ricercars exhibit some archaic features, especially in their harmonic texture; at the same time they present much that is novel and original, e.g., the various ostinati or the subjects shown in Fig.422, which are undoubtedly early Baroque experiments. His compositions contain many other stimulating details, e.g., the passage in Fig.423 from the *Ricercar secondo à 3,* which is wholly derived from tetrachords (cf. Torchi A, p.195, last measure). In the course of the piece this passage recurs two more times with the voices exchanged (i.e., in triple counterpoint), and involving hand-crossings.

Fig.423

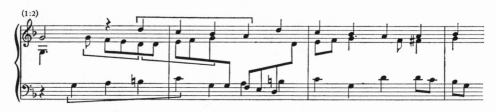

Banchieri

Adriano Banchieri was born in Bologna in 1567. He spent almost all his life in or near that city, and when he died he was the abbot of Monte Oliveto. Banchieri was enormously productive in many fields—church music, madrigal comedy, music theory, and literature, and in 1614 he founded the *Accademia de' Floridi* (later called *de' Filomusi* and finally *Filarmonica*). His main contribution to the history of keyboard music is his book *L'Organo suonarino*, which appeared in three different editions during his lifetime, in 1605, 1611, and 1622. It is mainly an extensive collection of *bassi continui* for the accompaniment of liturgical vocal music, and is divided in five *Registro:* Mass pieces (Kyries, Glorias, sequences, Credos), psalm tones, hymns, Magnificats, and Marian antiphons. A number of organ pieces are added to the thorough-basses, e.g., eight *Sonatas* at the end of the *Primo Registro*, which Banchieri says are "à proposito per il Graduale, Offertorio, Levatione e post Communione." The following is a list of the keyboard pieces:[11]

> 1605: 13 *Sonatas;* 4 *Capriccios* (in two parts); 2 *Ripienos per il Deo Gratias*
> 1611: 3 *Ricercatas;* 4 *Canzone;* 1 *Fantasia;* 2 *Dialogos, acuto e grave;* 2 *Sonatas;* 2 *Toccatas; La Battaglia; Ingressa di ripieno;* 2 *Ripienos al Deo Gratias*
> 1622: *Messa alla Domenica; Sonata grave;* 2 *Bizarias;* 2 *Fantasias* (all of these in two parts with occasional indications for *basso continuo*)[12]

Except for the somewhat longer ricercars, they are all brief pieces, some only a dozen measures long, but mostly about thirty to forty measures. The ricercars offer nothing worthy of note, nor do the canzonas. Several of the pieces called Sonata are cast as brief fugues, two as fuga triplicata (nos.2 and 6; the latter in Torchi A, p.357). Others are of greater interest because they are harmonically conceived and may be compared to the North German preludes of the same period: *Sonata terza Fuga grave, Sonata quarta Fuga cromatica,* and *Sonata settima Concerto enarmonico* from the *Primo Registro* (1605 edition); and *Prima sonata Ingresso d'un ripieno* and *Terza sonata in Dialogo* from the *Secondo Registro*. The first two pieces reappear in the 1611 edition under the titles *Toccata alla levatione del Santissimo Sacramento* and thus are predecessors of Frescobaldi's *Toccate per l'Elevazione* in fact as well as name.[13] Both are in *E*, the same key that Frescobaldi uses to express the mystic character of the transubstantiation. In the 1611 edition various notes are sharped—in order to stress further the character of the "elevation"? A typical passage is given in Fig.424 (the ♮ signs refer to the 1605 version).

Fig.424

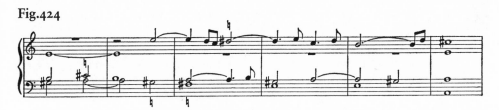

Fig.425

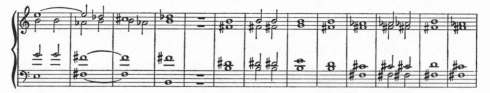

For a long time the *Sonata settima Concerto enarmonico* has caused excitement with its peculiar accidentals, such as those in Fig.425. Ambros took these accidentals literally, and thus understandably arrived at the conclusion that "the enharmonic concerto is the biggest nonsense."[14] On the other hand, Ritter recognized that the flats are in reality sharp signs, and indicate *D* sharp and *A* sharp not *D* flat and *A* flat.[15] His attempt to explain the curious notation is not convincing however. It is certainly connected with the construction of the arcicembalo that Banchieri used, and probably indicated that the key for the enharmonic *D* sharp was located to the left of the *D* key (i.e., above or to the right of the *C* sharp key), not to its right, and therefore, from the point of view of the player, it was quite correctly indicated by a flat sign, indeed had to be so indicated. Whatever the case, the *Concerto enarmonico* is by no means nonsense; like the two toccatas it is a beautiful prelude or postlude to a liturgical service. In the excerpt in Fig.425 note the appearance of two six-four chords in strongly stressed positions.

In addition to these fine compositions there are others that may not be of great artistic importance, but their originality deserves attention. The four capriccios in the 1605 edition, e.g., are brief pieces whose length is doubled by a *Da capo al fine*, and intimate a four-voiced imitation within a two-part texture. The beginning of the *Secondo Capriccio* is given in Fig.426. Banchieri invented something here that was used so often in Italian fugues around 1700 (and often in the German ones, too) that it ceased to be a successful idea.

Fig.426

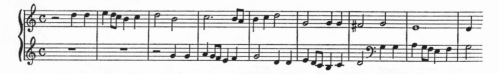

The *Bizaria del 1. tono* from the 1622 edition is a little two-part setting of eight measures. It is first presented in a moderate tempo, than *più presto,* and finally, reduced to just the beginning, *prestissimo*—one of the most successful jokes in musical literature.[16] The fact that such a piece could be heard during Mass— the piece carries the legend "al Graduale col Flauto, all' Ottava"—throws a significant light on the church services of the period, although we must be careful about generalizing.

Banchieri's *Moderna Armonia* (1612) contains 15 canzonas in two parts, which are interesting contributions to clavier literature. According to the title page they were composed "per suonare con facilità nell' Organo ò Clavacimbalo," but might also be used for "concertare uno et dui Stromenti." Each piece is to be repeated, presented first slowly, "in guisa di ricercare," and the second time "strettamente, rendendo tal varietà nuovo diletto (Avertenze a gli virtuosi suonatori)." This collection contains many entertaining pieces that can be used for unpretentious music-making even today. It is great fun to present such a composition first "in the guise of a serious ricercar" and then in its true form as a gay canzona.

Cima and Bottazzi

Milan was the home of Gian Paolo Cima (born about 1570?). Besides several volumes of vocal works, he published a collection of keyboard pieces entitled *Partito de ricercari et canzoni alla francese* (1606).[17] It contains 7 ricercars and 16 canzonas as well as an appendix with explanations and examples of transposition. The ricercars are based on two or more subjects, which are developed separately and then combined, making use of inversion and augmentation. The tenor of ricercar no.7, consists exclusively of ostinato-like repetitions of the main subject ($f\ a\ b\flat\ c'$) in various degrees of augmentation and diminution—a procedure that Frescobaldi imitated in two ricercars of 1615. The canzonas consist of two or three brief contrasting sections, and may thus be classed as contrast canzonas. It is quite certain that Pellegrini's canzonas served as the model, for he was active in Milan, too. As an example Fig.427 gives the beginnings of the three sections of Cima's Canzona No.2, *La Valeria*.

The appendix to Cima's print is of substantial theoretical interest for it presents the first complete treatment of transposition. The discussion is illustrated

Fig.427

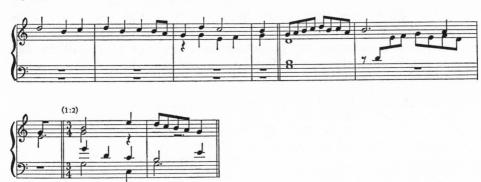

with the aid of a brief four-part setting in *D* minor, which is then notated "mezza voce più alto," "una voce più alto," "una terza minore più alto," etc. (cf. new edition, pp.63ff.). Each example is, moreover, accompanied by directions for tuning the clavichord. For the first transposition the half tones above *f*, *g*, and *c* (*diesis f fa ut*, etc.) were to be tuned as minor thirds above *e♭*, *f*, and *b♭*, and *b* as a minor third above *g♯*. The scale that results corresponds to the modern *E♭* minor: *e♭ f G♭ A♭ b♭ C♭ D♭ e♭* (the retuned strings are indicated by capitals). The writing of the accidentals is still quite different from modern usage, as Fig.428 shows (the accidental is valid only for the note immediately following it). Finally Cima offers two more rather extended ricercars, the first with a transposition "una voce più basso," the other "più alto uno semidiapente."[18]

Fig.428

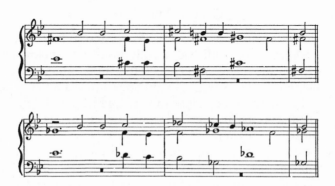

Nothing is known about the life of Bernardino Bottazzi except that he was a monk of the order of Brothers Minor in Ferrara. In a book entitled *Choro et organo* (1614) he tries to improve music for the services because, as he says in the foreword, of the "disordini e confusioni quali sogliono ben spesso occorrere nelle Chiese." The book contains the 3 usual Masses (*per gli Apostoli e feste doppie, Dominicale*, and *della Madonna*), 22 hymns for the entire year, and the 4 Marian antiphons. Under each work he lists both the monophonic choral chants and the interspersed organ pieces, thereby affording us a very clear idea of the practice of liturgical music. It deviates from the one generally held today, for the organ pieces do not replace the corresponding portions of the chant (as is supposedly the case in the so-called alternating organ Mass), but follow them. Thus the Kyrie is executed in the following manner:

Primus chorus:	Kyrie primus—*Organo:* Kyrie primus
Secundus chorus:	Kyrie secundus
Primus chorus:	Kyrie tertius—*Organo:* Kyrie tertius
Secundus chorus:	Christe primus
Primus chorus:	Christe secundus—*Organo:* Christe secundus
Secundus chorus:	Christe tertius

Primus chorus: Kyrie primus—*Organo:* Kyrie primus
Secundus chorus: Kyrie secundus
Primus chorus: Kyrie tertius—*Organo:* Kyrie tertius.

The two choirs truly alternate, while the organ has the role of paraphrasing the *Primus chorus.* The other portions of the Mass are treated in the same manner. The resulting execution is logical and suitable from the liturgical point of view, for no word of the sanctified text, no note of its melody is omitted. Was this execution also applied to other organ Masses? Should the organ Masses of Buchner, Cavazzoni, Merulo, and Frescobaldi not be regarded as alternating but as paraphrasing Masses?[19]

Bottazzi presents the first stanza of his hymns *choraliter,* then gives an organ arrangement of this stanza, e.g., *Deus tuorum militum* (chant)—*Deus tuorum militum* (organ). Whether the rather long organ pieces were also played after each of the succeeding stanzas or only after every odd stanza is not known. The intended execution of the Marian antiphons is even less clear since several portions of them are missing entirely. The following is an outline of the *Ave regina,* in which the omissions are indicated by parentheses and the organ piece by italics:

Ave. Regina caelorum—*Regina caelorum*—(Ave Domina Angelorum)—Salve radix . . . orta—(Gaude Virgo . . . speciosa)—Vale . . . exora

In the organ pieces the chant melodies are either set as *cantus plani* or only indicated in an initial imitation followed by a free continuation. As Bottazzi stresses repeatedly in his foreword, his main concern is that the choir and the organ correspond in "tone": "che i Cantori cantano, e l'Organista suona nell' istesso tuono."

Corradini and Picchi

Niccolò Corradini was active in Cremona, where he died in 1646. Until recently he was known through a number of vocal works and a collection of ensemble canzonas published in 1624. An essay by L. F. Tagliavini[20] brought news of the existence of a score print (probably 1615) containing twelve ricercars by the "forgotten musician from Cremona." The ricercars are designated *del primo tuono, del secondo tuono,* etc., and also carry legends such as *con due fughe, con tre fughe,* etc., which refer to the number of subjects used. These designations indicate that Corradini was familiar with the work of the Neapolitan composer Trabaci, who had employed very similar ones for his ricercars in 1603.

Corradini always employs several subjects—usually two to four, in one case five—and he presents them with the aid of the artifices introduced by Andrea Gabrieli (double subject, augmentation, diminution, inversion, etc.). Tagliavini's essay includes a table in which the formal outlines of the twelve ricercars are presented.[21] These compositions follow the strict polyphonic style of the 16th century, but occasionally one finds details of a more modern vintage. The *Ricercar del nono tuono, di due fughe,* e.g., begins with an interesting subject with two diminished fifths: (| *e'* | *f b* | *c' d* | *g♯* | *a* |).

Giovanni Picchi in Venice was contemporary with the great organists of St. Mark's and was *organista della Casa Grande.* Otherwise all that is known of his life is that he applied for the post of second organist at St. Mark's in 1624, but without success. He published an *Intavolatura di balli d'arpicordo* (1620) and a book of ensemble canzonas: *Canzoni da sonar con ogni sorte d' istromenti . . . con il basso continuo* (1625). An organ toccata is found in the *Fitzwilliam Virginal Book,* and the Turin tablature Foà 7 contains three unimportant passamezzi.[22]

Fig.429

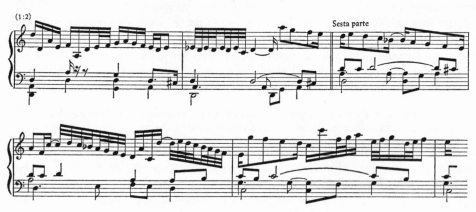

The *Balli d'arpicordo*[23] contains: *Pass'e mezzo* with *Saltarello, Ballo ditto il Picchi, Ballo detto il Steffanin, Ballo alla polacha, Ballo ongaro* with *Balletto, Todesca* with *Balletto,* and *Padoana ditta la Ongara* with *Altro modo.* Picchi's passamezzo has already been mentioned (cf.pp.271, 275). Fig.429 shows the transition from the *Quinta* to the *Sesta Parte* of this work, with the curious trill mentioned earlier and an equally unusual syncopation figure. Both the *Ballo ditto il Picchi* and *Ballo detto il Steffanin* are galliards in three sections with varied repetition of each section. In the latter work the first section is five 6/4 measures long, the other two are four measures each, and the concluding *Represe* consists of five repetitions of a two-measure phrase, with the harmonic progression dominant-tonic. The *Padoana ditta la Ongara* consists of three sections of four measures each, each of which is repeated in varied form (which is indicated by *Alio modo* in the third section only). A variation of the whole piece follows, as often occurs in the English pavanes. An interesting feature of Picchi's dances is the introduction of ideas from Poland and Hungary. They were already present in the German dance collections from the end of the 16th century, e.g., the *Ungarescha* by Jacob

Fig.430

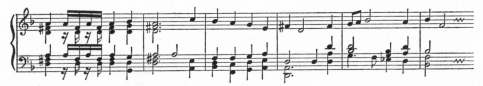

Paix (1583) and various Polish dances by Nörmiger (1598). The portrayal of local color at the beginning of the *Ballo alla polacha*, shown in Fig.430, is especially successful.

Picchi's toccata (*FW*, I, p.373) is just as interesting and unusual as his dances. Instead of the usual beginning with a few full, sustained chords, he starts with a sixteenth-note arpeggio that descends through three octaves from *d″* to *D*. The rest of the piece, which is purely toccata-like, i.e., without any fugal inserts, is highlighted by an extended pedal-point passage (p.375, staves 3–6) and the ending, which is given in Fig.431. Here the left hand sustains a *G* chord while the right hand executes running figures that end in an arpeggio of the dominant triad, which only at the last moment adapts itself to the *G* chord, in a typically early Baroque exhibition of conflict.

Fig.431

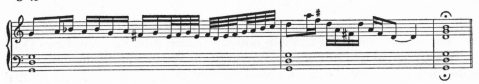

B. FIRST GENERATION, SOUTH ITALY

Ercole Pasquini

Ercole Pasquini, a curious and hitherto little-known organ master, was born in Ferrara about 1560, and taught there from 1583 to 1587. In 1597 he became the organist of the Cappella Giulia at St. Peter's in Rome, but was discharged in 1608 and replaced by Frescobaldi. He then lived on in Rome for some time (at most until 1620), apparently in unhappy circumstances. Until recently only one work of his was known, a *Canzona francese* printed by Torchi from an unidentified source.[24] Later research has brought to light 30 keyboard compositions, contained in manuscripts in Berlin (Staatsbibl. Mus. ms. 40615), Naples, Ravenna, Rome, and Trent.[25] The repertoire consists of 6 toccatas, 2 durezze, 10 canzonas, 2 fugal settings, 1 intabulation (*Anchor che co'l partire* by Cipriano de Rore), 5 variation sets, and 4 dances.

The toccatas are works of about thirty to fifty whole-note measures in toccata style throughout, i.e., without fugal sections. They contain a plethora of interesting features, novel figures, and curious chords. This is the first appearance of the type that may appropriately be called "experimental toccata" and plays a very important role in the keyboard music of the early Baroque. It was cultivated very intensively at the time throughout South Italy. Various details of Pasquini's toccatas are similar to those found in the works of the Neapolitan composers Macque, Mayone, and Trabaci, who exercised a decisive influence on Frescobaldi. Certainly Pasquini must be counted among those who created the basis for Frescobaldi's work. A more detailed characterization of the early Baroque toccata will be given in the next chapters; here we shall only point out some of the more interesting features in Pasquini's authenticated toccatas. The often uncertain way these pieces have been handed down makes this limitation necessary.

Fig.432

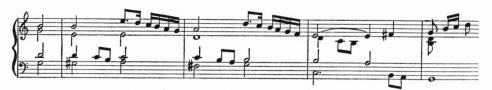

The excerpt from the toccata in *E* minor (Rome, Bibl. Vat. cod. Chigi Q IV 27, fol.90), reproduced in Fig.432, contains an interesting harmonic detail. Pasquini employs six-five chords and resolves them in a way that was not normal or usual until much later. On the whole the figurations in the toccatas are somewhat more conventional than those in the works by the Neapolitans, but there is no dearth of those turns and ideas that lend the toccatas of the period their peculiar forced, nervous tension. Fig.433 includes three such passages. Passage b. includes a figure of the type 2+3+3, that peculiar rhythmic motif that is frequently found in Spanish keyboard literature but only rarely in Italian. Passage c. shows a cadence form—a written-out trill above quick figuration—that is frequently used by Frescobaldi in his toccatas of 1627.

With the possible exception of the *durezze e ligature* by Giovanni Macque, Pasquini's are the earliest examples of a well-established type that appears repeatedly in the clavier literature of the 17th century, and which served as a proving ground for the then current burning problem of harmonic dissonance, the *seconda prattica*. Such compositions were written in a choral manner, extensively pervaded by dissonant harmonies (*durezze*) and suspensions (*ligature*). Fig.434 presents two typical passages (from Naples, Ms.34.5.28, fol.137v).

Fig.433

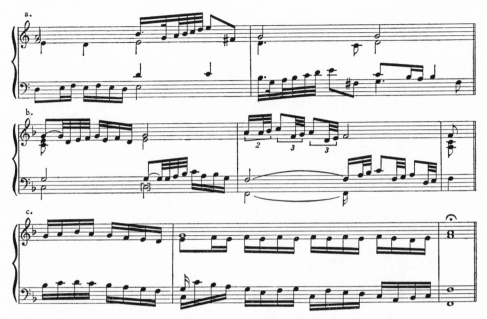

a. Chigi Q IV 27, fol.66v; b. ibid., fol. 87v; c. Trent Ms., fol.76v.

Pasquini's canzonas consist most often of three sections, with the middle one in triple meter. In several canzonas the first subject is also employed in the other sections; they are therefore early examples of the variation canzona, which emerges at the same time in Naples in Trabaci's works.

Two of Pasquini's variation sets are based on the passamezzo antico, two on the romanesca, and one on the ruggiero. His dances include two galliards and two correntes, the latter being the earliest known examples of the corrente in Italy. One of them consists of two sections of 13 and 14 measures, respectively, the other one of three sections of 12, 13, and 16 measures, respectively. Similar irregular structures are found in Frescobaldi's correntes.

Fig.434

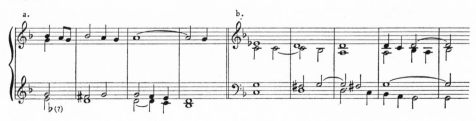

Macque, Stella, Lambardo, and Others

At the same time as Giovanni Gabrieli, Banchieri, and others were active in North Italy, a number of organ masters whose work and significance has been recognized only in the past twenty-five years were working in Naples. The North Italians took over and continued the tradition of the 16th century, while the South Italians attempted to find new formulations, which are of great interest in themselves, but gain even more importance because of their decisive influence on Frescobaldi.[26]

The earliest known representative of the Neapolitan keyboard school is Antonio Valente, whose ricercars, fantasies, variations, and organ verses (cf.pp. 187, 206, 276ff., 126ff.) are preserved in prints of 1576 and 1580. Alongside him worked the somewhat younger Rocco Rodio, whose ricercars and fantasies of 1575 occasionally exhibit early Baroque features (cf.pp.185ff., and 125f.). These features emerge more clearly in the works of Giovanni de Macque.

Recent research has shed light on Macque's life. Born around 1550 at Valenciennes (Belgium), he was a singer in the Vienna court chapel as early as 1563. From about 1568 to 1586 he lived in Rome, where he was quickly recognized as a madrigal composer. In 1586 he went to Naples, called there by Prince Fabrizio Gesualdo da Venosa, the father of Carlo Gesualdo (c.1560–1613), whose madrigals are famous for their bold chromaticism. In 1590 Macque left this position because of the tragedy of jealousy that befell the house of Venosa, and became the organist at Sta. Annunziata in Naples. In 1594 he became the organist and later the maestro di cappella at the court of the viceroy. He died in 1614. Among his students were Mayone, Trabaci, and Luigi Rossi (1589–1653).

Macque produced a voluminous output of madrigals, but only a small number of keyboard works. Most of them are preserved in a manuscript written by Luigi Rossi (Brit. Mus. Add. 30491); others are in the Neapolitan volume that also contains organ works by Ercole Pasquini (cf.p.496). In addition, there are four *Canzoni alla francese* in Woltz's *Nova musices organicae tabulatura* of 1617, but they are definitely ensemble works.[27] An *Intrada d'Organo* in a Naples manuscript (Bibl. del Conservatorio, Ms. 48, fol.55) and twelve ricercars at Florence (Bibl. naz. Magl. XIX, 106) remain unpublished.

Macque's clavier works are the first to exhibit clearly the characteristic traits of the early Baroque, those bold, conscious attempts to create a new tonal language, which today's musicians know from madrigals by Gesualdo and by Monteverdi. Two of his compositions are designated as *Stravaganze*, a title that implies the presentation of something extravagant, beyond the usual framework. A passage from the *Prime Stravaganze* (new ed., p.60) has scales in contrary motion and a novel figure that reappears particularly in Mayone's music (Fig.435). The title of a third piece, *Consonanze stravaganti* (new ed., p.37), is fitting, for its experiments in harmonic progressions anticipate and even outdo the chromatic audacities

Fig.435

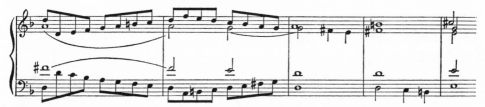

of Gesualdo's madrigals. Fig.436 shows a particularly remarkable passage. In his *Lamentations* Froberger still expresses the feeling of pain with the aid of similar, consciously forced turns.

Fig.436

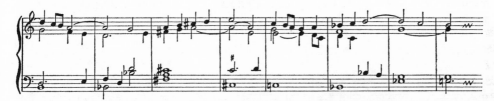

Macque also wrote four capriccios, one of which is called *Capricietto*. Like fantasy, capriccio is a term that is somewhat uncertain and changeable. In the 17th century "capriccio" often occurs as the title of collections that comprise all kinds of forms and types.[28] When it heads an individual piece of music, the composition may be based on some peculiar idea, an odd offspring of the fantasy, and not without reason, for the word derives from *capra* (goat). Macque's capriccios are definitely of this type. They start with a very individual subject and develop it in a special way. The very beginning of *Capriccio sopra re fa mi sol* (new ed., p.33) is unusual; it is a triple chordal fanfare, in which the subject is announced three times, first hidden in the lower parts, then clearly audible in the top voice. The last, triumphant annunciation is prepared by an arpeggio that descends to the lowest pitches and evokes a timpani effect. Passages like this one and many others that occur in the works of Macque and his followers are meaningful only when they are presented in a free tempo. This manner of playing is one of the many innovations of the Baroque. Frescobaldi was the first to describe and demand it, but he only made explicit what was implicit in the works of his Neapolitan precursors. Fig.437 offers the beginning of this capriccio (the tempo markings are mine). This introduction is followed by about seven sections, in some of which the subject appears in a varied form: in diminution, in a repeated four-fold stretto, and, at the end, four times in doubled note values embedded in an ornamented

425

Fig.437

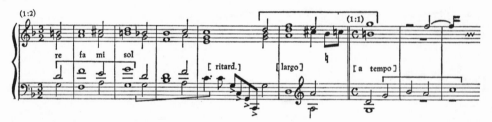

chordal texture. In one interesting passage the motif (*bb c′ f g*), which is probably somehow related to the *re fa mi sol*, descends precipitously, like a cascade, through several repetitions (new ed., p.35, brace 4, meas.5). The final cadence is one of the most fantastic passages in keyboard literature; despite all its apparent arbitrariness, it is definitely meaningful and effective, if it is correctly played—i.e., in a very free tempo and with strong stress on the dissonances (Fig.438a., b.).

Fig.438

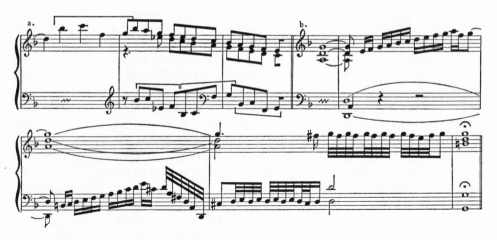

The *Capriccio sopra un soggetto* (new ed., p.39), is written throughout in imitative counterpoint. Here the title capriccio refers to the ingenious, capricious transformations of the double subject, which appears in the most diverse rhythmic variants, and occasionally in inversion. Fig.439 presents some of the most striking transformations. In a similar manner the *Capriccio sopra tre soggetti* (new ed., p.41) is constructed with three ideas—a subject and two countermotifs. In both capriccios almost the entire texture is derived from the subjects—a contrapuntal achievement that was again employed by Mayone as well as by Frescobaldi (cf. pp.430, 452). The *Capriccietto* (new ed., p.55) may be characterized as a musical

Fig.439

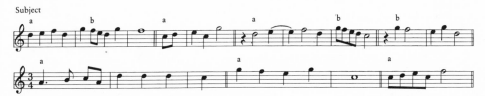

joke: A lively, almost merry, idea of four measures starts the piece and returns twice, lightly varied, as a refrain; in between various other ideas of a somewhat more serious kind appear, but the overall effect is one of a high-spirited mood.

Five of the eight canzonas (new ed., pp.43–49) are definitely ensemble pieces, and the other three (pp.57, 62, 65) probably derive from ensemble models, too. These works do not exhibit anything of special interest, nor do the two galliards (p.61). On the other hand, the *Toccata a modo di trombetta* (p.67) is noteworthy because its figurations are derived from trumpet fanfares, although with continued repetitions they soon lose their attraction.

In Macque's *Partite sopra Ruggiero*, the famous and much-discussed ruggiero theme, which was first found in Diego Ortiz's *Tratado de glosas* (1553), appears for the first time in keyboard music. Macque uses not only the bass line but also the melody of the theme. It can be traced more or less clearly in each variation, mostly in one of the middle parts. The variations tend more toward the ornamental type than toward the motivic. In the final variation Macque employs the peculiar scale runs in contrary motion that he uses in the *Prime Stravaganze*, and combines them with two sustained tones, while the ruggiero tune is sounded in the tenor.

The Rossi manuscript also contains a number of pieces by other composers. The authors named are Rinaldo, Scipione Stella, Franco Lambardo, and Ippolito and Fabritio Fillimarino, all of whom seem to have belonged to the same circle as Macque and Gesualdo.[29] There are two works by Rinaldo, a lively *Canzon* in five sections of varied meters and textures, and *Partite sopra Zefiro*.[30] The zefiro theme occurs earlier in the music of Valente. Rinaldo treats it in four variations, each of which develops another figuration motif in an imitative or complementary fashion. The skillful handling of this method, applied in a consistent manner to an entire set of variations, raises this work far above the level of Valente's variations. Fig. 440 presents an example.

Scipione Stella's four *Partite sopra la Romanesca* exhibit the same variation technique, involving complementary motifs, as Rinaldo's *Partite sopra Zefiro*. A *Prima canzon di Stella* consists of about eight sections, all, curiously, in triple meter. Several sections are purely homophonic, others chordal with figurations of complementary motifs. A third piece by Stella, *Seconda breve canzon*, is a normal canzona in three sections, probably intended for four instruments.

Fig.440

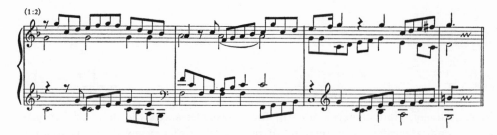

Franco Lambardo (c.1587–1642) is represented in the Rossi manuscript by a galliard, a brief toccata, and three *Partite sopra Fidele*, a theme that was also used by Mayone and Trabaci. The striking passage in Fig.441 is taken from the toccata.

Fig.441

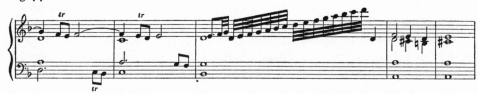

Like the *Prima canzon di Stella*, a *Canzon d'Ippolito* consists of a series of predominantly homophonic sections, all in triple meter. Probably both canzonas are based on a vocal model.

Another canzona preserved in the manuscript is by Fabritio Fillimarino. The first section develops a chromatic idea (g | e♭ e | f f♯ | g), with which livelier countersubjects are combined.

One of the most curious documents of the style of the period is preserved by Rossi in a piece entitled *Canzon francese del Principe*. The Principe is obviously Gesualdo, and the piece is probably an intabulation of one of his madrigals or canzonas. It would therefore seem to be of no special interest, but in six places it adds figures in special braces that are designated as *alternate* or *trillo galliardissimo* (very lively ornament). Inserted at various internal cadence points as well as at the end, these virtuosic passages artistically decorate and prolong a chord—like cadenzas in Mozart concertos. They are the clavieristic counterpart of the *gorgia*, the vocal ornamentation practice of the period, but go beyond its most extreme examples, just as cadenzas by Chopin or Liszt go beyond the coloraturas of Bellini or Donizetti. One of these cadenzas, in which a double trill at the interval of a fourth appears, is shown in one of my essays;[31] another one, hardly less curious, is given in Fig.442 (the added passage work is printed in small notes).

428

Fig.442

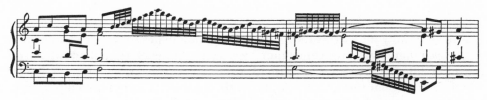

Mayone

Ascanio Mayone was one of Macque's students and served in the same organ positions as his teacher, at Sta. Annunziata (1593) and at the royal chapel (1602). He died in 1627. In contrast to his teacher, he is known primarily as a keyboard composer. His two prints of 1603 and 1609—*Primo* and *Secondo libro di diversi capricci per sonare*—are the first known Italian publications of the *opera-omnia-collecta* type, represented in the 16th century by Cabezón's *Obras de musica*. Their contents are as follows:[32]

	Primo Libro		*Secondo Libro*
Nos.1–4:	*Ricercar primo, . . . , quarto*	Nos.1–5:	*Recercari*
5–8:	*Canzon francese prima, . . . ,*	6–9:	*Canzon francese prima, . . . ,*
	quarta		*quarta*
9:	*Ancidetemi pur*	10:	*Io mi son giovinetta*
10–14:	*Toccata prima, . . . , quinta*	11–15:	*Toccata prima, . . . , quinta*
15:	*Partite sopra Rogiere*	16:	*Partite sopra il Tenore antico*
16:	*Partite sopra Fidele*		*ò Romanesca*

As in Rocco Rodio's print, the music is printed in a four-staff score. *Libro II* contains a preface "Alli studiosi," in which Mayone stresses, among other things, that ornamental passages will necessarily include some "wrong" notes "contra la regola del contrapunto." One should not get excited about them ("non si scandaliza") and think that the author is unfamiliar with the rules of counterpoint. But those who disagree with this procedure should keep to the ricercars, which Mayone "believes are *osservate.*"

Both books start with ricercars, four in the first book and five in the second. Six of them are ricercars in the usual sense, but the last three (II, nos.3–5) are built on *cantus firmi*. The ricercars of the first type all begin with a double subject (A_1, A_2), whose two portions are developed separately and combined with one another in various ways, just as Andrea Gabrieli had done. The ricercar II, no.1, is built exclusively on such a double subject; in the others a second (or a third, if one wants to call it that) subject is added, usually in a special section so that the structure $A_{1,2} \parallel A_1/A_2/B$ results. The ricercar I, no.2, is an exception, for all three subjects are introduced at the very beginning in the form of a triple subject:

A₁

A₁A₂

A₁A₂A₃

In all of Mayone's ricercars the first subject dominates the entire composition and gives it unity, while the contemporary ricercars of the North Italians often still consist of different sections, each with its own subject. Mayone's subjects no longer retain their original form, as was usual in the 16th century, but are employed in a large number of rhythmic and melodic variants. Thus many more possibilities open up for contrapuntal combinations, and the composer consciously exploits them with great dexterity, so much so that the entire contrapuntal texture consists almost exclusively of thematic material. This principle of formulation—which was perhaps even more consistently applied by Frescobaldi in his fantasies of 1608—contrasts sharply with the episodic approach practiced by Giovanni Gabrieli in some of his ricercars. In this procedure the principle of unity, the *omnia ex uno*, is perhaps carried too far, but one must not overlook the fact that unification necessarily includes the element of variety, which is manifested in the many alterations of the subject matter. To be sure, these fine points may escape the superficial listener; but they are all the more interesting for the "connoisseur and amateur," the "studioso delle regole del contrapunto e dello stile osservato."

Fig.443

(1:2)

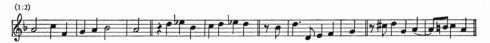

Some examples may serve to illustrate this argument. Fig.443 shows the main subject of ricercar II, no.1 and three of its variants. In all of them the characteristic triad motif is changed and only its direction is retained. Fig.444 is taken from ricercar I, no.3. It shows a., the beginning with a double subject A₁,₂; b., measures 21f., where subject B is introduced as a counterpoint to A₂; and c., measures 5off., in which the three subjects, in diverse variants and combinations, supply the material for the entire complex of voices. In this ricercar the subjects appear on various pitches (*e, a, d, f, c,* and *g*) but these transpositions have nothing to do with a trend toward modulation. In general, Mayone's ricercars, particularly those of the *Primo Libro*, exhibit a striking and, for the period, archaic indifference toward all things harmonic and chordal. The composer concentrates all his interest on the treatment of subject matter and counterpoint.

The last three ricercars of the *Secondo Libro* are built on *cantus firmi*: no.3 *sopra Ave maris stella,* no.4 *sopra il canto fermo di Costantio Festa,* and no.5 *sopra il canto fermo di Costantio Festa et per sonar all' Arpa.* The *canto fermo di Costantio Festa* is nothing but the famous old spagna melody, which for obscure reasons is ascribed to Costanzo Festa. With these compositions Mayone follows in

Fig.444

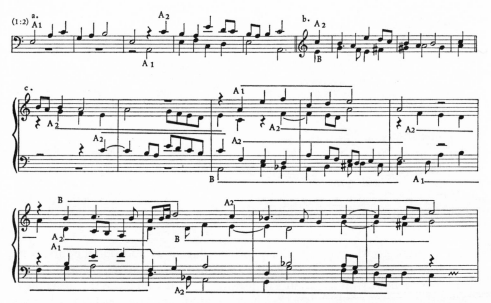

the footsteps of Rocco Rodio, whose print of 1575 contains four *cantus-firmus* fantasies, two of which are based on the above themes. Mayone, just like Rodio, treats the *cantus firmus* as a strict *cantus planus* in breves; in the *Ave maris stella* it is heard four times in the order tenor, alto, bass, and soprano; in each of the other two pieces it is heard once in the tenor. In the *Ave maris stella* and the first spagna setting Mayone composes the contrapuntal voices according to the same principles as in his free ricercars, by deriving the total texture from three subjects (in *Ave maris stella* from four times three subjects).

The second spagna setting carries the legend *per sonar all' Arpa*. In their publications "para tecla arpa y vihuela" Venegas de Henestrosa and Antonio de Cabezón had included the harp among the possible instruments, but compositions specifically written for harp occur for the first times in Mayone and Trabaci. In the meantime an extraordinary development in harp playing and harp technique must have taken place, although its traces are almost entirely lost. Nevertheless we know that in the Gesualdo circle of Neapolitan musicians there was a harp virtuoso of such fame that he was called Giovanni Leonardo dell' Arpa. Probably it is for him that Mayone wrote his harp piece,[33] which is indeed worthy of a great virtuoso, as can be seen from Fig.445.

Mayone's *Canzone francese* show the same tendency toward thematic unification as his ricercars, especially those in the *Primo Libro*. In fact, their general structures can be outlined in the same way as we have done several times for ricercars. Each canzona starts with a double subject (whose portions are symbol-

431

Fig.445

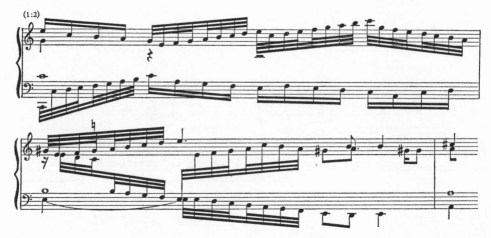

ized as A and B), to which one or several other subjects are added in the succeeding sections. Most canzonas have a middle section in triple meter, whose subjects often prove to be rhythmic variants of previously heard subjects; the principle of the variation canzona, which later becomes so important, emerges here. Schematic outlines of five of these canzonas follow:

```
I, no.5:  A/B ‖ C, A, B
I, no.6:  A/B ‖ C, A ‖ D ‖ A, E
I, no.7:  A/B ‖ A, C ‖ (3) A′, B′ ‖ A, D
I, no.8:  A/B ‖ C/B, Cⁱ/Bⁱ ‖ (3) Cⁱ/D ‖ A*
II, no.6: A/B ‖ (3) C, D, C/D ‖ A/B**
```

Mayone occasionally employs artifices in his canzonas that are normally the domain of the ricercar. In two of the pieces the subjects are inverted, and in canzona II, no.2, the first idea appears five times in augmentation, surrounded by rapid figurations. Thus the main difference between the ricercars and the canzonas is that the latter have much liverlier subjects. A few excerpts from I, no.8, given in Fig.446, will illustrate them.

In both books the canzonas are followed by an intabulated madrigal, Arcadelt's *Ancidetemi pur* (which was also arranged by Trabaci and Frescobaldi) in the first, and Domenico Ferrabosco's *Io mi son giovinetta* (arranged in collaboration with Giovanni Domenico Montella and Scipione Stella) in the second. The clavieristic ornamentation of the vocal setting of *Ancidetemi pur* consists mainly of scale passages, trills, and occasional complementary figures; but richer and more interesting means, such as motivic imitation and contrary scales, are applied

---

* C derives from A by omitting the repercussion motif with which A starts.
** The third section is a repetition of the first one. Canzona II, no.7, also shows this da capo form.

Fig.446

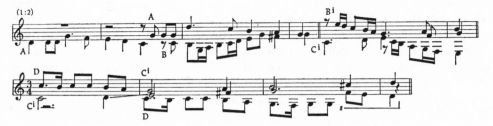

to the second piece, techniques that occur in even greater number and variety in Mayone's toccatas and variation sets.

Structurally the ten toccatas divide into two equal groups. Toccatas I, nos.10, 12, and II, nos.2, 3, 4 are written throughout in a chordal texture enlivened by figures and motifs, as was usual in the toccatas of the period. Three of the remaining five toccatas (I, nos.11, 13, and II, no.11) include imitative sections; however they do not appear in the middle of the composition, as in Merulo's toccatas, but at the end, and close with a full chord without a trace of a concluding toccata-like passage. Thus they represent an early, and in Italy probably singular, realization of the type that plays such an important role in the evolution of German music—the prelude and fugue. In fact, the imitative final portion of I, no.13 (*Toccata quarta*) is built on a single subject and may well be called a "fugue." In I, no.11 (*Toccata seconda*), as in all his ricercars, Mayone uses a double subject, but the imitative section of II, no.11 (*Toccata prima*) has the structure A || B || A/B, i.e., that of a fully developed double fugue. The two remaining toccatas (I, no.14, and II, no.15) are special cases. The former, *Toccata quinta*, is a very curious work, which may be described as a free fantasy on a single subject. We shall return to it below. The latter, entitled *Toccata 5. per il Cimbalo cromatico*, includes a purely chordal section in the style of the *durezze e ligature*, in which, by means of a stereotyped modulation, the tonal center moves from *E* to *C♯*, passing through all the intermediate keys and back again.

As to their content, Mayone's toccatas are among the most interesting representatives of a species that certainly does not lack for interesting and fascinating formulations. In the preserved repertoire they constitute the largest collection after Merulo's toccatas, and therefore suggest a comparison with them. Several similarities leave no doubt that Mayone was familiar with the North Italian toccata. On the whole, however, the predominant impression is one of novelty, of something grown in a different soil and created out of a different spirit. These toccatas differ from Merulo's not only in form but even more so in the figures and motifs that Mayone employs to enliven block chords and sustained tones. In Merulo's works the figurations, despite the variety in their details, are of a unified character, dominated everywhere by scale-wise motion, both ascending and descending. In

Mayone's case the principle of change, of contrast, rules. Scales in sixteenth notes occur only rarely, and where they do they do not constitute long, continuous chains, but clavieristic figures that appear successively in the various voices, like complementary motifs. In general, motivic enlivening of the chordal texture assumes a big role in his music. Each toccata contains several sections in which a motif half a measure or an entire measure in length—sometimes even longer—is taken up by one voice after another. In Fig.447 three such passages from the *Toccata terza* of the *Primo Libro* are reproduced.

Fig.447

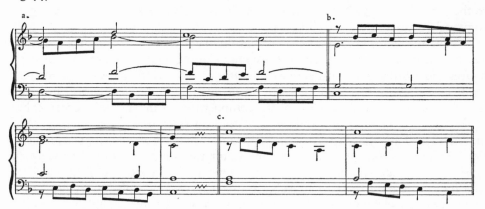

The zig-zag motif in b. appears so frequently in Mayone's music that it can be considered an earmark of his style. But it has an even wider significance: It is one among many figures in which a new musical tendency, a new spirit, manifests itself—a restless, flickering, nervous groping for tension, attracted by the consciously individual and the extraordinary. Forced dissonances, violent turns of harmony, jerky motifs, dotted and Lombardic rhythms, sudden directional impulses, steep ascents that end abruptly—all these, and many other features that cannot be expressed in brief terms, are unmistakable signs of the new musical language, that of the early Baroque. In keyboard music, at least, it emerges earliest and most clearly in South Italy. Men like Macque, Mayone, and Trabaci created this style, Frescobaldi led it to its apogee, and many of its traits are still found in the music of a later Neapolitan, Gregorio Strozzi.

To fill in the picture, let us begin by examining some of the peculiar trill figures found in Mayone's toccatas and variation works (for simplicity's sake they are all transposed to *c* as their main note in Fig.448). The last of these trills is of the type 3 + 3 + 2, which Mayone uses very often; but he makes little use of fast trills in thirty-second notes, much less than Merulo, who occasionally even writes

Fig.448

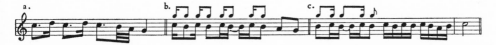

short trills in sixty-fourth notes. The ascending and descending scales of North
Italian provenance play a subordinate role in the toccatas. Their place is taken by
a great variety of figures with up-and-down motion, a few of which are shown in
Fig.449. The figure shown in c. occurs particularly often in Mayone's music, even
in thirty-second notes (in I, no.14). Mayone also employs scales in contrary motion;
like many other features, he acquired them from his teacher, Macque (cf.Fig.435).

Fig.449

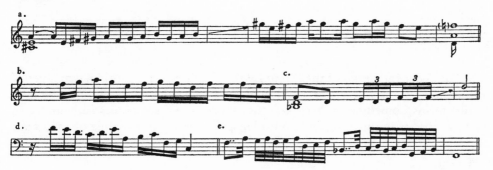

A striking harmonic feature that Mayone uses frequently is a formula in
which the raised and lowered third appear in close propinquity, separated only by
one step, e.g., *(g f♯ e | f)*. It suggests an abrupt change from major to minor—one
of the typical surprise effects of early Baroque style. This formula has a much
sharper effect than the abrupt chromatic progression *(g f♯ f)*, for it suggests a
common cadence formula *(g f♯ e | f♯)*—an expectation that is thwarted at the last
moment. Two instances from II, no.13, given in Fig.450, serve as illustrations.*
As may be expected from a disciple of Macque, there is no lack of bold dissonances,
without which, as Mayone says in the preface to his *Secondo Libro*, "é impossibile
che bello effetto faccia." Fig.451 shows two such "beautiful effects," one from the
beginning of I, no.10, the other from the conclusion of II, no.11.

---

* The absence of natural signs before the second *f* and *c* is characteristic of the notation
practice of the period, according to which an accidental is valid only for a note of the same pitch
that follows immediately. The second example in Fig.450, as well as hundreds of others in 17th-
century prints and manuscripts, prove this practice unambiguously. Bach still follows this principle; e.g., in the autograph of the *Fantasia super Komm Heiliger Geist*, in measure 6 the flat
before the *e* is given three times in the alto, but it is not given for the *e* in measure 7 because it
follows immediately after an *e* in measure 6.

Fig.450

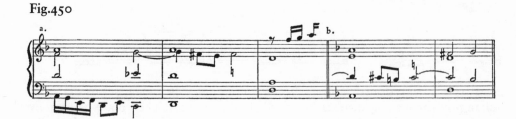

Fig.451

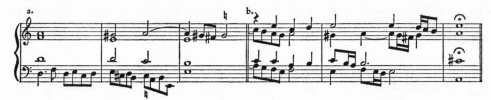

The *Toccata quinta* of the *Primo Libro* is based in a most original manner on the subject (| / *a a e* | *f — e —* |), which pervades the entire piece in the most varied forms, sometimes in brief imitative sections and sometimes surrounded by fast figurations in thirty-second notes. Fig.452 presents an example of each man-

Fig.452

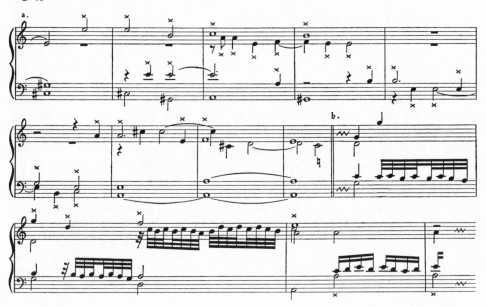

ner of treatment. Their contrast and immediate juxtaposition turn this piece into one of the most typical and most interesting products of the South Italian early Baroque.

Finally let us turn to Mayone's variation works. The following table is an analysis of the variation works of the period according to their subjects and number of variations:

Composer	Ruggiero	Zefiro	Fidele	Romanesca
Macque	4 var.			
Rinaldo		4 var.		
Lambardo			2(?) var.	
Stella				4 var.
Mayone	21 var.		10 var.	17 var.
Trabaci	15 var.	18 var.	20 var.	
Frescobaldi	12 var.			14 var.

It is apparent that Mayone (like Trabaci) treats the themes at much greater length than did his immediate predecessors.* This naturally leads him to a much greater variety of approaches. Most of his variations derive from complementary motifs or brief clavieristic figures, which wander from one voice to another; others are pervaded by ascending and descending scale passages; still others contain trill formulae of various kinds; a few are imitative, homophonic, or chromatic.

Among the motivic variations, variation XV of the ruggiero cycle has a striking zig-zag motif, which appears at the beginning in peculiar "flickering" impulses, and later in a more continuous manner, until toward the end it is replaced by a quieter motif. Fig.453 shows the beginning and end of this variation.

Fig.453

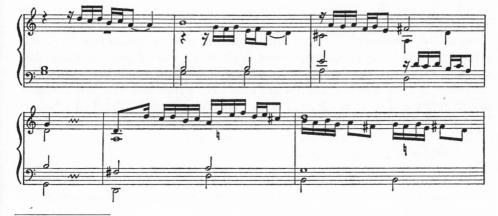

---

* Valente had already treated the zefiro theme in twelve variations, but his variation technique is so primitive that one cannot compare it with these works.

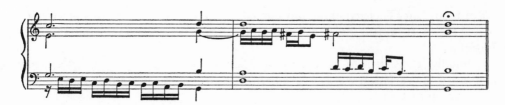

Even though very little is known about Mayone's life, a clear picture of his artistic personality emerges from his works: He was a musician of fiery, genuine South Italian temperament, whose lively imagination tended toward the fantastic, and predestined him to appropriate the new ideas of his time and realize them in an original way. His role in keyboard music is similar to that of Gesualdo's in the madrigal. But his work had a more fortunate fate than that of the Prince of Venosa. Gesualdo is a unique apparition, whose creations passed from memory with his passing, while Mayone found a companion in his work in Trabaci, and both were surpassed by their successor, Frescobaldi.

Trabaci

Giovanni Maria Trabaci was probably born about 1575, studied with Macque, was engaged as a singer at Sta. Annunziata in 1594, and as the organist of the royal chapel in 1601, where Mayone was associated with him in 1602 as second organist. Later he was given the office of maestro di cappella—in the title of his *Secondo Libro* of 1615 he calls himself "Maestro della Real Cappella." He died in 1647.[34]

Like Mayone, Trabaci published two books of keyboard music, the first in 1603, the second in 1615. Mayone modestly calls his collection of 1603 "primitie del mio ingegno." By that time Trabaci seems to have enjoyed a reputation that enabled him to boast of his capability and to make demands on his audience, for he says: "My *consonanze* are composed with much understanding [aggiustamento]—but if you, dear readers, do not apply study and diligence to them, they will not come up to my or your expectations. Therefore it will not be my fault but yours, if my intentions are not realized." He writes in a similarly assertive manner in the preface to the second book, and adds a special "Tavola dei passi et delle cose più notabile," i.e., a table of the most notable passages and details, which are also expressly noted in the various compositions.

The titles of the two prints are, respectively:

I: *Ricercate, canzone francese, capricci, canti fermi, gagliarde, partite diversi, toccate, durezze, ligature, consonanze stravaganti, et un madrigale passeggiato nel fine ... Libro primo ... 1603*

II: *Il secondo libro de ricercate, et altri varii capricci, con cento versi sopra li otto finali ecclesiastici ... 1615*

438

Their contents may be listed as follows:

Libro Primo

Nos.1–12: *Primo, ... , duodecimo tono* (ricercars)
   13–19: *Canzona francese prima, ... , settima*
   20–21: *2 Capriccios*
   22–25: *Canto fermo primo, ... , quarto*
   26–33: *Gagliarda prima, ... , ottava*
      34: *Partite sopra Rugiero*
      35: *Partite sopra Fidele*
   36–37: *Toccata prima, ... , seconda*
      38: *Durezze e ligature*
      39: *Consonanze stravaganti*
      40: *Io mi son giovinetto* [sic]

Libro secondo

Nos. 1–12: *Primo, ... , duodecimo tono* (ricercars)
   13–112: *Cento versi*
 113–16: *Toccata prima, ... , quarta*
 117–18: *2 Ricercar sopra il tenor di Costantio Festa 1–2*
 119–22: *Gagliarde (prima, ... , quarta) a quattro*
 123–27: *Gagliarde (prima, ... , quinta) a cinque*
    128: *Canzone francese a quattro per concerto de Violini o Viole ad arco*
    129: *Partite artificiose sopra il tenor di Zefiro*
    130: *Ancidetemi pur per l'arpa*

As was usual in the Neapolitan school, these works are notated in score on four staves. Curiously Trabaci (like Mayone) also employs this method of notation for toccatas, which naturally are much closer to free-voice writing than to a four-part texture. In the *Libro primo* Trabaci writes that his works may be performed "sopra qualsivoglia stromento, ma più proportionevolmente ne gli Organi e ne i Cimbali." The same remark is found in the second book, but the cembalo is named before the organ. This change is not an accident, for in the legend to his *Partite sopra Zefiro* (II, no.129) Trabaci adds that some variations are meant for the harp, but the cembalo should not be excluded, for "il Cimbalo è Signor di tutti l'istromenti del mondo, et in lei si possono sonare ogni cosa con facilità." Thus the stringed keyboard instrument acquires the same favored position it had been given fifty years earlier in England.

Both collections start with 12 ricercars, which carry legends such as *Primo tono con tre fughe* or *Secondo tono con quattro fughe*, expressly stating the number of subjects employed in each case. In all there are 2 ricercars *con una fuga sola* (I, no.10; II, no.5), 2 *con due fughe* (I, nos.7 and 11), 15 *con tre fughe*, and 5 *con quattro*. Several titles also contain special remarks on the manner of setting, e.g., *con tre fughe et inganni* (I, no.4) or *con tre fughe et suoi riversi* (I, no.6; II, nos.2 and 4). In the ricercars of the second book Trabaci goes even further in this direction and inscribes numerous passages with *due fughe insieme, riversi della terza fuga, moti contrarii della seconda fuga, inganni della seconda fuga*, etc. These

439

passages are the same as those he refers to in the "Tavola dei passi et delle cose più notabile." Thus Trabaci repeatedly stresses—because of scholarly pride, didactic zeal, or a mixture of the two—the special contrapuntal artifices he employs in his ricercars, and affords the modern analyst an especially valuable insight into the world of his thought and his method of composition. Since only the more important features can be presented here, we shall limit ourselves to the most representative type—the ricercar with three subjects.

Fig.454

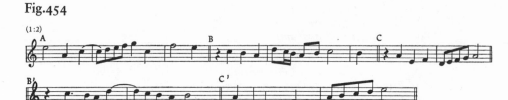

inganni della seconda fuga   inganni della terza fuga

These subjects are not offered in separate sections, as is usual in the North Italian school, but are introduced at the very beginning and treated continuously for about fifty to sixty breve measures. Occasionally a brief section in triple meter is inserted. Like Mayone, Trabaci endeavors to present the subjects repeatedly in ever changing combinations, but only rarely does he attempt to develop all the musical substance from the subjects. Next to passages of great thematic density there are others of looser texture, so that overall a normal balance between thematic and free polyphony obtains. In several ricercars Trabaci uses *riversi della fuga*, i.e., inversion of a subject, usually in such a way that the subjects appear several times in their inversion near the end. As in Mayone, the rhythm or the intervals of the subjects are often modified, and occasionally such variants are especially noted by the remark *inganni* [deceits] *della fuga*. Ricercar II, no.9 (*Nono tono con tre fughe*) contains two passages with the legends *inganni della seconda fuga* and *inganni della terza fuga*. Fig.454 shows the three subjects (A, B, C) of this ricercar with the variants that are called *inganni* (B', C'). Subjects A and C are quite similar, and the modern reader may well think that C is not the third subject but the *inganno della prima fuga*. That C is indeed an independent idea is evident from a passage inscribed *tre fughe insieme* (three themes simultaneously). It is shown in Fig.455, together with the final measures of this ricercar, in which, as usual, the three subjects again appear simultaneously but in another contrapuntal combination.

Trabaci's ricercars are among the most successful examples of the species and deserve thorough study. The many original references to technical details put the analysis on a sure footing and lend it a more authentic air than would otherwise be possible.

Fig.455

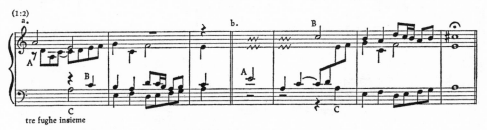

tre fughe insieme

In his canzonas Trabaci sets himself quite different goals. The place of thematic-contrapuntal elaboration is taken by a freer formulation, whose aims are the change of ideas and the diversity of approaches. A great variety of imitative, homophonic, figural, and motivic sections follow each other and form a total picture of spontaneous liveliness. The *Canzona franzesa quarta* (I, no.16) is especially diversified and interesting; it consists of eight sections, which may be characterized as follows:

1. overture in full chords (14 measures in 2/2)
2. fugal section (14 measures in 3/2)
3. homophonic phrase with echo-like repetition (8 measures in 3/2)
4. chordal texture with complementary motif (10 measures in 2/2)
5. like section 3, with a five-measure phrase (9 measures in 3/2)
6. short motif in multiple stretto with toccata-like ending (10+3 measures in 2/2)
7. one-measure complementary motif derived from section 4 (9 measures in 2/2)
8. toccata-like conclusion (16 measures in 2/2)

The introductory "overture" is particularly impressive, and reminds us of similar examples from ensemble music of the early 17th century. Is it possible to find such examples as early as 1603? In any case, this introduction is so significant that it is reproduced in full in Fig.456. The *Canzona sesta* (I, no.18)[35] is important in a different way. It consists of five sections, alternating duple and triple meter, which present the same subject in various rhythmic forms. This composition is not the first to present the principle of the variation canzona, but it does so with a clarity and consistency that are unusual if not unique for the time.

Fig.456

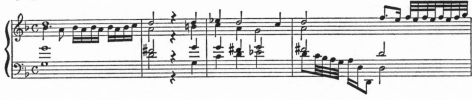

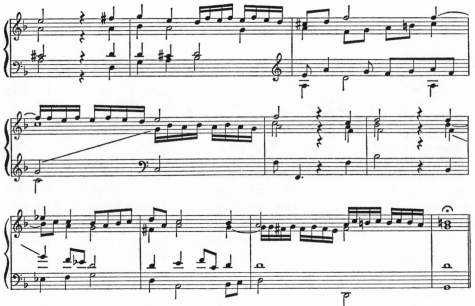

The canzonas are followed by two capriccios, *sopra un soggetto solo* and *sopra la fa sol la* (I, nos.20, 21). Even the title of the latter is reminiscent of Macque's *Capriccio sopra re fa mi sol*, after which it is obviously modeled. Like Macque's *Capriccio* (cf.Fig.437) it begins with three harmonizations of the subject, shown in Fig.457. Further on the subject is treated fugally in several sections, and appears not only in its normal form (*a f g a*), but also in other shapes near the end. These variants are derived from the solmization syllables in the various hexachords, e.g., *a bb g a* (*bb = fa* in the *hexachordum molle*), *a f g e* (*e = la* in the

Fig.457

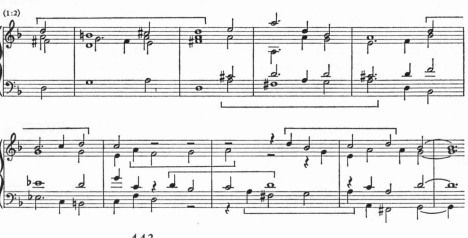

hexachordum durum), and *a b♭ c′ d′* (with *b♭*, *c′*, *d′* read in the *hexachordum molle*). Other four-tone motifs are heard, probably similarly derived from the solmization syllables (e.g., *d f g a*), even though the relationships are not always clearly recognizable.

The four pieces designated as *Canto fermo* (I, nos.22–25) and the two ricer-cars *sopra il tenor di Costantio Festa* (II, nos.117, 118) are all settings of the spagna melody. In principle Trabaci's treatment of the theme is the same as Rodio's and Mayone's (i.e., *cantus planus* in breve values), but he proves to be a more conservative master, in this and several other respects. He invents the three counterpoints in strict imitative polyphony, using imitations of several ideas in the four pieces from *Libro primo* and canons of two voices in the two from *Libro secondo*.

The earlier Italians did not cultivate dance music very much, but Trabaci wrote a number of galliards. They give the impression of not being genuine keyboard music but of being planned interchangeably for either an instrumental ensemble or a keyboard instrument. In the second book Trabaci says that the four galliards may be played in a four-part texture (on the clavier) or in five parts by viols or violins, with the aid of an additional voice, which is entered at the end of the volume.[36] Most of the galliards consist of two repeated sections. Curiously, some of these dances, which are normally in triple meter, include sections in duple meter, indicating that they belong to a late, stylized stage of this dance, as is the case with the English galliards, although they are very different.

Trabaci's *Libro primo* contains two variation works, on ruggiero and on fidele, both of unusual interest. The ruggiero variations by Macque often employ not only the bass but also the melody of the theme as stable elements. In Trabaci's set, on the other hand, there is no trace of a retention of the melody—whatever it may have been originally—and even the bass appears in the well-known form in the first variation only. The bass is altered so much in the others that sometimes the harmonies are affected. As an illustration Fig.458 gives the bass lines of variations I and XIV. Thus the theme is reduced more or less to its structural substance, i.e., to a series of four-measure phrases whose cadences fall on G, D, D, and G, respectively. Occasionally, however, even this basic structure is changed, either by changing the length of the phrases or the cadence tones. To illustrate this point, the following table first shows the normal structure and then lists the variations in which it is altered (4–G means: 4 measures ending on G):

basic structure:	4–G	4–D	4–D	4–G
variation IV:	4–G	4–D	5–A	3–G
VI:	4–G	5–D	4–D	4–G
VIII:	5–G	3–D	4–D	4–G
XI:	4–B	4–D	5–B	3–G
XII:	4–G	5–D	3–D	4–G

In five variations, i.e., one-third of the total, some phrases are lengthened or short-

Fig.458

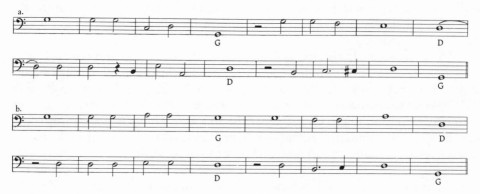

a. var. I; b. var. XIV.

ened by one measure, and usually the lengthening of one phrase is followed by the shortening of the next one, so that the structural change can also be described as a shift of the cadence point by one measure forward or backward. Only in one instance, in variation VI, is the lengthening of one phrase not compensated for, so that the total number of measures increases from sixteen to seventeen. In variation IV the third phrase concludes on A rather than on D, and in variation XI both the first and third phrases cadence on a B-minor chord. Since the phrase lengths are also altered, this variation represents an especially remarkable example of Trabaci's free treatment of thematic form.

The twenty variations on fidele are even more interesting. Although this theme was also set by Lambardo and Mayone, it is very difficult to recognize its essential features and reconstitute its melody or even its bass. Only the formal outline can be recognized: four four-measure (in Mayone's case two-measure) phrases, with cadences on F, D, F, and G.[37] Fig.459 shows the first half of Trabaci's *Partita prima*.

In the fidele variations the structure is treated even more freely than in the ruggiero set. The cadence tones always remain the same, but no less than half the variations exhibit deviations from the normal phrase lengths, and some are

Fig.459

(1:2)

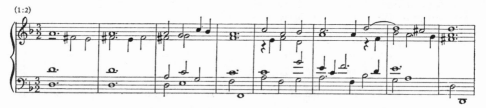

Fig.460

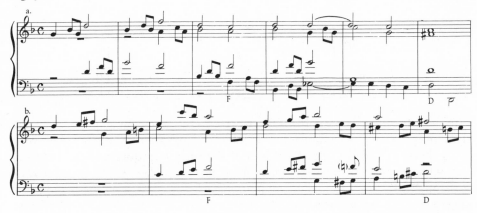

a. var. XIX; b. var. X.

rather substantial. If we signify the basic scheme by 4, 4, 4, 4 (an indication of the cadence tones is unnecessary, since they do not change), some variations exhibit structures such as 4, 4, 3, 3 (var.VI); 4, 6, 4, 4 (var.VII); 4, 4, 4, 7 (var.X); 3, 2, 3, 3 (var.XV); 3, 3, 4, 4 (var.XIX); and 3, 4, 3, 3 (var.XX). The triple meter of the theme is replaced by duple meter in four variations (IV, X, XV, XIX), always with the time signature C. Although a meter change in such an early variation work is remarkable in itself, it becomes even more interesting and complex when we discover that the length of the (normal) phrase is three or four whole notes in variations XV and XIX, and only four half notes in variations IV and X. Thus the latter two may be called allegro variations, in which the musical times is reduced to one half. Fig.460 reproduces the beginnings of variations X and XIX through the second cadence tones (note values and bar lines follow the original). Compared to the *Partita prima* in Fig.459, which is assumed to be rather close to the basic theme, these variations exhibit a freedom in matters harmonic, melodic, and structural that is not equaled until centuries later. Even Frescobaldi hardly ever treated the subjects of his variations as freely as Trabaci did in his *Partite sopra Fidele*. His tendency toward a texture of only a few voices emerges in both these variation works as well as elsewhere. It is reminiscent of Froberger's thin clavier texture.

Another variation of the fidele cycle, the *Partita ottava cromatica,* and the *Partita sesta cromatica* of the ruggiero set are the earliest instances of the chromatic variation, which was much in favor later on. The beginning of the former is given in Fig.461.*

---

* To cancel a previous accidental Trabaci employs the letter *l* (= *levar lo semitono*), or a tone letter such as *c* (after a *c♯*).

Fig.461

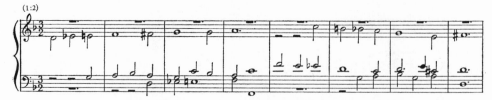

In the zefiro variations of 1615 Trabaci treats the theme much more conservatively than in his 1603 variations. Is this the first sign of a retreat from the overly great exuberance and desire for freedom of the early Baroque? Or did the zefiro theme, which is related to the romanesca (or, if one wishes, to the passamezzo), possess an "authority" that did not permit such liberties? It is interesting that among the twelve variations of this set there are three that are inscribed *per l'arpa*, and that these have faster figurations than the others.

Like Mayone, Trabaci constructs most of his variations with complementary motifs, but in quieter motion, rarely using note values smaller than eighths. The peculiar, forced trills so frequently used by Mayone do not occur in Trabaci's variations. Trabaci likes an unornamented contrapuntal texture, which hardly ever appears in Mayone's music.

All but one of Trabaci's toccatas (two in *Libro primo* and four in *Libro secondo*) are relatively short compositions of about fifty measures, and, like Mayone's, do not include imitative sections. The toccata I, no.1, like Mayone's *Toccata quinta* (cf.p.436), is a free fantasy on a subject (g eb d) that serves as the basis of brief imitations or rapid passage work. The toccata I, no.2 begins with a G-major chord, which is sustained through a full eleven measures while the hands alternate with various figurations, including an arpeggio that descends through three octaves. Fig.462 shows the first seven measures. The sustained chords continue through measure 26, where three brief contrasting sections begin abruptly. The first one (meas.27–36) is based on a clavieristic figure in 3/4 time; the second (meas.37–42) returns to duple meter and uses a brief complementary motif; and in the last one (meas.43–50) the left hand plays sixteenth-note figures while the right hand moves above them in quarter-note chords, executing a sequence of

Fig.462

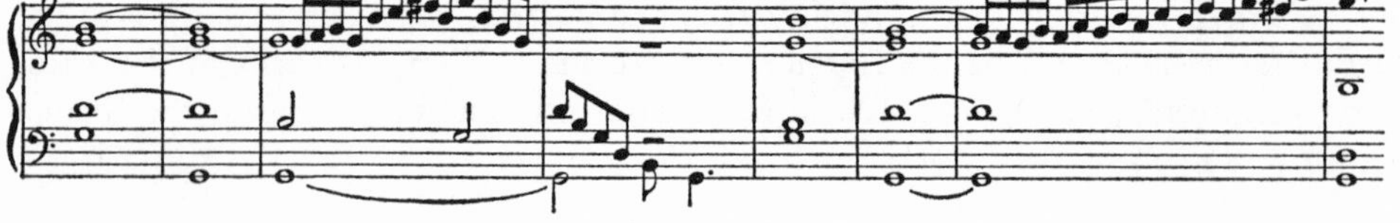

harmonies that is unusually rapid for the period. With its quick contrasts this toccata anticipates a characteristic feature of Frescobaldi's toccatas.

In the second book, toccata no.2 is written for the harp. The beginning is similar to that of the toccata just discussed: For thirteen measures the harmony is a sustained G-minor chord, which is enlivened by various figures, including another arpeggio—this one spans almost six octaves, from d^3 to G_1. Thus the harp again proves to be a highly developed virtuoso instrument of the period, and one that greatly exceeded the range of the harpsichord.*

Toccata terza et Ricercar sopra il Cimbalo cromatico, II, no.3, is a long work, consisting of a free introduction (*toccata*) of 35 measures and an imitative section (*ricercar*) of 90 measures. Trabaci employs the tonal possibilities of the arcicembalo, as he modulates from the *A* major of the beginning to the most distant sharp keys. The whole ricercar moves in the key areas of *F♯*, *C♯*, and *G♯*, occasionally even in *A♯* and *E♯*. The first three keys, moreover, often appear with raised thirds, i.e., with *a♯*, *e♯*, and *b♯*. In two passages Trabaci even uses the major third above *d♯*, the *f✕*, an innovation to which he refers in a lengthy preface to this toccata as "terze maggiore sopra *D* semitonato." Musically the ricercar is rather insignificant, but the toccata contains many interesting turns.

In addition to the various secular types and forms, Trabaci produced a large collection of liturgical music, the *Cento Versi sopra li otto finali ecclesiastici* (II, 13–112) in which each church mode is represented by twelve versets, with four additional ones for the last mode to make a full hundred. The title page states that these pieces were meant to "rispondere in tutti i Divini Officii, et in ogni altra sorte d'occasione." Trabaci was fully aware of the practical side of this enterprise, for all the pieces are written in the smallest format, hardly ever more than twelve measures in length, so that they could be used for responses even in small churches. Within this framework, Trabaci employs all the techniques at his disposal to ensure the greatest possible variety. Even the modern organist would find many a piece that would serve his purposes. Fig.463 shows the first half of verset no.11 of the sixth mode, in which an interesting chromatic idea is heard four times in imitation.

Fig.463

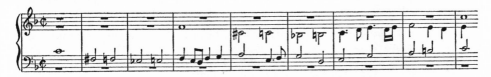

---

* *Ancidetemi pur per l'arpa,* at the end of *Libro secondo*, is also an extremely virtuosic setting.

C. FRESCOBALDI

Girolamo Frescobaldi was born in Ferrara in 1583 and died in Rome in 1643. About all that is known about his youth and student days is that he studied with Luzzascho Luzzaschi, whom he calls "organista si raro" in his various prefaces. By 1604 he was in Rome, first as a member of the *Accademia di S. Cecilia*, and four years later as the organist at the Cappella Giulia of St. Peter's, an office he occupied until his death. His life in Rome was interrupted by a journey to Flanders in 1607, a sojourn of two months at Mantua in 1615, where he waited in vain for employment as court organist to Duke Vincenzo II Gonzaga, and a five-year leave, 1628–33, which he passed as court organist at Florence.

To be employed as an organist at St. Peters at the age of twenty-five represents a recognition similar to the one given Claudio Merulo, when he was called to be an organist at St. Mark's. Doubtless it was due to Frescobaldi's extraordinary ability as an organist, but he soon received recognition and fame as an organ composer as well. In 1628, one of his students, Bartolomeo Grassi, brought out a score edition of his master's *Primo Libro delle Canzone*, which had appeared in part books in 1623. In the foreword he says that Frescobaldi's "volume of ricercars and the other one of capriccios . . . have found so much applause that it was found necessary to reprint them three times in a short time." Moreover, he reports that Frescobaldi had written a great number of books and was still continuing to write, but that they could not be published because of the high printing costs. Toward the end of his life Frescobaldi's fame had spread far beyond Italy's frontiers, particularly to France and Germany. It is only natural that such a strong personality would have adversaries (among them the antiquarian theorist Giovanni Battista Doni). Future generations never forgot Frescobaldi's name, but unfortunately falsified his work. Throughout the 19th century he was primarily known by four "fugues," which were obviously written in the second half of the 18th century. They were probably first published under his name in Clementi's *Selection of Practical Harmony* (1811–15) and then taken over in various collections of old keyboard music.[38]

Much of Frescobaldi's clavier music[39] reaches us in prints that appeared during his lifetime or shortly after his death; some even appeared in several editions—strong witness to the master's fame. A new edition by P. Pidoux comprises all these prints.[40] The following list of prints is in chronological order:[41]

I. *Il primo libro delle fantasie a quattro*, Milan, 1608: 12 fantasies (Pidoux F, I, pp.3–46)

II. *Recercari et canzoni francese fatte sopra diversi oblighi in partitura*, Rome, 1615; unchanged new edition, Rome, 1618: 10 ricercars, 5 canzonas (Pidoux F, II, pp.56–94)

III. *Toccate e partite d'intavolatura di cimbalo*, Libro primo, Rome, 1615; enlarged new edition, Rome, 1615–16: 12 toccatas, 4 partitas, 4 correntes (Pidoux F, III, pp.1–71)[42]

IV. *Il primo libro di capricci fatti sopra diversi soggetti et arie in partitura,* Rome, 1624: 12 capriccios (Pidoux F, II, pp.1–55)[43]

V. *Il secondo libro di toccate canzone versi d'hinni Magnificat gagliarde corrente et altre partite d' intravolatura di cimbalo et organo,* Rome, 1627: 11 toccatas, 6 canzonas, 4 hymns, 3 Magnificats, 2 arias (*Balletto, La Frescobalda,* both with variations), 5 galliards, 6 correntes, 1 intabulation (*Ancidetemi pur d'Archadelt passagiato*), 2 partitas (*sopra Ciaccona, sopra Passacagli*)(Pidoux F, IV)[44]

VI. *In Partitura Il Primo Libro delle canzoni a una, due, tre e quattro voci ... Con dui Toccate in fine ...* , Rome, 1628: This is chiefly a score print, edited by Bartolomeo Grassi, of 37 ensemble canzonas, which Frescobaldi had published in 1623 in five part books (*Canto I, Canto II, Basso I, Basso II, Basso generale*). *Toccata per Spinettina e Violino, Toccata per Spinettina sola,* and *Canzona per Spinettina sola detta la Vittoria* are added at the end.

VII. *Fiori musicali di diversi compositioni: toccate, Kirie, canzoni, capricci e ricercari in partitura a quattro utili per sonatori,* Venice, 1635: 3 organ Masses (consisting of toccatas, ricercars, and canzonas), 2 capriccios (*Bergamasca, Girolmeta*)

IIIa. *Toccate d'intavolatura di cimbalo et organo, partite di diverse arie e corrente, balletti, ciaccone, passaghagli,* Rome, 1637: new ed. of III with *Aggiunta* containing 3 capriccios (*Fra Jacopino, Battaglia, Pastorale*), 5 "suites" (cf.p.475), *Partite cento sopra Passacagli* (Pidoux F, III, pp.72–93)

VIII. *Canzoni alla francese in partitura ... Libro quarto,*[45] Venice, 1645: 11 canzonas (Pidoux F, I, pp.47–78)

More than sixty additional works reach us in manuscript, among them three courantes recently discovered in the Turin tablature Foà 6, and a toccata, ruggiero, and four hymns in Rome, Bibl. Vat. Chigi Q VIII 205.[46]

PRIMO LIBRO DELLE FANTASIE (1608)

Frescobaldi's first work in the field of keyboard music is the *Primo libro delle Fantasie a quattro,* which he published in 1608, when he was twenty-five. In the preface he calls these compositions "le mie prime fatiche," so that we have to assume that they were composed even earlier than the madrigals that came out in the same year (*Primo libro de madrigali a cinque voci*). The fantasies are printed in score on four staves. That they are meant for the keyboard is obvious from internal evidence and from the preface, in which Frescobaldi states that he "had played them sounding on the keys" before his patron Francesco Borghese.

The collection contains twelve fantasies, three each designated as *sopra un soggetto, sopra due soggetti, tre soggetti,* and *quattro soggetti.* Why Frescobaldi called these compositions fantasies—a term that he never used thereafter—is hard to tell. They are written in a strictly imitative counterpoint throughout, with none of the free improvising elements that are found in the English fantasies and in those by Sweelinck. Nor do they relate in form or content to the fantasies of

Antonio Valente and Rocco Rodio. On the other hand, in some details they are similar to Mayone's ricercars, especially in the tendency to derive the entire texture from the subjects. In the process the subjects are of necessity greatly modified, and perhaps it is this very free treatment of the thematic material that Frescobaldi wanted to express in the title *Fantasie*.

This first work shows that although Frescobaldi came from North Italy he already leaned on the Neapolitan school much more than on the Venetian one. Even the use of score notation for clavier works is South Italian. Frescobaldi's designations "sopra due, tre . . . soggetti" obviously derive from such titles as Macque's *Capriccio sopra tre soggetti* and Trabaci's *Primo tono con tre (quattro) fughe*. Internal features are even more decisive, especially the manner in which the subjects are introduced in a polythematic composition. In a ricercar of the North Italian school, except in instances where double subjects occur, they enter one after another in separate sections, so that an opportunity to combine them does not arise until later in the work. But Frescobaldi employs the same procedure as Trabaci, introducing all the themes at the very beginning and combining them in many ways. He makes extensive use of thematic variation, and uses this technique to derive the whole polyphonic web from the thematic substance.

However, while the South Italians develop their subjects in a single, unified section, Frescobaldi treats them in several clearly separated sections, which differ in the way the subjects are worked out and the type of transformations used. Diminution, augmentation, triple meter, chromaticism, and occasionally a sort of modulation are the most important, or at least the most easily recognizable, means he employs for this purpose. In many instances the characteristic difference of the new section can hardly be put into words. It merely consists in the fact that after a concluding cadence a new development of the subjects in new variants begins.

Let us scrutinize some of Frescobaldi's fantasies individually, although because of the extraordinary variability of the material, they can only be described here in outline. *Fantasia seconda, sopra un soggetto* consists of six sections, each of which starts with another version of the subject, as given in Fig.464 (all versions have been transposed to the same starting note). Variants II and V are syncopated, IV is a diminution, and VI a chromatic variant of the subject. The

Fig.464

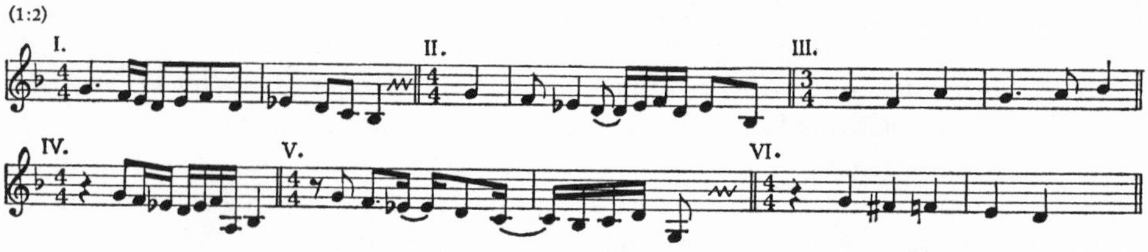

form of III is so completely different that we might be moved to call it a new idea.[47] But we can rely on Frescobaldi to use only one subject in a composition he designates as "sopra un soggetto." Indeed the variant in III is an inversion of the second half of the subject (beginning with the fifth note). The same form also occurs several times in the last section of this fantasy, sometimes abbreviated to the first four notes. The variants are not necessarily used throughout their respective sections; again and again new variants of the basic motif appear. To convey an idea of the variety of transformations as well as of the "density" of the thematic events, Fig. 465 presents the second section in full.

Fig.465

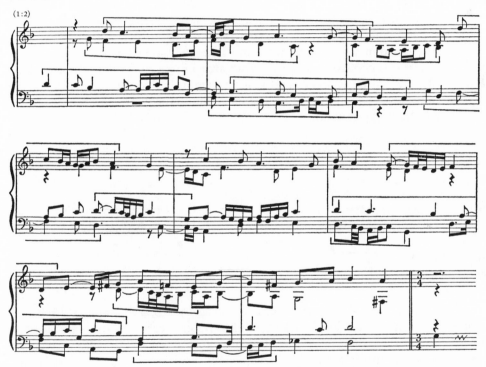

(1:2)

In the second section of *Fantasia quarta, sopra due soggetti* (meas.17–27) the beginning of the main subject (| a — d' c' | b♭ — |) appears in several solmization variants: (| a — d' g | f — |), (| a — b♭ f | g — |), and (| a — b♭ c' | a — |).*

In *Fantasia quinta* the second *soggetto* is nothing but a strict inversion of the first one, so that the composition is in fact based on only one idea. Obviously

---

* Cf. the discussion of Trabaci's *Capriccio sopra la fa sol la* of 1603, p.442.

Frescobaldi thinks of the inversion not as a variant but as an independent subject. Similar situations occur in fantasies nos.8 and 10, the former *sopra tre soggetti* (A, B, A¹); the latter *sopra quattro soggetti* (A, B, A¹, B¹). In the second section of *Fantasia quinta* (meas.30–97) the subject and its inversion appear in augmentation with note values multiplied by four, five, and six.

The *Fantasia nona, sopra tre soggetti* consists of three sections, the second of which (meas.36–67) is characterized more by tonal variants than by rhymthic ones, as the diatonic-modal steps *c* and *f* of the first section are replaced by *c♯* and *f♯*, and a *g♯* is occasionally introduced. In modern terms one could speak of a modulation from the Phrygian-Aeolian to a more or less clear *A* major.

The beginning of *Fantasia undecima sopra quattro soggetti* is outlined schematically in Fig.466 to demonstrate how the whole complex of voices is evolved from the subjects (unbroken lines indicate thematic material; dotted lines, free counterpoint; blank spaces, rests). In the second section (meas.27–51) the subjects are presented in diminution, in the third one in augmentation, in such a way that they appear successively in even *longa* values: first subject D in the alto, then B in the bass, A in the soprano, and C in the tenor. To conclude it all there are two measures in which all four subjects appear simultaneously—almost an antithesis of the preceding presentation.

Fig.466

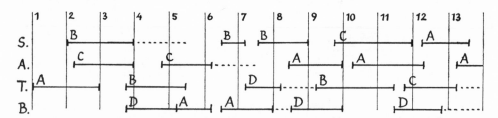

To sum up, we may say that in his fantasies Frescobaldi employs a method of composing that was developed by his Neapolitan predecessors, but he handled it even more brilliantly and exploited it more intensively, as he derived an entire composition from a basic substance. (This technique brings to mind Schönberg's twelve-tone method.) It is unavoidable that this procedure appeals more to the intellect than to the aural sense. It is not easy for the modern listener to relate to these compositions in which, with a fantastic onesidedness, everything is sacrificed to a single goal. But one cannot but admire a period and a musical culture in which such works could be created and appreciated by many (Cardinal Borghese was one), and especially a musician who tackled such a difficult task in his first work and solved it with a mastery that others only achieved toward the ends of their lives, if at all.

RECERCARI ET CANZONI (1615)

Seven years after the fantasies Frescobaldi's second collection of keyboard compositions appeared, containing 10 ricercars and 5 canzonas. The main difference between the ricercars and the fantasies (which also belong to the general ricercar type) lies in the abandonment of the interesting, but in the long run untenable, attempt to derive the entire texture from thematic material. Thematic substance and free counterpoint once more assume their natural, traditional position of alternation and balance, making it possible to concede a greater role to the sensuous element. In the fantasies the voices seem to be combined according to the rules of intervals only; in the ricercars one senses that the demands of harmony are observed, or at least not left entirely to chance.

Ricercars nos.1 and 9 follow the South Italian tradition, as their three and four subjects, respectively, are introduced at the very start and developed without any division of the work into subsections, as in Trabaci's ricercars. On the other hand, nos.2, 3, and 5 are modeled after the Venetian school, and divide into several sections that differ in their thematic content. Therefore they can be outlined schematically, like the ricercars by Andrea Gabrieli, Padovano, and other North Italians:

No.2: A/B ‖ C/D ‖ E/F (all the subjects occur in inversion also)
No.3: A ‖ B/A ‖ C/B/A
No.5: A, B, C, ‖ A ‖ B ‖ C ‖ A/B/C

Ricercar no.5 starts with a long section in two parts, in which the three subjects are presented by the soprano and tenor only. Then each subject is treated separately in four parts, and in the concluding section they are combined in various manners—a plan that is ingeniously thought out and equally masterfully executed.

Four other ricercars are given solmization titles: no.4 *sopra mi re fa mi*, no.6 *sopra fa fa sol la fa*, no.7 *sopra sol mi fa sol la*, and no.10 *sopra la fa sol la re*. The subject so denoted pervades the entire ricercar, mostly with extensive application of augmentations or diminutions in various degrees, and combined with additional subjects. No.4 can be outlined as follows: $A/B \parallel A^2/C/C^1 \parallel A^4/D/E/F$. Nos.6 and 7 are conceived in a particularly individual manner. Each has not only a main subject but also a main voice, which consists exclusively of this subject's repetitions. In no.6 it is the alto, which exhibits the following form: A (4 times), A^2 (3 times), $A^{3/4}$ (twice), $A^{1/2}$ (twice), $A^{3/2}$ (once), A^4 (once); and in no.7 it is the tenor, with the simpler formulation: A (7 times), A^2 (3 times), A^4 (once). Each work develops an entire voice part of about eighty measures from five notes, which are repeated in various proportions and often transposed (down a fourth in no.6, up a fourth in no.7).*

The last ricercar of the collection, no.10, also has a main voice that is de-

---

* Cf. the observations about a ricercar by Cima, p.417.

veloped from a solmization *soggetto*, but it is constructed in a different way and has a different function. Instead of the mathematically exact augmentations or diminutions entrusted to an inner voice, which therefore have a primarily structural function, irregular alterations are heard at irregular intervals in the soprano, and are clearly audible as an identical yet always changing leitmotif. The characteristic subject is heard more than twenty times, unaltered the first several times, then in constantly new variants, with one note or another shortened or lengthened, or the accent shifted. Fig.467 shows the beginning and a passage from the middle. The treatment is very similar to the *soprano ostinato* in the early English organ hymns by Redford and his successors. However, the subjective individuality with which the Italian master disposes of his ostinato and thereby bestows upon it its full measure of "obstinate" urgency is novel and typically Frescobaldian. Meanwhile the lower parts create three sections through their use of different secondary subjects (meas.1–25, 26–62, and 63–87).

Fig.467

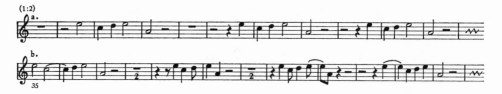

Ricercar no.8 carries the legend "obligo di non uscir di grado" (one must never proceed by steps). Frescobaldi's purpose is to lead the four voices in such a way that stepwise motion never occurs, that except for occasional tone repetitions, the voices move only in thirds, fourths, and larger intervals. Who else could have tackled such a difficult problem and carried it out with such mastery in turns that are always new and fascinating? Fig.468 shows the concluding measures.

In the canzonas in the 1615 print Frescobaldi deals for the first time with a form that interested him throughout his life. As much as the ricercar answered

Fig.468

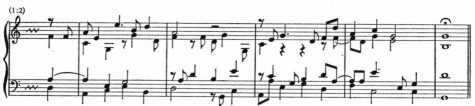

454

his need for intellectual activity and spiritual penetration, his heart really belonged to the canzona, whose lightness, vivacity, and changeability offered an especially appropriate field for his fiery temperament and inexhaustible imagination. The five canzonas of 1615 are followed by six more in the *Secondo libro di toccate* of 1627, five in the *Fiori musicali,* eleven in the posthumous *Canzoni alla francese,* and sixteen in manuscripts, as well as by numerous ensemble canzonas.

Earlier Italian composers had developed the contrast canzona with several contrasting sections. Trabaci was among the first to employ an opposite principle when he connected the various sections by employing the same subject throughout, though usually with slight variants (cf.p.441). The result was a new type known as the variation canzona. Frescobaldi cultivated this type primarily and led it to its culmination, although occasionally the older contrast canzona is found in his works.

All five canzonas of 1615 consist of five sections: Three long sections in duple meter with a fugal texture, in which two subjects are often contrapuntally combined, alternate with two shorter sections in triple meter, in a freer, occasionally almost homophonic, style. In the last canzona this scheme is reduced to three sections. This collection is still undecided about the use of the variation principle. In nos.1 and 5 it is totally absent. In no.4 the last section is built on the same (unaltered) subject as the first one, while the remaining sections are thematically independent. (Possibly the three middle sections are based on a common subject that is different from the first subject.) This cyclic form is found elsewhere in the canzona repertoire of the period. Nos.2 and 3, however, are genuine variation canzonas, in which a variant of the first subject is used in each of the four subsequent sections. In no.2 Frescobaldi goes even beyond this scheme, as he subdivides the first and third sections by introducing additional variants. Designating these variants of the subject as A_1, A_2, etc., the two canzonas can be outlined as follows (sections in triple meter are indicated by a 3):

No.2: A, A_1 || (3) A_2 || A_3/B, A_4/C, A_5/D || (3) A_6 || A_7
No.3: A || (3) A_1/B || A_2 || (3) A_3 || A_4/C

Fig.469 shows the variants that appear in no.2.

Fig.469

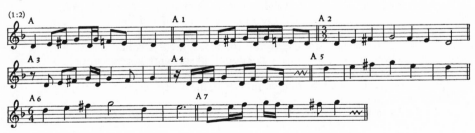

The ricercars, the first book of toccatas, and an enlarged new edition of the toccatas (on which the following observations are based) all appeared in the same year, 1615. For the first edition of the toccatas Frescobaldi wrote a foreword "Al Lettore," in which he gave a number of explanations about the execution of the toccatas and partitas. In the new edition this foreword appears in an expanded version, which was taken over into later reprints of this work as well as into the third edition of 1637. Since it is one of the most important documents on the presentation of old keyboard music almost all of it is reproduced here:

> To the reader:
>
> Since I well know how much the manner of playing that involves vocal affects and differentiation of sections [passi] is favored, I thought it right to prove my interest and sympathy therewith through this modest work, which I deliver to the printer together with the following remarks. . . .
>
> 1. This manner of playing must not always follow the same meter; in this respect it is similar to the performance of modern madrigals, whose difficulty is eased by taking the beat [battuta] slowly at times and fast at others, even by pausing with the singing in accordance with the mood or the meaning of the words.
>
> 2. In the toccatas I have seen to it not only that they are rich in varied sections and moods [passi diversi et affetti] but also that one may play each section separately, so that the player can stop wherever he wishes. . . .
>
> 3. The beginnings of the toccatas must be played slowly and arpeggiando. . . .
>
> 4. In trills as well as in runs, whether they move by skips or by steps [passagi di salto ò di grado], one must pause on the last note, even when it is an eighth or sixteenth note [croma ò biscroma], or different from the next note. Such a pause will avoid mistaking one passage for another.
>
> 5. Cadenzas, even when notated as fast [scritte veloce], must be well sustained [sostenerle assai], and when one approaches the end of a passage run or a cadenza, the tempo must be taken even more slowly [sostenendo il tempo più adagio].
>
> 6. Caesurae or ends of sections [passi] occur where both hands simultaneously play a consonance in half notes [minime]. Where a trill in one hand is played simultaneously with a run in the other, one must not play note against note, but try to play the trill fast and the run in a more sustained and expressive manner, otherwise confusion will result.
>
> 7. When there is a section with eighth notes in one hand and sixteenths in the other, it should not be executed too rapidly; and the hand that plays the sixteenth notes should dot them somewhat, not the first note, however, but the second one, and so on throughout, not the first but the second.
>
> 8. Before executing parallel runs [passi doppi] of sixteenth notes in both hands, one must pause on the preceding note, even when it is a black one; then one should attack the passage with determination, in order to exhibit the agility of the hands all the more.
>
> 9. In the variations that include both runs and expressive passages, it will be good to choose a broad tempo; one may well observe this in the toccatas also. Those variations that do not include runs one may play quite fast [alquanto al-

456

legre di battuta], and it is left to the good taste and judgement of the player to choose the tempo correctly.* Herein lie the spirit and perfection of this manner of playing and of this style.

These instructions are so clear that they hardly need additional explanations. But one detail deserves to be stressed. In 7. Frescobaldi states that a series of sixteenth notes played against eighth notes should not be executed evenly but in a dotted rhythm. This practice may seem affected and artificial to us, but it is described by Tomás de Sancta Maria in his *Arte de tañer fantasia* of 1565 (cf.Chap.8, note 53), and around 1700 it was in general use, especially in France, where it was called *notes inegales* (which were, however, executed long-short; cf.p.731).

The toccatas are Frescobaldi's most characteristic creative activity. They carry the stamp of his personality more than any of his other works. This is particularly true of the later toccatas, those in the *Secondo Libro* (1627) and the *Fiori musicali* (1635). But in many details even the twelve toccatas of 1615 show the unmistakable touch of his hand. A comparison with Claudio Merulo's toccatas, which they naturally suggest, shows differences in both formal construction and style. An important structural feature in Merulo's pieces is the insertion of imitative sections, which produce a clear three- or five-section form. Among the more than fifty toccatas by Frescobaldi in the various prints and manuscripts, there is only one of this type, no.9 of the collection of 1615. Even more important are the differences in style. Merulo's toccatas are invented wholly in the spirit of the Renaissance, but Frescobaldi's works are unmistakably informed by the spirit of the early Baroque: there sustained chords, which move with quiet dignity in modal progressions, here bold and often arbitrary turns of harmony, which result in surprising tonality changes; there articulations in broad plains that join together in an imposing architecture, here a splintering into small fragments, which seem to follow no other law but that of momentary inspiration; there figurations that ascend and descend in purposeful lines, here a plethora of nervous formulae, which change from moment to moment.

Doubtless Frescobaldi was stimulated to write in this new style by the works of the Neapolitan school. The remarks about Mayone's toccatas (cf.pp.433ff.) can be applied to Frescobaldi's without essential changes. But the latter avoids some of the more bizzarre features found in the works of the Neapolitans. And, as is to be expected from a great master, he possesses not only the talent to invent the most diverse figures but also the insight and the faculty to join them into an organic, meaningful whole.

One of the innumerable interesting details is the frequent use of brief, often

---

* In the preface to the first edition Frescobaldi seems to take a more conservative view with respect to the tempo of the partitas, for he says that they are all to be played in the same tempo ("non convenendo da principio far presto, et seguir languidamente; ma vogliono esser portate intere col medesimo tempo").

Fig.470

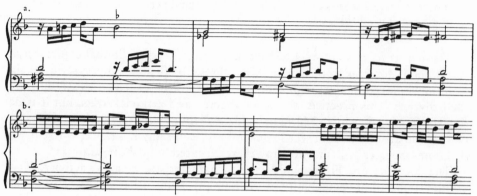

rhythmically nervous figures, which appear several times in succession as complementary motifs in various parts. Fig.470 shows two examples, the first from *Toccata seconda*, the second from *Toccata nona*. Technically these figures are similar to Sweelinck's clavieristic figures, but somehow this term, which is so applicable to the Netherlander, seems out of place with Frescobaldi. His figures are too tense, too "contrived" to relate them to the idea of virtuosic play, lightness, or weightlessness. Also the way in which the figures are used is very different: Sweelinck inserts them in an orderly, well-proportioned manner at the appropriate place in a lucid harmonic texture; in Frescobaldi's music they are irregular and fragmentary, carrying the harmony with them, often onto "devious" paths. Fig. 471 gives a lovely example, a passage from *Toccata settima* (Pidoux F, III, p.71, brace 1). Note how the motif appears in a hasty and changeable shape, and how,

Fig.471

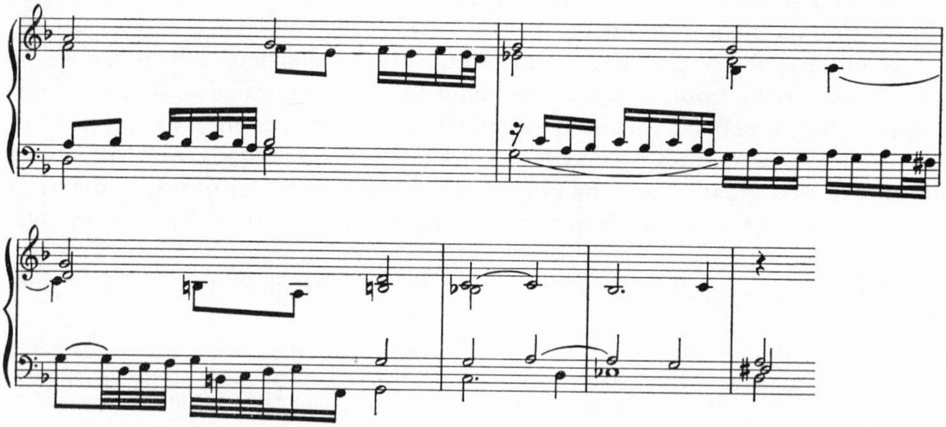

at the beginning of the second measure, it causes one of those curious turns of harmony that are so very characteristic of Frescobaldi's tonal language. Like this one, many are based on the interchangeability of the major and minor third, a phenomenon that occurred earlier in Mayone's music. Fig.472 shows a passage from *Toccata undecima*, where three such exchanges follow each other in close succession (Pidoux F, III, p.41, brace 1). The unprepared seventh chord is also an essential part of Frescobaldi's tonal language (cf.meas.4 in Fig.471). It is heard particularly often in its first inversion, as a six-five chord.*

Fig.472

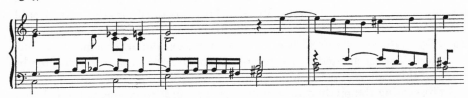

The last of the twelve toccatas of 1615 is completely devoted to problems of early Baroque harmony. It belongs to the *durezze e ligature* type, which occurred in the works of Ercole Pasquini, Macque, and Trabaci. Another interesting harmonic study is the very peculiar "prelude" at the beginning of the eleventh toccata, in which chords glide up and down above pedal points.

The first edition of *Toccate I* contains three variation sets: *Partite 12 sopra l'aria della Romanesca*, *Partite 6 sopra l'aria di Monicha*, and *Partite 8 sopra l'aria di Ruggiero*. In the second edition the number of variations is increased—to 14, 11, and 12, respectively—and a new set is added, the *Partite 6 sopra l'aria di Follia*. In the romanesca set several variations are replaced by new ones: the first four by five, and the last one (no.XII) by two (nos.XIII–XIV); altogether then there are nineteen variations, but the ones that are contained in the first edition only are not yet available in a modern edition.

The romanesca melody had already been used in the 16th century by various Spanish lute and organ composers—Narvaez, Mudarra, Valderrábano, Cabezón—as a theme for variations, mostly under the title *Guardame las vacas* or *Romanesca Guardame las vacas*. About 1600 Ercole Pasquini, Stella, and Mayone wrote variations on the same theme, now called romanesca. In Frescobaldi's music it appears in an expanded form, with an added ripresa that repeats the second half of the bass at the same time as the entire melody is played in diminution. Fig.473 shows the basic scheme. To give an idea of how Frescobaldi fills this twelve-measure

---

* Note that the six-five chord appears repeatedly in the works of Ercole Pasquini. Certainly this composer, whose works have become known only recently, must also be counted among the immediate predecessors of Frescobaldi. He, too was no doubt in some contact with the Neapolitan group.

Fig.473

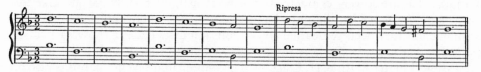

scheme with content, Fig.474 gives the beginning and end of the *Prima parte* (var. I).[48] Variations IV, VI, VII, and XII are identical in structure with the first one; so are those five variations in the first edition that are omitted from the second one. In variations III, XIII, and XIV the ripresa is reduced to its last two measures. In four successive variations, VIII–XI, Frescobaldi employs notes of double value, three whole notes, to represent each structural note of the theme;* in these "adagio" variations the ripresa is entirely omitted. On the other hand, the tempo of variation V is accelerated by the use of *proportio tripla.* Fig.475 shows the beginning of this "allegro" variation.

In discussing the method of variation it is natural to compare Frescobaldi's romanesca variations with those by Scipione Stella or Mayone. The latter (cf. p.437) may be divided into various groups, according to whether they are dominated by motifs (e.g., Stella's four *Partite sopra la Romanesca*), scale runs, trill fig-

Fig.474

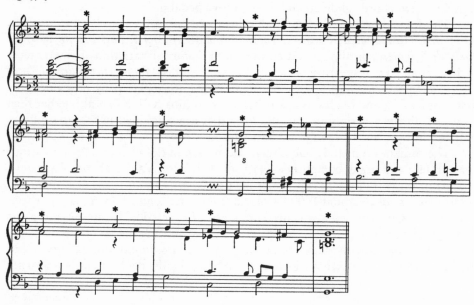

---

* In variations X and XI the fifth structural note is expanded from three to four whole notes.

Fig.475

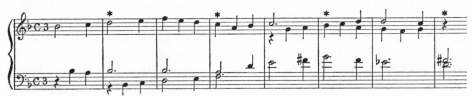

ures, etc. Such a classification is next to impossible for Frescobaldi's variations, for, like his toccatas, they change their approach from moment to moment. We have observed that in some of Byrd's variations, and even more so in Sweelinck's, changes of method occur. In Frescobaldi's work the approach does not change from section to section but just about all the time, not only in some variations but in all or most of them. Among his romanesca variations there are only two that are based on a single motif. The penultimate one (XIII) is reminiscent of one of Mayone's variations on the *Romanesca* (var.VII), whose first half employs an almost identical motif (cf.Fig.476). Of course, the primary interest of a comparison

Fig.476

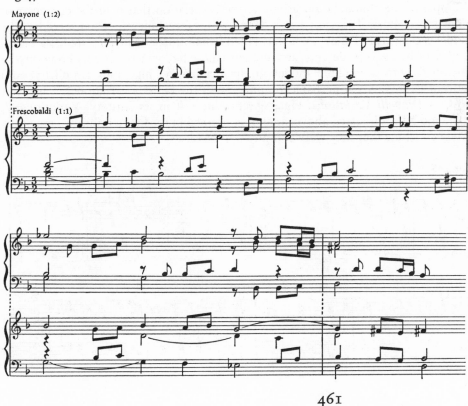

lies not so much in what is common to both pieces but what differentiates them. The small but decisive change, through which the motif exchanges its rhythmic character for a melodic one; the neutralization of the ascending motif by the melody, whose descent occasionally involves the motif also; the feminine ending at the conclusion of the phrase; the use of free voices and general loosening of the texture: all these mark Frescobaldi's variation as the work of a master of greatest sensitivity and great power of formulation. The motif technique is employed even more clearly and more insistently in the fourth variation of the first edition.

Fig.477

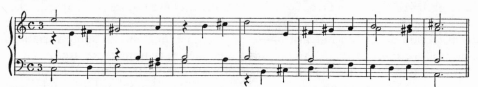

Two other variations, V and XIV, are unified, but in a completely new manner. The former, whose beginning was reproduced in Fig.475, may be the earliest example of the character variation, i.e., of a variation that is in the character of a particular musical species, e.g., a dance, or a funeral march. What served as the model is clear from Fig.477, which is taken from a corrente in *Toccate I*. Variation XIV also has a very definite and unified character, which cannot, however, be identified with a tangible model. In its originality, ingenious simplicity, and reticent expressivity it perhaps compares with the famous variation XX in Beethoven's *Diabelli Variations*. Fig.478 reproduces it in its entirety. Variations V, XIII, and XIV, discussed above, are not contained in the first edition; we may thus safely conclude that they were composed in 1615.

Fig.478

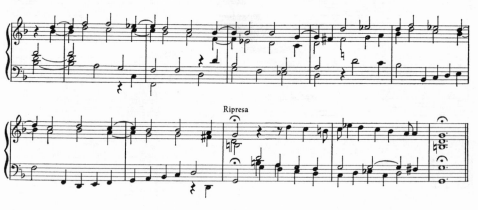

Frescobaldi's *Romanesca* is one of the very greatest creations in the field of variation, not only in its single variations but particularly as a whole. The basic character of the work is determined by the first and last variations: the first deeply expressive, the last of transcendent sublimity. In between others expand this framework in diverse and captivating ways, but never go beyond it. Nothing is mere decoration or pretty play; everything is expressive and meaningful.

None of the three other variation works of *Toccate I—Monicha, Ruggiero,* and *Follia*—can measure up to the *Romanesca* in artistic import. All of them suffer primarily from choppy phrasing and too regular structure and harmony. These faults are partly due to the themes, which, like so many popular tunes, divide into regular phrases of four or even two measures. But it is caused even more by the fact that instead of covering up or softening this articulation, which becomes particularly insistent and disturbing with continuous repetition, Frescobaldi actually seems to stress it, as he repeatedly brings a motion—often quite a lively one —to a sudden halt in a chord. This is all the more curious since his predecessors— Mayone, Trabaci, as well as others—recognized the danger involved, and learned to circumvent it by bridging such points with a continuation of the motion. That Frescobaldi did not "know" how to do this, would be a silly assumption. Obviously the alternation of stormy motion and sudden stops was intentional. Indeed, this principle plays an important role in the later toccatas, but there it is applied with much greater sensitivity and becomes a fascinating interplay of opposing forces. But in these three variation sets this technique merely results in monotony because of its completely regular, expected occurrence. Nevertheless these works offer many features of interest worthy of the master.

The *Partite sopra Monicha* are based on a popular melody, which occurs in a similar form as early as 1550 in Germany, and later as *Noël* (Christmas carol) in France.[49] In the earlier version the first phrase ends on the dominant, while in the Italian one it cadences on the tonic, but the change is certainly no improvement, as Fig.479 proves. In the *Partite sopra Follia* Frescobaldi uses a theme that has no recognizable connection with the famous folia. Two of the variations (III and V) are written in the style of a corrente. The twelve *Partite sopra Ruggiero* are based on the well-known theme that was also treated by Macque, Mayone, and Trabaci. Variation X, reproduced in Fig.480, follows the same idea as the final variation of the *Romanesca* set, but it does not equal its expressive power. The last variation is another corrente, in which the first three phrases are contracted from four measures to three. Such changes of the thematic structure are also found in Trabaci's *Ruggiero* variations (cf.pp.443f.).

Fig.479

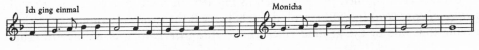

Fig.480

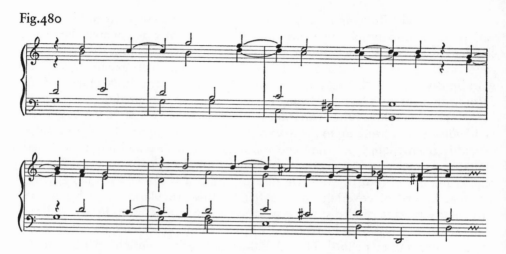

Toccate I is concluded by four correntes. Like Ercole Pasquini, Frescobaldi writes these dances in phrases of irregular length. *Corrente terza*, e.g., consists of two sections of twelve and twenty-five measures, respectively, *Corrente quarta* of sections of fourteen and seventeen measures.

PRIMO LIBRO DI CAPRICCI (1624)

The compositions in the two prints of the 1620s were created when Frescobaldi was a mature man of about forty. The *Primo libro di capricci fatti sopra diversi soggetti et arie in partitura* contains 12 capriccios, some of which are based on *soggetti* (e.g., *Ut re mi fa sol la, La sol fa re mi*), others on tunes (e.g., *Spagnoletta, Ruggiero*), and still others investigate special problems of composition (e.g., the *Capriccio cromatico di ligature al contrario*). In a preface "A gli studiosi dell' opera" Frescobaldi gives some directions as to the execution of the capriccios and mentions that they are not as simple in style as the ricercars (of 1615)—an observation that is confirmed on studying or playing these most interesting compositions.

Two of the capriccios differ from the others in their brevity and unity. *Capriccio di durezze* (no.9) is one of several works of the period that deal with the problem of dissonant harmony. While earlier compositions of this type, e.g., the *durezze e ligature* by Macque and Trabaci, were revolutionary experiments that went beyond their real aim—in a way this is also true of Frescobaldi's *Toccata duodecima* of 1615—Frescobaldi's capriccio represents an already clarified solution, which may be taken as the model of a new harmonic technique. The beginning of this expressive, sustained piece is given in Fig.481. In the *Capriccio cromatico di ligature al contrario* (no.8) Frescobaldi sets himself the problem, almost in jest, of proving that one of the ground rules of the *stile osservato* was wrong—the rule

464

Fig.481

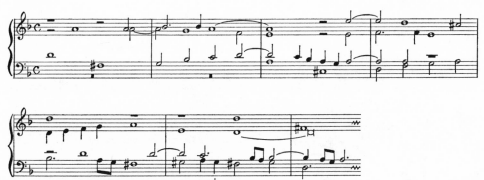

that dissonances must be resolved in descent. He shows that they may also be resolved "al contrario," i.e., in ascent, as in Fig.482.

The other capriccios are long compositions, which, like canzonas, divide into several contrasting sections. The first one, e.g., *sopra Ut re mi fa sol la,* consists of eleven sections, which are differentiated by the way the hexachord subject is presented or by the introduction of various counter-motifs. In the *Capriccio sopra La sol fa re mi* (no.4), the well-known *Lascia fare mi*—on which Josquin had already based one of his Masses—is treated in eight sections, in which it appears in diverse variants. Thematic variation, which Frescobaldi employed in his fantasies of 1608 in pursuing another aim, becomes a powerful technique here, masterfully handled. It enables him to develop an organism that is full of life from the driest substance. The aesthetic significance of the capriccios largely results from the combination or the dialectic coexistence of two contrary principles: identity and variety. "Semper idem, semper aliud" might be their motto.

One of Frescobaldi's most remarkable works is the *Capriccio sopra il Cucho* (no.3). The top part consists exclusively of the cuckoo call (*d″–b′*), which dominates the piece as a *soprano ostinato.* It is heard about eighty times at irregular intervals and in many rhythmic variants.* The lower parts fall into ten sections

Fig.482

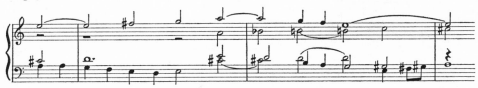

---

* Another *Capriccio sopra Cucchù,* similar in principle, appears in the manuscript Rome, Bibl. Vat. Chigi Q IV.25.

Fig.483

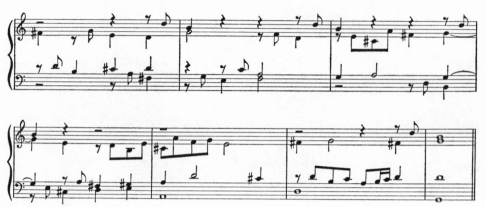

with different counter-motifs. In the third section, reproduced in Fig.483, the entire complex of voices is derived from the cuckoo call.

Capriccio no.10 is a kind of enigma canon; it is inscribed: "obligo di cantare la quinta parte senza toccarla sempre di obligo del soggetto scritto si placet" (it is necessary to sing the fifth voice without playing it, always following the *soggetto* exactly as it is written, if you please). The *soggetto* (*a c′ c′ b d′ c′ b a*) is written in whole notes at the beginning. The enigma for the player, who must also be a singer, is to find the places where this subject should or can be sung against the four lower parts, for they are not indicated.* A number of subjects appear in the lower voices; the first one is identical with the *soggetto*. Fig.484 presents the *soggetto* entrance at Pidoux F, II, p.42, measure 13.

Fig.484

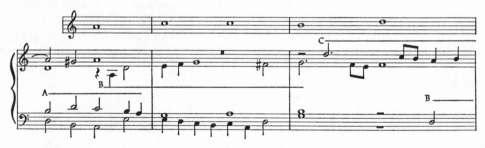

---

* In Pidoux F eight places are indicated, but at least two more may be added (at Pidoux F, II, p.42, middle of meas.13; p.45, meas.8). Even so, some long sections lack the *soggetto*. I am indebted to Mr. J. Burns for the suggestion that they may be partly enriched by transposing the *soggetto* to *d* (p.43, brace 2, middle of meas.1; p.44, brace 2, meas.2; p.45, brace 3, meas.3).

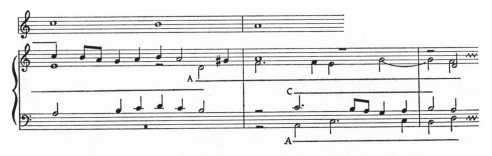

Finally, let us turn to the four "arioso" capriccios. Two of them, *sopra la Bassa fiamenga* and *sopra la Spagnoletta,* employ themes from which the otherwise apparently unknown tunes (or their beginnings) may be reconstructed with some confidence, as shown in Fig.485. The melodic ductus of the *Spagnoletta* leads Frescobaldi—or rather is exploited by him—to let the entire work be dominated and pervaded by the motif of the ascending third. The combination of artistic inspiration and technical skill makes this capriccio a masterpiece. A third "arioso" capriccio, *sopra l'aria di Ruggiero,* is constructed as a "quadruple fugue" based on the four phrases of the ruggiero bass. The thematic content of the eight sections of this piece may be presented schematically as follows:

I   II   III   IV   V   VI   VII   VIII
A, B, C, D, || (3) C/D || A, B, C, D || (3) B || B/C || A, B, C, D || A || C/D

Free counter-motifs are added to this basic scheme, e.g., the chromatic scale in VII, and a lively clavieristic figure and later rapid scales in VIII, which make for a spirited finale.

Fig.485

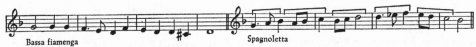

Bassa fiamenga   Spagnoletta

The capriccio on *Or chè noi rimena in partite* stands alone. It does not use imitative polyphony, but is a set of five variations on a theme. The print of 1626, which combines the capriccios with the ricercars and canzonas of 1615, omits it, probably because it is so different in character.[50] But it is one of the most interesting and most valuable variation works by Frescobaldi. The theme, which is heard most clearly in the *Prima, Terza,* and *Quarta parte,* is unfortunately unknown. It consists of two repeated sections, the first of six measures in triple meter, the second of eight measures in duple meter. The melody and bass may perhaps be reconstructed as shown in Fig.486. Each repetition is set differently. In the *Seconda parte* the basic structure is so altered that the six triple-meter measures are recast as four duple-meter measures, putting the whole variation in 4/4 time. In the final

Fig.486

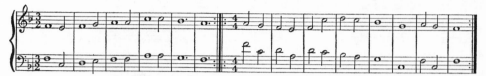

variation the entire section is omitted, and to make up for it, the variation of the second section is followed by a very interesting coda, which is reproduced in Fig. 487. It begins with the first two measures of the second section, so that it appears that another repetition of the whole section is iminent, but a sudden turn to a lively ending in triple meter transforms the threat into a successful jest.

Fig.487

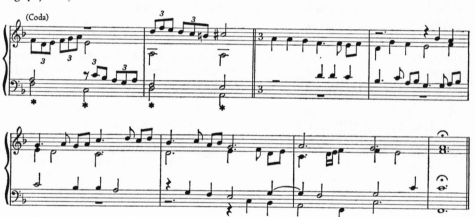

Several capriccios include a special feature, a brief postlude in toccata style, which is appended to one section or another. This feature is found for the first time in the *Ricercari e Canzoni* of 1615, but in only one piece, *Canzone quarta*. The second and fifth sections of this work (both in triple meter) conclude with postludes of this kind. They appear more frequently in the capriccios, and in the later canzonas (*Toccate II, Fiori musicali, Aggiunta* to *Toccate I*) the postludes acquire considerable length and become an integral part of the composition.

SECONDO LIBRO DI TOCCATE (1627)

Il secondo libro di toccate . . . appeared three years after the capriccios. It is an extensive, mixed collection of toccatas, canzonas, variations, dances, and a few liturgical compositions. This book may well be regarded as the central stage of Frescobaldi's keyboard output, the point at which the strands of his earlier opus are gathered together and joined to those that lead to his last works.

468

In the toccatas of 1615 Frescobaldi had created a very individual and personal type, which had hardly anything in common with Merulo's toccatas except the name. The toccatas of the *Secondo libro* are mostly of the same type, but in an even clearer format. The figures are even more diverse and individual, the expression more changeable, the formal articulation clearer. While the earlier toccatas give the impression of an uninterrupted, almost directionless drift, the later ones show an attempt to dam the flow, to halt the impulse of motion and bring it momentarily to a rest, before the energy is renewed. They are now divided into a number of sections, each of which usually concludes with a full final chord. Generally these sections are rather short, rarely longer than eight or ten measures. *Toccata prima*, e.g., divides into nine sections of 14, 3, 5, 8, 10, 5, 4, 9, and 7 measures, respectively*

This type is most clearly represented by *Toccata nona*, which may be divided into eighteen sections, some only two or three measures long, none longer than six. This piece represents a remarkable culmination of Frescobaldi's work. The inexhaustible wealth of ideas, the variety of figures is certainly admirable, but even more so is the alternation of force and counterforce, of impetus and braking, which is again and again effected in the smallest space, captivating the listener anew each time, never letting him rest. "Non senza fatiga si giunge al fine" (not without toil does one achieve one's end), writes Frescobaldi at the end of this piece, fully conscious of the great demands he has made, not only on the intellectual power of the listener but also on the technical ability of the player. It is not so much a matter of virtuosity in the usual sense, but of being able to solve rhythmic problems, such as three or six notes in one hand against four notes or dotted values in the other. Some of them are given in Fig.488.

Fig.488

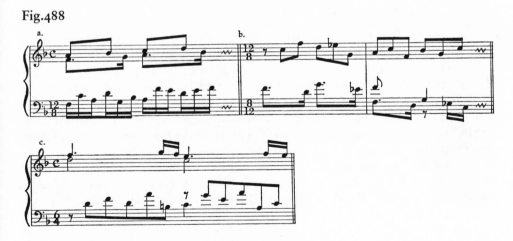

---

*I.e., whole-note measures; in the original print measures of double length are frequent.

Among the many interesting figures found in this toccata (as well as in others), two deserve special mention. The first is a written-out trill in sixteenth notes, played simultaneously with equally rapid but very different figures. The two motions lead to dissonant clashes, which Frescobaldi employs repeatedly to slow down the preceding motion and bring it to a halt. This highly effective device is found no less than four times in *Toccata nona,* and once more at the end of *Toccata undecima.* Fig.489 shows one of these passages from the former. Frescobaldi says in his foreword, "When one hand, be it the right or the left, executes a trill, while the other plays a run, one must not play note against note, but must see to it that the trill is rapid while the runs are sustained and expressive, for otherwise confusion would result." Does this remark refer to passages such as the one in Fig.489? It would seem so, and yet one would hope not, for it is exactly the simultaneity of the various motions that provokes the characteristic effect of clash and braking—with the cooperation of a strong ritardando. Indeed, it would be hard to say how Frescobaldi's direction could be applied here, since the same hand executes both the trill and the run.*

Fig.489

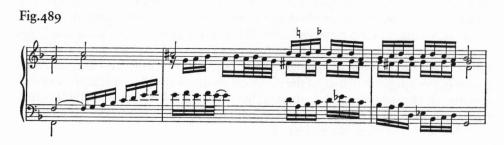

The second figure uses a short motif that, despite changing harmonization, is repeated like an ostinato on the same pitch and has the effect of a pedal point. The excerpt in Fig.490 is taken from *Toccata prima.* The application of the same idea is even bolder in *Toccata nona,* to which the reader is referred again and again.

Toccatas nos.3 and 4 are designated as "per l'organo da sonarsi alla levatione," and are expressly meant for the liturgical service during the transubstantiation of the Mass. Although they essentially belong to the type discussed above, they exhibit special qualities connected with their purpose. The sections are longer, the motion quieter, and the evolution more even. Several details seem to be directly connected with the sacrament during which the music is heard. It is therefore no accident that toccata no.3 contains several passages whose bold modulation may

---

* In the first book of toccatas, for which this foreword was originally written, the trills are in one hand against runs in the other. Such figures occurred earlier in Ercole Pasquini (cf. Fig.433).

Fig.490

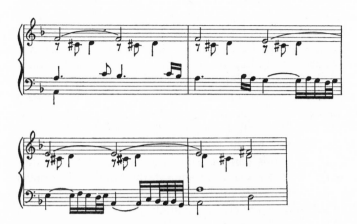

be interpreted as a symbol of the mystic transformation, e.g., the one given in Fig.491 (Pidoux F, IV, p.12, brace 2). Again, is it too bold to suggest that the flickering motifs that dominate the conclusion of the next toccata represent an expression of the ecstatic mood of the moment of Elevation? The elevation toccatas from the *Fiori musicali* surely have this intent.

Fig.491

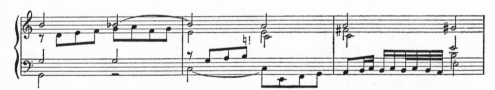

The two toccatas "sopra i pedali per l'organo, e senza" (nos.5 and 6) and the *Capriccio pastorale* from the *Aggiunta* of *Toccate I* are the only compositions in Frescobaldi prints that employ the organ pedals.* In all three pieces they serve only to sound long, sustained pedal points. The genuine use of the pedals, which was highly developed in Germany as early as the 15th century—in the Ileborgh tablature, the *Buxheim Organ Book*, and Schlick's *Ascendo ad patrem*, with its quadruple pedals—was never cultivated in Italy, not even by such a great organ master as Frescobaldi. Probably his organ at St. Peter's had only a rudimentary pedal keyboard, limited to the tones from C to A, for these pitches are the only ones used in these three pieces.

In comparison with the canzonas of 1615 the six in *Toccate II* represent a definite step in the direction of the variation canzona, which from here on dominates

---

* Three more pedal toccatas are contained in manuscripts; cf. p.482.

Frescobaldi's works in this field. Occasionally the subject is varied to such an extreme that the connection between it and the figures that emerge can only be recognized after detailed study. *Canzona quinta* is especially interesting in this regard; its fugal sections are based on the subjects shown in Fig.492. Subject b. is a simple transformation of a., but d. and e. are derived in a much more complicated way—with the aid of the inversion of a motif that is hidden in the second measure of a. (In a similar way the second and third subjects in the *Canzona quarta* are developed from the second measure of the main subject.) Subject c. does not seem to be connected with a. at all, but can probably be considered an ornamented variant of d., as indicated by the notes marked "x." It is certainly true that such far-fetched transformations cannot be heard, but as technical devices they are just as valid as the cancrizans of the theme in the finale of Beethoven's *Hammerklavier Sonata* or the variants of the (A S C H) motif in Schumann's *Carnaval*, not to speak of Schönberg's twelve-tone method.

Fig.492

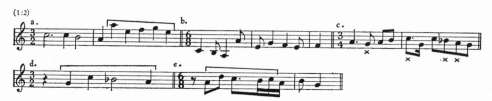

An important feature in the first four canzonas is the insertion of toccata-like postludes at the end of each section (cf.p.468). Such postludes are occasionally found in earlier works, but because of their considerable length and consistent use, they now become an integral part of the structure and style. The last two canzonas are very different, for all their sections are in triple meter, mostly alternating between 3/1 and 3/2, and they have no toccata-like postludes.

Toccate II also contains four variation works: *Aria detta Balletto* (8 variations), *Aria detta la Frescobalda* (5), *Partite sopra Ciaccona* (15), and *Partite sopra Passacagli* (32). The *Balletto* variations have no particularly interesting features. The title of the *Frescobalda* variations, on the other hand, indicates that the theme is Frescobaldi's own. This is the first variation work to be based on a melody written by the composer himself, rather than on a song or dance tune from the popular repertoire. Even the irregular structure of the theme proves that its origin is different: two sections of five plus four and three plus four measures, respectively. Moreover, the gracefulness and expressiveness of the melody are worthy of a great master. In the variations Frescobaldi renounces all virtuosic passage work and nearly all motivic work; instead, within the same basic harmonic framework, he creates ever new melodies whose beauty equals that of the theme. At the same time the structure is frequently altered by abbreviating or lengthening one phrase or

The *Magnificat secundi toni* has the usual number of six verses, the other two have only five. Their treatment is more varied than in the hymns. In some verses, e.g., the second and third verses of the *Magnificat primi toni,* the whole Gregorian melody is presented as a *cantus planus*. In most verses only the *initium* and the *terminatio* of the tone are employed, the former as the point of departure for the beginning, the latter similarly for the conclusion. All the first verses use only the *terminatio,* which indicates that the first word, *Magnificat,* was sung by the choir. These versets are also quite varied in their expression, some full of serious dignity, others approaching the lively style of the canzona.

AGGIUNTA (1637)

The pieces that were added to the 1637 edition of *Toccate I* under the title *Agguinta* closely follow *Toccate II* in content. The *Aggiunta* (Pidoux F, III, pp.72 ff.) starts with three suite-like compositions:[53]

1. *Balletto—Corrente del Balletto—Passachagli*
2. *Balletto secondo—Corrente del Balletto*
3. *Balletto terzo—Corrente del Balletto—Passachagli*

Nos.1 and 2 may be called variation suites, insofar as the beginning of the corrente is derived from that of the balletto. The two *Passachagli* differ from the variations in *Toccate II* in that the theme is in quadruple meter, mostly in some form of the descending tetrachord, as in the *Alio modo* of Fig.493, or in inversion as an ascent of a fifth (| g | a | b♭ c′ | d′). Two other pieces, later on in the *Aggiunta,* are similar, a *Balletto e Ciaccona* in G major and a *Corrente e Ciaccona* in A minor.

The fourth composition is entitled *Cento partite sopra passacagli*. It is a group (one might even call it a conglomeration), constituted as follows: *Passacagli* (20 var.), *Corrente* (12 meas.), *Passacagli* (22 var.), *Ciaccona* (10 var.), *Passacagli* (8 var.), *Ciaccona* (12 var.), *Passacagli* (5 var.), *Ciaccona* (19 var.), *Passacagli* (23 var.). It is certainly not a unified composition. The preface states, "Li Passacagli si potranno separatamente sonare . . . ," but how the piece has to be divided to arrive at the number of one hundred *partite,* as indicated in the title, is difficult to determine. Both the *Passacagli* and the *Ciaccona* are based on basic segments of four beats, which sometimes encompass four measures, sometimes two. An essential difference between the two types cannot be recognized. In style both are very similar to the *Passacagli* and *Ciaccona* variations in *Toccate II*. Both publications contain a total of over two hundred different settings of the same basic idea, every one interesting, and every one a testimony to the master's inexhaustible imagination.

Finally, there are three "capriccios" in the *Aggiunta*. The *Capriccio del soggetto scritto sopra l'aria di Roggiero* is not a capriccio in the usual sense of the word. Like the *Capriccio sopra l'aria Or chè noi rimena* from the *Capricci* of

1624, it is a set of six variations on the ruggiero theme, the same that underlies the *Partite 12 sopra l'aria di Ruggiero* in *Toccate I* (1615). Nevertheless it is a composition that certainly deserves its title, for, in a way that is as humorous as it is ingenious, a *soggetto scritto,* shown in Fig.496 is woven into it. The *soggetto* is written at the beginning of the work and labeled *Fra Jacopino*—obviously it is taken from Italian folk repertoire. This short song, or just its first or second section, is heard again and again in the variations, at times in the melody, at times in the bass or in an inner part, in various rhythmic variants, always in new and surprising combinations, while the ruggiero theme proceeds undisturbed, adding sparkling lights. In contrast to Ronga's view that "nessuna commozione nasce dallo sfruttamento un po' monotono del tema"[54] (no excitement at all arises from the exploitation of the rather monotonous theme), in my opinion the interplay between the two melodies and the juxtaposition of two basically different structures make this capriccio one of the master's most ingenious and stimulating works.

Fig.496

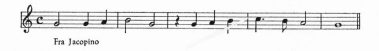

Fra Jacopino

The *Capriccio sopra la Battaglia* belongs to a different genre, which is of no interest today. Even so, with its frequent changes of ideas and tonality and merciful brevity, it is far superior to others of its type, such as those by Bull or Kerll.

On the other hand, Frescobaldi's *Capriccio pastorale* is a work of great interest; not only is it one of the earliest examples of this species (it may even be the earliest) but it is also one of the most beautiful. Most of its repeated sections are brief, and each one should probably be repeated in echo registration. It has the characteristic features of the Christmas pastorale: gracious melodies in a rocking triple meter and quiet harmony in major above real or suggested pedal points, which change at long intervals. The *Pastorale* contains four *pedali*—pedal points on G, D, A, and G. Frescobaldi shows a special sensitivity in not sustaining them throughout, but only long enough to clarify the tonal structure. The transition to the second main section, shown in Fig.497, is especially impressive; it is the only passage in which the prevailing major is momentarily darkened by the minor.

Fig.497

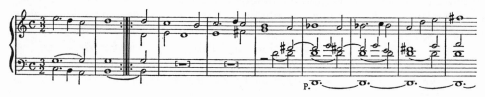

FIORI MUSICALI (1635)

With his last and most famous work, the *Fiori musicali* of 1635, Frescobaldi turned entirely to liturgical organ music, which he had touched on briefly only once before. In *Toccate II* he had written several pieces for the Daily Offices. In the *Fiori musicali* he devoted himself to the task of decorating the solemn service of the Mass with organ music.

The *Fiori musicali* include three organ Masses, *della Domenica* (feasts of the Lord), *delli Apostoli* (feasts of the Saints), and *della Madonna* (Marian feasts). Liturgically they are the same Masses that G. Cavazzoni and Merulo had set, but they have a completely different musical form. Frescobaldi retains only one section of the Mass ordinary, the Kyrie. To this he adds free compositions, which are heard at five points in the service: *avanti la Messa, dopo l'Epistola, dopo il Credo, per l'Elevazione,* and *post il Comunio* (before the Mass, after the Epistle, after the Credo, during the transubstantiation, and after the Communion). Except for the *Elevazione*, these pieces occupy the place of the Mass proper: introit, gradual and alleluya, offertory, communion. The following table is a synopsis of the *Fiori musicali*:[55]

	A. *Domenica*	B. *Apostoli*	C. *Madonna*
I. *avanti la Messa*	Toccata (1)	Toccata (19)	Toccata (35)
II. *Kyrie, Christe*	12 settings (2–13)	8 settings (20–27)	6 settings (36–41)
III. *dopo l'Epistola*	Canzon (14)	Canzon (28)	Canzon (42)
IV. *dopo il Credo*	Recercar (15) Recercar (16)	Toccata-Recercar (29–30); Recercar (31)	Recercar (43); Toccata-Recercar (44–45)
V. *per l'Elevazione*	Toccata (17)	Toccata (32); Recercar (33)	Toccata (46)
VI. *post il Comunio*	Canzon (18)	Canzon (34)	

The Masses are followed by two capriccios, on *Bergamasca* and *Girolmeta*. Because of their position they might form the conclusion of the third Mass, but their decidedly secular character makes such an interpretation questionable.

The Kyrie and Christe settings are the only pieces written on Gregorian melodies: in A. on *Kyrie Orbis factor* (no.XI of the modern ordinaries), in B. on *Cunctipotens genitor* (no.IV), and in C. on *Cum iubilo* (no.IX). They are all brief settings, which follow the 16th-century tradition in both style and treatment of the chant. In more than half the pieces Frescobaldi surprisingly uses the strict *cantus-planus* arrangement, which Cavazzoni had already abandoned as antiquated, but in some of them he takes the liberty of distributing the melody among two or three voices. In no.11, e.g., the beginning of the melody is heard in the bass and the rest in the soprano; in no.39 the first section lies in the tenor, the second in the alto, and the third in the bass. The *cantus planus* moves mostly in whole notes, but occurs once in half notes (no.5) and twice even in old-fashioned breves (nos.9, 10). Thus at the end of his creative life Frescobaldi consciously reverts to a tradition of a distant past, which he fills with new life. In the remaining settings an imitative texture prevails. In nos.7, 8, and 13 one part is sustained throughout as a pedal point, a technique employed earlier in Titelouze's *Hymnes d'Eglise* of 1623. Kyrie no.8 is particularly solemn; the alto presents the Gregorian melody three times (it is also intimated in the tenor once), while the high *d'* is heard above it, unwavering, almost like a voice from another world.

Let us now turn to the free pieces in the *Fiori musicali*, first of all to the toccatas. They are heard before the Mass (*avanti la Messa:* nos.1, 19, 35), during the elevation (nos.17, 32, 46), and before two ricercars (nos.29, 44). These eight pieces differ from the earlier toccatas above all in their brevity and, because of it, in their unified character. The introit and ricercar toccatas are preludes, both in function and content. A motif that generates the motion unfolds and completes itself within fifteen to twenty measures—just long enough to prepare the listener for the beginning of the Mass or the ricercar. They are similar in style to the earlier toccatas, and yet they are different—purified and sublimated, deepened and intensified, gems within the smallest framework.

The elevation toccatas are somewhat longer because of their function. It is no accident that all three are in *E* minor, i.e., in the Phrygian mode. According to 16th-century theory, this mode reflected the "unspeakable" or the mystic. The toccata of the first Mass is designated as *cromaticha;* it has a short introduction in the style of the *durezze e ligature*, followed by a lengthy ricercar on a chromatic subject. The other two elevation toccatas are much more beautiful. They are created without reference to definite ideas, out of free imagination, out of a religious passion. Nowhere in music has the spirit of the Catholic Baroque found as perfect an expression as in these toccatas. Their inspirational sounds are enlivened here and there by figures that symbolize almost pictorially the gestures of supplicating genuflection and devout invocation. Fig.498 shows the beginning of the elevation toccata from the *Messa delle Apostoli*.

Fig.498

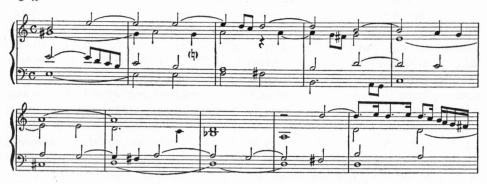

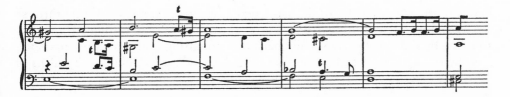

Lively canzonas occur at two points in the Masses, after the Epistle and after Communion. Like the earlier canzonas, they consist of a number of sections, which are frequently followed by a toccata-like or chordal postlude entitled *Adasio*. Curiously, canzona no.28 begins with an *Adasio* introduction. Thematic variation occurs repeatedly, but is not applied throughout.

The central part of the Mass, consisting of offering, transubstantiation, and communion, is opened by ricercars. The preparation of the offering requires some time and thus provided an opportunity for extended organ playing, which possibly replaced the liturgical offertory or was heard before or after it. Thus the ricercars of the *Fiori musicali* have the same function as the offertories of Redford, Preston, and Coxsun, or those of the French organ composers of the second half of the 17th century. Each of the three Masses contains two ricercars; two of them are preceded by short toccatas (nos.29–30, 44–45); and the *Messa delli Apostoli* contains an additional, rather lengthy ricercar after the elevation toccata (no.33).

Three ricercars have an interesting thematic formulation, which is quite similar to that of ricercars nos.2, 3, and 5 from the *Recercari et Canzoni* of 1615 (cf.p.453):

No.30: A ‖ A/B/C ‖ A²/D
No.31: A ‖ B ‖ C ‖ A/B/C
No.43: A/B ‖ A²/C/C¹

No.31 is a triple fugue, and nos.30 and 43 have bold chromatic subjects (Fig.499) that also appear in augmentation.

Fig.499

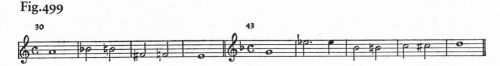

Ricercar no.33 is inscribed "con obligo del basso come apare" (with an obbligato bass, as will be seen). Its form is reminiscent of ricercars nos.6 and 7 from the *Ricercari* of 1615, in which there is "a main voice, which consists exclusively of the subject's repetitions" (cf.p.453). Here, too, there is such a main voice, the bass, in which a five-note subject ($|\ c\ |\ e\ |\ f\ |\ d\ |\ e\ |$) is heard fourteen times, interrupted by rests of two to five measures (during which it is sometimes heard in one of the upper parts). At the same time it is always transposed, first through the ascending circle of fifths from C to E, then back to C (omitting A), then descending by fifths to E♭, and finally back to C (omitting B♭). The upper parts follow the transpositions of the ostinato in corresponding modulations by fifths or fourths, so that in tonal respects the piece appears very progressive.

Fig.500

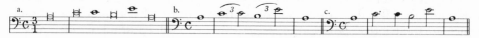

a. Original; b. Correct transcription; c. Modern edition.

Ricercar no.45 also contains an "obligo," "di cantare la quinta parte senza tocarla," the same as the one in capriccio no.10 from the *Capricci* of 1624 (cf.p. 466). The fifth voice consists of a brief *soggetto,* which is to be sung, not played, at various places to be puzzled out by the performer. Frescobaldi adds the remark, "Intendami chi puo che m'intend' io" (Understand me, who can, as long as I can understand myself). It probably refers not only to the problem of finding the correct places but also to the further complication that the *soggetto* must be sung in half-note triplets, which conflict with the rhythm of the organ texture. In some modern editions, however, the rhythm of the singing voice is adapted to that of the organ, as shown in Fig.500. Was this Frescobaldi's "intention"? Or is his proud, almost disdainful remark still valid today?

Fig.501

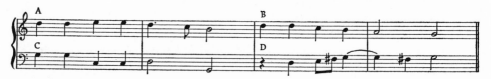

The *Fiori musicali* conclude with two capriccios on Italian folk songs, *Bergamasca* and *Girolmeta.* The former is treated with particular ingeniousness: Four subjects (shown in Fig.501), derived from the melody and its bass, are developed and contrapuntally combined with great variety in seven sections. As in his *Fantasie* of 1608, Frescobaldi derives almost the entire texture from these subjects, no longer with the fanaticism of youth but with the superiority of the mature master. In the earlier works the texture is complex and opaque, but now everything is clear and relaxed, every detail clearly audible. As an example Fig.502 gives the final measures of the first section. The subjects are easily recognized, and in the various sections Frescobaldi adds other figures, which, after careful scrutiny, prove to be related to them. "Chiquesta Bergamasca sonerà non pocho imparerà"

Fig.502

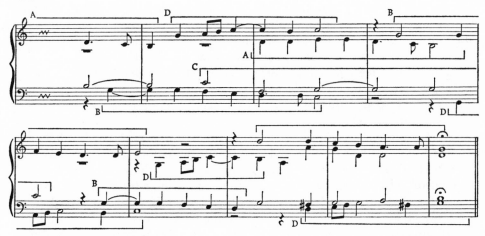

(Whoever plays this Bergamasca will learn not a little)—this remark of the master's is still valid today.

The *Capriccio sopra Girolmeta* is based on a melody that appears in *Libro primo delle laudi spirituali* by Fra Serafino Razzi (1563), in the form shown in Fig.503.[56] Frescobaldi makes use of the major variant of this melody (on C) and derives two subjects from it (A and B, and occasionally smaller fragments as well), which he works into his contrapuntal texture in many ways, as in his *Bergamasca*. The composition achieves a special attraction through the frequent recurrence of the refrain, which concludes both halves of the melody.

Fig.503

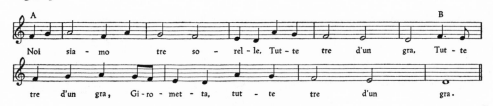

Noi sia - mo tre so - rel - le, Tut - te tre d'un gra, Tut - te

tre d'un gra, Gi - ro - met - ta, tut - te tre d'un gra.

THE POSTHUMOUS CANZONA PRINT AND THE MANUSCRIPT TRADITION

In 1645, shortly after Frescobaldi's death, the publisher Vincenti brought out a collection entitled *Canzoni francese, Libro quarto*, which contains eleven canzonas with dedicatory titles (such as *La Rovetta* and *La Sabbatina*). In the extensive employment of thematic variation and toccata-like postludes they closely resemble the canzonas in *Toccate II*.

In addition to Frescobaldi's printed compositions a rather large number of works are preserved in manuscript only (cf.p.449). Among them the toccatas are the most interesting, for they complement those in the prints. In the manuscript Rome, Bibl. Vat. Chigi Q. IV. 25,[57] e.g., there are three pedal toccatas, similar to those in *Toccate II*, but each one is followed by a canzona that belongs to it. The combination of a free and a fugal form was widely practiced in German organ music as prelude and fugue, but it rarely occurs in Italy. The only other instances in Frescobaldi's works are the two toccata-ricercar pairs in the *Fiori musicali* (nos. 29–30 and 44–45).

The Turin tablature Giordano 1 contains nine toccatas,[58] which differ from the printed ones in their smooth style, regular formulation, quiet harmony, and thinner texture. The forced turns and the turbulence of the works in *Toccate II* are completely absent. It is perhaps better to compare these pieces with *Toccate I*, i.e., look upon them as early works. But they include several features that are most easily understood if they are related to the musical discourse of the middle Baroque, as first indications of the evolution that leads from Frescobaldi to Bernardo Pasquini. Fig.504 shows two of them (new ed., Shindle; a., p.61, brace 5; b., p.69, brace 4). Are some of these toccatas works of Frescobaldi's last years?

Fig.504

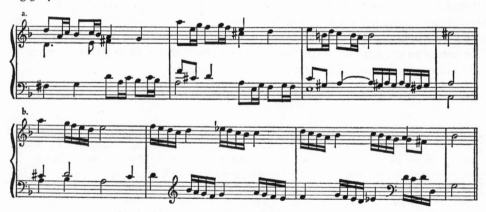

In contrast to these pieces, *Toccada Girolamo Frescobaldi* in the manuscript Berlin, Staatsbibl. 40316 (formerly 191; new ed., Shindle, I, p.86) unmistakably follows the intonations and toccatas of the Venetian school. It closely resembles Paolo Quagliati's toccata printed in Diruta's *Il Transilvano;* they both contain not only sustained chords and scales but also an extended passage of arpeggios. Since Quagliati worked in Rome from 1574 until his death in 1628, this toccata was most likely written during Frescobaldi's student days. Thus the manuscript sources

seem to document both the prelude and the epilogue to Frescobaldi's printed toccata repertoire.

D. SECOND GENERATION

Earlier in this chapter we pointed out the great importance of the Neapolitan keyboard school, whose representatives—Macque, Mayone, Trabaci, and others—
created the basis for Frescobaldi's works. Recent discoveries and research show
that this role was not their only one; they had other successors in South Italy, who
may not have been of the same epoch-making significance, but who were musical
personalities of rank and individuality.[59] The most important among them are
Giovanni Salvatore, Gioanpietro del Buono, Bernardo Storace, and Gregorio
Strozzi, as well as the two Scarlattis. Their works differ greatly from those of
their contemporaries in North Italy—Tarquinio Merula, Martino Pesenti, Antonio
Croci, and Giovanni Battista Fasolo—so that it would perhaps be best to treat the
developments in keyboard composition in the North and South as separate evolutions, as is usual for the German Baroque. Indeed, one could add a Central Italian,
i.e., Roman evolution, represented by Ercole Pasquini, Frescobaldi, Michelangelo
Rossi, and Bernardo Pasquini. But aside from the disadvantages of such a differentiation, the material that is known is not extensive and continuous enough to
make one absolutely necessary. Therefore it is preferable to treat this generation
of Italian composers as a single unit.

Merula

The first of the younger contemporaries and successors of Frescobaldi is Tarquinio
Merula. Born around 1590, he was active at Cremona and Bergamo, and also
at Warsaw at the court of King Sigismund III from 1624 to 1628. Like Ercole
Pasquini, he was known for a long time for a single organ composition—the *Sonata
cromatica* published by Torchi. Recently five more of his keyboard pieces have
been discovered: a *Capriccio cromatico* and a toccata in Lynar A 2, a capriccio in
Leipzig Ms. II. 2. 51, one canzona in a manuscript from Assisi, and another in a
Ravenna manuscript.[60]

The *Sonata cromatica* is based on the frequently used theme of the chromatically filled-in descending tetrachord. It is arranged in four sections, which are
contrasted with the aid of various counter-motifs. The formulation rests almost
exclusively on the principle of sequential repetition, which is employed in a consistent manner for the first time in the history of keyboard music (perhaps in music
in general). The result may be gathered from Fig.505, which shows the beginning
of a section of more than forty measures, in which the same figure (and later its
inversion) recurs about ninety times.

Fig.505

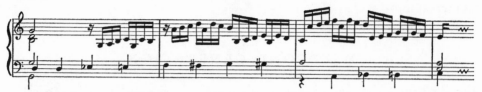

The result is as poor artistically as it is remarkable historically. Extended and regularly formed sequences belong to 18th-century music, and even in our time it is not easy to find a piece that is so completely beholden to this technique as the *Sonata cromatica*. Is it possible that this composition is spurious and is really the work of a musician who lived some fifty years later?

Merula's *Capriccio cromatico* from the Lynar tablature begins with a chromatic ascent from *d'* to *e''*, and later on it employs mostly chromatically filled-in fifths and fourths, ascending in the first half (meas.1–47) and descending in the second (meas.48–85). Here, too, the counterpoints are extensively formulated as sequences, but much less schematically and monotonously, and with frequent changes in motifs, so that as a whole this piece is much more attractive than the *Sonata;* it also fits better into the period around 1650.

The *Toccata 2ⁱ toni* (also from Lynar A 2) follows Merulo's toccatas in both form and detail. It consists essentially of two sections, one with chords enlivened by scale runs, and one in fugal style. In the former, complementary motifs are used here and there, as e.g., the one shown in Fig.506, where octaves are heard in syncopated position.

Fig.506

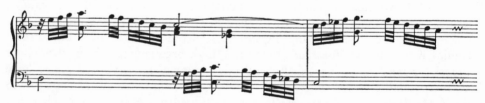

Merula's remaining pieces, a capriccio and two canzonas, offer nothing of great interest, except perhaps the subject of the Ravenna canzona, which starts with four broken triads descending stepwise (| *g'' e'' c''* | *f'' d'' b'* | *e'' c'' a'* | *d'' b' g'* |). The authorship of the other pieces in the new edition is either not authenticated or dubious.

Pesenti

Martino Pesenti is a curious phenomenon in Italian keyboard music of the 17th century. He was born about 1600 in Venice, blind (he is often called "cieco a nativitate" in his publications), and died there in 1647 or 1648. Between 1621 and 1648 about twenty prints appeared—madrigals, arias, Masses, motets, and four collections of keyboard music, containing only dances. Three of these collections are preserved: *Il primo libro delle correnti alla francese* (the first edition is lost; the second appeared in 1635); *Il secondo libro delle correnti* (1630); and *Correnti gagliarde e balletti ... libro quarto* (1645). Book I, which obviously appeared before 1630, contains 26 correntes, 3 voltas, and one balletto; book II, 22 correntes, and 2 voltas; and book IV, 8 correntes, 13 galliards, 10 ballettos, and 2 passamezzos. Curiously, only one balletto (in book I), 5 correntes in book II, and a balletto and a passamezzo in book IV are in three parts, the rest in two.

In book I the correntes and voltas are written in long measures mostly 3 x 3/4, as in the *Corrente detta la Ritza*, reproduced in Fig.507. In the other two books they are divided into 3/4 measures and consist more frequently of regular four-measure phrases.

Fig.507

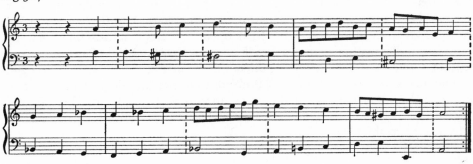

In the five three-part correntes at the end of book II each of the two sections is followed by a written-out repetition entitled "Prima (Seconda) parte spezzata," which proves to be a variant in arpeggiated style, the *style brisé* of French lute music. An example is given in Fig.508. This feature is so isolated in Italian keyboard music that it is undoubtedly due to a French influence.

Pesenti's *Libro quarto* is a remarkable experiment in expanding the sphere of tonalities. It contains the three-part balletto, a two-part and a three-part passa-

Fig.508

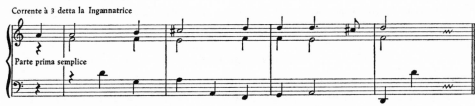

Corrente à 3 detta la Ingannatrice

Parte prima semplice

485

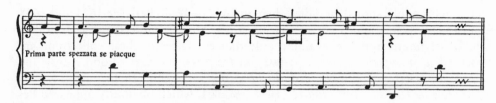

Prima parte spezzata se piacque

mezzo, and 30 dances, which, as the title *Correnti gagliarde e balletti diatonici, trasportati parte cromatici e parte henarmonici* indicates, are first presented *diatonico*, i.e., in one of the more usual keys, and thereafter transposed, the first eleven *cromatico* and the other nineteen *henarmonico*. The former transpositions comprise the flat keys, such as A♭ minor, E♭ minor, and D♭ major, the latter the sharp keys in a chromatic order: A♯, B, B♯, C♯, . . . , up to G♯, each one in major then in minor, omitting only the "common" keys of D minor, G major, and G minor. Curiously A major appears among the *cromatico* transpositions (in no.3). As much as this collection approaches Bach's *Well-Tempered Clavier*, it would be quite erroneous to think of a tempered instrument here. Indeed Pesenti says in the preface that this experiment was inspired by two harpsichords "col diatonico, cromatico ed henarmonico," which he happened to come across—one made by Domenico de Pesaro for Zarlino in 1548 and one made by Vido Transuntino in 1601, the former having twenty-four pitches to the octave, the latter twenty-eight. In comparison with the examples of transposition given by Gian Paolo Cima in 1606 (cf.p.417), the notation of the chromatic notes is much more logical, and essentially corresponds to the modern system. The beginning of the corrente no.22 is given as an example (Fig.509).

Fig.509

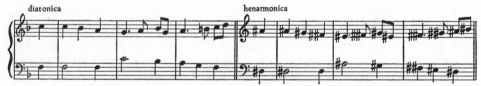

diatonica   henarmonica

    Musically this book is rather insignificant, but as a document of the theory of transpositions it is of interest, especially since it comes from a blind musician. It is well known that the blind possess particularly well-developed senses of hearing and touch, but it is surprising that Pesenti was also so intimately familiar with the notation that although he could not write the complicated chromatic alterations himself, he could dictate them correctly.

Michelangelo Rossi

Michelangelo Rossi was born around 1600 and apparently died about 1670. Only a few scattered facts about his life are known. In 1624 he was in the service of

Cardinal Maurizio di Savoia; he had a short stay in Turin in 1629, and one in Rome in 1633 in connection with the performance of his opera *Erminio sul Giordano*. In 1638 he was employed at the court of Modena and in 1639 he went to Forli as maestro di cappella. Finally, in 1670 his presence at Faenza is documented. Around 1640 he published a print of *Toccate e correnti d'intavolatura d'organo e cimbalo*, which came out in a new edition in 1657. This collection contains 10 toccatas and 10 correntes. A hand-written supplement in the copy at the Liceo-musicale in Bologna contains 4 more toccatas, *Partite sopra la Romanesca* (copied twice), and 2 *Versetti 5° tono*.[61]

More than any other composer Rossi follows in Frescobaldi's footsteps, taking over his frequent changes of idea, impetuous motion, and sudden halts. But Rossi's harmonic approach is generally more conservative and often already functional in orientation, as in the passage from the *Ottava Toccata*, given in Fig. 510.

Fig.510

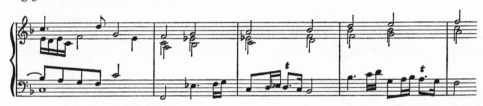

Even though Rossi's dependence on Frescobaldi is unmistakable, one must not overlook the fact that his toccatas deviate from those of his teacher in one essential detail, in the insertion of extended imitative sections. Possibly Merulo's Venetian toccata with its ricercar sections was the model, but in Rossi's case these often rather lengthy sections are not formulated like the ricercar or like the canzona; instead they are developed from fast, fugue-like motifs, which appear in many strettos as well as free variants. Very similar passages are found in Froberger's toccatas, as shown in Fig.511. Rossi's toccatas usually contain two fugatos

Fig.511

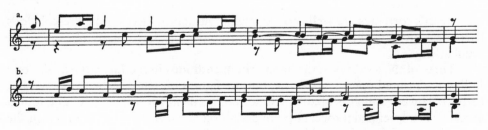

a. Rossi, Toccata No. 2; b. Froberger, Toccata No. 19.

in the order toccata—fugato—toccata—fugato, so that the overall form is one of four sections rather than three or five, as in Merulo's toccatas. The first of the two fugatos is longer and more clearly imitative, while the second is treated more freely and dissolves into passage work toward the end.

Rossi's toccatas offer figures that do not lag behind Frescobaldi's in originality and boldness—in particular the *tutto di salto* passages in toccatas nos. 1 and 7 (for the latter see Fig.512a.) and the final section of no.7, whose numerous chromatic motions culminate in a series of major thirds (Fig.512b.). In a passage at the start of no.6 (Fig.512c.) two voices are written in a faithful canon at the fifth, similar to the *Duett II* from Bach's *Clavierübung*, but with even less consideration for niceties.

Fig.512

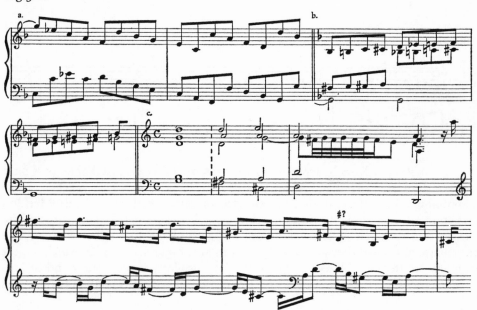

Rossi's correntes are well formed, melodious dance pieces. Like Frescobaldi's correntes, they are set essentially for three voices and have many phrases of irregular length.

Three of the toccatas in the handwritten additions in the *Liceo-musicale* copy follow the printed ones in structure, but the figuration tends to be smoother and better balanced, which probably justifies taking them for late works. The fourth toccata[62] is a brief pedal toccata (with pedals on C, G, A, D, and G), in which the musical discourse of the middle Baroque is quite unmistakable, e.g., at the very

Fig.513

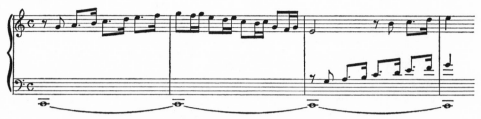

beginning, shown in Fig.513. The same is true of the four variations on the romanesca and especially of the two short versets.

Salvatore

In 1641 a print appeared in Naples entitled *Ricercari a quattro voci, canzoni francese, toccate, et versi per rispondere nelle Messe con l'organo al Choro composte dal R. D. Giovanni Salvatore, Organista nella Real Chiesa di San Severino de' RR. PP. Benedettini di Napoli.* Thus we know that Giovanni Salvatore was the organist at San Severino at Naples in 1641. From 1662 to 1673 he taught at the Conservatorio della Pietà dei Turchini, and from 1675 to 1668 (probably the year of his death) at the Conservatorio dei Poveri di Gesù Cristo, both in the same city.[63]

Salvatore's print contains 8 ricercars, 2 toccatas, and 3 organ Masses with versets for the pieces of the ordinary. Possibly he was a student of Trabaci. Like Trabaci he indicates the number of subjects in each ricercar by designations such as "con tre fughe" or "con due fughe e suoi riversi"; he also introduces all his subjects at the very beginning, and usually treats them in a single section of sixty to seventy breve measures. In the *Ricercar quarto con 4 fughe e canto fermo* the four subjects are introduced and developed in the usual way, but in a second section they are used as *canti fermi*, i.e., in long note values (each note as a breve) and distributed among the four voices, the first subject in the bass, the second in the soprano, etc.; this is followed by a third section in triple meter. The last ricercar, *con tre fughe sopra l'hinno d'Iste Confessor,* is constructed very much like Mayone's *Recercar sopra Ave maris stella* (cf.p.431). The hymn is heard four times—once in each voice—as a *cantus planus* in semibreves, while the counterpoints develop three subjects derived from it in a very ingenious manner. Fig.514 shows the passage where the hymn tune enters (in the original the text is added).

Salvatore's canzonas represent a significant step in formal construction, a step that may be regarded as a turn from the canzona to the sonata. The usual variety of short, frequently connected sections is replaced by a clear articulation into three extended sections, with the middle one in triple meter, and the last one taking up the subject of the first. The toccata-like codas and transitions of the Frescobaldi canzona are completely absent. Each section—one would almost like

Fig.514

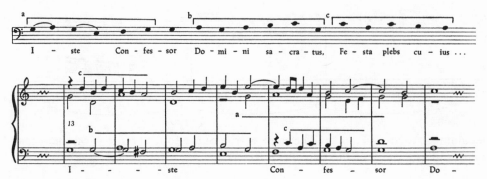

to say movement—is unified in itself and usually closes with a full chord. Canzonas nos.2 and 3 carry the legend "può sonarsi con il concerto di viole." Several short "chordal exclamations" in these canzonas are better suited to a string ensemble than to a harpsichord. One of them is the passage from the *Canzone seconda*, given in Fig.515, which also has an interesting harmonic progression. The last canzona, *sopra il ballo detto la Bergamasca*, is one of the most attractive compositions based on the favorite bergamasca theme, which is heard in ever new variants.

Fig.515

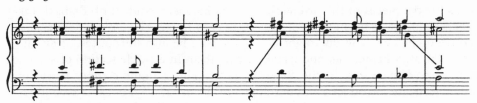

The two toccatas, with their truly Neapolitan surprise effects—dissonances, sweeping motions, unexpected shifts of harmony—are quite like Macque's, Mayone's, and Trabaci's, but they use somewhat softer, more restrained hues, rather like Froberger's way of expressing himself. As an example Fig.516 shows a passage from the second toccata. Both toccatas conclude with a pedal point on the dominant—one of eight, the other of ten measures—of a length that can hardly be found in earlier scores.

The last portion of the print is devoted to liturgical organ music. It consists of brief versets, about ten to fifteen measures each, for the three main Masses, *della Domenica, degli Apostoli e Feste Doppie,* and *della Madonna.* In each Mass there are 5 versets for the Kyrie, 9 for the Gloria, 2 for the Sanctus, and one for the Agnus Dei. Most of the pieces are fugal, some chordal with figurations.

Fig.516

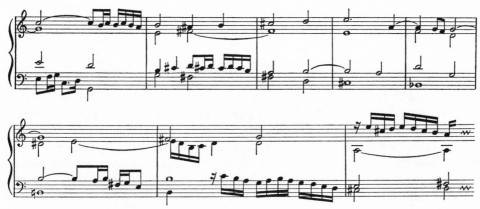

The manuscript Naples, Bibl. del Cons. ms. 34.5.28 contains several additional works by Salvatore: 2 toccatas (one is identical with the first half of the printed *Toccata prima*), a capriccio, a *Durezze*, and 2 correntes. The capriccio treats one of the common subjects of the period (| *a a a ga* | *b♭ f g a* |) like a variation canzona in three sections; the beginning carries the legend "Melanconico e largo" (which is without doubt contemporary, i.e., by Salvatore or by Cemino, the scribe of the manuscript). This shows that pieces such as these were not always played in a gay allegro, as we normally assume today. The *Durezze* is a lovely example of this species; its harmony exhibits neither the excesses of an earlier generation nor the routine turns of a later one. The two correntes have a 3/4 time signature, but the first one is divided regularly into measures of six quarter notes. Thus the indication 3/4 does not mean "three quarter notes, but refers in the spirit of the theory of proportions to the fact that three semiminims have the same duration as four of the *integer valor* (only in Germany were semiminims called quarter notes).

Del Buono

In the same year (1641) that Salvatore published his print in Naples, Gioanpietro del Buono in Palermo, Sicily, published *Canoni oblighi et sonate in varie maniere sopra l'Ave maris stella*, a voluminous collection of pieces, most of them vocal canons of great variety based on the hymn named in the title. At the end del Buono added *XIIII Sonate di cimbalo*, and it is these pieces that demand our attention.[64] They have nothing to do with the sonata, which is already rather clearly outlined in Salvatore's canzonas. Like the vocal canons, they are based on the melody of *Ave maris stella*, which lies in the tenor as a strict *cantus planus* of a four-part setting (it occurs once in the alto). Thus they belong to the same type as Rocco Rodio's fantasies, Trabaci's four *canti fermi* on the spagna melody, or Mayone's

491

Fig.517

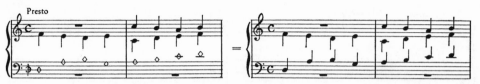

ricercars *sopra Ave maris stella* and *sopra il canto fermo di Costantio Festa*. What gives del Buono's collection its special importance is the great number of settings and the individuality of their treatment.

In seven sonatas the tenor is written in breves, in the other seven in semibreves. But the theory of proportions of the 15th and 16th centuries still plays a role, for in sonatas nos.6 and 11 the breves are reduced to semibreve values by the time signature ₵ (against C in the other parts), and in no.10 the semibreves are reduced to semiminims, i.e., to a quarter of their value (quarter notes) by the *proportio quadrupla* 𝄉 (Fig.517). Perhaps del Buono thought that notating a liturgical melody in quarter notes was not suitable (particularly in a presto), or perhaps he wanted to boast a little of his learning. Since the forty-two notes of the melody only fill about ten measures, del Buono extends the final note to a pedal point of twenty measures.

In the other sonatas the hymn is heard as a real *cantus planus* in sustained tones, contrasting with lively counterpoints derived from a well conceived start-

Fig.518

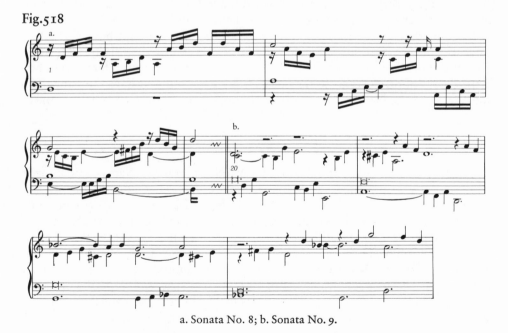

a. Sonata No. 8; b. Sonata No. 9.

492

ing motif. On the whole, the treatment is reminiscent of Rodio's fantasies or Trabaci's *Canti fermi*, but in their pieces the counterpoints are not so consistently derived from a single motif. Del Buono shows as remarkable a facility in inventing interesting motifs as he does a dexterity in their development and their adaptation to the *cantus planus*. Sonata no.8 is a study in individualized arpeggios, no.9 a veritable 17th-century hocket; both have a harmonic colorfulness that is almost impressionistic. Fig.518 shows a passage from each of these works.

In two sonatas del Buono tackles the problem of chromaticism, which was so acute for the 17th-century musician. In no.5, *Fuga cromatica*, the chromatic tetrachord of ancient Greek theory (*a f♯ f e*) serves as the subject of a ricercar-like work, while no.7, *Stravagante e per il cimbalo cromatico*, is a recherché study in chordal chromaticism, similar to Macque's *Consonanze stravagante*, but much longer and even more interesting because of the harmonic reinterpretations of the sustained tones of the *cantus firmus*. Fig.519 presents the final measures of this composition.

Fig.519

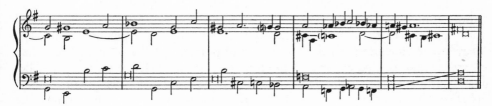

Del Buono's fourteen sonatas represent a document that is surprising, even within the South Italian evolution, which surely does not lack unusual phenomena. Abstruseness and ingeniousness, pedantry and caprice combine to form a product that seems possible only in the subtropical climate of Sicily.

Croci and Fasolo

Compared with the repertoire of the South Italians, the output of the contemporary North Italian organists looks rather conservative and conventional. In 1641 Fra Antonio Croci, who was active at two Modena churches, published his *Frutti musicali*—organ pieces for 3 Masses, 5 canzonas, and 3 ricercars, all with very modest requirements and of rather mediocre quality. The first Mass consists of a *Toccata per l'Introito* (mostly scale passages above parallel 1–5–8 chords), 8 brief versets for the Kyrie (the last three *alio modo*), a *Toccata* and 8 pieces for the Gloria, a *Toccata* and *Pleni* for the Sanctus, and one verset for the Agnus Dei. The other two Masses are formulated in a similar manner. Among the canzonas there are some "per quelli che non arrivano al'Ottava" (for those who cannot reach an octave), which include passages like the one given in Fig.520. The three ricercars are developed from chromatic subjects, and are written in a free-voiced texture, which only occasionally solidifies into real four-part writing.

Fig.520

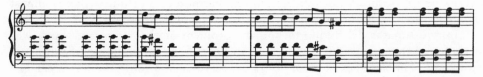

Giovanni Battista Fasolo's *Annuale* of 1645 is more significant. Fasolo came from Asti (between Turin and Genova), was a Franciscan monk, and, according to the title of his *Arie spirituali*, maestro di cappella of the Archbishop of Monreale (near Palermo) around 1659. His *Annuale* comprises versets for the *Te Deum*, 18 hymns, 3 Masses, 8 Magnificats, and a *Salve regina*, as well as 8 ricercars, 8 canzonas, and 4 fugues.[65]

For the *Te Deum* Fasolo wrote fifteen short organ versets, which alternate with portions that are sung. The hymns comprise three or four versets each, and in some instances an additional "altri più allegri" or "altri più moderni." The organ Masses include both the ordinary and portions of the proper. The *Missa in duplicis diebus*, e.g., consists of the following sections: Kyrie (5 versets)—Alleluya—Gloria (9 versets)—*Brevis modulatio post Epistolam*—*Gravis modulatio pro Offertorio*—Sanctus (2 versets) and *Elevatio* (during the Benedictus)—Agnus Dei (1 verset)—*Brevis modulatio post Agnus Dei*. The other two Masses omit the Alleluya, but are otherwise identical. The Magnificats include five settings for each tone, each followed by a *Modulatio loco Antiphonae*; thus the concluding antiphon is also replaced by organ playing. The *Salve regina* consists as usual of five versets.

The added ricercars, canzonas, and fugues are also meant for the service. The preface states that "If the graduals and offertories are too short, a ricercar or canzona may be played. . . . If the antiphon is too brief, one may play one of the fugues or a canzona, conforming with the mode."

The preface also gives some information about the musical intentions: "The hymns always employ the notes of the particular *cantus firmus*; some have both serious and cheerful short versets. Each hymn concludes with a *terzetto* verse, alluding to the Holy Trinity, to which the last stanza refers. Here one has to play the two lower parts with the left hand and the soprano with the right, an octave higher and in the choir measure (misura del choro, i.e., triple meter, which was usual for hymns at the time). The *versetti gravi* are mostly brief imitative settings of a traditional type; occasionally the *cantus-planus* technique is used, e.g., in *O lux beata Trinitas*, verse 1. A verset from the hymn *Ad coenam Agni providi*,

Fig.521

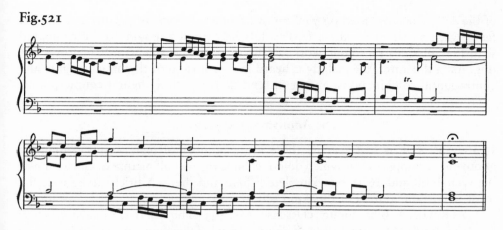

given in Fig.521, is an example of the style of the *versi più allegri*. The technique employed in the "Trinity stanzas" is illustrated by Fig.522, the final verset of the same hymn, which is inscribed "Terzetto alla forma del choro,* il soprano si puoi sonare all' ottava sopra."

Fig.522

(1:2)

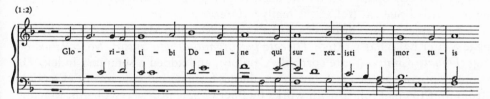

Glo- — ri-a ti – bi Do – mi – ne qui sur – rex – isti a mor – tu – is

In the Masses the more interesting pieces are the longer ones, which are heard after the Epistle, at the offering, during transubstantiation, and after the Agnus Dei. They represent what Frescobaldi calls *Canzon dopo l'epistola, Recercar dopo il Credo, Toccata per l'Elevazione,* and *Canzon post il Comunio* in the *Fiori musicali.* For these functions Fasolo employs the same musical types as Frescobaldi except for the Elevation, for which he uses a very slow chordal movement in the *ligature* style instead of a free toccata. At that place in the *Missa in duplicibus diebus* we read: "Ellevatio. Si suonera assai largo acciò si godano meglio li ligature" (this must be played very slowly so that the suspensions may be better enjoyed). The movements in canzona and ricercar style are entitled *modulatio,* meaning motet (i.e., fugal setting).

The term *Fuga,* designating fugal pieces—as it does here—is still rather unusual in Italy at the time. The four pieces called *Fuga* that are added at the end

---

* "Alla forma del choro" obviously means the same as "misura del choro."

of the collection are based on well-known themes, *Bergamasca*, *Girometta*, *Bassa fiamenga*, and *Ut re mi fa sol la*. Fasolo's *Bergamasca* should not be compared with Frescobaldi's ingenious work on the same theme, but with Salvatore's setting. As in the latter, the melody is heard in a profusion of rhythmic variants and contrapuntal combinations, and at the end there are lively figural counterpoints.

The Anonymous Repertoire

In Italy as well as in Germany there are a number of manuscripts containing anonymous compositions, which do not change the overall picture of clavier music between 1600 and 1650, but complete it here and there. A brief survey over the most important sources of this kind follows.

1. Ravenna, Bibl. comm. classense, Ms. 545. The title page reads: *Libro di Fra Gioseffo da Ravenna. Opere di diversi autori di Girolamo Frescobaldi, d'Ercol Pasquino, Cesare Argentini, Incert' Autore*. The manuscript consists of 116 folios in an oblong format and contains the following anonymous works: one Kyrie, one *Per la levatione*, 4 toccatas (the one on fol.8v is identical with A. Gabrieli's toccata in Diruta's *Il Transilvano* I), 7 ricercars, 2 capriccios, 6 canzonas, an *Aria di Fiorenze*, a *Monica*, and a few dance pieces. One piece, called *Romens* (fol.82), seems to be a ruggiero. The toccata on fol.5 contains various unusual and interesting ideas: syncopations after the beat, skipping figures, and arpeggios. Another piece, entitled ricercar (fol.12), is really a *durezze e ligature*.

2. Naples, Cons. di musica San Pietro a Majella, Ms. 34.5.28. On the title page a later hand has written: *Toccate per organo di vari autori. Miscellanea del Sigr. Donato Cimino* (more correctly Cemino), and added a summary index. The manuscript consists of 142 folios in an oblong format, and contains brief sections (from four to eight folios) with works by Boerio, Salvatore, Frescobaldi, Macque, Ansalone, and Pasquini, and two extended sections (fols.1–56 and 69–104) by Cemino, according to the index on the title page. But it is more likely that Cemino was the scribe of the manuscript and the pieces that were later ascribed to him were anonymous; indeed one of the canzonas (on fol.22v) proves to be by Ercole Pasquini, according to the manuscript Rome, Chigi Q VIII 206. In addition to toccatas, ricercars, canzonas, and three organ Masses this repertoire includes a number of pieces (mostly in the canzona style) with quasi-programmatic titles, such as *Maestà*, *Pace*, *Verità*, *Breve diletto* (which is particularly brief), *Farfalla* (butterfly), or with mottos, e.g., "Doppo lunga procella, comparisce nel ciel l'Iride bella" (fol.32v) or "Con sette fila Sanson della sua chioma, l'altiero stuol del Filisteo ci doma" (fol.33v: "With seven strands of hair Samson conquers the proud mass of Philistines"). Three unusual pieces are a pedal toccata (fol.6v) that unfolds above pedal points on G, D, A, F, C, D, G; a ricercata (fol.35v) whose formalistic figures are reminiscent of the Spanish tientos; and a *Per l'Elevatione* (fol.76) in F minor, which was a rather unusual key for the time.

3. Trent, owned by L. Feininger. This manuscript consists of 97 folios in an oblong format and contains 47 compositions, among them 9 by Ercole Pasquini (mostly with the signature "di Hᵉ," i.e., "di Hercole"); a *Toccata del sigʳ. Gio. P. G.*, which is identical with Giovanni Gabrieli's toccata printed in Diruta's *Il Transilvano* I; and a *Kirie a 5* and a *Benedictus a 3 di Palestrina*, which are intabulations from Palestrina's *Missa O magnum mysterium*.[66] The other pieces are all anonymous. Three pieces called *Entrata* (fols.13v, 16, 33) are each followed by a ricercar in the same key (*re, mi, b mol*). This is another instance of the combination of prelude and fugue, which is so very rare in Italy (cf.p.482). A trill that occurs in several pieces begins on the main note and goes on for seven or nine notes, like a 19th-century trill.

4. The Vatican Library's manuscripts Chigi Q IV 24–29 consist of six oblong volumes of keyboard works. Vol.25 contains only works by Frescobaldi, which were published by Santini (cf. note 57). Vol.27 includes some pieces by Frescobaldi and Pasquini. The remaining contents of these volumes—toccatas, canzonas, ricercars, correntes, passacaglias, etc.—are anonymous. In Vol.27 a group of passacaglias is arranged by ascending tonalities: C major (two), C minor, D major, D minor, E♭ major, E minor, E major, F major, G major, G minor, A minor (two), A major, B♭ major, and B minor. Most of the passacaglias are followed by a piece in the same key, in which an ostinato (| *c′ c′ c′ b* | *a g f e* | *d c g G* |) (appropriately transposed) or its inversion (| *c c c d* | *e f g a* | *g f g C* |) is repeated three or four times. Vol.24 contains two popular dance melodies with variations, and a *Corrente di Monsu della Bar* (cf.p.508) (probably Monsieur [Pierre] de La Barre).

5. Two additional manuscripts of the Vatican Library, Chigi Q VIII 205–206 (really a single volume, the former fols.1–127, the latter fols.128–233), present an extremely disordered collection of keyboard pieces, works for instrumental ensembles in six and twelve voices, and vocal compositions with figured bass. Some of the clavier pieces are by Ercole Pasquini; the remainder seem to be of minor importance.[67]

17

France

After Pierre Attaingnant's prints of 1530 the tradition of French keyboard music recedes into obscurity for almost a century. We know only one clavier piece from that period, a fantasy by Costeley;* the remainder is lost, including a *Premier livre de tablature d'espinette,* published by Simon Gorlier in 1560.

Around 1620 the veil lifts for both organ and clavecin music. Two prints by Jean Titelouze, who opens the series of French organ masters of the Baroque, appeared in 1623 and 1626. Until recently they were regarded as the earliest documents of French organ music after 1530, but a manuscript in the British Museum, which has hitherto been disregarded, enables us to push back this time limit and to enlarge our knowledge of the organ practice at the beginning of the 17th century. This manuscript, Add. Ms. 29486, contains an extensive collection of liturgical organ pieces, all anonymous, and ends with the entry "Finis tonorum 27 Septembris 1618." The legends "Ce vers est pour les registres coupez" and "Pour le cornet," which occur several times, indicate that this repertoire is French— or perhaps Belgian, succeeding Cornet?

The collection includes 8 preludes, 8 harmonized psalm tones, 3 alternation Masses, a *Te Deum,* a series of *Magnificat primi . . . octavi toni* with 6 versets each, a series of *Magnificat quarti . . . octavi toni quatuor pedum, Praeludia Giov. Gabrieli* (the intonations), and a large collection of *fugae* (about 70), apparently in the order of the church modes. The importance of this collection lies in the brevity and simplicity of this unpretentious functional music. It takes us into that

---

* Cf.p.208, where the fantasies by Eustache du Caurroy and Charles Guillet are also mentioned.

lower echelon of organ practice, which is the fundament for the great works of the masters and which is unfortunately too little known. Here we gain an insight into the kind of organ music that was heard in the smaller churches of France—and probably in other countries—around the turn of the 17th century. This music is simple and of modest dimensions, but certainly not provincial. The unknown organist who wrote these pieces was musically well-educated, had mastered the technique of his time, and employed his knowledge to decorate the religious services in a suitable fashion—not unlike the many unknown painters whose unpretentious pictorial presentations made the scenes of the sacred story available to the eyes of the faithful. The *Primi toni praeludium*, which opens the collection, is reproduced in Fig.523.

Fig.523

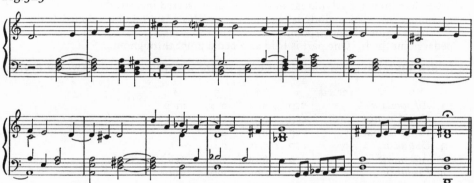

It is noteworthy that the consideration and explicit naming of the registers occurs in the earliest monument of 17th-century French organ music. The attention paid to registration is characteristic of the entire subsequent evolution of this art and differentiates it from that of other countries. The setting of the *Et laudamus* from the *Te Deum* carries the legend "Pour le cornet," and in the Magnificat collection, each *Gloria Patri* is followed by a "dernier vers" with the inscription "pour les registres coupez," apparently meaning "sharp registers." The designation "quatuor pedum," which is found consistently in the second Magnificat collection, may also be an indication of registration (4-foot?). In the *Liber Fratrum Cruciferorum* of 1617, which comes from neighboring Belgium, we similarly find the legend "pour trompette" (cf.p.344).

Titelouze

Jean Titelouze, born in 1563 at Saint-Omer, came from a family of English emigrants (Titlehouse). In 1588 he was appointed organist at the cathedral at Rouen, where he died in 1633. He was very famous as an organist and improviser, and was also sought as an expert in organ construction. He wrote only liturgical organ music. In 1623 he published his *Hymnes de l'Eglise pour toucher sur l'orgue, avec les fugues et recherches sur leur plain-chant,* and in 1626 *Le Magnificat ou cantique de la Vierge pour toucher sur l'orgue, suivant les huit tons de l'Eglise.*[1]

The first print contains organ settings for twelve hymns, each represented by three or four *Versets.* In these settings Titelouze utilized certain methods, which may be reduced to five basic types:

continuous *cantus planus* (ccp): The hymn melody lies continuously in one voice, mostly in the bass.

migrating *cantus planus* (mcp): The melody is laid out as a *cantus planus* distributed among several voices—e.g., phrase 1 in the tenor, phrase 2 in the soprano, phrase 3 in the tenor, and phrase 4 in the alto—with added imitative interludes.

motet-like (mot): Each phrase of the melody is treated imitatively.

canonic (can): The melody is laid out as a *cantus planus* and combined with two canonic counterpoints.

pedal point (ped): One part is held as a pedal point throughout.

The following table shows how these types are distributed in the twelve cycles:

versets:	1	2	3	4
1. *Ad coenam*	ccp	mot	mot	mcp
2. *Veni Creator*	ccp	ccp	can	mot
3. *Pange lingua*	ccp	mot	mcp	—
4. *Ut queant*	ccp	ccp	mot	—
5. *Ave maris*	ccp	mot	can	ped
6. *Conditor*	ccp	can	mot	—
7. *A solis ortus*	ccp	mot	mcp	—
8. *Exsultet*	ccp	ccp	mot	—
9. *Annue Christe*	ccp	mot	ped	—
10. *Sanctorum*	ccp	mot	mcp	—
11. *Iste confessor*	ccp	mot	mcp	—
12. *Urbs Jerusalem*	ccp	mot	mot	—

Titelouze proceeds very methodically. For the first setting of each hymn he always uses the traditional method of the uninterrupted *cantus planus,* and always puts the melody in the bass in a sequence of whole notes (semibreves), except in nos. 6 and 8, where breves and semibreves alternate. The counterpoints in the upper voices are developed imitatively from a number of subjects, the first of which is generally derived from the first few notes of the hymn tune. An especially instructive example is the first verse of *Iste confessor,* given in Fig.524.

In three cycles, nos.2, 4, and 8, type ccp is also employed for the second verse. In no. 2/2 (abbreviation for no.2, verse 2) and no. 8/2 brief fore-imitations precede the *cantus plani,* which lie in the soprano and alto, respectively. No. 4/2 starts out with a fore-imitation of nine measures, and the second phrase of the hymn melody is not presented as a simple *cantus planus,* but imitatively. This

Fig.524

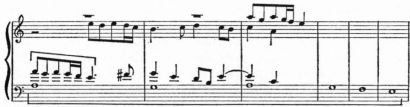

setting is the only one in the entire collection in which a particular type is not carried out purely.

Titelouze uses a migrating *cantus planus* in final verses only. It is again laid out in semibreves (whole notes) except for two instances: In no. 7/3 the first line is heard in breves, and in no. 10/3 the whole melody appears in half notes. Titelouze adds introductory sections to the various lines, often in the form of a fore-imitation.

In the motet-like settings each verse is transformed into a fugue subject (cf. two examples in Fig.525). The first fugue usually comprises two points of imitation, the others only one.

Fig.525

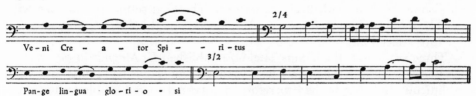

Three settings (nos. 2/3, 5/3, 6/2) add two canonic counterpoints to the *cantus planus,* and thus are Zarlino canons like those in Scheidt's works. These settings are the only three-part pieces in the collection; the others are all for four voices.

In no. 5/4 and no. 9/3 one voice is heard as a pedal point throughout. In the former the bass holds the tone *A* through 18 breve measures and 23 semibreve measures (a total of 59 notes), then moves up to *d* for the final 15 measures. In the other setting we hear a sustained *e″* in the soprano throughout the entire 56 measures. (Titelouze indicates that this note may be made to sound by putting a weight on the key.) Extended pedal-point settings as such are not so rare—examples such as Frescobaldi's and Bach's *Pastorale,* and Pachelbel's pedal-point toccatas come to mind. In Titelouze's pieces, however, the additional voices are not freely invented, but are derived from a pre-existent *cantus firmus.* Thus they solve the problem of writing a chorale motet to a pedal point, a problem that can hardly be denied the designation "recherché." In the verse from *Ave maris stella* (no.5/4) five of the subjects or motifs can be related to the hymn melody (e.g., the subject that enters on p.47, meas.10, of the new edition can be related to the notes that carry the syllable [*vir-*]*go*); only the relationship between the last phrase (*felix caeli porta*) and the conclusion of the motet remains obscure. Corresponding relationships seem to exist only for the beginning of the pedal-point setting from *Annue Christi* (no.9/3). Are even more devious "recherches" involved here?

It is obvious that Titelouze was a conservative musician. Unlike Sweelinck he was not a leader with novel aims, but a preserver of the tradition. He proves this in regard to harmony also. Its dark colors and the total absence of tonal drive remind us of Cabezón. His tendency toward continuity and interweaving in the motet-like settings is equally archaic, similar to Gombert's music. Nevertheless there are some features that show Titelouze to be a man of the 17th century—the occasional use of seventh chords, unprepared dissonances, and chromaticism (e.g., the conclusion of no. 5/2), and the employment of lively motifs (e.g., at the end of no. 3/2). Very definite modern tendencies are revealed in the final settings of nos. 1, 3, 7, 10, and 11. Here Titelouze frees himself from tradition and method; he presents the lines of the hymn tune in various parts and colors, expands the form with preludes, interludes, and postludes that are frequently quite extended, and furnishes some of them with lively figurations. The final setting of *Ad coenam* is probably the most impressive example and perhaps the artistic culmination of the entire collection.

Three years after the hymns Titelouze published *Le Magnificat ou cantique de la Vierge* (1626). In the preface he says that many people had found the hymns too difficult, and that he had therefore endeavored to reduce his technical demands. Each of the eight Magnificat cycles contains two settings for *Deposuit*, making a total of seven pieces instead of the usual six, and rendering the collection applicable also for the canticle *Benedictus*, which comprises fourteen verses and therefore requires seven organ versets.

In this work, too, Titelouze shows a conservative attitude, particularly when it is compared to the Magnificats in Samuel Scheidt's *Tabulatura nova* of 1624. Scheidt applies a great variety of techniques: two-, three-, and four-part settings; *choralis in cantu, alto, tenore,* or *basso;* figural, motet-like, or chordal texture, etc. (cf. the table on p.360). Titelouze, on the other hand, uses only a single method of approach, a four-part, motet-like texture. He derives one subject from each of the two halves of the reciting formula and presents them in imitations. Only very rarely does he deviate from this norm—in *IV. toni: Magnificat,* the first half of which is formulated as a pedal-point setting, while the second half is a *cantus-planus* arrangement, and in *V. toni: Suscepit* and *VII. toni: Suscepit,* the only three-part settings (see below).

In Magnificat cycles it is always interesting to observe how the same reciting formula gives rise to six or seven different fugue subjects, a point that was referred to in connection with Cavazzoni's Magnificats. Titelouze proves to be no less dexterous and imaginative. As an example Fig.526 presents the subjects of the first three settings of *III. toni*. Titelouze repeatedly employs the subject for inversion fugues as well, e.g., in *III. toni* the first subject of *Magnificat,* the first one of *Quia respexit,* the second one of *Suscepit,* and the first one of *Gloria patri.* Many pieces end with a free postlude.

Fig.526

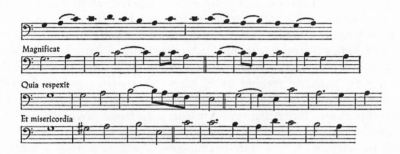

Compared to the hymns, the Magnificats are somewhat more forward-looking. There are more frequent chromatic progressions, though they keep within very modest limits, such as (*f f♯ g*) or (*g g♯ a*). Only in one piece does Titelouze venture into genuine chromaticism, in the second *Deposuit I. toni,* in which he moves three times through a fourth in chromatic semitone steps. There are other more progressive movements, such as the second *Deposuit VIII. toni,* in which all the voices move in sixteenth notes, though they are too constrained by contrapuntal necessities. The two three-part *Suscepits* are probably most successful in adopting new ideas. The *Suscepit V. toni* contains complementary motifs in eighth and sixteenth notes, as well as sixteenth-note figures in parallel thirds and tenths—devices that had long since acquired the status of common usage, but sound like audacious ventures with Titelouze. The surprise is even greater in the *Suscepit VII. toni,* when he abandons the fugal treatment after five measures, and moves to complementary motifs and then to a brief section in a ternary dance meter, as shown in Fig.527.

Fig.527

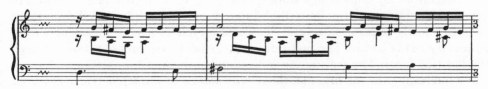

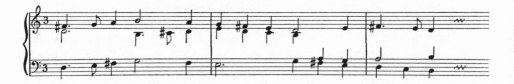

Racquet, Richard, and Anoymous Organ Music

Titelouze represents the end of an evolution, indeed of an epoch. He did have pupils, but could not form a school, for he was too far behind his time. Thus it is easy to understand why only a small number of French organ works reach us from the following decades. Only three bear the names of their composers: a fantasy by Charles Racquet (organist at Notre Dame in Paris from 1618 to 1643) and two preludes by Etienne Richard (organist at St. Jacques in Paris; died 1669).

Racquet's *Fantaisie* reaches us in Mersenne's own copy of the *Harmonie universelle*[2] (Racquet and Mersenne were close friends). It is unusually long for a French composition, more than 170 measures, and was obviously influenced by Dutch music. Like Sweelinck, Racquet develops one subject in several sections, in which he seems to follow different models. The first section is written in the traditional imitative style and employs several countermotifs. The second section (new ed., p.8, brace 2) is also imitative, but it is based on an ornamented version of the subject, and the other voices participate in the livelier motion (eighth notes). The third section (new ed., p.9) presents the subject in augmentation, once in each voice. Then (p.10) the subject appears in its basic form, combined contrapuntally with sixteenth-note figures, beginning with a *bicinium duplici contrapuncto* (at the fifth), like several that occur in Scheidt's works. The conclusion is formulated as a toccata-like section above a pedal point (bottom of p.11). Nothing like it was ever again written in France.

The two preludes by Etienne Richard[3] are among the most beautiful examples of this early 17th-century species. They combine a serious preoccupation with counterpoint and harmony with a first approach to that predilection for melody that gives later French organ music its special, often too secular character. The first *Prélude* consists of several sections of varying texture, among them two in triple meter (as in Titelouze's *Suscepit*, cf.fig.527). The second one is shorter, and made more unified by a pervasive chordal texture enlivened by expressive motifs. The beginning is given in Fig.528.

Several anonymous compositions, belonging to a slightly later period, are contained in the manuscript Paris, Bibl. Sainte-Geneviève 2348: a number of dance settings (mostly courantes), several duos, and a cycle of five arrangements of the hymn *Ave maris stella*.[4] The first three arrangements are *cantus-planus* settings, the last two fugal. The registration indications in the first four settings are especially interesting. In the first one the *cantus planus* in the tenor (*Plain chant en*

504

Fig.528

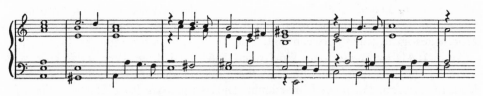

taille) is to be played as *Pédalles de trompettes*, and the other three parts as *Plain-jeu*. In the second setting, which is in three parts, the top voice carries the prescription *Positif: Fluste, Tremblant doux,* the hymn tune in the middle part *Pédale: Voix humaine,* and the lowest voice *Grand corps: Nazard.* In directions for registration French organ music is at least a century ahead of all the other countries.

Finally, there are the manuscripts Bibl. Sainte-Geneviève 2353, which includes a *Pange lingua,*[5] and Tours, Bibl. municipale 285, which was unfortunately destroyed during the Second World War. According to Pirro's detailed description[6] it contained versets for the eight church modes, fantasies in the same order, and "des versets sur les chants de l'office." Again it included indications of registrations such as *Le gros jeu de nazard avec le tremblant* or *Duo . . . pour deux différents jeux, comme le cornet et un jeu d'anches,* as well as *Dialogues,* much in favor with later organists, which demand the alternation of manuals. The penchant for melancholy, so characteristic of the period, emerges in such inscriptions as *Fugue mélancholique, bien grave et plaintive* or *Prélude plaintif.*

The Early Clavecinists

The first great master in the field of clavecin music is Chambonnières (c.1602–72). Until about thirty years ago he was also regarded as the creator of this genre, but in recent years a number of composers who prepared the way for his work have become known: Mézangeau, Pinel, Gaultier, La Barre, Monnard, and Richard. They wrote allemandes, courantes, and sarabandes—the dances that constituted the stock of France secular music until the early 18th century.

Toward the end of the 16th century and at the beginning of the 17th, the allemande, courante, and gigue were already extensively cultivated in England. In Italy the corrente appears in Ercole Pasquini's works and in Frescobaldi's *Toccate I* of 1615. In Germany, after a single example by Bernhard Schmid the Elder in 1577, it appears again in Scheidt's *Tabulatura nova* of 1624. The German area also produced the manuscript Copenhagen, Royal Library 376, which contains 7 allemandes, 12 courantes, and 12 sarabandes, as well as preludes, German chorales (*Vom Himmel hoch,* etc.) and songs (*Ich füle lauter Angst undt Schmerzen, Als Damon lang geplaget*).[7] In this source the sarabande appears for the first time in greater number.

One *Currant* in this manuscript, dated 1626, is signed "Ab.," and thus may be ascribed to David Abel. Two of the dances doubtless come from France, an *Allamande de Mr. Meschanson* and an *Allamande de Mr. Pinell*. The former is by René Mézangeau (died between 1636 and 1639), the latter either by Pierre Pinel (alive in 1641) or by Germain Pinel (died 1664). All three were active chiefly as lutenists, and it is quite possible that these allemandes are really lute pieces. Indeed, the Mézangeau piece in particular shows the *style brisé* of Denis Gaultier and his contemporaries, that peculiarly loose, arpeggiated texture, that only suggests polyphony, the style of writing that so strikingly differentiates 17th-century lute music from that of the 16th century. The first section of Mézangeau's allemande is given in Fig.529 with its original fingerings and signs for ornaments.

Fig.529

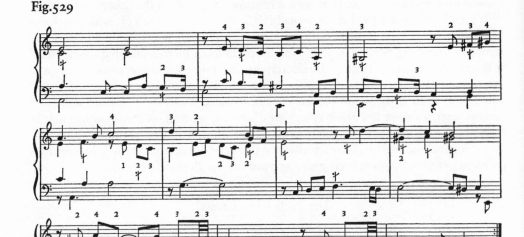

It does not matter whether this piece was originally written for the lute or the clavier. Despite the fact that it is an early work, it definitely shows all the peculiarities of the clavecin art in an especially beautiful and clear manner—broken texture, continuous melody, passing modulations, retarded cadences, musical flow, subtlety of expression, sublimation of feeling—in short what Tessier calls the "premier romantisme" in his edition of the works of Denis Gaultier. It seems that Tessier was right to relate this world of musical feeling to the English lutenist John Dowland, whom his contemporaries called "semper dolens," always lamenting. He and his fellow countryman Orlando Gibbons were the first to succeed in

506

opening for music that aura of gentle plaint, of restrained feeling, that appears again and again in the works of the clavecinists.

We also know two sarabandes by Mézangeau. Their style, too, closely approaches that of the lute, while a sarabande by Pinel shows a fuller, more clavieristic setting.[8] Notated in 3/2 measures, it exhibits the rhythmic sway of the hemiola (particularly in the bass), which is just as unusual in a sarabande as it is usual in a courante (Fig.530).

Fig.530

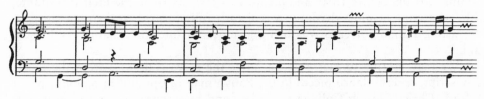

Names such as Ballard, Gaultier, La Barre, Monnard, and Richard belong to families that played a role in the musical life of France through several generations so that it is sometimes difficult to determine which one of several composers with the same name is the author of a given piece. There is no difficulty with Ballard, Gaultier, and La Barre since works of theirs are preserved in the Lynar tablature A I, which was written in the 1630s at the latest. Thus our Ballard is probably Pierre (died 1639), our Gaultier Ennemond (c.1580–1651, a cousin of Denis), our La Barre Pierre III (1592–1656). Our Monnard can only be Nicolas (died 1646?), and our Richard only Etienne (died 1669).

All the pieces in the Lynar tablature—one courante each by Ballard and Gaultier and three by La Barre—include varied repetitions, either of the individual sections (A A′ B B′) or of the entire piece, in form of a *Variatio* after the dance. In the dances of Chambonnières, Louis Couperin, and d'Anglebert the first method never occurs, and the second occurs only very rarely, under the designation *Double*. On the other hand such repetitions are almost indispensable in the works of the virginalists; their regular occurrence in these courantes may therefore be interpreted as a sign of English influence. It is not impossible, of course, that the repetitions represent a later addition by an English or German arranger. Fig.531

Fig.531

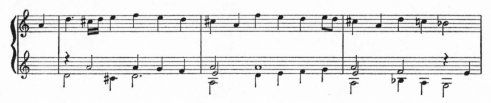

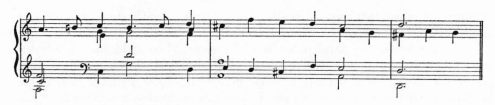

shows the beginning of Ballard's courante, in which the varied repetition is interestingly shifted to the lower octave. Even more important, in this piece, which was certainly written before 1630, and possibly as early as 1620, the French courante, with its swaying hemiola rhythms, was already fully formed; at the same time the contrasting Italian corrento was being given its distinct formulation by Frescobaldi.

We may ascribe to Pierre de La Barre the three courantes from the Lynar manuscript, several dance pieces in the Bauyn manuscript and in manuscripts at Oxford (Christ Church Coll. 1177, 1236), and two courantes and a sarabande signed "Monsu della Bar" in the manuscript Rome, Bibl. Vat. Chigi IV.24 (fol. 47ff.).[9] We also have two courantes and a sarabande by Monnard.[10]

Etienne Richard is the best known of the early clavecinists. His extant output comprises 2 preludes, mentioned earlier as organ works (cf.p.504), 4 allemandes, 3 courantes, 2 sarabandes, and 2 gigues.[11] The allemandes show the first signs of the more ornamented style that gradually increases as this species evolves. The two gigues are very curious: One (Bonfils P, no.9) is written in 3/2 time, but closes with a refrain in 2/2; the other (no.11) is written throughout in 2/2 and can hardly be told from an allemande. As a matter of fact, some of Froberger's gigues are also composed in even meter or with endings in even meter.

18

Spain and Portugal

Clavijo, Peraza, and Lacerna

WE KNOW VERY LITTLE about the development of keyboard music
in the Iberian peninsula from about 1560 to 1620. Who were the successors of
the great Cabezón? His son Hernando is the only representative we know from
the generation born around 1530. Bernardo Clavijo de Castillo seems to belong
to the following generation. Probably born around 1550, he became an organist
at the court of the Spanish viceroy of Naples in 1588, assumed the chair of music
at the University of Salamanca in 1593, and was active from 1619 on as an organist
at the court of Madrid, where he died in 1626. A contemporary account by Vicente Espinel reveals that Clavijo's house—like Count Bardi's *camera* at Florence
—served as the meeting place of a group of excellent musicians (among them
Bernardo's daughter Bernardina), who played various instruments and diligently
discussed "cuestiones acerca del uso de esta ciencia" (questions regarding the use
of music).[1]

Except for a motet book that was printed in 1588, Clavijo's extant creative
output is unfortunately limited to a single organ work. This *Tiento de segundo
tono,* which is preserved in an unnumbered manuscript of the Archivo de El
Escorial, is of great significance, both artistically and historically, and may perhaps throw some light on the questions discussed by the Madrid "camerata."[2]
In its formal aspects it follows Cabezón's tientos, since it consists of an initial
section in imitative style followed by an equally long one in free counterpoint; but
harmonically it opens a new field—what the Italians called *durezze e ligature* and
the Spaniards called *falsas.* In Cabezón's works there are also many dissonances
and turns that are inadmissible within the pure counterpoint of the 16th century,
but they hark back to the musical language of the late Middle Ages, while Clavijo's

509

tiento foreshadows the problems of the *stile moderno*, the *seconda prattica* of the 17th century. These problems may well have been the ones discussed by the "junta de excelentissimos músicos" in Madrid. Fig.532 offers a characteristic excerpt from Clavijo's tiento.

Fig.532

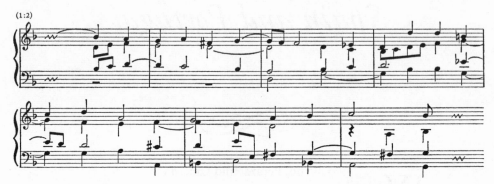

In the Escorial manuscript there is a counterpart to Clavijo's composition, a *Medio registro alto de Pedraza*,[3] which is remarkable, and, moreover, is the only preserved work of a very famous organ master. It is commonly, and certainly correctly, ascribed to Francisco Peraza, who was born in 1564 and died at an early age in 1598. His brother Jeronimo was probably ten years his senior, but outlived him. Both were organists at the cathedral of Seville, Jeronimo from 1572 to 1579 and Francisco from 1586 probably until his death. In 1599 the contemporary writer Pacheco published a *Libro de descripción de verdaderos retrados* (Book of Description of Truthful Portraits), in which he entered a detailed and highly laudatory presentation of the life and work of the recently deceased Francisco.[4] It reports that Guerrero, the master of Spanish vocal music (1528–99), "embraced" Francisco, "clasped his hands, and asked for his permission to kiss them"; that it was said of Clavijo that "an angel lived in his fingers"; that he "was the inventor of the *medios registros*"; and that on the keyboard he "played two thousand *flores* invented by himself with so much taste that to him alone [together with Felipe Rugier] Spain owed the grace and beauty of organ playing, the tasteful innovations together with the great variety of large fugues, such as had not been seen in Europe before him."

Even if this eulogy—after all, it represents a sort of necrologue for the youthfully deceased composer—is somewhat of an overstatement, it nevertheless shows that Francisco Peraza was without doubt an unusually outstanding organist and organ composer. It is regrettable that only one of his works reaches us—though it it is one that bears out Pacheco's description in many details and confirms it. The title, *Medio registro*, refers to an innovation introduced by Peraza, which acquired great importance in the later development of Spanish organ playing. The stops were divided into two independent halves, so that the upper and lower parts of the keyboard could be registrated differently. The Spanish organs of the period had only one manual, and this device made it possible to produce effects that would otherwise require two manuals. Organ pieces that were written with such an execution in mind were designated as *medio registro* (half register), and differentiated as *medio registro alto* or *de tiple* (*tiple* = soprano), and *medio registro baxo* or *de baxón*. In the former the upper portion of the keyboard was registrated soloistically, in the latter the lower part. Obviously this method required that each hand be limited to one half of the keyboard throughout the composition. The boundary lay between *c′* and *c♯′*. Thus in a *medio registro alto* the soprano never dips below *c♯′*, and the other voices never rise above *c′*.

In his *Medio registro* Peraza was not only a bold innovator in organ technique and registration, but also, quite in keeping with Pacheco's presentation, as a composer. The piece certainly belongs to the tiento species, but this type acquires an entirely new form here. The imitative element, which had been an essential part of the classical tiento, recedes into the background. The work does begin with a fourfold point of imitation, which, however, only serves as the jumping-off point for the real content, a *variedad de flores,* a colorful plethora of ornamental figures. For someone who had grown up and become familiar with the strict imitation style of the early Spanish school, this piece must have sounded completely novel, like something that "did not exist anywhere in Europe." Indeed, before 1598 there were not many organ compositions that are so completely devoted to the interplay of various figures. This approach emerges right away in the imitative "introduction," as the last presentation of the subject (*d f e d* in whole notes), in the soprano, is ornamented with eighth- and sixteenth-note passages. After this exposition of twelve measures the subject disappears. Most of the 79 measures of this work display a free contrapuntal texture, frequently enlivened by figurations. Several times clavieristic figures are repeated four or five times, accommodated to the changing harmonies. Such passages reveal a tendency

Fig.533

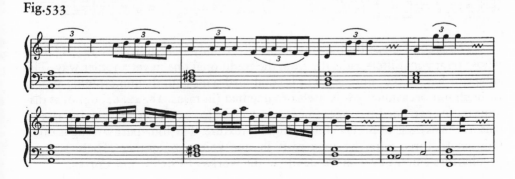

toward structural regularity and formalism, which is very characteristic of Spanish organ music of the 17th century. Peraza's *Medio registro* contains three such passages (meas.21–24, 43–48, and 63–73). The last one, which occurs near the end, is reproduced in Fig.533 (only the first few notes of the repeated figures are indicated).

Recently another *Obra de Perasa* has been found in a handwritten postscript to the copy of the *Libro de tientos* by Correa de Arauxo (1626) owned by the Real Biblioteca de Ajuda at Lisbon. It follows the 16th-century tradition rather closely, and was possibly written by Francisco's older brother, Jeronimo Peraza.[5]

Two tientos by Estacio de Lacerna (de la Serna)[6] in the same postscript are more interesting. Lacerna was born in Seville around 1565, served at the Royal Chapel at Lisbon from 1595 to 1604 as Coelho's predecessor, later emigrated to Peru, and died there around 1625. Like Peraza's *Medio registro*, Lacerna's tientos[7] point to the new ideas and methods of the 17th century: a more relaxed treatment of imitation and a strong stress on figuration.

The first tiento divides into three fugal sections, each with its own subject (the starting subject, $| f | f f | c e | d e | d |$, is similar to *Ein' feste Burg*), and in form may thus be called a ricercar; but several details show that the composer no longer took the principle of imitation too seriously. At two places, measures 18–27 and 38–48, the main subject occurs twice in immediate succession in the same voice (soprano), not imitated but merely repeated. Various passages in the second section are equally "inadmissible" (meas.91ff.), for the subject is heard simultaneously in two parts in parallel thirds or sixths, again not imitated but merely duplicated, as shown in Fig.534.

Fig.534

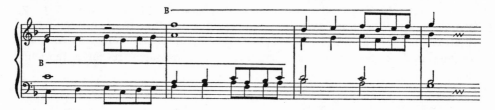

The second piece by Lacerna is based on only one subject ($| d | g a | b |$), whose treatment differs radically from the traditional one in yet another way. The subject is hardly ever imitated, but is combined with figural counterpoints almost throughout; occasionally it is itself ornamented (in meas. 18, 42, 62, 64) or it disappears for extended passages (meas. 22–30, 36–40, 52–60, 86–92), giving rise to episodic insertions of purely chordal-figural texture. The four-part writing is often reduced to three parts by long rests in one voice or another. These stylistic peculiarities emerge even more clearly in the works of Coelho and Correa.

Aguilera de Heredia

Sebastian Aguilera de Heredia is much better known than Clavijo, Peraza, or Lacerna. He must have been born around 1565, for in 1583, as a young man, he became an organist at the cathedral at Huesca (Aragon), a position he retained until 1603. Then he went to Sarogossa, where he is mentioned as "Portionarius et organis praeceptor." He died in 1627. The fact that some of his works were incorporated in collections as late as 1700—in the Portuguese *Libro de cyfra* and in a manuscript by Antonio Martin y Coll of 1709—is proof of his fame. Seventeen of his organ works are preserved, almost all in the Escorial manuscript: 2 *Pange lingua*, 2 *Salbe* (*Salve regina*), and 13 tientos.[8]

A piece inscribed *A tres sobre vajo* (for three voices with the *cantus firmus* in the bass), belongs to a group of three-part settings of the *Pange lingua* in the Escorial manuscript (most of them are by Jimenez), in which the old Spanish melody of the Corpus Christi hymn, which was already used by Cabezón, is laid out in one of the voices as a strict *cantus planus* in alternating long and short note values (either breves and semibreves or semibreves and minims). In Aguilera's arrangement it is heard in the bass, combined with a middle part, which is set to it almost note against note, and a sustained, ornamented melodic line in the soprano. The resulting setting is of noble beauty and restrained expression, a worthy continuation of the Cabezón tradition. Like all the *Pange lingua* in the group, the piece has no ending, but after twenty-one measures leads back to the beginning—proof that these settings are meant to accompany the singing of the various stanzas of the hymn. To illustrate this interesting practice Fig.535 gives the beginning and end of Aguilera's *Pange lingua*.[9] The other *Pange lingua*, in the manuscript Barcelona M. 450, is called "La reina [the queen] de los Pange lingua." Unfortunately my request for a photocopy was refused by the administration of the Biblioteca Central of Barcelona.

Fig.535

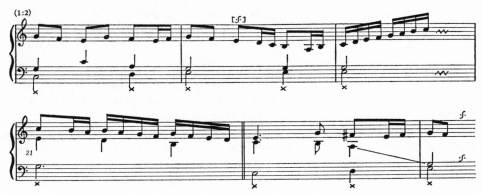

In the two *Salbe* Aguilera does not use the entire melody of the *Salve regina* but only its incisive starting motif (| *a* | *g♯* | *a* | *d* |), which serves as the subject of an extended imitative setting. This kind of treatment plays a very important role in the evolution of the Protestant organ chorale, and in this connection is called chorale fugue (or fughetta), but it is very rare in Catholic organ chorales in the 16th and 17th centuries. Pieces that consist of a single point of imitation on the head motif of the Gregorian melody do occur in the organ Masses of Girolamo Cavazzoni and Claudio Merulo, but Aguilera does not limit himself to a single point of imitation, but develops a complete fugue, in which the subject is heard again and again, fifteen times in one *Salbe*, sixteen times in the other. In the *Salbe de lleno* (*lleno* means full register, in contrast to *medio registro*) one voice or another adds to the sustained tones of the subject quietly flowing figures or motifs in eighth notes, which unify the texture. In the *Salbe de 1° tono*[10] the figurations are livelier and more varied, and begin to exhibit genuine Baroque features, such as the employment of unusual rhythmic figures that may be symbolized as 8 = 3+3+2. Figures of this kind occur earlier in a German prelude of about 1520 (cf.pp.215f.), a toccata by Pasquini (cf.p.422), and in the theme of Cabezón's *Diferencias sobre el canto del Caballero* (cf.p.265). In all these instances the motion is relatively slow, and the quarter note (or its equivalent in earlier notation) represents the unit of time. Aguilera uses a rhythm that moves twice as fast, with the eighth note as the unit, producing a characteristic clavieristic figure, which occurs very frequently in Spanish keyboard music of the 17th century. Fig.536 is a portion of an extended passage, in which such a formula is employed as a complementary motif.

Fig.536

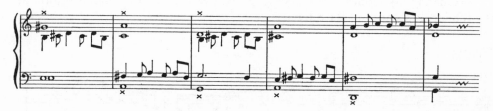

Finally let us turn to Aguilera's tientos. Three of them belong to the special *falsa* type, which occurs in Clavijo's work, but in Aguilera's hands they acquire a clearer formulation and are also called by this name for the first time (as far as we know at present).[11] The *falsas* differ from the normal tientos of the 17th century even in their visual aspect—if one wants to call it that: in their slow motion in half and quarter notes and in their strictly polyphonic texture. Completely free of figurations and chordal elements, they continue the 16th-century tradition, although they do not follow the rules of the *contrappunto osservato*. On the con-

Fig.537

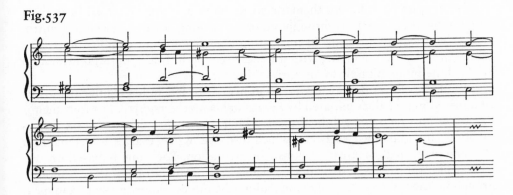

trary, these rules are consciously and consistently disregarded, as the voices are "incorrectly" led, exactly as in the contemporary *durezze e ligature* of the Italians. In the course of the 17th century, there sprang from these "incorrect" voice leadings those principles that determine, and are "correct" for, the counterpoint of Bach, although obviously much that the masters of the early Baroque indulged in in their over-enthusiastic reaction to their newly won freedom was later set aside. But it is interesting to observe that in Aguilera's *falsas,* in addition to typically early-Baroque passages, there occur occasional voicings that belong to the vocabulary of the late Baroque, which is so familiar to every musician. Note, e.g., the passage in Fig.537, taken from the second *Tiento de 4° tono de falsas.* Similar sequences, shown in Fig. 538, also occur in the *Falsas de 6° tono.* In measure 4 of this passage the original has an *eb* in the alto sounding simultaneously with an *e* in the bass. Both Villalba and Pedrell correct the latter without further ado into an *eb*, a procedure that will certainly be generally approved. And yet I cannot suppress a doubt, first of all because the employment of accidentals throughout the manuscript is generally very careful, and even more because of the demands of the voice leading. (A similar instance occurs in the first *Tiento de 4° tono*, measure 24, where a *c♯* in the tenor ascends to *d* against a *c′* in the alto that descends to *b*.) But what is decisive is that Correa de Arauxo, in his *Libro de Tientos* of 1626, expressly approves the simultaneous sounding of a tone and its chromatic variant —he calls it *punto intenso contra remisso*—and uses it repeatedly in his works cf.pp.528, 533f.).

Fig.538

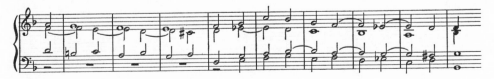

Aguilera uses a different thematic structure in each of the *falsas*. In the first one he employs two subjects throughout, one ascending and one descending, introducing them again and again in interesting alternations and combinations. The second *falsa* is monothematic, with a middle section in free counterpoint; and in the third, he limits himself to an initial imitation.

Aguilera follows Bernardo Clavijo in his *falsas*, but in his regular tientos he continues along the lines initiated by Peraza in his *Medio registro*. His four tientos that are *medios registros* will be discussed later. Let us turn first to the six tientos (or obras) for undivided registers, which also follow in Peraza's footsteps in at least one way—in their great emphasis on figuration. Each one is based on one ricercar-like subject, which reappears again and again in one voice or another throughout the rather extended composition (the pieces comprise 109 to 240 measures). But this thematic structure is no longer the chief aspect of the work; it serves rather as the basis or framework for the creation of figures whose lively motion and varied design seem to interest the composer more than the repetitions of the subject. Nevertheless he never crosses the borderline between inner life and superficial brilliance. The figuration is measured, often expressive, and combines with imitation in a balanced manner that may be called classical.

Like Sweelinck's fantasies, these tientos combine the monothematic approach with an articulation in several sections, but Aguilera employs different means to carry out this principle. In two of his tientos the articulation is brought about by a change in figuration. This method is exhibited particularly clearly in the *Obra de 1° tono* (Anglés A; I, no.III). The piece divides into four sections, with the first one (meas.1–71) moving in quiet half and quarter notes, the second (meas.72–107) in sixteenth-note runs and figures, the third (meas.108–26) in continuous eighth-note sextuplets, and the fourth (meas.127–33) in the same motion as the beginning, providing a quiet conclusion. The structure of the *Obra de 8° tono* (Anglés A; III, no.V) is similar, but the figurations within each section are less unified.

In three other tientos the articulation derives from the alternation of duple and triple meters. Cabezón used this idea in two late works, the *Tiento del cuarto tono* (Pedrell H; IV, 63), which presents a brief section in 3/2 near the end, and the *Tiento del sexto tono* (Pedrell H; VII, 2), whose *Segunda parte* begins with a lengthy section of this kind. But while Cabezón's sections in triple meter are thematically independent of the others, Aguilera uses them to present the main theme of the entire work in the rhythmic variant of the *proportio tripla*. Fig.539 shows the subject of the *tiento de 4° tono* (Anglés A; II, no.1) and its variant.

Fig.539

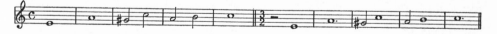

516

Fig.540

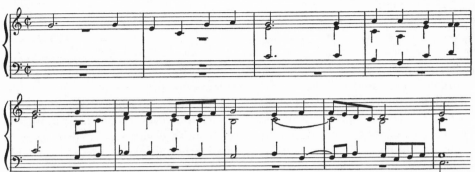

The work called *Obra de 8° tono, Ensalada* is a special case. The term *ensalada* (mixture) apparently refers to the fact that the piece, which runs to about 200 measures, consists of five extended sections, alternating duple and triple meters. The sections are thematically unrelated and exhibit a colorful, mixed content, partly imitative, partly motivic, partly homophonic, of vivid expression and playful character throughout. The work starts with an imitative section, given in Fig.540, which stands completely outside the stylistic limits of his other works in its gaily secular C-major subject and its regular phrasing in two- and four-measure groups.[12] In the conclusion of the third section of the *Ensalada* a ringing fanfare motif is heard four times. One has to imagine this played on one of the trumpet registers so characteristic of Spanish organs in the 17th century! The triplet figure in the section's penultimate measure recalls the fanfare motif in an abbreviated form, and it comes at the right moment to avoid the danger of too much symmetry (Fig.541). Nevertheless it is just this symmetric phrasing that is of great historical interest, for such passages, consisting of the modulating repetition of an idea, assume an ever-increasing importance later on in the evolution of Span-

Fig.541

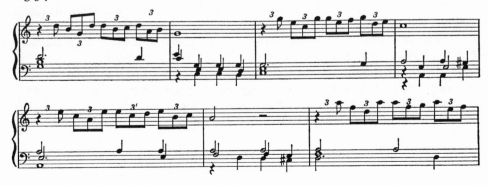

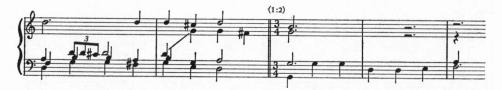

ish organ music, until they become the predominant principle of composition in Cabanilles. Aguilera's *Ensalada* includes several other passages of this type, one of which is given in Fig.542. Echo effects—which, however, do not play an important role in the subsequent development of Spanish organ music—also occur in Aguilera's *Ensalada*. This extraordinarily sprightly and varied piece is certainly one of the most valuable treasures of early organ music.

Fig.542

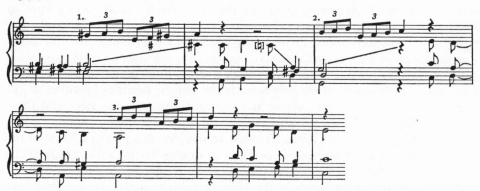

Finally, let us discuss the four *medios registros*.* Curiously Villalba did not incorporate them in his collection. Perhaps they looked too peculiar to him, and did not correspond to his views of what constituted valuable music. Indeed they contain many features that look rather strange at first glance, and only become intelligible when viewed within the historical evolution that leads from Aguilera to Cabanilles.

All four belong to the species of the *medio registro de bajo (vajo, baixo)*, in which the bass is treated soloistically—in one instance the two lowest parts are so treated. The left hand is busy with figurations almost throughout while the right hand adds chords. In contrast to this emphasis on figurations and chords, imitation is employed very laxly. Each piece starts with a point of imitation in the strict style of a ricercar in order to satisfy convention. In the rest of the piece the

---

* Because of its shallowness, one of them may well be regarded as spurious. It is preserved only in the *Libro de cyfra*.

subject occurs only once or twice more, just enough to preserve a minimum of politeness toward a cumbersome tradition. Aguilera's sole interest is figuration, which, indeed, exhibits very remarkable and novel features that emerge most clearly in the *Vajo de 1° tono*. From measure 37 to measure 127 (the whole piece contains 157 measures[13]) the bass is composed exclusively of seven brief formulae, each of which is repeated several times, shifted by fourths or fifths. In general there are four statements in a descending sequence followed by four in an ascending sequence, so that the same tonal space is traversed several times in the order of the descending and ascending circle of fifths, e.g.: E, A, D, G || C, G, D, A. Since such modulatory passages occur repeatedly in the evolution of Spanish organ music, we shall indicate them by symbols such as the following:

    4S(3m) = statement and 3 modulations to the subdominant of a 3-measure
             formula
    5D(2m) = statement and 4 modulations to the dominant of a 2-measure
             formula

With the help of these symbols the 91 measures described above can be outlined schematically as follows (omitting several rests):

   | 4S(3m) | 5D(2m) | 4S(3m) | 4D(3m) | 5S(2m) | 2D(6m) | 4S(2m) |

Fig.543 shows the first and second formulae in this scheme. Similar passages occur in Peraza's *Medio registro alto* (cf. Fig.533), but Aguilera's formulae are two or three times as long, and so lose their character of clavieristic figures and assume a structural significance.

Fig.543

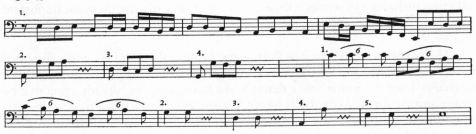

With his *falsas*, modulating figures, motifs in 3 + 3 + 2 rhythm, and other details, Aguilera becomes the founder of a school whose tradition leads via Jimenez, Bruna, Perandreu, and others to Cabanilles. His artistic importance is summed up in the last sentence of M. S. Kastner's article in *MGG:* "Above all Aguilera de Heredias' fame has remained alive in Aragon and Navarre until today; his works are heard there again and again."

Coelho

Manuel Rodriguez Coelho is the first organ master after Cabezón whose complete works are preserved in a print. Born around 1555 in Elvas, Portugal, he was an organist at the cathedrals of Badajoz (1573–77), Elvas (158?–1602), and Lisbon (1602–1603), and organist and *tangedor de tecla* (clavier player) of the Royal Chapel at Lisbon until 1633. He died at an advanced age in 1635. When he was about sixty-five he published a voluminous collection of organ works under the title *Flores de musica* (Lisbon, 1620), which he was permitted to dedicate to King Philipp III of Spain (and Portugal).[14] According to the original table of contents it includes the following:

A. Twenty-four *Tentos* (three for each church mode)
B. *Quatro Susanas grosadas sobre a de cinquo* (four ornamented *Susannas* on the five-part [*Susanna* by Lassus])
C. *Quatro Pange linguas sobre o canto chão de breves em cada voz* (four *Pange lingua* on the chant in breves, one in each voice)
D. *Quatro Ave Maris stellas sobre o canto chão de semibreves em cada voz* (...chant in semibreves...)
E. *Sinco Versos sobre os paços do canto chão da Ave Maris stella* (five versets on the sections of the ... *Ave maris stella*)
F. *Oito tons pera se cantarem ao orgão, acompanhandoos sempre a quatro et cinquo* (the eight psalm tones for singing to the organ, always accompanied by four and five parts)
G. *Outros oito tons sobre o canto chão de cada voz, pera se tangerem aos Benedictos et Magnificas* (another eight tones on the chant in each part, to be played at the Benedictus and Magnificat)
H. *Kirios ou versos por todos os sete sinos, começando de se sol fa ut até b fa negro* (Kyries or versets in all seven keys, from C to the black B♭)

Groups F, G, and H contain 23, 34, and 35 versets, respectively; thus the entire collection includes 133 works. Obviously we can only discuss the most important features of this rich content, which was surely composed over three or four decades.[15]

The twenty-four tientos (the Portuguese form of the word is *tento*), compositions of about 200 to 300 measures, occupy more than half the print. They complete the change from the Renaissance tiento to the Baroque types, already suggested by Peraza and Aguilera. Actually, "change" is not the correct word to describe this evolution. In contrast to the Italian ricercar, whose essential features were fully retained in the 17th century, the tiento was so fundamentally transformed that a completely new type resulted. The direction that this transformation took deviated radically from the central development. The 16th-century tiento, despite various idiomatic peculiarities, definitely kept within the framework of "European" music of the period, but the Baroque tiento, in the hands of Aguilera, Coelho, Correa, Jimenez, Bruna, and Cabanilles evolved into a national type, which cannot be likened to anything else. The peculiarity of the species consists in a wealth of formulae, which may best be called pictorial, for indeed these compositions acquire a picturesque, scenic quality. They represent a kind of drama, a colorful theater, on which certain figures appear, linger for a while, and then make room for others —all without real continuity or unification, but in a loose array whose meaning and attraction lies in its kaleidoscopic changes.

This attempt at characterization may be opposed on the grounds that Coelho's tientos are obviously planned thematically, usually so that they divide into three or four main sections, each based on a subject of its own, which unifies the section. As a theoretical, analytical fact this objection is definitely correct, but it does not correspond to the musical reality. For Coelho does not employ his subjects as means of unification but as a point of departure for creating variety; not as an organic seedling, but as a scaffolding for the presentation of colorful, changing figurations. Only rarely do the subjects occur in a genuine, tension-creating imitation; instead they are often regularly distributed, repeated immediately in the same voice, heard in parallel thirds, or arranged in sequences. Such methods, which also occur in Lacerna's tiento, point to a decay of imitative counterpoint, which seems to have begun much earlier in the Iberian peninsula than elsewhere. Fortunately it did not lead to the same decline in taste and content there as it later did in Italy, France, and England. For the musicians of the early Baroque the newly discovered techniques of figuration and motivic workmanship opened up a plethora of novel possibilities and a way to make up for the loss in contrapuntal substance. Coelho—like Sweelinck—employed these means to the fullest.

Coelho's tientos are very long compositions, some as long as 300 measures. Despite what has just been said, in trying to describe their contents, one has to start with their thematic plan. Several of them are monothematic, in the sense that one main idea reappears from beginning to end, although it appears together with or alternating with other materials that are thematic, figural, or motivic in character. One such piece is tiento no.9, a work of 206 measures, which divides into two sections. The first one is longer (meas.1–136), and is based on the subject (| *a* | — *f♯* | *f♯ g♯* | *a* |); it is introduced in a broadly conceived point of imitation with two episodes; but thereafter it is employed exclusively as scaffolding for varied figurations, as in Fig.544.* It is easy to see that the subject, despite its "learned" treatment in repeated strettos, plays a secondary role: The essential, life-giving element is the chain of figures with its changing formulae. Typical details are the figures in dotted rhythm and in triplets; both are unusual in the keyboard literature of the period, but occur very frequently in Coelho's music, often pervading entire sections (cf.new ed., pp.17–19, 103–105). Typical also are the long rests, which reduce the four-part texture to three voices for long stretches. This "fugal" first section of tiento no.9 is followed by a rather lengthy final section (meas.137–206), which is completely devoted to motivic figures. Its begin-

---

* At the places marked * Kastner adds editorial sharps, which I find justified.

Fig.544

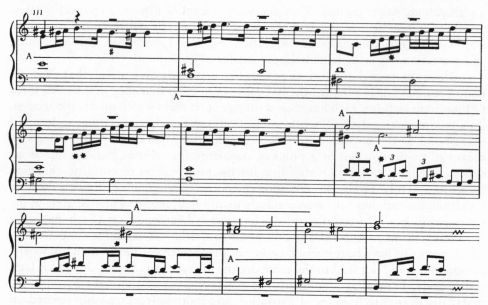

ning is given in Fig.545. The curiously capricious triplet figure that occurs three times in a row (in all it is heard about forty times!) is one of Coelho's most characteristic style traits. It was obviously invented by him, and he employed it repeatedly, even creating entire sections from it (cf. new ed., pp.13f., 51–53, 153f., 156f.).

Fig.545

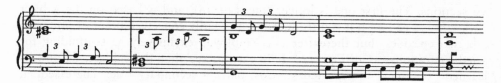

Another monothematic tiento, no.16, is interesting because its subject (| f | f g | a f | b♭ | a) appears in several degrees of augmentation and diminution, as in Sweelinck's fantasies, but they are not distributed among the sections so systematically. Thus we find diminution by one half in measures 72ff. and by one quarter in measures 109ff., augmentation by two in measures 51ff. and by three in measures 163ff.

Most of the tientos employ several subjects. The following is a schematic presentation of some of them:

No.7: A | A dim. | B | (3) C (var. of B?) | D | clav. fig.
     40   85 109   167 236–89

No.8: A | A aug. | B
     95 153–210

No.10: A | clav. fig. | B | C | clav. fig. | D
     28   52 73 108   144–64

No.21: A | clav. fig. | B | clav. fig. | A′ | A′ dim. | A′ aug. | clav. fig. |
     46   73 102 109 123 149 218

    A | (3) A/C,C
    232 251–307

The first subjects always move in long note values, like the ricercar subjects of the 16th and 17th centuries. Other subjects, e.g., B and C of no.10, have livelier motions in quarter and eighth notes, while still others, e.g., subjects D of no.10, resemble sprightly motifs. The longer the notes of the subject, the more opportunity they offer for figural counterpoints, especially in augmentations. In some instances the entries of the subject follow close upon one another (e.g., in the first section of no.21), while others are separated by shorter or longer interludes. In section C of no.10, e.g., several strettos of the subject (new ed., p.93, meas.73–84) are followed by an interlude of five measures, another entry of the subject (meas. 90), another interlude of eight measures, the subject again (meas.100), three free measures, and finally two more strettos of the subject (meas.104ff.). Additional examples of this method, which plays an even greater role in Correa's tientos, are found in many other pieces. Quite often subjects or motivic ideas are developed to an extent that exceeds the limits of taste. In tiento no.18, e.g., the first subject appears thirteen times and a second one (meas.139ff.) some twenty times, both with insertions of extended interludes, so that the first section alone runs to more than 100 measures. Each thematic section is followed by one pervaded by uniform figurations, the first comprising more than 30 measures (meas.102–35), the second nearly 40 (meas.207–46).

The harmonic language of the tientos is generally simple and clear. In any event, the experimental dissonances of the Neapolitans and the harmonic labyrinths of Fresobaldi are absent. The whole harmonic texture moves in the orderly paths of an intelligible tonality with occasional modal colors. In only one tiento, no.19, which differs from the rest in other traits of style as well, is there a sparing use of prepared dissonances, in the manner of a Spanish *tiento de falsas*. The passage shown in Fig.546—as far as I can see—represents the outer limit of harmonic boldness to which Coelho dared go (new ed., p.189, meas.82ff.). On occasion

Fig.546

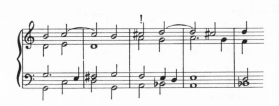

Coelho curiously still uses the archaic formula of the Lydian cadence, i.e., one with leading tones to both octave and fifth (*f♯–g* and *c♯–d* above a *G*), e.g., in no. 14, measure 19, and no.21, measure 38. In the harmonic discourse of the tientos Coelho repeatedly employs chord sequences as the fundament for repetitions of figures, e.g., in the passage from tiento no.14, given in Fig.547, (new ed., p.132, meas.100ff.).*

Fig.547

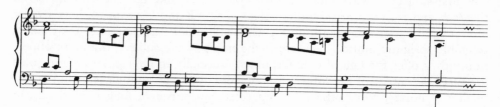

The tientos in the *Flores de musica* are followed by four *Susana grosada a 4 sobre a de 5*, in which Lassus' five-part *Susanna un jour* is reduced to four voices, and—as in Hernando de Cabezón's intabulations—decorated with varied and constantly changing figurations (*glosas*).

The rest of the *Flores* (new ed., vol.II) consists of versets for liturgical use. In four organ settings on *Pange lingua,* the hymn melody is heard successively in the soprano, alto, tenor, and bass as a strict *cantus planus* in breves, preceded in the first setting by an extended fore-imitation. Most of the counterpoints constitute a varied play of figurations, in which the motif shown in Fig.545 occurs repeatedly (e.g., new. ed., p.9, meas.17–18). Four settings of *Ave maris stella* follow (group D). They are again *cantus-planus* arrangements, but in shorter note values, half notes (minims) in the first setting and whole notes (semibreves) in the others. The counterpoints here are less ornamented than in the *Pange lingua* settings. Group E again consists of settings of the *Ave maris stella,* but they are formulated according to a different principle, as the hymn melody is divided into sections (*passos*) and each section is presented imitatively in an individual *verso.* Curiously, Coelho does not divide the tune into four sections according to its lines, but into five, splitting the first line (as shown in Fig.548), which probably seemed too long to

Fig.548

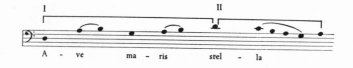

A - ve ma - ris stel - la

---

* Similar passages occur on p.94, meas.108–11; p.99, meas.19–21; p.108, meas.204–208; p.125, meas.169–71; p.136, meas.208–11.

him to serve as a fugue subject, and deriving from it the two subjects shown in Fig.549. In the *Segundo Verso* (new ed., II, p.38) the liturgical subject appears only twice (in meas.14 and 22), and then gives way to the countersubject, which had been introduced at the very start, and has a more striking contour.

Fig.549

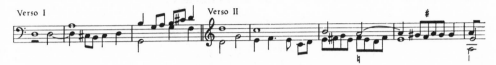

The next group is especially interesting. It consists of twenty-three versets, each with the annotation: "para se cantarem ao órgão; esta voz não se tange, as quatro abaixo se tangem" (for singing to the organ; this voice must not be played, the four below it should be played). Each verset consists of a vocal line set to a verse from the Magnificat plus a four-part organ accompaniment. They are thus examples of the concertato practice of the early Baroque, of which Viadana's *Concerti ecclesiastici* of 1602 are the first fruit. Fig.550 presents the beginning of the first verset. This group consists of two, three, or four versets for each tone, mostly for the even-numbered verses of the *Magnificat*. An exception is the *Sétimo tono*, for which Coelho writes only one verset, to which he adds the first verse of the *Nunc dimittis*. The melodies of the vocal line are generally related to the recitation formulae of the Magnificat, but occasionally freely invented melodies occur as well, especially in the third and fourth settings of the *Primeiro tom*. The organ accompaniment is chordal, but frequently enlivened by discreet figuration.

Fig.550

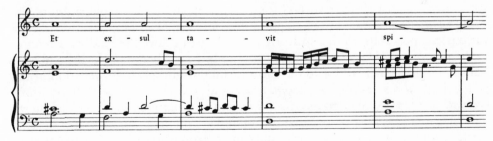

Et ex - sul - ta - - vit spi -

The next group (G) (new ed., II, pp.108ff.) consists of four versets for each tone (except for the first tone, which has six). As in the *Quatro Pange lingua*, the particular recitation formula is successively put in the soprano, alto, tenor, and bass. Often the entry of the *cantus firmus* is preceded by an extended introduction in imitative style.

The concluding collection (new ed., II, pp.165ff.) contains five settings each for seven Kyries, strangely designated as *Kyrio do primeiro tom, do quarto tom,* etc. A relationship to Kyrie melodies of the Roman Graduale can be recognized only in versets 1, 2, 3, and 5 of the first group, which derive from the Kyrie IV. Otherwise these settings are apparently freely imitative on subjects that even change within a given group. Compare, e.g., the beginnings of the *Primeiro* and *Segundo Kyrio do sexto tom por F fá ut,* given in Fig.551.

Fig.551

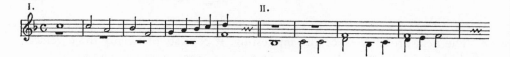

Correa de Arauxo

Six years after Coelho's *Flores de musica* there appeared an equally voluminous and even more important collection of Iberian organ music, the *Libro de tientos y discursos de musica practica y theorica de organo intitulado Facultad Organica* by Francisco Correa de Arauxo (Alcalá, 1626).[16] It may be assumed that Correa was born around 1575. The year of his death is often given as 1663, but it is doubtful that he lived that long. The question of where he was born, Spain or Portugal, must certainly be decided in favor of the former. All that is known is that in 1598 he was named organist of the church of San Salvador in Seville, a position he still held in 1633, and that like Bach and Mozart, he had difficulties with church authorities concerning the dignity of his office.

As the title indicates, Correa's *Facultad Organica* (Art of Organ Playing) contains not only musical works but also theoretical instructions. The latter consist of introductory "Advertencias" (new ed., I, pp.36–50), an explanation of the *Arte de poner por cifra* (new ed., I, pp.50–67), and explanatory notes added to the various compositions. In the "Advertencias" Correa draws the reader's attention to the many *curiosidades* and *cosas nuevas* to be found in the book: the explanations (*apuntamientos*) added to the various compositions; the classification of the pieces into *obras diatonicas, cromaticas,* and *enarmonicas* as well as *semicromaticas blandas, semicromaticas duras,* and *semienarmonicas duras;* a "nueva sentencia mia" (new assertion) that in certain keys no *discursos de medio registro* exist; "proporciones no conocidas" (unknown proportions), i.e., groups of 5, 9, 11, and 18 notes; "falsas y licencias" (dissonances and liberties) that do not seem to make for good music but which the reader will nevertheless admire and find satisfactory; pieces with twenty-four notes in an uneven meter and pieces with thirty-two notes in an even meter—"a new idea that until now has not been published in print by any Spanish author"; another "novel assertion" that *medios registros doblados* (with two upper or lower melody parts) must not be written for four voices but for five; the occasional use of the fourth as "consonancia perfecta parcial" or as "consonancia imperfecta"—"in order to impress you with the respect and honor in which the ancient musicians held this interval"; and finally "una nueva falsa de punto intenso contra remisso en cantidad semitono cromatico," i.e., the simultaneous employment of tones such as *c* and *c♯*.

These things and others are subsequently explained in more detail in separate sections, called "Primeiro punto," "Segundo punto," etc., and often mentioned again in annotations to the various pieces. This is followed by the *Arte de poner por cifra,* which explains the Spanish tablature with numbers, as used by Correa,[17] and contains instructions on the technique of playing, especially fingerings and ornaments. These rich theoretic and pedagogic materials deserve special study; a brief summary of the most important points follows.

Every composition belongs to one of four *generos: diatonico, semicromatico blando, semicromatico duro,* or *semienarmonico duro.* In modern terms, the *generos* differ in their key signatures. The *genero diatonico* has no key signature; the *semicromatico blando* has one flat; the *semicromatico duro* one sharp; and the *semienarmonico duro* three sharps, with the interval *g♯–a* evidently regarded as the enharmonic halftone. The *genero diatonico* is by far the most frequent, and includes about fifty compositions in *C, D, E, F, G,* and *A.* They are not at all purely diatonic, however, but employ various altered steps. The *genero semicromatico blando* is represented by 13 tientos: 6 on *F (por fefaut),* 3 on *G (por gesolrreut),* 2 on *C (por cesolfaut;* nos. 47, 64); one on *D (por delasolrre; no 36),* and one on *B♭ (por befabemi negro; no.44).* There is only one example for each of the two *generos duros:* no.7 on *A,* with *f♯* as the key signature, and no.9 on *F♯,* with *f♯, c♯,* and *g♯* as the key signature.

The "Undecimo punto" of the "Advertencias" contains interesting directions for the execution of triplets. Correa says that figures of 6, 12, 9, or 18 notes in the *proporción sexquialtera* may be played in two ways. The easier way is to play them evenly, not holding one note longer than another. The second way is to play them unevenly, with some liberty and gracefulness ("algo desguales, y con aquel ayrezillo y graciosidad"), by holding the first, fourth, seventh, tenth, etc., notes longer than those in between, i.e., playing the triplet rather like an eighth note and two sixteenths ("como haziendo una semiminima y dos corcheas"). Although this manner of playing was difficult, according to Correa it was the more usual one among organists. He differentiates the two methods of playing by the number "2" and "3," 2 indicating the "evenness of the figures as in bipartite division" and 3 the more refined execution. Fig.552 contains examples from tientos nos.1 and 5. In a. the sextuplets are thus to be played evenly (in modern notation they would have to be written as eighth-note triplets); in b. the triplets should be played with some lengthening of the first notes. Correa's treatise is another testimony for the practice of the *notes inégales,* which had been described by Tomás de Sancta Maria in

Fig.552

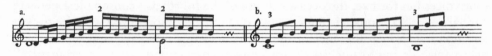

1565 (cf.Chap.8, note 53).[18] Correa expressly notes that this execution pertains only to the rapid figures in the *proporción menor;* triplets of quarter or half notes must be played evenly.

In the "Punto diez y siete" Correa addresses those who would disagree with the use of the *punto intenso contra remisso.* In its defense he cites works of earlier masters in which this dissonance occurs (mostly as *b♭* against *b*): a treatise by Francisco de Montanos; Nicolas Gombert's five-part canción *Ay me qui voldra,* which "Hernando Cabezón glossed and incorporated among the works of his father";[19] Gombert's motet *O gloriosa Dei genitrix;* and a three-part *Pleni sunt* by Josquin, the "autor antiguo e grave." Correa gives the passage in question from the last work in number tablature (Fig.553). He also cites three such passages from his own compositions, to which we shall return later.

Fig.553

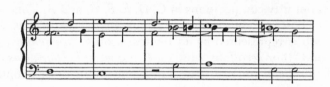

Finally, Correa describes four kinds of ornaments in the "Capitulo quinto" of the *Arte de poner por cifra* (new ed., I, p.54): the *quiebro senzillo* (simple) and *quiebro reiterado,* and the *redoble senzillo* and *redoble reiterado.* Fig.554 shows these ornaments, together with the fingerings given by Correa. In the music the *redobles* are frequently indicated by an "R,"[20] but they are surely intended to be inserted in other suitable places as well. Indeed, Correa says that a *redoble* is to be used for the leading tone of any clause that takes one measure or more, as well as on every *mi* leading directly to a *fa,* especially at the beginning of any large composition that starts with a *mi* and is played on a monochord. It must never be used in whole-tone progressions, such as *ut–re* or *re–mi,* but must be replaced by

Fig.554

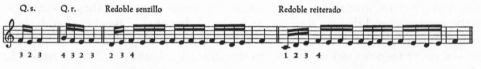

the *quiebro*. The *quiebro senzillo* is proper at the beginning of versets and other short compositions, as well as on all semibreves and minims in the course of a piece, in whichever hand is not engaged with *glosas*. In longer works one should use the *quiebro reiterado* in a similar manner, and either *quiebro*—in contrast to the *redobles*—may be employed on all steps. When a piece of music is entirely or for the most part unornamented (*llana*), it is to be decorated with these additions ("adornar con estos accidentes"), and some passages here and there should be left unornamented. The versions of the *quiebros* and *redobles* given by Correa represent only basic forms, which are capable of many variations. The annotation to tiento no.29 expressly states that these ornaments do not possess a definite number of notes. In measures 29 and 41 of this piece there are written-out *quiebros* that go considerably beyond the basic form.

The musical portion, the *musica practica* of the *Facultad organica*, is divided into a number of groups as follows:

A. Nos.1–12: Twelve tientos *de primer . . . duodécimo tono*
B. Nos.13–24: Siguese otro orden de tientos, de registro entero, por los tonos vulgares, mas faciles que los passados
C. Nos.25–51: Siguese otro nuevo orden de medio registro, célebre invención, y muy versada en los Reynos de Castilla, aunque en otros no conocida
D. Nos.52–57: Comiençan las obras de a cinco
E. Nos.58–61: Siguense quatro obras de a treinta y dos numeros [with thirty-second notes] al compas, a quatro voces
F. Nos.62–65: Siguense quatro obras de compás ternario de tres semibreves
G. Nos.66–69: Four separate pieces

The contents consist of 62 tientos, 2 intabulations of chansons (no.61: *Susana*; no.66: *Gay bergier*), 2 harmonizations of church songs (no.67: *Lauda Sion*; no.68: *Todo el mundo*), and 3 variation sets (no.64: *Dexaldos mi madre*; no.65: *Guárdame las vacas*; no.69: *Todo el mundo*). The first 24 tientos, the five-part tiento no.52, and the *compás-ternario* tiento no.62 are for *registro entero*; the other 36 are for *medio registro*, which Correa calls, in the title of group C, a "celebrated invention, very much used in Castilian lands, but unknown else-where." Eighteen of them are *de tiple*, 13 *de baxon*, 2 *de dos tiples*, and 3 *de dos baxones*.

Besides the term tiento, Correa employs the designation *discurso* in two ways: in the combination *tiento y discurso*, as in the title of the print and in nos.2, 3, and 57; and by itself, as in nos.55 and 56. There is no essential difference between the two terms, for many pieces that are entitled "tiento" are referred to in the annotations as "este discurso," e.g., nos.1, 22, 31, 33, 36, 41, etc. However, all of them are pieces that demand a well-developed technique. In the "Tabla de los tientos," at the beginning of the volume (new ed., I, p.32), the contents are arranged in the order of difficulty, starting "por los mas faciles" and rising to the "grado quinto y ultimo, el qual grado denota la mayor dificultad y perfección." In this table almost all the pieces in the "quarto" and "quinto grado" are designated as "discursos."

(Additional references to the degree of difficulty are given in connection with individual pieces, e.g., with nos.24, 30, and 36.)

Correa's tientos are shorter than Coelho's—most of them have fewer than 200 measures—and also differ in style and structure. Figurations play only a modest role in some of them, particularly those assigned to the "Primer grado" in the "Tabla." In this respect pieces such as tientos nos.24 (which is called "pequeño e facil") and 37 hardly go beyond what is occasionally found in Cabezón's music. At the other end of the scale there are pieces like tientos nos.58 and 59, which indulge in a profusion of figurations in thirty-second notes, quintuplets, septuplets, etc., or the "muy dificultoso" tiento no.30, with its complex texture.

While Coelho's tientos are mostly polythematic, almost half of Correa's— 28 to be exact—are monothematic. Of the remaining 34, 14 have two subjects, 12 have three, and 8 have four or more. Correa also approaches the treatment of the subjects differently. His sparing use of the subjects is particularly striking, in contrast to Coelho's tendency to enter them again and again. The result is that the free interludes occupy a much larger proportion of the piece. In Coelho's works the subject often serves as the scaffolding for figurations, but in Correa's case it rather has the function of a point of departure for long excursions into the domain of figurations. Correa almost always reuses his subjects in their original shape, without changing the rhythm or some other element, as Coelho often does. Even the elementary methods of variation by augmentation and diminution, which are almost as important in Coelho's works as in Sweelinck's, do not occur in Correa's, though occasionally he employs an ornamented variant, e.g., in no.3, measures 26, 29, 33, and in no.29, measure 15.

The formulations of several of Correa's tientos are diagrammed below, but the manner of presentation differs somewhat from that employed earlier. Since Correa's subjects appear only rarely and at long intervals after the first exposition, it is not only possible but even desirable to give the individual entries, while for Coelho's tientos—as well as in the works by the Italians and by Sweelinck—one must be satisfied with a summary treatment of the sections. In the following diagrams "A" always symbolizes one isolated subject entry, and two or more entries that follow one another without interruption are shown as "2A," "3A," etc. Thematic sections are indicated by lines, free episodes by dotted lines, whose lengths correspond approximately to the lengths of the sections.

No.10: | 3A ———— A — | ·············· | 4A | ·············· | 4A — | ··· ||

No.50: | 4A ——— | ········· | A | ·········· | A | ··············· ||

No.51: | 3A ——— A — | ····· | 4A ——— | B — B — 2B — | ······· | 4A — |
········· ||

No.56: | 5A — | ····· | A — A — A — A ····· | 5B — | ················ | 5B — |

```
        114           151
        ------------  ||
           23      32    40              64          86          105
No.6:  |  4A ——— | ----- | 2A | ----------------- | 6B ——— | 4C —— ---- | 4D |
       112           129
```

```
        112           129
        -----------   ||
           16       23   36      45 53   62        70    82        90
No.48: |  4A — | ---- | 3B — A — ---- | B 3C |  ----- | 2B --- 2B --- | A ---
        106     116       128
        2C, B — | -------------- ||
```

The following are a few explanatory notes. No.10 has a particularly simple structure. It consists of three full points of imitation on the subject, each followed by a long episode. In each point of imitation the subject appears once in each part; in the first one it is always heard as a "double subject" of six measures, in the other two as a three-measure phrase without the contrapuntal continuation. The second point of imitation is shortened to eight measures by a twofold stretto; in its second half the subject is ornamented by eighth-note triplets, which continue into the succeeding episode.

Tiento no.50 contains a single full exposition at the beginning. From measure 18 onward it consists of free polyphony, at times enlivened by passage work, within which the subject puts in only two more appearances, as though to satisfy the composer's feeling of responsibility toward the form.

In no.51 two subjects are employed in four full points of imitation, two for the main subject, one for the second one, and one more for the main subject. It is typical of Correa that each point of imitation is formulated differently. In the first one, the first three entries appear in stretto, while the fourth entry occurs after an episode of four measures; in the second one the entries follow each other without interruption, the second and third being in stretto while the soprano offers a figural variant; the third point (subject B) is treated very expansively, with episodes of six and eight measures; but the fourth one is condensed with the aid of strettos. The episodes that separate these points of imitation are relatively short in this tiento.

The five-part tiento no.56 is also based on two subjects, both of which are given two full points of imitation. The first, third, and fourth points are presented in stretto, while the second consists of four entries separated by episodes. The third and fourth points lead to long postludes with interesting figurations, including quarter-note quintuplets. The last two tientos in the diagram are exceptional rather than typical, no.6 because it uses four subjects (although D is hardly more than a figuration motif), and no.48 because it lacks extended episodes.

These analyses indicate that the terms and methods of analysis that suit Bach's fugues and were created for them can be applied naturally and appropriately to Correa's tientos as well as to Steigleder's ricercars, which were contemporary (cf.pp.398ff.). Far be it from me to arrogate the appellation "predecessors of Bach's fugues" for these works—an appellation that may be and has been applied to many types of imitative counterpoint with the same justification or lack of it—but it cannot be denied that one important aspect of the Bach fugues, the planned articulation into points of imitation and episodes, is clearly anticipated by Correa as well as by Steigleder. What is still missing is the meaningful coordination of these parts, the combination into a more unified whole. In this connection it is clear that Correa was quite aware of the significance of modulation. In the annotation to tiento no.57 he says that "the *digression en los modos* is as agreeable to the ear as the variety of dishes at a meal is to the palate." Indeed, this work, which is written in the eighth mode (Mixolydian on G), contains a brief section in *F* major (meas.58–64) and a somewhat longer one in *A* minor (meas.87–96).

Correa's harmonic language differs quite strikingly from that of Coelho. On the one hand, Correa tends to employ archaic, modal harmony, as his frequent use of the *genero diatonico* indicates, while on the other, his works offer a large number of bold dissonances of great variety, like those in the works of the Neapolitans. Both ingredients combine in a musical discourse, whose acerbity—even

Fig.555

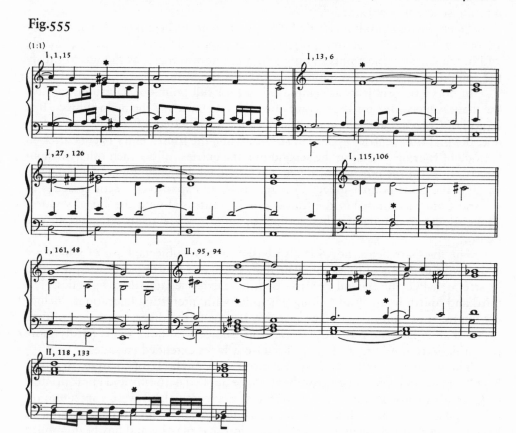

Fig.556

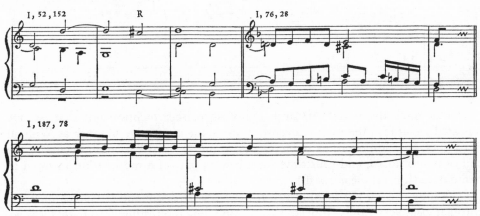

asperity—is more agreeable to the modern listener than the smooth formulations of the Portuguese Coelho. Fig.555 gives several particularly remarkable passages that use augmented fifths, diminished fourths, sustained exposed passing tones, and appoggiaturas (the numbers indicate volume, page, and measure in the new edition). The sharpness of these dissonances is even exceeded by Correa's *punto intenso contra remisso*: the simultaneous use of a note and its chromatic variant in notes of substantial length, such as quarter and half notes. As already noted, in his "Advertencias" Correa expressly notes this dissonance, defends it by references to works of the 16th century, and cites three passages in which it occurs in his own tientos. These passages are shown in Fig.556. It is not necessary (or perhaps it is?) to emphasize that such occurrences represent one of the strongest arguments against the still wide-spread practice of unjustified added accidentals. In a milder form, as a rapid passing tone, the *punto intenso contra remisso* (most often the *remisso* against the sustained *intenso*) is found in Correa's works very often, usually at the highest point of an ascending and then descending scale movement, but occasionally in other circumstances. Fig.557 provides a small selection of such passages. Interestingly, in his "Advertencias" Correa mentions only those three passages in which the *punto remisso* and *intenso* appear simultaneously as sustained tones, and not the many milder instances, such as the ones given here. He

Fig.557

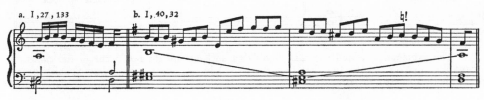

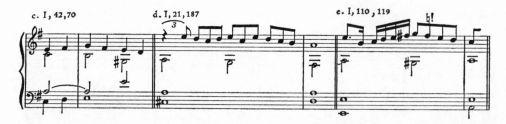

obviously finds them quite natural, requiring neither mention nor defense. He repeatedly employs the minor seventh in the same expressive manner as William Byrd does. In addition to example c. above, the "English" seventh occurs at the end of tiento no.20, and four times in a row as part of a modulation formula in tiento no.2 (I, p.11, meas.101ff.).

Despite this strong leaning toward the use of dissonances, Correa employs chromaticism very rarely. Indeed, there is only one interesting chromatic passage, measures 75–80 from tiento no.13, in which the motif (*bc c♯*) occurs several times.

In the figurations that fill so many pages of the *Facultad Organica*, sixteenth notes naturally predominate, but there are also many passages with triplets in various degrees of speed. Correa uses dotted eighth notes (e.g., in new ed., I, pp.42, 46, 125ff., 164) as well as dotted sixteenths (e.g., II, pp.135, 153f.). The figures in quintuplets and septuplets, the *proportio quintupla* and *septupla,* as he calls them in the preface, are probably unique in the literature of the 17th century. Fig.558 shows some of these passages.* Usually in such instances, two or three

Fig.558

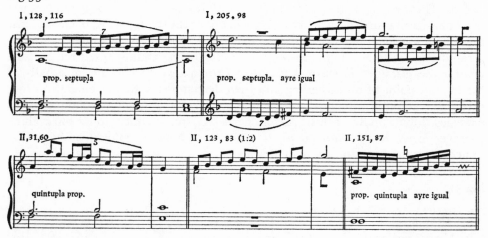

* The explanation added to no.22 states that such groups do not occur in the *canto de organo* (cf. note 17 above), but that they were used by the most outstanding Spanish organ masters in the *discursos de cifra.*

534

notes are played against a quintuplet or septuplet, and follow the main rhythm in such distributions as $5 = 3 + 2$ or $7 = 3 + 2 + 2$. Correa occasionally subdivides a group of nine notes in a similar manner, e.g., $4 + 5$ (rather than $3 + 6$) and $4 + 3 + 2$ (rather than $3 + 3 + 3$), as shown in Fig.559. These measures belong to an extended section of the "muy dificultoso" tiento no.30, which exhibits many more irregular and syncopated phrasings of the same type.

Fig.559

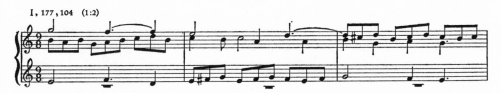

In a brief section of tiento no.16 (new ed., I, p.100, meas.90ff.) Correa employs the $3 + 3 + 2$ rhythm, whose importance in Spanish organ music was noted in connection with the works of Aguilera (cf.p.514).[21] It is surprising that Correa uses it only in this one passage, for it occurs very often in the works of Aguilera, Jimenez, and Bruna. There are only a few instances in Correa's music of passages of modulation, which is another specialty of Spanish keyboard music. The most conspicuous one occurs in tiento no.23 (new ed., I, p.131, meas.83–107), and consists of three presentations of an eight-measure echo phrase.

Several tientos deserve to be singled out because of certain individual features. In the annotations nos.19 and 43 are said to be "de mis principios," i.e., works of Correa's youth, and thus offer a small, but nevertheless welcome, clue to the chronology of his output. Both are written in a simple and moderately ornamented style ("facil y para principiantes"), and are monothematic and relatively short. After the initial exposition in no.19, the subject appears twice more in the middle (meas.43 and 48) and once toward the end (meas.96), while in no.43 it recurs clearly only once (meas.30).

Tiento no.16 is described in the annotation as "a modo de canción," which is surely to be interpreted as "in the manner of an Italian canzona." The composition consists of nine clearly articulated, contrasting sections, each about ten to twenty measures long. Like the normal tientos, the piece begins with a point of imitation, which does not continue as usual with figurations or other material, but ends with a full cadence after twenty measures. It is followed by a sixteen-measure section of song- or dance-like character, in regular four-measure phrases, that resembles nothing else in Correa's tientos. The next section, measures 36–44, consists of three similarly built phrases, each comprising ten quarter notes grouped in one 4/4 and two 3/4 measures. However, in the original notation this interesting construction is veiled by the employment of 4/4 measures throughout,

Fig.560

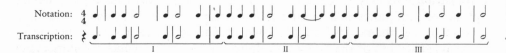

as in Fig.560. A brief, sustained section (meas.45–59) is followed by a lightly imitative section in triple meter, then by the one in 3+3+2 rhythm described above, another lightly imitative section in triple meter, and finally two more, whose beginnings are given in Fig.561. The first one has a modulatory character (the modulation continues for three more measures to reach F). The other has a boldly ascending motion, which continues up to d''', but since the highest notes were not available on the keyboard, the last portion is transposed down an octave (as occasionally happens in Beethoven's works!). This *Tiento a modo de canción* is certainly one of the most interesting and attractive of Correa's pieces. However, it is not typical of the master's overall output; in general layout and some details it is reminiscent of Aguilera's *Ensalada,* which is perhaps its model.

Fig.561

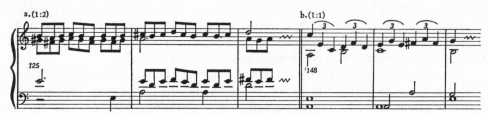

Tiento no.23 is very similar to this composition. As the annotation informs us, it is based "sobre la primera parte de la Batalla de Morales." With its 298 measures it is the longest piece in the *Facultad organica.* Although it is not as clearly articulated as the *Tiento a modo de canción* (to whose various meters Correa refers in his annotation), one can nevertheless differentiate ten sections rather clearly (beginning at meas.1, 29, 42, 67, 79, 113, 161, 198, 268, and 288). Sections 3, 5, 6, and 8 are written "op de Manier van een Echo," to refer to the situation in Sweelinckian terms; it is understandable that Correa employs this style in a composition that is derived from a battaglia. Sections 6 and 8 are formulated like chaconnes; the former is based on a four-measure idea, which is presented six times, and each setting is repeated by way of an echo (as usual, in the *lower* octave); the latter is set in the same manner, but includes seven presentations of a five-measure phrase.

The three *Tientos de a treinte y dos numeros al compas* (nos.58–60), with their extensive figurations in thirty-second notes, quintuplets, septuplets, etc., are

536

interesting as high points of virtuosic Spanish keyboard playing, and so is the arrangement of *Susanna* that follows them. The last two tientos, nos.62 and 63, are written in triple meter from beginning to end (*de compás ternario de tres semibreves*).

Let us now turn to the compositions that, except for nos.62 and 63, form the conclusion of the *Facultad organica*: liturgical pieces, variation sets, and intabulations. For the religious services Correa composed a *Prosa del Santissimo Sacramento* (no.67) and a *Canto llano de la Immaculada Concepción de la Virgen Maria* (no.68). The former is based on the sequence *Lauda Sion Salvatorem*, the latter on the Spanish church song *Todo el mundo en general*. Both are simple harmonizations, which have no special musical interest. The melody used for *Lauda Sion* (according to Correa it lies in the soprano) is completely different from the one employed in the Roman Catholic rite. In *Todo el mundo* the melody lies in the tenor.

Fig.562

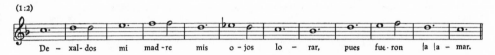

(1:2)

De – xal- dos   mi   mad -re   mis   o - jos   lo – rar,   pues   fue· ron   la la – mar.

Three of the final pieces are variation sets, on *Dexaldos mi madre* (no.64), *Guárdame las vacas* (no.65), and *Todo el mundo* (no.69). *Dexaldos mi madre* is based on the Spanish folk song reproduced in Fig.562. The theme is presented fourteen times without interruption, changing voices each time and transposed after every second appearance, from C to G, D, G, C, F, and back to C, but otherwise remaining unchanged. These repetitions act as the framework for figural-imitative variations, which, as in Cabezón, are connected by transitions and follow one another without interruption. The figurations start with quarter-note triplets (var.I–III), speed up to eighth notes (in var.IV–VI), to eighth-note triplets (var. VII–IX), and finally to sixteenth notes (var.X–XIV). Fig.563 shows the beginnings of one variation from each of these four groups.

Correa notes that the next set of variations, on the old melody of *Guárdame las vacas*, might more properly be called *Seculorum del primer tono* (cf.Chap.11,

Fig.563

(1:2) a.

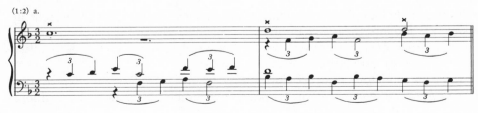

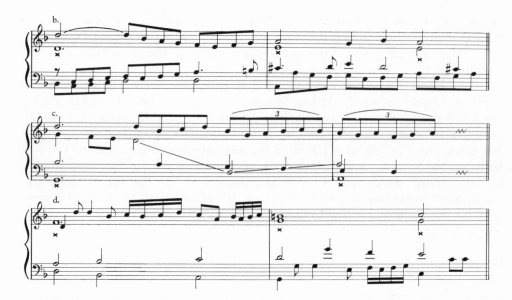

a. var. I, meas.1; b. var. V, meas.49; c. var. VII, meas.73; d. var. XII, meas.133.

note 2). The title reads "Dies y seis glosas" (sixteen variations), but the subject is actually heard seventeen times. This contradiction is explained by the fact that this is probably the first time in the literature of variations that the theme is presented first in a simple harmonization, and the sixteen *glosas* follow. The variations are based on the harmonic structure (one might also say on the bass) of the theme and are limited almost throughout to the ornamentation of one voice in continuous passage work, which soon becomes tiresome.

The *Facultad Organica* concludes with *Tres glosas sobre el Canto llano de la Immaculada Concepción*, i.e., variations on the church song *Todo el mundo*. The work consists of a simple harmonization of the melody, which lies in the soprano, and three variations in which the melody is surrounded by tasteful and often expressive figurations. Two parallel phrases of eight measures each (A, B) and a ripresa of four measures (C) constitute the theme. In the first variation, called "Copla segunda," the first phrase is repeated twice, for no apparent reason (A A A B C); it happens again in the second variation, but with the ripresa omitted (A A A B).

In the intabulation of Crecquillon's *Gay bergier* (no.66) Correa succeeds in infusing new life into the old chanson by means of varied and appropriate figurations, but he completely smothers Lassus' "muy celebre canción" under endless figurations in his intabulation of *Susanna* (no.61).

In his introductory study of Correa's "obra musical," Kastner characterizes the Spanish organ master and his work as the product of a period of transition:

"With one foot he is still completely chained to the art of the Renaissance; with the other, however, he steps over the threshold of the Baroque. . . . In his work the dignity, mysticism, clarity, and humanism of the Renaissance contrast with Baroque distortion [retorcimiento], pathos, exaggeration, dynamism, and subjectivity."[22] I certainly agree with this characterization, but I must stress that in this mixture of old and new the latter definitely prevails. In fact, Correa has stepped over the threshold of the Baroque with both feet, and only a loose thread, a faint memory ties him to the art of the 16th century. His art is essentially one of highly developed ornamentation, a game that is self-sufficient and finds its own justification and reason for being. Passages of simple and occasionally expressive character are certainly not missing, but Correa easily turns from them to devote himself to a pure enjoyment of figures, to afford his listener the pleasure and entertainment of a "variedad de mille flores." Together with his contemporary Aguilera he thereby establishes a type that originated in Peraza's music, and which became the model for the later development of Spanish clavier music. The roots of this art lie in pure music-making. Far from stressing expression and feeling, it serves entertainment, the pleasure of "playing" in the best sense of the word. What distinguishes it is the high level of the entertainment and the significance of the rules by which the game is played.

The Manuscript Tradition

During the half century that follows the publication of Correa's *Libro de Tientos* the evolution of keyboard music in Spain and Portugal is again obscured. The difficulties are quite different from those that affect the period between Cabezón and Correa or Coelho, when there was an almost total lack of sources. A plethora of material is extant from the period following Correa, but very little of it has been studied, and most of it is written by anonymous composers or by composers whose dates are unknown. The first firmly established Iberian personality thereafter is Juan Cabanilles, who was born in 1644, about seventy years after Correa. Who carried the evolution from one master to the other? What paths did this evolution take?[23]

The repertoire in question is preserved chiefly in the manuscript from the Escorial, an Oporto manuscript,[24] and in three manuscripts at the Biblioteca Central in Barcelona.[25] The following composers are represented:

Escorial Ms.: Clavijo, Peraza, Aguilera, Jimenez, Bruna, Diego de Torrijos, Perandreu, Sinxano, Joan Sebastian
Oporto Ms.: João da Costa, André (da Costa, d.1685), Gaspar dos Reis, Matéo Romero (El Capitán, d.1647)
Barcelona Mss.: Bruna, Cabanilles, Espelt, Menalt, Herváz, Tormo, and many others.

The Escorial and Oporto manuscripts definitely represent an older repertoire than the Barcelona manuscripts. They contain works by the earlier masters

Clavijo, Peraza, and Aguilera, but none by Cabanilles. It can therefore be assumed that they were written before Cabanilles had achieved general recognition, i.e., around 1660, and that the Barcelona manuscripts were penned at least thirty to forty years later. Thus the "younger" composers of the Escorial and Oporto manuscripts would be the ones who represent the transition between Correa and Cabanilles. The most important are Jimenez, who was probably the leader of the generation born around 1600, and Bruna, who probably belongs to the next generation, since most of his works are preserved in the Barcelona manuscripts. In the absence of further details, the other composers whose works appear in the Barcelona manuscripts must be considered contemporaries of Cabanilles.

Jimenez

All that is known about Joséph Jimenez (Ximenes) is that he was an organist at Saragossa in 1654 and that he died in 1672. The Escorial manuscript contains his *Versos de 6° tono sobre los Seculorum* (4 psalm versets), 8 *Pange lingua*, a *Sacris solemniis*, 8 rather extended pieces of the tiento type, mostly called *obra*, and 2 *Batallas*. A *Folias con veinte diferencias* is included in Barcelona M. 751.21 and about 10 versos are found in Barcelona M. 387 (888).[26]

The four psalm versets arrange the sixth psalm tone as a strict *cantus planus* (in whole notes) successively in the soprano, alto, tenor, and bass, each time combined with three counterpoints that imitate each other and occasionally exhibit moderate figurations. There are two occurrences of the English seventh in the 4° *Verso* (meas.5–10), shown in Fig.564. In the second half of the piece the figuration changes to quarter-note triplets, and finally to eighth-note triplets.

The eight settings of the *Pange lingua* are Jimenez' contribution to a type that has the same importance in Spain as the *In nomine* in England. There are about one hundred of these settings in the literature since almost every Spanish and

Fig.564

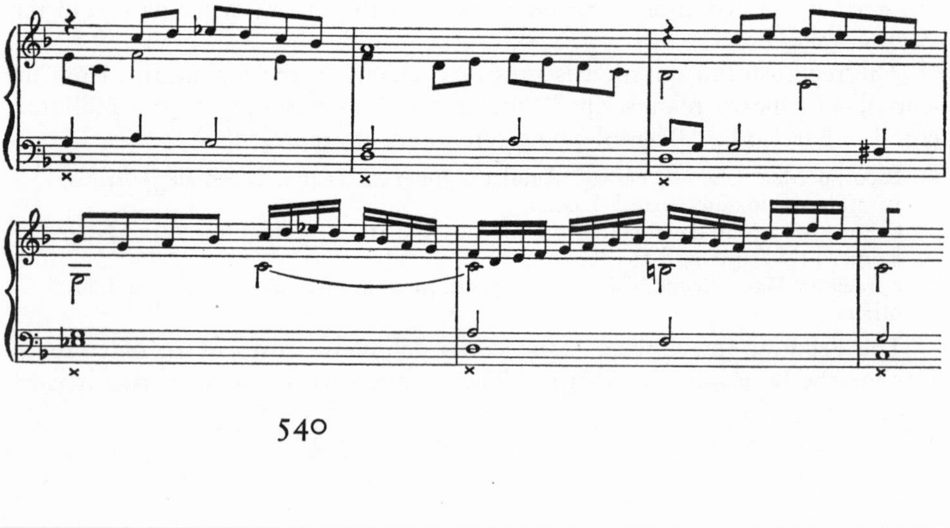

Portuguese organ master from Cabezón to Cabanilles wrote some. The Escorial manuscript contains a compact collection of 17 *Pange lingua*, which includes the 8 Jimenez settings as well as 2 that are anonymous, one by Aguilera, 4 by Perandreu, and 2 by Diego de Torrijos. They all show the same arrangement; cf. p.513 for the details. Jimenez' eight settings are grouped by key: The first four are *por delasolre*, i.e., in *D*, the others *por cesolfaut*, i.e., in *C*. The first setting is for four voices, the others for three, with the *cantus firmus* in the soprano (*sobre tiple*), the middle part (*sobre contralto*), or the bass (*sobre vajo*); the first piece, e.g., is entitled *Pange lingua a 4° sobre contralto por delasolre*. As in the psalm versets, some of the counterpoints are imitative and some figural. The *Pange lingua* are followed by a brief *Sacris solemniis* in a homophonic four-part setting, like Correa's *Lauda Sion*.

Jimenez' tientos (we shall retain this title, although it does not occur in any of these pieces) are all long compositions, mostly for a divided keyboard. They are listed here according to types:

Divided register, soprano:	*Obra de 8° tono, tiple*
	Obra de 1° tono, de tiple
Divided register, bass:	*Vajo, 1° tono*
	Medio registro vajo de 6° tono
	Registro vajo a tres
Divided register, two basses:	*Obra de 8° tono, dos vajos*
Full register:	*Obra de 1° tono, de lleno*
	Obra de lleno, 1° tono, sin paso

They are all written for four voices, except for no.5, which has three. The layouts of the *medio registro* works (nos.1–6) follow the corresponding works of Peraza, Aguilera, and Correa. They start with an imitative presentation of a ricercar-like subject, which merely serves as an introduction to the main portion, which is completely dominated by the idea of figuration. In some of them (e.g., nos.1 and 2) the subject, as in Correa's pieces, is heard a few more times at long intervals, in others (e.g., in nos.3 and 6) it disappears entirely. The two tientos for full register occupy a special place. No.7 is worked out in a thematically imitative style from beginning to end, almost devoid of figuration. In no.8 even the imitative introduction is omitted, and the piece starts with a few full chords. The work consists of series of chords, to which lively figures are added, at times in the soprano and at times in the bass. The words "sin paso" (without step or theme)* refer to the fact that no subjects exist anywhere. In its way, this composition is a counterpart to the Italian toccata, a type that was not cultivated as such in the Iberian peninsula.

The chief interest in Jimenez' tientos lies in the treatment of figurations. In his music, more so than in his predecessors', a tendency toward formalism can be

---

*This phrase is also found in the works of Cabanilles (Anglés C; III, p.168) and in the Portuguese *Libro de cyfra* (cf.pp.776f. below).

felt. Long sections of his tientos are almost exclusively constructed from sequences of brief figures and modulatory repetitions of longer phrases. Despite the formalism, many traits of earlier musical techniques are retained, which prevent the music from becoming dry and schematic and counteract a descent into triviality. With a sure instinct, Jimenez seizes the right moment to vary a figure, to abbreviate, to change—in short, to begin another game that captivates the listener anew. Another important feature is that the harmonic approach is still rooted in modality; the tonality often unexpectedly wavers between major and minor, and frequently retains a certain independence from the repetition scheme of the figurations. Unfortunately it is not possible to illustrate these procedures with examples, since they can only be recognized by studying or listening to the whole work. Fig.565, an excerpt from the *Obra de 1° tono, de tiple* (no.2), may, however, give a general impression of Jimenez' technique of composition. Typical details are the insertion of an effective measure of rest or transition before a phrase is repeated (see meas.4) and the abbreviation of the motifs in repetition.

Fig.565

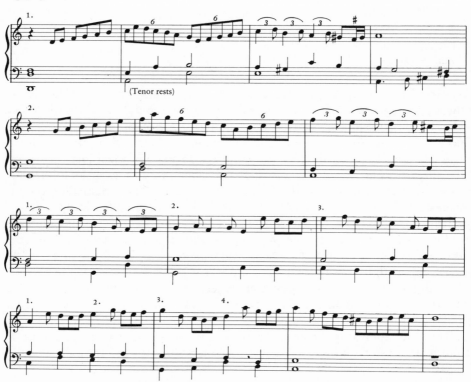

The Escorial manuscript also contains two *Batallas* by Jimenez,[27] which are of less artistic importance than the tientos proper. The second Batalla contains one of the many passages in the 3 + 3 + 2 rhythm that are found in Jimenez' works. His *Folias con veinte diferencias* is one of the earliest examples of folia variations in keyboard literature. Unfortunately the work was not available to me for study.

Perandreu and Others

Next to Aguilera and Jimenez, Perandreu is the most frequently represented composer in the Escorial manuscript, with four *Pange lingua* and five tientos. The *Pange lingua* form a group, in which the hymn melody appears successively in the bass, tenor, alto, and soprano, as a strict *cantus planus* (in alternating breves and semibreves), as is always the case in these works. The counterpoints are decorative and employ motifs that appear in a well-balanced distribution, sometimes in one voice, sometimes in another. Fig.566 shows a passage from the second setting that exemplifies the rhythmic complexities frequently found in Spanish organ music in pieces or sections in triple meter.

Fig.566

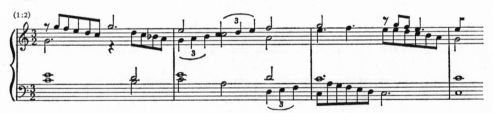

In contrast to the well-conceived *Pange lingua* settings, Perandreu's tientos are among the most disagreeable products of Spanish organ music. Even in their length they exceed the usual admissible measure: The shortest is 222 measures long,[28] the longest 414—figures that one gratefully accepts from the conscientious notes of the copyist ("finis. tiene 414 compases"). The content essentially consists of nothing but figurations in the soprano that go on and on in stereotyped and tiresome repetitions. Nevertheless some interesting details occur, e.g., the quintuplet figures shown in Fig.567.

Fig.567

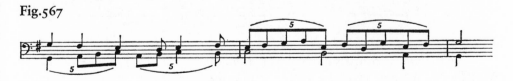

For completeness' sake three more composers, who are represented in the Escorial manuscript by one or two compositions each, should be mentioned: Diego de Torrijos (two *Pange lingua*), Joan Sebastian (*Tiento de 2° tono*), and Gabriel Sinxano (Tiento de 8° tono).[29]

Bruna

Pablo Bruna is another Spanish organ master whose work is preserved quite well. Born at Daroca in 1617, he was court organist to King Philip IV (1621–65), and died in 1679. In the title of some of his works he is called the "ciego de Daroca" (blind man from Daroca). Twenty-eight of his compositions are preserved: 7 *Pange lingua*, 17 tientos, and 4 separate works called *Psalmodia, Batalla, Gaytilla,* and *Clausulas.* Six of the tientos are included in the Escorial manuscript; the rest are in two of the Barcelona manuscripts (cf.p.539).[30]

The *Pange lingua* settings are all in three parts, and faithfully follow the tradition for this type. Some are particularly impressive examples of the species, such as the one given in Fig.568, in whose delicate counterpoint the classical tradition of Spanish organ music is both preserved and infused with new life.

Fig.568

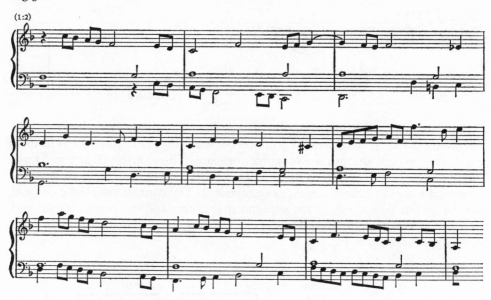

The *Psalmodia* consists of six *Versos 1° tono*, six *2° tono*, and four *3° tono*.[31] Actually they are not versets for psalms but for the Magnificat. This fact is obvious from the versets *2° tono*, whose *cantus firmus* begins with the Magnificat intona-

544

Fig.569

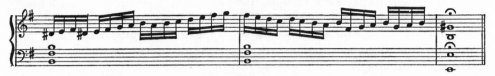

tion (*c d c f*), which is the Gregorian melody transposed up a whole tone, rather than with (*c d f*), the corresponding intonation for psalms. In the six *Versos 1° tono* the first Magnificat tone is used in *cantus-planus* fashion; all of the tone is used in the first four versets, but only the second half appears in the other two, where it is therefore played twice, in the soprano and then in the bass in one, and in the soprano and tenor in the other. In the other ten versets imitative treatment prevails, and the subject is either the intonation or the termination of the Magnificat tone. Three versets of the *2° tono* conclude with brief passages of figuration, which are interesting for their accidentals (or rather for the omission of accidentals), e.g., the one given in Fig.569. How absolutely "correct" are the raised seventh at the beginning and the raised third at the end, in combination with the purely diatonic passage work in between!

Bruna's tientos fall into two groups: five for undivided register and twelve for divided keyboard. The former are mostly contrapuntal-imitative, the latter predominantly chordal-figural. One of the former is the *Tiento de falsas, 1° tono,* a piece of about 90 measures, in which a sustained subject (| *d* | *d c♯* | *d e* | *f –e* | *d* |) is treated in an imitative setting. The quiet motion, mostly in half notes, is enlivened toward the end by modest figurations. The dissonances announced in the title keep within very modest limits. The harmonic approach is still strongly modal, as in the passage given in Fig.570, which is taken from the final section.

Fig.570

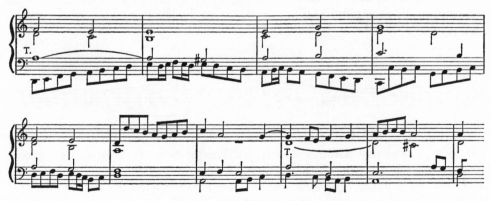

The *falsas* character emerges more clearly in the *Tiento de falsas 2° tono*, whose four parts move quietly within a tonal harmonic texture pervaded by suspensions, a texture that had already achieved wide-spread acceptance in central Europe. The piece is based on three subjects, which appear throughout in ever new combinations, exactly as in a polythematic ricercar of Italian provenance. Fig.571 shows the beginning.

Fig.571

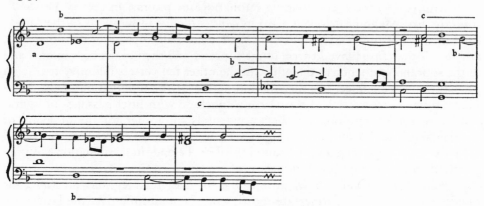

Three compositions inscribed *Tiento de lleno* differ from the ones just discussed in length (310, 239, and 252 measures, respectively) and in structure. They divide into several sections in which the main subject appears in different rhythmic variants. By analogy to the Italian variation canzona or variation ricercar, they may be called variation tientos. One has the hexachord as its subject, in both the ascending and descending forms. First it appears as a series of half notes; in a second section it is set forth in triple meter, in the rhythm (| o. | ♩o | ♩o | o. |), which the Spanish organ masters especially favored; and in later sections several new motifs and figural variants are derived from the hexachord, e.g., those shown in Fig.572.[32]

Fig.572

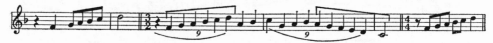

While almost all of Bruna's tientos for undivided keyboard suggest a more or less foreign, probably Italian influence, his *Tientos de medio registro* belong to a specific Spanish type, in which the thematic idea only serves as an introduction and point of departure for long sections entirely dominated by figurations. Five of the twelve compositions of this species are *de tiple* (or *mano derecha* = right hand), four *de baxo* (or *mano ysquierda* = left hand), and three for *dos tiples*. On the whole, these tientos follow the same paths as Jimenez' *medios registros*, but modulatory passages are even more frequent and more consistently developed. Again and again we find passages of various lengths in which an ornamented phrase of one, two, or three measures is repeated, transposed a fourth or a fifth. The following example, an especially extended passage from a *medio registro de baxo*, employs the symbols introduced for the modulatory passages in Aguilera's music (cf.p.519):

| 4S(3m) | 5D(2m) | 5S(2m) | 2D(2m) | 2S(2m) | 4S(1m) | 2D(2m) | 2S(1m) |
| 4D(1m) | 4S(1m) |

All the phrases involved here, thus the entire passage of more than 60 measures, move in 6/8 time, with a rather monotonous effect. However, Bruna often formulates such modulatory passages with some irregularities, such as the introduction of small variants in the figuration motif or in the harmonic scheme, e.g., by inserting a transposition of a third in a series by modulations of a fifth.

Fig.573

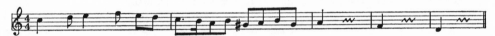

A *Tiento de 1° tono, mano derecha* provides one of the few instances of a series of modulations of a third. An excerpt from it (Fig.573) is another instance of the 3 + 3 + 2 rhythm, which Bruna employed much more often than any other Spanish composer. Occasionally a figure used in a modulatory passage is derived from the subject that was treated imitatively in the first section. Fig.574 presents an instance from the *Obra de 8° tono de tiple*.

Fig.574

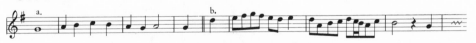

a. Subject; b. Modulation figure.

One of the compositions for *dos tiples* is entitled *Batalla*, another *Gaytilla*, but there seems to be no real reason for these titles. Fanfare and "tumult" motifs, which are used here and there in the two *Batallas* by Jimenez, are completely lacking in Bruna's *Batalla*, and the *Gaytilla* contains nothing that one could interpret as a reference to a *gaita* (bagpipe). In both pieces, rapid figures, like those that occur in his other tientos, play only a secondary role. The predominant features are rhythmically precise formulae, such as those shown in Fig.575.

In conclusion, the works of Aguilera, Jimenez, Perandreu, and Bruna have

Fig.575

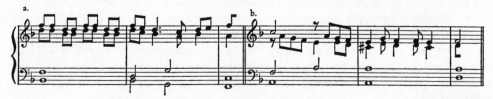

a. Batalla; b. Gaytilla.

certain things in common that are either absent from, or unimportant in, Correa's music—primarily the many settings of the *Pange lingua,* the *falsas,* the 3+3+2 rhythm, and the modulatory passages. Perhaps one may conclude from these penchants and from several other details that two schools existed in Spain—one Castilian, in the west, and the other Catalonian-Aragonese in the east. The former would be represented by Correa, who was active in Madrid, while the other composers worked in such northeastern places as Huesca (Aguilera), Saragossa (Aguilera, Jimenez), and Daroca (Bruna). Cabanilles, in Valencia, and Menalt and others in Barcelona should be included in the eastern school.

PART IV

THE SECOND HALF OF

THE SEVENTEENTH

CENTURY

19

Germany

A. SOUTH GERMANY

During the middle and second half of the 17th century Vienna developed into one of the most important centers of keyboard music. Froberger, Ebner, Kerll, Poglietti, Techelmann, Richter, Reutter, Fux, and others worked there, some only for a time, others throughout their lives. It is easy to understand that their compositions were greatly influenced by developments in Italy. They cultivated mainly the ricercars, canzonas, capriccios, toccatas, and versets, and occasionally the ostinato forms—passacaglias and chaconnes. The suite constitutes the main part of Froberger's output, but it is of secondary importance with the other composers. The Austrian emperors Ferdinand III (1608–57) and Leopold I (1658–1705) showed a lively interest in music, indeed actively engaged in composition.[1] Froberger's laments on the deaths of Ferdinand III and his son Ferdinand IV, who died early; Ebner's variations on the *Aria . . . Ferdinandi III;* Poglietti's *Rossignolo* autograph, which he presented to Emperor Leopold I and his wife; Froberger's and Techelmann's four autograph volumes that were dedicated to the two emperors; and Muffat's *Apparatus . . . invictissimo Leopold I . . . oblatus* of 1690 testify to the close relationship that existed between the court and the musicians of Vienna.

Froberger

Mid-17th-century South German clavier music was dominated by the personality of Johann Jakob Froberger. A descendant of a Halle family, he was born at Stuttgart in 1616. Nothing is known with certainty about his youth and education. In 1637 he was in Vienna, but at the end of that year he went to Rome, where he studied with Frescobaldi until 1641. Then he returned to Vienna, and from there undertook journeys to Dresden, Brussels, Paris, and London. Among his friends were Weckmann, Denis Gaultier, Chambonnières, Louis Couperin, and Sibylla, Princess of Württemberg, in whose castle at Héricourt (near Belfort) he spent his last years. He died there in 1667.

The cosmopolitan character of Froberger's life is reflected in his works, which represent a happy synthesis of German, Italian, and French elements. He was one of the few great masters who wrote almost exclusively for the keyboard, and the first, at least in Germany, to give equal interest to the organ and to the harpsichord. Many of his works are preserved in three precious manuscripts, which he penned between 1649 and 1658, and dedicated to the Emperors Ferdinand III and Leopold I.[2]

ORGAN WORKS

Froberger's organ works consist of 24 toccatas (not twenty-five, for nos.16 and 22 are identical), 18 capriccios, 6 canzonas, 8 fantasies, and 15 ricercars.[3] His toccatas are generally thought to imitate those of his teacher, Frescobaldi, but they differ in some essential details of form and style. However, they are remarkably similar in these very details to the toccatas of another Frescobaldi student, Michelangelo Rossi. Rossi's toccatas appeared in a first printing in 1640, when Froberger was studying with Frescobaldi in Rome, where he most probably met Rossi. In any event, Rossi's and Froberger's toccatas are very much alike and represent a new type. They differ from Frescobaldi's in that the rhapsodic structure of the many brief, abruptly ending sections is replaced by an articulation in a few extended sections, which alternate between improvisational and fugal writing. Thus in form these toccatas represent a return to the principles of Merulo, though the contents are completely different.

Froberger's toccatas are pieces of moderate length, about 50 to 60 measures, except for no.20 which comprises almost 100 measures. For the normal form we may take one that consists of two fugal and three toccata-like sections, the second and third of which are often just very brief flourishes. A few toccatas have only one fugal section (nos.21, 23), while others have three (nos.10, 19, 20, 25), and in still others there are none at all (nos.5, 6, 11, 17, 24). In the toccata-like sections the

Fig.576

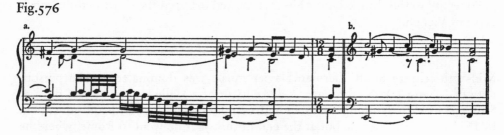

a. No. 1, meas.42–44; b. No. 10, meas.15–16.

musical language is generally the one developed by Frescobaldi, but in a milder, softer dialect: The forced shifts in harmony are usually replaced by more pleasing turns, like the ones shown in Fig.576. Some chords are sustained over two or three measures and their spans are filled with figurations that accommodate themselves to the chord. For such sustained harmonies Froberger often chooses the less affirmative sixth chord instead of a triad in root position, and sometimes even less stable harmonies, such as six-five and six-four chords. In the opening toccata section in no.21, after an initial *D*-major triad, no triads in root position appear for twenty-five measures. Fig.577 shows the harmonic skeleton of the first twelve measures.

Fig.577

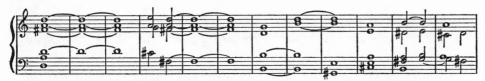

On the whole, Froberger's harmonic style represents a mixture, or rather a juxtaposition, of early-Baroque experimental harmony and late-Baroque functional harmony. Nos.1 and 10, e.g., both start with a classical series of dominant harmonies, until a sudden turn toward the unexpected occurs (Fig.578). The second example contains the change from the major to the minor third, which Froberger invokes very often, though not always in so obvious a fashion. Nos.5 and 6, both "da sonarsi alla Levatione," are particularly rich in bold turns; like Frescobaldi's elevation toccatas, they are written without fugal insertions. In measures 51–52 of no.5, Froberger modulates from *B* minor to *B* major by means of a seventh chord on *G*.

Fig.578

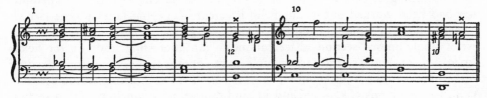

All the fugal portions of the toccatas employ lively subjects, which are treated in a light, free-voiced texture, more in the character of a playful fugato than of a fugue—this feature constitutes another similarity between Froberger's and Michelangelo Rossi's writing (cf.Fig.511). When the toccata has two or three fugal sections, they are often based on variants of the same subject, as, e.g., in no.4 (Fig. 579). Often the light fugato evaporates further into a superficial game with me-

553

chanically repeated motifs. In general, the fugal portions of Froberger's toccatas are rather unimportant; it is the free sections, with their bold formulations, that attract the listener's attention. Indeed, the toccatas in which Froberger omits the fugal interludes and gives his imagination free rein are probably his most successful: In the two elevation toccatas (nos.5 and 6) and in nos.11 and 24 a romantic pathos finds convincing expression in dissonant suspensions, unexpected turns of harmony, and expressive rhythmic-melodic gestures. They may well be compared to the Baroque paintings and sculptures of saints looking up to heaven with gestures of pain or expressions of ecstasy. No.17, which also exhibits toccata texture throughout, looks more like a work by Kerll.

Fig.579

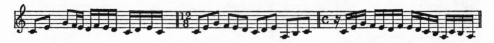

Froberger's canzonas are of the variation canzona type, which was developed by Frescobaldi in his *Toccate II* of 1627. Froberger does not distinguish between a canzona and a capriccio, whereas for Frescobaldi the two types mean quite different things. Froberger's canzonas flow more evenly and have a more melodious approach than Frescobaldi's, and his transitions and concluding passages in toccata style, which are usually limited to just a few measures, appear less regularly.

Froberger's ricercars and fantasies can hardly be differentiated either, again in contrast to Frescobaldi's works, in which a definite distinction is made between the two types. In both types Froberger employs slow subjects, without too much character, but they are appropriate for various contrapuntal treatments and for combinations with other subjects. All these compositions are monothematic, in the sense that the subject that begins the piece plays the main role, and is used from beginning to end. For their structure, Froberger employs various methods that had been worked out in this field. Ricercar no.11 and fantasy no.4 (which is based on a contrapuntal complex of *sol la re* against *Lascia fare mi*) both consist of single unified sections. Ricercars nos.1 (an interesting study on the hexachord),[4] 7, 13, and 15, and fantasy no.6 each contain two sections, one devoted to the main subject, and one in which it is combined with a countersubject (A ‖ A/B). Ricercars nos.5, 8, 9, 10, and 14, and fantasy no.3 conclude with a section that presents the subject in augmentation against a countersubject (which in the fantasy is the subject in diminution). In ricercars nos.5, 6, and 10, and fantasy no.5 the subject appears varied in one or several sections.

In ricercars nos.6 and 12 Froberger goes beyond the keys used in his day; the former is in C♯ minor, the latter in F♯ minor, and both conclude with a major triad. Fantasy no.8 is quite different from all the rest; it is an imitative duet similar to the *Ricercari a due voci* of Guami (1588), Metallo (1614 and later), Gentile (1642), and others. It is preserved only in the Bauyn manuscript, and may not be authentic.

Froberger's ricercars and fantasies are successful, often masterful, representatives of a type that includes much that is boring and purely mechanical. They are of exactly the right length and have sufficient variety to captivate the listener without tiring him. Good workmanship combines with refined taste, and neither intrusive learnedness nor empty figurations disturb the total impression.

SUITES

Froberger's suites are a particularly important part of his output. They are among the earliest examples, not of the suite as such, but of a special type to which the future belonged, in which allemande, courante, sarabande, and gigue were treated as a unit. The main accent here lies on the term "musical unit." Although the same dance types were already present in the works of Froberger's older contemporary Chambonnières (1602–72), they were not treated as a unit, but only as parts of a large group of pieces in the same key. The Bauyn manuscript, e.g., which was written shortly after 1650, preserves a group of pieces in C major by Chambonnières that consists of 5 allemandes, 11 courantes, 4 sarabandes, 2 gigues, 5 more courantes, and a chaconne, but these 28 pieces do not form a musical unit. It is, of course, possible to choose one representative of each species and connect them to form a suite, but whether this is in fact what happened, as has been variously stated, we do not know. And even if this were the case, the result would be an impermanent combination, dependent on the performer's fancy, and not a unity created by the will of the composer. If the idea of a real suite took root in France at all, it was very late. On the other hand, it was completely formulated in Germany as early as about 1620 in the ensemble suites of Schein and Peuerl. Froberger gave the form a new content, as he replaced the archaic paduanas, intradas, and galliards by the allemande, courante, sarabande, and later the gigue, and connected them to form a large musical structure.

Perhaps his fame should be divided with his contemporary Johann Erasmus Kindermann of Nuremberg (1616–55), from whom we have several manuscript suites, consisting of allemande (or ballet), courante, and sarabande. It is not possible to ascertain whether these composers influenced each other, and if so, which one influenced the other. The style of Kindermann's suites is much simpler than Froberger's, a fact that need not indicate an earlier date, but only the composer's Central German tendency toward simplicity and brevity. A more interesting, anonymous suite in A minor, consisting of an allemande, courante, and sarabande, appears as the final entry in the Lynar manuscript A 1. It is quite different from Kindermann's suites, for it is written in a free-voiced, refined style, which comes strikingly close to Froberger's, with its *style-brisé* effects and delicately dissolving endings. Is it a youthful work by Froberger? In the allemande and courante several groups of notes carry dots that can only mean staccato. The conclusions of the allemande and the sarabande are reproduced in Fig.580.

Fig.580

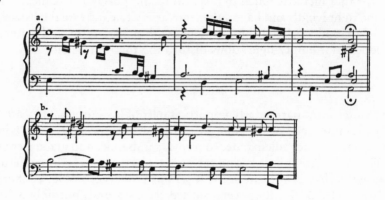

Let us turn to Froberger's 30 authenticated suites. For a better understanding we must refer to the tradition of the sources, which is unfortunately completely obscured and misrepresented in Adler's new edition. The earliest autograph volume (1649) contains six suites (new ed., nos.1–6). Except for no.2 all of them have the three-movement arrangement A C S (allemande courante sarabande), i.e., without a gigue. No.2 adds a gigue to these three basic movements, and in a later source, Vienna Nationalbibl. 16798 (1699), a gigue is added to nos.3 and 5 also. Another autograph volume, dedicated to Emperor Ferdinand III and therefore necessarily written before 1657, contains suites nos.7–12, all of which include a gigue, but inserted as the second movement, i.e., A G C S. The remaining suites (nos.13–30) come from later sources, e.g., a print by the Amsterdam publisher Mortier that appeared in the 1690s, which presents them as A C S G, an order that became standard after Froberger's death; the note "mis en meilleur ordre" on the title page shows that this order did not originate with Froberger. To summarize, Froberger began with the three-movement form A C S, which he later enlarged to A G C S. The sole exception is suite no.2, which already exhibits the classic order A C S G in the autograph of 1649. In three suites (nos.21, 23, 24) the allemande, courante, and sarabande are each followed by a double (a figural variation).[5]

All the dances consist of two repeated sections, but Froberger rarely employs the regular 8+8 measure structure; when he does so it is mostly in sarabandes. A number of dances, however, are built symmetrically, with schemes such as 6 + 6 measures (A 26);* 7+7 (C 11, G 11, C 17); 11+11 (G 20); 13+13 (A 12); 17+17

---

* "A 26" stands for allemande of suite no.26.

(G 2). In many others the second section is one or two measures longer or, more often, shorter than the first. The same situation obtains in Chambonnières, but with this difference: While Froberger employs the principle of irregular construction for sarabandes also, the French master's almost invariably consist of 8 + 16 measures.

It is also instructive to compare the stylistic details with works of French provenance. In Froberger's suites the allemande appears as a highly stylized type, in which the original dance rhythm of four quarter notes is completely veiled by figures and motifs, which appear in one part and then another. In this respect Froberger goes far beyond Chambonnières. In the latter's music eighth notes predominate, while the former employs the more rapid flow of sixteenth notes, but both composers avoid articulating internal cadences, which would break into the continuity. Froberger is intent on constantly changing the motif and avoiding everything that might give an impression of regularity. Even more than Chambonnières, he was influenced by the delicate and refined art of French lute music, whose chief master, Denis Gaultier (c.1600–72), was one of his friends. Everywhere there are figures in which the *style brisé*, the transparent and merely suggestive lute texture, is transferred to the harpsichord. In the harmony the seventh chord and its inversions play an important role. As an example Fig.581 presents the first section of the allemande in no.4.

The courantes, of course, are all in triple meter, which is interpreted in various ways. Most of them are in 6/4 time, into which occasional hemiola-like 3/2 measures are inserted. The hemiola is almost always found in the penultimate measure,

Fig.581

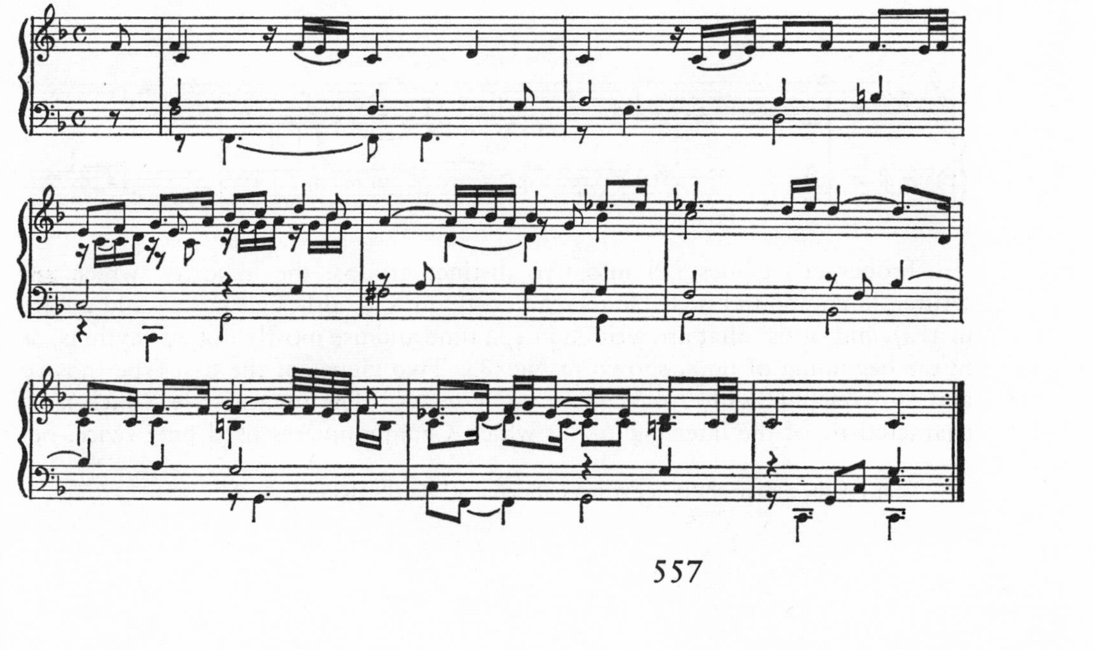

which is then followed by a final measure stressing the 6/4 accentuation, e.g., in no.8 (Fig.582). Nine courantes (in suites nos.2, 3, 4, 6, 14, 17, 21, 23, 30) move in a pronounced 3/2 time throughout, i.e., in a triple rhythm that is twice as slow as the usual 6/4 time. In these pieces, moreover, the eighth-note motion, so frequent in the other courantes, does not occur. Finally there are seven courantes (in suites nos.15, 24, 25, 26, 27, 29; no.29 includes two courantes) that are written in 3/4 time, therefore without hemiolas. These pieces resemble the Italian corrente, as cultivated by Frescobaldi and others. Thus there exist three types of courantes in Froberger's music, which may be differentiated as the 6/4, 3/2, and 3/4 types.

Fig.582

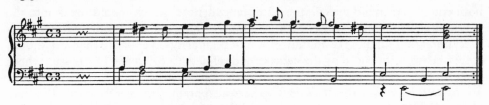

In his courantes Froberger occasionally uses the variation principle by deriving them from the respective allemandes. Except for the special case of the *Mayerin* suite, suite no.1 is the only one in which the entire courante is a free variation of the allemande. Elsewhere the relationship is limited to the first few measures, e.g., in suites nos.3 (10 measures), 4 (6 measures), and 24 (4 measures). As an example Fig.583 gives the beginning of the courante in no.4; compare it with the beginning of the allemande from the same suite, shown in Fig.581.

Fig.583

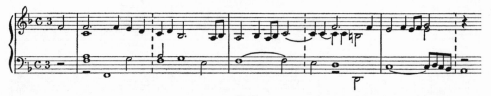

Froberger's gigues fall into two distinct groups: the majority, which are written in compound or triple meter (mostly in 6/8, although nos.23 and 29 are in 3/4), and twelve that are written in 4/4 time and use mostly dotted rhythms, as in the beginning of no.8, shown in Fig.584. Two gigues of the first type (nos.10 and 29) conclude with a passage in duple meter.* The fugato style, which is so characteristic of the later gigue, but which Chambonnières used only twice, be-

---

Cf.p.508 for similar shifts in rhythm in Etienne Richard's gigues.

Fig.584

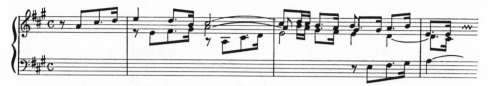

comes the rule with Froberger, though not without occasional exceptions (nos.12, 18, 30). The second section is frequently developed from a different motif (nos.8, 11, 19, 24, 28), occasionally from the same subject (nos.14, 17–21, and 26), and in several instances from its inversion, as was usual later on (nos.3, 9, 10, 20, and 29). A few details worth noting are the annotations *f* and *piano*, which occur twice in no.22, the only instances of an echo effect in Froberger's works; the passages marked "avec discrétion" near the end of nos.13 and 20; and the chromatic variant of the six-five chord in the penultimate measure of no.20, which, together with the preceding "avec discrétion" passage, creates an elegiac, romantic impression that is thoroughly alien to the gigue. This passage is shown in Fig.585.

Fig.585

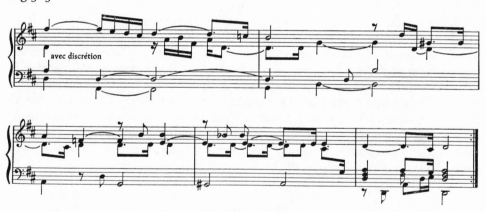

In comparison with the other dances, both Froberger's and Chambonnières's sarabandes are very unified and regular in structure. The 3/4 time preferred by Chambonnières is found in only five of Froberger's pieces (nos.11, 20, 22, 24, 26), all the others being in 3/2 time, which may well be interpreted as a slowing up of the type. Almost all have a feminine cadence on the third beat. The typical sarabande rhythm with the accent on the second beat, however, is clearly exhibited in only eight instances (nos.7–10, 12, 15, 17, 29), while in the others the rhythm | ♩ ♩ | predominates. Several sarabandes end with a *ripresa*, i.e., a repetition of the last three to five measures, which is indicated by the symbol $f.$ (e.g., in no.2) or is written out (e.g., in no.7). When it is written out the annotation *piano* (nos.10, 15, 18) or *doucement* (no.13) appears occasionally, not really indicating an echo effect but rather a soft dying away of the sarabande, and with it, the entire suite. Surely this execution should be applied even where it is not expressly called for.

Several of Froberger's other keyboard works deserve special mention, particularly suite no.6, entitled *Auff die Mayerin*. It is really a set of variations, starting with six "partite," which in a way represent the allemande, followed by a *Courante sopra Mayerin* with a double, and a *Sarabande sopra Mayerin*. Similar arrangements are found in Frescobaldi's works, especially in his *Aria detta la Frescobalda*, several of whose variations are written as suite movements. Froberger goes even further by applying this method to all the variations in the set. The *Mayerin* variations have appeared in several modern editions and are probably his best-known work, though surely not his best and certainly not one that fairly represents his delicate and refined art. The homey sentimental theme, the routine figurations of the first few variations, the forced chromaticism of the sixth variation, which leaves one in doubt whether to laugh or cry—all mark the composition as mediocre, a judgment that applies equally to many succeeding (and probably derivative) variation sets.

Among the most impressive of Froberger's keyboard works, on the other hand, are his three laments: one on the death of Emperor Ferdinand III (d.1657; vol.III, p.116), one for his son Ferdinand IV (d.1654; vol.II, p.32), and one for a friend, Monsieur Blancheroche (vol.III, p.114).* The first piece shows the three-section form of the pavane, the others the two-part structure of the allemande. All three exhibit a depth of feeling, a self-tortured expression of personally felt grief, that is not found again until the music of the 19th-century German Romantic composers, such as Schumann or Brahms. The lament on the death of Ferdinand III is especially beautiful. It begins in a sombre F minor, is filled with painful dissonances, and concludes, as shown in Fig.586, with an arpeggiated F-major triad, with which the redeemed soul of the deceased ascends to heaven.

Ebner and Kerll

Wolfgang Ebner was born in Augsburg in 1612. In 1634, at the age of twenty-two, he was already an organist at the cathedral in Vienna, and in 1637 was named court organist to Emperor Ferdinand III, a position he filled until his death in 1681,

---

* We may also include in this genre the allemande from suite no.20, which appears in the manuscript New Haven, Yale University (School of Music) Ms. 21. H. 59 (now M 1490. H 66; called the Hintze manuscript for a recent owner), with the title "Meditation faict sur ma Mort future laquelle se joue lentement avec discretion. di Gia: Gio: Frb:" and the postscript "Memento Mori" (cf. Riedel Q, p.97).

Fig.586

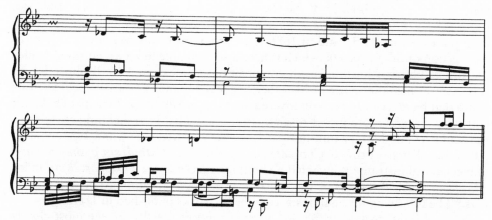

during the reign of Leopold I. We know only one keyboard work of his, entitled *Aria . . . Imperatoris Ferdinandi III, 36 modis variata ac pro cimbalo accomodata . . .* (printed in Prague, 1648).[6] The theme, possibly composed by the Emperor, is treated in thirty-six variations, articulated in three groups of twelve, of which the second group is entitled *Courante* and the third *Sarabanda*. As in Froberger's *Mayerin*, the first group thus represents the allemande. The last two variations of the courante group are called "gigue," and the standard 3/4 time of the courantes changes to 4/4. In Froberger's suites there are gigues in duple meter, but they at least maintain a connection with the skipping character of the dance by the frequent use of dotted rhythms, while Ebner's gigues move in a smooth eighth-note rhythm, and could more easily be regarded as allemandes. The second gigue is formed dexterously from the first one by an interchange of voices in double counterpoint. The sixth variation in the first group, like the sixth one in the *Mayerin* set, is pervaded by chromatic lines, but they sound much less forced than Froberger's. Indeed, Ebner treats the simple, rather pleasing theme with much ingenuity, taste, and imagination, which is more than can be said of Froberger's counterpart.*

Johann Kaspar Kerll was born in Adorf (southern Saxony) in 1627 and died in Munich in 1693. He came to Vienna as a youth and was sent to Rome for his education by Archduke Leopold Wilhelm. There he studied with Carissimi and probably with Frescobaldi, too. In 1656 Kerll accepted a call to the court of Munich, went again to Vienna in 1673, but returned to Munich after the siege of Vienna by the Turks in 1683. His works include a number of operas (whose music

---

* According to the introductory "Advertisement," François Roberday's *Fugues et Caprices* of 1660 contains a piece by Ebnert [*sic*]. Which composition is Ebner's, however, is not certain (cf.p.722).

is not preserved) and many compositions for the church, for instrumental ensembles, and for the keyboard. Of the keyboard pieces eight toccatas, six canzonas, *Capriccio Cucu*, *Battaglia*, *Ciaccona*, *Passacaglia*, and several dubious pieces have been published in *DTB*,[7] and in 1686 Kerll brought out his *Modulatio organica*, a collection of organ versets, which is now also available in a new edition.[8] Under the title "Subnecto initia aliarum compositionum mearum," Kerll appended to this print a thematic index of his other keyboard compositions. It includes four suites that have recently been discovered in a manuscript at the Benedictine Abbey Göttweig. Several more pieces reach us in the so-called Neresheim manuscript of the Munich State Library (mus.ms.5368), written between 1661 and 1682. Finally, Athanasius Kircher printed a *Toccata sive Ricercata in Cylindrum phonotacticum* [a mechanical instrument invented by him] *transferenda . . . a Gasparo Kerll* in his *Musurgia* of 1650; however, this piece is also preserved among Poglietti's ricercars.[9] The following discussion starts with the works published in *DTB*.

Of all the toccatas written in the 17th century, Kerll's are the most closely related to Frescobaldi's. Even Frescobaldi's immediate successor, Michelangelo Rossi, gave up the characteristic construction of the Frescobaldi toccata—the articulation in numerous brief sections of contrasting content—and Froberger followed him in this respect. Kerll, on the other hand, closely follows Frescobaldi. In toccata no.3, e.g., which is 75 measures long, fourteen or fifteen sections can be differentiated, each dominated by a particular motif or a particular manner of motif treatment, such as shifting it from the top voice to the bass. Like Frescobaldi, Kerll eschews fugal treatment; the only exception is a section of toccata no.1 (meas.14–22), in which a brief, lively motif is freely imitated in the manner of Rossi and Froberger.

The situation changes when it comes to style, although unmistakable echoes of Frescobaldi's highly individual musical language can be found here and there, e.g., in the passage from toccata no.1, given in Fig.587. Similarly, the repeated employment of contrasting rhythms (e.g., 4/4 and 12/8), exchanges of altered and diatonic steps (e.g., no.3, meas.10–14), and other details are taken over from the older master. But in general, Kerll's toccatas, which were written several decades after Frescobaldi's, exhibit the stylistic traits of the keyboard music of the middle

Fig.587

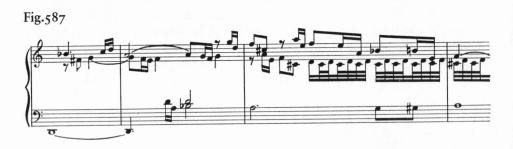

Baroque: rapid figurations, moving in smooth, sequentially repeated patterns and often assuming a virtuosic character, and a great emphasis on written-out trills, frequently even double trills, executed by both hands. Fig.588 offers a selection of such passages from no.8.

Fig.588

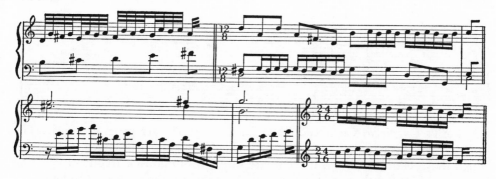

In toccata no.5, *tutta de salti*, Kerll tackles the same problem that Frescobaldi solved in his ricercar with "obligo di non uscir di grado" (the avoidance of all stepwise motion) (cf.p.454). Their solutions are, of course, very different—Frescobaldi's strict and inspired, Kerll's relaxed and rather trivial, insofar as he employs figurations in the form of arpeggios or broken octaves, while the main voices make extensive use of stepwise motion. He is more successful in imitating his model in toccata no.6, *per li pedali*, and most beautifully in no.4, *cromatica con durezze e ligature*, an impressive and lovely work; unfortunately the last section is tiresome because the same motif is repeated too often, but one might try to abbreviate it to enable the original conclusion to take its proper effect.

Kerll's canzonas consist of two or three sections, in which two or three subjects are treated fugally. Curiously, he uses thematic variation, which Frescobaldi had introduced into the canzona, only once, in the final section of *Canzona 2* (no. 10). In *Canzona 3* (no.11) three different subjects are presented, each in a separate section, and the second fugue is concluded by a lengthy toccata with thirty-second-note passages.* *Canzona 6* (no.14) consists of three thematically independent sections also, the first based on an interesting subject with large skips and the second on a contrapuntal combination of a new subject and its diminution. Fig.589 shows the beginnings of the three sections. In *Canzona 4* (no.12) the second section adds a countersubject to the subject of the first section, and both subjects are also heard in inversion. Here, as well as in most of the other canzonas, the contrapuntal work is achieved with dexterity and taste, without a tiresome involvement of pretentious learnedness.

---

* P. Heidorn wrote a parody on this canzona (cf.p.624).

Fig.589

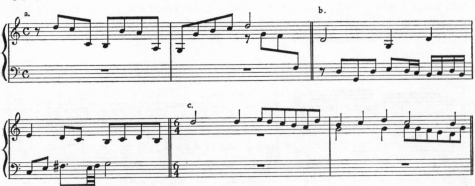

Kerll's *Capriccio Cucu* and *Battaglia* (nos.15, 16) are program music. The former is an attractive piece—it must be played on the harpsichord, though—in which the cuckoo's call and its echo are heard continuously, frequently passing from one step to another and supported by variegated passage work. The *Battaglia*, as is expected of such a piece, is very bombastic, especially toward the end. A third character piece, *Halter, Der steyrische Hirt* (no.20), is held to be dubious, but is also ascribed to Kerll in the Neresheim Ms., where it is entitled *Canzon 8vi toni* (fol.106v). However, it is even less worthy of fame than the *Battaglia*.

The *Passacaglia* is by far the longer and the more remarkable of the two ostinato compositions. It consists of forty variations on the well-known tetrachord bass (*d c B♭ A*), which is retained in pure or varied form in most variations, but is occasionally reinterpreted to yield new melodic or harmonic progressions. A number of variations employ one-measure formulae from beginning to end, whose repetitions are accommodated to the harmonic progressions. This technique of the formula variation occasionally appears in earlier works (first in Valente's, 1576; cf.p.277), but occurs with increasing frequency from about 1650 onward. Fig.590 includes three examples from Kerll's *Passacaglia*.

Let us now turn to the *Modulatio organica*, which Kerll had printed in 1686, seven years before his death. As Frescobaldi does in his *Fiori musicali*, Kerll turns

Fig.590

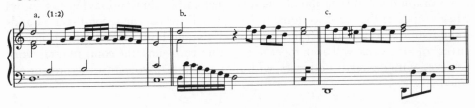

a. var. IV; b. var. XXXI; c. var. XXXIV.

Fig.591

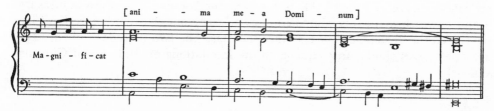

from the secular to the spiritual, from entertainment to edification. The collection comprises 56 versets for the Magnificat, seven for each of the eight toni. The first six versets of each group represent, as usual, the odd verses of the Magnificat, to which is added a *Versus ultimus loco Antiphonae*. The *Versus primus* always begins with the monophonic choral intonation ("Magnificat"), and continues with the melody in the soprano of a setting of four to six measures, as e.g., in the *Quartus tonus*, shown in Fig.591. The final versets *loco antiphonae* are brief settings in toccata style. Versets 2–6 are mostly fugal, all well worked out, showing the hand of an experienced and mature master. Kerll's handling of the varied formulation of the subjects is especially apt: canzona-like, chromatic, repercussive, in gigue rhythm, etc. Some particularly interesting subjects are assembled in Fig.592. In a few exceptional instances the chant melody is used in middle versets also: in verset 4 of the *Secundus tonus* (whole notes in the bass), verset 3 of the *Sextus tonus* (half notes in the tenor), and verset 3 of the *Septimus tonus* (as the subject of an imitative setting).

Fig.592

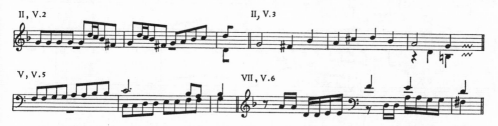

A number of other compositions by Kerll that have recently been discovered but not yet published reach us in the Neresheim manuscript.[10] In addition to some pieces that are printed in *DTB*, it contains 5 versets, 3 toccatas, 2 preludes, and, at the end (fol.155), an *Aria Casp. Kerll* with two variations. The versets are short fugal pieces, very similar to those in the *Modulatio organica*. The toccatas are definitely less virtuosic than those published in *DTB*, and this is to their advantage. The *Toccata primi toni* (fol.17v) is a masterpiece of deep expression and noble pathos, one of the best created in this field in South Germany. At least its beginning must be given here (Fig.593). Not only the formal disposition but also the stylistic details recall Frescobaldi, particularly the Lombardic rhythms in measures 4 and 5, which mark this composition as an early one, written before Kerll had developed the "brilliance" of his other toccatas. The two preludes (fol.20, 145v) are brief pieces similar in character to the intonations of Andrea and Giovanni Gabrieli.

Fig.593

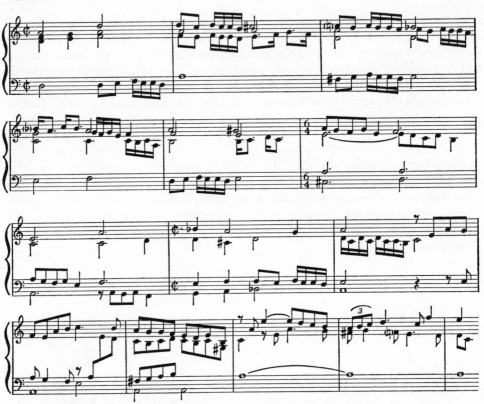

The Göttweig manuscript[11] shows another side of Kerll, as a composer of suites and follower of Froberger. One of the five preserved suites has the arrangement A C S, but the others already show the "classic" form A C S G. In style these pieces keep to a modest, occasionally popularizing level. Fig.594 presents the beginning of an allemande.

Poglietti

Very little is known about Alessandro Poglietti's life. His name clearly points to Italian extraction. The first trace of him comes in January 1661, when he was the

Fig.594

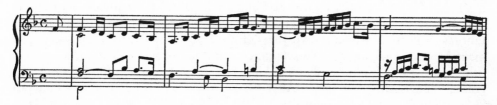

organist and musical director of the Jesuit church at Vienna. In July of the same year he was an organist of the court chapel of Emperor Leopold I, who bestowed on him the title of "comes palatinus" and probably raised him to the nobility. Poglietti died in 1683 during the siege of Vienna by the Turks.

His reputation as a great composer is borne out not only by the honors bestowed on him by the Emperor but also by the numerous copies by which his works spread, though only in Vienna and its environs. Works by other composers were frequently ascribed to him, not only those by his friend Kerll but also toccatas by Frescobaldi and, in several sources, even a hexachord fantasy by John Bull.* The following works are regarded as authentic:[12]

1. An autograph collection of pieces, which he presented to Emperor Leopold I and his wife Eleanora in 1677, entitled *Rossignolo*.
2. A kind of suite *sopra la ribellione di Ungheria*
3. A canzona and capriccio *über das Henner und Hannengeschrey*
4. A collection of twelve ricercars
5. Two toccatas, two canzonas, and three suites in a New Haven manuscript[13]
6. An autograph pedagogic volume entitled *Compendium oder kurtzer Begriff und Einführung zur Musica . . . ,*[14] which, in addition to the theoretical discourses, contains a collection of preludes, cadenzas, and fugues, a *Toccatina per l'Introito*, and the beginnings of many program pieces
7. A suite in *F* major in a collective print, published by Roger in Amsterdam in 1698/99, entitled *Toccates et suites pour le Clavessin de Messieurs Pasquini, Poglietti et Gaspard Kerll*

The pieces in the autograph (1.) are often called the *Rossignolo* suite, probably because they are all written in *D* major; but the volume contains much more than a genuine suite: a toccata and canzona followed by a suite, consisting of an allemande with two doubles, a courante with a double, a sarabande with a double, and a gigue with a double; an *Aria Allemagna* with twenty variations; a *Ricercar per lo Rossignolo* followed by a *Syncopatione* (variant) and a *Capriccio sopra il Ricercar;* and an *Aria bizarra del Rossignolo* with *Imitatione del medesimo uccello*.

The toccata, canzona, and suite exhibit no special features, except that the doubles in the suite exceed the ornamental treatment usually employed in such movements and approach the genuine variation, with occasional touches of virtuosic style.

---

* Cf.Chap.13, note 15; cf. also Chap.16, note 38, and p.562.

The *Aria Allemagna con alcuni variazioni sopra l'età della Maestà Vostra* is a kind of birthday offering for the Empress, in which the number of variations is supposed to equal her age. (The work consists of twenty variations, but the Empress was already twenty-two years old in 1677). Poglietti is in his special element here, that of amusing entertainment and humorous caricature. With such titles as "Lyra," "Böhmisch Dudelsakh" (Bohemian bagpipe), "Holländisch Flagolett," "Bayrische Schalmei," "Alter Weiber Conduct" (Old Women's Funeral), "Hanacken Ehrentanz" (Honor Dance), "Französische Baiselmens" (French Hand-Kisses), "Polnischer Sablscherz" (Polish Sabre Joke), "Soldaten Schwebelpfeif" (Soldiers' Small Flute), "Ungarische Geigen" (Hungarian Fiddles), and "Steyermarkher [Styrian] Horn," and several similar ones he enters the field of program music. Folk musicians and other figures from the Austrian provinces and neighboring countries are combined in a colorful wedding procession in honor of the young Empress. The "Alter Weiber Conduct" of variation XIII (Fig.595a.) and the "Französische Baiselmens" of variation XV (Fig.595b.) bear vivid witness to Poglietti's gift for humorous and accurate caricature.

Fig.595

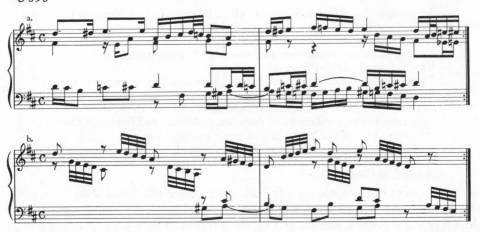

The *Ricercar per lo Rossignolo* and its *Syncopatione* are expanded and rhythmically altered variants of the twelfth ricercar in 4. in the above list. The subject on which they are based (| d | e | $f\sharp$ g | $-f\sharp$) is employed again in the subsequent *Capriccio sopra il Ricercar*, where it is enlivened by rapid repeated notes, which lend it a jocular character (Fig.596).

The collection concludes with an *Aria bizarra del Rossignolo* and an "imitation of the same bird." The latter, particularly, is a virtuosic exhibition piece, whose brilliant and sometimes bizarre effects are written as specifically for the

Fig.596

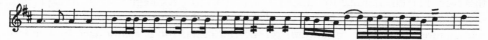

harpsichord as the thundering passages of a Liszt rhapsody demand the grand piano. Acciaccaturas are employed repeatedly, and (as far as I know) this is their first occurrence (Fig.597). Such passages express the same propensity for curiosity, distortion, and malformation as the deformed figures in the Salzburg "Zwerglgarten" (dwarf garden), which gave the nobility of the period so much pleasure.

Fig.597

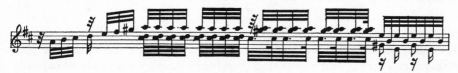

Another piece of program music is a suite (2. in the above list) whose movements depict the course of a revolution in Hungary in 1671: A toccatina describes the cavalry attack (*Galop*) and the flight (*Fuge*), the allemande the prison (*La Prisonnie*), the courante the trial (*Le Procès*), the sarabande the sentence (*La Sentence*), the gigue the chaining in the dungeon (*La Lige*), and two postludes the decapitation (*La Decapitation, avec discretion*) and the funeral bells (*Les Kloches*). A passacaglia inserted between the postludes probably does not belong to the set; in fact, parts of it are copied from Frescobaldi's *Passacagli* in E minor (*Toccate I, Aggiunta* of the 1637 edition). As is so often the case with jokes from a much earlier period, it is difficult to understand all the allusions or to find them amusing. If we disregard them and approach the work as pure music, it proves to be Poglietti's most impressive composition—except for the first and last movements, which are somewhat cheap. The allemande and gigue, with their evolving lines and chromatic digressions, are especially beautiful.

Other program pieces by Poglietti are the well-known canzona and capriccio on the cries of the hens and cocks (3. in the list), and a *Toccata fatta sopra Cassedio* [a misspelling of *l'assedio*] *di Filipsburgo* (the siege of Philippsburg on Rhine,

Fig.598

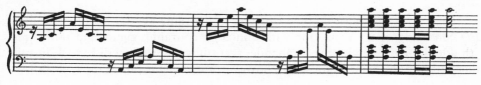

1676) as well as a *Canzon Teutsch Trommel* and *Franzoik Trommel,* all part of the New Haven manuscript (listed as 5.). The toccata begins with an arpeggio, shown in Fig.598, which also occurs elsewhere in Poglietti's works, and may represent cannon shots here. In the *Canzon* the German drum is symbolized by a repercussive motif with reinforcing octaves below, which is varied in triple meter for the French drum (Fig.599).

Fig.599

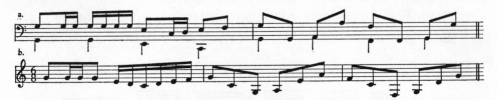

Poglietti's views on program music are expressed in the following passage from his *Compendium:* "Music has now arrived at so much substance and perfection that it cannot become any better, therefore I have set a number of caprices that imitate the harmonies of the birds and other sounds on the instrument" (p. 101). As reinforcement he lists the beginnings of each of the following pieces on a separate sheet: *Bergwerckh oder Schmidten Imitation; Der Khüehalter* (preserved completely as *Capriccio sopra pastorale* in Ms.XIV. 717 of the Vienna monastery of the Brothers Minor); *Die welsche Kinderwiegen, sonst Piva genannt; Imitation von dem Canari Vogl;* and other jocular trifles.

Only a few of Poglietti's harpsichord pieces do not depend on a program. In one of them, a *Toccata* in the New Haven manuscript,[15] we have the first appearance of arpeggio passages like those in Bach's *Chromatic Fantasy,* which one is never sure how to execute. They are given in Fig.600.

Fig.600

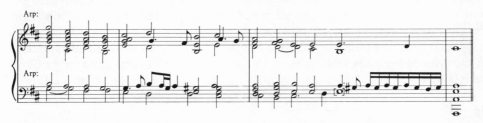

This toccata is followed by a canzona in the same key (*D* major), and by a suite consisting of an allemande with double, a courante, gigue, and sarabande with double—closing with the sarabande, according to Froberger's model. In two other suites in the same manuscript, however, the gigue is put at the end.

Poglietti's pieces that are meant primarily for the organ show the composer in a completely different light from that of the amusing, bizarre program pieces. His chief works in this field are the twelve ricercars (4. in the above list), which were copied again and again and used to teach strict counterpoint until the 19th century. They are indeed very appropriate for that purpose, for they most successfully combine, within the appropriate limits of about 60 measures, the solid counterpoint and the traditional treatment of the 16th century with the harmonic innovations of the 17th. Ricercars nos.1, 5, 6, and 7 are essentially monothematic; no.1 uses the augmentation of the subject, and no.6 the inversion. In nos.8, 9, and 12 a second subject is added (A || A/B), and in nos.2, 3, 4, and 10 there is a third one (A || A/B || A/B/C). No.11 stands alone; it is an arrangement of the first few lines of the chorale *Der Tag der ist so freudenreich.* "The style of the other ricercars is so difficult to recognize [in this piece] that one would rather think of another composer, perhaps of N. A. Strunck."[16] No.4 is identical with the *Toccata sive Ricercata in Cylindrum phonotacticum transferenda*, which Kircher had published in his *Musurgia* (1650) as a work by Johann Kaspar Kerll. No.12 is the model for the ricercar of the *Rossignolo* collection (cf.p.568).

Poglietti inscribed some liturgical organ music in his *Compendium* of 1676: a number of *Praeludia, Cadenzen und Fugen . . . über die acht Choral Ton . . . zu Vespern wie auch Ämbtern sehr tauglich zu schlagen.* The collection consists of three brief pieces for each tone, a prelude (or toccatina) in toccata style, a cadenza written in chordal style, and a fugal setting. The three pieces of the *Tertii Toni* are reproduced in Fig.601. Note the diatonic, modal g at the passages marked *. The omission of the accidental for the f♯ (when it is preceded and followed by a

Fig.601

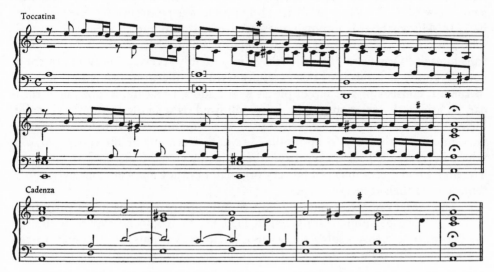

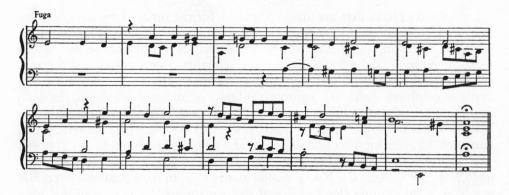

g♯) in the final measures of the *Toccatina* and the *Cadenza* accords with the practice observed from the beginning of the 16th century (Kotter, Kleber) until the end of the 17th.

The *Toccatina per l'Introito della Messa con il pedale* in the *Compendium* has a pedal part that is unusually active for South German music. It consists of a series of whole notes (*a b♭ a g a d*, etc.), and is probably an introit melody from the *Editio Medicea*. Poglietti says that the piece is "in dem Pedal auf den Choral gericht."

Techelmann

Another representative of the Viennese keyboard school is Franz Mathias Techelmann. Born around 1649 in Hof (southern Moravia), he was an organist at St. Michael's in Vienna between 1683 and 1685, and then second court organist (as a colleague of F. T. Richter and later Draghi). He was pensioned in 1713, and died in 1714. His keyboard output is preserved in an autograph (Vienna, Nationalbibliothek Cod. 19167) dedicated to Emperor Leopold I, in which Techelmann calls himself "Organista di S. Michele." He probably received his appointment as court organist as a result of this carefully written collection, penned presumably in 1685. It consists of a group of pieces in *A* minor: a toccata, a canzona, a ricercar, an aria with variations, and a suite, followed by a similar group in *C* major, but without the variation set. Obviously Techelmann wanted to prove that he was familiar with every form popular in South Germany at the time, a plan in which he succeeded well, even from the point of view of the modern observer. The individual pieces may not be very original, but they are well-conceived representatives of their respective types.

The toccata of the *A*-minor group contains three sections in a lightly fugal texture, whose beginnings are given in Fig.602. As would be expected, the following canzona treats a subject in various rhythmic variants. Next comes a ricercar whose strict style expresses itself even in the scoring, which is in four staves

Fig.602

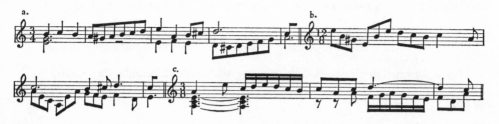

(partitura), while the other pieces are written in the usual keyboard score of two staves. The theme of the *Aria semplice con trenta variationi seguenti*, consists of two repeated sections of four measures each; the individual variations are not without charm, but they follow the recipe of the formula variation too closely to be tolerable in such large numbers. The first half of the theme and the first two measures of two variations appear in Fig.603. The A-minor group concludes with a suite of the form A C S (with *Variatio*) G.

Fig.603

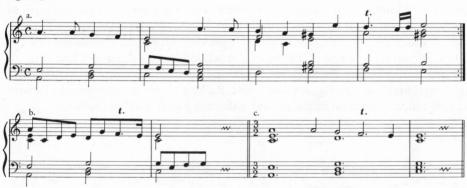

a. Theme; b. var. VIII; c. var. XXIII.

The pieces in C major are rather similar to the corresponding ones in A minor. The suite starts with an *Alamand dell' Allegrezze alla Liberazione di Vienna*, i.e., written to celebrate the liberation of Vienna from the Turkish siege in 1683.[17]

Richter and Reutter

Two other Viennese composers are Ferdinand Tobias Richter (1649–1711) and Georg Reutter (1656–1738). Four compositions by Richter are published in

DTÖ,[18] the first three of which are suites with more or less extended introductions, consisting of a free section and a fugal one, i.e., a kind of prelude and fugue:

No.1: *Toccatina* (prelude)—*Capriccio* (fugue)—*Allemande—Courante—Menuet*
No.2: Untitled (prelude and fugue)—*Allemande—Bourrée—Sarabande—Menuet
—Gigue*
No.3: Untitled (prelude)—*Adagio* (fugue)—*Allemande—Courante—Passacaglia*

Fig.604

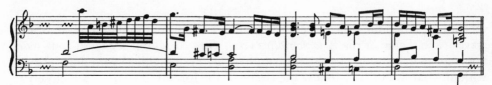

These works are obviously intended for harpsichord or clavichord, a fact that is confirmed by stylistic details, especially by the repeated use of full chords that are repeated repercussively. The free form goes hand in hand with a lively and agreeable content, in which a variety of ideas follow each other in a relaxed but well-conceived manner. In the first movement from no.3, e.g., several measures of thirty-second-note passages are followed by a phrase, reproduced in Fig.604, which is modeled after the recitative of opera or oratorio. The subject of the *Capriccio* from no.1 is one of the most attractive ideas in the entire literature of keyboard music before Bach. From beginning to end this piece is written in a dotted rhythm, shown in Fig.605, for which Richter shows a preference in various places. It reflects the taste of the period, influenced as it was by France.

Fig.605

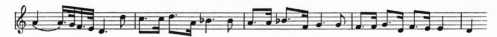

The fourth composition consists of a toccata of fourteen measures and ten fugal versets of similar brevity. It may have served as organ music for psalmody or perhaps for the Magnificat, with the toccata as a prelude and the versets, or some of them, in alternation or in connection with verses that were sung. Here, too, Richter proves to be a musician of ability and good taste, who knows what suits the organ and does not give it anything that could disturb the mood of the service.

Georg Reutter is represented by a goodly number of keyboard pieces in the same *DTÖ* volume, but on the basis of recent research, most of them have turned out to be works by Nicolaus Adam Strunck.[19] Only a canzona (p.80), a fugue (p. 86), and a toccata (p.92) remain as Reutter's works, on the basis of a not too reliable manuscript collection of 1837.[20] The canzona might have been written by a South German composer at the end of the 17th century, but the fugue shows signs of decadence, so that it is better ascribed to the younger Georg Reutter (1708–72). The *E*-minor toccata consists of a pompous introduction that shows the influence of the French opera overture, a fugue, a double fugue, and a conclusion that is similar to the introduction.

Nicolaus Adam Strunck and Others

Nicolaus Adam Strunck, a versatile and much traveled musician, was born at Brunswick in 1640, the son of Delphin Strunck. As early as 1661 he was in Vienna, and between 1661and 1682 he was a violinist at Celle, Hannover, and Hamburg. Thereafter he journeyed to Rome and Vienna, became the orchestral director at Dresden in 1688, and in 1696 director of the opera at Leipzig, where he died in 1700. As a keyboard composer he is known by seven capriccios and two ricercars, most of which, according to the testimony of the manuscript New Haven E. B. 1688, were composed between 1683 and 1686, i.e., when he lived in Rome and Vienna. Indeed, they are very close to the Italian-South German tradition. Six capriccios and a ricercar were erroneously published in *DTÖ* as works by Georg Reutter.[21]

All of Strunck's compositions are written in a strict contrapuntal style, generally employing two or three subjects. The capriccio in *G* minor, e.g., which is dated 1678 (*DTÖ*, p.67), has the form A/B, and the capriccio in *A* minor of 1681 (p.78) is an inversion fugue: A ‖ A^1, A. The capriccio in *E* minor (1683) (p.60) is a double fuge: A ‖ A/B; and the capriccio in *F* major, also written in 1683, is a triple fugue; A ‖ B ‖ A/B/C, in which the chromatic subject C is anticipated at the end of the second section. Another composition dated 1683, a ricercar (p.89), is based on a subject of five sustained notes (| *g* | *f♯ b* | *a* | *d* |). In a second section (*Stanza 2da a 3 suietti*) it is combined with two other subjects, one of which was occasionally heard in the first section (meas.23–26). An undated capriccio in *A* minor (p.70) is a variation canzona in two sections. It has a particularly lively subject, which is shown with its variant in Fig.606.

Fig.606

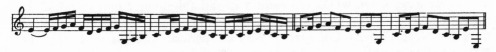

One of Strunck's capriccios is found in no fewer than seven manuscripts: the *Capriccio sopra il Corale Ich dank dir schon durch deinen Sohn* of 1684 (p.74). Indeed, this work must have attracted attention because of its theme, and even more so because of its treatment, which is both artful and lovely. In the first section a subject formed from lines 1 and 2 of the chorale is treated fugally; the second section develops line 3, transformed in a siciliano rhythm; and in the last one, line 4 is combined with line 1 and a vivacious countersubject to form a triple fugue.

In Venice, on December 20, 1685, Strunck wrote a *Ricercar sopra la Morte della mia carissima Madre Catharina Stubenrauen morsa a Brunsviga il 28 d'Augusto ao. 1685.*[22] This work is another that is very artfully wrought in three sections, whose scheme may be outlined as A/A¹ || (3) A/B || A/C/D/E. Although it is in G major, the descending seventh and the chromatic continuation of the main subject, along with the sustained tempo, create an impression of dignified funeral music. The beginnings of the three sections are reproduced in Fig.607.

Fig.607

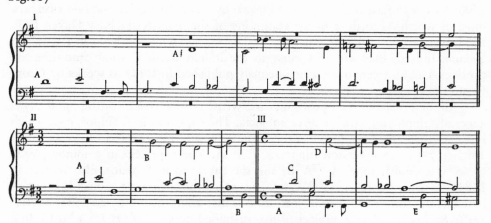

A *Capriccio primi toni*, composed in Vienna in 1686, consists of two sections, in which a chromatic subject and its 12/8 variant are developed and combined with various countersubjects. This work, too, testifies to Strunck's great contrapuntal artistry. Finally, a canzona that is published in *DTÖ* (p.82) as a work by Georg Reutter should certainly be ascribed to Strunck; actually it is a chorale setting of *Christ ist erstanden*.

These nine or ten works represent a remarkably unified output, which betrays an intensive preoccupation with problems of the *stile osservato*, for which there is practically no counterpart during the period. Such problems were not taken up again for fifty years, when Bach tackled them.

The New Haven manuscript in which Strunck's works are preserved also contains a toccata by Bartholomäus Weissthoma, who, it is believed, "came from the southeastern section of Germany."[23] Another toccata by this composer is found in the manuscript XIV. 717–722 of the Vienna monastery of the Brothers

Minor. Other organists represented in this manuscript are Johann Ludwig
Wendler, Kaspar Jäger, and Kaspar Schmidt.

Scherer, Provintz, and Spiridio

Let us now move from the southeastern corner of the German-language area to
the southwestern one, to the Ulm cathedral (where Adam Steigleder had been
active earlier) and the organist Sebastian Anton Scherer (1631–1712). In 1664
he published his *Operum musicorum secundum* (his *Opus primum* containing
Masses, psalms, and motets appeared in 1657), a print consisting of two parts, a
Tabulatura in Cymbalo et organo Intonationum brevium per octo tonos and a
Partitura octo Toccatarum usui apta cum vel sine pedali. The first part, which he
himself engraved in copper, is notated in a two-staff system of six and eight
lines, respectively; the second part is written in a *partitura* of four systems.[24]

Fig.608

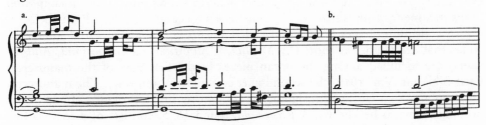

The *Tabulatura* consists of a collection of organ versets, four for each psalm
tone, arranged according to a strictly homogeneous plan. In each group the first
verset is a brief toccata supported by three or four pedal notes (mostly in the
sequence tonic, subdominant, dominant, tonic), the second is a short fugue, the
third is again toccata-like but without pedals, and the fourth again fugal. The
Frescobaldian influence on the style is unmistakable, e.g., in the employment of
Lombardic rhythms and in the sequence of major and minor triads on the same
root, as shown in Fig.608 (a. *Intonatio prima septimi toni;* b. *Intonatio tertia
septimi toni*). Naturally, everything moves on the smooth surfaces of the harmony
of the period, "Ad modernam suavitatem concinnatum," as the title page reads.
The fugal movements are based on lively, canzona-like subjects, two of which are
reproduced in Fig.609. (*Int. quarta tertii toni; Int. quarta octavi toni*). The second
one is possibly a conscious allusion to the bergamasca theme.

Fig.609

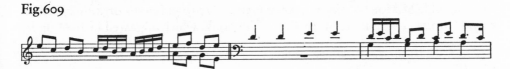

The *Partitura* contains eight toccatas, all worked out according to the same recipe—over a series of pedal notes, about eight on the average, each of which is sustained for fifteen to twenty measures. Curiously, these toccatas, like those by Trabaci and Mayone, are notated on four staves, a method that seems ill-suited to toccatas. The figurations that are spread over the pedal notes are varied rather well: Scale fragments, trills, dotted rhythms, chromatic passages, and imitative motifs alternate and effectively infuse life into the broad harmonic plains of the pedal notes. All the toccatas except nos.5 and 7 contain sections in different meters (e.g., no.4: C − 6/4 − C − 3/2 − C − 12/8 − C).

I cannot quite agree with the negative judgment applied to Scherer's organ pieces by many scholars.[25] He certainly exhibits a very conservative approach, working according to a recipe whose uniformity becomes all too clear when one contemplates his entire output. But if one looks at these works from the point of view of the musician and considers the compositions individually (which is only right), they prove to be quite respectable achievements that are not antiquated even today. At least one must admit that Scherer shows much more imagination in his treatment of sustained pedal points in his toccatas than, e.g., Pachelbel.

A collection of very brief pieces called *Versus aut fuga brevis* and some canzonas that are almost as short (*La Marina, L'Albertina, La Gregoriana, Ambrosiana*) are included among the organ pieces in the first part of the manuscript Paris Bibl. nat. Vm[7] 1817 (the second part contains vocal music). The manuscript also contains two works of insignificant content by Franz Provintz, about whom nothing seems to be known. A *Ricercada*, dated 1675, consists of a toccata-like introduction and a *Fuga*, followed by a *Variatio precedentis fugae*. An *Intonatio sexti toni*, dated 1677, traverses the circle of fifths from *F* to *B* forward and backward with the aid of stereotyped figures. This procedure, which is employed here for the first time in German music,* is not without interest, and a sample of it is given in Fig.610.

Fig.610

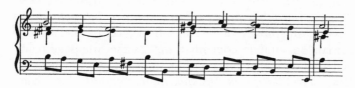

Bertoldo Spiridio (1615–85), a monk in the Bamberg monastery of the Carmelites, published four books of a *Nova instructio pro pulsandis organis, spinettis, manuchordiis . . .* beginning in 1670. A "fifth book, which appeared in 1683 under

---

* Cf. similar procedures among Spanish composers; discussions will be found on pp.519, 547, 772f.

the title *Musicalische Erzgruben*," mentioned by Riemann and Frotscher, cannot be traced.[26] The *Nova instructio* is a voluminous pedagogic work containing more than one thousand didactic examples, most of them based on scale fragments, like those in Paumann's *Fundamentum organisandi*. In each instance only the first two or three measures are worked out, the others being left for the student to continue. For the series (*c d e f e g f a*), e.g., Spiridio gives the elaboration shown in Fig.611 (*Pars* III/IV, p.56).

Fig.611

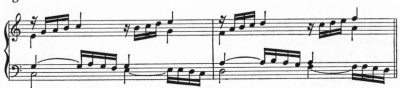

The didactic examples are accompanied by a large number of brief pieces, canzonas, toccatinas, correntes, galliards, etc. In *Pars* I (pp.28ff.), e.g., there are canzonas of about ten measures, among them an especially short *Canzone La Bartholina*, reproduced in Fig.612. Under the title "Adiunctum Frescobaldicum," Spiridio appends a number of longer compositions to *Pars* IV: canzonas, a *Hymnus de Dominica, Partite sopra Passacagli, Ciaccona, Aria* with six variations, and others.

Fig.612

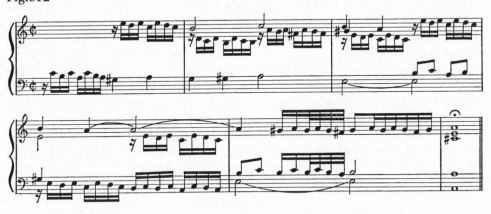

Georg Muffat

Georg Muffat was the descendant of a Scottish-English family that emigrated during the time of Queen Elizabeth, probably because they were Catholics. His mother

(Margarita Orsy) was French, and he was born at Mégève (Savoy) in 1653. As a child he lived in Schlettstedt (Alsace), studied in Paris from about 1663 to 1669 (probably with Lully), and became an organist at Molsheim (Alsace) in 1671. To escape the strains of war he traveled to Vienna and Prague, and became a court organist of the Salzburg archbishop in 1678. From Salzburg he journeyed to Rome (1681, 1682), where he became personally acquainted with Pasquini and Corelli. In 1690 he became the musical director at the episcopal court of Passau, and retained this position until his death in 1704. His creative estate consists chiefly of orchestral suites (*Armonico tributo*, 1682; *Florilegium* I/II, 1695/96) and keyboard pieces, which he published in 1690 under the title *Apparatus musico-organisticus*, as well as a few dance movements in the manuscript XIV. 743 of the Vienna monastery of the Brothers Minor.

Like Froberger, Muffat led a migratory existence, which brought him into contact with French, Italian, and German music and resulted in a synthesis of musical forms and styles. In the preface to the *Apparatus* he writes, "Although I know that something like this was printed seventy years ago, at the time of Frescobaldi, it seems to me that the significant difference in my style justifies the publication of a new work: . . . a style that is the result of the experience I have acquired in my contacts with the outstanding organists in Germany, Italy, and France, and which is hitherto not known." Although Muffat did not possess a strong enough personality to fuse the various elements into something quite new, he succeeded in absorbing them and coordinating them with good taste and a disciplined technique.

The *Apparatus* contains twelve toccatas, a chaconne, a passacaglia, and two other works under the title *Nova Cyclopeias Harmonica*: an *Aria* and a variation set entitled *Ad malleorum ictus allusio*.[27] The toccatas consist of five or six sections of varying length, which often carry such tempo designations as grave, adagio, allegro, vivace, and presto. The term adagio also occurs several times at ritardando endings of allegro movements. To give content to these sectional structures, Muffat resorts to the most varied approaches: toccata-like running passages combined with sustained chords; fugatos based on brief motifs; occasionally even complete fugues, which usually fade into other textures, however; and one-measure figures that are accommodated to the harmonic progressions and repeated many times. He makes extensive use of the pedals, to which he entrusts not only long pedal points but also independent melodic lines—probably for the first time in the South—e.g., in the final section of toccata no.1 (meas.51–62). Muffat indicates obbligato pedals by the terms *Pedale, Ped.,* or *P. s.* (i.e., *pedale solum*), and *ad libitum* doublings of the left hand by the abbreviation *P. m.* (*pedale ad manuale*). Double trills occur frequently, often introduced by Lombardic rhythms. Toccata-like introductions are often repeated by exchanging the materials of the two hands (cf. toccatas nos.3, 5, and 9). Muffat's toccatas also contain features that did not develop in keyboard music. The introductions to nos.7 and 10 are modeled after Lully's overtures, the latter using a formula that reappears in var.XVI of Bach's *Goldberg Variations*. Corelli's trio sonatas may have served as the archetype of the first allegro in no.8 and the first adagio in no.11. Other passages recall the style of the violin sonata (no.12, the adagio before the presto), of the aria (no.9, the adagio before the presto), or of the *recitativo accompagnato* (no.5., first and second adagios). Fig.613 shows some of these passages (the page numbers refer to De Lange's edition, those in parentheses to Walter's).

Fig.613

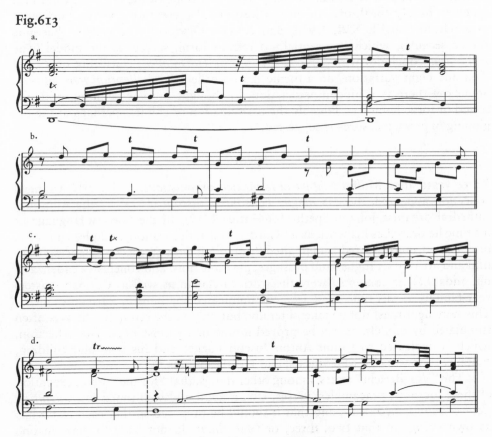

a. p.49(64); b. p.38(50); c. p.46(60); d. p.22(31).

Despite his eclecticism Muffat succeeds in unifying the various materials in his toccatas to form impressive and well written entities. Only now and then are there disturbing passages, which announce the decadence of organ music with sequential or modulatory repetitions of cheap formulae, e.g., the passage from no.1, shown in Fig.614.

Fig.614

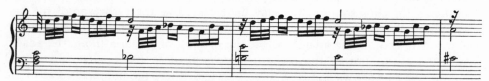

Among the other compositions in the *Apparatus* the passacaglia is particularly worthy of mention. It contains twenty-four renditions of the eight-measure idea (one can hardly speak of a theme), whose initial presentation recurs four times as a refrain (var.VI, XVI, XVIII, and XXIV). Obviously the French chaconne (or passecaille), which is essentially a refrain form, served as the model. The *Apparatus* concludes with a *Nova Cyclopeias Harmonica*, consisting of a brief *Aria* and eight variations on a theme that is called *Ad malleorum ictus allusio*. Somehow there is a hidden association, in thought or tone-painting, with the sound of forge hammers. Possibly the participation of chimes—perhaps at the beginning of every measure—is suggested.

Speth

Three years after Muffat's *Apparatus musico-organisticus*, a similarly arranged collection appeared, the *Ars magna consoni et dissoni* (1693) by the Augsburg cathedral organist Johann Speth (1664–after 1719). In the flowery language of his time he describes his work as a "Garden of art, decoration, and pleasantry . . . ornamented, embroidered, and planted throughout with pretty consonances, beautiful and artfully set fugues and passages, pleasant runs, and conclusive cadenzas," but adds that its contents "were the work of Italian as well as German masters very famous at this time" and are "communicated [by him] in a friendly spirit." This statement must not be taken literally, but only in the sense that he was often stimulated by models, as can be proved in one or two instances. The collection, which is dedicated to Count Anton Joseph Fugger and his wife and children, contains 10 toccatas, 8 Magnificats, and 3 variation sets.[28]

The "Vor-Bericht" states, among other things, that "for the correct execution of these toccatas, praeambles, verses, etc., a good and well-tuned *instrument* or *clavicordium* is necessary, and that it should be prepared so that each *clavir* has its own string, so that two, three, or four *clavir* do not have to play on one [string]." Thus the unfretted clavichord is demanded as early as 1693, although even in the most recent literature, its invention is ascribed to the "Crailsheim organist D. T. Faber in 1725."[29]

Speth's toccatas are shorter and more unified in style than Muffat's. Except for the first one, which contains two fugal sections, and no.5, which is toccata-like throughout, they all follow the scheme T F T. The toccata-like sections often consist of figurations above pedal points (e.g., no.1, beginning and end; no.2, end; no.3, end; all of no.5; no.6, beginning), or of chord progressions in the *durezze* style (no.2, beginning). As often occurs in Muffat, instrumental ensemble music served as the model for the *Toccata quarta;* its conclusion, given in Fig.615, fades out in a pianissimo. In the fugal sections, the subjects are usually answered at the fourth or lower fifth, occasionally at the octave, but only once (in no.10) at the fifth. Speth's toccatas are well-conceived works, simpler than Muffat's, but free of disturbing commonplaces and massed ornaments, whose application is left to the players' or "their teachers' dexterity."

Fig.615

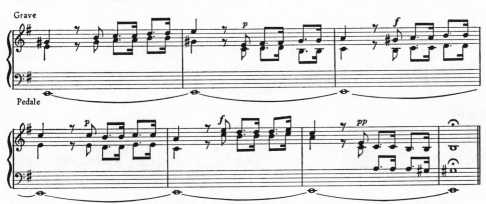

The Magnificat collection in Speth's *Ars magna* shows some similarity to the one in Kerll's *Modulatio organica* (cf.p.564). Both consist of seven versets for each of the eight toni, and in both the concluding versets (Speth calls them *Finale,* Kerll *Versus ultimus loco Antiphonae*) are toccata-like postludes. But while Kerll introduces the chant melody in the first versets, Speth opens each cycle with a free praeamble in toccata style. Fig. 616 shows the beginning of the cycle *Quinti toni.* The five middle versets are mostly brief fugatos on freely invented subjects, which are occasionally related to each other as variants, e.g., in the versets 4–6 *Tertii*

Fig.616

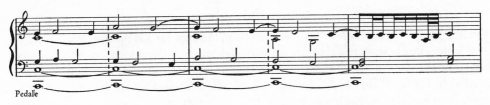

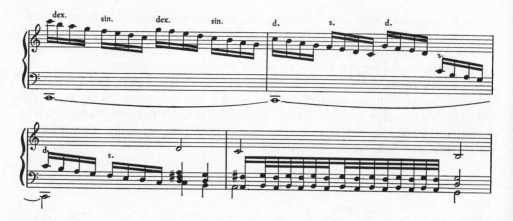

toni (Fig.617). ℣3 *Quinti toni* is a simplified and shortened version of the *Canzon Teutsch Trommel*, by Allessandro Poglietti, who is one of the "very famous masters" of whom Speth speaks in the preface.

Fig.617

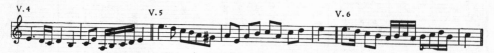

The *Ars magna* concludes with three variation sets on *L'aria detta la Todescha, L'aria detta la Pasquina,* and *La Spagnioletta,* each with six *partite.* The theme of the second set is obviously by Pasquini. The *Spagnioletta* has a passacaglia bass, reproduced in Fig.618, which shows a distant relationship with the bass of Bernardo Storace's *Spagnioletta* of 1664 (cf.p.682) as well as with the romanesca and other traditional themes.

Fig.618

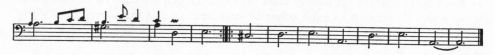

Fux

Johann Joseph Fux (1660–1741) has long been famous for his operas, instrumental ensemble works, and his *Gradus ad Parnassum,* but the fact that he was also active in the field of keyboard music has only become known through a recent edition in *DTÖ.*[30] This collection, which is called a selection in the introduction, contains 7 sonatas, 3 single pieces, 4 suites, and 12 minuets.[31]

The sonatas are doubtless ensemble works that were merely copied in keyboard score. A significant clavier piece is a *Ciaccona* in which the traditional four-measure theme (almost always expanded to eight measures by repetition) is varied thirty-three times. Var.I–XXVII are in *D* major, XXVIII–XXXII in *D* minor, and the first variation is repeated as a conclusion. The motivic formulae show great variety and the reinterpretations of the basic harmonic scheme are ingenious, e.g., in var.VII, XIX, XXVI, XXVIII, and XXXII. The second single piece is a prelude and fugue, whose first section (called *Harpeggio*) consists of arpeggiated chords interspersed with recitative-like passages, in the manner of Bach's *Chromatic Fantasy*. The third single work, *Aria passeggiata*, is a song that is varied by sixteenth-note passages.

Fig.619

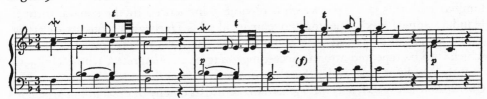

Suites nos.1, 3, and 4 exhibit the classic form A C S G, expanded by the insertion or addition of currently fashionable dances, while no.2 consists of *Aria, Rigaudon, Passepied, Echeggiata, Gigue,* and *Menuett,* and belongs to the ballet suite type. The traditional dances have an impressive wealth of contrapuntal-motivic workmanship, while the others depend on the natural charm of their melodies. In no.2 Fux repeatedly uses the echo effect, especially charmingly in the *Echeggiata,* shown in Fig.619. The frequent application of written-out or symbolized ornaments (generally the same ones used by D'Anglebert) reveals a French influence, which is also found in the works of earlier South German clavier masters, e.g., Georg Muffat. Fux shows a special predilection for the ornament called *tirata* in the Italian terminology of the early 17th century. It consists of a rapid run, either ascending or descending, and passing through a large interval, mostly an octave. The *Gigue* of no.1, from which Fig.620 is drawn, is particularly

Fig.620

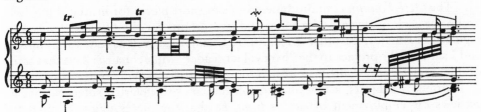

rich in such ornaments. According to Schenk's explanation the twelve minuets that conclude the volume represent a "well-organized cycle," in which one finds suggestions of the "stamping rhythm of the Alpine Yodel," the ländler, and other traits from the realm of "popular-Alpine" music.[32]

A volume of *Werke für Tasteninstrumente* appeared in 1964 as part of a complete Fux edition.[33] In this volume the sonatas are correctly omitted, and the real keyboard repertoire is enlarged by two works, an *Ouverture* in G major (in two versions, nos.5a and 5b) and a *Capriccio* in G minor (no.6). The *Ouverture* is a suite, which starts with a movement in the style of the French overture and concludes with a series of dance movements. In the *Sarabande* Fux's favored *tirata* is symbolized by an oblique dash above a dot. The *Capriccio* represents a novel type of suite, in which the dance movements are replaced by freely invented pieces, characterized mostly by tempo indications. The modern musician is familiar with this late type, which is obviously influenced by the sonata, through Handel's suites. Fux's opening movement, like his *Harpeggio,* consists of arpeggiated chords interspersed with recitative-like passages. It is followed by a *Fuga,* which is to be repeated after a succeeding *Adagio;* an *Allegretto,* whose character is aptly put by a title added by the copyist: *La Superbia;* a little piece entitled *Gustuoso* (or *Arietta*); a *Tempo giusto* that consists chiefly of descending arpeggios and for this reason was probably inscribed by the copyist as *L'Humilta;* an *Affettuoso* (or *La vera pace*); and finally an *Allegro-Finale.* The whole work is richly varied and captivating—probably the most outstanding preserved keyboard composition by Fux.

Murschhauser

Franz Xaver Murschhauser was born at Zabern (Alsace) in 1663, but went to Munich in 1676, where he spent the rest of his life. He was first active as a singer at St. Peter's, and from 1691 on was the choir director at the parish church of Unser Lieben Frau. He died in 1738. With his theoretical treatise *Academia Musico-Poetica Bipartita* (1721) he became enmeshed in a polemic with Mattheson, which, as would be expected, ended with his defeat. His contribution to keyboard music consists chiefly of two prints, the *Octi-Tonium novum organicum* of 1696 and the *Prototypon Longo-Breve organicum* (*Prima pars* 1703, *Pars secunda* 1707).[34]

The *Octi-Tonium* contains nine groups of short pieces for liturgical use—one group for each of seven psalm tones and two groups for the *Quintus tonus,* one *regularis* in F major, the other *irregularis* in C major—as well as four variation sets and a suite. In the preface to the "benevolent reader" Murschhauser says that some of the versets are written in the "cromatico stylo gravi," others on lighter ("laetoribus") subjects, a few on two subjects or with inverted subjects; that he eschews the employment of *cantus firmi,* so that the pieces might be used for

Fig.621

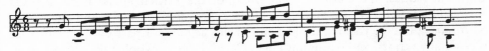

psalmody as well as for the Magnificat; that instead of the grandiose ("gloriosi") terms toccata and canzona he chooses the simpler names prelude and fugue; and that his teacher Kerll is his model.

In the general arrangement of the *Octi-Tonium* the similarity with Kerll's *Modulatio organica* is unmistakable. Like Kerll, Murschhauser writes seven pieces for each tone: a praeamble, five fugues, and a finale. The main difference is that Kerll works out his first piece on the basis of the Magnificat tone, while Murschhauser (like Speth) conceives it as a free prelude. The preludes and postludes are mostly movements of fifteen to twenty measures, composed of the usual figurations, complementary motifs, arpeggios, and trill cadences, and several have pedal points. Some of the fugues are miniatures of only five or six measures, others are twice as long, but only a few reach a length of twenty measures (e.g., the *Fuga 5ta, Sexti toni*). The subjects are hardly weighty, but are well-designed; the answers are made mostly at the fourth or lower fifth. One of the few fugues with an answer at the fifth and a modulation to the dominant is no.4, *Quinti toni irregularis,* shown in Fig.621. Fugue no.3, *Septimi toni* is an example of the *cromaticus stylus gravis*. It has the interesting subject (| *d' a f♯ f* | *b♭ a* |). Fugue no.5, *Secundi toni,* is also chromatic, but not in the *stylus gravis*. A chromatic counter-motif leads to a particualrly interesting final passage, which is reproduced in Fig.622. Fugue no.4, *Sexti toni,* is a prime example *en miniature* of an inversion fugue.

Fig.622

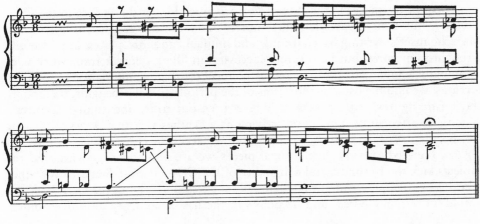

The four variation sets added to the verset collection are based on popular Christmas songs, the German counterpart of the French noëls: *Lasst uns das Kindelein wiegen, Aria pastoralis, Gegruest seyest du O Jesulein,* and again *Aria pastoralis,* all in the rocking triple meter of the siciliano or pastorale. The first set is especially attractive; "per imitationem Cuculi," the cuckoo's call is heard again and again, e.g., in the beginning of the second variation, shown in Fig.623. The suite that concludes the print consists of the four traditional movements, with the sarabande followed by a variation (*Partita*) and a minuet (*Menue*).

Fig.623

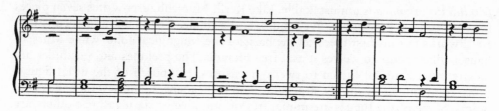

Like the *Octi-Tonium*, Murschhauser's *Prototypon* consists of key cycles, the "frequentiores toni" appearing in the first part (1703), and the others in the second (1707). Among the "more usual modes" Murschhauser counts the first (*D minor*), second (*G minor*), third (*E minor*), and seventh (*G major*); in the others he includes the eighth (*G major*), tenth (*A minor*), eleventh (*C major*), and twelfth (*F major*). Confusion and uncertainty in the concept of keys reaches its absolute zenith here. Each cycle consists of free settings and fugues, in a varied, often illogical order. The *Primus tonus*, e.g., consists of an *Intonatio, Praeambulum, Fuga I, Fuga II, Fuga finalis,* and *Praeambulum;* the *Septimus tonus* of a *Finale, Fuga I, Praeambulum,* and *Fuga II;* the *Undecimus tonus* of a *Toccata pro pedali, Fuga brevis, Fuga sive Canzon II, Praeambulum,* and *Arpeggiata.*

Most of the pieces in the *Prototypon* are much longer than those in the *Octi-Tonium,* but their greater length is not to their advantage. In a small format Murschhauser's writing is charming and unified, and his pieces are carefully wrought miniatures, but he is rarely successful in filling a larger framework with meaningful content. In the free pieces of the *Prototypon,* intonations, preludes, toccatas, we find the usual mannerisms of the period—trivial arpeggios, threadbare clavieristic figures, scale passages, long written-out trills, and similar features—added one after another without arriving at a synthesis. A few *Arpeggiate* (new ed., pp.133, 151, 162) use suspension and acciaccatura chords such as those in Fig.624 (new ed., p.151). In the fugal pieces we are immediately aware that the subjects lack the freshness and originality of the *Octi-Tonium*. Seiffert says[35] that "the devices of counterpoint that were only suggested briefly [in the *Octi-Tonium*] unfold more richly here," and he points to the use of contrary motion, counter-

Fig.624

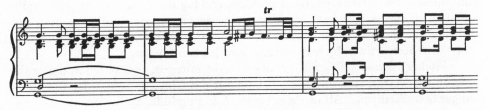

subjects, rhythmic-melodic transformations, and in one piece (p.132), a combination of contrary motion, augmentation, diminution, and transformation of the subject. From the technical point of view Seiffert's statement is quite correct, but aesthetically the result is unsatisfactory in many instances, especially in the longer fugues. The beginning of the fugue on p.132, given in Fig.625, is an illustration.

Fig.625

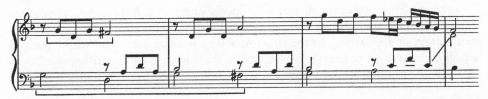

In the longer preludes and fugues, Murschhauser, a practical man, often writes "NB" to indicate places where the player may stop or turn to a final chord if he wishes to shorten the piece. A table of ornaments added to the preface is also noteworthy. It contains some unusual symbols, and shows the Italian trill starting on the main note. Murschhauser often uses this trill in written-out form as well (e.g., on pp. 142, 150).

Fischer

Despite much research the date and place of birth of Johann Caspar Ferdinand Fischer are still unknown. He was probably born about 1670 (certainly not around 1650) in Bohemia. From the title page of his first publication, *Journal du Printemps,* we learn that in 1695 he was the musical director for Margrave Ludwig of Baden at his residence at Schlackenwerth (north of Karlsbad). He later followed the Margrave to his new residence at Rastatt, and died there, probably in 1746. Four prints of his keyboard works are known:

1. *Les Pièces de Clavessin . . . Oeuvre II* (Slacoverde = Schlackenwerth, 1696); second edition, entitled *Musicalisches Blumen-Büschlein* (Augsburg, 1699[?])
2. *Ariadne musica* (1702[?]; preserved only in a new print, Augsburg, 1715)
3. *Blumen-Strauss* (Augsburg, undated; R. Sietz in *MGG* gives the date as 1732)
4. *Musikalischer Parnassus* (Augsburg, undated; *MGG* gives the date as 1738)[36]

The *Blumen-Büschlein* and the *Parnassus* are collections of suites, the *Ariadne* and the *Blumen-Strauss* mainly of preludes and fugues. A number of other, rather amateurish pieces that have been preserved in manuscript and have been published under the title *Notenbüchlein für Clavier*[37] are certainly not by Fischer, but may have been written by his youngest son, Johann Caspar.

Fischer's *Blumen-Büschlein* contains eight suites or, as is stated in the dedication to the Margravine of Baden, "allein auf das Clavicordium, oder Instrument eingerichte Parthyen." All of them begin with a prelude, but otherwise they vary in organization. Only two, nos.1 and 6, approach the usual type, the first with the order A C S followed by a gavotte and minuet, the other with A C S G plus a bourrée and minuet. Nos.2, 3, 4, and 7 consist of fashionable French dances—ballet, canarie, passepied, gavotte, and others—and thus belong to the ballet suite type, which is only occasionally found in Germany, e.g., Fux and Böhm each wrote only one. Nos.5 and 8 can hardly be called suites, for in addition to the prelude the former contains only an aria with eight variations and the latter a lengthy chaconne.

Some of the preludes are veritable jewels of musical miniatures, developing a simple idea or an attractive motif in twenty or thirty measures, with the harmony modulating and returning to the tonic in a very natural way. The whole piece is a polite yet serious conversation, in which the various voices participate freely. The prelude to no.3, whose beginning is given in Fig.626, is particularly beautiful.

Fig.626

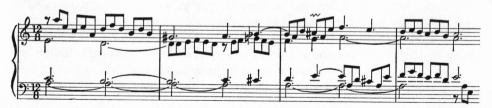

The strong prevalence of fashionable French dances is easily explained by the geographic position of the court of Baden. However, keyboard suites written in France continue to be based on the traditional four dances until the early 18th century, e.g., those by d'Anglebert (1689), Gaspard le Roux (1705), and François Couperin (*Livre I*, 1713). The ballet suite seems to have developed in German orchestral music. The earliest examples are found in the works of Kusser (*Composition de musique,* 1682), Georg Muffat (Florilegium, 1695/96), and Fischer (*Journal de Printemps,* 1695). The inspiration came from Lully, who frequently arranged overtures and dances from his operas for concert performances. Fischer was among the earliest composers to transplant this type to the clavier. His gavottes, bourrées, and passepieds represent a combination of French and German spirit, which he achieved as successfully as Bach.

Fischer's *Ariadne musica* is the most important predecessor of Bach's *Well-Tempered Clavier*. The first edition is supposed to have appeared in 1702. Just as Ariadne, in Greek mythology, used a thread to lead Theseus out of the Cretan labyrinth, this work leads the organist out of the difficulties and errors of his art to sure fame—thus Fischer describes the purpose of his work in the ponderous Latin of his preface. His "errorum gravissimorum pericula" are the dangerous province of keys, which grew to ever greater numbers during the period, and replaced the traditional church modes. The seventeen anonymous suites printed in *DTB* II.1[38] represent seventeen keys. Fischer adds two more, *F* minor and *B* major, so that only five are missing from the complete circle of fifths, *C♯* major, *E♭* minor, *F♯* major, *A♭* minor, and *B♭* minor. Curiously, *E* minor appears twice, once without a key signature and once with two sharps (no.VII). The order is the same as in the *Well-Tempered Clavier,* except that the minor always precedes the major and *C* minor is shifted to the end of the collection (no.XX).

Fig.627

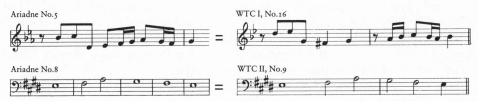

Each key is represented by a prelude and fugue, exactly as in Bach's work. Bach certainly knew the *Ariadne* and used it as his model. Not only does the identical planning bear out this assumption but there are also many corresponding details, which are too striking to be ascribed to coincidence. Two particularly obvious examples are shown in Fig.627. In contrast to Bach's substantial preludes and fugues in the *Well-Tempered Clavier*, Fischer preserves the small format of the South German verset collections, such as Kerll's *Modulatio organica* (1686) or Murschhauser's *Octi-Tonium* (1696). The preludes in *Ariadne* tend to be more unified and concentrated than those in the *Blumen-Büschlein*. They have the admirable quality of being able to say what is needed within the smallest framework. The same is true of the fugues, which, in contrast to many fugues of the period, preserve the appropriate contrapuntal texture throughout. Almost all of the subjects are significant, whether they are of the ricercar type (nos.8, 9), more canzona-like (nos.4, 20), or dance-like (nos.10, 12), or, without leaning on recognizable models, freely and almost as well invented as Bach's fugue subjects. The word "almost" here is decisive. Nothing marks Bach's preeminence over his predecessors in the field of keyboard music as palpably as the absolutely "right" and convincing formulation of his fugue subjects, and it is borne out with particular clarity in these instances where a certain similarity can be recognized.

In addition to the twenty preludes and fugues that constitute the main content, the *Ariadne* includes five *Ricercaras super . . . Ecclesiasticas Cantilenas,* i.e., compositions on spiritual songs. The first one, *Ave Maria klare,* is a Catholic melody, while the others are well-known Protestant chorales—*Der Tag der ist so freudenreich, Da Jesu an dem Creutze stund, Crist ist erstanden,* and *Kom heiliger Geist*—all of which, however, derive from Latin hymns. Each ricercar is a fugue of moderate length based on the initial line of the respective melody, and each involves a countersubject, which is woven into the texture as an obbligato counterpoint.

The two other publications by Fischer belong to a period that lies beyond the limitations of this volume, and they do not add anything particularly new to the picture established by the two earlier works. The *Musikalischer Parnassus* contains nine suites (*Parthien*), each of which carries the name of one of the muses. Here, too, each suite starts with a prelude, with such titles as *Praeludium harpeggiato, Ouverture, Toccatina,* or *Tastada.* Two suites follow the classical pattern: no.1 (*Clio*) with allemande—courante—sarabande—ballet—minuet—gigue, and no.9 (*Uranie*) with allemande—courante—sarabande—gavotte—gigue—rigaudon—minuet —passepied. The others generally have an allemande after the prelude and then continue with other dances, sometimes including a gigue. Several times the minuet appears in the alternativo arrangement of minuet I—minuet II—minuet I, which reappears in the works of the Viennese classicists as minuet—trio—minuet. The final movement of the last suite is a long passacaglia.

Like the *Ariadne,* the *Blumen-Strauss* consists of preludes and fugues, and therefore belongs to the organ more than to stringed keyboard instruments. In arrangement this collection is not a predecessor of the *Well-Tempered Clavier,* but is obviously an imitation of Murschhauser's *Octi-Tonium.* It contains only eight cycles, though, and also differs in that six fugues, instead of the five in the *Octi-Tonium,* are inserted between the prelude and the finale. There are many attractive pieces, but nothing that indicates real artistic progress over the *Ariadne.* A comparison of the two suite collections yields the same judgment: The later one is perhaps of equal stature with the earlier one, but definitely not superior to it.

B. NORTH GERMANY

During the first half of the 17th century an outstanding artistic evolution was initiated in North Germany by a surprisingly large number of important masters. The three Praetoriuses, Scheidt, Scheidemann, Schildt, Delphin Strunck, and Morhardt constitute a group that is without equal in the organ music of the period. In the succeeding period as well, each decade produced one or two major organ masters: Tunder, Weckmann, Reincken, Buxtehude, Lübeck, Böhm, Hanff, Bruhns, and several others who take a worthy place beside them. They primarily cultivated three species: the prelude, the toccata, and the organ chorale. What they created in these fields outshines all the other keyboard music that was produced during the second half of the 17th century. It constitutes an organ repertoire of magnificence and of grandiose pathos, filled with dramatic gestures, and sustained by a spirit of visionary mysticism which has been compared, justifiably, with the transcendentalism of the late Gothic era. Traits pointing to this style can be found in the works of Michael Praetorius, Scheidemann, Schildt, and Delphin Strunck, but the style emerges fully formed for the first time in the works of Tunder.

Tunder

Born in 1614 in Burg on the Baltic island of Fehmarn, Franz Tunder played the organ at the court of Gottorp in Schleswig from 1632 to 1641. In 1641 he was chosen to play at the Marienkirche at Lübeck, and died there in 1667. The Lüneburg tablatures preserve four preludes and seven organ chorales; two additional chorale settings are in the Pelplin tablatures; and there is a canzona in Uppsala, Univ. Libr., Ihre Ms.285.[39]

The preludes consist—as Scheidemann's occasionally did—of a free introduction, a fugal section, and a free postlude, and are really toccatas in a smaller framework. The fugues are somewhat awkward, and too filled with subject matter; by contrast the free sections are all the more convincing and magnificent. Characteristic of the North German style are the dramatic gestures at beginnings. With a movement that is both erratic and purposeful, they introduce the first full chord, and, in a manner of speaking, "apostrophize" it (cf.p.370), as e.g., in the G-minor prelude (Fig.628).

The North German display style manifests itself even more impressively in Tunder's organ chorales. Ordered by species, they may be divided into six chorale fantasies (*In dich hab ich gehoffet, Komm Heiliger Geist, Herr Gott dich loben*

Fig.628

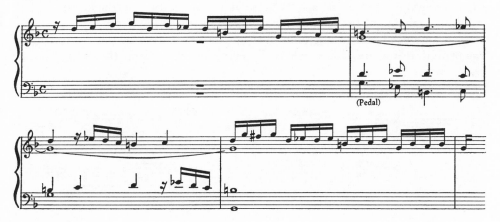

wir, Was kann uns kommen an für Not I and II, *Christ lag in Todesbanden*—the last two in the Pelplin tablatures), two chorale variations (*Auf meinen lieben Gott, Jesus Christus unser Heiland*), and a chorale motet (*Jesus Christus wahr Gottes Sohn*). Among Scheidemann's known organ chorales, the fantasy is still secondary numerically, but in Tunder's output it occupies first place, and he develops this type of chorale setting into a well-defined species, which became a kind of standard or at least a model. It is therefore valuable to go into some detail here about the methods applied. As a basic principle each chorale line is heard twice in its entirety: once in the soprano, ornamented, and once in the bass, unornamented. Occasionally the line is shifted into the tenor, but only when the pedal basses pause, causing the tenor to function as the lowest part. The full chorale line is very rarely imitated in all voices, and fore-imitation occurs only once or twice. Fragmentation, however, is very important. Usually the six to eight notes of the line plus the ornamentation of the first and last notes yield two motifs, which are extensively developed in a lengthy section using imitation, complementary treatment, echo repetitions, or similar devices. Sometimes several figures ornament the beginning or end of the line, as, e.g., in measures 137f. and 142f. of *Herr Gott dich loben wir* (Fig.629).

Fig.629

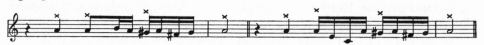

For the ornamentation of the entire chorale line Tunder at times still uses the older method of connecting the individual notes with even running passages, as, e.g., in *Herr Gott dich loben wir*, measures 108ff. But elsewhere there appears a new kind of figuration (which had already been anticipated by Scheidemann), in which a note is stressed expressively by an individual figure only here and there. A lovely example, interesting also because of its bold gestures at the beginning and end, is the opening of *In dich hab ich gehoffet*, shown in Fig.630.

Various echo effects not only play an important role in the course of the fragmentation but are also occasionally employed to enliven the entire chorale

Fig.630

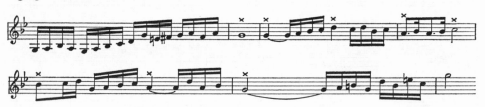

line. Two examples, are given in Fig.631: a. *Komm Heiliger Geist,* measures 100ff., b. *Was kann uns kommen an für Not* I, measures 121f. (R = Rückpositive; O = Organ).

Fig.631

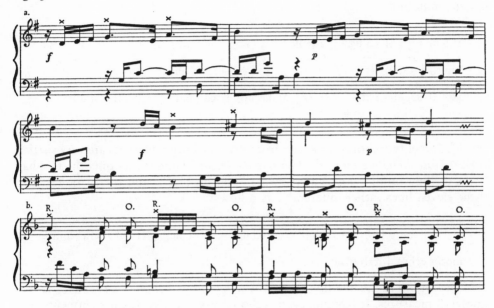

The way these methods are employed in the course of the composition may be shown schematically. Numbers 1, 2, 3, etc., indicate full chorale lines, 1a or 1b fragments derived from the beginning or end of the line. The symbols in parentheses indicate the voice that carries each chorale line (S = soprano, B = bass), the note value when a diminution is involved (e.g., ♩), and figuration when it applies (fig.); F stands for fore-imitation.

In dich hab ich gehoffet. The chorale consists of five lines. For the last line Tunder does not use the melody given in the new edition (g | f g b♭ c' | b♭ a g |) but the variant (g | f g a d' | b♭ a g |). Especially interesting are the passages starting in measures 22 and 64, which alternate between two motifs, sometimes in imitation and sometimes in echo-like repetition.

meas.1   6   11   18   22
1 (S fig.) | 1 (B) || 2 (S fig. and B in stretto) || 3 (S fig.) | 3a, 3b (imit., echo) |

    33   39   44   48   53   57   61   64
| 3 (B) | 3 (S fig.) || 4 (S fig.) | 4 (B) || 5a (imit.) | 5b (imit.) | 5 (S♩) | 5, 5b

           78   83   87–93
(imit. echo) | 5 (B) | 5 (S fig.) || coda

Komm Heiliger Geist. The chorale divides into nine lines. The composition starts with a single ornamented presentation of the first three lines. The other lines are more extensively treated, except for line 7, which appears only in fore-imitation and discant figuration. Note especially the section beginning with measure 19, where line 4 is heard three times in a row with different figuration as well as in canonic imitation.

meas.1   7   13   19   26   29   34
1 (S fig.) || 2 (F+S fig.) || 3 (S fig.) || 4 (♩ fig. and imit.) | 4 (B♩) | 4 (S fig.) || 5a

       47   51   55   59   61   73   76
(imit.) | 5 (S♩) |5 (S fig.) || 6 (B) | 6 (S♩) | 6a, 6b (imit.) | 6 (S fig.) || 7 (F+S

      87   100   107   114
fig.) || 8a, 8b (imit.) | 8 (S♩ fig. and echo) || 9a (imit.) | 9 (S echo and fig.) ||

120   132–140
8 and 9 (S fig.) || coda

The other two chorale fantasies from the Lüneburg tablatures are very similar. In *Herr Gott dich loben wir,* the German *Te Deum,* Tunder uses only the first half of the melody (until "Gott Vaters ewger Sohn du bist"), and treats the last two of the eleven lines rather differently, as follows:

103   108   113   117   125   131   137
10 (S) || 11 (S fig.) || 10 (B) || 11 (F+S fig.) | 11 (T fig.) | 11 (B) | 11a (comp.

            146   148–154
motifs echo) | 11b (B♩) || coda

The setting of the five-line chorale *Was kann uns kommen an für Not* is very long, 258 measures. It has numerous echo effects and two fugal treatments of a whole line (meas.101–20 and 145–60), a method that Tunder employs only rarely in his chorale fantasies. The two chorale fantasies from the Pelplin tablatures are very long also: *Christ lag in Todesbanden* has 239 measures, and a second setting of *Was kann uns kommen an* has 180, but seems to be incomplete. Fig.632 shows a passage from the former in which the two hands alternate with brief motifs between the two manuals, while the pedals play the chorale tune.

Fig.632

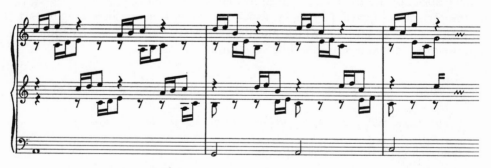

The chorale variation is represented in Tunder's works by *Auf meinen lieben Gott* and *Jesus Christus unser Heiland,* each consisting of three variations. The former, set "auf 2 Claviere manualiter," includes two presentations in the manner of the discant chorale, the first ornamenting the melody, the second (meas. 17–35) unadorned, and a variation in the form of an extended fantasy (meas. 36–145).

In contrast to this composition, which is almost lyrical in effect, the variation set on *Jesus Christus unser Heiland* is the most grandiose and dramatic of Tunder's works. The first variation, which is in five parts with double pedals, begins with an apostrophe that is entrusted to the pedals; it leads to the chorale, which is heard in the upper pedal part. In the second half of this variation a characteristic scale motif is introduced (Fig.633a.), which may be recognized as having a pictorial-symbolic meaning referring to the text phrase "der von uns den Gotteszorn wandt," all the more so, since similar "averting" motifs recur in the other two variations (Fig.633b., c.). In the second variation the melody appears in the tenor, played by the left hand, while the two upper voices and the pedal part are developed from motif b., whose relentless, warning repetitions imbue the piece with

Fig.633

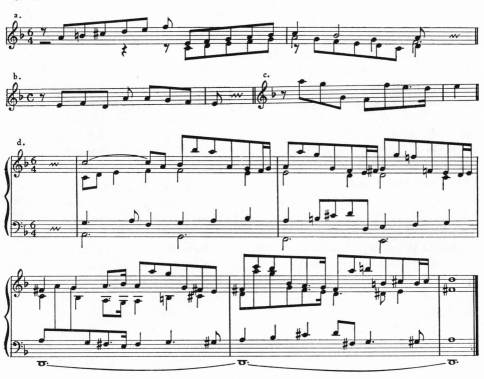

tragic greatness. In the third variation the chorale is the lowest part and is played by the pedals. Above it motif c. is heard again and again, in both its original and inverted forms, one of the boldest and most dramatic gestures in the entire literature of Baroque organ music. The tension increases continually, until it reaches its climax in a concluding passage of apocalyptic sublimity. The massed leading tones of the last measures are the highest achievement of the "Gothic" organ style of the 17th century (Fig.633d.). This composition deviates so strikingly from Tunder's other works that only two explanations can account for it: Either it is a singular work from the last years of his life or it is the work of a younger composer—but whose? In any event, it is the only Tunder piece in Lüneburg KN 209 that is not signed "F. Tunder" but only "F. T."

Finally we turn to Tunder's chorale motet, *Jesus Christus wahr Gottes Sohn*. The chorale melody is one of the few in 3/2 time. Its six lines are treated in six imitative sections, in a purely contrapuntal setting of great simplicity, a simplicity that presupposes a sovereign technique. Certainly this work, too, is mature and late, although it is completely different in character from *Jesus Christus unser Heiland*. It also concludes with massed leading tones—with a Lydian cadence in which both octave and fifth are reached by half-tones steps (*f♯–g, c♯–d*).

Weckmann

Information about Matthias Weckmann's life comes primarily from the report in Mattheson's *Ehrenpforte*. Born in 1619 (or 1621?) in the little town of Niederdorla (Thuringia), he came to the Dresden Court in 1630 as a boy singer under the direction of Heinrich Schütz; but because his voice was weak, he was sent to Hamburg to become an organist. There he studied with Jacob Praetorius from 1637 to 1640, and also became acquainted with Scheidemann. Mattheson writes, "Since he also had the good fortune to hear the agreeable Scheidemann at St. Catherine's and to visit his Vespers, he was able to moderate the Praetorian seriousness with a Scheidemannian grace, and to introduce many *galant* ideas." From 1641 Weckmann was active as court organist at Dresden, and for a while at Copenhagen also, until he took over the office of organist at St. Jacobi at Hamburg in 1655, a position he retained until his death in 1674. Toward the end of his Dresden period, he was declared victorious in a competition with Froberger in keyboard virtuosity, though local pride may have played a role in the decision. But more importantly it was the beginning of a lasting relationship, as Mattheson says: "The two artists continued an intimate correspondence afterwards, and Froberger sent Weckmann a suite in his [Froberger's] own hand, in which he set all the ornaments, so that Weckmann became familiar with Froberger's manner of playing."

Weckmann's preserved keyboard works include 9 compositions on chorale melodies, 8 fugal pieces, 6 toccatas, 5 suites, and a variation set. Let us begin with the chorale settings, most of which were probably written during or soon after his student years with Praetorius and Scheidemann. They follow the older tradition, as is shown by the fact that all of them are chorale variations, i.e., of the type that predominates in Sweelinck and Scheidt, but was already largely abandoned by Jacob Praetorius and Scheidemann and only rarely used by Tunder. The works are: *Magnificat secundi toni* (4 var.), *Komm heiliger Geist* (3 var.), *Gelobet seist du* I (4 var.), *O lux beata Trinitas* (11 var.), *Es ist das Heil* (7 var.), *Nun freut euch* (3 var.), *Gott sei gelobet* (3 var.), *Gelobet seist du* II (3 var.), and *Ach wir armen Sünder* (3 var.).[40]

Fig.634

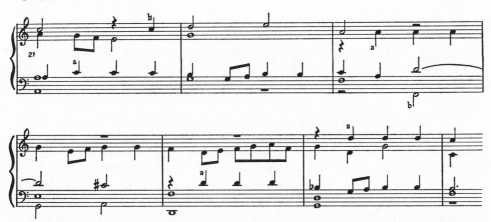

As in the overall formulation, Weckmann also follows the older tradition in details of construction and style. A number of features in his chorale variations are strikingly conservative for the time in which they were written. This is especially true of *O lux beata Trinitas,* a long composition in six *Versus,* of which the *Quartus versus* comprises four connected variations and the *Quintus versus* three, making a total of eleven variations. In the first seven variations (*Versus* I–IV) the hymn melody is treated in the antiquated manner of a strict *cantus planus* in whole notes. In the first three variations counterpoints are added to it, which evolve throughout from a freely invented countersubject (two such subjects in the first variation), so that one may describe these pieces as combinations of *cantus planus* and fugue. Fig.634 shows a passage from the first variation (the two countersubjects are marked "a" and "b"). This interesting and very dexterously employed technique has practically no counterparts in German organ chorales. The four variations of the *Quartus versus* are written entirely in the "old German" manner, i.e., modeled after Samuel Scheidt. The first two variations are bicinia, in which the sustained notes of the *cantus planus* are contrasted with continuous sixteenth-note passages, while in the other two it is combined with a two-part Zarlino *Canon post semiminimam*. In the *Quintus versus* the hymn tune is presented three times as an ornamented melody, first in the soprano, then (meas.31) in the tenor, and finally (meas.57) in the soprano again, mostly with brief fore-imitations for the individual lines. The figuration is often very schematic and dry, indeed threatens to smother the chorale instead of enlivening it, as Scheidemann's, and especially Tunder's, do. Fig.635 presents a particularly crass case. The *Sextus versus* is of the same type as the first three. Above the *cantus planus* in the bass four counterpoints intone a fugal texture, which is based on a syncopated subject in the first half and on a chromatic subject (which perhaps is a variant of the former) in the second half.

Fig.635

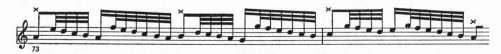

The cycle on *Es ist das Heil uns kommen her*, which consists of seven variations, called *Versus*, is almost as long as *O lux beata Trinitas*. The first and last variations belong to the *cantus-planus*-plus-fugue type mentioned above; the former combines a kind of four-part fugue with the chorale in the bass, the latter a kind of inversion fugue in five parts, ingeniously accommodated to the chorale, which is placed in a middle voice. Variations II, IV, and V are Zarlino canons, like the canonic variations VI–VII in *O lux beata Trinitas*. The *Sextus versus* is a chorale fantasy, which is not devoid of interesting details, such as the fragmentation applied in the first section (meas.1–63) or the extended pedal point at the end; however, with its 238 measures it far exceeds the admissible bounds of a variation set.

Weckmann's other chorale settings have only three or four variations, and keep more within the proper framework. The three main treatments observed above—the *cantus-planus* bicinium, the Zarlino canon, and the combination of chorale with fugue—do not occur in them. Their place is taken by freer and more contemporary methods, though the chorale motet is surprisingly absent. Several times Weckmann employs the chorale, either in its unadorned form or lightly paraphrased, as the basis of an impressively artful contrapuntal setting of four, five, or in one instance, even six voices, e.g., in variations I, III, and IV of the Magnificat and in variation I of *Nun freut euch*. In the initial variation of *Komm heiliger Geist*, the chorale, which is heard in the soprano, is enlivened here and there by expressive melodic lines, similar to what we hear in many of Buxtehude's chorales. Four sets (*Komm heiliger Geist, Nun freut euch*, and the two *Gelobet seist du*) conclude with a tricinium in which two upper parts with lively ornamentation are combined with the chorale in the bass, a method that Pachelbel often used later on. The tricinium from *Nun freut euch* is particularly interesting for the variety of its figurations and especially for the chromatic figures toward the end. In *Gelobet seist du* I (Ilgner, p. 70; cf. note 40 above) the second variation is a long chorale fantasy with many changes of registration and echoes; in the third variation the chorale tune is heard twice in the tenor with different ornamentation.

Weckmann, even more often than Tunder, employs triplet figures, mostly to embroider the chorale tune (cf. Ilgner, pp.59, 96, 113) but occasionally in the counterpoints, too (cf.p.125). In several variations quarter-note triplets are introduced by changing the time from 4/4 to 6/4 (cf.pp.61, 62). Weckmann tends to superficial and somewhat cheap effects, particularly in the chorale fantasy in *Gelobet seist du* I with its arpeggios and trills (p.75). In general, many of Weckmann's chorale settings suffer from his penchant for pedantry and dry schematism. Especially where figurations occur, whether they are in the chorale or in the counterpoints, a lack of inspiration and *élan* is felt, a lack that, to be sure, occasionally emerges in Sweelinck's and Scheidt's music, but is even more disturbing here because Weckmann aspires to more but is unable to attain it—quite in contrast to Tunder, where aspiration and capability are equally great. Nevertheless there are several fine, impressive pieces among the unornamented settings, especially among the initial variations of the cycles.

There is one exception to these general remarks, the variations on *Ach wir armen Sünder*. This composition is the only one of Weckmann's nine chorale works that is not preserved in the Lüneburg tablatures, but is found in a much later manuscript, Berlin Staatsbibl. P.802. It consists of three variations, which form a very unified, lyrical whole. The chorale tune is heard throughout in a "song-like" line of quarter notes—unadorned in the tenor in variation I, occasionally ornamented in the soprano in variation II, and similarly treated in the bass in variation III. Free of all schematism and formalism, the voices unfold in gently flowing lines and attractive harmonies, in a style very different from that of the other chorales. Dietrich explains the striking individuality of this work by pointing to Mattheson's remark about the "Scheidemannian grace," but Hedar tends to dispute Weckmann's authorship and "to look for the author in the circle of Buxtehude."[41] I agree with Hedar unhesitatingly. The lyrical character of this especially beautiful

Fig.636

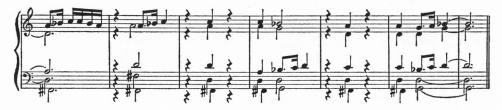

work has nothing to do with Scheidemannian grace, but unmistakably points to a period perhaps even later than 1700, long after Weckmann's death.

Fig.637

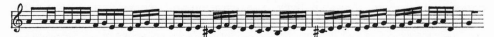

We will discuss only a few details of Weckmann's secular compositions—fugal pieces, toccatas, and suites.[42] In fantasy no.1 there is a passage that anticipates an effect that Buxtehude employed frequently, the insertion of dramatic rests, see Fig.636. A new type of fugue subject, which came into much favor during the second half of the 17th century, makes its first appearance in canzona no.7. It consists of long stretches of running sixteenth notes, often starting with a tone repetition, as shown in Fig.637. Toccata no.12 in *E* minor, which is well-suited to either organ or harpsichord, is especially impressive. It proceeds throughout in a freely improvising manner, its dreamy, romantic expression unmistakably showing the influence of Froberger. It starts with an *E*-minor chord, which rises in a slow arpeggio from the lowest to the highest register (Fig.638a.). This is followed by faster chordal figures, which are occasionally interrupted by recitative-like exclamations (Fig.638b.), then by a lengthy section that elaborates an idea derived from the contemporary trio sonata (Fig.638c.), and finally by a few measures of figurations that conclude with a very individual cadence that sounds like a question (Fig.638d.).

Fig.638

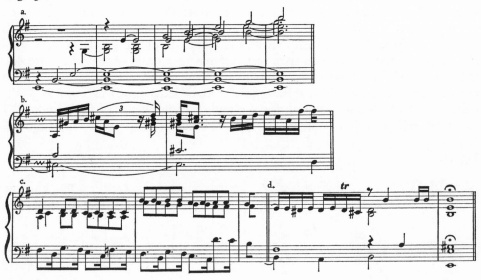

Weckmann's five suites, if they are really his, also point to his acquaintance with Froberger. Two of them (Buchmayer K, II, p.37 and III, p.28) exhibit the Frobergerian order A G C S, with the gigue in second place; two others (Buchmayer K I, p.32 and Ilgner p.135) show the later arrangement of A C S G (the first of these even includes an introductory prelude); and the fifth suite (Ilgner, p.138) consists of A G S, but it is probably incomplete. The beginning of the second suite, given in Fig.639, illustrates how much the style of these suites resembles Froberger's.

Fig.639

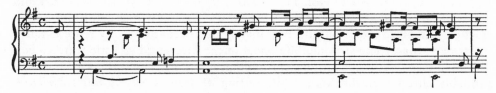

Finally, there is a secular variation set (Buchmayer K, I, p. 35). It is based on a charming student song, *Die lieblichen Blicke,* which is treated to four rather attractive variations. The theme is lightly ornamented in the first one and variously embroidered in the others.

Wilhelm Karges, Lorentz, N. Hasse, and Kortkamp

Wilhelm Karges was born in 1613 or 1614 and died in 1699 at Berlin, where he had been active since 1646 as a chamber musician at the Brandenburg court and as a cathedral organist. It is clear from purely chronological observations that he is not identical with the W. Karges who appears in the Lynar tablature B 1, written around 1630 (cf.p.376), and it is proven unambiguously by comparing W. Karges' *Allein Gott in der Höh* with the three pieces by Wilhelm Karges, *Capriccio G, Praeludium quarti toni,* and *Fantasie* (dated 1664),[43] which are preserved in a much later source (Berlin, Amalienbibl. Ms.340). The *Capriccio* and the *Fantasie* are unimportant, but the *Praeludium* is an impressive composition in *E* minor in the sustained *durezze* style; even today it is appropriate for serious liturgical services.

Johan Lorentz, born in Flensburg in 1610, the son of a famous organ builder of the same name, was called to Copenhagen in 1629 to play the organ at the Vor Frue Kirke. In 1631 he obtained a leave of two years to study in Italy, and in 1634 he became the organist at St. Nicholas' in Copenhagen, where he died in 1689. In a report from the year 1670 he is called "Organista ipse nulli in Europa secundus." Strangely none of his organ works are preserved. There are only about 30 harpsichord pieces (in Uppsala, Univ. Bibl. Mss. Ihre 284, 285; Copenhagen, Royal Libr.

Ms. Add. 396. 4to; Berlin, Staatsbibl. Ms. 40623), but most of them prove to be intabulated dances, with titles such as "Saraband In Tavolat. Joh. Laurent." Four brief preludes and four dance settings may be considered original compositions, but they are very modest miniatures without much interest.[44]

Nicolaus Hasse, born in Lübeck around 1617, the son of Peter Hasse the Elder, became an organist at St. Marien at Rostock in 1642, as the successor of David Abel (Ebel), and died there around 1672. He has long been known as a composer of instrumental chamber music (*Delitiae musicae,* 1656) and solo songs (*Geistliche Seelenmusik,* 1659), but only recently four of his organ works were discovered in the Pelplin tablatures (along with a few chorale settings by Scheidemann and Tunder): *Allein Gott in der Höh, Jesus Christus unser Heiland* I and II, and *Komm heiliger Geist Herre Gott.*[45] Surely these works constitute only a fraction of a much larger output. Fortunately they seem to be very representative of Hasse's works. The striking differences in the forms and stylistic features employed in these pieces constitute a chronological outline. The earliest in style, and probably chronologically, too, is the setting of *Jesus Christus unser Heiland:* (I) *Pleno.* It consists of three *Versus,* in each of which the chorale is heard once each in the soprano, tenor, and bass, without any ornamentation and with strict counterpoints, whose motion seldom exceeds eighth notes. In *Allein Gott in der Höh* the individual lines of the chorale are treated imitatively, as in a chorale motet; when they appear in the soprano they are generally ornamented. The second *Jesus Christus (unser Heiland): pro 3 Clav.* is also a chorale motet, but it is much longer (161 measures) and approaches the chorale fantasy in the use of echoes and motivic fragments. Finally, *Komm Heiliger Geist,* with almost 300 measures and a fantastic wealth of figures, ranks equal to the chorale fantasies of Tunder and Reincken.

Jacob Kortkamp (died 1677?) was an organist at Kiel. His son Johann (about 1643–1721) reports in his chronicle of organists that he was a student of Jacob Praetorius', along with Weckmann, and that "these two children of Jacob were

Fig.640

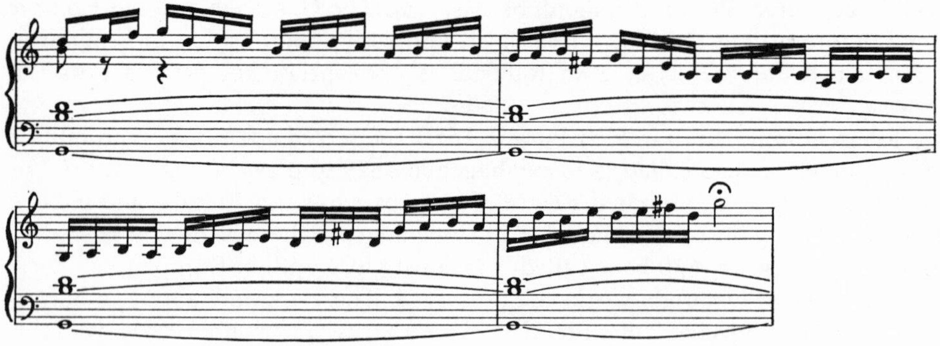

united in brotherly love until the end." A setting of *Herr Gott dich loben wir,* preserved in Lüneburg KN 207,[46] consists of six *Versus.* Nos.1 and 2 are set imitatively, no.3 (*Dein göttlich Macht*) is an extended fantasy with figurations and echoes, and nos.4–6 are brief *cantus-planus* movements. Fig.640 shows the final cadenza of the *Tertius versus.*

Reincken

Jan Adam Reincken was born in Wilshausen (Alsace) in 1623, and moved with his parents to Deventer in the Netherlands in 1637. From 1654 to 1657 he studied with Scheidemann at Hamburg, became his assistant in 1659, and his successor at St. Catherine's in 1663. He died in 1722, almost a centenarian, having lived from the days of Scheidt to those of J. S. Bach, who often walked from Lüneburg to Hamburg to hear Reincken. Very little of his keyboard output is preserved, only two chorale settings, a toccata, two variation works, a fugue, and three suites.[47]

Both chorale settings, *Was kann uns kommen an für Not* and *An Wasser-flüssen Babylon,*[48] are long fantasies, the first comprising 221 measures, the second 330. Each line is extensively treated, and all the technical means of the North German organ art are employed: motet-like development, figuration of the chorale in the soprano, fore-imitation in diminished note values, introduction of counter-motifs, virtuosic passage work, double pedals, fragmentation, and echo effects.

Fig.641

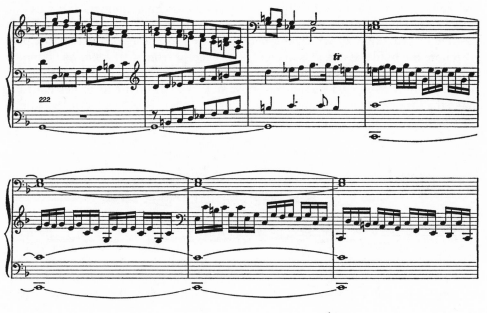

Fig.642

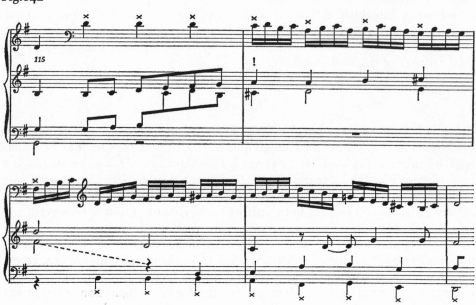

The arrangement of *An Wasserflüssen Babylon* shows a particular wealth of brilliant ideas and individual figures, which make this composition one of the most outstanding creations of its type. Reincken repeatedly uses hand-crossings, which are really quite natural on the organ, with its two or three manuals, but was only rarely employed by other North German organ masters. Fig.641 shows a typical passage of crossings, in which the pedals as well as the two hands participate. Also note the bold passing dissonances. The excerpt from *Was kann uns kommen an* (third chorale line) given in Fig.642, is even more remarkable in this respect. At the point of crossing a *c* sounds against a *c♯*; the requirements of voice leading make the former as justified and necessary as the latter. Here is a German example for Correa de Arauxo's *punto intenso contra remisso*.

Fig.643

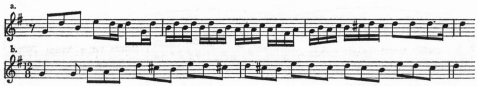

The toccata is another very long work, with 150 measures, but unfortunately its content does not justify its length.[49] As usual, it is arranged in five sections alternating between toccata and fugue writing, but here the second fugue employs a gigue-like variant of the first fugue subject. Both subjects are shown in Fig.643. The second of the three toccata sections exhibits briefly articulated figures (Fig.644a.) and a passage in which a series of harmonies is enlivened by the varied repetition of an arpeggio motif (Fig.644b.)—the same technique that Bach uses in the fourth section of his *F♯-minor* Toccata (Ed. Peters, vol.XIII, p.10).

Fig.644

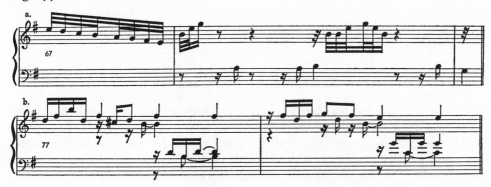

A *G-minor* Fugue[50] is based on a subject (Fig.645) that may represent the peak of the "motoric" type so much in favor at the time. Despite the superficiality of the subject, a fugue in a fascinating *perpetuum mobile* evolves from it, anticipating the Vivaldi style, to which Bach owes so many inspirations.

Fig.645

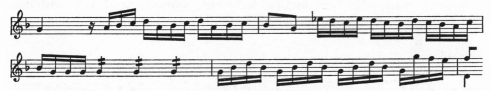

Reincken's three suites[51] have the classic order A C S G. Two of the gigues are fugal, and use the inversion of the subject in the second section, e.g., in the *Suite ex G♮* (Fig.646).

Fig.646

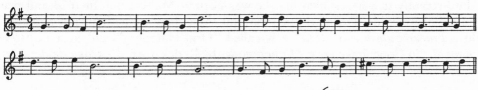

The *Partite diverse sopra l'Aria: Schweiget mir vom Weiber nehmen, altrimente chiamata La Meyerin*[52] employs the *Mayerin* tune that Froberger used earlier. Reincken writes eighteen variations on this theme. Seiffert is correct in assuming "that this reveals close relations to the Viennese school." He points out that, as in Froberger's work, "the last three variations exhibit the definite traits of courante, sarabande, and gigue."[53] Like Froberger, Reincken applies the figurative method of variation almost exclusively, and because of the greater number of variations, this method unfolds with particular richness and brilliance.

Reincken's other variation set consists of eleven variations on a *Ballet ex Eg* (i.e., *E* with *g* = *E* minor).[54]

Flor, Radek, Bölsche, Erben, and Fabricius

Christian Flor was born at Neukirchen near Eutin in 1626. He worked in Lüneburg from 1652 on, and died in 1697. In his *Neues musikalisches Seelenparadies* (1660, 1662) he set many poems by his good friend Johann Rist. His preserved keyboard works comprise a chorale prelude on *Eine feste Burg*, two preludes, and two suites.[55] The chorale prelude, an early work dated 1652, is a brief three-part setting, in which some of the lines are presented with ornaments by the right hand, and some by the left without ornaments. The piece does not rise above the technical average and is closer to the Central German tradition than to the North German. In the penultimate line the hands cross, as in Reincken's organ chorales, e.g., in the passage given in Fig.647. The preludes are short, but attractive, functional music. One of the suites (*ex Df*, i.e., D minor) begins with a variation canzona in three sections, called *Fuga*,[56] and continues with A C S G. The other (in C major) consists of prelude, aria (with double), courante, sarabande (with double), and gigue—all of moderate length and rather inconsequential content.

Fig.647

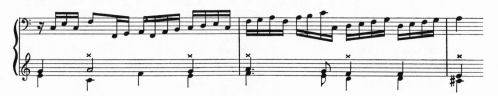

Compositions by Martin Radek (Radex) are preserved in several manuscripts. Until recently it was assumed that he was born at Mühlhausen in 1623 and was buried at Roskilde (Denmark) in 1683, but these data are perhaps not tenable.[57] In a *Praeambulum noni toni* he is called "Org. Hamburg" and in a *Canzone manual.* "in Copenhagen org." Other works by Radek are a *Chiacona del pasegal*, a suite, a *Fuga tertii toni*, and two settings of *Jesus Christus unser Heiland*.[58] The *Praeambulum* consists of a full-sounding introduction, a simple fugue, and a brief postlude. In the introduction phrases in dotted rhythm appear frequently, suggesting an acquaintance with the French overture. The subject of the fugue (| / g c' c' | bb g a — |) is a transposition of the subject of Kerll's *Ricercata* printed in Kircher's *Musurgia* (|a—d' d' | c' a bb— |) (cf.p.562), and is possibly borrowed from it.[59] Fig.648 shows the beginning of this composition. One setting of *Jesus Christus unser Heiland*, "in ordinari Contrapunkt gesetzt," is a chorale motet in strict, somewhat archaic counterpoint, with little attention paid to its playability. The other, "in doppeltem Contrapunkt," is a shorter arrangement in which the four voices are exchanged in four "Evolutiones." There is a similar study in learned counterpoint in Buxtehude's work (cf.p.622).

Fig.648

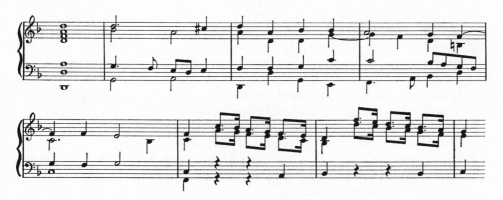

In contrast to the compositions of Flor and Radek, which continue the Central German tradition in many details, a *Praeambulum ex E Sig. Jacobus Bölsche Org. ad Bürgedorff 1683 pedaliter* exhibits North German traits. Bölsche was an organist at Burgdorf near Hannover until 1669, and then at Brunswick, where he died in 1684. Riedel, who published the piece,[60] opines that it was composed before 1669 and that 1683 is the year in which it was copied (in New Haven E. B. 1688). The piece is in *E* major, a key which was used in only one other piece during the period, in a prelude and fugue by Buxtehude. It consists of an introductory section of 38 measures, followed by a simple fugue of similar dimensions. The opening manual passage, given in Fig.649, uses the Lydian fourth (a♯) in its rising scale run.

Balthasar Erben (1626–86) and Werner Fabricius (1633–79) belong to this group of secondary masters, who were five to fifteen years older than Buxtehude. Erben was active at St. Mary's at Danzig (Gdansk). Three of his pieces are in the

Fig.649

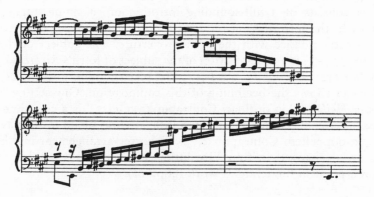

Hintze Ms. (cf. footnote, p.560): a short *Passacaglia* with four presentations of the traditional tetrachord ostinato (*c' b♭ a g*), a courante, and a sarabande.

Fabricius came from Itzehoe (Holstein), studied under Scheidemann in Hamburg, worked there as well as in Leipzig as an organist, and died in Hamburg. His organ works were only recently discovered in a manuscript that surfaced in the American book market and was bought by the Newberry Library in Chicago. The manuscript opens with a collection of very simple, short, mostly homophonic preludes, inscribed as "Kurtze Praeambula vor Incipienten durch alle Claves manualiter und pedaliter zu gebrauchen Werneri Fabricii." They are followed by a number of figured basses, brief three-part exercises (all in 3/4 and with fingerings for the bass), and several chorales (in a later hand) in purely homophonic settings. This manuscript probably originated at Weimar, where, according to a statement by A. Adrio,[61] organ tablatures by Werner Fabricius were once located. The Uppsala tablature mentioned by the same author contains intabulations of vocal and instrumental ensemble compositions only. In the Möller Ms. a *Gigue belle*, *Sig^re Guernero Fabricio* is preserved on fol.67v/68.

Buxtehude

The evolution of North German organ music reaches its peak with Dietrich Buxtehude. Little about his life is known with certainty. He was born about 1637, in either Helsingborg (Sweden) or Oldesloe (Holstein). In 1660 he obtained the position of organist at St. Mary's at Helsingör (Denmark), and in 1668 was elected to succeed Tunder (who had died the year before) as organist of the Marienkirche at Lübeck, a position he held until his death in 1707. Because he may have been born in Helsingborg, he has been claimed for Sweden, but it now seems rather certain that his family was of German descent. The end of a notice of his death in the *Nova literaria Maris Balthici et Septentrionis* of 1707 reads "Patriam agnoscit Daniam," but these words do not mean much because both southern Sweden and

Holstein then belonged to Denmark. Whatever his national or political background, musically he belongs to Germany, even as the Italian Poglietti does, and even as England is justified in counting the German Handel among her own.

The first edition of Buxtehude's collected organ works was published by Ph. Spitta in 1876/8. New finds led to an enlarged edition in 1903 and to a supplementary volume in 1939, both published by M. Seiffert; and a new complete edition by W. Kraft in 1952 combined all three. In the same year there appeared a four-volume edition by J. Hedar, *Sämtliche Orgelwerke*, which is based on a critical study of the complete sources and which alone reflects the state of research today. The following observations are based on this edition.

In the 1930s a manuscript containing suites and variations by Buxtehude was discovered in the private possession of the Danish family Ryge. It was published by E. Bangert (W. Hansen Verlag, 1941) under the title *Dietrich Buxtehude, Klavervaerker*. A manuscript from Uppsala (cf. my article cited in note 39) contains four suites, which appear in Bo Lundgren's *Buxtehude: Vier Suiten für Clavichord oder Laute* (Copenhagen, 1955). Two of them are also preserved in the Danish manuscript. Buxtehude's works for organ comprise a passacaglia, 2 chaconnes, more than 20 preludes and fugues, 4 toccatas, about 10 canzonas (or fugues), and 45 chorale settings. A survey of the rather complicated state of the sources may be found in Riedel Q, pp.194ff. A detailed study of the organ compositions with a treatment of the evolution that leads up to them was published by J. Hedar under the title *Dietrich Buxtehudes Orgelwerke* (Stockholm, 1951).

FREE ORGAN WORKS

As far as we can tell today the later Baroque masters did not differentiate between the terms passacaglia and chaconne. Buxtehude's passacaglia and two chaconnes are each based on a four-measure subject. In the *Passacaglio* it always appears in the bass and never changes, while in the *Ciaconas* it is altered in many ways and is shifted to a higher voice at times (as in Bach's *Passacaglia*). The *Passacaglio* is constructed in a very regular fashion, articulated in four equally long sections. In each section the subject ($d \mid a - c\sharp \mid d - A \mid B\flat - \mid A -$) is presented seven times, on D, then on F, on A, and on D again. The regularity of the structure is further reinforced by the unification of the last three variations in each section by means of the same figuration motif, and in several instances the first four variations are similarly related in pairs. This $2+2+3$ articulation is particularly clear in the first and third sections. Of the various figures with which Buxtehude builds his superstructure, the one at the beginning of the third section, given in Fig.650, illustrates the dramatic-declamatory style of rests, which was used in a fantasy by Weckmann (cf.Fig.636) and which Bach took over for the beginning of his *Passacaglia*.

The *Ciacona* in C minor consists of 38 variations on the ostinato subject ($\mid c - a\flat \mid g - B \mid c - e\flat \mid d - G \mid$), which is heard in the bass unchanged for the

Fig.650

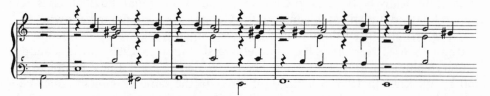

first seven variations and then freely varied in other voices. Sometimes the transformation of the subject goes so far that its contour is entirely lost and only the
harmonic scheme remains, as, e.g., in variations VIII, IX, and X. Fig.651 shows
variation VIII and the transition to variation IX, in which even the C-minor
cadence is replaced by one that goes to E-flat major. Variation XX is also very
free, as Buxtehude modulates to G minor. In order to return to C minor, he inserts a fifth measure. Beginning with variation XXI each variation is literally or
almost literally repeated (XXI = XXII, XXIII = XXIV, etc.). Thus this chaconne
falls into three main sections of seven, thirteen, and eighteen variations, respectively, the first marked by a strict ostinato, the second by a particularly free treatment of the subject, and the third by paired variations.

Fig.651

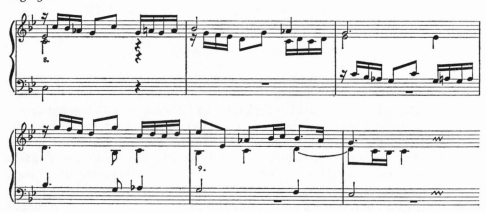

The 31 variations of the *Ciacona* in E minor are based on a variant of the
tetrachord ostinato introduced by Frescobaldi (| e − | d − B | c − A | B − |), which
is treated as a strict basso ostinato in the first ten variations, but then appears in
varied forms. Each variation is repeated, except for variations XI and XXIV–
XXIX. Attempts to divide this work into three sections (as in Hedar B, p.78)
are not convincing. At most one may see the beginning of a concluding section in
variation XXIV, where the paired repetitions are given up except for the last
two variations, XXX–XXXI.

Except for Radek's *Chiacona* and Erben's *Passagaglia,* Buxtehude's *Passacaglio* and two *Ciaconas* are the only ostinato compositions in the North German organ repertoire. Their model may well have been Frescobaldi's *Passacagli,* or perhaps Biber's violin chaconnes, with their virtuosic treatment of form. In any event, Buxtehude's works differ from Frescobaldi's, as well as from those by such South German masters as Kerll or Muffat, in their magnificence and *élan.* The loftiness of the total effect is occasionally disturbed by routine figures, especially by arpeggio forms, which are always somewhat cheap and unfortunately find more and more favor in the keyboard music of the second half of the 17th century. None of these works can stand the obvious comparison with Bach's *Passacaglia,* mainly because they still employ a four-measure ostinato, while Bach's subject is eight measures long.

A number of Buxtehude's preludes and fugues, however, definitely measure up to corresponding works by Bach,[62] i.e., Bach's toccatas, for almost all of Buxtehude's so-called preludes and fugues are in reality toccatas or are more closely related to this species than to what is commonly referred to as prelude and fugue. We shall call them toccatas, no matter what they are called in the manuscripts or in the modern editions.

No.16 of the Hedar edition is the only genuine prelude and fugue.[63] The others consist of alternating sections in toccata-like and fugal style. The simplest structure, with only one fugue, T F T, is found in nos.7, 11, 15, 18, 26, and 27. No.1, which concludes with a chaconne rather than a toccata section, can be included in this group. The form with two fugues, T F T F T, occurs in nos.8, 10, 17, 19, and 24. A form T F F T, which omits the middle toccata section, is used in nos.4, 5, 6, and 13, as well as in no.22, which concludes with an ostinato setting. Others exhibit variants of these structures or even contain three fugues and two or four toccata sections: T F F T F in no.9, T F T F F in no.14, and T F T F T F T in no.25. In this analysis short transitions or conclusions in a free style (as in no.4, meas.64–66) are not noted.

The content of these pieces is not easily summarized. Passage work of great brilliance, dramatic pedal solos, breath-taking rests, obstinate ostinatos, expressive recitatives, boldly traced fugue subjects, massive chords, and sustained pedal points as bases for lively motivic play or for gently flowing sicilianos are some of the multifarious ideas that come and go, carried forward by a magnificent *élan* and embedded in a harmonic framework that is as firm as it is elastic. Among the most outstanding details are introductory pedal solos in nos.1, 7, and 10, which are probably the earliest instances of this effect, except for Tunder's chorale setting of *Jesus Christus unser Heiland,* which is not definitely authenticated. Very often Buxtehude breaks off a rapid motion in the right hand and seems to catch it in a low-lying pedal tone. This effect is especially dramatic in a passage from no.1, shown in Fig.652, in which all the voices are suddenly interrupted by rests (cf. Weckmann's *Fantasia,* Fig.636). The foot trills in nos.14 (*trillo longo*) and 23 and

Fig.652

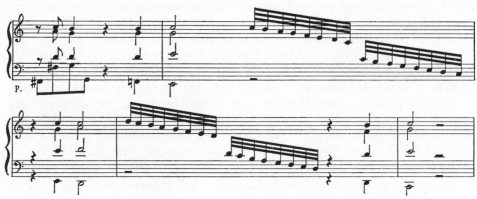

the passage in no.17 (meas.121f.) that has skips of tenths are examples of the virtuosic pedal treatment. Curiously, in contrast to Reincken, no passages of double pedals can be found. There are many pedal points, however. The one at the beginning of no.13 demonstrates with particular clarity the change in meaning of this device: The held tone no longer serves as the natural carrier of consonant, pastoral chords, as it does, e.g., for Frescobaldi, but as a forceful hold for a dynamic progression of conflicting harmonies (Fig.653).

Fig.653

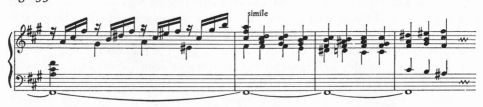

Many times the pedals are employed for *bassi ostinati* or *quasi-ostinati*, e.g., in no.10 (meas.16ff.), no.11 (meas.77ff.), no.14 (meas.104ff.), no.19 (meas.112ff.), and no.24 (beginning). In no.3 (meas.70ff.) the upper parts present an ostinato against a moving bass. Nos.1 and 22 conclude with an extended ostinato movement, which is particularly interesting because the subject regularly alternates between the bass and one of the upper parts. Only at the beginning (meas.3–4) is this not so, for the subject is missing. Has it been omitted in error? In any event, as Fig.654 proves, it can easily be fitted in. At the sixth entrance of the ostinato Buxtehude modulates to B♭ major and remains in this key until shortly before the end; not until the antepenultimate measure does he return to the main key of G minor. Quite a number of toccatas show this tendency to stay in a secondary key

Fig.654

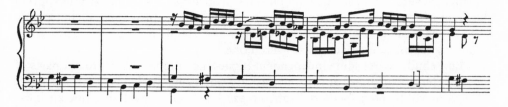

(mostly the subdominant) and return to the tonic only at the last moment. Toward the end of the *D* minor toccata no.19 a clear *G*-minor ostinato (*G d G*) appears, which dominates the music until the penultimate measure.

In the first or single fugal sections of his toccatas Buxtehude uses many novel ideas, in addition to more or less traditional subjects. Some may be called pedal subjects because their regular alternation of ascending and descending intervals is designed to be played by alternate feet. Such subjects are found, e.g., in nos.1, 9, 14, and 16. In another type the course of the subject is effectively interrupted by rests, as in nos.17, 18, and 19. The fugue subject of no.15 is particularly bold and dramatic. It begins with three identical trill figures, separated by quarter rests, and extends over three more measures. The whole six-measure subject, moreover, is couched in the zigzag motion of a pedal subject. The repercussion subjects in nos.4, 22, and others, which are characterized by tone repetitions, are purely of historical interest. In the second half of the 17th century this type achieved a popularity that is difficult to explain and hardly justified aesthetically. The repercussion subjects of nos.13 and 22 exhibit the striking skip of a diminished seventh, which Bach used in various fugue subjects (e.g., in the *A*-minor Fugue from the *WTC* II). Fig.655 offers some of these subjects. The above observations refer to the first fugues in the respective toccatas. When a work contains more than one fugue, Buxtehude often uses variants of the first fugue subject, e.g., in nos.4, 5, 6, 8, 10, 19, and 24, but Hedar definitely goes too far in his analyses when he considers every such subject a variant of the main subject.

Fig.655

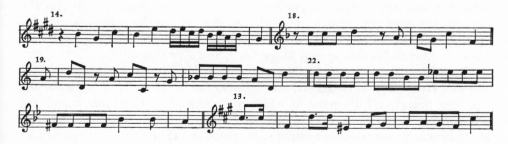

Artistically the fugal sections of Buxtehude's toccatas are inferior to the free sections. Nevertheless they usually fill their proper role well, that of interrupting the flight of free fancy from time to time and in a sense providing anchor points from which it can take off again. Buxtehude was certainly not a great master of the organ fugue, but until Bach there were none.

Buxtehude wrote some independent fugues, i.e., fugues that were not parts of toccatas. Nine canzonas (or canzonettas) are published in Hedar, vol.I, nos.4–12. A *Fuga* in vol.II, no.3 (Seiffert-Kraft, no.22), however, is probably not an independent composition but the final section of the toccata.[64] Canzonas nos.5 and 12 approach the genuine fugue, insofar as a single subject is developed within a single section. Compatible with the title "canzona," the other compositions consist of two or three sections based on different subjects or on variants of the main subject and occasionally its inversion. A number of subjects (nos.4, 6, 7, 11, 12) belong to the "motoric" type, which may have been introduced in keyboard music by Weckmann; with its mostly insignificant liveliness it condemns the counterpoints to mere sham activity, if not inactivity. The subject of the canzonetta in *E minor* (no.9) is one of the few fugue subjects of the 17th century that could have been invented by Bach. It is developed in two well-wrought sections, by itself in the first one, and combined with a countersubject that is no less significant in the second. Subject and countersubject appear in Fig.656. Both sections conclude with a "rhetoric gesture," which is unobtrusive but therefore all the more effective. Hedar rightly says that with its "elegiac subject" and its "unified structure stressing melody and discant" this canzonetta holds a "special place not only among Buxtehude's organ compositions but also in the entire 17th century."[65]

Fig.656

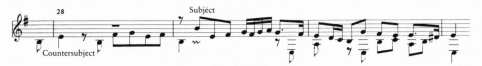

CHORALE ARRANGEMENTS

In number, and even more in variety and artistic value, Buxtehude's organ chorales represent the most important contribution to this field in the 17th century. This repertoire consists of 6 chorale variations, 2 chorale motets, 3 large chorale fantasies, 30 shorter chorales, several *Magnificats*, and a *Te Deum*.[66]

Buxtehude uses mostly traditional forms in his chorale variations on *Ach Gott und Herr* (only in Hedar III, no.1), *Danket dem Herrn, Nun lob mein Seel* (two sets, nos.4a and 4b, parts of which are identical[67]), *Vater unser*, and *Auf meinen lieben Gott*. Thus, for example, he follows older models in the frequent use of bicinium and tricinium settings, in which the chorale is accompanied by one or two ornamental voices. Nevertheless, like Goethe's lovely aphorism on "ererben und erwerben" (inheriting and making one's own), the old form is filled with new meaning. The bicinia, in particular, differ from Sweelinck's, Scheidt's, or Weckmann's, not only because the strict *cantus planus* is replaced by a naturally flowing chorale rhythm, articulated by rests, but also in the vitality of the figural counterpoints, which are free of schematism and formalism. Buxtehude frequently writes a fore-imitation in the counterpoints during the rests in the chorale tune, e.g., in the third line of variation II of *Vater unser*, given in Fig. 657. Only a few variations do not belong to this type; e.g., variation I of *Nun lob mein Seel* II (Hedar no.4b; Seiffert no.7b), in which most of the chorale lines are heard first in the bass and then in the soprano; and especially variation III of *Vater unser*, which is a beautiful example of the ornamented discant chorale, a type that Buxtehude employed very often in his shorter chorale settings.

Fig.657

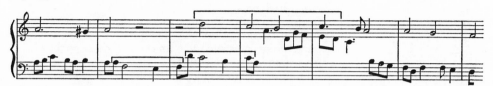

The variations on *Auf meinen lieben Gott* are most curious. The chorale is treated very differently, in the form of a variation suite, which consists of allemande with double, sarabande, courante, and gigue. This combination of the spiritual and the secular is reminiscent of the 13th-century motets with their amorous French texts, or of the 15th- and 16th-century masses that were based on *L'homme armé* or *Ma maitresse*. The question of sacrilege is just as unthinkable in Buxtehude's compositions as in the earlier ones, and surely we may assume that Buxtehude's chorale suite was not heard on the church organ but on the harpsichord or clavichord for domestic edification.

Among the single chorale settings the chorale motet is represented by *Ich dank dir schon*. The four lines of the chorale are fugally treated in four sections, which are clearly differentiated through their time signatures: ¢, C, 3/2, C. The first section, given in Fig.658, is a fine example of a modernized *durezze e ligature* style. The third section is also much pervaded by suspensions.

Fig.658

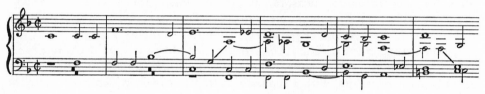

A freer treatment of the motet structure is exhibited by the arrangement of *Ich dank dir, lieber Herre*. The first and last lines, e.g., are not imitative but chordal. They form a firm framework for the imitative treatment of the middle lines, to which Buxtehude tries to give a free and varied formulation. The following is an outline of this chorale motet:

Line	Measure	
1	1	Homophonic with melody in the soprano
2	4	*Allegro:* melody with inserted notes, in dotted rhythm and canonically imitated
3 = line 1, meas.12		*Lento:* fugal treatment of the melody in diminution; augmentation in the pedals at the end
4 = line 2, meas.24		*Allegro:* like line 2, but in triple canon; ascending scale passage as concluding apostrophe
5	38	Three-part phrase of two measures, fashioned from the canonically imitated melody plus a counterpoint, presented five times on various pitches
6	55	Similar to line 5
7	74	Phrase of two 6/4 measures consisting of the melody plus two counterpoints plus its repetition in inverted counterpoint, presented five times on various pitches, also expanded to four parts
8	101	Homophonic with melody in the bass

Changing the treatment from section to section compensates for repetitions that go on too long in some sections, especially the penultimate one.

The arrangements of *Gelobet seist du*, *Wie schön leuchtet*, and *Nun freut euch* belong to the species of the large chorale fantasy, which was founded by Tunder. Its chief characteristic is the application of the most varied methods, especially fragmentation and, connected with it, echo effects. With lengths of 155, 196, and 256 measures, respectively, these fantasies far exceed the length of the chorale motets. In *Gelobet seist du* the four lines of the chorale are treated in sections of 37, 30, 31, and 40 measures. In the first section, line 1 and, later on, its starting motif are treated in free fugatos. A concluding apostrophe in form of an arpeggiated C-major triad leads to the second section, which starts with several repetitions of a three-part phrase (similar to lines 5 and 7 in *Ich dank dir, lieber Herre*) and continues with lively passage work above fragments of the tune in the pedals. Line 3 is first combined with a countersubject, then (meas.87) exposed twice in the soprano in rich ornamentation. Line 4 is extensively treated to fragmentation, with echoes and sometimes even double echoes (e.g., in meas.103–107). A free postlude starting in measure 139 perhaps refers briefly to the "kyrieleis" refrain (*f g a g*) of the chorale (in meas.143–45). Fig.659 shows passages from the third and the fourth sections (R = Rückpositiv; O = Organ).

In the arrangement of *Wie schön leuchtet der Morgenstern* the chorale is set twice. In measures 1–135 it appears in its original form combined with various decorative counterpoints, with a separate section in 6/8 in which the melody of

Fig.659

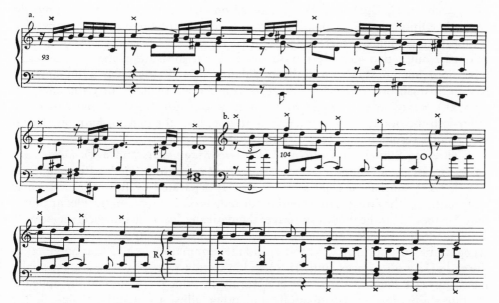

the last line ("hoch und sehr prächtig erhaben") is presented several times. In the second setting, in 12/8, the melody is presented ornamented and fragmented. The almost exclusive use of triplet rhythms gives the work a gentle, idyllic character, which is underscored by mostly limiting the number of voices to two or three and by using the pedals in the last four measures only.

The following list of the main sections of *Nun freut euch* may serve as a guide to this particularly long fantasy:*

1. Lines 1–2 (meas.1)	6. Line 6 (meas.131)
2. Line 3 (= 1; meas.13)	7. Line 6 (meas.149)
3. Line 4 (= 2; meas.45)	8. Line 7 (meas.167)
4. Line 5 (meas.83)	9. Line 7 (meas.192)
5. Line 5 (meas.109)	10. Coda (meas.238–56)

The first two lines are treated briefly, the others at great length; and the last three lines each receive two long presentations. Section 1 is ornamented; sections 2, 4, and 8 are fugal; and all four use the entire chorale line. The content of the other sections is not easily summarized. In most of them the ornamented version of a melodic fragment is combined with a countersubject to form a complex that is repeated several times, often with echoes or double echoes. Modulation to the dominant or subdominant plays an important role. Section 3, e.g., begins with

---

* The measure numbers refer to Hedar's new edition; in Seiffert's measures 63–64 are repeated, probably erroneously.

21 presentations of a three-part complex of one measure, which is heard four times each on *G*, *D*, *A*, and *D*, then twice on *A*, and three times (five times in Seiffert's edition) on *G*. Similarly, section 6 consists of three presentations of a six-measure complex, which cadence on *G*, *D*, and *G*. Measures 206–19 are developed from a two-measure phrase (really a one-measure group with an echo repetition). Such passages recall the modulatory passages that play a fundamental role in Spanish organ music of the 17th century, particularly in Cabanilles (cf. pp.772f.), Buxtehude's younger contemporary. It is not suggested that either one influenced the other, but it is interesting to note how the logic of harmony led to very similar results in two very distant places.

Three of Buxtehude's organ works, two *Magnificats* and a *Te Deum*, are based on Gregorian tunes. His large *Magnificat primi toni* (Hedar III, p.59; Seiffert II, p.18) consists of eight sections, clearly separated by full cadences. Their relationship to the Gregorian recitation formula is often problematic; Hedar thinks that "neither Magnificat fantasy derives thematically from the liturgical melody."[68] This generality is not correct; the Gregorian intonation (*f g a b♭ a*) is clearly recognizable in sections 1, 4, 5, and 7, and the termination (*a g f e d*) is apparent at the end of section 4 (meas.69ff., *lento*) and in section 8 (meas.125ff., and especially meas.139–41). Fig.660 shows several forms in which the intonation appears. Despite these clear transformations and other allusions, a unified plan in the sequence of the sections does not seem to exist. The second *Magnificat primi toni* (Hedar III, p.8; Seiffert II, p.25) consists of a four-measure introduction, in which the first three notes of the Magnificat tone (*f g a*) are freely paraphrased, and two fugatos whose subjects are possibly related to these notes, too. An additional *Magnificat noni toni* in three *Versus* (Hedar III, p.10; Seiffert-Kraft I, p.163) was put together by Seiffert, but incorrectly. *Versus I* has nothing to do with the *tonus peregrinus*, but is perhaps related to the *primus tonus*; *Versus II* has the *tonus peregrinus* as a *cantus planus* in the bass; and *Versus III* uses its *initium* (*a c′ a*) in various voices and on various pitches.

Fig.660

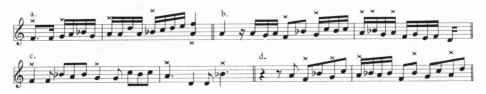

a. sec. 1, meas.2; b. sec.4, meas.64; c. sec.5, meas.77; d. sec.7, meas.103.

With its 268 measures the *Te Deum* is Buxtehude's longest organ work, and suggests a comparison with Tunder's fantasy with the German title *Herr Gott dich loben wir* (cf.p.596). While Tunder treats the first eleven lines in a continuous movement, Buxtehude limits himself to four lines (not in the original order)—*Te Deum Laudamus*, *Te martyrum candidatus*, *Tu devicto mortis*, and *Pleni sunt coeli*—and presents each in a separate section of great length. The work is introduced by a *Praeludium*, which is in fact a prelude and fugue. This magnificent, gigantic work represents a kind of synopsis of organ music from Sweelinck to Buxtehude, from the archaic *cantus-planus* setting to the most modern methods of composition: fugue, pedal point, echo, virtuosic pedal playing, fragmentation, and double trills. Fig.661 shows the Lydian cadence at the end of the first section,[69] and a similar passage from the *Prelude* and *Fugue* in *E* minor (Hedar no.9; Seiffert no.6).

Fig.661

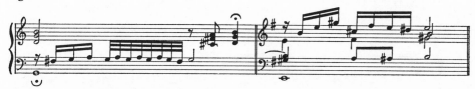

In addition to the large chorale variations, motets, and fantasies Buxtehude wrote many short chorale settings, commonly called chorale preludes, because their brevity and clarity make them suitable for introducing singing by the congregation. Most of them are ornamented discant chorales. The melody is heard in the soprano, sporadically furnished with expressive ornamentation, and extended rests clearly separate the lines. This kind of paraphrase differs essentially from the earlier one, in which the chorale tune is ornamented throughout, and which often employs an obbligato motif. In his chorale fantasies Tunder occasionally employs "a new kind of figuration, in which a note is stressed expressively by an individual figure only here and there" (p.594). Buxtehude goes still further in this direction, for he is even more sparing with ornamental figures and makes them even more expressive. The lovely example in Fig.662 occurs in the repetition of the a-section in *Ach Herr, mich armen Sünder*. It would be nice to have a better term than ornamentation or coloration for such affective, gesture-like figures, which are so closely related to the vocal art of the period. Indeed, they are similar to the ones Buxtehude uses in his solo cantatas.[70]

Fig.662

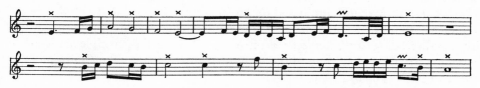

The rests between the chorale lines are sometimes used to announce the melody in the lower voices, mostly in the bass. In *Durch Adams Fall*, e.g., there are three such announcements, before lines 3, 4, and 7, while the other lines are connected by freely formed transitions. Genuine fore-imitations, i.e., several fugal announcements of the succeeding line, are found only rarely, e.g., in the last two lines of *Erhalt uns Herr*.[71]

In several of these chorales Buxtehude attempts to symbolize the effect of the text in music. Perhaps the most impressive instance is *Durch Adams Fall*, with its falling fifths in the bass of the first line, the descending sequence in the transition to the next one, and the chromatic basses in the third and fourth lines. The pathos-laden formulation of the conclusion (given in Fig.663) suggests the gesture of despair, the darkness of damnation, and the ray of hope for salvation.

Fig.663

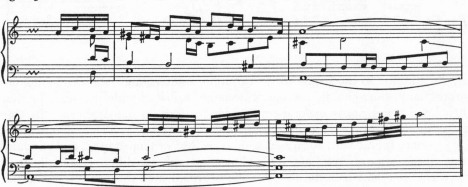

The ornamented discant chorale represents Buxtehude's most significant contribution to the evolution of the organ chorale. In it he created a type in which simplicity of presentation and forceful expression are most beautifully combined. He firmly established it in numerous compositions and made it a symbol of the subjective, emotional faith of his time. With it he built the basis for Bach's discant chorales.

Four movements in a learned four-part counterpoint may in a sense be included in Buxtehude's organ works. They were printed in 1674 under the title *Fried- und Freudenreiche Hinfarth* . . . as memorial music on the death of his father, Hans.[72] These movements, entitled *Contrapunctus I, Evolutio, Contrapunctus II,* and *Evolutio,* are based on the chorale *Mit Fried und Freud fahr ich dahin,* whose four text stanzas are printed underneath. Each *Evolutio* is derived from the preceding *Contrapunctus,* the first one following the principle of invertible counterpoint, the second one in the form of a mirror fugue, like *Contrapunctus* 16–18 of Bach's *Art of Fugue.*

SUITES AND VARIATIONS

The privately owned Ryge manuscript, discovered in the 1930s (cf.p.611), contains, among other compositions, 19 suites and 6 variation sets by Buxtehude.[73] They offer a welcome addition to the picture of the master's creative activity, although their contents are disappointing when compared to his organ works. Almost all the suites have the arrangement A C S G, which was generally adopted around 1680. One might expect to find among them the seven suites that, according to Mattheson's report, Buxtehude wrote "on the nature and properties of the planets," but there are no indications to this effect. A manuscript at Uppsala (Ihre 285, dated 1679) also contains four suites by Buxtehude (signed D.B.H), two of which are also found in the Ryge manuscript (Bangert edition, nos.XI and XIII). The other two, however, are further additions to Buxtehude's output of suites. Fig.664 gives the beginnings of the movements of the C-major suite. The dotted upbeat is employed by Buxtehude in most of his allemandes and courantes, and a variational relationship usually exists between these two dances.

Fig.664

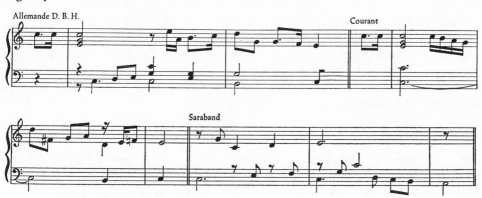

The themes of two variation works in the Ryge manuscript are of special interest: an *Aria More Palatino* and *La Capricciosa* (Bangert, nos.21 and 25). The former appears in a much earlier variation set, which Seiffert has included among Sweelinck's works, not without justification;[74] the latter proves to be the well-known bergamasca tune, which had served Sweelinck, Scheidt, and others. To vary his themes Buxtehude generally uses a method that became more and more dominant in the second half of the 17th century; because of the repetitive employment of a clavieristic formula, it may be called the formula variation.

Heidorn, Kneller, Ritter, and Werckmeister

Several keyboard composers who are not so well-known were born in the 1640s, and occupy a kind of middle position between Reincken and Buxtehude, on the one hand, and the later masters of North German organ music, Lübeck, Böhm, and Bruhns, on the other.

Fig.665

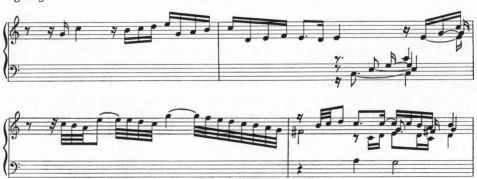

A toccata and three fugues by P. Heidorn, who is called "Heidorn a Crempe" (i.e., Krempe in southern Schleswig-Holstein) are preserved in the New Haven manuscript E.B. 1688. The toccata is a long piece of about 220 measures, consisting of a prelude, fugue, interlude, fugue on the varied subject, and postlude. The free sections contain impressive passages in the rhapsodic style of Buxtehude, e.g., at the very beginning (Fig.665). The fugue, with its motoric subject and reduction of the counterpoints to pure chords (Fig.666) shows the decay of contrapuntal writing.

Fig.666

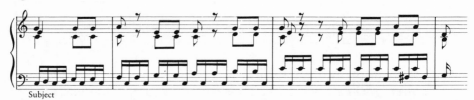

Subject

In the Möller manuscript (Berlin Staatsbibl. Mus. Ms. 40644) there is a *Fuga ex Gb* (G minor; fol.35v) and a *Fuga, Thema Reinckianum a Domino Heydornio elaboratum* (fol.33v). The latter is based on a repercussion subject, a type that was much favored during the period; in a second section this subject is treated in a 12/8 variant. Heidorn may have been a student of Reincken. Another fugue by Heidorn in the New Haven manuscript (fol.147) is closely related to South German organ music, for it is a clever parody of Kerll's canzona no.3.[75] Heidorn takes over the beginning of the canzona without much change, but later on, when Kerll introduces two new subjects (cf.p.563), Heidorn retains the main subject, and subsequently varies it in 12/8 time. To the two fugatos he adds two toccata-like sections in North German style, from which the ostinato passage given in Fig.667 is taken.

Fig.667

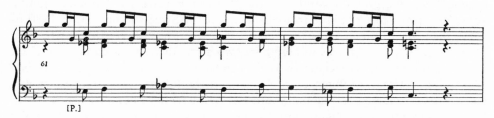

Andreas Kneller (not to be mistaken for A. Kniller, cf.p.380) was born in Lübeck in 1649, and became Melchior Schildt's successor at Hannover in 1667. In 1685, sponsored by his father-in-law, Reincken, he became an organist at St. Petri in Hamburg, where he died in 1724. His preserved works consist of three preludes and fugues in the Mylau manuscript of about 1730 (in which he is called Knüller),[76] eight variations on *Nun komm der Heiden Heiland*, and possibly two additional preludes (signed A.K.) in Berlin Staatsbibl., Mus. Ms. 30439. The Berlin manuscript collection was put together from various fragments by F. W. Riedel, and unfortunately it is often very difficult to read. Variations IV and V of the chorale are also found in Berlin, Staatsbibl. Mus. Ms. 22541 (Walther autograph).

Fig.668

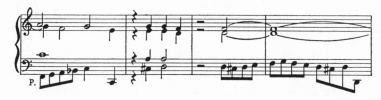

The Mylau *Praeludium ex D. f.*[77] is a toccata with three fugues, whose subjects are interrelated by variation (the second one in the 12/8 time of the siciliano), plus the usual prelude, interludes, and postlude. Its style is very reminiscent of Buxtehude, e.g., in the "eloquent" rests of the prelude, as shown in Fig.668. The whole work is rather significant, and tends more to lyric than to dramatic expression. The other two pieces from Mylau, a *Praeludium ex F und Fuga* and a *Praeludium ex Gb*, are similarly constructed but are less important. Only variations IV and V on *Nun komm der Heiden Heiland* have been published.[78] In the first setting the chorale is heard in the discant, lightly ornamented in the Buxtehude manner, and combined with an ostinato-like counterpoint in the pedals. In the second variation the chorale is in the pedals and is combined with various motifs in the upper parts, among them a chromatic counterpoint. Kneller's tendency toward gentle, lyrical expression emerges again in these settings.

Christian Ritter is a curious personality, difficult to characterize. He was born around 1645, and probably studied with Christoph Bernhard at Dresden. He was active as an organist at Halle from 1672 on, at the Swedish court from 1680 to 1682, then for a time at Dresden, and again at the Swedish court from 1688 to 1689. From 1700 on he was in Hamburg, where he died, apparently after 1725. Three keyboard works reach us, two suites and a toccata, which is called *Sonatina*. The suites are clearly influenced by Froberger, the toccata by Buxtehude.[79] Ritter may be considered as much a South German keyboard composer as a North German one, but he is classed with the latter because of his long activity in the North, where the suite had found another center of cultivation.

Ritter's *Sonatina* is a toccata in three sections, whose middle section is occupied by a long fugue in strict style. The regularity of various passages in the prelude and postlude makes them appear trivial in comparison with those in the Buxtehude circle; but they contain the seeds of the late-Baroque musical language, which is the basis of Bach's works. Take, e.g., the chordal passage, shown in Fig. 669, with which the prelude concludes.

Fig.669

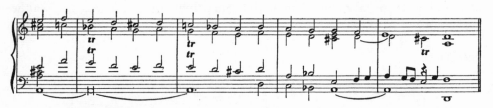

In the title of the F♯-minor suite published by Buchmayer, Ritter is called "Maistre de Chapelle de S. Maj. de Svecia"; this means that it must have been composed between 1680 and 1699. It consists of A C S (with two variations) G. Except for the very hackneyed sarabande, this work is beautiful and impressive,

Fig.670

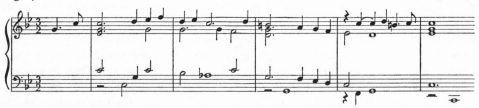

and definitely superior to Buxtehude's suites. The gigue is particularly noteworthy, with its lively fugato subject, which is used in inversion for the second half. Another suite by Ritter, not considered until now, is found in the Möller manuscript, with the inscription "Allemanda in discessam Caroli XI Regis Sveciae" (Carl died in 1697). The allemande is followed by C S G, all in C minor. Fig.670 presents the beginning of the courante.

Fig.671

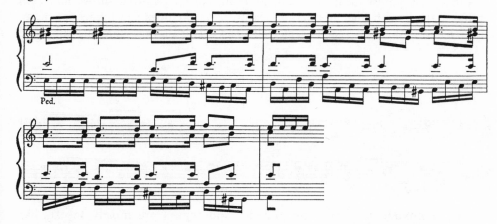

Andreas Werckmeister (1645–1706), organist at Hasselfelde, Quedlinburg, and Halberstadt, is known for various books, among them the *Musicalische Temperatur* of 1691, which has given him the not entirely deserved fame of having invented equal temperament. But he also composed occasionally. A canzona (in Leipzig, Ms.II.2.51) is based on a *perpetuum-mobile* idea, a favorite treatment at the time; its fourth entrance, in the pedals, is shown in Fig.671. In the second section this subject is presented in 3/4 time. The following postlude is based on an unchanging arpeggio motif (Fig.672), a technique used by Reincken (cf.Fig.644) and Böhm (cf.Fig.677c.), as well as by Central German masters such as Kuhnau (cf.Fig.723) and Zachow (cf.Fig.728). A *Praeludium ex G und Fuga* in the Mylau

Fig.672

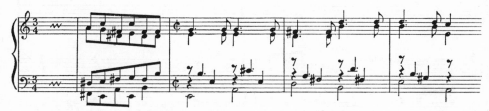

manuscript is a toccata with two fugues, whose themes are related by variation, and three free sections (T F T F T). The music is rather insignificant.

Lübeck

Vincent Lübeck belongs to the last generation of North German organ masters. He was born in Paddingbüttel near Bremen in 1654, became an organist at Stade in 1675, and was called to the Nikolaikirche in Hamburg in 1702, where he held the office of organist until his death in 1740. An oil painting shows him as a septuagenarian, with fine, aristocratic features. Six preludes and fugues for organ and two chorale settings reach us, as well as a *Clavier Übung*, which he published in 1728.[80]

Fig.673

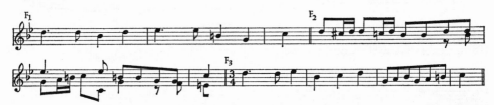

As in Buxtehude's case, the preludes and fugues are mostly toccata-like compositions of great length and variable structure. The most complex in structure and the most significant is the one in G minor (Keller no.4). It has the form T F F[1] T F[2], like Buxtehude's toccata no.9. The first fugue is based on an interesting subject, which is varied in the other two and combined with an effective countersubject in the middle fugue. All the subjects are shown in Fig.673. The introductory toccata is bold and magnificent, and measures up to Buxtehude's toccatas. It starts with a grand invocation, given in Fig.674. The last nine measures

Fig.674

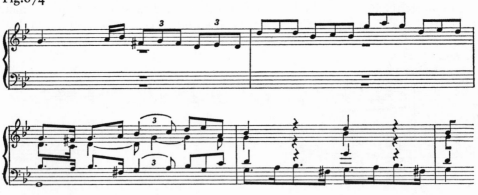

are written in five parts, and the pedals (if one may trust the modern editions) participate with two voices. The first fugue is also in five parts with double pedals, a feature that occurs in Reincken's works but not in Buxtehude's.

Lübeck's other toccatas have either two fugal sections (Keller, nos.2, 6) or only one (nos.1, 3, 5). None of them equals the G-minor toccata in musical value. The fugue of no.1 is based on a repercussion subject on the pitches (*a d b♭ c♯*), i.e., of the same contour as the subjects in Buxtehude's toccatas nos.22 and 13 (cf.Fig.655). In the free sections there are extended pedal solos (in nos.1, 2, 6) and occasionally fast fugatos (in nos.2, meas.75ff., and 6, meas.6off.). In no.4, meas.111, there is a cadence with two leading tones (*c♯–d, g♯–a*).

The chorale *Ich ruf zu dir* is treated in a grandiose fantasy of 271 measures, in which the right hand dips far below the left several times (e.g., meas.36ff., 51ff.). These passages also remind one of Reincken, in whose chorale fantasies hand-crossings are frequently employed. In contrast to earlier works of this type, Lübeck uses the echo sparingly, to the benefit of the whole piece. He presents the chorale *Nun lasst uns Gott dem Herren* in six variations, which surround the melody with rich figurations as counterpoints or as ornaments, and sometimes retain only the harmonic framework rather than the melody.

The *Clavier Übung*, which Lübeck published in 1728 at the age of seventy-two, "auff Ersuchen einiger Freunde," contains a prelude and fugue, a suite, and, as the title says "eine Zugabe von dem Gesang Lobt Gott ihr Christen allzugleich in einer Chaconne." The praise and extravagant words with which the modern editor tries to introduce today's listener to these works—he speaks of an "iron-bound consequence and fateful course" of the prelude and fugue and of a "mighty breath, a single, unprecedented motion toward a climax" in the suite—can hardly be accepted even with the best of wills. For its length the prelude is rather conventional and lacking in content, and the fugue, despite its lively repercussion subject, is rather tiresome because of the many repeated passages. The suite, consisting of A C S G, presents many interesting and individual features, though they are not always significant. The gigue is the best and most unified movement, spirited and lively. The chaconne is a little two-part piece that combines the chorale melody *Lobt Gott ihr Christen allzugleich* with an eight-measure *basso ostinato*, which is heard four times, first alone, then three times as the basis of the chorale.

Böhm

George Böhm was born in Hohenkirchen near Ohrdruf (Thuringia) in 1661. He was educated at the Latin school at Goldbach (1675–78), the gymnasium at Gotha (1678), and the University of Jena (1684). In 1690 he went to Hamburg and in 1698 to Lüneburg, where he held the office of organist at the Johanniskirche until his death in 1733.

In the new edition[81] Böhm's keyboard works are arranged in three groups: I. free compositions, II. suites, and III. chorale settings. This division is retained here, the only exception being the *Partita über Jesu du bist allzu schöne*, which Wolgast adds to the suites, and which we shall include in the chorale settings. Accordingly, Böhm's keyboard works consist of 6 free compositions, 18 chorale arrangements, and 11 suites plus a single minuet. Several of the free compositions and the chorale settings are as obviously meant for the organ as the suites are for the harpsichord or clavichord.

FREE COMPOSITIONS

In his free compositions Böhm generally follows the North German tradition. Two of them (I, 1 and 2) consist of a prelude and fugue with a short postlude. The prelude and fugue in D minor (I, 4; merely called *Praeludium* in the original) is constructed like a toccata, with two thematically related fugues embedded in a longish prelude, a short interlude, and a short postlude. The *Capriccio* in D major (I, 5) consists of three thematically related fugues, which are connected by two brief interludes, reminiscent of Froberger's variation canzona, which was also cultivated by Weckmann and Buxtehude. Similarly the *Praeludium, Fuge und Postludium* in G minor (I, 6) derives its formal aspect from North German models, although its musical substance exhibits other, very personal traits. Only the *Praeludium* in F major (I, 3) comes from a different background, for all its details are modeled after the French overture of Lully, so much so that it almost seems to be an arrangement of an orchestral piece. French elements occur repeatedly in other works by Böhm.

Fig.675

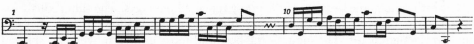

The *Praeludium und Fuge* in C major (I, 1) begins with a full C-major chord, followed by an extended pedal solo, in which cadences are formed by means of descending octave skips, as shown in Fig.675. The formula was taken from the *basso-continuo* aria of the period. Manual passages, full chords, ostinato basses, and rhetorical exclamations follow—all in effective variety and within a well-planned structure. In one passage the modulation leads as far as B major, while at the end, with genuine Baroque deception, the brilliant C major passes into minor. The succeeding fugue is based on one of the most characteristic subjects in pre-Bach organ music (Fig.676). The cadence formula of the pedal solo in the prelude is cleverly used as the starting point of the fugue subject. For the conclu-

Fig.676

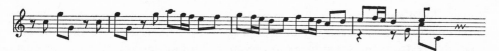

sion of the fugue, Böhm employs the dramatic effect of the deceptive cadence, so frequently employed by Bach: The dominant of C major is followed by an A-minor chord, which serves as the starting point for a brief, toccata-like ending leading to the final C major.

Fig.677

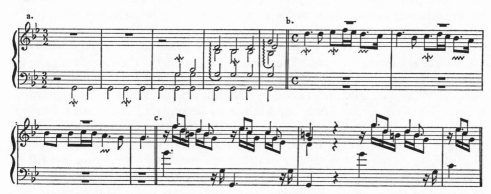

The content of the *Praeludium, Fuge und Postludium* in G minor (I, 6), is very different. It is a very curious and subjective creation, pursuing the opposites of brilliance and magnificence—romantic dreaminess and meditation. Spitta[82] characterizes it as "a mood so deep, so melancholy, a dreaming and reveling in bittersweet harmonies, such as only a German is capable of." The prelude consists entirely of chords, which rise slowly at the beginning from the low register to the high one. The postlude is also purely chordal, but uses a repeated arpeggio motif —a technique also found in Reincken's music (cf.Fig.644). Between them there is a fugue whose peculiar, winding, descending subject gives a curiously tired, almost melancholy impression. To speak of a French gracefulness here, as Spitta does, hardly seems appropriate. Fig.677 shows the beginnings of the three sections. French influence is however, shown by the various ornaments that Böhm uses in this composition as well as in others: *tremblement, pincement, coulé, arpègement,* etc. (cf. the table of ornaments from the Möller manuscript on p.XXIII of the new edition). The intimate character of this work makes it particularly suitable for performance on the clavichord, on which the arpeggios of the postlude, especially, sound much more beautiful than on the harpsichord or organ.

CHORALE ARRANGEMENTS

Böhm adds a new type, the chorale partita, to the traditional species of chorale variations. In the 17th century partita always means variation, so that the two types derive from the same idea—to present a chorale several times in the form of a cycle. But they differ essentially in their methods. In chorale variations the melody is treated in many different ways: as a motet, bicinium, *cantus planus* with figural counterpoints, free fantasy, etc.; in the chorale partita, on the other hand, it is handled like a secular song, usually employing only various kinds of figuration. The former are dominated by contrapuntal texture; the latter employs counterpoint only to enliven the homophony. In the former the harmonic and structural features of the theme, such as the length of the individual phrases, have no importance; in the latter they are retained strictly. In chorale variations the melody is often freely treated, put in a lower voice, diminished, augmented, ornamented, or fragmented; in a partita it is always heard in its original form and almost always in the soprano. The former are meant for the church organ; the latter is just as easily executed on a house instrument. Thus the chorale partita is closer to what is usually understood by variations than a set of chorale variations is, but this term is too firmly established to be replaced by another (such as chorale cycle).

The following works by Böhm are chorale variations: *Auf meinen lieben Gott* (III, 3; 4 verses), *Aus tiefer Not* (III, 4; 2 verses), *Christe der du bist* (III, 5; 3 verses), *Herr Jesu Christ* (III, 10; 6 verses), and *Vater unser* (III, 12.i; 2 verses). In several of these settings Böhm employs more or less traditional methods; thus *Aus tiefer Not*, var.I, *Christe*, var.II, and *Herr Jesu*, var.V, are motets; *Christe*, var. III, has the chorale in the bass; *Herr Jesu*, var.V, is an ornamented chorale; and *Vater unser*, var.II, is a motet or a fantasy. Other settings exhibit more novel ideas, such as expanding the lines of an ornamented discant chorale by insertions or continuations. In Buxtehude's discant chorales one occasionally finds the penultimate and sometimes also the antepenultimate note doubled in value, so that it occupies a whole measure rather than just a half, e.g., in line 3 of *Ein feste Burg*. Böhm goes much farther in this direction. In var.III of *Herr Jesu Christ*, e.g., the last line is expanded from its normal length of four measures to ten, and an even greater expansion occurs in the following verse. In addition, the melody is so freely treated in some variations that it is difficult to recognize it.

A very peculiar and personal approach informs the second variation of *Aus tiefer Not*.[83] It is very difficult to describe it intelligibly. Fig.678 shows how the first line of the tune is treated—it is the tune that Morhardt used (cf.p.379), but in major. The influence of the aria style is unmistakable. This very lively arrangement resembles a tenor aria from a chorale cantata more than an organ chorale, and this impression is reinforced by the motto beginning in measure 10.

Fig.678

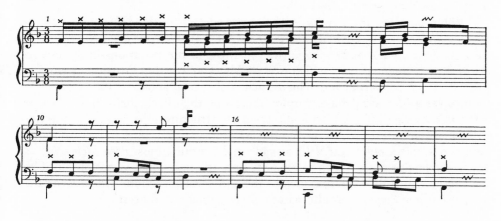

The aria influence is no less obvious in a number of variations that represent a new type, the thorough-bass bicinium. Böhm's works include four instances of this type: *Auf meinen lieben Gott*, var.III; *Christe der du bist*, var.I; *Herr Jesu Christ*, var.II; and *Vater unser*, var.I. In these pieces the lower voice is formulated like a genuine *basso continuo*, while the upper part presents the chorale, freely expanded by echo repetitions, insertions, and continuations. Here, too, the motto beginning, so characteristic of the aria of the period, is employed regularly. Fig. 679 shows the beginning of *Auf meinen lieben Gott*, var.III. J. S. Bach applies this

Fig.679

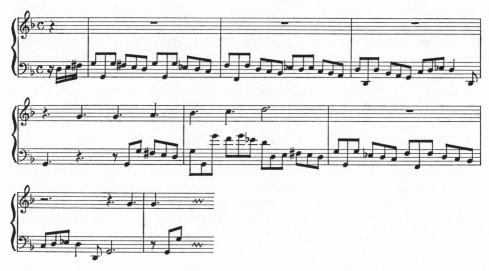

method of variation in two early works, in the variations on *O Gott du frommer Gott* and on *Sei gegrüsset, Jesu gütig.*

Böhm employs the new type of the chorale partita in *Ach wie nichtig* (III, 1), *Freu dich sehr* (III, 8),[84] *Gelobet seist du* (III, 9.i), *Wer nur den lieben Gott* (III, 14), and *Jesu du bist allzu schöne* (II, 13). Most of the variations in these works are of the ornamented type, which was clearly established in Froberger's variation suite *Auff die Mayerin*, and which Pachelbel transplanted to the chorale. But Böhm's variations are definitely more interesting than Pachelbel's. In the last several variations he often expands the thematic structure in one way or another—with echo-like insertions, as in *Ach wie nichtig,* var. VII, preparatory announcements, *Ach wie nichtig,* var. VIII, or cadential continuations, *Freu dich sehr,* var. XI. In the last of these, given in Fig.680, note the individual variation motif and the altered chord that is heard toward the end of each section. The last variation of *Wer nur den lieben Gott* alternates between adagio and presto.

Fig.680

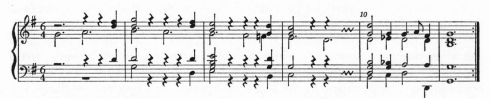

Böhm also wrote eight single chorale settings. Except for two that are written fugally (*Allein Gott,* III, 2, and *Christ lag,* III, 6.i), they all belong to the Buxtehude type of the ornamented discant chorale, but they have longer and more fully developed fore-imitations. The combination of imitation and ornamentation is especially impressive in *Gelobet seist du* (III, 9.ii). *Vater unser* (III, 12.ii) has a singular approach; above a *basso continuo* in the pedals and homophonically reinforcing middle parts, the chorale is heard in a high Baroque, over-rich decoration with numerous suspensions, mordents, trills, and even free ornaments written in small notes. Fig.681 presents line 4 of this setting.

SUITES

Except for suite no.2, Böhm's suites belong to the type that was usual around 1700: A C S G. However in no.9 the gigue is omitted, in no.8 it is replaced by a chaconne, and suite no.10 is introduced by a short prelude, perhaps inspired by Kuhnau's suites of 1693 (*Clavier Übung* II). In suites nos.5 and 7 the gigue is written in duple meter, as Froberger sometimes does. No.5 is very reminiscent of Froberger in other respects, especially in the allemande with its sixteenth-note rests and *brisé* effects. In suites nos. 3, 6, and 9 some of the movements are related

Fig.681

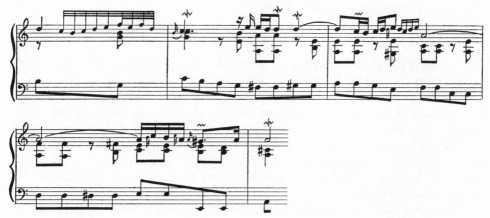

by starting with variants of the same idea; in no.4 this variation principle relates all the movements.

Suite no.2 represents a very different type. It is probably the first example in keyboard music of a fully developed French ballet suite or, as Bach called it, the French overture (cf.pp.585, 590). The cycle consists of overture, air, rigaudon and trio, rondeau, minuet, and chaconne. The overture reflects the plan and style of Lully's ballet and opera overtures with three sections, the first and last gravely pompous adagios, and the second a quasi-fugal allegro. Like the others, this movement shows a thorough familiarity with the French style and is a successful imitation of it. The rigaudon is especially charming; part of it is given in Fig.682.

Fig.682

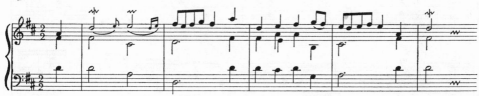

Various stylistic tendencies meet in Böhm's keyboard works: North German, Central German, South German, and French. Froberger, Buxtehude, and Lully were his models, perhaps Pachelbel and some others as well. Should one therefore call him eclectic? Surely not in a pejorative sense. Even though his output does not exhibit obvious personal traits, it nevertheless represents a successful synthesis, a well-rounded whole. Indeed it contains things of real originality, particularly in several chorale settings, in which he transplants the aria style to the organ. His most personal work is the *Praeludium, Fuge und Postludium* in G minor, a romantic creation, which occupies in his output a position similar to that of the *Chromatic Fantasy and Fugue* in Bach's.

Hanff

Johann Nikolaus Hanff was born in Wechmar (Thuringia) in 1665, but lived in North Germany: in Hamburg (1688), where he taught Mattheson for four years, Eutin (1696), Schleswig (?), and again in Hamburg (1706), where he died in 1711. He is known as an organ composer by six chorale preludes, almost all of which belong to the Buxtehude type of the expressively ornamented discant chorale.[85] This form probably suited a native of Thuringia better than the typically North German toccata or extended chorale fantasy. All his chorales reach us in manuscripts by Walther, who did not include anyone born in North Germany in his voluminous collections.

The chief means of presentation in Hanff's chorales is the expressive and affective figuration of the chorale in the soprano. In addition, he uses the imitative treatment of the lower parts in preludes and interludes, which Buxtehude employed only rarely and lightly in his discant chorales. Thus Hanff's chorales combine the Central German chorale fugue technique with the expressive ornamentation of the North German school to form a new type, which Bach may have taken over from Hanff (or Böhm) and used in many of his works. Hanff's symbolic and poetic interpretation of the text may also have influenced Bach. *Ach Gott vom*

Fig.683

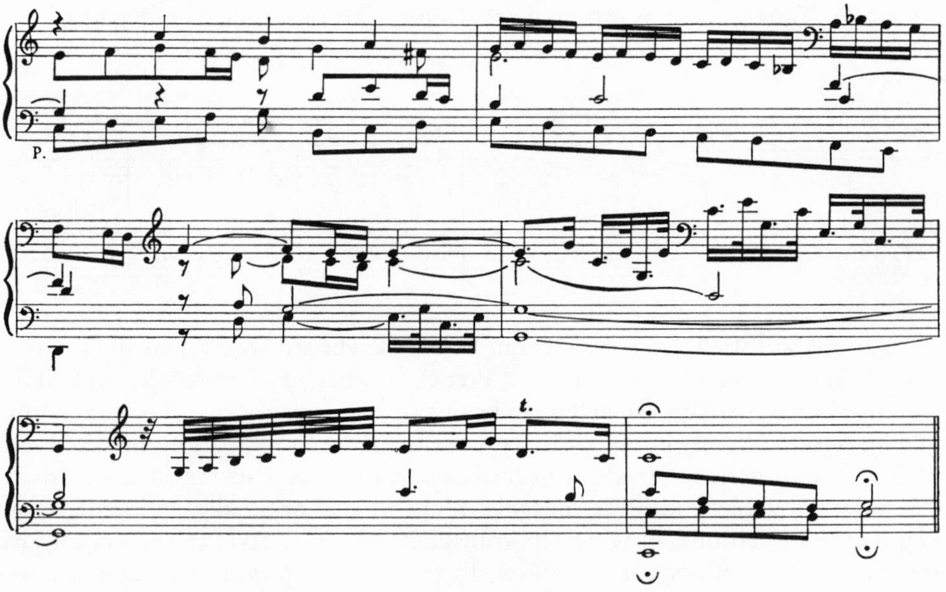

Himmel sieh darein clearly expresses a supplication for mercy, *Auf meinen lieben Gott* reveals a childlike faith, and *Ein feste Burg* proclaims the certainty of victory. The end of this last chorale is given in Fig.683.

The setting of *Erbarm dich mein, o Herre Gott* is somewhat different from the other chorales. It consists of two sections: an extended, almost motet-like presentation of the entire chorale; and a *Versus secundus*, in the manner of the Central German chorale fugue, which develops only the first line imitatively and concludes with a single presentation of the second line. In both sections, reflecting the affect of the chorale, Hanff transforms the first line into a chromatic subject. In the second section the subject is inverted, and in descent it is even more expressive of lamentation (Fig.684).

Fig.684

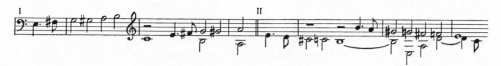

All Hanff's known works prove him to be a "musicus poeticus," whose purpose was not the dramatic gesture but a heartfelt and true expression. As Ritter says,[86] "with others what appears to be only an accidental result—the poetic interpretation of the song—he consciously achieved, not only in general terms but also in very definite physiognomic features."

Bruhns

Nicolaus Bruhns was born in the same year as Hanff, 1665, in Schwabstedt near Husum. He was the son of the local organist, Paul Bruhns. In 1681 he went to Lübeck, where he studied organ and composition under Buxtehude. On Buxtehude's recommendation he then went to Copenhagen, and in 1689 became an organist at the church at Husum. There he stayed, although the city of Kiel tried to engage him, and died in 1697 at the age of thirty-two. He is said to have produced compositions in various fields, but only twelve church cantatas and four organ works are preserved. The latter are typical products of the North German organ art of the end of the 17th century: three long toccatas, called prelude or prelude and fugue, and a fantasy on *Nun komm der Heiden Heiland*.[87]

Like so many North German toccatas, the G-major toccata consists of a prelude, fugue with repercussion subject, interlude, fugue on a triple-meter variant of the first subject, and postlude. Both fugues are written in five parts, using the pedals, and in the first one there is a passage in six parts with double pedals (Fig. 685). In the free sections Bruhns uses figures like Buxtehude's: rapidly ascending octaves, arpeggios, and pedal solos. The other two toccatas are in *E minor*. One

637

Fig.685

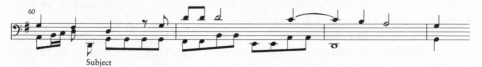

(Stein, no.3; Seiffert, no.3) has only one fugal section, based on a strong, energetic subject. Unfortunately the prelude and postlude contain many routine, superficial passages, e.g., five measures in the prelude in which the pedals execute an octave alternation (murky bass) on *B–b*. The other *E*-minor toccata (Stein, no.2; Seiffert, no.1) is Bruhns's most significant work. Like Schubert's *C*-major Symphony, it raises expectations whose fulfillment was rendered impossible by an early death. It consists of two independent fugues plus the usual prelude, interlude, and postlude. The first fugue is based on a ricercar-like subject (| *e b* | *a♯ a* | *g♯ g* | *f♯ d′* | *c♯′ b* | − *a♯* | *b* |), whose seriousness is most successfully enlivened by a repercussive countersubject and various additional sixteenth-note motifs. The subject of the second fugue, given in Fig.686, with its rests and syncopations, is one of the

Fig.686

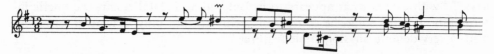

most original ideas in the fugue literature of the 17th century. The infinitely varied figures of the free sections that are associated with these fugues go from one extreme to another and create the impression that the organ, with its unlimited means of sound, is presenting a musical show or a magic theatre, in which ever new personages are entering, crossing the stage, and disappearing again. Fig.687 indicates five successive scenes of this very exciting drama.

Nun komm der Heiden Heiland is a long work in four sections, corresponding to the four lines of the chorale, and separated by descending cadential passages. The first line is heard seven times, mostly alternating between discant and bass, and combined with an obbligato counterpoint which, like the main sub-

Fig.687

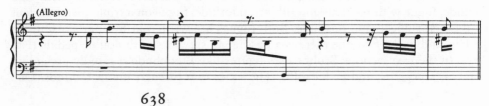

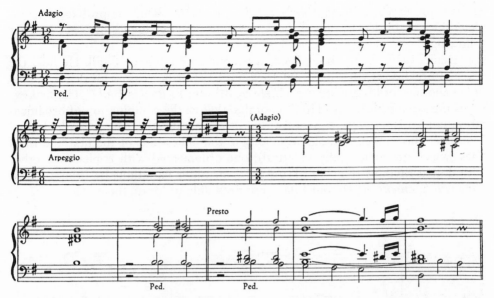

ject, is variously ornamented when it appears in the soprano. Fig.688 shows this contrapuntal complex. The frequent use of ornamentation symbols is reminiscent of Böhm, but these signs may not be original.[88] In the second section Bruhns works with fragmentation. On several occasions he uses the first few notes of the line together with an obbligato countermotif as the fore-imitation of the entire line. In the two remaining sections the use of obbligato countermotifs continues to play an essential role, and the result is that too much of the work is constructed according to the same recipe. Two echo passages in the second section are not much more than a superficial attempt to counteract the uniformity of approach. Bruhns owes his place of honor in the history of organ music to his great *E*-minor toccata, an admirable work of genius and originality.

Fig.688

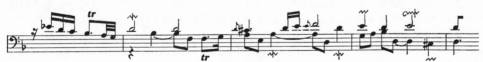

P. Hasse the Younger, Erich, Leiding, Brunckhorst, and Saxer

Let us now round out the picture of North German organ music with the works of some less important composers. Peter Hasse the Younger (1659–1708), son of Nicolaus, and grandson of the elder Peter Hasse, was probably a pupil of Buxtehude and became the organist of St. Jacobi at Lübeck, in 1686. Only one work of his is preserved, a *Praeludium ex d fis con pedale*, which is probably incomplete, since it consists of only a toccata section, without fugues or other sections following.[89]

Daniel Erich, born about 1660, was another Buxtehude pupil. He held the office of organist at Güstrow from 1679 until 1712 (the year of his death?). Two organ chorales of his are known, *Allein zu dir* and *Es ist das Heil*.[90] The first exhibits the same features as Hanff's chorales, that is, the combination of ornamentation (which is not very expressive) with fore-imitations of the individual lines. The other shows considerable originality in the figurations of the first and third lines (which are melodically identical), one ornamented with triplets, the other with dotted rhythms (Fig.689). Frotscher[91] mentions variations by Erich on *Von Gott will ich nicht lasse*n, but I have not been able to locate them.

Fig.689

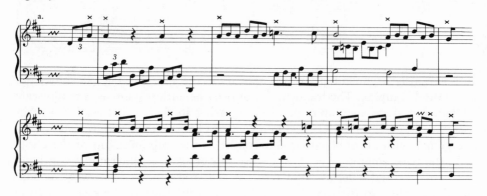

a. line 1; b. line 3.

Georg Dietrich Leiding (Leyding) was born in 1664 in Bücken near Hoya on the Weser. In 1679 he went to Brunswick to study with Bölsche. He studied further with Reincken at Hamburg and with Buxtehude at Lübeck. After Bölsche's death in 1684 Leiding became his successor in Brunswick, and died there in 1710. Of his organ works two preludes and two chorale settings are preserved.[92] The preludes are mediocre and favor homophonic sound effects. The first one, in E flat major, even omits the fugal section.[93] I am acquainted with only one of the chorale settings, *Von Gott will ich nicht lassen*, which is the last work in the Berlin Ms. P.802 and obviously incomplete. Only two variations are extant, the first one an ornamented discant chorale and the second a bicinium with continuous sixteenth notes (often in arpeggios) in the left hand. For the arrangement of *Wie schön leuchtet der Morgenstern* see Frotscher's description.[94]

Arnold Melchior Brunckhorst, born about 1670, was the organist of the community church at Celle from 1697 until his death in 1720. A prelude in E minor, consisting of an extended prelude, fugue, and brief postlude, is modeled after Buxtehude, but is no more than a solid student work.[95]

George Wilhelm Dietrich Saxer was the last representative of the North German school. He was an organist at St. Jacobi at Lübeck from 1737 to 1740 (the year of his death?). The Leipzig manuscript collection II.2.51 (part III—which also contains the prelude by Brunckhorst and Werckmeister's compositions) preserves three organ pieces by him that have not yet been printed: *Prelude ex E.* ♮, *Praeludium ex F*, and *Praeludium ex D. fis*, each consisting of a prelude and fugue. These pieces are quite brilliant, if sometimes rather dry. The most successful is probably the *D*-major prelude, whose beginning is given in Fig.690.

Fig.690

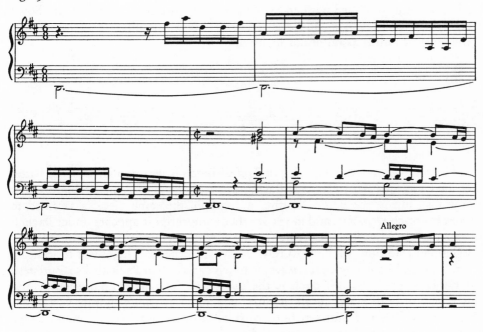

C. CENTRAL GERMANY

Heinrich Bach, Ahle, Briegel, Wecker, and Keller

The repertoire of Central German keyboard music in the first half of the 17th century, as it is preserved in the prints of Michael, Klemm, and Kindermann, consists chiefly of preludes, fugues, and dance movements. In Kindermann's *Harmonia organica* of 1645, the chorale fugue, the type that plays a central role in the later evolution, makes its first appearance. It is a brief, simple treatment of the

Protestant organ chorale, which employs only the first line of the melody and presents it in the form of a chorale fugue. Kindermann concerned himself with this species only occasionally and more or less accidentally, when he based some of his fugues on ecclesiastic subjects, but it constitutes an essential part of the output of the later Central German composers, and many of them, especially the older members of the Bach family, are known almost exclusively through works in this field.

Johann Sebastian's great-uncle Heinrich Bach was born in Wechmar in 1615. He was called to play the organ at Arnstadt in 1641, and worked there until his death in 1692. Only one organ piece can be ascribed to him with certainty, a setting of *Erbarm dich mein, o Herre Gott*, which is found in one of the famous Walther autographs, signed HB.[96] The first line is extensively developed in imitative writing and combined with an expressive chromatic countersubject, as shown in Fig.691. In its strict style and serious, devout expression, this composition is one of the most beautiful examples of its kind.

Fig.691

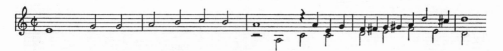

The arrangement of *Christ lag in Todesbanden* is very similar in style. Ritter published it as a work by Heinrich Bach,[97] probably from a Weimar tablature that is now lost, but in the Berlin Walther autograph, the same piece is ascribed to Johann Heinrich Buttstett, and in yet another manuscript it appears under Pachelbel's name.[98] In cases like this, which occur very frequently, especially in the Central German tradition, we have to rely on stylistic criteria. They seem to indicate that this piece, like *Erbarm dich mein,* is much earlier than Pachelbel or Buttstett, and rather suggest that H. Bach is the composer. The strict counterpoint and slow tempo of both pieces recall the first sections of Scheidt's chorale variations, whereas Pachelbel and Buttstett both work with ornamental counterpoints. One exception is the setting of *Da Jesus an dem Kreuze stund*, which Seiffert included among Pachelbel's works, but with the remark that the style of the piece is more like that of Heinrich Bach.[99]

Johann Rudolf Ahle, born in Mülhausen in 1625, became an organist at the local church of St. Blasien in 1654, and later town councilor and mayor, offices he held until his early death in 1673. In addition to a large number of liturgical and secular vocal works (about 200?), he wrote many organ pieces, of which only a few have been preserved. A. Adrio, in *MGG*, mentions a collection of 64 organ compositions. A copy of Grobe's tablature (1675, now lost), made by A. G. Ritter and now held at Beuron Archabbey, contains 23 organ chorales, 12 of them expressly attributed to Ahle. The remaining ones (nos.9–11, 13, 14, 16, 18–20, 22, 23) are probably also by Ahle.

Fig.692

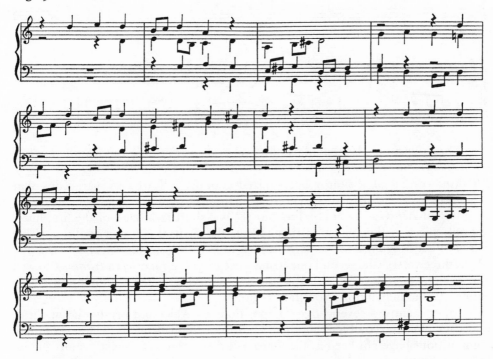

In contrast to many other Central German composers, Ahle almost always bases his organ chorales on the entire chorale tune. In several very interesting, unique settings the lines are presented in quarter-note diminution and in manifold strettos. In order to introduce the subject as often as possible fragmentation is also employed, and Ahle does not even mind forcing the chorale melody into alien rhythms to serve this purpose. Fig.692 shows the first two lines from *Komm heiliger Geist* (no.3 of the above collection). Almost the entire chorale is presented in this manner; only two of its nine lines are treated differently, being heard once only in their proper note values (half notes). The arrangements of *Gott der Vater* (no.1), *Nun lob mein Seel* (no.4), *Allein zu dir* (no.8), and *Christ unser Herr zum Jordan kam* (no.12) are more or less of the same type. The extensive, artificially forced imitations hark back to an earlier time; so do most of the chorales that Ahle sets, for they were no longer in general use in the second half of the 17th century. The employment of Sweelinck-like clavieristic figures above *cantus-firmus* lines, such as those in Fig.693, from *Mensch willtu leben* (no.7), is similarly archaic.

Fig.693

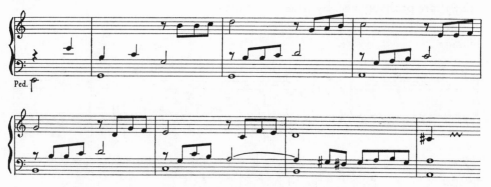

The collection also contains three chorale variations, on *Komm heiliger Geist* (no.5), *Allein Gott in der Höh* (no.6), and *Mensch willtu leben* (no.23[100]). All three consist of a simply harmonized chorale, followed by variations that are mostly of the ornamented type—one each in nos.5 and 6, and four in no.23. A setting of *Ach Gott vom Himmel* (no.18) is a short treatment of the first line— the only piece in the collection that reflects the Central German tradition. Ahle also wrote a *Magnificat 8vi toni* (no.19) in four verses, a *Magnificat 9ni toni* (no. 20) in three verses (the second one being a bicinium), a *Lux beata trinitas* (no.21), and a *Vita sanctorum* (no.22), the last two testifying to the continuation of the Roman Catholic hymn in Protestant regions.

Ritter mentions several free compositions by Ahle, and prints one of them, a toccata,[101] which combines South and North German elements. The rest of these compositions have not been available to me; they seem to be mostly short fugues of insignificant content.[102]

Wolfgang Carl Briegel, born in 1626 (in Pomerania?), worked as organist and orchestral director at Gotha from 1650 on. In 1671 he was called to Darmstadt to be the director of the court orchestra, and died there in 1712. Like Ahle, he is primarily known as a vocal composer, indeed so exclusively that his clavier works are not mentioned in any of the usual reference books (including *MGG*). They were preserved (together with Ahle's) in Grobe's lost tablature, from which G. W. Körner and A. G. Ritter published several pieces, including a *Fuga tertii toni*,[103] a *Fuga sexti toni*, and two chorale settings.[104] The *Fuga tertii toni* is noteworthy for its chromatic subject (| b c′ a b | e e′ d♯′ d′ | c♯′ c′ b a | b . . .) and two clearly differentiated interludes of three measures each. In the *Fuga super: Diess sind die heil' gen zehn Gebot* each chorale line is fugally treated. The arrangement of *Christ lag in Todesbanden* begins with a full chordal presentation of the first two lines, with the first three notes (*a g♯ a*) heard in the bass and the others in the soprano. Then the whole chorale is offered as a *cantus planus* in the discant, accompanied by two lower parts, which show figurations similar to Pachelbel's.

Georg Kaspar Wecker (1632–95) lived and worked exclusively in Nuremberg, where Kindermann was his teacher, and Johann Krieger and Pachelbel his pupils. A short fugue in *D* minor[105] shows all the signs of a solid, but moderate, Central German gift.

Heinrich Michael Keller (1638–1710), who was active at Berka and Frankenhausen, left several fugues and an organ chorale on *Gelobet seist du*, in which the individual lines are presented at great length, a very unusual treatment for Central Germany, but unfortunately not too inspired.[106] Thus the piece is of interest only as a curious example of a "Thuringian chorale motet."

Johann Christoph Bach and Johann Michael Bach

More precise information is available for Heinrich Bach's two sons, Johann Christoph and Johann Michael. The former was born at Arnstadt in 1642. In 1665 he was called to Eisenach as an organist, and later worked there as a harpsichordist of the ducal court chapel also. He died in Eisenach in 1703. Around 1700 a manuscript collection of 44 of his chorale preludes was put together under the title: *Choraele welche bey wärenden Gottes Dienst zum Praeambulieren gebrauchet werden können, gesetzet und herausgegeben von Johann Christoph Bachen, Organ: in Eisenach.*[107] In addition he wrote a prelude and fugue and two or three variation works.

The 44 chorales are particularly suited "zum Praeambulieren bey wärenden Gottes Dienst," for they are brief and simply set. Few are longer than 35 measures and many are only about 20. Their style is unified and limited; the texture is essentially one of three parts, the motion rarely exceeds eighth notes, and the role of the pedals is limited to brief passages that end in pedal points. Such works could be used in the smallest churches as preludes and suitable introductions to congregational singing.

Johann Christoph employs a variety of methods to present the chorale melody. Sometimes he constructs the entire piece as an imitative development based on the first line, i.e., as a chorale fugue or, as it may be called because of its brevity, a chorale fughetta (nos.10, 21, 37, 38). In other compositions the second line is also used, either sounding in the soprano (nos.11, 13, 31, 35) or treated in a second fugato, which is often compressed into strettos, (nos.1, 8, 15, 20). Occasionally a later line of the chorale is sounded toward the end, e.g., the third line in no.39 (*Wie schön leuchtet*) and the fourth one in no.42 (*Christ der du bist*). Many times the entire chorale is presented, with the first line as always in a fugato and the others heard only briefly (nos.12, 14, 16, 19, 22, 29, etc.). Quite often Johann Christoph Bach employs fragmentation, which is really more at home in North German organ music. As an example, a passage from no.21 (*Dies sind die heiligen zehn Gebot*) is reproduced in Fig.694.

Fig.694

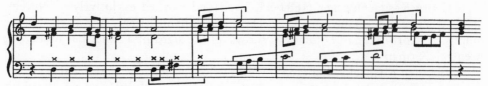

Since all forty-four chorales start with imitation, we have another opportunity to investigate the comparative frequencies of the answer at the fifth and at the fourth. In Johann Klemm's fugue collection of 1631 (cf.p.386) the older principle of imitation at the fourth (or lower fifth) still predominated, but in Johann Christoph's pieces the balance has clearly shifted in favor of the answer at the fifth. Only about a dozen of the chorales begin with an answer at the fourth.

The most important of Johann Christoph Bach's remaining compositions is the *Praeludium und Fuge ex Dis* (i.e., in E flat major). It consists of a prelude, a fugue, and a toccata-like postlude, and in its formal disposition as well as in various details it is unmistakably influenced by Froberger.[108] The fugue is based on the chromatic subject (| *eb bb a ab* | *g gb f bb* |), and the note *cb*, which is written as a *b* in the original, is used several times, e.g., in the passage given in Fig.695.

Fig.695

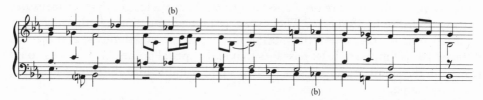

Finally there are several variation works. In a sarabande with twelve variations[109] Johann Christoph relies completely on formula variation, which became more and more popular toward the end of the 17th century. A new figure is introduced in the first measure of each variation, and is repeated in every measure thereafter, with adaptations to the underlying harmony. This technique is not attractive in itself, and it becomes particularly tiresome when it is applied to such an empty subject as this sarabande. Another variation set is preserved as *Aria Eberliniana pro dormente Camillo variata,*[110] and dated "Mens. Mart. 23, 1690." It is based on a brief, song-like theme, probably by Daniel Eberlin (1630–92), which is treated in fifteen variations of a less formulary character than those of the sarabande. Variation IX stands out, because it moves chromatically throughout, like the "Alter Weiber Conduct" in Poglietti's variations on the *Aria allemagna* (cf.p.568).

Johann Christoph's younger brother Johann Michael was born in Arnstadt in 1648, became an organist at Gehren in 1673, and died there in 1694 at the age of forty-six. His daughter Maria Barbara was Johann Sebastian's first wife. In his *Lexikon*, Gerber reports that Johann Michael possessed "seventy-two different fugues and ornamented chorales, some of them with six, eight, or ten variations and of great variety and diversity." Of this large output only eight pieces exist today: 1. *Allein Gott in der Höh*, 2. *Dies sind die heiligen zehn Gebot*, 3. *In dich hab ich gehoffet*, 4. *Nun freut euch*, 5. *Von Gott will ich nicht lassen*, 6. *Wenn mein Stündlein*, 7. *Wenn wir in höchsten Nöten sein*, 8. *Wo Gott der Herr*.[111]

Fig.696

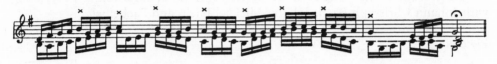

No.7 consists of three brief variations in the older style, the last of which is constructed as a bicinium of the ornamented chorale plus a note-against-note counterpoint (Fig.696). No.2 presents the chorale lines in half notes in the discant, each line with its more or less completely worked out fore-imitations, all within a four-part setting of traditional counterpoint. In no.6 a fore-imitation of the first line introduces the entire chorale in quarter notes, with lines 1–2 in the soprano, lines 3–4 in the bass, and lines 5–7 first in the soprano and then in the bass. Nos.3, 4, 5, and 8 belong to the type frequently employed by Pachelbel, in which the chorale is heard in half notes in the discant, accompanied by two lightly ornamented counterpoints. In no.1 each line is first presented fugally on the *Rückpositiv* and then in a four-part harmonization on the swell organ; Fig.697 shows the line "Ein Wohlgefalln" (R = Rückpositiv; O = Organ).

Fig.697

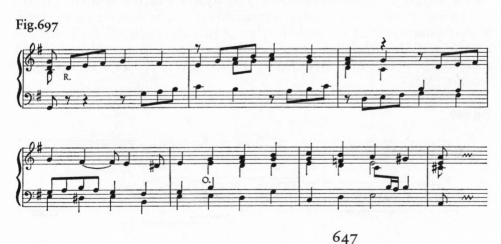

Even in the incomplete form that Johann Michael Bach's output reaches us, it bears out the correctness of Gerber's appraisal: "There is great variety and diversity in these preludes, and none is really unworthy of the name of Bach."[112] Geiringer says that "the compositions of Johann Michael and Johann Christoph are to each other as promise and fulfillment."[113] This is certainly true of their cantatas and motets, but not of their organ works—Johann Michael's are definitely superior to his older brother's, particularly his beautiful prelude to *Wenn mein Stündlein Vorhanden ist* (no.6).

Alberti, Kittel, Pestel, Schultheiss, and Others

Several lesser masters belong to the generation born around the mid-century, along with Johann Christoph Bach, Johann Michael Bach, and Pachelbel.

Fig.698

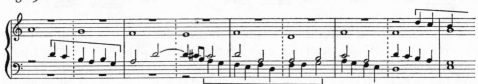

Johann Friedrich Alberti (1642–1710) comes from Tönning (Schleswig) and worked as an organist at Merseburg. Four chorale settings of his have been preserved: *O lux beata Trinitas, Te Deum laudamus, Gelobet seist du,* and *Herzlich lieb hab ich dich*.[114] In *O lux beata Trinitas* the chorale is arranged in three contrapuntal variations, which use only the first line of the melody. In *Versus 2, cum contrapuncto fracto,* the chorale line is heard four times in whole notes, combined with its diminution by four, as shown in Fig.698. In the *Te Deum* Alberti devotes the first section to a strict double fugue in the style of a ricercar based on the first two lines of the tune. In the second section, *Alio modo,* he creates a double fugue of more modern character from the first line and a lively countersubject. In *Gelobet seist du* and *Herzlich lieb* he combines the first line with two freely invented countersubjects to create triple fugues. Fig.699 gives a passage from *Gelobet seist du.*

Fig.699

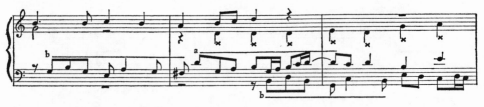

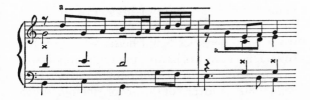

All these compositions exhibit a preference for—and also a very dexterous handling of—the strict contrapuntal style, which was unusual in Central and North Germany. This tendency of Alberti's is corroborated by Mattheson's report about "twelve ricercate . . . in which he applied all species of counterpoint."[115] It is quite apparent that Alberti had somehow become acquainted with the South German-Italian tradition.

Several decades ago a number of keyboard pieces by the Dresden court organist Johann Heinrich Kittel (1652–82) were discovered in the Brasov (Rumania) library, in a *Tabulatura 12 Praeambulorum und einem Capriccio von eben 12 Variationen; durch alle Claves und Tonos auff Clavichordien und Spinetten zu gebrauchen,* written by Daniel Croner in 1682. E. H. Müller reports that this collection contains one prelude in each of the twelve most usual major and minor keys and twelve variations on a two-measure ostinato, and that it "belongs to the series of predecessors of J. S. Bach's *Well-Tempered Clavier.*"[116]

The Mylau tablature book preserves seventeen preludes by Gottfried Ernst Pestel (1654–1732), organist at Weida and Altenburg. Most of them (some barely legible) are transcribed in Shannon M. They are all sustained preludes, written in a modernized *durezze* style, and obviously meant for introducing a festival occasion on the church organ. The beginning of a *Praeludium ex D.f.* is given in Fig.700. The so-called Andreas-Bach Book (Leipzig, Ms.III.8.4) contains a *Partie di J. E. Pestel,* consisting of *Entré, Menuet, Bouré, Bassepied, Gavotte,* and *Sarabande* (with two variations), i.e., an early example of a ballet suite; and in a collection (Berlin, Staatsbibl. Ms. 40268) written by Heinrich Nicolaus Gerber (1702–75), there occurs a *Menuet di Gottfried Ernst Besset* (= Pestel?).

Fig.700

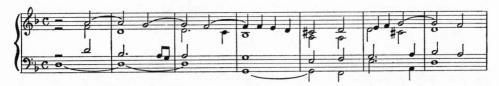

David Heinrich Garthoff of Weissenfels appears in the Mylau tablature book with a *Praeludium di Garthoff* (really a fugue on a repercussion subject). A D-minor fugue by Johann Anton Coberg (1650–1708) from Rotenburg on the

649

Fulda is preserved in the Möller manuscript, but a suite of his is probably lost with Grimm's tablature book.

Nuremberg figures in our survey with Benedict Schultheiss, who was the organist at St. Egidius' and died in 1693. His organ works are apparently unknown, but he published eight suites in his *Muht- und Geist-ermuntrender Clavier-Lust Erster Theil* (1679) and *Anderer Theil* (1680). A lover "of the art of etching, which is never praised enough," he himself "etched [the plates] in copper." In Kindermann we saw a tentative beginning of the suite in Central Germany (cf.p.388). Here it appears firmly established in a form that shows two important innovations when compared to Froberger's suites: The gigue is always placed at the end, and all four suites of 1679 begin with a prelude. Only in a very distant place can we find earlier instances of clavier suites with introductory preludes, in Matthew Locke's *Melothesia,* which appeared in London in 1673. It would of course be wrong to speak of an "influence" in this case and in several similar ones. Curiously, the four suites of the *Anderer Theil* do not have preludes.

Schultheiss' preludes are rather extensive movements, generally in several sections, designated as adagio or allegro. The fourth prelude, e.g., consists of 8 measures *Adagio* in *durezze* style, 12 measures *Allegro* in arpeggios, and 5 final *Adagio* measures. Fig.701 provides some excerpts from it. It is interesting that in this piece, which was written shortly before 1700, the notation is still dominated by the 15th- and 16th-century theory of proportions. The time signature 9/8 of

Fig.701

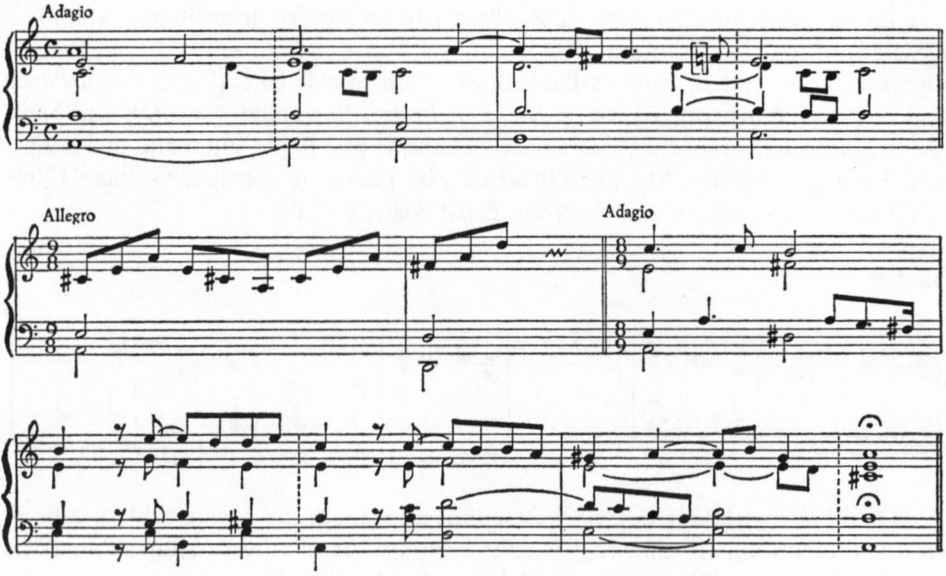

the *Allegro* implies that nine eighth notes fill the same time span as eight notes of the preceding *Adagio;* but the title *Allegro* means a diminution of 1:2, so that in the bass, half notes are given (instead of whole notes) and quite correctly. The signature 8/9 for the final *Adagio* then serves to reverse the proportion in the same way as Tinctoris and Gafori did.[117]

Seiffert is rather negative in his appraisal of Schultheiss' dance movements, and among other things says that they "look like dwarfs next to the dance forms of Froberger, not to speak of Poglietti."[118] This judgment is unjustified, for no one would think of relating Schultheiss' dances to Froberger's epochal creations, and they do not fall far behind Poglietti's (if we exclude the virtuosic froth that the Viennese master develops in his doubles). In short, they come close to the general level of the suite in Germany at the time, whether written by Buxtehude, Böhm, Krieger, or Pachelbel.[119] To hear something really fine, we have to turn to France, to d'Anglebert—or wait for Bach.

Pachelbel

Johann Pachelbel was born in Nuremberg in 1653, and studied with Schwemmer (and Wecker?). He played the organ at Eisenach (1677), Erfurt (1678), Stuttgart (1690), Gotha (1692), and, from 1695 until his death in 1706, back at Nuremberg at the Sebalduskirche. His position as auxiliary organist at St. Stephen's, the cathedral of Vienna, in 1673, and his appointment at Oxford have recently been questioned.

During his lifetime three prints of keyboard works appeared: *Erster Theil etlicher Choräle,* containing eight organ chorales, was apparently printed in 1678, during his stay in Erfurt.[120] (It is usually called *Acht Choräle zum Praeambulieren,* after a new edition of 1693.) *Musicalische Sterbensgedancken,* 1683, is lost. According to Walther's *Musicalisches Lexikon,* it contained four chorale variations. *Hexachordum Apollinis,* with six variations sets on song (arias), appeared in 1699. In addition there is a very extensive manuscript tradition, but it includes many uncertain and doubtful pieces. The total output is published in three *DTB* and *DTÖ* volumes, arranged by types, as follows:[121]

> Vol. I.   Organ works: 24 free compositions (preludes, toccatas, and fantasies, nos.1–24); 2 preludes and fugues (nos.25, 26); 19 fugues (nos.27–45); 3 ricercars (nos.46–48); 72 chorale settings (nos.1–72)
> Vol. II. 94 Magnificat fugues
> Vol. III. Works for harpsichord or clavichord: 13 variation sets on songs (nos. 1–10) and chorales (nos.11–13); 6 chaconnes (nos. 14–19); 4 fantasies (nos.20–23); 16 suites (nos.24–42); 7 fugues (nos. 43–49)

In addition, there are a number of hitherto unpublished works: a prelude and fugue in New Haven E. B. 1688 (p.66), a fugue in Leipzig II.2.51 (part II, p.24; three other pieces from this manuscript have been printed), a *Toccata ex C* in the

Möller manuscript, two preludes and fugues in the Mylau manuscript, and several others.

FREE ORGAN WORKS

Except for no.6, which is unimportant, the six preludes that open vol.I are successful prologues of ten to twenty measures, which project their respective keys with the aid of toccata-like figurations, short pedal points, modulations to closely related keys, and carefully prepared suspensions. The three toccatas (nos.7–9) and the two fantasies (nos.10–11) that follow fulfill the same function within a somewhat broader scope; fantasy no.11, e.g., is in the *durezze e ligature* style, with modulations that lead from *G* minor to *A* flat major and *E* flat minor, as shown in Fig.702.

Fig.702

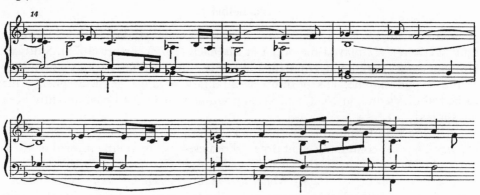

Toccatas nos.12–23 derive from Frescobaldi's pedal toccatas (*Toccate II*, nos.5–6). Like the latter they consist of figurations above long, sustained pedal points. Sebastian Anton Scherer had already cultivated this type, using Frescobaldi as a model for his figurations (cf.p.577). Pachelbel differs here, for his figurations no longer carry out the principle of change and contrast, but are unified throughout or over substantial sections, though unfortunately in a rather uniform manner. They ripple away softly in conventional, frequently repeated formulae—somewhat like a conversation that does not offend anybody because it does not say anything. Toccata no.24, entitled *Praeludium*, goes a little beyond this routine, for it includes two pedal solos reminiscent of the North German toccata. Later on, though, it lapses into trivialities again, as exemplified by the excerpts in Fig.703.

Pachelbel's contributions to the fugue are much more significant. The three monument volumes contain 120 examples of the species, and a number remain unpublished. In only two instances does a prelude precede the fugue in vol.I, (nos.

Fig.703

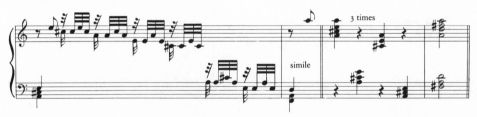

25–26), but additional preludes and fugues are preserved in the New Haven and Mylau manuscripts, and the publisher W. M. Endter announced a print of *Fugen und Praeambuln über die gewöhnlichsten Tonos figuratos* by Pachelbel for the fall fair of 1704; however the print probably never appeared.[122]

Most of the nineteen fugues published as organ compositions (vol.I) start with a four-part exposition. At the fourth entry, however, one of the voices disappears, so that a three-part texture results, which is only occasionally expanded to four parts, especially in the concluding measures. The subjects—and therefore the fugues—excel in variety of design and expression, in comparison with those of earlier composers. Some flow quietly, others are lively; some are short, others rather long. Fig.704, taken from nos.27 and 36, indicates the approximate limits.

Fig.704

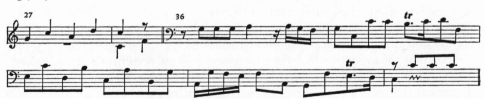

The subject is still occasionally answered at the fourth, but mostly at the fifth, supported by a modulation to the dominant, e.g., in nos.30, 33–35, 37, 39, 42, and 44. Most of the longer fugues, such as no.33, have three sections, separated by episodes, but the subject is heard only on the steps on which it was placed in the exposition. There is practically no trace of the idea of treating the middle section in a modulatory manner. Fugues nos.28 and 29 are somewhat exceptional, for they have only two voices, and the subject is answered only at the octave. Perhaps they served as models for Bach's *Two-Part Inventions*. The beginning of no.29 (its subject is similar to that of the "March of the Armed Men" from *The Magic Flute*) is given in Fig.705.

Seven more fugues are published among the harpsichord (clavichord) works (vol.III, nos.43–49). There is no particular reason for separating them from the organ fugues, for they have some features in common—their vivacious subjects

Fig.705

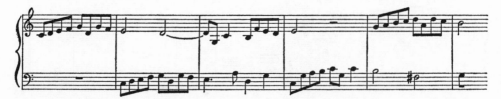

and frequent employment of repercussion formulae. One of the three ricercars (vol.I, no.47) gives the impression of being a school assignment modeled on a Sweelinck hexachord fantasy or something similar, but the other two (nos.46 and 48) are mature works, whose strict style and learned technique reveal a South German influence. The inversion of the subject plays an important role in both; it is an artifice that, along with augmentation, diminution, and stretto, does not appear anywhere else in Pachelbel's fugues.

MAGNIFICAT FUGUES

Pachelbel's Magnificat fugues (vol.II) present two problems concerning their liturgical function. First of all, most of these pieces do not show any relationship to the liturgical melodies, and secondly, they appear in very irregular groupings—23 pieces for the first tone, 10 for the second, 11 for the third, etc. The first difficulty resolves itself when we remember that freely composed versets are found as early as the end of the 16th century in the music of Antonio Valente, and more recently in Kerll's *Modulatio organica* of 1686. As for the second point, it should be noted that the order in which the monument volume presents the pieces is completely different from that of the original sources. The chief source for Pachelbel's Magnificat fugues is a manuscript of the Berlin Institute for Church Music, now lost, which contained sixty-four versets in a very regular order—in two collections of four versets for each tone. These collections were reprinted in the same order by F. Commer,[123] but later, when additional manuscripts were discovered, increasing the repertoire by about one half, this material was combined with the pieces from the Berlin manuscript in the monument volume, and "the combination was freely handled"; the order of the pieces within the eight groups was determined by "the more or less close motivic relationship of the individual fugue subjects."[124] It is obvious that this procedure produced a completely erroneous impression.

In general, the Magnificat fugues are similar to the other organ fugues, but because there are more of them they exhibit the same features more clearly and more richly. The limits of expression are thus even more expanded, from the serious ricercar to the light-footed repercussion fugue, as exemplified by Fig.706. Relationships to Gregorian tunes are recognizable in only a very few instances, most clearly in versets III, 1; III, 2; and VII, 1, where after an initial fugal section,

Fig.706

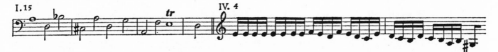

the melody of the respective Magnificat tone (or at least its second half) is heard in sustained tones in the pedals and combined with figurations in the upper parts. Several fugue subjects may be derived from the intonation formulae, e.g., VI, 3 and VI, 4 from (*f g a f*) or VII, 1 and VII, 2 from (*c' b c' d'*).

Nos.I, 12; VI, 1; and VIII, 8 are double fugues in three sections, of the type A ‖ B ‖ A/B. Only no.VI, 1 appeared in the verset collection of the Berlin manuscript, but as three separate versets, accounting for three of the regular group of four (the fourth is VI, 2). It is also included in the London manuscript, Brit. Mus. Ms. 31221, which contains most of the remaining versets, among them VIII, 8. The three sections of I, 12 occur separately in three different German manuscripts.

The Magnificat fugues, as well as the other organ fugues, include several two-part works, some of which (nos.I, 17; III, 8, marked "Für zwey Clavier") are formulated archaically as *Bicinia contrapuncto duplici*. A number of others (nos.I, 3; I, 10; VIII, 2: III, 12) may be regarded as additional models for Bach's *Two-Part Inventions*. Verset I, 3 is unusual, for it divides into three sections, the second of which modulates from the basic *D* minor to the related key of *F* major.

CHORALE SETTINGS

Pachelbel wrote almost as many organ chorales as fugues. Seventy-two chorale settings are included in vol.I, and about half a dozen remain unpublished. There are about twelve examples of the traditional type of Central German organ music, the short chorale fugue. In some the treatment is limited to the fugal presentation of the first line, e.g., in *Christe der du bist* (no.12) and *Dies sind die heil'gen zehn Gebot* (no.19). Others involve the second line as well, using it as an "answer" to the first, as in *Ach Herr mich armen Sünder* (no.3) and *Der Herr ist mein getreuer Hirt* (no.17), or sounding it here and there in the course of the piece, as in *Ach Gott vom Himmel* (no.1). Fig.707 shows the beginning of no.3.

Among the settings that employ the entire chorale tune, the ornamented

Fig.707

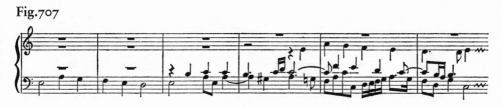

treatment of the melody, which plays such an important role in the North German tradition, occurs in only one example, *Wir glauben all* (no.66), one of the *Acht Choräle zum Praeambulieren* printed in 1693. However, this attempt to appropriate a strange technique has a rather awkward result, for the ornamentation merely replaces the half and whole notes of the chorale with continuous conventional sixteenth-note figures. The motet-like treatment also occurs in only one piece, *Erhalt uns Herr* (no.25), but it is not certain that this piece is Pachelbel's; it may be Buxtehude's or Böhm's.[125]

With these two exceptions, the melodies are laid out throughout as "Protestant *cantus plani*," i.e., in the simple form in which they occur in the songbooks of the 17th century. Pachelbel combines the melodies with one or several counterpoints to arrive at two-, three-, or four-part settings. There are four two-part settings (bicinia), one of which (no.26), however, is not by Pachelbel but by Sweelinck or Scheidemann.[126] The others (nos.20, 42, 61) also sound rather archaic, especially *Jesus Christus unser Heiland*, another of the *Acht Choräle*, where the chorale, in half and whole notes, is heard twice, first in the upper part, then in the lower, combined almost throughout with sixteenth-note figures in the other voice.

The three-part arrangements, on the other hand, have originality; at the same time they show a definite tendency toward crystallizing of types. The great majority of these settings present the chorale in half notes (occasionally in whole notes) in either the soprano or the bass, while the two counterpoints move predominantly in sixteenth-note figures, which employ complementary motifs or join in parallel runs. In addition, there are short fore-imitations in diminished note

Fig.708

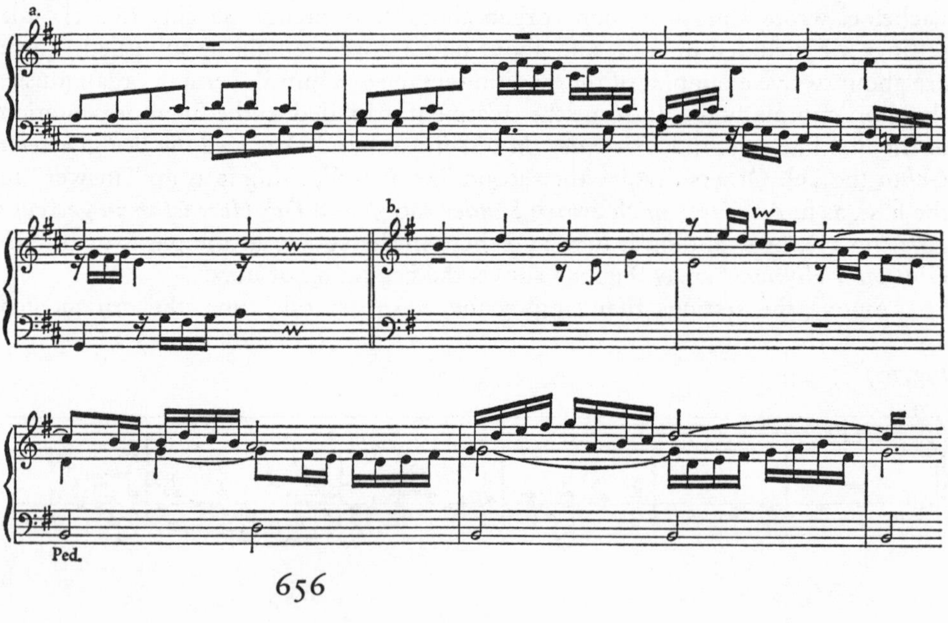

values, usually in eighth notes when the chorale is in the soprano, and in quarter notes when it is in the bass. The discant type is very clearly represented by nos.6, 21, 31, 37, 40, and 46, the bass type by nos.35, 41, 45, 48b, 62, and 65, as well as by nos.24 and 49, in which the chorale is reinforced by octave doublings. Fig.708 shows the beginnings of *Gott der Vater wohn'uns bei* (no.31) and *Meine Seele erhebt den Herren* (no.48b). Several settings deviate somewhat in their treatment by using quieter motion in the counterpoints (nos.30, 59), presenting the chorale in quarter notes (nos.14, 67), or omitting the fore-imitations (no.57). Only in one piece does the chorale appear in the middle voice (no.52).

The four-part settings (nos.11, 32, 33, 43, 47, 51, 55) are even more unified in method. They generally begin with an extensive fore-imitation, and present the chorale in half notes in the discant. The motion of the counterpoints in the other voices rarely exceeds eighth notes. The *Vater unser* from the *Acht Choräle* (no.55) deviates somewhat from this norm, having only a two-measure fore-imitation and counterpoints in a livelier tempo.

Another curious form, found only among Pachelbel's works, is called "combination form" by Seiffert. It combines two of the above types: the chorale fugue on the first line and the three- or four-part setting of the entire chorale. The two sections are about equal in length and are connected by a transition. The first section is always formulated like the individual chorale fugues described above; the second is either in four voices, with the chorale in the discant (nos.2, 4, 5, 10, 18, 22, 27, 53, 60, 63, 64, 69), or in three parts, with the chorale in the bass (nos. 9, 13, 23, 34, 38, 50, 56, 58), mostly with octave doublings. The treatment is exactly the same as in the pieces that consist of only one of these types. An exception is *Allein Gott in der Höh sei Ehr* (no.7), whose chorale fugue is based on an ornamented version of the first line, and whose second section deviates from the norm by the frequent use of full chords and other details. This piece is probably not by Pachelbel but by Buttstett.

The combination form introduced by Pachelbel obviously did not spring from purely musical considerations, but resulted from some external circumstance. Seiffert[127] connects it with an official obligation incurred by Pachelbel at Erfurt, according to which he had to "play on the entire organ for half an hour once a year at the end of the service." Consequently Seiffert sees these pieces as intended for an organ recital during which "the congregation did not sing the chorale after the introductory fugue, but listened to its echo, produced by the organ with greater art and in richer harmonies." To me it seems more plausible that the second section of these pieces does not represent pure organ performance but an artfully worked out organ accompaniment for the singing by the congregation or more likely by the church choir, which entered after the organ solo in the first section. Depending on whether the melody was heard in the bass or soprano, the men's or boys' voices of the choir would sing the melody, and the congregation could join in, if it wished.

In 1683, shortly after the plague left him bereft of wife and child, Pachelbel published his *Musicalische Sterbensgedancken, aus 4 variierten Chorälen bestehend*. The print is lost, and a manuscript of the Hamburg Staatsbibliothek, which probably contained these variations, was a victim of the Second World War.[128] Three series of variations have been preserved: on *Ach was soll ich Sünder machen, Werde munter mein Gemüthe,* and *Alle Menschen müssen sterben.* They have been published (vol.III, nos.11–13) as the probable content of the *Sterbensgedancken,* although the second one is the exact opposite of thoughts on death. In contrast to the chorale variations of Sweelinck or Scheidt, all three belong to the type that is more aptly called chorale partita, and which occurs in the music of Pachelbel's contemporary Georg Böhm. The variations are mostly figural, similar to those in Froberger's *Auff die Mayerin,* but many features recall earlier models, e.g., the employment of the bicinium style (no.12, var.IV; no.13, var.III and V), the shifting of the theme into a lower voice (no.11, var.VI; no.13, var.II and III), and the changing of the motif of figuration (no.11, var.III, V, and VI; no.12, var. IV). Awkward figures like the ones in Fig.709 suggest that these variation sets are early works.

Fig.709

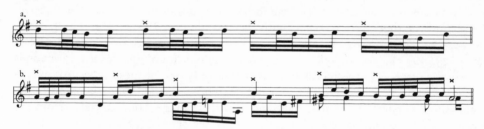

a. No. 11, var. III; b. No. 12, var. IV.

SECULAR COMPOSITIONS

Six variation sets based on secular songs are preserved in the *Hexachordum Apollinis* of 1699, and four others are found in manuscripts (III; nos.1–10). All the themes are called *Aria,* and all of them were probably composed by Pachelbel himself, except perhaps for the *Aria Sebaldina* (no.6), whose title suggests a connection to the tradition of Nuremberg's Sebalduskirche. Pachelbel was probably one of the first to take the step from writing variations on an existing theme to using an original one—Frescobaldi's *Aria detta la Frescobalda* represents an earlier, but singular, instance. This innovation was in the air at the time, for a number of Bernardo Pasquini's variation works also seem to have been based on his own themes.

Fig.710

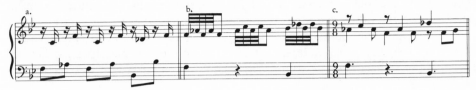

a. var. III; b. var. V; c. var. VII.

Pachelbel's themes are song-like little pieces with attractive melodies, all in two sections with four measures in the first section and four or eight in the second. The variations in the *Hexachordum* exhibit a greater maturity and a more even technique than his chorale variations. One must not expect anything magnificent or deep from them, but many are well made and attractive in their modesty and lack of pretension. There are many kinds of figurations and arpeggios, and chord intervals played after the beat, which produce particularly fine sound effects on the harpsichord and clavichord, especially in the *Aria Sebaldina,* from which Fig. 710 draws some samples. The fourth variation of the *Aria quarta* contains an early instance of the left-hand arpeggios known as the Alberti bass.

The six chaconnes (III, nos.14–19) should also be counted as variation works. The first three, obviously intended for the harpsichord or clavichord, are unpretentious pieces for home use, and border on humdrum, bourgeois contentedness. They approach the song variation, insofar as both bass and melody of the theme are generally retained. The other three chaconnes are more significant. They require the organ pedals—throughout in no.17, at the end of no.18, and in the middle of no.19 (var.XV). All three works are genuine chaconnes (or passacaglias), in which new ideas are introduced above a never-changing bass. They contain a number of details that may have served as models for Bach's *Passacaglia,* such as the figures shown in Fig.711.

Pachelbel's most interesting works are his fantasies (vol.III; nos.20–23), mainly because their contents are very different from what one would expect after

Fig.711

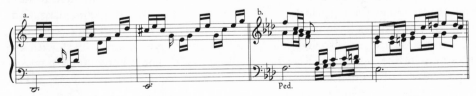

a. No. 17, var. X; b. No. 19, var. XV.

Frescobaldi or Froberger. Fantasy no.20 is still somewhat traditional, for it is a fugue in three sections, with the subject entering in the fourth measure. Fantasies nos.21–23, on the other hand, represent quite another type. All three are written in 3/2 time and consist—without any suggestion of imitation—of homophonic and figural passages of varied length (four, five, six, or eight measures), which are very similar to chaconne variations. Fig.712 shows the first and last sections of fantasy no.21.

Fig.712

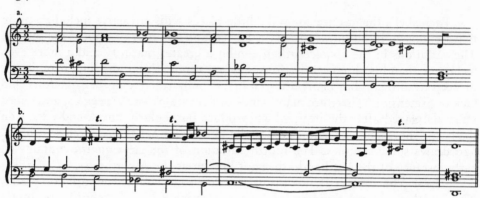

The imprecise use of the term *fantasy*—for pieces that are obviously canzonas or toccatas, and appear as such in other sources—can be traced to the beginning of the 17th century, particularly in French and Belgian manuscripts, such as the *Liber Cruciferorum* of 1617. Thus its employment for compositions that are really brief toccatas (vol.I, nos.10 and 11) is understandable, though unusual. On the other hand, fantasies nos.21–23 are exceptional, not only for their titles but also for their content. Can they be regarded as predecessors of the modern fantasy, in which—as in Bach's *Chromatic Fantasy*—the free treatment, the improvisational continuation of an idea is of fundamental importance?

Let us now turn to the suites (vol.III, nos.24–42). Only three of them, nos.29, 32, and 33B, are established as Pachelbel's compositions. The rest were included in Seiffert's edition on the basis of circumstantial evidence, which he held to have been "zu sicherem Ende geführt,"[129] but which is really not very conclusive. The three authentic suites have only the traditional movements—allemande, courante, and sarabande (no.29 also has a gigue)—and their style is on a level with the suites of Schultheiss, Johann Krieger, and Buxtehude. The other suites are mostly simpler, especially in the more song-like allemandes (e.g., in nos.25, 28, 31, 34, 35, 36), which lack the sixteenth-note figures that are usual in this type. They expand the classic form for the first time by the insertion of a more recent dance, taken from the French ballet, usually a gavotte, but occasionally a bourrée or an air. Usually these inserted dances (symbolized here by I) are placed in the middle, between the courante and sarabande (A C I S G). There is a clear contrast in style between the traditional and the inserted dances, which is still recognizable in Bach's suites. In the long evolution the former have largely lost their original character and have become stylized types, while the latter preserve their individuality as dances. The first section of the *Gavotte* from the *Suite ex Fis* (no.41), reproduced in Fig.713, is as a good example.

Fig.713

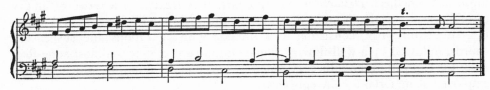

Each of the seventeen anonymous suites is in a different key, thus constituting one of the many antecedents of the full circle of keys of the *Well-Tempered Clavier*. The seven keys that are still omitted are *F* minor, *B* major, *B* minor, *E* flat minor, *A* flat minor, *F* sharp major, and *C* sharp major. *F* minor and *B* major, however, are included in Fischer's *Ariadne musica* of 1702.

Although Pachelbel's role in the evolution of the suite is uncertain, in other fields, particularly the fugue and the organ chorale, he created works that are historically important and artistically significant. They do not offer the magnificence and power of Tunder or Buxtehude, or the fascination and excitement of Frescobaldi or Froberger; they excel, instead, in a sense of order and carefulness, in a balance between intent and ability, in the expression of a heartfelt piety and contemplative attitude. Many pieces are too modest to stand up under the judgment of history, but many others belong to the permanent keyboard repertoire.

Johann Philipp Krieger and Johann Krieger

An important musical personality of the period was Johann Philipp Krieger. He was born in Nuremberg in 1649, and after various trips (to study with Rosenmüller in Venice and Pasquini in Rome, among others), he became a chamber musician and chamber organist at Halle in 1677. In 1680 he was called to Weissenfels as orchestral director, and worked there until his death in 1725. As a composer of many operas, cantatas, and trio sonatas he plays an important role in German vocal and instrumental music before Bach. His younger brother, Johann, was born in Nuremberg at the end of 1651 (he was baptized on January 1, 1652) and was a pupil of Schwemmer's and Wecker's. From 1672 to 1677 he worked as a court organist at Bayreuth, and in 1681 he was called to Zittau as choir director and organist at the Johanniskirche. He died in Zittau in 1735.

The relationship between the brothers Krieger is similar to the one between J. Christoph and J. Michael Bach. In both cases the older brother excels in vocal and instrumental music, the younger in keyboard music. Only three clavier works by Johann Philipp are preserved.[130] A *Passagaglia,* written before 1676, consists of forty-five variations on a six-measure series of harmonies and is close in style to Kerll's passacaglias. Fig.714 offers three of the many figuration formulae. An *Aria* with twenty-four variations uses an unpretentious, song-like theme similar to those in Pachelbel's *Hexachordum Apollinis.* It is treated in a series of empty formula variations that is much too long. On the other hand, a *Toccata* in A minor is a successful work, consisting of a prelude with figurations and suspension chords, followed by a well-flowing fugue with a subject that is almost song-like. After the exposition the subject is joined by two figuration motifs, which are also employed as material for the episodes.

Fig.714

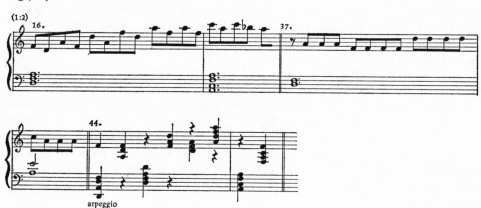

arpeggio

The keyboard output of Johann Krieger (or Krüger jun., as he is called in some manuscripts) is much larger and more significant. It includes two prints, *Sechs musicalische Parthien* (Nuremberg, 1697) and *Anmuthige Clavier-Übung* (Nuremberg, 1698). The former contains a fantasy and 6 suites, the latter 9 preludes, 5 ricercars, 7 fugues, 2 toccatas, a fantasy, and a chaconne. A number of other pieces are preserved in manuscripts—preludes, fugues, ricercars, and chorale settings.[131]

The problem of which pieces might belong together becomes acute at times. The *Anmuthige Clavier-Übung,* e.g., begins with a prelude in *E* and a ricercar in *E,* which may well form a single work in E minor. A ricercar in *F* and a prelude in *F* (nos.3–4) follow, but their position should be inverted if they are to be connected. The same is true of nos.17–18 (ricercar and prelude in G minor), 19–20 (fugue and fantasy in D minor), and the group nos.7–10 (ricercar in A, ricercar in B♭, prelude in A, prelude in B♭). Similarly, prelude in C (no.16) seems to belong before the thematically related fugues nos.11–15 rather than after. In the *Sechs Parthien,* on the other hand, there is a question of whether the initial *Fantasia e Partita C* actually belong together. The fantasy is much too long and independent to function as a prelude to the ensuing suite; moreover, none of the other suites begins with an introductory piece. The relationships in the group of four manuscript pieces offered as a musical unit in *DTB* XVIII under no.4 (p.193) and in the three offered as no.5 (p.199) are equally doubtful. It will therefore be best to treat all these compositions as single pieces. If so, Johann Krieger's known keyboard output is as follows: 9 ricercars, 8 fugues, 4 fantasies, 14 preludes, 5 toccatas, 9 chorale settings, 6 suites, and several single pieces (*Durezza, Giacona, Passacaglia, Battaglia*).

In his imitative compositions Krieger exhibits a definite penchant for learnedness, which is quite unusual for his time. The ricercars, which clearly differ from the fugues in their sustained subjects, almost all employ inversion of the theme, either in a separate section or right at the beginning in the answer to the subject. Nos.3 and 7 of the *Clavier-Übung* follow the first scheme, and have the structure A ‖ A^i ‖ A, A^i. No.7 even has a countersubject that is inverted. The other type, that of the inversion fugue, is represented by nos.2, 8, and 17 of the *Clavier-Übung*. All three are long and, after a first section in ¢, treat the subject and its inversion in a section in 3/2. Ricercar no.2 is actually part of a larger work; ricercars nos.5a and 5b (called *Fuga* in the manuscript), which F. W. Riedel published from the New Haven manuscript, constitute the rest of it. All three pieces are based on the same subject, no.5b on its original form, no.5a on its inversion, and no.2 of the *Clavier-Übung* on both forms and, in the second section, on its variants in triple meter. The beginnings of these pieces are given in Fig.715 with

Fig.715

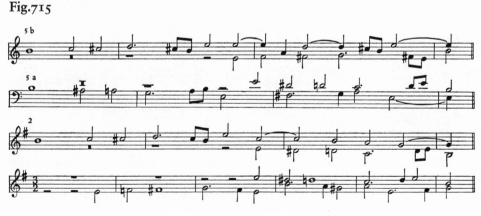

those of nos. 5a and 5b transposed from *D* to *E*. Another ricercar (*DTB*, p.200), entitled *Thema,* has the form A || A/B || (6/4) A || A/B, thus combining the principle of the double fugue with that of the rhythmic variation. A *Fuga* in the New Haven manuscript (new ed., Riedel, p.6) should also be counted as a ricercar. Its main subject is combined with two obbligato countersubjects, as shown in Fig. 716 (meas.18–22).

Fig.716

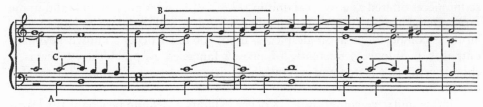

Fugues nos.11–15 from the *Clavier-Übung* are entitled *Fuga aus C Thema I, Thema II, Thema III, Thema IV,* and *à 4 Themati,* and form a cycle in which each of the four subjects is developed in an individual fugue, and then all the subjects are combined in a quadruple fugue. Each fugue concludes with a free, predominantly chordal postlude of four to eight measures. The postlude is an indication that the fugue (but not the ricercar) was not yet firmly established at the time, and needed a final, external confirmation.

One of the four pieces entitled *Fantasia* (*DTB*, p.204) is a kind of *perpetuum mobile* in 12/8 with a fugal beginning. The other three (*DTB*, pp.5, 59; Riedel, p.13) belong to the same curious type as those by Pachelbel. The one that opens the *Sechs Parthien* begins with an eight-measure song theme, which later returns as a refrain. Like Pachelbel's fantasy no.21 (cf.Fig.712), the second fantasy is in 3/2 and in *D* minor and begins with a chaconne idea of six measures, which is repeated at the end (Fig.717). The third one resembles a French chaconne even more.

Fig.717

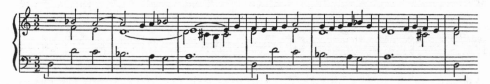

Krieger's preludes (eleven in *DTB*, three more in Riedel's new ed.) are brief pieces, which make use of passage work, complementary motifs, full chords, short fugatos, and similar elements. A particularly interesting one is a *Preludio* (*DTB*,

Fig.718

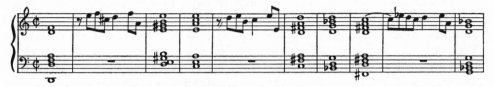

p.193), in which full chords—among them many seventh chords and their inversions—are connected by brief recitative-like formulae, similar to Bach's *Chromatic Fantasy*. Fig.718 reproduces measures 14–23.

Fig.719

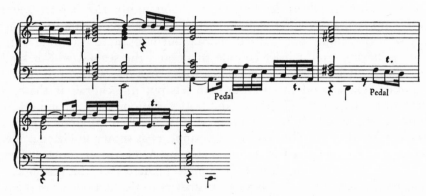

One of the toccatas (Riedel, p.5) contains only a short prelude, but two others (Riedel, pp.1, 16) consist of prelude and fugue. Details in the two toccatas in the *Clavier-Übung* definitely point to a North German influence. Near the end of the first one (*DTB*, p.61) two passages in thirty-second notes end abruptly with a rest, as often occurs in Buxtehude's music. The second one (*DTB*, p.70), entitled *Toccata mit dem Pedal aus C,* is perhaps the only fully-developed toccata written in Central Germany before Bach. It starts with a purely North German pedal solo, which is followed by a chordal section intermingled with recitative-like figures, as exemplified by Fig.719. This introduction is followed by a lengthy movement of song-like character in 3/4 time, an interlude in chordal-recitative style, and a fugue, whose lively subject, shown in Fig.720, is heard twice in the pedals and is fashioned, according to North German practice, for alternating feet.

Fig.720

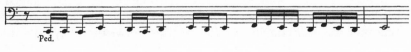

Finally, the *Clavier-Übung* includes a *Giacona aus Gb* (G minor), which is the first instance of an eight-measure (not four- or twice four-measure) ostinato (Fig. 721). This subject is presented in twenty-nine extremely varied and inventive variations, which form several pairs (var.I–II, III–IV, V–VI, XIII–XIV, XVII–XVIII, etc.). As in Muffat's passacaglia (cf.p.582) the first setting returns as a refrain three times (in var.X, XIX, and XXV). A passacaglia by Krieger preserved in manuscript (*DTB*, p.197) treats a four-measure subject in sixteen variations.

Fig.721

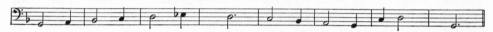

Krieger's chorale settings are preserved exclusively in manuscripts. Two variation sets, on *Herr Christ der einig Gottes Sohn* and *In dich hab ich gehoffet, Herr* (*DTB*, pp.208, 210), differ from Pachelbel's chorale partitas in that they do not start with the simply harmonized chorale but with more elaborate settings. The first set begins with a brief chorale fugue and the second with a kind of prelude, which concludes after six measures with a free quotation of the final line of the chorale. The second variation in both sets puts the chorale in the bass as the carrier of the harmony. The third (and last) variation of the second set treats the chorale in an unusually free manner—at least for Central Germany: in 6/8 time and in a free rhythm. The first line, e.g., appears as shown in Fig.722. Several chorale settings are preserved in a copy made by A. G. Ritter (now at Beuron Archabbey).[132] These settings are short, simple fughettas on the first line. Occasionally the second line is also used, as an answer to the first one or in the form of a concluding quotation.

Fig.722

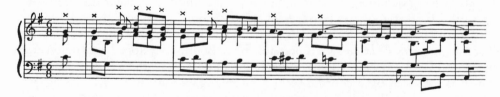

Finally we come to Krieger's suites, which he published in 1697 under the German and Italian title *Sechs musicalische Parthien, Sei Partite musicali*. They consist of A C S G (the sarabande generally with doubles or variations), the final order that came into general use around 1680. Most of the suites are followed by additional dances—minuet, bourrée, gavotte, or rondeau—which are added only to fill space—"wo einig *Spatium* oder Raum vorgefallen," as we read in the preface. The fact that they are occasionally in different keys shows that they do not really

666

belong to the suites. Thus the C-major partita is followed by a minuet, bourrée and gavotte in G major, and the B flat-major partita is followed by a rondeau in B flat major and a minuet and bourrée in A minor. Two of the gigues are still in duple meter, obviously reminiscent of Froberger.

Kuhnau

Johann Kuhnau was born in Geising (Saxony) in 1660 and died in Leipzig in 1722. After studying at the Dresden Kreuzschule, he went to Zittau in 1680 to work as the choir director and organist at the Johanniskirche, and to Leipzig in 1682, where he stayed for the remainder of his life. There he studied law, worked as a lawyer from 1688 to 1700, and held the office of organist at the Thomaskirche from 1684 on. From 1701 until his death, he was the cantor at the Thomaskirche, an office that was just as vexatious and difficult for him as for his successor, J. S. Bach. He wrote literary works of various kinds—even today his satirical novel *Der musikalische Quacksalber* (1700) is worth reading as a document of the period—as well as numerous church cantatas, works for festivals, and motets, much of which is lost. His keyboard works are preserved in four prints:

1. *Neuer Clavier Übung erster Theil. Bestehend in sieben Partien aus dem Ut, Re, Mi, oder Tertia majore eines jedweden Toni . . .* 1689.
2. *Neuer Clavier Übung Andrer Theil, das ist: Sieben Partien aus dem Re, Mi, Fa, oder Tertia minore eines jedweden Toni, benebenst einer Sonata aus dem B . . .* 1692.
3. *Frische Clavier Früchte oder Sieben Suonaten . . .* 1696.
4. *Musicalische Vorstellung einiger Biblischer Historien in 6 Sonaten . . .* 1700.[133]

Clavier Übung I contains seven suites in the major keys of C, D, E, F, G, A, B♭, and *Clavier Übung II* seven more suites in the minor keys of C, D, E, F, G, A, B. In both prints the suites are called *Partien,* a term probably derived from the French word *partie* (part). This is the first time that it has the meaning of suite. Johann Krieger applied it in the same sense in his *Sechs musicalische Parthien* of 1697 and equated it with the Italian word *partita*. The basic arrangement of Kuhnau's suites is A C S G, but the sarabande is replaced once by an aria (I, no.6) and the gigue several times by a minuet, bourrée, or aria (I, 3; II, 2; II, 4; II, 6). In the last suite (II, 7) a gavotte is inserted between the sarabande and gigue. Each suite begins with a substantial prelude; this is the expanded suite form that had appeared in Schultheiss' works. Suite II, 7 is probably the earliest instance of the sequence P A C S I G, which was employed by Bach in his *English Suites* and *Partitas*.

For his preludes Kuhnau generally chooses the form of a short toccata-like introduction followed by a fugal movement. In the preface to *Clavier Übung II* he draws attention to the fact that the fugues "usually involve countersubjects, so that not only beginners but also those who are adept at the clavier and at composition will find a challenge." Occasionally the preludes take a different approach;

e.g., suite I, 4 begins with a *Sonatina* consisting of a chordal introduction and a fugato, and suite II, 4 starts with a *Ciacona* of about twenty variations on the ostinato (*f eb db c*). Four preludes (in I, 3; I, 5; II, 3; II, 7) are quite novel in their formulation—chordal throughout with an identical arpeggio figure repeated within each harmony. The excerpt from I, 5, given in Fig.723, is a very likely model for Bach's famous C-major prelude from the *Well-Tempered Clavier*.

Fig.723

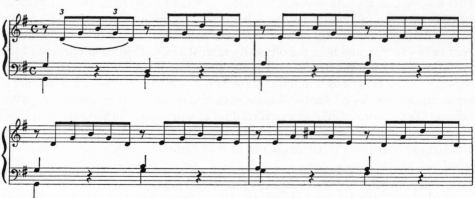

The allemandes are less unified in their formulation than is usual in this species, for sixteenth-note figurations and eighth-note motion occur side by side. Occasionally the allemande and the courante are related as variations, e.g., in I, 3 and I, 5. Most of the gigues consist of two fugatos, with the second one based on the inverted subject. The gigue in I, 4 is an exception; the entire piece consists of the relentless repetition of a two-measure phrase, whose melodic content is as trivial as its harmonic foundation. The beginning is shown in Fig.724, and the

Fig.724

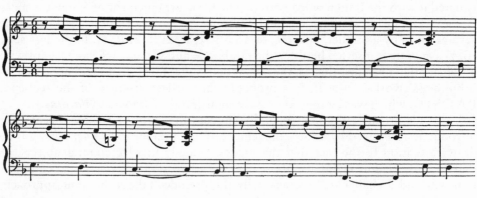

piece continues for forty measures in the very same manner, descending to the lowest imaginable level of banality. At least this is how it appears to the modern observer, who is all too familiar with this phenomenon from the cheap hackwork of the 18th and 19 centuries. The music lover of 1700 was probably not so negatively affected by this novelty, and Kuhnau himself may have been rather proud of his invention, since he had no idea how far astray he was going.

Kuhnau's fame derives not so much from his suites as from his sonatas—compositions that have earned him the title of "inventor of the clavier sonata," a title that is not quite justified yet not unjustified. If what is meant by "sonata" is not just a "sound piece," but a special form consisting of several movements, which had been evolving in Italian violin music since about 1650, Kuhnau may indeed have been the first to transplant this species to the keyboard. "Denn warumb sollte man auff dem Claviere nicht eben, wie auff andern Instrumenten, dergleichen Sachen tractiren können?" he says with respect to his *Sonate aus dem B,* which he added to the *Clavier Übung II.* Five years earlier Gregorio Strozzi had published three sonatas of several movements each in his *Capricci da sonare cembali et organi* (1687), but Kuhnau certainly had no knowledge of this work, which was printed in Naples. Moreover, Strozzi did not take the violin sonata as his point of departure but used the keyboard canzona, which had been in existence for a long time, and merely gave it a new, more suitable name (cf.p.685). Pasquini's clavier works include some sonatas in several movements, but they represent singular and special cases, for they are notated in the form of thoroughbasses, sometimes with two such basses, for two claviers (cf.p.699).

Kuhnau's *Sonate aus dem B* consists of four freely formed movements, which contrast with each other in changing styles, tempos, meters, and other properties. A *da capo* at the end signals a repetition of the entire first movement, which is modeled after a trio sonata, but is so long—or rather, long-winded and boring—that it is rather laborious to find one's way through it. Here, as in many other sonata movements Kuhnau develops the entire movement from a single formula, which unfortunately is too empty to justify so many repetitions. The same is true of the other movements, a lively fugato, an "arioso" adagio, and a fugal allegro, the last two in triple meter.

Despite its shortcomings, this sonata must have found enough applause to spur Kuhnau on to further attempts in this field. His *Frische Clavier Früchte* of 1696 contain seven more sonatas, of which he says in the preface that he "wrote them in a heat . . . , so that I completed one every day and thus completed the work, which I had started on the Monday of one week, on the Monday of the following one." Consequently he warns that "nobody should expect a great 'rarity' from it." On the whole, these sonatas are more agreeable than the first one, although here again several movements are too long and can only be made bearable by large cuts. The peculiar style of one movement of the *Suonata sesta* (Fig.725), was employed again in the first *Biblische Historie* (cf.Fig.727).

Fig.725

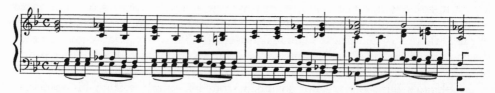

The form of the sonatas is very variable with respect to both the number and style of the individual movements. Probably their models must be sought in the works of Legrenzi or Cazzati, and not in Corelli's trio sonatas with their rather fixed form of alternating adagios and allegros. Some movements are successful, e.g., the first ones of nos.1, 5, and 7, or the last one of no.6. Others exhibit Kuhnau's frequent tendency to loquacious repetition of insignificant formulae.

Kuhnau's last keyboard work is the *Musicalische Vorstellung einiger Biblischer Historien* of 1700, in which he develops the novel idea of imbuing a keyboard sonata with a program, a purpose well suited to this form, with its many movements of contrasting character. In the six sonatas he presents some of the most dramatic episodes from the Scriptures, each prefaced by a detailed explanation, whose picturesque language and apt characterization give as clear proof of Kuhnau's literary gift as his *Musikalischer Quacksalber*. The Biblical stories are: 1. The Combat of David and Goliath, 2. Saul Cured by David with the Aid of Music, 3. Jacob's Wedding, 4. Hiskias, Who Was Deathly Sick and Regained His Health, 5. Gideon, the Savior of Israel, and 6, Jacob's Death and Burial. The following are his presentations of two of these stories:

The Combat of David and Goliath explained
1. The stamping and challenge of Goliath.
2. The trembling of the Israelites and their prayer to God when facing this horrible adversary.
3. The bravery of David, his desire to break the giant's pride, and his child-like faith in God's assistance.
4. The words of challenge exchanged between David and Goliath and their combat, when the rock is hurled at Goliath's forehead and he thus falls and dies.
5. The flight of the Philistines and how the Israelites pursue them and slay them with the sword.
6. The jubilation of the Israelites on their victory.
7. The concert performed in praise of David by all the women.
8. And finally the general joy expressed in dancing and hopping.

Saul cured by David with the aid of music
1. Saul's sadness and madness
2. David's life-giving harp playing
3. The king's quieted soul

In the preface Kuhnau shows a good understanding of the problems of program music. He recognizes that it is relatively easy in vocal music "to induce a special effect in souls, because the words contribute much, indeed the most to their being moved." In instrumental music it is easy to represent certain effects—the song of birds, the pealing of bells, the crash of the cannon—in such a way "that the listener can grasp the composer's intention, even if it has not been suggested by words." In other instances one must "aim at analogies, and arrange the music in a manner that it may be compared to the object represented by some *tertium comparationis*, and in such instances words are indeed necessary." Thus in the first sonata he represents "the snarling and stamping of Goliath by the low-lying subject, which sounds defiant because of the dots, and by additional noises; the flight of the Philistines and their pursuit by a fugue in fast notes"; and in the third sonata he depicts "Laban's deceit by misleading the ear with the unexpected progression from one key into another (which the Italians call *inganno*)." In the emotions of sadness and joy "words are unnecessary, unless one has to indicate a certain individual, as happens in these sonatas, so that one would, e.g., not take the lament of a sad Hiskias for a crying St. Peter, a distressed Jeremiah, or any other grieving person."

The realistic scenes include the combat between David and Goliath, in which the hurling of the rock and the fall of Goliath are represented by appropriate musical motions (no.1, *Il combattere*), the musical concert in David's honor (no. 1, *Il concerto*), the sounding of the trumpets in Gideon's camp (no.5, *Il suono delle trombe*), and the flights of the Philistines (no.1, *La fuga de' Filistei*) and of the Midianites (no.5, *La fuga dei nemici*). Dance-like rhythms represent David's bravery (no.1, *Il coraggio di David*), the joy and jubilation of the Israelites over David's victory (no.1, *La gioia* and *Il giubilo comune*), the joy over Gideon's victory (no.5, *La loro allegrezza*), and the consolation of Jacob's survivors (no.6, *L'animo consolato*). Descending seconds depict the distress over Jacob's death (no.6, *La sepoltura*); and for the representation of fright, Kuhnau uses the operatic recitative (no.5, *Il di lui paura*), reinforcing the desired effect by several "terrible" dissonances (note especially the $b\flat$ against the $g\sharp$ in measure 5 of Fig.726). Where the tortured soul turns to God with a prayer, a Protestant chorale is heard: *Ich ruf zu dir* (no.1, *Il tremore degl' Israliti e la loro preghiera*) and *Heil du mich, lieber*

Fig.726

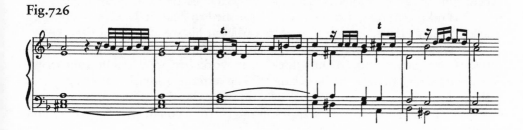

Herre (from *Ach Herr mich armen Sünder; no.4, Il lamento di Hiskia e le sue preghiere*). The first of these chorales uses the *bebung* effect that also occurs in the sixth sonata of the *Clavier Früchte* (Fig.727; cf.Fig.725). Several times, in depicting an affect, Kuhnau introduces suggestions of its contrast. In no.3 Jacob's laborious period of service is made easier by the memory of Rachel and the "amorous pleasantry," and in no.4 Hiskias' joy over his restoration is temporarily darkened by the memory of his earlier illness.

Fig.727

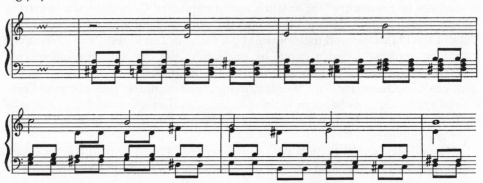

In his Biblical Histories, just as in his non-programmatic sonatas, Kuhnau places successful and impressive pieces next to insignificant and pedantic ones. This happens most clearly in the second History, *Der von David vermittels der Music curirte Saul*. The first movement is a really ingenious depiction of insanity, a deep psychological study of a state of the soul, in which despair, fits of rage, rays of sanity, and resignation alternate. David's "life-giving" harp playing follows, but after eight measures it lapses into such endless repetition that the most one can see in it is the healing power of boredom. In the final movement, which describes the calmed soul of the king, nothing occurs but the continuous repetition of a brief formula in dotted rhythm. The sonata about David and Goliath is probably the only wholly successful one. The one on Jacob's Wedding contains many fine passages, such as the wedding song and the description of Laban's deceit, which is as ingenious as the depiction of the insane Saul. Unfortunately the work has no real ending, for who will be satisfied to hear at Jacob's wedding to Rachel the same music heard seven years earlier at his wedding to Leah?

Although Kuhnau played the organ of the Thomaskirche, he was not very active as an organ composer. Only three organ works are preserved in manuscript, two preludes and fugues and a toccata.[134] The latter is a long, interesting work; with its virtuosic passage work, pedal solos, massive chords, well worked-out fugue in 3/4 time, and rhapsodic postlude, it follows North German models, like Johann Krieger's C-major toccata (cf.p.665).

672

Kuhnau is a curious, unique phenomenon in the history of keyboard music. The character and artistic significance of his musical output are as varied as his abilities and interests were, for he was a lawyer, man of universal knowledge, novelist, satirist, music theorist, and composer. His music is a peculiar mixture of novel ideas, ingenious inventions, smug loquaciousness, and occasionally a rather painful banality.

Zachow

Halle, the city in which Samuel Scheidt worked at the beginning of the 17th century, was also the place where Friedrich Wilhelm Zachow was active. Born in Leipzig in 1663, he was called to Halle as the organist of the Marktkirche in 1684. He died there in 1712, not yet fifty. From about 1694 to 1697 he taught Handel, who was devoted and grateful to his teacher and his widow ever after. Zachow's collected works comprise a number of cantatas and 52 keyboard compositions: 8 fugal pieces and 44 chorale settings.[135] A suite is preserved in the Möller manuscript (fol.80v).[136]

Fig.728

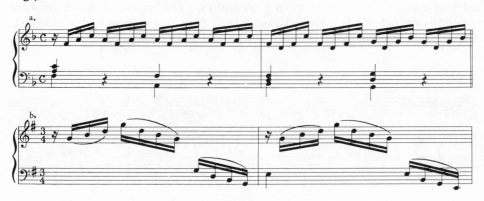

a. Prelude No. 2; b. Prelude No. 3.

Parts of two of the preludes found among the fugal pieces are given in Fig.728. Along with similar pieces by Kuhnau, they are of interest as predecessors of Bach's C-major prelude from the *Well-Tempered Clavier*. Similiarly, the beginning of a *Capriccio* (no.8), shown in Fig.729, anticipates the subject of Bach's great organ fugue in G minor, but only in the general curve, not in its details.

Fig.729

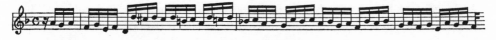

Zachow's organ chorales suggest a comparison with Pachelbel's. In general, Zachow's settings are shorter and simpler in style. In ornamented counterpoints, e.g., he limits himself mostly to eighth notes, while Pachelbel usually writes sixteenth-note figures against the chorale melody. A number of Zachow's organ chorales belong to the chorale fugue type (nos.12, 18, 24, 28, 34–36, 45–48). These settings are about thirty measures long and treat the first line of the chorale fugally, mostly with an obbligato counter-motif, as in *Nun komm der Heiden Heiland* (no. 36), whose beginning appears in Fig.730. In a few instances (nos.9, 20, 40, 44) each line is fugally developed as in chorale motets, but much more briefly than is usual in that type. Like Pachelbel, Zachow prefers the type in which the chorale is heard in the form of a "Protestant *cantus planus*," as discant chorale. Several settings contain two verses, with the melody in the soprano and bass, respectively (nos.11, 17, 41). Settings such as *Christ lag in Todesbanden* and *Komm Gott Schöpfer* (nos.17, 31), with their tight formulation and their employment of an obbligato motif in the counterpoints, may be regarded as predecessors of Bach's *Orgelbüchlein*. In several instances each chorale line is introduced by a more or less elaborate fore-imitation in diminished note values, especially in *Nun lasst uns Gott* (no.38), while in others Zachow limits himself to a fore-imitation of the first line, e.g., in *Auf meinen lieben Gott* (no.15). The setting of *Ach Herr mich armen Sünder* (no.10) is a special case; it is a pure trio setting with continuous sixteenth-note figurations in the middle part and a supporting bass.

Fig.730

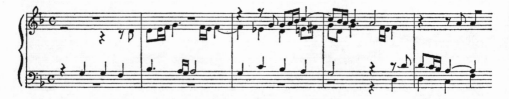

Buttstett

Johann Heinrich Buttstett (Buttstedt) was born in Bindersleben near Erfurt in 1666, and died in Erfurt in 1727. A pupil of Pachelbel's and the teacher of Johann Gottfried Walther, he is known in music history chiefly as the author of *Ut Mi Sol, Re Fa La, Tota Musica et Harmonia Aeterna* (1716), with which he engaged in a fight, as heroic as it was futile, against Mattheson's first publication, *Das Neueröffnete Orchestre* of 1713. He is known as a keyboard composer by about forty organ chorales preserved in manuscripts[137] and a printed collection, *Musicalische Clavier-Kunst und Vorraths-Kammer* (1713, 1716).

In general Buttstett's chorale settings follow Pachelbel's approaches. There are a few short chorale fugues such as *Gelobet seist du* (Keller A) and *Nun komm der Heiden Heiland* (Berlin Walther autograph), as well as a number of three-part pieces, in which the chorale is heard in the discant or the bass against counterpoints with varied figurations—complementary motifs, parallel thirds, and occasional arpeggios and double trills—or above full chords. Two settings, a second one of *Nun komm der Heiden Heiland* (Berlin Walther autograph) and *Vom Himmel hoch* (Frotscher O, p.34), show that Buttstett was familiar with the North German technique of chorale figuration, which appears only rarely in Central Germany. In this setting of *Nun komm der Heiden Heiland* the chorale is first performed simply, with two counterpoints below it, then ornamented—as in Buxtehude's works—with energetic figures carrying some of the chorale notes to the octave above (Fig.731).

Fig.731

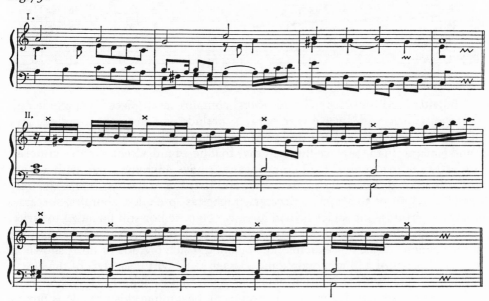

The chorale *Ich ruf zu dir* (Hague Walther autograph) is the basis of a partita of six variations; the tremolo figures shown in Fig.732 occur at the end of variation III. Passages like this one are characteristic of Buttstett's style and prove *ex contrario* that Buttstett could not have written such strictly contrapuntal works

Fig.732

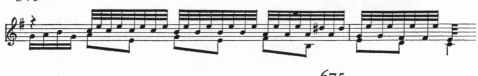

as the chorale fugues in *Erbarm dich mein* and *Christ lag in Todesbanden* (cf. notes 96 and 98 above). They must be works of Heinrich Bach, who was about fifty years his senior.

Some of Buttstett's settings of chorales that reflect the joyful mood of Christmas are especially successful. In *Vom Himmel kam der Engel Schar* (Straube C) lively figurations symbolically depict the flapping of the angel's wings, and in a setting of *Gottes Sohn ist kommen* (Berlin Walther autograph) the arrival of the Savior is expressed most realistically by descending motions of various kinds. Fig.733 provides an excerpt from this work (meas.11–14).

Fig.733

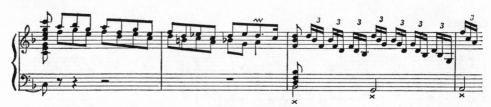

Buttstett's *Musicalische Clavier-Kunst* contains seven pieces: 1. prelude and capriccio, 2. aria with twelve variations, 3. prelude and ricercar, 4. prelude and fugue, 5. prelude and canzona (followed by two minuets), 6. and 7. two suites, in D and F major. In the preface Buttstett says that he would accept possible criticism from a *Theoreticus* only, "for I do not want to have anything to do with a mere *Practicus* (though I do not despise any)"; and that this collection represents only a small fraction of the fugues, ricercars, fughettas, preludes, chorales, toccatas, sonatas, overtures, and suites he had already composed or still intended to write. The contents offer a curious mixture of dry pedantry and interesting, even bizzare and ingenuious ideas. For example, the opening of the prelude of no.1, shown in Fig.734, consists of a long monophonic passage in the virtuosic style of the North German toccata, with abrupt exclamations separated by long rests. Although its continuation does not live up to this promising beginning, this prelude is one of

Fig.734

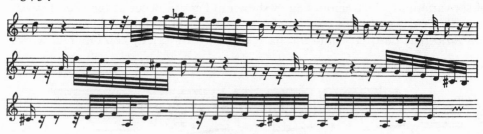

the most remarkable keyboard pieces of Bach's time. A pedal passage further on unmistakably shows that this composition—along with several others—is intended for the organ. The capriccio that follows is based on a virtuosic, rushing subject, given in Fig.735. It closes with a toccata-like section modeled on the final part of the prelude. The prelude from no.3 of the *Clavier-Kunst* is short, well-wrought, and quiet. It sounds like an anticipation of the *F*-major prelude from vol. II of the *Well-Tempered Clavier*. The prelude and fugue (no.4) reveal a North German influence in many of their details. The short *Air* from the second suite (no.7) seems to have French rather than Thuringian affinities.

Fig.735

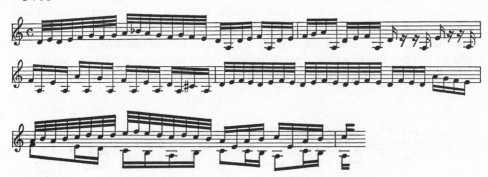

A *Fuga ex E♮* preserved in the so-called Andreas-Bach Book at Leipzig, whose subject is given in Fig.736, employs repercussion to an extreme degree, and contains a skip of a diminished seventh. At the end the repercussion in sixteenth notes is even applied to full chords in both hands. This composition proves again that Buttstett was familiar with the North German organ music of Reincken and others.

Fig.736

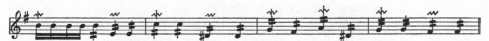

Witte, A. N. Vetter, D. Vetter, Armsdorff, and Beyer

The output of several minor masters completes the picture of Central German keyboard music in the 17th century.

Christian Friedrich Witte (about 1660 to 1716) studied in Nuremberg (under Wecker), Salzburg, and Vienna, and then became court organist and orchestral director at Altenburg. "His few preserved chorale settings are not unusual," according to Ritter,[138] and Frotscher agrees, mentioning *Herr Christ der einig Gottes*

677

Fig.737

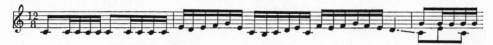

Sohn, Nun komm der Heiden Heiland, and *Aus tiefer Not.*[139] The first (Frotscher O, p.95) is a three-part setting with the chorale in the bass and two ornamented counterpoints, like many of Pachelbel's and Buttstett's chorales. Three fugues and a *Praeludium ex D fis* with a fugue are preserved in the Mylau tablature book.[140] The subject of no.23 (Fig.737) is another example of a repercussion subject. A *Capriccio C.F.W.*, found in the Andreas-Bach book at Leipzig (fol.72v), consists of a series of four- and eight-measure sections in the style of a sarabande, clearly modeled after Pachelbel's so-called fantasies (cf.p.660). In addition, there are two suites, a minuet, and a short prelude in Gerber's Clavier Book, and a *Passegaglie* of thirty variations on the traditional *basso ostinato d c B♭ A*, which was given the undeserved honor of being included in J. S. Bach's works.[141]

Fig.738

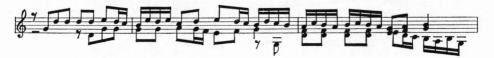

Andreas Nicolaus Vetter (1666–1734) was born in Königssee, and studied with Wecker (1681) and Pachelbel (1688). He took over Pachelbel's office at Erfurt in 1690, and then went to Rudolstadt in 1691 to be court organist. About a dozen organ chorales and a number of fugues are preserved in manuscripts.[142] Several chorales are fugally treated; others employ the entire melody in the discant or in the bass. For *Allein Gott in der Höh* (Dietrich O, no.7; the first section also in Keller A, p.6) Vetter uses Pachelbel's combination form. A modest suggestion of originality appears in his chorale fugue on *Lobt Gott* (Frotscher O, p.91), when he derives a lively fugue subject (Fig.738) from the chorale and treats it more fully than is usual in this genre. The Mylau tablature book contains an aria with variations and about ten fugues, several of which have subjects of the popular repercussion type, e.g., the one given in Fig.739 (Shannon M, no.22).

Apparently Daniel Vetter from Breslau (Wroclaw) was not related to Andreas Nicolaus. From 1679 until his death in 1721 (?) Daniel Vetter was the organist

Fig.739

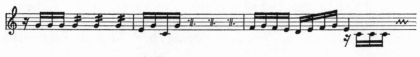

at the Nikolaikirche at Leipzig. He published two prints, *Musicalische Kirch- und Hauss-Ergötzlichkeit* (I: 1709, 1716, II: 1713), in which more than one hundred chorale tunes (several with different texts) are offered. The title page states "that the whole chorale is heard [first] on the organ, then in an ornamented variation on the harpsichord or clavichord." The organ version is a simple harmonization, which is lightly varied by arpeggios and modest figurations in the succeeding *Variatio*. As an example Fig.740 gives two excerpts from the setting of *An Wasserflüssen* (I, nos.31–32).

Fig.740

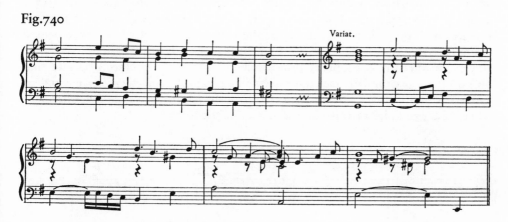

Another representative of the Central German school is Andreas Armsdorff, who was born at Mühlberg near Gotha in 1670, was an organist at Erfurt, and died in 1699. Despite his early death he must have earned a widespread reputation, for we know about twenty-five chorale preludes by him.[143] As late as 1758 Adlung mentions him in his *Anleitung zu der musikalischen Gelahrtheit*, noting that his chorales "are not very artful but rather agreeable to the ear." In addition to the usual Central German types, Armsdorff occasionally employs an ornamented discant chorale, e.g., in his *Allein zu dir* (Frotscher O, p.14), and the rare form of the chorale canon in two pieces, *Allein Gott in der Höh* (Frotscher O, p.13) and *Es spricht der Unweisen Mund* (Berlin, Staatsbibl., Ms.30245). Fig.741 gives the beginning of the latter.

Fig.741

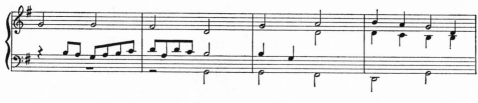

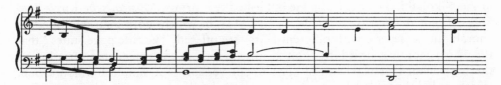

Finally there is Johann Samuel Beyer from Gotha (1669–1744), who worked as a cantor at Weissenfels and Freiberg. Under the title *Musikalischer Vorrath Neu-varriierter Fest-Choral-Gesänge auf dem Clavier im Canto und Basso* . . . (three parts, 1716–19), he published a collection of 97 chorales, each of which is first presented in a simple harmonization and then in several (mostly four) ornamented variations. All the settings are for two voices—melody and figured bass. The "clavier" in the title is probably the clavichord, for in the preface it is said that "on no other [instrument] can the affects be so rapidly and correctly evoked or changed as on this one." The excerpts from *Christ lag in Todesbanden*, offered in Fig.742, are examples of this modest music for the home.

Fig.742

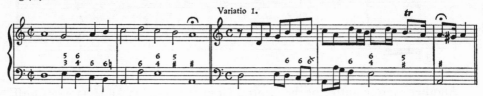

20

Italy

Giovanni and Storace

THE PRINT *Intavolatura di cembalo et organo, Toccate, Hinni sopra il canto fermo, Corrente, Balletti, Ciaccone e Passacagli diversi. Libro primo di D. Scipione Giovanni, organista e maestro di capella in S. Pietro di Gubbio* appeared in Perugia in 1650. Two years later a *Partitura di cembalo et organo*, with a similarly mixed content, appeared in Venice. In the title the same author calls himself a *Cremonense* and an organist and orchestral director in Mont' Oliveto at Florence. Unfortunately both prints seem to be lost. Old copies of the title pages and prefaces are all that are preserved.[1] They contain instructions similar to those in Frescobaldi's prefaces, e.g., that one may begin and end at various places in the toccatas, and that one may perform the pieces in a free tempo. The author says that he had not endeavored to provide the capriccios with "stravaganze insonabili" but only with "vaghezza di armonia" (beauty of harmony). Thus Scipione Giovanni—or Giovanni Scipione, as he is usually called in modern writings— seems to have been among the first to leave the harmonic experiments and audacities of the early Baroque behind.

The first Italian keyboard print preserved from the second half of the 17th century, the *Selva di varie compositioni d'intavolatura per cimbalo ed organo* of 1664 by Bernardo Storace, is another interesting monument of the South Italian school.[2] On the title page the otherwise unknown composer calls himself a "vice maestro di cappella" of the Senate of the city of Messina. The print contains mostly variations on the *Passo e mezzo* (3 sets), *Romanesca, Spagnoletta, Monica, Ruggiero, Cinque passi, Follia, Passagagli* (4 sets), *Ciaccona,* and *Balletto.* It concludes with a *Ballo della battaglia,* two correntes, two toccatas with canzonas, two ricercars, and a pastorale.

The first passamezzo is a *moderno* in A major, and the others are *anticos* in C minor and E minor. Each consists of eight *parte*, of which nos.5 and 6 are designated and written as galliards and nos.7 and 8 as correntes. Thus they are examples of the mixed type of suite variations, which were already completely formulated in Wolfgang Ebner's variations of 1648 (cf.p.561). The structural tones are two measures apart, except in the galliards and correntes, where they are four measures apart, and in most of the variations Storace employs a basic formula, which is repeated measure for measure to fill the intervals between the structural tones. This method was used by the early Neapolitan Valente, and in the second half of the 17th century it became the dominant variation technique in both Germany and Italy. A great master like Bach can use it and create the *Goldberg Variations*, but Storace still uses the recipe too schematically. Fig.743 shows an excerpt from the C-minor passamezzo (var.II).

Fig.743

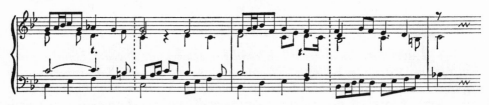

The variation sets on the *Spagnoletta* and the *Cinque passi* have unusual themes. The former is based on a long theme of twenty-four measures in 6/4 time, which is found in a Florentine manuscript (Magl. XIX 138; cf.p.245) about one hundred years earlier; there it appears in G major, but Storace puts it in A minor. It is not related to Farnaby's *Spagnioletta* (FW, I, 199), a dance song in two sections (|| : 4 : || : 8 : ||) in duple meter, or to Frescobaldi's *Spagnoletta*.

A *Cinquepass* appears as early as the *Mulliner Book* among the pieces in lute tablature.[3] It is in 6/4 time and looks like a galliard, bearing out Michael Praetorius' explanation that the name refers to the five steps of the galliard. Storace's *Cinque passi*, on the other hand, is based on a song-like theme of six 4/4 measures, which clearly divide into a main section of five measures and a one-measure ritornello. Storace employs this unusual and attractive melody, shown in Fig.744, for a series of fifteen variations connected by transitions.

In his variations on the *Follia* Storace uses the same theme as Frescobaldi did in his *Partite sopra l'Aria di Follia* (*Toccate I*). All that this theme has in common with the famous folia is the name, however.

The passacaglia theme inspired Storace to even greater lengths than Frescobaldi. Altogether his four sets contain 320 different presentations of the descending tetrachord. Each set is divided into a number of long sections, which are called *prima, seconda*, etc., *partita* (*parte*). They greatly expand the tonal field, for each

Fig.744

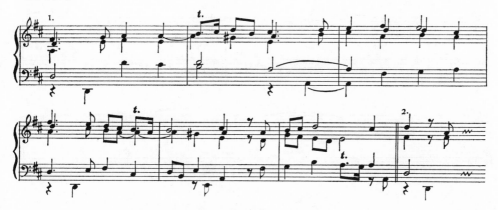

Passagaglia is in a different key: *A* minor, *C* minor, *D* major (at the beginning), and *F* minor, and the last two contain modulatory transitions, designated as *Passa ad altro Tono*. Thus no.3 consists of:

I. *Prima Partita–Seconda Partita Modo Pastorale:* 27 variations in *D* major
II. *Passa ad altro Tono. Prima Partita Modo Pastorale–Seconda Partita altro Modo–Terza Partita, Vario–Quarta Partita, Ordinario:* 24 variations in *A* major
III. *Passa ad altro Tono. Prima Partita–Seconda Partita, altro modo Pastorale:* 20 variations in *E* major.
IV. *Passa ad altro Tono. Prima Partita, A tempo–Seconda et ultima Partita:* 20 variations in *B* minor

No.4 consists of only three sections: 21 variations in *F* minor, 15 in *B♭* minor, and 36 in *E♭* major. The key signature for this piece contains an *E* flat and an *A* flat, but no *B* flat, which was obviously considered self-evident.

The two toccatas are brief pieces of 36 and 12 measures, respectively, in the usual ornamented chordal texture, but with novel features in both harmony and figures. Instead of the forced dissonances and chord progressions, the harmonic texture is smoothed-out, tonally oriented, and based almost entirely on tonic, dominant, and subdominant. The passage work, which in earlier toccatas often stressed the dissonant tones—the sixth, the seventh, and the second—now relies completely on the third, the fifth, and the octave, and so takes on the function of filling out the chords. A comparison of the excerpt from Salvatore's toccata, which was written about twenty-five years earlier (Fig.516, p.491), with Fig.745, the beginning of Storace's first toccata, clearly shows the fundamental differences between keyboard music before and after 1650 and the basic innovations of the middle Baroque. Nevertheless the memory of the earlier style lives on in several details, e.g., in the irregular grouping of the figures at the beginning or in the modal scales in measures 4–5.

Fig.745

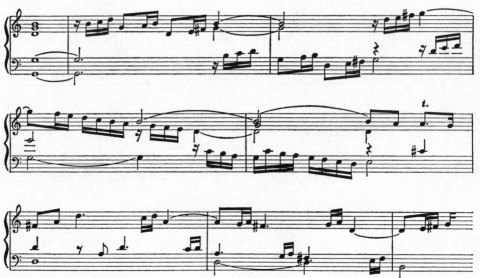

In the last piece of the *Selva di varie compositioni*, a *Pastorale*, Storace improvises with great dexterity for about 200 measures above a pedal point on *D*. One of the many interesting passages is shown in Fig.746. It is curiously reminiscent of the bird calls in Beethoven's *Pastoral Symphony*.

Fig.746

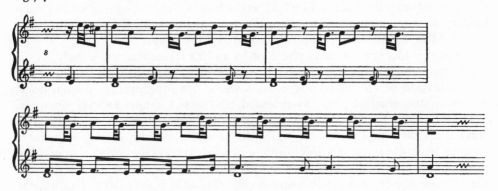

Strozzi and Pistocchi

Storace's publications were followed by another South Italian print, Gregorio Strozzi's *Capricci de sonare cembali et organi, op. 4*, published in Naples in 1687. In the title Strozzi calls himself "Dottor Napolitano dell'una e l'altra legge e

Protonotario Apostolico," and in his dedication to the Archangels Michael, Gabriel, and Rafael, he says that the work was written "nella mia cadente età" (in my old age). Thus his dates are probably about 1610 to about 1690.[4] In addition to the *Capricci*, we also have his *Responsoria, Lamentationes . . .* (Rome, 1655) and *Elementorum musicae praxis, op. 3* (Naples, 1683), a collection of two-part canons for instructional use.

The *Capricci* contain 3 capriccios, 3 ricercars, 3 sonatas, 4 toccatas, an *Ancidetemi diminuito*, a romanesca, 3 galliards, 8 correntes, a balletto, *Eufonia con partite*, and *Toccata de passagagli*. These pieces, like those by Salvatore and del Buono, are printed in open score, whereas Storace's *Intavolatura* uses the keyboard score.

The first piece, *Capriccio primo con partite sopra ut re mi fa sol la*, is a long contrapuntal work on the hexachord, perhaps the last composition on this famous subject. It divides into nine sections, each of which treats the subject differently: in larger or smaller note values, varied rhythms, chromatic filling in, stretto, new countersubjects. The other two capriccios each fall into three thematically related sections. The ricercars, on the other hand, are polythematic—with four, three, and three subjects, respectively—but without articulation into clearly separated sections.

The three compositions called *Sonata* are more interesting. The first one carries the legend "detta da altri impropriamente Canzona francese," a contemporary testimony to the well-known fact that the Baroque sonata developed from the canzona. In contrast to earlier keyboard pieces that were entitled sonata (by Banchieri and del Buono), Strozzi's are indeed sonatas in content as well as title. Each consists of three thematically interrelated movements, with the middle one in triple meter. In nos.2 and 3 an additional free movement is inserted before the last movement—a toccata in no.2 and a homophonic largo in no.3. Fig.747 shows the beginning of each movement of *Sonata* no.2.

Fig.747

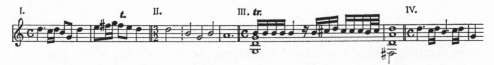

Strozzi's four toccatas represent the last of the Neapolitan-Roman toccatas. Varied passage work, intermingled with trill figures and Lombardic rhythms, is spread above and below chords, and there are still occasional suggestions of the harmonic experiments of the early Baroque. The first toccata (*con pedarole e senza*) is a pedal toccata of about 130 measures with pedal points on A, E, G, B_1 ("si tocchi b mi gravissimo"), D_1 ("si tocchi de sol re gravissimo"), and E_1 ("si tocchi e la mi gravissimo") a remarkable downward extension of the organ pedals.

The section above the pedal point on *G* is written in the form of a pastorale. The last toccata is called *per l'elevatione*. Toccatas nos.2–4 are interesting as illustrations of Italian ornamentation practice, which is so different from the contemporary French practice. Here, e.g., *tr* probably means a trill starting on the main note, while the French *tremblement* starts on the upper auxiliary note. Frequent use is made of a genuine tremolo, an exclusively Italian ornament, which Caccini designates as *trillo* in the preface of his *Nuove musiche* of 1602. The legends *arpeggiando*, *gruppegiando*, and *accentando* are always found in connection with Lombardic rhythms. Whether they are simply intended to draw attention to these rhythms or to indicate, in addition, a particular manner of playing is uncertain. A few examples are given in Fig.748.

Fig.748

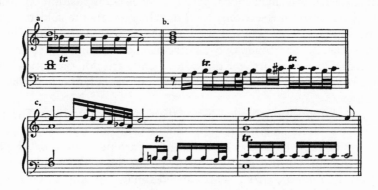

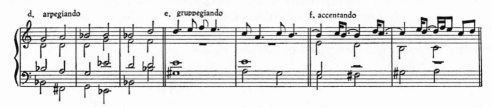

In his *Romanesca con partite tenori e ritornelli* Strozzi once more proves to be the last preserver of a tradition, in both his choice of theme, which goes back to the early 16th century, and his treatment, which is still largely beholden to the musical language of the early Baroque. This very long composition consists of 15 variations (*Parte prima to decimaquinta*), followed by an additional 18 *Ritornelli nel binario*, which may apparently be repeated *ad libitum*. This basic structure is further expanded by three ritornelli, added to variations I, IV, and VII, and by four sections called *Tenore* that follow variations III, V, X, and XIII. The work is notated in a very antiquated manner, moreover; each structural note of the theme comprises three semibreves, exactly as in Cabezón's works, but the bar lines are

Fig.749

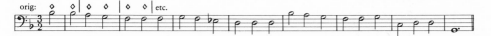

often set like Frescobaldi's, two semibreves apart. To clarify the structure, it is necessary to reduce the note values and group them in 3/2 measures. Then the basic form of the bass is as given in Fig.749. However, Strozzi does not follow this rhythmic form strictly; in every variation he expands or contracts individual 3/2 measures to 4/2 or 2/2 measures, and in the last few variations the theme is subjected to even more radical metric changes. In many variations Strozzi works with brief motifs or with virtuosic formulae that wander from voice to voice, as in Mayone's and Trabaci's variation works from the beginning of the 17th century. In fact, in the first variation all the mannerisms of the early Neapolitans are revived in morbid exaggeration: passionate gestures, flickering movements, flashing lights. Fig.750 presents the first few measures. The four sections called *Tenore* prove to be additional variations in the style of Giovanni Macque's *consonanze stravaganti*. The term *Tenore* probably refers to the sustained, unornamented chords, for no other meaning of this term is recognizable. The example in Fig.

Fig.750

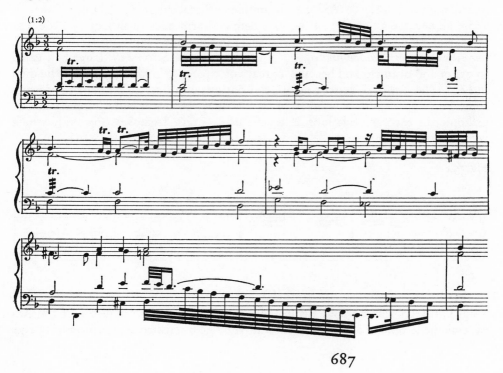

Fig.751

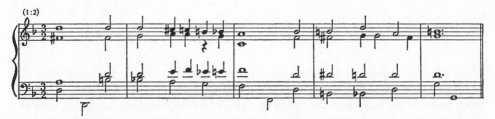

751, the second half of the *Tenore primo*, introduces a chromatic substitution toward the end that is as bold as it is successful—a *B♭*-major triad is replaced by a *B*-major triad.

Among the remaining pieces in Strozzi's print are the *Toccata de passagagli*, which is a series of fifty variations on the tetrachord bass (| *d* | *c* | *B♭* | *A* |), and thus should not be entitled toccata; and the *Ancidetemi dell' Arcadelt*, which is probably the last representative of the once flourishing intabulation.

Like Thomas Tomkins in England, Strozzi represents an anachronism in Italy. They both preserved the memory of a bygone era in a time that had long since turned to new aims; and both earned an appreciation from later generations that their contemporaries denied them.

A child prodigy now completes the curious picture of South Italian keyboard music, Francesco Antonio Mamiliano Pistocchi from Palermo. Born in 1659, he became a member of the Accademia Filarmonica of Bologna in 1667, at the age of eight, and published a print there in the same year—*Capricci puerili . . . per suonarsi nel Clavicembalo, Arpa, Violino, et altri Stromenti*. Later he turned to opera and oratorio and became a great voice teacher in Bologna, where he died in 1726. The *Capricci,* consisting of 40 variations of a *Basso d'un balletto,* despite some naiveté, contain a number of details that are historically interesting. For example, in several variations Pistocchi uses octave tremolos (Fig.752), which were in great favor later on.

Fig.752

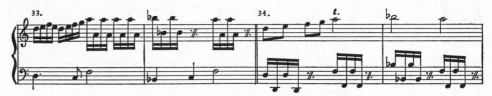

Battiferri and Fontana

Luigi Battiferri was born in Urbino, and was the orchestral director of the Accademia dello Spirito Santo at Ferrara. In 1669 he published a collection of twelve ricercars, ten in four parts and one each in five and six parts (nos.11 and 12), under the title *Ricercari a quattro, a cinque, e a sei*. The first three are "con un soggetto solo," the next three "con due soggeti," the next three "con trè soggetti," and the last three "con quattro," "cinque," and "sei soggetti." They are obviously modeled on Frescobaldi's fantasies of 1608, which are quite similarly arranged in four groups of three pieces with one, two, three, and four subjects, respectively. However, internally they differ greatly from Frescobaldi's fantasies; their extreme variation technique and thematic density are the normal methods of imitative writing that were used in the ricercars by Frescobaldi, Salvatore, Fasolo, and others. The *Ricercar quinto a due soggetti*[5] is a well-formulated double fugue of the type A ‖ B ‖ A/B. In the ricercars with four, five, and six subjects, the subjects are introduced at the very start, each in a different voice, and then developed in various combinations. Battiferri's ricercars were much appreciated; J. J. Fux, e.g., copied them for his own study and use. Is it possible that Bach knew them, too, and that the idea for his six-part ricercar in the *Musical Offering* derived from them?

Fabritio Fontana's *Ricercari* of 1677 also testify to an intensive occupation with problems of counterpoint. Born at Turin, Fontana was active as an organist in Rome from 1650 until his death in 1695. His collection contains twelve ricercars,[6] in which the main subjects are usually combined with countersubjects. In ricercar no.8 the subject ($|\,d - d\,e\,|\,f\,d\,a\,b\,|\,c'\,|$) appears in triple meter in a second section. Ricercar no.11 is entitled "con due soggetti rivoltati," while no. 12 carries the legend "L'istesso soggetto con tre altri, e tutti quattro rivoltati." Fig.753 offers a passage from no.12 in which all four subjects occur, three of them in both their original and inverted forms.

Fig.753

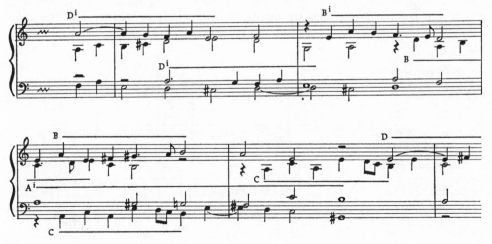

Three preludes preserved in a Hamburg manuscript (ND VI, no.3270) were not available to me. A manuscript at the Library of Congress at Washington (M 21. M. 185) contains a *Toccata dell Sign. Fabritio Fontana*, which starts with three introductory chords and continues with smooth and conventional passage work.

The Bolognese Circle

Battiferri and Fontana are probably the last representatives of the strictly contrapuntal school in Italy. New directions emerged at Bologna, the city that became a center of violin music under Cazzati (c.1620–77), Vitali (1632–92), Pietro degli Antonii (1648–1720), Bassani (c.1657–1716), and others. Keyboard music was also cultivated there, but to a much more modest extent. Foremost among the keyboard composers was Giulio Cesare Aresti (Arresti). He spent his entire life, from 1617 to 1692 (or 1694?), in Bologna, helped found the Accademia dei Filarmonici in 1666, and was an organist at San Petronio from 1685 until his death. He published a *Partitura di modulationi percettive sopra gl'hinni del canto fermo gregoriano, con le riposte intavolate in sette righe per l'organo*, which appeared after 1665, probably even later than 1685.[7] The collection contains short settings of nine hymns in a very curious order. The settings of *Veni Creator Spiritus P[rim]us* appear in a three-part score on page 1, and two additional settings in a clavier brace of two staves of seven lines ("in sette righe") appear opposite on page 2. The first two apparently represent the "modulationi precettive," i.e., teaching pieces, the other two the "riposte intavolate per l'organo." Four settings of a *Veni Creator Spiritus S[ecund]us* follow on the next two pages, and all the other hymns are similarly presented in eight settings in the same order, four didactic ones in open score and four for the organ. The beginnings of two settings of *Veni Creator Spiritus* are given in Fig.754. In several instances the beginnings of the teaching pieces and the organ settings are identical. The whole procedure and the style

Fig.754

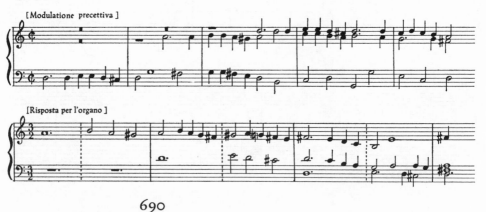

[Modulatione precettiva]

[Risposta per l'organo]

are very antiquated for the time in which the print appeared. I suspect that this collection was written in the first half of the 17th century, but for some reason it was not published until much later.

Fig.755

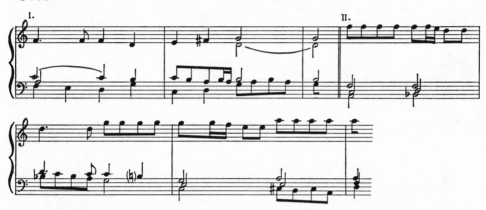

The *Sonate da organo di varii autori* is an important printed collection, probably from the 1680s. It may have been initiated by Aresti, for it contains a dedication by him to Cardinal Antonio Vidman.[8] The collection consists of eighteen "sonatas," one each by Ziani, Pollaroli, Cherli (= Kerll), Bassani, Giustiniani, Schiava, and N. N. di Piacenza, two by Colonna, and three each by Monari, N. N. di Roma, and Aresti, who appears here as a kind of Nestor among composers twenty to forty years his junior. His own contributions, which he places at the end of the collection, with a modesty that does him honor, consist of an *Elevazione sopra il Pange lingua*,[9] a *Sonata cromatica*, and a *Sonata piena*. The *Sonata cromatica* is a traditional ricercar on the subject (| e | g g♯ | a f | f♯ g | e |). The other two pieces exhibit more modern features. In the *Elevazione* the Corpus Christi hymn is first presented in the soprano like a song or a Protestant chorale. Later, freely ornamented and paraphrased, it exhibits some gay, secular passages, similar to contemporary French organ music. Finally, a short section in 3/2 time merely suggests the hymn tune here and there. Fig.755 gives the last line (*fructus ventris generosi*), as it appears in the first and second sections. The *Sonata piena* is a lively piece of about fifty measures. After a pedal point on *A*, various motifs are briefly touched upon, and toward the end four Allegro measures lead to a more sustained concluding section of eleven measures in 3/2 time (Fig.756), with arpeggio figures as well as several other details that clearly derive from violin music.

Several other Bolognese composers are represented in Aresti's collection: Giovanni Paolo Colonna (1637–95), Giovanni Battista Bassani (c.1657–1716),

Fig.756

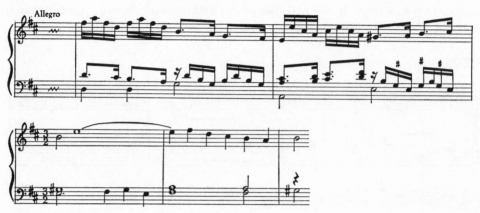

and Monari da Bologna. Monari's three pieces are written in a pure organ style. The first two obviously belong together as a prelude and fugue in *A* major; the third one, called *Elevatione*,[10] is a short movement whose quiet motion suits its liturgical function. By contrast the pieces by Colonna and Bassani obviously stem from violin music. In Bassani's sonata[11] a melodious and occasionally aria-like violin line is transferred to the organ and accompanied by suitable progressions in the left hand. A passage with a fully formed Neapolitan sixth chord is reproduced in Fig.757. Almost all the sixteenth-note passages are written in dotted rhythm, conforming to the widespread preference of the period for the *notes inégales*.

Fig.757

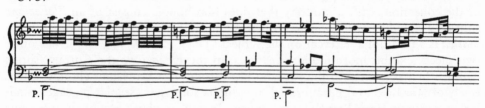

Carlo Francesco Pollaroli (Polaroli), another composer in Aresti's collection, was born in Brescia in 1653 and studied under Legrenzi. In 1690 he became organist and in 1692 maestro di cappella at San Marco in Venice, where he died in 1722. He wrote numerous operas, most of which are known only by their names today. He left four pieces for the keyboard, which are called either capriccios or sonatas in the sources, but are really monothematic fugues. They are generally based on lively subjects that are treated, as is often the case during the period, in a texture that no longer has much connection with polyphony or counterpoint.[12]

Its goal is a busy vivacity that engages the listener's attention in a way that differs greatly from a Bach fugue. The most successful of Pollaroli's fugues from Aresti's collection is probably the one in *D* minor, whose subject, shown in Fig.758, has something of the vitality and incisiveness of a Vivaldi concerto.

Fig.758

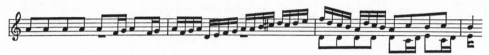

The N. N. di Roma whose three pieces appear in the Aresti print is most certainly Bernardo Pasquini, for one of them (no.12) is called *Sonata 7° tono Bernardo Pasquini* in the manuscript Bologna DD 53 (fol.68v).

The Bolognese circle also includes the brothers Pietro and Giovanni Battista degli Antonii, both of whom were mainly active in instrumental music. Pietro (1648–1720) was elected president of the Accademia dei Filarmonici six times. In 1712 he published a collection *Sonate e versetti . . . per l'organo*, in which the pieces are written for two parts with occasional thorough-bass figures added. The collection contains 81 pieces, the first and last of which are designated as sonatas and the rest as versetti. The concluding sonata carries the legend *Organo serato* [closed] *e col flauto: Pastorale, per il SS Natale*. Fig.759 gives the beginning. The slurs that appear in several passages throughout the piece are characteristic of the violinistic approach of the Bolognese composers.

Fig.759

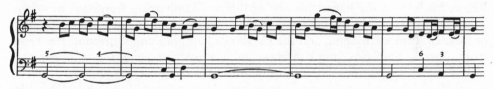

Pietro's younger brother, Giovanni Battista (born c.1660), was an organist at S. Giacomo Maggiore at Bologna. In addition to chamber music works (balletti, correntes, etc.), he published two collections of *Versetti per tutti li tuoni* (op. 2, 1687; op. 7, 1696), in which he used thorough-bass figures not only for the bass but occasionally for the upper part, too. In the preface to the first print he claims that his procedure is his own invention. As an example Fig.760 gives the beginning of the *Verso sesto del primo tuono* from the 1696 collection (the notes indicated by the figures are added in small print).

For almost all of these composers keyboard music was a sideline. This is also true of Alessandro Stradella, who was born in Naples about 1645, led an adventurous life, and was murdered in Genoa in 1682. He owes his place of honor

Fig.760

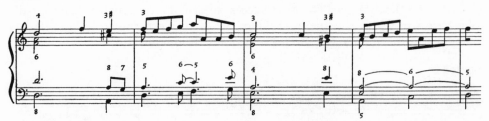

in the history of music to his operas, oratorios, and cantatas. As a keyboard composer he is known by only one work, a toccata in *A* minor, more than eighty measures long, which is preserved in the manuscript Rome, Conservatorio S. Cecilia A/400.[13] This piece may be the earliest example of the type of toccata from which the 18th-century etude evolved. The entire piece is a continuous *perpetuum mobile*, with sixteenth notes in one hand or the other, and occasionally in both simultaneously. All the elements that were valued at the time—melody, harmony, counterpoint, expression—are sacrificed to the ideal of motion, which is carried out as fanatically as by Vivaldi or by many a 20th-century composer.

Bernardo Pasquini

Bernardo Pasquini was born in Massa di Valdinievole near Lucca in 1637, came to Rome in 1650 to study with Cesti, and lived there until his death in 1710. In 1663 he became an organist at S. Maria Maggiore, and in the following year at S. Maria in Aracoeli as well. He played a very important role in the musical life of Rome, for he was the harpsichordist of Prince Giambattista Borghese, in whose palace he lived, and he participated in the musical programs of Queen Christina of Sweden, Prince Colonna, and the Cardinals Pamphili and Ottoboni. He wrote many operas, oratorios, and cantatas, but in most cases only the texts are preserved. Later generations know him mainly as a composer of keyboard pieces, most of which reach us in four autographs written toward the end of his life. The most important one, entitled *Sonate per Gravicembalo, composte del Sig. Bernardo Pasquini e scritto di sua mano in questo libro. A.D. 1702*, belongs to the Berlin Staatsbibliothek; the other three are located in the British Museum (Add. Ms.31501). Several other pieces are contained in manuscript collections and early prints.[14]

Pasquini's keyboard works include 11 pieces in the field of imitative counterpoint (capriccio, fantasy, ricercar, canzona, fugue, sonata), 35 toccatas, 22 variation sets, 17 suites, 8 single dances, 4 bizzarias, 22 arias, 28 sonatas written only as figured basses (14 for one harpsichord and 14 for two), and a dozen secondary or dubious pieces. A sketchy survey of this large output is all that is possible here, and we shall discuss only the more individualistic pieces.

One of the imitative compositions, a *Ricercare con fuga in più modi* (new ed., I, no. 5), is a very long variation ricercar of 345 measures. It divides into nine sections, each of which treats the subject in a different manner.[15] Aresti's printed collection contains three sonatas by N. N. di Roma (i.e., Pasquini), the second and third of which (I, nos.10 and 11) are fugues on lively subjects, written in the usual decadent style of the period.

Fig.761

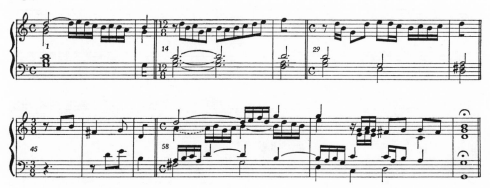

Pasquini's output in the field of the toccata or, as he occasionally calls it, *tastata,* is more interesting, although the structures are more interesting than the contents. Only a few of them (IV, nos.70, 98–101) exhibit the usual articulation in sections with varied content and change of key, but they do not include anything that might be called a fugue or a fugato. The most subdivided is no.98, which presents five sections within its sixty measures. The beginnings of the sections are reproduced in Fig.761. Except for no.70 these toccatas belong to a group (IV, nos.95–102) that is not preserved in the autographs but in a manuscript (Brit. Mus. Add. Ms. 36661) that mostly contains works by earlier composers: Gibbons, Bull, Bevin, and Frescobaldi. It is obvious that the toccatas copied in the manuscript are much earlier than those in Pasquini's autographs, the earliest of which is dated 1691. The autograph toccatas are almost all short pieces of about forty measures, and consist of a single section or occasionally of two sections of passage work, prefaced in several instances by a few chordal measures. The figurations with which Pasquini works are basically always the same: simple complementary motifs, sequential passages, scales, and parallel tenths. Individually the pieces are quite attractive, in large part because of the agreeable, though by no means trivial, harmonic texture that serves as the framework for the figurations. Fig.762 shows the beginning and end of toccata no.76. Toccata no.71 is a lengthier piece (132 measures), in which smooth figurations spread over six long pedal points (on C, G, D, F, G, C), in a manner similar to the toccatas by Sebastian Scherer (cf.p.578)

Fig.762

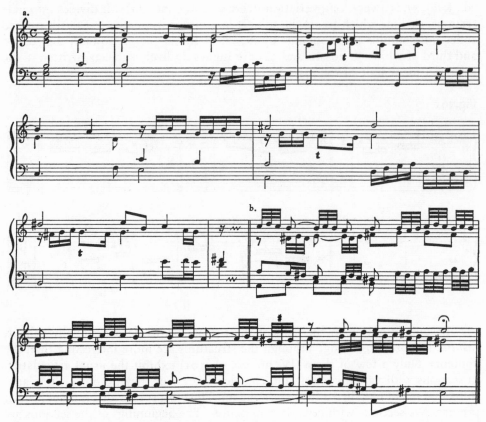

and Pachelbel (cf.p.652). No.81, *Toccata con lo Scherzo del Cucco,* which is available in several modern reprints,[16] bears a striking similarity to Kerll's *Capriccio Cucu.*

Pasquini's gift and individuality unfold much more clearly and freely in his variations, suites, and song- and dance-like pieces than in his ricercars or toccatas. The harpsichord, rather than the organ, was the instrument on which he felt at home and for which he wrote many attractive works. Many of them excel in their natural simplicity and "correctness" of melodic invention, and represent a novel departure. For the first time in Italian keyboard music we have a suite in the form of two, three, or four dances in the same key that follow one another. In most cases there are titles for the first one or two dances, but the character of the remaining pieces is not always too clear. The following are some examples (original titles are italicized):

696

II, no.13: *Alemanda,* Corrente
II, no.14: *Alemanda, Bizzaria*
II, no.15: *Alemanda,* Giga
II, no.17: *Alemanda, Corrente,* Giga
II, no.22: *Alemanda,* Corrente, Giga, Gavotte

Only two suites (nos.17, 18) clearly exhibit the three-movement arrangement A C G, which Seiffert (and others following him) suggests as Pasquini's chief type.[17] The complete absence of the sarabande is striking; it is not only missing in the suites but also among the single dance movements.

The model for Pasquini's suites is not to be found in those by Froberger or the French clavecinists, but rather in the numerous dance collections of Italian ensemble music, which after about 1660 frequently exhibit groupings of various kinds, e.g., ballo—corrente (Cazzati, 1660), balletto—corrente (Prioli, 1665), allemanda—giga (Vitali, 1668), corrente—giga—sarabanda (Vitali, 1668), allemanda—corrente—sarabanda (Bononcini, 1671), and finally allemanda—corrente—giga, the grouping that occurs several times in Corelli's *Sonate da camera,* op.2 (1685).[18] Pasquini's clavier suites fit into this evolution not only in arrangement but also in style. What characterizes his movements is not the pseudo-counterpoint of the *style-brisé* type, not unexpected turns of harmony or exciting irregularities of form, but the attractive melodies in which the *galant* style of the 18th century announces itself. The first section of a *Bizzaria* (II, no.40), given in Fig.763, is an example.

Fig.763

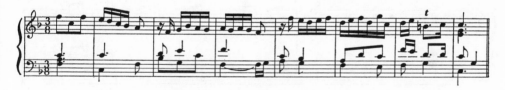

No other composer of the 17th century was as active in the field of variations as Pasquini. He wrote twenty-two such works (III, nos.48–69). The first four merely consist of a dance—a *Bizzaria, Allemande, Corrente,* and *Sarabande,* respectively—with one or two variations; the others, however, are mostly full sets, with eight, ten, or more variations. Pasquini uses the *Follia* twice, the *Bergamasca* or its saltarello three times, and the *Passagagli* four times—in B♭ major, C major, D minor, and G minor, with 20, 17, 12, and 24 variations, respectively. The remaining sets are based on freely invented song- or dance-like themes. Three of them are clearly gavottes (nos.57–59), which could easily come from Lully's operas, as, e.g., the one reproduced in Fig.764. No.53 is entitled *Variationi a inventione,* which may mean that the theme (this theme only?) is Pasquini's own invention.

Fig.764

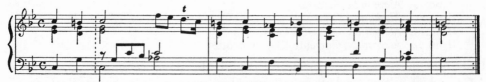

Pasquini's gift for melodic invention, which distinguishes his suites, is again displayed in the individual variatons. More often than one would expect in the 17th century, he keeps the harmonic and structural features of a theme as the basis for a new melody, which is no less attractive than the one it replaces. The first variation of the gavotte above is given in Fig.765. Frequently there are variations "in Correnta," and occasionally in the style of the sarabande (no.52, var. IV; no.55, var.XII). In the *8ᵃ Partita* from the *Variationi a inventione* (no.53) Pasquini utilizes a formula which he obviously borrowed from Frescobaldi's *Toccata nona* of 1627; compare the beginning of this variation in Fig.766 with the excerpt from the Frescobaldi toccata given in Fig.488c. A detailed comparison of the two passages will reveal the changes in harmonic procedure between the early and the middle Baroque. The same material that Frescobaldi connects in unforeseeable ways is expanded by Pasquini with the aid of the smooth chord progressions of functional harmony.

Fig.765

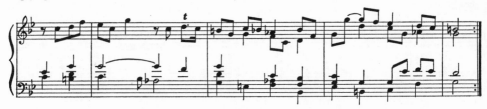

Pasquini's best known variation work is his *Partite diversi di Follia* (III, no. 61), in which the famous folia theme is presented fourteen times. Several variations, especially nos.VII–XII, are based on the repeated use of a characteristic two-

Fig.766

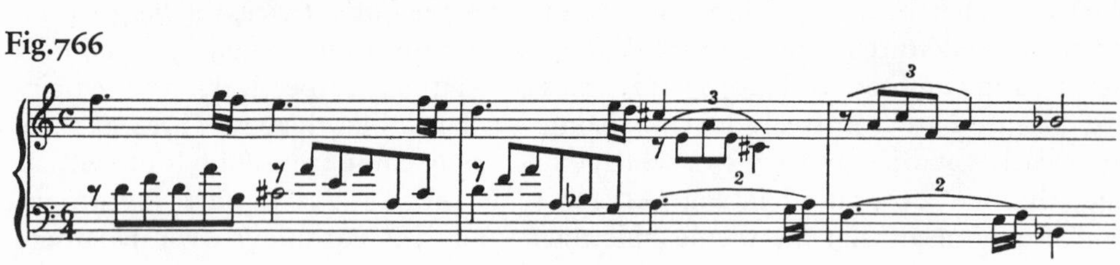

measure formula, but it is treated with enough freedom to avoid the danger of monotony. The first half of variation VIII is given in Fig.767.[19] Here as well as elsewhere Pasquini exhibits a tendency toward precise, energetic formulations, which derive from the violin music of the late 17th century and find their most perfect expression in the works of Antonio Vivaldi (c.1678–1741).

Fig.767

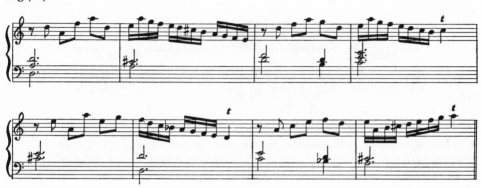

The influence of violin music emerges even more clearly in Pasquini's sonatas, those curious pieces, unique in keyboard literature, that are preserved in the autographs at the British Museum. These twenty-eight compositions, each in several movements, are written as mere figured basses, fourteen of them for one harpsichord and the other fourteen for two instruments. The latter are almost all in three movements—mostly Allegro, Adagio, Allegro—while the sonatas for a single harpsichord vary from two to five movements. They are the only compositions in Pasquini's autograph that are entitled *Sonata*. The first one is dated 1704. Here and there brief sections of the upper part are inserted in the thorough-bass, usually with the legend *Solo*. As an illustration Fig.768 gives an excerpt from the first movement of no.114.

Alessandro Scarlatti

Alessandro Scarlatti's fame and historical significance are so deeply rooted in vocal music that his output for the keyboard, although not inconsiderable, plays a secondary role. This was also true of Giovanni Gabrieli. In Sweelinck's case, however, even though his vocal works greatly outnumber his keyboard works, the latter nevertheless surpass the former in historical and artistic significance.

Scarlatti was born in Palermo in 1660, and died in Naples in 1725. In addition to more than 100 operas, 150 oratorios, 600 cantatas, and many other vocal works, he wrote about 50 keyboard compositions, of which about 40 toccatas are the most significant. Twenty-nine of them reach us in a manuscript that was

Fig.768

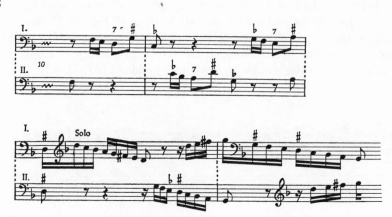

in private English hands (H. M. Higgs) at the beginning of this century and is now at Yale University. J. S. Shedlock described and then published it under the original title, *Toccate per Cembalo . . . del Sig.° Cavaliere Alessandro Scarlatti*,[20] and our observations will be based on it.

Fig.769

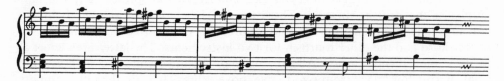

Almost every toccata consists of several more or less clearly separated sections, and almost every one contains at least one section in the *perpetuum-mobile* style employed in Alessandro Stradella's toccata (cf.p.694). This style crystallizes even further in Scarlatti, assumes an even more elementary manner, and comes even closer to the character of an etude. Passages like the one shown in Fig.769 (new ed., p.53) occur repeatedly, in addition to scales, octave tremolos, and arpeggios of various kinds. The Italian toccata is now far removed from the monumental character of Merulo's pieces and the expressive power of Frescobaldi's! What lends interest to this motoric toccata style, despite all its routine (and differentiates it from the later etude), is that it still retains elements of the middle Baroque: irregular phrases, sequences that are not continued consistently, unprepared and therefore surprising changes from one figure to another, and similar details.

Another ingredient of Scarlatti's toccatas are fugues, which usually serve as concluding sections. They, too, are to a large extent motoric. Scarlatti limits most of the *Fuga* sections to two parts, introducing the subject in one hand or the other from time to time, and combining it with "counterpoints" that consist of accentuated single tones or chords; toward the end they tend to lapse more and more into free passage work. The beginning of the fugue from toccata no.6 is given in Fig.770 (new ed., p.39). A few fugues are written more or less in three parts, e.g., the one from toccata no.19 (new ed., p.133); and the fugue from toccata no.17 (new ed., p.123), which has a quiet, ricercar-like character.

Fig.770

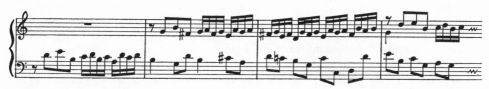

A third element that occurs in several toccatas are short passages with arpeggiated chords, which often form a dramatically effective contrast with the preceding and succeeding passage work. In such sections Scarlatti often uses seventh chords and similar dissonances, such as occur in Bach's *Chromatic Fantasy*. One of these sections (new ed., p.60) is reproduced in Fig.771.

Fig.771

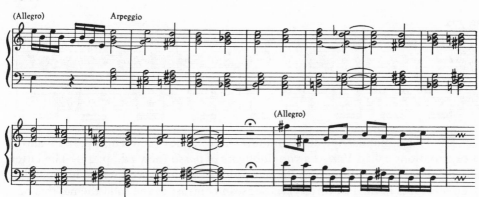

Such chordal passages—which appeared earlier in Pasquini's toccatas, but more briefly—fit organically into the overall structure as introductions and transitions; but the occasionally appended dances—a minuet at the end of the *Toccata quarta*, a corrente at the end of the *Toccata quinta*—are heard as purely external additions, which are possibly not authentic. In toccata no.25 the combination of a minuet followed by a fugue seems similarly unconvincing, particularly since the minuet is in *C* major and the fugue starts in *G* major and ends in *D* major. Some of these things must be the fault of a careless copyist.

The overall structure of the toccatas is very variable. Some consist essentially of only one section, others of four, five, or more sections, e.g. (original titles are italicized):

No. 12: Allegro
No. 24: Allegro—*Fuga*
No. 26: *Fuga*—Allegro
No. 6: Allegro—*Arpeggio*—*Fuga*
No. 15: Introduction, Moderato (?) — Allegro — *Allegro* — *Lento* — *Andante* — *Adagio assai* — *Andante* — *Adagio* (recitative) — *Fuga: Allegro assai*
No. 29: *Primo tono Preludio: Presto* — *Adagio* (recitative) — *Presto* — *Fuga* — *Adagio: Appogiato cantabile*—*Follia*

Toccata no.29, entitled *Toccata per cembalo d'ottava stesa, Napoli 1723*, is by far the longest, and in some ways the most interesting. The first *Adagio* is a kind of recitative above chromatic harmonies, which contrasts dramatically with the mechanically repeated hammer blows of the following *Presto*. The second *Adagio* concludes with a passage in which the hands alternate in playing chords, some of which include various *acciaccaturas,* as in the passage given in Fig.772. The toccata concludes with twenty-nine variations on the folia, all of which are written as formula variations, but often involve very noteworthy and original formulae.

Fig.772

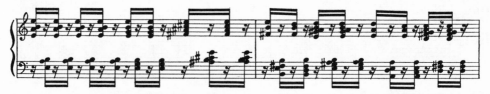

The Higgs manuscript also contains three fugues (new ed., pp.88ff.) and a set of variations called *Varie Partite obbligate al basso* (new ed., p. 47). The latter consists of twelve variations on a thematic idea of six measures, which is expanded to ten measures in the last three variations. In contrast to the folia theme, this one is subjected to ornamentation, but Scarlatti's figures are hardly more than routine.

Very few compositions from other sources have been published. The best known is a fugue in *F minor* with a syncopated subject, which has been included in many collections,[21] occasionally as a work by Domenico Scarlatti. A manuscript of the Milan Conservatory (Noseda n.8802) contains ten toccatas, of which three have been published by M. Esposito.[22] The *Toccata settima* is in fact a variation set in which a chaconne-like subject (the descending *C*-minor scale) is treated in a very ingenious manner. Esposito says, not without justification, that its dramatic effects remind one of Beethoven.[23]

Additional manuscripts of Alessandro Scarlatti's keyboard music are held by the Biblioteca del Conservatorio at Naples. One of them, entitled *Primo e secondo libro di toccate del sig.r Alessandro Scarlatti* (n.34.6.31), contains ten toccatas, which have been published by R. Gerlin.[24] All of them, however, are also contained in Shedlock's new edition, some in variant versions. The Naples manuscript 22.1.22 contains three toccatas and *Partite sopra basso obligato* (dated 1716), which are published by G. Pannain.[25] The manuscript 34.4.40 (*Toccate per cembalo di diversi autori*) contains works by Pasquini and Handel ("del Sassone") and eight (or nine?) compositions by Scarlatti. Three of them appear in Shedlock's edition (nos.12, 17, 19), while the others do not seem to have been published yet.[26]

21

France

Wᴴᴇɴ ᴡᴇ ᴛᴜʀɴ to French keyboard music of the second half of the 17th century we enter the period of the Sun King, Louis XIV. Born in 1638, he came to the throne in 1643, and until his death in 1715, dominated not only his country's policies but also its culture, and indeed that of all Europe. Along with literature, theater, the visual arts, and architecture, music also flourished: opera and ballet under Lully, cantata and motet under Charpentier, and especially keyboard music under a long series of important masters.

In France, more so than in other countries, music for the organ is separated from that for stringed keyboard instruments. Even the usual titles of the prints, *Livre d'orgue* and *Livre de clavecin,* indicate this fact. The former contain pieces for the church service, the latter explicitly secular music, mostly dances. The border types, which are so frequent in other countries and which may be assigned almost as well to either instrument—the toccata, the fugue, variations—rarely occur in France, and when they do other circumstances usually indicate on which instrument they are to be played. This differentiation also applies largely to the composers. The output of Nivers, Raison, Gigault, Jullien, and Boyvin is just as exclusively devoted to the organ as that of Chambonnières, Louis Couperin, and d'Anglebert is to the clavecin; only a few were equally active in both fields, e.g., Lebègue and Marchand. The clavecinists worked exclusively in Paris and at the court of Versailles, the organists both within and outside the capital, at the cathedrals of Chartres (Jullien), Rouen (Boyvin), and Reims (Grigny). Thus it seems convenient to discuss the two repertoires in separate sections, for they are as different from one another as they are unified within themselves.

A. CLAVECIN MUSIC

Chambonnières

Jacques Champion called himself de Chambonnières after his mother's country estate, where he loved to live. On the basis of his parents' marriage in 1601 his birth date is usually given as 1602, but he may have been born somewhat later. He died between 1670 and 1672. As early as 1638 he is mentioned as "joueur d'épinette de la chambre du roi." He was very famous, gave many concerts at the court and in noble circles, and assembled a large number of students, among them Louis Couperin, Cambert, d'Anglebert, and Hardel.

We know 142 pieces by Chambonnières, all of them dances.[1] More than 120 are contained in the Bauyn Manuscript Paris, Bibl. nat. Vm⁷ 674, a collection devoted exclusively to this composer. Shortly before his death Chambonnières published two books of *Pièces de clavecin* (1670), containing sixty pieces, fifteen of which do not appear in this manuscript. His compositions are distributed among the dance types as follows: 15 allemandes, 67 courantes, 28 sarabandes, 14 gigues, 4 pavanes, 4 chaconnes, 3 galliards, 2 brusques, a canaris, a minuet, a rondeau, a volte, and a drôlerie. In the Bauyn manuscript the dances are grouped according to keys, in the following sequence: 28 pieces in C major, 15 in D minor, 16 in D major, 27 in F major, 15 in G major, 8 in G minor, 14 in A minor, and 4 in B♭ major. Within each group the dances are mostly grouped according to types, usually in the order allemandes, courantes, sarabandes, gigues, but frequently other dances are inserted or the order is changed somewhat, as in the following four examples:

C major: 5A 11C 4S 2G 5C 1 chaconne
D major: 1A 7C 2S 2C 4G
G major: 6C 1S 1C 3S 1G 1 canaris 1G 1 chaconne
B♭ major: 1A 1C 1S 1 galliarde

Since the Bauyn manuscript was written in Paris during Chambonnières's lifetime (around 1660), it stands to reason that the overall order originated with him, but this is not certain. In any event, his two printed collections are ordered very differently, each one in six small groups that are unified musically as well as by key, and form genuine suites. As a basic sequence Chambonnières uses the order A 3 (or 2) C S, which occurs five times in this simple form, twice with a galliard added (as the last or penultimate movement), and once expanded at the end by a courante and two gigues. Four of these eight groups open *Livre I* and four open *Livre II*. The last two groups of both volumes are less regularly formed, e.g., pavane G C G and A G 3C S minuet. The significant change from the voluminous key groups to suites was undoubtedly due to the influence of Froberger, who regularly employed the three-movement form A C S or the four-movement form A G C S in his autographs of 1649 and 1656. Chambonnières took this form over, but gave the courante the numerical superiority that it had always held in the French dance literature and that it still occupies in some of Bach's suites.

Very few symbols for ornaments appear in the manuscript pieces, but in the prints they appear with the same richness and variety as they do in all other French publications, beginning with this generation. Thus, pavane no.24, e.g., has sixty-two *agréments* in the print (mordents, trills, and arpeggios), while there is only one in the Bauyn manuscript—at the end of the second section there is a trill above the *c″* at the end of the measure, but it is missing in the print. What is the historical reason for this difference? Did Chambonnières introduce systematic ornamentation into French clavier music only toward the end of his life?*

Let us now discuss the various dance types in some detail. Chambonnières still retains the pavane and the galliard from the 16th-century repertoire. The pavanes (nos.24, 50, 87, and 128) all follow the English tradition in having three sections and in their carefully worked style, dark sound, and serious expression (three are in G minor and one in D minor). The galliards (nos.6, 34, and 141) are less traditional; they are all in two sections and vary in technique and expression. No.34 is one of Chambonnières's most beautiful pieces, also one of the few in which the *coulé sur une tierce* (cf.meas.3 in Fig.773) and the turn (in meas.15) are added to the three ornaments mentioned above.

Fig.773

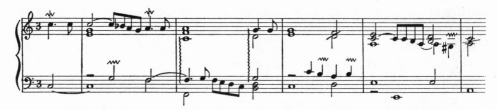

With Chambonnières the allemande reaches the same state of artistic stylization that the pavane and galliard reached in England around 1600. At that time Morley could still speak of the allemande as a "heavy dance fitly representing the nature of the people whose name it carrieth." This characterization is quite apt for the allemandes of his day, e.g., for William Byrd's *The Queens Alman*, shown in Fig.774. But the process of change from a dance to an art form began with the early clavecinists, Mézangeau and Richard. How far Chambonnières carried this process is shown most palpably by the fact that only one of his allemandes (no.31) exhibits the regular eight-measure structure, which is proper and necessary for

---

* As far as I know the earliest systematic explanation of the French *agréments* is found in Nivers' *Livre d'orgue* of 1665, where the preface lists three ornaments with their symbols and execution: *agrément, cadence,* and *double cadence.* In Lebègue's *Pièces de clavecin* of 1677 we find *cadence ou tremblement, pincement, coulé,* and *harpègement.* In d'Anglebert's print (1689) the number of ornaments rises to twenty-nine (cf.p.717).

Fig.774

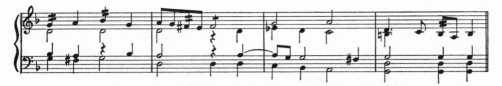

the dance. All the others have sections of nine to fourteen measures in which the music continues in uninterrupted lines, flowing on without any articulating internal cadences. A particularly beautiful example of such continuous flow is the beginning of the *Allemande la Rare* (no.1), reproduced in Fig.775.

Fig.775

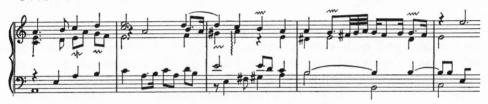

This continuous flow is also typical of the courantes. Regularly built and articulated sections are very much in the minority, too, and first sections with only seven measures are very frequent. Chambonnières's courantes and those of his successors alternate between 3/2 and 6/4 time, a peculiarity that occurs in an early example by Ballard (cf.Fig.531). It lends the music a subtle ambiguity and uncertainty, which has been compared by Écorcheville to the movements of a fish that continually changes direction, now appearing at the surface, now disappearing in the depths.[2]

In the sarabandes, on the other hand, regularity predominates. Most of them have the form || : 8 : || : 16 : ||. Sections and phrases usually end with a feminine concluding formula, which is occasionally found earlier in the sarabandes of Pinel and Mézangeau. The prevailing rhythm is that of the dotted first note, but at times the dotting, and with it the accent, is shifted to the second beat. In several sarabandes the latter rhythm predominates, e.g., in no.23 shown in Fig.776. Sarabande

Fig.776

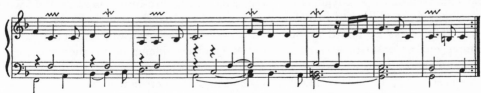

no.75 is identical with galliard no.34 (cf.Fig.773), except that it is notated in halved values, 3/4 instead of 3/2.

Some of the gigues are written in 3/2 time and some in 3/4. The sections are often irregularly formulated, e.g., || : 10 : || : 13 : || (no.17) or || : 14 : || : 14 : || (no.18). In nos.98 and 99 a prime characteristic of the later gigue is employed; both sections start imitatively and the second section uses the inverted subject. In no.99, e.g., the two sections begin as shown in Fig.777.

Fig.777

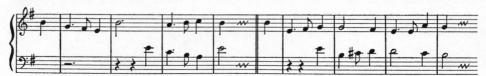

Chambonnières's four chaconnes (nos.81, 113, 116, 123) represent a type that was cultivated exclusively in France, and that was essentially different from the one usual elsewhere (Italy, Germany, England). The ostinato structure is replaced by a rondeau form, in which a refrain alternates with a number of couplets: R C$_1$ R C$_2$ R C$_3$ . . . R. Nos. 81 and 113 have two couplets, no.116 has five, and no. 123 apparently three. The refrain of no.116 has a low, full sound, and the couplets have enchanting melodies; it is one of Chambonnières's most beautiful works and deservedly one of his most famous. He used the rondeau form, to which later clavecinists were very partial, in yet another piece, the *Rondeau* no.106, whose nimbleness is a presentiment of the Rococo. So is the *Menuet* no.60, one of the earliest preserved examples of the type, which exhibits all the traits of the *style galant*.

Dumont

Henri Dumont was born in Villers-l'Evêque (Belgium) in 1610. After having been active as an organist at Maastricht for a short time, he went to Paris and became an organist at Saint-Paul in 1639 (or 1643?), an office that he apparently held until his death in 1684. In addition, he was made organist and clavecinist for the Duke of Anjou in 1652, and orchestral director for the Queen in 1662 and for the King in 1663.

Dumont is chiefly known as the originator of the *plain-chant musical*, a Baroque treatment of Gregorian Masses. His motets are more important, however; they were published in 1686 "par exprès Commandement de Sa Majesté." Very little of his keyboard output reaches us. The new edition,[3] collected from printed and manuscript sources, consists of 17 pieces, including 11 allemandes, a courante, and a pavane, to be performed on either the harpsichord or the organ. These serious, grave pieces follow Chambonnières's; their melodies are also con-

Fig.778

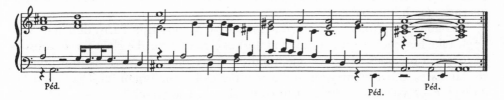

tinuously spun out over sections of irregular length (e.g., 15 and 17 measures in no.I and 11 and 13 measures in no.II). The pavane (no.XV), in the usual three sections, is one of the last examples of the type. It is set in a serious *D* minor and pervaded by appoggiatura dissonances. Like many pavanes of the 17th century, it may be taken as a *plainte*, as music of mourning. Fig.778 shows the end of the first section.

The four remaining pieces (nos.IV–VII) carry the title *Prélude en façon d'Allemande à 2 parties* and the additional legend "serviront aussi pour les Dames Religiouses qui touchent l'Orgue en façon de Duo."* Here secular music intrudes upon the Church, a tendency that gets continually stronger in the subsequent evolution of French keyboard music. The *en Duo* also occurs repeatedly later on. It represents the French counterpart of the bicinium in German organ music, although the two-part texture assumes a very different character. The usual contrast in the bicinium between a *cantus planus* and a rapid figuration is replaced in the *en Duo* by contrapuntal equivalence and occasionally—particularly at the beginning of the piece—by imitation. Fig.779 provides an example from the beginning of no.IV.

Fig.779

Gayement

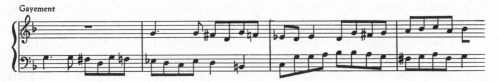

Louis Couperin

Louis is the first member of the large Couperin family of musicians to be known as a composer. He was born about 1626 at Chaumes (Brie), and in 1650 Cham-

---

* They are found in a print *Meslanges . . . contenant . . . plusieurs chansons . . . préludes et allemandes pour orgue et pour les violes* (1657) and are really ensemble pieces in two parts, which were expanded to three parts by an additional print *Troisième partie adjoustée aux Prèludes . . .* (1661). The original version may also be played on the organ, but not the three-part version.

bonnières induced him to come to Paris to study with him. In 1653 Couperin was called to be the organist at the church of Saint-Gervais, an office he held until his early death in 1661.

Couperin's output is preserved in the Bauyn Manuscript (Paris, Bibl. nat. Vm⁷ 675). Like his teacher's it is written almost exclusively for the clavecin. It consists of fourteen preludes and over one hundred dance pieces, as well as four *doubles* to dances by other composers and a few pieces for the organ (cf.p.723) and for ensembles—a voluminous output for one who died so young.[4]

The dances are distributed as follows: 17 allemandes, 30 courantes, 31 sarabandes, 4 gigues, 3 galliards, 10 chaconnes, 2 passacaglias, 2 minuets, and several single pieces (pavane, canaris, volte). As in the Chambonnières Bauyn manuscript, most of them are grouped by keys, in the following order: 15 pieces in C major, 5 in C minor, 23 in D minor, 5 in D major, 3 in E minor, 16 in F major, 10 in G major, 6 in G minor, 13 in A minor, 3 in A major, 3 in B minor, and 2 in B♭ major. Four keys have been added to those used by Chambonnières: C minor, E minor, A major, and B minor. A single pavane (no.121) is in F♯ minor. The order within these groups is more regular than in the older master's. Each group begins with one or several allemandes, followed by courantes, sarabandes, and finally various dances. In the shorter groups—mostly those in the new keys—each type is represented by a single piece, so that real suites result: A C S G chaconne in C minor, A C S gaillarde chaconne in D major, and A C S in E minor and B minor. The two suites in three movements have the same arrangement that Froberger used in 1649. There is some doubt as to who was the initiator and who was the follower, but it must be noted that Froberger was ten years Couperin's senior, and that the latter was only twenty-three in 1649. The other suites, consisting of the classic suite with optional dances added (not inserted), represent a type that played a passing role in the German evolution toward the end of the 17th century, and that occurs again in Lebégue's works. In the French tradition, however, it seems to be more incidental, and was as unimportant as the A C S suites, which reappear only in Chambonnières's prints of 1670.

The individual dance types follow Chambonnières in their essential features. However, the courantes show more preference for eight-measure sections. The ten chaconnes belong to the French rondeau type; usually four or five couplets alternate with the refrain, which is called the "grand couplet." The same form also appears in the *Passacaille* no.27, in which both the refrain and the couplets are based on the tetrachord ostinato (| *c′* | *b♭* | *a* | *g* |), while in the chaconnes the couplets are more or less independent of each other and of the refrain. This *Passacaille* suggests Italian models, and *Passacaille* no.99 even more so, for it has no refrain and consists of a series of forty variations on the tetrachord bass, often with repetitions by pairs. It is not clear why no.95 is called *Chaconne ou Passacaille*.

Couperin's dances are often somewhat threadbare in melodic invention and rather thin in texture. Sometimes he employs contrapuntal features, such as brief imitations or an individualized bass line, perhaps under Italian influence again, but these features do not quite fit into the whole. All in all, his art is not quite on the same level as that of the master he tried to emulate.

On the other hand, the group of fourteen *Préludes* that opens the collection of Louis Couperin's works is a highly original and significant achievement. Even their appearance is remarkable, for each tone is symbolized by a whole note, with no differentiation into longer and shorter note values. This notation does not mean that all the notes are equally long; on the contrary, it indicates a variety and variability of rhythm that cannot really be expressed in conventional notation. Even more curious are the many slurs that in subtle fashion connect groups of notes or more important notes that are perhaps to be sustained somewhat longer and suggest points of support in the flow of melodic lines. Fig.780 shows the beginning of the first prelude.

Fig.780

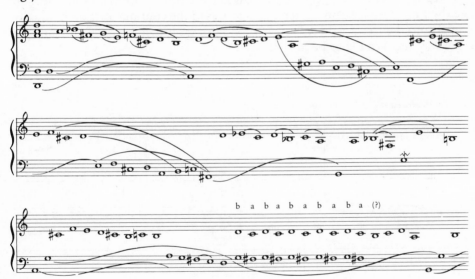

It is almost impossible to "transcribe" this music into customary notation with fixed relative note values.[5] But it is not at all impossible to empathize with the music and perform it in a free, improvising manner as a result of this empathy. At first the sequence of tones seems almost meaningless, but it emerges essentially as a progression of chords connected by a continuous flow, varied ornaments, transitions, and arpeggiations, as exemplified in Fig.781. In the execution of this style Couperin shows an admirable gift of invention and imagination. The music flows freely from beginning to end with always new and attractive turns. The inspiration for these works came from the improvisational preludes of the French lutenists, like the one that opens Denis Gaultier's *La Rhétorique des dieux,* which is also written without bar lines and rhythm symbols.

Fig.781

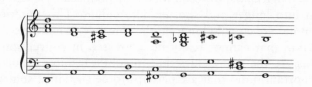

Preludes nos.1, 3, 6, and 12 each contain a section designated as "changement de mouvement," which is written in a precise triple meter, approximating the style of a courante, and generally followed by another improvisational section in free rhythm. In prelude no.3 the final measures of the courante section gradually lead back into the free postlude, as shown in Fig.782, providing a valuable insight into the way the latter is to be played.

Fig.782

Changement de Mouvement

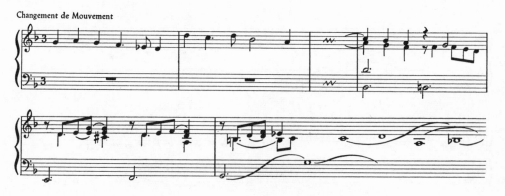

J. de la Barre, Hardel, and Thomelin

Joseph de la Barre, the son of Pierre de la Barre (cf.p.507), lived from 1633 to 1678. Only one composition can be ascribed to him with certainty, a *Gigue de M^r. Joseph De la Barre* in the second Bauyn manuscript, which reappears anonymously elsewhere in the same manuscript as an "allemande," a title that suits its character much better. The same manuscript contains three more pieces by La

Barre, at least one of which, an allemande (which also reappears elsewhere—as a gigue) may be attributed to Joseph on the basis of its style.[6]

The Bauyn manuscript also contains a group of seven pieces by Hardel (Hardelle, c.1640–79). The first six—an allemande, three courantes, a sarabande, and a gigue—are all in D minor and thus represent a key group, which may be called a suite. The beginning of the strikingly simple, but deeply expressive allemande is given in Fig.783. The suite is followed by a gavotte in A minor, which is probably the earliest example of this species preserved in the sources of keyboard literature. Louis Couperin wrote a *Double* (variation) for it.[7]

Fig.783

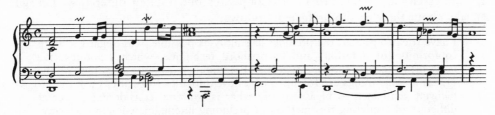

Finally, there is an allemande by Jacques-Denis Thomelin (c.1640–93)[8] that is overly rich and rather tasteless in its flourishes and ornaments.

Lebègue

Nicolas Antoine Lebègue was born in Lâon in 1630, became an organist at the church of Saint-Merry in Paris in 1664, court organist in 1678, and died in 1702. He is one of the few French keyboard masters who composed as much for the clavecin as for the organ. A first book of *Pièces de Clavecin* appeared in 1677, a *Second livre de Clavessin* in 1687.[9]

Book I presents five key groups, each beginning with a *Prélude*. In the first group the prelude is in D minor and is followed by seven dances in the same key (allemande, two courantes, sarabande, gavotte, minuet, canaris), and then by six more dances in D major, beginning with a courante. The second group consists of a prelude and six dances in G minor, followed by five dances in G major. The other three groups are all in one key, A minor, C major, and F major, respectively, with the prelude followed by six to eight dances as follows (omitting the *doubles*):

A minor: A 2C S G 2 minuets
C major: A 2C chaconne bourrée G gavotte minuet
F major: A 2C G S gavotte

Book II consists of six such groups, each of which is called a *Suite*. This is probably the first appearance of this term, which is such a common one today. The introductory preludes are omitted here. Some of the suites have ten or eleven movements; others, however, show a tendency toward brevity and standardization:

    Suite no.1: A C S G minuet
    Suite no.3: A C S gavotte minuet
    Suite no.4: A C S G bourrée canaris

These three suites with optional dances added at the end represent a type that occurs in Louis Couperin's works, and later makes a brief appearance in Germany. In contrast to Book I, the courante occurs only once in each of them, and no doubles are added.

Let us now turn to the music itself. The preludes, which occur only in Book I,[10] are essentially similar to Louis Couperin's but notated differently. Lebègue speaks about them in the preface as follows:

> I have tried to present the preludes as simply as possible, with regard to both conformity [of notation] and harpsichord technique, which separates [the notes of] or repeats chords rather than holding them as units as is done on the organ; if some things are found to be a little difficult or obscure, I ask the intelligent gentlemen to please supply what is wanting, considering the great difficulty of rendering this method of preluding intelligible enough for everybody.

Indeed Lebègue tries to alleviate the "great difficulty of this method of preluding" somewhat by notating the pieces in definite note values, which indicate the desired rhythm at least within certain limits of certainty. To be sure, Lebègue's preludes are much less intricate than Louis Couperin's, and can therefore be more easily represented by measured note values. Moreover, they are much shorter and do not contain any "changement de mouvement." The beginning and a later section of the prelude in A minor are given in Fig.784.

Fig.784

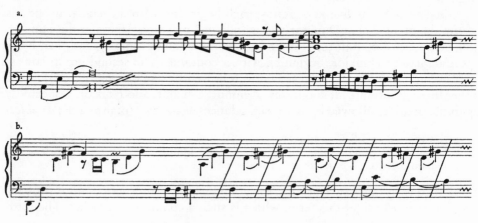

The traditional dance movements—allemande, courante, sarabande, and gigue—follow the Chambonnières and Couperin model. The lively *Gigue d'Angleterre* from Book I (new ed., p.18), is inscribed "Fort viste" (very fast). It is written in the refrain form borrowed from the French chaconne, with a main couplet and three intermediate couplets. The bourrée is often found among the extra dances, probably for the first time in keyboard literature. The bourrée from the last suite in Book II (new ed., p.87) is especially pretty; its beginning is given in Fig.785.

Fig.785

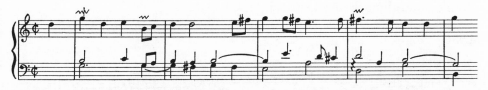

Three of the five chaconnes (new ed., pp.10, 34, 82) are composed in the form of the French rondeau. In the last one the refrain is not repeated literally, but in a varied form and shortened in various ways. The two remaining chaconnes (new ed., pp.76, 90), on the other hand, are genuine ostinato chaconnes (or passacaglias) of the Italian type, such as Louis Couperin wrote. The first one consists of twenty-six variations on the bass ($| f - - | c - - | d - Bb | c - - |$) and the second one (*Petitte Chaconne*) of twelve variations on the subject ($| g - d | e - c | d - - | g - - |$), which appears in various figurations. The designation "petitte" is apt not only for the length of the piece but also for its gay, playful character, so very different from the heavy magnificence of Chambonnières's famous chaconne.

D'Anglebert

Jean Henri d'Anglebert was born in Paris in 1628, and was a student of Chambonnières. In 1661 he became the court organist of the Duke of Orleans and in 1664 his teacher's successor as court clavecinist at Versailles. Shortly before his death in 1691 he published a collection of *Pièces de clavecin* (1689), dedicated to the "Princess de Conty, fille du roy." He says in the foreward, "I have included in this collection pieces in only four modes, although I have composed in all the others as well. I hope to publish the rest in a second volume. Here I have added several *Airs* by Monsieur de Lully. . . ." The second volume never appeared, but a few additional pieces are preserved in manuscript.[11]

The print contains pieces in four groups: G major, G minor, D minor, and D major. The first three are suites introduced by *Préludes;* an allemande, several courantes, a sarabande, a gigue, and various other pieces follow, among them arrangements of works by Lully, such as the *Ouverture de Cadmus, Ritournelle*

715

des Fées de Rolland, Menuet dans nos bois, and *Chaconne de Phaeton,* with which we shall not concern ourselves. The last group includes six organ compositions, five *Fugues pour l'orgue sur le mesme sujet,* and a *Quatuor sur le Kyrie à trois sujets tirés du plein chant.* As an appendix d'Anglebert offers instructions on the *Principes de l'Accompagnement.*

D'Anglebert, like Lebègue, tries to render the rhythm of his preludes precisely, but he does so in a different manner. In principle he symbolizes the tones as whole notes but inserts groups of eighth notes (and occasionally sixteenths) here and there. The beginning of the prelude of the second group is given in Fig. 786. Two preludes that reach us in manuscript (new ed., pp.143, 151) are written in whole notes throughout like Couperin's.

Fig.786

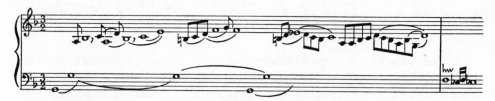

The compositions that follow the preludes include, in addition to the four main dances, 5 examples of the ancient galliard, 3 gavottes, 2 minuets, 3 chaconnes, a *Passacaille,* a *Folies d'Espagne,* and a *Tombeau de Mr de Chambonnières.* The chaconnes exhibit the usual rondeau form, but the *Passacaille* consists of twenty variations of the well-known four-measure tetrachord subject. The *Variations sur les folies d'Espagne* is the earliest example of the song variation in France, perhaps the only one except for the 18th-century noëls. Most of the twenty-two variations keep to the limits of the French style, but a few are composed according to the formula variation recipe, which d'Anglebert probably received from Italy. Pasquini's variations on the same subject may be the immediate model for the one in Fig.787. The *Tombeau,* d'Anglebert's music of mourning for his teacher, could not be more beautiful. It is quite different from Froberger's laments, which indulge

Fig.787

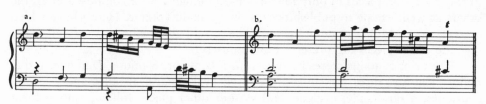

a. D'Anglebert, var. XVI; b. Pasquini, var. VII.

716

Fig.788

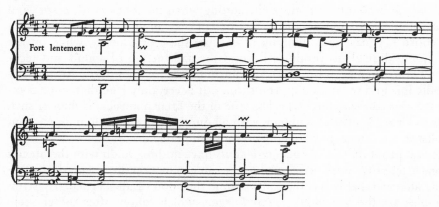

in veritable outbursts of despair. D'Anglebert preserves his calm and dignity—as behooves a Frenchman—and does not write a lament but a salute, in *D* major, part of which is given in Fig.788.

Fig.789

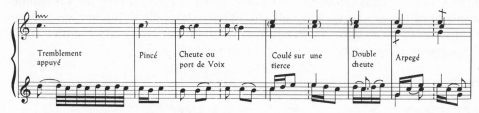

D'Anglebert's variety of ornaments goes far beyond his predecessors'. The table appended to his print contains twenty-nine "marques des agréments," some of which are given in Fig.789. Thus the beginning of the *Tombeau* (Fig.788) should be executed as shown in Fig.790. The explanation in vogue until recently, that these ornaments are a means of overcoming the brevity of the harpsichord tone, is not taken seriously today. Certainly they are very well suited to the harpsichord,

Fig.790

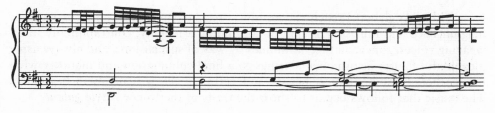

not because of the thinness of its sound, but rather because of its fulness and magnificence, which becomes even more enchanting when the tones swirl, rustle, and purl. The technical possibilities of the instrument play an important role also. On a harpsichord it is easy and fulfilling to execute these ornaments, while on the piano they are difficult to produce. Beyond the satisfaction of sound and technique, however, they are also musically meaningful, for they serve to intensify the melodic line and to stress important tones. It is certainly true that some composers have abused them, but this is less true of the French musicians than of such Germans as Georg Muffat or Kuhnau, with whom the ornaments do not grow out of the musical substance, but are added as a fashionable decoration.

The best proof that the French *agréments* have nothing to do with the brevity of the tone is that they were performed to the same extent on the organ, the instrument that unquestionably has the longest tone duration of all. Particularly striking examples are the five *Fugues pour l'orgue*, which follow after the clavecin pieces in d'Anglebert's print. They are strict four-part fugues, each based on a different rhythmic variant of the same melodic idea (*d' a c' b a bb a*). They are not small, song-like pieces, as often occur in French organ music, but spaciously conceived works of strict, indeed of learned, counterpoint. Nevertheless all the voices are furnished with ornaments to the same extent as the allemandes and the other dances. In the passage from the first fugue, given in Fig.791, note the euphonious suspensions (meas.21–25). The collection concludes with a *Quatuor sur le Kyrie à trois sujets tirés du plein chant*, which is meant primarily as a contrapuntal study. It is notated in four staves and carries no ornaments.

Fig.791

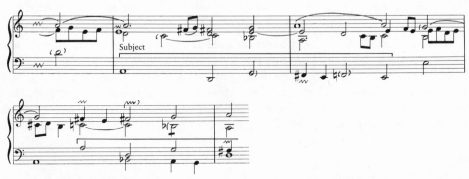

With d'Anglebert French clavier music reaches its highest point of Baroque magnificence and fulness. His skill in continuing a melody, contrapuntally interweaving voices, concatenating harmonies by way of suspensions, and always using meaningful figures as ornaments brings to a final culmination and maturity what his teacher, Chambonnières, began—and certainly his was no mere beginning. The music that follows begins to show the traits of the Rococo *style galant*.

Marchand and Le Roux

Louis Marchand was born in Lyons in 1669. At age 15 he was already an organist at Nevers. He was later an organist at Auxerres and from 1689 on he was active at several churches in Paris, including the *Chapelle royale*, where he succeeded Nivers in 1706. His unrestrained way of life and intrigues of all kinds led to his banishment from France in 1717 (?) and a journey to Germany. It was during this trip that his well-known competition with J. S. Bach was to have taken place at Dresden, which, it is generally assumed, he avoided by flight. He then returned to Paris, where he soon regained his former fame as an organist and teacher, and died in 1732.

Fig.792

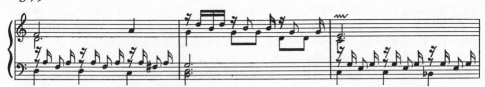

Marchand's two prints of *Pièces de Clavecin* (*Livre premier*, 1702; *Livre second*, 1703) each contain one suite.[12] The first one, in D minor, consists of a prelude, allemande, two courantes, sarabande, gigue, chaconne, gavotte, rondeau, and minuet; the second one, in G minor, of prelude, allemande, courante, sarabande, gigue, gavotte, minuet, and minuet rondeau. In contrast to earlier preludes, the prelude of the first suite is written entirely in exact note values. It is probably the first example of the type that François Couperin calls *mesuré* in his *L'Art de toucher le clavecin* (1717), but which must nevertheless be played "d'une manière aisée sans trop s'attacher à la précision des mouvements." Along with measurement, another spirit enters this very beautiful prelude, a more straightforward character that suggests the *galant* style here and there. The chaconne, as usual, is cast in the form of a rondeau with recurring refrain and four couplets. The last couplet is written in the "goût italien," with fast figurations and even a passage with Alberti basses, as shown in Fig.792. In the prelude to the second suite Marchand curiously returns to the largely unmeasured notation of d'Anglebert. Fig.793 reproduces its beginning.

Fig. 793

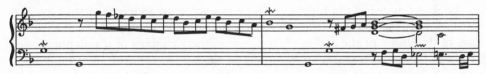

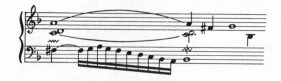

The report of Marchand's dealings with Bach tends to make one imagine him as the very opposite of the German master, i.e., as a facile composer of the fashionable Rococo. Seiffert may well have succumbed to this influence when he says that Marchand's "keyboard writing no longer possesses the sweep of forceful, orchestral magnificence, but flows along in a specifically clavieristic elegance and gracefulness."[13] In reality both suites, and particularly the first one, are still completely within the high Baroque style, as it had evolved in the hands of d'Anglebert. The softening of the basically serious and severe character of his music by the gentleness of the *galant* style makes it even more attractive. To be sure, both suites are rather early works, composed when Marchand was about thirty. By the time of his encounter with Bach his taste may well have changed, influenced by the new tendencies, which are most clearly recognizable in François Couperin's suites. In his organ works, some of which come from a later period, there are various indications of such a style change.

The print *Pièces de Clavecin composées par Gaspard Le Roux* appeared in Paris in 1705.[14] Nothing is known about the composer except a few archival entries from the time between 1690 and 1696. He seems to have been born around the same time as Marchand and François Couperin or perhaps somewhat earlier. His print contains seven suites (more correctly, key groups), each of which is constituted differently in number and selection of movements and in sequence. The first group, e.g., consists of prelude, allemande, courante, sarabande, minuet, passepied, and courante, while the fourth has only allemande, courante, and gigue. Four suites begin with preludes, for which Le Roux returns to the old method of notation in whole notes, as Louis Couperin used it, but he adds thorough-bass figures. The seven suites are followed by a gigue for two clavecins and by five "contre parties," which turn five pieces from the suites into pieces "à deux clavecins." The second clavecin plays the same basses as the first one, but enriches the upper texture with parallel thirds or dexterously added passages in contrary motion. The beginning of the gavotte from the third suite (new ed., pp.17, 72) is given in Fig.794. Finally, most of the movements are also presented *en trio*, i.e., for two melody instruments (violins, flutes) and figured bass, generally in a somewhat simplified form.

Le Roux, more so than Marchand, proves to be an adherent of the new era, which aims at the simplification of style. Even the allemande, which always appears in the music of the earlier clavecinists in the rich garb of a polyphonic (or pseudo-polyphonic) texture, appears here in the simple form of an accompanied

Fig.794

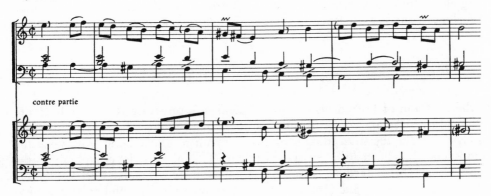

melody, which leaves something to be desired in strength and continuing tension. The *Allemande grave* of the fifth suite, e.g., begins as shown in Fig.795. The remaining contents of the print move on the same level, containing little of special importance. The sarabande of the seventh suite is presented as a theme with variations in twelve *couplets*, but the variation form is really alien to French clavecin music. Where it appears, e.g., in d'Anglebert's folia variations, it shows some Italian influence in the employment of characteristic and formulary figurations. In Le Roux's sarabande, this influence emerges more and more clearly as the set approaches the end.

Fig.795

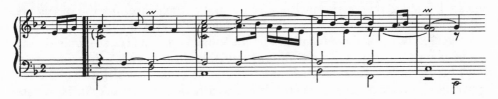

A work of considerably more significance than Le Roux's print, the *Premier livre de pièces de clavecin* by Rameau, appeared one year later. It was followed by two more volumes in 1724 and 1731, and by François Couperin's four books, of 1713, 1717, 1722, and 1730. These works lie beyond this study's limits. To be sure, Couperin's first volume contains some works that still follow the 17th-century tradition and represent it most impressively (e.g., the allemande that opens the *Second Ordre*), but in addition there is much that belongs to a new world of sensibility and musical style (e.g., the *Diane* and *Florentine* of the same group). In his later books there are only sporadic reminiscences of the severe musical language of the Baroque, e.g., in the passacaille of the *Huitième Ordre* or the allemande for two claviers in the *Neuvième Ordre* (both in the *Second Livre*); everything else combines to create a colorful picture, in which the scintillating world of feeling of the French Rococo achieves its expression in the most enchanting manner

B. ORGAN MUSIC

In the tradition of French organ music Titelouze's prints of 1624 and 1626 are followed by a lacuna which is not as long as the one preceding them, but long enough to make the succeeding evolution difficult to understand. Who were the composers who effected the decisive turn from Titelouze's strict polyphony to the richly ornamented Baroque style that appears forty years later in Guillaume Nivers' first *Livre d'orgue* (1665)? True, we know a goodly number of organists who were active during the intervening years—Pacquet, Thomelin, La Barre, Richard, Dumont—but the small amount of their output that is preserved mostly belongs to the field of secular music, and is certainly not adequate to clarify the evolution succeeding Titelouze.

The *Fugues et Caprices* of 1660 by François Roberday (1624–95) do not help us here, for they do not really represent a link in the national evolution, but an attempt to transplant Italian organ music onto French soil.[15] The print contains twelve compositions that are called *Fugue*. According to the introductory "Advertissement" one is by Frescobaldi, one by Ebnert [*sic*] (cf.p.561), and one by Froberger. Roberday says that the subjects of all the other compositions were given to him by La Barre, Couperin, Cambert, d'Anglebert, Froberger, Bertali, and Cavalli, but which themes or pieces were written by which composers is not indicated. Roberday is very much under the Italian influence, for the pieces are notated in open score, in what he calls "la manière d'escrire la plus utile et la plus avantageuse." One of the advantages he mentions is that pieces so notated may also be played "sur les violles ou autres semblables instruments." Roberday thus strays far from the idea of French organ music, with its typical instructions for registration, which occur in a manuscript as early as 1618 (cf.p.498). He treats the subjects he received in accordance with Frescobaldi's variation principle, in four or five sections, first in quiet motion as *Fugue,* then in lively transformations as *Caprice.* As illustrations Fig.796 gives the subjects of no.9. The last three

Fig. 796

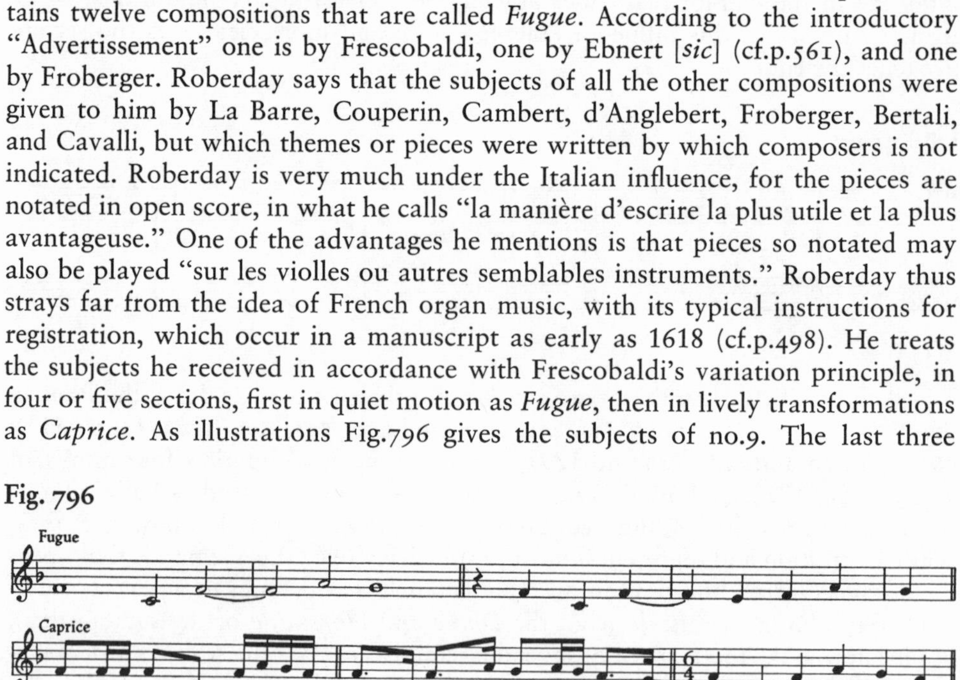

works in the collection are also constructed around varied subjects but without *Caprice* sections. These pieces are probably the three by Frescobaldi, Ebner, and Froberger.

The six organ works by d'Anglebert, discussed earlier (cf.p.718), similarly stand outside the mainstream of late 17th-century organ music.

Several pieces by Louis Couperin more or less belong to the organ: a *Fantasie*, in which the right hand plays long, sustained chords in several places; two brief pieces called *Pseaume*, whose function is not quite recognizable; and three *Carillons*, the third of which—a three-part version of the first one—dexterously imitates the simultaneous sound of high and low bells.[16]

Types of French Organ Music

Several other organists contemporary with Roberday were pursuing quite different aims. Instead of abstract ricercars and fugues, they wrote hundreds of short pieces for liturgical use, which tended more and more toward a simple, easily grasped texture and an attractive, melodious style. Gigault (1624–1707), Lebègue (1630–1702), Nivers (1632–1714), and their successors gave French organ music a completely new character. Their compositions for the organ are so uniform that they suggest the influence of an external power. The first to come to mind is the Jesuits, one of whose aims was to bring the church service closer to the faithful and to formulate it according to the taste of the time. These aims are well served by these many short, attractive, yet dignified pieces.

The most striking characteristic of French organ music is the development of well-defined types, which are largely determined by the sound qualities of the French Baroque organ. The beginnings of this evolution can be found in the first half of the 17th century—in directions such as *pour le cornet* and *pour trompette* or in such titles as *Duo pour différents jeux* and *Dialogue* (cf.pp.499, 505). Later the terminology for the various sound effects was formulated in the greatest detail. The most important types are the following:

1. *Récit*. A piece in which one voice emerges soloistically and is played with a special registration, e.g., *Récit de Cromorne, de Voix humaine*. The soloistic voice is usually in the soprano, sometimes indicated by a legend such as *Dessus de Cromorne*. Titles like [*Récit de*] *Cromorne* (or *Tierce*) *en taille* indicate that it is

Fig.797

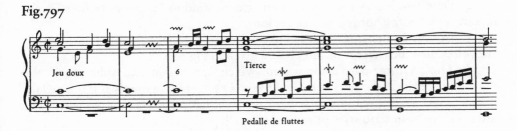

723

in the tenor (*taille*). Solos for the bass appear under legends such as *Basse de Trompette*. The entry of the richly ornamented solo voice is usually preceded by a few measures played on the *Jeu doux* (soft stops). Fig.797 gives an example of a *Tierce en Taille* by Lebègue.[17]

Fig.798

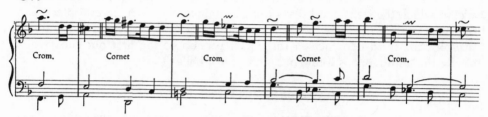

2. *Dialogue*. Two different registrations are employed in alternation for phrases of varying length. Nivers differentiates between *Dialogue de récits* (e.g., cromorne and cornet) and *Dialogue à deux choeurs* (alternation between *positif* = choir organ and *grand jeu* = full reed stops). An excerpt from his *Dialogue de récits* from the *Troisième livre d'orgue* appears in Fig.798.

3. *Echo*. Phrases of various lengths are repeated as echoes. The end of the *Echo* from Nivers' *Livre III*, reproduced in Fig.799, is particularly lovely.

Fig.799

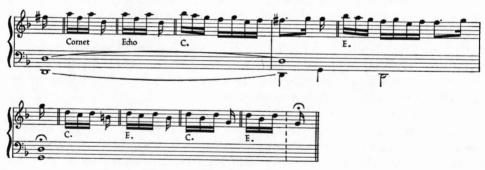

4. *Plein jeu*. Pieces for a particular, clear-sounding mixture, written in the *durezze* style, with chords and suspensions.

5. *Duo*. A composition consisting of two similar, occasionally lightly imitative voices, like the excerpt from Lebègue given in Fig.800.[18]

6. *Trio*. A three-part composition, which appears in two subtypes in the works of Lebègue and others: *a trois claviers*, i.e., for two manuals and the pedals, or *à deux dessus*, i.e., with two parts for the right hand and one for the left.[19] The latter is close to the trio style of Lully or Corelli.

Fig.800

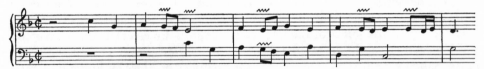

7. *Fugue*. Three- or four-part compositions in a more or less strict imitative style. When the subject is of a sustained character, the piece is called a *Fugue grave*. The beginning of one of Nivers' *Fugues graves* is shown in Fig.801.

Fig.801

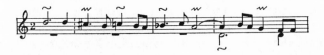

Let us now turn to the individual composers in the chronological order of their printed publications.

Nivers

Guillaume-Gabriel Nivers was born near Paris in 1632 (not, as once believed, in 1617). In 1654 he became an organist at Saint-Sulpice, Paris, an office he held until his death in 1714. He was also active at the court, as organist of the *Chapelle royale* (1678) and music teacher of the Queen (1681), and as organist and voice teacher at the *Maison royale de St.-Louis* at St.-Cyr, a school for young ladies of the nobility. He wrote church music and participated in the reform of the Gregorian chant. His numerous organ works were published in three prints: *Livre d'orgue contenant cent pièces de tous les tons de l'Eglise* (1665), *Second livre d'orgue contenant la Messe et les Hymnes de l'Eglise* (1667), and *Troisième livre d'orgue des huit tons de l'Eglise* (1657).[20]

The first book contains one hundred pieces arranged in twelve key groups: first the eight usual church modes and then four transposed ones, e.g., "1. transposé en E." The first two groups each contain ten pieces, the others eight, e.g., *Prélude du 3. Ton, Fugue, Récit de Cromhorne, Basse Trompette, Cornet, Duo, Grand jeu*, and *Plein jeu*. All the types that dominate and characterize French organ music until the early 18th century emerge here for the first time. The *Troisième livre* is similarly arranged. It consists of eight groups of thirteen pieces each. Each group consists of a *Prélude* and two groups of six pieces each, both starting with a fugue, e.g., *Prélude du 1er Ton; Fugue, Récit, Duo, Basse, Echo, Dialogue à deux choeurs; Fugue grave, Récit, Duo, Basse, Dialogue de Récits, Dialogue à deux choeurs*.

The arrangement according to church modes suggests that the pieces in books I and III were probably used primarily for the singing of psalms and Magnificats. The second book contains compositions for the Mass—a number of hymns, three sequences, and the *Te Deum*. Nivers' organ Mass consists of five versets for the Kyrie, nine for the Gloria, an *Offerte*, three versets for the Sanctus (and Benedictus), and two for the Agnus. For the first movements in the Kyrie, Gloria, Sanctus, and Agnus Nivers uses the melodies of Mass IV in the bass or in the tenor (e.g., *Agnus: le plain chant en taille*). Most of the other movements— *Récit, Fugue, Duo,* etc.—are freely composed. During the offertory the *Offerte en fugue et dialogue* is played; it is a longer piece in which a subject is first presented as a fugue and then in alternate hands on the *Grand jeu*.

Nivers writes two or three settings for each hymn. In the first one the melody lies in the bass as a strict or lightly ornamented *cantus planus* in whole or half notes. In the other settings the melody is either treated as a short fugato on the beginning (*Fugue sur le mesme sujet*) or as an ornamented discant chorale (*Récit*). As an illustration of the technique of ornamentation Fig.802 reproduces the third line of the *Récit de Voix humaine* from the hymn *Ave maris stella* (new ed., *Livre II*, p.65).

Fig.802

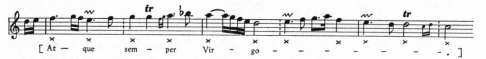

[At — que sem — per Vir - go - - - - - - - -.]

Nivers' *Second livre* also contains organ versets for three sequences (*Proses*): *Victimae paschali laudes, Veni Sancte Spiritus,* and *Lauda Sion Salvatorem*. The added text beginnings show that the organ always played in the odd verses, either replacing them (according to the usual assumption) or following them as postludes, as described by Bottazzi (cf.418). The versets rarely comprise more than twelve measures and often employ the chant melody in the bass or soprano, mostly in lightly ornamented versions. In several settings for *Lauda Sion* Nivers uses the rhythmic formula ♩. ♪♪. ♩, an interesting attempt at representing *notes inégales*.

Nivers is certainly not an extraordinary artistic personality, but he does not quite deserve the negative judgment applied to him by Pirro ("very mediocre"), Frotscher ("hardly goes beyond mediocrity"), and others.[21] Despite his obvious striving to please, he definitely keeps away from a too secular, song- or dance-like flavor, and though his pieces may no longer accord with today's ideas of what is suitable for services, they nevertheless maintain dignity and a suitable posture. Quite apart from the question of suitability, most of them are interesting and quite attractive musically. Nivers avoids stereotyped turns or tiring repetitions, changes the length of the phrases, and occasionally inserts measures in 3/4 (as his contemporary Lully does). He writes lively melodies, gives sufficient consideration to the contrapuntal element, and last but not least observes a proper limitation of length. These features and others distinguish Nivers' organ pieces; it is regrettable that they can no longer be employed today.

Lebègue

A few details about Lebègue's life are given on p.713. Like Nivers, he published three *Livres d'orgue* (1676, 1678/79, c.1685).[22] Book I contains eight groups (*Premier, . . . , Huitième Ton*), each consisting of a *Prélude* and six to ten pieces similar to those in Nivers' third book: *Duo, Trio, Dialogue, Récit, Basse de trompette*, etc., ending with a *Plein jeu*. But Lebègue's tendency toward secular music is quite manifest in four-measure phrases of a song-like or dance-like character, which becomes more and more dominant in the later evolution of French organ music. The beginning of the *Dialogue du 2. Ton* (new ed., p.65) given in Fig.803, is an illustration. Lebègue exhibits an inexhaustible inventiveness in the creation of such somewhat superficial but always attractive and graceful melodies. But he also writes pieces of a different kind, particularly a number of *Tierces* (or *Cromhornes*) *en taille* in which the left hand executes an energetic, declamatory solo part, accompanied by the right hand and an obbligato pedal part (cf.Fig.797). This is the most peculiar, most interesting type of French organ music, and the only one that has no counterpart in any other country. Lebègue seems to have introduced it, and almost all of his successors until Du Mage (1708) appropriated it. The *Trios à 3 claviers* demand the pedals, too, and Lebègue was probably the first to entrust individual tasks to them.

Fig.803

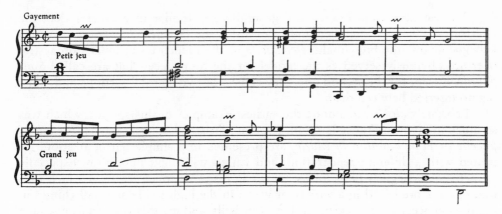

His *Second livre* contains an organ Mass of the same disposition as Nivers'

(but without the offertory), and nine groups of seven or eight versets each for the Magnificat. In comparison with the first book, the contents of this volume are somewhat disappointing, probably because of external circumstances. In the preface the publisher says that the first book was written "pour les sçavans," and the second for those who possess only "science mediocre." He adds that Lebègue "a voulu se rendre intelligible à tous" and that he "a esté mesme contraint d'abandonner ce grand feu qui accompagne d'ordinaire son jeu." Probably it was the church authorities that caused him to "become intelligible for everybody" and forced him "to abandon the fire of his playing." Most of the pieces are shorter and more simply written than those in the *Premier livre*, completely without pedals, and some are rather trivial, e.g., the *Basse de Trompette* of the *Magnificat du 8e. Ton* (new ed., p.159).

The *Troisième livre*, according to the publisher's notice, contains "des grandes Offertoires et des Elévations sur l'Orgue et le Clavecin." The offertories are rather extended pieces in several sections, but neither the changes in ideas nor those of registration can hide the rather empty and trivial contents. Lebègues does not hesitate to accompany the offertory with bellicose fanfares or with song-like phrases that would be more suitable for amorous shepherd scenes. The last two offertories are based on chants, one on the *Stabat Mater,* the other on *O filii et filiae.* In the former there is a brief prelude, after which the melody of the hymn (originally a sequence) appears as shown in Fig.804.

Fig.804

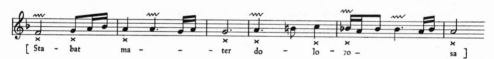

The elevations are briefer and generally less secular in character than the offertories. The most dignified and beautiful is the *Première Elévation*, in which Lebègue adapts the Frescobaldi *elevazione* to the French taste. Lully's orchestral overture obviously served as the model for the four pieces that are called *Simphonie.* Except for the second one, they consist of two chordal sections and a fast fugato inserted between them.

Lebègue's *Noëls* are among the earliest examples of this species, which was so much in favor in France later on. Popular Christmas songs, such as *Une vierge pucelle* or *Pour l'amour de Marie*, are presented in a simple harmonization, repeated with a different registration, and varied with light figuration. Especially attractive is Lebègue's *Les Cloches* (new ed., p.232), a tone picture in which four tones *f e d c* are heard in a variety of ways: in the high treble as small chimes in rapid sequence, in a low register as big, slow bells, and in other combinations, such as *f d e c*, or in an alternation of *c* and *d* only, as in William Byrd's *The Bells*.[23]

Gigault

Nicolas Gigault was probably born in Paris in 1624 or 1625 and was active as an organist at several Parisian churches, chiefly at Saint-Nicolas-des-Champs, an office he held from 1652 until his death in 1707. In 1683 he published a *Livre de musique dedié à la Très Ste. Vierge*, and in the title he says that it might be employed for the organ and the harpsichord as well as for lutes, viols, or flutes. It is divided into two parts and contains ten noëls, two *Conditor* (one each at the beginning of each part), several short versets for the sequence *Mittit ad virginem* (for the Annunciation), and several other pieces.

The noëls—apparently the earliest examples of this species that are preserved —consist, as usual, of variations in which Gigault mostly follows a rigid outline: *à 2 p[arties]; à 2; à 3; à 3, dialogue; à 3, 2 dessus; à 4, 2 Ceurs* (choirs)—i.e., the subject first in two parts, then a two-part variation, etc. This plan suggests a tendency toward pedantry, which is confirmed by a rather thin, schematic variation technique. Interestingly, the Christmas songs still appear in an older rhythm, which was changed by Lebègue for a more intelligible form two years later and was subsequently entirely modernized. The three versions of *O dites nous Marie*, given in Fig.805, clearly indicate the change from a grave stride to a dance-like élan.

Fig.805

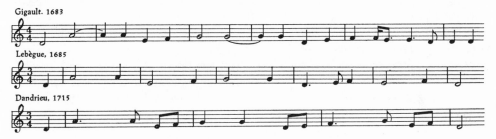

Gigault's *Livre de musique pour l'orgue*[24] published in 1685 is more significant. The preface states that it contains about 180 pieces, which may be played on one, two, three, or four claviers, and,with the aid of added signs, may be shortened or divided into separate settings; that there are several pieces "à cinque parties, ce qui n'a encore jamais paru pour l'orgue," "une fugue pursuivie et diversifiée à manière italienne," and another "dont les vers sont fuguez à la manière de feu Monsieur Titelouze." The collection opens with three organ Masses. The first and third each include more than twenty versets in two to five parts. The second is much shorter and simpler, with seven three-part settings (new ed., pp. 28–30). The Masses are followed by numerous pieces arranged in six groups, according to the church modes, a *Te Deum* of twenty-one versets, and four additional pieces in the eighth church mode.

For the three organ Masses Gigault generally (if not always) uses the chant melodies of Mass IV, either as *cantus plani* in half notes or transformed into fugue subjects. There are several *cantus-planus* settings in five parts, in which the chant tune is played in the pedals, not as the bass but as a middle voice, e.g., the *Kyries* on pp.6 and 10 of the new edition or the *Et in terra* on p.12. In a *Fugue grave recherchée sur le Kyrie* on p.32 the melody of the Kyrie IV is transformed into the remarkable subject given in Fig.806. The versets of the *Te Deum* are also based on a chant tune, but it is different from the one in the Roman *Antiphonale*.

Fig.806

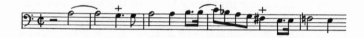

The pieces that are arranged according to the church modes include *Préludes, Dialogues, Récits, Echos*, a few hymn settings (e.g., a *Veni Creator spiritus* and a *Pange lingua*), and numerous fugues. In the preludes dissonant harmony is often employed with ingenuity and taste, e.g., in the *Prélude du 3. et 4. tons* (p.109), given in Fig.807. As was usual in France during the period, Gigault is satisfied in his fugues with mere suggestions of the subject within a texture that is more homophonic than contrapuntal wherever it is not limited to two parts. Even in the *Fugue grave recherchée sur le Kyrie* the complete subject (cf.Fig.806) appears only twice, at the beginning, and thereafter it is merely suggested by its opening. The *Fugue poursuivie à la manière italienne* (p.77), specially mentioned in Gigault's preface, together with the next fugue on *Le mesme subjet d'un autre mouvement*, represents an extended and strict treatment of a subject and its variant. The fugue *à la manière de . . . Titelouze*, also mentioned in the preface, is probably the *Fugue sur Pange lingua* (p.107), in which several subjects, derived from the hymn melody, are successively developed.

Fig.807

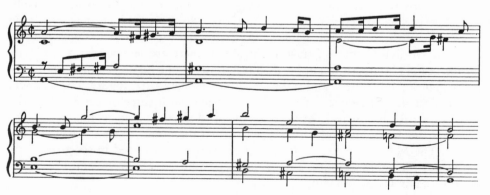

French scholars like Pirro, Dufourcq, and Bonfils have judged Gigault's organ compositions rather negatively.[25] Of course he should not be compared to Buxtehude, as Pirro does in discussing a subject that was used by both composers. Within the field of French organ music such a judgment does not seem justified. It is true that his organ pieces lack the melodious invention that constitutes the charm—and at the same time the danger—of Lebègue's music, but this lack is balanced by the more serious attitude, more suitable for the church, in which Gigault follows Nivers. What is most disturbing is that Gigault, more than anyone else, surrendered to the dotted rhythms, the modish *notes inégales*. Today many of his pieces are no longer bearable as they are written, but one may approach them— as well as the numerous *agréments* of d'Anglebert—with some discretion and play, e.g., the subject that is reminiscent of Buxtehude (prelude and fugue in F♯ minor, new ed., p.84; cf.Fig.655, no.13) as shown in Fig.808 (the small notes indicate the original version).

Fig.808

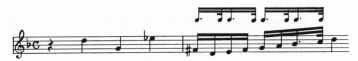

Raison

Little is known about the life of André Raison. He must have been born in the 1640s, for he was an organist at the Abbey of Sainte-Geneviève from 1666 to 1716. For a time (1714) he was also an organist at the church of the Jacobins of the rue St.-Jacques. He died in 1719, having published two *Livres d'orgue*, in 1688 and 1714.[26]

The *Premier livre d'orgue* contains versets for five organ Masses, which are only nominally related to the Masses of the Roman *Graduale*. This fact is even shown externally, for the versets are arranged according to church modes, a principle that is quite alien to the Gregorian Masses. However, it makes it possible for Raison to say in the preface that the Masses might also "servir en Magnificat pour ceux qui n'ont pas besoin de Messe." He also says that in each piece one should pay attention to its "rapport à une Sarabande, Gigue, Gavotte, Bourrée, Canaris, Passacaille et Chaconne, mouvement de Forgeron etc." and should give it the same "Air" as on the clavecin, except that the pieces should be played more slowly "à cause de Sainteté du Lieu"—a candid acknowledgment that shows how much music destined for the services had fallen victim to secular dance music.

Many of the settings therefore can barely be differentiated from dances, e.g., the *Dernier Agnus* of the second Mass (new ed., Guilmant, p.57), whose beginning appears in Fig.809. The *Second Agnus* of the first Mass is probably one of those pieces referred to in the preface as "mouvement de forgeron," i.e., an imi-

Fig.809

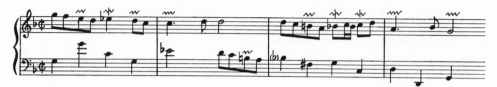

tation of forge hammers. In their melodious, dance-like character these pieces follow Lebègue; others of a more organ-like and eccleciastic approach are similar to
Nivers'. Often they are the first versets of the various sections of the Ordinary—
the first Kyrie, the Et in terra, the first Sanctus, and the first Agnus. The following movements deserve to be singled out: the five-part *Autre premier Kyrie* of the
first Mass; the *Second Kyrie, Fugue grave* of the third Mass, which for French
music is unusual because of its fully imitative style; the *Tu solus altissimus* of the
fourth Mass, with its interesting *Dialogue* between *Cromorne* in 3/4 time and
Cornet in 4/4; the *Glorificamus* of the last Mass, with its alternation between
Cornet and *Eco;* and the *Christie, Trio en Passacaille* of the second Mass, whose
ostinato subject is identical with the first half of the subject of Bach's *Passacaglia* (Fig.810).

Fig.810

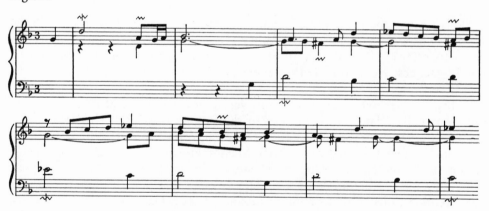

The five Masses are followed by an *Offerte du 5. ton,* modeled after the
French overture and written as a salute to the King ("Vive le Roy des Parisiens")
on his entrance into the city hall on January 30, 1687.

In 1714 Raison published his *Second livre d'orgue sur les acclamations de
la Paix tant desirée,* which obviously refers to the Peace of Utrecht (1713) or of
Rastatt (1714). The collection begins with a setting of the peace antiphon *Da
pacem Domine* (*cantus planus* with two ornamented upper parts) together with

a *Fugue sur Da pacem Domine.* They are followed by a *D*-major prelude with a long fugue and an *Ouverture.* The end of the fugue degenerates into a superficial play with sounds on the exclamation "la paix," and the second section of the *Ouverture* repeats the text "Vive le Roy" about one hundred times. An excerpt from the prelude is given in Fig.811. The volume concludes with an *Allemande grave* and a number of noëls with variations—all quite insignificant and superficial.

Fig.811

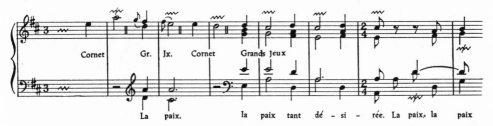

Boyvin

Jacques Boyvin was born about 1653, and was made an organist at the Rouen cathedral in 1674, an office that Titelouze once held. In 1683 the organ was destroyed in a storm, and Boyvin supervised the construction of a new one. He died in Rouen in 1706. His organ works are preserved in two *Livres d'orgue,* of 1689 and 1700.[27] In the preface to the *Premier livre* he gives instructions for the "Mélange des jeux" and explanations of the ornaments. He does not represent the *tremblement* by the usual figure, ♩♪♪♪♪♪♪ , but as ♪♪♪♪♪♪♪♪ . The second volume opens with a treatise on thorough-bass, entitled "Traité abregé de l'accompaniment"—a treatise that was also known in Holland, Germany, and Italy.

Both books are arranged according to the church modes. For each mode there are six to ten pieces typical of French organ music of the period: *Duo, Trio, Récit, Dialogue, Fugue grave, Plein jeu.* When he published his first volume, Boyvin already had the new organ of the Rouen cathedral at his disposal, and was therefore especially concerned with displaying his art of registration, the "sçavoir bien marier les jeux," as he calls it in the preface, in full brilliance. As in other French organ music, ecclesiastic and secular, successful and rather trivial

Fig.812

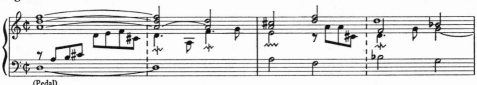

(Pedal)

733

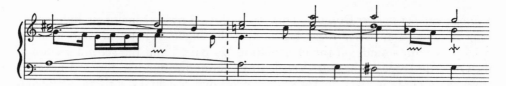

pieces appear side by side. In the *Récits en taille* (p.5) the solo voice (played by the left hand) is formulated as a freely improvising organ recitative with many ornaments and figurations, as shown in Fig.812.

The art of registration is most richly exploited in the *Grands Dialogues*, although the effects are superficial and bombastic. The *Dialogues* are extended pieces in several sections, in which Boyvin occasionally works with four choirs, e.g., with *Grand corps, Positif, Cornet,* and *Eco.* The beginning of the *Grand Dialogue à quatre choeurs* is given in Fig.813. The *Prélude facile du 4. ton* (new ed. p.35), with its chromatic *durezze* harmony, is rather lovely. On the other hand, the *Grand Prélude avec des pedalles de Trompettes meslées* (p.34) is something of a curiosity. The pedals encompass the entire gamut from A_1 to f' in large skips, which are really cheap arpeggios. Such a piece may have been sensational around 1680, but today it cannot be taken seriously.

Fig.813

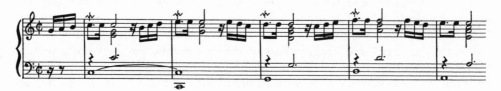

Jullien and Chaumont

At the same time as Boyvin was transplanting Parisian organ music to Rouen, Gilles Jullien was bringing it to Chartres. He was born about 1653, and is mentioned as early as 1668, at the age of fifteen, as an organist of the cathedral of Chartres. He died there in 1703, "50 ans ou environ." In 1690 he published a *Premier livre d'orgue,* which contains eighty pieces arranged according to the church modes.[28] Like Boyvin and others, he gives some instructions in his preface on the "meslanges ordinaires des jeux de l'orgue," a matter which he says was already "tant de fois dite et rebatue." He claims that his five-part compositions are a new invention, but such works are found earlier in Gigault (1685) and Raison (1688). He indicates the dotted rhythm in only one of the pieces, with instructions to follow this example in the others as well and dot them more or less lightly ("pointer les autres de mesme plus ou moins légèrement").

Although Jullien was honored by being called to one of the most famous organs in France while still an adolescent, the book's contents are rather disappointing. Most of the works are mediocre, and some are even inferior, particularly his *Dialogues*, in which a continuous series of four-measure phrases, one as empty as the next and some bordering on vulgarity, succeed one another without interruption; even the most dexterous registration cannot bring them to life. Some of the *Récits de dessus* are comparatively successful, as melodies that are not too inspired but rather dexterously continued are heard on the various solo stops (cromhorne, tierce, trompette, cornet, voix humaine). The five-voiced preludes with *Pedalle de trompette en taille* (new ed., pp.35, 65) may even be used today to fill a church with festive sounds. In general Jullien's preludes are his best works.

A contemporary of Raison's at Rouen and Jullien's at Chartres, Lambert Chaumont worked in neighboring Belgium. He was born around 1635(?), probably near Liége, and played the organs of two Carmelite churches at Huys—at St. Martin, from 1672 to 1688, and then at St. Germain, until his death in 1712. In 1695 he published a collection of organ pieces entitled *Pièces d'orgue sur les 8 tons*, which he called "2d ouvrage du R.P.L. Chaumont Curé de St. Germain a Huy."[29] Each of the eight church modes is represented by twelve to fifteen pieces, beginning with a prelude, continuing with the usual *Duo, Trio, Basse de Cromorne*, etc., and concluding with an allemande and sometimes a gigue or chaconne as well.

The modern editor (R. Bragard) says in the preface: "Quand on parcourt ces Pièces écrites dans les huit Tons, on reste stupéfait non seulement devant leur richesse et leur pureté mélodiques mais aussi devant la solidité indéniable de leur écriture." Even though the term "stupéfait" is somewhat exaggerated, it is nevertheless true that Chaumont is a composer of melodious imagination, good taste, and solid technique. His organ pieces are certainly superior to Jullien's. Occasionally he, too, employs cheap methods, e.g., in the *Echos* of the first and fifth tones (new ed., pp.9, 58), but they are exceptions. All his pieces carry tempo instructions, such as *Gravement, Andante, Très gaiement, Légèrement, Allegretto*.

In most of the *Récits* the melody is entrusted to the discant, and generally articulated in phrases of varied length, which contribute greatly to the attractiveness of the pieces. The 2e. *Cornet* of the first tone (p.8), e.g., has phrases of 5, 4, 9, 3, 3, 2, and 8 measures, and the *Voix humaine* of the second tone (p.17) has phrases of 5, 9, 4, 5, 7, 8, and 6 measures. In both pieces, as well as in others of the same type, Chaumont develops the melody from a basic motif, which recurs at the beginning of every phrase, but is continued differently each time. It is only in the *Dialogues* that the changeover from one registration to another is made in regular four-measure sections, but the monotony of this regularity is somewhat relieved by changing the tempo along with the timbre, e.g., from allegro to moderato or from andante to grave.

735

The two chaconnes (pp.22, 69) are genuine ostinato chaconnes rather than the rondeau type, which was usual in the French tradition. The second one consists of ten variations on an eight-measure ostinato bass, while the first is written above the eleven-measure subject shown in Fig.814. Such long and freely formed ostinatos are not infrequent in the vocal and violin music of the 17th century, but in keyboard music they appear only very rarely. In Chaumont's chaconne the bass subject is varied seven times. In the last variation it is divided into two sections of seven and four measures, respectively, each of which is repeated.

Fig.814

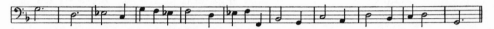

At the conclusion of his *Pièces d'orgue*, Chaumont, like many other French organists, gives instructions on the "Meslanges des jeux" and an explanation of the *agréments*. Included in the latter is the *port de voix*, which he (and some others) usually writes out fully in the form of two sixteenth notes on the same pitch.

François Couperin

In the same year that Jullien's *Livre d'orgue* was published, there appeared another volume, entitled *Pièces d'orgue consistantes en deux Messes . . . par François Couperin Sieur de Crouilly*, which is interesting for several reasons, quite apart from its contents. This work "appeared" in 1690, not in print, but apparently only in manuscript copies with a printed title page, of which only a single copy seems to be extant (at Carpentras). At one time this volume was generally attributed to the older François Couperin (1630–1701), Louis Couperin's brother. Frotscher still held this opinion when he said that "the various attempts to attribute this work to the great François Couperin (1668–1733) as an early opus are not convincing."[30] Today there no longer seems to be any doubt that Couperin "le Grand" is indeed its author. I share this opinion, but not without reservations.

The collection consists of organ pieces for two Masses, one for secular churches ("paroisses pour les fêtes solemnelles"), the other one for abbey churches ("couvents de religieux et religiouses").[31] Both exhibit the traditional order, with 5 pieces for the Kyrie, 9 for the Gloria, 3 for the Sanctus, and 2 for the Agnus, to which are added an *Offertoire* and a concluding *Deo gratias*. In the first Mass Couperin, like Nivers and Lebègue before him, uses the *plein chant* of Mass IV for the initial piece of each movement. The first setting for the Sanctus (p.145; p.49) is especially striking, for after a fore-imitation the chant tune is heard as a canon in the pedals, as shown in Fig.815. Couperin follows his predecessors in the treatment of the second Kyrie setting also. He formulates it as a fugue on the begin-

Fig.815

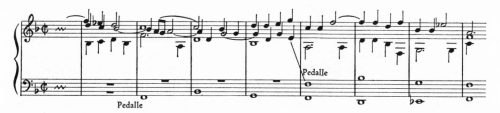

ning of the chant melody, but he differs from them in also employing the chant for the last Kyrie verset.

The remaining pieces of the first Mass as well as all of the second one are freely composed. In these versets Couperin falls back on the usual types of French organ music, but fills them with a new content, giving them a superior musical substance. In the *Récits* the solo voices lose their former character of organ recitatives and become well-formulated, strictly rhythmical melodies: The arioso is replaced by the aria. The difference is striking when one compares Couperin's *Récit de cornet* (new ed., p.146; p.50) in Fig.816 with, e.g., Boyvin's *Tierce en taille*, whose beginning is given in Fig.812. In both pieces the solo part starts with almost the same idea, but Boyvin continues it in freely formulated, magnificently ornamented phrases, while Couperin writes simple lines that flow naturally from the beginning, and later he even continues it in a sequential manner. This music shows a sense of natural order, a vitality, and an immediacy of feeling that breaks into French organ music like a fresh wind. Couperin surely learned from Lully, but the simplicity and grace of his melodies go far beyond Lully. One of the pieces with a solo part in the tenor, a *Tierce en taille* (p.127; p.29), has a descending scale motif that repeatedly recurs and is also woven into the accompanying

Fig.816

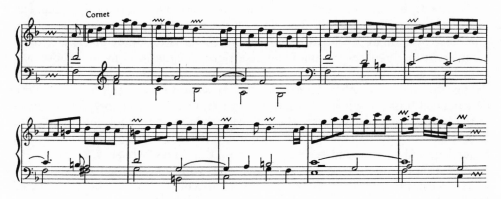

parts. Boyvin uses the same motif in a smaller framework in a *Cromhorne de taille*,[32] also with great ingenuity.

In his *Dialogues* Couperin proceeds in a similar manner from a basic motif that pervades the entire piece. It is heard once in a high register, then in a low one, in one registration here, in another there. At the same time Couperin avoids the banal regularity of articulation that was usual in this species. In the *Dialogue* for the *Domine Deus* of the first Mass (p.122; p.24), the subject is presented first in D major and then in D minor, but unfortunately Alberti basses enter toward the end and greatly disturb the total impression. In the *Dialogue* for the Agnus of the same Mass (p.153; p.57), the subject is developed imitatively, resulting in a very lively if not a really "regular" fugue, which also carries detailed instructions about registration. One excerpt is given in Fig.817. The subject shows Italian influence, which also appears in other details in Couperin's music, particularly in the rather frequent sequential passages, which appear here for the first time in French organ music.[33]

Fig.817

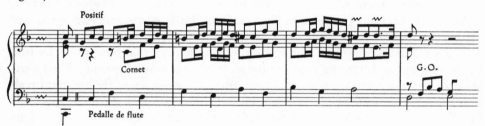

The principal pieces and the show pieces in the two Masses are the offertories. The *Offertoire sur les grands jeux* of the first Mass (p.137; p.40) is one of the longest compositions in the entire repertoire of French organ music. Like Raison's *Offerte*, it is constructed like a French overture, but enormously expanded. It is a very significant work. The first of the three main sections is a festive, grandiose prelude in a brilliant C major, which turns to minor in the last measures and thus prepares for the second section, a fugue in C minor whose sustained subject, chromatic progressions, and severe dissonances lead the spirit of the faithful toward another world. But the last section returns to this world, with an extended fugue in gigue-like rhythms, written in a gay C major. The offertory of the second Mass also consists of three sections in major, minor, and major, but it is mediocre music, a thing that does not occur too often with Couperin. In general he did not expend the same care for this Mass, which was written for modest abbey churches, as for the other one, which he himself certainly presented on important holidays on the organ of Saint-Gervais, where he played from 1685 on.

Grigny

The work of innovation that the twenty-two-year-old Couperin began was continued and brought to its culmination by another youthful master Nicolas de Grigny. He was born in 1672, into a family of musicians in Reims. In his early years he went to Paris, where he probably studied with Lebègue, and became an organist of the Abbey of Saint-Denis in 1693. In 1695 (or a little later?) he returned to Reims to take over the organist's position at the cathedral, which he held until his early death in 1703. His organ works reach us in a *Premier livre d'orgue,* which he published in 1699, and which appeared in a new printing in 1711.[34] It contains an organ Mass, five hymns with three to five settings each, and a concluding *Point d'orgue sur les grands jeux.*

The arrangement of the organ Mass follows those by Nivers (1667), Lebègue (1678), and Couperin (1690). There are 5 versets for the Kyrie, 9 for the Gloria, 3 for the Sanctus, and 2 for the Agnus, to which the usual offertory as well as an *Elévation* and a *Communion* are added. Some of the settings are based on chant melodies, which are taken from Mass IV. From the hymns Grigny chooses *Veni Creator, Pange lingua, Verbum supernum, Ave maris stella,* and *A solis ortus,* all of which also appear in Nivers' larger collection. Except for the offertory and the concluding *Point d'orgue,* all the pieces belong to the usual types, distributed as follows: 9 *Plain chants* (*cantus-planus* settings), 9 *Fugues,* 10 *Dialogues,* 9 *Récits,* 3 *Duos,* 3 *Trios* (one of them "en dialogue"), and a *Plein jeu.* *Echos,* once so favored, are strikingly lacking. *Duos* and *Trios* are also rather sparingly represented, but among the *Dialogues* and *Récits* there are eight more three-voice settings. However, the large number of five-part pieces is surprising. Gigault (1685), Raison (1688), and Jullien (1690) had already used five-part texture on occasion, but in Grigny's volume it is so frequent that it replaces the four-part setting as the leading type: of the movements that have a constant number of voices there are eleven with four parts and fifteen with five.

The volume divides into nine groups, four for the versets of the Mass movements and five for the hymns. For the first piece in each group Grigny regularly employs the chant melody, which, as a strict *cantus planus* in whole or half notes, becomes the basis of a four- or five-part setting. In the five-part pieces (*Kyrie, Gloria, Sanctus, Veni Creator,* and *Ave maris stella*) the melody is presented in the pedals as a tenor part, in the others it is mostly played on a manual as a bass. The counterpoints combine with it in a basically chordal texture, enlivened by quiet passing tones which sometimes assume the character of motifs. The opening verset of *Ave maris stella* (p.80; p.82), is given in Fig.818.

There are also nine examples of the fugue, most of them occupying the second place in each group. Grigny employs five-part texture in six of the fugues not only for the first time* but also with special predilection. Considering how

---

* Except for a very dry *Fugue renversie un 5 parties* by Jullien; new ed., p.28.

Fig.818

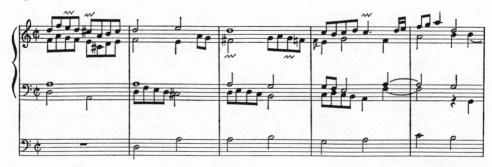

rarely Bach (who, by the way, copied Grigny's book for his own use) invokes five voices, this approach is really unusual. The subjects are derived from the chant tunes, mostly from their beginnings, but in *Veni Creator* (p.55; p.56) it is derived from the second line. The very impressive subject, given in Fig.819, is derived from *A solis ortus* (p.90; p.93). Grigny creates a fugue from it, in which the subject is consistently developed, while the counterpoints move freely and sometimes combine with the sustained tones of the subject to form chords. Nevertheless everything is joined into an impressive whole, proving that it is possible to write fugues without observing "the rules."

Fig.819

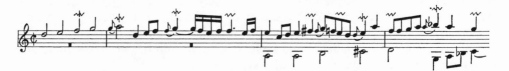

In the *Dialogues* Grigny follows two different models. Some unfold in regular phrases of song-like character, such as are frequently found in Lebègue's music; others, as in Couperin, use an initial motif as the point of departure, and develop it in different ways in several sections.[35] The *Dialogue sur les grands jeux* for *Veni Creator* (p.62; p.63) employs the form of the French overture, with a slow prelude, a fugato in the rhythm of a gigue, and a postlude similar to the prelude. The *Dialogue sur les grands jeux* for *Ave maris stella* (p.86; p.88) begins with a virtuosic introduction and concludes with echo-like repetitions of a rather trivial formula.

In one of the *Récits*, the *Cromorne en taille à 2 parties* from the Kyrie (p.5; p.8), the left hand executes the solo in two parts. The *Récit du chant de l'hymne* from the *Pange lingua* (p.70; p.72) opens with a fore-imitation; then the hymn tune is heard as an ornamented melody in the tenor—one of the few examples of the

Fig.820

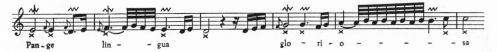

Pan - ge   lin - - gua   glo - ri - o - - - - - sa

ornamented chorale in French organ music. Grigny, to be sure, limits himself
almost entirely to the addition of mordents, trills, and turns, while Nivers paraphrased the melody of *Ave maris stella* in a somewhat freer manner (cf.Fig.802).
Fig.820 reproduces the beginning of this hymn in Grigny's version. The most
beautiful of the *Récits*, indeed one of the most impressive of Grigny's compositions,
is the *Récit de tierce en taille* for the verse *Domine Deus, Rex caelestis* from the
Gloria. While in Couperin's Mass a bellicose fanfare motif is employed for this
verse, which seems to place the King of Heaven on an equal footing with the Sun
King, Grigny writes music that does not lack for brilliance and magnificence or
for seriousness and dignity. The first section of Grigny's piece is dominated by
a triad motif that is both musically and allegorically meaningful, and the second
section presents glorious, triumphant passage work. Fig.821 offers excerpts from
both.

Fig.821

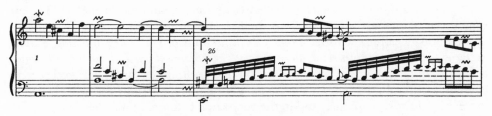

Grigny's offertory is as expansive as Couperin's, but is mostly oriented toward
superficial effects and cannot compare with it in artistic significance. In the final
piece of the collection, the *Point d'orgue sur les grands jeux* (p.95; p.98), Grigny,
with remarkable ingenuity, solves a problem that is none too simple: Above pedal
points on *A* and *E*, he develops the upper parts from several well-conceived ideas,
without employing the cheap means of figuration that predominate in the pedal
toccatas of Pachelbel and other composers. Not far from the end, the *punto intenso
contra remisso* appears (Fig.822)—perhaps for the last time.

Grigny's compositions represent the culmination of French organ music, the
most significant achievement that this art could attain within its limited scope.
Neither Grigny nor his successors were able to break through these limitations, to
free themselves from the traditional types, or to liberate the musical imagination
from the fetters of the art of registration. But in several of his pieces he created
works of high rank and lasting significance.

Fig.822

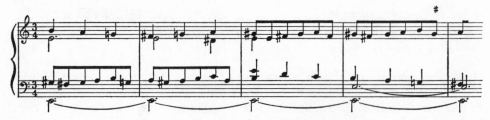

Dandrieu, Marchand, Corrette, and Guilain

The rest of French organ music written at the turn of the century needs only brief mention, for organ music in France, as in other countries, was in a decline. In the era in which the *style galant,* the frivolous elegance of the Rococo, became dominant, the instrument that in the past had inspired so many great creations retained only the role of surrounding harmless songs with colorful finery, and squandered its enchanting sounds on trivialities. To be sure, not every composition was of this kind, and many fugues, récits, or dialogs recall a more glorious past, but the principal effort was directed at inventing pretty and unpretentious melodies that flatter the ear. The model was Lebègue, not Nivers, Couperin, or Grigny.

Lebègue's influence shows very clearly in Pierre Dandrieu (c.1660–1733), an organist at Saint-Barthelémy in Paris. In 1715 he published (apparently in a second edition) a volume entitled *Noëls, O filii, Chansons de saint Jacques, Stabat mater et Carillons, le tout revu, augmenté et extrêmement varié et mis pour l'orgue et le clavessin.*[36] It consists of variations on noëls and other songs, half ecclesiastic and half secular. In the noël *Une jeune pucelle* he treats the same theme as Lebègue did in his *Une vierge pucelle*, and in the very same fashion. In a rather lovely, suitable manner he writes the old cradle song *Puer nobis nascitur* in form of a "Muzette," in a canon above a pedal point, as shown in Fig.823.

Fig.823

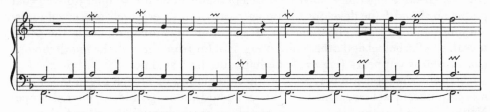

Louis Marchand (cf.p.719) wrote a number of organ pieces, several of which appeared after his death under the title *Pièces choisies, Livre premier,* and others that are preserved in manuscripts, chiefly one at Versailles.[37] They are on the

742

border between past and future. The *Cromorne en taille* (new ed., vol. V, p.252), which concludes the manuscript collection, and most of the *Pièces choisies* (which indeed present a choice of the very best of the work of the "Grant Marchand," as he is called in the title) remind us of the older tradition. In the six-voiced *Plein jeu* (III, p.61) virtuosic double pedals are employed for the first time in French organ music. Marchand probably intended to use a work like this one for his competition with Bach. A *Tierce en taille* (III, p. 72) ranks with similar works by earlier masters, with its energetic, at times virtuosic, solo part. Most of his pieces, however, are song-like, pretty, and rather insignificant, like the excerpt in Fig.824. At least they are never sentimental or frivolous, and irregular phrasing in three, five, and seven measures prevent them from sinking into triviality.

Fig.824

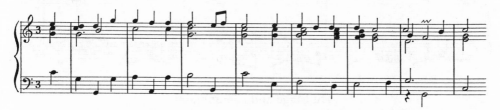

In 1703 Gaspard Corrette, the organist of the church of Saint-Herbland at Rouen, published a *Messe du 8.ᵉ ton pour l'orgue,* consisting of the usual movements for the four parts of the Ordinary, to which he added two *Graduels,* an *Offerte,* and two *Elévations.*[38] He seems to be the last French organist to compose music for the Mass. Pirro characterized his pieces quite aptly by saying that they start with rather fine ideas, but then bog down in the repetition of empty formulae.[39] His offertory, which comprises more than 200 measures, is even longer than Couperin's, but consists chiefly of repetitions of trivial formulae, e.g., the one given in Fig. 825, which recurs five times.

Fig.825

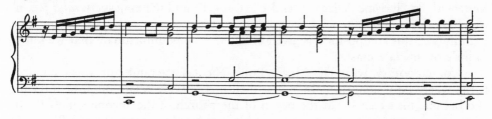

The name Guilain apparently hides a German, Wilhelm (= Guilain) Freins-berg, who acquired a fine reputation in Paris as a harpsichord teacher and who was a friend of Marchand. In 1706 he published *Pièces d'orgue pour le Magnificat,*

which contains a "Suite" of seven pieces for each of the first four church modes.[40] In some of these compositions Guilain follows the French tradition, especially in a *Tierce de taille* (new ed., p.126), a *Cromorne de taille* (p.147), and in a *Quatuor* (p.136), every detail of which is modeled after a *Quatuor* by Marchand.[41] Other pieces show that he must have been acquainted with Italian instrumental music; e.g., the entire *Basse de trompette* (p.141) develops from an energetic motif, in an inexorable manner that is quite alien to French music, but is reminiscent of sonata movements of Scarlatti or Vitali. *Basso-continuo* lines, such as the one given in Fig.826 (p.152), are also unmistakably Italian.

Fig.826

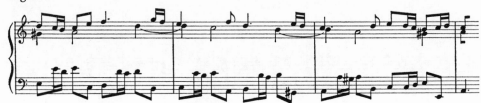

Du Mage and Clérambault

Du Mage and Clérambault may be called the last representatives of French Baroque organ music. Pierre Du Mage was born in 1676, probably in Beauvais, came to Paris at an early age, and there became a student of Marchand. Lebègue also took him under his wing by procuring for him a position as organist at the convent church of Saint-Quentin. In 1710 he was called to the cathedral of Lâon, where he worked until his death in 1751. A *Premier livre d'orgue* appeared in 1708; a second one from 1712 is unfortunately lost.

The print of 1708 contains a *Suite du premier ton*, consisting of eight pieces: *Plein jeu, Fugue, Trio, Tierce en taille, Basse de trompette, Récit, Duo,* and *Grand jeu*.[42] Each piece shows the hand of an important master. The most striking are the *Tierce en taille,* whose rhapsodic solo voice solidifies in a second section; the *Récit* with its "lyrisme délicat et tendre" (Raugel); and the majestic *Grand jeu,* in which the form of the French overture is once again transferred to the organ. The beginning of this composition is given in Fig.827. How unfortunate that we know so little of this late master!

Contemporary with Du Mage, Louis-Nicolas Clérambault was active in Paris, where he was born in 1676 and died in 1749. He was a pupil of Raison's and became his successor at the organ of the church of the Jacobins in 1719. In addition to numerous cantatas and motets, he wrote a collection of *Pièces de clavecin* (cf. note 14 above) and a *Premier livre d'orgue* (1710?), dedicated to Raison.[43] The latter contains *Suites du premier* and *du second ton,* each with seven pieces. The fugue from the first suite (new ed., p.98; p.8), with its expressive

744

Fig.827

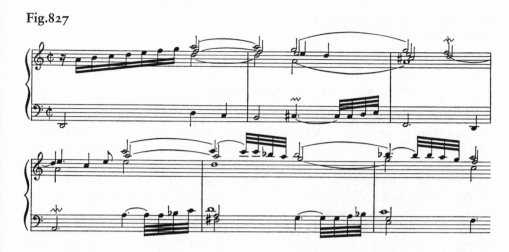

subject and consistent development, is one of the best of this species created in France. In the *Récits de Cromorne et cornet séparé* (p.107; p.16) Clérambault operates with a five-measure ostinato, which recurs several times without being strictly repeated. The upper part starts with a motif that is reminiscent of Beethoven's *Variations in C minor* for piano, although because of the legend "doucement et gratieusement" and its ornaments it assumes quite a different character (Fig.828).

Fig.828

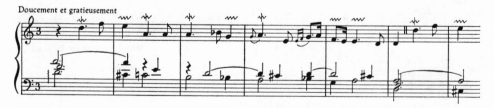

The same ostinato appears twice in a piece for flute stops in the second suite (p. 120; p.28), a soft, plaintive idyl, which one could easily imagine as accompanying an opera or ballet scene. The *Récit de nazard* that follows is modeled after the Italian siciliano. The collection concludes with a *Caprice sur les grands jeux*, whose beginning is given in Fig.829. Its driving rhythms and sequential phrases

Fig.829

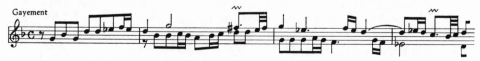

also disclose Italian provenance. Other pieces, especially the *Duos* and *Trios,* already show the features of the *galant* style. Again it is the frequent irregular phrases of five or seven measures that keep the music from descending to triviality.

The Anonymous Repertoire

The unusually complete picture transmitted by the numerous prints of well-known French organ masters is supplemented by several manuscripts with anonymous contents. The manuscript Paris Conservatoire, Rés.476 (formerly 24827) preserves on eighty-eight leaves nine noëls, an organ Mass, four offertories, organ accompaniments for psalm singing, and other pieces—all anonymous except for a few transcriptions from Lully operas.[44] Apparently following A. Gastoué, the manuscript is attributed to a member of the Geoffroy family, either Nicolas or Jean-Nicholas, who lived from 1633 to 1694 and died at Perpignan,[45] but there is nothing to support this assumption. The contents of the manuscript keep within the limits of what was usual around 1680. The organ accompaniment for the psalms and other vocal music of the church are particularly interesting, for they reveal a field of organists' activities that is not represented in the prints. On fol. 19v, e.g., we find organ accompaniments for various verses of Psalm cxxxi, together with an introductory *Prélude* and several insertions, such as *Fugue, Récit,* etc. Fig.830 conveys an idea of this liturgical type of functional music.

Fig.830

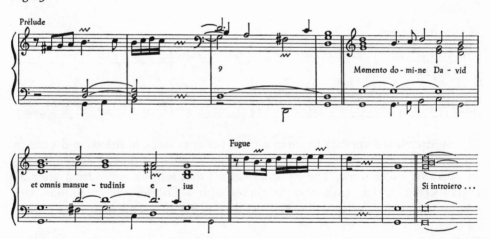

A manuscript at Tours, Bibl. mun. Ms. 1772, contains several works that throw light on French organ music for the country church around 1700. The *Trompete 4. ton* (Fig.831), on fol.9v, shows how an organist of a small church went about presenting a fugue.[46]

Fig.831

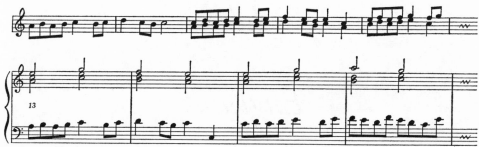

The manuscript Paris Conservatoire 2094 belonged to Marguerite Thiéry about 1680, who in 1683 became the second wife of the famous organ builder Alexandre Thierry (1647–99). This collection was probably written for her by her organ teacher, who (I believe) was probably Nivers, because the "repercussion ornament" shown in Fig.832 occurs with equal frequency in Nivers' music, but rarely occurs elsewhere in French organ music. The manuscript contains two Masses, three Magnificats, and versets to *Veni Creator, Pange lingua,* and *Te Deum.*[47]

Fig.832

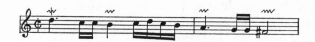

A collection that has apparently been neglected until now (Rome, Bibl. del Conservatorio di S. Cecilia A/400, fol.40–54) consists chiefly of brief but rather attractive organ pieces, arranged in eight key groups, e.g., for the 3.me ton: *Plain Jeu, Récit, Duo, Plain Jeu pour finir,* or for the 4.me ton: *Plain Jeu Verset, Verset, Pour le Cornet, Dessu, Plain Jeu pour finir.* The group for the 8.me ton begins with *Plain Jeu* and *Jeu de Cornet,* then continues with a gavotte, a sarabande, and other dances.

22

England

VERY LITTLE IS KNOWN about the evolution of English keyboard music
from the 1620s to the mid-century, i.e., in the decades following the deaths of the
great virginalists; for what Thomas Tomkins wrote during those years is too conservative to qualify as evolution. Only around 1650 does the picture become
clearer, with the keyboard compositions of Benjamin Rogers (1614–98), Christopher Gibbons (1615–76), and Matthew Locke (1630–77). In what has been
preserved of their works and those of a few others, two fields emerge almost as
sharply as in France: suites or single dances for harpsichord, and the so-called
voluntaries and verses for organ. The former are unmistakably influenced by
French and possibly also by German music (Froberger sojourned in London),
while the latter exhibit peculiar and interesting national features. However, the
sources of English keyboard music around 1650 and thereafter—chiefly manuscripts at the British Museum and the Christ Church College Library at Oxford—
are still mostly uninvestigated. The following observations therefore are not necessarily complete.

Harpsichord Music in the Mid- and Late 17th Century

While on the Continent harpsichord literature includes many different forms and
types, in England it is limited almost exclusively to suites. They emerge just before
1650. One of the earliest examples is an A C S suite by William Lawes (d.1645),
which is found in one of the virginal manuscripts at the Paris Conservatory (Rés.
1184–85). In a later manuscript, Oxford, Christ Church Ms.1236, an allemande
and courante by Lawes are preserved under the title *The Golden Group*. In his
Musicks Hand-maide (1663) the publisher John Playford prints a faulty version

of the allemande, together with another courante, under the similarly faulty title "The Golden Grove." The beginning of the allemande exhibits a peculiarity of English harpsichord music that clearly differentiates it from French clavecin music: While the French composers knew how to extract deep and sonorous sounds from their instrument, the English pieces frequently contain passages in which a high lying upper part is separated by several octaves from the accompaniment. Thus the allemande of the *Golden Group* begins as shown in Fig.833. The accent that appears above several notes probably indicates the so-called *backfall*, a descending appoggiatura like the French *accent*. Later it was written as an oblique stroke descending from left to right (cf.Fig.836).

Fig.833

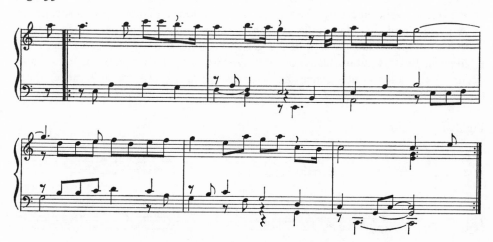

Hardly anything is known about the lives of some of the other English keyboard composers. One of the earlier ones is Henry Loosemore, who is represented by two pieces, a *Coranto* and *The Nightingale,* in Paris Conserv., Rés.1186 (formerly 18546, dated 1635–38), and a courante from the Oxford Manuscript (Christ Church Ms.1236). This manuscript also contains about ten dances (allemandes, sarabandes, etc.) by William Ellis and five pieces (four courantes and an

Fig.834

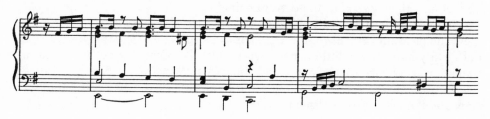

Ayre) by Jonas Tresure. A more remarkable work, an A C S suite by Jonas Tresor, is contained in the Hintze manuscript. The first movement, called *Allemande plörant,* begins as shown in Fig.834. An *Allemand Tresoor* in the Clavier Book of Anna Maria van Eijl (cf.p.767) is probably by the same composer. Various other composers appear in the manuscripts of the Christ Church Library and the British Museum, each with a few pieces: Batis, Bryan (Albertus?; born around 1620?), Mark Coleman, T. Holmes (d.1638), Richard Portman (1610?–56), and John Roberts.[1]

Benjamin Rogers is the first personality to emerge more clearly. He was active as an organist in Dublin 1639–41, later at Windsor, Eton (around 1660), and at Magdalen College at Oxford (1664). He wrote much church music (anthems, services) as well as works for viols and violins. The Oxford manuscript mentioned above contains six pieces by "Ben. Rogers of London": a courante and sarabande in *A* minor, and an allemande, courante, sarabande, and gigue, which form a suite in *C* major.[2] Like some of Froberger's, the gigue is in 4/4 time. Its beginning is given in Fig.835; note the syncopated entrances of the upper part, which also occur in the allemande. Other manuscripts contain about twenty more dance pieces by Rogers.

Fig.835

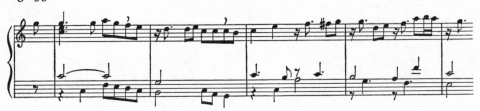

The manuscript Brit. Mus. Add. 10337, known as *Elizabeth Rogers' Virginal Book,* and dated 1656, contains, in addition to 19 songs, 81 keyboard compositions, mostly simple dances. There are almaynes, corrants, selebrands (sarabandes), and maskes, as well as titled pieces, such as *Prince Ruperts March, The Nightingale,* and *My Delight.* Most of the pieces are anonymous, but the names of William Byrd, Orlando Gibbons, Robert Johnson, Nicholas Lanier, and William Lawes can be supplied from other sources. Six dances are ascribed to Thomas Streightfeild, among them two almayne-corrant pairs.[3]

In 1663 John Playford published his *Musicks Hand-maide,* a collection of "new and pleasant Lessons for the Virginals or Harpsycon." They are unimportant and mostly anonymous little dances, with which he obviously addressed an unpretentious audience of beginners and dilettants. The *Second Part of Musick's Hand-maide* (1678, 1689) is on the same level, despite a few contributions by Blow and Purcell, clearly written for this publication.

The content of a print that Matthew Locke published in 1673 under the title *Melothesia* is more significant. Locke, born at Exeter around 1630, apparently went to London as a young man and died there in 1677. His chief creativity lay in the field of church music, but he also composed for instrumental ensembles. After an insignificant dedication the *Melothesia* begins with "Advertisements to the Reader," in which the most important ornaments of English keyboard music are listed by symbol and name, but without indicating their execution. They are reproduced in Fig.836, along with the execution as given in Purcell's *Lessons for the Harpsichord* (1696). (Note that the last ornament, which is found mostly if not exclusively in organ pieces, does not occur in Purcell's music. But its designation as *forefall and shake* leaves no doubt about its execution.)

Fig.836

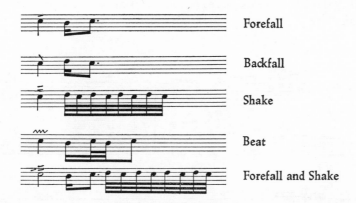

Forefall

Backfall

Shake

Beat

Forefall and Shake

The *Melothesia* starts with four suites by Locke, continues with compositions by various contemporaries, and closes with seven organ pieces by Locke. Locke's suites[4] have no unified formulation, such as was usual at the time on the Continent. The first one is a C-major group of prelude, sarabande, prelude, allemande, courante, gavotte, and country dance, which is rearranged in the new edition as P P A C S gavotte country dance, with the two preludes designated as "alternative." This is followed by a G-minor suite A S Virago Round; a C-major suite P A C S G; and an A-major suite P A C S Rant. Note that each suite starts with a prelude—an expansion of the form that was apparently first recorded in the lute suites of Esaias Reusner (*Deliciae testudinis*) of 1667. The prelude of the third suite, with its *style-brisé* passages, is probably the most interesting piece musically. For curiosity's sake the beginning of *Virago* (quarrelsome woman) is reproduced in Fig.837. Other sources preserve a number of small and generally rather unimportant dances by Locke. (His organ compositions will be discussed later.)

The *Melothesia* contains several other suites—by William Gregory (d.1663), John Moss, Christian Preston, and John Roberts. The one by Moss begins with an

Fig.837

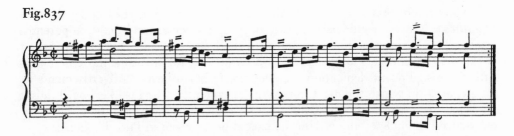

Almaine that makes extensive use of *notes inégales*; the first few measures are given in Fig.838. Other musicians who contributed to the *Melothesia* are John Banister (c.1630–79), Gerhard Diesner (Diessener), who probably emigrated from Kassel to London,[5] and William Hall (d.1700). According to the preface by William Thatcher, the anonymous pieces in this print are by "a known and esteemed Master in this City."

Fig.838

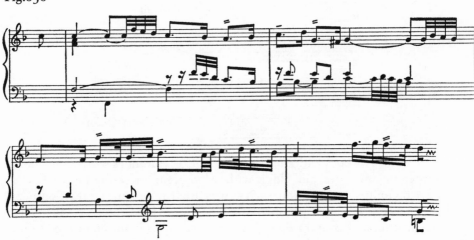

The manuscript Washington, Library of Congress, M 21.M.185, contains three suites and some separate pieces by Francis Forcer (c.1650–c.1705). The first suite, in C minor with B♭, E♭ and A♭ in the key signature, consists of A S gavotte G; the second one, in F major, of A C S G; and the third of A C gavotte G, possibly with an additional minuet. The two gavottes, in which Forcer dexterously appropriates the French style, are probably the most successful. Some of the other pieces are rather dilettantic, e.g., the sarabande of the second suite, shown in Fig.839.

Giovanni Battista Draghi (brother of Antonio Draghi?) was an Italian who can be traced in London from 1667 to 1706. About 1700 he published *Six Select*

752

Fig.839

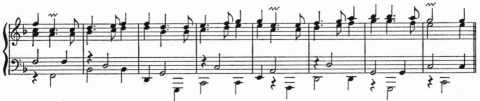

Suites of Lessons for the Harpsichord, in which preludes are combined with the four traditional dances and other pieces in several ways. The first suite, in *E* minor, consists, e.g., of P A C *The Complaint Aire* G; the second suite, in *G* major, of P A C S *Aire The Hunting Tune;* and the fifth suite, in *D* minor, of P A C S *Bore Aire* minuet. In the prelude of the first suite Draghi uses a particular arpeggiation, which recurs very similarly in Purcell's suites. Fig.840 offers the beginning of this piece of only nine measures. The rather extended allemande that follows is of

Fig.840

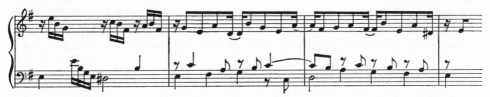

interest, for it shows that this dance type was very differently stylized in England and on the Continent: In the French and German allemandes evenly flowing sixteenth-note passages succeed one another, while the English allemandes are dominated by sharply dotted rhythms (cf. Moss's *Almaine,* Fig.838). The Washington manuscript mentioned above contains two more pieces by Draghi, a *Toccata* and a *Trumpet Tune.*

John Eccles is also one of the composers born around 1650. He obtained the position of "Master of the King's Musick" in 1700, and died in 1735. As a keyboard composer he is known by only a few pieces, including *Trumpet Air, Minuet, Jigg,* and *Round O* (= rondo), which he published in *A Set of Lessons* (1702), together with several anonymous pieces and some by Daniel Purcell. The book was reprinted several times during the 18th century.[6]

Organ Music in the Mid- and Late 17th Century

While English harpsichord music in the late 17th century evolved entirely under French influence, the organ music of the same period exhibits a peculiar national character that clearly differentiates it, despite occasional relations and similarities, from what was written on the Continent. One difference, an external one, is that such structural titles as ricercar, canzona, capriccio, toccata, and fugue hardly ever occur in the English repertoire. The purely functional designations *Verse* and *Voluntary* that appear in their places do not imply anything about the character of the compositions, but only that they are meant to be used during religious services. Both terms appear as early as 1560 in the *Mulliner Book*. Thomas Tomkins used them occasionally, but after 1650 they dominate the field almost exclusively, except for pieces that carry the even less definite legend "For the Organ" or "For the Double Organ" (an organ with two manuals). The difference between Verse and Voluntary is not clear. Possibly the Verse had a more definite function, perhaps in connection with the Mass, while the Voluntary was played at the beginning or end of the services, as an introduction to the anthem or in its place. Quite often, however, the same piece is called a Verse in one source and a Voluntary in another.

Unfortunately not very much organ music from around 1650 is preserved because many church organs were destroyed during Cromwell's Commonwealth (1649–60). Nevertheless a careful sifting of the sources brings to light enough material to give us an idea of the evolution of English organ music during the middle Baroque. The first name that must be mentioned is that of Christopher Gibbons, the second son of Orlando Gibbons. He was born in 1615, became an organist at Winchester Cathedral in 1638 and at Westminster Cathedral in 1660, received the title of Doctor of Music from Oxford University in 1663, and died in 1676. Five of his organ works are preserved and are available in a new edition.[7]

A *Verse* [or *Voluntary*] *for the Double Organ* (new ed., no.2),[8] like many other English organ pieces, consists of two fugal sections, the first one on a sustained subject, the second on a livelier one, and concludes with a free postlude. The first fugue, with its syncopated subject entrances and unexpected contrasts

Fig.841

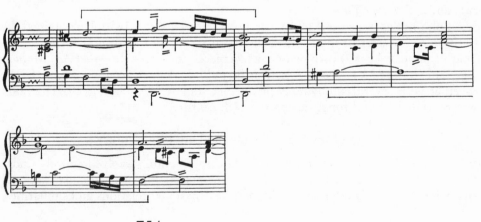

between sustained tones and quick figures, gives the impression of broad, dark planes that are suddenly lit by flashing lights. Various unusual harmonic progressions reinforce the impression of unusualness, as in Frescobaldi's music. Fig.841, taken from a manuscript of the British Museum (Add.34695), is an illustration (meas.9–16). An effective contrast is provided by the second section, a light, quick-moving fugato on a motif of descending thirds, shown in Fig.842. A rather virtuosic postlude concludes the composition. This is a significant work; as Pirro says, it represents a "musique ample, aérée et impérieuse jusqu'à la violence."[9]

Fig.842

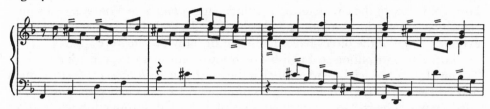

A *Voluntary for double Organ* in A minor (new ed., no.1) is an equally important work. It is similarly constructed, but on an even larger scale. Its beginning is given in Fig.843. As Figs.841–43 show, ornaments, whether written out, indi-

Fig.843

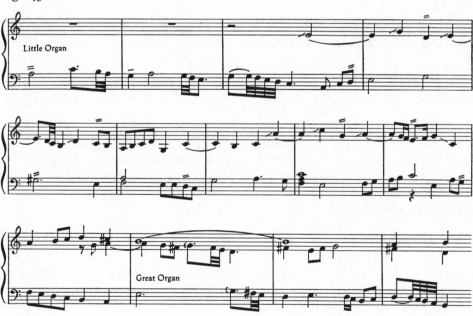

755

cated by symbols, or added by improvisation, are almost as important in English organ music as in the French. However, they hardly ever occur in Germany or Italy.

Another of Christopher Gibbons' organ works is formulated in two fugal sections and a postlude (new ed., no.4), a second (no.3) lacks the postlude, and a third one (no.5), which is only twenty measures long, is rather like a contrapuntal fantasy without a genuine subject. Two or three dance pieces by Gibbons are also known, but they do not contribute anything extraordinary to the field.

Benjamin Rogers, a composer of dances and suites, also wrote organ works. There must surely be more than the three pieces that are known to me: a prelude, a short Voluntary in the character of a prelude, and a *Fugue or Voluntary*—a somewhat longer piece in C major that begins fugally and then lapses into a freer texture.[10] None of the pieces have significant or individual features.

Locke's contribution to English organ music consists of seven compositions "For an Organ," which he had printed at the end of his *Melothesia*.[11] Four of them (new ed., nos.1, 2, 3, 5) are brief fugues of about fifteen to twenty measures, each based on one subject. No.7, which consists of a chordal introduction and a short fugato interspersed by passage work, indicates an Italian influence. No.6, "For a Double Organ," begins with a double fugue that is reminiscent of French models. After twenty measures it reaches a free postlude containing various figurations as well as two echo measures, which are given in Fig.844. Only one of Locke's pieces

Fig.844

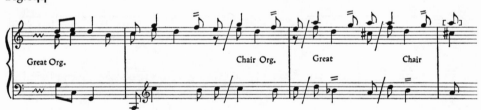

(no.4) exhibits the form introduced by Christopher Gibbons, consisting of two fugal sections and a postlude. The first subject has bold interval skips, and becomes even more audacious when the added ornaments are translated into actual notation, as shown in Fig.845. This composition is Locke's most remarkable contribution to English organ music.

Blow

John Blow is the first master after the Elizabethans whose keyboard output is so significant in both volume and content that it deserves, indeed requires, separate treatment. He was born in 1649, and is supposed to have studied with Christopher

Fig.845

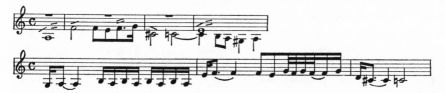

Gibbons. As a boy he was a singer in the Chapel Royal, and from 1674 until his death, he held the position of "Master of the Children" there. In 1676 he was made the organist at Westminster Cathedral, but transferred the office to his pupil Purcell three years later. He took it over again after Purcell's early death in 1695, and held several other important and honorable positions until he died in 1708. Most of Blow's keyboard works are preserved in manuscripts, quite often in several copies that differ in details, especially with regard to titles and ornaments. The organ works are available in a complete edition,[12] but the harpsichord pieces are scattered among several new publications that encompass a large part of the preserved output, but not all of it and not always reliably.

Blow's extant organ works comprise thirty compositions, which may be divided into several types, according to their contents. A number of them (new ed., nos.2, 7–9, 17, 19–21, 23) may be called preludes; they usually start with a brief imitation and then continue freely. No.2 begins with nine measures taken almost literally from a Frescobaldi toccata (*Toccate I*, no.12). Today this would be called plagiarism, but people thought differently then. Handel, for example, was a frequent "borrower"!

A second group consists of pieces worked out as fugues with one subject. Some of them have the character of a ricercar, others that of a canzona. Fig.846 shows an example of each type. Canzona no.3—it is called *Verse* in one manuscript and *Fugue* in another—is mostly in three parts, with loose-knit points of imitation separated by several interludes, which are easily recognizable and audible as such by their continuous sixteenth-note motion. Thus Blow consciously develops an important formal principle of the later fugue, though still somewhat superficially. Like many English fugal pieces, this one closes with a section in free style. Such

Fig.846

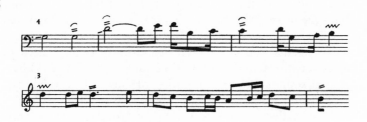

fugues with postludes are found almost exclusively in England, and contrast inter-estingly with the Continental type of prelude and fugue.

Blow wrote several works of the type created by Christopher Gibbons, con-sisting of a pair of fugues, the second one livelier than the first (particularly new ed., nos. 5, 10, 16, 22, 29). In no.29 (*A Double Vers,* i.e., a piece for an organ with two manuals) the two fugues are separated by an extended interlude, which begins with lively passage work and then suddenly (meas.45–57) moves to a passage from a Frescobaldi toccata (*Toccate I*, no.8, meas.18–24). In this piece, as well as in many others for the organ, Blow has no sense of stylistic unity. His organ pieces reflect the pragmatic idea, widespread in England at the time, that the justifica-tion and aim of music is exclusively sensuous satisfaction. "Music hath two ends, first to please the sense . . . and secondly to move ye affections or excite passions," as Roger North says in his *Musicall Gramarian* (c.1728). Blow realizes this philos-ophy of music in a series of organ compositions that are not really great works of art, but nevertheless contain many interesting and stimulating ideas.

Although not all of Blow's harpsichord compositions have been published, enough of them are available to give an adequate idea of his creativity in this field.[13] While his predecessors limited themselves to dances and suites, Blow expanded the scope of English harpsichord music with fugues and preludes, and brought the traditional 16th-century ground to life again.

Fig.847

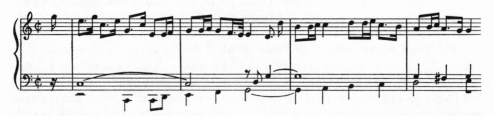

Among his clavier dances there are allemandes, courantes, sarabandes, min-uets, gavottes, and ayres. They are probably mostly single pieces except for a suite in *D* minor, consisting of allemande, courante, and minuet, which reaches us in a print of 1700 (Fuller I, p.2). In any event, in contrast to Purcell, Blow does not seem to have contributed much to the evolution of the English suite. Several allemandes exhibit the usual stylization of this species (e.g., Oesterle, p.127), while others exhibit a tendency toward song-like formulation, as in the excerpt given in Fig.847 (Fuller I, p.7). This tendency is even clearer in the other dances, for which Blow often invents very attractive tunes. One courante (Fuller I, p.15) has a gentle Rococo melody that sounds like a premonition of Gluck. It also has an unusual form. The four measures given in Fig.848 function as a refrain that recurs four times after various episodes, exactly as in a French rondeau. The *Corant II* that

Fig.848

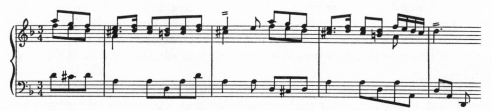

follows obviously belongs to the same composition and represents a fifth and longer interlude. Among Blow's many attractive dance pieces this one occupies a very special place because of its unusually developed form and its loveliness. It almost seems to come from the dramatic or opera repertoire, rather than being an original clavier piece.

New editions are available of three preludes (Fuller II, pp.3, 7; Oesterle, p. 128) and of two fugues (Fuller II, p.1; Oesterle, p.130); the first fugue is also included in Blow's organ works (Shaw, no.22). His grounds, however, are of greater interest. *The Hayes: a Ground, Morlake's Ground,* and *Chacone* are all based on simple ostinatos of four 3/4 measures. The *Ground* in G minor (Fuller II, p.14), on the other hand, has a running bass of four 6/4 measures as its subject. The first

Fig.849

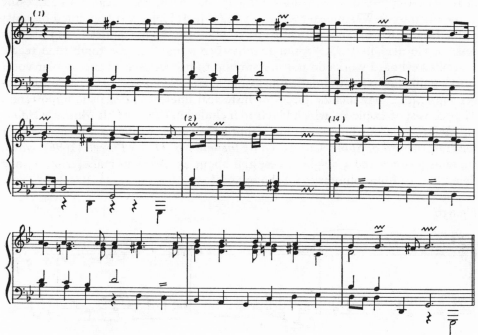

and last variations from this piece are reproduced from the original (Oxford, Christ Church Ms.1177) in Fig.849. In the interesting dissonant figures of the last variation, Blow is still beholden to the tradition of the early Baroque, for Frescobaldi may have served as a model here. Later authors, such as Burney, who have criticized Blow unjustly for such "crudities" were bowing to the taste of their own times.

The other two grounds (Fuller II, p.17; Oesterle, p.122) are in 4/4 time, and are based on ostinatos of irregular length, five and seven measures, respectively, but they are not genuine grounds in the strict sense of the word, since the bass is more or less varied. The second one, *Ground in C faut*, still shows signs of the virginal style, which occurs elsewhere in Blow's works, e.g., in a *Vers for the Double Organ* (Shaw, no.27).

All in all Blow's keyboard works show a curious mixture of various influences. It is an output in which contemporary elements combine with reminiscences of John Bull, quotations from Frescobaldi, and intimations of Gluck. The repertoire is uneven in part because it was written at different periods of Blow's life, but it also reflects a basically eclectic approach.

Purcell

Henry Purcell, the most famous English composer of the 17th century, was born in 1658 or 1659, studied with John Blow in the 1670s, and became his successor as the organist at Westminster Abbey in 1679. In 1682 he was appointed organist of the Chapel Royal, and in 1683 court composer to King Charles II and his successors. He died in 1695, "Anno Aetatis suae 37mo," as his tombstone reads. Purcell's keyboard works do not measure up to his ecclesiastic and secular vocal works (anthems, odes, dramatic music, the opera *Dido and Aeneas*) or his chamber music, but they include pieces of historical interest and artistic importance. They consist of 12 pieces, which Playford included in Part II of his *Musick's Handmaide* (1678); a posthumous volume entitled *A Choice Collection of Lessons for the Harpsichord or Spinet Composed by the late Mr. Henry Purcell* (1696), which contains 8 suites and 5 single pieces; and about 25 pieces in manuscript, among them three or four voluntaries for the organ.[14]

Fig.850

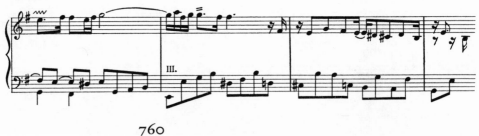

Most of the pieces from *Musick's Hand-maide—Song Tune, March, Minuet, A New Irish Tune, Rigadoon*—are short and rather insignificant. An exception is the single longer piece, *A New Ground* (new ed., p.30). Above a running bass of three 4/4 measures in eighth notes, which is heard ten times, Purcell sets a remarkably inventive and varied melody, whose phrase structure does not coincide with that of the bass, but deliberately crosses its periodic repetitions. Fig.850 shows a characteristic passage, the transition from the second to the third presentation of the ostinato. The third measure of this example is an instance of the syncopated displacement of the melody, which Purcell employs very often, and which also occurs in a prelude by Draghi (cf.Fig.840).

Fig.851

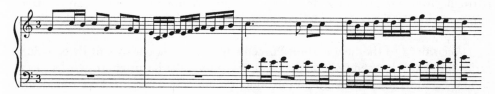

The eight suites in the posthumous print have the basic outline P A C S, which is occasionally varied by replacing the sarabande by a minuet or hornpipe, or by adding some dances after the sarabande. In principle, it is Froberger's three-movement suite expanded by a prelude, as Locke had already done in his *Melothesia*. Most of Purcell's preludes, however, are much more developed than those of his predecessor. In the fifth suite, the first half of the prelude is written in an imitative two-part texture that is strikingly similar to Bach's *Two-Part Inventions* (Fig.851). In the dance movements Purcell frequently uses the syncopated displacement technique, which is a somewhat superficial but nevertheless effective means of increasing the rhythmic activity. Like all English composers, he favors dotted rhythms. Phrases here and there are modeled after the musical language of his vocal works, e.g., the affective sigh in the allemande of Suite II (Fig.852a.) or the dramatic declamation in the courante of the same suite (Fig.852b.). The five pieces added to the suites in the print of 1696 are taken from Purcell's theater music, e.g.,

Fig.852

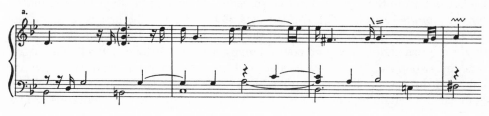

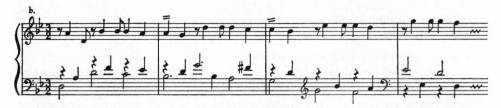

the *March* (new ed., p.23) from *The Married Beau,* the *Chaconne* (p.24) from *Timon of Athens.*

Among the pieces preserved in manuscripts (pp.33ff.) we may single out a *Ground* in C minor (p.39), which exhibits traits similar to the *New Ground* in *Musick's Hand-maide;*[15] a brief, melodically very attractive *Hornpipe* (p.47); and particularly a *Toccata* in A major (p.42), an extended, virtuosic composition, which obviously derives from Italian models by Pasquini or perhaps by Alessandro Scarlatti.[16]

According to the new edition Purcell's organ music consists of three voluntaries (pp.59ff.), but the *Prelude* that appears among the harpsichord works (p.53) should be added. It consists of an introduction, modeled after the Frescobaldi elevation toccatas, and a fugue of a more modern character. The *Voluntary on the 100th Psalm Tune* (p.59) is probably the only English organ piece from the second half of the 17th century that is based on a liturgical melody.[17] Like many German organ chorales it begins with an imitative treatment of the first line of the psalm tune, after which the whole melody is heard twice, first in the bass, then in the soprano. The legend "Half stop," which appears in the bass melody four times, means the same thing as *medio registro* in Spanish organ music: The four lines of the chorale lie in the lower half of the manual (which was probably reinforced by a 16-foot stop), the interludes in the upper half.

Fig.853

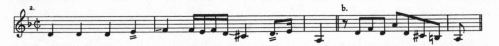

The second *Voluntary* (p.61) belongs to the type that appears so frequently in English music: a pair of fugues with a sustained subject in the first one and a livelier subject in the second. The two subjects are given in Fig.853. The *Voluntary for the Double Organ* (p.64) also consists of two fugues, the first of which is an expanded variant of the first fugue of the preceding work. Both compositions are works of great significance and contain many details worthy of Purcell. The fugue that the two pieces share includes several episodes in rapid figurations, which interrupt the sustained presentations of the subject matter in an unexpected but quite effective manner, one that is very characterisic of English organ music. The two measures from the first episode given in Fig.854 echo the early Neapolitans, and again prove that Purcell was familiar with the organ works of Frescobaldi, not only with the *Fiori musicali* but also with the toccatas.

Fig.854

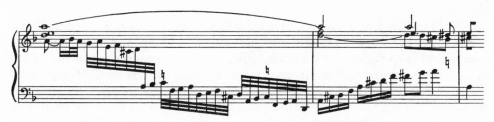

The *Voluntary* that concludes the new edition (p.68) is a dubious work. It is a rather diffuse and noisy *battaglia*, which one would rather not connect with Purcell's name, although some of its details are more interesting than the usual piece in this genre.

Henry Purcell's younger brother Daniel (1660–1717) is represented by an apparently posthumous print, *The Psalms set full for the Organ or Harpsichord*, which contains "harmonizations of psalms that are no less dry than Continental ones. The ornamentation of the chorale tones retains in a surprising manner the materials of the ancient technique of the virginalists and colorists."[18] On the other hand, several dance pieces exhibit quite modern tendencies.[19]

Clarke and Croft

Jeremiah Clarke (1673/74–1707) and William Croft (1678–1727), like Purcell, were Blow's pupils. A few keyboard pieces by Clarke were printed in the collections *A Choice Collection of Ayres for the Harpsichord* (Young, 1700) and *The Harpsichord Master* (Walsh, 1700), and six of his suites are included in the posthumous volume *Choice Lessons for the Harpsichord or Spinett, Mr. Jeremia Clarke* (1711).[20] A *Jigg* from *Choice Lessons* (new ed., p.11) is manifestly modeled after Continental gigues (such as Froberger's). Both halves of the piece start with a light imitation, the second half using the inversion of the subject, as shown in Fig.855.

Fig.855

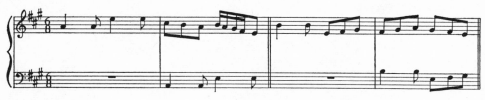

As far as I know, this is the only English example of this treatment of the gigue. Although this dance represents England's contribution to German, French, and Italian suites, it is comparatively rare in English suites. In the rest of the dances Clarke largely follows the English tradition in the use of dotted rhythms, syncopated displacements of the melody, and a thin texture with wide spacing between the hands.

William Croft is known for twelve suites,[21] most of which have the basic form A C S, but some begin with a prelude or end with an *Aire* or *Rondo*. Some movements keep within the tradition, others suggest the approach of the *galant* style with its attractive, but also precarious innovations. One of Croft's prettiest pieces is the *Aire* of the last suite, written in the form of a rondeau; its refrain is reproduced in Fig.856. The roguish ending pleased him—justifiably—so much that he used it again in the two couplets. The *Ground* in C minor from Suite III is based on a running *basso ostinato* of three and one-half measures and has the refrain form of the French chaconnes. In similar fashion the allemande that follows consists of a refrain and two couplets.

Fig.856

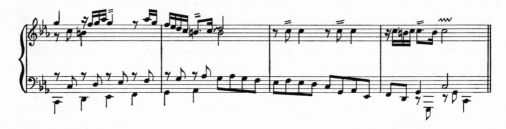

23

The Netherlands

Our knowledge of dutch music of the 17th century is very incomplete. This is probably not due so much to the loss of sources as to the large decline in musical activity. The great era of Dutch music had come to an end, and its place was taken by painting. Sweelinck was the last great composer in Holland, Cornet the last one in Belgium. During the next century only three musicians emerge clearly: the Dutchmen Anthoni van Noordt (d.1675?) and Gisbert Steenwick (d. 1679), and the Belgian Abraham van den Kerckhoven (1627–1702). A number of anonymous pieces, mostly unpretentious dances and songs, can be added to their outputs.

Van Noordt

Anthoni van Noordt was an organist in Amsterdam. In 1659 he published the only printed volume of the period, the *Tabulatuur-Boeck van Psalmen en Fantasyen.*[1] It contains ten psalm settings, intended primarily for the organ, and six fantasies, which are more suited to the harpsichord. The psalm settings consist of three to eight verses, i.e., different settings of the same melody, except for the first psalm (Psalm xv), which is represented by a single verse. Thus they are counterparts of the German chorale variations. The Lutheran tunes are replaced by the melodies of the French psalter of 1562 (texts by Marot and Beza, music by Bourgeois), which had been introduced in the Netherlands in 1566 and had already been used by Sweelinck for his organ compositions on Psalms cxvi and cxl and by Speuy for his psalm settings of 1610.

Van Noordt's psalm settings sound rather antiquated for the time in which they were written, or at least printed. In all 41 arrangements the psalm tune is entrusted to a single voice: 25 times to the soprano, 13 times to the bass, and 3 times to the tenor. It is almost always heard in the same sustained note values in which it is notated in the psalter, i.e., partly in whole notes and partly in halves, as a sort of "Calvinist *cantus planus*." The only exceptions are two discant settings in which the melody is partly ornamented (Psalms vi, verse 2; cxix, 3), and two others in which it is entirely resolved into smaller note values (cxix, 2; xxiv, 2). To these *cantus firmi* van Noordt adds one, two, or three counterpoints, creating 24 three-part settings, 13 four-part ones, and 4 bicinia. In most of the three-part pieces the two counterpoints are formed from a series of somewhat vivacious motifs and clavieristic figures, which are often connected by brief imitations. In the four-part settings a quieter motion predominates, as may be expected with three counterpoints. The counterpoints occasionally form rudimentary fore-imitations that anticipate various chorale lines. Fig.857 shows how the same passage—Psalm vii, beginning of the line "Et ne me desrompe"—is treated in a three-part setting (verse 2) and in a four-part one (verse 3). The most striking deviation from these methods is found in Psalm xxiv, verse 2, where the psalm tune appears as a *cantus coloratus* in sixteenth-note motion, as often occurs in Scheidt and Scheidemann. Among the bicinia Psalm cxix, verses 1 and 2 represent two different types of two-part texture. In the first one the sustained tones of the chorale are combined with a rapidly moving counterpoint, while in the second one the entire chorale is re-solved into an eighth-note motion, to which a similarly formulated counterpoint is added.

Fig.857

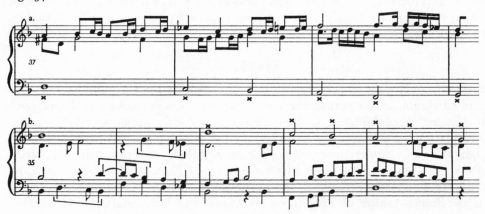

Van Noordt's six fantasies are of greater interest than these conservative psalm settings. Like Sweelinck's fantasies, they are based on one subject each, which is developed in several sections (usually three), but much more briefly and in a more uniform style than Sweelinck's. They are true ancestors of the genuine fugue, and van Noordt was very conscious of the significance of episodes as articulating factors in the course of such a work. The subjects, too, belong to neither the ricercar nor the canzona type, but are distinguished by a fine sense of individual contour and dynamic linearity. Two of these subjects (Seiffert, nos.12, 13) are given in Fig.858. In the second section of no.12, van Noordt introduces a chromatic countersubject, which is added in small notes. The subject of the fugue in Bach's C-major *Sonata* for solo violin has a very similar contour, and is also combined with a chromatic countersubject. Around 1650 there are very few pieces that announce the principles of the subsequent fugue as clearly as van Noordt's fantasies.

Fig.858

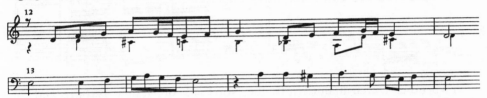

Steenwick and Others

Gisbert van Steenwick was an organist at Arnheim from 1665 to 1674 and then went to Kampen, where he died in 1679. In 1671 he wrote a notebook with thirty-three pieces, nine of them his own, for his pupil, fifteen-year-old Anna Maria van Eijl.[2] Like many provincial organists, his ability as a composer is limited to arranging well-known melodies for the clavier and varying them. Among others he arranged the Christmas songs *Puer natus* and *Heiligh saligh Bethlehem* and the student song *More Palatino* (which Sweelinck and Buxtehude also arranged), as well as a few dances and folk tunes. An "ingenious variation technique" attributed to Steenwick by F. Noske[3] is nothing of note, even if one is being charitable. An otherwise unknown composer, Georg Berff, who is called "Organist der Stadt Deventer" in German, is represented in this notebook by two dance songs with variations (*Ballet* and *La Princesse*). An *Allemand Tresoor* (no.IV) is probably by the English composer Jonas Tresure (cf.p.750). The rest of the manuscript is not very interesting from the general historical point of view.

The same is more or less true of some other Dutch manuscripts from the second half of the 17th century, which have been published under the designations "Leningrad Manuscript," "Camphuysen Manuscript," and "Gresse Manuscript."[4] The first one contains some anonymous dances and three short pieces (*Fantazia, Toccata, Malle Sijmon;* new ed., nos. XLV–XLVII) by Mr. Jan Pijtters (probably Sweelinck). The last manuscript includes among other compositions four works by Jacob Gresse (two allemandes and two suites; nos.LX–LXVII), some arrangements from Lully's operas *Alceste* (1674) and *Isis* (1677), and a

Preludium and *Canzon* (nos.LVII-LVIII). The *Preludium* and *Canzon* are both in A minor and perhaps belong together. Whether they are of Dutch origin is doubtful. The canzona closes in the Frescobaldi manner, with a sixteenth-note trill against which the left hand executes a descending passage in equally rapid note values (Fig.859). The Camphuysen manuscript preserves among other things a *Daphne* with three variations (no.LVI), which is a very pretty arrangement of a dance song that appears first among Farnaby's works (*FW*, no.CXII). This composition, too, seems not to have originated in the Netherlands.

Fig.859

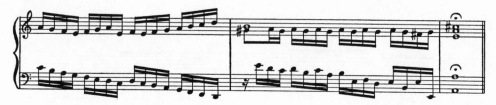

Two other Dutch manuscripts, the Notebook of Gesina Terburg and the Broeckhuizen book, are lost. According to what is known about them, they did not contain anything of special interest.[5] Recently a print by Pieter Bustijn, *IX Suites pour le Clavecin* (1710) has become known.[6] Bustijn was an organist at Middelburg and died in 1729.

Kerckhoven

Abraham van den Kerckhoven belongs to a family of musicians who were active in Belgium, chiefly in Brussels, from the 16th until the 18th century. Born in 1627, he worked at the Court Chapel of Governor Archduke Leopold Wilhelm of Austria from 1647 on, and was its organist from 1656 to at least 1673. He died in 1702. A manuscript at Brussels, Bibl. Royale, II 3326, contains more than 35 organ works by Kerckhoven, most of which are available in a new edition,[7] but unfortunately they are intermingled with many anonymous pieces. According to statements in the preface of the new edition,[8] the preserved organ works of Kerckhoven comprise 23 versets (new ed., nos.1–9, 20, 36–40, 71–74, 86, 89–91), 10 settings for the *Salve regina* (nos.97–106), an organ Mass (nos.107–123), 7 fantasies (nos. 128–33, 135), a fugue (no.134), and 2 preludes and fugues (nos.136–37).

The versets are short pieces of about ten to twenty measures, which were probably used in conjunction with the singing of psalms or the Magnificat. Musical relationships with the corresponding chant tones are barely recognizable; the pieces are freely composed, like so many of that period, and even today might well be used in services. In contrast to these versets, the pieces for the Marian antiphon employ the beginnings of the *Salve regina, Ad te clamamus*, etc., as subjects for fugal settings. The organ Mass, called *Missa duplex*, comprises 5 versets for the Kyrie, 10 for the Gloria, 2 for the Sanctus, and one for the Agnus, all using the melodies of Mass IV. Fig.860 shows an excerpt from the first verset (meas.7–11), in which Kerckhoven makes an effective and convincing use of the English cross relation (at *).

Fig.860

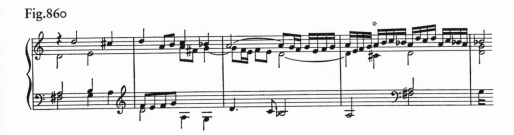

Kerckhoven's fantasies and fugues are works of larger scope and greater significance. He always shows estimable ability and good taste, and employs the stylistic elements of his day with ingenuity, without exaggeration or pedantry. One fantasy (new ed., no.128) begins with a kind of free prelude, in the second measure of which a "motto" is heard ($| f f | g g | a |$), which is expanded into a subject ($| f f g g | a f b♭ a g f |$) in measures 29ff.; beginning with measure 113 this subject appears four times in augmentation. In contrast to this extended contrapuntal composition, the short fantasy that follows (no.129) represents a quiet prelude in an expressive C-minor setting. Its beginnings appears in Fig.861. The piece is filled with an introspective warmth that recalls the works of an earlier Belgian organ master, Pieter Cornet. The next piece (no.130), *Fantasia pro duplici organo*, is a lively work in D major, which continues through more than 150 measures with-

Fig.861

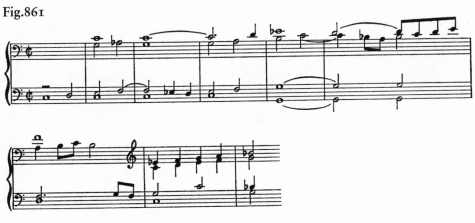

out a genuine subject, but with frequent "changes of scenery"—among them echo effects—like the fantasies of the English virginalists, especially William Byrd. The next fantasy (no.131) is similarly free. It is a particularly impressive work in C minor, for which Kerckhoven's authorship is not expressly stated. It includes several passages in Lombardic rhythms, a feature that does not occur in his authenticated compositions.

24

Spain and Portugal

Cabanilles

The outstanding personality in Spanish music of the late 17th century is Juan Cabanilles. He was born in Algemesi (Valencia) in 1644, chosen as organist of the Valencia Cathedral in 1665 (to succeed Jeronimo de la Torre), and died in 1712. He was very famous in France as well as in Spain. In 1722 his pupil Joseph Elias made a copy of his numerous organ works. Elias called himself "uno de los menores dicípulos del Grande Maestro," and opened his collection with the verses "Ante ruet mundus quam surget Cabanilles secundus" (the world may vanish before a second Cabanilles comes). Cabanilles' fame is matched by the number of his organ compositions preserved in manuscripts. It has been estimated that a complete new edition would comprise some 1200 pages. About half of his output has been published in four volumes by H. Anglés.[1] They contain 70 tientos, 6 toccatas, and about 20 other compositions, mostly variation sets. In addition there are numerous unpublished works for use at services—versets, hymns, etc.

Several types may be differentiated in Cabanilles' tientos; essentially they are the same ones that had already been cultivated by his predecessors. Twelve of the published compositions are *Tientos de falsas*, relatively short, quietly moving pieces in which—as in the Italian *durezze e ligature*—the harmonic texture is pervaded by multiple suspensions. Cabanilles' masterful handling of the technique and expressiveness of this style is shown by an excerpt from *Tiento* no.1 (new ed., vol.I, p.1, meas.27–36), given in Fig.862. The other tientos belong to the florid type, which also plays the main role in the works of Correa de Arauxo, Jimenez, and Bruna. Some are written for undivided keyboard (*lleno, pleno*) others for divided registers, e.g., "partit de mà dreta" (III, p.4; Catalan for "right hand"),

Fig.862

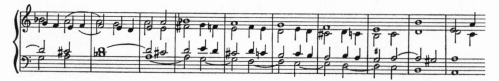

"partido de mano izquierda" (I, p.67; "left hand"), "de dos tiples" (VI, p.89),
"partido de dos bajos" (IV, p.8), "de dos tiples i dos baixos" (III, p.114), etc. The
term "de contras" is new; it is found in three tientos (I, p.25; III, p.63; IV, p.70),
and apparently refers to the employment of the pedals for sustaining long pedal
points.

Most of the tientos are extended fantasies, in which the various elements of
17th-century style are used in free succession: imitation, motivic development,
ornamented counterpoint, toccata-like passage work, and thematic variation. An
especially important role is played by modulatory passages, those peculiar sequences that occurred earlier in the music of Aguilera de Heredia and Pablo Bruna.
In the course of the tiento Cabanilles frequently arrives at a phrase (mostly of
four measures) that fascinates him so much that he repeats it four or five times,
or even more often, transposing it by successive fifths or seconds. He goes far beyond his predecessors in applying this method, fortunately not only quantitatively
but also qualitatively. In Bruna's music the modulatory passages rarely rise above
a chordal setting with an ornamented upper or lower voice, but Cabanilles invents
many different phrases of captivating individuality and originality. Fig.863 shows
two examples from *Tiento* no.16 (I, pp.102, 103), and there are hundreds more like
it. Moreover, in the repetitions the original formula is often somewhat altered, e.g.,

Fig.863

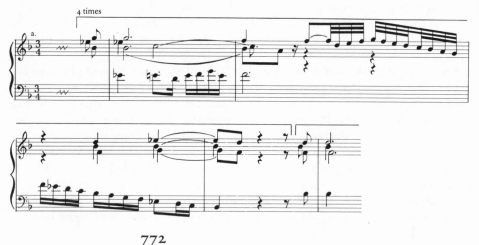

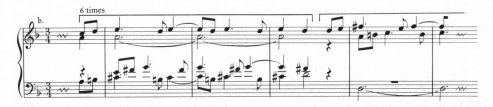

by interchanging the voices, as in Fig.863b. This method is driven to extremes in a few tientos that consist exclusively of modulatory repetitions of a single formula. The three *Tientos de contras* belong to this type. They each consist of just one long section based on a pedal point (55, 43, and 49 measures, respectively), which is repeated four, four, and three more times, transposed to different steps. It has been said of the last *Tiento de contras* that "as important a master as Cabanilles cannot possibly mean this in a formal sense," and that one must assume he intended it either as an "adjustment to differently tuned organs" or as "pedagogical instructions for pupils or playing instructions for organists."[2] But for anyone who is familiar with Cabanilles' works as a whole there is no doubt that these pieces are indeed meant as they are preserved. Whether such procedures coincide with our ideas of an "important master" is another question. Cabanilles' works contain much that is significant and valuable, but it sometimes slips into triviality—a fault that can hardly be avoided in such a voluminous opus.

Most of the tientos—like those of Correa de Arauxo—begin with an imitative presentation of the subject, which is reintroduced occasionally later on, often in rhythmic variants. But there are also other formulations, e.g., a *Tiento pleno* (III, p.31), that consist of a prelude, a fugal middle section, and a postlude. In a *Tiento sobre Ave maris stella* (I, p.12), the individual lines of the hymn are imitatively developed, as in a chorale motet, and often combined with lively, florid counterpoints. The concluding section (meas.135–81), which is apparently freely invented, includes a modulatory passage that is heard four times (meas.150ff.). About fifteen tientos have no subjects, including one entitled *sin passo* (no.50; III, p.168), the strikingly song-like *Tiento a modo de Italia* (no.57; IV, p.17), and the *Coreado o de ecos* (no.70; IV, p.136), a piece of 404 measures that is filled with many modulatory passages, echo effects, and other trifling techniques. Finally, in *Tiento* no.13 (I, p.80) Cabanilles develops a single subject in diminution, augmentation, and a triple-meter variant, manifestly in imitation of a central European model, such as a monothematic fantasy by Sweelinck.

Cabanilles' *Tocatas* are in no way similar to the Italian toccatas. One of them (new ed., n.28, II, p.168) is essentially a song-like subject and its modulatory repetition, accompanied by virtuosic repercussion phrases. Another one, No. 29 (II, p. 170) consists of four *discurs*, which may be compared to the various sections of a variation canzona.

Finally, there are a number of compositions by Cabanilles in vol.II of the new

Fig.864

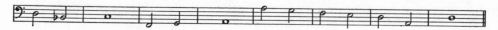

edition whose titles suggest dances: 5 pasacalles, 5 gallardas, 4 paseos, and one xácara. They are not dances in the true sense but sets of continuous variations on short subjects comparable to passacaglias, chaconnes, or grounds. The pasacalles and paseos are all based on four-measure harmonic progressions, I I IV V. *Pasacalles* I (p.40) and *Paseos* II and IV (pp.123,128) are in triple meter, which is normal in central European passacaglias and chaconnes, while the others are in duple meter. All the gallardas are in duple meter and thereby differ fundamentally from the galliard in French, Italian, and English sources of the 16th century. They are based on subjects of greater length—eight, ten, or sixteen measures—and of individual formulation, mostly ostinatos that are largely retained throughout the variations. In *Gallardas* I (p.62), e.g., the subject may be abstracted, as shown in Fig.864.

The *Xácara* (or *Jácara*) is described in various literary sources of the 16th and 17th centuries as a kind of popular, often rather plebeian, comedy, perhaps comparable to the Viennese Hanswurst comedy of the 18th century. The songs and dances that were interspersed were on a rather low level. Cervantes, e.g., says in *El Rufián dichoso*: "The music is not sublime; for I can see from the notes that it is of a rather low type, similar to a *jacarandina*."[3] Cabanilles' *Xácara* (II, p.146) rises above this level, just as the chaconne in European art music shed the wild, erotic character this dance had in Mexico, where it originated. Cabanilles' work is based on a four-measure subject, which is repeated in many variants, some of them very interesting, in the manner of a chaconne.

In these works Cabanilles proves to be a great master of the variation technique. He is not satisfied with an unaltered sequence of harmonies masked by formulae, which was usual at the end of the 17th century, but often evolves from the thematic substance novel phrases with many original and individual features, which are not just superficial variants but genuine reformulations of the subject.

The manuscripts at Barcelona contain organ works by many other composers: Gabriel Menalt, Francisco Espelt, Vicente Herváz, Antonio Tormo, Juan de San Augustín, Francisco Llussá, Juan Bazea (Baseya), Francisco Vilar, Pablo Nassarre, and about a dozen others.[4] The first five names seem to be the most important, for each of them is represented in these manuscripts by a respectable number of works. I therefore asked the administration of the Barcelona Biblioteca Central to make a selection of their compositions available to me in photographic copies for the purposes of this study. Unfortunately my request was denied on the grounds that a comprehensive publication from these manuscripts was planned by the library for the celebration of the fiftieth anniversary of its founding. Let us hope that this plan will soon be realized. Until then we must be satisfied with a

774

reference to the few works that are available in modern reprints: three versets by Llussá; four tientos by Menalt, who was an organist at Santa Maria del Mar at Barcelona from 1679 until his death in 1687; two tientos by Bazea; and one each by Bernabé and Xarara.[5] The other organists named above were probably active mainly in eastern Spain.

Three Portuguese Manuscripts

M. S. Kastner[6] was the first to draw attention to three Portuguese manuscripts from the end of the 17th century. One of them is entitled *Livro de obras de orgão juntas pello curiosidade do P. P. Fr. Roque da Conceição, Anno de 1695.*[7] It contains about 130 versos, 26 obras, 5 meyo registos, 4 batalhas, and a Susana, all written in a score of four staves. The following composers are named: D. Agostinho (one tento), Pedro de Araujo (two tentos and a batalha), Antonio Correa Braga (one batalha), Fr. Diego da Conceição (a collection of versos, a meyo registo, and a batalha), Joseph Leyte de Costa (one tento), and Fr. Carlos de S. Joseph (one tento). The rest of the manuscript is anonymous and part of it may be by Fr. Roque da Conceição.

The versos are brief pieces, mostly of five to ten measures, just long enough for a fugal presentation of the subject. The subjects are occasionally derived from a psalm tone, but are most often freely invented. As an example Fig.865 reproduces a *Verso* by Diego da Conceição.

Fig.865

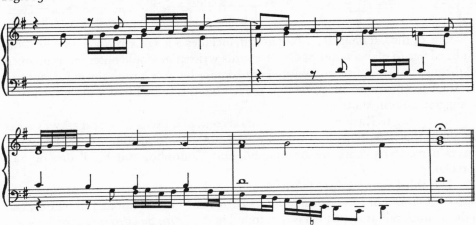

The obras are longer compositions, often designated as *Tento* or *Phantasia*. Musically they are of several types. Some are rather brief, about sixty measures in length, and limited to a normal contrapuntal texture, which hardly goes beyond quarter-note motion. Others are longer and begin with a ricercar-like subject, which combines further on with fairly vivacious motifs, similar to the tentos of Coelho. A few start with a free polyphonic introduction of about ten measures, e.g., a *Phantasia de 4° tom* (Speer, no.27), whose beginning is given in Fig.866.

Fig.866

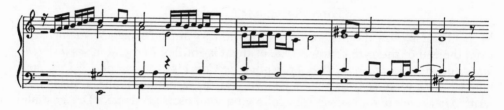

Among the *meyo registo* (= *medio registro*) there is one *de tres tiple* (no.26), which means the same as "meyo registo de un contrabaixo": Three voices move in the upper half of the keyboard (*b* and above) and one in the lower half (*b♭* and below). The *meyo registo* are ornamented more richly and with more variety than the other obras. Fig.867 offers a passage in 3 + 3 + 2 rhythm from a *Meyo registo de dous contrabaixos* (the two upper voices have rests).

Fig.867

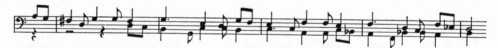

One of the batalhas, *Batalha famoza,* includes a lengthy passage in which the left hand has to play a series of C–g–c chords written in whole notes, accompanied by the annotation: "Esta mão esquierda sempre ha de estar abolir em quanto se dexara a arcabuziara," meaning that the left hand is to be lifted rapidly each time to suggest cannon shots.

According to Kastner's description a second manuscript, at Braga,[8] was written about the same time, and is also notated in a score of four staves. The composers named are Pedro de Araujo, Fr. Luis Coutinho, and Fr. Pedro de San Lorenzo.

The third manuscript, *Libro de cyfra adonde se contem varios Jogos de Versos é Obras é outras coriosidades de varios autores,*[9] is notated in figures, i.e., in the Spanish tablature, which is first found in the *Libro de cifra nueva* of Venegas de Henestrosa (1577), and which continued to be used until the beginning of the 18th century.[10] The manuscript includes more than 260 versos (grouped in six *Jogos* or "games"), 16 obras, 28 registos, 14 canções, 8 entradas, and one each of *Pange lingua, Sacris solemniis,* batalha, xácara, marizápalos, paraletas, espan-

776

holetas, folias, galharda, and toada. Except for fourteen rather short pieces, all the works carry a composer's name. Fr. Bertolomeu de Olague is particularly well represented with two obras, ten registos, three jogos de versos, three entradas, a canção, and the *Pange lingua, Sacris solemniis,* xácara, and toada. There are two better-known names—Aguilera de Heredia and Pablo Bruna—as well as Jacinto Bacelar (one canção); Antonio Brocarte, organist at Saragossa (two obras, two registos); João Correa (two obras); Alessandro Cuevaz (one registo); Sebastián Durón, court organist at Madrid in 1691 and a famous opera composer, who died in Bayonne in 1716 (two registos); Martino Garcia de Olague (one jogo); Lucas Puxol (one obra); Andre de Sola (one jogo, one obra, two registos); Miguel de Supuerta (one obra, one registo); Joséph Torrelhas (one obra, nine registos, three canções, one batalha); Joséph de Torres (1665–1738), court organist at Madrid (one canção); Joséph Urros, organist at Avila and in 1710 at Santiago de Compostela (one jogo, three cançãos); and Juan del Vado, in 1635 violinist and later organist and orchestral director at the Madrid court (four obras). Some of these composers were Spaniards or were active in Spain.

In a few of the versos the usual imitational texture of this genre is replaced by a homophonic setting. Most of these pieces are found in the collections of the two Olagues, often carrying such titles as *registo alto corneta, trompeta alta, clarim, trompeta baixa, de corneta e eco.* Fig.868 presents the beginning of a *Verso de clarim* by Bertolomeu de Olague (Hudson II, p.51).

Fig.868

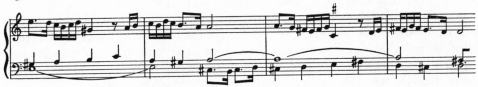

The numerous tientos are called either *Obra de ambas as mãos* (works for two [equal] hands) or *Registo (de tiple, baixo).* In many of them the typical modulatory passages of Spanish organ music play an important role. This aspect and several others indicate that this repertoire is not essentially Portuguese but Spanish, especially Catalan. In the tientos of the *Livro de obras* discussed above, there are practically no instances of this technique.

The fourteen cançãos are mostly short pieces in which an attractive, folk-like melody is offered in a simple harmonization, very similar to the themes in Pasquini's variation sets or in the French noëls. A *Canção de 7. tom* by Joséph Urros (Hudson, no.46), reproduced in Fig.869, is an illustration. A few cançãos are longer, especially two by Joséph Torrelhas (Hudson, nos.64, 66), which begin with song-like themes that are then taken up in very attractive free fantasies.

777

Fig.869

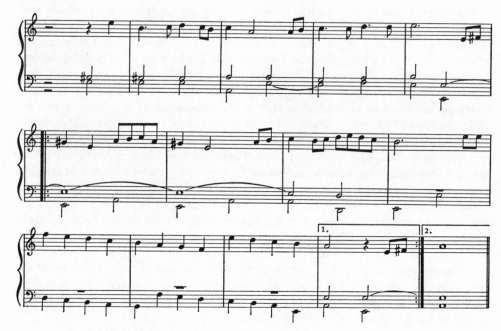

The entradas are very peculiar. Some of them are short, song-like pieces like the canções; others are continuous variations on four-measure bassi ostinati. The spirit of a festive introduction, which characterizes the German and Italian intradas, is nowhere in evidence. Similarly, a *Xácara* by Bertolomeu de Olague—like Cabanilles' *Xácara*—consists of continuous variations on a four-measure subject. The anonymous *Paraletas, Espanholetas,* and *Folias* (Hudson, nos.33, 32, 35) are of the same type. The last one consists of four simple presentations of the well-known theme. The *Marizápalos* (Hudson, no.37) is a brief movement of sixteen measures, whose harmonic structure is very similar to that of the folia. In the two marizápalos in the collection of Martin y Coll the same theme is varied several times.

The Collections of Martin y Coll

Antonio Martin y Coll (c.1660–c.1740) comes from Catalonia. As a young man he was named organist of the Franciscan monastery San Diego at Alcalá de Henares (northeast of Madrid). Later he moved to the monastery San Francisco el Grande at Madrid, and occupied the office of first organist there until his death. He is known as the author of several theoretical treatises (1714, 1734), and his collection of Spanish keyboard music is by far the largest in this field. The first four volumes contain more than 1850 works by other composers, while the fifth contains Coll's own works.[11] The individual volumes carry the following titles:

I. *Flores de música, obras y versos de varios organistas, escriptas por F. Antonio Martin Coll, Organista de San Diego de Alcalá,* 1706

II. *Pensil deleitoso de subabes flores de música, recogidas de varios organistas por F. Antonio Martin, Organista . . . de Alcalá,* 1707

III. *Huerto ameno de varias flores de música recogidas de muchos organistas por Fray Antonio Martin,* 1708

IV. *Huerto ameno de varias flores de música recogidas de varios organistas por Fray Antonio Martin,* 1709

V. *Ramillete oloroso* [Fragrant Flower Bouquet] *suabes flores de música para órgano compuestas por Fray Antonio Martyn,* 1709

It will only be possible to discuss this enormous repertoire in very general terms. Even though the material is very comprehensive, most of the "varios organistas" referred to in the titles of volumes I–IV unfortunately remain anonymous. The only compositions for which the composers are named are two *Pange lingua de Urreda,* a *Marche de Gautier, Tocatas alegres de Coreli,* and a *Jaboste* (gavotte) *de Ardel,* all in vol.IV. Through comparisons with other manuscripts three pieces have been identified as works by Aguilera and four as works by Cabanilles, all also in vol.IV.[12] As sparse as this information is, it gives an idea of the many sources Martin y Coll drew upon: His *varios organistas* include Denis Gaultier, Hardel, and Corelli!

The music comprises almost all forms and types cultivated in Spain, France, and Italy: obra, registro partido, juego de versos de todos tonos, canción, entrada, xácara, españoleta, marizápalos, pasacalles, chacona, batalla, favordones, pavana, alamanda, corrent, zarabanda, gigue, matassins, minué, folia, tocata ytaliana, as well as settings for the Mass ordinary, the Magnificat, and hymns (*Pange lingua, Veni Creator, Sacris solemniis, Ave maristela,* etc.). The notation is in keyboard score, except for the first half of vol.II, which employs the Spanish tablature with figures.

Twenty-five tientos are entered as an uninterrupted group in vol.II, fol.10–38. In both form and style they are similar to one another, suggesting that they are all by the same composer, and there is an unmistakable relationship, at least in form, with the tientos of Correa de Arauxo. The ninth piece of the group, *Tiento de 8.° tono,* is strictly contrapuntal, but all the rest exhibit the same alternation of brief expositions of the main subject and long ornamented or motivic interludes that occurs in Correa's monothematic tientos (cf.p.530). On the other hand, the elaborate modulatory passages characteristic of the eastern Spanish school are absent, and, as in Correa's works, there is only one instance of a phrase in $3+3+2$ rhythm, in no.14 of the group, *Otro* [tiento] *de un baxo, mano izquierda.* These tientos are of interest mainly because they furnish evidence of the continuation (and also the decline) of the Castilian school, which is otherwise known only through Correa de Arauxo.

779

Fig.870

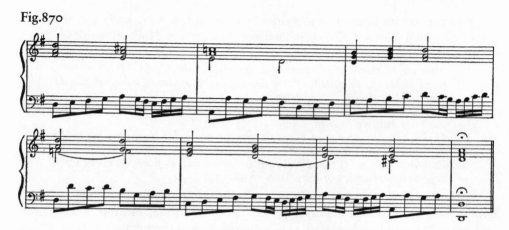

Martin y Coll's own compositions, contained in vol. V, include a large number of versos, about fifteen canciós, an obra, and a *Pange lingua*. The versets appear mostly in *Juegos de todos tonos*, i.e., in collections for all psalm tones, usually six for each tone. Fig.870 provides an example, the *6. Verso de 8° tono por De la sol re*. Coll's versets keep within the framework of suitability and the customs of the period, but his canciós are trivial concoctions of the cheapest kind. Usually the left hand plays only sustained tones in octaves, while the right hand presents a popular tune, and when the tune ends the right hand moves on to routine figurations "alla battaglia." Some of these pieces may be interesting as folkloric documents, however, e.g., the excerpt from *Canción catalana mui aprisa* [very fast], given in Fig.871. The only work that is somewhat more pretentious is an *Obra de lleno 1° tono*, a tiento of about 125 measures, which divides into several partly imitative sections.

Fig.871

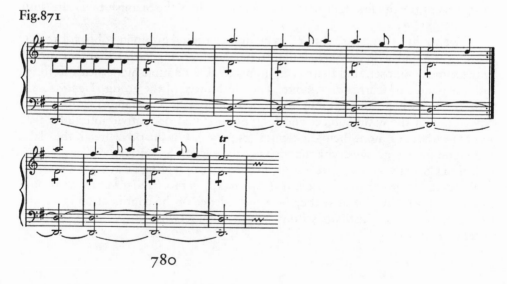

NOTES

The abbreviations used to designate the various periodicals and monument editions are given on p.818 (e.g., *MGG* = *Die Musik in Geschichte und Gegenwart*). Works referred to frequently are cited by means of abbreviations that generally consist of the author's name plus a key letter from the title of the work (e.g., Apel N = Apel, W. *Die Notation der Polyphonen Musik, 900 bis 1600).* These abbreviations are given in bold type following the full references in the Selected Bibliography, pp.818–31.

INTRODUCTION

1. General Observations on Keyboard Instruments and Keyboard Music

1. Cf. J. A. Burns, "L'impiego della partitura e l'Arte della Fuga di J. S. Bach," *L'Organo,* II (1961), pp.163ff.
2. Kinkeldey O, p.98.
3. J. Wolf, *Handbuch der Notationskunde,* II, p.305, note 3.
4. Kinkeldey O, p.141.

2. The Evolution of Keyboard Instruments

1. For more details, particularly for sources concerning the following explanations, see W. Apel, "Early History of the Organ," *Speculum,* XXIII (1948), pp.191ff.
2. This is still maintained in H. Neupert's article "Clavichord," in *MGG,* II, p.1471.
3. Bermudo, fol.69v.

PART I. CLAVIER MUSIC BEFORE 1500

3. Antiquity and Early Middle Ages

1. Cf. C. Sachs, *The Rise of Music in the Ancient World* (New York, 1943), p.256.
2. Cf. A. Lavignac, *Encyclopédie de la Musique* (1914), I, 1, p.572.
3. Cf. Frotscher G, p.52.

4. The Fourteenth Century

1. Cf. the facsimile in H. E. Wooldridge, *Early English Harmony* (1897), plates 42–

45; new ed. in Apel K. For the question of provenance (English, Italian or French?) cf. Apel N, p.44.

2. In earlier writings (J. Wolf, *Geschichte der Mensuralnotation* I, p.363; Frotscher G, p.62) these pieces were erroneously called preludes. Cf. J. Handschin, "Uber Estampie und Sequenz," *ZfMw*, XII (1929/30), pp.1ff.

3. Paris, Bibl. nat. fr. 146; new ed. in L. Schrade, *Polyphonic Music of the Fourteenth Century* I (1956), pp.54,60.

4. At one time called *Codex Bonadies* (cf. Ch. van den Borren's article "Bonadies" in *MGG*). Cf. D. Plamenac's articles: "Keyboard Music of the 14th Century in Codex Faenza 117," *JAMS*, IV (1951), pp.179ff.; "New Light on Codex Faenza 117," *Kongress Report Utrecht*, 1952, pp.310ff.; and "Faenza, Codex 117" in *MGG*. Facsimile edition in *MD*, XIII–XIV (1959–60), and separately in *An Early 15th-Century Italian Source of Keyboard Music* (Amer. Inst. of Musicology, 1961).

5. For the vocal settings cf. Th. Marrocco, *The Music of Jacopo da Bologna* (1954).

6. This Kyrie and the one with five movements mentioned above are transcribed in Plamenac's articles mentioned in note 4.

7. Cf. Th. Dart, "A New Source of Early English Organ Music," *Music and Letters*, XXXV (1954), p.201ff.

5. The Fifteenth Century

1. For early organ construction cf. Y. Rokseth, *La musique d'orgue du XVe siècle et au début du XVIe* (1930).

2. The alphabetic designations are taken from the new ed. in Apel K. In the preface of that edition references to special studies will be found. Regarding a few recently discovered pieces cf. Th. Göllner, "Notationsfragmente aus einer Organistenwerkstatt des 15. Jahrhunderts," *AfMw*, XXIV (1967), pp.170ff.

3. New ed. of the last-named in Apel K, nos.16, 18.

4. Wynsem probably means the village of Windsheim near Lüneburg. Another Windsheim existed near Nuremberg (cf. K. Ameln, *Locheimer Liederbuch*, p.6), but the spelling "Wynsem" is obviously North German. Moreover, in the sermons mention is made of a Ludolf Wilkin, which is also a North German name.

5. New ed. in Apel K, no.27.

6. Cf. Baumann L.

7. New ed. in Apel K, nos.31, 32.

8. Cf. W. Apel, "Die Tabulatur des Adam Ileborgh," *ZfMw*, XVI (1933–34), p.193. New ed. in Apel K, nos.33–40.

9. New ed. in Apel K, no.30.

10. Cf. Th. Göllner, *Formen früher Mehrstimmigkeit* (1961), pp.61, 157.

11. Cf. L. Schrade, *Die handschriftliche Überlieferung der ältesten Instrumentalmusik* (1930), pp.95f.

12. E.g., Ganassi, *Opera intitulata Fontegara* (1935); Ortiz, *Tratado de glosas* (1553); etc.

13. Formerly Wernigerode, Fürstl. Stolbergsche Bibl. Zb 14; now Berlin, Staatsbibl. Ms. 40613. Facsimile in K. Ameln, *Locheimer Liederbuch und Fundamentum organisandi des Conrad Paumann* (1925). Transcriptions in F. W. Arnold, *Das Locheimer Liederbuch . . .* , *Jahrbücher für mus. Wiss.*, II (1867), and in Apel K, nos.41–57. Cf. Chr. Wolf, "Conrad Paumanns Fundamentum organisandi und seine verschiedenen Fassungen," *AfMw* 25 (1968), pp. 196ff.

14. Here a folio is apparently lost. The complete series of *redeuntes* is preserved in the *Fundamentum M. C. P. C.* (*Magistri Conradi Paumanni Caeci*) of the *Buxheim Organ Book* (New ed., vol.II, p.248).

15. New ed. in Apel K, no.41a.

16. Three pieces (Apel K, nos.51, 53, 54) carry names of composers, namely, Georg de Putenheim, Wilhelmus Legrant, and Paumgartner. No.53 marks the beginning of an appendix written by a later hand.

17. Compare this with the analysis in A. Schering's *Studien zur Musikgeschichte der Frührenaissance* (1914), pp.37ff., according to which various notes of the *cantus firmus* appear, not in the tenor, but in the discant, or in both voices simultaneously. We prefer to avoid this somewhat artificial interpretation wherever possible, and to explain occasional missing notes by variant tradition or free paraphrase.

18. Substantial deviations between song and organ tenor occur at the end of the main section (before the *repeticio*) and at the end of the *repeticio*. Schering (p.31) reads the first tenor note of *Benedicite* as an F and therefore shifts the starting note of the song, A, into the upper part. The setting in the *Fundamentum*, however, clearly shows an *A*. A number of settings of *Benedicite* are listed in a table in Baumann L, *Beispiele*, no.1.

19. In K. Ameln, *Locheimer Liederbuch*, pp.18f.; cf. the new ed. by F. W. Arnold, p.113.

20. In O. Koller's new ed. in *DTÖ* IX.1, p.200.

21. Cf. E. Closson, *Le Manuscrit dit des Basses Danses* (1912), no.24.

22. We owe the identification to F. Ludwig; cf. his edition *Guillaume de Machaut, Musikalische Werke* II (1928), p.27. There is a new edition of the ballata in S. Clercx, *Johannes Ciconia*, II (1954), p.63. In the commentary on p.11 the Wernigerode manuscript is not mentioned.

23. Cim. 352b; formerly Ms. mus. 3725.

24. B. A. Wallner, *Das Buxheimer Orgelbuch*, facsimile ed. (1955); B. A. Wallner, *Das Buxheimer Orgelbuch, Das Erbe deutscher Musik*, vols. XXXVII–XXXIX (1958–59).

25. Cf. W. Schrammek, "Zur Numerierung im Buxheimer Orgelbuch," *Mf*, IX (1956), pp.298ff.; and E. Southern, "An Index to *Das Buxheimer Orgelbuch*," *MLA Notes*, XIX (1962), pp.47ff. Let us note two later studies: H. R. Zöbeley, *Die Musik des Buxheimer Orgelbuches* (1964), and E. Southern, *The Buxheim Organ Book* (1963), pp.132ff.

26. In the new edition the sign *pe*, which is added to the entire contratenor of nos.226 and 227, is omitted.

27. Although Schering quotes this rule in full (*Studien . . .*, p.145), he concludes that "the contratenor was in general looked upon as the regular pedal part," which is not correct.

28. Cf. H. Funck, "Eine Chanson von Binchois . . . ," *AM*, V (1933), pp.3ff.

29. Munich, Staatsbibl. Ms. mus. 3232; new ed. in R. Eitner, *Das Deutsche Lied des 15. und 16. Jahrhunderts*, vol.II (Supplement to *Monatshefte für Musikgeschichte*, 1880). For what follows cf. the concordances in Baumann L.

30. New eds.: 1. C. Mazzi, *Il libro dell' Arte del Danzare di Antonio Cornazano, La Bibliofilia*, XVII (1916), pp.1ff.; 2. E. Closson, *Le Manuscrit dit des Basses Danses* (1912); 3. V. Scholderer, *L'Art et instruction de bien dancer* (facsimile edition, 1936), Cf. E. Southern, "Some Keyboard Dances of the Fifteenth Century," *AM*, XXXV (1963), pp.114ff.; in this article several other settings from the *Buxheim Organ Book* are also discussed, but their relationship to *basse-danse tunes* cannot be considered fully proved.

31. New ed. in Apel K, no.43.

32. Cf. G. Reese, *Music in the Renaissance* (1954), p.94.

33. Cf. *DTÖ*, vol.53, p.85. This identification is found in E. Southern, *The Buxheim Organ Book* (1963), p.146.

34. In "Die Messe in der Orgelmusik des 15. Jahrhunderts," *AfMf*, I (1936), pp.129ff.

35. The division of this enormously large collection into four sections, adopted by the new edition, is unjustified and misleading. The collection should be broken into six subdivisions, if at all, each of which is coordinated with one of the six steps of the hexachord: 1. *super ut:* ascensus-descensus, clausulae, redeuntes, praeambulum, ascensus-descensus, clausulae, redeuntes (vol.III, pp.287–308); 2. *super re:* clausulae, redeuntes, praeambulum, clausulae, redeuntes (pp.308–23); 3. *super mi:* clausulae, redeuntes, praeambulum, clausulae, redeuntes (pp.324–33); 4. *super fa:* ascensus-descensus, clausulae, redeuntes, praeambulum (pp. 333–37); 5. *super sol:* clausulae, redeuntes (pp. 338–40); 6. *super la:* clausulae, redeuntes (pp.340–42).

36. In the new edition, vol.III, p.356; counted as the continuation of no.236.

PART II. THE SIXTEENTH CENTURY

6. General Observations

1. Cf. R. Lunelli, "Contributi trentini . . . ," *AM*, XXI (1949), p.48.

2. New ed. in G. Harms, *Arnolt Schlick, Tabulaturen . . .* (1924); for unconvincing reasons all the compositions are transposed down a fourth and the note values are doubled. A better new edition by R. Walter is in preparation.

3. New ed. in M. S. Kastner, *Arnolt Schlick, Hommage à l'empereur Charles-Quint* (1954).

4. New ed. in Moser H and Moser F.

5. Zurich, Stadtbibl. Cod. 284; the library also has in its collection a German translation, *Fundament und gründliche Anweisung*, with almost identical contents.

6. Basel, Univ. Bibl. F. I. 8.

7. Cf. K. Päsler, "Fundamentbuch von Hans von Constantz," *VfMw*, V (1889), pp.1ff.; W. Nagel, "Fundamentum Authore Johanne Buchnero," *MfM*, XXIII (1891), pp.71ff.; E. von Werra, "Johann Buchner," *KmJb*, 20 [30], (1895), pp.88ff.

8. New ed. in Merian T.

9. Cf. W. R. Nef, *Der St. Galler Organist Fridolin Sicher und seine Orgeltabulatur* (1938), pp.47f.

10. New eds. of the *Mulliner Book* in Stevens M; of Redford's collected works (including several uncertain ones) in Pfatteicher R.

11. New ed. in Benvenuti M and in Jeppesen O².

12. New eds. of the first collection in H. Anglés, *La Música en la corte de Carlos V* (1944); of the second collection (not quite complete and with many mistakes) in Pedrell H, vols.III, IV, VII, VIII (1894–98); and in a corrected new ed. of the latter by H. Anglés: *Antonio de Cabezón,* 3 vols. (1966).

13. New ed. in D. Stevens, *Thomas Tallis: Complete Keyboard Works* (1953).

14. New ed. by P. Pidoux, 5 vols. (1941–52).

15. New ed. by S. Dalla Libera (1959). It is only in recent years that the Turin tablatures have become generally known. They consist of sixteen volumes written in German organ tablature; eight of them belong to the *Collection Giordano* and eight to the *Collection Foá*. Cf. Schierning Ü, p.125; complete inventory in Mischiati T.

16. New eds. of the *Libro primo* in Torchi A; of both books in *I Classici della musica italiana,* Quad. 23–27 (G. Benvenuti, ed., 1919), and (better) in O. Mischiati, *Girolamo Cavazzoni, Orgelwerke,* 2 books (1958).

17. Cf. K. Jeppesen, *AfMw,* XII (1955), p.191. In the article "Cavazzoni" in *MGG* we read that Girolamo was born in 1525, but Mischiati, in the preface to vol.I of his new edition, puts the year of his birth between 1506 and 1522; moreover, he gives 1577 as the date of "last mention."

18. The *Primo libro de ricercari of 1556* (new ed. by N. Pierpont and J. P. Hennebains) is a part-book print, and thus belongs to the field of ensemble music.

19. New eds. of the Masses by J. B. Labat, *Livre IV des Oeuvres d'orgue de Claude Merulo* (1865); of the canzonas by P. Pidoux (1941); of the toccatas by S. Dalla Libera (1959) in three volumes, the last of which contains nine additional toccatas from the Turin tablatures.

20. Three additional publications of *Ricercari* (1574, 1607, 1608) are part-book prints "da cantare." The Turin tablature Giordano 3 contains 56 versets "di Ms. Claudio" (cf. Mischiati T, pp.37ff., nos.31–87; cf. note 15 above).

21. New editions of *My Ladye Nevells Booke* in Andrews N; of the *Fitzwilliam Virginal Book* (*FW*) by Fuller-Maitland and Barclay Squire (1899); of the *Parthenia* by K. Stone (1951); of the additional compositions in Tuttle B. Thus the master's total output of keyboard compositions is available in new editions.

7. Liturgical Organ Music

1. In Kleber's tablature we find the note "Judica 1520" at the end of the piece (fol.127v), but it surely refers to the date of writing rather than of composition.

2. For the *Festum Septem dolorum B. M. V.* (*Graduale Romanum,* p.600). Cf. Moser H, p.138.

3. Cf. *Antiphonale Romanum,* p.144*.

4. Also in Obrecht's *Missa super Maria zart.* Cf. the references in Baumann L, pp.110ff., where, however, a "second melody type" is erroneously invoked for Schlick's lute setting. To Baumann's references a setting by Senfl should be added; cf. A Geering and W. Altweig, eds., *Ludwig Senfl, Sämtliche Werke,* vol.II, no.5.

5. Cf. the presentation by G. Reese in *Music in the Renaissance* (1954), p.193, where sections 11–12 are combined into a single section.

6. New ed. by M. S. Kastner; cf. Chap.6, note 3. A facsimile is found in K. Berg-Kotterba's article "Schlick" in *MGG.*

7. Cf. *Ant. Rom.,* p.492.

8. This is the total content of the Zurich *Fundamentum* and the Basel copy. Päsler (cf. Chap.6, note 7) refers only to the latter.

9. Cf. the survey in *MD,* VI (1952), pp.173f. by D. Stevens. The Gloria by Philip ap Rhys is erroneously printed as a work by Redford in Pfatteicher R, p.84; it starts with the second half of V2: *Hominibus bonae voluntatis.* Cavazzoni's and Merulo's troped and therefore somewhat differently treated Glorias of the *Missa de Beata Virgine* are not considered here.

10. In Basel, Univ. Bibl. F. I. 8, p.80.

11. In Zurich, Stadtbibl. Cod. 284, fol.15v–16.

12. *Recordare* and *Sancta Maria* are reprinted in Moser F. The latter is not (as is stated there) from Kleber's tablature but from Sicher's, where it is ascribed to Johann Schrem. Schrem may perhaps have to be identified with Buchner; cf. W. R. Nef, *Der St. Galler Organist Fridolin Sicher und seine Orgaltabulatur* (1938), p.63f., note 3. The

Lutheran contrafactum of *Sancta Maria* is not (as Moser states) *Dies sind die heilgen zehn Gebot,* but *Gott der Vater wohn uns bei* (cf. Baumann L, p.141).

13. Most of them are published in Moser F with a number of errors, e.g., the tablature letters c and e are often mistaken for one another.

14. In his *Geschichte des deutschen Orgelchorals im 17. Jahrhundert* (1932).

15. Ibid., p.14.

16. For what follows cf. Ritter G, pp.113f., and W. Apel, "Die Celler Orgeltabulatur von 1601," *Mf,* XIX (1956), pp.142ff. Note that the chorale settings 1571, no.1 (*Wo Gott der Herr*) and 1583, no.10 (*Gelobet seistu*) are by Johann Walther (cf. *Sämtliche Werke,* O. Schröder, ed. (1953–61), I, pp.41, 19).

17. For tables of contents and more detailed references cf. Merian T.

18. New ed. in Ritter B, no.71.

19. Cracow, Acad. of Sciences, Ms. 1716. Cf. A. Chybinsky, "Polnische Musik und Musikkultur des 16. Jahrhunderts . . . , *SIMg,* XIII (1912), pp.463ff., and J. R. White, "The Tablature of Johannes of Lublin, *MD,* XVII (1963), pp.137ff., with a "Revised Catalogue." New ed. by J. R. White in *CEKM,* no.6, vols.I–VI (1964–67).

20. With regard to the Sanctus, cf. P. J. Thannabaur *Das einstimmige Sanctus* (1962), p.117, melody 19.

21. At my suggestion the photos were bought by the Isham Memorial Library of Harvard University in 1940. Cf. Z. Jachimecki, "Eine polnische Orgeltabulatur aus dem Jahre 1548," *ZfMw,* II (1919–20), pp.206ff.; and W.M. Inski, *The Cracow Tablature* (diss., Indiana University, 1964).

22. Ms. I/220; a photographic copy is preserved in the Isham Memorial Library of Harvard University.

23. M. Grafczýnski, *Über die Orgeltabulatur des Martin Leopolita* (diss., Vienna, 1919).

24. "Tabulatura Warszawskiego . . . ," *Muzyka Kwartalnik,* VI (1961), pp.60ff.; and "Il Manoscritto I/220 della Società di Musica di Varsavia," *L'Organo* II (1964), pp.129ff. New ed. of four pieces (by J. Golos and A. Sutkowski) in *CEKM* no.10, vol.IV (1967); complete new ed. by J. Golos, *The Organ Tablatures of Warsaw, Musical Society, Antiquitates Musicae in Polonia,* vol.15 (1968).

25. New ed. in Rokseth D.

26. Cf. Rokseth D, p.8, meas.6–13; p.23, meas.3–7; as well as the photographic reproduction (following p.XII) of a Kyrie, Gloria, etc., from a 14th-century manuscript.

27. This order is also found in a Kyrie by Andrea Gabrieli (cf. p.121).

28. It appears also in one Magnificat verse (*octavi toni, secundus versus*), which, however, is a transcription of a vocal setting by Richafort (cf. Rokseth D, p.XI).

29. The fundamental differences in the construction of the German and Latin organs are also important in this regard; for the French organs, cf. Rokseth D, for the Italian, cf. Jeppesen O, pp.24ff.

30. New ed. partially in Jeppesen O.

31. New ed. in Jeppesen O and Benvenuti M.

32. Cf. Jeppesen O, pp.102f.

33. Attempts in this direction in Benvenuti M, pp.91f., do not appear convincing.

34. Cf. K. Jeppesen, "Eine frühe Orgelmesse aus Castell' Arquato," *AfMw,* XII (1955), pp.187ff. H. C. Slim reports on several additional fascicles in "Keyboard Music at Castell' Arquato by an Early Madrigalist," *JAMS,* XV (1962), pp.35ff. New edition partially in Benvenuti M and Jeppesen O^2; a complete edition (by H. C. Slim) in *CEKM* is in preparation.

35. New ed. in Jeppesen O^2, vol.II, p.82.

36. Cf. *AfMw*, XII (1955), p.197.

37. For the original prints and the new ed. cf. p.79 and Chap. 6 note 16.

38. In Gardano's reprint of the Masses, as well as in Mischiati's new edition, the *Chirie quartus* is changed to *Chirie tertius;* obviously only the organ verses are counted here.

39. The old melody is found in A. Schering, *Geschichte der Musik in Beispielen,* no.103, and in R. Gerber, *Dufay: Sämtliche Hymnen, Das Chorwerk,* vol.14, no.7.

40. Cf. the melody on p.[49] of the *Ant. Rom.*

41. New ed. by Labat (cf. Chap.6, note 19).

42. Cf. W. Apel, "Neapolitan Links Between Cabezon and Frescobaldi," *MQ,* XXIV (1938), pp.419ff.

43. For commentary on the peculiar notation of this print cf. Apel N, p.53.

44. The new edition in Kastner R contains the ricercars and the first fantasy.

45. Cf. the table of 361 settings in O. Gombosi's *Compositione di Messer Vincenzo Capirola* (1955) (Lute Book of Capirola of 1517), pp.XXXVIff.

46. Cf. Titelouze's remark in the preface to his *Hymnes de l'Eglise* (1623): "J'ay employé en quelques lieux la dixiesme par ce qu'il y a peu d'organistes qui ne la prennent" (Guilmant A, vol.I, p.5).

47. New ed. in I. Fuser, *Antonio Valente: Versi spirituali* (1958); a selection in Torchi A, pp.45ff.

48. New ed. in M. S. Kastner, *Altitalienische Versetten* (1957). Cf. also his article "Una intabulatura d'organo italiana del 1598," *Collectanea Hist. Mus.,* II (1956), pp.237ff. In 1596 the Verona organist Gio. Matteo Asola published a print, *Canto fermo sopra Messe . . .*, which has been mentioned in connection with the history of the Italian organ versets (cf. Frotscher G, p.219); actually it contains only Gregorian melodies.

49. Cf. Anglés M, Commentary, p. 175; also H. Anglés, "El Pange lingua de Johannes Urreda," *Annuario musical,* VII (1952), pp.193ff.

50. Nor can they with the aid of M. Melnicki, *Das einstimmige Kyrie des lateinischen Mittelalters* (1954).

51. Pedrell's titles are not always authentic, but they are retained here for simplicity's sake. His transcriptions are very unreliable and are corrected here according to the original print.

52. Cf. Pedrell H III, p.LIX.

53. Facsimile edition by M. S. Kastner in *Documenta musicologica*, XI (1597). New ed. of the organ settings in Froidebise B; several also in Kinkeldey O, pp.229ff., and in Pirro A, pp.1199f. Cf. Kinkeldey O, pp.9–25; and R. Stevenson, *Juan Bermudo* (1960).

54. "Pero he sido importunato de amigos, que imprimesse alguna hecha aposta para tañer, mayormente que de Indias me han rogado por ella" (fol.113v).

55. Cf.p.6, footnote.

56. New ed. in Apel S, no.1, and Pedrell H, III, 14.

57. New ed. in Stevens M.

58. Cf. D. Stevens in *JAMS*, IX (1956), p.2; also D. Stevens' article "Preston" in *MGG.*

59. New ed. in Pfatteicher R; this edition contains a number of errors, such as calling *Felix namque* a responsory, printing several pieces twice, and giving inadequate references to the Gregorian melodies.

60. Many of them are said to be by Redford because they appear in the first fascicle of the manuscript Brit. Mus. Add. 29996, which is often considered to be a Redford autograph, though without justification.

61. The chant model of this antiphon is found in the *Antiphonale Sarisburense* (W.

Frere, ed.), vol.III, pl.287. The end of the melody as given in Pfatteicher R no longer belongs to it, but is the beginning of the succeeding canticle, *Nunc dimittis*. The end of the organ composition is given a third too low by Pfatteicher (cf. the correct transcription in Stevens M, no.39).

62. This contradicts Pfatteicher's opinion that "for the most part . . . the scheme is not carried out consistently" (p.55). Pfatteicher's frequently irregular distribution of crosses (x) results mostly from the use of inapplicable versions of the chant. Thus one finds, e.g., the correct model for Redford's *Felix namque* in the organ composition of the same name by Thomas Preston (new ed. in Stevens M), who treats the chant in strict *cantus-planus* fashion.

63. Here, too, the end is incorrectly transcribed by Pfatteicher (cf. Stevens M, no.34).

64. Cf. Pfatteicher R, p.55; also H. M. Miller, "Sixteenth-Century English Faburden Compositions for Keyboard," *MQ*, XXVI (1940), p.50.

65. E.g., in the verse *Te orbem* from Redford's *Te Deum* (Pfatteicher R, p.79).

66. Cf. Miller, note 64 above.

67. Instead of the chant melody given there, Redford actually used the version given in Fig.133, as is apparent from ℣ 2–3 of this composition.

68. Cf. the so-called *Eton Choir Book*, F. L. Harrison, ed., *Musica Britannica*, X–XI.

69. *Miserere mihi*, the last antiphon of the Sunday Compline, was a favorite subject of English organ composition; cf. Stevens M, Commentary, p.36. In a collection "Forty Wayes of 2 Pts. in One of Thomas Woodson" it serves as the basis for contrapuntal teaching examples; cf. H. M. Miller in *JAMS*, VIII (1955), pp.14ff.

70. The meaning of the term "meane" (middle part?) is not clear; cf. Pfatteicher R, Introduction, pp.63ff.

71. A *Gloria* printed in Pfatteicher R, p.84, belongs to the organ Mass by Philip ap Rhys (cf.p.154).

72. Cf. this list of sources given on p.140; the second and fourth manuscripts contain only works by Redford.

73. New ed. in Stevens A, p.3, where, however, section C is strangely omitted.

74. The latter is reproduced in facsimile in J. Wolf's *Musikalische Schrifttafeln* (1923).

75. From the communion for Marian feasts; *Grad. Rom.*, p.[80].

76. The designation *In nomine* for these pieces is explained by the fact that their ancestor was the section *in nomine* from the Benedictus of Taverner's *Missa Gloria tibi trinitas*. This section is found as a keyboard setting with the title *In nomine* in the *Mulliner Book* (no.35). Cf. W. Coates, "In Nomine," in *MGG*.

77. This is the offertory for the feast of Trinity; in the manuscript it is erroneously entitled *Benedicta*.

78. In Stevens A, p.21, a *Veni redemptor* from the anonymous hymn collection "upon the faburden" (cf.p.143) is ascribed to Preston without apparent justification. On the other hand, the interesting *Uppon la mi re* (cf.p.284) may well be by Preston, since it appears within the offertory collection ascribed to him.

79. Cf. D. Stevens, "Thomas Preston's Organ Mass," *ML*, XXXIX (1958), pp.29ff. New ed. (but in a partially incorrect transcription) in E. Kraus, *Cantantibus organis*, book 8 (1962).

80. Cf. the detailed discussion in H. M. Miller, "Fulgens praeclara," *JAMS*, II (1949), pp.97ff., and D. Stevens, "Further Light on Fulgens praeclara," *JAMS*, IX (1956), pp.1ff.

81. New ed. in Stevens A, p.24. Cf. D. Stevens, "A Unique Tudor Organ Mass," *MD*, VI (1952), pp.167ff.

82. New ed. in Stevens A, p.38.

83. New ed. in Stevens A, p.36.

84. There the composition is rather arbitrarily ascribed to Thomas Preston.

85. New ed. in Stevens M.

86. Cf. Stevens M, nos.97–102, 104, 105. These settings are also available in a new ed. in Stevens T.

87. Cf. (M.) S. Kastner, "Parellels and Discrepancies between English and Spanish Keyboard Music . . . ," *Anuario musical,* VII (1952), pp.77ff.

88. New ed. in *FW,* nos.109, 110, and in Stevens T, pp.10ff. In the following discussion we refer to the latter edition, where the note values are reduced and the bar lines are inserted more regularly.

89. Borren A, p.102, erroneously states: "Son second Choral est écrit après une autre version mélodique du Felix namque." As used in England, the melody deviates from the Roman version in two places; at *sol (c d e e c)* and at *(De)us noster (d dcefd d)*; cf. note 62 above.

90. Borren A, p.102, erroneously calls the two initial passages of I "deux courts préludes en style de ricercar ou de voluntary."

91. Cf. C. Ott, *Offertoriale sive versus offertoriorum* (1935), p.188; however, there both offertory and verse have other melodies.

92. Here, too, Borren A, p.102, speaks of "deux préludes d'un charactère imitatif."

93. E. Lowinsky, in "English Organ Music of the Renaissance," *MQ,* XXXIX (1953), p.532, interprets *melos suave* as an organ stop.

94. The third setting is found in *FW,* I, p.181, entitled *In nomine.*

95. Cf. Stevens M, Commentary, p.54.

8. Imitative Forms

1. Frotscher O, p.181. Thoughts along the same lines are expressed in O. Deffner's *Über die Entwicklung der Fantasie für Tasteninstrumente bis Sweelinck* (1927), where the fantasia is explained as an improvisatory imitation of the ricercar. Cf. also H. H. Eggebrecht's article "Terminus 'Ricercar'," *AfMw,* IX (1952), pp.137ff.

2. Cf. A. Einstein, "Vincenzo Galilei and the Instructive Duo," *ML,* XVIII (1937), pp.36off.

3. In contrast to the title of this part-book print, all the pieces except for two *Regina caeli* are called ricercars in the table of contents.

4. Cf. Jeppesen O, p.55.

5. As asserted in Jeppesen O, p.108.

6. Ibid., p.111.

7. New ed. in Benvenuti M; most of the pieces are also in Jeppesen O², II. Several ricercars by Claudio Veggio are also preserved in a manuscript from Castell' Arquato; cf. H. C. Slim, "Keyboard Music at Castell' Arquato by an Early Madrigalist," *JAMS,* XV (1962), p.35ff.

8. Cf. K. Jeppesen, *AfMw,* XII (1955), p.195. Thirteen ensemble ricercars by Julio Segni appear in an incompletely preserved part-book print, *Musica nova accomodata per cantar et sonar sopra organi* (1540). With the aid of a completely preserved part-book print of largely the same content, *Musique de Joye,* H. C. Slim has published a new edition in *Monuments of Renaissance Music* I (1964).

9. *AfMw,* XII (1955), p.195.

10. *Musik-Lexikon,* 11th ed., 1929, p.1509.

11. *Frotscher G,* p.178.

12. New ed. in *I classici della musica italiana* I (G. Benvenuti, ed., 1919); and (better) in Mischiati C. The latter contains at the end two ensemble ricercars by Girolamo, which are extant in part books. Comparison with his organ ricercars points up the difference between the two types.

13. Cf. W. Apel, "Die menschliche Stimme als Instrument," *Stimmen*, vol.15 (1949), pp.404ff.

14. Kinkeldey O, pp.245ff.

15. We read, e.g., in J. Schmidt-Görg's article "Buus" in *MGG:* "The selection of four pieces . . . ;" and in G. Sutherland's article "The Ricercari of Jacques Buus," *MQ*, XXXI (1945), p.449: "four of these ten in organ tablature." The correct facts were examined by M. S. Kastner in his edition *Jacques Buus, Ricercari III° e IV°* (1957). The Portuguese manuscript Coimbra no.48 contains several ricercars by Buus notated in open score, which may possibly be taken from the part-book prints; cf. M. S. Kastner, "Los manoscritos musicales n.ˢ 48 y 242 de la Biblioteca General de la Universidad de Coimbra," *Anuario musical*, V (1950), pp.78ff.

16. *Geschichte der Instrumentalmusik im XVI. Jahrhundert* (1878), pp.122–25.

17. *Musikgeschichte in Beispielen* (1911), pp.70ff.

18. His earliest publication, *Sacre cantiones*, appeared in 1562.

19. New ed. of the *Libro Secondo* is published in Pidoux G, vol.I, except for nos.4 and 5 (*terzo* and *quarto tono*) which appear, together with the ricercars of the *libro terzo*, in vol.II (pp.26ff).

20. A detailed treatment of the double subject will be found in E. Emsheimer's study *Johann Ulrich Steigleder* (1928), in which it is held to be the "original creation of the south German school, particularly of Erbach" (p.37). For what follows cf. W. Apel, "The Early Development of the Ricercar," *MD*, III (1949), pp.139ff.

21. New ed. (unfortunately with many errors) in Torchi A, pp.79ff. A new edition of the keyboard works of Padovano and Bertoldo in *CEKM*, 34 (K. Speer, ed., 1969). Eight ricercars that earlier authors generally ascribed to Padovano's famous contemporary, Palestrina (1524/5–94; new ed. in F. X. Haberl, *Palestrina*, vol.XXII, p.80ff.) are today held to be anonymous. In K. Jeppesen's article "Palestrina" in *MGG* they are not included in the list of works. Moreover, they are not genuine organ compositions but ensemble ricercars.

22. New ed. of these two ricercars in Torchi A, pp.55ff. For the complete new edition of Bertoldo's keyboard works cf. note 21.

23. New ed. of the *Ricercar XII. tono* in Tagliapietra A, II, p.17.

24. Some of these appear in a new ed. in Torchi A (pp.149, 161, 353).

25. Cf. Frotscher G, p.223.

26. Cf. Mischiati T, p.63; cf.Chap.6, note 15.

27. New ed. in Kastner R.

28. This is not quite correctly transcribed in Kastner R.

29. Cf. Kastner R, p.12a.

30. Ibid., p.10a.

31. New ed. in Anglés M, to which the numbers in the text refer. Nos.40 and 47 are designated "Antonio" in the table of contents (p.VI), but "Anonimo" in the musical portion; I agree with the latter. No.49 is anonymous in Venegas' collection, but it ascribed to de Soto in Ms.84 at Coimbra (cf. M. S. Kastner in *Anuario musical*, V (1950), p.83, no.84). The anonymous nos.45 and 46, and no.52, which is ascribed to Cabezón, are found in the *Musica nova* of 1540 (cf. note 8 above) as ensemble ricercars by Julio Segni.

32. Anglés M, p.173.

33. New ed. in Pedrell H, the first nine in vol.IV, pp.46–71, the last three in vol.VII,

pp.1–10; also in M. S. Kastner, *Antonio de Cabezón: Tientos und Fugen* (1958), which avoids the many errors of Pedrell's edition, but in which the order of the pieces differs from that of the original.

34. It probably also contains a number of disturbing printer's errors. The first note in measure 3 must surely be *g* (not *a*), and in the last measure on p.7 the first four notes in the alto are certainly intended to be read a fourth lower. In the coda the single measure in sixteenth notes (p.8, brace 3, meas.6) should probably be read in note values of double length.

35. New ed. in Froidebise B, pp.12ff; no.1 also in Pirro A, p.1200, nos.2 and 3 in Kinkeldey O, p.229. "Resabio" means vice or error, here probably "deviation" or modulation to another key.

36. Pirro A, p.1198.

37. New ed. in Anglés M, nos.38 and 39. In Pedrell A and in Muset E, Vila is represented by a tiento which is really by Cabezón (Venegas no.32).

38. Cf. Anglés M, commentary to nos.38–39, pp.172f.

39. Cf. note 31. A whole group, which in the original table of contents is designated as *Tientos de vihuela* (nos.56–73), are transcriptions from lute pieces; cf. J. Ward, "The Editorial Methods of Venegas de Henestrosa," *MD*, VI (1952), pp.105ff.

40. Cf. M. S. Kastner, "Los manuscritos musicales . . . de Coimbra," *Anuario musical*, V (1950), pp.78ff. New ed. in M. S. Kastner, *Antonio Carreira: Drie Fantasieën*, Ed. Harmonia, Hilversum (n.d.).

41. New ed. of the Passereau chanson in H. Expert, *Maîtres musiciens de la Renaissance française* (separate edition no.30); of Josquin's in A. Smijers, *Josquin des Prés: Werken*, Secular Works no.15.

42. *Petit Jacquet* is probably by Courtois, *Le bergier* (= *Un gay bergier*) by Crecquillon, *Con lei foss'io* by Giaches Ponte.

43. Gioseffo Guami of Lucca (c.1540–1611) published several collections of canzonas. At best the *Partitura per sonare delle canzonette alla francese* (1601) may have been intended for the keyboard. It contains twenty pieces, written in only two parts, soprano and bass, but the first one, *La Guamina* is found in four parts in Woltz's tablature (new ed. in Ritter B, no.5).

44. New ed. of two of these in Torchi A, pp.49ff.

45. New ed. in G. Benvenuti, *Istituzioni e Monumenti dell' Arte Italiana* I (1931), p.86.

46. Cf. Merian T, p.262. A *fuga* by Brignoli, printed in Ritter B, no.6, shows the unmistakable character of ensemble music, except for the clavieristic coda, which is surely Schmid's work.

47. New eds. of some of the fugues in Ritter B (nos.68, 69), Pirro A (p.1223), Gauss O, and Metzger O. The *Fuga prima* is also found in Lynar B 1; new edition in Moser C, I, p.18, as a work by David Abel.

48. New ed. in Ritter B, no.70.

49. New ed. of two in Merian T, p.278. In Frotscher G, p.169 (". . . Reihe von Fugen . . . über die zwölf Töne . . ."), the fugues are confused with the collection of *Zwölf toni oder modi* (cf.p.220) that follow them.

50. New ed. in Merian T, p.58.

51. New ed. of one in Ritter B, no.62, of the other in *MfM*, XX (1888), Beilage (R. Eitner), p.109.

52. New ed. in Pidoux G, IV, p.3.

53. New ed. in P. Froidebise, *Tomas de Santa Maria . . .* (Orgue et Liturgie no.49); some also in Villalba A, Kinkeldey O, Kaller L (vol.III). Tomás' explanations and ex-

amples of the practice of *notes inégales* (cf. Kinkeldey O, p.41) are especially interesting.

54. In Paris, Bibl. nat. frç. 9152, containing many errors; facsimile in *MGG*, II, p. 1707.

55. Several sections of the first fantasy appear in Pirro A, p.1203.

56. New ed. of five fantasies by H. Expert in *Edition populaire française*, nos.2645– 49. Cf. also H. Quittard in A. Lavignac, *Encyclopédie . . .* I,3, p.1215.

57. Cf. Frotscher G, p.667.

58. New ed. of twelve fantasies in *Monumenta musicae Belgicae*, IV.

59. New ed. by J. Golos and A. Sutkowski in *CEKM*, no.10, vol.III (1967).

60. Cf. Ritter G, p.107.

61. Cf. Frotscher G, p.161.

62. New ed. in Stevens M, p.9.

63. New ed. in Stevens T, p.8.

64. New ed. of the original edition in *Shakespeare Association Facsimiles*, XIV (London, 1937), p.180.

65. Cf. the fine description in Borren A, p.188.

66. Cf. H. Grace's article "Voluntary" in Grove's *Dictionary of Music and Musicians*.

67. New ed. in Andrews N, pp.243, 156, 140.

68. Cf. the commentary in Andrews N.

9. Free Forms

1. In the manuscript we find the added legend "O. Zellis Mariae," probably meaning "organist at Mariazell."

2. New ed. in Merian T, pp.60ff.

3. Cf. H. J. Moser in *Festschrift für Guido Adler* (1930), p.84.

4. Cf. W. Apel, "Drei plus Drei plus Zwei = Vier plus Vier," *AM*, XXXII (1960), pp.29ff.

5. New ed. by A. Wilhelmer in *Music alter Meister*, book 9 (Graz: Akad. Verlagsanstalt, 1958). Cf. H. Federhofer, "Eine Kärntner Orgeltabulatur . . . ," (*Carinthia* I, Jahrgang 142, pp.330ff. The tablature is written entirely in letters; it is the earliest instance of the so-called new German organ tablature.

6. New ed. in *Cantantibus organis*, book 9, edited by E. Kraus, who calls the manuscript *Neresheim Organ Book*.

7. New ed. in J. R. White, *Johannes of Lublin: Tablature of Keyboard Music, CEKM*, no.6, vol.I (1964).

8. New ed. in Libera G, vol.I.

9. Cf. Anglés M, p.215.

10. Cf.Chap.8, note 49.

11. An exception is no.59, which, as the editor himself notes (vol.I, p.171), is not by Bull.

12. Cf. L. Schrade, "Ein Beitrag zur Geschichte der Tokkata," *ZfMw*, VIII (1925/26), pp.610ff.

13. Two more toccatas by Andrea are found in Diruta's *Il Transilvano;* cf.p.225.

14. New ed. in Pidoux G, vol.I, pp.11, 18.

15. New ed. of the first one in Kinkeldey O, p.301; of the second one in Tagliapietra A, vol.I, p.99. Cf.Chap.8, note 21.

16. Nos.4 and 5 are ricercars by Padovano; cf.p.182.

17. In Krebs's study of *Il Transilvano, VfMw*, VIII (1892), pp.344ff., as well as in Frotscher G (pp.194, 217), incorrect figures are given regarding the number of toccatas

(seventeen instead of thirteen). This error apparently stems from a superficial reading of the page titles, which are in part erroneously printed. New ed. of nos.1, 2, and 13 by Krebs; of nos.1 and 7–13 in Torchi A.

18. New ed. in Libera M in three books, which are referred to in what follows as I, II, and III; some also in Torchi A; Ritter B; Tagliapietra A, II; Guilmant A, vol.X (from the *Liber Cruciferorum*); etc.

10. Dance Music

1. Cf.Chap.5, note 30.

2. A genuine *bassa danza*, also based on the spagna tune, is found in Petrucci's *Intabolatura de lauto* (1507).

3. W. Merian, *Die Tabulaturen des Organisten Hans Kotter* (1916), p.37.

4. Two other keyboard arrangements of the spagna were written by Antonio de Cabezón (Anglés M, no.5) and by Rocco Rodio (cf.p.125).

5. Cf. O. Gombosi, "Der Hoftanz," *AM*, VII (1935), pp. 50ff.

6. The designation derives from the song "Wie es dem Bentzenauer zu Kopfsteyn ergangen ist" (referring to the battle of Kopfstein, 1504); cf. F. Böhme, *Altdeutsches Liederbuch* (1877), p.47.

7. Cf. K. Jeppesen, "Ein altitalienisches Tanzbuch," *Festschrift für K. G. Fellerer* (1962), pp.245ff. I cannot agree with the opinion proposed there that the last two pieces are something like "liturgical dances." They are simple hymn settings that have nothing to do with dances. New ed. in K. Jeppesen, *Balli antichi veneziani* (1962).

8. New ed. of *Recercade IV* and *VIII* in M. Schneider, *Diego Ortiz . . .*, pp.117, 130.

9. *Pavana con su glosa*, by Antonio de Cabezón; new ed. in Anglés M, p.191.

10. The second form is also found in Attaingnant's print; cf.Fig.236.

11. Cf. L. Schrade, "Tänze aus einer anonymen italienischen Tabulatur," *ZfMw*, X, (1927/28), pp.499ff. New ed. by D. Heartz in *CEKM* no.8 (1965).

12. New ed. by D. Heartz in *CEKM*, no.8 (1965), to which the numbers in the text refer. The meters and phrases cited refer to the original print, indicated in the new edition by small bars. Cf. W. Apel, "Attaingnant: Quatorze Gaillardes," *Mf*, XIV (1961), pp. 361ff.

13. In the new edition all the galliards are presented in 6/4.

14. The print includes two more dances of the passamezzo-antico type, pavanes nos. 23 and 26. Cf. W. Apel, "Attaingnant: Quatorze Gaillardes," *Mf*, XIV (1961), pp.367ff.

15. Cf., e.g., Claude Gervaise, *Livre de danceries* of 1550 (new ed. in H. Expert, *Maîtres musiciens de la Renaissance*, vol.23, p.28); also *FW*, I, p.299 (Philips); *FW*, II, p.111 (Byrd); *FW*, I, p.99 (Bull).

16. New ed. in A. Chybinski, *36 Tancóv . . .* (1948), containing some mistakes. In what follows the numbers cited correspond to this edition.

17. Cf. R. Schwartz, *Ott. Petrucci, Frottole* (1935), p.37. Dances nos.7 and 19 employ the same melody a third higher (or is this the tenor of the frottola?).

18. New ed. by W. Apel in *CEKM*, no.2 (1963). Cf. W. Apel, "Tänze und Arien . . . ," *AfMw*, XVII (1960), pp.51ff. Mr. A. Curtis has pointed out to me a *Passamezzo antico* (twelve variations) and a *Pavane la Paganina* from Facoli's *Libro Primo*, which appear to have been preserved in manuscript.

19. The *clamatione* of Diruta; cf. C. Krebs in *VfMw*, VIII (1892), p.348.

20. Cf. "Die Wiener Tanzkomposition . . . ," *Studien zur Musikwissenschaft*, VIII (1921), pp.45ff.

21. New ed. by R. E. M. Harding (1949). A highly irregular, often confused way of

inserting bar lines in the original print was unfortunately taken over into the new edition, and renders the recognition of structural details rather difficult. It is necessary to replace these bar lines with regularly drawn ones to understand the structure of the dances.

22. Tables of contents for 2–7, as well as numerous transcriptions, are given in Merian T. Note that all of Merian's transcriptions from these sources are reduced 1:4, a reduction that is not to their advantage.

23. Cf. Ritter G, p.111.

24. New ed. in F. Dawes, *Schott's Anthology of Early English Keyboard Music*, book 1. The first piece in this book, *La Belle fyne*, is originally for an ensemble.

25. New ed. in J. Wolf, *Music of Earlier Times* (1946). A somewhat abbreviated edition is given in Apel M, vol. II, p.5. In Andrews N, p.XXIII, this composition is called a "crude piece" (!).

26. On "dompe" ("dump," Irish for lament) cf. J. Ward in *JAMS*, IV (1951), pp.111ff.

27. The *Kyngs Pavyn* occurs as a four-part ensemble piece, entitled *Pavane Lesquercade*, in Jean d'Estrée's *Tiers livre de danseries* (1559); cf. Ward D, p.XII.

28. New ed. in Stevens M, no.116.

29. In the new edition (ibid.), the sharp before the F is interpreted as a natural sign for the E♭ in the final chord (cf. Commentary, p.66), a conjecture that seems completely unjustified.

30. New ed. in Ward D.

31. Cf. the commentaries in Ward D.

32. The double bar at the end of measure 39 belongs to measure 40. In the commentary in Ward D this dance is related to a tune known as *Chi passa per questa strada*, but the reasons for the connection are not too convincing.

33. *My Ladye Nevells Booke*, written in 1591, offers a date *ante quem* for a number of the pavanes and galliards. Facoli's and Radino's prints appeared in 1588 and 1592, respectively.

34. E. H. Meyer, "Allemande," in *MGG*.

35. New ed. by R. A. Harman, p.297.

36. New ed. by A. Curtis in *Monumenta musica Neerlandica* III (1961). The clavier book of Elizabeth Eysbock of Frankfurt am Main, containing German and English dances, dates from the same time; cf. Th. Dart's article in *Svensk tidskrift för Musikforskning*, 44 (1962), pp.5ff.

11. Variation Forms

1. Cf. R. Haas, *Aufführungspraxis der Musik* (1930), pp. 103f. The title does not mean "The Windmills of Paris," but refers to the Parisian composer Pierre de Moulins. New edition of the rondeau with the ornamental versions (taken from other sources) in F. Kammerer, *Die Musikstücke des Prager Kodex XI E 9* (1931), p.145.

2. Correa de Arauxo, *Libro de tientos* (1626), adds the following note to his glosas on *Guardame las vacas*: "o por mejo dezir sobre el seculorum del primero tono" (cf. Kastner L, vol.II, p.213).

3. In measures 10–12 and 15–17 the notes should probably not be dotted but should have simple values that form hemiolas, as can be seen in the glosa.

4. Cf.pp.215f. and the article mentioned in Chap.9, note 4.

5. In Ward D, p.11, this piece is called "Variations on the Romanesca," but in the original it is untitled. Its interpretation as a passamezzo antico is borne out by its duple meter, which to my knowledge does not occur in the romanesca. On the other hand, the

theme and all the variations do not start with the tonic (*G minor*) but, as in the romanesca, with the mediant (*B flat* major).

6. New eds. in Chilesotti P and in Tagliapietra A, vol.V, p.80.

7. New ed. of the *Romanesca* in M. S. Kastner, *Silva Ibérica* (1954), p.4.

8. Cf. W. Chappell, *Old English Popular Music* (rev. ed., H. E. Wooldridge, 1892).

9. The chanson is printed in Smijers' edition of Josquin's works, *Missen* I, p.105, as an anonymous composition. The attribution to Busnois is found in a manuscript of the Segovia cathedral; cf. H. Anglés, "Un Manuscrit inconnu . . . ," *AM*, VIII (1936), p.12, no.110.

10. New ed. in A. Schering, *Geschichte der Musik in Beispielen* (1931), no.86.

11. Both may be found in the Montpellier codex; new ed. in Y. Rokseth, *Polyphonies de XIIIe siècle* (1935–39), nos.328 and 267.

12. New ed. in *DTÖ* VII, vol.15 (G. Adler and O. Koller, eds.), p. 105.

13. New ed. in Stevens A, p.13; cf. Chap.7, note 78.

14. Cf. the observations on Gibbons' variations on *The Hunt's up*, p.323.

12. Intabulations

1. In Pedrell's new edition most of these pieces are omitted (Pedrell H, vol.VII, p.IV). Some of them are published in M. S. Kastner, *Antonio de Cabezon: Claviermusik* (Ed. Schott 4286).

2. New ed. in Apel S, nos.3, 2, 4, 5.

PART III. THE FIRST HALF OF THE SEVENTEENTH CENTURY

13. England

1. New ed. in Th. Dart, *Keyboard Works, Thomas Morley*, 2 vols. (1959). Some pieces are also in *FW*.

2. No.1 is also in *FW*, II, p.209; no.2 in *FW*, II, p.173. The latter is a *Pavana Lachrymae*, i.e., an arrangement of Dowland's famous lute air *Flow my tears*. Other arrangements of this air are by Byrd (*FW*, II, p.42), G. Farnaby (*FW*, II, p.472), Sweelinck, and Melchior Schildt.

3. Th. Dart regards the raising of the g to g♯ as a scribe's error.

4. In Uppsala, Univ. Bibl. 408 (formerly J. Mus. 408, also known as the Düben Ms.) this composition is called *Pavana Scharlabaget* (obviously Charles Paget). Philips was in the service of Lord Thomas Paget, Charles's older brother, from 1585 to 1590.

5. In *FW* the title reads *Pavana Doloroso Treg. set by Peter Philips;* Tregian is usually considered the penman of the *FW*.

6. The fame of the *Pavana Doloroso* can be seen from the fact that it reappears in three German manuscripts: Berlin Staatsbibl. 40316 (formerly mus.191), Uppsala Univ. Bibl. Ms.408, and Lynar Tablature A 1. The first of these manuscripts also contains four galliards that do not appear in the *FW* (fol. 7v, 8v, 30v, 31) and a galliard to the passamezzo (fol.4v), which is somewhat different from the one in *FW*, I, p.306.

7. New ed. in Guilmant A, vol.X, p.11.

8. New eds. in Ritter B, p.51, and in Guilmant A, vol.X, pp.83, and 155, where it is

given with the vocal setting and a variant from a print of 1615. Two more variants of the intabulation may be found in *FW*, I, p.312, and in Lynar A 1.

9. The index of *FW* lists two more fantasies, but they are intabulations of two of his *Canzonets* (*FW*, II, p.333 = *The Wavering Planet; FW*, II, p.340 = *Daphne on the Rainbow*); this is also true of *FW*, II, p.330 (= *Ay me poore heart*).

10. A fine characterization of Farnaby's work is given in Borren A, p.228. This reference seems particularly necessary because of a more recent study in which—and it is hard to believe one's eyes—Farnaby is called "medieval" and "archaic" (cf. W. Mellers' article "Farnaby" in *MGG*).

11. New ed. of the last two pieces in F. Dawes, *Two Elizabethan Keyboard Duets* (London: Schott, no.10110). In Seiffert G, p.36, a ricercar for two instruments by A. Gabrieli is mentioned, but I have not been able to locate it.

12. The manuscript Brit. Mus. Add. 23623 was prepared shortly after Bull's death by Guilelmus à Messaus at Antwerp, and was apparently based on material he found in Bull's estate. But he proceeded carelessly and uncritically, and included pieces by Byrd, Frescobaldi, Macque, and others, along with Bull's. Nevertheless, in H. H. Miller, "John Bull's Organ Works," *ML*, XXVIII (1947), pp.25ff., the unsigned pieces of the manuscript are regarded as Bull's. For the Vienna manuscript cf. J. H. van der Meer, "The Keyboard Works in the Vienna Bull-Manuscript," *TVer*, XVIII (1965), pp.72ff.; for the Paris manuscript cf. M. C. Mass, "Seventeenth-Century English Keyboard Music . . ." (diss., Yale University, 1969); and M. C. Maas, ed., *Songs and Dances for Keyboard from 17th-Century England* (New Haven: Yale University Press, 1970).

13. They are, respectively, Glyn E, pp.128–34; and M. H. Glyn, *Complete Keyboard Works of John Bull* (London, 1930), of which only two books appeared.

14. This edition also contains some things that are doubtful and open to question, but this can hardly be avoided because of the complex source situation. A particularly crass case is *God save the King* (no.32). On the basis of a 19th-century copy, it is ascribed to Bull, but in Lynar A1 it is signed Joann Pieters, and is therefore published correctly in Seiffert S (I, no.12) as a work by Sweelinck. Cf. M. Reimann, *Die Autoren der Fuge No. 23 . . .*, *Mf*, XVI (1965), pp.166ff.

15. Near 1700 this composition appears as a work by Poglietti in several manuscripts, among them a luxury print entitled *Musica Aulica Authore Alexandro de Poglietti*; cf. Riedel Q, pp.142ff.

16. Cf. the note in *FW*, I, p.183, and Borren A, p.209.

17. Other instruments of this type are described in a print of 1645 by Martino Pesenti (cf.p.486).

18. Cf. Borren A, p.140.

19. Two pieces by Bull entitled *Pavana Sinfoniae* are extant, but the one discussed here is not included in the new edition because the editor ascribes it, without sufficient reason, it seems to me, to Jacques Champion (cf. Th. Dart in *ML*, XL, 1959, p.279). It is published in H. F. Redlich, *Harpsichord Pieces from Dr. Bull's Flemish Tablature* (1958).

20. Three pieces are printed in J. A. Fuller Maitland, *Twenty-five Pieces . . . from Benjamin Cosyn's Virginal Book* (1923); four others in M. H. Glyn, *Thirty Virginal Pieces* (1927). A catalog of Cosyn's works may be found in Glyn E, pp.141f.

21. This manuscript also contains pieces from Frescobaldi's *Toccate, Libro primo* of 1616.

22. The prelude, the *Verse of four Parts*, and *Upon the Sharpe* are published in *Schott's Anthology of Early Keyboard Music*, book 4 (1951).

23. New ed. by H. Ferguson, *Complete Keyboard Works of William Tisdall* (London, 1957). I believe that *Coranto no.6* is a jig.

24. New ed. by H. M. Glyn, *Th. Weelkes, Pieces for Keyed Instruments* (London, 1924). The second voluntary is anonymous in the source (New York Public Library, Drexel 5612).

25. *Three Voluntaries for Double Organ* (Novello, 1956) and *Two Toys and a Jigg* (Schott, 1958), both edited by S. Jeans and J. Steele.

26. *Thomas Tomkins: Keyboard Music* (S. Tuttle, ed.) in *Musica Britannica*, V (1955).

27. It is possible that the dates refer to the time of copying, and that the works were written a little earlier.

28. For the older portions, cf. the observations on pp.147, 154–56, and 318.

29. No. 57 does carry a date, which Tuttle reads as 1647, but which may be read equally well as 1617 or 1627.

30. In the manuscript no.40 carries the designation "Arthur Philips," and is therefore ascribed to this otherwise unknown composer in *Schott's Anthology of Early Keyboard Music*, book 5. Tuttle is probably justified in ascribing it to Tomkins and assuming that the subject may be by A. Philips.

31. One of these is reproduced in A. T. Davison and W. Apel, *Historical Anthology of Music*, vol.I (1946), no.176.

32. Cf. facsimile no.3 in Apel N.

33. This stylistic relationship is another reason that I doubt the date of 1647 (cf. note 29).

34. H. M. Glyn, *Orlando Gibbons, Complete Keyboard Works*, 5 books (1925–26).

35. G. Hendrie, *Orlando Gibbons: Keyboard Music, Musica Britannica*, vol.XX.

36. I would consider some of the "spurious" pieces to be genuine, especially no.58 (Glyn IV, no.13), because of its source and its style.

37. New ed. nos.5 and 6, the latter given in Glyn IV, no.3, as *A short Prelude*. The two "voluntaries" in Glyn IV, nos.1 and 2, do not appear in the *Musica Britannica* edition.

38. In the *Musica Britannica* edition a variation set on a *Sarabrand* (Glyn II, p.4) is justifiably held to be a work by Gibbons' pupil Richard Portman (cf. the commentary to no.52).

14. The Netherlands

1. A *Bergamaska* with nine variations and an *Allemande de chapelle* with five variations were recently published by J. H. Schmidt in *Exempla Musica Neerlandica*, II (1965), from the *Celle Klavierbuch* (1662). Three additional, rather unimportant pieces from the so-called Leningrad manuscript have been published in *Mon. Mus. Neerlandica* III, pp.67–69. The fundamental study in the field is B. van den Sigtenhorst Meyer, *Jan P. Sweelinck en zijn instrumentale muziek*, 2nd ed. (1946); his stylistic analysis (pp.119ff.) is particularly valuable as a supplement to our observations. A more recent study by R. L. Tusler, *The Organ Music of Sweelinck* (1958), goes rather astray in its remarks on history and style, but offers valuable pictorial material on Dutch organs. The latest study, Alan Curtis' *Sweelinck's Keyboard Music* (1969), is excellent, but was published too late to be considered here.

2. Regarding no.12 cf.Chap.13, note 14.

3. For an echo fantasy wrongly attributed to Giovanni Gabrieli cf.pp.411f.

4. Cf. Schierning Ü, p.71, and W. Breig, "Der Umfang des choralgebundenen Orgelwerkes von Sweelinck," *AfMw*, XVII (1960), pp.258ff. The latter also reports on a few new discoveries (p.264). No.55 is by Henderick Speuy (cf.p.338).

5. For the hymn cf. *Variae preces* (1901), p.29; for the antiphon cf. *Antiphonale Romanum*, p.144*, also p.87 above.

6. In Lynar B 1 these 4 settings commence a series of 17 arrangements of this chorale —among them settings by Andreas Düben, Peter Hasse, and Gottfried Scheidt. They are published in Gerdes C, p.130, and in Moser A. The first 4 settings are signed M. J. P., which is erroneously interpreted as Magister Jacob Praetorius by Moser. M. J. P. is found in many manuscripts as the abbreviation for Magister Jan Pieterszon (Sweelinck). Another 6 settings of *Allein Gott* are found in the Celle tablature of 1601 (cf.pp.347f.).

7. Cf. the discussion on p.266. For two recently discovered variation works cf. note 1 above.

8. Van den Sigtenhorst Meyer (cf. note 1 above), p.187.

9. The same melody is used by Farnaby under the title *The New Sa-Hoo* (FW, II, p.161).

10. This has been pointed out by Sigtenhorst Meyer, p.187 (cf. note 1 above).

11. Cf. *FW*, pp.42, 173, 472.

12. Cf. New ed., p.LXII.

13. Cf. Ritter G, p.50.

14. Cf. Borren P, p.148.

15. Cf. Pirro A, p.1249.

16. New ed. by F. Noske, *Henderick Speuy, Psalm Preludes* (1962).

17. New ed. in *CEKM*, no.26 (1969).

18. According to Ritter G, pp.49 and 52, Philips was court organist to the Governor, Archduke Albrecht, and Cornet served his wife, Infanta Clara Eugenia, in the same capacity.

19. Cf. Borren P, p.184. This author devotes a fine and well-conceived presentation to Cornet (pp.175–85).

20. Cf. Seiffert G, pp.89f.

21. Liége, Bibl. de l' Université Ms.888; new ed. in Guilmant A, vol.X.

22. Clearly this is an English composer. A few courantes of his are also preserved in the manuscript Berlin Staatsbibl. 40316.

15. Germany

1. Two pieces appear in Ritter G, p.107, and Ritter B, nos.72–73. The original manu-script is lost (last known to be in the private collection of Miss Eva Richter), but a rather complete photographic copy is preserved in the Berlin Staatsbibliothek (Bü 84). Cf. W. Apel, "Die Celler Orgeltabulatur von 1601," *MF*, XIX (1966), pp.142ff. New ed. by W. Apel in *CEKM*, no.17 (in preparation).

2. Cf. Frotscher G, p.383, note. 1.

3. Cf. Schierning Ü, p. 5, note 5.

4. Ritter B, no.73 reproduces only 60 measures.

5. Selections appear in *DdT*, vol.23, H. Leichtentritt, ed. (1905).

6. The usual designation of this manuscript as the Johan-Bahr tablature is misleading, especially when the name is corrupted to Bähr (as in Frotscher G, p.431). Cf. Hedar B, p.18, and Schierning Ü, p.24.

7. New ed. by C. G. Rayner in *CEKM*, no.4: *Hieronymus Praetorius: Magnificats for Organ* (1963).

8. New ed. by W. Gurlitt in *AfMw*, III (1946), pp.135ff., and in K. Matthaei, *Michael Praetorius, Sämtliche Orgelwerke* (1930). The latter also includes a sinfonia that is cer-tainly meant for an ensemble. Cf. p.6, footnote.

9. Cf. C. Ott, *Offertoriale sive versus Offertoriorum* (1935), p.122.

10. Matthaei (cf. note 8) calls these pieces fantasies, but in this book this term is reserved for another type (cf.p.355).

11. New eds. of the chorales in Gerdes C, of the preambles in Seiffert O, book 2. Regarding the settings that are signed M. J. P. in Lynar B 1, cf.Chap.14 note 6.

12. In Gerdes C, p.166, this is changed to a dotted rhythm: (♩.♫)

13. In Kotter's *Fantasia in ut;* cf.p.205.

14. New ed. in Seiffert O, book 21; one also in Moser C, I, p. 18, combined with a fugue that is anonymous in the manuscript but is actually by Simon Lohet (cf.Chap.8, note 47).

15. New ed. by M. Seiffert in *DdT*, vol.I (1892), and in G. Harms and C. Mahrenholz, *Samuel Scheidts Werke*, vols.VI–VII.

16. New ed. in Harms and Mahrenholz, vol.V, called suppl. in what follows. An *Alamanda* with variations occurs in the Turin tablature Foà 8 (cf. Mischiati T, p.115; and Chap.6, note 15).

17. Cf.Chap.63: *Delli contrapunti a tre voci, che si fanno con qualche obbligo.* Such canons are also found in the hymn cycle "uppon the faburden" in Brit. Mus. Add.29996 (cf.p.156) and in vocal music by Isaac and Josquin.

18. Two of them are nos.4 and 5 in the suppl.; nos.6 and 7 in the suppl. are doubtful.

19. A more detailed classification of the four-part settings is given by M. Seiffert in *VfMw*, VII (1891), pp.206f.; but I do not agree with his statement that in these settings "all forms are represented." In G. Kittler, *Geschichte des protestantischen Orgelchorals* (1931), pp.55f., the two- and three-part settings are also considered.

20. This technique occurs earlier in Buchner under various titles; cf.p.94.

21. Cf. Scheidt's remark on the *imitatio violistica* at the end of Part I (in Seiffert's new ed., p.84).

22. Scheidt's cycle of Magnificats includes the *tonus peregrinus* in addition to the usual eight tones. With this tune and with the translation *Meine Seele erhebet den Herrn,* the Magnificat became part of the repertoire of the Protestant chorale. Cf.pp.376ff.

23. The same canon appears on a sheet of music that Scheidt holds in his hand in his portrait at the beginning of the *Tabulatura nova.*

24. New ed. by C. Mahrenholz, *S. Scheidt, Das Görlitzer Tabulaturbuch* (1940).

25. Cf. *Grundlage einer Ehrenpforte* (1740), pp.329, 394.

26. New ed. of 11 preludes and 4 imitative pieces in Seiffert O, book 1; of 10 organ chorales in Gerdes C; of the 4 organ chorales from the Pelplin tablatures in J. Golos and A. Sutkowski, *Keyboard Music from Polish Manuscripts, CEKM,* 10, vol.II (1967). New ed. of 35 organ chorales in G. Fock, *Scheidemann: Choralbearbeitungen* (1966), several of which are preserved anonymously and have not been authenticated; some have been transposed "at the discretion of the publisher" (cf.p.149), and this is rather irritating. The Magnificat settings from the Calvör manuscripts, which are apparently very significant, have not been published yet.

27. New ed. in Reimann L, p.76.

28. In the new ed. in Moser C II, p.43, the note values are halved, and two original measures are contracted into one.

29. Cf. her study "Pasticcios and Parodien in norddeutschen Klaviertabulaturen," *MF*, VIII (1955), pp.265ff.

30. New ed. by Bo Lundgren (n.d.).

31. In Gerdes C two measures are omitted after measure 44.

32. W. Breig describes these compositions as "works signed in the sources with Scheidemann's initials but of doubtful authenticity" (cf.p.111, nos.75, 76, 77, 79). But his

arguments (pp.15f.) are not convincing, and in any event, are not sufficiently specific. In general, it seems to me that original ascriptions, except for obvious errors, deserve greater weight than "style-critical" ones in anonymous works, such as Breig's group B, pp.110f.

33. New ed. in Reimann L, p.4.

34. An *Alleluia* printed in Reimann L, p.86, is an intabulation of a double-choir setting by Hassler.

35. Cf. H. Panum, "Melchior Schild oder Schildt," *MfM*, XX (1888), pp.27ff.

36. New ed. by F. Noske in *Monumenta Musica Neerlandica*, vol.II (1959), p.40.

37. New ed. in Pirro A, p.1234.

38. New eds. in Gerdes C and in Moser C, vol.I. Moser also prints a *Nun komm der Heiden Heiland* under Siefert's name (p.36), but it is really anonymous.

39. New ed. in Seiffert O, book 20.

40. Cf. the remark in Schierning Ü, p.40.

41. New ed. in Seiffert O, book 21.

42. New ed. of nos.1–3 in Gerdes C and Moser C; of nos.4–5 in Seiffert O, book 21. Moser also ascribes the anonymous variations VIII and IX of *Allein Gott in der Höh* to Andreas Düben, without justification.

43. This technique is also found in Scheidemann's works, e.g., in *In dich hab ich gehoffet* (cf. Gerdes C, p.187, brace 1).

44. New eds. of the preludes in Seiffert O, book 2; of the chorale settings of Gerdes C, nos.43–45. Two additional pieces, *Gleichwie das Feuer* and *Paduana lagrime* (after Dowland), are preserved in the Copenhagen copy of Voigtländer's *Odes* (cf. note 35 above). Cf. also below, note 57.

45. New ed. in Moser A, p.42. The next arrangement, *Per fugas*, may also be by Karges.

46. New ed. of the first three in Seiffert O, book 2. Neunhaber's *Ich ruf zu dir*, a lovely chorale motet for three manuals and pedals, is found in Lynar B 8.

47. Modern editions of these works are almost all limited to excerpts, which do not afford a satisfactory insight. Pirro A, pp.1289ff., offers six substantial sections from the *Toccata*. Only the first verse of the Magnificat (the excerpt in Straube C is obviously not taken from the Lüneburg Ms. but from a "modernized" version in the Walther Ms.) and the first verse of *Ich hab mein Sach* (M. Seiffert in *Allgemeine Musik-Zeitung* 21, 1894, p.619) are available. Concerning *Lass mich dein sein* cf. note 49 below.

48. Cf. note 47.

49. New ed. in Ritter B, p.207; in Straube A, p.98; and by M. Seiffert in *Algemeine Musik-Zeitung*, 21 (1894), p.619 (as *Herzlich tut mich verlangen*).

50. A substantial excerpt from *Was fürchst du*, in Pierro A, p.1305, is all that is available in a modern edition.

51. Cf. note 6, above.

52. New ed. of four pieces in Pirro A, pp.1232ff.

53. They once belonged to Count Lynar of Lübbenau and are also called Lübbenau tablatures, e.g., in *MGG*. Tables of contents are given in Schierning Ü, pp.27ff. M. Seiffert's assertion (*J. P. Sweelinck, Werken* I, pp. IIf.) that Lynar A 1 is a Weckmann autograph has no basis in fact, nor does his date of 1637. Cf. also W. Breig, "Die Lübbenauer Tabulaturen Lynar A 1 and A 2," *AfMw*, XXV (1968), pp.96ff., 223ff., especially pp.227, 232.

54. With some justification some of these pieces have been incorporated in Seiffert's Sweelinck edition. Others have been published in Moser C, though with very questionable interpretations of the initials. B. D. H., e.g., is interpreted as Georg Wolfgang Drucken-

meier Hallensis, and M. W. C. B. M. as Magister Wilhelm Carges Berolinensis Marchicus, whom Moser identifies as Wilhelm Karges, born 1613 (vol.I, p.6), although the setting of *O Mensch bewein dein Sünde gross*, which is attributed to him, is dated 1628. The two pieces ascribed to Johan Lorentz do not bear the monogram J. L., but are anonymous.

55. A table of contents appears in Schierning Ü. Cf. also *Katalog der Musikalien der Ratsbücherei Lüneburg*, F. Welter, ed. (1950), although it is rather poorly arranged.

56. Reimann L, and John R. Shannon, *The Free Organ Compositions from the Lueneburg Tablatures,* 2 books (1958).

57. In Shannon's new ed. nos.17–24 are said to be "probably by Melchior Schildt," but in Welter's catalog only nos.22, 23, and 29 of the edition are cited under Schildt; in both cases the ascriptions appear to be entirely arbitrary. Manuscript KN 149 contains six short preludes signed C. S. (Shannon, nos.60–65); Welter (*Katalog*, pp.156f.) resolves this monogram most questionably as Samuel Capricornus.

58. A lovly setting of *Ach Gott vom Himmel* is available in Straube C.

59. Cf. J. H. Schmidt, "Eine unbekannte Quelle . . . ," *AfMw*, XXII (1965), pp.1ff.

60. A partial new ed. is available in P. Rubardt, *Spielstücke des 17. und 18. Jahrhunderts,* vol.I (1940). In the copy in the Berlin Staatsbibliothek (the only preserved one?) the first page, which contains the first prelude, is lost, but it is reprinted in R. Wustmann's *Musikgeschichte Leipzigs* (1909), p.223.

61. New ed. by F. Schreiber and B. A. Wallner, in *DTB*, XXI–XXIV (vol.30, 1924); and of some pieces in Ritter B and Metzger O. New ed. of the *Harmonia organica* by R. Walter (1966). Cf. also R. Baum, *Kindermann: Stücke für Klavier* (1929).

62. Cf. E. Epstein, *Der französische Einfluss auf die deutsche Klaviersuite im 17. Jahrhundert* (1940), Musical Appendix nos.26a, 26b.

63. New ed. by J. Watelet in *Monumenta Musicae Belgicae* IV, pp.73ff. Nos.5 and 8 are anonymous, but no.5 uses the same subject as the *Fuga suavissima*. In J. Robijns's article "Luython" in the *MGG*, the authenticity of no.7 (Hassler?) and no.8 is questioned.

64. Cf. M. Schuler, "Eine neu entdeckte Komposition von Adam Steigleder," *MF*, XXI (1968), pp.42ff.

65. New eds. in Pirro A, pp.1228ff., and by L. Schrade in *ZfMw*, VIII (1925/26), pp.633ff.

66. *DTB*, IV. 2 (1903), E. von Werra, ed.

67. Why Werra published them as works of Hassler's is not known.

68. *DTB*, IV. 2 (1903), E. von Werra, ed.

69. A new ed. by C. Rayner in *CEKM* is in preparation. One especially important source is a (partial) autograph, which is added to the Wolfenbüttel copy of Melchior Neusiedler's *Teutsch Lautenbuch* (1574).

70. Cf. "Die Entwicklung der Toccata im 17. und 18. Jahrhundert" (diss., Vienna, 1930), p.90.

71. Cf. "Ein Beitrag zur Frühgeschichte der Toccata" *ZfMw*, VIII (1925/26), pp.610ff.

72. Cf. Mischiati T, p.64.

73. New eds. of nos.37 and 40 of the *Vater-unser* cycle in Ritter B, pp.139f.; of four ricercars by E. Emsheimer (1928). Cf. also E. Emsheimer, *J. U. Steigleder: Sein Leben und seine Werke* (1928). New ed. of both prints by W. Apel and U. Siegele, in *CEKM*, no.13, 2 vols. (1969).

74. Cf. *AfMf*, II (1937), pp.92ff.

75. Cf. H. P. Schanzlin, review of M. Zulauf's *Johannes Benn: Missae concertatae*, *Mf*, XVII (1964), p.459.

16. Italy

1. Bedbrook omits the first ricercar from the *Ricercari* of 1595; his list of sources is not clear and it contains several errors.

2. The print consists of five part books entitled *Canzoni per sonare con ogni sorta d'istrumenti con il suo basso generale per l'organo.* Cf. the new ed. by A. Einstein, *G. Gabrieli: Canzoni per sonar a 4* (1933).

3. Cf. Mischiati T, p.55, no.8.

4. It contains seven, in fact, but one is identical with the canzona *La Spiritata* from the Raverii print, and another with the *Ricercar del 10° tono* from the *Ricercari* of 1595.

5. Cf. Mischiati T, pp.78f., nos.2, 18, 19.

6. New ed. in Pirro A, pp.1224ff. In the fourth measure before the end of p.1225 the chords should be twice as long as they are in Pirro's transcription.

7. Cf. *ZfMw*, XVI (1933/34), pp.126f.

8. Cf. *Mf*, XII (1959), p.373.

9. New ed. by W. Apel in *CEKM*, no.9 (1965); three ricercars are also in Torchi A, pp.153ff. Woltz's *Tabulatura* of 1617 contains 15 canzonas by Antegnati, but they are most certainly arrangements of ensemble pieces.

10. New ed. of three pieces in Torchi A, pp.191ff., unfortunately with many errors; measures 17–18 on p.195 are particularly corrupt.

11. In the 1611 and 1622 editions the organ pieces are all placed at the end. New ed. of ten pieces in Torchi A, pp.354ff.; of a ricercar from *Il Transilvano* II, ibid., p.353; of the *Battaglia* and one *Bizaria* in Apel M, I, p.27.

12. In the appendix, there are, in addition, 4 sonatas for organ, violino, and trombone.

13. In Torchi A the first piece is entitled *Suonata terza*, according to the 1605 edition, and the second one *Toccata*, according to the 1611 edition.

14. Cf. *Geschichte der Musik*, vol.IV (^{2}1881), p.437.

15. Cf. Ritter G, p.28.

16. The middle voice added in Apel M, measures 4, 8, etc., is indicated in the original by the thorough-bass figures 4–♯3.

17. New ed. by C. Rayner in *CEKM*, no.20 (1969); one ricercar in Torchi A, p.141. The *Ricercate . . .* , a 1602 print mentioned in K. G. Fellerer's article in *MGG*, cannot be located.

18. At this point let us note two prints, *Ricercari e canzoni francese, Libro primo* and *secondo* (both 1619), by Antonio Cifra (1584–1629), which obviously contain ensemble music. *Libro primo* appeared in both part books and score, *Libro secondo* in score only. Cf. Frotscher O, pp.225f.

19. Cf.p.30, footnote.

20. Cf. "Un musicista cremonese dimenticato," *Collectanea Historiae Musicae*, vol. II (1957), pp.413ff.

21. Ibid., p.429.

22. Cf. Mischiati T, p.110.

23. New ed. in Chilesotti P. Chilesotti takes over the dividing bars of the original, which serve for purposes of orientation only, but by adding time signatures such as 6/4, 5/4, or 9/4, he gives them the misleading meaning of irregularly set bar lines. In reality, each dance is in a regular time, 4/4 or 6/4, with the original dividing bars often placed in the middle of these measures.

24. Cf. Torchi A, p.257; the source remains unidentifiable.

25. New ed. by W. R. Shindle in *CEKM*, no.12 (1966); for the manuscripts cf.pp. 496f.

26. Cf. W. Apel, "Neapolitan Links between Cabezon and Frescobaldi," *MQ*, XXIV (1938), p.419.

27. New ed. of all these pieces by J. Watelet in *Monumenta Musicae Belgicae*, vol.IV (1938), pp.33–96.

28. Indeed, Mayone's two books *di diversi capricci* do not include a single capriccio (cf. the table of contents on p.429).

29. New ed. by R. Jackson, *Neapolitan Keyboard Composers circa 1600*, *CEKM*, no.24 (1967).

30. This work is printed in the new ed. of Macque's works (cf. note 27 above). R. Jackson, p.ix, suggests that the composer was Rinaldo dall' Arpa (d.1603).

31. Cf. "Die süditalienische Clavierschule des 17. Jahrhunderts," *AM*, XXXIV (1962), pp.128ff.

32. The study of Mayone's and Trabaci's prints has been considerably facilitated by their complete transcription, which Dr. Roland Jackson has accommodatingly put at my disposal. New ed. of Mayone's *Secondo Libro* by M. S. Kastner in *Orgue et Liturgie*, vols. 53 and 65 (1964, 1965).

33. M. S. Kastner conjectures that this is also true of Rocco Rodio's fantasies (cf. Kastner R, p.9). The cultivation of harp playing in South Italy is perhaps another sign of the connection with Spain, which is stressed in the essay cited in note 26 above.

34. Cf. U. Prota-Giurleo, "Giovanni Maria Trabaci e gli organisti della Real Cappella di Palazzo di Napoli," *L'Organo*, I (1960), pp.185ff. A complete new edition by O. Mischiati has begun to appear (vol.I, containing 12 ricercate from book I, in *Monumenti di Musica Italiana*, vol.III, Kassel, 1964).

35. New ed. in A. T. Davison and W. Apel, *Historical Anthology of Music*, II (1950), no.191. Several pieces are also reprinted in Torchi A.

36. Actually an additional voice for only three galliards is found at the end of the volume.

37. According to A. Einstein, "Die Arie di Ruggiero," *SIMg*, XIII (1912), pp.444ff., fidele is a later name for the ruggiero melody, but this identification does not apply in the present instance.

38. Cf. G. Benvenuti, *Rivista musicale italiana*, XXVII (1920), pp.133ff. One of these fugues is found in the manuscript Berlin Staatsbibl. 30112 (formerly P 407; a collection made by Alois Fuchs) under Poglietti's name, who cannot have composed it either. Redlich's *Meister des Orgelbarock* (1931) contains a number of other spurious pieces.

39. A catalog of works in L. Ronga, *Gerolamo Frescobaldi* (1930), p.291, is unreliable and insufficient with respect to Frescobaldi's keyboard music. Cf. also monographs by F. Morel, *G. Frescobaldi, Organista di S. Pietro di Roma* (1945), and G. Machabey, *G. Frescobaldi, La vie, l'oeuvre* (1952).

40. Pidoux F. The *Fiori musicali* have been available in various editions for a long time (by Haberl, Keller, Bonnet and Guilmant, and Germani).

41. The chronology is not clear in Pidoux's edition since he always cites the prints with reference to their last edition; e.g., he lists the *Toccate . . . Libro primo* of 1615 as *Das erste Buch der Toccaten . . . 1637*.

42. This work appeared in several new editions, about which both Eitner and Ronga give misleading information. The true circumstances are as follows: 1st ed., 1615 (with a preface "Al Lettore," dated Dec. 22, 1614), contains 12 toccatas and 3 partitas (*sopra Romanesca, Monicha,* and *Ruggiero*); 2nd ed., 1615 (with expanded preface and the remark

"Christophorus Blancus sculpsit 1616"), contains enlarged and partly altered versions of the partitas and adds the *Partite sopra Folia* and 4 correntes; unchanged new editions of 1616 and 1628 (the latter with the title "di cimbalo et organ"); 3rd ed., 1637, contains the pieces of the 2nd ed. and a number of additional works under the heading "Aggiunta." Complete information on titles, publishers, and prefaces can be found in Sartori B. In the present listing on p.448 the 1st and 2nd editions are combined (as III) because of their closeness in time, and the 3rd edition is listed subsequently (as IIIa).

43. Prints II and IV appeared in 1626 in a combined edition entitled *Il primo libro di capricci, canzon francese, e recercari*, which omitted *Capriccio Or chè noi rimena*. The frequently repeated statement (it even appears in M. Reimann's article "Frescobaldi" in MGG) that this capriccio was replaced by a new one *sopra un soggetto* is erroneous. The *Capriccio sopra un soggetto* had already appeared in the 1624 print.

44. This collection appeared in a new edition in 1637, with the two partitas omitted.

45. On the basis of the preserved prints the designation of this posthumous volume as *Libro quarto* cannot be explained unequivocally. A *Primo libro delle Canzoni* (in five part books) appeared in 1623, and was reprinted several times.

46. For about fifty of these pieces cf. my article "Die handschriftliche Überlieferung der Klavierwerke Frescobaldis," *Festschrift Karl Gustav Fellerer* (1962), pp.40ff. New ed. of all manuscript pieces by W. R. Shindle, *Girolamo Frescobaldi, Keyboard Compositions Preserved in Manuscripts*, CEKM, no.30, 3 vols. (1968).

47. Tagliapietra A, vol.4, p.1, reproduces this fantasy, and an explanatory note calls this variant a "motivo secondario."

48. Frescobaldi divides these and most other variations into measures of four half notes (two semibreves), usually with an upbeat in the first measure. (The same meter is found in many of Mayone's romanesca variations, but without the upbeat.) Groupings such as these, that deviate from and obscure the true rhythm, are not rare in the 16th and 17th centuries. Cf. Apel N, p.73.

49. The varying titles are: *Einmal ging ich spazieren; Von Gott will ich nicht lassen* (cf. J. Zahn, *Die Melodien der evangelischen Kirchenlieder*, III, p.352, no.5264b); *Une vierge pucelle* (Lebègue); *Une jeune pucelle* (Dandrieu).

50. In Pidoux F, II, p.53, it is placed at the end.

51. The most recent contributions to this discussion are K. von Fischer, "Chaconne and Passacaglia," *Revue Belge de musicologie*, XII (1958), pp.19ff; Th. Walker, "Ciaconna and Passacaglia," *JAMS*, XXI (1968), pp.300ff.; and R. Hudson, "The Development of Italian Keyboard Variations on the Passacaglio and Ciaccona from Guitar Music in the 17th Century" (diss., University of California at Los Angeles, 1967; Univ. Microfilm 68–219), and "Further Remarks on the Passacaglia and Ciaccona," *Jams*, XXIII (1970), pp.302ff.

52. Both compositions are omitted in the second printing of 1637 and therefore do not appear in Pidoux F. *Partite sopra Passacagli* is numbered from 1 to 30 in the original, but the unlucky number 13 is omitted, and the last three *partite* are not numbered.

53. In Italian ensemble music, suites first appear in Buonamente's *Il 5° libro de varie sonate . . .* (1629).

54. Cf. L. Ronga, *Gerolamo Frescobaldi* (1930), p.129.

55. The pieces are numbered consecutively, as in the edition by Haberl. In H. Keller's edition no.18 is counted as two pieces (no.18: *Canzona*; no.19: *Alio modo*), so that after no.18 all of Keller's designations are one number higher than those given here.

56. Cf. D. Alaleona in *Rivista musicale italiana*, XVI (1909), p.36.

57. New ed. by A. Santini in *Musica veterum* (R. Casimiri, ed.), vol.3 (n.d.); new ed. Shindle, I; nos.1–3.

58. New ed. in S. Dalla Libera, *Girolamo Frescobaldi: Nove Toccate inedite* (1962); new ed. Shindle, I; nos.11–19.

59. Cf. W. Apel, "Die süditalienische Clavierschule des 17. Jahrhunderts," *AM*, XXXIV (1962), pp.128ff.

60. Cf. A. Curtis, "L'Opera cembalo-organistica di T. Merula," *L'Organo*, I (1960), pp.141ff., in which six more pieces from Lynar A 2 are ascribed to him. New ed. by A. Curtis, *Tarquinio Merula, Composizioni per organo e cembalo* (1961). The recently discovered Pelplin tablatures (cf. A. Sutkowski and O. Mischiati, *L'Organo*, II, 1961, p.62) contain twelve canzonas by Merula, but they are probably intabulated ensemble canzonas. For Merula's many other instrumental and vocal compositions cf. D. Arnold's article in *MGG*.

61. New ed. of the print in Torchi A; new ed. of all the pieces in *I Classici della musica italiana*, 26 (1920), A. Toni, ed. Both editions are rather inadequate and are superseded by the new ed. in *CEKM*, no.15 (1966), J. R. White, ed. Cf. O. Mischiati's article "Rossi" in *MGG*, particularly with reference to the various editions of the *Toccata*. In several collections of "old masters" several Rococo pieces are printed as compositions by Michelangelo Rossi, but they are really by Lorenzo de Rossi (1720–94).

62. This toccata is erroneously and misleadingly inscribed *Andante* by Toni (p.22); cf. note 61 above.

63. Cf. U. Prota-Giurleo, "Due camioni della scuola napoletana del sec. XVII," *L'Organo*, III (1962), pp.115ff. New ed. of the ricercars by B. Hudson, *CEKM*, no.3 (1964).

64. Cf. W. S. Newman, "The XIII Sonate di Cimbalo by Giovanni Pietro del Buono," *Collectanea historiae musicae*, II (1957), pp.297ff.

65. New ed. in Ritter B; Kaller L, IV; Tagliapietra A, VII; and Gauss O.

66. These three identifications were discovered by Mr. R. Shindle.

67. New ed. of 62 pieces from the various Chigi manuscripts listed under 4. and 5. (excluding those by E. Pasquini, cf. note 25, and Frescobaldi, cf. note 46), in H. B. Lincoln, *Seventeenth-Century Keyboard Music in the Chigi Manuscripts of the Vatican Library*, *CEKM*, no.32, 3 vols. (1968); cf. H. B. Lincoln, "I manoscritti chigiani . . . ," *L'Organo*, V (1967), pp.63ff.

17. France

1. New ed. in Guilmant A, vol.I; various pieces also in Kaller L, vols.I and II.

2. New ed. in Raugel M, vol.II. This volume also includes some duos by Racquet, which were excerpted from a group of twelve teaching examples in Mersenne's work that "ne sont point destinés pour l'orgue" (Pirro A, p.1268).

3. New ed. in Bonfils P, nos.5, 12; the former also in Pirro A, p.1272.

4. New ed. in Bonfils P, nos.25–29; the duos and dances appear in the *Supplément*.

5. New ed. in Bonfils P, no.30.

6. Cf. Pirro A, p.1269.

7. Cf. P. Hamburger, "Ein handschriftliches Klavierbuch aus der ersten Hälfte des 17. Jahrhunderts," *ZfMw*, XIII (1930/31), pp.133ff., as well as the instructive presentation in Pirro A, p.1232, which was obviously unknown to Hamburger.

8. All three sarabandes occur in the so-called Bauyn manuscript (Paris, Bibl. nat. Vm⁷ 674/675; written about 1660), the chief source of early clavecin music. New ed. of Mézangeau's sarabandes in Raugel M, vol.I, pp.3, 4 (curiously without the original designation "sarabande").

9. Seven pieces by La Barre are printed in Bonfils P (nos.18–24). No.23 is identical

with one of the courantes in Lynar A 1. The allemandes nos.18 and 20, both also in Raugel M (vol.II, pp.31, 32), are surely not by Pierre but by his son Joseph (1633–78).

10. New ed. in Bonfils P, nos.2–4; the first two also in Raugel M, vol.I, pp.4, 5.

11. New ed. in Bonfils P, nos.5–17.

18. Spain and Portugal

1. Cf. the study in Villalba A, pp.10ff.

2. New ed. in Anglés A, II, no.I; Apel S, no.9; Pedrell A; and Villalba A. Except for the prints of Coelho and Correa, the Escorial manuscript is the chief source of Spanish organ music before 1650. For what follows, cf. W. Apel, "Spanish Organ Music of the Early 17th Century," *JAMS*, XV (1962), pp.174ff.

3. New ed. in Apel S, no.8, as well as in Pedrell A and Villalba A, with many mistakes in both.

4. Cf. the study in Villalba A, pp.8ff. (earlier in *La Ciudad de Dios*, Madrid, vol.40, 1896, pp.193–206, 285–97).

5. New ed. in Kastner L, vol.II, p.268, and in Apel S, no.6.

6. Cf. R. Stevenson, "Serna," in *MGG*.

7. New ed. in Kastner L, vol.II, pp.246, 251; the first also in Apel S, no.7. The second tiento is anonymous, but according to Kastner F, vol.I, p.XXV, it is also by Lacerna.

8. New ed. in Apel S, nos.10–25a; most of these pieces are also in Villalba A, Pedrell A, and in Anglés A, where he is also credited with several anonymous pieces from Madrid, Bibl. nac. Ms. M 1360.

9. New ed. in Anglés A II, no.II.

10. New ed. in Anglés A I, no. I.

11. New ed. of one *de 4° tono* in Anglés A I, no.II; another *de 4° tono* in Anglés A III, no.IV, and in Muset E, pp.23ff.; and one *de 6° tono* in Gauss O, pp.20ff.

12. This composition is disfigured in Villalba A by especially disturbing mistakes. E.g., measures 136 and 176 are omitted, and measure 139 is printed twice. The same mistakes occur in the reprint in J. Bonnet, *Historical Organ Recitals*, vol.VI.

13. The Escorial manuscript, which indicates the number of measures for most pieces, says at the end, "tiene 150 compases."

14. New ed. in Kastner F, which is referred to in the following discussion.

15. In his preface ("Advertencias Particulares") Coelho says, "I have cultivated these flowers since the spring time of my life" (desda Primavera de meus anuas cultivey).

16. New ed. in Kastner L, which is referred to in the following discussion.

17. This tablature is essentially the same as the one used in the 16th century by Venegas de Henestrosa and Cabezón. At the very beginning of his book, in a "Prólogo en alabança de la cifra" (Prologue in Praise of the Number), Correa stresses the advantages of this notation, invented "by the genius of our Spaniards," over the usual notation, which he calls *canto de organo*.

18. Kastner (p.73) tries to explain "detenire" as an accent, not as a lengthening, but this meaning contradicts the unambiguous explanations in the original text, which are briefly recapitulated in connection with tiento no.1.

19. One of the hitherto unpublished intabulations from the *Obras*.

20. In Kastner L they are often realized (in small notes) in various ways, probably with a greater liberty at times than would seem admissible.

21. The rhythm of this passage is somewhat problematic; cf. Kastner L I, p.74 (the version adopted by Bonnet mentioned there is also found in Pirro A, p.1216). I believe the above interpretation to be the most plausible one.

22. Cf. Kastner L, pp.24f.

23. For what follows cf. W. Apel, "Spanische Orgelmusik vor Cabanilles," *Anuario musical*, XVII (1962), pp.15ff. Some statements made there need correction, e.g., the one about the number of compositions by Bruna.

24. Oporto Ms.1576 Col.B/5 has only recently become known through a new edition by C. R. Fernandes in *Portugaliae Musica*, vol.VII (1963). Under such titles as *Exercicios, Fugas, Concertos, Liçõnes, Tençõnes* (themes?), the manuscript contains more than one hundred pieces. Some are brief contrapuntal studies of five to six measures; some are longer compositions. Figural technique is completely absent in the thirty-four works that have been published. The prevailing style is the normal contrapuntal texture with a somewhat freer treatment of dissonance, which may have been generally accepted around 1630.

25. Tables of contents for these manuscripts may be found in Anglés C, vol.I, pp. XLIVff. (nos.3, 4, and 7).

26. New ed. of a psalm verset and the two *Batallas* in Pedrell A, vol.I, pp.40ff., where Jimenez is erroneously called a composer of the 16th century; new ed. of the *Folias* in Anglés A I, no.VII, and of one tiento lleno in Anglés A II, no.IV.

27. New ed. in Pedrell A, vol.I, pp.41ff., 47ff.

28. New ed. in Anglés A I, no.VIII.

29. Muset E includes *Tres versillos de primer tono* by Diego de Torrijos from a source that I do not know. Sebastian's *Tiento* appears in Anglés A II, no.VIII.

30. The following discussion is based on photocopies from M 751.21 and M 387 (888), which the administration of the Biblioteca Central at Barcelona helpfully put at my disposal. New ed. of ten tientos in Anglés A I–III.

31. The *Psalmodia* is written at the end of a manuscript, and since a number of folios are missing, it is probably incompletely preserved.

32. Another *Tiento de lleno,* which consists of eight sections, is briefly presented in the study cited in note 23.

PART IV. THE SECOND HALF OF THE SEVENTEENTH CENTURY

19. Germany

1. Cf. G. Adler, *Musikalische Werke der Habsburgischen Kaiser* (1892).

2. New ed. in DTÖ, IV. 1; VI. 2; and X. 2 (G. Adler, ed.), cited in the following pages as vols.I, II, and III. A special edition in two volumes, *Johann Jakob Frobergers Werke für Orgel und Clavier* (G. Adler, ed., 1903), contains the same material with the addition of a ricercar (no.15). For the sources cf. Riedel Q, pp.75ff., 121ff.

3. Part of this repertoire is printed in vol.I of the new edition, the remainder in vol.III.

4. This piece is preserved in the second Bauyn Ms. with the inscription "fait à Paris."

5. Suites nos.1–28 are printed in vol.II, nos.29–30 as an appendix to vol.III. No.28 was compiled by Adler from dances preserved as single pieces. Nos.25 and 27, both consisting of only allemande and courante, may be preserved incompletely.

6. New ed. in G. Adler, *Musikalische Werke der Habsburgischen Kaiser* (1892), and in Tagliapietra A, vol. VII. In F. W. Riedel's new ed., *Fux, Werke für Tasteninstrumente*, p.IX, mention is made of "mehrere handschriftlich überlieferte Stücke (Wien, Minoritenkonvent; Ottobeuren)" by Ebner, with which I am not acquainted.

7. Vol.II. 2 (1901; A Sandberger, ed.).

8. By R. Walter, 1956.

9. In the manuscript Bologna, Lic. mus. DD 53, it is ascribed to Frescobaldi.

10. This manuscript is so named because of the entry "In usum F. F. Neresheimensium 1661"; cf. H. Schmid, "Una nuova fonte di musica organistica del secolo XVII," *L'Organo*, I (1960), pp.107ff.

11. Cf. F. W. Riedel, "Eine unbekannte Quelle zu Kerlls Musik für Tasteninstrumente," *Mf*, XIII (1960), pp.310ff. Four of these suites are listed in Kerll's "Subnecto" index (cf. Riedel Q, p.132), but without the doubles, which may have been added by another hand.

12. 1., 2., and 3. of the list have been published in *DTÖ*, XIII. 2 (vol.27, 1906; H. Botstiber, ed.); no.4 in *Die Orgel*, series II, nos.5 and 6 (F. W. Riedel, ed.); 5. in W. E. Nettles, *Alessandro Poglietti: Harpsichord Music* (1966); the rest have not yet appeared in modern reprints.

13. New Haven (Yale University), School of Music E. B. 1688; cf. Riedel Q, pp. 99ff.

14. Kremsmünster, Regenterei of the Benedictine Monastery, I. 146.

15. Cf. Riedel Q, p.110, no.77.

16. Cf. Frotscher G, p.481.

17. This suite is also found as part of a group of fifteen anonymous suites in the Göttweig manuscript mentioned in connection with Kerll (cf.pp.562, 566, and note 11 above). H. Knaus states in "Franz Mathias Techelmann, Sein Leben und seine Werke" (diss. Vienna, 1959) that the other suites are also by Techelmann, but that is doubtful. I am grateful to Prof. E. Schenk and Mr. F. W. Riedel for information concerning Techelmann and for furnishing photographic reproductions.

18. *DTÖ*, XIII, 2 (vol.27, 1906; H. Botstiber, ed.).

19. Cf. F. Berend, "Nicolaus Adam Strunck" (diss., Munich, 1913); also Riedel Q, p.184.

20. Berlin, Staatsbibl. Mus. Ms. 30112 (formerly P.407), written by Alois Fuchs.

21. Cf. notes 18 and 19 above.

22. New ed. in Seiffert O, book 18.

23. Cf. Riedel Q, p.91, note 274.

24. New ed. in Guilmant A, vol.VIII.

25. Cf., e.g., Pirro A, p.1326b.

26. Cf. *Riemanns Musik-Lexikon* and Frotscher G, p.498.

27. New ed. of the *Apparatus* by S. de Lange (1888) and by R. Walter (1957); the latter omits the *Nova Cyclopeias Harmonica*, but otherwise it is more faithful to the original.

28. New ed. of the toccatas in Kaller L, vol.IX (G. Klaus, ed.).

29. E.g., in H. Neupert's article "Clavichord" in *MGG*; cf.p.16 above.

30. *Werke für Tasteninstrumente*, *DTÖ*, vol.85 (1947), E. Schenk, ed.

31. Three fugues published in Gauss O, nos.106-108, are probably spurious. The same is true of a "number of fugues and preludes" mentioned in Frotscher G, p.484.

32. Cf. *DTÖ*, vol.85, pp.XXVf.

33. *Johann Joseph Fux: Sämtliche Werke*, published by the Johann-Joseph-Fux Society, Series VI, vol.1; F. W. Riedel, ed.

34. New eds. of both prints in *DTB*, XVIII, vol.30 (1917; M. Seiffert, ed.). The versets of the *Octi-Tonium* and the *Prototypon* also appear in a new ed. by R. Walter (1961, 1969). In his article "Murschhauser" in *MGG*, L. Hoffman-Erbrecht mentions twelve toccatas in a Hamburg manuscript that is now lost.

35. Cf. *DTB*, XVIII, p.LVII.

36. New ed. by E. von Werra (1901).

37. F. Ludwig, ed. (1940).

38. *Pachelbel: Klavierwerke*, M. Seiffert, ed. (1901); cf.pp.66of. above.

39. New eds. of the preludes in Seiffert O, book 6; of the Lüneburg organ chorales in R. Walter, *F. Tunder, Sämtliche Choralbearbeitungen für Orgel* (1956); of one organ chorale each in Straube C and Straube AN, vol.II; of the two chorales from the Pelplin tablatures (cf.Chap.15, note 26) in *CEKM* no.10, vol.II (J. Golos and A. Sutkowski, ed., 1967). For the canzona, cf. W. Apel, "Neu aufgefundene Clavierwerke von Scheidemann, Tunder, Froberger, Reincken und Buxtehude," *AM*, XXXIV (1962), pp.65ff.

40. New ed. of the first seven works in R. Ilgner, *M. Weckmann, Gesammelte Werke* (1942); of the eighth in Dietrich O; of the last in Straube C. The final variation of *Gott sei gelobet* II is incomplete; cf. Ilgner, p.160.

41. Cf. Dietrich G, p.59; Hedar B, p.235.

42. New ed. of 14 preludes, fugues, and toccatas in Seiffert O, book 3, to which the numbers in the text refer; seven of these pieces are also available in Buchmayer K, vols. I–III, along with several others. Most of the secular pieces (five canzonas, five toccatas, and five suites) are preserved anonymously in Lüneburg KN 147, but are generally considered autographs (cf. Buchmayer K; I, p.V); I consider them authentic.

43. New ed. in Seiffert O, book 21.

44. Cf. the articles by B. Lundgren in *Kongressbericht Köln* (1958), pp.183ff., and in *Svensk tidskrift för musikforskning* (1961), pp.249ff.; also my paper, mentioned in note 39. Some of the pieces published in Moser C under Lorentz's name are anonymous and some are by Sweelinck; the authentic works have been edited by Bo Lundgren (Lund, 1960).

45. Cf. the article by Sutkowski and Mischiati mentioned in Chap.15, note 26. New ed. by J. Golos and A. Sutkowski in *CEKM*, no.10, vol.I (1965), together with a very remarkable chorale motet on *Allein zu dir* (also preserved in the Pelplin tablatures) by Ewaldt, an otherwise completely unknown composer.

46. This setting is signed Jacobus Kurtzkampff, not Johann as stated in Schierning Ü, pp.43, 48.

47. New ed. by W. Apel in *CEKM*, no.16 (1967).

48. *Was kann uns kommen an* is preserved in Berlin, Staatsbibl. P.802, *An Wasserflüssen Babylon* in a Lübeck copy from the 19th century. New ed. by H. Winter (1963; ed. Sikorski 234, 235); substantial excerpts are also found in Pirro A, pp.1299ff., probably following the now lost copies at the Berlin Institut für Kirchenmusik (cf. Dietrich G, pp. 91ff.). These settings were apparently studied by Ph. Spitta also (cf. his *J. S. Bach*, 1873–80, p.194).

49. New ed. in Buchmayer K, vol.III, and in Seiffert O, book 5 (following Leipzig, Stadtbibl. III. 8.4).

50. New ed. in Buchmayer K, vol.III, following Darmstadt, Landesbibl. Ms. No.51 (4061).

51. Two suites are contained in Berlin, Staatsbibl. 40644, the so-called Möller Ms.; one in Uppsala, Ihre Ms.285 (cf. my article cited in note 39).

52. New ed. in *Vereeniging voor Nord-Nederlands Muziekgeschiedenis*, vol.14, and in Tagliapietra A, vol.VII.

53. Cf. Seiffert G, p.256.

54. New ed. in Buchmayer K, vol.IV. The prelude mentioned in Riedel Q, p.191, can barely be deciphered.

55. The chorale prelude is found in Lüneburg KN 209; the preludes appear in Lüneburg KN 207 (new ed. in Seiffert O, book 2), the suites in Berlin, Staatsbibl. 40644.

56. This canzona appears independently in Berlin, Staatsbibl. P.230, and is printed in Körner and Ritter, *Der Orgelvirtuose* (no.44).

57. Cf. H. Kümmerling, "Radek," in *MGG*.

58. The *Praeambulum* and *Canzone* are found in the manuscript New Haven, E. B. 1688, the *Chiacona* and suite in the Wenster Collection (cf. Hedar B, p.72), the *Fuga* in the Album of J. V. Meder (cf. J. Bolte in *VfMw*, VIII, 1892, p.502), and the chorale settings in Berlin, Staatsbibl. Mus. Ms. 6473 (cf. Riedel Q, p.182).

59. Cf. Riedel Q, p.194, note 410.

60. In *Die Orgel*, series II, no.4.

61. In his article "Fabricius" in *MGG*.

62. Cf. H. Pauly, *Die Fuge in den Orgelwerken Dietrich Buxtehudes, Kölner Beiträge zur Musikforschung*, XXXI (1964); review by B. E. Nielsen, *MF*, XX (1967), pp.345f.

63. The following discussion refers to the Hedar edition, which may be equated to the Seiffert-Kraft edition by employing the following concordance for the toccatas and the preludes and fugues (H = Hedar, vol.II, S = Seiffert-Kraft, vols.I–II):

H	S	H	S	H	S	H	S
1	4	8	—	15	15	22	5
2	20	9	6	16	19	23	7
3	22	10	13	17	26	24	14
4	9	11	11	18	27	25	16
5	18	12	21	19	10	26	28
6	17	13	12	20	30	27	29
7	—	14	8	21	—		

64. Cf. Hedar B, p.180.

65. Ibid., p.118.

66. Hedar puts most of the longer settings into vol.III and the shorter ones into vol. IV; Seiffert puts them into vol.II, sections 1 and 2, respectively. In Hedar's new edition and in Hedar B, pp.262ff., the chorale motets are called fantasies.

67. Hedar erroneously includes no.5 among the chorale variations.

68. Cf. Hedar B, p.282.

69. In Hedar III, p.82, the *c♯* is changed to *c*.

70. Cf. Hedar B, p.305.

71. Hedar IV, no.6. Another arrangement (Hedar IV, no.26; Seiffert-Kraft, p.90) is possibly spurious; cf. Hedar's commentary, p.VI.

72. New ed. in *Dietrich Buxtehude, Werke*, vol.II (Ugrino Edition, 1926). For similar compositions cf. Riedel Q, p.182; one by Radek is mentioned on p.609.

73. These works may be ascribed to Buxtehude with reservations, for nos.8 and 16 are identical with Lebègue's *Second livre de clavecin* (1677), nos.1 and 2.

74. Cf. Seiffert S, no.61.

75. New ed. in *Die Orgel*, series II, no.4. Cf.p.563, footnote.

76. Cf. M. Seiffert "Das Mylauer Tabulaturbuch von 1750," *AfMw*, I (1944), pp. 607ff., and the detailed study with transcriptions in Shannon M.

77. New ed. in Seiffert O, book 7.

78. In Straube C, with the wrong attribution to Anton Kniller; the manuscript is signed "A. Kniller."

79. New eds. of one suite and of the *Sonatina* in Buchmayer K, vol.5, and of the *Sonatina* in Seiffert O, book 5. Cf. R. Buchmayer "Christian Ritter," *Riemann Festschrift* (1909), pp.354ff.

80. New ed. of the organ works by H. Keller (1941), of the *Clavier Übung* by H.

Trede (1940). There are also four preludes in Seiffert O, book 9, and an organ chorale in Straube C.

81. F. Wolgast, *Georg Böhm, Sämtliche Werke*, vol.I, according to which the works will be cited in the following pages. Several pieces also appear in Ritter B; Straube A; Straube AN, vol.I; Straube C; Seiffert O, book 4; Buchmayer K, vol.5; Keller A; and elsewhere.

82. Cf. *J. S. Bach*, vol.I, p.206.

83. In Straube C, no.10, this work appears under the title *Herr wie du willst.*

84. In Pirro A, p.1313, this work appears under the title *Treuer Gott, ich muss dir klagen.*

85. New ed. in Straube C; two are also in Ritter B, nos.118 (incomplete) and 119. The dates 1630–1706, which appear in most reference works, are wrong; cf. Th. Holm in *Mf*, VII (1954), p.455.

86. Cf. Ritter G, p.172.

87. New ed. in F. Stein, *Bruhns, Orgelwerke* (separate printing from the complete edition in *Das Erbe deutscher Musik*, Landschaftsdenkmale Schleswig-Holstein I–II); the toccatas are also in Seiffert O, book 8, and one toccata and the organ chorale are in Straube AN, vol.I.

88. Cf. F. W. Riedel in *Mf*, XI (1958), pp.381f., who also suggests possible relationships with J. S. Bach, who copied Bruhns's keyboard pieces and used them as "models."

89. New ed. in Seiffert O, book 21.

90. New ed. of the first one in Straube C, of the second in Dietrich O.

91. Cf. Frotscher G, p.452.

92. According to F. W. Riedel in his article "Leiding" in *MGG*. New ed. of the preludes in Seiffert O, book 7; a third one seems to have been lost with the manuscript Berlin, Staatsbibl. 40295, the so-called Plauen Organ Book.

93. G. Frotscher (G, p.451) sees it as similar to an intrada; F. W. Riedel (in *MGG*) likens it to an orchestral overture.

94. Cf. Frotscher G, p.452.

95. New ed. in Seiffert O, book 7.

96. This autograph is preserved in the Art Museum at The Hague, and is known as the Frankenberger or Scheurleer manuscript after previous owners. New ed. of the work in Ritter B, p.169. It has been ascribed to Johann Heinrich Buttstett (cf. note 98 below); however this manuscript always uses the monogram JHB for Buttstett.

97. Körner and Ritter, *Der Orgel-Freund*, vol.VI, p.13.

98. In Frotscher O, p.27, it is printed as a work by Buttstett. The arrangement printed there on p.29 is probably a separate composition from a later period; cf. Frotscher's comment on p.102.

99. *DTB*, IV. 1, no.15 and p.XVIII.

100. New ed. in Frotscher O.

101. In Ritter B, no.117; cf. Ritter G, p.169.

102. Cf. Frotscher G, p.578.

103. New ed. in Ritter B, no.123.

104. The *Fuga sexti toni* and the chorale settings are printed in Körner and Ritter, *Der Orgel-Freund*, vol.VI.

105. New ed. in Ritter B, no.79.

106. New ed. of the chorale in Frotscher O. The fugues, which are said to be included in Ritter's copy at Beuron, were not available to me.

107. New ed. in M. Fischer, *44 Choräle zum Präludieren*, together with a study, *Die organistische Improvisation im 17. Jahrhundert* (1929).

108. New ed. in Ritter B, p.172; also as a "doubtful" work in the Old Bach-Gesell-schaft edition, vol.36, no.12.

109. New eds. by H. Riemann (Steingräber Verlag, 1892), and in Tagliapietra A, vol.IX.

110. New ed. in the New Bach-Gesellschaft edition (J. S. Bach, *Neue Ausgabe sämtlicher Werke*, Kassel, 1954–   ), Jahrgang 39 (1940), book 2. R. Benecke, "Joh. Christoph Bach," *MGG* (I, 955) mentions a lost *Arie mit 15 Variationen* in A minor.

111. New eds. of nos.2 and 3 in Frotscher O; no.4 in *Orgeljournal* (Mannheim), vol. I, book 7; no.5 in Straube C; no.6 in Ritter B, p.175; no.7 in Dietrich O. Cf. the catalog of openings in M. Schneider, "Thematisches Verzeichnis der musikalischen Werke der Familie Bach," *Bach-Jahrbuch* (1907), pp.127ff. An aria with variations, attributed to Johann Michel Bach, is said to exist only in an arrangement for the harmonium, and may not be authentic; cf. K. Geiringer, *The Bach Family* (1954), p.45, note 2.

112. Cf. *Neues Lexikon der Tonkunst* (1812), I, p.213.

113. Cf. *The Bach Family* (1954), p.39.

114. New ed. of no.1 in Straube C (under the title *Der du bist drei in Einigkeit* and with variations II and III changing places); of no.2 in Frotscher O; no.3 in Dietrich O; no.4 in Gauss O and Keller A.

115. Cf. his *Grundlage einer Ehrenpforte . . .* , p.7, quoted in Frotscher G, p.588.

116. Cf. "Eine Tabulatur des Dresdner Hoforganisten Kittel," *ZfMw*, XIII (1930/31), pp.99ff.; also J. H. Baron, "A 17th-Century Keyboard Tablature in Brasov," *JAMS*, XX (1967), pp.279ff.

117. Apel N, p.175. Similar examples are frequently found in the music of Fres-cobaldi and other 17th-century composers.

118. Cf. Seiffert G, p.195.

119. I am referring here to the three suites by Pachelbel that are definitely genuine, and not to the others, which are of inferior quality (cf.pp.660f.).

120. Cf. H. H. Eggebrecht's article "Pachelbel," in *MGG*.

121. The three volumes, to be cited as vols. I, II, and III in the following pages, are: *DTB* IV.1 (1903; M. Seiffert, ed.); *DTÖ* VIII.2 (vol.17, 1901; H. Botstiber and M. Seiffert, eds.); and *DTB* II.1 (1901; M. Seiffert, ed.).

122. Cf. Riedel Q, p.168.

123. In *Musica Sacra* I (1839).

124. Cf. vol. II, p.105. According to Riedel Q, p.168, some of these fugues seem to have been connected with preludes.

125. It is found in the new eds. of Buxtehude (II, p.90) and Böhm (p.142). Cf. also the catalog in H. H. Eggebrecht's article "Pachelbel," in *MGG*.

126. Cf. W. Breig, "Der Umfang des choralgebundenen Orgelwerkes von Jan Pieterszon Sweelinck," *AfMw*, XVII (1960), p.274, footnote 1.

127. Cf. vol. I, p.XIV.

128. Cf. F. Wolgast, *Georg Böhm, Sämtliche Werke*, vol.I, p.XII (under no.3).

129. Cf. vol. III, p.XXXIII.

130. New ed. in *DTB*, XVIII, vol.30 (1917; M. Seiffert, ed.), pp.175ff.

131. New eds. of the two prints and some manuscript pieces in *DTB*, XVIII, vol.30 (1917; M. Seiffert, ed.), of other manuscript pieces in *Die Orgel*, series II, no.3 (F. W. Riedel, ed.) and in Frotscher O.

132. New ed. of one in *DTB*, XVIII, p.213 (after Ritter B, p.121) and six more in Frotscher O.

133. New ed. in *DdT*, IV (1901; K. Päsler, ed.).

134. New ed. by M. Seiffert in *Organum IV*, no.19. In Straube C, Kuhnau is repre-

sented by two pieces: *Ach Herr mich armen Sünder,* taken from the Biblical History of the sick Hiskias, and *Auf meinen lieben Gott,* which may be ascribed to Kuhnau with reservation.

135. New ed. in *DdT,* XXI–XXII (1905; M. Seiffert, ed.).

136. Frotscher G, p.595, mentions a toccata that I have not been able to locate.

137. New eds. in Dietrich O (1 piece), Frotscher O (6), Keller A (1), Ritter B (2), Straube C (1), and elsewhere; cf. F. Blume's article "Buttstett," in *MGG.* For the manuscript tradition of Buttstett's chorales (and those of other organ masters) the catalog in Dietrich G, pp.89ff., is very useful. Several of the sources named there have since been lost or are inaccessible, particularly the Walther autograph at Kaliningrad (Königsberg).

138. Ritter G, p.169b.

139. Frotscher G, p.604.

140. New ed. in Shannon M, nos.23, 55, 57, 76.

141. In the Old Bach-Gesellschaft edition, vol.42, no.15; cf. R. Buchmayer's article "Drei irrtümlich J. S. Bach zugeschriebene Klavier-Kompositionen," *SIMg,* II (1901) pp.265ff.

142. New eds. in Dietrich O, Frotscher O, Keller A, Ritter B; several others are listed in Dietrich G, pp.89ff.

143. Cf. the catalog in Dietrich G, pp.89ff. A number of the pieces are lost or at present inaccessible. New eds. in Dietrich O (1 piece), Frotscher O (4), and Keller A (1).

20. Italy

1. Reprinted in Sartori B, pp.411, 414.

2. Cf. the article mentioned in Chap.16, note 59. New ed. of the *Selva* by B. Hudson in *CEKM,* no.7 (1965).

3. Cf. Stevens M, *Commentary,* Musical Appendix no.7.

4. Cf. the articles mentioned in Chap.16, notes 59 and 63. New ed. of the *Capricci* by B. Hudson in *CEKM,* no.11 (1967). Cf. B. Hudson, "Notes on Gregorio Strozzi and his *Capricci,*" *JAMS,* XX (1967), pp.209ff.

5. New ed. in Ritter B, p.46.

6. New ed. of nos.3, 5, and 9 in Torchi A; of nos.2, 10, and 11 in Tagliapietra A, vol.VI; of the conclusion of no.12 in Pirro A, p.1141.

7. For the dating cf. Sartori B, p.434; Riedel Q. p.72, note 164; K. G. Fellerer's article, "Arresti," in *MGG,* and his "Zur italienischen Orgelmusik . . . ," in *Jahrbuch Peters* 1938, p.71, note 3. The "numerous organ works" mentioned in the *MGG* article cannot be identified at present (according to a communication from Prof. Fellerer).

8. Several dates for this print appear in the literature, but no particular reasons are adduced, e.g., 1680 (Tagliapietra A, vol.VIII, under Pasquini), 1687 (Fellerer in *MGG* and in *Jahrbuch Peters* 1938, p.70), 1700 (Eitner).

9. New ed. in Ritter B, no.24.

10. New ed. in Ritter B, no.23.

11. New ed. in Ritter B, no.22.

12. New ed. in Tagliapietra A, vol.IX. The sonata from the Aresti print is also found in the manuscript Bologna, Ms. DD 53 (cf. Torchi A, p.341). According to *Riemanns Musik-Lexikon* (Gurlitt edition), several of these pieces may be by Pollaroli's son Antonio (1680–1746).

13. New ed. by F. Boghen in *Antichi maestri italiani: Toccate* (Ricordi, 1918), unfortunately with many deviations, which may be due to another source.

14. New ed. of twenty pieces in Tagliapietra A, vol. VIII. Complete new ed. in *CEKM*, no.5, vols.I–VII (1964–68; M. B. Haynes, ed.). In what follows we shall refer to this edition, in which all of Pasquini's compositions are numbered continuously.

15. Cf. Seiffert G, p.270.

16. E.g., in Tagliapietra A, vol.VII.

17. Cf. Seiffert G, p.277.

18. Detailed information about these prints is found in Sartori B.

19. Cf.p.716 and Fig.787.

20. Cf. "The Harpsichord Music of Alessandro Scarlatti," *SIMg*, VI (1904), pp. 16off.; addendum, ibid., p.418 (new ed., London: Bach & Co., 1908).

21. E.g., in L. Köhler, *Les Maîtres du Clavecin*, vol.II, p.90.

22. In his collection *Early Italian Piano Music* (Boston, 1906).

23. Tagliapietra A, vol.IX, p.129, includes a toccata from the same Milan manuscript (no.1 of the manuscript) whose *galant* style, however, indicates that it is a later composition.

24. R. Gerlin, *I Classici musicali italiani*, vol.13 (1943).

25. This volume has not been available to me; cf. Gerlin's edition, p.142.

26. For other sources cf. Gerlin, pp.140f., and E. Hanley's article, "Scarlatti, Alessandro," in *MGG*.

21. France

1. New ed. by Brunold and Tessier, *Oeuvres complètes de Chambonnières* (1925). Cf.pp.505ff., above, and M. Reimann, *Untersuchungen zur Formgeschichte der französischen Klavier-Suite* (1940).

2. Cf. J. Écorcheville, *Vingt Suites d'Orchestre du XVIIe Siècle français* (1906), vol. I, p.66.

3. By P. Bonfils (1956).

4. New ed. by P. Brunold (1936), revised by Th. Dart (1959), and by A. Curtis in *Le Pupitre*, vol.18 (1970).

5. Cf. the transcription in Tagliapietra A, vol.VIII, p.43, and similar attempts in Lavignac, *Encyclopédie*, I, 3, pp.1235, 1242 (by Quittard), or in the new ed. of the keyboard works of Gaspard Le Roux, by A. Fuller (1959).

6. New ed. of the two allemandes in Raugel M, vol.II, and Bonfils P.

7. According to a remark in J. Vigué's article, "Hardel," in *MGG*, it was varied by several composers of the 18th century.

8. New ed. in Bonfils P, no.1.

9. New ed. by N. Dufourcq (1956); one suite in Tagliapietra A, vol.VIII.

10. In the Möller manuscript several of these suites appear without the prelude.

11. New ed. by M. Roesgen-Champion (1934).

12. New ed. of the first suite in Tagliapietra A, vol.IX, pp.90ff.

13. Seiffert G, p.290.

14. New ed. by A. Fuller, *Gaspard Le Roux, Pieces for Harpsichord* (1959). A *Livre de Pièces de Clavecin* by Clérambault (1704) was not available to me.

15. New ed. in Guilmant A, vol.III; several also in Tagliapietra A, vol.VII; Raugel M, vol.II; Kaller L, vol.II.

16. New ed. of these compositions in P. Brunold's edition of L. Couperin's works (1636), nos.97, 124, 125, and 135–37; the second *Carillon* is also in J. Wasielewski's *Geschichte der Instrumentalmusik* (1878).

17. New ed. in Guilmant A, vol.IX, p.52.

18. New ed. in Guilmant A, vol.IX, p.74.

19. Cf. Guilmant A, vol.IX, pp.12, 32.

20. The new ed. of the *Livre I* by Vervoitte (1900) is all but unavailable today; the new ed. of *Livres II* and *III* by N. Dufourcq (1956, 1958) is to be followed by that of *Livre I*.

21. Cf. Pirro A, p.1337; Frotscher G, p.682.

22. New ed. in Guilmant A, vol.IX.

23. The pieces from the manuscript Paris, Bibl. nat. Vm⁷ 1823 that are added to the new edition can be attributed to Lebègue only with reservations, and sound more like student works.

24. New ed. in Guilmant A, vol.IV.

25. Cf. Pirro A, p.1339; N. Dufourcq, *La musique d'orgue française*, p.71; and J. Bonfils, "Gigault," in *MGG*.

26. New ed. of the *Premier livre* in Guilmant A, vol.II, and by N. Dufourcq (1962); of the *Second livre* by Bonfils (n.d.).

27. New ed. in Guilmant A, vol.VI.

28. New ed. by N. Dufourcq, *Premier livre d'orgue de Gilles Jullien* (1952); nine pieces also in Raugel M, vol.II, pp.36ff.

29. New ed. by Ch. Hens and R. Bragard, *Livre d'orgue (1695) de Lambert Chaumont*, in *Monumenta Leodiensium musicorum* (1939).

30. Cf. Frotscher G, p.680.

31. New ed. in Guilmant A, vol. V, and in P. Brunold, *François Couperin, Pièces d'orgue* (1952). Pages in both editions are given in the following discussion.

32. Guilmant A, vol.VI, p.119.

33. Cf. Guilmant A, vol. V, pp.123, 134, 159; Brunold, pp.24, 37, 63.

34. New ed. in Guilmant A, vol. V, and in N. Dufourcq and N. Pierront, *Premier livre d'orgue de Nicolas de Grigny* (1953). Pages in both editions are given in the following discussion.

35. For the former cf. Guilmant A, pp.23, 45, 46, 75, and Dufourcq and Pierront, pp.25, 46, 48, 78; for the latter Guilmant A, pp.7, 30, and Dufourcq, pp.10, 32.

36. New ed. of three noëls in Raugel M, vol.II.

37. New ed. in Guilmant A, vol.III (the print) and vol.V (the manuscript collection).

38. New ed. in Howell F; three pieces also in Raugel M, vol.II.

39. Cf. Pirro A, p. 1343.

40. New ed. in Guilmant A, vol.VII.

41. Guilmant A, vol.III, p.68.

42. New ed. in Guilmant A, vol.III; of the *Grand jeu* also in Raugel M, vol.II.

43. New ed. in Guilmant A, vol.III, and in N. Dufourcq, *Premier livre d'orgue . . . par Louis-Nicolas Clérambault* (1954). Pages in both editions are given in the following discussion.

44. New ed. of the Mass in Howell F, pp.40ff; of seven noëls in J. Ter Hasselt, *Noëls pour l'orgue de Nicolas Geoffroy* (n.d.).

45. Cf. the statements in the article "Geoffroy" in *Larousse de la musique* (1961), which, however, are not necessarily reliable. There, as well as in D. Launay's article "Geoffroy" in *MGG*, a *Livre de pièces de clavessin . . . de Jean-Nicolas Geoffroy* (Bibl. du Cons., Rés.475; formerly 24827) is also attributed to this composer. Its very interesting contents, however, point to a later time, about 1730–40. Various pieces give the impression that an 18th-century Satie is involved. I am grateful to M. Norbert Dufourcq for detailed communications about his studies of the two manuscripts and of the Geoffroy family.

46. Several other pieces are cited in Pirro A, p.1347.

47. New ed. by P. Hardouin, *Le livre d'orgue de Marguerite Thiéry* (*L'Organiste liturgique*, no.25); the Masses also in Howell F, pp.18ff., 28ff.

22. England

1. New ed. of a courante by Coleman in Fuller C, book VI. A sarabande with variations, at one time attributed to Orlando Gibbons, is now justifiably held to be by his pupil Portman (cf. J. Steele's article, "Portman," in *MGG*); new ed. in M. H. Glyn, *Orlando Gibbons,* II, p.4. Cf. Chap.13, note 38, above.

2. New ed. of the sarabande in Fuller C, book VI.

3. Mr. George Sargent has studied this manuscript and has completely transcribed the keyboard repertoire.

4. New ed. by Th. Dart, *Keyboard Suites: Matthew Locke* (1959).

5. New ed. of a *Ground* in Fuller C, book VI, p.2.

6. New ed. in Fuller C, book VI, pp.9–22.

7. New ed. by C. Rayner in *CEKM,* no.18 (1967).

8. New ed. also in West O, no.28.

9. Cf. Pirro A, p.1245.

10. New ed. of the *Prelude* in West O, no.27. The other two works are found in manuscripts at the Royal College of Music in London.

11. New ed. in Th. Dart, *Organ Voluntaries: Matthew Locke* (1957); two pieces also in West O, nos.14 and 20.

12. New ed. in W. Shaw, *John Blow, Complete Organ Works* (1958); a partial new ed. in A. V. Butcher, *John Blow, Selected Organ Music* (Hinrichsen Ed., n.d.).

13. New eds. in Fuller C, books I, II; K. Oesterle, *Early Keyboard Music*, vol.I (1904). Not all the pieces attributed to John Blow in E. Pauer, *Old English Composers* (n.d.) can be called his with certainty.

14. New ed. in vol.VI of the *Complete Edition* by the Purcell Society, to which the following discussion refers; the harpsichord works also in W. Barclay Squire, *Henry Purcell, Original Works for Harpsichord*, 4 vols. (1908).

15. Another *Ground* in C minor (p.51) may be by Croft; cf. Fuller C, book III, p.10.

16. This piece was included among the doubtful works of Bach in the Old Bach-Gesellschaft Edition, vol.42, p.250.

17. It was also included, though hardly with justification, among Blow's organ works; cf. new ed., Shaw, no.30.

18. Cf. Frotscher G, p.812.

19. Preserved in Eccles' *A set of Lessons* (cf.p.753); new ed. in Fuller C, book VI, pp.9–14.

20. A partial new ed. in Fuller C, book V.

21. New ed. in Fuller C, books III–IV.

23. The Netherlands

1. New ed. by M. Seiffert, *Anthoni van Noordt, Tabulatuur-Boeck* (in *Vereeniging voor Noord-Nederlands Muziekgeschiedenis*, Uitgave XIX, 1896); new ed. of the psalms in P. Pidoux, *Anthoni van Noordt, Psalmenbearbeitungen für Orgel* (1954).

2. New ed. by F. Noske in *Monumenta Musica Neerlandica*, vol. II (1959).

3. Cf. his article "Steenwick," in *MGG*.

4. In A. Curtis, *Nederlandse Klaviermuziek uit de 16e en 17e eeuw*, in *Monumenta Musica Neerlandica*, vol.III (1961).

5. Cf. *Monumenta Musica Neerlandica*, vol.III, p.IX.

6. New ed. of three suites by A. Curtis in *Exempla Musica Neerlandica* I (1964).

7. By J. Watelet, in *Monumenta Musicae Belgicae*, vol. II (1933).

8. Cf. p.XX; but Watelet's statements may not be completely reliable; cf. E. Lowinsky's review in *MQ*, XL (1954), p.600.

24. Spain and Portugal

1. In *Musici organici Iohannis Cabanilles opera omnia* (1927–56).

2. Cf. M. Reimann in *Mf*, XI (1958), p.538.

3. I owe this reference and various others to personal communications from Dr. Robert Stevenson.

4. Cf. the tables of contents in Anglés C, vol. I, pp.XLIXff. (nos.3, 4, and 7).

5. New ed. of the versets under the title *Versillos de sexto tono para Sanctus* in Pedrell A, vol.II, p.11 (where Llussá is erroneously called Llissá), and under the title *Versets de segon to,* in Muset E, p.66; new ed. of one tiento by Menalt in Muset E, p.48, and of five others in Anglés A, I–II, and of two tientos by Bazea and a few others in Anglés A, II–III.

6. Cf. *Carlos Seixas* (Coimbra: Coimbra Editora, 1947), pp.26, 40, 35.

7. Oporto, Bibl. mun. No.1607; complete transcription and commentary by K. Speer, "A Portuguese Manuscript of Keyboard Music . . ." (diss., Indiana University, 1956); printed new ed. in *Portugaliae Musica*, vol.XI (1967).

8. Cf. note 6; Braga, Bibl. pública No.964.

9. Oporto, Bibl. mun. No.1577; complete transcription and commentary by B. Hudson, "A Portuguese Source of 17th-Century Iberian Organ Music" (diss., Indiana University, 1961).

10. The Library of Congress holds a *Libro de cifra,* whose contents (*Folias, Xácara, Rigodon, Seguidilla, Minuets,* etc.) point to the early 18th century.

11. All the volumes are in Madrid. Detailed tables of contents appear in *Catálogo musical de la Biblioteca Nacional de Madrid* (H. Anglés and J. Subira, eds.), vol.I, pp. 295ff.; the original "Indice de lo contenido" (arranged by *tonos*) is also in Anglés C, vol.I, pp.LVIIff. Cf. M. Querol's article, "Martin y Coll," in *MGG*.

12. Cf. Anglés C, vol.I, p.LIX.

BIBLIOGRAPHY

Periodicals and Monument Editions

AfMf	*Archiv für Musikforschung*
AfMw	*Archiv für Musikwissenschaft*
AM	*Acta Musicologica*
CEKM	*Corpus of Early Keyboard Music*
DdT	*Denkmäler deutscher Tonkunst*
DTB	*Denkmäler der Tonkunst in Bayern*
DTÖ	*Denkmäler der Tonkunst in Österreich*
JAMS	*Journal of the American Musicological Society*
KmJb	*Kirchenmusikalisches Jahrbuch*
MD	*Musica Disciplina*
Mf	*Die Musikforschung*
MfM	*Monatshefte für Musikgeschichte*
MGG	*Die Musik in Geschichte und Gegenwart*
ML	*Music and Letters*
MQ	*Musical Quarterly*
SIMg	*Sammelbände der Internationalen Musikgesellschaft*
TVer	*Tijdschrift der Vereeniging voor Nederlandsche Muziekgeschiedenis*
VfMw	*Vierteljahrsschrift für Musikwissenschaft*
ZfMw	*Zeitschrift für Musikwissenschaft*

Selected Bibliography

The following list is not intended to be a complete bibliography of early keyboard music, but contains only books, articles, and editions cited in the text. Those that occur very often are cited in the abbreviations given in bold type following the full references. When several publications are listed for the same author they are given in chronological order. Encyclopedia articles are not listed, nor are works referred to in the text but which do not deal with keyboard music.

Abbiati, F. *Storia della musica* (1943).

Adler, G. *Musikalische Werke der Habsburgischen Kaiser* (1892).

——, ed. *J. J. Froberger: Orgel- und Klavierwerke* (DTÖ, IV. 1, VI. 2, X. 2, vols.8, 13, 21, 1897, 1899, 1903).

——, ed. *Trienter Codices*, I (DTÖ, VII, vols.14/15, 1900).

Adlung, J. *Anleitung zu der musikalischen Gelahrtheit* (1758).

Alaleona, D. "Le laudi spirituali nei secoli XVI e XVII e il loro rapporto coi canti profani" (*Riv. mus. it.*, XVI, 1909, 1ff.).

Altwegg, W., ed. *L. Senfl, Sämtliche Werke*, II (1962).

Ambros, A. W. *Geschichte der Musik* (1881²).

Ameln, K., ed. *Das Locheimer Liederbuch . . .* (1925).

Andrews, H., ed. *My Ladye Nevells Booke* (1926) [**Andrews N, AN, Nev**].

Anglés, H., ed. *Musici organici Johannis Cabanilles . . . Opera omnia . . .* , 4 vols. (1927–58) [**Anglés C**].

—— "Un Manuscrit inconnu avec polyphonie du XVᵉ siècle conservé à la Cathédrale de Ségovie" (*AM*, VIII, 1936, 6ff.).

—— *La musica en la Corte de Carlos V . . .* (1944) [**Anglés M**].

——, ed. *Catálogo musical de la Biblioteca Nacional de Madrid* (1946–   ).

—— "El Pange lingua de Johannes Urreda" (*Anuario Musical*, VII, 1952, 193ff.).

——, ed. *Antologia de Organistas Españoles del siglo XVII*, 3 vols. (1965–67) [**Anglés A**].

——, ed. *Antonio de Cabezón*, 3 vols. (1966).

Annegarn, A. *Supplement* (1958) to Seiffert, M., *J. P. Sweelinck: Werken voor Orgel en Clavicimbel* (1943).

Apel, W. Review of Tagliapietra, G., *Antologia di Musica . . . per Pianoforte* (*ZfMw*, XVI, 1933/4, 126f.).

—— "Die Tabulatur des Adam Ileborgh" (*ZfMw*, XVI, 1933/34, 193ff.).

——, ed. *Musik aus früher Zeit für Klavier*, 2 vols. (1934) [**Apel M**].

—— "Du nouveau sur la musique française pour orgue au XVIᵉ siècle" (*Revue musicale*, XVIII, 1937, 96ff.).

—— "Neapolitan Links between Cabezon and Frescobaldi" (*MQ*, XXIV, 1938, 419ff.).

—— *Historical Anthology of Music*, 2 vols. (1946/50). Cf. Davison.

—— "Early History of the Organ" (*Speculum*, XXIII, 1948, 191ff.).

—— "Die Süditalienische Clavierschule des 17. Jahrhunderts" (*AM*, XXXIV, 1948, 128ff.).

—— "The Early Development of the Ricercar" (*MD*, III, 1949, 139ff.).

—— "Die menschliche Stimme als Instrument" (*Stimmen*, XV, 1949, 404ff.).

—— "Die Celler Orgeltabulatur von 1601" (*Mf*, XIX, 1956, 142ff.).

—— "Drei plus Drei plus Zwei = Vier plus Vier" (*AM*, XXXII, 1960, 29ff.).

—— "Tänze und Arien für Clavier aus dem Jahre 1588" (*AfMw*, XVII, 1960, 51ff.).

—— "Attaingnant: Quatorze Gaillardes" (*Mf*, XIV, 1961, 361ff.).

—— *Die Notation der Polyphonen Musik, 900 bis 1600* (1962) [**Apel N**].

—— "Die handschriftliche Überlieferung der Klavierwerke Frescobaldis" (*Festschrift K. G. Fellerer*, 1962, 40ff.).

—— "Neu aufgefundene Clavierwerke von Scheidemann, Tunder, Froberger, Reincken und Buxtehude" (*AM*, XXXIV, 1962, 65ff.).

—— "Spanish Organ Music of the Early 17th Century" (*JAMS*, XV, 1962, 174ff.).

—— "Die spanische Orgelmusik vor Cabanilles" (*Anuario Musical*, XVII, 1962, 15ff.).

——, ed. *Keyboard Music of the Fourteenth and Fifteenth Centuries* (CEKM, 1, 1963) [**Apel K**].

——, ed. *Marco Facoli, Collected Works* (CEKM, 2, 1963).

——, ed. *Costanzo Antegnati, L'Antegnata intavolatura* (CEKM, 9, 1965).

——, ed. *Adam Reincken, Collected Keyboard Works* (CEKM, 16, 1967).

——, and Siegele, U., eds. *Johann Ulrich Steigleder, Compositions for Keyboard*, 2 vols. (CEKM, 13, 1968/9).

——, ed. *Pieter Cornet, Collected Keyboard Works* (CEKM, 26, 1969).

——, ed. *Spanish Organ Masters after Cabezon* (CEKM, 14, 1971) [**Apel S**].

——, ed. *The Tablature of Celle* (CEKM, 17, forthcoming).

Arnold, F. W. "Das Locheimer Liederbuch" (*Jahrbücher für musikalische Wissenschaft*, II, 1867, 1ff.).

Bangert, E., ed. *Dietrich Buxtehude, Klavervaerker* (1941).

Barclay Squire, Wm., ed. *The Fitzwilliam Virginal Book* (1899) [**FW**]. Cf. listing under Manuscript Sources.

——, ed. *Henry Purcell, Original Works for Harpsichord* (1908).

Baron, J. H. "A 17th-Century Keyboard Tablature in Brasov" (*JAMS*, XX, 1967, 279ff.).

Baum, R., ed. *Kindermann, Stücke für Klavier* (1929).

Baumann, O. A. *Das deutsche Lied und seine Bearbeitungen in den frühen Orgeltabulaturen* (1934) [**Baumann L**].

Bedbrook, G. S., ed. *Giovanni Gabrieli, Werke für Tasteninstrumente* (1957).

Benvenuti, G., ed. *Girolamo Cavazzoni detto d'Urbino dal I e II libro di Intavolature per Organo . . . (I Classici della musica italiana*, I, 1919).

—— "Noterella circa tre fughe attribuite al Frescobaldi e alcune ristampe moderni" (*Riv. mus. it.*, XXVII, 1920, 133ff.).

——, ed. *Istituzioni e Monumenti dell' Arte Italiana*, I (1931).

——, ed. *Marco Antonio Cavazzoni, Jacobo Fogliano, Julio Segni (ed Anonimi). Ricercari e Ricercate (I Classici musicali italiana*, I, 1941) [**Benvenuti M**].

Berend, F. "Nicolaus Adam Strunck" (diss., Munich, 1913).

Boghen, F., ed. *Antichi maestri italiani, Toccate* (1918).

Böhme, F. *Altdeutsches Liederbuch* (1877).

Bolte, J. "Das Stammbuch Johann Valentin Meder's" (*VfMw*, VIII, 1892, 499ff.).

Bonfils, J., ed. *Henri Dumont, L'oeuvre pour clavecin* (1956).

——, ed. *Les Pré-Classiques français . . . (L'Organiste liturgique*, 18, 1957; 31: *Supplément*) [**Bonfils P**].

——, ed. *André Raison, Second livre d'orgue (L'Organiste liturgique*, 39/40, 43/44, 1963).

——, ed. *Chansons françaises pour orgue (Le Pupitre*, 5, 1968).

Bonnet, J., ed. *Historical Organ Recitals*, 6 vols. (1917–45).

——, ed. *G. Frescobaldi, Fiori musicali (Les grands maîtres anciens de l'orgue*, 1922).

Borren. Cf. van den Borren.

Botstiber, H., ed. *Joh. Pachelbel, 94 Kompositionen, zumeist über das Magnifikat (DTÖ*, VIII. 2, vol.17, 1901).

——, ed. *A. Poglietti, Klavier- und Orgelwerke (DTÖ*, XIII. 2, vol.27, 1906).

Breig, W. "Der Umfang des choral-gebundenen Orgelwerkes von Sweelinck" (*AfMw*, XVII, 1960, 258ff.).

——, ed. *Die Orgelwerke von H. Scheidemann* (1967).

—— "Die Lübbenauer Tabulaturen A1 und A2" (*AfMw*, XXV, 1968, 96ff., 223ff.).

Brunold, P., ed. *Oeuvres complètes de Chambonnières* (1925).

——, ed. *Oeuvres complètes de Louis Couperin* (1936).

——, ed. *François Couperin, Pièces d'orgue* (1952).

Buchmayer, R. "Drei irrtümlich J. S. Bach zugeschriebene Klavier-Kompositionen" (*SIMg*, II, 1901, 265ff.).

—— "Christian Ritter" (*Riemann Festschrift*, 1909, 354ff.).

—— *Aus Richard Buchmayers Historischen Konzerten*, 5 vols. (1927) [**Buchmayer K**].

Burney, Ch. *A General History of Music* (1776–89).

Burns, J. A. "L'impiego della partitura e l'Arte della Fuga di J. S. Bach" (*L'Organo*, II, 1961, 163ff.).

Butcher, A. V., ed. *John Blow, Selected Organ Music* (n.d.)

Casimiri, R., ed. *Musica veterum* (n.d.).

Chappell, Wm., ed. *Old English Popular Music*, 2 vols. (1892²).

Chilesotti, O., ed. *'Balli d'arpicordo' di Giovanni Picchi* (*Biblioteca di raritá musicali* II, c.1885) [**Chilesotti P**].

Chybinsky, A. "Polnische Musik und Musikkultur des 16. Jahrhunderts . . ." (*SIMg*, XIII, 1912, 463ff.).

——, ed. *36 Tancόw . . .* (1948).

Closson, E., ed. *Le manuscrit dit des Basses Danses . . .* (1912).

Commer, F., ed. *Musica Sacra* I (1839; Pachelbel's Magnificat Fugues).

Curtis, A. "L'Opera cembalo-organistica di T. Merula" (*L'Organo*, I, 1960, 141ff.).

——, ed. *Nederlandse Klaviermuziek uit de 16ᵉ en 17ᵉ eeuw* (*Monumenta Musica Neerlandica*, III, 1961).

——, ed. *Exempla Musica Neerlandica*, I (1964; 3 suites by Pieter Bustijn).

—— *Sweelinck's Keyboard Music* (1969).

——, ed. *Louis Couperin: Pièces de Clavecin* (*Le Pupitre*, 18, 1970).

Dalla Libera, S., ed. *G. Gabrieli, Composizioni per organo*, 2 vols. (1956/7) [**Libera G**].

——, ed. *C. Merulo, Toccate per organo*, 3 vols. (1958) [**Libera M**].

——, ed. *A. Gabrieli, Tre messe per organo* (1959).

——, ed. *G. Frescobaldi, Nove Toccate inedite* (1962).

Dart, Th. "A New Source of Early English Organ Music" (*ML*, XXXV, 1954, 201ff.).

——, ed. *Organ Voluntaries: Matthew Locke* (1957).

——, ed. *Keyboard Suites: Matthew Locke* (1959).

—— P. Brunold, *Oeuvres complètes de Louis Couperin*, rev. ed. (1959).

——, ed. *Keyboard Works: Thomas Morley*, 2 vols. (1959).

—— "John Bull's 'Chapel' " (*ML*, XL, 1959, 279ff.).

—— "Elisabeth Eysbock's keyboard book" (*Svensk Tidschrift för Musikforskning*, 44, 1962, 5ff.).

Davison, A. T., and Apel, W., eds. *Historical Anthology of Music*, 2 vols. (1946–50).

Dawes, F., ed. *Schott's Anthology of Early English Keyboard Music* (n.d.).

——, ed. *Two Elizabethan Keyboard Duets* (n.d.).

Deffner, O. *Über die Entwicklung der Fantasie für Tasteninstrumente bis Sweelinck* (1927).

De Lange, S., ed. *Georg Muffat, Apparatus musico-organisticus* (1888).

Dietrich, F. *Geschichte des deutschen Orgelchorals im 17. Jahrhundert* (1932) [**Dietrich G**].

—— *Elf Orgelchoräle des 17. Jahrhunderts* (1932; musical supplement to Dietrich G) [**Dietrich O**].

Dufourcq, N. *La musique d'orgue française* (1949).

——, ed. *Premier livre d'orgue de Gilles Jullien* (1952).

——, ed. *Premier livre d'orgue de Nicolas de Grigny* (1953).

——, ed. *Premier livre d'orgue . . . par Louis-Nicolas Clérambault* (1954).

——, ed. *N. A. Lebègue, Oeuvres de Clavessin* (1956).

——, ed. *G.-G. Nivers, Livre d'orgue* (2 and 3, 1956/8).

——, ed. *André Raison, Premier livre d'orgue* (*Orgue et Liturgie*, no.58/59, 1962).

Écorcheville, J., ed. *Vingt Suites d'Orchestre du XVIIe Siècle français* (1906).

Eggebrecht, H. H. "Terminus 'Ricercar' " (*AfMw*, IX, 1952, 137ff.).

Einstein, A. "Die Arie di Ruggiero" (*SIMg* XIII, 1912, 444ff.).

——, ed. *G. Gabrieli, Canzoni per sonar a 4* (1933).

—— "Vincenzo Galilei and the Instructive Duo" (*ML*, XVIII, 1937, 36off.).

Eitner, R. *Das deutsche Lied des XV. und XVI. Jahrhunderts*, 2 vols. (1876/80; also *MfM*, VIII–XV).

——, ed. *L. Kleber, Fantasia in Re* (*MfM*, XX, 1888, Beilage).

Emsheimer, E. *Johann Ulrich Steigleder, sein Leben und seine Werke* (1928).

Epstein, E. *Der französische Einfluss auf die deutsche Klaviersuite im 17. Jahrhundert* (1940).

Esposito, M., ed. *Early Italian Piano Music* (1906).

Expert, H., ed. *Edition populaire française* (n.d.).

——, ed. *Anthologie chorale des Maîtres musiciens de la Renaissance française* (1938).

Feder, G., ed. *Die Orgel, Reihe II: Werke alter Meister* (1957–   ).

Federhofer, H. "Eine Kärntner Orgeltabulatur . . ." (*Carinthia*, I, Jahrgang 142, 33off.).

Ferguson, H., ed. *Complete Keyboard Works of Wm. Tisdall* (1957).

Fellerer, K. G. "Zur italienischen Orgelmusik des 17./18. Jahrhunderts" (*Jahrbuch Peters*, 1938, pp.7off.).

Fernandes, C. R., ed. *Portugaliae Musica* VII (1967; Oporto Ms.).

Fischer, K. v. "Chaconne und Passacaglia" (*Revue Belge de Musicologie*, XII, 1958, 19ff.).

Fischer, M., ed. *44 Choräle zum Präludieren & Die organistische Improvisation im 17. Jahrhundert* (1929).

Fock, G., ed. *Scheidemann: Choralbearbeitungen* (1966).

Froidebise, P., ed. *J. Bermudo, Oeuvres d'orgue . . .* (*Orgue et Liturgie*, 47, 1960) [**Froidebise B**].

——, ed. *Tomas de Santa Maria, Oeuvres transcrites de L'Arte de tañer Fantasia* (*Orgue et Liturgie*, 49, 1961).

Frotscher, G. *Geschichte des Orgelspiels und der Orgelkomposition*, 2 vols. (1935) [**Frotscher G**].

——, ed. *Orgelchoräle um J. S. Bach* (*Das Erbe deutscher Musik, Reichsdenkmale 9*, 1937) [**Frotscher O**].

Fuller, A., ed. *Gaspard Le Roux, Pieces for Harpsichord* (1959).

Fuller-Maitland, J. A., ed. *Fitzwilliam Virginal Book* (1899) [**FW**]. Cf. listing under Manuscript Sources.

——, ed. *Contemporaries of Purcell*, 7 books (1921) [**Fuller C**].

——, ed. *25 Pieces . . . from Benjamin Cosyn's Virginial Book* (1923).

Funcke, H. "Eine Chanson von Binchois . . ." (*AM*, V, 1933, 3ff.).

Fuser, I., ed. *Antonio Valente: Versi spirituali per organo* (1958).

Gastoué, A. "La Musique byzantine et le chant des églises d'Orient" (Lavignac's *Encyclopédie de la musique* I. 1, 1913, 541ff.).

Gauss, O., ed. *Orgelkompositionen aus alter und neuer Zeit* (4 vols.) I (1913⁴) [**Gauss O**].

Geering, A., ed. *Ludwig Senfl, Sämtliche Werke* II (1962).

Geiringer, K. *The Bach Family* (1957).

Gerber, R., ed. *Dufay: Sämtliche Hymnen* (*Das Chorwerk*, 14, 1937).

Gerdes, G., ed. *46 Choräle für Orgel von J. P. Sweelinck und seinen deutschen Schülern* (1957) [**Gerdes C**].

Gerlin, R., ed. *Al. Scarlatti: Primo e secondo libro de Toccate (I classici musicali italiani,* 13, 1943).

Germani, F., ed. *G. Frescobaldi, Fiori musicali* (1936).

Glyn, M. H. *About Elizabethan Virginal Music and Its Composers* (1924) [**Glyn E**].

——, ed. *Th. Weelkes, Pieces for Keyed Instruments* (1924).

——, ed. *O. Gibbons, Complete Keyboard Works,* 5 books (1925–6).

——, ed. *30 Virginal Pieces* (1927).

——, ed. *Complete Keyboard Works of John Bull* (1930).

Göllner, Th. *Formen früher Mehrstimmigkeit* (1961).

Golos, J. (G.), ed. *Keyboard Music from Polish Manuscripts,* 4 vols. (*CEKM,* 10, 1965–7).

——, ed. *The Organ Tablatures of Warsaw, Musical Society (Antiquitates Musicae in Polonia,* 15, 1968).

Gombosi, O. "Der Hoftanz" (*AM,* VII, 1935, 50ff.).

——, ed. *Compositione di Meser Vincenzo Capirola* (1955).

Grafczyński, M. "Über die Orgeltabulatur des Martin Leopolita" (diss., Vienna, 1919).

Guilmant, A. *Archives des maîtres de l'orgue,* 10 vols. (1898–1910) [**Guilmant A**].

——, ed. *G. Frescobaldi, Fiori musicali* (*Les grands maîtres anciens de l'orgue,* 1922).

Gurlitt, W. "Die Orgelwerke des Michael Praetorius" (*AfMw,* III, 1930, 135ff.).

Haas, R. *Aufführungspraxis der Musik* (1930).

Haberl, F. X., ed. *G. P. da Palestrina: Werke,* 33 vols. (1862–1907).

——, ed. *G. Frescobaldi, Fiori musicali* (1889).

Halbig, H. *Klaviertänze des 16. Jahrhunderts* (1928).

Hamburger, P. "Ein handschriftliches Klavierbuch aus der ersten Hälfte des 17. Jahrhunderts" (*ZfMw,* XIII, 1930/1, 133ff.).

Harding, R. E. M., ed. *G. M. Radino: Il primo libro d'intavolatura di balli d'arpicordo* (1949).

Hardouin, P., ed. *Le livre d'orgue de Marguerite Thiéry* (*L'Organiste liturgique,* 25, n.d.).

Harman, R. A., ed. *Thomas Morley: A Plaine and Easie Introduction to Practicall Musicke* (1952).

Harms, G., ed. *Gesamtausgabe der Werke Samuel Scheidts* (1923–   ).

Hawkins, J. *A General History of the Science and Practice of Music,* 5 vols. (1776).

Haynes, M. B., ed. *Bernardo Pasquini, Collected Works for Keyboard,* 7 vols. (*CEKM,* 5, 1964–8).

Heartz, D., ed. *Keyboard Dances from the Earlier 16th Century* (*CEKM,* 8, 1965).

Hedar, J. *Dietrich Buxtehudes Orgelwerke* (1951) [**Hedar B**].

——, ed. *Dietrich Buxtehude, Sämtliche Orgelwerke,* 4 vols. (1952).

Hendrie, G., ed. *Orlando Gibbons: Keyboard Music* (*Musica Brittanica,* XX, 1961).

Hens, Ch., and Bragard, R., eds. *Livre d'Orgue (1695) de Lambert Chaumont* (*Monumenta Leodiensium musicorum,* 1939).

Hirtler, F. "Neu aufgefundene Orgelstücke von J. U. Steigleder und Johann Benn" (*AfMf,* II, 1937, 92ff.).

Howell, A. C., ed. *Five French Baroque Organ Masses* (1961) [**Howell F**].

Hudson, B. "A Portuguese Source of 17th-Century Iberian Organ Music" (diss., Indiana University, 1961).

——, ed. *Giovanni Salvatore: Collected Keyboard Works* (*CEKM,* 3, 1964).

——, ed. *Bernardo Storace: Selva di varie compositioni . . .* (*CEKM,* 7, 1965).

——, ed. *Gregorio Strozzi: Capricci . . . op.4* (*CEKM,* 11, 1967).

—— "Notes on Gregorio Strozzi and his Capricci" (*JAMS,* XX, 1967, 209ff.).

Hudson, R. "The Development of Italian Keyboard Variations on the Passacaglio and Ciaccona from Guitar Music in the 17th Century" (diss., University of California at Los Angeles, 1967; University Microfilm 68–219).
—— "Further Remarks on the Passacaglia and Ciaccona" (*JAMS*, XXIII, 1970, 302ff.).

Ilgner, R., ed. *M. Weckmann, Gesammelte Werke* (1942).

Jachimecki, Z. "Eine polnische Orgeltabulatur aus dem Jahre 1548" (*ZfMw*, II, 1919/20, 206ff.).
Jackson, R., ed. *Neapolitan Keyboard Composers circa 1600* (*CEKM*, 24, 1967).
Jeans, S., ed. *3 Voluntaries for Double Organ* (1956).
——, ed. *Two Toys and a Jigg* (1958).
Jeppesen, K. *Die italienische Orgelmusik am Anfang des Cinquecento* (1943[1]; 1960[2], 2 vols., enlarged ed.) [**Jeppesen O, O²**].
—— "Eine frühe Orgelmesse aus Castell' Arquato" (*AfMw*, XII, 1955, 187ff.).
——, ed. *Balli antichi veneziani* (1962).
—— "Ein altitalienisches Tanzbuch" (*Festschrift K. G. Fellerer*, 1962, 245ff.).

Kaller, E., ed. *Liber organi,* 9 books (1931–54) [**Kaller L**].
Kammerer, F., ed. *Die Musikstücke des Prager Kodex XI E 9* (1931).
Kastner, M. S. *Carlos Seixas* (1947).
——, ed. *Libro de tientos . . . compuesto por Francisco Correa de Arauxo*, 2 vols. (1948) (1952) [**Kastner L**].
—— "Los manuscritos musicales . . . de Coimbra" (*Anuario musical*, V, 1950, 78ff.).
—— "Parallels and Discrepancies between English and Spanish Keyboard Music . . ." (*Anuario musical*, VII, 1952, 77ff.).
—— *Silva Ibérica* (1954).
——, ed. *Arnolt Schlick, Hommage à l'empereur Charles-Quint* (1954).
—— "Una intabulatura d'organo italiana del 1598" (*Collectanea Hist. Mus.*, II, 1956, 237ff.).
——, ed. *Juan Bermudo, Declaración de instrumentos musicales* (1555) (*Documenta musicologica*, XI, 1957).
——, ed. *Altitalienische Versetten für Orgel und andere Tasteninstrumente* (1957).
——, ed. *Jacques Buus, Ricercari III° e IV°* (1957).
——, ed. *Rocco Rodio: Cinque ricercate una fantasia* (1958) [**Kastner R**].
——, ed. *Antonio Cabezón: Tientos und Fugen* (1958).
——, ed. *Manuel Rodrigues Coelho: Flores de musica*, 2 vols. (*Portugaliae Musica* I/III, 1959/61) [**Kastner F**].
——, ed. *Ascanio Mayone: Secondo libro di diversi capricci per sonare* (*Orgue et Liturgie*, 63, 65, 1964/5).
——, ed. *Antonio Cabezón: Claviermusik* (n.d.).
Keller, H., ed. *80 Choralvorspiele deutscher Meister des 17. und 18. Jahrhunderts* (1937) [**Keller A**].
——, ed. *Vincent Lübeck, Orgelwerke* (1941).
——, ed. *G. Frescobaldi, Fiori musicali* (1943).
Kinkeldey, O. *Orgel und Klavier in der Musik des 16. Jahrhunderts* (1910) [**Kinkeldey O**].
Kittler, G. *Geschichte des protestantischen Orgelchorals* (1931).
Klaus, G., ed. *Johann Speth, 10 Toccaten* (*Liber organi* IX, 1954).
Knaus, H. "Franz Matthias Techelmann, Sein Leben und seine Werke" (diss., Vienna, 1959).

Köhler, L., ed. *Les maîtres du clavecin*, 13 books (1860–67).
Körner, G. W., ed. *Der Orgel-Freund* (1841–   ).
——, ed. *Der Orgelvirtuose* (1845–   ).
Kraft, W., ed. *Buxtehude, Orgelwerke*, 2 vols. (1952).
Kraus, E., ed. *Cantatibus organis 8/9* (1962).
Krebs, C. "Girolamo Diruta's Transilvano" (*VfMw*, VIII, 1892, 344ff.).

Labat, J. B., ed. *Livre IV des Oeuvres d'orgue de Claude Merulo* (1865).
Lange, S. de. Cf. De Lange.
Leichtentritt, H., ed. *H. Praetorius, Ausgewählte Werke* (*DdT*, 23, 1905).
Libera, S. dalla. Cf. Dalla Libera.
Lincoln, H. B., ed. *17-Century Keyboard Music in the Chigi Manuscripts of the Vatican Library*, 3 vols. (*CEKM*, 32, 1968).
Lowinsky, E. "English Organ Music of the Renaissance" (*MQ*, 39, 1953, 373ff., 528ff.).
—— Review of J. Watelet, *Monumenta Musicae Belgicae* (*MQ*, 40, 1954, 595ff.).
Ludwig, Franz, ed. *J. C. F. Fischer: Notenbüchlein für Clavier* (1940).
Lundgren, Bo. ed. *Buxtehude, 4 Suiten für Clavichord oder Laute* (1955).
——, ed. *H. Scheidemann, Tokkata* (n.d.).
—— "Johann Lorentz in Kopenhagen . . ." (*Kongressbericht Köln*, 1958, 183ff.).
—— "Johann Lorentz" (*Svensk Tidskrift för Musikforskning*, 43, 1961, 249ff.).
Lunelli, R. "Contributi trentini alle relazioni fra l'Italia e la Germania nel Rinasciamento" (*AM*, XXI, 1949, 41ff.).

Maas, M. C. "Seventeenth-Century English Keyboard Music: A Study of Manuscripts Rés. 1185, 1186, and 1186bis of the Paris Conservatory Library" (diss., Yale University, 1969).
——, ed. *Songs and Dances for Keyboard from Seventeenth-Century England* (*Collegium Musicum: Yale University*, ser. 2, vol. III, 1971).
Machabey, G. *G. Frescobaldi, La vie, l' oeuvre* (1952).
Matthaei, K., ed. *M. Praetorius, Sämtliche Orgelwerke* (1930).
Mattheson, J. *Grundlage einer Ehrenpforte . . .* (1740).
Mazzi, C. *Il libro dell' Arte del Danzare di Antonio Cornazano* (*La Bibliofilia*, XVII, 1916, 1ff.).
Meer, J. H. van der. Cf. Van der Meer.
Merian, W. *Die Tabulaturen des Organisten Hans Kotter* (1916).
—— *Der Tanz in den deutschen Tabulaturbüchern* (1927) [**Merian T**].
Metzger, H.-A., ed. *Orgelwerke alter Meister aus Süddeutschland* (1954) [**Metzger O**].
Miller, H. M. "Sixteenth-Century English Faburden Compositions for Keyboard" (*MQ*, XXVI, 1940, 50ff.).
—— "John Bull's Organ Works" (*ML*, XXVIII, 1947, 25ff.).
—— "Fulgens praecalara" (*JAMS*, II, 1949, 97ff.).
—— "Forty Wayes of 2 Pts. in One of Tho(mas) Woodson" (*JAMS*, VIII, 1955, 14ff.).
Mischiati, O., ed. *Girolamo Cavazzoni: Orgelwerke*, 2 books (1958).
—— "L'intavolatura di Pelplin" (*L'Organo*, II, 1961, 53ff.).
—— "L'intavolatura d'organo tedesca della Biblioteca Nazionale di Torino" (*L'Organo*, IV, 1963, 1ff.) [**Mischiati T**].
——, ed. G. M. Trabaci, *Composizioni per organo e cembalo* (*Monumenti di Musica Italiana*, III, 1964–   ).
Morel, F. *G. Frescobaldi, Organista di S. Pietro di Roma* (1945).

Moser, H. J., ed. *91 gesammelte Tonsätze Paul Hofhaimers und seines Kreises* (1929) [**Moser H**].
—— *Paul Hofhaimer* (1929).
——, ed. *Frühmeister der deutschen Orgelkunst* (1930) [**Moser F**].
——, ed. "Eine Trienter Orgeltabulatur aus Hofhaimers Zeit" (*Adler Festschrift*, 1930, 84ff.).
——, ed. *Allein Gott in der Höh sei Ehr: 20 Choralvariationen der deutschen Sweelinck-Schule* (1953) [**Moser A**].
——, ed. *Choralbearbeitungen und freie Orgelstücke der deutschen Sweelinck-Schule*, 2 books (1954/5) [**Moser C**].
Müller, E. H. "Eine Tabulatur des Dresdner Hoforganisten Kittel" (*ZfMw*, XIII, 1930/1, 99ff.).
Muset, J., ed. *Early Spanish Organ Music* (1948) [**Muset E**].

Nagel, W. "Fundamentum Authore Johanne Buchnero" (*MfM*, XXIII, 1891, 71ff.).
Nef, W. R. *Der St. Galler Organist Fridolin Sicher und seine Orgeltabulatur* (1938).
Nettl, P. "Die Wiener Tanzkomposition in der zweiten Hälfte des 17. Jahrhunderts" (*Studien zur Musikwissenschaft*, VIII, 1921, 45ff.).
Nettles, W. E. *Alessandro Poglietti: Harpsichord Music* (1966).
Newman, Wm. S. "The XIIII Sonate di Cembalo by G. P. del Buono" (*Collectanea Hist. Mus.*, II, 1957, 297ff.).
Nielsen, B. E. Review of H.-J. Pauly, *Die Fuge in den Orgelwerken Dietrich Buxtehudes* (*Mf*, XX 1967, 345f.).
Noske, F., ed. *Klavierboek Anna Maria van Eijl* (*Monumenta Musica Neerlandica*, II, 1959).
——, ed. *Henderick Speuy, Psalm Preludes* (1962).

Oesterle, K., ed. *Early Keyboard Music*, 2 vols. (1904).

Pannain, G., ed. *A. Scarlatti: 3 Toccate e Partite sopra basso obligato* (n.d.).
Panum, H. "Melchior Schild oder Schildt" (*MfM*, XX, 1888, 27ff.).
Päsler, C. "Fundamentbuch von Hans von Constantz" (*VfMw*, V, 1889, 1ff.).
——, ed. *Johann Kuhnau: Musicalische Vorstellung einiger biblischen Historien . . .* (*DdT*, IV, 1901).
Pauer, E., ed. *Old English Composers* (n.d.).
Pauly, H.-J. *Die Fuge in den Orgelwerken Dietrich Buxtehudes* (*Kölner Beiträge zur Musikforschung*, XXXI, 1964).
Pedrell, F., ed. *Hispaniae Schola Musica Sacra*, 8 vols. (1894–6) [**Pedrell H**].
——, ed. *Antologia de organistas clásicos españoles*, 2 vols. (1908) [**Pedrell A**].
Pfatteicher, C. F. *John Redford . . .* (1934) [**Pfatteicher R**].
Pidoux, P., ed. *Claudio Merulo: Canzoni d'intavolatura d'organo* (1941).
——, ed. *Andrea Gabrieli: Intonationen* [etc.] *für Orgel*, 5 books (1941–53) [**Pidoux G**].
——, ed. *G. Frescobaldi: Orgel- und Klavierwerke*, 5 books (1948–53) [**Pidoux F**].
——, ed. *Anthoni van Noordt, Psalmenbearbeitungen für Orgel* (1954).
Pierront, N., and Hennebains, J. P., eds. *Annibale Padovano: 13 Ricercari for Organ 1556* (1934).
Pierront, N., ed. *Premier livre d'orgue de Nicolas de Grigny* (1953).
Pirro, A. "L'Art des organistes" (Lavignac's *Encyclopédie de la musique . . .*, II. 2, 1181ff.) [**Pirro A**].

Plamenac, D. "Keyboard Music of the 14th Century in Codex Faenza 117" (*JAMS*, IV, 1951, 179ff.).

—— "New Light on Codex Faenza 117" (*Kongressbericht Utrecht*, 1952, 310ff.).

—— *An Early 15th-Century Italian Source of Keyboard Music* (1961; also in *MD*, XIII/ XIV, 1959/60).

Prota-Giurleo, U. "Giovanni Maria Trabaci e gli organisti della Real Cappella di Palazzo di Napoli" (*L'Organo*, I, 1960, 185ff.).

—— "Due campioni della scuola napoletana del sec. XVII" (*L'Organo*, III, 1962, 115ff.).

Quittard, H. "Musique instrumentale jusqu'à Lully" (Lavignac's *Encyclopédie de la musique* . . . , I. 3, 1913, 1176ff.).

Raugel, F., ed. *Les Maîtres français de l'orgue*, 2 books (n.d.) [**Raugel M**].

Rayner, C. G., ed. *Hieronymus Praetorius, Magnificats for Organ* (*CEKM*, 4, 1963).

——, ed. *Christopher Gibbons, Keyboard Compositions* (*CEKM*, 18, 1967).

——, ed. *Giovanni Paolo Cima: Partito de Ricercari & Canzoni alla francese (1606)* (*CEKM*, 20, 1969).

——, ed. *Christian Erbach, Organ Works* (*CEKM*, forthcoming).

Redlich, H. F., ed. *Meister des Orgelbarock* (1931).

——, ed. *Harpsichord Pieces from Dr. Bull's Flemish Tablature* (1958).

Reese, G. *Music in the Renaissance* (1954).

Reimann, M. *Untersuchungen zur Formgeschichte der französischen Klavier-Suite* (1940).

—— "Paticcios und Parodien in norddeutschen Klaviertabulaturen" (*Mf*, VIII, 1955, 265ff.).

——, ed. *Die Lüneburger Orgeltabulatur KN 208¹ᐟ²* (*Das Erbe deutscher Musik*, 36/40, 1957/68) [**Reimann L**].

—— Review of H. Anglés, *Musici organici Joannis Cabanilles . . . opera omnia* (*Mf*, XI, 1958, 537f.).

—— Review of G. S. Bedbrook, *G. Gabrieli: Werke für Tasteninstrumente* (*Mf*, XII, 1959, 373).

—— "Die Autoren der Fuge Nr.23 in Lüneburg KN 208¹ . . ." (*Mf*, XVI, 1963, 166ff.).

Riedel, F. W., ed. *Jakob Bölsche: Praeambulum, Peter Heidorn: Fuga* (*Die Orgel*, II. 4, 1957).

——, ed. *A. Poglietti, 12 Ricercare* (*Die Orgel*, II. 5/6, 1957).

—— Review of M. S. Kastner, *Jacques Buus, Ricercari III° e IV°* . . . (*Mf*, XI, 1958, 381f.).

—— *Quellenkundliche Beiträge zur Geschichte der Musik für Tasteninstrumente in der 2. Hälfte des 17. Jahrhunderts* (1960) [**Riedel Q**].

—— "Eine unbekannte Quelle zu Kerlls Musik für Tasteninstrumente" (*Mf*, XIII, 1960, 310ff.).

——, ed. *Fux, Werke für Tasteninstrumente* (*Sämtliche Werke*, Serie VI, 1964).

Riemann, H., ed. *Joh. Christoph Bach, Variationen über eine Sarabande* (1892).

——, ed. *Musikgeschichte in Beispielen* (1911).

Ritter, Aug. G., ed. *Der Orgel-Freund* (1841–).

——, ed. *Der Orgelvirtuose* (1845–).

—— Copies of manuscripts at Beuron Archabbey (incl. copy of Grobe's tablature).

—— *Zur Geschichte des Orgelspiels* . . . , I (1884) [**Ritter G**].

—— Idem, vol.II: *Musikalische Beispiele* (1884) [**Ritter B**].

Roesgen-Champion, M., ed. *Pièces de Clavecin composées par J. Henry d'Anglebert* (1934).

Rokseth, Y., ed. *Deux livres d'orgue parus chez Pierre Attaingnant en 1531* (1925) [**Rokseth D**].
——, ed. *Treize Motets et un Prélude* (1930).
—— *La Musique d'orgue au XVᵉ siècle et au début du XVIᵉ* (1930).
——, ed. *Polyphonies du XIIIᵉ siècle*, 4 vols. (1935–9).
Ronga, L. *Gerolamo Frescobaldi* (1930).
Rubardt, P. *Spielstücke des 17. und 18. Jahrhunderts* (1940).

Sachs, C. *The Rise of Music in the Ancient World . . .* (1943).
Sandberger, A., ed. *J. K. Kerll, Ausgewählte Werke* (*DTB*, II. 2, 1901).
Santini, A., ed. *Frescobaldi, Girolamo: XIV Composizioni inedite* (*Musica veterum*, III, n.d.).
Sargent, G. *A Study and Transcription of Ms. Brit. Mus. Add.10337* (1968).
Sartori, C. *Bibliografia della musica strumentale italiana* (1952) [**Sartori B**].
Schanzlin, H. P. Review of M. Zulauf: *Johannes Benn, Missae concertatae* (*Mf*, XVII, 1964, 459f.).
Schenk, E., ed. *J. J. Fux, Werke für Tasteninstrumente* (*DTÖ*, 85, 1947).
Schering, A., ed. *Alte Meister der Frühzeit des Orgelspiels* (1913).
—— *Studien zur Geschichte der Frührenaissance* (1914).
——, ed. *Geschichte der Musik in Beispielen* (1931).
Schierning, L. *Die Überlieferung der deutschen Orgel- und Klaviermusik aus der 1. Hälfte des 17. Jahrhunderts* (1961) [**Schierning Ü**].
Schmid, H. "Una nuova fonte di musica organistica del secolo XVII" (*L'Organo*, I, 1960, 107ff.).
Schmidt, J. H., ed. *Werken voor orgel of clavicimbel uit het "Celler Klavierbuch 1662"* (*Exempla Musica Neerlandica* II, 1965).
—— "Eine unbekannte Quelle zur Klaviermusik des 17. Jahrhunderts" (*AfMw*, XXII, 1965, 1ff.).
Schneider, Marius. "Thematisches Verzeichnis der musikalischen Werke der Familie Bach" (*Bach-Jahrbuch* 1907, 127ff.).
Schneider, Max, ed. *Diego Ortiz: Tratado de glosas* (1913).
Scholderer, V., ed. *Michel Toulouze: L'Art et instruction de bien dancer* (1936).
Schrade, L. "Ein Beitrag zur Geschichte der Tokkata" (*ZfMw*, VIII, 1925/6, 610ff.).
—— "Tänze aus einer anonymen italienischen Tabulatur" (*ZfMw*, X, 1927/8, 449ff.).
—— *Die handschriftliche Überlieferung der ältesten Instrumentalmusik* (1931).
—— "Die Messe in der Orgelmusik des 15. Jahrhunderts" (*AfMf*, I, 1936, 129ff.).
Schrammek, W. "Zur Numerierung im Buxheimer Orgelbuch" (*Mf*, IX, 1956, 298ff.).
Schreiber, F., ed. *J. E. Kindermann, Ausgwählte Werke* (*DTB*, XXI–XXIV, vol.30, 1924).
Schröder, O., ed. *Johann Walther, Sämtliche Werke* (1953–61).
Schuler, M. "Eine neu entdeckte Komposition von Adam Steigleder" (*Mf*, XXI, 1968, 42ff.).
Seay, A., ed. *Pierre Attaingnant: Transcriptions of Chansons for Keyboard* (1961).
Seiffert, M. "J. P. Sweelinck und seine direkten deutschen Schüler" (*VfMw*, VII, 1891, 145ff.).
——, ed. *S. Scheidt: Tabulatura nova* (*DdT*, I, 1892).
——, ed. *J. P. Sweelinck, Werken I* (1894).
—— "Alte Orgelmeister" (*Allgemeine Musik-Zeitung*, 21, 1894, 617–19).
——, ed. *Anthoni van Noordt: Tabulatuur-Boeck* (*Vereeniging voor Noord-Nederlands Muziekgeschiedenis*, XIX, 1896).
—— *Geschichte der Klaviermusik I* (1899) [**Seiffert G**].
——, ed. *Johann Pachelbel: Klavierwerke* (*DTB*, II. 1, 1901).

——, ed. *Johann Pachelbel: Orgelkompositionen* (*DTB*, IV. 1, 1903).

——, ed. *Dietrich Buxtehude: Orgelwerke* (revision of Spitta's edition, 1903; Supplement, 1939).

——, ed. *F. W. Zachow: Gesammelte Werke* (*DdT*, XXI–XXII, 1905).

——, ed. *F. X. Murschhauser: Gesammelte Werke für Klavier und Orgel* (*DTB*, XVIII, vol.30, 1917).

——, ed. *J. und J. Ph. Krieger: Gesammelte Werke für Klavier und Orgel* (*DTB*, XVIII, vol.30, 1917).

—— *Organum, Vierte Reihe* (*Orgelmusik*), 21 books (n.d.) [**Seiffert O**].

—— *J. P. Sweelinck: Werken voor Orgel en Clavicimbel* (1943) [**Seiffert S**].

—— "Das Mylauer Tabulaturbuch von 1750" (*AfMw*, I, 1944, 607ff.).

Shannon, J. R., ed. *The Free Organ Compositions from the Lueneburg Tablatures*, 2 books (1958).

—— "The Mylau Tabulaturbuch" (diss., University of North Carolina, 1961) [**Shannon M**].

Shaw, W., ed. *John Blow: Complete Organ Works* (1958).

Shedlock, J. S. "The Harpsichord Music of Alessandro Scarlatti" (*SIMg*, VI, 1904, 160ff., 418).

Shindle, W. R., ed. *Ercole Pasquini: Collected Keyboard Works* (*CEKM*, 12, 1966).

——, ed. *Girolamo Frescobaldi: Keyboard Compositions Preserved in Manuscripts*, 3 vols. (*CEKM*, 30, 1968).

Sigtenhorst Meyer. Cf. Van den Sigtenhorst Meyer.

Slim, H. C. "Keyboard Music from Castell' Arquato by an Early Madrigalist" (*JAMS*, XV, 1962, 35ff.).

——, ed. *Keyboard Music from Castell' Arquato* (*CEKM*, forthcoming).

Southern, E. *The Buxheim Organ Book* (1963).

—— "Some Keyboard Dances of the 15th Century" (*AM*, XXXV, 1963, 114ff.).

Speer, K. "A Portuguese Manuscript of Keyboard Music . . ." (diss., Indiana University, 1956).

——, ed. *Annibale Padovano, Sperindio Bertoldo: Compositions for Keyboard* (*CEKM*, 34, 1969).

Spitta, Ph. *J. S. Bach*, 2 vols. (1873/80).

——, ed. *Dietrich Buxtehude: Orgelwerke*, 2 vols. (1876/78).

Steele, J., ed. *Thomas Tomkins: Three Voluntaries for Double Organ* (1956).

——, ed. *Thomas Tomkins: Two Toys and a Jigg* (1958).

Stein, F., ed. *Bruhns: Orgelwerke* (*Das Erbe deutscher Musik, Landschaftsdenkmale, Schleswig-Holstein* I/II, 1939).

Stevens, D., ed. *The Mulliner Book* (*Musica Britannica* I, 1951; *Commentary*, 1952) [**Stevens M**].

—— "A Unique Tudor Organ Mass" (*MD*, VI, 1952, 167ff.).

——, ed. *Thomas Tallis: Complete Keyboard Works* (1953) [**Stevens T**].

——, ed. *Altenglische Orgelmusik* (1953) [**Stevens A**].

—— "Further Light on *Fulgens praeclara*" (*JAMS*, IX, 1956, 1ff.).

—— "Thomas Preston's Organ Mass" (*ML*, XXXIX, 1958, 29ff.).

Stevenson, R. M. *Juan Bermudo* (1960).

Stone, K., ed. *Parthenia . . .* (1951).

Straube, K., ed. *Alte Meister: Eine Sammlung deutscher Orgelkompositionen . . .* (1904) [**Straube A**].

——, ed. *Choralvorspiele alter Meister* (1907) [**Straube C**].

——, ed. *Alte Meister des Orgelspiels: Neue Folge*, 2 vols. (1929) [**Straube AN**].

Subirá, J., ed. *Catálogo musical de la Biblioteca Nacional de Madrid* (1946–   ).
Sutherland, G. "The Ricercari of Jacques Buus" (*MQ*, XXXI, 1945, 448ff.).
Sutkowski, A. "L'Intavolatura di Pelplin" (*L'Organo*, II, 1961, 53ff.).
——, ed. *Keyboard Music from Polish Manuscripts*, 4 vols. (*CEKM*, 10, 1965–7).

Tagliapietra, G., ed. *Antologia di musica antica e moderna per pianoforte,* 18 vols. (1931–3) [**Tagliapietra A**].
Tagliavini, L. F. "Un musicista cremonese dimenticato" (*Collectanea Hist. Mus.*, II, 1957, 413ff.).
Ter Hasselt, J., *Noëls pour l'orgue de Nicolas Geoffroy* (n.d.).
Tessier, A., ed. *Oeuvres complètes de Chambonnières* (1925).
Toni, A., ed. *Michelangelo Rossi: Composizioni* (*I Classici della musica italiana*, 26, 1920).
Torchi, L., ed. *L'Arte musicale in Italia*, III: *Composizioni per organo o cembalo* (1899) [**Torchi A**].
Trede, H., ed. *Vincent Lübeck: Clavier Übung* (1940).
Tusler, R. L. *The Organ Music of Sweelinck* (1958).
Tuttle, S. D., ed. *William Byrd: 45 Pieces for Keyboard Instruments* (1939) [**Tuttle B**].
——, ed. *Thomas Tomkins: Keyboard Music* (*Musica Britannica*, V, 1955).

Valentin, E. "Die Entwicklung der Tokkata im 17. und 18. Jahrhundert" (diss. Munich, 1930).
Van den Borren, Ch. *Les Origines de la musique de clavier en Angleterre* (1912) [**Borren A**].
—— *Les Origines de la musique de clavier dans les Pays-Bas* (1919) [**Borren P**].
Van den Sigtenhorst Meyer, B. *Jan P. Sweelinck en zijn instrumentale muziek* (1946²).
Van der Meer, J. H. "The Keyboard Works in the Vienna Bull-Manuscript" (*TVer*, XVIII, 1965, 72ff.).
Vervoitte, C., ed. *G.-B. Nivers: Livre d'orgue (1665)* (1900).
Villalba-Muñoz, L., ed. *Antologia de organistas clásicos* (2 vols.), I (1914) [**Villalba A**].

Wallner, B. A., ed. *J. E. Kindermann: Ausgewählte Werke* (*DTB*, XXI–XXIV, vol.30, 1924).
——, ed. *Das Buxheimer Orgelbuch* (*Das Erbe deutscher Musik*, 37–39, 1958–59).
Walter, R., ed. *Franz Tunder: Sämtliche Choralbearbeitungen für Orgel* (1956).
——, ed. *J. K. Kerll: Modulatio organica* (1956).
——, ed. *Georg Muffat: Apparatus musico-organisticus* (1957).
——, ed. *F. X. Murschhauser: Octi-Tonium Novum Organicum* (1961).
——, ed. *J. E. Kindermann: Harmonia organica* (1966).
——, ed. *F. X. Murschhauser: Prototypon Longo-Breve organicum* (1969).
——, ed. *Arnold Schlick: Tabulaturen etlicher Lobgesang und Lidlein uff die Orgeln und Lauten* (in preparation).
Ward, J. "The 'Dolfull Domps' " (*JAMS*, IV, 1951, 111ff.).
—— "The Editorial Methods of Venegas de Henestrosa" (*MD*, VI, 1952, 105ff.).
——, ed. *The Dublin Virginal Manuscript* (1954) [**Ward D**].
Wasielewski, J. F. v. *Geschichte der Instrumentalmusik im XVI. Jahrhundert* (1878).
Watelet, J., ed. *A. Kerckhoven: Werken voor Orgel* (*Monumenta Musicae Belgicae*, II, 1933).
——, ed. *Ch. Guillet, Giov. de Macque, C. Luyton* (*Monumenta Musicae Belgicae*, IV, 1938).

Bibliography

Welter, F., ed. *Katalog der Musikalien der Ratsbücherei Lüneburg* (1950).
Werra, E. v. "Johann Buchner" (*KmJb*, 20[30], 1895, 88ff.).
——, ed. *J. C. F. Fischer: Musikalischer Parnassus* (1901).
——, ed. *Chr. Erbach: Ausgewählte Werke* (*DTB*, IV.2, 1903).
——, ed. *H. L. Hassler: Werke für Orgel und Klavier* (*DTB*, IV.2, 1903).
West, J. E., ed. *Old English Organ Music*, 35 books (c.1903–c.1910) [**West O**].
White, J. R. "The Tablature of Johannes of Lublin" (*MD*, XVII, 1963, 137ff.).
——, ed. *Johannes of Lublin: Tablature of Keyboard Music*, 6 vols. (*CEKM*, 6, 1964–7).
——, ed. *Michelangelo Rossi: Keyboard Works* (*CEKM*, 15, 1966).
Wilhelmer, A., ed. *Musik alter Meister*, 9 (1958).
Winterfeld, C. v. *Johannes Gabrieli und sein Zeitalter*, 3 vols. (1841).
Wolf, Chr. "Conrad Paumanns Fundamentum organisandi und seine verschiedenen Fassungen" (*AfMw*, 25, 1968, 196ff.).
Wolf, J. *Geschichte der Mensuralnotation von 1250 bis 1460*, 3 vols. (1904).
—— *Handbuch der Notationskunde*, 2 vols. (1913/19).
——, ed. *Music of Earlier Times* (1946).
Wolgast, F., ed. *Georg Böhm: Sämtliche Werke* I (1927).
Wooldridge, H. E., ed. *Old English Popular Music*, 2 vols. (1892).
——, ed. *Early English Harmony* (1897).
Wustmann, R. *Musikgeschichte Leipzigs* (1909).

Zöbeley, H. R. *Die Musik des Buxheimer Orgelbuches* (1964).

SOURCES CITED

Numbers at the end of an entry indicate the pages in this book where the source is cited; a *"see"* citation in parentheses refers to a modern edition listed in the Bibliography; other *"see"* notes refer to entries elsewhere in this list.

Amsterdam, Vereeniging voor Nederlandse Muziekgeschiedenis Ms., 408f.
Andreas-Bach Book, *see* Leipzig, Ms.III.8.4
Anleitung zur musikalischen Gelahrtheit, Adlung (1758), 679
Antwerp Ms., *see* London, B.M., Add.23623
Apparatus musico-organisticus, Muffat (1690), 551, 580f., 666
Ariadne musica, Fischer (1702?), 589f., 591f., 661
L'Art de toucher le clavecin, Couperin (1717), 719
Arte de tañer fantasia, Sancta Maria (1565), 206f., 457
L'Arte organica, Antegnati (1608), 412
Assisi Ms., 483
Attaingnant prints, 105ff., 289

Joh. Bahr tablature, *see* Visby tablature
Balli d'arpicordo, Picchi (1620), 420f.
Barcelona, Bibl. Central, Mss.: M 387 (888), 539f., 540, 543, 774f.; M 450, 513, 539f., 774f.; M 751.21, 539f., 540, 543, 774f.
Basel, Univ.-Bibl., Mss.: F.I.8 (c.1520; Buchner), 77, 784n6, 785n8; F.IX.22 (Kotter), 77, 288; F.IX.49 (Mareschal), 204; F.IX.58 (Kotter), 77, 288
Basse-danse Ms., *see* Brussels Ms. 9085
Bauyn Mss., *see* Paris, B.N., Vm^7 674, 675
Belvoir Psalter (13th cent.), 15, 22
Berkeley Ms. (Parville Ms.), 814n4

Berlin, Amalien-Bibl., Ms.340, 603

Berlin, Institut für Kirchenmusik, lost Ms., 654

Berlin, Öffentl. wissenschaftl. Bibl., Ms. 40098, *see* Glogau Song Book

Berlin, Staatsbibl.: Celle tablature of 1601, *see* Celle tablature; Lübbenau tablatures, *see* Lynar tablatures; Ms. theol. lat. quart. 290 (Wynsem Ms., Ms. H), 33, 34, 36f., 38; Michael print (1645), 384f., 801n60; P.230, 810n56; P.802, 601, 640; Pasquini autograph (1702), 694

—Ms.mus.: 6473, 810n58; 22541, *see* Walther Mss.; 30112 (formerly P.407; Fuchs), 803n38, 808n20; 30245, 679; 30439, 625; 40034 (1585; Löffelholtz), 246f.; 40089 (1598; Nörmiger), 246ff.; 40115 (1593), 99, 246ff.; 40147 (lost), 388, 389; 40268 (Gerber's Clavier Book), 649, 678; 40295 (Plauen Organ Book; lost), 811n92; 40316 (formerly 191), 795n6, 339, 798n22, 389, 394, 408, 482; 40613 (formerly Wernigerode, Fürstl. Stolbergsche Bibl., Ms.Zb 14), *see* Fundamentum organisandi, Lochamer Song Book; 40615, 398, 421; 40623, 604; 40644 (Möller Ms.), 809n51,n55, 610, 624, 625, 631, 650, 651f., 673; Z.26 (Kleber), 77, 288

Bern treatise, *see* De fistulis organicis

Beuron Archabbey Ms., *see* Grobe's tablature

Bologna, Lic.mus., Ms.DD53, 808n9, 813n12, 693

Bonadies codex, *see* Faenza Ms.

Braga, Bibl.pública, Ms.no.964, 776, 817n8

Brasov (Kronstadt), Mus. Ms.808 (1682; Croner), 649

Breslau (Wroclaw), Staatsbibl.; lost tablature (c.1565), 97f., 98

—Mss.: I F 687 (Ms.I), 33f., 34, 39ff., 52; I Qu 42 (Ms.E), 33, 34, 38, 69; I Qu 438 (Sagan fragment, Ms.D), 33, 34, 35f.

Broeckhuizen book (lost), 768

Brussels, Bibl.Roy., Mss.: 9085 (Basse-danses; *see* Closson), 54f., 783n21, 65, 66; II 3326, 768

Buxheim Organ Book (Munich, Cim 352b.; c.1470; *see* Wallner), 7, 30, 33, 34, 40, 41, 783n14, 55, 55ff., 93, 95, 107, 141f., 213, 217, 230, 262, 288, 389, 471

Calvörsche Bibl. at Clausthal-Zellerfeld (Scheidemann), Mss.: Ze 1, 349, 368, 799n26, 369f.; Ze 2, 368, 799n26, 369f., 375

Camphuysen Ms., 767, 816n4 (bottom), 768

Castell' Arquato, Bibl.Capitolare, Mss. (*see* Slim), 77, 93, 111ff., 117, 168ff., 236f., 324

Celle Klavierbuch (1662; *see* Schmidt), 797n1, 372, 384

Celle tablature (Berlin, Staatsbibl.; 1601; *see* Apel), 798n6, 347ff., 376

Chicago, Newberry Library, Ms.VM 7 F 126 (Fabricius Ms.), 610

Clausthal-Zellerfeld, *see* Calvörsche Bibl.

Coimbra, Univ.Libr., Mss.: no.48, 790n15,n31; no.242, 188, 195

Copenhagen, Royal Libr.: Mss.: 376, 372, 382, 505; Add.396.4to, 603f

—Voigtländer print (1642), 372, 800n44

Cosyn's Virginal Book (London, Royal Libr., Ms.23.L.4; *see* Fuller), 259, 311f.

Cracow, Academy of Sciences, Ms.1716 (1537–48; Joh. of Lublin; *see* White), 101, 786n 19, 217f., 241f.

Cracow, Holy Ghost Order tablature (1548; lost; photo copy at Harvard Univ., Isham Libr.), 103f., 786n21, 217, 218, 289

Danzig Ms., *see* Gdansk Ms.

Darmstadt, Landesbibl., Ms.51 (4061), 809n50

Declaración de instrumentos musicales, Bermudo (1555), 6fn, 7, 16, 138, 194

De fistulis organicis (10th cent.; Bern treatise), 13, 15

Musicks Hand-maide, Playford (1663, 1678), 748f., 750, 760, 762
My Ladye Nevells Booke (1591; *see* Andrews N), 80, 212, 254ff., 276, 278, 285f.
Mylau Ms. (1750), 625, 627f., 649, 652, 678

Naples, Bibl.del Cons. San Pietro a Majella, Mss.: 22.1.22, 703; 34.4.40, 703; 34.5.28, 421,
    423, 424, 491, 496; 34.6.31, 703; 48, 421, 424
Neresheim Organ Book, *see* Munich, 5368
New Haven (Yale University), School of Music; Mss.: E.B.1688, 808n13, 569, 570, 576,
    810n58, 609, 624, 651, 663; M 1490.H 66 (formerly 21.H 59; Hintze Ms.), 560fn,
    609f., 749; A. Scarlatti (H. M. Higgs Ms.), 699f., 702
New York, Public Library, Ms.Drexel 5612, 797n24
Le nuove musiche, Caccini (1602), 686

Old Hall Ms. (15th cent.), 6fn, 315
Oporto, Bibl.mun., Mss.: 1576 Col.B/5 (*see* Fernandes), 807n24; 1577 (Libro de cyfra;
    c.1700), 513, 518fn, 541fn, 776ff.; 1607 (Livro de obras de orgão; 1695), 775f., 817n7
L'Organo suonarino, Banchieri (1605, 1611, 1622), 415ff.
Ottobeuren Ms., 807n6
Oxford, Christ Church College Libr., Mss.: 371 (Redford), 140, 788n72; 1113 (formerly
    1175), 299f., 311, 312f., 319; 1177, 508, 759; 1236, 508, 748f.

Padua, Univ.Libr., Ms.1982, 328f., 392, 395
Paris, Bibl.nat., Mss.: frç.9152, 792n54; Vm^7 574 (Bauyn Ms.; c.1660; Chambonnières),
    555, 705, 710; Vm^7 575 (Bauyn Ms.; c.1660), 805n8, 508, 807n4, 700, 712f.; Vm^7
    1817, 578; Vm^7 1823, 815n23
Paris, Conservatoire, Mss.: 2094 (Thiéry organ book; c.1680; *see* Hardouin), 747; Rés.
    475 (formerly 24827), 815n45; Rés.476 (formerly 24827), 746, 815n44,n45; Rés.1122
    (Tomkins autograph), 315; Rés.1184/85 (formerly 18548), 303, 796n12, 311, 748;
    Rés.1186/86b (formerly 18546), 796n12, 749
Paris, Ste.Geneviève, Mss.: 2348, 504f.; 2353, 505
Parthenia (1611; *see* Stone), 80, 221, 253, 254, 293, 303, 320, 321, 322
Parville Ms., *see* Berkeley Ms.
Pasquini autographs, *see* Berlin, Staatsbibl., Pasquini autograph; London, Brit.Mus., Add.
    31501
Pelplin tablatures, 368, 799n26, 371, 805n60, 594, 596f., 809n45
Petri tablature, *see* Visby tablature
Plaine and Easie Introduction to Practicall Musicke, Morley (1597), 259, 293, 311
Plauen Organ Book, *see* Berlin, Staatsbibl., 40295
Pommersfelden, Gräfl.Schönborn'sche Bibl., Cod.2776 (11th cent.), 14

Ravenna, Bibl.comm., classense Ms.545, 421, 483, 496
Regensburg, Fürstl.Thurn- und Taxis'sche Hofbibl., Ms. FK 21, 217
Robertsbridge fragment (London, Brit.Mus., Add.28550; c.1325), 22, 24ff., 28, 43, 51, 288
Elizabeth Rogers' Virginal Book, *see* London, Brit.Mus., Add.10337
Le Roman de Fauvel, Chaillou de Pesstain (Paris, Bibl.nat., frç.146; 1316), 25f.
Rome, Bibl.del Conservatorio di S.Cecilia, Ms.A/400, 747
Rome, Bibl.Vat., Chigi Mss. Q IV 24–29 and Q VIII 205/206 (*see* Lincoln), 421, 422f.,
    449, 465fn, 482, 496, 497
Rossi Ms., *see* London, Brit.Mus., Add.30491
Ryge Ms. (Buxtehude), 611, 623

Sagan fragment, *see* Breslau, I Qu 438
St.Etienne Bible (Dijon, Bibl.mun.; 11th cent.), 14, 21

St.Gall, Stiftsbibl., Ms. Cod.530 (Sicher), 77, 288f.
Schedel's (Schedelsches) Song Book (Munich, Ms.mus.3232; c.1460), 63f., 783n29, 64
Scheurleer Ms., *see* Walther Mss., The Hague
Schönborn'sche Bibl., *see* Pommersfelden
Segovia, Bibl.de la Catedral, Ms., 795n9
Soldt Clavier Book, *see* London, Brit.Mus., Add.29485
Spiegel der Orgelmacher und Organisten, Schlick (1511), 76, 87
Syntagma musicum, Praetorius (vols.II-III, 1619), 4, 14, 165f., 307, 352, 389

Tabulatura nova, Scheidt (1624), 6, 276, 356ff., 376, 392, 398, 404, 504
Tabulatur-Buch hundert geistlicher Lieder und Psalmen (Görlitz Tabulatur), Scheidt
    (1650), 98, 356, 365f., 376
Gesina Terburg's Notebook (lost), 768
Thiéry organ book, *see* Paris, Conservatoire, 2094
Torun (Thorn), Church archive (Arch. woj. w Torunin), Ms. Rps.XIV 13 a (1595; Jo-
    hannes Fischer of Mohrungen), 289
Tours, Bibl.mun., Mss.: 285, 505; 1772, 746f.
Il Transilvano (*see* Diruta, Index of Names)
Trento, Archivo di Stato, Organ tablature, 215; Ms.Sez.ted.N.105, 76, 89ff.
Trento, Feininger Ms., 421, 422, 497
Turin tablatures (collections Foá and Giordano), Mss. F, 3, 6, 7, 8 and G, 1, 2, 3, 5, 6, 8,
    78, 784n15, 785n20, 121, 185, 226, 227, 325, 332, 799n16, 391, 391ff., 394f., 395,
    397, 409, 410f., 802n4, 449, 482

Uppsala, Univ.Libr., Mss.: 408 (J.Mus.108; Düben Ms.), 795n4,n6 (bottom), 315, 372,
    372; Ihre 284, 369, 603; Ihre 285, 593, 603, 809n51, 611, 623
—tablature, 610
Utrecht Psalter (8th or 9th cent.), 21

Venice, Bibl.Marc., Ms. it.Cl.IV.No.1227, 234ff., 238; 1598 print (Intavolatura d'organo
    facilissima), 128
Versailles, Marchand Ms., 742
Vienna, Monastery of the Brothers Minor, Mss.: XIV.714 (formerly Mus.ms.8), 373, 389;
    717–722, 570, 576f.; 743, 580; number unknown, 807n6
Vienna, Nationalbibl., Mss.: 2856 (Mondsee Ms.), 52; Cod.3617 (Ms. C), 33, 35; 16798,
    556; 17771, 303, 796n12, 306; Cod.18491 (Regina Clara Im Hoff Clavierbuch; 1629),
    388f.; Cod.19167, 572
Visby tablature (Bahr or Petri tablature; 1611), 350, 798n16 (top), 380, 381

Walther Mss.: Berlin, Staatsbibl., Ms.mus.22541, 376, 378f., 625, 636, 642, 674f., 676; The
    Hague (Frankenberger or Scheurleer Ms.), 636, 642, 811n96, 675; Kaliningrad (Kö-
    nigsberg), Univ.Libr., Sec.Gotthold No.15839, 813n137
Warsaw, Musicological Soc., Ms.I/220 (Leopolita tablature; c.1580; lost; photo copy at
    Harvard Univ., Isham Libr.; *see* Golos), 104f., 786n22,n23
Washington, Library of Congress: Ms. M 21.M.185, 690, 752, 753; Libro de cifra, 817n10
Wenster Collection, 810n58
Wernigerode Ms. Zb 14, *see* Berlin, Staatsbibl., 40316
Wolfenbüttel, Herzog August Bibl.: Erbach autograph, 801n69; Ms. Helmstadt 1055, 381
Wroclaw, *see* Breslau
Wynsem Ms., *see* Berlin, Staatsbibl., Ms.theol.lat.quart., 290

Zellerfeld, *see* Calvörsche Bibl.
Zürich, Stadtbibl., Ms.Cod.284, 784n5, 96

INDEXES

INDEX OF NAMES

Only persons directly connected with the production or description of keyboard music, musical techniques, instruments, and scores are listed in this Index, except those active after the middle third of the 18th century; composers discussed in the text are given in bold type. When several page references follow a name those in bold type refer to major discussion of music; references that include musical examples are followed by an asterisk; ² indicates two or more distinct references on the same page, e.g., 123².

INDEX OF WORKS

This Index lists all titles of individual works mentioned in the text as well as types of works, except for compositions written after approximately 1710; works by J. S. Bach will be found under J. S. Bach in the Index of Names. A reference to the Index of Terms is indicated by t; an asterisk indicates a musical example; 2 after a page number signifies two or more references on that page; where a work appears under several titles or includes several subtitles, such titles may carry superscripts 1, 2, etc., and these numbers also follow the names of the composers using the respective titles.

The following abbreviations are used: ant = antiphon, can = canzona, c.b. = clavier book, ch = chorale, d = dance, ds = dance song, E = the Elder, h = hymn, in = introit, o.b. = organ book, off = offertory, s = song, s.b. = song book, t. = tablature(s), var = variations, v.b. = virginal book, Y = the Younger. Titles that start with an article—*a, der, die, el, il, la, le, the, un,* etc.—are alphabetized under the article.

INDEX OF TERMS

References in this Index are to discussions of types of music, of techniques of composition and performance, and of instruments, not to particular works; these are listed in the Index of Works, references to which are symbolized by ᵂ. Names of ornaments are marked °; particularly significant passages appear in bold type; and page references to musical examples carry an asterisk. Where two or more distinct references occur on a page this is indicated by ².